Ci-Cz Volume 4

The World Book Encyclopedia

94184MS

World Book, Inc.

a Scott Fetzer company

Chicago London Sydney Toronto

The World Book Encyclopedia

CIA. See Central Intelligence Agency.

Ciardi, *chee AHR dee,* **John** (1916-1986), was an American poet. Unlike the work of many modern poets, Ciardi's poetry usually is not difficult or surprising. Critics have praised his verse for its musical grace and ease. According to Ciardi, style should serve the purposes of the subject rather than express the individuality of the writer. Critics sometimes accused him of sentimentality, but he achieved the highest excellence in many of his poems and in his translations of Dante's *Divine Comedy* (*Inferno,* 1954; *Purgatorio,* 1961; *Paradiso,* 1970). Collections of Ciardi's poetry appear in *As If: Poems New and Selected* (1955) and *For Instance* (1979).

AP/Wide World
John Ciardi

Ciardi was born in Boston. He taught at Harvard University from 1946 to 1953, and at Rutgers University from 1953 to 1961. He served as poetry editor for *Saturday Review* from 1956 to 1977. Ciardi has written several children's books. He also wrote *How Does a Poem Mean?* (1960), a critical introduction to the study of poetry at the college level.

Bonnie Costello

Cibber, Colley. See Poet laureate; Pope, Alexander.
Cibola, *SEE boh lah,* **Seven Cities of,** were seven legendary cities in what is now the Southwestern United States. Early Spanish explorers in Mexico believed they were rich in gold, silver, and precious jewels.

During the 1530's, Indians in northern Mexico told stories to the Spanish explorers about a rich civilization to the north. These stories led to an expedition in 1539 led by Marcos de Niza, a Spanish priest, to explore the land in the north. Niza sent a black guide named Estevanico ahead to seek information from the Indians. They told Estevanico about seven rich cities in a land they called Cibola. Estevanico reached Hawikuh, the largest of six Zuni villages near what is now Gallup, N. Mex. The Zunis killed him outside Hawikuh.

Niza claimed that he saw Hawikuh from a distance and said the village appeared large and wealthy. His report led to an expedition headed by Francisco Coronado in 1540 to conquer the villages and claim their wealth for Spain. Coronado captured the six villages and called them Cibola. He found no riches there, however, and returned to Mexico in 1542.   Charles Gibson

See also **Coronado, Francisco Vásquez de; Estevanico.**
Cicada, *suh KAY duh* or *suh KAH duh,* is a heavy-bodied insect with four thin wings that it folds over its body like a roof. The cicada is a darkly colored insect from 1 to 2 inches (2.5 to 5 centimeters) long. It has a wide head and short, bristlelike *antennae* (feelers). Most cicadas live in tropical and subtropical areas, but many types live in North America.

Cicadas are commonly known for the buzzing song the male makes. The male makes two drumlike *membranes* (thin sheaths of skin) on the abdomen vibrate rapidly to produce the sound. The sound attracts fe-

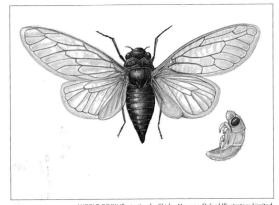

WORLD BOOK illustration by Shirley Hooper, Oxford Illustrators Limited
A cicada emerges as an adult insect after shedding its skin, *right.* The periodical cicada shown above takes 17 years to develop and is often called a *17-year locust.*

males or calls large numbers of males together. Each *species* (kind) of cicada has its own song. Many types of male cicadas often assemble in large groups and produce a loud chorus of sounds. Most cicadas produce a short "protest" sound if they are disturbed.

Types of cicadas. Two common groups of cicadas are the *dog-day cicadas* and the *periodical cicadas.* Dog-day cicadas are large, very dark, and often have greenish markings. They appear each year in July and August. It takes from four to seven years for a dog-day cicada to develop from an egg into an adult. But some adults are seen each year, because different *broods* (groups of young) develop at different times.

Periodical cicadas are dark, and have red eyes and wing veins. They appear in late May and early June. Periodical cicadas take either 13 years or 17 years to develop, depending on where they live.

Cicadas that take 17 years to develop are sometimes called *17-year locusts.* Adult periodical cicadas thus appear in a region only once every 13 or 17 years. But so many broods exist that they appear somewhere in the United States nearly every year.

Development. A female cicada lays her eggs in the twigs of trees and shrubs. She places the eggs in small holes that she makes with a sawlike organ near the tip of her abdomen. The twigs usually are so badly injured by the process that the tips of the twigs die. In a few weeks, the eggs hatch and young cicadas called *nymphs* appear. They fall to the ground, enter the soil, and feed on roots. A nymph remains in the ground until it is full-grown. Then it comes out of the ground and climbs a tree or some other object. It sheds its skin, and emerges as an adult. The adult cicada has a life span of only a few weeks.

Scientific classification. Cicadas belong to the order Hemiptera and the cicada family, Cicadidae. The most common dog-day cicadas belong to the genus *Tibicen.* The periodical cicadas belong to the genus *Magicicada.*   Candace Martinson

Cicely. See Sweet cicely.
Cicero, *SIHS uh ROH,* **Marcus Tullius,** *TUHL ee uhs* (106-43 B.C.), was a great Roman orator and statesman. His written orations and philosophical and religious essays made him one of the most influential authors in

Latin literature. In his writings, Cicero translated ideas and technical terms into Latin that had previously existed only in Greek. Cicero so improved Latin that it served as the international language of intellectual communication for centuries.

Marble sculpture by an unknown Roman artist; Uffizi Gallery, Florence (Alinari from Art Reference Bureau)

Marcus Tullius Cicero

His life. Cicero was born of middle-class parents in Arpinum, Italy. He studied philosophy, rhetoric, and Greek and Latin literature in Rome, Athens, and Rhodes.

Cicero gained fame in 70 B.C., when he successfully prosecuted Gaius Verres, a corrupt former governor of Sicily. Cicero's victory in this trial earned him the approval of the Roman aristocracy. With the support of the aristocracy, Cicero attained the position of consul, Rome's highest elected political office, in 63 B.C.

The First Triumvirate of Julius Caesar, Gnaeus Pompey, and Marcus Licinius Crassus banished Cicero from Rome in 58 B.C. because he opposed their rule. However, Cicero was allowed to return to Rome in 57 B.C. The Second Triumvirate of Octavian (later the Emperor Augustus), Marcus Aemilius Lepidus, and Mark Antony would not tolerate Cicero's opposition. They had him killed.

His works. Cicero composed more than 100 orations. They are known for their precise choice of words; attention to grammatical structures; and skillful use of descriptions, narration, and prose rhythms. Two series of orations reflect Cicero's support for the republican form of government. In 63 B.C., he delivered four speeches against a Roman named Catiline who plotted to overthrow the Roman government. These speeches led to the defeat and death of Catiline and his followers (see **Catiline**). In 44 and 43 B.C., Cicero composed 14 speeches called the *Philippics.* In them, he attacked Mark Antony because he believed Antony intended to rule Rome with absolute power.

Cicero composed two major works on oratory, *Brutus* and *De Oratore.* He described the advantages of a serene old age in *De Senectute,* and he analyzed friendship in *De Amicitia.* Cicero examined ethical behavior in *De Finibus* and the nature of the gods in *De Natura Deorum.* Cicero discussed the attainment of happiness in *Tusculan Disputations* and one's duties in life in *De Officiis.* The influence of the Greek philosopher Plato appears in a book on law called *De Legibus* and a study of various forms of government called *De Republica.* Cicero was also an active letter writer. His correspondence reveals his informal side. Cicero's letters also provide valuable accounts of Roman life.   Joseph R. Tebben

See also **Education** (Ancient Roman education); **Oratory; Latin literature** (The age of Cicero).

Additional resources

Lacey, Walter K. *Cicero and the End of the Roman Republic.* Barnes & Noble, 1978.
Stockton, David. *Cicero: A Political Biography.* Oxford, 1971.

Cid, *sihd,* **The** (1043?-1099), also called El Cid, is one of Spain's national heroes. His real name was Rodrigo Díaz de Vivar. *The Cid* comes from the Arabic *El Sayyid,* meaning *the lord.* The Cid served in the armies of Sancho II and Alfonso VI of Castile. Alfonso banished The Cid in 1081 after The Cid was unjustly accused of disloyalty. The Cid then gathered a small army and fought for anyone who hired him. He was successful in war and gained great power and wealth. In 1094, he conquered Valencia from the Moors, who had controlled much of Spain since the 700's.

The Cid's story became a legend in *Poem of the Cid,* written in the 1100's or early 1200's, and in many later ballads. His story inspired a drama by the French playwright Pierre Corneille. The Cid was born near Burgos and is buried there.   James W. Brodman

See also **Spanish literature** (The Middle Ages).

Cider is a beverage made from the juice pressed out of apples. There are two kinds of cider—hard cider and sweet cider. *Hard cider* is an alcoholic drink. Most hard ciders contain 5 to 7 per cent alcohol. *Sweet cider* is nonalcoholic apple juice.

Cider is produced by grinding apples and squeezing out the juice with mechanical presses. To make hard cider, the juice is then allowed to *ferment.* In this process, the juice is stored until yeasts convert sugar in the juice to alcohol. Sweet cider is made from juice that is not allowed to ferment. To prevent spoiling, manufacturers pasteurize some hard cider and all sweet cider, and sometimes add chemical preservatives. Hard cider may be made into *cider vinegar* by allowing bacteria to convert the alcohol to *acetic acid.* This acid gives the vinegar its sour taste. See **Vinegar.**   Henry P. Fleming

Cigar is a tight roll of dried tobacco used for smoking. Cigars range in size and shape from short, slim *cigarillos* to long, slender *panetelas* and large, fat *coronas.* The majority of cigars are made by machines, but the more expensive ones are hand-rolled.

Most cigars consist of three parts and three types of tobaccos. Folded *filler tobacco leaves* make up most of the body of a cigar. The filler is held together and surrounded by a *binder leaf.* A *wrapper leaf* is wound around the binder. Some inexpensive cigars have as their binders or wrappers *reconstituted tobacco sheets.* These sheets are made of coarse or damaged tobacco leaves that have been ground up and mixed with adhesive.   J. H. Smiley

See also **Cuba** (picture); **Smoking; Tobacco.**

Cigarette is a roll of shredded tobacco wrapped in paper. Nearly all cigarettes smoked in the United States are a blend of tobaccos grown inside the country or imported. They contain chiefly flue-cured tobacco, which is grown in Florida, Georgia, North Carolina, South Carolina, and Virginia; burley tobacco, which is grown mainly in Kentucky and Tennessee; imported oriental tobacco, which mostly is grown in Greece and Turkey; and a small amount of Maryland tobacco. Some cigarettes contain flue-cured and burley tobaccos imported from Argentina, Brazil, Canada, and Malawi. They may also contain reconstituted sheet tobacco, which is made from ground leaf stems and leaf pieces. The tobacco blend is sprayed with flavorings and a chemical that preserves moisture. Most cigarettes have a filter at one end.

Hand-rolled cigarettes achieved limited popularity in

the United States between 1855 and 1885. They contained either oriental tobacco, flue-cured tobacco, or a blend of the two. The first practical cigarette-making machine was invented in the early 1880's.

During the 1960's, scientists reported that *tar* and *nicotine,* which are inhaled in cigarette smoke, could cause lung cancer, heart disease, and other illnesses. In 1965, Congress passed a law requiring manufacturers to label packages and cartons of cigarettes with a health warning. Since 1971, radio and television commercials on cigarettes have been banned. In 1972, manufacturers agreed to include a health warning in all cigarette advertising. In 1984, a system of four different warning labels was adopted. In 1988, Canada passed several anti-smoking laws and banned cigarette advertising.

Since the 1970's, the consumption of cigarettes with reduced tar and nicotine has increased. Today, manufacturers reduce the amount of tar and nicotine inhaled through changes in blending and cigarette design. These changes include filtration to trap some of the tar and a ventilation process that dilutes the smoke.

W. David Smith

See also **Smoking; Cancer** (Causes of cancer); **Filter; Nicotine; Tobacco.**

Cilia, *SIHL ee uh,* are tiny, hairlike structures that project from certain kinds of cells. Cilia are slender and move constantly. They can be seen only under a microscope. In higher animals, cilia are found in cells of the membranes of the nose, the ear, and the tubes leading toward the lungs. The wavy motion of the cilia in these organs pushes out dust, bacteria, and mucus, and keeps the passages clean. In a clam, cilia-containing cells fan water containing food and oxygen into the animal. Many one-celled organisms have cilia that serve as sense organs and provide a means of locomotion. See also **Protozoan** (Ciliates).   Lawrence C. Wit

Cimabue, *CHEE mah BOO eh,* **Giovanni** (1240?-1302?), an Italian painter, was the first famous painter of the city of Florence. He began an era of famous Florentine painters that included Leonardo da Vinci.

Cimabue's art does not show obvious originality. He painted in a traditional style based on the medieval art of the Byzantine Empire, and his paintings show little of the realism used by the later Florentine painters. His faces and figures are the formalized types of the Byzantine period. But his works have great personal force and effect, even though the forms are traditional.

Five or six of Cimabue's works exist today. The most famous include the altarpiece of the *Madonna and Child with Angels* in the Uffizi Gallery in Florence and religious frescoes in the church of Saint Francis at Assisi. Cimabue's church frescoes show great power and grandeur. His *Crucifixion* in the church combines those qualities with dramatic impact.   Donald Rabiner

See also **Renaissance** (picture: Medieval and Renaissance art).

Cimmerians were nomads who lived in what is now southern Ukraine from about 1200 B.C. to 700 B.C. They inhabited an area north of the Caucasus Mountains, near the Black Sea. They used horses and the bow and arrow and were known as fierce warriors. They were one of the first nomadic groups to invade Asia Minor (now Turkey) from the north.

Scholars have not found written records left by the

Tempera on wood (1295?); formerly in the Church of Santa Croce, Florence, now in the Uffizi Gallery, Florence (Art Reference Bureau)

Cimabue's *Crucifixion* shows the influence of Byzantine art. A 1966 flood in Florence, Italy, badly damaged the painting.

Cimmerians and know little about the group. The Greek historian Herodotus wrote that they were driven from their homeland into Asia Minor by nomads called the Scythians. About 700 B.C., the Cimmerians fought the Assyrians and destroyed the kingdom of Phrygia in what is now central Turkey. About 690 B.C., they began to raid Lydia, in what is now western Turkey. The Cimmerians were defeated by the Assyrians during the mid-600's B.C.

Andrew C. Hess

Cimon, *KY mohn* or *SY muhn* (507?-450 or 449 B.C.), was a military and political leader in ancient Athens. In 478 and 477 B.C., he helped form the Delian League of Greek city-states to wage war against Persia. During most of the 470's and 460's B.C., Cimon commanded the league's Athenian forces. Cimon also led the aristocrats in Athens. In 461 B.C., a quarrel between Athens and Sparta led democratic leaders in Athens to banish Cimon because he favored friendly relations with the Spartans. Cimon probably returned to Athens in 451 B.C. That year, he arranged a truce between the two city-states.   Jennifer Tolbert Roberts

Cinchona, *sihn KOH nuh,* is the name of a group of valuable South American trees and shrubs. The bark of a cinchona is called *Jesuits' bark, cardinal's bark,* or *sacred bark.* The bark is used to make the drugs quinine, quinidine, and cinchonidine, with which doctors treat malaria. The cinchona is an evergreen. Cinchona plants were first found in Peru and Ecuador. They are now grown in India, Sri Lanka, eastern Asia, tropical America, and parts of Africa. The flowers are usually fragrant. They vary from rose-purple to greenish-white and look like lilac blossoms.

Scientific classification. Cinchona belongs to the madder family, Rubiaceae. Cinchona makes up the genus *Cinchona.*

Frank Welsch

See also **Bitters; Quinine.**

Cincinnati, a major commercial and industrial center, lies on the Ohio River in southwestern Ohio. Riverfront Stadium, *center,* is home to the city's professional baseball and football teams.

Cincinnati, *SIHN suh NAT ee,* is a major industrial and commercial center of the Midwest. It leads the world in the production of soap and playing cards and produces more machine tools than any other city in the United States. Cincinnati is one of the largest cities in Ohio. It lies on the Ohio River in the southwestern part of the state. It is one of the most beautiful cities in the nation and was once called the *Queen City of the West.*

In 1788, settlers established a village called Losantiville on what is now the site of Cincinnati. In 1790, General Arthur St. Clair, the first governor of the Northwest Territory, changed the name to Cincinnati. He did so to honor the Society of the Cincinnati, an organization that was formed by Army officers of the Revolutionary War in America (see **Cincinnati, Society of the**).

River trade accounted for much of Cincinnati's growth during the 1800's. Steamboats linked the city with many major ports. Later, after railroads became the chief method of transportation, Cincinnati lost much trade to other cities. Since the late 1800's, its economy has relied largely on manufacturing.

Metropolitan Cincinnati

Cincinnati lies on the north bank of the Ohio River. The Great Miami and the Little Miami rivers flow into the Ohio on two sides of the city. Cincinnati covers 79 square miles (205 square kilometers), or about a fifth of Hamilton County. The Cincinnati metropolitan area occupies 3,342 square miles (8,656 square kilometers) and extends over Hamilton, Brown, Clermont, and Warren counties in Ohio; Boone, Campbell, Gallatin, Grant, Kenton, and Pendleton counties in Kentucky; and Dearborn and Ohio counties in Indiana.

The city. A flat plain called the *basin* extends north into Cincinnati from the Ohio riverfront. In this area are the city's central business district, some manufacturing sections, and several old residential areas. Hills surround the basin on three sides.

Downtown Cincinnati centers around Fountain Square Plaza, between Vine and Walnut streets. The 48-story Carew Tower, the city's tallest building, rises west of the square. Fourth Street, the heart of Cincinnati's financial district, lies south of the square. A convention center stands at the western edge of the business district. In 1986, the city completed an expansion of the convention center that doubled the meeting rooms and exposition space. The expanded facility was named the Albert B. Sabin Cincinnati Convention Center in honor of the doctor who developed oral polio vaccine in Cincinnati in the 1950's. The birthplace of U.S. President William Howard Taft lies north of the business district. Riverfront Stadium overlooks the Ohio River.

The metropolitan area. Residential areas occupy the hillsides surrounding the basin. Cincinnati suburbs include Madeira, Norwood, and Saint Bernard. Freeways connect some of the suburbs with downtown Cincinnati. The metropolitan areas of Cincinnati and of Hamilton-Middletown, Ohio, form the Cincinnati-Hamilton Consolidated Metropolitan Area.

The people

About 97 per cent of Cincinnati's people were born in the United States. Blacks make up about 38 per cent of the city's population. Most blacks live north and east of downtown. But since about 1980, increasing numbers have moved to areas throughout the city and the sub-

Facts in brief

Population: *City*—364,040. *Metropolitan area*—1,526,092. *Consolidated metropolitan area*—1,817,571 (1,456,769 in Ohio, 316,652 in Kentucky, and 44,150 in Indiana).

Area: 79 sq. mi. (205 km²). *Metropolitan area*—3,342 sq. mi. (8,656 km²). *Consolidated metropolitan area*—3,810 sq. mi. (9,868 km²), excluding inland water.

Altitude: 550 ft. (168 m) above sea level.

Climate: *Average temperature*—January, 36 °F (2 °C); July, 79 °F (26 °C). *Average annual precipitation* (rainfall, melted snow, and other forms of moisture)—39 inches (99 centimeters). For the monthly weather in Cincinnati, see **Ohio** (Climate).

Government: Council-manager. *Terms*—2 years for the nine council members; manager appointed.

Founded: 1788. Incorporated as a city in 1819.

urbs. About 15 per cent of the people have German ancestry. Other major groups include people of English, Irish, and Italian descent. In Cincinnati, as in other cities, poverty is a problem—especially among blacks.

Economy

Industry and commerce. The Cincinnati metropolitan area has about 2,000 manufacturing companies. They employ over 165,000 workers and produce about $7\frac{1}{2}$ billion worth of goods yearly. The city ranks as the world's leading manufacturer of soap and playing cards and the nation's chief producer of machine tools. Other major Cincinnati industries produce automobiles and automobile parts, chemicals, clothing, cosmetics, jet engines, leather goods, and pianos. About a third of the area's workers are employed in manufacturing. About a fourth are employed in wholesale and retail trade, and most of the rest work in other service industries.

Cincinnati's port handles about 16 million short tons (14 million metric tons) of cargo yearly. Much of the cargo is *bituminous* (soft) coal.

Transportation. Cincinnati links Ohio and the other north-central states with the South. Railroad passenger trains and rail freight lines serve the city. Several major highways, including three interstate routes, pass through Cincinnati.

Many commercial airlines use the Greater Cincinnati International Airport, which lies 10 miles (16 kilometers) outside the city in Boone County, Kentucky. The city-owned Lunken Airport, at the city's southeastern edge, handles about 200,000 take-offs and landings a year. The steamboats *Delta Queen* and *Mississippi Queen* provide service between Cincinnati and other Ohio and Mississippi river ports.

Communication. Cincinnati has two daily newspapers, the *Enquirer* and the *Post.* More than 30 suburban

newspapers also serve the Cincinnati metropolitan area. The city has 6 television stations and 30 radio stations.

Education

The Cincinnati public school system includes about 100 elementary and high schools with a total of approximately 52,000 students. Blacks make up about 52 per cent of the enrollment. About 75,000 students attend private and parochial schools in the area.

The University of Cincinnati was founded in 1819. Other schools in the area include the College of Mount St. Joseph, a liberal arts college; the Hebrew Union College—Jewish Institute of Religion, the oldest Jewish theological school in the United States; and Xavier University, a Roman Catholic institution.

The Public Library of Cincinnati and Hamilton County has about 40 branches. It circulates about $6\frac{1}{2}$ million books, films, and other materials annually.

Cultural life

The arts. The Cincinnati Symphony Orchestra, the Cincinnati Summer Opera, and the Cincinnati Ballet Company perform in the Cincinnati Music Hall. The annual Cincinnati May Music Festival is also held in the hall. A local theater company presents stage dramas at the Playhouse in the Park, which is located in Eden Park.

Museums. The Cincinnati Art Museum, in Eden Park, has more than 100 galleries of famous art works, including American Indian and ancient Egyptian collections. The Taft Museum features English, Flemish, and French paintings. The Cincinnati Museum of Natural History has a full-scale model of an underground cave.

Recreation

The Ohio River provides a setting for many recreational areas in the Cincinnati area. During the summer,

WORLD BOOK map

City of Cincinnati

Cincinnati is a leading Midwest commercial center. The map shows the city, located on the Ohio River, and its main points of interest.

	City of Cincinnati
	Area outside Cincinnati
- - -	State boundary
— —	County boundary
≡≡≡	Expressway
——	Other street
+++	Railroad
▪	Point of interest

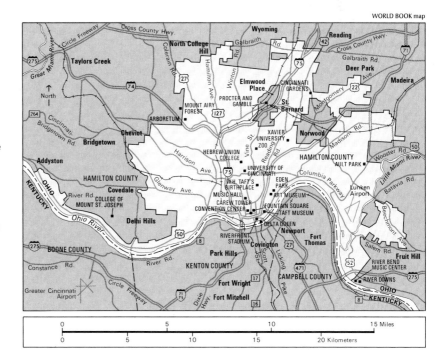

excursion boats operate on the river. Many people also enjoy the several artificially created lakes near the city.

Parks and playgrounds in the area cover about 5,000 acres (2,000 hectares). Mount Airy Forest, the largest park, has about 1,500 acres (607 hectares) of camping grounds, picnic areas, and woods. Eden Park includes the Krohn Conservatory, which is famous for its tropical and seasonal plant displays. Ault Park offers open-air dancing. The Cincinnati Zoo owns one of the nation's largest collections of animals. The Cincinnati Nature Center, located near the city, has more than 500 acres (200 hectares) of rare flowers and plants. The center sponsors nature study programs in summer.

Sports. The Cincinnati Reds, the nation's first professional baseball team, meet their National League opponents in Riverfront Stadium. The Cincinnati Bengals of the National Football League also play in the stadium.

Government

Cincinnati has a council-manager form of government. The nine-member City Council selects the city manager, who is the chief administrative officer. The council also chooses a mayor from among its members. Council members are elected to two-year terms. The city gets most of its revenue from a payroll tax.

In 1971, the council elected two men to split the two-year term for mayor. One of the men, Theodore M. Berry, was the first black mayor of Cincinnati. In 1979, Sylvester Murray became the first black city manager.

History

Early days. The powerful Miami Indians once hunted in what is now the Cincinnati area. In 1788, settlers arrived there and founded a village called Losantiville. In 1790, General Arthur St. Clair, governor of the Northwest Territory, renamed the settlement Cincinnati.

Many settlers came to the village during the late 1700's. They opened new businesses or set up farms in the surrounding area. Cincinnati was incorporated as a town in 1802. By 1810, it had more than 2,500 people.

The 1800's. Much of the town's growth during the early 1800's resulted from river trade. Steamboat service, which began on the Ohio River in 1811, permitted goods to be transported quickly and inexpensively. Cincinnati soon became an important river port and, in 1819, received a city charter. In 1827, workers completed the first section of the Miami and Erie Canal. This canal, which connects Cincinnati with northern Ohio communities, greatly increased local trade. By 1830, the city's population had risen to nearly 25,000.

During the 1830's and 1840's, thousands of Germans left their country and settled in Cincinnati. They included people who were seeking economic improvements and people escaping political persecution. A large German-speaking community, known as the *Over-the-Rhine* area, grew up north of the business district. Germans contributed greatly to the cultural and economic development of the city. In the 1840's, many Irish immigrants came to Cincinnati after fleeing a potato famine in their homeland.

A number of slaughterhouses and pork-packing plants opened in Cincinnati during the 1830's and 1840's. Farmers sent their livestock, especially hogs, to be processed in the city. The meat was then shipped down the Ohio River to other ports. By 1850, Cincinnati had become the nation's chief pork-packing center.

During the mid-1800's, Cincinnati became an important point on the underground railroad, which helped runaway slaves escape to the North. Harriet Beecher Stowe gathered much material in Cincinnati for her famous antislavery novel, *Uncle Tom's Cabin.* Trade between Cincinnati and the South ended during the Civil War (1861-1865). But several merchants made up their losses by establishing arms and ammunition factories and selling their products to the government.

After the Civil War, trade expanded from Cincinnati into the Southwest, and the city's river traffic increased. The Art Museum, Fountain Square, and the Music Hall were built. Cincinnati also annexed more than 20 neighboring communities during the 1860's. By 1870, the population of the city had reached about 216,000.

Cincinnati's position as an important commercial center declined during the 1870's. River trade dropped because railroads were carrying more and more freight to Chicago and other cities. Cincinnati revived its Southern markets in 1880, when the Cincinnati Southern Railway, built by the city, reached Chattanooga.

During the late 1800's, manufacturing became one of the city's main sources of income. With the growth of Procter & Gamble and other soap companies, Cincinnati's population rose to more than 325,000 by 1900.

The 1900's. During the early 1900's, many wealthy Cincinnati residents moved from the basin area to the surrounding hillsides. The riverfront became the site of factories, railroads, and shipping facilities, and the houses near the river turned into slum dwellings.

World War II (1939-1945) brought defense industries to the area. Great numbers of rural people moved to the city to take factory jobs. Most of these workers remained after the war, and the government built many low-rent apartment projects to house them. The government also rebuilt parts of the riverfront district.

Recent developments. Traffic jams on the city's expressways became a serious problem during the late 1960's. In 1971, the U.S. Department of Transportation granted the city federal funds to start an express bus service between the suburbs and downtown Cincinnati.

During the 1950's and 1960's, more and more middle-class Cincinnatians moved from old residential neighborhoods to newer areas on the hillsides. But in the late 1960's, private developers began to build new housing in the basin area and to repair old housing. This construction helped slow the moving trend. Other improvements in the central business district included elevated walkways, high-rise office buildings, and parking garages. Construction projects continued through the 1970's and into the 1980's.   James P. Delaney

Cincinnati, Society of the, is an organization of men descended from commissioned officers who served in the Continental Army or Navy during the Revolutionary War in America (1775-1783). Continental Army officers founded it in 1783. George Washington was its first president-general. The name *Cincinnati* comes from Lucius Quinctius Cincinnatus, a Roman statesman and general who was a legendary model of patriotism. General Arthur St. Clair, a member and the first governor of the Northwest Territory, named the city of Cincinnati, Ohio, for the society.

Today, the Society of the Cincinnati has about 3,500 members in the United States and France. Headquarters are at 2118 Massachusetts Avenue NW, Washington, DC 20008. The society operates a museum and reference library relating to the Revolutionary War at the headquarters.   Critically reviewed by the Society of the Cincinnati

Cincinnatus, *SIHN suh NAY tuhs,* **Lucius Quinctius,** *LOO shuhs KWIHNGK tee uhs* (519?-439? B.C.), a Roman statesman and general, was a legendary model of patriotism. In 458 B.C., Rome was threatened by the Aequi, a tribe of central Italy. The Senate sent messengers to tell Cincinnatus that he had been named commander in chief. The messengers found him plowing his fields. He joined the army at once, and marched to rescue a *consul* (chief government official) who was in great danger. Cincinnatus defeated the enemy, marched his army back to Rome, and resigned. He returned to his farm 16 days after he took office.

George Washington was sometimes called the "American Cincinnatus" because he also held his office only as long as necessary. After the Revolutionary War in America (1775-1783), a group of former officers formed the patriotic Society of the Cincinnati. The city of Cincinnati, Ohio, is named after this organization.

Arther Ferrill

Cinema. See Motion picture.

Cineraria, *SIHN uh RAIR ee uh,* is a group of herbs that belong to the composite family. They grow wild in the Canary Islands, but are cultivated in gardens throughout the world. The flower heads are usually purple, red, or purple and white, with dark centers. Cinerarias are easily grown from seed. They make fine window plants, but must be grown at a temperature less than 65 °F (18 °C).

Scientific classification. Cinerarias belong to the genus *Senecio* in the composite family, Asteraceae or Compositae.

David J. Keil

WORLD BOOK illustration by Robert Hynes

Cineraria blossoms

Cinnabar is a bright red mineral consisting of mercury and sulfur. It provides most of the world's supply of mercury. The chemical formula for cinnabar is HgS. Cinnabar crystals are six-sided, either hexagonal or rhombohedral (see **Crystal** [Classifying crystals]). Cinnabar rarely appears as large crystals. However, mines in the Hunan Province of China have produced large, gemlike crystals since the early 1980's. Cinnabar usually occurs in earthy masses or scattered in opal. It is found mostly near the earth's surface, close to volcanic rocks and hot springs. In addition to China, deposits occur in Italy, Slovenia, and Spain, and in California, Nevada, and Oregon. See also **Mercury** (element).

Robert B. Cook

Cinnamon is a popular spice used in cooking and for flavoring candies and preserves. It comes from the inner bark of the cinnamon tree. The tree grows in Sri Lanka, the principal source of the spice, and in Brazil, India, Jamaica, Java, Madagascar, and Martinique. The cinnamon tree grows as high as 30 feet (9 meters) and has oval leaves and tiny yellow flowers. The fruit of the cinnamon tree looks like an acorn.

WORLD BOOK photo

Cinnamon is sold in both powdered and stick form.

Workers cut off the tops of cinnamon trees near the lower buds so that strong, straight shoots grow up from the base. The shoots are gathered, and the inner bark is peeled off. The bark then turns brown and curls up as it dries. The dried bark is sold as stick cinnamon or is ground up to make powdered cinnamon. Oil of cinnamon is made from the fruit, leaves, and roots of the tree.

An oil similar to that of the cinnamon tree comes from a related plant, commonly called cassia. Cassia oil and bark are often used instead of cinnamon.

Scientific classification. The cinnamon tree belongs to the laurel family, Lauraceae. Its scientific name is *Cinnamomum zeylanicum.* The cassia plant is *C. cassia.*   Lyle E. Craker

Cinquefoil, *SIHNGK foyl,* is the name of about 500 species of plants that belong to the rose family. Cinquefoils grow wild in most cool and cold regions of the world. Most species are herbs. A few species are erect or creeping shrubs. The leaves of cinquefoils consist of

WORLD BOOK illustration by Robert Hynes

The cinquefoil grows in most cold regions.

three, five, or more leaflets in a fingerlike or featherlike arrangement. Some species are called *five-finger* because of the shape of their leaves. The blossoms are bright yellow, orange, white, or reddish in color. Some cinquefoils are troublesome weeds. Other types are grown in gardens. See also **Flower** (picture: Flowers of the Arctic tundra).

Scientific classification. Cinquefoils belong to the rose family, Rosaceae. They make up the genus *Potentilla.*

Kenneth R. Robertson

CIO. See Congress of Industrial Organizations.
Cipher. See Codes and ciphers.
Circadian rhythm. See Biological clock.
Circe, *SUR see,* a beautiful enchantress in Greek mythology, had the power to turn men into beasts. She lived on an island in the Mediterranean Sea. When Odysseus (Ulysses in Latin) landed on her island, Circe turned most of his men into pigs and drove them into a pigsty. But the god Hermes had given Odysseus a magic herb which protected him from Circe's power (see

Hermes; Ulysses). Odysseus forced Circe to give his men their human form again.

After that, Circe became friendly. She loved Odysseus and persuaded him to stay with her on the island for a year. When he prepared to leave, she warned him about the dangers that awaited him, and told him how to overcome them. For example, Circe told Odysseus that by plugging his sailors' ears with wax he could safely pass the island where the Sirens lived (see **Siren**).

Cynthia W. Shelmerdine

See also **Odyssey; Scylla**.

Circle is a closed curve on a plane. All points of the curve are the same distance from a point that lies within the curve. This point is called the *center*. There are 360 degrees in a circle.

Many common objects have a circular shape, including rings, hoops, and wheels. You can easily draw a circle with an instrument called a *compass*. A compass looks like a pair of scissors with a pencil where one point should be. To draw a circle, place one point of the compass at the point chosen as the center, and rotate the pencil around it.

Parts of a circle. Sometimes people use the words *disc* or *circle* to mean the area inside the curve. They call the curve itself the *circumference*. The length of the curve is also called the circumference. An *arc* is any connected part of the circumference.

A *chord* is a straight line between two points on the circumference of a circle. If a chord goes through the center, it forms a *diameter*. A diameter is the longest chord of a circle, and divides the circle into two equal parts called *semicircles*.

The *radius* is the distance from the center to the circumference. It equals half the length of a diameter. The word *radius* is also used to mean any line that joins the center to the circumference.

A *secant* is a straight line that intersects a circle at two points. A line that just touches the circle, or meets the circle at just one point, is called a *tangent*. If you move a secant away from the center of the circle so that it always lies parallel to its previous position, the two points at which it touches the circle will get closer to each other. When the points come together, the secant has reached the position of a tangent. The point where the tangent touches the circle is the *point of tangency*. The radius at the point of tangency makes a right angle with the tangent.

The use of pi. The Greek letter *pi* (written π) stands for the number by which the diameter of a circle (d) must be multiplied to obtain the circumference (c). That is, $c = \pi d$ or $2\pi r$, where r is the radius. The area of a circle (A) is given by the formula $A = \pi r^2$.

You cannot write π exactly as a decimal. But by increasing the number of digits, you can get a number as near to it as you want. Common estimates used for π include $\frac{22}{7}$, 3.14, 3.1416, and 3.14159.

History. The ancient Chinese used 3 as the value of π. About 1650 B.C., the Egyptians improved on the approximation. The astronomer Ptolemy of Alexandria calculated a value for π that was the equivalent of 3.1416. After decimals came into use in the 1600's, an exact value for π, with either repeating or a limited number of decimal places, was sought. Mathematicians now know that this is impossible.   Colin C. Graham

See also **Degree; Pi; Radian**.

Circuit, Electric. See Electric circuit.

Circuit, Electronic. See Electronics (Devices and circuits).

Circuit breaker is an automatic switch. It protects electric motors, household wiring, long-distance power lines, and other electric circuits against damage caused by too much electric current. Too much current may flow in a circuit as a result either of a fault in the circuit or of an outside event, such as lightning.

Every circuit breaker is designed to allow a specific maximum amount of electric current to pass. If the current exceeds this limit, an automatic mechanism inside the circuit breaker throws open a *set of contacts* (switch) and stops the current. Mechanisms used to open the switch include electromagnets and temperature-sensitive devices similar to a thermostat.

As the switch opens, an electric arc leaps across the open contacts. Electricity continues to flow through this arc until it is extinguished. In an *oil circuit breaker,* the switch is immersed in an oil that extinguishes the electric arc. In an *air-blast circuit breaker,* a blast of compressed air blows out the arc. In a *magnetic arc-suppression circuit breaker,* a magnetic field deflects and breaks the arc.

A circuit breaker called a *ground fault circuit interrupter* (GFCI) helps prevent electric shocks. Most electric shocks occur when people use faulty appliances. Such appliances can produce slight variations in the electric current entering and leaving the circuit. A GFCI detects these changes, which are too small to activate an ordinary circuit breaker. It then automatically shuts off the electricity to the defective appliance.

Some circuit breakers are about as small as an ordinary light switch. But some are as large as a small two-story house. A large circuit breaker can interrupt currents up to 40,000 amperes at 345,000 volts. It can open a circuit in less than $\frac{1}{30}$ of a second, and reclose it in less than $\frac{1}{3}$ of a second.   Donald W. Novotny

See also **Saint Lawrence Seaway** (picture: Huge circuit breakers).

Circuit rider was an important figure in pioneer times in America. There were two kinds of circuit riders. One was a religious man who rode a *circuit* (regular route) conducting services. The other was a judge who rode a circuit hearing cases. Either kind of circuit might cover great distances.

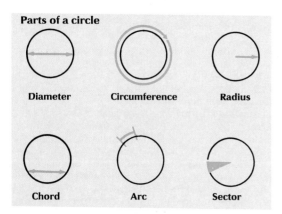

Parts of a circle

Diameter   Circumference   Radius

Chord   Arc   Sector

Preachers, often called *backwoods preachers,* began riding circuits in what is now the United States during the 1760's. John Wesley, founder of the Methodist movement in Great Britain, sent several *lay preachers* (people not ordained as ministers) to preach the gospel in America. Famous early circuit riders included Francis Asbury, one of the first Methodist bishops in the United States, and Peter Cartwright, a pioneer preacher in Kentucky and Illinois.

Judges began riding circuits in 1790. Congress divided the 13 states into three circuits, with two Supreme Court justices appointed to hear cases in each circuit. This system was changed when more states joined the Union and the Supreme Court had more work to do. Many state judges also rode circuits. Lawyers usually traveled with the judges and would argue cases brought to the court. Abraham Lincoln spent several years riding circuits as a lawyer in Illinois.   Odie B. Faulk

Related articles in *World Book* include:

Asbury, Francis
Lincoln, Abraham (Riding the circuit)
Pioneer life in America (Religion)
Western frontier life (Religion)

Circulation. See Circulatory system.

Circulatory system is a network that carries blood throughout the body. All animals except the simplest kinds have some type of circulatory system.

In some *invertebrates* (animals without a backbone), the circulatory system consists of a simple network of tubes and hollow spaces. Other invertebrates have pumplike structures that send blood through a system of blood vessels. In human beings and other *vertebrates* (animals with a backbone), the circulatory system consists primarily of a pumping organ—the heart—and a network of blood vessels.

The human circulatory system supplies the cells of the body with the food and oxygen they need to survive. At the same time, it carries carbon dioxide and other wastes away from the cells. The circulatory system also helps regulate the temperature of the body and carries substances that protect the body from disease. In addition, the system transports chemical substances called *hormones,* which help regulate the activities of various parts of the body. This article discusses mainly the human circulatory system.

Parts of the circulatory system

The human circulatory system has three main parts: (1) the heart, (2) the blood vessels, and (3) the blood. A watery fluid called *lymph,* and the vessels that carry it, are sometimes considered a part of the circulatory system (see **Lymphatic system**).

The heart is a hollow, muscular organ that pumps blood. It consists of two pumps that lie side by side. These pumps relax when taking in blood and contract as they send out blood. The left side of the heart is a stronger pump than the right side. The stronger pump receives blood from the lungs and sends it to cells throughout the body. The weaker pump receives blood from the cells throughout the body and sends the blood to the lungs.

The blood vessels form a complicated system of connecting tubes throughout the body. There are three major types of these vessels. *Arteries* carry blood from the heart. *Veins* return blood to the heart. *Capillaries* are extremely tiny vessels that connect the arteries and the veins.

The blood consists chiefly of a liquid called *plasma* and three kinds of solid particles known as *formed elements.* Plasma is made up mostly of water, but it also contains proteins, minerals, and other substances. The three types of formed elements are called *red blood cells, white blood cells,* and *platelets.* Red blood cells carry oxygen and carbon dioxide throughout the body. White blood cells help protect the body from disease. Platelets release substances that enable blood to clot. Platelets thus aid in preventing the loss of blood from injured vessels.

Functions of the circulatory system

The circulatory system performs many vital functions. It plays an important role in respiration. The circulatory system is also important in nutrition, in the removal of wastes and poisons, and in several other body processes.

In respiration. The circulatory system plays a part in respiration by delivering oxygen to the cells and removing carbon dioxide from them. During this process, the blood follows two routes called the *systemic circulation* and the *pulmonary circulation.*

From the left side of the heart, blood full of oxygen is

The human circulatory system

A person's circulatory system consists chiefly of a pump—the heart—and a network of blood vessels. These vessels—arteries, veins, and capillaries—carry blood throughout the body.

WORLD BOOK illustration by Colin Bidgood

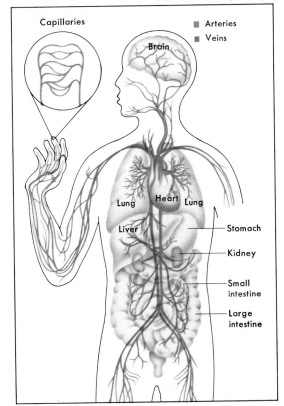

Capillaries   ■ Arteries   ■ Veins

Brain

Lung   Heart   Lung

Liver

Stomach

Kidney

Small intestine

Large intestine

Some functions of the circulatory system

WORLD BOOK illustrations by Colin Bidgood

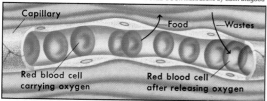

Capillary — Food — Wastes

Red blood cell carrying oxygen — Red blood cell after releasing oxygen

In maintaining body tissues. The circulatory system supplies tissues of the body with essential food and oxygen, and carries away carbon dioxide and other wastes. Substances leave and enter the bloodstream through thin capillary walls.

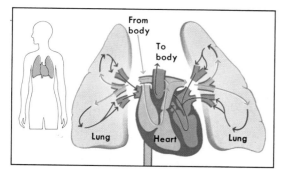

From body — To body — Lung — Heart — Lung

In respiration. Blood carrying carbon dioxide, *blue,* flows to the heart. The heart pumps it to the lungs, where it gives up carbon dioxide and picks up oxygen. The oxygen-rich blood, *red,* returns to the heart and is pumped to all parts of the body.

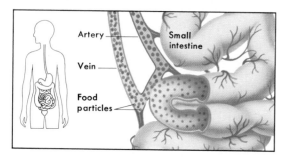

Artery — Small intestine — Vein — Food particles

In nutrition. The circulatory system carries digested food particles to the cells of the body. These particles enter the bloodstream through the walls of the small intestine.

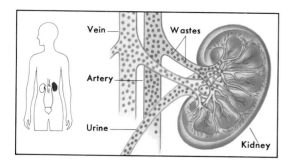

Vein — Wastes — Artery — Urine — Kidney

In removal of wastes. Waste products from body tissues are carried by the blood to the kidneys. The kidneys filter out these substances and expel them in the urine.

pumped into the systemic circulation. This blood leaves the heart through the *aorta,* the main artery of the body. A number of major arteries branch off the aorta. These arteries, in turn, branch into smaller and smaller vessels, finally emptying into the tiny capillaries. There, oxygen leaves the blood and enters the tissues through the thin capillary walls. In a similar way, carbon dioxide leaves the tissues and enters the blood. The blood, now carrying carbon dioxide, leaves the capillaries and flows through larger and larger veins. Eventually, the blood enters the right side of the heart through two large veins—the *superior vena cava,* which carries blood from the head and arms, and the *inferior vena cava,* which carries blood from the trunk and legs.

From the right side of the heart, the blood is pumped into the pulmonary circulation. *Pulmonary arteries* carry the blood that contains carbon dioxide to capillaries in the lungs. The carbon dioxide passes through the capillary walls into the lungs and is then exhaled. Oxygen that has been inhaled passes from the lungs into the blood in a similar way. The blood returns through the *pulmonary veins* to the left side of the heart and begins its journey again.

In nutrition. The circulatory system carries digested food substances to the cells of the body. These nutrients enter the bloodstream by passing through the walls of the small intestine into the capillaries. The blood then carries most of the nutrients to the liver.

The liver removes certain nutrients from the blood and stores them. It later releases the nutrients into the blood when the body needs them. The liver also changes some nutrients into substances needed by the body. Blood leaving the liver contains nutrients that the cells use in the production of energy, enzymes, and new building materials for the body.

In removal of wastes and poisons. The circulatory system helps dispose of waste products and poisons that would harm the body if they accumulated. These substances include carbon dioxide, salts, and *ammonia,* a by-product of the cell's use of protein.

The liver removes ammonia and other wastes, and various poisons that enter the body through the digestive system. The liver converts the wastes and poisons into water-soluble substances, which are carried by the blood to the kidneys. The kidneys filter out these and other water-soluble wastes and expel them from the body in urine.

Other functions. The circulatory system helps protect the body from disease. White blood cells engulf and destroy bacteria, viruses, and other harmful invaders. As the blood circulates, it also helps keep the body temperature stable by absorbing heat from the cells' production of energy.

If the temperature of the body begins to rise, the flow of blood into vessels in the skin increases. The heat from cells deep in the body is thus carried to the skin, from where it passes out of the body. If the temperature of the body begins to drop, the flow of blood to the skin is restricted. This action enables the body to retain as much heat as possible.

The circulatory system also carries hormones. These chemical substances affect or control the activities of various organs and tissues. Hormones are produced by the endocrine glands, including the thyroid, pituitary, adrenal, and sex glands. These glands release their hormones into the bloodstream.

Disorders of the circulatory system

The circulatory system can be damaged by disease or injury. One of the most common diseases of the system is *arteriosclerosis,* which results from the accumulation of fatty deposits in the arteries. Such deposits stiffen and thicken the walls of the arteries. As a result, the flow of blood is restricted. In some cases, blood clots develop in vessels affected by arteriosclerosis. Such clots may lead to a heart attack or a *stroke,* a condition in which the brain does not receive enough blood.

Another disease, *hypertension,* commonly called *high blood pressure,* is often associated with arteriosclerosis. Hypertension makes the heart work harder and may lead to such complications as a heart attack, a stroke, or kidney failure.

Treatment for arteriosclerosis and hypertension includes rest, exercise, and changes in the diet. Physicians may prescribe various drugs to lower the blood pressure, strengthen the heart, or prevent infection and blood clots. In extreme cases, a surgeon may remove clots or replace one or more diseased blood vessels.

Other disorders result from damage or defects in the heart or blood vessels. For example, bacteria may harm or destroy the valves that control the flow of blood through the heart. Incomplete development of the heart or its blood vessels before birth may produce defects called *congenital heart disorders.* Many cases of damage or defects can be corrected by surgery.

The circulatory system in other animals

Vertebrates all have a *closed* circulatory system. In this type of system, the blood flows only in the vessels and remains separate from the fluid in the body tissues. Mammals—including human beings—and birds have a heart with two separate pumps. In these animals, the blood in the systemic and pulmonary circulations almost always remains separate. In amphibians and most reptiles, the pumps of the heart are only partly separated, and the systemic and pulmonary blood mixes together somewhat. In fish, the heart has only one pump. The pump collects the blood and sends it to the gills and then to the rest of the body.

Invertebrates have circulatory systems that range from complex to simple. Some invertebrates, such as earthworms and octopuses, have a closed circulatory system. Other invertebrates have an *open* circulatory system, in which the blood is only partially confined to the vessels. It fills the hollow spaces of the body as well. Animals with an open circulatory system include insects, spiders, and most shellfish.

In many invertebrates, the blood is pumped by contracting vessels or by *pumping centers* (contracting portions of vessels), or by both. Among insects, for example, the "heart" consists of an internal contracting vessel that extends almost the length of the back.

The simplest animals with a true circulatory system include certain kinds of worms. Earthworms, leeches, and a variety of sea worms have contracting vessels that pump the blood. A group of simpler worms, called *ribbon worms* or *proboscis worms,* have a circulatory system with no pumping centers and no contracting vessels. The movements of the animal keep the blood flowing through the body.   Francis L. Abel

See also **Blood; Heart; Lung; Lymphatic system;** and their *Related articles.* For a *Reading and Study Guide,* see *Circulatory system* in the Research Guide/Index, Volume 22.

Circumcision is the surgical removal of the skin that covers the tip of the penis. An uncircumcised penis has a loose fold of skin called the *foreskin* or *prepuce* that covers the *glans* (tip of the penis). A surgeon removes the foreskin by cutting around the penis where the foreskin is attached. The word *circumcise* means *cut around.*

In the United States, most circumcisions are performed within a few days of birth. The circumciser gets the parents' permission before performing this minor surgery. When circumcision is performed on newborn boys, an *anesthetic* (painkilling drug) generally is not used. Older boys and adult males may receive an anesthetic for the operation. In a less frequently used circumcision method called *electrocautery,* an electrically heated needle is used to cut the foreskin or to stop bleeding that occurs. But electrocautery has caused serious injury to some patients, and many doctors object to its use.

At one time, most United States physicians recommended routine circumcision of newborn males. They felt the operation made the glans easier to clean and thus helped prevent infections of the penis. They also believed circumcision reduced the risk of developing cancer of the penis. Research shows uncircumcised males are more prone to infections of the *urinary tract,* the organs and tubes that produce and eliminate urine. But many physicians argue that proper hygiene can be just as effective in preventing such infections and that routine circumcision is not medically necessary.

Today, circumcision is performed largely for cultural or religious reasons. Many parents choose to have their sons circumcised because the father is circumcised, or because the operation is common where they live. Many parents feel it would be undesirable for the child if his penis did not look like that of other males.

For thousands of years, various religious rituals have included circumcision. The ancient Jews, Egyptians, and other Middle Eastern peoples performed it when a boy was maturing into a young man. Circumcision was a sign that the youth should be ready to assume his religious duties in the adult community.

The Old Testament of the Bible includes many references to circumcision as a sign of initiation and membership into the Jewish community. Circumcision became an important rite of Judaism. A traditional Jewish circumcision takes place on the eighth day after birth.

Muslims also regard circumcision as part of their religion. Some Muslims celebrate circumcisions with feasts and parades. Muslim boys are circumcised sometime between infancy and about 14 years of age.

A procedure called *female circumcision* is practiced by many ethnic groups, particularly in Africa and the Middle East. This procedure involves the partial or complete removal of the *clitoris,* a sensitive part of the female genitals, or the *labia,* the folds of tissue covering the clitoris. The operation is done for cultural reasons.

Martin Weisberg

Circumference. See Circle.

Ringling Bros. and Barnum & Bailey (WORLD BOOK photo)

A colorful circus parade called the *spectacle* begins the show. Animals and circus performers march around the arena while the circus band, shown at the far end, plays lively music.

Circus is a variety show that features daring and graceful acts by trapeze artists, acrobats, horseback riders, animal trainers, and other performers. Trained animals play an important part in most circuses. Clowns in funny clothes provide comedy for the show while the circus band and performers in bright costumes add to the color and excitement.

The word *circus* comes from a Latin word for *circle* or *oval.* For thousands of years, circus-type entertainments have been put on in circular structures. Today, circuses are held in tents and arenas.

At the circus

For many years, circus shows were held in large canvas tents. The main circus acts appeared in the *big top,* the largest tent. The Ringling Brothers and Barnum & Bailey Circus had a big top 500 feet (150 meters) long and 200 feet (61 meters) wide. In 1956, the Ringling circus gave up its tent and began to perform indoors. But many smaller circuses still perform in tents.

The circus performance may include a parade called a *spectacle.* As the band plays a lively tune, circus performers and animals march around the arena. The elephants wear bright velvet or satin ornaments. Each elephant may have a pretty girl perched on its head, or riding in a large saddle called a *howdah.* Beautiful horses with shiny coats prance by proudly. Sometimes dozens of dancers in colorful costumes take part.

As the circus performers pass in review, the clowns make the audience laugh with their funny tricks. A dozen of them may pile out of a tiny car. Others may set a toy house on fire, then put out the flames with water from a miniature fire truck.

Most circus acts take place in round areas called *rings.* A small circus may have only one or two rings. Large circuses have three rings where three acts go on at the same time.

In one act, elephants stand on their hind legs and dance. In another, trained seals balance big rubber balls on their noses. Trained horses *canter,* or gallop gently, in a circle while riders jump from horse to horse. A family of riders stand on each other's shoulders on the backs of horses cantering side by side around the ring. A lion trainer enters a cage and cracks a whip. The big cats leap onto platforms upon command.

Some performers hang by their teeth from a rope and twirl around. Others, called *flyers,* leap through the air from one trapeze to another. They perform daring somersaults in the air before being caught by other members of the act. Other acts feature performers on the high wire, riding bicycles or doing acrobatics.

The circus band plays throughout the show. The band helps keep the acts running on time. By playing faster or slower, or by changing tunes, it signals the performers when to finish the various parts of their acts. The music keeps up the feeling of excitement and pride in the performance that is as old as the circus itself.

Many people visit the menagerie to see the circus animals up close. Fierce lions and tigers pace back and forth in cages. Elephants stick out their trunks for peanuts. Monkeys jump and climb around their cages, chattering at the crowds.

Life in the circus

On tour. Most circuses travel by truck, giving performances in a different city or town every day. The Ringling Brothers and Barnum & Bailey Circus is the only one that continues to travel by railroad. This circus may perform in a city for several days or weeks.

The Ringling Brothers and Barnum & Bailey Circus actually consists of two separate and complete shows, called the Red and the Blue Units. Each unit travels on its own railroad train, covering about 25,000 miles (40,000 kilometers) a year and performing in about 45 cities throughout the United States and Canada. The performers and workers travel and live in railroad coach cars. The animals ride in stock cars, and special cars carry the wagons of equipment.

On the shows that travel by truck, most performers and workers live in trailers. Most performers prepare their own meals. The circus provides meals for the workers. A circus may also have its own blacksmith, barber, post office, and doctor and first-aid unit.

Before the circus comes to town, publicity people put up brightly colored posters advertising the show. As soon as the circus arrives, workers called *roustabouts* begin to unload the equipment and set it up. If the circus uses tents, machines help unload great sections of canvas and drive the tent stakes into the ground. The roustabouts have plenty of work even if the show is given in a building. After the last performance on the final day, the roustabouts quickly take everything down so it can be moved on to the next city.

Circus people work together like members of a huge family. Sometimes even the stars of the show perform in acts besides their own, or help with the everyday circus chores. For example, a trapeze artist may ride an elephant in the elephant act. A clown may spend some time every day brushing the circus horses.

Circus stars often teach their acts to their children. When the children grow up, they carry on the traditional family acts. Sometimes aunts, uncles, cousins, and other relatives become members of a family act.

Winter quarters. Most truck circuses travel about 7 months, while the railroad circuses stay on tour about $10\frac{1}{2}$ months before heading for their winter quarters. But the busy life of the circus people does not slow down for long. Soon they are hard at work preparing for

Susan Ylvisaker, Jeroboam, Inc.

Clowns in funny costumes and comic makeup entertain the audience with their playful antics and humorous stunts. The clowns often perform between acts.

© Michael Philip Manheim

Daring aerialists perform acrobatic feats high above the ground. One member of this team hangs from a trapeze, ready to catch his partner.

Wild animal acts provide great excitement for audiences. These tigers do tricks on command from their trainer. To protect the spectators, the tigers perform inside a wire cage.

Robert H. Glaze, Artstreet

Gerald L. French

Performing elephants are among the most popular attractions at many circuses. Trainers work for months teaching the huge animals difficult tricks.

the next season. Wild animal trainers begin to train new jungle beasts. The flyers, acrobats, and other circus stars practice every day. The clowns plan new stunts. Other circus workers design and sew costumes, purchase and mend equipment, and take care of the circus animals.

The circus winter quarters look like a small city. They have streets and shops, large storehouses, barns for the animals, and a ring where the circus stars practice their acts. Many circus people live nearby in houses and trailers. The Ringling Brothers and Barnum & Bailey Circus has winter quarters at Venice, Fla.

Famous circus performers

Many circus stars have become world famous. Poodles Hanneford and his family combined clowning with skillful bareback riding. Arthur Concello and his wife Antoinette won fame on the flying trapeze. Antoinette Concello became the first woman to perform a triple somersault, the most difficult trapeze stunt. Clyde Beatty

and Mabel Stark became known for their acts with wild jungle animals. Gunther Gebel-Williams also gained fame as an animal trainer. Famous circus clowns have included Felix Adler, Otto Griebling, Lou Jacobs, and Emmett Kelly.

Franz Furstner, known as "Unus," stood on top of a pole on one finger. His daughter, Vicki, became famous for doing one-armed swings while hanging from a rope high in the air. Chrys Holt performed a juggling act while hanging by her hair at the top of the tent.

Some circus acts are dangerous, and the performers risk their lives at each show. Lillian Leitzel became world famous for her breathtaking aerial act. She hung by one wrist from a rope and swung her body around and around. She fell to her death during a performance in 1931 when part of her equipment snapped. The Wallendas, a famous circus family, developed the most spectacular high wire act in history. Seven of them stood on each other's shoulders, then walked along the wire. Four

Bradley Smith

Jugglers perform a tricky balancing act while tossing clubs back and forth. Skilled jugglers use a variety of objects, including delicate dishes and flaming torches.

A high-wire team performs on a cable far above the ground. The men on the bottom use poles to help keep their balance.

At the winter quarters of a circus, the art of applying makeup is demonstrated at a school for clowns.

members of the act were killed and one was paralyzed in falls from the high wire during the 1960's and 1970's.

History

Circus-type acts and performers go back thousands of years. In ancient Rome, games featured chariot races and men standing on the bare backs of two horses racing around a track. During the Middle Ages, various performers and clowns called *jesters* entertained on the streets and in the royal courts of Europe.

The modern circus developed in England. In 1768,

Philip Astley staged a show that featured trick horseback riding and live music. Astley later added other acts, such as acrobats, a clown, and a band to his performances. He presented his show in a circular structure and it became popularly known as "Astley's Circus."

The first Astley-type circus in America was opened by John Bill Ricketts in Philadelphia in 1793. Ricketts' circus featured a rope walker, a clown, and riding acts. Most early circuses had acts similar to the Ricketts' circus.

During the late 1700's and early 1800's, traveling menageries of exotic animals toured parts of the North-

Horseback riders perform dangerous acrobatic stunts while their horses canter around the ring. Such acts require careful teamwork between the horses and the acrobats.

eastern United States. People flocked to see exhibits of animals that were new to North America. The first elephant arrived in the United States in 1796. Menageries traveled by horse and wagon, and were often shown in a barn or canvas-wall enclosure. Circuses adopted many characteristics of these shows. By 1835, many circus acts included wild animal exhibits.

By 1850, circuses already had many of the elements that are associated with them today. These included brass bands, bright costumes, and colorful circus posters. About 1857, a musical instrument called the *steam calliope* was introduced to the circus (see **Calliope** [picture]). Established American circuses before the Civil War (1861-1865) included Dan Rice's Circus, Van Amburgh's Circus, Yankee Robinson's Circus, Spalding & Rogers Circus, and John Robinson's Circus.

For many years, circuses paraded through the streets before a performance. The brightly painted wagons, saddle horses, and elephants made a colorful sight. The circus band played spirited music. But the parades had to be discontinued in most places because city streets became crowded with traffic.

Many circuses once featured a *side show,* which was a smaller, separate show near the big top. The side show offered such exhibits as a snake charmer, a sword swallower, a fire eater, and a tattooed man. Also on display were such curiosities as midgets, giants, a bearded lady, or a fat lady. Circus people called *talkers* told the crowd about the wonders to be seen in the side shows. Side shows were popular in tent circuses. However, they are rarely seen today.

The golden age of the American circus began about 1870. Several large circuses toured the United States. Each circus boasted it was the biggest or the best and tried to outdo the others with new acts and new kinds of animals. In 1872, circuses began traveling in colorful circus trains. Trains remained the chief form of circus transportation until the 1920's, when many circuses switched to trucks.

One of these large circuses was Barnum's circus, started in 1871 by P. T. Barnum and two partners. The next year, the show toured the country on between 60 and 70 railroad cars. In 1881, Barnum joined his show

with James A. Bailey's circus. Beginning in 1888, it operated under the name of Barnum & Bailey's Greatest Show on Earth. In 1882, the five Ringling brothers started a variety show in Baraboo, Wis. In 1884, they joined with Yankee Robinson to open their first circus. The Ringlings bought the Barnum and Bailey show in 1907. They joined the two circuses in 1919 to form the Ringling Brothers and Barnum & Bailey Combined Shows. This circus became the world's largest and most famous. The Ringling family sold it in 1967 to Irvin Feld and his associates. Irvin's son Kenneth Feld continued the family's leadership of the circus.

Several circus museums display historic circus posters, wagons, and equipment. These include the Circus Galleries of the John and Mable Ringling Museum of Art in Sarasota, Fla., and the Circus World Museum in Baraboo, Wis.   Robert L. Parkinson

Related articles in *World Book* include:

Barnum, P. T.	Lion (Training lions)
Buffalo Bill	Ringling brothers
Clown	Rome, Ancient (Recreation)
Hagenbeck, Karl	Stratton, Charles S.
King, Karl	Wisconsin (Places to visit)

Additional resources

Hippisley Coxe, Antony. *A Seat at the Circus.* Rev. ed. Shoe String, 1980. A study of the circus for older readers.
Hubbard, Freeman, and Farley, L. V. *Great Days of the Circus.* Am. Heritage, 1962.
Krementz, Jill. *A Very Young Circus Flyer.* Knopf, 1979.

Circus Maximus. See Hippodrome.

Cirque. See Glacier (How glaciers shape the land).

Cirrhosis, *suh ROH sihs,* is a disease of the liver in which scar tissue forms throughout the organ. Groups of cells called *regenerative nodules,* surrounded by sheets of scar tissue, replace the normal spongy tissue of the liver. The diseased organ may be unable to perform such vital functions as manufacturing proteins and removing harmful substances from the blood. The affected tissue may block the flow of blood, causing high pressure in blood vessels that serve the liver. Internal bleeding may then result. The blockage also may lead to the accumulation of fluids in the abdomen.

Many people with severe cirrhosis become weak and

Circus World Museum, Baraboo, Wis.

Early circuses paraded through a town before the show began. This 1908 scene shows a crowd watching the animals and circus wagons pass by.

A **citadel** is a fortress built to defend a city. Most citadels stand on a hill overlooking the city they protect. The citadel at the left is Dover Castle, which stands on a cliff near Dover, England, facing France across the Strait of Dover.

Edmond Nagele, The Photo Source

disoriented. Severe cases can cause death. But some cases do not even cause noticeable symptoms.

Cirrhosis results from injury to the liver. Excessive use of alcoholic beverages or *hepatitis* (inflammation of the liver) may cause such injury. Inhaling the fumes of certain chemicals, such as carbon tetrachloride, also may cause cirrhosis. After scar tissue forms, the liver cannot regain its sponginess. Some cases of cirrhosis can be controlled by proper diet and by avoiding liquor.

Charles S. Lieber

Cirrus. See Cloud.

Cisneros, *sees NAY rohs,* **Henry Gabriel** (1947-), became the first Hispanic American to serve as United States secretary of housing and urban development. A Democrat, he was appointed to the post in 1993 by President Bill Clinton. Before serving as secretary, Cisneros had become the first Mexican American to win election as mayor of a major U.S. city. He was first elected mayor of the city, San Antonio, in 1981 and won reelection three times. He served as mayor until 1989.

Cisneros was born in San Antonio. He earned bachelor's and master's degrees at Texas A&M University. Cisneros also received graduate degrees from Harvard University and George Washington University. In 1974, he joined the faculty of the Division of Environmental Studies at the University of Texas at San Antonio.

Cisneros was elected to San Antonio's city council in 1975 and was reelected twice. As a council member, he emphasized economic development and cooperation between the city's Hispanic and white residents. Hispanic Americans formed the largest ethnic group in San Antonio. In the 1981 mayoral campaign, Hispanic Ameri-

© Franco Cernero

Henry Cisneros

cans cast most of the votes Cisneros received, but many whites also supported him. As mayor, Cisneros helped strengthen the urban and business communities of downtown San Antonio.　　　Homer D. C. Garcia

Cistercians are monks and nuns who belong to two Roman Catholic religious orders throughout the world. Their daily routine follows a *rule* (set of guidelines) established by Saint Benedict of Nursia. This rule emphasizes prayer, study, and manual labor.

There are two orders of Cistercians—the Common Observance and the Strict Observance. Monks of the Common Observance sometimes teach and provide spiritual guidance in their communities. Nuns lead secluded, prayerful lives. The order of the Common Observance was formerly called the *Sacred Order of Cistercians.* Both monks and nuns in the Strict Observance lead secluded lives. The monks are popularly called *Trappists* and nuns, *Trappistines.* See **Trappists.**

Cistercian orders trace their history to a French monastery founded in 1098 at Cîteaux (Cistercium) by the abbot Saint Robert of Molesme. Orders of Cistercian nuns were founded about 1120.　　　E. Rozanne Elder

Citadel, *SIHT uh duhl,* is a high, walled fortress built to defend a city. A citadel usually stands on a high hill overlooking a city. In early days, its walls surrounded the palace of the ruler.

The citadels of Mycenae and Tiryns in Greece were important ancient fortresses. The citadel known as Acrocorinth, built on a hill more than 1,800 feet (549 meters) high, guarded the Greek city of Corinth. The French citadel of Carcassonne was an important stronghold during the Middle Ages. The best-known citadel in North America stands atop Cape Diamond in Quebec, Canada. The French built it about 1665, and the British rebuilt it from 1823 to 1832.　　　A. J. Busch

See also **Acropolis; Carcassonne; Quebec** (city), the section *The city.*

Citibank is one of the largest banks in the world. It has more than 290 branches in the New York City metropolitan area and about 3,000 offices in 93 countries. The bank's history dates from June 16, 1812, when the New York state legislature granted a charter to the City Bank of New York. The bank entered the national system in 1865. In 1955, the National City Bank merged with the First National Bank of the City of New York to form the First National City Bank of New York. The name of the bank was changed to Citibank in 1976. The bank is a subsidiary of Citicorp, a multinational financial services organization.   Critically reviewed by Citibank

Cities. See City.

Cities of refuge were six cities of ancient Palestine. They were set apart as places of refuge for people who had killed other persons either accidentally or in self-defense. They included Bezer, Ramoth-Gilead, and Golan, on the east side of the Jordan River, and Kedesh, Shechem, and Hebron on the west side of the river (Josh. 20). Persons who fled to one of these cities were protected from avengers until a trial could be held. If found not guilty of willful murder, they were allowed to continue living in the city. If declared guilty, they were returned for punishment to the place from which they had fled. See also **Hebron.**   H. Darrell Lance

Citizen King. See Louis Philippe.

Citizens band radio is a method of short-distance communication used by private citizens. It operates on the *citizens band* (CB), a group of radio frequencies that many nations reserve for private use.

CB radio is most frequently used for conversations between places that are not linked by telephone. Many motorists and truck drivers use it to talk with other highway travelers or people who are in an office or at home.

Most CB sets are devices called *transceivers,* which consist of a transmitter and a receiver. Some CB devices receive radio signals but do not transmit them.

Most CB transmitters broadcast for distances of fewer than 5 miles (8 kilometers) in cities and up to 20 miles (32 kilometers) in rural areas. The broadcast range varies with the atmospheric conditions, the terrain, the design and height of the set's antenna, and the amount of power supplied to the transmitter. Government regulations in the United States and Canada limit the power of a CB transmitter to a maximum of 4 watts. In both countries, CB radio has 40 channels, with frequencies of

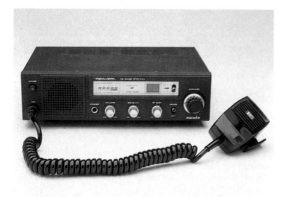

WORLD BOOK photo by Ralph Brunke

Citizens band radio often serves as a communication link between motorists. For example, truckers and other drivers keep one another informed about road conditions and the weather. They also use citizens band radios during emergencies.

26.965 to 27.405 megahertz. The Canadian CB is called *General Radio Service.*

In the United States, there are no licensing requirements for the operation of citizens band radios. But Canada requires a CB transmitter of more than one-tenth watt to be licensed. A Canadian citizen may obtain a General Radio Service license from the nearest district office of the Department of Communications.

Remote controls for such devices as model airplanes and automatic garage-door openers also operate on CB radio frequencies. For more information on remote control, see **Remote control.**   Stanley R. Alten

Additional resources

CB Radio. Comp. by the Howard W. Sams Editorial Staff. Sams, 1977.
Chilton's CB Handbook—40 Channel: Guide to Choosing, Installing & Operating Citizens Band Radio, Cars, Trucks, RV's, Vans, Marine, Base. Rev. ed. Chilton, 1977.
Smelser, Newt. *Beginner's CB and Two-Way Radio Repairing.* Nelson-Hall, 1981.

Citizenship is full membership in a nation or in some other unit of government. Citizenship is also called *nationality.* Almost all people have citizenship in at least one country. Citizens have certain rights, such as the right to vote and the right to hold public office. They also have certain duties, such as the duty to pay taxes and to serve on a jury.

Not all the people in a nation are citizens of that country. For example, many countries have noncitizen nationals. The word *national* is often used as another word for *citizen.* In some cases, however, *national* means *a person who owes loyalty to a country but lacks full membership in it.* Noncitizen nationals of the United States include the people of American Samoa, a group of Pacific islands controlled by the United States. The people of American Samoa have the protection of the U.S. government but lack some of the special rights of citizens.

People who are neither citizens nor noncitizen nationals of a country are *aliens* there. Most aliens are citizens or noncitizen nationals of one country who are traveling or living in another. Many aliens have a permit called a *visa* allowing them to visit or live where they do not hold citizenship. *Illegal aliens* are noncitizens living in a country without proper papers.

The laws or beliefs of a country might deny some rights to certain citizens. Such people are sometimes called *second-class citizens.* Many have a language, race, or religion different from that of the country's largest or most powerful group. For example, the South African government has made blacks second-class citizens. Under South African law, blacks lack the right to vote in national and provincial elections. In 1948, South Africa established a policy of rigid racial segregation called *apartheid.* Under apartheid, blacks and other nonwhites faced official discrimination in education, employment, and other areas. In 1991, the government repealed the last of the laws that had formed the legal basis of apartheid. But nonwhites in South Africa still face much unofficial segregation and discrimination.

Under the Constitution and other laws, no American may be made a second-class citizen. Citizens receive equal protection of the law, no matter what their race, color, or religion. But some Americans treat certain groups as second-class citizens despite the law.

Voting

©Shepard Sherbell, Picture Group

Jury duty

Jim Pickerell, FPG

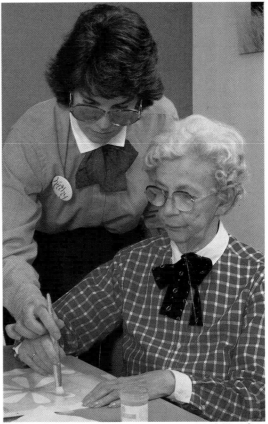

Volunteer work

©Ira Wyman, Sygma

Citizenship involves both rights and responsibilities. Citizens are guaranteed such privileges as the right to vote, the right of free speech, and freedom of religion. Citizens are also expected to obey laws, serve on juries, help in their communities, and perform other duties.

The word *citizen* comes from the Latin word *civitas,* which in ancient times meant *membership in a city.* Today, citizenship refers mainly to membership in a nation.

What it means to be a citizen

The rights of citizens differ from nation to nation. The Constitution of the United States provides the basic rights of American citizens, and laws passed by Congress give additional rights. These rights are called *civil rights.* They include freedom of speech, freedom of religion, and *freedom of assembly* (the right to gather peacefully for political or other purposes). American citizens have the right to vote for the President and members of Congress and to run for government office themselves. U.S. citizens have the right to travel throughout the United States. American citizens, unlike those of some countries, cannot be forced to leave their homeland. American citizenship cannot be taken away, except for certain serious actions.

Aliens and noncitizen nationals share many of the rights of U.S. citizens. But they cannot vote, hold public office, or do certain other things that citizens can do.

The rights of citizens have certain limits. For example,

U.S. citizens must be at least 18 years old to vote. States also can limit voting rights to people who have registered to vote. Freedom of speech does not allow a person to tell lies that damage someone's reputation. Many other civil rights also have limits.

The duties of citizens, like citizens' rights, differ from nation to nation. Most governments demand that citizens pay taxes, defend their country, and obey its laws. Some governments require certain citizens to serve on juries.

Many people believe that citizens also have duties not demanded by law, such as voting, learning about public problems, and trying to help other people. Many of these duties go along with rights. For example, the duty to vote comes with the right to vote. The duty to learn about public problems comes with freedom of speech and of the press, which protect the open discussion of public events and the exchange of ideas.

Aliens must obey the laws of the country in which they are traveling or living, except for those that bind only citizens. In addition, aliens must obey some of the laws of their homeland. For example, some foreigners who work in the United States must pay taxes both to the U.S. government and to the government of their own

A naturalization ceremony, *left,* is the final step in the legal process by which foreigners become citizens of a country they have adopted. In the United States, many naturalization ceremonies take place on Citizenship Day, September 17.

Andrew Sacks, Black Star

country. Travelers who break the laws of a country they are visiting may be put on trial and fined or imprisoned. Many nations grant *diplomatic immunity* to aliens who represent foreign governments. Diplomatic immunity is a set of special rights granted to the representatives of foreign governments and to the representatives' families and staffs. In many countries, these rights include freedom from arrest, search, and taxation.

Ways of becoming a citizen

Nations have various laws that govern the granting of citizenship. People become citizens in two ways: (1) by birth and (2) by naturalization.

Birth. Most people become citizens of a country simply by being born there. The right to citizenship in the country of one's birth is called *jus soli* (pronounced *juhs SOH ly*), a Latin phrase that means *right of soil.* The laws of most nations, including Canada, the United Kingdom, and the United States, grant citizenship based on jus soli. Some nations limit jus soli to children whose parents already have citizenship in that nation. Some nations also deny jus soli to certain groups of persons. Such persons include children who are born in a country where their parents are serving as diplomatic representatives. Persons denied jus soli also include babies born to *refugees* (persons who have been forced from their homeland by war or some other difficulty).

Some countries use another rule of citizenship instead of jus soli—or in addition to it. This rule provides that the citizenship of children is determined by the na-

tionality of their parents, no matter where the children are born. The right to citizenship in the country of one's parents is called *jus sanguinis* (pronounced *juhs SANG wuh nuhs*). This phrase is a Latin term that means *right of blood.* Canada, France, the United States, and a number of other nations grant jus sanguinis to children born abroad if one or both parents are citizens.

Naturalization is the legal process by which foreigners become citizens of a country they have adopted. Each nation sets requirements that aliens must meet to become naturalized. For example, aliens cannot undergo naturalization in Canada or the United States unless they have lived in their new country for a number of years. On the other hand, Israel allows Jewish immigrants to become Israeli citizens the day they arrive under a rule called the Law of Return. Many nations naturalize only people who understand the rights and duties of citizenship and can use the national language. The United States and certain other countries require aliens to give up citizenship in their homelands to become naturalized.

Naturalization usually takes place in a ceremony in which qualified aliens promise loyalty to their new country. In the United States, many naturalization ceremonies take place on Citizenship Day, September 17.

Treaties or the passage of special laws may naturalize groups of people without the usual naturalization process. For example, an act of Congress naturalized the people of Puerto Rico in 1917. The United States had taken over Puerto Rico through the treaty that ended the Spanish-American War in 1898.

The United States oath of allegiance

Every alien applying for American citizenship must, as the final step, take the following oath of allegiance to the United States:

"I hereby declare, on oath, that I absolutely and entirely renounce and abjure all allegiance and fidelity to any foreign prince, potentate, state, or sovereignty of whom or which I have heretofore been a subject or citizen; that I will support and defend the Constitution and the laws of the United States of America against all enemies, foreign and domestic; that I will bear true faith and allegiance to the same; that I will bear arms on behalf of the United States when required by the law; or that I will perform noncombatant service in the armed forces of the United States when required by the law; or that I will perform work of national importance under civilian direction when required by the law; and that I take this obligation freely without any mental reservation or purpose of evasion; so help me God."

Dual citizenship

Some people hold citizenship in two nations. The condition of being a citizen of two nations is called *dual citizenship* or *dual nationality.*

Some people gain dual citizenship by birth. For example, a baby born to a French family visiting the United States would have U.S. citizenship by jus soli. The baby also would have French citizenship by jus sanguinis. People whose parents are citizens of two countries might have dual nationality by jus sanguinis.

Some people have dual citizenship as a result of naturalization. For example, a nation might allow its naturalized citizens to keep their original citizenship. Such persons could claim citizenship in two countries. Or, a nation might refuse to allow its people to give up their citizenship. People who declared that they no longer were citizens of such a country and became naturalized in another still would be claimed as citizens by the original nation.

The loss of citizenship

Expatriation is the act of giving up one's citizenship in a country. Such countries as Canada and the United States allow citizens to expatriate themselves. The term *expatriation* also means the act of taking away a person's citizenship in a country.

United States law provides that citizens might be expatriated if they willingly commit certain acts. Such acts include becoming naturalized in another country, promising loyalty to another country, and serving in another country's armed forces or government. An American may also be expatriated for trying to overthrow the United States government by force. U.S. law provides a process by which expatriated Americans can become citizens again.

Statelessness is the lack of citizenship in any country. Children of alien parents are born stateless if the country of their birth does not grant jus soli and the parents' homeland does not grant jus sanguinis. People can become stateless by giving up citizenship in one country without gaining citizenship in another.

Some people become stateless as a result of government action. For example, a government might punish citizens by expatriating them, leaving them stateless. In 1935, the German government led by the Nazi dictator Adolf Hitler expatriated all Jews living in Germany. Many other people become stateless when their homelands are destroyed by war.

In the United States, a stateless person is considered an alien. Unlike other aliens, however, stateless persons have no government from which to ask protection.

U.S. citizenship laws

The Constitution, as it was first written, did not clearly say how citizenship would be granted. The writers of the Constitution probably believed that citizens of the 13 original states would keep their state citizenship after they became citizens of the United States. Later, the United States followed the British practice of granting jus soli. In 1790, Congress adopted laws that provided jus sanguinis to children born to American parents abroad if the father had lived in the United States.

Today, the Constitution protects citizenship mainly through the 14th Amendment. This amendment establishes jus soli for nearly everyone born in the United States. It guarantees citizenship to "all persons born or naturalized in the United States, and subject to the jurisdiction thereof." Only children of foreign diplomats and other persons not *subject to the jurisdiction* (under the authority) of the United States lack jus soli. Under the 14th Amendment, United States citizens automatically become citizens of a state as well, simply by living in that state. A special law grants citizenship to Indians on reservations.

The Supreme Court of the United States has used the Eighth Amendment to limit Congress's powers of expatriation. The Eighth Amendment forbids cruel and unusual punishments. The court has ruled that citizens cannot be expatriated for deserting U.S. military forces during wartime or for avoiding military duty by living abroad during a war.

Other constitutional amendments protect the voting rights of certain groups of citizens. For example, the 15th Amendment states that citizens cannot be denied the right to vote because of their race. The 19th Amendment gives women the vote. The 26th Amendment provides that citizens who are at least 18 years old cannot be denied voting rights because of their age.

The first 10 amendments, known as the Bill of Rights, protect the civil rights of citizens, noncitizen nationals, and aliens. The Bill of Rights provides freedom of speech, religion, and the press. In addition, it safeguards the rights of persons accused of crimes and promises fair treatment by the government in several other matters.

Laws passed by Congress regulate the granting of citizenship by birth and by naturalization. Under jus sanguinis, children born abroad have U.S. citizenship if one or both parents are citizens. If only one parent is a citizen, that parent must have lived in the United States or one of its possessions for 10 years, 5 of them after the age of 14.

Naturalization is limited to aliens who are at least 18 years old. Applicants for naturalization must have lived in the United States for a certain number of years. In addition, they must prove that they understand the U.S. political system, follow generally accepted moral standards, and can use the English language. They also must show that, in the 10 years before naturalization, they have not supported any disloyal political belief or group. Congress often passes laws that excuse certain aliens from one or more of the requirements for naturalization. In many cases, alien children under the age of 18 automatically become U.S. citizens if one or both of their parents become naturalized. Naturalized citizens cannot serve as President or Vice President of the United States. However, naturalized citizens have all the other rights and duties that citizens by birth have.

The McCarran-Walter Act establishes the basic laws of U.S. citizenship and immigration. This act, also known as the Immigration and Nationality Act of 1952, has undergone several changes since its adoption. Originally, the law admitted only a certain number of immigrants of each nationality. But a law passed by Congress in 1965 gave preference to immigrants with skills needed in the United States and to close relatives of U.S. citizens. A 1990 law continued these preferences. Aliens must be admitted as legal immigrants to get U.S. citizenship. People who flee to the United States after being officially certified as refugees may receive immigrant status.

Canadian citizenship

Canada regulates citizenship through the Citizenship Act, which took effect in 1977. Under this law, a person can become a citizen of Canada in any of three ways:

The Canadian oath of allegiance

Every alien applying for Canadian citizenship must, as the final step, take the following oath of allegiance to Canada:
"I swear that I will be faithful and bear true allegiance to Her Majesty Queen Elizabeth II, Queen of Canada, her heirs and successors according to law, and that I will faithfully observe the laws of Canada and fulfill my duties as a Canadian citizen."

(1) by being born in Canada, (2) by having at least one parent with Canadian citizenship, and (3) by being naturalized.

The right to acquire citizenship has certain limits. For example, children born in Canada to foreign diplomats do not automatically become Canadian citizens. Canadian citizens born abroad must fulfill certain requirements to keep their citizenship. To become naturalized in Canada, aliens must be at least 18 years old and must have lived in Canada for at least three years on a permanent basis. They also must know about Canadian history, geography, and government and be able to use French or English. Naturalized Canadian citizens have the same rights and duties as citizens by birth. The rights of Canadian citizens include voting and holding positions in the government.

Canada belongs to the Commonwealth of Nations, an association of independent countries and other political units formerly under British rule. Citizens of Commonwealth nations, including Australia, Great Britain, and New Zealand, have citizenship in the Commonwealth as well as in their own country.

History

The idea of citizenship developed in the cities of ancient Greece and Rome about 700 B.C. The early Greeks and Romans thought of cities mainly as communities, rather than as geographic places. These communities consisted of citizens linked by such ties as friendship, family relationships, and participation in government. Not all the people of cities had citizenship. For example, ancient Greek and Roman cities denied citizenship to slaves.

The rights of Greek citizens included owning land and taking part in government. Their duties included voting, attending the government assembly, sitting on juries, and giving military service.

The special rights of Roman citizens included owning property, making contracts and wills, and suing for damages. As the Roman government expanded its rule, Roman citizens traveled to other lands to fight wars, rule territories, and conduct business. They kept all their special rights when they traveled anywhere in the Roman Empire. The government also began to grant Roman citizenship to people who had never lived in Rome. In A.D. 212, the government granted Roman citizenship to most people throughout the empire, except for slaves.

During the Middle Ages, which lasted from about the late 400's to about 1500, citizenship remained connected with cities. By this time, people thought of cities mainly as geographic places where people lived. During the 1500's and 1600's, nations ruled by kings or queens developed. As a result, people began to think of citizenship as membership in a nation. The people of these nations gave their loyalty to their monarch and were often called *subjects*.

During the 1700's, democracies began to develop. People living in democracies gave their loyalty to the nation instead of to the nation's ruler. As a result, the terms *citizen* and *national* began to replace *subject.*

Robert J. Pranger

Related articles in *World Book* include:

Alien   Bill of rights

Civil rights   Nationality
Illegal alien   Naturalization
Immigration   Patriotism
Nationalism   Voting

Additional resources

Level I

Atkinson, Linda. *Your Legal Rights.* Watts, 1982.
Boy Scouts of Am. *Citizenship in the Community.* Rev. ed. 1984. *Citizenship in the Nation.* Rev. ed. 1984. *Citizenship in the World.* Rev. ed. 1984.
Kahn, Charles R., and Howard, R. C. *Government and You.* McClelland (Toronto), 1979.
Snyder, Gerald S. *Human Rights.* Watts, 1980.

Level II

Barber, Benjamin R. *Strong Democracy: Participatory Politics for a New Age.* Univ. of California Pr., 1984.
Kettner, James H. *The Development of American Citizenship, 1608-1870.* Univ. of North Carolina Pr., 1984. First published in 1978.
The Supreme Court and Individual Rights. Ed. by Elder Witt. Congressional Quarterly, 1980.
U.S. Immigration and Naturalization Service. *Citizenship Education and Naturalization Information.* U.S. Government Printing Office, 1987.

Citizenship Day is celebrated in the United States each year on September 17. The day honors native-born citizens who have reached voting age and naturalized foreign-born citizens. Citizenship Day celebrations include pageantry and speeches to impress Americans with the privileges and responsibilities of United States citizenship.

A movement to recognize new citizens began in 1939. William Randolph Hearst gave it national prominence through his chain of daily newspapers. In 1940, Congress passed a resolution designating the third Sunday in May as I Am an American Day. It authorized the President to issue an annual proclamation urging its celebration.

On February 29, 1952, President Harry S. Truman signed a bill establishing September 17 as Citizenship Day. This act of Congress replaced I Am an American Day and moved the celebration to the date on which the United States Constitution was signed in 1787. Many cities continue to observe I Am an American Day in May.

Jack Santino

Citlaltépetl. See Orizaba, Pico de.

Citrange, *SIHT ruhnj,* is a hybrid plant derived from the sweet orange and the trifoliate orange. Although the fruit of the trifoliate orange is not eaten, the plants are hardier than ordinary oranges. Plant breeders developed the citrange to be raised in Georgia and in

—WORLD BOOK illustration by James Teason

The citrange looks and tastes like an orange.

other regions of the South where the climate and soil do not allow oranges to grow. Commercial citrus plants have been grafted to the *rootstocks* (underground stems) of some types of citranges, especially Carrizo, Rusk, and Troyer varieties. The rootstocks provide a hardy, disease-resistant system for citrus plants. The citrange orange may grow from 2 to 3 inches (5 to 8 centimeters) in diameter. It has an acid, orangelike taste. The citrange is used in cooking and to flavor various kinds of beverages.   Wilfred F. Wardowski

Citrate. See Citric acid.

Citric acid, *SIHT rihk,* is a common organic acid that gives lemons, oranges, and other citrus fruits their sour taste. Lemon juice contains 5 to 8 per cent of the acid. The name *citric* comes from the Latin word *citrus,* which means *citron tree* (similar to lemon and lime trees). Carl Wilhelm Scheele, a Swedish chemist, first isolated citric acid from lemon juice in 1784.

Citric acid is used as a flavoring for soft drinks and pharmaceuticals. Industry uses it in chemicals, alkyd resins, plasticizers, inks, and as a *mordant* (dye-fixative). It is also used to clean and polish steel, and to preserve color and flavor in canned and frozen fruits and fish. Citric acid is prepared commercially from fermentation of sugar, and by extraction from lemon juice, lime juice, and pineapple canning residues.

Pure citric acid forms colorless, odorless crystals that have a pleasant, sour taste. It is very soluble in water. Its chemical formula is $C_3H_4(OH)(COOH)_3$, and it melts at 153 °C. Citric acid combines with metals to form salts called *citrates.*   David C. Armbruster

See also **Acid; Scheele, Carl Wilhelm.**

Citrin, *SIHT rihn,* is a chemical substance that belongs to a group of chemicals called *flavonoids.* Scientists do not know exactly what citrin is, or whether it is essential to the health of human beings. However, they have found that flavonoid substances help to control bleeding from the *capillaries* (tiny blood vessels) in the body. Citrin affects the capillary walls, making them less likely to hemorrhage. The citrin used in medicine is usually prepared from paprika and lemon peel. Citrin was once called *vitamin P,* but it is not a vitamin.   Richard A. Ahrens

Citron, *SIHT ruhn,* is a large, usually sour fruit much like the lemon. It ranks among the largest citrus fruits. The citron tree grows wild in northeastern India. It is also grown commercially in Corsica, Greece, Israel, and southern Italy, and the fruit is exported to other countries. The thorny citron tree has leaves that range from 4 to 7 inches (10 to 18 centimeters) in length. The edges of the leaves are slightly toothed.

The fruit is 6 to 10 inches (15 to 25 centimeters) long, or longer, and shaped like an egg. It has a thick, firm *rind* (peel) that is preserved and candied for use in cakes, puddings, and candies. The rind also furnishes fragrant oils. The *etrog,* a variety of citron with small fruits, is grown for use in a Jewish ceremony called the Feast of the Tabernacles.

Scientific classification. The citron belongs to the rue family, Rutaceae. It is classified as *Citrus medica.*

Wilfred F. Wardowski

Citronella, *SIHT ruh NEHL uh,* is an oil used in perfumes and in citronella candles. It is also a source of two other ingredients used in perfumes: *citronellal* and *geraniol.*

Citronella comes from various citronella grasses, which are cultivated in many tropical regions. Workers obtain citronella by cutting the grass, leaving it in the sun for a few days to dry, and then distilling it (see **Distillation**).   Patricia Ann Mullen

Citrus, *SIHT ruhs,* is the name of a group of trees and shrubs which belong to the rue family. Some citrus fruits are oranges; grapefruits; lemons; mandarins, including tangelos, tangerines, tangors, and their hybrids; kumquats; bitter oranges; limes; citrons; shaddocks; and bergamots. Citrus trees grow wild in parts of India and southeastern Asia. The Chinese were the first to cultivate citrus trees, more than 4,000 years ago. These trees and shrubs have been grown in other parts of the world for their fruits for many years.

Citrus trees are thorny, but usually attractive. They are evergreen, with long, shiny, pointed leaves. The flowers are fragrant. Ripe citrus fruits may be green or yellow to orange-red in color. All citrus fruits are a type of berry that scientists call a *hesperidium.*

Citrus fruits all grow in rather warm climates. They grow best where there is almost no frost or wind. All grow in tropical regions, but produce better fruit in a slightly cooler climate. Citrus plants grow best in Arizona, California, Florida, and Texas in the United States. Citrus fruits are grown in greater quantity than any other fruit in the United States. Citrus fruits are valuable foods. They contain large amounts of vitamins and minerals. Citrus fruits are usually high in vitamin C.

Scientific classification. Citrus plants are members of the rue family, Rutaceae. This family consists of six genera: *Fortunella, Eremocitrus, Poncirus, Clymenia, Microcitrus,* and *Citrus.*

Wilfred F. Wardowski

Related articles in *World Book* include:

Bergamot	Mandarin
Citron	Orange
Grapefruit	Tangelo
Kumquat	Tangerine
Lemon	Tangor
Lime	

WORLD BOOK illustration by Kate Loyd-Jones, Linden Artists Ltd.

The citron is a citrus fruit that resembles a large lemon. A citron is shaped like an egg and has a thick, firm pale yellow rind. The fruit grows on the small, thorny citron tree.

Mireille Vautier, Woodfin Camp, Inc.

City

Crowded street scenes—like this one in Lima, Peru—are common in cities throughout the world. Cities occupy only a small portion of the world's land. But more than 40 percent of all people now live in or near cities, and the percentage continues to grow.

City is a community where thousands—or even millions—of people live and work. Cities are the world's most crowded places. New York City, for example, has an average of about 19,900 persons per square mile (7,700 persons per square kilometer). The United States as a whole averages only about 68 persons per square mile (26 persons per square kilometer). Similarly, other large cities of the world have population densities that are hundreds or thousands of times as large as their average national population densities.

The percentage of the world's people living in *urban places* (cities and their surrounding areas) keeps growing. In 1800, only about $2\frac{1}{2}$ percent of the world population lived in urban places. This figure reached 45 percent in 1990, and it is expected to grow to 55 percent by about the year 2010. In 1800, the United States classified only about 5 percent of its population as urban. This figure has reached about 75 percent and might reach 80 percent by 2010.

Cities offer a variety of activities for their residents and visitors. Art museums display works by famous artists, and musicians perform in classical recitals or rock concerts. Motion pictures from around the world play at

local theaters. Restaurants offer food from diverse cultures, and department stores sell a wide range of products. Huge stadiums enable thousands of people to attend sporting events.

Nevertheless, many cities are overcrowded, dirty, and noisy. Traffic jams delay people who are trying to travel to work, stores, or other places. Automobiles and electric power plants dirty the air with fumes that endanger people's health. Motor vehicles, factories, sirens, and construction equipment create bothersome noise. Many cities have a high crime rate, and violence sometimes breaks out between racial or religious groups.

People choose to live in or near cities for several reasons. Many people enjoy the rapid pace and bustling activity of city life. However, the main reason people choose cities is the number and variety of jobs available. The cities of most industrialized nations serve as manufacturing centers. A manufacturing company might provide jobs to many people, such as factory workers and accountants. Far fewer jobs are available in the cities of developing nations, including most of the countries of Africa, Asia, and Latin America. Even so, large numbers of people flock to these cities searching for work.

No rule states the number of people a community must have to be classified as a city. In fact, some communities are called cities for reasons that have nothing to do with their population. In the United States, for example, one definition of *city* is any community—regardless of population—that has some form of city govern-

The contributors of this article are Henry C. Binford, Associate Professor of History at Northwestern University; and Terry Nichols Clark, Professor of Sociology at the University of Chicago.

The business center of a city is packed with tall buildings where people work and shop. In Lagos, Nigeria, *above,* and other cities, residential areas stretch beyond the center.

Georg Gerster, Comstock

Trade and industry provide jobs for millions of city dwellers. An open-air grain market in Kabul, Afghanistan, *above,* helps make that city an important trading center.

S. E. Hedin, Carl Östman

ment. But most people use the word for large urban communities. This article uses the word *city* in that sense.

Population standards, however, help distinguish urban places and rural places. In general, all communities in the United States with 2,500 or more people, and smaller communities near big ones, are considered urban. Farms, and communities in uncrowded areas with fewer than 2,500 people, are considered rural. The population standard varies among other nations of the world, and ranges from about 2,500 to 10,000 people for urban places. The United Nations considers as urban only those communities that have a population of 20,000 or more.

This article explains how cities began and developed. It describes cities and city life throughout history. It also discusses urban problems, cultural groups in cities, and cities of the future.

How cities began and developed

Human beings have probably lived on the earth about 2 million years. But they began to live in permanent settlements only between 13,000 and 10,000 years ago. Before this time, people wandered from place to place, hunting animals and gathering plants for food. But eventually people noticed seasonal supplies of fish and plants in certain regions. They remained near the avail-

Terry Farmer, Tony Stone Images

City governments provide such services as fire fighting and sewage disposal for the people of their cities. The photograph above shows a meeting of the city council of Springfield, Ill.

Comparing the sizes of cities

A city determines its population by counting the people who live within its political boundaries. But cities of the world define their city limits differently, making population comparisons difficult. United States cities fix their limits so that they do not overlap or include other cities and towns. Some foreign cities include other urban and rural areas.

Countries also determine metropolitan areas in various ways. In the United States, metropolitan area boundaries follow county lines. Each metropolitan area includes a county with a large city and perhaps nearby counties. But in most countries, a metropolitan area does not have definite political boundaries.

In these countries, metropolitan areas include the major city and urban and rural areas that are socially or economically identified with the city.

São Paulo has the largest population of any city in the world. Mexico City has the largest metropolitan area population in the world.

Some governments do not report separate city and metropolitan area populations in their censuses and population estimates. In such cases, the same city proper figure appears in both the cities and the metropolitan areas tables, *below,* to show the existence of a metropolitan area.

50 largest cities in the world

1. São Paulo	11,128,848	26. Bogotá	3,982,941
2. Mexico City	10,263,275	27. Ho Chi Minh	
3. Seoul	9,645,932	City	3,934,395
4. Moscow	8,769,000	28. Sydney	3,538,970
5. Bombay	8,227,332	29. Pusan	3,516,807
6. Shanghai	8,214,436	30. Los Angeles	3,485,398
7. Tokyo	8,163,573	31. Berlin	3,433,695
8. Beijing	7,362,425	32. Wuhan	3,340,000
9. New York		33. Calcutta	3,305,006
City	7,322,564	34. Madras	3,276,622
10. Jakarta	6,761,886	35. Yokohama	3,220,331
11. Istanbul	6,620,600	36. Guangzhou	3,220,000
12. London	6,378,600	37. Madrid	3,123,713
13. Hong Kong	6,055,000	38. Hanoi	3,058,855
14. Cairo	6,052,836	39. Melbourne	3,022,157
15. Rio de		40. Lahore	2,952,689
Janeiro	6,042,411	41. Alexandria	2,917,327
16. Baghdad	5,908,000	42. Buenos	
17. Tianjin	5,855,068	Aires	2,908,001
18. Teheran	5,734,199	43. Rome	2,830,569
19. Lima	5,493,900	44. Chicago	2,783,726
20. Karachi	5,208,170	45. Chongqing	2,730,000
21. Bangkok	5,153,902	46. Pyongyang	2,639,448
22. Delhi	4,884,234	47. Taipei	2,637,100
23. Santiago	4,385,481	48. Osaka	2,623,801
24. St. Petersburg	4,295,000	49. Kiev	2,616,000
25. Shenyang	4,130,000	50. Harbin	2,590,000

50 largest metropolitan areas in the world

1. Mexico City	19,150,000	26. Delhi	5,729,283
2. São Paulo	17,112,712	27. Karachi	5,208,170
3. Shanghai	13,341,896	28. Bangkok	5,153,902
4. Tokyo	11,927,457	29. Philadelphia	4,922,175
5. Rio de		30. St. Petersburg	4,827,000
Janeiro	11,205,567	31. Santiago	4,385,481
6. Beijing	10,819,407	32. Madras	4,289,347
7. Cairo	10,000,000	33. Detroit	4,266,654
8. Buenos Aires	9,927,404	34. Washington,	
9. Seoul	9,645,932	D.C.	4,223,485
10. Calcutta	9,194,018	35. Shenyang	4,130,000
11. Moscow	8,967,000	36. Bogotá	3,982,941
12. Los Angeles-		37. Ho Chi Minh	
Long Beach	8,863,164	City	3,934,395
13. Tianjin	8,785,402	38. Toronto	3,893,046
14. Paris	8,706,963	39. Belo Horizonte	3,615,234
15. New York		40. Sydney	3,538,970
City	8,546,846	41. Pusan	3,516,807
16. Bombay	8,227,332	42. Berlin	3,433,695
17. Chicago	7,410,858	43. Dhaka	3,430,312
18. Jakarta	6,761,886	44. Wuhan	3,340,000
19. Manila	6,720,050	45. Houston	3,322,025
20. Istanbul	6,620,600	46. Boston	3,227,707
21. London	6,378,600	47. Yokohama	3,220,331
22. Hong Kong	6,055,000	48. Guangzhou	3,220,000
23. Lima	6,053,900	49. Montreal	3,127,242
24. Baghdad	5,908,000	50. Madrid	3,123,713
25. Teheran	5,734,199		

50 largest cities in the United States

1. New York City	7,322,564	25. New Orleans	496,938
2. Los Angeles	3,485,398	26. Denver	467,610
3. Chicago	2,783,726	27. Austin	465,622
4. Houston	1,630,553	28. Fort Worth	447,619
5. Philadelphia	1,585,577	29. Oklahoma City	444,719
6. San Diego	1,110,549	30. Portland, Ore.	437,319
7. Detroit	1,027,974	31. Kansas City,	
8. Dallas	1,006,877	Mo.	435,146
9. Phoenix	983,403	32. Long Beach	429,433
10. San Antonio	935,933	33. Tucson	405,390
11. San Jose	782,248	34. St. Louis	396,685
12. Indianapolis	741,952	35. Charlotte	395,934
13. Baltimore	736,014	36. Atlanta	394,017
14. San Francisco	723,959	37. Virginia Beach	393,069
15. Jacksonville,		38. Albuquerque	384,736
Fla.	672,971	39. Oakland	372,242
16. Columbus,		40. Pittsburgh	369,879
Ohio	632,910	41. Sacramento	369,365
17. Milwaukee	628,088	42. Minneapolis	368,383
18. Memphis	610,337	43. Tulsa	367,302
19. Washington,		44. Honolulu	365,272
D.C.	606,900	45. Cincinnati	364,040
20. Boston	574,283	46. Miami	358,548
21. Seattle	516,259	47. Fresno	354,202
22. El Paso	515,342	48. Omaha	335,795
23. Nashville	510,784	49. Toledo	332,943
24. Cleveland	505,616	50. Buffalo	328,123

50 largest cities and towns in Canada

1. Montreal	1,017,666	28. St. Catherines	129,300
2. Calgary	710,677	29. Richmond	126,624
3. Toronto	635,395	30. Oakville	114,670
4. Winnipeg	616,790	31. Halifax	114,455
5. Edmonton	616,741	32. Thunder Bay	113,946
6. North York	562,564	33. Vaughan	111,359
7. Scarborough	524,598	34. Nepean	107,627
8. Vancouver	471,844	35. East York	102,696
9. Mississauga	463,388	36. Gloucester	101,677
10. Hamilton	318,499	37. St. John's	95,770
11. Laval	314,398	38. Saanich	95,577
12. Ottawa	313,987	39. Sudbury	92,884
13. Etobicoke	309,993	40. Cambridge	92,772
14. London	303,165	41. Gatineau	92,284
15. Surrey	245,173	42. Delta	88,978
16. Brampton	234,445	43. Guelph	87,976
17. Windsor	191,435	44. Montreal-Nord	85,516
18. Saskatoon	186,058	45. Coquitlam	84,021
19. Regina	179,178	46. Brantford	81,997
20. Kitchener	168,282	47. Sault Ste.	
21. Quebec	167,517	Marie	81,476
22. Burnaby	158,858	48. Richmond Hill	80,142
23. Markham	153,811	49. Sherbrooke	76,429
24. York	140,525	50. Kelowna	75,950
25. Longueuil	126,874		
26. Burlington	129,575		
27. Oshawa	129,344		

Sources: 1990 census for the United States cities; 1991 census for Canadian cities; 1980-1991 censuses and estimates for other cities.

able food for years at a time. About 11,000 years ago, according to most scientists, people in the Middle East began to cultivate the land. These men and women, called *Neolithic people,* became the first farmers.

Between about 8000 and 3500 B.C., some Neolithic villages had developed into small cities of a few thousand people. Since these first cities appeared, people have built cities for many reasons. The cities have differed in size and layout, and they have had a variety of economic, governmental, and social systems. But all permanent settlements—from Neolithic village to giant city—needed four main features to begin and to grow. These features were (1) advances in technology, (2) a favorable physical environment, (3) social organization, and (4) population growth.

Advances in technology. The word *technology* refers to the tools, knowledge, and inventions that help people satisfy their needs and improve their way of life. Technological advances that helped cities develop include farming skills and improved transportation.

Neolithic people learned how to grow crops and invented tools that improved farming methods. Neolithic people also tamed animals, which they used for food or agricultural tasks. All these developments helped many Neolithic families produce more food than they needed.

Because of this surplus food, a number of people switched to jobs other than farming. Some became skilled at crafts and made baskets, cloth, leather goods, tools, or other products. Others became miners and dug for flint, metal, and stone. The nonfarmers traded the items they made to the farmers in exchange for food.

Through the years, people in distant cities began to trade with one another. In addition, technological advances enabled more people to become nonfarmers. They worked as warriors, record keepers, and religious and political leaders. These people founded and populated the cities of the world.

Technological advances have influenced city life throughout history. For example, the development of the steam engine in the 1700's gave people the power source they needed for large-scale manufacturing. Many cities became giant manufacturing centers partly because of this development. Sometimes industrial expansion led to the construction of new cities. In the early 1900's, the United States Steel Corporation (now USX Corporation) planned and built Gary, Ind., around the company's new mills. During the 1900's, thousands of suburbs grew up around big cities. The automobile and the railroad train—two technological advances in transportation—helped make these suburbs possible. Many people who lived in the suburbs needed cars and trains to travel to work in the cities.

Physical environment of a city includes its location, its climate, and the availability of water and food. Cities have been founded in many kinds of environments, but their development has depended on certain favorable environmental features. All cities, for instance, must have enough drinking water. Early communities, which depended on farming, needed enough rainfall to grow crops. Good soil was also essential for growing crops, and nearness to other food—animals and edible plants—was helpful. Other favorable environmental features included a reasonably mild climate and a location near materials for making clothes and building shelters.

Early people found many favorable environmental features in river valleys with hot weather. Some chose to settle in the Tigris-Euphrates Valley of what is now Iraq and the Nile Valley of what is now Egypt. Other early people settled in the Huang He (Yellow River) Valley of present-day China and the Indus Valley of what are now northwestern India and Pakistan.

Through the years, other environmental features have also helped cities develop. Since ancient times, for example, people have traveled in ships to trade with peo-

Drawing by Alan Scorell, British Crown Copyright; reproduced by permission of the Ministry of Public Building and Works, Edinburgh

The University Museum, University of Pennsylvania

Neolithic villages were the ancestors of cities. An artist's conception, *right,* shows how the Neolithic village of Jarlshof in the Shetland Islands may have looked. A wall surrounded the houses and a tall watchtower. Many people stored food in large jars. A painted storage jar, *above,* was found in Pakistan's Indus Valley. It stands about $2\frac{1}{2}$ feet (76 centimeters) high.

ple of other nations. Many cities that lay near large bodies of water became important trading centers. They included Istanbul, Turkey; London, England; Shanghai, China; and Venice, Italy. Chicago, in the United States, and Toronto, in Canada, developed partly because they lay along important land and water transportation routes. Many cities, including Manchester, England, gained importance as manufacturing centers because of nearby minerals or other raw materials needed for manufacturing. Some cities owe their development chiefly to climate. For example, the warm, healthful climate of parts of Florida and the Southwestern United States attracted many people.

Social organization. Certain rules of behavior are needed to maintain order, peace, and security in any community. Since Neolithic times, most people have agreed that it is wrong to steal from or harm others in their group. In turn, people expect that their own rights to safety and property will be respected by other members of the group. People also have duties toward their group as a whole. They have often fought to protect their group from enemies.

The maintenance of order in groups also requires some system of authority. In the family, the most basic social group, parents have authority over their children. In larger social groups, including cities, citizens must accept the authority of government.

Neolithic villages had a simple social organization. People were required to respect each other's rights, and children had to obey their parents. But most villages had few government officials as we think of such officials today. Someone probably took care of the surplus food,

and there may have been a chief planner for defense against outsiders. As cities grew, the duties of family members and neighbors toward each other remained basically the same. But to keep order in cities, governments took on a greater role in managing community affairs and providing services for the people. Government officials organized trade, planned military action, and conducted religious worship. The number of workers employed by cities also increased. Today, these workers include mayors, city planners, garbage collectors, police officers, and teachers.

Population growth. Only about 10 million people existed at the beginning of the Neolithic Period. The population of the world reached about 500 million by A.D. 1650 and about $5\frac{1}{3}$ billion by 1990. This *population explosion* led to an increase in both the size and number of cities.

Two other trends also have aided the development of cities. One trend—sometimes called *population implosion* or *population urbanization*—is the increasing concentration of people in small parts of the earth. These parts are the cities and their surrounding areas. The other trend—sometimes called *population displosion* or *population diversification*—is the movement to cities by people of a variety of cultural backgrounds. Through the years, cities came to include people of different racial, religious, national, and language groups. This mixing of people brought about *cultural diffusion,* a process by which people of different backgrounds learn from each other by exchanging ideas. Cultural diffusion ranks among the most important factors in the development of civilization.

Ancient cities

Thousands of years passed before the Neolithic villages developed into cities. The first cities had appeared by 3500 B.C. in the Tigris-Euphrates Valley. The valley was located in the lower part of Mesopotamia, in what is now Iraq. The first Chinese cities probably began to develop by the mid-1600's B.C. Cities developed in east Africa by about 500 B.C. and in Central America by about 200 B.C.

Ancient cities differed from Neolithic villages in several ways. The cities covered more land than the villages, with large public buildings for worship and storage of grain or weapons. More people lived in cities than in villages, including more people from different backgrounds. The work of the city people also differed from the work of the village people. Almost all village workers were farmers, but most city people had nonfarm jobs. Merchants became a new group of workers in early cities, and the number of craftworkers and government officials continued to grow.

Description. An early ancient city covered less than 1 square mile (2.6 square kilometers). Most of its people lived near the city's water supply because they had to get their own water and carry it home themselves. Technological advances enabled some ancient cities to grow. Rome, for example, built structures called *aqueducts* for transporting water over long distances and grew to more than 4 square miles (10 square kilometers).

Many ancient cities had walls surrounding them for

protection against enemies. Hills also helped protect some ancient cities. Rome was built on hills, and Athens was built around a hill where the people could go if enemies attacked the city. The central area of most cities included a place of worship, the ruler's palace, and a storehouse for food. In some cities, a wall surrounded this central area to keep out both enemies and hungry citizens. Houses stood crowded together around the central area.

Sanitation presented a major problem in ancient cities, most of which had no system for getting rid of wastes. The people simply threw garbage and other wastes into the streets or piled them up outside the city wall. As a result, disease spread quickly and death rates were high. The narrow, unpaved streets often turned into seas of mud when rain fell.

Some ancient cities reached a more advanced degree of development. Rome, for example, had a sewer system and a water supply system. Teotihuacán, in what is now Mexico, contained a planned street system and apartment buildings. Other advanced ancient cities included Athens, Babylon, and several cities of Egypt. See **Athens; Babylon; Egypt, Ancient; Jerusalem; Maya** (The Classic Period); **Rome.**

The people. Ancient cities had more people than did Neolithic villages but far fewer than cities of today. Most of the cities had populations of under 10,000, though other cities were much larger. For instance, Athens,

© American Museum of Natural History

Ur was one of the first cities. The Sumerians founded it about 3500 B.C. in what is now Iraq. They built a *ziggurat* (temple), *background above,* in the shape of a mountain—perhaps because they once worshiped on mountaintops. The plan of Ur is shown at the right.

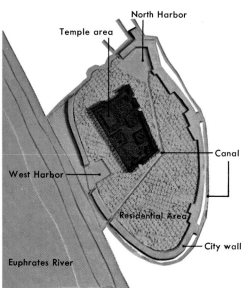

WORLD BOOK illustration by George Suyeoka

Drawing (1908) by A. Zippelius; Deutsches Archäologisches Institut, Istanbul

Priene, an ancient Greek city, lay in what is now western Turkey. The wall around the city helped keep invaders out. The marketplace, consisting of long, narrow buildings and a large yard, dominated the center of Priene. Government buildings, houses of worship, and an outdoor theater stood nearby. A huge gymnasium and a stadium stood along the near wall. The houses, as in many cities today, were laid out in rectangular blocks.

Savio Oscar Fotografo

Rome, one of the largest ancient cities, reached a size of more than 4 square miles (10 square kilometers) and a population of nearly 1 million. Aqueducts carried water from mountain springs. One of these long wall-like structures appears at the lower right of the model of Rome above. Rome had huge public buildings. These included the oblong Circus Maximus, *left,* and the circular Colosseum, *right,* where people were entertained, and many government buildings.

Greece, had about 25,000 people in 1200 B.C. Its population reached about 155,000 by 430 B.C.

The first peoples of the first cities formed *homogeneous societies.* That is, they had the same racial and geographic backgrounds and shared the same religious beliefs and other cultural characteristics. But the cities soon began to draw people from a variety of backgrounds. Many people moved from the countryside in search of a better life in the city. Others had been captured in war and were brought to cities to serve as slaves. The arrival of newcomers gave the cities *heterogeneous societies,* made up of people of many different backgrounds.

The formation of heterogeneous societies caused cultural diffusion, but it also had undesirable effects. In many cities, the original group and the newcomers distrusted each other. Their distrust often led to *discrimination,* the unfair treatment of people from different cultures.

The people of ancient cities were divided into classes. The upper class included government and military officials, rulers, and high priests. The lower class consisted of farmers, craftworkers, and merchants. At the bottom of society were the newcomers, especially slaves and people from greatly different backgrounds than those of the native citizens. The newcomers were called *outcasts,* and most of them were forced to live in separate areas of the cities. The outcasts had the poorest housing, little food and clothing, and no education.

Upper-class families lived in large houses. Most other people lived in small one- or two-room houses. In many families of all classes, children, parents, grandparents, and other relatives lived in the same house.

In most ancient cities, only boys from upper-class families got a formal education. Other boys learned a craftworker's trade—usually that of their father—or received no education at all. Girls of all classes learned various household duties from their mothers.

Most people worshiped a number of gods. Many thought that angry gods caused personal misfortune. Festivals were held to honor and to please the gods. Many ancient peoples, including the Egyptians, Greeks, and Romans, built beautiful temples and monuments and dedicated them to the gods. Some Indians of Central and South America also followed this practice. For example, ancient Indians constructed the famous religious buildings at Monte Albán, in what is now Mexico.

Economy. Just as technological progress in agriculture had made Neolithic villages possible, further advances in farming spurred the development of ancient cities. The invention of new farm tools and the discovery of new methods of cultivation, irrigation, and animal raising helped increase food surpluses. As the surpluses increased, more people stopped farming and went to cities in search of other work.

Craftworkers became an important group in the cities. The first craftworkers wandered from place to place because no one community had enough work for them.

But as cities grew large enough to support them, craftworkers began settling permanently.

The first craftworkers sold the products they made. Later, city life grew more complex and a new group of working people, the merchants, appeared. This group sold the products made by others.

The merchant class was a result of technological advances in transportation. The wheel, invented in the Tigris-Euphrates Valley about 3500 B.C., gradually came into general use during ancient times. Wheeled vehicles and vastly improved roads enabled people to move large amounts of goods within cities and from city to city. Improvements in water transportation enabled merchants to trade their goods both in nearby places and in distant lands. Foreign trade became important to the economy of some ancient cities. For example, trade networks connected cities throughout the Middle East with cities in northern and eastern Africa. The Phoenicians played a leading part in the development of trade over large bodies of water. The Phoenician city of Tyre became an important shipping port (see **Phoenicia**).

Government. Religious leaders performed most duties of government in the earliest communities. The people believed that their leaders' authority came from the gods. Therefore, the leaders were responsible to the gods, not to the people. As communities developed, emperors, kings, and other nonreligious rulers took over the power to govern. These rulers developed laws that could be enforced by military and police power. But many people still believed that the right to govern came from the gods. As a result, rulers had both the divine right to rule and the civil power to enforce laws.

Local administrators from the upper class governed most ancient cities. They were responsible to the emperor, the king, or some other higher authority. Some cities, including Athens, were independent of any higher authority. Their rulers governed the city and its outlying area. Such regions were called *city-states* (see **City-state**).

The local rulers taxed the craftworkers, farmers, and merchants heavily to pay the costs of operating the government, constructing public buildings, and carrying out other projects. The people had little or no voice in the government. Athens and some other Greek city-states were important exceptions. In those communities, all adult males who were not slaves helped determine government policy. See **Democracy** (Origins of democracy).

Medieval cities

The Middle Ages began after the fall of the Roman Empire in the A.D. 400's and lasted until the 1500's. The Roman Empire ruled a vast region that, at its height, included most of Europe, the Middle East, and the northern coastal area of Africa. Rome was its capital.

The Romans helped build cities throughout their empire. They also built a network of roads that served as trade routes between the cities. The empire declined during the 400's, and Germanic tribes conquered it and divided it into many kingdoms. These tribespeople were

Brian Brake, Rapho Guillumette

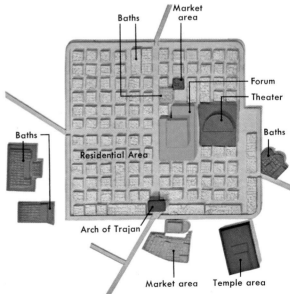

Baths
Market area
Forum
Theater
Baths
Baths
Residential Area
Arch of Trajan
Market area
Temple area

WORLD BOOK illustration by George Suyeoka

Timgad, part of the giant Roman Empire, was built about A.D. 100 in what is now Algeria. Military engineers planned Timgad and many other cities in the empire as camps for Roman soldiers. The ruins of Timgad, *left,* and a plan of the city, *above,* show the orderly arrangement of buildings and streets that was typical of the work of these military planners.

warriors, hunters, and farmers with little interest in trade. After the fall of the Roman Empire, trade among European cities almost stopped. Thousands of people left the cities and went to work on farms. Between the 400's and 1000's, the populations of existing cities decreased and few new cities appeared. Trade regained importance after about 1000, and cities began to grow again.

Description. Many European medieval cities had a similar layout. A typical city covered less than 1 square mile (2.6 square kilometers) and had walls around it for protection against invaders. The city's main church—in many cases a magnificent, towering Gothic cathedral—stood in the central area. The church was the city's biggest and most expensive building and a symbol of the medieval emphasis on religion. The chief government buildings and the marketplace were near the church. Wealthy people lived near the center of the city, and the poor lived away from this area. Some poor people lived in huts outside the walls.

Medieval cities, like ancient cities, were dirty and unhealthful. Disease spread rapidly, partly because the people had no sanitary method for disposing of garbage and other wastes. From time to time, disease wiped out a large part of a city's population.

The walls around medieval cities limited the amount of living space. Land was expensive, so people began to construct five- and six-story buildings. Overcrowding became a problem during the late Middle Ages. Some cities solved this problem by knocking down the walls and rebuilding them farther out. Florence, in Italy, increased its size three times in this way. Other cities let their walls stand but built new cities nearby.

Scholars believe that Eastern medieval cities had the same general layout as European cities. But Eastern trade did not decline, and many Eastern cities were large and prosperous throughout the Middle Ages. African cities also continued to grow, and their trade networks extended to people in nearby forests and to Middle Eastern merchants. Such American Indian cities as Tenochtitlan in what is now Mexico and Cusco in modern-day Peru prospered until the 1500's.

The people. Many medieval cities contained only 300 or 400 people. Even Lübeck, Germany, an important city in northern Europe, had a population of only about 10,000 during the 1200's. In that same period, London, with about 40,000 people, Venice, with about 100,000, and Paris, with about 150,000, ranked among the biggest cities in Europe. Many Asian cities had more people. In the mid-1200's, Hangzhou (also spelled Hang-chou), China, had a population of about 320,000. Guangzhou (also called Canton), China, had about 250,000 people.

European medieval cities attracted people from a variety of backgrounds. But the people tended to settle in *quarters* (neighborhoods) with people of their own group. Some quarters resembled separate cities. They had their own markets, water supplies, and churches or synagogues. The system of separate quarters helped limit conflicts between various groups, but it also limited the exchange of ideas. Some quarters, called *ghettos,* were used to persecute certain groups. For example, many cities in Europe forced Jews to live in ghettos and to pay extra taxes.

Upper-class medieval people lived in large houses that had separate rooms for bathing, cooking, eating, sleeping, and religious and social activities. Most

Medieval Europe had many small, walled cities. Magnificent churches rose above the other buildings, symbolizing medieval society's emphasis on religion. The Cathedral of Notre Dame in Reims, France—marked "A" above—was one of the biggest, most beautiful medieval buildings.

Cities in Flanders—including Bruges, *left,* and Ghent, Liège, and Ypres—grew prosperous from trade during the Middle Ages. Flemish merchants shipped large quantities of wool across the North Sea to England. They also carried on a heavy overland trade in France, Germany, and other countries. Flanders was sometimes called the marketplace of Europe.

Illustration from an illuminated manuscript (1500's) by an unknown Flemish artist; The Bodleian Library, Oxford, England

Engraving from *L'Ambassade de la Campagnie Orientale* by Pierre de Goyer and Jacob de Keyser; Newberry Library, Chicago

Many Eastern cities prospered, even while European cities were struggling to survive in the early Middle Ages. Guangzhou (also called Canton), China, *above,* was among the busiest medieval trading centers. It became one of the first Eastern cities to trade with the West.

people in the middle and lower classes continued to live in homes with one or two rooms, which they used for all purposes. Few people in a medieval city had much comfort or privacy.

During the Middle Ages, children, parents, grandparents, and other relatives continued to live in the same house. Some medieval households also included servants and workers associated with the family's economic activity. For example, some young people worked as personal servants to nobles and lived in the nobles' houses. Many *apprentices* (young people learning a craft) lived in the homes of the skilled workers who taught them.

Religion played a vital role in medieval life. Major religions included Christianity in Europe, Islam in the Middle East, and Buddhism and Hinduism in the East.

In Europe, the Christian church had great influence. Church officials owned much land and could tax the people. The church also performed such important activities as baptism, marriage, and burial services. The church could ban people from religious services through its power of *excommunication.* An excommunicated person was a public disgrace. In addition, people who did not belong to the Christian church were often treated harshly. For example, Jews in the Christian cities of medieval Europe suffered much persecution.

In the late Middle Ages, the Christian church also influenced religious life in the cities of Africa, North America, and South America. Missionaries from Europe traveled to these continents and converted many of the original inhabitants to Christianity.

As in ancient times, formal education was largely restricted to boys of the upper class. In Europe, the Christian church played an important part in medieval education and ran most of the schools. Priests taught in these schools and also in many government schools.

Economy. During the Middle Ages, much land in Europe was divided into large rural estates called *manors.* Lords and bishops owned most of the land, and peasants farmed it for them. This economic system, called *manorialism,* began to decline during the 1000's. Many peasants began moving to cities to earn a living. Some became merchants or craftworkers. Others farmed land outside the cities and helped supply food to the city dwellers.

The growth of trade played the leading part in the economic progress of medieval cities. Trade had declined after the fall of the Roman Empire. But Venice, an Italian city, traded with Constantinople (now Istanbul), Turkey, throughout the Middle Ages. Venice remained prosperous even after other European cities declined. After those cities began to grow again, Venice traded with them. These less prosperous cities also traded with one another. The increased trade brought further growth and prosperity to European cities.

In addition to Venice, several European cities played an important part in the economic revival. They included Genoa and Pisa in Italy, Bruges in Flanders, and the

Illustration from an illuminated Latin manuscript by an unknown artist (1300's); Bibliothèque Nationale, Paris

Trade fairs were held each year in many European cities during the Middle Ages. Merchants traveled from fair to fair, buying and selling goods and exchanging ideas about new products and production methods. In the scene at the right, a bishop blesses a trade fair while merchants discuss prices and a man on horseback prepares to amuse fairgoers with acrobatic tricks. Trade fairs became part of the general revival of trade that spread through Europe after about 1000. This revival helped cities prosper and grow. Most European cities had lost importance and stopped growing after the Roman Empire fell and trade almost stopped in the late 400's.

French cities of Nantes, Orleans, Paris, and Rouen. Other important trading centers were Antwerp in what is now Belgium, and Cologne, Hamburg, and Lübeck in what is now Germany. The Chinese cities of Guangzhou, Hangzhou, Kaifeng, Beijing (also called Peking), and Suzhou (also spelled Su-chou) became leading Asian centers of trade.

Technological advances also aided the economic progress of medieval cities. New products included barrels and tubs, gunpowder, mechanical clocks, paper, printing presses, and soap. The use of water and wind power to make products increased production, thus raising standards of living and stimulating city growth. The invention of the printing press about 1440 enabled people to receive information about business and government more quickly than ever before. Newspapers and printed books increased the exchange of ideas among people.

Craftworkers and merchants benefited greatly from the economic progress. Craftworkers could make more goods—and merchants could sell more products—because of expanding trade and technological advances. The new prosperity drew even more people to the cities, providing additional markets for the craftworkers and merchants.

The craftworkers and merchants formed a new economic class—the middle class. To ensure their continued prosperity, they established organizations of workers called *guilds*. There were guilds for merchants and craft guilds for bakers, brewers, goldsmiths, tailors, weavers, and other workers. By banding together, the guild members increased their profits. In groups, they could buy large quantities of materials and goods at low prices. The guilds allowed only their members to make and sell products. They kept memberships from growing too large so each member could prosper. See **Guild**.

Government. A system of government called *feudalism* developed in Europe during the Middle Ages. The feudal system divided kingdoms into sections called *fiefs*, each ruled by a lord or bishop. Feudalism weakened the power of kings because a king ruled only the land he owned, rather than an entire kingdom. Cities were governed by the lord or bishop who owned the land on which they stood. See **Feudalism**.

As cities gained importance during the 1000's and 1100's, many city people began to resent the interference of lords and bishops in local affairs. Led by the merchant and craft guilds, citizens fought for the right to govern themselves.

Numerous cities succeeded in their struggle for self-government, though women and many other groups could not participate. In Milan and other Italian cities, male citizens won the right to elect *consuls* (officials who ran the city government). The practice of electing consuls then spread to other parts of Europe. Cities in Flanders and northern France achieved a high degree of independence. The citizens made their own laws and elected their own officials. Guild members ran many of the cities. Some kings supported the people in their fight for self-government because strong city governments weakened the power of the lords and bishops.

During the 1400's and 1500's, many kings gained power over large regions. They set up strong central governments, which reduced the power of cities.

In the East, government remained centralized throughout the Middle Ages. The king or emperor appointed local officials, who had to prove their leadership capabilities. In China, a candidate for office had to pass a civil-service examination. Government inspectors oversaw the performance of appointed officials.

Industrial cities

Between the 1500's and the 1700's, cities throughout the world grew and gradually changed. But the basic pattern of cities and city life remained much the same until the 1700's and early 1800's, when a period of rapid industrialization called the Industrial Revolution took place. During this time, many cities in Europe and North America changed greatly. These communities—called *industrial cities*—became centers of large-scale manufacturing. The manufacturing boom resulted chiefly from the invention of steam engines and new machines. The machines could do the work of many people, and the steam engine easily powered the machines as well as railroads and ships. The expansion of trade among the nations of Europe and North America also aided the growth of manufacturing. See **Industrial Revolution**.

The Industrial Revolution caused dramatic changes in city life. Skilled craftworkers had trouble finding work because machines could make the same products quickly and cheaply. Instead, people in many cities worked in large factories, lived near the factories, and depended on manufacturing jobs for their livelihood. They were often overworked and poorly housed, though living conditions improved during the 1800's and early 1900's. Even people in cities with few factories became dependent on manufacturing. They often sold materials to the industrial plants or shipped finished products abroad.

The Industrial Revolution had little immediate effect on cities outside Europe and North America. But in the late 1800's and 1900's, many cities throughout the world became involved in the growing networks of manufacturing and trade created by industrialization. Some cities of Africa, Asia, Australia, and South America became industrial centers, though others have never industrialized.

Description. Some industrial cities developed from medieval cities. When a city became too crowded, the walls were knocked down and the city expanded. Other industrial cities grew up where there had been a fort, a trading post, a village, or open land. Development in open areas occurred most commonly in North America.

Factories, warehouses, and railroad yards stood near the center of an industrial city. Nearby, poor people lived in cheap houses and apartment buildings. The poor had no means of transportation, and so they needed to live within walking distance of their jobs. As cities grew, the central areas became crowded and unhealthful. Many wealthy merchants and factory owners built big houses in the outer sections of the city. They used horse-drawn carriages for travel to the central area. In the 1800's, some people began to move to communities just outside the city, called *suburbs.* They rode to work on railroads or streetcars. See **Suburb.**

Industrial cities had sanitation problems similar to those of earlier cities. Garbage and other wastes produced health hazards because of inadequate sanitation systems. In addition, a new problem—pollution from industry—became a health hazard. Factories polluted the waterways with chemical wastes and polluted the air with harmful gases. They also created huge dumps of garbage, rusting metals, and other wastes.

The *gridiron pattern* of city blocks, which remains common today, came into widespread use in industrial cities. In this pattern, buildings are spaced more or less evenly apart, and groups of them form rectangular blocks. Streets, generally of the same width, separate the blocks from each other. Most earlier cities had a more irregular arrangement of buildings and many winding streets. The regular pattern made it easy to ex-

tend a city in any direction. But it also gave a city a monotonous appearance.

The people. City populations increased greatly during the Industrial Revolution for two main reasons. First, the population of the world was increasing faster than ever before. Second, improvements in agricultural methods had reduced the need for farmworkers. These workers flocked to the cities and took jobs in factories.

Chicago and Manchester, England, provide two examples of the tremendous growth of industrial cities. Manchester's population grew from about 6,000 in 1685 to about 303,000 in 1851. Chicago's population jumped from about 4,000 in 1840 to more than 1 million in 1890.

In the early years of the Industrial Revolution, most city people lived under miserable conditions. Men and women—and even many children—worked 12 or more hours a day in dark, dirty factories. They held monotonous, tiring jobs, such as tending a machine or carrying heavy materials. The factories had few safety rules, and

Engraving (1872) by Gustave Doré; The Mansell Collection

The Industrial Revolution increased the production of goods, but it also brought miserable living conditions at first. Farm people in Europe and North America flocked to cities to take newly created jobs in factories. But like the Londoners above, most of them lived crowded together near the factories.

Carnegie Library of Pittsburgh

Factories, such as those in Pittsburgh, *above,* turned out products quickly and cheaply. Factory workers, underpaid at first, later shared more in the profits that resulted from the factory system.

accidents killed or injured many workers.

The workers earned barely enough money to feed themselves and their families. During economic slumps, factories laid off large numbers of workers who had nowhere to turn for relief. They could no longer farm the land for food, and governments had not yet begun to provide relief for the needy. Sometimes workers organized protests against their living conditions.

The workers lived in poorly built, dirty *tenements* (crowded apartments), *row houses* (groups of houses without space between them), and cellars. In 1842, for example, about a fifth of the people in Liverpool, England, lived in cellars. The early industrial cities had widespread disease and high death rates. Pollution filled the air and the waterways, and rats and insects spread illness. The rich and the poor alike fell victim to pollution and disease. Until the 1830's, the homes of even most of the rich lacked plumbing for toilets and bathtubs. Most workers did not have these facilities until the late 1800's or the early 1900's. In the industrial cities of some developing nations, many workers still do not have indoor plumbing.

In time, the standard of living in most industrial cities improved. The mass production method used in the factories reduced the cost of making goods and thus cut the cost of the goods to customers. Many factory workers formed labor unions and threatened mass strikes to support their demands for higher wages and better working conditions. Finally, governments passed wage and welfare laws that helped the workers. The governments also took steps to improve sanitation.

A small percentage of people had great wealth throughout the Industrial Revolution. Factory owners made huge profits from the business boom and paid their workers little. Bankers and financiers invested money in the new industries and made big profits on their investments. Merchants sold more and more goods as city populations grew. These rich people lived in large houses and could afford many luxuries.

During the 1700's and 1800's, charitable organizations and governments started tuition-free schools in many

Aerofilms

Letchworth, England, *above,* was designed in the early 1900's along principles laid down by Ebenezer Howard. Howard and many other people tried to eliminate the crowded, dirty conditions of industrial cities. The plans for this town near London called for open space and for the separation of industrial and residential areas. Howard's ideas influence city planners today.

cities. These schools gave some poor children a chance to have a formal education. But many of the teachers lacked good training, and the schools often did not have enough textbooks. Also, many children could not go to school because they had to support their families. Children from wealthy families attended private schools or studied in their homes under tutors.

As in medieval times, the cities included people from a variety of backgrounds. People still tended to settle in neighborhoods with others of the same background. But various groups had much more contact with each other than they had in medieval cities. People from all groups worked together in factories, and children from many groups attended schools together. The influence of the family on the behavior and ideas of the individual remained strong. But the influence of people outside the family—fellow workers, friends, teachers, and others—increased greatly.

Economy. The flow of workers from farms to cities rose tremendously during the Industrial Revolution. The manufacturing boom provided more jobs in cities than ever before. At the same time, technological advances in agriculture reduced the number of jobs available on farms. The invention of the reaper, for example, enabled one farmer to do the work of many.

Large numbers of craftworkers became unemployed or went to work in factories. Craftworkers made their products slowly, and usually used hand tools. But factory workers could make many of the same products with machines. These mass-produced goods were easier to make, and they could be sold more cheaply than the craftworkers' goods. Many craftworkers found that they could not compete with the factories, and they were forced out of business.

The factory system of manufacturing began the greatest economic boom in history. With machines, people turned out products more quickly and cheaply than ever before. The savings in production costs—together with fairer policies toward workers—resulted in greater earnings for workers. As their earnings increased, workers could buy more goods. The increased demand for goods led to increased production. Businesses built new factories and expanded existing ones. The new

business created jobs for more people, and the new jobs meant that people had more money to spend. Thus, the demand for products increased again. This process of economic expansion is still going on.

Technological advances in transportation and communication aided the economic boom. The development of the steam-powered railroad train in the early 1800's gave businesses a way to send extremely heavy loads of products and raw materials over long distances. The railroad became—and remains—the chief method of transporting goods across land. The invention of the telegraph about 1837 and the invention of the telephone in 1876 made communication more efficient than ever before. With these inventions, buyers could send and receive orders for goods more quickly than by using the mail.

Business executives had to spend enormous amounts of money to obtain raw materials, build factories, and make and operate machines. The cost was met in part through the use of the economic system called *capitalism*. Under this system, bankers and private investors put up money to help pay for business operations. Their investments entitle them to share in the business profits. In early industrial cities, only the wealthiest people could invest in businesses. But as time went on, many more people took part in the system.

Government. The rapid growth of city problems during the 1700's and 1800's forced governments to take steps to improve city life. Governments of some industrial nations passed laws during the late 1800's and early 1900's that were designed to help workers. These laws included measures that regulated child labor and provided income for injured workers and for families of workers who were killed on the job. Other laws improved public health care and provided food and shelter for the unemployed.

In most countries, the central government passed the laws that benefited city people. In the United States, the federal government generally left city affairs to the state governments. Reform bills had to be approved by the state legislatures. But the majority of the legislators represented farmers and business owners. For this reason, reform for U.S. cities often came about slowly.

Metropolitan cities

Cities have grown more than ever in the 1900's. In the early 1990's, about 2,900 cities had more than 100,000 people, and about 225 cities had over 1 million people. São Paulo, the world's largest city, has a population of about 11 million. New York City, the largest city in the United States, has about $7\frac{1}{2}$ million people.

An even more striking growth has taken place in the suburban areas that lie near big cities. Large numbers of people have settled in suburbs during the 1900's. The great masses of people that had filled the cities are now crowding both the cities and the land that surrounds them. Besides homes, many suburbs today contain offices and shopping centers. Suburban residents can work and buy the goods they need without traveling to the city.

A city with suburbs is a *metropolitan city,* and the city and the developed area around it is a *metropolitan area.*

The word *metropolitan* comes from Greek words meaning *mother city.* The Mexico City metropolitan area is the largest metropolitan area in the world. It has about 19 million people. The largest cities are all metropolitan cities. See **Metropolitan area.**

The population explosion has played an important part in the development of metropolitan areas. By 1990, the world's population was about five times as large as it was in 1850. This rapid growth led to overcrowded cities, causing large numbers of people to move to outlying areas. The population implosion, in which people moved from rural to urban areas, also helped build up metropolitan areas. The population displosion, in which people of various racial, religious, and national backgrounds moved into cities, was an important trend in the growth of metropolitan areas. After poor people moved into central cities, many wealthy people moved

A **metropolitan city** is a giant community with suburbs nearby. In Los Angeles, *above,* and other American metropolitan cities, expressways connect the center of town and surrounding communities. These high-speed highways enable millions of people to travel from their homes in the suburbs to their jobs in the city.

out of the cities and into the suburbs.

In addition, economic growth aided the development of metropolitan areas. The booming economies of industrial nations helped millions of people achieve a high living standard. As a result, more people could afford expensive homes in the suburbs. In many nations, governments helped pay for roads and transportation systems in new areas. People could easily travel to the city on streetcars, subways, and railroads.

Motor vehicles, a major technological advance of the 1900's, also helped metropolitan areas develop. The automobile made it possible for millions of people to live far from jobs, schools, and shopping. By the early 1990's, there were about 450 million passenger cars in the world. Motor trucks became cheaper than railroads for transporting goods over long distances. The lower costs encouraged many factories and stores to locate in the suburbs.

Description. Today's cities are much larger than those of earlier times. In the late 1400's, for example, Paris covered about 3 square miles (8 square kilometers). The city now covers 41 square miles (105 square kilometers), and its metropolitan area stretches about 185 square miles (479 square kilometers).

The layouts of most metropolitan cities in the United States resemble one another. The original business section lies downtown, in the center of the city. It contains banks, museums, government buildings, and company headquarters. People throughout the metropolitan

area work in offices there and shop in downtown stores. The business section covers a small area. But it can serve thousands of people daily because many offices and stores are in large skyscrapers.

In the past, most business people worked downtown and lived nearby. But many metropolitan areas today are *decentralized.* They contain various centers of business and housing in addition to the original city center.

An industrial region of factories, warehouses, and shipping yards lies next to or encircles the downtown section of many cities. The residential areas, where most of the people live, begin beyond the industrial region. The oldest and most run-down houses are in the residential area closest to the city center. Most of the city's poor people live in this area, often called the *inner city.* In the mid-1900's, local and federal governments began urban renewal projects in many inner cities. These projects replaced some of the worst buildings with new, low-cost housing. In the United States, a large portion of this new housing consisted of high-rise apartment buildings.

The neighborhoods become newer away from the inner city, and the newest homes stand in the distant suburbs. Each residential area has its own stores or other businesses. In the suburbs, shopping centers may contain many stores—and several restaurants and movie theaters—in one building.

The main streets of cities and suburbs are often jammed with automobiles, buses, and trucks. At such times, traffic creeps along slowly. As a result, many wide expressways have been built to help carry the traffic. However, the number of motor vehicles has increased so greatly that traffic jams occur on expressways as well as on streets.

In the largest metropolitan areas, many people no longer spend much of their time downtown. They can live, work, shop, and find entertainment in the suburbs. In some cities, this suburban way of life led to the closing of old stores and businesses in the city center. But in the late 1970's and the 1980's, some suburbanites who worked downtown grew tired of constantly traveling between the suburbs and the city. In response, builders began to construct new luxury apartments and homes near downtown.

Many cities have a serious pollution problem. Motor vehicles, factories, and other sources create so much air pollution that it may hang in the air like dirty fog. Air pollution threatens the health of the people who live in cities. City wastes cause water pollution when they are poured into waterways. These wastes kill fish and make some areas unfit for swimming. In addition, many large cities have difficulty disposing of their refuse. The amount of refuse grows each year, but places to put it are quickly filling up.

The people. The population of urban places has continued to increase since the Industrial Revolution. Today, about two-fifths of the people of the world live in urban areas. The United States classifies about 75 percent of its population as urban. In Canada, too, about 76 percent of the population lives in urban places. Since 1945, suburban growth has been even more spectacular than the growth of cities has been. In the United States, more people now live in the suburbs than in the central cities.

On the whole, the people in the metropolitan areas of North America, Western Europe, and Japan have the highest standard of living in history. There are many more wealthy people and middle-income people than ever before.

Most of the people who live in metropolitan areas have good housing, send their children to well-equipped schools, and can afford the necessities—and many luxuries—of life. Workers in all occupations have benefited from the booming economy and from the increased strength of the labor movement during the 1900's. However, as has been true throughout history, many people live in poverty.

The existence of poverty ranks among the chief problems of today's cities. The poor are often unable to find the jobs they need to better themselves. They may lack the education or training to help them find good jobs. Discrimination on the basis of race, religion, sex, or nationality also limits opportunities for many people. In the United States, targets of discrimination in the 1800's and early 1900's included the Chinese, Irish, Italians, Jews, and Poles. Blacks, Hispanic Americans, American Indians, and Asian Americans are among the many groups that still suffer from discrimination in U.S. cities.

Many poor people live in the inner city. This area is characterized by run-down apartment buildings that are crowded and close together. Many of the apartments have been divided, so that more than one family lives in quarters originally intended for a single family.

A large percentage of the people in neighborhoods just beyond the inner city are classified by sociologists as lower middle class. These people live more comfortably than the poor people but not nearly so well as the people farther out. Most of the houses are old and small. But they are in better condition and are less crowded than housing in the inner city.

Most middle-class and wealthy people live on the edges of the city or in the suburbs. However, some live in apartment buildings downtown. Their homes are bigger and newer than those in the inner city. Many houses have large backyards where families can play and relax in privacy.

Since the mid-1900's, the movement to the suburbs has increased dramatically. People move out to find better housing and cleaner, quieter, and safer living conditions. They seek a better education for their children than that available in the inner city. Many schools in the inner cities rank low on various measures of educational achievement.

Metropolitan areas are becoming more culturally diverse. People from many backgrounds live in the city and suburbs. However, residents with similar incomes, nationalities, and religions often live near each other.

Economy. The economic boom that began during the Industrial Revolution of the 1700's and 1800's is still going on, and the markets for products made in cities continue to grow. The population explosion has created more buyers for more goods, and higher standards of living make it possible for people to buy an increasing volume of products. Many nations have expanded their trade with other nations, creating new markets for their products. Technological advances have also made many new products available. The economies of advanced nations rely heavily on sales of such products as automobiles, computers, refrigerators, and television sets.

Metropolitan cities, like industrial cities, are manufacturing centers that provide jobs for thousands of factory workers. But today's cities also have large numbers of jobs for workers in hundreds of other fields. Salespeople sell the products of industry, and transportation workers move the products from place to place. Office workers help keep businesses running smoothly. Construction workers build offices, factories, and housing units.

Many people who work in metropolitan cities have jobs in *service industries,* which provide services instead of agricultural products or manufactured goods. Examples of workers in service industries include psychologists, lawyers, and secretaries. To manage the affairs of cities, governments employ such service workers as accountants, fire fighters, and tree trimmers.

Major technological advances have helped economic growth in the 1900's. These advances include the use of electricity and gasoline to run machines and the development of plastics and other materials to make new products. Other technological advances have been radio, TV, and the space satellite for communication; the automobile and airplane for transportation; and the computer to handle information needed by complex economies. Jobs created by technological progress include those of airplane pilots, computer operators, electricians, mechanics, and service station attendants.

Economic activity in metropolitan areas has become increasingly decentralized due to technological advances. Many business firms have built factories or warehouses in the suburbs while keeping their main offices in the city.

Government. The governments of metropolitan cities have grown into large, complex organizations. They face the challenging tasks of providing services for thousands or millions of people and of helping rebuild aging, decaying parts of cities. They are hard-pressed to obtain the funds they need to do their work, and their problems increase as urban populations continue to grow. For further information, see the *Governmental problems* section of this article.

City problems

Cities are the cultural, economic, governmental, population, transportation, and communication centers of the world. They are places where most people can find a job and earn a living and where some people can accumulate moderate or great wealth. In cities, people can also choose from a variety of cultural and recreational activities that add to the enjoyment of life. Nevertheless, cities have many physical, social, economic, and governmental problems.

Physical problems of cities include substandard housing, pollution, and traffic congestion. The term *substandard housing* refers to poorly constructed, run-down, unsanitary, or overcrowded dwellings. In developing nations, millions of people live in crude shacks or other dwellings that barely provide shelter. The people of advanced nations are better off. Even so, some housing in advanced nations is also substandard. Many governments have set up programs to improve housing for needy families. However, population growth, lack of funds, the high cost of construction, and other factors continue to cause a worldwide housing crisis. Substandard housing and attempts to solve the problem are discussed in detail in the **Housing** article.

Motor vehicles, factories, and other sources pollute the air with fumes that endanger the health of the people in cities. Urban wastes pollute waterways. City residents and industries produce extraordinary amounts of refuse. A government might want to end pollution by eliminating sources of contamination. But the government would need to close factories and prohibit almost all automobiles to do so, thus crippling the economy and inconveniencing the people.

Instead, citizens, governments, industry, scientists, and business people must work together to gradually reduce pollution. For example, most cities have introduced recycling programs, which cut down on refuse and the space needed to store it. Residents separate recyclable products from garbage, and city governments provide drop-off sites or pick up the products from homes. See **Environmental pollution; Recycling.**

At any time—but especially during the morning and evening rush hours—the main streets of cities and suburbs can become jammed with motor vehicles. Such traffic jams delay and anger people trying to get to and from work and other places. Governments have built expressways, tried to improve public transportation, and taken other steps to relieve traffic congestion. Even so, getting from place to place in a metropolitan area continues to become more and more difficult, because of population growth and the ever-increasing use of automobiles.

Social problems in today's cities include crime, juvenile delinquency, alcoholism, drug addiction, and friction between people of different backgrounds. Poverty—which is both a social and an economic problem—is discussed in the *Economic problems* section of this article.

Crime, alcoholism, drug addiction, and juvenile delinquency do not occur only in cities. But these social problems affect many people who live in cities. Social scientists point out that some individuals come to feel they have no place in society. These individuals may turn to crime or delinquency as a way of making money or lashing out at society. Or they may seek escape from their problems through the abuse of alcohol or drugs. Young people in the inner city sometimes turn to crime or drugs because they have grown up without enough guidance from adults.

Stricter law enforcement might help reduce crime. However, the problems will reappear unless their causes are eliminated. Private and governmental organizations try to reduce social problems. These groups publicize the dangers of turning to crime, alcohol, or drugs. They also work with people to help them overcome their problems.

The population displosion has led to conflicts between groups of people. Often, groups with different cultural backgrounds fear and distrust each other and view each other's way of life as inferior. Such attitudes have caused violence between groups. Examples in the 1900's include conflicts between Protestants and Roman Catholics in Northern Ireland; Hindus and Muslims in India and Pakistan; blacks and whites in South Africa and the United States; and language groups in India. In some places, governments have passed laws to protect minority groups from injustices. However, group conflicts will continue until people learn to live together peacefully.

S. E. Hedin, Carl Östman

Substandard housing is one of the most serious city problems. In spite of government efforts to improve housing, many dwellings like the shacks in New Delhi, India, *above,* remain.

Pictorial Parade

Travel in cities is often difficult. People must crowd into trains and buses and drive on jammed roads. In Tokyo, *above,* workers called *pushers* cram passengers into the trains.

Economic problems. Most people in the cities of advanced nations enjoy a high standard of living. But even in the best times, a city has many poor people. Poverty has existed since ancient times, but the wealth of some people in cities highlights the problem. Most of the new jobs, spacious homes, and good schools are in the suburbs. Residents of the inner city cannot share in these opportunities. In some inner cities, the loss of jobs and housing has left poor people homeless. When poor people also suffer discrimination, their anger has occasionally led them to riot.

Governments, individuals, and charitable and social action organizations work to eliminate poverty. They try to improve educational and job opportunities for the needy, and they provide many poor people with financial aid. For a detailed discussion of the problem and steps taken to solve it, see **Poverty**.

Complex economic and social factors sometimes lead to business slumps. During a slump, many workers lose their jobs and the number of needy people in cities increases. The workers can sometimes collect unemployment pay from the government, but this pay is much less than their usual income. Unemployed workers cut down on their buying, and business suffers further.

Governmental problems. Through the years, the job of governing cities has become increasingly complex. Today, city governments must find ways to rebuild aging, decaying areas and to provide satisfactory schools, police protection, and other necessary services. Population growth contributes to the difficulty of governing cities. Urban governments also lack the funds that would help solve their problems.

Governments throughout metropolitan areas must provide services for populations that are continually increasing. Also, many people who move into cities are poor, and many who move out are wealthy. This development means that city governments must provide financial assistance for a larger part of the population. It also means that the people who live in the cities are less able to pay for services that are provided by the government. Wealthy people who move to suburbs may continue to earn a living in the city, but these people may no longer pay taxes to support the city's government. A city's tax base also shrinks when industries move to suburbs. State and federal governments contribute to the cost of operating cities. Even so, cities face serious financial problems.

Suburban governments also face challenging problems. They must find the money to pay for new schools and for fire and police protection. They must also install expensive sewerage and water systems.

A city government is part of a complex authority system. Each city government is subject to the regulations of its central government. In some countries, cities are also subject to the regulations of regional governments, such as those of states and provinces.

In the United States, state legislatures set up city governments to provide local services. Almost all of the states grant cities *home rule*. That is, a city may—within the general laws of the state—adopt its own *charter* (form of government) and have considerable freedom in local matters. In a state without home rule, the state legislature decides what form of government a city will have. It also decides many city government policies, such as the kind of and rate of taxation. See **Home rule**.

Many separate governmental units operate within most metropolitan areas in the United States and Canada. These units include city, suburban, county, and township governments; school districts; and special districts. Special districts include units that provide for garbage collection, mosquito control, sewage disposal, and park management. No one governmental unit has authority over the entire area. Therefore, no one unit has the authority or the responsibility for dealing with such areawide problems as pollution and the flow of mass transportation. *Metropolitan governments* have been established in a few metropolitan areas to provide an overall authority. A metropolitan government is responsible for an entire metropolitan area's police protection, water supply, mass transportation, and other services. The Miami, Fla.; Nashville, Tenn.; and Toronto, Ont., areas have metropolitan governments. Many people oppose this form of government. They fear that it results in higher taxes, and they believe only small local governments can remain close to the people.

For more details on the functions and problems of local governments today, and of their relations with higher levels of government, see **Local government**. For a discussion of how city governments operate and are organized, see **City government**.

Solving city problems. Cities have made some effort to solve their problems, but much remains to be done. More money than is now available could partially solve some of the problems. In some countries, the funds would come from taxes paid by citizens and businesses. Some people favor extensive use of tax money for social improvement, but others oppose it. Government regula-

Metropolitan area governmental units

This diagram shows some of the governmental units that operate within a metropolitan area. Solutions to areawide problems are difficult, partly because no one unit has areawide authority.

County	School districts
Township	Division of two sanitary districts
Towns	Park district

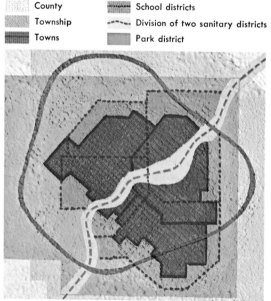

WORLD BOOK illustration by George Suyeoka

tion can also be used to help solve problems. For example, governments can demand that car manufacturers make cars that pollute the air less than today's vehicles do. Again, some people favor extensive government regulation as a solution, but others oppose it.

But money and government cannot solve all city problems. Some are too complex and too poorly understood to be solved rapidly. Also, government efforts to combat such problems as crime and pollution need help from citizens and businesses.

Cultural variety in cities

Metropolitan cities are filled with people from many different cultures, and this variety makes them interesting places to live. People who arrive from other countries often settle in cities. They bring many ideas about religion, food, language, and government to their new homes. For this reason, cultural contrasts are often more dramatic in cities than in smaller towns.

Many people choose to live in cities because they enjoy the variety of cultures found there. But cultural differences can add to urban conflict. Discrimination often occurs between cultural groups. In addition, older groups sometimes dislike newcomers because they do not welcome a challenge to their own culture.

Neighborhoods. Immigrants tend to settle near others with similar cultural backgrounds. Neighborhoods often develop with stores, restaurants, and houses of worship for people from certain cultures. In these neighborhoods, people may speak, read, and hear the language of their original country. They may buy books in Polish or rent videotapes from India. Many cities have an area called "Chinatown," where visitors can sample Chinese foods and buy imported products.

Immigration patterns often shape the neighborhoods and cultures found within a city. In the 1800's, for example, many neighborhoods in the United States attracted immigrants from Ireland or Eastern Europe. Today,

many immigrants come from Latin America and Asia, especially Cambodia, Korea, and Vietnam. The Asians bring Buddhism and other non-Western religions to the United States. Latin Americans bring a tradition of large, close-knit families.

Political culture. One important way in which the cultural groups within a city may differ from one another is in their views on government. Social scientists use the term *political culture* to describe such views. For example, most people in some cultural groups believe strongly that citizens should actively participate in government. A majority from other groups feel that a low level of citizen participation is not a problem. Different cultural groups also tend to have different views on how a city's government should be organized, which services it should provide, and which problems it should try to solve first.

The existence of a variety of political cultures within a city can lead to friction. However, many people point out that a city can be strengthened by the existence of a wide range of viewpoints among its residents. For example, a city's immigrants may have lived under various types of governments and observed many different solutions to urban problems. As a result, they may bring to their adopted city new ideas and experiences that can help solve the city's problems.

Future cities

Sociologists have made various predictions about urban communities of the future. They believe that metropolitan areas will continue to grow in both population and area. In 1990, about $2\frac{1}{4}$ billion people in different parts of the world lived in urban places. By the year 2010, the number is expected to rise to about 4 billion people. In the United States in 1990, about 187 million people lived in urban places as defined by the U.S. government. By the year 2010, the number is expected to reach 225 million.

Some new urban communities have already been built in the 1900's, and more will be built in the future. Like today's suburbs, the new communities will provide living space and ease the overcrowding problem caused by the population explosion and implosion. City planners hope that—unlike most suburbs—the new communities will also provide jobs for most of their residents. If the communities do so, the overcrowding of cities will be eased even more.

Communities that have such a self-supporting feature are called *new towns* or *new cities*. The United Kingdom and the Scandinavian countries have been leaders in the development of new towns. The governments of these nations provided much financial aid for this development. In the United States, where private enterprise

plays the major role, only a few new towns have been developed. They include Columbia, Md., and Reston, Va.

Brazil built a new capital city, Brasília, in the mid-1900's. The Brazilian government located this city in the thinly populated interior of the country. It hopes that an important, modern city there will lead to further development of the interior.

The development of new towns and cities is a slow, costly process. Private developers are reluctant to take on such projects because of the uncertainty of—and the long wait for—profits. Many governments have been unable or unwilling to finance such projects. For these reasons, sociologists predict that almost all the additional millions of people who will live in urban places in the future will crowd into existing communities. More and more of the land around central cities will be filled by people. The suburbs will spread out so far that some metropolitan areas will run together with no rural areas between them. Such a continuous stretch of metropolitan areas is called a *megalopolis*. For example, a megalopolis has formed between Boston, New York City, Philadelphia, Baltimore, and Washington, D.C.

Sociologists also foresee physical changes in metropolitan areas. To absorb the increasing population, governments may permit tall buildings in areas where they are now prohibited. Governments may also set aside much more land for parks and other recreational areas. They may try to solve traffic problems and improve safety by expanding public transportation and by creating separate roadways for automobiles, trucks, and pedestrians. See City planning; Urban renewal.

The effort to free cities of pollution seems sure to continue. Entire urban communities may be enclosed in plastic domes. Temperature and humidity inside the domes would be controlled, and electronic filters would keep the air clean and fresh. It is hoped that future cities and suburbs will offer the advantages of urban life without the disadvantages.

Henry C. Binford and Terry Nichols Clark

Study aids

Related articles. *World Book* has separate articles on hundreds of cities. Lists of U.S. cities appear at the end of the articles on the states, and Canadian cities appear at the end of the province articles. Cities of other countries are listed at the end of the articles on those countries. See also the following articles:

History

Athens	Guild
Babylon	Industrial Revolution
City-state	Middle Ages
Egypt, Ancient	Phoenicia
Free city	Rome (The ancient city)
Greece, Ancient	Rome, Ancient

City problems

Air pollution	Riot
Crime	Segregation
Drug abuse	Traffic (Traffic problems)
Environmental pollution	Waste disposal
Juvenile delinquency	Water pollution
Poverty	

Other related articles

Architecture	Park (Kinds of parks)
City government	Playground
City planning	Population
Communication	Public health
Community	School
Education	Street
Housing	Suburb
Local government	Technology
Megalopolis	Transportation
Metropolitan area	Urban Coalition, National
National League of Cities	Urban renewal

Outline

I. How cities began and developed
  A. Advances in technology C. Social organization
  B. Physical environment D. Population growth
II. Ancient cities
  A. Description   C. Economy
  B. The people   D. Government
III. Medieval cities
  A. Description   C. Economy
  B. The people   D. Government
IV. Industrial cities
  A. Description   C. Economy
  B. The people   D. Government
V. Metropolitan cities
  A. Description   C. Economy
  B. The people   D. Government
VI. City problems
  A. Physical problems C. Economic problems
  B. Social problems   D. Governmental problems

  E. Solving city problems
VII. Cultural variety in cities
  A. Neighborhoods
  B. Political culture
VIII. Future cities

Questions

What are some of the reasons that so many people live in and near cities?
What are some of the problems of cities?
What city was founded by a steel company?
What is the *population explosion*? The *population implosion*? The *population displosion*?
How did medieval cities solve the problem of overcrowding?
How did people of ancient cities try to please the gods?
What is a *megalopolis*?
What northern Italian coastal city remained a trading center throughout the Middle Ages?
How did the decline of manorialism contribute to the growth of cities?
Why can a city business section that covers a small area serve thousands of people daily?

Reading and Study Guide

See *City* in the Research Guide/Index, Volume 22, for a *Reading and Study Guide.*

Additional resources

Level I
Gay, Kathlyn. *Cities Under Stress: Can Today's City Systems Be Made to Work?* Watts, 1985
Kalman, Bobbie. *Early City Life.* Crabtree (Toronto), 1983.
Pringle, Laurence P. *City and Suburb: Exploring an Ecosystem.* Macmillan, 1975.
Splendors of the Past: Lost Cities of the Ancient World. National Geographic Soc., 1981.

Level II
After the Developers. Ed. by James Lorimer and Carolyn MacGregor. James Lorimer (Toronto), 1981. Essays on Canadian urban problems.
Braunfels, Wolfgang. *Urban Design in Western Europe: Regime and Architecture, 900-1900.* Univ. of Chicago Pr., 1988. First published in Germany in 1976.
Cities of the World: A Compilation of Current Information on Cultural, Geographical, and Political Conditions in the Countries and Cities of Six Continents. Ed. by Margaret W. Young. 4 vols. 3rd ed. Gale Research, 1987.
Hanmer, Trudy. *The Growth of Cities.* Watts, 1985. Evolution of American cities.
Hibbert, Christopher. *Cities and Civilizations.* Weidenfeld & Nicolson, 1986.
Mumford, Lewis. *The City in History: Its Origins, Its Transformations, and Its Prospects.* Harcourt, 1968. First published in 1961.

City government manages the affairs of and provides services for cities, towns, villages, and other communities. Some states also have units of local government called *boroughs,* which resemble towns. Cities and other communities with their own government are known as *municipalities,* and city government is also called *municipal government.*

About 62 per cent of the people of the United States live in municipalities. State legislatures set up city governments to provide services for the people. These services include education, police and fire protection, recreational facilities, street maintenance, and health and welfare services. Most of the states grant cities *home rule.* That is, the cities may, within the general laws of the state, adopt their own *charter* (form of organization) and have considerable freedom in local matters. See Home rule.

The United States has about 19,000 *incorporated* municipalities. An incorporated municipality is a corporation under the law and has a charter from the state defining its powers, responsibilities, and organization. Illinois leads the states with about 1,280. Hawaii, on the other hand, has no incorporated cities. All of the cities and towns in Hawaii are governed as part of the county in which they are located. Nevada, New Hampshire, and Rhode Island have fewer than 20 incorporated municipalities each.

Municipalities vary greatly in size. The largest municipality in the United States is New York City, with more than 7 million people. The smallest municipalities may have only a few hundred residents.

All municipal governments perform similar functions and have similar organization. These governments are the principal providers of such services as police and fire protection, sanitation, water supply, and public health programs. All city governments are organized into three branches: (1) legislative, (2) executive, and (3) judicial. Legislative responsibilities are carried out by a lawmaking body called the *city council,* sometimes known as the *board of aldermen* or *city commission.* The council makes laws for the city in the form of *municipal ordinances.* The executive branch is headed by the mayor or city manager, who administers the city government and coordinates its public services. Courts, which make up the judicial branch, try people accused of violating municipal ordinances. In small municipalities that do not have their own courts, county or district courts handle most cases.

For information on city and other local governments, see the article on **Local government.** To learn about city government in Canada, see the section on *Local government* in each province article in *World Book.*

Forms of city government

There are two major forms of city government in the United States: the *mayor-council* form and the *council-manager* form. A small and steadily decreasing number of cities use a third type called the *commission* form.

The mayor-council form is the oldest type of city government in the United States. The first city governments in the American Colonies were patterned after those in England. They had a council, which was the chief organ of government, and a mayor, who was a member of the council and presided over it.

Under most mayor-council systems today, the mayor operates from a separate office and is not a member of the council. The people elect both the mayor and the council. More than one-third of the cities in the United States with populations of 25,000 or more have the mayor-council system.

There are two main types of mayor-council government: (1) the weak-mayor system and (2) the strong-mayor system. The weak-mayor system developed in the late 1700's and is the most popular type of government in small cities. The strong-mayor system developed in the late 1800's and is especially popular in large cities.

The weak-mayor system gives the mayor only limited executive authority. The council, on the other hand, has executive as well as legislative powers. In most cities, the mayor does not prepare the city budget and has little veto power over council decisions. In the weak-mayor system, the mayor appoints few, if any, of the city's top administrative officials, and these appointments may be subject to the approval of the council. Other administrative officials are chosen by the city council, the governor, the state legislature, the voters, or independent boards and commissions.

The chief criticism of the weak-mayor system is that responsibility is not centralized but divided among many officials. The mayor does not have a voice in selecting many department heads, and consequently has difficulty coordinating the administration of city services. However, some persons favor such decentralization of authority because they fear too much power vested in a single individual.

The strong-mayor system gives the mayor broad

Mayor-council form of government

The council is the chief governing body of the city. Under the strong-mayor system, the mayor appoints most department heads and has direct control over them. Under the weak-mayor system, the mayor appoints few, if any, top administrative officials and has only limited control over them.

WORLD BOOK chart

Strong-Mayor System

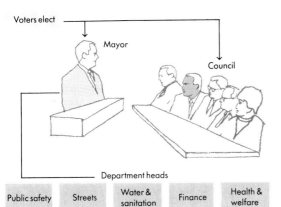

Weak-Mayor System

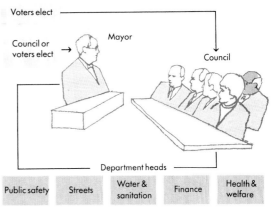

powers. The mayor can appoint and dismiss most department heads, veto acts of the council, prepare the budget, plan various programs, and direct the operation of all city departments. The mayor serves as the leader in city government and proposes legislation to the city council. However, the council determines basic government policy and raises revenue for the city.

Most experts on city government consider the strong-mayor system superior to the weak-mayor system. The centralization of authority in the office of the mayor assures better coordination of the services of city government. One of the chief weaknesses of the strong-mayor system is that conflicts often arise between the mayor and the council because they share policymaking powers. One reason most of the largest cities in the United States use the strong-mayor system is that satisfying the conflicting demands of a wide variety of social groups requires strong political leadership.

The council-manager form of government is also called the *city manager plan.* Under this form of government, a professional administrator called a *city manager* supervises all municipal affairs. An elected city council hires the city manager. Most councils have from five to nine members. The council-manager plan is the most common form of city government in the United States for cities with populations of 25,000 or more. More than half of all such cities use the council-manager system.

In most cities that use the council-manager form, the council members are elected on nonpartisan ballots. The mayor is a member of the council. He or she is either elected to the office by the people or selected by the other council members. The mayor presides at council meetings but seldom has more power than other members. The council is the chief governing body of the city. It determines policies and passes ordinances. The city manager carries out the policies set by the council. The council may dismiss the city manager if it is dissatisfied.

A chief feature of the council-manager plan is the

Council-manager form of government

The council determines city policies and appoints a city manager to carry them out. The city manager, in turn, appoints department heads and manages all city services.

WORLD BOOK chart

Voters elect

Council

City manager

| Public safety | Streets | Water & sanitation | Finance | Health & welfare |

centralization of administrative responsibility. The city manager appoints the heads of all departments and is responsible for managing all city services.

Council-manager government is modeled on the organization of a business firm. The city council corresponds to the board of directors of a corporation, and the city manager to a corporation's general manager. City managers, who have experience and special training in city administration, perform many of the governmental activities. Politics is supposed to play little or no part in their administrative decisions because they are appointed, not elected. However, some scholars believe that city managers lack the ability to handle political conflicts between races, economic groups, or neighborhoods. They argue that council members selected in nonpartisan elections lack political experience and do not work well together. In addition, some cities have tended to blame all political weaknesses on the city manager and therefore have had high rates of turnover in managers.

The council-manager plan developed in the United States during the early 1900's. It was promoted by a businessman named Richard S. Childs and by the National Short Ballot Organization, a nonpartisan political group he founded. In 1908, Staunton, Va., hired a general manager to handle its administrative affairs under a mayor-council system. In 1912, Sumter, S.C., became the first city to adopt a complete council-manager government. The first large city to do so was Dayton, Ohio, in 1914.

The commission form of government combines legislative and executive authority in an elected group of commissioners. The number of commissioners varies from city to city, but most commissions are made up of five commissioners. Each commissioner heads a city department—such as public works, finance, or public safety—and is separately responsible for the administration of his or her department. The commission as a body has the power to pass ordinances, impose taxes, distribute funds for city needs, and appoint officials. One of the members may be designated as mayor for ceremonial functions and for presiding over commission meetings.

The chief objection to commission government has been that disagreements among commission members on issues involving more than one department make effective coordination difficult. Today, only about 50 U.S. cities with populations of 25,000 or more have a commission form of government.

Administering city government

City governments employ many people to provide services to residents. These employees are organized into many separate departments and agencies, such as the police department and the public library. Each department is headed by an administrator who is responsible to the mayor, city manager, or commissioners. These agencies and their employees are called the city *bureaucracy.*

Patronage is the practice of awarding jobs and government contracts based on people's service to the party in power. The patronage system was widely used during the 1800's. Chicago and a few other cities still fill some government jobs on the basis of patronage. During the late 1800's, many reformers charged that the patronage system produced dishonest and inefficient city workers. The reformers urged that more city jobs should be filled by a civil service system based on merit. They also called for *nonpartisan elections,* in which candidates for city office are listed on the ballot with no indication of their political party. Today, about 70 per cent of all municipalities in the United States hold nonpartisan elections for city offices.

Civil service includes all city government employees who are appointed rather than elected. The term *civil service* is usually used, however, for a system in which appointments are based on merit rather than on political connections. Applicants for such civil service jobs take an examination, and those with the highest scores are hired. Civil servants are protected against being fired from their jobs for political reasons.

In many cities, municipal employees have joined labor unions in an effort to obtain higher pay and better working conditions. Strikes by police, fire fighters, and other city workers affected many cities during the 1970's and 1980's.

City finances

Sources of revenue. City governments have traditionally relied on property taxes to finance city services. The city collects these taxes from homeowners, businesses, and other owners of taxable property. The amount of tax is based on the estimated value of the property.

City governments rely in part on financial aid from state and federal governments. Much of this assistance comes in the form of *grants-in-aid.* Grants-in-aid are funds made available under certain conditions or for a certain program. Most grants from state governments may be used for general purposes, but the city must meet certain standards established by the state. Most federal aid consists of grants for such specific purposes as airport construction or improvements in city sewerage systems.

Expenditures. About 40 per cent of a typical municipal budget goes to pay city workers. The rest is used for such lasting improvements as parks and museums, and for such specific purposes as buying library books and maintaining roads.

Budget problems. During the 1970's and 1980's, many cities in the United States faced serious budget difficulties. For example, New York City suffered a financial crisis in 1975. City officials had borrowed heavily to meet basic city expenses and lacked enough money to pay the bills. The state and federal governments loaned money to the city to enable it to pay its expenses. As a result of its budget problems, New York City had to reduce city services and eliminate many city jobs. In 1978, Cleveland *defaulted on* (failed to pay) its debts. Many other cities avoided serious financial problems only by cutting back on city services and laying off city employees.

There are many reasons for city budget problems. Many urban residents are eager for more services but are unwilling to pay more taxes. When city employees receive higher salaries, officials often are reluctant to pass the added costs on to the taxpayers. In some older cities, the *tax base* (total value of property that can be taxed) has decreased as people and businesses have

moved to the suburbs. Inflation also strains municipal budgets.

Influencing city government

People can influence their city government in many ways. They can act individually by voting in municipal elections and by writing or talking to city officials. They can join with others to organize and participate in political parties and other groups.

Municipal elections are held every four years in most cities. Elections enable citizens to vote for the officials and proposals of their choice. However, the number of people voting in city elections is small in comparison with the number voting in state or national elections. Only about 29 per cent of the eligible voters cast their ballots in municipal elections.

Parties and other groups. During the late 1800's, political parties were extremely active in local government. They developed strong organizations called *machines,* which did favors for citizens in return for votes cast for party candidates. Party machines began to disappear during the early 1900's, when municipal governments adopted nonpartisan elections and other reform measures. Chicago and a few other cities still have powerful political machines.

Groups called *special-interest groups* are probably the major influence on city government today. Business groups and downtown merchants call for policies to attract new industries. Minority groups may demand more jobs and better community services. Taxpayer organizations attempt to limit city spending and taxes. Neighborhood organizations support programs to reduce crime rates and to improve neighborhood conditions. Environmental groups may oppose the construction of nuclear power plants and other projects that they believe threaten the environment or people's health.

Robert L. Lineberry

Related articles in *World Book* include:

Services of city government

City planning	Public health
Fire department	Sanitation
Health, Board of	Sewage (Urban sewerage systems)
Housing (Local housing controls)	Street
Library (Public libraries)	Urban renewal
Park	Waste disposal
Police (City police)	Water (City water systems)

Other related articles

Assessment	Property tax
Borough	Revenue sharing
City	Suburb
Local government	Town
Mayor	Town meeting
Metropolitan area	Traffic
Patronage	Village

Additional resources

City Politics in Canada. Ed. by Warren Magnusson and Andrew Sancton. Univ. of Toronto Pr., 1983.
Gay, Kathlyn. *Cities Under Stress: Can Today's City Systems Be Made to Work?* Watts, 1984. Also suitable for younger readers.
Martin, David L. *Running City Hall: Municipal Administration in America.* Univ. of Alabama Pr., 1982.

City manager. See City government (The council-manager form).

Skidmore, Owings & Merrill (WORLD BOOK photo by Ralph Brunke)

City planning involves the work of many people, including city planners, architects, and economists. City planners work to improve existing communities and to develop new ones. The experts shown here are reviewing the design of a Japanese city.

City planning

City planning is the process of preparing programs to guide the development of cities and towns. City planners—the people who direct the process—advise local governments on ways to improve communities. They also advise governments and real estate developers who are planning entirely new neighborhoods and communities.

City planners deal chiefly with the physical layout of communities. They make proposals designed to beautify communities and to make life in them comfortable, enjoyable, and profitable. Their proposals include slum-clearance programs, projects to replace run-down housing, recreation areas, shopping centers, and plans to improve transportation and parking facilities.

Many city planners work for local governments. Others work for developers or groups of citizens who propose plans to the government. A city planner's day-to-day work chiefly involves improvements in parts of a community. But a planner views a community as a single system in which all the parts are dependent on one another. A planner may create a *master plan* (overall plan for the community) and use it as the basis for all the work. Such a plan shows the entire community both as it is and as the planner believes it should be. The city planner's suggestions for changes in any part of a community must follow the master plan. For example, the plan might restrict the height of buildings in residential areas. City planners must follow this restriction whenever they design changes for any residential area.

City planners try to predict the future. They attempt to forecast such developments as large changes in population and industrial activity. The predictions of city planners help a government plan for the future.

City planning began with the first cities—about 3500 B.C. Ancient peoples set aside areas for housing, worship, and other activities. They built walls around their communities for protection against enemies. Throughout history, people have done some planning for their communities. But the planning has not kept pace with the tremendous growth of urban communities. Many have become dirty, noisy, overcrowded, and run-down. City planners work to redevelop these communities and to manage new development in places that are rapidly growing. During the 1900's, governments have greatly increased city planning activities in an attempt to help solve the many problems of cities and towns. For a discussion of these problems, see the *World Book* article on **City** (City problems).

The master plan

The preparation of master plans ranks among the most important duties of city planners. A master plan, also called a *comprehensive plan,* includes diagrams and models that show a community as it is and as the planner believes it should exist in the future. The plan includes reports and statistical information that support the planner's proposals.

A master plan shows how land should be used. It also shows how public facilities and services—such as schools, roads, fire and police stations, and water, sewerage, and transportation systems—should be improved or expanded. Planners call these services and facilities a community's *infrastructure.* In some cities, new developments are permitted only when a master plan allows the developments and when the infrastructure can provide certain levels of expanded service. In some states of the United States, a master plan is required before a city can proceed with development.

Preparing the plan. A professional city planner may consult many other professional experts in preparing a master plan. These experts might include architects, economists, educators, engineers, finance specialists, geographers, lawyers, political scientists, statisticians, and specialists in air and water quality. The city planner also seeks advice from nonprofessional people who will be affected by the plan. These people include business persons, homeowners, and members of citizens groups. The general public may also be allowed to participate in the preparation of the plan.

Today, many city planners use computers in their work. Computers process information that planners analyze in forming a plan. Planners also use computers to create maps and designs.

Many communities—mostly small ones—hire a private planning firm that prepares a master plan and submits it to the local government for approval. In many other communities, an agency of the local government does the planning job. In some communities—especially big cities—the government includes a department of city planning. This department prepares the master plan. The city planner and other department members are responsible to the top executive.

Proposals of the plan. A master plan aims to make community life more comfortable, enjoyable, safe, and profitable. A good plan provides transportation facilities that enable people to get to and from stores, offices, and factories quickly and easily. It also provides enough recreation areas, schools, and shopping facilities.

The major part of a master plan recommends how the community's land should be used. The plan divides the community into sections. It classifies some sections as residential areas, others as commercial and industrial areas, and the rest as public facility sites. It divides these major sections into smaller districts, each with certain building restrictions. For example, the plan reserves some parts of residential areas for houses only and some for both houses and small apartment buildings. It may propose construction of high-rise apartment buildings in other neighborhoods. The master plan may permit retail trade, wholesale trade, and light manufacturing in some commercial and industrial districts but forbid heavy manufacturing there. The plans may allow *mixed-use* development in some areas, with a combination of residential, commercial, and industrial sites.

A master plan may suggest ways to improve the appearance of a community. For example, it may propose treelined boulevards, parks, and a new civic center.

Skidmore, Owings & Merrill

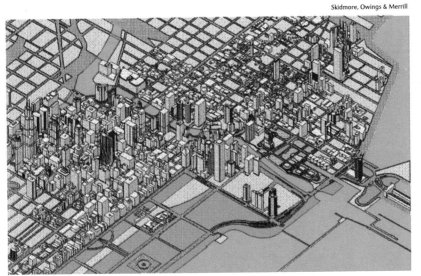

A computer-generated drawing may be used by city planners to show proposed changes in the arrangement of buildings and other features of an urban area. The computer-generated drawing at the left shows downtown Chicago.

Improving an existing community

City planning may involve rebuilding sections of a community according to a master plan. The illustrations below show how Philadelphia city planners worked to improve one section of the city. The model shows what they planned, and the photograph shows the finished project.

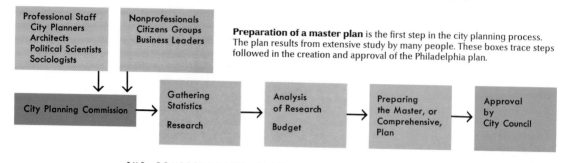

Professional Staff City Planners Architects Political Scientists Sociologists	Nonprofessionals Citizens Groups Business Leaders

Preparation of a master plan is the first step in the city planning process. The plan results from extensive study by many people. These boxes trace steps followed in the creation and approval of the Philadelphia plan.

City Planning Commission → Gathering Statistics / Research → Analysis of Research / Budget → Preparing the Master, or Comprehensive, Plan → Approval by City Council

THE COMPREHENSIVE PLAN
THE PHYSICAL DEVELOPMENT PLAN FOR THE CITY OF PHILADELPHIA

RESIDENCE
under 20
20 to 39
40 to 59
60 and over
COMMERCE
CENTERS
FREE STANDING
RECREATION
PLAYGROUNDS & PLAYFIELDS
PARKS
INSTITUTIONS
CEMETERIES
INDUSTRY
TRANSPORTATION &
UTILITIES
EXPRESSWAYS
ARTERIALS

A land-use map is a major part of a master plan. The land-use map at the left shows which sections of Philadelphia should be commercial, industrial, recreational, and residential areas.

© John McGrail

Lawrence Williams, Philadelphia City Planning Commission

A planner's model shows how a section of the city would look according to the master plan. The model above calls for construction of three tall apartment buildings, *center,* and a nearby expressway above the ground.

Philadelphia City Planning Commission

An aerial photograph shows how planners revised their design during construction of the project. The three apartment buildings, called Society Hill Towers, have been completed as planned, but the expressway runs below the ground.

Such improvements are sometimes called *urban design.*

The plan may include proposals for major changes in citywide facilities, such as sanitation and transportation systems. It may recommend a more complex sanitary drainage system for heavy manufacturing areas than for residential and commercial districts. The plan also may call for such developments as the widening of streets and the construction of a new expressway to ease travel between residential, commercial, and industrial areas.

City planners are still chiefly concerned with the physical layout of communities. But since the mid-1900's, many planners have also dealt with economic and social problems. Today, a city plan may include proposals for economic development, education, and health-care and welfare programs for the needy.

Making city planning work

City planners need both money and authority to carry out their programs. They get much of the money from local and federal governments. But governments get their money by taxing the people, so much of the money a city planner uses actually comes—indirectly—from the people. Local, state or provincial, and federal governments give city planners the authority they need to carry out their plans.

Gaining support for the plan. Strong public opposition can cause a government to refuse to act on proposals of a master plan. Proposals may lose support if the public believes they are too costly or would benefit only a small part of the population.

City planners are likely to gain public support with proposals that capture the imagination of the people. Such proposals include the development of housing, office buildings, and other facilities that can make a city more enjoyable. Sometimes a plan gains public support because it includes proposals for solving problems of deep concern to most of the people. For example, a proposal to improve roads may get wide support in a community that constantly has bad traffic jams.

Governmental authority. To carry out their plans, city planners must have influence over development and other activities that affect the layout of a community. They rely on the government's power of *eminent domain* and its authority to enforce zoning laws, subdivision regulations, and building and housing codes.

The term *eminent domain* describes a government's right to buy private property—even when the owner does not want to sell it. City planners must often rely on this power to get the land they need for major rebuilding projects. In the United States, governments have used it to carry out urban redevelopment programs and to build roads and other parts of a community's infrastructure. See **Eminent domain; Urban renewal.**

Zoning laws designate the kinds of buildings permitted in each part of a community. If a zoning law allows only houses and apartment buildings in a certain area, city planners know they can plan that area as completely residential. Zoning laws also allow planners to regulate sizes of lots, heights of buildings, the number and location of parking and loading areas, and the use of signs. See **Zoning.**

Other regulations control the subdivision and development of large, open land areas. Private real estate developers often buy large areas and subdivide them into lots. They either sell the empty lots or construct buildings on the lots before selling. Subdivision regulations designate the size of lots and other aspects of physical layout. For example, they cover the location and width of streets and the amount of land that must be used for public buildings, schools, and open space.

Building and housing codes regulate the safety and quality of construction. They also include rules that govern the number of occupants per building and the quality of electric wiring and plumbing.

Building new communities

The term *city planning* usually refers to attempts to improve existing communities. But it can also mean the development of entirely new communities. These communities, called *new cities* and *new towns,* differ from suburbs in at least one important way. Most suburbs are designed chiefly as residential communities for people who work in nearby cities. Planners of new communities try to make them fully or partly self-supporting by attracting businesses, thus providing places for the residents to work.

New cities and new towns differ from each other in location and in the degree to which they are self-supporting. Planners of new cities try to ensure that the communities have enough facilities and job opportunities for all the residents. Thus, new cities can be built far from existing cities. In the mid-1900's, the Brazilian government built Brazil's new capital, Brasília, far from the country's population center. New cities are extremely costly projects, and Brasília and Canberra, Australia, are among the few ever completed.

New towns provide jobs for many of their residents, but most rely on neighboring cities for many jobs. Most new towns are built within commuting distance of a big city. Others are communities within such a city.

The United Kingdom and the Scandinavian countries rank among the leaders in the development of new towns. The governments of these nations provide aid for new town development, including money and the authority to purchase the needed land. In the United States, private business is the major source of funds for new town development. But the development of a new town is a slow, costly process, and many private devel-

Rouse Company

Columbia, Md., one of the first *new towns* built in the United States, was begun during the early 1960's. New towns are completely new communities designed by city planners.

opers are reluctant to take on such a project.

Two of the first new towns built in the United States were Columbia, Md., and Reston, Va. By the early 1990's, an estimated 100 new towns were planned or under construction. Some private developers of several large-scale new towns received federal funds, technical assistance, and bond guarantees. These communities included Park Forest South (now University Park), near Chicago; St. Charles, near Waldorf, Md.; Soul City, near Henderson, N.C.; and Woodlands, near Houston. Today, all new towns are privately funded.

Criticism of city planning

Although most people favor the goals of city planning, some criticize the methods used to achieve those goals. Major criticisms include the length of time needed to implement plans, the high cost of planning, government control of city planning, and what opponents feel is a wrong emphasis on certain goals.

Length of time required for city planning is the most common criticism. Some political leaders argue that the results of city planning often come too late to solve the problems that the planning was intended to address. Some private developers believe that planning causes delays that result in higher costs.

High cost is another common criticism of city planning. Critics claim that the cost of carrying out a master plan places too great a burden on the taxpayers. They argue that city planners try to do too much at one time.

Government control. Some people object to a government's power to force individuals to sell their property and to regulate its use. They view this power as a violation of owners' rights. Some people also object to the city planner's role as a decision maker because the planner is not an elected official.

Wrong emphasis. Some critics complain that city planners care more about beautifying communities and helping businesses than about solving such social problems as overcrowding and pollution. These critics also charge that changes made for a community's physical improvement sometimes increase the social problems. For example, a loss of low-cost housing results when luxury apartments replace run-down buildings.

Some people believe that city planners put too much emphasis on the future of cities and towns and not enough on present problems. Yet others criticize city planners who assist in trying to solve day-to-day problems. They believe that planners should concentrate on long-range programs because the planners are the officials most directly concerned with the future development of communities.

Reducing criticism. City planners need the public's support, and so they work to reduce criticism against their methods. More and more cities are scheduling planning projects farther and farther apart to reduce the financial burden on taxpayers and developers. Planners also hope that more and more people will become convinced of the value of city planning as they see the completed projects.

History of city planning

People have done some city planning ever since the first cities appeared about 3500 B.C. This section traces some of the highlights of city planning. For a detailed description of cities and their development through the ages, see **City.**

Ancient times. People of ancient cities set aside certain areas for meetings, recreation, trade, and worship. Many ancient peoples built walls around their cities to keep invaders out. Groups of public buildings and monuments are among the major examples of city planning in ancient times. Athens and Rome were especially famous for their public buildings and monuments. See **Athens; Rome** (The ancient city).

Historians believe that Hippodamus, an ancient Greek architect, developed the first systematic theories about city planning. His work included plans for the use of land and the location of streets and buildings in the cities of Miletus and Piraeus.

The Middle Ages. Many peoples built protective walls around their cities during the Middle Ages—from the A.D. 400's to the 1500's. Population growth caused a number of cities to become overcrowded. Some cities solved this problem by knocking down the walls. Other cities let the walls stand and built new cities nearby.

Religion played a major role in medieval European life and was reflected in the planning of many cities. The main church stood in the center of the city and was the biggest and most expensive building.

The Renaissance, a period of great artistic development, began near the end of the Middle Ages and lasted into the 1600's. Several leading artists of the Renaissance, including Gian Lorenzo Bernini, Leonardo da Vinci, and Michelangelo, helped beautify cities.

During the Renaissance and for many years after it, city planners designed parts of cities on a grand scale. They created open spaces to overcome the overcrowding of earlier days. Examples of this trend include the huge plazas in front of the Cathedral of Saint Mark in Venice and Saint Peter's Church in Vatican City. Another is the beautiful palace and gardens at Versailles, near Paris. Perhaps the high point of the trend toward city planning on a grand scale was Georges Eugene Haussmann's plan for Paris in the mid-1800's. Haussmann de-

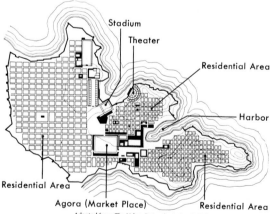

Adapted from *The Urban Pattern* by Arthur B. Gallion and Simon Eisner, copyright 1950, 1963, by Litton Educational Publishing, Inc., by permission of Van Nostrand Reinhold Company

Miletus, an ancient Greek colony, was one of the first cities to have the regular arrangement of city blocks called the *gridiron pattern.* Hippodamus, the man who planned Miletus, is sometimes called the father of city planning.

signed wide boulevards and plazas and helped make Paris one of the world's most beautiful cities.

In colonial America, most cities and towns were smaller and less elaborate than the European communities. Early planned cities included Charleston, S.C.; Philadelphia; Savannah, Ga; and Washington, D.C. Washington was probably the most elaborately planned early American city. George Washington hired Pierre Charles L'Enfant, a French architect, to plan it.

The Industrial Revolution of the 1700's and early 1800's marked the beginning of the factory system of manufacturing. In Europe and North America, the population of many cities increased rapidly as thousands of workers left farms to take manufacturing jobs in cities. Cities became overcrowded, dirty, and noisy. Many people lived in crowded, run-down, unsanitary housing near the factories.

Social reformers began calling on governments to improve city life. They proposed new housing areas with gardens and open spaces and new communities with industry and housing in separate areas. Governments took some steps to regulate the quality of housing and to otherwise improve cities. But the cities continued to grow, and city planning failed to keep pace.

Planners tried to show what the ideal city could look like at the World's Columbian Exposition, held in Chicago in 1893. American architect Daniel Burnham planned and arranged most of the buildings at the exposition, which marked the beginning of the City Beautiful movement in the United States. Plans influenced by the movement were characterized by wide boulevards, spacious parks, and large, graceful public buildings.

The 1900's. Until the early 1900's, city planning in the United States was largely the responsibility of architects who were hired by private organizations or, in some cases, by governments. The rapid increase in urban problems during the late 1800's forced governments to take a greater part in city planning.

Between 1900 and 1930, many local governments in the United States established city planning commissions and introduced zoning laws. Among the most famous redevelopment plans of the early 1900's was Burnham's plan for Chicago, which reflected the style of the City Beautiful movement. The urban population explosion that followed World War II (1939-1945) caused severe housing shortages, more slums, and heavier traffic than ever. To meet the challenge of growing cities, planning agencies had to expand their programs to provide for new housing projects, parks and recreation areas, and better industrial and commercial districts.

Today, city planning is usually done by a partnership of government planning agencies and private developers. Such partnerships have redeveloped many rundown urban areas, including Faneuil Hall Marketplace in Boston, South Street Seaport in New York City, and Harborplace in Baltimore.

Careers in city planning

A professional city planner needs certain personal and educational qualifications. City planners have a special interest in design, social planning, and economic development. Most planning positions are available only to people who have a master's degree in city planning. Many colleges offer this degree.

People with a master's degree in city planning may have a bachelor's degree in any of a number of fields. These fields include architecture, computer programming, economics, engineering, finance, law, political science, statistics, and sociology. *Anthony James Catanese*

Related articles in *World Book* include:

Architecture	Eminent domain	Soleri, Paolo
Brasília	Housing	Street (How streets
Building permit	Landscape architec-	are built)
Burnham, Daniel H.	ture	Tapiola
Canberra	Le Corbusier	Urban renewal
City	L'Enfant, Pierre C.	Zoning
City government	Sociology (Careers)	

Outline

I. **The master plan**
    A. Preparing the plan   B. Proposals of the plan
II. **Making city planning work**
    A. Gaining support for the plan
    B. Governmental authority
III. **Building new communities**
IV. **Criticism of city planning**
    A. Length of time   D. Wrong emphasis
    B. High cost   E. Reducing criticism
    C. Government control
V. **History of city planning**
VI. **Careers in city planning**

Questions

What does a master plan for a city include?
Who probably developed the first theories about city planning?
What is the power of *eminent domain*?
Why is public support important to a city planner?
What was the City Beautiful movement?
Why are there few new towns in the United States?
Who planned Washington, D.C.?
How do zoning laws help city planners?
What are some criticisms of city planning?
How did the Industrial Revolution increase the need for city planning?

Additional resources

Cities: The Forces That Shape Them. Ed. by Lisa Taylor. Rev. ed. Rizzoli, 1982.
Hall, Peter. *Cities of Tomorrow.* Basil Blackwell, 1988. Discusses urban planning in the 1900's.
Urban Planning. Ed. by Anthony J. Catanese and J. C. Snyder. Rev. ed. McGraw, 1988. First edition published as *Introduction to Urban Planning.*

City-state is an independent or nearly independent state in which political and cultural activities are concentrated in a single urban center. City-states were often ruled by a king, by a dictator, or by a small group of powerful citizens. In some cases, political life was controlled by city dwellers, and in other cases by people of both the countryside and the city. The city-state had its fullest development in ancient times. The most famous examples were Athens and Sparta in Greece, and Rome before the formation of the Roman Empire in 27 B.C. During the Middle Ages, which lasted from about A.D. 500 to 1500, some German and Italian cities in the Holy Roman Empire became self-governing and almost entirely independent. They included Florence, Genoa, Milan, and Venice in Italy, and Bremen, Hamburg, and Lübeck in Germany. *Ronald P. Legon*

Related articles in *World Book* include:

Athens (Earliest times)	Hittites (History)
Ebla	Italy (Rise of the city-states)
Free city	Phoenicia (Government)
Greece, Ancient	Sparta

Ciudad Bolívar, *syoo DAHD boh LEE vahr* (pop. 225,846; met. area pop. 247,593), is a major port and commercial city on the Orinoco River in eastern Venezuela. For the location of Ciudad Bolívar, see **Venezuela** (political map). The port at Ciudad Bolívar has a large floating pontoon dock. Such goods as animal skins, cashews, latex, lumber, and palm fibers pass through the port. The city also ships gold and diamonds from the Guiana Highlands in southern Venezuela.

The Spanish founded what is now Ciudad Bolívar in 1764. They named it Angostura. In 1819, under the leadership of General Simón Bolívar, the Congress of Angostura organized the republic of Gran Colombia, which included what are now Venezuela and Colombia. Venezuela was liberated in 1821, and Angostura was renamed *Ciudad Bolívar,* which is Spanish for *Bolívar City.*

William J. Smole

Ciudad Trujillo. See Santo Domingo.

Civet, *SIHV iht,* is a furry mammal that looks somewhat like a long, slender cat. But a civet has a more pointed snout, a fluffier tail, and shorter legs than a cat. Civets live in Asia from India to Indonesia, and in Africa. The spotted skunk, found in most parts of the United States, is sometimes called a civet cat, though it is not a civet.

Civets vary in color and size. Their fur may be black, brown, gray, or tan. Most species, including the *banded palm civet* of Asia and the *African civet,* have dark spots or splotches, and the tail has rings of light and dark fur. A few species—such as the *masked palm civet* and the *small Indian civet,* both found in Asia—have a plain coat or only faint spots.

Civets range from about 13 inches (33 centimeters) to about 38 inches (97 centimeters) long. In addition, their muscular tail is sometimes as long as the rest of the body. Civets use their tail to grasp branches and to steady themselves while climbing trees.

Civets live within a specific area called a *territory.* Most kinds of civets climb well and spend much of their time in trees. Some civets sleep in tree holes or among tangled branches. A few species live mostly on the ground and dig burrows. Civets move about chiefly at night. They live alone, except for females and their young. Most civets eat birds, frogs, insects, rodents, and small reptiles. Excellent hearing, sight, and smell help civets hunt their prey. Civets also eat fruit and other

parts of plants and the eggs of various animals. Palm civets feed chiefly on plants.

Some civets live near farmhouses and in villages. They help people by feeding on mice and rats, but they also may eat chickens and raid fruit orchards.

Civets mark their territory with a foul-smelling liquid from a gland near the base of the tail. Perfume manufacturers have used the liquid, called *civet musk,* from several species, especially the *African civet.* Civet musk makes the odor of perfume last longer.

Scientific classification. Civets belong to several genera in the family Viverridae.   Bruce A. Brewer

See also **Mongoose.**

Civics is the study of the rights and responsibilities of citizens. Many middle schools and junior and senior high schools offer courses in civics, also called *citizenship education.* Civics students in the United States and many other countries learn about such subjects as democracy, freedom, and individual rights. They study the structure, function, and problems of government on the local, state, national, and international levels. The students also learn about other economic, political, and social institutions.

Civics teachers encourage students to participate in student government, school publications, and other school organizations. Students may also become involved in such community programs as voter registration drives and conservation projects.   Francis P. Hunkins

See the **Government** article and its list of *Related articles.* See also **Social studies.**

Civil Air Patrol (CAP) is the volunteer civilian auxiliary of the United States Air Force. The CAP's three main missions are emergency services, aerospace education, and a cadet program. The CAP is not a government agency but operates with the advice and assistance of Civil Air Patrol-U.S. Air Force Headquarters at Maxwell Air Force Base, Ala.

The CAP has about 22,000 cadets from 13 to 18 years old and 35,000 senior members over 18. Members are organized into 52 wings—one for each state, plus Washington, D.C., and Puerto Rico—and about 1,750 local groups, squadrons, and flights. Members wear uniforms similar to those of the U.S. Air Force, but with distinctive CAP insignia and badges. The CAP has about 530 corporate-owned and 5,300 member-owned aircraft. It oper-

© Anthony Bannister, NHPA

A civet has a long, slender body, short legs, and a long, muscular tail. Civets live in Africa and in parts of Asia. The *African civet, left,* has grayish fur with dark spots or splotches.

ates a radio network of about 18,150 fixed, mobile, and airborne stations.

Civil Air Patrol
Civil Air Patrol emblem

Each year, CAP members fly more than 80 per cent of the hours flown on search and rescue missions directed by the Air Force Rescue Coordination Center at Scott Air Force Base, Ill. CAP pilots fly thousands of hours yearly, searching for missing aircraft and lost persons or doing relief work during disasters.

The CAP sponsors aerospace education courses in high schools. It also conducts workshops for training teachers in aviation-related subjects. The CAP awards scholarships and educational grants to selected members. It participates in an International Air Cadet Exchange program with more than 20 member countries and offers training in aerospace developments.

The Civil Air Patrol was established in 1941 as part of the Office of Civilian Defense. It organized and directed the activities of volunteer civilian pilots using their own aircraft and equipment for wartime tasks. The CAP was transferred to the War Department in 1943 as an auxiliary of the Army Air Forces. In 1946, Congress chartered it as a nonprofit private organization. The CAP became the civilian auxiliary of the U.S. Air Force in 1948. Civil Air Patrol headquarters are at Maxwell Air Force Base, AL 36112-5572.   Critically reviewed by the Civil Air Patrol

Civil code. See Code Napoléon.

Civil defense is a nonmilitary program designed to save lives and property if an enemy attacks a country. Civil defense also provides assistance in such emergencies as blizzards, earthquakes, floods, hurricanes, tornadoes, explosions, and fires, and it is intended to reduce the consequences of major terrorist incidents.

In the United States, the federal, state, and local governments share the responsibility for civil defense. Local agencies develop and carry out civil defense plans for their communities with the guidance and assistance of state and federal agencies.

The first U.S. civil defense agency, the Council of National Defense, was created in 1916, during World War I. The council directed the nation's civil defense program until 1918, the year the war ended. In 1941, the Office of Civilian Defense was established to coordinate civil defense activities during World War II. In 1945, U.S. airplanes dropped atomic bombs on the Japanese cities of Hiroshima and Nagasaki, and the war ended. American leaders recognized the need for a continuing civil defense program after the Soviet Union tested its first atomic bomb in 1949. The Federal Civil Defense Act of 1950 established the forerunner of the present civil defense system. The system has been reorganized several times. In 1979, the Federal Emergency Management Agency (FEMA) began to administer the nation's civil defense program.

Nuclear weapons have made civil defense more difficult than ever before. A missile can carry nuclear explosives from continent to continent in about 30 minutes and cause massive destruction. Some Americans believe civil defense is unnecessary. They question whether any nation would attack the United States at the risk of being destroyed in a nuclear counterattack. Others believe the destructive power of nuclear weapons, combined with the speed at which they can be delivered, makes civil defense useless. Some experts argue that civil defense could save at least half the U.S. population if a nuclear attack occurred, but other experts strongly disagree with that view. Supporters of civil defense say the program keeps communities prepared to protect lives and property in severe storms and other disasters.

Civil defense in action

The first task of a civil defense agency in an emergency is to warn the public of danger and provide instructions on how to avoid hazards. People may be able to protect themselves from an enemy attack or other disaster in one of two ways. They can (1) evacuate the area or (2) remain and take shelter. Civil defense agencies advise the public about the best action to follow in a particular situation. They also coordinate rescue efforts and other emergency services. In most disasters, however, people usually reach safety without help and take care of their own needs.

Warning. Most civil defense agencies in the United States warn communities of danger by means of the *attack warning signal* and the *attention,* or *alert, signal.* Both signals last for three to five minutes.

The attack warning signal consists of a wavering sound from a siren or a series of short blasts on a factory whistle or other device. This signal means that an enemy has attacked the country and that people should act immediately to protect themselves. The attention signal is a long, steady sound from a siren, whistle, or other device. It means that the community is threatened by a peacetime disaster. After either signal has sounded, radio and television stations broadcast information about the danger and give instructions for the public to follow.

Evacuation. Floods and hurricanes are the most common disasters for which communities are evacuated. Unlike many natural disasters that strike suddenly, most floods and hurricanes can be predicted in time for people to safely leave the area. If time permits, individuals should board up windows and disconnect all electric appliances before leaving home. Then they should go to the location directed by the civil defense agency, using the route specified. Citizens also may be asked to evacuate an area after an industrial accident to protect them from such hazards as leaking gasoline or poisonous fumes.

No nation could evacuate its cities in time to prevent the massive loss of life from a surprise missile attack. However, most U.S. defense experts believe that a nuclear war would begin only after a period of extreme tension between enemy nations. Some of these experts predict that the people of major cities

Civil defense symbol

could be moved to rural "host areas" before a war started. Other experts believe that such evacuations would be rendered futile by the widespread havoc created by nuclear war.

Shelter. Earthquakes, tornadoes, and other emergencies that occur suddenly give people little or no time to evacuate a community. If a tornado approaches, people should immediately take shelter in a storm cellar or basement. In an earthquake, they should stand under a doorframe or crouch under a table or chair until the shaking stops. If caught outdoors during such emergencies, they should get away from such objects as telephone poles, power lines, or anything else that might fall or be blown down. In a tornado, people should lie facedown—in a ditch if possible—for protection against flying debris.

People must also take cover immediately in an enemy attack. After a nuclear attack, they may have to remain in a fallout shelter for two weeks or longer. Such shelters provide protection from radioactive fallout that has been scattered into the air by a nuclear explosion. Particles of fallout can cause illness or death and may settle on an area hundreds of miles or kilometers from the explosion. As a result, even people who have been evacuated from the blast area must remain in shelters.

The basements of office buildings, factories, and schools, plus mines and subway tunnels, could serve as public fallout shelters in a nuclear attack. People also could use the basement of their home as a fallout shelter. Fallout loses much of its radioactivity after a few days. Following an attack, civil defense officials would measure the amount of radiation and announce when people could safely leave their shelters.

Emergency services. When a natural disaster strikes, civil defense agencies coordinate the efforts of fire fighters, police officers, and other community employees to save lives and property. These workers—often with help from the National Guard, Red Cross volunteers, and others—evacuate people who have been stranded in hazardous areas. They also provide medical care for the injured and food and shelter for people who have had to leave their homes. Officials may find it necessary to close off certain areas to prevent looting of unattended buildings.

If a nuclear war appeared likely, efforts would be made to stock public fallout shelters with food, water, and other supplies that were locally available. Civil defense officials would supervise survival operations in the shelters if war broke out.

Communities begin recovery activities as soon as possible after an emergency. Workers clear away garbage and other debris, and utility companies restore telephone communications and water, gas, and electrical service. Welfare organizations help victims of the tragedy who have been left homeless. Some communities have counseling programs to meet the emotional needs of individuals who suffer psychological damage as a result of a major disaster.

How civil defense is administered

In the United States, the Federal Emergency Management Agency coordinates the nation's nonmilitary preparations for an enemy attack. The agency also has the chief responsibility for the federal programs that fol-

What to do in a nuclear attack

1. **Take cover immediately after hearing the attack warning signal.** Go to a fallout shelter if possible. If a flash from a nuclear explosion occurs before you reach a fallout shelter, take whatever cover you can find, preferably in a ditch or other low-lying area. Instant action may prevent serious burns and other injuries caused by the heat and blast waves of the explosion.
2. **Do not look at the nuclear flash.** It can cause temporary or permanent blindness.
3. **Move to a fallout shelter after the blast.** Any structure with thick walls that block radiation can serve as a fallout shelter. Possible shelters include basements of houses and other buildings, corridors in the center of large buildings, and subway tunnels.
4. **Bring necessary supplies to the fallout shelter.** Such necessities include water, ready-to-eat food, sanitation equipment, medicine and first-aid supplies, and a flashlight, a battery-powered radio, and spare batteries.
5. **Do not leave the fallout shelter until advised by authorities.** Radio broadcasts will tell you when it is safe to go outside. In most areas, people could leave the shelter for short periods after two or three days. In areas of heavy fallout, they probably could leave after a week or two to perform such tasks as obtaining food or water.

low peacetime disasters. FEMA works with industries, national organizations, and state and local governments to improve civil defense preparedness.

FEMA administers a nationwide system of public fallout shelters and thousands of *emergency operating centers.* The centers are protected places where top officials can meet to direct operations in an emergency situation.

In a major peacetime disaster, such as an especially destructive flood or storm, the President may declare a region to be a *disaster area.* Such a declaration makes the area eligible to receive funds and other assistance from the federal government to help deal with the disaster. FEMA coordinates this relief program.

Every state has a civil defense director and provides assistance to the civil defense agencies of its cities and counties. Most cities and counties also have a civil defense director. This official coordinates emergency preparations made by the local government and by individuals and private organizations.

In Canada, a federal agency called the National Emergency Planning Establishment, also known as Emergency Planning Canada, administers civil defense. It coordinates emergency planning by all federal agencies and departments. It also helps the cities, provinces, and territories plan for major emergencies.

In other countries. Civil defense programs are conducted by the governments of many other countries, including Denmark, Norway, Russia, Sweden, Switzerland, and the United Kingdom. For example, the United Kingdom Warning and Monitoring Organization is set up to warn the public of an enemy attack and measure the level of nuclear fallout.   James Fallows

See also **Fallout; Fallout shelter; Geiger counter; Radiation.**

Additional resources

Andrews, Elaine K. *Civil Defense in the Nuclear Age.* Watts, 1985. For younger readers.
Civil Defense: A Choice of Disasters. Ed. by John Dowling and E. M. Harrell. American Institute of Physics, 1987.

Vale, Lawrence J. *The Limits of Civil Defence in the USA, Switzerland, Britain and the Soviet Union: The Evolution of Policies Since 1945.* St. Martin's, 1987.

Civil disobedience is the deliberate and public refusal to obey a law. Some people use civil disobedience as a form of protest to attract attention to what they consider unjust or unconstitutional laws or policies. They hope their actions will move other people to correct the injustices. Other people regard civil disobedience as a matter of individual religious or moral conviction. They refuse to obey laws that they believe violate their personal principles.

Most lawbreakers try to escape punishment. On the other hand, people who practice civil disobedience accept willingly their punishment for breaking the law. In this way, people who practice civil disobedience can dramatically demonstrate their deep concern about the situation they are protesting.

Many lawbreakers use violence. But most acts of civil disobedience are nonviolent. Civil disobedience is usually distinguished from riot, rebellion, and other types of violent opposition to law and authority.

Is civil disobedience ever justified? Throughout history, there has been widespread disagreement concerning the use of civil disobedience in a society based on law and order. Some people claim that citizens are obligated to disobey laws they consider unjust, such as laws segregating the races. They say that such lawbreaking may be the best way to test the constitutionality of a law. Some defend the use of civil disobedience by pointing to Nazi Germany's laws calling for extermination of Jews and other groups.

Other people claim that it is never right to break a law deliberately. They argue that defiance of any law leads to contempt for other laws. Any act of civil disobedience, they believe, weakens society and may lead to violence and *anarchy* (no government or law).

Many people approve civil disobedience only in extreme circumstances, and then only if it is nonviolent. They argue that injustices can usually be corrected legally through democratic processes. Free elections give people a chance to choose their leaders and express their views. Various constitutional provisions also protect the right of dissent and protest.

History of civil disobedience. People have practiced civil disobedience for hundreds of years. When the disciples of Jesus Christ were ordered by the state to stop their teachings, they replied that they would obey God rather than mortals. In the A.D. 1200's, the Christian theologian Saint Thomas Aquinas argued that people must disobey earthly rulers when the laws of the state disagree with the laws of nature, or God.

During the 1600's and 1700's, certain religious sects became known for civil disobedience. For example, the Quakers in colonial America refused to pay taxes for military purposes because they disapproved of war. In the 1850's, abolitionists in the United States disobeyed the Fugitive Slave Law, which sought to compel the return of runaway slaves.

Many leaders of the women's rights movement used civil disobedience to call attention to their demands. In 1872, for example, Susan B. Anthony was arrested for voting before it was legal for American women to vote. Her trial attracted nationwide attention.

The American writer Henry David Thoreau was one of the most influential spokesmen for civil disobedience. In 1846, he spent a night in jail for refusing to pay taxes. He argued that he did not owe allegiance to a government that captured runaway slaves and waged war on Mexico to expand its area of slavery. In his essay "On the Duty of Civil Disobedience" (1849), Thoreau declared that people should refuse to obey any law they believe is unjust.

Thoreau's essay strongly influenced Mohandas K. Gandhi of India. Led by Gandhi, the Indian people used such nonviolent acts as strikes and protest marches to free themselves of British rule. They gained independence in 1947.

In the United States, during the 1950's and 1960's, Martin Luther King, Jr., and other civil rights workers deliberately violated Southern segregation laws as a means of fighting racial injustice. Many opponents of the Vietnam War (1957-1975) committed various illegal acts in attempts to change U.S. policy. Some refused to pay their taxes. Others refused to register for the draft. During the 1980's, nonviolent protests were directed at the repressive racial policy of *apartheid* (segregation) of the minority white government in South Africa.

Leon F. Litwack

See also **Gandhi, Mohandas K.; India** (Gandhi's leadership); **King, Martin Luther, Jr.** (The early civil rights movement); **Thoreau, Henry David** (His beliefs and works).

Additional resources

Civil Disobedience. Ed. by Paul Harris. Univ. Pr. of Am., 1989.
Civil Disobedience in America: A Documentary History. Ed. by David R. Weber. Cornell Univ. Pr., 1978.
Revolutionary and Dissident Movements of the World: An International Guide. 3rd ed. comp. by Longman's Current Affairs Division. Gale Research, 1992.

Civil engineering. See Engineering (The branches of engineering).

Civil law is a term with several meanings. The term is often used to describe the rules of private law and to set them apart from the rules of criminal law. When used in this way, civil law covers such matters as contracts, ownership of property, and payment for personal injury. These matters usually involve private citizens. But the state may become party to a civil suit when it enters into a contract or causes personal injury. Criminal law deals with actions that are harmful to society and that society has made a crime.

The term *civil law* can also mean the law of most European countries, as opposed to the *common law* of the United Kingdom and every state of the United States except Louisiana. Under this type of civil law, *codes* (sets of rules) approved by legislatures are the primary sources used by judges to decide cases. Under common law, judges base their decisions chiefly on previous court decisions in similar cases. See **Common law; Louisiana** (Courts).

Originally, civil law referred to the code of laws collected by the Roman emperor Justinian in the A.D. 500's. These laws were used to govern the Roman Empire. A new civil law became popular in most of Europe after it took effect in France in 1804. This law, called the *Code Napoléon* or *Code Civil,* combined the Roman law and the law of northern France. It is the basis of present law in Quebec, Mexico, and some South American nations.

In the United States, many areas of law have been arranged into codes. Examples include the law of business and the law of crimes.   Sherman L. Cohn

Related articles in *World Book* include:

Code	Justinian Code
Code Napoléon	Law (Private law;
Contract	The development of law)
Court	Negligence
Damages	Suit
Equity	Tort
Fraud	Trespass

Civil liberties. See Civil rights.

Civil Liberties Union, American. See American Civil Liberties Union.

Civil rights are the freedoms and rights that a person may have as a member of a community, state, or nation. Civil rights include freedom of speech, of the press, and of religion. Among others are the right to own property and to receive fair and equal treatment from government, other persons, and private groups.

In democratic countries, a person's civil rights are protected by law and custom. The constitutions of many democracies have *bills of rights* that describe basic liberties and rights. Courts of law decide whether a person's civil rights have been violated. The courts also determine the limits of civil rights, so that people do not use their freedoms to violate the rights of others.

In many nondemocratic countries, the government claims to respect and guarantee civil rights. But in most of these countries, such claims differ greatly from the actual conditions. In some Communist countries, for example, the people are denied such basic rights as freedom of speech and of the press. Yet their constitutions guarantee these rights.

Some people draw sharp distinctions between *civil liberties* and *civil rights*. These people distinguish between *freedom from* certain actions and *freedom to* be treated in certain ways. They regard civil liberties as guarantees that a person will enjoy *freedom from* government interference. They think of civil rights as guarantees that all people will have the *freedom to* be treated equally. For example, civil liberties would include freedom from government interference with a person's right to free speech. Civil rights would include everyone's freedom to receive equal protection of the law. In this article, the term *civil rights* refers to both civil liberties and civil rights.

Limits of civil rights

All civil rights have limits, even in democratic countries. For example, a person may be denied freedom of speech in a democracy if it can be shown that his or her speech might lead to the overthrow of the government. A person may not use civil rights to justify actions that might seriously harm the health, welfare, safety, or morals of others. In 1919, U.S. Supreme Court Justice Oliver Wendell Holmes, Jr., wrote: "The most stringent protection of free speech would not protect a man in falsely shouting fire in a theatre and causing a panic."

A person may be denied a civil right if that right is used to violate other people's rights. Freedom of expression, for example, does not permit a person to tell lies that ruin another person's reputation. Property owners have the right to do what they choose with their property. However, this right may not allow a person legally to refuse to sell property to a person of a certain race or religion. This is because the property owner would be denying the other person equal freedom of choice.

The specific limits of civil rights vary with the times. In time of war, a government may restrict personal freedoms to safeguard the country. Changing social and economic conditions also cause changes in the importance that people give certain rights. During the late 1800's, most people in the United States valued property rights more than personal freedoms. But since the late 1930's, most Americans have shown greater concern for personal freedoms and equality of opportunity.

Civil rights in the United States

The United States Constitution describes the basic civil rights of American citizens. The first 10 amendments to the Constitution are usually regarded as the U.S. Bill of Rights. However, civil rights are also mentioned in the main body of the Constitution and in later amendments. Each state constitution also has a bill or declaration of rights. Since the mid-1950's, the federal, state, and local governments have passed several civil rights laws. But the courts—especially the Supreme Court—have probably done the most to define civil rights. When Americans raise questions about the extent and limits of civil rights, they turn to the Supreme Court's decisions for the answers. The court often defines the limits of a right by balancing the right of the individual against the rights of society in general.

For a detailed description of the constitutional rights of Americans, see **Constitution of the United States**. For information on the Supreme Court's part in protecting civil rights, see **Supreme Court of the United States** (Civil rights).

The First Amendment is the basis of the democratic process in the United States. The First Amendment forbids Congress to pass laws restricting freedom of speech, of the press, of peaceful assembly, or of petition. Many people consider freedom of speech the most important freedom and the foundation of all other freedoms. The First Amendment also forbids Congress to pass laws establishing a state religion or restricting religious freedom. The Supreme Court has ruled that the 14th Amendment makes the guarantees of the 1st Amendment apply to the state governments.

Due process. Many parts of the Constitution, congressional and state laws, and court decisions require the government to treat individuals fairly. These requirements reflect a basic principle in the American legal system called *due process*. The 5th and 14th amendments forbid the government to deprive a person of life, liberty, or property "without due process of law."

Various statements in the Constitution guarantee due process. For example, the Constitution forbids the government to suspend the *writ of habeas corpus* except during an invasion or rebellion. This right protects citizens against arrest and detention without good reason. Neither Congress nor the states may pass *bills of attainder*. Such bills declare a person guilty of a crime and take away the person's property and civil rights without a trial. The Constitution also prohibits *ex post facto laws*. Such laws make a particular act a crime and punish people who committed the act before it was a crime.

Due process of law also includes court procedures

that protect individuals accused of wrongdoing. For example, a person may not be tried for a major federal crime unless a grand jury has first decided that enough evidence exists against the individual. Persons accused of a crime also must be informed of their constitutional rights and of the charges against them. They may demand a jury trial, which must be held soon after the charges are filed. Persons on trial may cross-examine their accusers and may force witnesses to testify.

Other constitutional guarantees. The Constitution also guarantees that accused persons may not be tried twice for the same crime, and they may not be forced to testify against themselves. If they cannot afford a lawyer and want one, the government must provide one. Persons accused of crimes must not be required to pay excessive bail. In addition, those convicted of crimes must not be fined excessively nor made to suffer cruel or unusual punishment.

The Constitution also provides for the security of people and their property. The government may not conduct "unreasonable searches and seizures" of persons or property. It may not take a person's property without due process of law. If it takes private property for public use, it must pay the owner a fair price.

The Constitution forbids the states to pass laws interfering with contracts made between persons or groups. Each state must recognize the legislative acts, public records, and court decisions of other states. A state must extend its legal protections to the citizens of any other state while they are within its jurisdiction.

Protecting the rights of minorities. The United States has many minority groups. These minorities include blacks, Jews, Asian Americans, European immigrants, Hispanic Americans, American Indians, and handicapped people. Members of these groups often have not had an equal chance for economic, political, or social advancement. Members of some minorities have been denied the right to vote. Many persons have been discriminated against in housing, education, and employment, and have been denied equal access to restaurants, hotels, and other public accommodations and facilities. A main goal has been to end such discrimination and guarantee equal rights and opportunities for all people.

The struggle for the rights of blacks. Black Americans, who make up the largest minority group in the United States, have been denied their full civil rights more than any other minority group.

Black Americans made significant gains in their struggle for equal rights during *Reconstruction,* the 12-year period after the Civil War. The 13th Amendment, adopted in 1865, abolished slavery in the United States. In 1868, the 14th Amendment made the former slaves citizens. It also provided that the states must grant all people within their jurisdiction "equal protection of the laws." The 15th Amendment, which became law in 1870, prohibited the states from denying people the right to vote because of their race. During Reconstruction, Congress passed several laws to protect blacks' civil rights. See **Reconstruction.**

During the late 1870's, white Americans increasingly disregarded the newly won rights of black Americans. The government itself contributed greatly to denying blacks their rights. In 1883, the Supreme Court ruled

that congressional acts to prevent racial discrimination by private individuals were unconstitutional. In 1896, in the case of *Plessy v. Ferguson,* the Supreme Court upheld a Louisiana law requiring separate but equal accommodations for blacks and whites in railroad cars. For over 50 years, many Southern states used the "separate but equal" rule established in this case to segregate the races in public schools, and in transportation, recreation, and such public establishments as hotels and restaurants. Many states also used literacy tests, poll taxes, and other means to deprive blacks of their voting rights. See **Voting** (Restrictions on voting).

Since the 1930's, blacks have had fairer hearings on civil rights cases in the federal courts. The high point came in 1954 in *Brown v. Board of Education of Topeka.* In this case, the Supreme Court ruled that segregation in public schools is unconstitutional. In time, this decision broke down the "separate but equal" principle.

In 1955, the Supreme Court ordered that public school desegregation be carried out "with all deliberate speed." But many Southern school districts continued to have segregated schools. In 1969, the court departed from its "all deliberate speed" doctrine and ordered the integration of all school systems "at once." By the 1980's, public schools in the South were more integrated than those in many Northern and Western states.

In 1957, Congress passed the first federal civil rights law since Reconstruction. The Civil Rights Act of 1957 set up the Commission on Civil Rights to investigate charges of denial of civil rights. It also created the Civil Rights Division in the Department of Justice to enforce federal civil rights laws and regulations.

During the 1960's, black Americans' voting rights received increased protection. The Civil Rights Act of 1960 provided for the appointment of referees to help blacks register to vote. The 24th Amendment, adopted in 1964, barred poll taxes in federal elections. The Voting Rights Act of 1965 outlawed literacy tests in many Southern states. A 1970 law made literacy tests illegal in all the states. In 1966, the Supreme Court prohibited poll taxes in state and local elections.

The Civil Rights Act of 1964 was the strongest civil rights bill in U.S. history. It ordered restaurants, hotels, and other U.S. businesses that serve the general public to serve all people without regard to race, color, religion, or national origin. It also barred discrimination by employers and unions, and established the Equal Employment Opportunity Commission to enforce fair employment practices. In addition, the act provided for a cutoff of federal funds from any program or activity that allowed racial discrimination.

The Civil Rights Act of 1968 aimed chiefly at ending discrimination in the sale or rental of housing. Also in 1968, the Supreme Court ruled that the federal government had the power to enforce housing-discrimination laws even in cases involving only private individuals. Before the court's ruling, such laws had been applied only to cases that involved government agencies.

The struggle for women's rights in the United States at first concentrated on gaining the right to vote. A proposed constitutional amendment granting women the vote was introduced in every session of Congress from 1878 to 1919. In 1920, it finally became law as the 19th Amendment to the Constitution.

During the mid-1900's, women gained increased protection against job discrimination. In the 1940's, the U.S. government established a policy of equal pay for equal work. Under this policy, the government forbade businesses with federal contracts to pay a woman less than a man for the same job. The Civil Rights Act of 1964 prohibited job discrimination on the basis of sex. In 1972, Congress approved the Equal Rights Amendment. It failed to become law because only 35 of the necessary 38 states approved it by the deadline of June 30, 1982. The amendment would have guaranteed equal rights for all citizens, regardless of sex.

Major changes in the field of civil rights occurred during the 1970's. Earlier civil rights efforts had involved lawsuits and other attempts to protect individual rights. In the 1970's, the emphasis shifted from individual rights to group rights.

The federal government began to enact laws designed to assure rights for groups that formerly had suffered discrimination. For example, the government began a program of *affirmative action.* Affirmative action consists of efforts to counteract past discrimination by giving special help to disadvantaged groups. Typical measures included recruiting drives among women and minority groups, and special training programs for minority workers. The government required such plans to be set up by businesses that had government contracts, by many other employers, and by all schools receiving federal funds.

Efforts to help groups that had suffered discrimination raised a number of new civil rights issues. Many people felt the government violated the principle of equality under the law by giving preference to certain groups at the expense of others. Some white men complained of *reverse discrimination,* saying they were treated unfairly because of their race and sex. Other individuals believed such efforts were necessary to help the disadvantaged overcome past discrimination and eventually compete on an equal basis with white males.

In 1990, Congress passed the Americans with Disabilities Act to protect handicapped people from discrimination by private employers. The law also requires that public buildings and mass transportation systems be accessible to disabled people. In addition, the act orders telephone companies to provide telephone relay services that enable people with speech or hearing disorders to make and receive calls.

The Civil Rights Act of 1991 made it easier for workers to win job discrimination suits. Under this law, if an employer's hiring or promotion practices seem fair but result in discrimination, the employer must prove the practices are necessary to his or her business. Such practices may include tests of strength or of education. The law also gave victims the right to sue for money damages—in addition to back pay and lost benefits—in cases of intentional job discrimination based on sex, religion, national origin, or disability. Previously, such additional damages were awarded only to victims of racial discrimination.

Civil rights in Canada

The Canadian and U.S. governments apply the same broad principles in dealing with civil rights. Generally, Canadian courts have protected individual liberties, and most of the provinces have civil rights laws similar to those in the United States. In 1960, Canada's Parliament passed an act establishing the Canadian Bill of Rights. An expanded version of the bill, called the Canadian Charter of Rights and Freedoms, became part of Canada's Constitution in 1982. The charter is similar to the U.S. Bill of Rights. It guarantees the same basic freedoms and most of the same protections.

As in the United States, the main civil rights problems in Canada involve assuring equal rights for members of minority groups. In the past, Canadian Eskimos and Indians were sometimes denied their full civil rights. French Canadians of the province of Quebec have long struggled against what they consider discrimination by Canada's English-speaking majority. Many French Canadians claim they have been denied jobs because they speak French rather than English. The French Canadians fear that if they give up the French language, they will lose their national identity, culture, and customs.

Development of civil rights

Natural law. The idea that people have certain rights that cannot be taken away probably began thousands of years ago with the theory of natural law. This theory states that a natural order exists in the universe because all things are created by nature, or God. Everything has its own qualities and is subject to the rules of nature to achieve its full potential. According to this theory, anything that detracts from a person's human qualities, or prevents their full achievement, violates natural law.

The ancient Greek philosophers and the writers of the Old Testament stressed that there is a higher law than human law. In the first century B.C., the Roman philosopher Cicero insisted that this higher (natural) law is universal and can be discovered through human reason. This idea led to the belief that governmental power has limits, and that people and governments everywhere are bound by natural law.

Some of the most historic English legal documents are based on natural law. The earliest and most famous was Magna Carta, which the king approved against his will in 1215. The document placed the king himself under the law. In 1628, the English Parliament drew up a Petition of Right. The petition claimed that certain actions of the king, such as levying taxes without the consent of Parliament, were unconstitutional.

Natural rights. Natural law had always stressed duties over rights of government and individuals. But in the late 1600's, natural law began to emphasize natural rights. The change was brought about largely by the writings of the English philosopher John Locke.

Locke argued that governmental authority depends on the people's consent. According to Locke, people originally lived in a state of nature with no restrictions on their freedom. Then they came to realize that confusion would result if each person enforced his or her own rights. People agreed to live under a common government, but not to surrender their "rights of nature" to the government. Instead, they expected the government to protect these rights, especially the rights of life, liberty, and property. Locke's ideas of limited government and natural rights became part of the English Bill of Rights (1689), the French Declaration of the Rights of Man (1789), and the U.S. Bill of Rights (1791).

Today, many scholars reject the natural law and natural rights theories. They believe that all laws—including those guaranteeing civil rights—are simply devices that people find convenient or useful at a particular time. Nevertheless, nearly all civil rights laws have resulted from the theories of natural law and natural rights.

Civil rights today. Civil rights have long been protected in the constitutional democracies of Western Europe. These nations include France, Great Britain, Switzerland, and the Scandinavian countries. Personal liberties are also secure in such newer democracies as Australia, New Zealand, Canada, and the United States. Many new nations of Africa and Asia have adopted constitutions that guarantee basic civil rights. But in many of these countries, unstable governments and inexperience with self-rule have often led to political arrests, censorship, and other denials of civil rights.

Most nondemocratic governments claim to protect civil rights. But in practice, they grant civil rights only when they find it politically convenient to do so. The civil rights tradition is weak in many Latin-American countries. Most of the Communist nations have constitutions that guarantee the people basic rights and liberties, but the governments seldom enforce these rights. China's Constitution, for example, guarantees the right to vote and assures freedom of speech, of the press, and of assembly. But China's Communist Party completely controls the government, and the people may be punished if they publicly criticize the party. The Chinese government controls the newspapers and other forms of communication.

The United Nations General Assembly adopted a Universal Declaration of Human Rights in 1948. It states that all people are born free and are equal in dignity and rights. Many experts in international law believe that the declaration lacks legal authority, but most agree that it has high moral authority.   Bruce Allen Murphy

Related articles in *World Book* include:

Affirmative action	Freedom of speech
American Civil Liberties Union	Freedom of the press
Attainder	Habeas corpus
Bakke case	Human Rights, Universal Dec-
Bill of Rights	laration of
Black Americans (The civil	Jury
rights movement)	Magna Carta
Brown v. Board of Education of	Minority group
Topeka	National Association for the
Censorship	Advancement of Colored
Citizenship	People
Civil Rights, Commission on	Northern Ireland (History)
Civil Rights Act of 1964	Open housing
Class action	Petition of Right
Constitution of the	Privacy, Right of
United States	Rights of Man, Declaration of
Declaration of Independence	the
Democracy	Scottsboro Case
Due process of law	Search warrant
Equal Employment Opportunity	Segregation
Commission	Student Nonviolent Coordi-
Equal Rights Amendment	nating Committee
Feminism	Trial
Fifth Amendment	Wiretapping
Fourteenth Amendment	Woman suffrage
Freedom	Women's movements
Freedom of religion	(Legal gains)

See also *Civil rights* in the Research Guide/Index, Volume 22, for a *Reading and Study Guide.*

Additional resources

Level I

Kronenwetter, Michael. *Taking a Stand Against Human Rights Abuses.* Watts, 1990.
McKissack, Patricia and Fredrick. *The Civil Rights Movement in America from 1865 to the Present.* 2nd ed. Childrens Pr., 1991.

Level II

The Encyclopedia of Human Rights. Comp. by Edward H. Lawson. Taylor & Francis, 1991.
The Eyes on the Prize Civil Rights Reader: Documents, Speeches, and Firsthand Accounts from the Black Freedom Struggle, 1954-1990. Ed. by Clayborne Carson and others. Penguin, 1991.
Graham, Hugh D. *The Civil Rights Era: Origins and Development of National Policy, 1960-1972.* Oxford, 1990.
Weisbrot, Robert. *Freedom Bound: A History of America's Civil Rights Movement.* Norton, 1990.

Civil Rights, Commission on, is an independent agency of the United States government. It works to guarantee the civil rights of women and of American Indians, black Americans, and members of other minority groups. The commission attempts to protect voting rights and the right to equal opportunities in education, employment, housing, and other areas. It also investigates charges of denial of civil rights; studies how government policies affect such rights; and makes recommendations to the President and to Congress.

The commission was created in 1957. It originally had six members. Congress expanded the commission to eight members in 1983. The President appoints four members, and the *president pro tempore* (temporary president) of the U.S. Senate and the Speaker of the U.S. House of Representatives each appoint two. Commissioners serve six-year terms and may not be dismissed for their political opinions. No more than four members may belong to the same political party.   Jacob Cohen

Civil Rights Act of 1866. See **Reconstruction** (The Civil Rights Act).

Civil Rights Act of 1964 is a United States law that bans discrimination because of a person's color, race, national origin, religion, or sex. The act primarily protects the rights of blacks and other minorities. It is one of the nation's strongest civil rights laws.

The rights protected by the act include a person's freedom to seek employment; vote; and use hotels, parks, restaurants, and other public places. An individual who is discriminated against by an employer can file a complaint with the Equal Employment Opportunity Commission (EEOC), which was established by the act. The EEOC will take the complaint to court. The U.S. Department of Justice handles other complaints of discrimination. Before the law was passed, people had to take such complaints to court themselves, but few could afford to do so.

The Civil Rights Act also forbids discrimination by any program that receives money from the federal government. The government may cut off financing for a program that does not end discriminatory policies or practices. In addition, the act authorizes the Office of Education (now the Department of Education) to direct school desegregation programs in areas specified by the government. The government can sue any school system that refuses to desegregate, or any system whose desegregation program it considers inadequate.

President John F. Kennedy proposed the act in 1963.

After Kennedy's assassination later that year, President Lyndon B. Johnson continued to support it. The law was passed after a 75-day *filibuster* (lengthy debate to block legislation) in the Senate. The debate was one of the longest in Senate history.   Charles V. Hamilton

See also **Equal Employment Opportunity Commission; Civil Rights, Commission on.**

Civil Rights Act of 1968. See Open housing.

Civil rights movement. See Civil rights.

Civil service consists of most civilian government employees who are appointed rather than elected to their jobs. Most civil service employees are appointed under a merit system, which is a program designed to hire and promote the best person to do each job, without regard to race, religion, sex, or political loyalty. Civil service systems form important parts of national and lower levels of government, and they exist in many countries throughout the world.

Civil service in the United States

Federal employment. The United States government hires and assigns civil service workers in all parts of the country, in the territories and possessions, and in many other lands. Fewer than 10 per cent of such employees work in the nation's capital, Washington, D.C.

The federal government is the nation's largest single employer. It has more than 2,800,000 civilian employees in over 100 agencies. Most of these employees work in the 14 executive departments of the executive branch. Nearly half of them, not including members of the armed forces, work for the Department of Defense. Nearly a fourth work for the U.S. Postal Service.

Almost any occupation may be found in the civil service. Skilled artists and engravers design and print government maps, books, and currency. Plant and animal experts help improve the quality and nutritional value of foods. Engineers, scientists, and technicians conduct research on road materials, missiles, ceramics, and aeronautical safety devices. Air traffic controllers guide aircraft at airports.

Services. There are two classifications for government jobs: the *competitive service* and the *excepted service.* Competitive service positions are subject to civil service laws. Applicants must generally take an examination to be eligible for jobs. Almost 90 per cent of all federal workers are in the competitive service.

Excepted service positions are outside the scope of civil service laws. They are mostly top-level jobs filled by appointment without an examination. High excepted service positions, for example, are held by Cabinet members. A few government agencies, such as the Foreign Service, have their own separate career systems. Finding the correct balance between the competitive and excepted services is a continuing concern of those who make personnel policy.

Examinations are given for jobs in the competitive service at all levels of government. Information about such examinations may be obtained from federal job information centers throughout the country as well as from state employment offices and local government personnel offices. Newspapers and television stations often publicize information about the tests. Some of the examinations are written. Others are oral. Some include performance tests. For many jobs, the examiner simply evaluates applicants on education, training, and experience in that particular occupation.

Questions have been raised over the effectiveness of civil service examinations. Some critics doubt the examinations test for skills that are related to the job. Others question whether examinations are fair in the way they test minority group members. In addition, workers and administrators continue to debate whether governments should make a special effort to recruit and promote women and members of minority groups. People in these groups make up a large proportion of government employees, but most have jobs with lower pay and status than the jobs of other civil service employees.

Appointments. Applicants who pass the civil service test for a particular job are placed on a list in order of their grades. The government grants extra points to the ratings of veterans, disabled veterans, and certain dependents of veterans. Some people object to the policy of awarding extra points to nondisabled veterans. They believe this practice works against women, who are much less likely to be veterans than men and therefore are less likely to get extra points added. However, veterans maintain that the hiring preference is an earned reward for previous national service.

When a vacancy occurs, an agency's hiring officer may select any of the three highest-rated people on the list for that job. Some reformers think that this "rule of three" is too restrictive. They favor allowing the hiring officer to choose from a greater number of people.

Civil service jobs. Government employees belong to a career system and may get better jobs by being promoted or transferred. Generous benefits also attract many people to civil service work. Such benefits include vacations, sick leave, low-cost life insurance, health insurance, and pensions.

Federal government workers, however, must accept certain restrictions that do not apply to others in the labor force. For example, certain people in the excepted service face some restrictions about doing business with the government for a period of time after they leave the civil service. Some civil service employees must publicly reveal all their sources of income. Government employees are encouraged to exercise their political rights, but the Hatch Political Activities Act bars most of them from involvement in party politics (see **Hatch Political Activities Act**).

Compensation. The government has a number of pay plans, depending on the nature of the work. Each plan has a series of *grades* (levels), with a range of salary steps within each grade. The pay of federal office workers is reviewed annually. Mechanics and laborers in the civil service have their pay set on the basis of private-industry wage rates in the area where they work. This practice often leads to high wages in parts of the country where unions are strong. Some federal workers are paid for overtime and receive travel and uniform allowances. Most state and local government employees and some federal government workers have the right to *collective bargaining*—that is, they can negotiate wages. Most government workers can negotiate working conditions. Federal workers, however, do not have the right to strike. In addition, their bargaining rights are more limited than those of nongovernment workers who belong to unions.

Evaluation. Administrators regularly evaluate the work of civil service employees. But the civil service has been criticized for failing to reward excellent work and for failing to fire unsatisfactory employees. Congress responded to these issues when it passed the Civil Service Reform Act of 1978. This act made it easier for government managers to reward superior employees and discipline inefficient ones. Firing procedures also became more flexible, but career employees still have many rights that make dismissal or discipline difficult.

Management. The Office of Personnel Management (OPM) manages the federal civil service. The OPM receives much direction from the President and top White House aides. The agency sets standards, administers civil service examinations, helps government agencies find and train qualified people, and supervises the personnel system. The Merit Systems Protection Board, an independent government agency, initiates investigations, hears complaints from federal employees, and reviews firings if the worker involved requests a review. The Federal Labor Relations Authority, also an independent agency, oversees relations among unions of government employees.

State and local civil services have more than four times as many employees as the federal civil service. Most states and almost all major cities have civil service systems. These systems face many of the same issues and concerns as the federal system. Even in states without a merit system, a 1940 federal law requires that employees who administer certain federal funds be placed under a merit system. These funds include federal grants under the Social Security Act and grants for public health, child welfare, public employment, and vocational rehabilitation.

History. The earliest Presidents generally sought qualified individuals for jobs, though they tended to favor their own political supporters. By the mid-1820's, government jobs were commonly used as political rewards. An incoming President would dismiss a large number of government workers originally hired by the opposition party and replace them with members of his own party. This practice was done to enhance the President's control of the bureaucracy. It was based on the ideas that government work was not complicated, and that all people in a democracy should be eligible for it. This practice also reflected the idea that "to the victor belong the spoils." It led to much corruption and was called the *spoils system* (see **Spoils system**).

Many people hired through the spoils system had little or no training for their work and no interest in it. Many were dishonest. As government activities grew, a serious need for qualified workers developed. The government passed laws in 1853 and 1855 requiring clerk examinations to make sure that new employees would be qualified to do the work. In 1871, Congress gave the President authority to establish tests for people seeking government jobs. But this merit-system trial ended in 1875, because Congress failed to fund the system.

However, reform leaders continued to press for a more thorough merit system in the federal, state, and local governments. In 1881, Charles J. Guiteau, a disappointed office seeker, shot and killed President James A. Garfield. Garfield's death brought public demands for civil service reforms and led to a bill introduced by Senator George H. Pendleton of Ohio. The bill became the Civil Service Act of 1883. About the same time, New York and Massachusetts began merit programs.

The Civil Service Act called for examinations open to all citizens. It provided for selection of new workers from among those making the highest grades on these examinations. It banned the firing or demoting of workers for political reasons. The law also relieved government workers from any obligation to give political service or payments. The act established the United States Civil Service Commission to enforce the law.

At first, the Civil Service Act covered only about 10 per cent of the federal positions. By 1940, 90 per cent of all federal jobs were covered. Additional laws have sought to make civil service a true career service. They have authorized advancement based on merit and similar benefits to those offered by progressive private employers. For example, the Retirement Act of 1920 set up a pension system for civil service workers. The Classification Act of 1923 provided that all executive department jobs in Washington, D.C., be analyzed and classified so that workers would be paid according to the requirements of their jobs. A law passed in 1940 extended the provisions of the Classification Act to many federal positions outside Washington, D.C.

The Civil Service Reform Act of 1978 included many far-reaching reforms. For example, it abolished the U.S. Civil Service Commission and created the Office of Personnel Management, the Merit Systems Protection Board, and the Federal Labor Relations Authority.

Civil service in other lands

Civil service systems have been established in many countries. The idea of a civil service based on merit has long been practiced in China. Civil service systems developed in Europe more than 200 years ago. Developing nations in Africa, Asia, and Latin America have also begun to operate modern personnel programs.

Germany has one of the oldest civil service systems in Western Europe. It dates from the Prussian system of the late 1700's. The merit system occupies a strong position in France. Each local government unit there either must have its own merit system or accept the system developed for local administration by the national government. The British Civil Service Commission, established in 1855, became part of the Civil Service Department in 1968. The department runs the British merit system.

Canada set up its first examining system for government employees in the Civil Service Act of 1908. This law covered most government positions in Ottawa, Canada's capital. A law passed in 1918 established a competitive examination system and extended the number of positions covered to include most jobs in government service. The Canadian civil service has more than 200,000 competitive positions, not including those positions in public corporations. The Canadian Public Service Commission shares management of the personnel system with the Treasury Board. Canada's retirement system provides an annuity for government workers who reach age 65 or who serve 35 years. Canada grants preference to veterans with overseas service.

Gerald Benjamin

Civil Service Commission, United States. See **Civil service** (History).

Detail of *The Gettysburg Cyclorama of 'Pickett's Charge'* (1884), a painting by Paul Philippoteaux; Gettysburg National Military Park, Gettysburg, Pa. (Walter B. Lane)

The Battle of Gettysburg was fought between Union and Confederate forces at Gettysburg, Pa., in July 1863. The South's retreat, following terrible losses, marked a turning point in the Civil War. Never again would the Confederate Army be able to mount a major attack against the North.

Civil War

Civil War (1861-1865) took more American lives than any other war in history. It so divided the people of the United States that in some families brother fought against brother. The Civil War was between the Southern States, trying to preserve slavery and an agricultural way of life, and the Northern States, dedicated to a more modern way of life and to ending slavery. The terrible bloodshed left a heritage of grief and bitterness that declined only slowly and, even today, has not fully disappeared.

The Civil War is also known by such names as the War Between the States and the War of Secession. It started on April 12, 1861, when Southern troops fired on

Gabor S. Boritt, the contributor of this article, is Robert C. Fluhrer Distinguished Professor of Civil War Studies and Director of the Civil War Institute at Gettysburg College.

Fort Sumter, a U.S. military post in Charleston, S.C. The war ended four years later. On April 9, 1865, Confederate General Robert E. Lee surrendered his ragged army to Union General Ulysses S. Grant at Appomattox Court House, a small Virginia settlement. The other Confederate armies gave up soon after.

Probably far more people are interested in the Civil War era than in any other period in United States history. Interest in the war appeared soon after peace came. Veterans' organizations were formed, and later civilian discussion groups and clubs arose. Over the years, the Civil War has been the subject of numerous novels, histories, plays, poems, paintings, sculptures, songs, movies, and television programs. Civil War monuments stand in parks and squares of big cities and small towns. Battlefields and the homes and tombs of such people as President Abraham Lincoln, Confederate President Jefferson Davis, and Generals Lee and Grant are popular tourist sites. Some Civil War figures are among the nation's most beloved heroes. Lincoln in particular became a respected figure throughout the world.

In 1861, the United States consisted of 19 *free states,* in which slavery was prohibited, and 15 *slave states,* in which it was allowed. Abraham Lincoln called the nation "a house divided." Americans had much in common, but the free and slave states also had many basic differences besides slavery.

Historians have long debated the causes of the Civil War. Many of them maintain that slavery was the root cause. In his second inaugural address in 1865, Lincoln said of slavery: "All knew that this interest was, somehow, the cause of the war." But most historians agree that the war had a number of causes. They note especially the *sectional division* between North and South— that is, the differences in economies, ideals, and ways of life. They also point to the disputes between the federal government and the states over what rights and powers the states possessed. Historians further mention the blunderings of politicians and the disorder in the American political party system during the 1850's. Yet all explanations for the causes of the war have always involved or revolved around the issue of slavery.

The sectional division

The sectional division between North and South began in colonial times and resulted from geographical differences. In the South, the earliest settlers found the warm climate and fertile soil ideal for growing tobacco. They started many tobacco plantations and brought in black slaves from Africa to provide most of the labor. In time, other plantation crops, especially cotton, sugar

cane, and sugar beets, were found to thrive in the South. The South thus quickly established a rural way of life supported by an agricultural economy based on slave labor.

The cooler climate and rocky soil in the North were not suitable for establishing plantations or large farms. As a result of those and other factors, the North's economy came to depend more on trade than on agriculture. Such an economy favored the growth of cities, though most Northerners still lived in rural areas during the colonial period.

The sectional division between North and South had widened enormously by the mid-1800's. By that time, the United States had expanded all the way to the Pacific Ocean and was rapidly becoming a major industrial and commercial nation. However, industry and commerce were centered in the North. Many factories using mass-production methods had sprung up there, and cities grew rapidly. Great advances in transportation and communication aided the economic growth.

The Northerners, or *Yankees* (a name applied to the Northerners by U.S. Southerners), welcomed modernization and the constant changes it brought to their way of life. The ideals of Yankee Protestantism encouraged modernization. Those ideals included hard work, education, economic independence, and the belief that the community had the right and responsibility to decide whether an action was moral or immoral. While Northerners looked forward to a different and better future, Southerners held the present and past dear. They

The divided nation   Before the start of the Civil War in 1861, the United States consisted of 19 free states, 15 slave states, and several territories. Eleven slave states withdrew from the Union and made up the Confederate States of America. The remaining 23 states and the territories fought for the Union.

WORLD BOOK map

enjoyed a prosperous agricultural economy based on slave labor and wished to keep their old way of life.

The conflict over slavery

In colonial times, most Americans regarded slavery as a necessary evil. The Founding Fathers of the United States had been unable to abolish slavery and compromised over it in writing the Constitution (see **Constitution of the United States** [The compromises]).

By the early 1800's, many Northerners had come to view slavery as wrong. Abolitionists in the North began a movement to end it. An antislavery minority also existed in the South. But most Southerners found slavery to be highly profitable and in time came to consider it a positive good. From a fourth to a third of all Southern whites were members of slaveholding families. About half the families owned fewer than 5 slaves, though less than 1 per cent of the families owned 100 or more. Even many of the white Southerners who did not own slaves supported slavery. They accepted the ideas that the South's economy would collapse without slavery and that blacks were inferior to whites.

In 1858, Senator William H. Seward of New York, who later became Lincoln's secretary of state, referred to the differences between North and South as "an irrepressible conflict." He placed slavery at the heart of that uncontrollable conflict. Indeed, an almost continuous series of debates over slavery raged in Congress between Northern and Southern lawmakers during the 1850's.

The Compromise of 1850 was a group of acts passed by Congress in the hope of settling the slavery question by giving some satisfaction to both the North and the South. The Compromise allowed slavery to continue but prohibited the slave trade in Washington, D.C. It admitted California to the Union as a free state but gave newly acquired territories the right to decide for themselves whether to permit slavery. The Compromise also included a strict fugitive slave law that required Northerners to return escaped slaves to their owners.

Northerners resisted the fugitive slave law in several ways. Abolitionists disobeyed the law by operating the *underground railroad,* a system of escape routes and housing for runaway slaves. The routes led from the slave states to the free states and Canada. Abolitionists also rescued or tried to rescue fugitive slaves after they had been recovered in the North by their owners. A number of rescue attempts, such as those in Christiana, Pa., in 1851 and in Boston in 1854, resulted in riots and several deaths. One of the most effective attacks on the fugitive slave law—and on slavery as a whole—was Harriet Beecher Stowe's best-selling antislavery novel *Uncle Tom's Cabin* (1851-1852).

The Kansas-Nebraska Act was passed by Congress in 1854. Like the Compromise of 1850, it dealt with the problem of slavery in new territories. The act created the territories of Kansas and Nebraska and allowed slavery in them. The act also provided that when the people of each territory organized as a state, they could decide by popular vote whether to permit slavery to continue. The decision process was called *popular sovereignty.* Many Northerners opposed the act. They feared that once slavery was in a territory, it was there to stay.

The first test of popular sovereignty came in Kansas, where a majority of the population voted against becoming a slave state. However, proslavery forces refused to accept the decision. The situation quickly erupted into violence. The violence spread to Washington, D.C., where in 1856 an antislavery senator, Charles Sumner of Massachusetts, was beaten unconscious by Preston Brooks, a proslavery representative from South Carolina. In the end, Kansas joined the Union as a free state in 1861.

The Dred Scott Decision. In 1857, the Supreme Court of the United States tried to settle the slavery issue with its Dred Scott Decision. The case involved Dred Scott, a slave who claimed freedom because he had lived for a time in a free state and territory. The court denied Scott's claim and declared that no black could be a United States citizen. It further ruled that Congress could not prohibit slavery in the territories. The ruling aroused anger in the North and showed that the conflict over slavery was beyond judicial solutions.

The raid at Harpers Ferry. In 1859, an extreme abolitionist named John Brown and his followers attempted to start a slave rebellion by seizing the federal arsenal in Harpers Ferry, Va. (now W. Va.). Brown was captured 28 hours later by troops under Colonel Robert E. Lee. Within a few weeks, he was convicted of treason and hanged. Many Southerners saw the raid as evidence of a Northern plot to end slavery by force.

Developments in the political party system

Anger over the Kansas-Nebraska Act led to the founding of the Republican Party in the North in 1854. The Republicans considered slavery evil and opposed its extension into Western territories. Many Whigs and Democrats—members of the nation's two largest parties—joined the new party. They included Abraham Lincoln, a former Whig. Some other Americans belonged to the Know-Nothing Party, which blamed immigrants and Roman Catholics for the country's problems. The Republican Party's first presidential candidate, John C. Frémont, won most of the Northern vote and almost the presidency in 1856.

In 1858, the Democratic Party was divided over a constitution that proslavery Kansans hoped to have adopted when the Kansas territory became a state. Two of the party's leaders, Senator Stephen A. Douglas of Illinois and President James Buchanan, took opposite positions on the constitution. Douglas opposed it, and Buchanan favored it. The conflict between proslavery and antislavery Democrats caused the party to split into Northern and Southern branches in 1860.

The Republicans chose Lincoln as their candidate in the 1860 presidential election. Douglas ran on the Northern Democratic ticket. Vice President John C. Breckinridge was the Southern Democratic candidate. Some former members of the Whig and Know-Nothing parties—which had disbanded by 1860—formed the Constitutional Union Party and nominated former Senator John Bell of Tennessee.

Lincoln won all the electoral votes of every free state except New Jersey, which awarded him four of its seven votes. He thus gained a majority of electoral votes and won the election. However, Lincoln received less than 40 per cent of the popular vote, almost none of which came from the South. Southerners feared Lincoln would restrict or end slavery.

Secession

Before the 1860 presidential election, Southern leaders had urged that the South *secede* (withdraw) from the Union if Lincoln should win. Many Southerners favored secession as part of the idea that the states have rights and powers which the federal government cannot legally deny. The supporters of states' rights held that the national government was a league of independent states, any of which had the right to secede.

In December 1860, South Carolina became the first state to secede. Five other states—Mississippi, Florida, Alabama, Georgia, and Louisiana—followed in January 1861. In February, representatives from the six states met in Montgomery, Ala., and established the Confederate

States of America. They elected Jefferson Davis of Mississippi as president and Alexander H. Stephens of Georgia as vice president. In March, Texas joined the Confederacy. Lincoln was inaugurated two days later.

In his inaugural address, Lincoln avoided any threat of immediate force against the South. But he stated that the Union would last forever and that he would use the nation's full power to hold federal possessions in the South. One of the possessions, the military post of Fort Sumter, lay in the harbor of Charleston, S.C. The Confederates fired on the fort on April 12 and forced its surrender the next day. On April 15, Lincoln called for Union troops to regain the fort. The South regarded the move as a declaration of war. Virginia, Arkansas, North Carolina, and Tennessee soon joined the Confederacy.

Virginia had long been undecided about which side to join. Its decision to join the Confederacy boosted Southern morale. Richmond, Virginia's capital, became the capital of the Confederacy in May.

Mobilizing for war

When the Civil War began, about 22 million people lived in the North. About 9 million people, including $3\frac{1}{2}$ million slaves, lived in the South. The North had around 4 million men from 15 through 40 years old—the approximate age range for combat duty. The South had only about 1 million white men from 15 through 40. The North began to use black soldiers in 1863. The South did not decide to use blacks as soldiers until the closing days of the war.

How the states lined up

Eleven states fought for the Confederacy. They were Alabama, Arkansas, Florida, Georgia, Louisiana, Mississippi, North Carolina, South Carolina, Tennessee, Texas, and Virginia. Twenty-three states fought for the Union. They were California, Connecticut, Delaware, Illinois, Indiana, Iowa, Kansas, Kentucky, Maine, Maryland, Massa-

chusetts, Michigan, Minnesota, Missouri, New Hampshire, New Jersey, New York, Ohio, Oregon, Pennsylvania, Rhode Island, Vermont, and Wisconsin. The territories of Colorado, Dakota, Nebraska, Nevada, New Mexico, Utah, and Washington also fought on the Union side.

Each side included slave states that lay on either side of the border between the North and the Deep South. Some people in those *border states* supported the North, but others believed in the Southern cause. The heaviest fighting of the war occurred in the border states. Border states on the Southern side were Virginia, North Carolina, Tennessee, and Arkansas. However, Virginians in the western part of the state remained loyal to the Union and formed the new state of West Virginia in 1863. Border states that stayed in the Union were Delaware, Maryland, Kentucky, and Missouri. But secession-

Bombardment of Fort Sumter, Charleston Harbor, a color lithograph by Currier & Ives (SCALA/Art Resource)

Fort Sumter, in Charleston Harbor, was the site of the first battle of the Civil War. Confederate troops under the command of General Pierre G. T. Beauregard attacked the U.S. Army post on April 12, 1861. On April 14, the Union defenders surrendered to the rebels.

ist groups in Kentucky and Missouri set up separate state governments and sent representatives to the Confederate Congress.

In both the North and the South, some families were torn by divided loyalties to the Union and the Confederacy. One of Kentucky Senator John J. Crittenden's sons, Thomas, became a Union general. Another son, George, became a Confederate general. George H. Thomas, one of the Union's best generals, was born in Virginia. Admiral David Farragut, who defeated Southern forces at New Orleans and Mobile Bay, was born in Tennessee. Three half brothers of Mary Todd Lincoln, Lincoln's wife, died fighting for the Confederacy. The husband of one of her half sisters was a Confederate general who was also killed.

Building the armed forces

At the beginning of the Civil War, neither the North nor the South had a plan to call up troops. The Regular Army of the United States at that time consisted of only about 16,000 men, most of whom fought for the North. Both sides tried to raise their armies by appealing to volunteers. That system worked at first. Individual states, rather than the Union or Confederate governments, recruited most volunteers and often equipped them. Any man who wanted to organize a company or a regiment could do so. In the North, especially late in the war, volunteers often received a *bounty* (payment for enlisting). The bounty system encouraged thousands of *bounty jumpers,* who deserted after being paid. Many bounty jumpers enlisted several times, often using a different name each time.

The draft. As the Civil War went on, enthusiasm for it faded and volunteer enlistments decreased. Both sides then tried drafting soldiers. The first Southern draft law was passed in April 1862 and made all able-bodied white men from ages 18 through 35 liable for three years' service. By February 1864, the limits had been changed to 17 and 50. The Northern program, begun in March 1863, drafted men from ages 20 through 45 for

three years. Exceptions to the draft were made in the North and South, however, and both sides allowed a draftee to pay a substitute to serve for him. In addition, a draftee in the North could pay the government $300 to avoid military service. The system seemed unfair, and many soldiers grumbled that they were involved in "a rich man's war and a poor man's fight." But on the whole, both armies had a fair representation of soldiers from the various social groups of their regions.

The draft worked poorly and was extremely unpopular in many areas of both North and South. In some isolated hill country of the South, it could not be enforced. In July 1863, armed antidraft protesters in New York City set fire to buildings and took over parts of the city before police and the Army restored order. However, the Northern and Southern draft succeeded in its main purpose, which was to stimulate volunteering.

No one knows exactly how many men served in the Civil War. The totals on both sides included many short-term enlistments and *repeaters* (men who served more than once). According to the best estimates, 2,100,000 men served in the Union Army, and 800,000 men served in the Confederate Army. A little more than half the men of military age served for the North. A larger proportion of eligible men—almost four-fifths—served for the South. In the South, black slaves performed most of the labor, thereby freeing a greater percentage of eligible whites for military duty. Immigrants made up about 24 per cent of the Union Army and about 10 per cent of the Confederate Army.

The Confederate Army reached peak strength in 1863, then declined. But the Union Army grew. In the last year of the war, the North had over a million soldiers. The South probably had no more than 200,000. About 10 per cent of the soldiers on both sides deserted. Desertion from the Confederate Army became most common in the last months of the war, when Southern morale began to collapse and defeat seemed certain.

The commanding officers. As commander in chief of the U.S. armed forces, Abraham Lincoln had to

Library of Congress

Abraham Lincoln was President of the United States during the Civil War. His strong leadership helped preserve the Union and led to the end of slavery throughout the nation.

Granger Collection

Jefferson Davis served as president of the Confederate States during the Civil War. He was firmly dedicated to the Southern cause but lacked the North's resources.

choose the Union's top military officers. Jefferson Davis had the same task in the Confederacy. Davis fortunately had General Robert E. Lee to take command of the Eastern Confederate Army. Lee's able officers included Generals Stonewall Jackson and James Longstreet. Confederate commanders in the West—Generals Albert Sidney Johnston, Pierre G. T. Beauregard, Braxton Bragg, and Joseph E. Johnston—were less successful.

Lincoln tried several commanders for the Eastern Union Army, which came to be called the Army of the Potomac. They were, in turn, Generals Irvin McDowell, George B. McClellan, John Pope, McClellan again, Ambrose E. Burnside, Joseph Hooker, and George G. Meade. All had serious weaknesses. Lincoln's Western generals—Henry W. Halleck, Don Carlos Buell, and William S. Rosecrans—also failed to meet his expectations. But as the war progressed, four outstanding generals emerged to lead the Union armies to victory. They were Ulysses S. Grant, William T. Sherman, Philip H. Sheridan, and George H. Thomas.

Leading Civil War generals

National Archives · Valentine Museum, Richmond, Va. · Bettmann Archive · Bettmann Archive

Ulysses S. Grant (North)   **Robert E. Lee (South)**   **William T. Sherman (North)**   **Stonewall Jackson (South)**

Major Civil War weapons

Civil War soldiers used the first *breech-loading rifles,* which were loaded at the *breech* (rear) of the barrel instead of the muzzle. *Mortars* fired cannonballs in a high arc. *Rifled-barrel cannons* had spiral grooves inside the barrel that sent cannonballs spinning accurately toward targets.

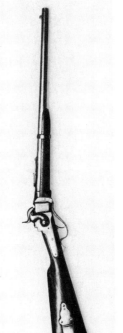

Chicago Historical Society

Mortar mounted on a railroad flatcar

Chicago Historical Society

Chicago Historical Society

Breech-loading rifle   **Rifled-barrel cannon mounted on wheels**

The enlisted men. Civil War soldiers were much like American enlisted men of earlier and later wars. They fought well but remained civilians, with a civilian's dislike of military rules. In most regiments, the men all came from the same area. Many units elected their own officers. Northern troops called the Southern soldier *Johnny Reb* or *Reb,* after *rebel.* Southerners called the enemy *Billy Yank* or *Yank.*

Civil War soldiers received more leaves and furloughs than did soldiers of previous wars, and they had better food and clothing. But compared with today's standards, they had a hard life. Both sides paid their soldiers poorly. Food supplies consisted mainly of flour, cornmeal, beef, beans, and dried fruit. Many soldiers made their own meals. Armies on the march ate salt pork and hard biscuits called *hardtack.* Poorly made clothing of *shoddy* (rewoven wool) often fell apart in the first storm. Southern soldiers at times lacked shoes and had to march and fight barefoot.

Most Civil War soldiers carried muzzleloading rifles. Because the guns could fire only one shot at a time, they seem primitive today. But they had an accurate range of nearly 400 yards (366 meters), far longer than earlier muskets. Civil War infantrymen often marched in close-order formation, as soldiers had done in other wars, and so were an easy target. A determined force in a strong position could resist almost any head-on attack by men approaching in close-order formation.

Many Civil War battles took a terrible toll in human lives. An army often had 25 per cent of its men killed, wounded, captured, or otherwise lost in a major battle. Among some regiments at the Battle of Gettysburg and other battles, the death rate alone ran as high as 25 per cent or more. The heavy death toll led Civil War soldiers to devise the first dog tags for identification in case they were killed. A soldier would print his name and address on a handkerchief or a piece of paper and pin it to his uniform before going into battle.

Uniforms of the Civil War

At the start of the Civil War, the militia units that largely made up the Union and Confederate armies wore a variety of uniforms. Both sides soon established regulation uniforms, such as the Union blue and Confederate gray examples shown below. But certain regiments called *zouaves* wore distinctive Oriental-style uniforms throughout the war.

WORLD BOOK illustration by H. Charles McBarron, Jr.

North

Cavalry Corporal in Winter Overcoat

Infantry Private

Cavalry Captain in Full-Dress Uniform

Navy Captain

Seaman

Zouave of the 5th New York Infantry

South

Cavalry Sergeant, 1862

Infantry Private, 1861-1862

Infantry Private, 1863-1865

Navy Captain

Seaman

Artillery Gunner

Early black participation. Early in the war, Northern blacks who wanted to fight to end slavery tried to enlist in the Union Army. But the Army rejected them. Most whites felt the war was a "white man's war."

As Northern armies drove into Confederate territory, slaves flocked to Union camps. After a period of uncertainty, the Union government decided to allow them to perform support services for the Northern war effort. In time, as many as 200,000 blacks worked for Union armies as cooks, laborers, nurses, scouts, and spies.

The Emancipation Proclamation. Black leaders, such as the former slave Frederick Douglass of New York, saw the Civil War as a road to *emancipation* (freedom) for the slaves. However, the idea of emancipation presented problems in the North. For one thing, the Constitution recognized slavery. In addition, most Northerners—even though they may have opposed slavery—were convinced of black inferiority. Many of them feared that emancipation would cause a mass movement of Southern blacks into the North. Northerners also worried about losing the border states loyal to the Union because those states were strongly committed to slavery. Skillful leadership was needed as the country moved toward black freedom. Lincoln supplied that leadership by combining a clear sense of purpose with a sensitivity to the concerns of various groups.

On Sept. 22, 1862, Lincoln issued a preliminary order to free the slaves. It declared that all slaves in states in rebellion against the Union on Jan. 1, 1863, would be forever free. It did not include slave states loyal to the Union. On Jan. 1, 1863, Lincoln issued the final order as the Emancipation Proclamation. The Emancipation Proclamation, though legally binding, was a war measure that could be reversed later. Therefore, in 1865, Lincoln helped push through Congress the 13th Amendment to the Constitution, which abolished slavery throughout the nation. For his effort in freeing the slaves, Lincoln is known as the "Great Emancipator."

The use of black troops. The Emancipation Proclamation also announced Lincoln's decision to use black troops, though many whites believed that blacks would make poor soldiers. About 180,000 blacks served in the Union Army. Two-thirds of them were Southerners who had fled to freedom in the North. About 20,000 blacks

Important events during the Civil War

1861

April 12	Confederate troops attacked Fort Sumter.
April 15	Lincoln issued a call for troops.
April 19	Lincoln proclaimed a blockade of the South.
May 21	Richmond, Va., was chosen as the Confederate capital.
July 21	Northern troops retreated in disorder after the First Battle of Bull Run (Manassas).

1862

Feb. 6	Fort Henry fell to Union forces.
Feb. 16	Grant's troops captured Fort Donelson.
March 9	The ironclad ships *Monitor* and *Merrimack (Virginia)* battled to a draw.
April 6-7	Both sides suffered heavy losses in the Battle of Shiloh, won by the Union.
April 16	The Confederacy began to draft soldiers.
April 18-25	Farragut attacked and captured New Orleans.
May 4	McClellan's Union troops occupied Yorktown, Va., and advanced on Richmond.
May 30	Northern forces occupied Corinth, Miss.
June 6	Memphis fell to Union armies.
June 25-July 1	Confederate forces under Lee saved Richmond in the Battles of the Seven Days.
Aug. 27-30	Lee and Jackson led Southern troops to victory in the Second Battle of Bull Run.
Sept. 17	Confederate forces retreated in defeat after the bloody Battle of Antietam (Sharpsburg).
Sept. 22	Lincoln issued a preliminary Emancipation Proclamation.
Oct. 8	Buell's forces ended Bragg's invasion of Kentucky in the Battle of Perryville.
Dec. 13	Burnside's Union forces received a crushing blow in the Battle of Fredericksburg.
Dec. 31-Jan. 2, 1863	Union troops under Rosecrans forced the Confederates to retreat after the Battle of Stones River (Murfreesboro).

1863

Jan. 1	Lincoln issued the Emancipation Proclamation.
March 3	The North passed a draft law.
May 1-4	Northern troops under Hooker were defeated in the Battle of Chancellorsville.
May 1-19	Grant's army defeated the Confederates in Mississippi and began to besiege Vicksburg.

July 1-3	The Battle of Gettysburg ended in a Southern defeat and marked a turning point in the war.
July 4	Vicksburg fell to Northern troops.
July 8	Northern forces occupied Port Hudson, La.
Sept. 19-20	Southern troops under Bragg won the Battle of Chickamauga.
Nov. 19	Lincoln delivered the Gettysburg Address.
Nov. 23-25	Grant and Thomas led Union armies to victory in the Battle of Chattanooga.

1864

March 9	Grant became general in chief of the North.
May 5-6	Union and Confederate troops clashed in the Battle of the Wilderness.
May 8-19	Grant and Lee held their positions in the Battle of Spotsylvania Court House.
June 3	The Union suffered heavy losses on the final day of the Battle of Cold Harbor.
June 20	Grant's troops laid siege to Petersburg, Va.
July 11-12	Early's Confederate forces almost reached Washington but retreated after brief fighting.
Aug. 5	Farragut won the Battle of Mobile Bay.
Sept. 2	Northern troops under Sherman captured Atlanta.
Sept. 19-Oct. 19	Sheridan led his troops on a rampage of destruction in the Shenandoah Valley.
Nov. 8	Lincoln was reelected President.
Nov. 15	Sherman began his march through Georgia.
Nov. 23	Hood invaded Tennessee.
Nov. 30	Schofield's Union forces inflicted heavy losses on Hood in the Battle of Franklin.
Dec. 15-16	The Battle of Nashville smashed Hood's army.
Dec. 21	Sherman's troops occupied Savannah, Ga.

1865

Feb. 6	Lee became general in chief of the South.
April 2	Confederate troops gave up Petersburg and Richmond.
April 9	Lee surrendered to Grant at Appomattox.
April 14	Lincoln was assassinated.
April 26	Johnston surrendered to Sherman.
May 4	Confederate forces in Alabama and Mississippi surrendered.
May 11	Jefferson Davis was captured.
May 26	The last Confederate troops surrendered.

Black troops fought in nearly 500 Civil War engagements. Twenty-three blacks won the Medal of Honor, the highest U.S. military award, for heroism. Nearly all black soldiers served in the Union Army. They were organized into segregated units like this one.

Bettmann Archive

served in the Union Navy, which had been open to blacks long before the war. Black troops formed 166 all-black regiments, most of which had white commanders. Only about 100 blacks were made officers.

Blacks fought in nearly 500 Civil War engagements, including 39 major battles. About 35,000 black servicemen lost their lives. Altogether, 23 blacks won the Medal of Honor, the nation's highest military award, for heroism. A black regiment was one of the first Northern units to march into Richmond after it fell. Lincoln then toured the city, escorted by black cavalry.

At first, black soldiers received only about half the pay of white soldiers and no bounties for volunteering. In 1864, Congress granted blacks equal pay and bounties. However, other types of official discrimination continued. For example, most black soldiers were allowed to perform only noncombat duties. But some blacks who had the opportunity to go into combat distinguished themselves. The bravery of blacks in the 1863 Mississippi Valley campaign surprised most Northerners. But protests against the use of black troops went on.

Later in 1863, the 54th Massachusetts Volunteers—the first black troops from a free state to be organized for combat in the Union Army—stormed Fort Wagner in Charleston Harbor. Their bravery turned the tide of Northern public opinion to accept black troops. Lincoln wrote that when peace came "there will be some black men who can remember that, with silent tongue, and clenched teeth, and steady eye, and well-poised bayonet, they have helped mankind on to this great consummation; while, I fear, there will be some white ones, unable to forget that, with malignant heart, and deceitful speech, they have strove to hinder it."

Reaction in the South. The Confederacy objected strongly to the North's use of black soldiers. The Confederate government threatened to kill or enslave any captured officers or enlisted men of black regiments. Lincoln replied by promising to treat Confederate prisoners of war the same way. Neither side carried out its threats, but the exchange of prisoners broke down mainly over the issue of black prisoners.

The North's success in using black soldiers slowly led Southerners to consider doing the same. In the spring of 1865, following a strong demand by General Lee, the Confederate Congress narrowly approved the use of black soldiers. However, the war ended soon thereafter.

The home front

The Civil War became the first war to be completely and immediately reported in the press to the people back home. Civilians in the North were especially well informed of the war's progress. Northern newspapers sent their best correspondents into the field and received their reports by telegraph. Winslow Homer and many other artists and illustrators produced war scenes for such magazines as *Harper's Weekly.* Mathew Brady, Alexander Gardner, and other pioneer photographers captured the horrors of the battlefield and the humanity of the soldiers in thousands of news pictures.

The Civil War inspired a flood of patriotic songs. Northern civilians and soldiers sang such songs as "The Battle Cry of Freedom," "Marching Through Georgia," and "John Brown's Body." Early in the war, Julia Ward Howe wrote "The Battle Hymn of the Republic" to the tune of "John Brown's Body." Southern soldiers marched to war to the stirring music of "Dixie" and "The Bonnie Blue Flag." Some Northern songs, such as "Tenting on the Old Camp Ground" and "When Johnny Comes

Marching Home," also became popular in the South. And some Southern songs—for example, the mournful "Lorena" and "All Quiet Along the Potomac Tonight"— were also popular in the North.

In the North

Government and politics. After the attack on Fort Sumter, Lincoln boldly ordered troops to put down the rebellion, increased the size of the U.S. Army, proclaimed a naval blockade of the South, and spent funds without congressional approval. He became the first President to assume vast powers not specifically granted by the Constitution. He suspended the right known as *habeas corpus* in many cases in which people opposed the war effort. Habeas corpus guarantees a person under arrest a chance to be heard in court. Its suspension received bitter criticism. Yet many traditional American freedoms continued to flourish, even though the nation was in the midst of a civil war.

Opposition to the war and Lincoln's policies came

chiefly from the Democratic Party, especially from a group known as the Peace Democrats, who wanted the war stopped. Republicans considered the Peace Democrats disloyal and treacherous and called them Copperheads, after the poisonous snake. Other protesters of the war joined secret antigovernment societies, such as the Knights of the Golden Circle. The Lincoln Administration was also criticized by so-called Radical Republicans. They wanted the government to move more rapidly to abolish slavery and to make sweeping changes in the Southern way of life. Such disputes continued throughout the war.

Economy. The Civil War brought booming prosperity to the North. Government purchases for military needs stimulated manufacturing and agriculture. The production of coal, iron and steel, weapons, shoes, and woolen clothing increased greatly. Farmers vastly expanded their production of wheat, wool, and other products. Exports to Europe of beef, corn, pork, and wheat doubled. Factories and farms made the first widespread use of labor-saving machines, such as the sewing machine and the reaper.

Although the Civil War brought prosperity to the North, financing the war was difficult. Taxes and money borrowed through the sale of war bonds became major sources of income. The government also printed more paper money to meet its financial needs. But by increasing the money supply, the government promoted inflation. Wages did not keep up with inflation through much of the war, and factory workers struck for higher pay. But as the war went on, war production—and finally victory—helped the North grow ever stronger.

During the Lincoln Administration, Congress passed the most important series of economic acts in American history to that time. It established the national banking system, a *uniform* (standard) currency, and the Department of Agriculture. The Pacific Railroad Act of 1862 provided for the building of the nation's first transcontinental rail line. The Homestead Act of 1862 granted settlers public land in the West free or at low cost. The Land-Grant, or Morrill, Act of 1862 helped states establish agricultural and technical colleges. Under Lincoln, Congress also passed the first federal income tax. Altogether, the economic progress in the North brought about by and during the Civil War helped put the United States on the road to becoming the world's greatest industrial power by the late 1800's.

In the South

Government and politics. During the Civil War, the South tried to bring political power under the control of a single authority. But it was not very successful. Southerners had long opposed a strong central government. During the war, some of them found it difficult to cooperate with officials of both the Confederacy and their own states and cities. States' rights supporters backed the war but opposed the draft and other actions needed to carry it out. And Jefferson Davis lacked Lincoln's leadership abilities. For example, Lincoln believed he had the power to suspend the law if necessary, and he did so. Davis asked the Confederate Congress for such power but received only limited permission.

Economy. As in the North, manufacturing and agriculture in the South were adapted to the needs of war. Factories converted from civilian to wartime production. For example, the Tredegar Iron Works in Richmond became the South's main source of cannons. Cotton cultivation dropped sharply, while food production was greatly increased.

The South thus tried to adjust to meet wartime needs, but its economy became strained almost to the breaking point. The attempt to finance the war by taxation and borrowing from the people failed. The Confederacy's solution to the problem was to print large amounts of paper money, which led to an extremely high inflation rate. By the end of the war, prices were 10 times higher than they were at the start. In 1865, flour cost up to $300 a barrel, and shoes $200 a pair. In time, Southerners had to make clothes of carpets and curtains and print newspapers on the back of wallpaper.

Confederate troops were never as well equipped as their Northern foes. As resources were used up and the tightening naval blockade severely reduced imports, matters got worse. The Confederate government then passed the Impressment Act of 1863. The act permitted government agents to seize from civilians food, horses, and any other supplies the Army needed. The civilians received whatever the agents decided to pay.

Relations with Europe. At the beginning of the Civil War, Southern leaders hoped that European countries—especially Great Britain and France—would come to the aid of the Confederacy. Southerners believed that Britain and France would be forced to support the Confederacy because their textile industries depended on Southern cotton. The efforts of Southern statesmen to persuade the European powers to help the Confederacy came to be called "cotton diplomacy."

As a result of cotton diplomacy, Britain and France allowed the Confederacy to have several armed warships built in their shipyards. But the South never won Euro-

Library of Congress

Magazine illustrators, as well as reporters and photographers, traveled to Civil War battlegrounds. Alfred R. Waud, a *Harper's Weekly* artist, is shown sketching at Gettysburg.

pean recognition of the Confederacy as an independent nation or obtained major aid. Northern grain had become important in Europe, which had suffered several crop failures. At the same time, Southern cotton was increasingly replaced by cotton from India and Egypt. The Emancipation Proclamation made the Civil War a fight against slavery. The proclamation deeply impressed those Europeans who opposed slavery. Such skillful Northern diplomats as Charles Francis Adams also helped persuade the European powers not to recognize the Confederacy. But most important, Britain and France would not fight on the side of the South unless the Confederacy could show that it might win final victory. And that never happened.

Major battles of the Civil War

Battle	State	Date	Commanders		Casualties*		Results
			North	South	North	South	
Antietam (Sharpsburg)	Md.	Sept. 17, 1862	McClellan	Lee	12,500	13,700	Confederate retreat gave Lincoln the occasion to announce the preliminary Emancipation Proclamation.
Bull Run (Manassas) First	Va.	July 21, 1861	McDowell	Beauregard	3,000	2,000	The North first realized the seriousness of the war.
Second		Aug. 27-30, 1862	Pope	Lee	16,100	9,200	The South regained almost all of Virginia.
Chancellorsville	Va.	May 1-4, 1863	Hooker	Lee	16,800	12,800	Confederate forces were victorious, but Stonewall Jackson was killed.
Chattanooga	Tenn.	Nov. 23-25, 1863	Grant	Bragg	5,800	7,700	Union win put most of Tennessee in Northern hands.
Chickamauga	Ga.	Sept. 19-20, 1863	Rosecrans	Bragg	16,200	18,500	Southern victory trapped Rosecrans in Chattanooga.
Cold Harbor	Va.	June 1-3, 1864	Grant	Lee	12,000	1,500	Heavy losses forced Grant to change his tactics.
Fair Oaks (Seven Pines)	Va.	May 31-June 1, 1862	McClellan	Johnston	5,000	6,000	Confederate forces were driven back.
Fort Donelson	Tenn.	Feb. 13-16, 1862	Grant	Buckner	2,800	15,800	The North won its first important victory.
Fort Henry	Tenn.	Feb. 6, 1862	Grant	Tilghman	50	20	Initial success encouraged Grant's Western campaign.
Franklin	Tenn.	Nov. 30, 1864	Schofield	Hood	2,300	6,300	Hood's Tennessee campaign failed to draw Sherman from Georgia.
Fredericksburg	Va.	Dec. 13, 1862	Burnside	Lee	12,700	5,300	A terrible defeat left the North discouraged.
Gettysburg	Pa.	July 1-3, 1863	Meade	Lee	22,800	22,600	Northern victory marked a turning point in the war.
Kennesaw Mountain	Ga.	June 27, 1864	Sherman	Johnston	2,100	400	In spite of Confederate success, Davis replaced Johnston with Hood.
Mobile Bay	Ala.	Aug. 5, 1864	Farragut	Buchanan	320	300	The North closed one of the major Southern ports.
Nashville	Tenn.	Dec. 15-16, 1864	Thomas	Hood	3,100	6,000	Northern victory practically ended Southern resistance in the West.
Perryville	Ky.	Oct. 8, 1862	Buell	Bragg	4,200	3,400	Confederate troops abandoned Kentucky.
Petersburg, Siege of	Va.	June 20, 1864-April 2, 1865	Grant	Lee	42,000	28,000	Months of trench warfare pinned Lee to a defensive.
Seven Days	Va.	June 25-July 1, 1862	McClellan	Lee	15,800	20,100	Richmond was saved from capture, and Northern forces retreated.
Shiloh (Pittsburg Landing)	Tenn.	April 6-7, 1862	Grant	Johnston, Beauregard	13,000	10,700	Grant pushed back Southern forces.
Spotsylvania Court House	Va.	May 8-19, 1864	Grant	Lee	17,500	10,000	Grant continued to hammer at Lee's resistant forces.
Stones River (Murfreesboro)	Tenn.	Dec. 31, 1862-Jan. 2, 1863	Rosecrans	Bragg	12,900	11,700	Southern forces failed to follow up an initial victory.
Vicksburg, Siege of	Miss.	May 19-July 4, 1863	Grant	Pemberton	10,000	10,000	Northern victory proved decisive in winning the Mississippi and the West.
Wilderness	Va.	May 5-6, 1864	Grant	Lee	17,700	11,000	Heavy losses failed to halt Grant's progress southward.

*Figures are approximate totals of dead, wounded, missing, and captured.

The Appalachian Mountains divided the Civil War into two main *theaters of operations* (military areas). The Eastern theater stretched east of the mountains to the Atlantic Ocean. The Western theater lay between the mountains and the Mississippi River. A third theater, west of the Mississippi, saw only minor action.

Many Civil War battles have two names because the Confederates named them after the nearest settlement, and Northerners named them after the nearest body of water. In such battles described in this article, the North-

ern name is given first, followed by the Confederate name in parentheses.

Opening battles

Fort Sumter. The Civil War began on April 12, 1861, when Confederate forces under General Pierre G. T. Beauregard attacked Fort Sumter, a U.S. Army post in the harbor of Charleston, S.C. The Union troops evacuated the fort on April 14, and the Confederates occupied it until almost the end of the war.

Battles and campaigns of the Civil War

This map locates important battles and campaigns of the Civil War. Most of the fighting in the East occurred in Virginia. Fighting in the West centered in Tennessee and along the Mississippi River. Union strategy succeeded in dividing the Confederacy and blockading its harbors.

WORLD BOOK map

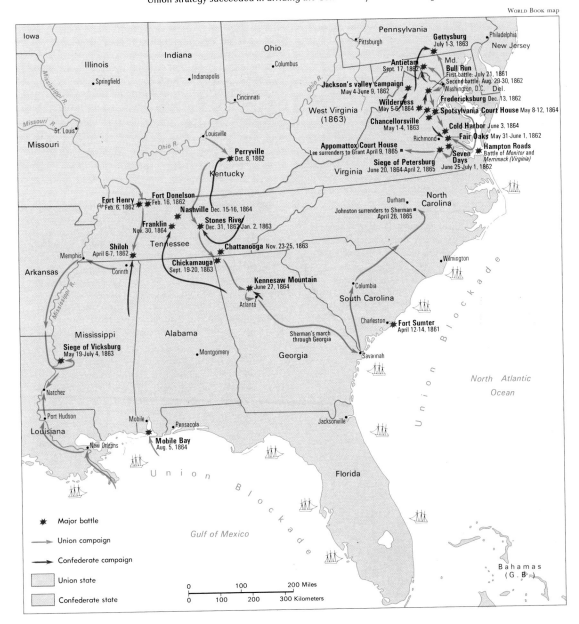

Following the fall of Fort Sumter, a Union army of about 18,000 men under General Robert Patterson held the northern end of the fertile Shenandoah River Valley, which lay in Virginia west of the rival capitals of Washington and Richmond. Another Union force of about 31,000 under General Irvin McDowell moved into eastern Virginia to attack Southern forces. A Confederate army under Beauregard faced McDowell at Manassas, Va., about 25 miles (40 kilometers) southwest of Washington. General Joseph E. Johnston commanded Confederate troops in the Shenandoah Valley. Those forces, along with other scattered troops, added up to about 35,000 Confederates ready for action.

First Battle of Bull Run (or First Battle of Manassas). In July 1861, McDowell approached Manassas, which lay on a creek called Bull Run. McDowell thought his troops could destroy Beauregard's forces while the Union troops in the Shenandoah Valley kept Johnston occupied. But Johnston slipped away and traveled by rail to join Beauregard just before the battle.

The opposing forces, both composed mainly of poorly trained volunteers, clashed on July 21. The North launched several assaults. During one attack, the Confederate General Thomas J. Jackson stood his ground so firmly that he received the nickname "Stonewall." After halting several assaults, Beauregard counterattacked. The tired Union forces fled to Washington, D.C., in wild retreat. After the battle, some Southerners regretted not moving on to capture Washington. But such an attempt would probably have failed.

The North realized that it faced a long fight. The war would not be over in three months, as many Northerners had predicted. Confederate confidence in final victory soared and remained high for the next two years.

The drive to take Richmond

After Bull Run, Lincoln made General George B. McClellan commander of the Army of the Potomac in the East. During the winter of 1861-1862, McClellan assembled a force with which he planned to capture Rich-mond from the southeast. He wanted to land his men on the peninsula between the York and James rivers and advance along one of the rivers toward the Southern capital. But before McClellan could move, a naval action changed his plans.

First battle between ironclads. In 1861, the Confederates had raised a sunken federal ship, the *Merrimack,* off Norfolk, Va., and covered the wooden vessel with iron plates. The South used the ironclad ship, renamed the *Virginia,* to stage the South's greatest naval challenge to the North. On March 8, 1862, the *Virginia* attacked Northern ships at Hampton Roads, a channel that empties into Chesapeake Bay. It destroyed two Northern vessels and grounded three others. When the ship returned the next day to finish the job, it faced the *Monitor,* an ironclad ship designed especially for the Northern Navy. History's first battle between ironclad warships followed. Although neither ship won, the *Monitor* proved to be the superior vessel. Later, the U.S. Navy built a large ironclad fleet modeled after it.

The peninsular campaign. After the battle of the ironclads, McClellan landed on the peninsula between the York and James rivers with more than 100,000 men. He occupied Yorktown and advanced along the York River. He could not follow the James River because the *Virginia* was on the river. By late May 1862, McClellan was within 6 miles (10 kilometers) of Richmond. Johnston led an attack against McClellan on May 31. But the Confederates failed to follow up their success and were driven back toward Richmond. In the two-day fight, called the Battle of Fair Oaks or Battle of Seven Pines, Johnston was wounded. General Robert E. Lee was given command of Johnston's army, which Lee called the Army of Northern Virginia.

Jackson's valley campaign. The Confederacy feared that McClellan would receive reinforcements from the numerous troops that had stayed behind to protect Washington. Stonewall Jackson therefore launched a campaign in the Shenandoah Valley. He planned to make the Northerners think he was going to attack

Bettmann Archive

The battle of the ironclads pitted the Northern *Monitor,* against the Southern *Merrimack (Virginia)* in March 1862. Neither ship won, but the event marked the first time that ships were fitted with armor for battle.

The Battle of Antietam was waged between Confederate forces under General Robert E. Lee and Union forces under General George B. McClellan on Sept. 17, 1862, near the town of Sharpsburg, Md. The savage battle ended with Lee's retreat, giving Lincoln the opportunity to issue the preliminary Emancipation Proclamation on September 22.

Bettmann Archive

Washington. In a series of brilliant moves from May 4 through June 9, 1862, Jackson advanced about 350 miles (560 kilometers) up the Shenandoah Valley and beyond, toward the Potomac River. His 17,000 men received the name "foot cavalry" because they marched so fast. Jackson won four battles against the Union armies. He reached the Potomac but soon had to retreat. However, he had forced the Union to withhold the powerful reinforcements that McClellan had counted on.

Stuart's raid. While Lee planned his strategy as the new commander of the Army of Northern Virginia, Confederate General Jeb Stuart led a remarkable cavalry raid. In June 1862, Stuart and about 1,200 men galloped completely around McClellan's army of 100,000 in three days, losing only one man. Stuart's raid gained information about Union troop movements and boosted Southern morale.

Battles of the Seven Days. Lee planned a daring move to destroy McClellan's army, which lay straddled over the Chickahominy River. With his forces reinforced by Jackson's men to about 95,000 men, Lee fell on McClellan in a series of attacks, called the Battles of the Seven Days, from June 25 through July 1, 1862. The advantage shifted from side to side during the battles, but McClellan believed that his forces were hopelessly outnumbered. He finally retreated to the James River, and Richmond was saved from capture. McClellan's army was ordered to northern Virginia to be united with a force under General John Pope. McClellan was to command the combined army.

The South strikes back

Second Battle of Bull Run (or Second Battle of Manassas). Lee moved rapidly northward to attack Pope, stationed at Manassas, before McClellan's men could join him. Lee sent Jackson ahead to move behind Pope's army and force a battle. On Aug. 29, 1862, Pope attacked Jackson, sending in McClellan's troops as fast as they arrived. Meanwhile, Lee and General James Longstreet had joined Jackson. Pope attacked Lee's army on August 30, but a Confederate counterattack swept the Union forces from the field. The beaten Northern troops plodded back to Washington.

Battle of Antietam (or Battle of Sharpsburg). The South hoped to gain European recognition by winning a victory in Union territory. Lee invaded Maryland in September 1862. He divided his army, sending about half with Jackson to capture Harpers Ferry, Va., which Union troops occupied. McClellan moved to meet Lee with about 90,000 men. On September 13, a Union soldier found a copy of Lee's orders to his commanders wrapped around three cigars at an abandoned Confederate campsite. Lee learned of the loss and took up a position at Sharpsburg, a town on Antietam Creek in Maryland. But McClellan did not immediately attack, giving the Confederate forces time to reunite after Jackson's success at Harpers Ferry. On September 17, McClellan launched a series of attacks that almost cracked the Southern lines. But then, the last of Lee's absent troops, headed by General A. P. Hill, arrived and saved the day. Lee's force of about 40,000 men suffered heavy losses and had to retreat to Virginia.

Antietam was the bloodiest day of the Civil War. About 2,000 Northerners and 2,700 Southerners were killed. Approximately 19,000 men from both sides were wounded, of which about 3,000 later died. Because Lee retreated, the North called Antietam a Union victory. On September 22, Lincoln issued the preliminary Emancipation Proclamation. He had been waiting for a Northern victory as a good time for the proclamation.

Battle of Fredericksburg. As bloody as Antietam was, McClellan had more fresh troops under him after the battle than Lee had left in his entire army. Yet McClellan permitted the Army of Northern Virginia to retreat with almost no interference. Lincoln, who had long felt that McClellan was not aggressive enough, replaced him with General Ambrose E. Burnside as commander of the Army of the Potomac.

Burnside decided to attack Lee at Fredericksburg, Va. The Confederates, about 73,000 strong, established a

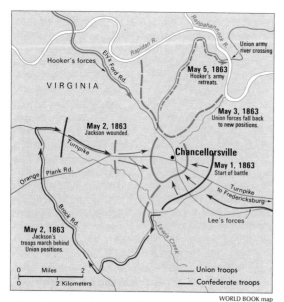

WORLD BOOK map

The Confederate victory at Chancellorsville was won by Lee with Jackson's help. Lee struck Hooker's Union forces in front, while Jackson attacked the right flank. But Jackson was fatally wounded by accident in the battle.

line of defense along fortified hills called Marye's Heights. On Dec. 13, 1862, Burnside's men tried to storm the hills in a brave but hopeless attack. The Union suffered nearly 13,000 *casualties*—soldiers killed, wounded, missing, or captured—and retreated. Burnside was relieved of command at his own request.

Battle of Chancellorsville. General Joseph Hooker replaced Burnside. In the spring of 1863, the Army of the Potomac numbered about 138,000 men. Lee's forces totaled about 60,000 and still held the line of defense at Fredericksburg. Hooker planned to keep Lee's attention on Fredericksburg while he sent another force around the town to attack the Confederate *flank* (side).

The flanking movement began on April 27, 1863, and seemed about to succeed. But then, Hooker hesitated. On May 1, he withdrew his flanking troops to a defensive position at Chancellorsville, a settlement just west of Fredericksburg. The next day, Lee left a small force at Fredericksburg and boldly moved to attack Hooker. He sent Stonewall Jackson to attack Hooker's right flank, while he struck in front. The attack, on May 2, cut the Northern army almost in two, but Union troops managed to set up a defensive line. Hooker retreated three days later. During the battle, Jackson was shot accidentally by his own men. His left arm had to be amputated. Lee told Jackson's chaplain: "He has lost his left arm; but I have lost my right arm." Jackson died on May 10.

Battle of Gettysburg. In June 1863, Lee's army swung up the Shenandoah Valley into Pennsylvania. The Army of the Potomac followed it northward. Both armies moved toward the little town of Gettysburg. When it appeared that the battle was about to begin, Lincoln put General George G. Meade, a Pennsylvanian, in com-

mand of the Union troops. The shooting started when a Confederate brigade, searching for badly needed shoes, ran into Union cavalry near Gettysburg on July 1. For the first three days of July, a Northern army of about 85,000 men fought a Southern army of about 65,000 in the greatest battle ever fought in the Western Hemisphere.

On the first day, the two armies maneuvered for position. By the end of the day, Northern troops had been pushed from west and north of Gettysburg to south of the town. They settled into a strong defensive location that resembled a fishhook. Culp's Hill and Cemetery Hill, at the right, formed the barb of the hook. The front ran about 3 miles (5 kilometers) along Cemetery Ridge and ended at two hills called Little Round Top and Round Top. Confederate forces occupied Gettysburg and then Seminary Ridge, to the west.

On the second day, July 2, Lee tried to crack the Union flanks and roll up Cemetery Ridge. He aimed his main assault at the left flank. Lee managed to crush a Northern corps. Other Union troops, however, held on to Cemetery Ridge and to Little Round Top, perhaps the most important point in the entire Union line. The Confederate attack on the right flank at Culp's Hill and Cemetery Hill came too late to succeed.

On July 3, Lee decided to attack the Union center. After a fierce artillery duel, he ordered General George E. Pickett to prepare about 13,000 men to charge the Union lines. The men, marching in perfect parade formation, swept across an open field and up the slopes of Cemetery Ridge, ignoring enemy fire. Only a few troops reached the top of the ridge, where they were quickly shot or captured. Barely half the soldiers involved in the assault returned to Lee, who took complete responsibility for the attack's failure. Pickett's charge showed the

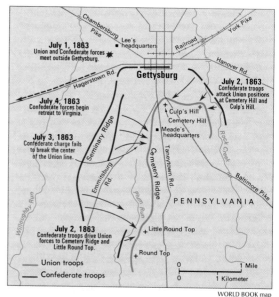

WORLD BOOK map

The Battle of Gettysburg started with Union armies taking up defensive positions south of Gettysburg. Confederate forces attacked both ends of those positions, then failed to break the Union center, turning the battle into a Union victory.

hopelessness of *frontal* (head-on) assaults over open ground against a strong enemy. Lee's attempt to pierce the Union rear with Stuart's cavalry, which had arrived the night before, also failed.

Lee withdrew his battered army to Virginia after the battle. Much to Lincoln's disgust, Meade made little effort to follow him, even though Meade had about 20,000 fresh reserves and had received further reinforcements. Lee's army thus escaped. Gettysburg became a turning point in the war. Casualties among Lee's men numbered nearly 23,000. Never again would he have the troop strength to launch a major offensive.

The war in the West—1862-1864

In the Western theater, the North attacked early and hard to seize the Mississippi River. Northern forces in the West totaled about 100,000 men, and Southern forces about 70,000. General Henry W. Halleck led Union forces in Arkansas, Illinois, Iowa, western Kentucky, Minnesota, Missouri, and Wisconsin. General Don Carlos Buell led the Northern forces in Indiana, eastern Kentucky, Michigan, and Ohio. General Albert Sidney Johnston led Southern forces in Arkansas, western Mississippi, and Tennessee. His command included General Earl Van Dorn's troops in Arkansas.

Fight for the Mississippi Valley

Battles of Fort Henry and Fort Donelson. The center of the Confederate line in the West rested on two forts about 12 miles (19 kilometers) apart in western Tennessee. They were Fort Henry on the Tennessee River and Fort Donelson on the Cumberland River. If Union forces could capture the forts, the Confederate position in Kentucky and western Tennessee would collapse. Gunboats under orders from General Ulysses S. Grant, commanding officer under Halleck in western Kentucky, took Fort Henry on Feb. 6, 1862. Grant himself moved against Fort Donelson. The Confederate commander, General Simon Bolivar Buckner, asked for "the best terms" of surrender. Grant replied: "No terms except an unconditional and immediate surrender can be accepted." On February 16, about 13,000 of the Confederate troops stationed at Fort Donelson surrendered. Grant gained the nickname "Unconditional Surrender" Grant and became a Northern hero.

Grant's army lay between the two flanks of the Confederate forces. To escape destruction, Johnston pulled his troops back to Corinth, Miss., a major railroad center. The Confederacy had lost Kentucky and half of Tennessee. West of the Mississippi River, a Union army under General Samuel R. Curtis defeated Van Dorn at Pea Ridge, Ark., on March 6 through 8. The defeat put Missouri solidly in Northern hands.

Battle of Shiloh. Halleck, who had become commander of most Union forces from Ohio to Kansas, ordered Grant to move down the Tennessee River and told Buell to join Grant. Grant and some 40,000 men moved to Pittsburg Landing, Tenn., a village about 20 miles (32 kilometers) north of Corinth. Johnston and his co-commander, General Beauregard, decided to strike Grant before Buell arrived. They planned to destroy Grant's forces with their army of some 44,000 troops. The Battle of Shiloh, named after a church on the battlefield, occurred on April 6 and 7, 1862. The battle is also called the Battle of Pittsburg Landing.

On the first day, Confederate troops surprised and almost smashed Grant. But Grant held his lines. Johnston was killed in the battle. The next day, Grant received about 25,000 reinforcements, including some 18,000 troops led by Buell. The Confederate army received only about 700 reinforcements. Grant used his now much larger army to force a Southern retreat to Corinth. The Union suffered about 13,000 casualties, and the Confederacy nearly 11,000. Many Northerners urged Lincoln to replace Grant because of the heavy losses. But Lincoln refused, saying, "I can't spare this man—he fights!"

After Shiloh, Halleck took command of Grant's and Buell's forces. He moved southward and forced Beauregard to evacuate Corinth. By early June, the Union held the Mississippi River as far south as Memphis.

Capture of New Orleans. Meanwhile, Northern forces were moving up the Mississippi River from the South. In April 1862, a naval squadron under Captain David G. Farragut appeared at the mouth of the river. Farragut steamed through the weak Confederate defenses and captured New Orleans on April 25. On May 1, Northerners took control of New Orleans and southern Louisiana, which they held for the rest of the war.

Raids. Some of the most daring actions of the Civil War occurred behind the front lines. In April 1862, a Union spy named James J. Andrews led 21 men through the Confederate lines to Marietta, Ga., where they captured a railroad engine named the *General*. They ran it northward toward Chattanooga, Tenn., destroying telegraph communications as they went. But Confederate troops in another engine, the *Texas*, pursued the *General* and caught it after an exciting chase. The Confederacy hanged Andrews and 7 of his men.

In the spring of 1863, Colonel Benjamin Grierson took a Union cavalry force of about 1,700 men on daring raids between Vicksburg, Miss., and Baton Rouge, La. They tore up about 50 miles (80 kilometers) of railroad track and lured Confederate cavalry and infantry regiments away from Union troops massing near Vicksburg.

Confederate Generals Nathan Bedford Forrest and John Hunt Morgan led many daredevil cavalry raids into enemy territory. In 1864, for example, Forrest's men galloped as far north as Paducah, Ky., destroying Union supplies and communications lines. Morgan led his men, called Morgan's Raiders, on a spectacular dash into Ohio in July 1863. They destroyed property worth about $576,000 before being captured. Morgan escaped in November but was killed a year later in Tennessee.

Battle of Perryville. After Corinth fell to Union forces, Halleck went to Washington to act as Lincoln's military adviser. He assigned Grant to guard communications along the Mississippi and ordered Buell, who had yet to prove himself, to capture Chattanooga. Before

Buell could advance, General Braxton Bragg, the Confederate commander in Tennessee, suddenly invaded Kentucky. Buell raced to meet him, and the two armies clashed on October 8 at Perryville. Neither side won, but Bragg retreated to Murfreesboro, Tenn.

Battle of Stones River (or Battle of Murfreesboro). Lincoln felt that Buell was too cautious and replaced him with General William S. Rosecrans. Rosecrans advanced south from Nashville toward Bragg's army at Murfreesboro on Stones River. The hard-fought battle dragged on from Dec. 31, 1862, to Jan. 2, 1863, when Bragg retreated. The battle had the highest casualty rate of the war, with each side losing about a third of its men.

Siege of Vicksburg. In the winter of 1862-1863, Grant proposed to capture Vicksburg, the key city that guarded the Mississippi River between Memphis and New Orleans. Grant tried several times to take Vicksburg by approaching from the north. But the ground north of the city was low and marshy, and the Union army bogged down. In April 1863, Grant launched a new plan. At night, Union gunboats and supply ships slipped past the Confederate artillery along the river and established a base south of the city. Grant's troops then marched down the west side of the river and crossed over by ship to dry ground on the east side south of the city. In a brilliant campaign, Grant scattered Confederate forces in the field and drove toward Vicksburg. After direct attacks failed, he began a siege of the city in mid-May. Vicksburg finally surrendered on July 4, the day after the Southern defeat at Gettysburg.

Four days later, forces under General Nathaniel P. Banks took Port Hudson, La. The North controlled the Mississippi River, splitting the Confederacy in two.

The Tennessee campaign

Battle of Chickamauga. In September 1863, Rosecrans advanced on Chattanooga with a force of about 55,000 men. Bragg, who was seeking to keep his army free for action, evacuated the city and withdrew to Georgia. Rosecrans recklessly pursued him. Bragg had received reinforcements by rail from Virginia, and his forces numbered approximately 66,000. He fell on Rosecrans savagely at Chickamauga, Ga., on September 19 and 20. The Northern right flank broke completely. Only the Union left flank fought on under General George H. Thomas, who earned the nickname "The Rock of Chickamauga" for holding his line. In the end, Rosecrans' entire army had to retreat to Chattanooga. The Battle of Chickamauga was the Confederacy's last important victory in the Civil War.

Battle of Chattanooga. Bragg did not follow up his victory at Chickamauga immediately. In late September 1863, he finally advanced on Chattanooga. Bragg's army occupied Lookout Mountain, Missionary Ridge, and other heights south of the city. From these points, Confederate artillery commanded the roads and the Tennessee River, by which Chattanooga received its supplies. Starvation threatened Rosecrans' army. But the North had enough troops available in the West to meet any threat. In October 1863, Grant was given command of all Union forces in the West. He replaced Rosecrans with Thomas. Grant then went to Chattanooga with part of his own army.

From November 23 through 25, the Union troops dealt Bragg an immense blow in the Battle of Chattanooga. Lookout Mountain and some other heights fell on the first two days in the so-called Battle Above the Clouds. On November 25, Thomas' army, anxious to make up for its defeat at Chickamauga, swept up Missionary Ridge without orders. The successful charge ended the Battle of Chattanooga in an hour. The Union had won Chattanooga. From that base, Northern armies could move into Georgia and Alabama and split the eastern Confederacy in two.

Behind the lines

Hospitals. During the Civil War, many wounded and sick soldiers were treated in hospitals in Northern and Southern cities. But most received care in temporary facilities. Such facilities included field hospitals on or near battlegrounds, hospital ships and barges, and civilian buildings converted for medical use.

By today's standards, the medical care was primitive during the Civil War. More than twice as many soldiers died of disease—especially of dysentery, malaria, or typhoid—as were killed in battle. Doctors did not yet understand the importance of sanitation, a balanced diet, and sterile medical equipment and facilities. But medical care within the military made some progress with the introduction of horse-drawn ambulances and a trained ambulance corps. The first such corps, begun in 1862, served under Union General McClellan.

Women performed a key role in providing medical care. Mary Walker served as a surgeon with the Union Army. She became the only woman ever to receive the Medal of Honor. Dorothea Dix, famous for her earlier work in mental institutions, was superintendent of U.S.

Bettmann Archive

Medical care during the Civil War was given in temporary facilities and in city hospitals like this one in Washington, D.C. Temporary facilities included field hospitals on battlegrounds.

Army nurses. Thousands of volunteer nurses served the Union and Confederate forces. One of the North's volunteer nurses, Clara Barton, later founded the American Red Cross.

Private organizations also helped care for ill and wounded soldiers. One organization was the United States Sanitary Commission, created in June 1861. It operated hospitals and distributed food, clothing, medicine, and other supplies. The organization cared for both Union and Confederate soldiers.

Prisons. About 194,000 Union soldiers and about 214,000 Confederate soldiers were held prisoner during the Civil War. The North and the South had about 30 major prison camps each. Both sides also set up temporary prison quarters. Prison conditions were generally miserable because the camps were overcrowded and officials could not provide adequate care. In the South, where such necessities as food and clothing were in short supply for the Confederacy's own soldiers and civilians, prisoners had an especially difficult time.

One of the best-known prisons was Andersonville, a Confederate camp in Georgia. It was horribly overcrowded, and prisoners were deliberately abused and neglected. At Andersonville, as many as 33,000 Northern prisoners at a time were crowded into a log stockade that enclosed only $16\frac{1}{2}$ acres (6.7 hectares). After the war, the graves of nearly 13,000 Union prisoners were discovered there. The officer in charge of Andersonville, Henry Wirz, became the only Confederate soldier to be tried and executed for war crimes after the war.

At first, no official prisoner exchange took place between North and South. The Union government refused to extend such a degree of recognition to the Confederacy. A successful prisoner exchange agreement was reached by the middle of 1862. However, the agreement broke down in 1863, chiefly because the Confederacy resented the Union's use of black soldiers and refused to treat them as prisoners of war. After the Confederate government itself authorized the use of black soldiers in 1865, large-scale prisoner exchange started again.

The final year—1864-1865

All signs pointed to victory for the Union in early 1864. The size of Southern armies had dwindled because of battle losses, war weariness, and Northern occupation of large areas of the Confederacy. Southern railroads had almost stopped running, and supplies were desperately short. But the South, still capable of tough resistance, fought on for over a year before surrendering.

Grant in command

Since 1862, Lincoln had wanted the Union armies to have a unified command and a coordinated strategy. Lincoln favored a *cordon offense*—a strategy in which the Union armies would advance on all fronts, pitting the vast Northern resources against the South. In Grant, Lincoln felt that he had finally found the leadership needed to carry out such an offensive.

On March 9, 1864, Lincoln promoted Grant to lieutenant general and gave him command of all Northern armies. Grant planned three main offensives. The Army of the Potomac, under Meade, would try to defeat Lee in northern Virginia and occupy Richmond. Grant intended to accompany and direct that army. An army under General William T. Sherman would advance from Chattanooga into Georgia and seize Atlanta. Banks would move his men from New Orleans to Mobile, Ala., and later join Sherman. The third offensive never developed because of a crushing defeat suffered by Banks on April 9 in a battle at Pleasant Hill, La.

Battle of the Wilderness. In May 1864, the Army of the Potomac moved into a desolate area of northern Virginia called the Wilderness. Grant, with about 118,000 men, planned to march through the Wilderness and force the Confederates into a battle that would have a clear winner. Lee, with only about 62,000 troops, met Grant on May 5, and the Battle of the Wilderness raged for two days. Troops stumbled blindly through the forest, where cavalry proved useless and artillery did little

good. The underbrush caught fire, and wounded men died screaming in the flames. Both sides suffered heavy losses, and neither could claim it had won.

Battle of Spotsylvania Court House. In spite of his losses, Grant was determined to push on to final victory or defeat. He moved off to his left toward Richmond. Lee marched to meet him, and the great opponents clashed again at Spotsylvania Court House, Va., on May 8 through 19, 1864. Spotsylvania, like the Wilderness, brought large losses but no victory for either side.

Battle of Cold Harbor. Grant again moved off to his left toward Richmond, and again Lee marched to meet him. By June 1, 1864, Grant had reached Cold Harbor, a community just north of the Confederate capital. There, on June 3, he made another attempt to smash Lee. About 50,000 attackers faced 30,000 defenders in trenches across a 3-mile (5-kilometer) line. Northern troops charged in a frontal assault. Murderous gunfire cut down some 7,000 of them, chiefly in the first minutes of the charge. Grant later said, "I regret this assault more than any one I have ever ordered."

Cold Harbor forced Grant to change his strategy. Lee had shown superb defensive skill, and Northern losses had been enormous. In a month of fighting, Grant had lost almost 40,000 men. Newspapers began to call him "butcher Grant." Grant felt that if he repeated his moves, Lee would fall back to the Richmond defenses, where the Confederates could hold out against a siege. Grant therefore made one more attempt to force a quick and final win-or-lose battle.

Siege of Petersburg. Concealing his movement from Lee, Grant marched south and crossed the James River. His men built *pontoon* (floating) bridges across the river. Grant then advanced on Petersburg, a rail center south of Richmond. All railroads supplying Richmond ran through Petersburg. If Grant could seize the railroads, he could force Lee to fight in the open. But a small Confederate force under Beauregard held him off until Lee arrived. Grant then realized that he could not destroy Lee's army without a siege. His men dug trenches around the city. Lee's weary troops did the same. The deadly siege of Petersburg began on June 20, 1864. It lasted more than nine months, until the Confederate troops withdrew at the war's end.

Cavalry maneuvers. While Grant was moving toward Richmond, he had sent his cavalry ahead under Sheridan to attack the city's communications. Confederate cavalry led by Jeb Stuart opposed Sheridan. The two forces met at Yellow Tavern, Va., on May 11, 1864. Stuart was fatally wounded in the battle.

In June, Lee sent an infantry force under General Jubal A. Early through the Shenandoah Valley to raid Washington, D.C. He hoped that Grant would send some of his troops to guard the Northern capital. Early attacked one of the forts on the outskirts of the city. Lincoln stood on a low wall atop the fort and watched the attack as bullets spattered around him. Early was not strong enough to take the capital and retreated to Virginia. But he remained a threat in the valley.

Although the Confederates could not take Washington, their ability to threaten the capital after three years of war weakened Northern morale. Grant thus put all Union forces in the Shenandoah Valley under Sheridan and ordered him to follow Early to the death. Sheridan's forces outnumbered the Confederates 2 to 1 and drove them from the valley in a series of victories. His greatest success came at Cedar Creek, Va., on Oct. 19, 1864, when Early made a surprise attack while Sheridan was returning from a conference in Washington. Riding to the field from nearby Winchester, Sheridan rallied his men and won the battle. Sheridan then laid waste to the valley to flush out ambushers and to prevent its resources from being used by any Confederate army that might try again to attack Washington.

Battle of Mobile Bay. The North's blockade of Southern ports grew more effective. Union forces worked steadily to seize the main ports still open to ships that slipped through the blockade. In August 1864, a naval squadron under Farragut sailed into the bay at Mobile, Ala., which was defended by forts; mines (then called *torpedoes*); gunboats; and an ironclad. After the Union lead ship, an ironclad, was blown up, Farragut ordered his own wooden commander's ship, the *Hartford,* into the lead. "Damn the torpedoes! Full speed ahead!" was the cry he reportedly bellowed. The Union sailors captured the forts and took control of the bay, though they did not occupy Mobile. In February 1865, another main port, Wilmington, N.C., fell to Northern ships. But Charleston, S.C., still held out.

Closing in

The Atlanta campaign. In May 1864, while Grant drove into the Wilderness, Sherman's army of about 100,000 men advanced on Atlanta, Ga., from Chattanooga. General Joseph E. Johnston opposed him with a force of about 62,000. Johnston planned to delay Sherman and draw him away from his base. The Atlanta campaign developed into a gigantic chess game. Sherman repeatedly moved forward, trying to trap Johnston into battling on open ground. Each time, Johnston and his troops slipped away into prepared trench positions. The two armies clashed frequently in small battles. The largest battle occurred on June 27 at Kennesaw Mountain, an isolated peak near Atlanta.

As Sherman reached the outskirts of Atlanta, President Davis, perhaps more for political than military reasons, decided Johnston fought too cautiously. He replaced him with General John B. Hood. Hood attacked the Union columns as Sherman approached Atlanta. But Hood's attacks failed, and he took up a position in the city. Sherman first tried siege operations. But because he did not want to be delayed, he wheeled part of his army south of Atlanta and seized its only railroad to cut Hood's supply line. Hood evacuated the city on Sept. 1, 1864. Sherman occupied it the next day.

North to Nashville. Sherman's victory was not as complete as it seemed. Hood's army had escaped and begun hit-and-run raids on Sherman's railroad commu-

Sherman's march through Georgia was aimed at destroying any civilian and industrial property that might help the South continue fighting. His troops tore up railroad tracks and burned property as they swept across the state on a path 50 miles (80 kilometers) wide. Atlanta was left in flames, *above.*

nications with Chattanooga. Sherman thought it would be useless to chase Hood along the railroad. Instead, he sent Thomas back to Tennessee to take command and gave him some 32,000 men under General John M. Schofield. He ordered Thomas, at Nashville, to assemble more troops in Tennessee and keep Hood out of the state. With his remaining men, Sherman planned to cross Georgia to Savannah, near the Atlantic coast.

Hood boldly decided to invade Tennessee in the hope that Sherman would follow him. He felt sure that he could beat Sherman in the mountains. He would then either invade Kentucky or cross into Virginia and join Lee. But Hood's plan was too big for his army.

Battle of Franklin. Hood might have won a partial success if he had moved into Tennessee immediately. But he delayed and met Schofield's force at Franklin, Tenn., on Nov. 30, 1864. Hood, an aggressive commander, had complained that his army had retreated so much under Johnston that it had forgotten how to attack. His generals seemed determined to prove him wrong. In six reckless charges, the Confederates suffered about 6,300 casualties, including 6 generals killed.

Battle of Nashville. Hood had no chance of success after his defeat at Franklin. He took a position south of Nashville and waited. In the city, Thomas had time to gather an army of about 55,000. He attacked Hood on Dec. 15 and 16, 1864, and won one of the biggest victories of the war. The Confederates beat a bitter retreat to Mississippi.

Sherman's march through Georgia began on Nov. 15, 1864, when he left Atlanta in flames. His army, numbering about 62,000 men, swept almost unopposed on a 50-mile (80-kilometer) front across the state. Advance troops scouted an area. The men who followed stripped houses, barns, and fields and destroyed everything they could not use. Sherman hoped the horrible destruction would break the South's will to continue the war.

Sherman occupied Savannah on December 21 and sent a message to Lincoln: "I beg to present to you as a Christmas gift the city of Savannah with 150 heavy guns and plenty of ammunition and also about 25,000 bales of cotton." From Savannah, Sherman swung north into South Carolina. There, on the breeding ground of the Southern independence movement, his army seemed bent on revenge. They burned and looted on a scale even worse than in Georgia. When Charleston surrendered, it was spared. Although Sherman tried to prevent it, most of Columbia, the state capital, was burned.

Sherman and his troops then moved on into North Carolina. Johnston tried to oppose them, but he had only one-third as many men. The Northerners drove on toward Virginia to link up with Grant.

The South surrenders. In Virginia, Grant at last achieved his goal. In April 1865, he seized the railroads supplying Richmond. The Confederate troops had to evacuate Petersburg and Richmond. Lee retreated westward with nearly 50,000 men. He hoped to join forces with Johnston in North Carolina. But Grant overtook him and barred his way with an army of almost 113,000 troops. Lee realized that continued fighting would mean useless loss of lives. He wrote Grant and asked for an interview to arrange surrender terms.

On April 9, 1865, the two great generals met in a house owned by a Southern farmer named Wilmer McLean in the little country settlement of Appomattox Court House, Va. The meeting was one of the most dramatic scenes in American history. Grant wore a mud-spattered private's coat, with only his shoulder straps indicating his rank. Lee had put on a spotless uniform, complete with sword. Grant offered generous terms, and Lee accepted them with deep appreciation. The Confederate soldiers received a day's rations and were released on parole. They were allowed to keep their horses and mules to take home "to put in a crop." Officers could keep their side arms.

Five days later, on April 14, Lincoln was assassinated. Northerners cried out for revenge for Lincoln's death and for the hundreds of thousands killed in the war. But before his death, Lincoln had advised "malice toward none . . . charity for all" to heal the country's wounds.

Culver Pictures

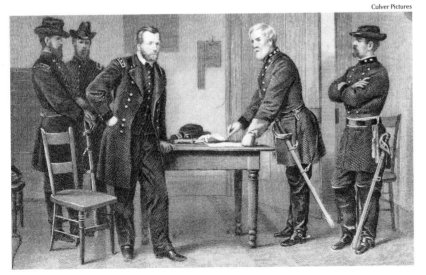

Lee surrendered to Grant, *left,* at a house in Appomattox Court House, Va., on April 9, 1865. With Lee's surrender of the main Confederate army, the Civil War soon ended.

Although feelings were strong, no major incidents occurred.

With Lee's army gone, Johnston surrendered to Sherman on April 26 near Durham, N.C. Confederate President Davis fled southward and was captured in Georgia.

General Richard Taylor surrendered the Confederate forces in Alabama and Mississippi on May 4. On May 26, General Edmund Kirby Smith surrendered the last Confederate army still in the field. The war to preserve the American Union was over.

Results of the war

The tragic costs. About 620,000 soldiers died during the Civil War, almost as many as the combined American dead of all other wars from the Revolutionary War (1775-1783) through the Vietnam War (1957-1975). The Union lost about 360,000 troops, and the Confederacy about 260,000. More than half the deaths were caused by disease. About a third of all Southern soldiers died in the war, compared with about a sixth of all Northern soldiers.

Both the North and the South paid an enormous economic price as well. But the direct damages caused by the war were especially severe in the South. The destruction in the South extended from the beautiful Shenandoah Valley in the north to Georgia in the south and from South Carolina in the east to Tennessee in the west. Towns and farms, industry and trade, and the lives of men, women, and children were ruined throughout the South. The whole Southern way of life was lost.

Terrible bitterness between the people of the North and South followed the Civil War and continued for generations. The South was given almost no voice in the social, political, and cultural affairs of the nation. With the loss of Southern control of the national government, the more traditional Southern ideals no longer had an important influence over government policy. The Yankee Protestant ideals of the North became the standard for the United States. However, those ideals, which stressed hard work, education, and economic freedom, helped encourage the development of the United States as a modern, industrial power.

The beginning of modern warfare. The Civil War changed the ways of waging war. It has been called the first modern war. The conflict introduced tactics and weapons that, in improved forms, were used widely during wars of the late 1800's and 1900's. Civil War soldiers were the first men to fight under a unified command, to battle from trenches, and to wage a major cordon offense. They also were the first soldiers to use

repeating arms, which could fire several shots without reloading, and *breechloading arms,* which were loaded from behind the barrel instead of at the muzzle. The Civil War introduced observation balloons, ironclad ships, mines, and submarines. Railroads and telegraphy were used for the first time in warfare.

The Civil War is also considered a modern war because of the vast destruction it caused. It was a *total war,* in which all the resources of the opposing sides were used. The Civil War could perhaps have ended only in the complete defeat and unconditional surrender of one side or the other.

The end of slavery. The Declaration of Independence, which gave birth to the United States in 1776, stated that "all men are created equal." Yet the United States continued to be the largest slaveholding nation in the world until the Civil War. Americans tried to make equality a reality soon after the war by *ratifying* (approving) the 13th Amendment to the Constitution, which officially abolished slavery throughout the United States. The place of blacks in American society, however, remained unsettled.

The preservation of the Union. In a fundamental sense, the Civil War may have been the greatest failure of American democracy. The war, in Lincoln's words, was an "appeal from the ballot to the bullet." From 1861 to 1865 in the United States, the calm reason that is basic to democracy gave way to human passions.

Yet democracy in the United States survived its "fiery trial." The nation's motto was *E Pluribus Unum,* a Latin term meaning *out of many, one.* It referred to the creation of one nation, the United States, out of 13 colonies. But for a long time, Americans could not decide whether they wanted to be "many" or "one." The Northern victory established that no state had the right or power to end the Union. Furthermore, the outcome of the war paved the way for the rise of the United States as a major global power.   Gabor S. Boritt

Study aids

Related articles in *World Book.* See the *Places to visit* and *History* sections of the articles on those states that fought in the Civil War, such as **Virginia** (Places to visit; History). See also the following articles:

Northern military leaders

Burnside, Ambrose E.	Hooker, Joseph
Butler, Benjamin F.	Kearny, Philip
Doubleday, Abner	Logan, John A.
Farragut, David G.	McClellan, George B.
Foote, Andrew H.	Meade, George G.
Frémont, John C.	Miles, Nelson A.
Grant, Ulysses S.	Porter, David Dixon
Halleck, Henry W.	Porter, Fitz-John
Hancock, Winfield S.	Rosecrans, William S.
Sheridan, Philip H.	Wallace, Lew
Sherman, William T.	Wilkes, Charles
Shields, James	

Southern military leaders

Beauregard, Pierre G. T.	Jackson, Stonewall
Bragg, Braxton	Johnston, Albert S.
Breckinridge, John C.	Johnston, Joseph E.
Buckner, Simon Bolivar	Lee, Robert E.
Early, Jubal A.	Longstreet, James
Ewell, Richard S.	Morgan, John H.
Forrest, Nathan B.	Mosby, John S.
Hampton, Wade	Pickett, George E.
Hood, John B.	Polk, Leonidas

Semmes, Raphael
Smith, Edmund Kirby
Stuart, Jeb

Watie, Stand
Wheeler, Joseph

Other biographies

Barton, Clara
Beecher, Henry Ward
Benjamin, Judah P.
Bickerdyke, Mary A. B.
Boyd, Belle
Brady, Mathew B.
Brown, John
Buchanan, James
Chase, Salmon P.
Crane, Stephen
Davis, Jefferson
Douglas, Stephen A.
Edmonds, Sarah E. E.
King, Thomas Starr
Lincoln, Abraham

Mallory, Stephen R.
Mason, James M.
Ruffin, Edmund
Seddon, James A.
Seward, William H.
Slidell, John
Smalls, Robert
Stanton, Edwin M.
Stephens, Alexander H.
Stowe, Harriet Beecher
Walker, Leroy P.
Walker, Mary E.
Welles, Gideon
Whitman, Walt

Causes and background

Abolition movement
Black Americans (The years of slavery)
Compromise of 1850
Crittenden Compromise
Dred Scott Decision
Fugitive slave laws
Kansas-Nebraska Act
Missouri Compromise

Nullification
Popular sovereignty
Proslavery movement
Slavery
States' rights
Uncle Tom's Cabin
Underground railroad
Wilmot Proviso

Events

Alabama (ship)
Emancipation Proclamation
Fort Sumter
Gettysburg, Battle of
Gettysburg Address

Hampton Roads Conference
Harpers Ferry
Monitor and Merrimack
Trent Affair

Other related articles

Appomattox Court House
Balloon (Balloons in war)
Confederate States of America
Copperheads
Dixie (song)
Flag (Changes in the United States flag; pictures)

Frietchie, Barbara
Grand Army of the Republic
National Park System
Reconstruction
Sons of Liberty
United States, History of the (The irrepressible conflict)

Outline

I. Causes and background of the war
  A. The sectional division
  B. The conflict over slavery
  C. Developments in the political party system
  D. Secession
II. Mobilizing for war
  A. How the states lined up
  B. Building the armed forces
III. Blacks and the war
  A. Early black participation
  B. The Emancipation Proclamation
  C. The use of black troops
  D. Reaction in the South
IV. The home front
  A. In the North
  B. In the South
V. The war in the East—1861-1863
  A. Opening battles
  B. The drive to take Richmond
  C. The South strikes back
VI. The war in the West—1862-1864
  A. Fight for the Mississippi Valley
  B. The Tennessee campaign
VII. Behind the lines
  A. Hospitals
  B. Prisons
VIII. The final year—1864-1865
  A. Grant in command
  B. Closing in
IX. Results of the war
  A. The tragic costs
  B. The beginning of modern warfare
  C. The end of slavery
  D. The preservation of the Union

Questions

Why has the Civil War been called the first modern war?
How did economic conditions in the North and South differ during the Civil War?
Why was the Battle of Gettysburg a turning point in the war?
How did Northerners resist the fugitive slave law?
What were some ways black soldiers were discriminated against during the Civil War?
Why was the outcome of the Battle of Antietam important to Abraham Lincoln?
What are some examples of the sectional division between North and South before the Civil War?
What two victories did the North win within a day of each other?
Why do many of the battles fought during the Civil War have two names?
All explanations for the causes of the Civil War have always involved or revolved around what issue?

Reading and Study Guide

See *Civil War* in the Research Guide/Index, Volume 22, for a *Reading and Study Guide.*

Additional resources

Level I
Batty, Peter, and Parish, Peter. *The Divided Union: The Story of the Great American War, 1861-1865.* Salem Hse., 1987.
Jordan, Robert P. *The Civil War.* 5th ed. National Geographic Soc., 1982.
Ray, Delia. *A Nation Torn: The Story of How the Civil War Began.* Lodestar, 1990. *Behind the Blue and Gray: The Soldier's Life in the Civil War.* 1991.

Level II
Catton, Bruce. *The Army of the Potomac.* 3 vols. Anchor Bks., 1990. First published in 1951-1953. Pulitzer Prize winner. *The Centennial History of the Civil War.* 3 vols. 1961-1965.
Foote, Shelby. *The Civil War: A Narrative.* 3 vols. Random Hse., 1958-1974.
Hattaway, Herman, and Jones, Archer. *How the North Won: A Military History of the Civil War.* Univ. of Illinois Pr., 1983.
Long, Everette B. *The Civil War Day by Day: An Almanac, 1861-1865.* Da Capo, 1985. First published in 1971.
McPherson, James M. *Battle Cry of Freedom: The Civil War Era.* Oxford, 1988.
Ward, Geoffrey C., and others. *The Civil War: An Illustrated History.* Knopf, 1990.

Civilian Conservation Corps (CCC) was an agency authorized by the government to hire unemployed young men for public conservation work. The corps was set up as part of the New Deal program in 1933. It provided training and employment. The CCC conserved and developed natural resources by such activities as planting trees, building dams, and fighting forest fires. More than 2 million men served in the corps before Congress abolished it in 1942. See also **Conservation** (The rise of the conservation movement; picture).   James T. Patterson

Civilization is a way of life that arose after people began to live in cities or in societies organized as states. The word comes from the Latin word *civis,* which means *citizen of a city.*

A civilization consists of the art, customs, technology, form of government, and everything else that makes up the way of life in a society. In this respect, civilization is similar to culture. But culture refers to any way of life and includes both simple and complex life styles. The word *civilization* refers only to life styles that feature complex economic, governmental, and social systems.

Therefore, every human being lives within a culture, but not everyone lives within a civilization. See **Culture.**

Throughout history, individual civilizations have arisen and collapsed, but the basic features of civilization do not disappear. Ideas and inventions spread from one civilization to another. In many cases, similar developments occur independently in different civilizations.

How civilizations develop. During most of the prehistoric period, people lived in small groups and moved from place to place in search of food. They hunted, fished, and gathered wild plants. These early people had a simple social organization based on close family ties. Between 13,000 and 10,000 years ago, some societies of hunters and gatherers in the Middle East adopted more settled ways of life and developed social organizations based on larger, more formal groups. All of these societies developed in areas with predictable seasonal supplies of such foods as fish and easily gathered plant foods. Some archaeologists believe that the social changes occurred in part because certain grain plants became more plentiful near the end of the last ice age, about 10,000 years ago. The technology and social organizations of some of these more advanced societies served as a foundation for later farming societies.

About 9000 B.C., people in the Middle East began to cultivate cereal grasses and other plants. They also domesticated goats and sheep at about this time, and they later tamed cattle. In Southeast Asia, people had begun raising crops by about 7000 B.C. People in what is now Mexico also learned to grow crops by about 7000 B.C.

The rise of agriculture was a major step in the development of civilization. Farmers settled in permanent villages, which had enough food to support a few craftworkers and priests. Periodic food shortages led to increased trade among villages. The villagers exchanged grain, pottery, and various raw materials.

By about 3500 B.C., people in the Middle East had learned to smelt copper and make bronze tools and weapons. The demand for metal ore increased, and priests and chieftains gained greater control over trade. Gradually, villages in the Middle East grew into cities. Religious shrines and sacred places, which flourished as ceremonial sites, became the centers of economic and political power in the emerging cities.

Several civilizations developed independently in various parts of the world. The first one arose about 3500 B.C. in the Tigris-Euphrates Valley in the Middle East. Other civilizations developed in the Nile Valley in Egypt, the Indus Valley in what are now Pakistan and northwestern India, the Huang He Valley in China, and the Andes Mountains of present-day Peru. These ancient civilizations grew up in widely different natural environments. The people developed systems of writing and new forms of government, made advances in science and technology, and excelled in crafts and art. For a description of these and other early civilizations, see **World, History of the.**

Why civilizations rise and fall. Philosophers, historians, and archaeologists have suggested many reasons for the rise and fall of civilizations. Georg W. F. Hegel, a German philosopher of the early 1800's, compared societies to individuals who pass the torch of civilization from one to another. During this process, according to Hegel, civilization develops through three stages: (1) rule by one person, a dictator; (2) rule by one class of society; and (3) rule by all the people. Hegel believed the process eventually results in freedom for all people.

The German philosopher Oswald Spengler thought civilizations, like living things, are born, mature, and die. In *The Decline of the West* (1918-1922), he wrote that Western civilization is dying and will be replaced by a new Asian civilization.

The British historian Arnold Toynbee proposed his theory of *challenge and response* in *A Study of History* (1934-1961). Toynbee believed that civilizations arise only where the environment challenges the people, and only when the people are ready to respond to the challenge. For example, a hot, dry climate makes land unsuitable for farming and represents a challenge to people who live there. The people may respond to this challenge by building irrigation systems to improve the land. Toynbee suggested that civilizations collapse when the people lose their creativity.

Most archaeologists attribute the rise of civilizations to a combination of causes, including the structure of political and social life, the ways people modify their environment, and changes in population. In many cases, civilizations may have appeared because local chieftains took deliberate steps to strengthen their own political power. Many scientists believe that political forces and the misuse of land and other natural resources resulted in the economic and political collapse of early civilizations.   Brian M. Fagan

For a discussion of the history of civilization, see **World, History of the.** See also **City.**

Civitan International, *SIHV ih tan,* is an association of service clubs dedicated to good citizenship. The clubs strive to provide their members with fellowship and increased knowledge and to render service to the community and nation. Civitan projects include aid to developmentally disabled persons, civic improvement programs, scholarship programs, and sponsorship of awards for citizenship and service.

About 38,000 men and women belong to the approximately 1,200 Civitan clubs. There are clubs in the United States, Canada, Mexico, South Korea, Japan, Norway, Sweden, Germany, and Austria. The organization was chartered in 1920. The mailing address is P.O. Box 130744, Birmingham, AL 35213.

Critically reviewed by Civitan International

CLA. See **Canadian Library Association; Catholic Library Association.**

Claiborne's Rebellion, *KLAY bohrnz,* was a series of conflicts in the 1630's and 1640's in which William Claiborne, a Virginia fur trader, refused to accept the authority of Leonard Calvert, the governor of Maryland. Claiborne came to Virginia from England in 1621. He explored Chesapeake Bay and became interested in the Indian fur trade. Claiborne went to England and obtained a trading license in 1631. When he returned to the bay area, he set up a trading post on Kent Island in the bay.

According to a charter issued to the Calvert family in 1632, Kent Island lay within the boundaries of Maryland. Claiborne refused to acknowledge the authority of the Calverts, and war broke out. Claiborne was forced to leave the island. However, in 1644, with some Puritan settlers, he drove Calvert out and seized control of the colony. Oliver Cromwell ordered the restoration of the

Calvert government in 1657, and Claiborne returned to Virginia. Claiborne played a prominent role in the affairs of the Virginia colony until he died in 1677.

Marshall Smelser

See also **Maryland** (Colonial days).

Clair, René, *ruh NAY* (1898-1981), was a French motion-picture director. He gained his first acclaim with the silent comedy *An Italian Straw Hat* (1927). He won praise for his creative use of sound in the early sound films *Under the Roofs of Paris* (1929), *A Nous la Liberté (Give Us Liberty,* 1931), and *Le Million* (1931).

Clair was born in Paris. His real name was René-Lucien Chomette. During World War II (1939-1945), he worked in the United States and directed the comedy fantasies *I Married a Witch* (1942) and *It Happened Tomorrow* (1944). He returned to France in 1946. In 1960, Clair became the first moviemaker to be elected to the French Academy.

Gene D. Phillips

Clairvoyance, *klair VOY uhns,* is an awareness of events, objects, or people without the use of the senses of hearing, sight, smell, taste, or touch. It is a major form of *extrasensory perception (ESP).* A person who can locate a lost child or perform similar acts without using known senses might be considered clairvoyant.

Clairvoyance supposedly is not affected by time or distance. A person may "see" an accident in a dream before it happens or sense an event taking place far away. Awareness of an event before it occurs is known as *precognitive clairvoyance.* Clairvoyance is under scientific investigation, and the question of its existence remains open. However, most scientists are skeptical. The relationship of clairvoyance to telepathy, if any, is not known.

James E. Alcock

See also **Extrasensory perception; Telepathy; Mind reading; Parapsychology; Psychical research.**

Clam is an animal whose soft body is covered with a protective shell. Clams live on the bottoms or along the shores of oceans, lakes, and streams in many parts of the world. Clams are a type of *mollusk,* a group of soft-bodied animals that have no bones (see **Mollusk** [Bivalves]).

The body of a clam. Clams use a large, muscular organ called a *foot* to burrow in mud or sand. The clam's shell is made up of two parts called *valves.* A *ligament* connects the valves. *Adductor muscles* cause the valves to open and close.

The *mantle,* a thin, fleshy part of the body just inside the shell, produces substances that form the shell. Clam shells are composed chiefly of *calcium carbonate,* a major component in limestone. In many shells, a smooth, shiny substance called *mother-of-pearl* or *nacre* forms an inner layer.

The space between the main body of the clam and the mantle is called the *mantle cavity.* Clams have gills that hang into the mantle cavity. In most clams, water filled with food and oxygen passes into the mantle cavity through two openings called *siphons.* Water enters through the *incurrent siphon,* passes through the gills, and exits through the *excurrent siphon.*

Small hairs called *cilia* cover the gills. Food particles are usually trapped on the gills and are carried by the cilia to a small mouth. The mouth leads to the stomach, where food is partly digested. The clam completes digestion in *digestive glands,* which hang off the stomach.

Some kinds of clam

Clams live on the botton[m] in many areas of the wo[rld] shape. Four important k[inds]

are in the family Ve[ ]
Myidae, giant cla[ ]
clams are in th[ ]

See als[o]
duck (p[ ]
Cla[ ]
co[ ]

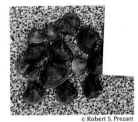
© Robert S. Prezant
Asian clams

© Robert S. Prezant
Hard-shell clams

George Whiteley, Photo Researchers
Soft-shell clam

Kjell B. Sandved
Giant clam

Waste travels out through the clam's intestine. Clams have a heart, blood vessels, and kidneys.

The life of a clam. Most clams feed on tiny water organisms called *plankton.* Some clams obtain food from the mud or sand in which they live. Other clams feed on small, shrimplike animals.

Clams reproduce sexually. In most species, each clam is either male or female. Males release sperm, and females release eggs. The sperm unite with and fertilize the eggs in the surrounding water or in the gills of the female. Fertilized eggs of most clams develop into tiny, swimming larvae called *veligers.* Veligers eventually become mature clams. In some species of clams, the same individual produces both sperm and eggs.

Types of clams. Several types of clams are valuable as food. These types include such saltwater species as the *hard-shell clam* and the *soft-shell clam.* Hard-shell clams are harvested along the Atlantic coasts of Canada and the United States. Soft-shell clams have a smooth, thin shell. They are found on tidal flats from South Carolina to Greenland. Soft-shell clams from the mudflats of New England are especially popular.

The *giant clam,* another major type of saltwater clam, lives on coral reefs in the Red Sea, the Indian Ocean, and the western Pacific Ocean. These clams can grow to a length of more than 4 feet (1.2 meters). Many people have collected giant clams for their shells, greatly reducing the population of these animals.

The *Asian clam* is an abundant type of freshwater clam. It was brought to North America from China in the 1930's. Today, many Asian clams live in cooling systems of power plants. Sometimes there are so many that they slow the necessary waterflow and cause severe damage.

Scientific classification. Clams belong to the phylum Mollusca. They are members of the class Bivalvia. Hard-shell clams

eridae, soft-shell clams are in the family
ns are in the family Tridacnidae, and Asian
e family Corbiculidae. Robert S. Prezant

Aquaculture; Biology (picture); Cockle; Geo-
cture); Shell (picture).

is a group of people who are related through a
mmon ancestor. Some clans are *matrilineal* (related
through the female line). Others are *patrilineal* (related
through the male line). Although they may live far apart,
members of a clan feel a close relationship to each
other and usually have a strong spirit of unity. They
often share property or special privileges. Most clans
are *exogamous*. That is, the members must marry outside of the clan. Clans are often named after a *totem* (a
symbolic animal or plant). American Indian tribes had
clans such as the Bear clan or Tobacco clan.

The word *clan* also refers to groups of people in early
Scotland and Ireland who had common ancestors and a
common name, and were organized under the rule of a
chief. These clans were *bilateral* (related through both
men and women), and marriage within the clan was customary. The Scottish clans began about A.D. 1000. They
carried on feuds in the Highlands, and clan members
were expected to defend one another. Most clans lost
power after the rebellion of 1745, but a spirit of clan loyalty remains among Scots. They are distinguished by
their names—such as MacDonald and Campbell—and by
their *tartans*, the plaids worn as emblems of clan membership (see **Tartan**). Jennie Keith

Clarendon, Earl of (1609-1674), played a leading part
in restoring the monarchy in England in 1660. Clarendon
originally sided with Parliament in its dispute with King
Charles I, who tried to keep all political power for himself. But when civil war broke out in 1642, Clarendon
joined the *Royalists* (supporters of the king). He insisted
that the king represented the entire kingdom, not just a
royal group. Named lord chancellor in 1660, he tried to
restore England to, in his words, "its old good manners,
its old good humor, and its old good nature." But he was
forced into exile in 1667. In exile he wrote the 10-volume
History of the Rebellion, which defends the Royalist activities during the civil war. Clarendon was born Edward
Hyde in Dinton, England. He studied at Oxford University. Lacey Baldwin Smith

Clarinet is a woodwind instrument. Most clarinets are
made of wood. The instrument consists of a tube with a
mouthpiece at one end and a bell-shaped opening at
the other end. A clarinet has open *tone holes* and other
holes covered by small metal levers called *keys*. The musician places his or her fingertips on the holes and keys
and blows on a flat cane reed attached to the mouthpiece. The reed vibrates, producing a full, rich tone. The
musician plays different notes by covering or uncovering various holes. Clarinets are manufactured in five
pitches. The B-flat soprano clarinet is the most popular.

Johann Christoph Denner, a German instrument
maker, invented the clarinet about 1700. It has been an
important instrument in bands and orchestras since the
mid-1700's. Thomas C. Slattery

See also **Music** (pictures: Wind instruments).

Clark is the family name of two Americans—father and
son—who held important government positions.

Tom Campbell Clark (1899-1977), the father, served
as an associate justice of the Supreme Court of the
United States from 1949 to 1967. He generally voted with
the conservative group on the court, though he regularly supported the government in antitrust cases. He
also took an active part in movements to improve the
U.S. judicial system.

Clark was born in Dallas, Tex. He received A.B. and
LL.B. degrees from the University of Texas. He joined the
Department of Justice in 1937, and became assistant attorney general of the United States in 1943. President
Harry S. Truman appointed Clark attorney general in
1945. He served in that position until 1949, when Truman
named him to the Supreme Court.

Ramsey Clark (1927-   ), the son, was attorney general of the United States from 1967 to 1969, under President Lyndon B. Johnson. Clark had been assistant attorney general from 1961 to 1965 and deputy attorney
general from 1965 to 1967. In 1974, he ran as the Democratic nominee for U.S. senator from New York, but lost.
He then practiced law in New York.

Throughout his career, Clark has been identified with
liberal causes. As attorney general, he supported civil
rights initiatives and favored reform of criminal procedure. In private practice, Clark attacked the death penalty and represented many individuals involved in protest activity.

William Ramsey Clark was born in Dallas, Tex. He received a B.A. degree from the University of Texas, and
A.M. and J.D. degrees from the University of Chicago. He
wrote *Crime in America* (1970). Owen M. Fiss

Clark, Abraham (1726-1794), was an American political leader during the Revolutionary War in America
(1775-1783) and a New Jersey signer of the Declaration
of Independence. He served in the Second Continental
Congress, the Congress of the Confederation, and the
U.S. Congress.

Clark was born in Elizabethtown, N.J. He was called
the *Poor Man's Counselor* because he defended poor
farmers in land cases. Clarence L. Ver Steeg

David R. Frazier

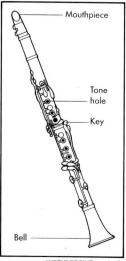

Mouthpiece

Tone
hole

Key

Bell

WORLD BOOK illustration by
Oxford Illustrators Limited

The clarinet is a popular woodwind instrument. A musician
blows through the mouthpiece and produces different notes by
pressing keys and covering or uncovering tone holes.

Charles Joseph Clark

**Prime Minister of Canada
1979-1980**

Trudeau
1968-1979

Clark
1979-1980

Trudeau
1980-1984

Photo Features from Miller Services Ltd.

Clark, Charles Joseph (1939-   ), became the youngest prime minister in the history of Canada. He was only 39 years old when he succeeded Pierre Elliott Trudeau in June 1979. Clark took office after leading the Progressive Conservative Party to its first national victory since 1962. But Clark's popularity fell rapidly, and Trudeau became prime minister again in March 1980.

Joe Clark, as he preferred to be called, rose to national fame quickly during the 1970's. He first held public office in 1972, when voters in western Alberta elected him to the House of Commons. In 1976, the Progressive Conservative Party selected the 36-year-old Clark as its leader. Although he had only a few years of experience in public office at that time, Clark was no newcomer to politics. During the 1960's, he had held leadership positions in student political groups and worked in campaigns for Conservative candidates. From 1967 to 1970, he had served as an assistant to Robert L. Stanfield, the party leader.

Clark became known as a careful thinker who was more concerned with practical solutions than with political theories. His associates respected him for his political strategy and skill as a debater. Clark had little time for recreation, but he liked to relax by reading a mystery novel or watching a movie.

Clark became prime minister at a troubled time in Canada's history. Since 1976, the provincial government of Quebec had been controlled by the Parti Québécois, a political party that favored the separation of Quebec from Canada. Many French Canadians supported separation as a way to guarantee the preservation of the French language and culture in Quebec. Clark also faced the problems of high rates of unemployment and

inflation. His first challenges as prime minister were to find solutions to these and other difficulties that threatened Canada's national unity and its economic stability.

Early life

Boyhood. Charles Joseph Clark was born on June 5, 1939, in High River, Alta., a farming community about 30 miles (48 kilometers) south of Calgary. His father, Charles A. Clark, published a weekly newspaper, the *High River Times.* Joe Clark's grandfather had started the paper in 1905, shortly after coming to the area from Kincardine, Ont. Charles Clark met Grace Welch while both were students at the University of Alberta, and they were married in 1937. Joe was their first child. They had one other son, Peter, born in 1942.

Joe enjoyed camping, horseback riding, and the outdoors. He rarely participated in sports, but he reported on local sporting events for his father's paper. In high school, Joe showed talent for writing and public speaking. He made his first public speech at the age of 16. It won him a trip to Ottawa, where he observed Parliament in session and met John G. Diefenbaker, who later became prime minister of Canada. The trip stimulated Joe's interest in politics. His mother recalled that he returned home saying, "We don't have democracy in this country. It's run by one party, and it should have an effective and strong opposition."

College years. In 1957, Clark entered the University of Alberta, where he majored in history. He soon became active in the campus Progressive Conservative club and campaigned door-to-door for Conservative candidates in the 1958 election. In 1959, he gained valuable political experience by serving as secretary and

Joe Clark raises his hands in triumph as he greets supporters on the night of the 1979 election. His wife, Maureen, stands by his side. Clark led the Conservatives to their first national victory since 1962.

Canapress

chauffeur to the leader of the Progressive Conservative Party in Alberta.

In spite of his interest in politics, Clark devoted most of his time and energy to the student newspaper, the *Gateway.* During his third year at the university, he served as editor of the *Gateway.* In his editorials, he frequently criticized the provincial government and commented on national political issues. Clark's studies suffered because he gave so much time to journalism and politics. He graduated in 1960. He hoped to study political science at Georgetown University in Washington, D.C. But Georgetown rejected his application, and he set out on a tour of Europe in the fall of 1961.

Political career

Political worker and student. Clark returned to Canada early in 1962 to accept a job at Progressive Conservative headquarters in Ottawa. There he prepared campaign literature, wrote speeches for members of Parliament, and organized conventions. In the fall, he left his job to enter law school at Dalhousie University in Halifax, N.S. After one year, he transferred to the University of British Columbia Law School in Vancouver.

Clark disliked law school, however, and he devoted most of his time to politics both at Dalhousie and in Vancouver. In 1962, he was elected president of the Progressive Conservative Student Federation. In Vancouver, Clark also worked in an unsuccessful Conservative election campaign to gain control of the provincial government. His absorption in politics caused Clark to neglect his schoolwork. He failed his final exams in 1964, and his law school career ended.

Important dates in Clark's life

1939	(June 5) Born in High River, Alta.
1960	Graduated from University of Alberta.
1962	Elected president of Progressive Conservative Student Federation.
1972	Elected to House of Commons.
1973	(June 30) Married Maureen McTeer.
1976	Chosen leader of Progressive Conservative Party.
1979	Became prime minister of Canada.
1980	Liberals defeated Progressive Conservatives. Clark resigned as prime minister on March 3.
1983	Succeeded as party leader by Brian Mulroney.

In the fall of 1964, Clark began the first of three years as a graduate student in political science at the University of Alberta. From 1965 to 1967, he supported himself by working part time as a teaching assistant and journalist. But politics continued to claim a major share of his time. In 1964, he helped found the Canadian Political Youth Council and served as secretary of the National Conference on Canadian Goals. From 1965 to 1967, Clark worked for Peter Lougheed, the Conservative leader in Alberta. Clark played a major role in developing campaign strategies that led to the election of Lougheed and five other Conservatives to the Alberta legislature in 1967.

Also in 1967, Clark himself sought election to public office for the first time. He ran for the Alberta legislature against a candidate whom political experts considered unbeatable. Clark lost, but by a remarkably small margin—only 461 votes out of nearly 13,000.

From 1967 to 1970, Clark worked in Ottawa as an assistant to Robert L. Stanfield, the leader of the Progressive Conservative Party. In his spare time, he studied French and began to develop a good command of the language. This ability later became a valuable political asset because French is the native language of more than a fourth of Canada's people.

In May 1970, Clark resigned from his job with Stanfield and began another visit to Europe. During his stay, he observed British politics, worked on his thesis for his master's degree, and continued his study of French. When he returned to Canada late in 1970, he was determined to run for Parliament as soon as possible.

Member of Parliament. In 1971, Clark decided to seek election to the Canadian House of Commons from the *riding* (district) of Rocky Mountain in western Alberta. After a hard-fought campaign, he defeated his Liberal opponent by more than 5,000 votes in the election in October 1972. Clark quickly gained a reputation in Parliament as a skilled speaker who could be both witty and aggressive in attacking Liberal Party policies.

Late in 1972, Clark hired a research assistant named Maureen McTeer, a student at the University of Ottawa. She had been active in Progressive Conservative politics. Clark and McTeer began to date in March 1973, and they were married on June 30 of that year. She and Clark have one daughter, Catherine, born in 1976.

In the election of 1974, the voters reelected Clark to

the House of Commons by a wide margin. But overall, the Conservatives did poorly in the election. As a result, Stanfield decided to resign as party leader. Clark announced his candidacy in November 1975. His wife interrupted her studies at the University of Ottawa Law School to help him campaign. She became a public figure known for her support of women's rights.

Party leader. Clark faced 10 opponents in the race for party leader, and few political observers thought he would win. But his tireless campaigning and youthful, popular image carried him to victory at the party convention held in February 1976.

In his acceptance speech, Clark committed the Progressive Conservative Party to a positive style of campaigning. He declared that "Canadians today don't want to know what we're against. They want to know what we are for." As party leader, Clark called for decreased government spending, restrictions on the right of public employees to strike, and fewer economic controls.

The 1979 election. In March 1979, Prime Minister Trudeau called a general election for May. During the campaign, Clark criticized the Liberals for their failure to solve Canada's economic problems, which included inflation and high unemployment. The Progressive Conservatives pledged that a Conservative government would cut taxes, reduce government spending, and encourage private investment in the Canadian economy. Clark also proposed that the government allow homeowners to deduct part of their mortgage interest and property tax payments from their income tax.

Trudeau and the Liberals concentrated on the issue of national unity. Trudeau, a French Canadian, favored the preservation of French language and culture in Canada but firmly opposed independence for Quebec.

Clark believed the problem of national unity could not be solved by seeking a common national identity among French- and English-speaking Canadians. Instead, he urged Canadians to recognize their nation as a collection of regional cultures.

The election of 1979 ended 16 years of Liberal government. The Progressive Conservatives won 135 of the 282 seats in the House of Commons, and Clark became prime minister. The Liberals won 115 seats, and the rest went to smaller parties.

Prime minister. Clark took office as prime minister on June 4. Shortly after the election, Conservative officials indicated that they no longer favored a tax cut and that they needed to revise the deduction plan for homeowners. Opposition to Clark's government soon became widespread. The government was defeated on a vote concerning its budget, which called for a sharp increase in gasoline taxes. On Dec. 13, 1979, the House of Commons passed a motion of no-confidence in Clark's government, and the government fell from power.

Clark called a general election for February 1980. In the election, the Liberals won a majority of the seats in the House of Commons, and Trudeau again became prime minister. Opposition to Clark's leadership of the Progressive Conservative Party increased. In June 1983, the party chose Brian Mulroney to replace Clark as its leader. Mulroney became prime minister in September 1984.

Later years. Clark continued working in government after serving as prime minister. From 1984 to 1991, he was secretary of state for external affairs under Mulroney. In 1991, Clark became Mulroney's minister of constitutional affairs and president of the Privy Council. He resigned from those positions in 1993, after being appointed a special representative of United Nations Secretary-General Boutros Boutros-Ghali.

Andrew Snaddon

See also **Prime Minister of Canada**.

Clark, George Rogers (1752-1818), was an American frontiersman and soldier who won important victories in the Northwest Territory during the Revolutionary War in America (1775-1783). The Northwest Territory was a vast tract of land lying north of the Ohio River, south of Canada, west of Pennsylvania, and east of the Mississippi River. Clark's victories helped the American negotiators claim this area during peace talks with Britain that ended the Revolutionary War.

Clark was born near Charlottesville, Va. He became a surveyor as a young man and began exploring and surveying the western frontier. When the Revolutionary War broke out, Clark was living in Kentucky. Although

The Fall of Fort Sackville, detail of an oil painting by Frederick C. Yohn; William Henry Smith Memorial Library, Indiana Historical Society, Indianapolis

George Rogers Clark captured Vincennes in 1779 by forcing the British to surrender the fort that controlled the town.

this region was claimed by the Colony of Virginia, the Virginia colonial government at first refused to send military aid to protect the Kentucky settlers from raids by the Indian allies of the British. In response, Clark argued, "if a country is not worth protecting, it is not worth claiming." Virginia officials yielded. They sent valuable supplies of gunpowder to the settlers.

In 1777, Clark convinced Governor Patrick Henry of Virginia that the British were supplying weapons to the Indians to fight the Kentuckians. Britain sought to control all the region west of the Appalachian Mountains. Clark was commissioned a lieutenant colonel in the Virginia militia and pulled together about 175 men to carry the fight into the Northwest Territory. In 1778 and 1779, he and his men captured Kaskaskia, Cahokia, and Vincennes, three key settlements in what are now southern parts of Illinois and Indiana. In 1783, Britain formally surrendered the region to the United States. See **Northwest Territory**.

In 1783, Thomas Jefferson, who was then a member of Congress, asked Clark to explore the land west of the Mississippi River. But Clark refused. His younger brother, William, agreed to take part in a similar project in 1803 and became a leader of the Lewis and Clark expedition (see **Clark, William**).   James Kirby Martin

Clark, Jim (1936-1968), became one of the world's greatest automobile racing drivers. Clark won 25 Grand Prix races. Grand Prix races are road races held in many countries in which points are awarded to the top drivers. Clark won world racing titles in 1963 and 1965 by earning the most points in Grand Prix races. In 1963, he became the youngest driver ever to win the world title. He won the 1965 Indianapolis 500-mile race. Clark was born in Fife County, Scotland. He was killed in a race in Hockenheim, Germany.   Sylvia Wilkinson

Clark, Kenneth Bancroft (1914-   ), an American educator and psychologist, became known for his studies on school segregation and its effects on students. The Supreme Court of the United States referred to his work in its 1954 desegregation ruling, which declared that "separate but equal" schools for blacks are actually unequal and therefore unconstitutional.

From 1939 to 1941, Clark participated in a study of black Americans by the Swedish sociologist and economist Gunnar Myrdal. Clark became the first black to receive a permanent appointment as a professor at the City College of New York, where he taught psychology from 1942 to 1975. He has served since 1950 as a consultant to the National Association for the Advancement of Colored People (NAACP).

Clark was born in the Panama Canal Zone. He earned a Ph.D. degree from Columbia University in 1960. Two of his books are *Desegregation: An Appraisal of the Evidence* (1953) and *Dark Ghetto* (1965).   Gerald L. Gutek

Clark, Mark Wayne (1896-1984), was a leading United States general of World War II (1939-1945). He also had a major role in the Korean War (1950-1953).

Clark was born in Madison Barracks, N.Y. He graduated from the U.S. Military Academy in 1917 and served in World War I (1914-1918).

In 1942, during World War II, Clark became a lieutenant general after leading a secret submarine mission to North Africa. He acquired information that was vital to the success of the 1942 Allied invasion of North Africa. Clark commanded the U.S. Fifth Army in its invasion of Italy at Salerno in 1943, during the hard-fought battles at Cassino and Anzio, and during its entrance into Rome in 1944. In 1945, Clark was promoted to general. In May 1945, in northern Italy, he accepted the first major German surrender.

During the Korean War, Clark commanded the United Nations Forces and the U.S. Army in the Far East in 1952 and 1953. He took part in the signing of the armistice that ended the fighting in July 1953. Clark retired from the Army in 1953.   James L. Stokesbury

Clark, Ramsey. See Clark (family).
Clark, Tom Campbell. See Clark (family).
Clark, William (1770-1838), was an American explorer. With Meriwether Lewis, he led the famous Lewis and Clark expedition, which explored the Louisiana Territory and the Pacific Northwest from 1804 to 1806.

President Thomas Jefferson appointed Lewis to lead the expedition, and, in 1803, Lewis invited Clark to join

it. Lewis and Clark privately agreed to share command of the expedition.

The expedition started out from a camp near St. Louis in May 1804 and followed the Missouri River west. The men crossed the Rocky Mountains in 1805 and reached the Pacific coast in November that same year. They arrived back in St. Louis in September 1806.

In addition to sharing command, Clark also had record-keeping duties. Especially important were the maps he made of the party's route. After Lewis' death in 1809, Clark became responsible for the publication of the expedition journals.

Clark was born in Caroline County, Virginia. His brother, George Rogers Clark, became a hero in the Revolutionary War in America. After the expedition with Lewis, Clark held several public offices in St. Louis, including that of superintendent of Indian affairs.

Gary E. Moulton

See also **Lewis and Clark expedition**.

Clarke, Arthur C. (1917-   ), is a British-born author of science fiction and related nonfiction. His novels are noted for their blend of scientific accuracy and spiritual optimism, and many of them describe the exploration of other worlds. The novels include *Childhood's End* (1953), his finest single work; *The City and the Stars* (1956); *Rendezvous with Rama* (1973); and *The Fountains of Paradise* (1979). With film director Stanley Kubrick, Clarke wrote the screenplay for the motion picture *2001: A Space Odyssey* (1968). He continued the series with the novels *2010: Odyssey Two* (1982) and *2061: Odyssey Three* (1988). Excellent examples of his short fiction were collected in *The Other Side of the Sky* (1958).

Arthur Charles Clarke was born in Somerset County, England, and settled in Ceylon (now Sri Lanka) in the mid-1950's. He was the first person to propose communications satellites. Clarke's book *The Exploration of Space* (1951) helped make the idea of space travel popular in the 1950's. His nonfiction works include *Interplanetary Flight* (1950), *The Challenge of the Sea* (1960), *Profiles of the Future* (1962), *The View from Serendip* (1977), and *Astounding Days: A Science Fiction Autobiography* (1990).   Neil Barron

Class, in biology. See **Classification, Scientific**.
Class, Social. See **Social class**.
Class action is a judicial proceeding in which one or more individuals sue on behalf of a group having similar claims. Such a group is called a *class.* Suppose that many consumers had to pay an unreasonably high price for a product because its few producers agreed illegally to charge similar prices. Most purchasers could not afford an individual lawsuit to recover the overcharge. But they might pool their claims and file a class suit to collect damages from the companies.

In the United States, people first used class suits to recover money owed them in bankruptcy cases. During the 1950's and 1960's, civil rights groups used class action to fight school segregation, job discrimination, and housing and voting restrictions. Since the 1960's, the use of class actions has expanded to all types of consumer actions, including price fixing. Environmental protection groups also have filed class actions to protest oil spills and other public nuisances.   Jean Appleman

Classic car. See **Automobile** (Classic cars [with pictures]).

Owen Franken, Stock, Boston

A performance of classical music in a concert hall features highly skilled musicians. Many classical music concerts involve both instrumental music and singing. In the picture above, a large orchestra and chorus perform at Harvard University's Sanders Theatre in Cambridge, Mass.

Classical music

Classical music is music written chiefly for concerts, for religious services, and for opera and ballet. It includes music for groups of instruments—such as symphony orchestras—for voices, and for both instruments and voices. Classical music is sometimes called *art music.* Most classical music is more complex than *popular music,* which includes country music, rock music, and jazz.

Classical music varies greatly. Many compositions are extremely long and have a variety of *tempos* (speeds) and styles. Others are short and have the same tempo and style throughout. Some classical music deals with a specific subject. For example, it may tell a story, express an idea, or describe a mood.

There are two principal kinds of classical music. These two kinds are *instrumental music* and *vocal music.* Composers write instrumental music to be performed by one instrument, a small *ensemble* (group of instruments), or an orchestra. Vocal music may be written for one singer, for several singers, or for a large chorus. Many works of classical music combine both instrumental parts and vocal parts.

Most performances of classical music feature highly skilled and extensively trained musicians. A conductor directs performances that involve an orchestra or chorus. The conductor selects the music, rehearses it with the musicians, and guides them during the performance of the work.

The beginnings of Western classical music date from ancient times. Certain styles, forms, and principles of composition became popular during different periods of history. The spread of Christianity played an important part in the early growth of Western classical music. Many forms of classical music were created to be performed during church services. Later, royalty and wealthy nobles promoted the advancement of classical music by encouraging composers to produce particular types of music.

This article deals with the major forms and styles of Western classical music. It also traces the history of Western classical music. To read about other kinds of Western music, see such *World Book* articles as **Country music, Jazz,** and **Popular music.** For information on

F. E. Kirby, the contributor of this article, is Professor and Chair, Department of Music, Lake Forest College.

the music of non-Western cultures and the basic elements of music, see **Music.**

Instrumental music

There are three main kinds of instrumental music: (1) solo, (2) chamber, and (3) orchestra. They differ chiefly according to the number of musicians who perform the music. Solo music is played by only one musician. A small group of musicians—in most cases, from 2 to 5—performs chamber music. A large group—as many as 100 musicians or more—plays orchestra music.

Solo music can be composed for any instrument, but much of it has been written for the piano. This instrument enables a musician to play more than one melody at a time and to give the music richness and depth. The organ and the harpsichord are also used. Solo music written for the cello, clarinet, flute, French horn, guitar, harp, oboe, trumpet, viola, and violin often includes accompaniment by a keyboard instrument.

A long solo composition may consist of a number of sections, called *movements.* The most common form of long composition is the *sonata.* The movements of a sonata vary in speed and style. Many sonatas have a fast first movement, a slow second movement, a dancelike third movement, and a vigorous fourth movement. The rousing final movement is called the *finale.* Some of the best-known piano sonatas were written by Ludwig van Beethoven of Germany and Wolfgang Amadeus Mozart of Austria. Johann Sebastian Bach of Germany composed well-known sonatas for the violin and the cello.

The most common short type of solo music is the *character piece,* a simple, lyrical composition that expresses a certain characteristic. The characteristic may be a mood, a thought, or an emotion.

A type of solo music composed chiefly for keyboard instruments is called the *prelude and fugue.* The *toccata* is a form of solo composition written primarily for the organ. The *chorale-prelude,* another important type of organ solo, precedes the singing of a hymn.

Chamber music is chiefly written for 2 to 5 musicians. But music for as many as 20 players may also be called chamber music. In most chamber music, each musician plays a different part. Chamber music was originally performed in the chambers, or rooms, of private homes, rather than in churches or public halls.

Almost all chamber music is composed for one of several types of ensembles. These groups include the *string trio* (violin, viola, and cello); the *piano trio* (piano, violin, and cello); the *string quartet* (two violins, viola, and cello); the *string quintet* (two violins, two violas, and cello; or two violins, viola, and two cellos); and the *piano quintet* (piano, two violins, viola, and cello). Ensembles of six or more musicians vary in makeup.

Most chamber music consists of four movements. Compositions are named according to the instruments involved, such as a string quartet or a piano quintet.

Orchestra music is written to be performed for large audiences. The size of an orchestra ranges from about 15 to more than 100 musicians. The musicians are organized into groups, called *sections,* according to the instruments they play.

An orchestra has four main sections. They are (1) string, (2) woodwind, (3) brass, and (4) percussion. The string section of an orchestra consists of violins, violas,

Ken Firestone

A string quartet has two violinists, a viola player, and a cello player. It is one of the most common chamber music groups. Music written for such a group is also called a string quartet.

cellos, and string basses. The woodwind section includes flutes, oboes, clarinets, and bassoons. An orchestra's brass section consists of such instruments as trumpets, French horns, and trombones. The percussion section includes bells, cymbals, and various kinds of drums. The string, woodwind, and brass sections of most orchestras have two or more musicians who play the same kind of instrument and the same part.

The chief forms of orchestra music are *symphonies, concertos, suites,* and *symphonic poems.* Most symphonies consist of three or four movements that follow the structure of the sonata. Symphonies express a variety of ideas and emotions. For example, the German composer Robert Schumann dealt with his happiness at being married in his symphony *Spring* (1841).

A concerto highlights a particular instrument, such as the piano or violin. Composers have written concertos for nearly every instrument. Most concertos have three movements, of which the first and third are fast and the second is slow. A type of concerto called a *concerto grosso* features more than one instrument. The Italian composer Antonio Vivaldi wrote many such concertos, chiefly for stringed instruments.

During the 1700's, a suite consisted chiefly of a collection of dances. But in the 1800's, it began to include a series of contrasting movements. Well-known suites include the *Peer Gynt Suite* (1876) by the Norwegian composer Edvard Grieg and the *Nutcracker Suite* (1892) by Peter Ilich Tchaikovsky of Russia. A suite may consist of various pieces of music written for certain parts of a play. Such a suite is known as *incidental music.*

A symphonic poem expresses the theme of a story or some other literary work. The form of the model determines how the composer organizes the music. Tchaikovsky based his symphonic poem *Romeo and Juliet* (1870) on William Shakespeare's famous play.

Some orchestra music, including the *overture,* has only one movement. Such a composition may serve as the introduction to an opera or a play.

Vocal music

There are four chief types of vocal music: (1) songs, (2) choral music, (3) operas, and (4) oratorios.

Songs are compositions for vocal soloists. In classical music, the works are sometimes known as *art songs*. Many song composers select a poem of literary merit and set the words to music. The music strengthens and emphasizes the meaning of the words. Originally, most singers performed without accompaniment. Today, the majority of singers are accompanied by a pianist. A chamber ensemble or an orchestra may also provide the accompaniment.

The best-known songs are the *lieder* written by German composers during the late 1700's and the 1800's. *Lieder* is a German word for *songs*. Most lieder have a piano accompaniment and are set to a romantic poem. For example, Franz Schubert based his song "Gretchen at the Spinning Wheel" (1814) on a love poem by Johann Wolfgang von Goethe. Schubert probably ranks as the most noted composer of lieder. Other composers known for their lieder include Johannes Brahms, Robert Schumann, and Hugo Wolf.

A song may be short or long, simple or complex. The melody may be repeated throughout the composition, or it may follow no pattern at all. Some composers write *song cycles*. Such works are sets of songs about the same subject.

Songs called *part songs* are written for two or more performers. Each singer has a different part, or two or more performers sing each part. Most such songs written before 1600 have parts for four to six singers and are sung *a cappella* (without accompaniment). The majority of part songs by later composers have a piano accompaniment. Sacred part songs, called *motets* or *anthems,* are based on religious texts and are performed during church services. The most important type of nonreligious part song is the *madrigal* (see **Madrigal**).

Choral music is written for a chorus. Most choral music written since the 1400's has parts for four voices—soprano, alto, tenor, and bass. A chorus may sing a cappella or with accompaniment by an orchestra, a chamber ensemble, an organist, or a pianist. Operas, symphonies, and other musical productions may feature choral music. For example, Beethoven's famous ninth symphony includes a chorus.

Most choral music has been written for religious services. The principal form of such choral music is the *mass,* a series of pieces composed for the Roman Catholic Mass. In the 1560's, the Italian composer Giovanni Palestrina wrote *Missa Papae Marcelli,* which became a model for masses. Palestrina wrote this composition for a small, unaccompanied chorus. Later composers, including Bach, Beethoven, and Schubert, wrote masses with parts for vocal soloists and orchestra accompaniment. The *requiem,* which is a mass composed for funerals, also involves choral singing. Important requiems were written by such composers as Mozart, Hector Berlioz of France, and Giuseppe Verdi of Italy.

Operas combine drama with vocal and instrumental music. The music, which is set to the *libretto* (text) of an opera, highlights the dramatic, tragic, or comic aspects of the story. Many operas involve an orchestra, vocal soloists, a chorus, and ballet. The greatest opera composers include Mozart; Verdi, Claudio Monteverdi, and Giacomo Puccini of Italy; and Richard Strauss and Richard Wagner of Germany.

The most important kinds of opera vocal music are *recitatives* and *arias.* Recitatives, which performers sing in a simple, speechlike style, carry the action of the opera forward by giving the audience information about the characters or plot. Arias are vocal solos with much more complex melodies than those of recitatives. These solos express the feelings and thoughts of characters in an opera. See **Opera** (Recitative and arias).

Most operas consist of a series of arias, duets, and choruses connected by recitatives. Such operas are known as *number operas.* Other operas, called *music dramas,* have no breaks between episodes or scenes. Wagner developed this kind of opera in the 1800's.

Oratorios, like operas, use an orchestra, vocal soloists, and a chorus to tell a story. However, an oratorio has no stage action. Most oratorios have a religious subject. Famous religious oratorios include *Messiah* (1742) and *Judas Maccabaeus* (1747) by the German-born composer George Frideric Handel, *The Creation* (1798) by Joseph Haydn of Austria, and *Elijah* (1846) by Felix Mendelssohn of Germany. Among the most important nonreligious oratorios are Haydn's *The Seasons* (1801) and *Joan of Arc at the Stake* (1935) by the French composer Arthur Honegger.

A short oratorio is called a *cantata.* Most cantatas

Ken Firestone

Choral singing plays an important part in many works of classical music. At the left, the audience joins in singing the *Messiah,* a famous oratorio by the German-born composer George Frideric Handel. This work also has parts for vocal soloists and orchestra accompaniment.

are composed for church services. Bach wrote more than 200 cantatas, most of them based on hymns.

Classical music forms

Composers of classical music give form to their works by using three main techniques—*repetition, variation,* and *contrast.* A composer develops a *theme* (main melody) for a work and repeats it throughout. At times, the composer varies the theme slightly or uses a completely new melody to provide contrast with the theme.

The most important patterns involving repetition, variation, and contrast include (1) simple forms, (2) the sonata form, (3) the variation form, and (4) fugue. Some pieces of classical music have no pattern of repetition, variation, and contrast. They are written in *free form.*

Simple forms include the *binary form* and the *ternary form.* Music written in the binary form has two parts. Suppose that *A* represents the theme of a piece, *A'* a variation of the theme, and *B* a contrasting section. The two parts of a composition in the binary form would have a sequence of AA' or AB. Many composers of the 1600's and 1700's used binary form in minuets and other music written for dancing.

The ternary form, also known as *song form,* consists of three parts. This form has a *reverting* pattern—that is, the composer repeats the theme or a variation of it after a contrasting part. The three parts have a sequence of ABA or ABA'. Many songs have the ternary form. The dancelike third movements of sonatas, concertos, and symphonies also have this form.

Composers sometimes create a more elaborate pattern from the ternary form by adding more contrasting parts. Such a pattern is called a *rondo.* The sequence of parts in a typical rondo is ABACABA, with *B* and *C* representing the new contrasting sections.

The sonata form, also known as the *sonata structure,* developed in western Europe during the mid-1700's. The sonata form received its name because composers used it for the movements of sonatas. The sonata form was the most common musical form from the late 1700's to the mid-1900's. Composers used it not only for sonatas but also for the first movements of string quartets, symphonies, and other instrumental compositions. Beethoven, Haydn, and Mozart became famous for their work with this form.

A movement in the sonata form has three parts. The first part, called the *exposition,* introduces the main theme or group of themes. In the second part, the *development,* the composer varies the themes, combines them, breaks them into smaller sections, or plays them in different keys. The third part of the movement, the *recapitulation,* restates the original theme or themes.

The composer may give the movement an *introduction* and a concluding section called the *coda.* The introduction comes before the exposition. The coda follows the recapitulation.

The variation form, also known as the *theme and variation form,* consists of a theme and a series of different versions of it. Each of these versions is known as a variation. Composers use this form throughout a composition or in a movement of a work. A variation may be based on the entire theme, on a certain part of it, or on its accompaniment. Some variations also involve a change of key or of rhythm.

Fugue is a form of musical composition in which several instruments or singers repeat a series of melodies with slight variations. Generally, however, the word *fugue* refers to a work written in this form. The fugue is the chief type of music with *counterpoint,* a combination of two or more melodies. Bach composed the most famous fugues.

Many fugues have been written with four parts, called *voices.* A fugue begins with the first voice presenting the basic melody, called the *subject.* The second voice then gives the *answer,* a melody that is very similar to the subject but at a higher or lower pitch. During the answer, the first voice may present a second subject, known as the *countersubject.* Next, the third voice joins the first two voices with a restatement of the subject. The fourth voice completes the group by repeating the answer. A fugue contains passages called *expositions,* in which each voice states the original subject. In most cases, the expositions in a fugue are linked by brief sections called *episodes.* An episode does not include statements of the subject in all parts.

Free form gives the composer the greatest freedom of all. A composition written in free form has no standard pattern of theme, variation, and contrast. Each section of a free-form composition is completely different. The composer gives the work a sense of unity by means of the harmony and orchestration used. Instrumental compositions in free form include *fantasias, improvisations,* and *rhapsodies.* Many symphonic poems also have this form. The French composer Claude Debussy used free form in *Jeux* (*Games,* 1912), an orchestra piece for ballet.

History

Beginnings. Scholars know little about the music of the earliest civilizations. Musicians and their instruments appear in many ancient works of art. However, early people did not write down music, and so we know almost nothing about how it sounded.

The music of the Greeks was the most influential music of ancient times. The systems of music theory that the Greeks worked out helped shape the development of later Western music. To the Greeks, the word *music* had a much broader meaning than it does today. For example, it included poetry.

According to Greek mythology, the gods invented music. The ancient Greeks associated certain music with certain gods. Such Greek philosophers as Plato and Aristotle believed that music had emotional qualities and influenced human behavior. They thought that people who listened to a certain type of music acquired the qualities associated with it. For example, a slow, steady style of music played on a type of lyre called the *kithara* was believed to have a calming effect. The Greeks associated such music with Apollo, the god of light, purity, reason, and the sun. A passionate style of music played on the *aulos,* a wind instrument, was associated with Dionysus, the god of wine. This music supposedly caused wild, unpredictable behavior.

Music had an important role in many Greek public events, especially dramas, athletic competitions, and religious ceremonies. All Greek music, both instrumental and vocal, was probably *monophonic*—that is, it consisted of a single melody throughout. The Greeks based their music on scales called *modes,* which resembled the major and minor scales used today.

The ancient Romans continued the musical theories and performing techniques of the Greeks. In addition, the Romans developed such instruments as the trumpet and pipe organ.

The Middle Ages. From the A.D. 400's to the 1500's, music became much more structured and complicated. The oldest known Western music was *plain song,* used in Christian church services. This vocal music developed gradually from early Jewish religious music. Much plain song was set to the words of *psalms,* lyrical poems from the Old Testament. A soloist or choir sang the melody without accompaniment. The most important type of plain song was the *Gregorian chant,* organized during the reign of Pope Gregory I, who died in 604.

Music remained monophonic until about 800. Composers in western Europe then began to create *polyphonic* music by putting two or more melodies together. The earliest form of this music, known as *organum,* was created by adding a new part to an existing piece of plain song. At about the same time, a means of writing down notes of different lengths was developed.

Beginning about 900, more *secular* (nonreligious) songs began to appear. During the 1100's and 1200's, French nobles composed many secular songs and poems. These poet-musicians became known as *troubadours* in southern France and *trouvères* in northern France. A similar group, called *minnesingers,* flourished in Germany. See **Minnesinger; Troubadour; Trouvère.**

New forms of polyphonic music appeared during the 1100's and 1200's. The most important of these forms,

the motet, developed from organum. A motet consisted of a piece of plain song and two or more additional parts, each with different words.

Music grew increasingly complex during the 1300's as rhythm became more varied. The motet and other forms of polyphony continued to develop. The French composer Guillaume de Machaut wrote a Mass that was the first polyphonic setting of the entire Mass written by one person. Italian and English composers also produced important music.

The Renaissance period in music lasted from about 1450 to 1600. It occurred during the second half of the Renaissance, a time of outstanding cultural achievement in Europe. Composers of the Renaissance period experimented with new arrangements of tones and simpler rhythm. As a result, they produced fuller and richer sounds. Most music continued to be polyphonic and vocal, though instruments occasionally accompanied or replaced one or more of the voice parts. Many of the new developments in music occurred in Flanders, a region that included parts of what are now Belgium, the Netherlands, and northern France.

In the late 1400's, composers began to use a style called *imitative counterpoint.* In this style, which became known as *fugue,* different voices or instruments followed one another and repeated the same melody with slight variations. Imitative counterpoint became the most common form of composition in the 1500's. Composers of this period included Orlando di Lasso of the Netherlands and Giovanni Palestrina of Italy.

In Italy, imitative counterpoint led to the development of the madrigal, a polyphonic secular song with three to

Highlights in the history of classical music

The Sumerians played music on harplike instruments.	Western European composers started to create polyphonic music.	Composers in Paris introduced the earliest system for writing down rhythmic values.
About 3000 B.C. About 500 B.C.	A.D. 400's About 800	1100's and 1200's
The Greeks began to develop systems of music theory.	Plain song became the chief music of Christian worship.	

Raymond V. Schoder, S.J.

The kithara was an important stringed instrument of ancient Greece. The Greeks believed that music played on the kithara had a calming effect on listeners.

Historical Pictures Service

Guido d'Arezzo, *left,* an Italian monk, developed a revolutionary system of notation and method of sight-singing in the A.D. 1000's.

Granger Collection

Troubadours often performed for royalty during the 1100's and 1200's in southern France. These poet-musicians helped popularize nonreligious songs.

six parts. Madrigals were written by such composers as Luca Marenzio of Italy, Ciprian de Rore of the Netherlands, and William Byrd and Thomas Morley of England.

Composers of the 1500's also created new forms of instrumental music. Some of these forms, including *canzoni* and *ricercari,* came from vocal music. Other forms were composed for one or more specific instruments. For example, the toccata was written for keyboard instruments. During the late 1500's, composers in Venice developed the concerto.

The baroque period, which lasted from about 1600 to 1750, featured elaborate, vividly expressive music. During this period, composers introduced several important vocal forms, including the cantata, oratorio, and opera. Instrumental music also flourished, especially chamber and orchestra music.

The modern system of major and minor scales, with 12 different tones, gradually came into use. This system is called *tonality.* Another feature of baroque music was the *continuo,* an accompaniment played by a bass instrument and a keyboard instrument.

Most of the new musical ideas of the period developed in Italy. Composers in other countries copied the styles and forms of Italian music. Leading composers during the 1600's included Claudio Monteverdi of Italy, Jean-Baptiste Lully of France, Heinrich Schütz of Germany, and Henry Purcell of England.

In the late 1600's Italian composers created the *opera seria.* This form of opera was based on stories of ancient monarchs and of gods and goddesses from various myths. Recitatives and arias became standard parts of operas during this period. The leading composer of

opera seria was Alessandro Scarlatti of Italy, whose works became famous throughout Europe.

In instrumental music, the *trio sonata* became a popular style of chamber music during the baroque period. The trio sonata featured two melody instruments—usually violins—and a continuo played by a cello and a keyboard instrument. Orchestras played a new form of music known as the concerto grosso, which featured solo instrumentalists.

Baroque music reached its greatest heights in the work of two German composers, Johann Sebastian Bach and George Frideric Handel. Bach's works included cantatas and organ compositions written for church services. His music overflows with rich harmonies and elaborate counterpoint. Musicians still study Bach's use of harmony in the *Well-Tempered Clavier,* a collection of 48 preludes and fugues, and in other works. Handel wrote more than 40 operas and over 30 oratorios.

The classical period. During the 1700's, the European middle class grew in size and importance. More and more people acquired an interest in music. Public concerts became increasingly popular, and composers wrote light, simple music that audiences could enjoy easily. Such *galant* music gradually developed into the classical style, which dominated composition before 1750 to about 1820. This style emphasized balance and contrast among the movements of a work. Galant music expressed emotions in a refined, elegant way.

The sonata form appeared during the classical period, and composers used it in all types of instrumental music. Another important development was the *opera buffa,* a comic form of opera.

Guillaume de Machaut of France wrote the first polyphonic Mass composed by a single person.

The modern system of major and minor scales came into use.

Johann Sebastian Bach of Germany completed Book I of the *Well-Tempered Clavier.*

| 1300's | 1597 | 1600's | 1722 |

Jacopo Peri of Italy composed *Dafne,* probably the first opera.

Jean-Philippe Rameau, a French music theorist, published *Treatise of Harmony.*

Detail of a relief sculpture (1431-1438) by Luca della Robbia (SCALA/Art Resource)

During the Renaissance period, choirs consisted entirely of male singers. This marble sculpture shows a choir of boys singing a psalm.

Detail of *Psalms of Penitence* (1565-1570), a miniature painting on parchment by Hans Mielich; Bayer. Staatsbibliothek, Munich, Germany

Chamber music flourished during the 1500's. The chamber orchestra above featured composer Orlando di Lasso of the Netherlands at the keyboard.

Detail of a German engraving (1732) (Granger Collection)

Johann Sebastian Bach composed many masterpieces during the first half of the 1700's. He is shown here conducting a performance of chamber music.

The greatest composers of the classical period were Joseph Haydn and Wolfgang Amadeus Mozart, both of Austria, and Ludwig van Beethoven of Germany. Haydn's works included symphonies, string quartets, sonatas, and operas. His instrumental music consisted of four movements that both contrasted with and balanced one another. Haydn built his movements on phrases that consisted of three or four notes. These phrases are called *motives*. Haydn's style became a model for later composers of the period.

Mozart composed in a greater variety of styles and forms than Haydn did. Mozart created much instrumental music, including sonatas, chamber music, symphonies, and piano concertos. He also wrote operas, some of which combined serious and comic elements. Mozart's *The Marriage of Figaro* (1785), *Don Giovanni* (1787), and *The Magic Flute* (1791) rank among the great operas of all time.

Beethoven composed most of his works during the classical period. He specialized in piano sonatas, string quartets, and symphonies. Many of Beethoven's works emphasize nonmusical ideas. For example, his ninth symphony expresses the ideal of human brotherhood. Beethoven wrote longer compositions than did Haydn and Mozart. His later piano sonatas and string quartets have an extraordinary range and power of expression.

The romantic era began about 1820. Composers of this period believed music should be highly imaginative and emotional. A number of them developed characteristic personal styles.

Many shorter and simpler forms, such as German lieder, became popular during the romantic period. New instrumental forms, including overtures, character pieces for piano, and symphonic poems, also flourished.

Beethoven composed his later works during the first years of the romantic era. Franz Schubert, an early romantic from Austria, wrote more than 600 lieder, as well as piano solos, chamber music, and symphonies. Felix Mendelssohn, also of Germany, was noted for his piano and orchestra music. Still another German composer, Robert Schumann, wrote expressive symphonies, character pieces, and vocal music. Hector Berlioz of France became known for inventive types of orchestra compositions, many of them based on literary works. The Polish-born composer Frédéric Chopin wrote magnificent piano pieces.

In the mid-1800's, Franz Liszt of Hungary and Richard Wagner of Germany gained fame for their extremely complex music. Liszt wrote brilliant piano music and established the symphonic poem as an important form. Wagner combined music, poetry, dance, and other arts in his revolutionary music dramas, which he based on various myths and legends. He used recurrent themes, called *leitmotifs*, that were associated with various characters and other aspects of the dramatic action.

Composers of the late 1800's used a wide variety of forms and styles. Anton Bruckner of Austria composed symphonies that had both religious and secular elements. Johannes Brahms of Germany wrote music in the classical tradition. Giuseppe Verdi created some of Italy's finest operas. The Bohemian composer Gustav Mahler wrote symphonies to be performed by a large orchestra. Many of these works involve vocal soloists and choruses. Richard Strauss of Germany became fa-

---

Messiah, an oratorio by George Frideric Handel of Germany, was first performed.

The Austrian composer Joseph Haydn completed his "London" Symphonies.

| 1742 | 1787 | 1794 | Early 1800's |

Wolfgang Amadeus Mozart of Austria wrote the opera *Don Giovanni.*

Ludwig van Beethoven of Germany composed many of his greatest works.

Detail of *Leopold Mozart with His Two Children* (about 1765), an oil painting on canvas by Louis Carrogis; Carnavalet Museum, Paris (Giraudon/Art Resource)

As a young boy, Mozart showed extraordinary musical talent. This painting portrays him playing the piano, accompanied by his father and sister.

Historical Pictures Service

Beethoven's studio. Beethoven worked in this studio in his home during his final years. Although he became totally deaf, he continued to compose great music.

Granger Collection

Franz Schubert of Austria wrote brilliant piano solos, chamber music, and symphonies. Here he is sitting at the piano, *lower left,* in a friend's home.

mous for his symphonic poems and operas.

About 1850, composers in eastern and northern Europe began to express the feelings of their people in music. They used elements of folk songs and folk dances in works that became known as *nationalistic music*. Nationalistic composers included Edvard Grieg of Norway; Alexander Borodin, Modest Mussorgsky, and Nikolai Rimsky-Korsakov of Russia; and Bedřich Smetana and Antonín Dvořák, both Czechs. Nationalistic elements are also important in the music of Peter Ilich Tchaikovsky, the most popular Russian composer of the 1800's. He became famous chiefly for his symphonies.

The 1900's have brought a number of new developments in classical music. For example, composers introduced harmonic principles that differed from the traditional system of harmony. Composers also often rejected the emotionalism of romantic music.

The first principal new musical approach was *impressionism*, a vivid, descriptive style that had originated in France in the late 1800's. Impressionism became widespread during the early 1900's. Claude Debussy of France, the leading impressionist composer, introduced new ideas in harmony and musical structure. Some of his works have sounds that suggest certain images, such as those of moonlight, wind, and the sea.

During the early 1900's, Austrian composer Arnold Schoenberg began writing *atonal music*. In atonal music, there is no feeling of key. Schoenberg eventually developed *serialism*, a method of composition that uses all 12 notes of the scale in a predetermined series as the basis for a composition. Schoenberg used serialism in string quartets, symphonies, and other traditional forms.

At first, his innovative music aroused protests from audiences and from conservative composers and critics. Schoenberg's students included two other noted Austrian composers, Anton Webern and Alban Berg.

Musical nationalism continued to flourish in the 1900's. The leading nationalistic composer was Béla Bartók of Hungary, who wrote piano pieces, string quartets, two ballets, and an opera. Among the other nationalistic composers were Charles Ives and Aaron Copland of the United States and Sergei Prokofiev and Dimitri Shostakovich of Russia.

Styles of popular music influenced many classical composers. For example, elements of jazz appeared in the works of such French composers as Maurice Ravel and Darius Milhaud.

A movement known as *neoclassicism* affected much of the music written after 1920. Neoclassical composers based their compositions on musical forms of the 1700's or earlier. The leading early neoclassical composers were the Russian-born Igor Stravinsky and Paul Hindemith of Germany. The early works of Stravinsky included such nationalistic ballets as *The Firebird* (1910) and *Petrouchka* (1911). From the early 1920's to the early 1950's, however, he modeled his works on the music of Bach and various other composers of the past. After 1952, Stravinsky began to compose in the style of Schoenberg. Hindemith composed in a variety of forms.

Since 1950, a number of composers have experimented with untraditional styles and with new methods of making sounds. The French-born Edgard Varèse became known for his *electronic music*. In this kind of music, the composer uses electronic equipment to

---

The Polish-born composer Frédéric Chopin wrote outstanding compositions for solo piano.

Johannes Brahms of Germany composed brilliant symphonies in the style of Beethoven.

Mid-1800's   Late 1800's

Richard Wagner of Germany created operas that featured *leitmotifs* (recurrent themes).

A vivid musical style called *impressionism* developed in France.

Granger Collection

Hector Berlioz ranked as the leading French musician of the romantic period. He became famous throughout Europe as a composer, conductor, and music critic.

Bettmann Archive

The Ring of the Nibelung, a group of operas by Wagner, was first performed in its entirety in 1876. This painting shows a scene from that performance.

All-Union Association Vneshtorgizdat, Moscow

Swan Lake, one of the world's great ballets, premiered in Moscow in 1877. Peter Ilich Tchaikovsky of Russia composed the music for this ballet.

create sounds that have any desired pitch, loudness, tone, and duration. Another American composer, John Cage, helped develop *aleatory music*. In such music, all or part of the sounds depends on chance. The composer provides only a general outline of the composition. Musicians are largely free to create melodies and rhythms that vary with each performance.

Since the mid-1960's, *minimalism* has become an important musical style in classical music. Minimalism uses short melodic, rhythmic, and harmonic patterns that are repeated again and again. These patterns often create a hypnotic effect. Composers of minimalism include Philip Glass, Steve Reich, and Terry Riley.

Today, classical music consists of compositions that vary widely—from traditional to revolutionary—in style and form. Composers of the late 1900's include Elliott Carter, George Crumb, David Del Tredici, George Rochberg, and Charles Wuorinen of the United States; Alberto Ginastera of Argentina; Pierre Boulez and Olivier Messiaen of France; Carl Orff and Karlheinz Stockhausen of Germany; Luciano Berio of Italy; and Krzysztof Penderecki of Poland. F. E. Kirby

Related articles in *World Book*. See the *Arts* section of the articles on various countries, such as **Mexico** (Arts). See also:

Biographies

For biographies of other persons relating to classical music, see the lists of *Related articles* at the end of **Hymn; Opera; Piano;** and **Violin.** See also:

American composers

Barber, Samuel
Bernstein, Leonard
Billings, William
Blitzstein, Marc
Bloch, Ernest
Cage, John
Carter, Elliott
Copland, Aaron
Cowell, Henry
Crumb, George
Dello Joio, Norman
Gershwin, George
Glass, Philip
Gottschalk, Louis M.
Gould, Morton
Grofé, Ferde
Hanson, Howard
Harris, Roy
Hovhaness, Alan
Ives, Charles E.
MacDowell, Edward Alexander
Menotti, Gian Carlo
Moore, Douglas S.
Piston, Walter
Schuman, William
Sessions, Roger
Thomson, Virgil
Varèse, Edgard
Zwilich, Ellen T.

Austrian composers

Berg, Alban
Bruckner, Anton
Czerny, Karl
Haydn, Joseph
Kreisler, Fritz
Mahler, Gustav
Mozart, Wolfgang
Schoenberg, Arnold
Schubert, Franz P.
Strauss, Johann, Sr.
Strauss, Johann, Jr.
Webern, Anton

British composers

Britten, Benjamin
Byrd, William
Delius, Frederick
Dowland, John
Elgar, Sir Edward W.
Gibbons, Orlando
Holst, Gustav
Morley, Thomas
Purcell, Henry
Sullivan, Sir Arthur S.
Tallis, Thomas
Vaughan Williams, Ralph
Walton, Sir William

French composers

Berlioz, Hector
Bizet, Georges
Boulez, Pierre
Couperin, François
Debussy, Claude
Delibes, Léo
Dukas, Paul A.
Fauré, Gabriel U.
Franck, César
Gounod, Charles
Honegger, Arthur
Ibert, Jacques
Lully, Jean-B.
Massenet, Jules
Messiaen, Olivier
Milhaud, Darius
Offenbach, Jacques

Arnold Schoenberg of Austria developed *serialism,* a method of composition based on all 12 notes of the scale.

Edgard Varèse, a French-born composer, produced *Poème Electronique,* the first major work of electronic music.

| 1920's | 1930's | 1958 | 1977 |

Dimitri Shostakovich developed a sophisticated modern style of Russian music.

The American composer Elliot Carter completed *A Symphony of Three Orchestras.*

Historical Pictures Service

The Firebird, a ballet by Igor Stravinsky of Russia, was first performed in 1910. The production starred Michel Fokine and Tamara Karsavina, *above.*

Historical Pictures Service

Wozzeck, an opera by Alban Berg of Austria, caused a sensation at its premiere in 1925. This picture shows a performance in Germany in 1931.

WORLD BOOK photo by Dan Miller

Electronic music is composed with special electronic equipment. The composer above is using a *synthesizer,* an instrument that makes a wide variety of sounds.

Poulenc, Francis
Rameau, Jean-Philippe
Ravel, Maurice

Saint-Saëns, Camille
Satie, Erik

German composers

Bach, Carl Philipp Emanuel
Bach, Johann Christian
Bach, Johann Sebastian
Beethoven, Ludwig van
Brahms, Johannes
Bruch, Max
Buxtehude, Dietrich
Gluck, Christoph Willibald
Handel, George Frideric
Henze, Hans Werner
Hindemith, Paul

Humperdinck, Engelbert
Mendelssohn, Felix
Meyerbeer, Giacomo
Orff, Carl
Schumann, Clara
Schumann, Robert
Stockhausen, Karlheinz
Strauss, Richard
Telemann, Georg Philipp
Wagner, Richard
Weber, Carl Maria von

Italian composers

Bellini, Vincenzo
Boccherini, Luigi
Boito, Arrigo
Cherubini, Luigi
Clementi, Muzio
Corelli, Arcangelo
Dallapiccola, Luigi
Donizetti, Gaetano
Leoncavallo, Ruggiero
Mascagni, Pietro
Monteverdi, Claudio

Paganini, Niccolò
Palestrina, Giovanni
Pergolesi, Giovanni B.
Puccini, Giacomo
Respighi, Ottorino
Rossini, Gioacchino A.
Scarlatti, Alessandro
Scarlatti, Domenico
Tartini, Giuseppe
Verdi, Giuseppe
Vivaldi, Antonio

Russian composers

Borodin, Alexander
Glinka, Mikhail I.
Khachaturian, Aram I.
Mussorgsky, Modest
Prokofiev, Sergei S.
Rachmaninoff, Sergei V.

Rimsky-Korsakov, Nikolai
Rubinstein, Anton G.
Scriabin, Alexander
Shostakovich, Dimitri
Stravinsky, Igor
Tchaikovsky, Peter I.

Other composers

Albéniz, Isaac
Bartók, Béla
Chávez, Carlos
Chopin, Frédéric F.
Desprez, Josquin
Dvořák, Antonín
Falla, Manuel de
Ginastera, Alberto
Grainger, Percy A.
Grieg, Edvard

Janáček, Leoš
Kodály, Zoltán
Lasso, Orlando di
Liszt, Franz
Nielsen, Carl A.
Paderewski, Ignace J.
Penderecki, Krzysztof
Sibelius, Jean
Smetana, Bedřich
Villa-Lobos, Heitor

Conductors

Barbirolli, Sir John
Barenboim, Daniel
Beecham, Sir Thomas
Bernstein, Leonard
Boulez, Pierre
Caldwell, Sarah
Damrosch, Leopold
Damrosch, Walter
Fiedler, Arthur
Furtwängler, Wilhelm
Karajan, Herbert von
Klemperer, Otto
Koussevitzky, Serge
Levine, James
Maazel, Lorin
MacMillan, Sir Ernest C.

Mahler, Gustav
Masur, Kurt
Mehta, Zubin
Mitropoulos, Dimitri
Monteux, Pierre
Ormandy, Eugene
Ozawa, Seiji
Previn, André
Reiner, Fritz
Solti, Sir Georg
Stokowski, Leopold
Szell, George
Toscanini, Arturo
Walter, Bruno
Zukerman, Pinchas

Elements of music

Counterpoint
Harmonics
Harmony

Key
Pitch
Rhythm

Sound
Tone

Instrumental musical forms

Concerto   Étude   Fantasia   Fugue   Intermezzo

March
Overture
Rondo
Scherzo

Serenade
Sonata
Suite
Symphonic poem

Symphony
Variation
Waltz

Vocal music

Ballade
Barcarole
Bard
Canon
Cantata
Chorale

Lieder
Madrigal
Mastersinger
Minnesinger
Minstrel
Passion music

Singing
Song
Troubadour
Trouvère
Voice

Other related articles

Aleatory music
American Society of Compos-
 ers, Authors and Publishers
Ballet
Baroque (Baroque music)
Cecilia, Saint
Chamber music
Composer
Electronic music
Greece, Ancient (The arts)
Hymn
Metronome
Music Clubs, National Federa-
 tion of

National anthem
National Music Camp
Opera
Operetta
Oratorio
Orchestra
Pulitzer Prizes (Music)
Romanticism (Romanticism in
 music)
Suzuki method
Treble
Tuning fork
Western frontier life (Music)

Outline

I. Instrumental music
 A. Solo music
 B. Chamber music
 C. Orchestra music
II. Vocal music
 A. Songs
 B. Choral music
 C. Operas
 D. Oratorios
III. Classical music forms
 A. Simple forms
 B. The sonata form
 C. The variation form
 D. Fugue
 E. Free form
IV. History

Questions

What are the characteristics of baroque music?
What are the three main techniques that composers use to give
 structure to their music?
How do a symphony and a concerto differ?
What is *aleatory music? Electronic music?*
What are the principal kinds of instrumental music? Of vocal
 music?
What instruments make up a string quartet?
What is *serialism* and who developed it?
What is the major difference between an oratorio and an opera?
How did chamber music get its name?
What is the chief form of religious choral music?

Additional resources

Gammond, Peter. *The Harmony Illustrated Encyclopedia of Clas-
 sical Music.* Rev. ed. Harmony Bks., 1988.
Griffin, Clive D. *Classical Music.* Dryad Pr., 1988. For younger
 readers.
Grout, Donald J., and Palisca, C. V. *A History of Western Music.*
 4th ed. Norton, 1988.
Heritage of Music. 4 vols. Ed. by Michael Raeburn and Alan Ken-
 dall. Oxford, 1992. First published in 1989.
The New Harvard Dictionary of Music. Ed. by Don M. Randel.
 Belknap, 1986.
The Norton/Grove Concise Encyclopedia of Music. Ed. by Stan-
 ley Sadie. Norton, 1988.
Rubin, Mark. *The Orchestra.* Firefly Bks., 1992. First published in
 1984. For younger readers.
Wade, Graham. *The Shape of Music: An Introduction to Form in
 Classical Music.* Allison & Busby, 1982. Also suitable for
 younger readers.

Classicism is a philosophy of art and life that emphasizes order, balance, and simplicity. The ancient Greeks were the first great classicists. Later, the Romans, French, English, and others produced classical movements. Each group developed its own unique characteristics, but all reflected certain common ideals of art, humanity, and the world.

The qualities of classicism

Classicism contrasts with the philosophy of art and life called *romanticism*. Classicism stresses reason and analysis, while romanticism stresses imagination and the emotions. Classicism seeks what is universally true, good, and beautiful. Romanticism seeks the exceptional and the unconventional. Classical art looks to the past for its models. It often revives ancient Greek and Roman values, and is then called *neoclassicism*. Romanticism is often sympathetic to revolutions in society and art. Classical artists follow formal rules of composition more closely than romantic artists do. See **Romanticism.**

Classicists know that reality is complex. But they try to approach it through simple structures. For example, the classical playwright concentrates on essentials by restricting a play to a single line of action that could happen within one day, in one place, or in nearby places.

The Italian artist Raphael and the French artist Nicolas Poussin painted pictures illustrating the finest qualities of classical art. Many of their pictures have a poetic mood, but the organization of the subject matter is always balanced, harmonious, and orderly. These qualities can be seen in Raphael's *Madonna of the Goldfinch* and Poussin's *St. John on Patmos.* Both of these pictures are reproduced in the **Painting** article. The works of the Italian composer Giovanni Palestrina and the French composer Jean-Philippe Rameau show the classical qualities of balance and clarity.

Great classical movements

The first important classical movement developed in ancient Greece and Rome. Another such movement appeared in Western Europe in the 1600's and 1700's.

Greece. The first classical period in the West arose in ancient Greece, and reached its height in the 400's and 300's B.C. The Greeks praised reason and denounced emotionalism and exaggeration. They tried to see all reality within a unified system that gave it meaning and direction. Greek artists showed the beauty of the human form. The sculptures of Phidias and Praxiteles are magnificent examples of proportioned human figures. Aeschylus, Sophocles, and Euripides wrote tragedies about the power of fate and the danger of excessive pride. See **Greek literature; Greece, Ancient** (The arts).

Rome. Roman classicism developed in two stages. These stages occurred during the age of Cicero from 80 to 43 B.C., and the age of Augustus from 37 B.C. to A.D. 14. The Romans adopted the Greek classical values, and added a unique emphasis on civilization as an organized, cooperative undertaking. Under the influence of the statesman and orator Cicero, civic responsibility gained a new importance. Rome's literature reached its highest achievement during the reign of Augustus. The classical poet Virgil wrote works on the development of civilization and on the heritage of Rome. The works of the classical poet Horace exemplify civilized attitudes

The Father of Psyche Sacrificing at the Temple of Apollo (1670);
an oil painting on canvas (Jeremy Witaker, National Trust Photographic Library)

A French classical landscape of the 1600's by Claude reflects the movement's admiration for balance, harmony, and order. The idealized rural setting and the subject matter taken from Greek mythology were also typical of French classical painting.

toward society and life. See **Latin literature.**

France. The French classical movement of the 1600's developed the most diverse expression of classical values ever seen in the Western world. French classicists placed especially strong emphasis on reason and the intellect in analyzing ideas and human actions. The most important people in the intellectual and literary history of the French classical period include the mathematician-philosophers Blaise Pascal and René Descartes; the moralist writer Duc de La Rochefoucauld; the writer of fables Jean de La Fontaine; and the dramatists Pierre Corneille and Jean Racine. See **French literature** (The classical age).

England. The English classical period followed French classicism. It arose in the late 1600's and reached its height during the first half of the 1700's. The English modeled their movement on the classicism of France, Greece, and Rome. They strove for good taste and truth to nature. For a more detailed discussion of English classicism, see **English literature** (The Augustan Age).

Germany. In Germany and in German-speaking Austria, music rather than literature best expressed classical ideals. Joseph Haydn, Wolfgang Amadeus Mozart, and Ludwig van Beethoven rank among the great classical composers (see **Classical music**). In the late 1700's in Germany, a classical literature flourished side by side with romantic literature. Johann Wolfgang von Goethe is often regarded as the finest classical and the finest romantic German writer.   Lawrence Lipking

There is a separate article in *World Book* for each person discussed in this article. See also **Russian literature** (The classical movement).

Classification, Scientific. Scientific classification is a method scientists have developed to arrange all of the world's organisms in related groups. It is the orderly arrangement of all living things. Scientific classification indicates certain relationships among all organisms. Detailed scientific classifications also show how ancient and extinct biological groups fit into this arrangement. The classification of organisms is a science called *taxonomy* or *systematics.*

Scientific classification is an interpretation of facts. It is based on the opinion and judgment a biologist forms after studying many living and preserved dead organisms. Most biologists use the same basic framework for classification. But not all biologists agree on how different groups of organisms fit into this scheme, and so classifications often differ in details.

The language of classification. Latin and Greek words are used in scientific classification, because early scholars used these languages. Every known organism belongs to a particular *species.* Each species has a two-part scientific name. Most of these names come from Greek or Latin words. We call this system of names the *binomial system of nomenclature,* or *binomial nomenclature.* These are Latin terms that mean *two-name naming.* The two names identify an organism by indicating which species it belongs to.

Organisms are known by different common names in different regions of the world. However, each organism has only one correct scientific name, and scientists anywhere in the world can recognize the organism by its scientific name. For example, the same large member of the cat family may be known in various parts of North America and South America as a puma, cougar, mountain lion, panther, or león. The cat's scientific name is *Felis concolor.* Scientists can identify the animal by that name no matter what language they speak.

International commissions of scientists establish the rules for adopting scientific names. Some scientific names are descriptive. The scientific name of the spotted skunk, for example, is *Spilogale putorius,* which means *smelly, spotted weasel.* But many scientific names have no descriptive meaning.

Groups in classification. Seven chief groups make up a system in scientific classification. The groups are: (1) kingdom, (2) phylum or division, (3) class, (4) order, (5) family, (6) genus, and (7) species. The kingdom is the largest group. The species is the smallest. Every known organism has a particular place in each group.

Kingdom is the largest unit of biological classification. Until the 1960's, most biologists formally recognized only two major kingdoms—Animalia, the animal

How organisms are classified

The illustrated tables below are simplified examples of classification. They show how a red squirrel (*Tamiasciurus hudsonicus*) and a common buttercup (*Ranunculus acris*) can be separated from any other species of animal or plant. As you go down the tables, from kingdom to species, the animals and plants in each group have more and more features in common. The captions list these features. Individuals in a species have so many similar features that they look alike.

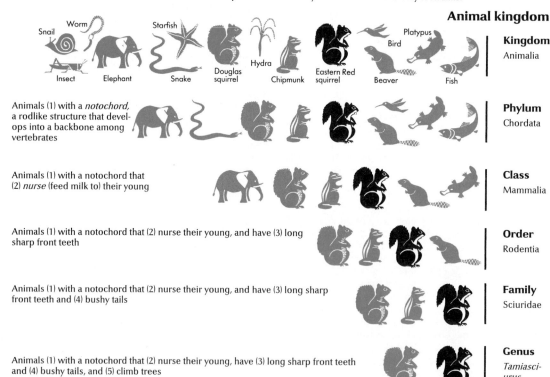

Animal kingdom

Kingdom
Animalia

Animals (1) with a *notochord,* a rodlike structure that develops into a backbone among vertebrates

Phylum
Chordata

Animals (1) with a notochord that (2) *nurse* (feed milk to) their young

Class
Mammalia

Animals (1) with a notochord that (2) nurse their young, and have (3) long sharp front teeth

Order
Rodentia

Animals (1) with a notochord that (2) nurse their young, and have (3) long sharp front teeth and (4) bushy tails

Family
Sciuridae

Animals (1) with a notochord that (2) nurse their young, have (3) long sharp front teeth and (4) bushy tails, and (5) climb trees

Genus
Tamiasciurus

Animals (1) with a notochord that (2) nurse their young, have (3) long sharp front teeth and (4) bushy tails, (5) climb trees, and (6) have brown fur on their backs and white fur on their underparts

Species
Tamiasciurus hudsonicus

kingdom, and Plantae, the plant kingdom. But as more information about the microscopic structure and biochemistry of organisms became known, scientists realized that a two-kingdom classification system was not exact enough. Today, most biologists use a system that recognizes five kingdoms of organisms. These kingdoms are Animalia, Plantae, Fungi, Protista, and Monera.

The kingdom Animalia is the largest kingdom. It has more than 1 million named species. These species include the organisms that most people easily recognize as animals, such as human beings, deer, fish, insects, and snails. The kingdom Plantae consists of more than 350,000 species. It includes those organisms that most people easily recognize as plants, such as magnolias, sunflowers, grasses, pine trees, ferns, and mosses. The kingdom Fungi has more than 100,000 species. These species include fungi, such as mushrooms and bread molds, as well as the lichens. The kingdom Protista has more than 100,000 species. This kingdom includes green, golden, brown, and red algae; ciliates; sporozoans; sarcodines; and flagellates. The kingdom Monera, also called *Prokaryotae,* consists of bacteria, including blue-green algae or cyanobacteria. There are more than 10,000 known species in this kingdom.

Division, or *phylum,* is the second largest group. The kingdoms Protista, Fungi, and Plantae are classified into *divisions.* In the animal kingdom, the term *phylum* is used instead of division. Scientists disagree on which term should be used for the kingdom Monera.

The animal kingdom may be divided into 20 or more phyla. All animals with backbones belong to the phylum Chordata. The plant kingdom has 10 divisions. All plants that have flowers belong to the division Anthophyta.

Class members have more characteristics in common than do members of a division or phylum. For example, mammals, reptiles, and birds all belong to the phylum Chordata. But each belongs to a different class. Apes, bears, and mice are in the class Mammalia. Mammals have hair on their bodies and feed milk to their young. Reptiles, including lizards, snakes, and turtles, make up the class Reptilia. Scales cover the bodies of all reptiles, and none of them feed milk to their young. Birds make up the class Aves. Feathers grow on their bodies, and they do not feed milk to their young.

Order consists of groups that are more alike than those in a class. In the class Mammalia, all the animals produce milk for their young. Dogs, moles, raccoons, and shrews are all mammals. But dogs and raccoons eat flesh, and are grouped together in the order Carnivora, with other flesh-eating animals. Moles and shrews eat insects, and are classified in the order Insectivora, with other insect-eating animals.

Family is made up of groups that are even more alike than those in the order. Wolves and cats are both in the

Plant kingdom

WORLD BOOK illustrations by John M. Bolt, Jr., and Trudy Rogers

Kingdom
Plantae

Cattail   Fern   Larkspur   Sunflower   Common buttercup   Pine   Grass   Water crowfoot   Magnolia   Hornwort   Maple   Moss

Division
Anthophyta

Plants that have (1) flowers with reproductive organs called *ovaries* that protect *ovules* (structures that can develop into seeds)

Class
Dicotyledonae

Plants that (1) have flowers with ovaries and (2) develop from plant embryos with two *cotyledons* or *seed leaves*

Order
Ranales

Plants that have (1) flowers that have ovaries, (2) embryos with two cotyledons, and (3) *floral parts* (petals, sepals, stamens) that grow from beneath the ovary

Family
Ranunculaceae

Plants that have (1) flowers that have ovaries, (2) embryos with two cotyledons, (3) floral parts growing from beneath the ovary, and (4) many spirally arranged stamens

Genus
Ranunculus

Plants that have (1) flowers that have ovaries, (2) embryos with two cotyledons, (3) floral parts growing from beneath the ovary, (4) many spirally arranged stamens, and (5) all petals identical

Species
Ranunculus acris

Plants that have (1) flowers that have ovaries, (2) embryos with two cotyledons, (3) floral parts growing from beneath the ovary, (4) many spirally arranged stamens, (5) all petals identical, and (6) yellow flowers

order Carnivora. But wolves are in the family Canidae. All members of this family have long snouts and bushy tails. Cats belong to the family Felidae. Members of this family have short snouts and short-haired tails.

Genus consists of very similar groups, but members of different groups usually cannot breed with one another. Both the coyote and the timber wolf are in the genus *Canis*. But coyotes and timber wolves generally do not breed with one another.

Species is the basic unit of scientific classification. Members of a species have many common characteristics, but they differ from all other forms of life in one or more ways. Members of a species can breed with one another, and the young grow up to look very much like the parents. No two species in a genus have the same scientific name. The coyote is *Canis latrans,* and the gray wolf is *Canis lupus.* Sometimes groups within a species differ enough from other groups in the species that they are called *subspecies* or *varieties.*

Development of classification. For thousands of years people have tried to classify living things. Early human beings divided all organisms into two groups: (1) useful, and (2) harmful. As people began to recognize more kinds of living things, they developed new ways to classify them. One of the most useful was suggested by the Greek philosopher and naturalist Aristotle, who lived during the 300's B.C. Only about a thousand organisms were known in his time. He classified animals as those with red blood—animals with backbones—and those with no red blood—animals without backbones. He divided plants by size and appearance as herbs, shrubs, or trees. Aristotle's scheme served as the basis for classification for almost 2,000 years.

During the 1600's, the English biologist John Ray first suggested the idea of species in classification. But the basic design for modern classification began with the work of the Swedish naturalist Carolus Linnaeus in the 1700's. Linnaeus classified organisms according to their structure and gave distinctive two-word names to each species. Many of Linnaeus' groupings from species through orders still are accepted today. But his higher groupings often were based on superficial physical resemblances. Modern classifications are based on more microscopic structural and biochemical characteristics, as well as on presumed evolutionary relationships among the organisms. Classifications continue to change as more information becomes available.

Theodore J. Crovello

Related articles in *World Book* include:

Animal (table: A classification)
Botany
Flower (How flowers are named and classified; table: Representative families of flowers)
Fungi
Kingdom
Linnaeus, Carolus
Moneran
Plant (table: A classification of the plant kingdom)
Protist

Claude (1600-1682) was a French painter who established a tradition of landscape painting that influenced artists in Europe and America for 200 years. Claude's full name was Claude Gellée, but he is often called Claude Lorrain, after his native province of Lorraine. Claude settled in Rome in 1627 and lived there the rest of his life.

Claude's landscapes show the Italian countryside bathed in golden light. They have a feeling of calm and peace, sometimes tinged with sadness. Peasants and their farm animals appear in some of his paintings. In others, characters from mythology contribute to the mood. Claude also painted seaport or river scenes with the setting sun reflected in the water.

Like other artists of his time, Claude went into the countryside to make sketches but completed his paintings in his studio. Patrons would have been insulted to receive a mere copy of nature that the artist had not bothered to idealize. Claude's landscapes were immediately popular and continued to be influential for generations. His work was especially popular in England in the 1700's. There it influenced garden design and helped shape the style of the great English landscape painter J. M. W. Turner. Ann Friedman

See also **Classicism** (picture).

Claudel, *kloh DEHL,* **Paul** (1868-1955), was a French writer and diplomat. He became one of the foremost French poets and playwrights in the early 1900's and helped provide a new religious focus to the literature of his time. His writings are examples of the Roman Catholic revival in French literature and philosophy.

Early in his life, Claudel lost his religious faith. But on Christmas Day in 1886, he had a spiritual experience while listening to evening prayers in the Cathedral of Notre Dame in Paris. This experience led to the return of his faith and to his acceptance of orthodox Catholicism.

Claudel expresses his religious faith in such lyric poems as *Cinq Grandes Odes* (1910). But he is best known as a playwright. His most famous play, *The Tidings Brought to Mary* (1912), portrays the triumph of divine love. It illustrates themes common throughout his work: the relationship between human love and salvation, the link between humanity and divine will, and the necessity of self-sacrifice for the redemption of others.

Claudel was born in Villeneuve-sur-Fère, near Soissons, France. Between 1893 and 1935, he worked in several countries as a French diplomat. He served as France's ambassador to Japan, the United States, and Belgium. Claudel was elected to the French Academy in 1946. Dora E. Polachek

See also **French literature** (The four masters).

Claudius (10 B.C.-A.D. 54) was the emperor of Rome from A.D. 41 to 54. Claudius was a capable but eccentric ruler. He built aqueducts, drained marshes, and made a harbor near Ostia at the mouth of the Tiber River. However, he became unpopular for executing senators and for giving secretaries who had been slaves great influence in his court. Claudius began the conquest of Britain in A.D. 43 and made the Balkan Peninsula (then called Thrace) a Roman province in A.D. 46. He also granted citizenship to many people from Rome's provinces.

Claudius was born in Lugdunum (now Lyon), France. His full name was Tiberius Claudius Nero. Lame and a stutterer, Claudius was kept from public view in his youth. He spent his time studying and writing histories of Etruria and Carthage. Claudius married several times. After he married his niece Agrippina the Younger, he adopted her son Nero. It is generally believed that Agrippina murdered Claudius so that Nero could become emperor (see **Nero**). F. G. B. Millar

Clause is a group of words with a subject and a predicate. A complete sentence is called a *main,* or *independent,* clause. For example, *we were practicing* is a main clause. A *subordinate,* or *dependent,* clause begins with a relative pronoun, such as *which, who,* or *that;* or with a subordinating conjunction, such as *although, if, because, so that, unless,* or *while.* Thus, *when we were practicing* is a subordinate clause.

Subordinate clauses are classified as *restrictive* or *nonrestrictive.* A restrictive clause is binding upon the word it modifies. To omit it would alter the meaning of the sentence. In "The man *who was coming toward me* suddenly stumbled," the subordinate clause is restrictive because it tells us who stumbled. A nonrestrictive clause can be omitted without changing the sentence's essential meaning. In "George, *who was coming toward me,* suddenly stumbled," the clause is nonrestrictive. The word "George" tells us who stumbled. The clause places no restrictions upon the subject. It merely adds information. Nonrestrictive clauses are enclosed by commas. Restrictive clauses are not. William F. Irmscher

See also **Sentence.**

Clausewitz, *KLOW zuh vihts,* **Karl von** (1780-1831), was a Prussian army officer and military theorist. His theories and observations about war, published in the book *On War* (1832-1834), influenced military strategy for more than 100 years.

Clausewitz was born in Burg, Prussia. He joined the army in 1792 and fought in numerous battles against the French armies of Emperor Napoleon I. These battles included the campaign of 1815, when Napoleon was finally defeated. In 1818, Clausewitz became director of the War College in Berlin.

In his writings, Clausewitz observed that armies of citizens fighting for their nation showed greater determination than professional soldiers fighting only for territory. Clausewitz' most original contribution was his analysis of the close relationship between the army and the nation. To Clausewitz, war was merely "the pursuit of diplomacy by other means." Thus, it was necessary to consider the political interests of the nation as more important than military goals. He also stressed that a nation at war must take risks and act boldly to obtain a decisive and total victory. Charles W. Ingrao

Clausius, *KLOW zee uhs,* **Rudolf Julius Emmanuel** (1822-1888), a German physicist, helped establish thermodynamics as a science. In 1850, he stated the second law of thermodynamics: "Heat cannot of itself pass from a colder to a hotter body" (see **Thermodynamics**). He derived an equation that relates the saturated vapor pressure of a liquid to the temperature. He also developed a theory to explain electrolysis (see **Electrolysis**). Clausius was born in Köslin, Germany (now Koszalin, Poland). Richard G. Olson

Claustrophobia. See **Phobia.**

Clavichord, *KLAV uh kawrd,* is a keyboard musical instrument that was a forerunner of the piano. The clavichord's tone is produced by metal blades that strike the instrument's wire strings when keys are pressed down. The blades, called *tangents,* remain in contact with the strings as long as the keys are held down. This action allows the player to control the tone after the first attack by making slight changes in pitch. This is an important feature of the instrument. The word *clavichord* comes from the Latin words *clavis,* which means *key,* and *chorda,* which means *string.*

The clavichord dates from the 1400's. It produces soft tones, and so it was used for musical practices and en-

tertaining small gatherings instead of for playing in public concerts. The instrument became especially popular in Germany. During the 1700's, the piano was developed and began to replace the clavichord. F. E. Kirby

See also **Piano** (History).

Clavicle. See **Collarbone.**

Claw. See **Animal** (How animals protect themselves; picture).

Clay is a substance present in most kinds of soil. Geologists define clay as extremely small particles of soil that measure less than 4 microns, or 0.000157 inch, in diameter. The word *clay* also refers to earthy material composed of certain kinds of silicate minerals that have been broken down by weathering.

Clay consists mainly of tiny, sheetlike particles of alumina and silica bound together by water. Various other materials in clay may give it different colors. For example, iron oxide may color clay red. Clays that contain various amounts of carbon compounds may be different shades of gray.

The clay in soil has a vital role in farming. For example, it absorbs ammonia and other gases needed for plant growth. Clay also helps soil retain minerals necessary for plant growth. Without clay, soil would not keep its fertility from year to year. However, too much clay makes soil stiff and heavy and prevents the movement of air and water through soil.

There are two general types of clay, based on how the substance reacts when mixed with water. *Expandable clay* swells when water is added to it. Expandable clay can absorb so much water that the clay itself becomes a liquid. *Nonexpandable clay* becomes soft but not liquid when mixed with water.

The petroleum industry uses expandable clays called *bentonites* to make drilling mud. The petroleum industry also uses another kind of expandable clay as a chemical agent in the process of oil refining.

Ceramics industries use nonexpandable clay in mak-

WORLD BOOK photo by Ralph Brunke

An artist uses clay to model an earthenware vase. Sculptures, dishes, and other objects may also be created from clay.

ing bricks, pottery, tile, and many other products. For example, pottery makers mold moist clay into almost any shape and bake it in hot ovens called *kilns*. Heat removes the water from the clay, which becomes permanently hard and cannot be softened by adding water to it. The whitest kind of clay, *kaolin* or *china clay*, is used in making porcelain. The paper industry also uses kaolin, which serves as a filler that adds whiteness and strength to paper. In addition, kaolin gives some kinds of paper a smooth, shiny surface. *Fire clay* contains a large percentage of silica and can stand high temperatures. It is used in making firebrick and furnace linings.

Taylor J. Johnston

Related articles in *World Book* include:

Alumina	Feldspar	Marl	Soil
Bentonite	Fuller's earth	Porcelain	Terra cotta
Brick	Kaolin	Pottery	Tile
Ceramics	Loam	Silica	

Clay, Cassius. See Ali, Muhammad.

Clay, Cassius Marcellus (1810-1903), was an American politician and abolitionist. He was the son of a slaveholder, but he learned to despise slavery and preached against it. In 1845, he founded an antislavery newspaper, *True American,* in Lexington, Ky. After moving to Louisville, he called it the *Examiner.* His views on slavery and his fiery nature earned him a reputation as a rebel and a brawler. He carried two pistols and a knife because of threats on his life, and he guarded his office and his home with a cannon.

Clay was born in Madison County, Kentucky, and studied at Yale. He served in the Kentucky legislature in 1835, 1837, and 1840. He worked for Abraham Lincoln's election in 1860 and was minister to Russia in 1861 and 1862 and from 1863 to 1869.   Frank L. Klement

Clay, Henry (1777-1852), was a leading American statesman for nearly 50 years. Clay became known as the Great Compromiser because he repeatedly helped settle bitter disputes over slavery between the Northern and Southern states. His compromises did much to hold the nation together during the first half of the 1800's. Clay's charm, generosity, and eloquent speeches made him one of the most idolized figures of his time.

Clay served as Speaker of the U.S. House of Representatives, a U.S. senator, and a U.S. secretary of state. He campaigned for President unsuccessfully five times. Through the years, Clay showed great devotion to principle. Once, after taking a controversial stand on slavery, he told an associate, "I had rather be right than be President."

Early career. Clay, the son of a Baptist minister, was born on April 12, 1777, in Hanover County, Va. He received little formal schooling, but he had a sharp mind and liked to read. Clay studied law and, at the age of 20, set up a successful law practice in Lexington, Ky.

In 1803, Clay was elected to Kentucky's state legislature. The legislature greatly admired Clay and elected him to fill an unexpired term in the U.S. Senate in 1806. At that time, state legislatures elected U.S. senators. Clay was not quite 30 years old, the minimum age required by the Constitution of the United States. But the Senate did not investigate Clay's age. From 1810 to 1811, Clay filled another unexpired term in the U.S. Senate.

National leader. Clay was elected to the U.S. House of Representatives in 1811. He had become known as an

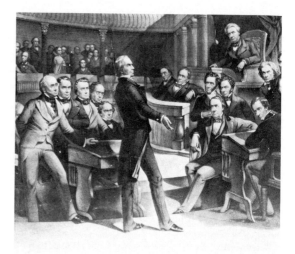

Engraving by R. Whitechurch; Library of Congress, Washington, D.C.

Henry Clay spoke eloquently before the United States Senate in support of the Compromise of 1850, *above*. His ability to bring about compromises between the North and South earned him the title the Great Compromiser.

outstanding leader and was chosen Speaker of the House on the first day of the session. Clay was reelected to the House and to the office of Speaker five more times. He became head of the "War Hawks," a group that helped influence Congress to declare war against Great Britain in 1812. But Clay also helped negotiate peace with Great Britain and was a signer of the Treaty of Ghent. See **War of 1812.**

After the war, Clay proposed a national economic plan called "the American System." The plan included a protective tariff to aid American manufacturers, a national bank, and government support of improvements in transportation. Clay became the most important leader of the National Republican Party, which endorsed his economic program.

The Missouri Compromise. In 1820, Clay helped settle a dispute between the North and South over the expansion of slavery. He helped win congressional approval of a plan that became known as the Missouri Compromise. The compromise permitted slavery in the new state of Missouri and banned it in the new state of Maine. The compromise also prohibited slavery in most of the Louisiana Territory, a huge area west of the Mississippi River. See **Missouri Compromise.**

Clay also played a key role in settling a dispute over the federal tariff. The dispute arose in 1832, when South Carolina *nullified* (declared unconstitutional) two U.S. tariff laws. South Carolina threatened to *secede* (withdraw) from the United States if the federal government tried to enforce the tariff in the state. But in 1833, Clay persuaded Congress to pass a compromise bill that gradually lowered the tariff. His measure helped preserve the supremacy of the federal government over the states.

Candidate for President. Clay ran for the presidency five times, but never won. In the presidential election of 1824, Clay's first attempt, no candidate received a majority of the votes in the Electoral College. As a result, the U.S. House of Representatives had to choose the

President from among the three candidates who received the most electoral votes. Clay had come in fourth in the voting, behind Andrew Jackson, John Quincy Adams, and William H. Crawford. He gave his support to Adams, who was then elected President. Clay served as Adams' secretary of state from 1825 to 1829.

In 1832, Clay ran as the candidate of the National Republican Party. He opposed President Andrew Jackson, the Democratic-Republican candidate. Jackson won easily, partly because Clay supported efforts to renew the charter of the unpopular Bank of the United States. Clay and other National Republicans helped form the Whig Party in 1834. Clay ran for President again in 1840 as a Whig, but he dropped out of the race when the Whig Party made William Henry Harrison its nominee.

Clay became the Whig Party's presidential candidate in 1844. He opposed James K. Polk of the Democratic Party. Annexation of the then independent Republic of Texas became a major campaign issue. Clay opposed annexation and warned that it would provoke war with Mexico and reawaken the controversy over slavery in the United States. Polk favored annexation and narrowly won the election. Clay's warnings came true. A border dispute led to the Mexican War (1846-1848), and the North and South later clashed over the question of extending slavery into the territory gained from the war. Clay sought the presidency again in 1848. He ended his campaign when the Whigs nominated Zachary Taylor, a general who had become a hero in the Mexican War.

The Compromise of 1850. Clay retired to Ashland, his plantation in Lexington, in 1848. In 1849, the Kentucky legislature again elected him to the U.S. Senate. Clay helped settle another dispute between Northern free states and Southern slave states sponsoring a plan known as the Compromise of 1850. Parts of this plan allowed slavery in the New Mexico and Utah territories and prohibited it in California. The Compromise of 1850 helped delay the Civil War for 11 years. See **Compromise of 1850.**

Personal life. In 1799, Clay married Lucretia Hart, the daughter of a wealthy Lexington land speculator and merchant. The Clays suffered several tragedies in their home life. Their oldest son, Theodore, was confined to a mental institution. Their six daughters died young, and their son Henry was killed during the Mexican War.

Clay died in Washington, D.C., in June 1852 and was buried in Lexington. A marker by his grave has a quotation from one of his speeches: "I know no North—no South—no East—no West." Daniel Walker Howe

Additional resources

Clay, Henry. *The Papers of Henry Clay.* 9 vols. Univ. Pr. of Kentucky, 1959-1988.
Remini, Robert V. *Henry Clay: Statesman for the Union.* Norton, 1991.

Clay, Lucius Dubignon (1897-1978), served as commander in chief of the United States armed forces in Europe and as military governor of the U.S. zone in Germany from 1947 to 1949. In 1948, the Soviet Union blockaded all supply routes to the Western section of Berlin, hoping to drive out of Berlin the forces of the United States, Britain, and France. But the Berlin airlift, directed by Clay, flew food and other supplies into the city.

Clay was born in Marietta, Ga., and graduated from the United States Military Academy in 1918. He served as an Army engineer. During World War II, Clay directed the delivery of supplies to invasion fronts. He retired from the Army in 1949, and became associated with several civilian firms. Clay served as an adviser to the Office of Defense Mobilization in 1951. In 1961 and 1962, he served as the personal representative of President John F. Kennedy in Germany. From 1968 to 1974, Clay was chairman of Radio Free Europe (see **Radio Free Europe/Radio Liberty**). He wrote a book, *Decision in Germany* (1950), based on his experiences in military government. Maurice Matloff

Clayton, John Middleton (1796-1856), was an American political leader. He served as United States secretary of state from 1849 to 1850, under President Zachary Taylor. As secretary of state, he negotiated the Clayton-Bulwer Treaty of 1850. In this pact, the United States and Britain agreed to protect the neutrality of a canal to be built through Central America. The treaty helped the two countries avoid war over the proposed canal. See **Clayton-Bulwer Treaty.**

Clayton was born in Dagsboro, Del. He served as chief justice of Delaware from 1837 to 1839 and represented Delaware in the U.S. Senate from 1829 to 1836, 1845 to 1849, and 1853 to 1856. For most of his career, Clayton belonged to the Whig Party. A statue of him represents Delaware in the U.S. Capitol. Michael F. Holt

Clayton Antitrust Act. See **Antitrust laws.**

Clayton-Bulwer Treaty, signed by the United States and Britain in 1850, gave both countries an equal share in the protection of a canal to be built through Central America. Both countries agreed to maintain the neutrality of the canal and the land on either side of it. The treaty was named for John M. Clayton, American secretary of state, and Sir Henry Bulwer (1801-1872), British minister to the United States. It became unpopular in the United States. In 1901, the Hay-Pauncefote Treaty replaced the Clayton-Bulwer Treaty. It granted the United States the right to build and manage the canal. See also **Hay-Pauncefote Treaty.** Robert F. Dalzell, Jr.

Clearinghouse is an institution used by banks to exchange checks and to establish claims against each other that result from financial transactions. Clearinghouses may be formal institutions with written rules and regulations, or they may consist of informal arrangements among banks. Nearly every city in the United States with more than two banks has a clearinghouse operated by an association of local banks. Formal clearinghouses operate in most large U.S. cities. Banks collect most checks drawn on out-of-town banks through Federal Reserve Banks or through commercial banks called *correspondent banks.* The rest of these checks are exchanged directly with banks in other cities.

A clearinghouse allows banks to settle their debts with one another with the smallest possible exchange of funds. Suppose you have a checking account at Bank A and write a check for $75 at a grocery store. The grocery store deposits the check in its account at Bank B. The grocery store then sends a check for $300 to the power company, which deposits the check in its account at Bank A. The banks send the two checks to the local clearinghouse.

The clearinghouse would examine the checks and

How a clearing-house works   A clearinghouse is an institution used by banks to settle their debts with one another. For example, suppose Bank B has a check for $75 from a customer of Bank A, and Bank A has a check for $300 from a customer of Bank B. Instead of paying the checks separately, the banks send them to a clearinghouse. It would find that both debts could be settled at once if Bank B paid $225 to Bank A.

WORLD BOOK diagram

Pay to Grocery $75.00 Mary Doe
Check from Bank A

Grocery store

Bank B

Clearinghouse

Pay to Bank A $225
Bank B
Payment to Bank A

Pay to Power Co $300.00 Grocery
Check from Bank B

Power company

Bank A

find that Bank A owes $75 to Bank B, and Bank B owes $300 to Bank A. Both debts could be settled at once if Bank B paid $225 to Bank A. Actually, a clearinghouse may handle thousands or millions of checks and other transactions daily. The dollar amounts tend to offset each other, leaving much smaller amounts to be transferred between the banks.

Almost all U.S. banks that use a formal clearinghouse have an account at their district Federal Reserve Bank. The clearinghouse gives the Federal Reserve Bank information that allows settlement between banks through their Federal Reserve accounts. In some cases, banks that use a particular clearinghouse settle claims against each other through accounts at one of the user banks.

The first clearinghouse was formed in London in the late 1700's. In 1853, New York City banks formed the first clearinghouse in the United States. In 1970, the Clearing House Interbank Payments System (CHIPS) began operating in New York City. This system handles electronic fund transfers that are related to international financial transactions. Its computer network provides settlement information to the Federal Reserve Bank of New York.

Joanna H. Frodin

Cleary, Beverly (1916-   ), is an American author of books for children. She is best known for her series of books about the adventures of two youngsters named Henry Huggins and Ramona Quimby. The two characters and their friends live in a middle-class suburb of Portland, Ore. Cleary's books are noted for their humor and for their realistic and natural dialogue.

Cleary's first book was *Henry Huggins* (1950). Ramona first appeared as a major character in *Beezus and Ramona* (1955). Cleary's other children's books include *Ellen Tebbits* (1951), *The Mouse and the Motorcycle* (1965), and *Runaway Ralph* (1970). Cleary was born in McMinnville, Ore. In 1975, she received the Laura Ingalls Wilder Award for her contributions to children's literature. Cleary won the 1984 Newbery Medal for *Dear Mr. Henshaw* (1983). She wrote an autobiography, *A Girl from Yamhill* (1988).   Marilyn Fain Apseloff

Cleaver, Eldridge (1935-   ), became known for preaching the doctrine of *Black Power*. According to

this doctrine, blacks must organize politically so they can deal with white society from a position of strength. Cleaver became best known for his book *Soul on Ice* (1968). Critics praised the book's insights into black attitudes toward American society.

Leroy Eldridge Cleaver was born in Wabbaseka, Ark., and grew up in California. As a youth, he spent several years in prison. In 1958, he was convicted of assault with intent to kill and given a 2- to 14-year sentence. He was paroled in 1966 and joined the Black Panther Party (see **Black Panther Party**).

In 1968, Cleaver ran as the United States presidential candidate of the Peace and Freedom Party. Later that year, he fled to Algeria after he became involved in a shooting incident in California. Cleaver returned to the United States in 1975. He said he had experienced a "religious conversion" and gave up many of his earlier political beliefs. He described his conversion in his book *Soul on Fire* (1978). Cleaver then was arrested for parole violation. He was released on probation in 1980. In 1986, Cleaver sought the Republican nomination for the United States Senate in California but was not successful.   Hanes Walton, Jr.

Cleft lip. See Cleft palate.

Cleft palate, *PAL iht,* is a birth defect in which there is a split in the roof of the mouth. Many people born with a cleft palate also have a *cleft lip*—a split through the upper lip. Cleft lip—with or without cleft palate—occurs in about 1 out of every 700 births. Cleft palate alone occurs in about 1 out of every 2,500 births.

Clefts result when the tissues that form the roof of the mouth or the lip fail to unite in the unborn baby. Research indicates that this may be caused by a combination of environmental and hereditary factors.

A cleft palate starts at the rear of the mouth. In some cases, it involves only the *soft palate*—the muscular tissue that forms the rear part of the roof of the mouth. In other cases, it extends into the *hard palate*—the bony tissue that makes up the front part of the mouth's roof. It may even extend through the gum.

Speech defects are one of the chief problems caused by a cleft palate. During normal speech, the soft palate rises to separate the mouth and nasal cavities. Such separation cannot be attained with a cleft palate, and certain sounds cannot be formed properly. Another serious problem is chronic ear infections. These result if the cleft palate interferes with the drainage of fluids through the *Eustachian tube*. This tube connects the middle ear with the back of the throat.

A cleft in the lip can be *complete* (extending into the nostril) or *partial* (stopping before the nostril). It may occur on one or both sides of the lip, and alone or along with a cleft palate. A cleft lip is sometimes called a *harelip*, because it resembles the split lip of a hare. By itself, a cleft lip is chiefly a defect in appearance.

Cleft palates and lips can be repaired by surgically joining the split structures. Surgical repair of a cleft lip often produces almost normal appearance. Repair of a cleft palate greatly improves speech ability. However, some patients require speech therapy, additional surgery, or both to obtain usable speech. If clefts extend into the gum, orthodontia may be needed to correct the angle of the teeth.   David W. Furnas

Cleisthenes, *KLYS thuh neez,* was a statesman in ancient Athens. He established a democratic constitution there after Hippias, who held complete political power, was overthrown in 510 B.C. Cleisthenes was the head of the noble Alcmaeonid clan. This clan had an *oracle* (prophet) persuade Cleomenes, the king of Sparta, to overthrow Hippias. After that, Cleisthenes gained public support and set up a democratic form of government. He then reformed the Athenian tribal organization, ending the political control of the noble clans. The government had a council of 500 members who were chosen each year in a drawing. Membership in the council was open to any citizen. Some scholars believe that to protect the new democracy, Cleisthenes enacted a law providing for *ostracism* (banishment) of politicians the people thought were dangerous.   Donald Kagan

See also **Athens** (History).

Clematis, *KLEHM uh tihs,* is any one of a group of perennial herbs or woody vines that grow throughout North America, Europe, and Asia. Several small-flow-

WORLD BOOK illustration by Robert Hynes

An American clematis, *above,* has violet blossoms that grow in clusters.

ered kinds are called *virgin's-bower.* The most popular American species include a large group of hybrid varieties. These vines may climb 10 feet (3 meters) high and have flowers 6 inches (15 centimeters) wide. Clematis flowers may be blue, violet, white, pink, or red. After the flowers fade, the plant bears small dry fruits. The fruits often have long feathery tufts attached.

Scientific classification. Clematis is in the crowfoot family, Ranunculaceae. The scientific name for the best-known American vine is *Clematis jackmanii.*   Melinda F. Denton

Clemenceau, *KLEHM uhn SOH* or *kleh mahn SOH,* **Georges,** *zhawrzh* (1841-1929), a French statesman, led France triumphantly through the last and most difficult period of World War I. In 1917, at age 76, he became premier of France for the second time. He exercised powerful leadership with his slogan, "I make war!" and became known as "The Tiger of France." He presided over the Paris Peace Conference, where he insisted on severe terms for Germany and sought to protect France by creating an independent state out of German territory west of the Rhine River. Clemenceau ran for president of France in 1920 but lost to Paul Deschanel. He resigned as premier the day after his defeat.

Keystone

Georges Clemenceau

Clemenceau was born in Mouilleron-en-Pareds, near La Roche-sur-Yon, France. Trained as a doctor, he traveled and taught for a time in the United States, where he married an American. When he returned to France, he became mayor of Montmartre, a section of Paris. He helped defend Paris against the Germans in 1870. Clemenceau served as a deputy from 1876 to 1893 and as premier from 1906 to 1909.   Marc Trachtenberg

Clemens, Samuel Langhorne. See **Twain, Mark.**

Clement I, Saint (? - about A.D. 101), was elected pope about A.D. 92. He is traditionally regarded as the third in succession to Saint Peter as bishop of Rome. Clement is most famous for a letter he wrote to the church in Corinth, probably in A.D. 96. The letter strongly condemned pride and arrogance within the church and clarified the order of succession from bishop to *presbyter* (elder) to *deacon* (assistant). In later years, Clement's letter was regarded as the first exercise of papal authority in the affairs of a Christian church outside Rome. But Clement's concerns in writing the letter were spiritual and fraternal, not legal. The letter is the oldest surviving Christian text except for the Scriptures.

Clement was a citizen of Rome. He may have been the Clement who worked with Saint Paul at Philippi. Many legends surround Clement's life. According to one, he was martyred by being thrown into the sea with an anchor tied to his neck. None of the legends can be verified. His feast day is November 23.   Thomas F. X. Noble

Clement VII (1342-1394) was an *antipope*—that is, a man determined to have improperly claimed to be or served as pope. His reign began in 1378 and marked the beginning of a period in church history known as the

Great Schism. See **Roman Catholic Church** (The Great Schism).

Clement was born in Geneva (now Geneva, Switzerland) and was known as Robert of Geneva before being elected pope. Pope Gregory XI made him a cardinal in 1371. Gregory sent Robert to Italy to make arrangements for the return of the pope to Rome after the long papal residence in Avignon, in what is now France. Gregory died in 1378, shortly after returning to Rome. Robert and the other cardinals elected a new pope in April 1378 who took the name Urban VI. Urban had an unstable personality and soon antagonized many cardinals. The French cardinals claimed Urban's election was illegal because they argued it had been held under threat of violence. They withdrew their allegiance and elected Robert pope in September 1378.

Many European countries recognized Clement as the true pope. However, the church now considers Urban VI and his successor, Boniface IX, as the legitimate popes during Clement's reign.   Kenneth Pennington

Clement VII (1478-1534) was elected pope in 1523 and reigned during a stormy period in European religious and political affairs. Clement was born in Florence, Italy. His given and family name was Giulio de' Medici. His cousin, Pope Leo X, made him a cardinal in 1513. The Medici were a powerful family in Florence and after his election, Clement determined to preserve his family's control of the city. This control was threatened by struggles between the Holy Roman Empire and France for dominance in Italy. Clement shifted sides repeatedly. This policy proved disastrous when the forces of Holy Roman Emperor Charles V captured King Francis I of France in 1525. They then raided Rome in 1527, forcing the pope to take refuge in the Castel Sant'Angelo.

Clement's concentration on Italian politics interfered with any effective papal response to the emerging Protestant Reformation. Lutheranism spread in Germany and was winning over Scandinavia. Clement's weak handling of the divorce case of King Henry VIII of England led to the split from Rome by the English church and the start of the Reformation in England.   Charles L. Stinger

Clement VIII (1536-1605) was elected pope in 1592, during the time of renewal and reform in the Roman Catholic Church known as the Counter Reformation. As pope, Clement typified the spiritual ideals of Catholic reform. A pious man, he fasted rigorously, practiced extensive devotions, and regularly visited on foot the pilgrimage churches of Rome. He issued a corrected edition of the Vulgate Bible and also revised the main church liturgical books. In 1595, Clement recognized Henry of Navarre, a convert from Protestantism, as King Henry IV of France. Clement presided over the Jubilee of 1600, which attracted millions of pilgrims to Rome.

Clement was born in Fano, Italy. His given and family name was Ippolito Aldobrandini. He studied law and held positions on several key papal commissions. He became a cardinal in 1585.   Charles L. Stinger

Clemente, *kluh MEHN tee,* **Roberto** (1934-1972), a Puerto Rican athlete, was one of the greatest baseball players in history. He won four National League batting titles and had a lifetime batting average of .317. Clemente won the league's Most Valuable Player award in 1966. He played on 12 National League All-Star teams during his 18-year career.

Wide World
Roberto Clemente

Clemente, who played right field for the Pittsburgh Pirates, won fame for his fielding, throwing, and hitting. He helped lead the Pirates to World Series victories in 1960 and 1971. Clemente never went hitless in a World Series game. He was named the outstanding player of the 1971 series. On Sept. 30, 1972, three months before his death, he became the 11th man in major-league history to get 3,000 hits.

Roberto Walker Clemente was born in Carolina, Puerto Rico. He died in a plane crash off the coast of Puerto Rico while flying to aid earthquake victims in Nicaragua. Clemente was elected to the National Baseball Hall of Fame in 1973 in a special election, without the traditional waiting period of five years after a player has retired.   Thomas H. Barnidge

Clementi, *klay MEHN tee* or *kluh MEHN tee,* **Muzio,** *MOO tsyoh* (1752-1832), was an Italian composer best known for his piano music. Clementi was also a successful pianist, conductor, and manufacturer of pianos. His most important composition, *Gradus ad Parnassum* (1817-1826), is a collection of 100 piano studies still used by students to develop their technique. Clementi's works also include more than 60 piano sonatas and almost 40 sonatas for piano and other instruments. His compositions helped establish techniques for playing the piano, which was replacing the harpsichord as the most important keyboard instrument in the late 1700's.

Clementi was born in Rome. At the age of 14, he was taken to England to study music. In 1773, he made his London debut as a pianist and composer. In 1780 and 1781, he toured Europe as a piano soloist. Clementi performed against Wolfgang Amadeus Mozart in 1781 in a test of skill at the court of the Austrian Emperor Joseph II. Clementi lived in England from 1810 until his death.
    Reinhard G. Pauly

Cleopatra, *KLEE oh PAT ruh* or *KLEE oh PAY truh* (69-30 B.C.), was a queen of ancient Egypt and one of the most fascinating women in history. She lacked beauty, but became known for her intelligence, charm, wit, and ambition. At times, Cleopatra was ruthless. However, she took a great interest in her subjects' welfare and won their affection. Cleopatra loved and developed loyal relationships with Julius Caesar and Mark Antony, two of the greatest Roman leaders of her day.

Cleopatra was the last ruler in the *dynasty* (series of rulers in the same family) founded by Ptolemy I in 323 B.C. Ptolemy was a general in the army of the Macedonian conqueror Alexander the Great. Cleopatra is also known as Cleopatra VII because she was the seventh Egyptian queen of Macedonian descent with that name.

Cleopatra and Caesar. Cleopatra became queen in 51 B.C. after the death of her father, Ptolemy XII. Her 10-year-old brother, Ptolemy XIII, became her co-ruler and husband. Marriage between a brother and a sister was a common practice in Egyptian royal families.

In 48 B.C., young Ptolemy's guardians seized power

for him and drove Cleopatra from the throne. At the same time, Julius Caesar arrived in Alexandria, Egypt's capital. He came in pursuit of Pompey, a Roman general and rival in Caesar's struggle to become the ruler of Rome. Caesar and Cleopatra met and fell in love.

Caesar defeated Cleopatra's opponents. Ptolemy XIII drowned while trying to escape. Caesar then put Cleopatra back on the throne along with another brother, Ptolemy XIV. In 47 B.C., Cleopatra gave birth to a boy, Caesarion, who she claimed was Caesar's son. In 46 B.C., at Caesar's invitation, she went with Caesarion and Ptolemy XIV to Rome. She stayed there until 44 B.C., when a group of Roman aristocrats assassinated Caesar. After returning to Egypt, Cleopatra had Ptolemy killed so that Caesarion could rule with her.

Cleopatra and Mark Antony. In 41 B.C., Mark Antony invited Cleopatra to Tarsus in Asia Minor (now Turkey). Antony was then one of the rulers of Rome, with Gaius Octavian and Marcus Lepidus. Antony had met Cleopatra when she stayed in Rome as Caesar's guest. Antony wanted to rule Rome alone and hoped to obtain financial aid from Cleopatra. Antony and Cleopatra fell in love. In 40 B.C., Cleopatra gave birth to twins, Alexander Helios and Cleopatra Selene. Antony loved Cleopatra and their children. But he left them to marry Octavia, the sister of his co-ruler Octavian (see **Octavia**). The marriage was a wise political move, but Antony missed Cleopatra. He left Octavia in 37 B.C., returned to Cleopatra, and soon married her. In 36 B.C., she had another son by him, Ptolemy Philadelphos.

Antony and Cleopatra worked closely to achieve their ambitions. He believed that the wealth of Egypt would help him become the sole ruler of Rome. She wished chiefly to put her children, especially Caesarion, in line to rule Rome. In 34 B.C. Antony appointed Cleopatra ruler of Egypt, Cyprus, Crete, and Syria. He gave his sons and daughter by Cleopatra much of the land once ruled by Alexander the Great. These actions angered Antony's co-rulers and rivals. Octavian regarded Cleopatra as greedy and ambitious, and felt that she had turned Antony into a helpless puppet.

In 32 B.C., Octavian and Antony went to war. In 31 B.C., forces of Antony and Cleopatra lost the Battle of Actium off the west coast of Greece (see **Actium, Battle of**). Cleopatra and Antony then returned to Alexandria. A few months later, Octavian came after them. In 30 B.C., after Octavian reached Egypt, Cleopatra spread a report that she had committed suicide. Antony heard the report and stabbed himself out of grief. Before he died, Antony learned that Cleopatra was alive. His followers carried him to Cleopatra, and he died in her arms.

Cleopatra believed that Octavian would publicly humiliate her in Rome. She tried to make peace with him, but failed. In despair, Cleopatra took her life by placing an asp, a poisonous snake, on her chest or arm. After her death, the Romans executed Caesarion because they feared he would claim to be Caesar's heir and the rightful ruler of Rome's empire.

Cleopatra's reputation in history comes largely from the views of Octavian, who described Antony as the lovestruck victim of a wicked temptress. The Roman poets Virgil and Horace also adopted this version. Cleopatra's story has been told many times in literature. It is dramatized in the famous plays *Antony and Cleopatra*

(1607) by William Shakespeare, *All for Love* (1677) by John Dryden, and *Caesar and Cleopatra* (1901) by George Bernard Shaw.   William G. Sinnigen

See also **Antony, Mark; Augustus; Caesar, Julius; Egypt, Ancient** (picture).

Additional resources

Hoobler, Dorothy and Thomas. *Cleopatra*. Chelsea Hse., 1986. Suitable for younger readers.
Langley, Andrew. *Cleopatra and the Egyptians*. Bookwright, 1986. For younger readers.

Cleopatra's Needles, *KLEE oh PAT ruhs* or *KLEE oh PAY truhs,* are two famous *obelisks* (tall pillars of stone) from ancient Egypt. One stands in Central Park in New York City. The other stands along the River Thames in London. The obelisk in New York rises 69 feet (21 meters) and weighs 200 short tons (180 metric tons). The one in London is $68\frac{1}{2}$ feet (20.9 meters) tall and weighs 180 short tons (160 metric tons). Egypt gave the obelisks to the United States and Great Britain in the 1870's.

Kings of ancient Egypt erected such obelisks as Cleopatra's Needles as monuments to the sun god Re. The kings built the largest of these monuments at Memphis, Heliopolis, and Thebes between 1500 and 1200 B.C.

Cleopatra's Needles bear the name of Thutmose III, who ruled Egypt during the 1400's B.C. They also include markings added by Ramses II, an Egyptian ruler of the 1200's B.C. Cleopatra's Needles originally stood at the temple of Re at Heliopolis. About 10 B.C., the Roman rulers of Egypt moved them to Alexandria to decorate a palace. Scholars do not know why the obelisks became associated with Queen Cleopatra of Egypt.   Leonard H. Lesko

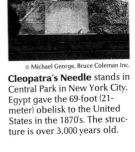

© Michael George, Bruce Coleman Inc.

Cleopatra's Needle stands in Central Park in New York City. Egypt gave the 69-foot (21-meter) obelisk to the United States in the 1870's. The structure is over 3,000 years old.

Clepsydra. See **Water clock.**

Clerestory, *KLIHR stawr ee,* is an architectural term for the row of windows in a wall that rises above adjacent roofs. The word is most often applied to churches where the clerestory above the main aisles admits light to the interior. Clerestory windows in many cathedrals and churches are made of beautiful stained glass.

William J. Hennessey

See also **Architecture** (Romanesque architecture).

Clergy. See **Minister; Priest; Rabbi; Deacon.**

Clerk of court is an officer of a court of justice who performs many important administrative duties. The

Cleveland, a leading U.S. industrial center, lies along Lake Erie. The picture at the left shows downtown buildings and Cleveland Municipal Stadium, *foreground.* The stadium is the home of the Cleveland Indians of the American Baseball League and the Cleveland Browns of the National Football League.

Mort Tucker Photography

clerk keeps the court records, such as the *docket* (list of cases awaiting hearing). The clerk issues the *summons* that calls a person into court and the *judgment* that orders the unsuccessful party to do what the court has directed. The clerk also keeps the court seal and certifies as correct any court records that are needed in other legal proceedings.   Jack M. Kress

Clermont was the first commercially successful steamboat. Designed by Robert Fulton, it sailed in regular passenger service on the Hudson River. Fulton sailed the wood-burning *Clermont* up the Hudson from New York City to Albany in 1807 on its first trip. Registered as the *North River Steam Boat,* the ship was generally called the *Clermont* after the home of Fulton's business partner, Robert Livingston. It was 142 feet (43 meters) long and 14 feet (4.3 meters) wide. An English-built engine drove its side paddle wheels. The ship was dismantled in 1815. See also **Fulton, Robert** (with picture); **Ship** (The *Clermont*).   Philip Chadwick Foster Smith

Cleveland is Ohio's second largest city and one of the leading industrial centers of the United States. Columbus is the state's largest city. Cleveland lies on the southern shore of Lake Erie, at the mouth of the Cuyahoga River. These waterways and the city's location near huge supplies of coal and iron ore helped make Cleveland an important steel producer. The city also ranks as a transportation, medical, and cultural center of the Midwest and a chief port of the Great Lakes.

Moses Cleaveland, a surveyor for the Connecticut Land Company, founded Cleveland in 1796. This company had bought the site of present-day Cleveland from Connecticut. The site formed most of an area called the Western Reserve, which Connecticut had reserved for settlement. The village was named after Cleaveland, but a newspaper printer misspelled the name in 1831 and it has been known as Cleveland ever since.

The city

Cleveland covers 76 square miles (197 square kilometers), or about a sixth of Cuyahoga County. The Cleveland metropolitan area covers 2,708 square miles (7,014 square kilometers). It extends over six counties—Ashtabula, Cuyahoga, Geauga, Lake, Lorain, and Medina.

Cleveland proper. The valley formed by the Cuyahoga River divides the city of Cleveland into an East Side and a West Side. Iron and steel mills, and other plants operate in the valley, which is known as the *Flats.*

Cleveland's chief public buildings border the Mall, a park that extends from Lake Erie into downtown Cleveland. These buildings include the Cuyahoga County Court House, City Hall, the Public Auditorium and Convention Center, and the Public Library.

Monumental Park, commonly called Public Square, lies nearby in the center of downtown Cleveland. Moses Cleaveland set aside the 4.4-acre (1.8-hectare) square for use as a park. The Civil War Soldiers and Sailors Monument and a statue of Cleaveland stand in the square. The Terminal Tower Building, one of the tallest buildings in the United States, rises 768 feet (234 meters) at the southwest corner of Monumental Park.

The city's main streets branch out from Public Square. The best-known street, Euclid Avenue, extends from the

Facts in brief

Population: *City*—505,616. *Metropolitan area*—2,202,069. *Consolidated metropolitan area*—2,859,644.
Area: *City*—76 sq. mi. (197 km²), excluding inland water. *Metropolitan area*—2,708 sq. mi. (7,014 km²), excluding inland water. *Consolidated metropolitan area*—3,613 sq. mi. (9,358 km²).
Altitude: 660 feet (201 meters) above sea level.
Climate: *Average temperature*—January, 27 °F (−3 °C); July, 73 °F (23 °C). *Average annual precipitation* (rainfall, melted snow, and other forms of moisture)—32 inches (81 centimeters). For the monthly weather in Cleveland, see **Ohio** (Climate).
Government: Mayor-council. *Terms*—4 years for the mayor and the 21 council members.
Founded: 1796. Incorporated as a city in 1836.

Symbols of Cleveland. The city flag's red, white, and blue stripes represent patriotism. The flag, adopted in 1895, has a shield that resembles the city seal, *right.* The seal bears Cleveland's founding date and symbols for its industry and waterways.

square through the eastern suburbs. The city's main downtown shopping district lies along Euclid Avenue from Public Square to East 22nd Street.

Cleveland's residential areas spread outward from the downtown district. Like many other industrial cities, Cleveland has large slum areas. These run-down areas present a sharp contrast to Cleveland's clean and modern suburbs.

Metropolitan Cleveland. Parma, Cleveland's largest suburb, has a population of about 88,000. Other suburbs of the city include Cleveland Heights, East Cleveland, Euclid, Garfield Heights, Lakewood, Maple Heights, North Olmstead, Shaker Heights, and Strongsville. The metropolitan areas of Cleveland-Lorain-Elyria and Akron form the Cleveland-Akron Consolidated Metropolitan Statistical Area.

The people

About 95 per cent of Cleveland's people were born in the United States. Blacks make up approximately 45 per cent of the population, and almost all the blacks live on the East Side. Other groups include people of German, Hungarian, Italian, or Slavic ancestry. These people live on both sides of Cleveland. The city also has about 1,500 American Indians, most of whom live on the East Side.

High unemployment among blacks is a major problem in Cleveland. In 1966, a riot in the all-black Hough ghetto increased racial tension. Race relations improved

City of Cleveland

Cleveland lies on Lake Erie in northeastern Ohio. The map at the right shows the metropolitan area of Cleveland. The map below shows the city and its major points of interest. The Cuyahoga River divides Cleveland into two parts.

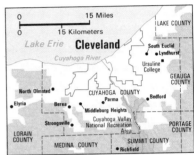

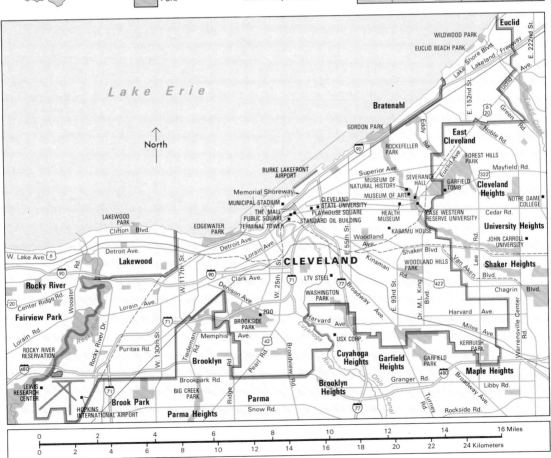

WORLD BOOK maps

Cleveland's harbor is one of the busiest on the Great Lakes. This ship carries iron ore for use in the city's steel mills.

in 1967 after Carl B. Stokes, a black state legislator, was elected mayor. In 1968, a series of gun battles between blacks and police in the Glenville area again increased tension. Since then, city programs have done much to ease the tension. These efforts include a fund-raising program called *Cleveland: Now,* which has helped finance projects to train the unemployed and find jobs for them. The city also set up child day-care centers and has helped blacks develop their own businesses.

Another problem in Cleveland is a lack of good low-cost housing for the poor. During the late 1960's, the city built about 5,000 units of low-rent public housing. A dispute developed in 1970 over plans to build similar housing projects throughout the city. Many middle-class Clevelanders—both blacks and whites—protested against projects planned for their communities. These people charged that the projects would create traffic jams, crowded schools, and other problems. The protests led to debates in the Cleveland City Council and delayed construction of the housing. Less than half of the planned units were built.

Economy

Industry. The Cleveland area's 4,200 factories produce about $30 billion worth of goods yearly. About 45 per cent of the city's workers are employed in manufacturing. The production of transportation equipment is Cleveland's chief industry, and the city ranks high in the manufacture of motor-vehicle parts. Cleveland is also a chief producer of machine tools. Other goods manufactured in the city include clothing, chemicals, electrical equipment, paint, and petroleum products.

Manufacturing has brought prosperity to Cleveland, but the city's many factories have also created problems. During nationwide economic slumps, for example, Cleveland usually has a higher percentage of unemployed workers than do some other major urban centers. In addition, some Cleveland industries pollute the

city's air and water. Industrial wastes dumped into Lake Erie have, at times, made swimming unsafe at some of Cleveland's beaches.

Like many other large industrial cities, Cleveland has experienced a loss of jobs, particularly in the steel and machine tool industries. But much of the loss has been offset by an increasing number of jobs in service industries. The city has become an important health care center. The Cleveland Clinic Foundation is now the city's largest employer. It occupies a large complex of buildings on the city's East Side.

Several new office towers were built in the downtown area in the early 1980's. The 46-story headquarters for the Standard Oil Company was finished in 1985.

Shipping. Cleveland's harbor, one of the busiest on the Great Lakes, handles about 13 million short tons (12 million metric tons) of cargo annually. Between 1940 and 1959, the city spent over $20 million to widen, deepen, and straighten the Cuyahoga River. Today, ore and coal vessels can travel more than 5 miles (8 kilometers) inland to steel mills. The opening of the St. Lawrence Seaway in 1959 made Cleveland an international seaport. Oceangoing ships sail via the seaway from the Atlantic Ocean to the Great Lakes.

Transportation. Cleveland Hopkins International Airport lies in the southwestern section of the city, and Burke Lakefront Airport is near downtown Cleveland. Passenger trains and four freight rail lines serve Cleveland. The Regional Transit Authority provides the chief means of local transportation. Its buses and rapid-transit lines serve the city and many suburbs. In 1968, Cleveland opened a rapid-transit line between the downtown area and Hopkins Airport. It was the first U.S. city to offer downtown-to-airport train service.

Communication. Cleveland has one daily newspaper, the *Plain Dealer.* WHK, Ohio's oldest radio station, began in Cleveland in 1922. The state's first television station, WEWS-TV, opened in Cleveland in 1947.

Education

Cleveland's public school system includes about 130 schools, with a total enrollment of about 73,000. Blacks make up about 70 per cent of this enrollment. About 20,000 students attend parochial and private schools.

Universities and colleges in Cleveland include Case Western Reserve University, the Cleveland Institute of Art, Cleveland State University, John Carroll University, Notre Dame College, and Ursuline College.

The Cleveland Public Library owns more than $2\frac{1}{2}$ million books and operates over 30 branches. During the 1880's, the library became one of the first in the nation to adopt the open-stacks plan. This plan allows the public to select books directly from the shelves.

Cultural life

The arts. The world-famous Cleveland Orchestra performs in Severance Hall. The orchestra gives outdoor summer concerts in the Blossom Music Center near Cuyahoga Falls. The city is also the home of the Cleveland Ballet and two opera companies. The Cleveland Play House, a resident professional theater group, gives plays at three theaters in the same building—the Bolton, Brooks, and Drury. Karamu House opened in 1915 as an experiment in racial understanding through the arts.

Today, its two theaters present integrated casts in dance and drama programs. Renovation of the Playhouse Square Center was completed in 1988. The downtown complex includes three theaters with a combined seating capacity of 7,400.

Museums. The Cleveland Museum of Art owns one of the nation's finest collections of American, Asian, and European paintings and sculpture. The Cleveland Museum of Natural History has exhibits on the development of life on the earth. It also has a planetarium. The Cleveland Health and Education Center, which opened in 1940, was the nation's first permanent health museum. The Western Reserve Historical Society displays items from the settlement of the Western Reserve.

Recreation

Parks. Cleveland's park system covers about 2,600 acres (1,050 hectares) and includes about 40 parks. The largest park, 273-acre (110-hectare) Rockefeller Park, was given to the city by the industrialist John D. Rockefeller, Sr. It includes the Cleveland Cultural Gardens, a series of gardens that represent the city's nationality groups. Brookside Park is the site of the Metroparks Zoo. The Metroparks District, which circles Greater Cleveland, covers about 15,000 acres (6,070 hectares).

Sports. The Cleveland Indians of the American League play baseball in Cleveland Municipal Stadium, which is also the home of the Cleveland Browns of the National Football League. The Cleveland Cavaliers meet their National Basketball Association opponents in Richfield Coliseum in nearby Richfield. The Indians and the Cavaliers planned to move to new home fields in downtown Cleveland in 1994.

Government

Cleveland has a mayor-council form of government. The voters elect the mayor and the 21 members of the City Council—all to four-year terms. Property taxes are Cleveland's largest single source of revenue. Other sources include local bond issues and federal grants.

Like most big cities, Cleveland has difficulty raising enough money to pay for increasingly costly city services. In 1967, the city began to tax the incomes of everyone—including suburbanites—who worked there.

History

Early settlement. The Chippewa, Erie, and Iroquois Indians lived in the Cleveland region before the first white settlers arrived. In 1796, Moses Cleaveland, a surveyor, led a group of Connecticut settlers to the site of what became Cleveland. During the early 1800's, settlers from New England came to the area. Cleveland became the seat of Cuyahoga County in 1810 and was incorporated as a village in 1814.

Industrial growth. The opening of the Erie Canal in 1825 provided a cheap transportation route for manufactured goods traveling to the Northwest and for raw materials going to the East. The canal helped Cleveland become a commercial center. In 1836, the Ohio legislature granted Cleveland a city charter. The city had a population of about 6,000 at that time.

During the last half of the 1800's, Cleveland changed from a commercial to an industrial center. The first railroad came to the city in 1851 and connected it with Columbus, the state capital. In 1852, the first boatload of iron ore from the Lake Superior region entered Cleveland's harbor. Shipments of iron ore from Minnesota and coal from Pennsylvania helped the city become a major producer of locomotives and other iron products. Between 1850 and 1870, Cleveland's population grew from 17,034 to 145,281. The city also became the chief refiner for Pennsylvania oil. In 1870, John D. Rockefeller organized the Standard Oil Company in Cleveland.

During the 1880's and 1890's, the city's rapid industrial growth attracted many settlers from other countries. Most came from Hungary, Lithuania, Poland, or Russia. By 1900, 381,768 people lived in Cleveland.

The 1900's. During Tom L. Johnson's term as mayor, from 1901 to 1909, Cleveland became one of the best-governed U.S. cities. Johnson improved the police department and brought about lower streetcar fares. He also developed a system of taxing owners of commercial property at a higher rate than homeowners.

The development of the automobile industry during the early 1900's greatly aided steel manufacturing in Cleveland. After the United States entered World War I in 1917, the city made airplanes, ships, and tanks for the Allies. The rapid growth of the steel industry after the war helped Cleveland's population hit 900,429 by 1930.

During World War II (1939-1945), the city again produced war materials. Thousands of people from other parts of the United States, including great numbers of blacks from the South, came to Cleveland seeking work in the defense industries. Most of the newcomers remained in the city after the war. By 1950, Cleveland's population had risen to 914,808.

A trend toward suburban living developed during the 1950's, and thousands of white middle-class Clevelanders moved to newly built areas outside the city. Cleveland's population fell to 876,050 by 1960 and continued to drop in the 1960's.

The city faced serious racial problems in the 1960's. In July 1966, 4 people were killed and 50 were injured during a five-day riot in the Hough area. Racial tension decreased in 1967 after voters elected Carl B. Stokes mayor. Stokes, a Democrat, was the first black mayor of a major U.S. city. He served until 1971. Another riot occurred in the Glenville area in July 1968. It resulted in 11 deaths and property damage of about $2 million.

Recent developments. Cleveland's population continued to drop in the late 1900's. It stood at about 751,000 in 1970. By 1980, it had fallen to less than 574,000, and by 1990, to about 500,000.

Cleveland encountered severe financial difficulties during the 1970's. In 1978, Cleveland became the first U.S. city to *default on* (fail to pay when due) its loans since the Great Depression of the 1930's. In 1979, voters approved an increase in the city income tax to help raise funds. Cleveland emerged from default in 1980 after city leaders and eight banks reached an agreement that enabled the city to repay its overdue loans.

In 1985, Cleveland began the North Coast Harbor project, a recreation, education, and tourist area along the lakefront. In 1988, workers completed a harbor and park. By the late 1990's, North Coast Harbor is scheduled to include museums, walking and jogging paths, and a retail and restaurant complex.   John Griffith

See also **Stokes, Carl B.; Western Reserve.**

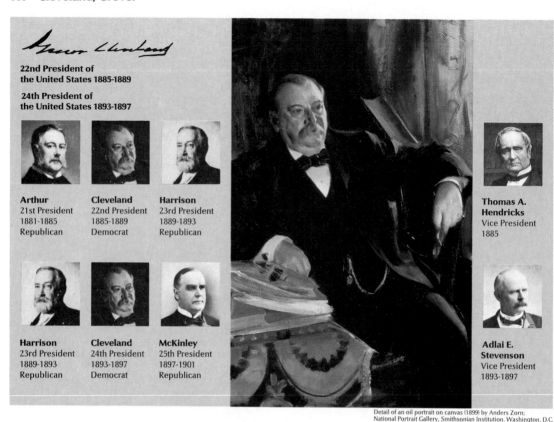

**22nd President of
the United States 1885-1889**

**24th President of
the United States 1893-1897**

Arthur
21st President
1881-1885
Republican

Cleveland
22nd President
1885-1889
Democrat

Harrison
23rd President
1889-1893
Republican

Harrison
23rd President
1889-1893
Republican

Cleveland
24th President
1893-1897
Democrat

McKinley
25th President
1897-1901
Republican

**Thomas A.
Hendricks**
Vice President
1885

**Adlai E.
Stevenson**
Vice President
1893-1897

Detail of an oil portrait on canvas (1899) by Anders Zorn;
National Portrait Gallery, Smithsonian Institution, Washington, D.C.

Cleveland, Grover (1837-1908), was the only President who served two terms that did not directly follow each other. He won the presidency in 1884, but lost it four years later to Benjamin Harrison. He ran against Harrison again in 1892 and won a second term.

Cleveland was the first Democratic President elected after the Civil War. This very fact showed that the emotions of the war had cooled enough to permit the return to a two-party system. Cleveland's victory also was a protest against the waste and corruption that had disgraced Republican administrations after the war. His honesty and common sense helped restore confidence in the government. These qualities had served him in his earlier successes as a lawyer, sheriff, and mayor, and as governor of New York.

As President, Cleveland had the courage to say "No." He said it often—to farmers who sought easy money to pay their debts, to manufacturers who wanted high protective tariffs, and to veterans who wanted bigger pensions. These "No's" made Cleveland unpopular in his time, but have added to the respect with which history holds him.

This big, good-humored man, called "Uncle Jumbo" by his relatives, occupied the White House during a time of swift social and economic change. The growing strength of labor unions and farm organizations created new problems for government. Cleveland lacked the experience and vision to find completely satisfactory answers to all the problems. He attempted to settle labor strikes by force—the legal force of court injunctions and the physical force of army troops. He clung steadfastly

to his faith in "sound" money and a low tariff as a cure for the nation's other economic ills. Although Cleveland's intentions were good, his methods fell short of success.

The era of the western frontier was drawing to a close when Cleveland took office. Settlers in the Southwest breathed easier when federal troops captured Geronimo, the fierce Apache leader. Jacob Riis shocked a complacent public with newspaper stories of how "the other half" lived in run-down slums.

During Cleveland's second term, the Duryea brothers built America's first automobile. A Kansas preacher, Charles Sheldon, wrote *In His Steps,* one of the world's all-time best sellers. Americans of the Gay Nineties enjoyed Victor Herbert's early operettas. At the World's Columbian Exposition in Chicago, they applauded John Philip Sousa's band and rode the first and largest Ferris wheel ever built.

Early life

Boyhood. Stephen Grover Cleveland was born on March 18, 1837, in Caldwell, N.J. He dropped his first name while still a boy. Grover was the fifth child in a family of four brothers and five sisters. His father, Richard Falley Cleveland, was a Presbyterian minister and a relative of Moses Cleaveland, the founder of Cleveland, Ohio. His mother, Ann Neal Cleveland, was the daughter of a publisher.

The family of a country minister led a hard life. The Clevelands had little money and moved several times. Grover attended schools in Fayetteville and Clinton, N.Y.,

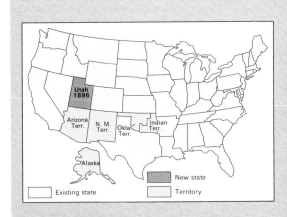

There were **38 states** throughout Cleveland's first term. During his second term, Utah joined the Union in 1896, bringing the number of states to 45.

The United States flag had 38 stars when Cleveland took office in 1885. The flag had 44 stars when Cleveland began his second term in 1893. One star was added to the flag, *left,* in 1896.

The world of President Cleveland

The last spike of the Canadian Pacific Railway (now CP Rail) was driven at Craigellachie, B.C., in 1885. This railroad was the first to cross Canada.

The American Federation of Labor was founded in 1886.

The Statue of Liberty, a gift from France to the United States, was dedicated by President Cleveland in 1886.

Queen Victoria of Great Britain celebrated the golden jubilee of her reign in 1887.

The Interstate Commerce Act, approved by Congress in 1887, became the first federal law to regulate railroads and other forms of transportation in the United States.

The United States Department of Agriculture became a Cabinet-level agency in 1889.

Women's voting rights were granted by New Zealand in 1893. New Zealand was the first nation to give female citizens the complete right to vote.

The Pullman strike, a violent labor dispute in Chicago in 1894, was ended by government troops sent by President Cleveland.

X rays were discovered in 1895 by Wilhelm K. Roentgen, a German physicist.

A practical wireless telegraph system was produced in 1895 by Guglielmo Marconi, an Italian inventor.

The Red Badge of Courage, Stephen Crane's classic novel about the Civil War, was published in 1895.

Sir Wilfrid Laurier in 1896 became the first French-Canadian prime minister of Canada.

Henry Ford's first automobile appeared in Detroit in 1896. Three years earlier, the Duryea brothers had built the nation's first successful gasoline-powered car.

WORLD BOOK map

and went to work at the age of 14 as a clerk in a Fayetteville general store. He was only 16 when his father died, leaving him and his brothers to support his mother and sisters. Cleveland joined an older brother who was teaching at the New York Institution for the Blind in New York City. He taught there for a year.

Lawyer. When Cleveland was 17, he decided to go west to look for better opportunities. He planned to settle in Cleveland, Ohio, which attracted him because of its name. But he stopped in Buffalo, N.Y., to visit his mother's uncle, Lewis F. Allen, who persuaded him to stay there. Grover worked for his uncle for six months, then decided to become a lawyer. He worked as a clerk in the law office of Rogers, Bowen, and Rogers, and studied there. The serious, quiet youth worked hard for his $4 a week, which paid for room and board at the home of a fellow law clerk.

After being admitted to the bar in 1859, Cleveland continued to work for the same law firm. Two of his brothers served in the Union Army during the Civil War, but Cleveland's help was needed to support his mother

and the other children. He paid a substitute to take his place in the army. Although this was legal and a common practice, the fact that he had not served in the war was later used against him by his political enemies.

Political career

Minor offices. Cleveland entered politics as a ward worker for the Democratic Party in Buffalo. He served as ward supervisor in 1862 and later as assistant district attorney of Erie County. He was elected sheriff in 1870.

Important dates in Cleveland's life

1837	(March 18) Born in Caldwell, N.J.
1881	Elected mayor of Buffalo, N.Y.
1882	Elected governor of New York.
1884	Elected President of the United States.
1886	(June 2) Married Frances Folsom.
1888	Defeated for reelection by Benjamin Harrison.
1892	Elected to second term as President.
1908	(June 24) Died in Princeton, N.J.

Gene Collerd

Cleveland's birthplace was the parsonage of the First Presbyterian Church of Caldwell, N.J., where his father was minister.

During his term, the county had to hang two convicted murderers. Most sheriffs had delegated this distasteful task to deputies, but Cleveland sprang the traps himself. He explained that he would not ask anyone else to do what he was unwilling to do.

Cleveland returned to the practice of law after three years as sheriff. He relaxed by hunting and fishing with fellow lawyers. To relatives who wondered whether their stout "Uncle Jumbo" had ever thought of marrying, he replied: "A good many times; and the more I think of it the more I think I'll not do it."

Mayor of Buffalo. Like many cities, Buffalo suffered from a corrupt administration. In response to a growing demand for reform, Democratic leaders chose Cleveland to run for mayor in 1881. He won the election, and gave his political backers more reform than they had bargained for. Cleveland vetoed so many padded city contracts that he became known as the "veto mayor."

Governor of New York. Cleveland's reputation for honest administration became a valuable political asset. The Democrats nominated him for governor in 1882 as a candidate not owned by any political faction. He won easily.

Cleveland gave New York the same conscientious administration he had given Buffalo. He vetoed padded appropriation bills regardless of political pressure. He aroused a storm of protest when he killed a bill that would have lowered streetcar fares in New York City. Cleveland explained that the bill violated the terms of a previous transit contract. Theodore Roosevelt, then a member of the state legislature, had advocated the bill, but later admitted that Cleveland had been right. When Cleveland later cooperated with Roosevelt to pass laws reforming the government of New York City, he earned the undying hatred of Tammany Hall, the Democratic political machine that controlled the city.

Election of 1884. Cleveland's reputation for good government made him a national figure. The Republican Party nominated James G. Blaine for President in 1884, even though he had been implicated in a financial scandal (see **Blaine, James G.**). Many influential Republicans were outraged. They thought the time had come for a national reform administration. These Republicans, called *mugwumps,* withdrew from the convention and declared that they would vote for the Democratic candidate if he were an honest man (see **Mugwumps**). The Democrats answered by nominating Cleveland. They chose Governor Thomas A. Hendricks of Indiana for Vice President.

Good political issues were available to both parties in the campaign. Farmers were growing poorer, private interests were grabbing public lands and resources, and labor was becoming more dissatisfied. But neither party faced these issues. Instead, each attacked the other's nominee with scandalous personal stories.

The basic unrest of the people, their lack of faith in the honesty of previous administrations, and a series of campaign blunders by Blaine turned the tide. One of the most costly mistakes was made by a supporter of Blaine at a Republican rally in New York City. Samuel D. Burchard, a Presbyterian clergyman, declared that a vote for Cleveland would be a vote for "rum, Romanism, and rebellion." This remark appealed to popular prejudices that linked the Democrats with whiskey, Roman Cathol-

icism, and the Southern cause in the Civil War. Roman Catholics deeply resented the statement. Blaine later repudiated it, but the damage had been done. Cleveland, by 25,685 votes, became the first Democratic President to be elected since James Buchanan in 1856.

First Administration (1885-1889)

Cleveland, who faced a Republican Senate, made effective use of the presidential powers of veto, appointment, and administrative control. With these weapons, rather than with any strong legislative program, he moved to restore government efficiency.

Reforms. Cleveland ordered the members of his Cabinet to eliminate "abuses and extravagances" in their departments. As a result, the Department of the Navy tightened its supervision of shipbuilding and added several new vessels to the fleet, including the battleship *Maine.*

The Department of the Interior forced western railroads to return to the public domain vast acreages of excess right-of-way land that the railroads had held illegally. This land was forfeited because the railroads had failed to carry out their earlier agreements to extend their lines. The forfeited land equaled the combined areas of New York, New Jersey, Pennsylvania, Delaware, Maryland, and Virginia.

The spoils system had continued to flourish in spite of the Civil Service Act of 1883 (see **Spoils system**). Cleveland, like other Presidents of his era, was besieged by office seekers. He tried to steer a middle course between the reformers, who wanted him to extend civil service, and party politicians, who were hungry for jobs. He more than doubled the number of workers who held jobs through the merit system, although the total still included fewer than a fourth of all government employees. But his moderation satisfied neither the reformers nor the politicians.

Labor problems were among Cleveland's gravest concerns. Farmers had heavy debts, and the Grange and Farmers' Alliances demanded reforms. Laborers suffered from low wages and harsh working conditions. Employers in those days felt little sense of responsibility for their employees. The Knights of Labor, a labor group, grew to 700,000 members by 1886. This labor group's strike at the McCormick-Harvester plant in Chicago led indirectly to the bloody Haymarket Riot (see **Haymarket Riot**).

Cleveland distrusted workers' movements, but he acted for the best interests of the nation as he saw them. He was the first President to devote an entire congressional message to the subject of labor, although nothing came of his proposal for a permanent government arbitration board.

Cleveland's first election

Place of nominating convention	Chicago
Ballot on which nominated	2nd
Republican opponent	James G. Blaine
Electoral vote*	219 (Cleveland) to 182 (Blaine)
Popular vote	4,874,621 (Cleveland) to 4,848,936 (Blaine)
Age at inauguration	47

*For votes by states, see **Electoral College** (table).

Vice President and Cabinet

Vice President	*Thomas A. Hendricks
Secretary of state	Thomas F. Bayard
Secretary of the treasury	Daniel Manning
	Charles S. Fairchild (1887)
Secretary of war	William C. Endicott
Attorney general	Augustus H. Garland
Postmaster general	William F. Vilas
	Don M. Dickinson (1888)
Secretary of the navy	William C. Whitney
Secretary of the interior	*Lucius Q. C. Lamar
	William F. Vilas (1888)
Secretary of agriculture	Norman J. Colman (office
	established in 1889)

*Has a separate biography in World Book.

Veterans' affairs. Cleveland opposed many pension measures, defying the Grand Army of the Republic and other powerful pressure groups. The pension rolls had become full of fraud. Many healthy veterans claimed to be unfit for work, and widows continued to collect government money after they had remarried. Cleveland vetoed hundreds of dishonest claims. He also vetoed the Dependent Pension Bill, which would have extended pension coverage to all disabled veterans, whether or not their disabilities were connected with military service. This bill was later passed in 1890.

The currency and the tariff were the most important issues facing Cleveland during his first term. Dissension was growing between the bankers and industrialists of the East, and the farmers of the South and West. The industrialists wanted a high tariff to protect high prices. They also wanted what they called a "sound" money system, based on gold. Farmers wanted a low tariff so they would not have to pay high prices for imported manufactured goods. They had heavy debts, and wanted money to be "cheap" in comparison with goods. That is, the farmers wanted *inflation,* so they could pay their debts with less farm produce.

The currency of the United States at this time was based on gold. But the Bland-Allison Act of 1878 required the Treasury to buy and coin at least $2 million worth of silver a month. The coins were minted on a standard that made 16 ounces of silver equal in value to 1 ounce of gold. Meanwhile, new silver mines had been discovered, and the world price of silver fell. Since the actual value of a silver dollar was less than that of a gold dollar, people exchanged their silver dollars for gold dollars. As a result, gold was drained from the Treasury.

Cleveland believed in a gold standard (see **Gold standard**). He asked Congress to repeal the Bland-Allison Act, but it refused. The government then issued bonds and sold them to banks for gold. But this helped matters for only a short time, because the drain on the Treasury's gold continued.

The tariff. Cleveland felt that tariffs should be reduced, mainly because the government was collecting more money than it spent. His supporters advised him not to bring up this controversial subject. But, in his annual message in 1887, he dared to ask Congress to lower tariffs. Congress refused, but Cleveland focused national opinion on this problem.

Other actions. The Presidential Succession Act of 1886 settled questions regarding succession to the presidency (see **Presidential succession**). One of the most important bills of Cleveland's first term was the Interstate Commerce Act of 1887. This act allowed the federal government to regulate interstate railroads.

Cleveland's family. In June 1886, Cleveland delighted the nation with his marriage to Frances Folsom (July 21, 1864-Oct. 29, 1947). The 21-year-old bride had been Cleveland's ward since her father died in 1875. He had been one of Cleveland's law partners. Cleveland was the only President to be married in the White House, and reporters pried into every detail with what he called "colossal impertinence."

The Clevelands had five children: Ruth (1891-1904), Esther (1893-1980), Marion (1895-1977), Richard F. (1897-1974), and Francis (1903-   ). Esther Cleveland was the first and only child of a President to be born in the White House.

Five years after Cleveland's death, Mrs. Cleveland married Thomas J. Preston, Jr., a Princeton professor.

Life in the White House. During Cleveland's first year in office, his younger sister Rose acted as his hostess. After his marriage, his young wife performed these official duties with ease and charm.

Cleveland was a hard-working President, particularly because he was unwilling to delegate responsibility. "He would rather do something badly for himself than have somebody else do it well," grumbled a political colleague. The President often stayed up until 2 or 3 A.M. going over official business, and sometimes answered the White House telephone himself.

As the Clevelands left the White House in 1889, Mrs. Cleveland told the servants: "I want you to take good care of all the furniture and ornaments in the house, for I want to find everything just as it is now when we come back again . . . four years from today."

Election of 1888. The tariff became the main issue in the election of 1888. Benjamin Harrison, the Republican candidate, opposed tariff reduction. Neither Cleveland nor the Democratic Party waged a strong campaign.

Harper's Weekly, The Newberry Library, Chicago

The youngest First Lady in the nation's history was Frances Folsom Cleveland. She was 21 years old and the President was 49 when they were married in 1886 in the White House.

Cleveland's attitude toward the spoils system had antagonized party politicians. His policies on pensions, the currency, and tariff reform had made enemies among veterans, farmers, and industrialists. Even with these enemies, Cleveland had more popular votes than Harrison. However, Harrison received a larger electoral vote and won the election. See **Harrison, Benjamin** (Election of 1888).

Between terms

New York attorney. Cleveland moved to New York City in 1889 and returned to the practice of law. The Harrison Administration reversed many of Cleveland's stringent policies. It boosted the tariff, increased the purchase of silver, and extended pension coverage. Both prices and government expenditures reached new heights. Cleveland, on the sidelines, sharply criticized Harrison's program.

Election of 1892. By the end of Harrison's term, many Americans were ready to return to Cleveland's harder policies. In 1892, the Democratic National Convention nominated Cleveland and chose Adlai E. Stevenson, a former Illinois congressman, as his running mate. The Republicans renominated Harrison and nominated Whitelaw Reid for Vice President.

The campaign centered mainly on the issue of a sound currency. The new Populist Party, formed by groups from the Grange, the Farmers' Alliances, and the Knights of Labor, polled more than a million votes. But Cleveland won easily.

Second Administration (1893-1897)

Cleveland enjoyed greater popularity at the beginning of his second term than at any other time during his presidency. He had made no promises to anyone in order to become President again. He was free to handle the country's problems as he saw fit, with Democratic majorities in both houses of Congress. But a severe financial panic swept the country only two months after he took office. Its causes included a farm depression, a business slump abroad, and the drain on the Treasury's gold reserve.

At this crucial time, physicians found that Cleveland had cancer of the mouth. Government leaders feared that the nation's shaky financial situation would become worse if the public knew of the President's illness. To keep it a secret, Cleveland boarded a friend's yacht in New York Harbor in July, and a team of surgeons removed his left upper jaw while the ship steamed up the East River. The operation was completely successful. Cleveland wore an artificial jaw made of rubber, which changed his appearance only slightly. News of the operation gradually became public, although great efforts were made to keep it secret.

Cleveland's second election

Place of nominating convention	Chicago
Ballot on which nominated	1st
Republican opponent	Benjamin Harrison
Electoral vote*	277 (Cleveland) to 145 (Harrison)
Popular vote	5,551,883 (Cleveland) to 5,179,244 (Harrison)
Age at inauguration	55

*For votes by states, see **Electoral College** (table).

Vice President and Cabinet

Vice President	*Adlai E. Stevenson
Secretary of state	Walter Q. Gresham
	Richard Olney (1895)
Secretary of the treasury	John G. Carlisle
Secretary of war	Daniel S. Lamont
Attorney general	Richard Olney
	Judson Harmon (1895)
Postmaster general	Wilson S. Bissell
	William L. Wilson (1895)
Secretary of the Navy	Hilary A. Herbert
Secretary of the interior	Hoke Smith
	David R. Francis (1896)
Secretary of agriculture	*Julius Sterling Morton

*Has a separate biography in *World Book*.

Labor unrest grew more serious with the business slump. Cleveland was not hostile to labor. But his strong belief in order and his limited understanding of changing conditions led him to use force rather than to seek constructive solutions to the new problems that faced his Administration.

One sign of discontent was "Coxey's Army," a group of unemployed men who demonstrated for government aid (see **Coxey, Jacob S.**). The Pullman strike of May, 1894, had far greater importance. Workers of the Pullman Company went on strike, and members of the American Railway Union, led by Eugene V. Debs, supported them by refusing to handle Pullman cars (see **Debs, Eugene V.**). A general railroad strike resulted. A federal court issued an injunction against the strikers because mail service had been interrupted. Disorders broke out near Chicago, and Cleveland sent federal

Library of Congress

"Coxey's Army," a group of unemployed men led by Jacob S. Coxey, marched into Washington, D.C., in 1894 during a depression. They demanded that the government create jobs.

troops, saying: "If it takes the entire army and navy of the United States to deliver a postal card in Chicago, that card will be delivered." The government broke the strike. Most people approved Cleveland's action. But Governor John P. Altgeld of Illinois, who had state militia standing ready to take action, argued that the disorders were not serious enough to warrant federal troops. Some historians believe that Cleveland exceeded his constitutional powers and violated states' rights. See **Pullman strike.**

Tariff defeat. Cleveland resumed his campaign for tariff reform, and again asked Congress to lower import duties. While the Wilson-Gorman Bill was being debated, the President issued a statement accusing uncooperative Democrats of "party perfidy and party dishonor." His comments outraged many party members, and the bill as passed in 1894 fell far short of Cleveland's goal. He let it become law without his signature because it also provided for a federal income tax. The Supreme Court later declared the income tax provision unconstitutional.

Foreign affairs. Many Americans in the 1890's felt that the United States should build a colonial empire. Cleveland wanted the United States to respect the rights of smaller, weaker nations. Events in Hawaii and Venezuela tested his principles.

Hawaii. At the end of Benjamin Harrison's Administration, American settlers in Hawaii had brought about a revolution and asked the United States to annex the islands. Cleveland's second term began before the Senate could ratify the treaty of annexation. Cleveland felt that Americans in Hawaii had involved the United States in a dishonorable action, and he withdrew the treaty from the Senate. The islands continued independent until 1898.

Venezuela. Cleveland's most popular action during his second term was his firm stand in a boundary dispute between Great Britain and Venezuela. Britain had refused for several years to allow its claim to be decided by a board of arbitration. In 1895, Secretary of State Richard Olney sent a sharp note to Britain declaring that "the United States is practically sovereign on this continent, and its fiat is law upon the subjects to which it confines its interposition." In a message to Congress, Cleveland hinted that armed force might be necessary to settle the matter. England agreed to submit the Venezuela boundary to international arbitration, and a settlement was reached in 1899. But historians have criticized Cleveland's intervention as extreme and provocative.

Saving the gold standard. A severe financial panic in 1893 caused 15,000 business failures and threw 4 million people out of work. Cleveland felt that a basic cause of the panic was the Sherman Silver Purchase Act of Harrison's Administration. In June 1893, he called a special session of Congress to repeal the act. Congress did so, but the nation's gold reserves had dwindled alarmingly. The government floated four bond issues in the next three years to replenish the gold reserves. J. P. Morgan and other financiers bought three of these bond issues, and Cleveland's opponents charged that Cleveland had betrayed the nation to Eastern bankers.

Meanwhile, the silver interests grew stronger. By the time of the Democratic convention in 1896, the "silverites" outnumbered the "goldbugs." To the dismay of

Cleveland, who did not seek a third term, William Jennings Bryan won the Democratic presidential nomination. Bryan's famous "cross of gold" speech swung the party to the silver cause (see **Bryan, William Jennings**). Cleveland preferred the sound money policies of William McKinley, the Republican candidate, but he took no part in the campaign. Cleveland's popularity had reached a low ebb at the end of his term, and he spoke of his "poor old battered name" when he left the White House in 1897.

Later years

Cleveland spent his last years in Princeton, N.J. Public opinion about him gradually changed, and he regained respect. Cleveland served Princeton University as lecturer and as trustee, and enjoyed the company of Woodrow Wilson, president of the university. He wrote several magazine articles, and in 1904 published some of his lectures under the title *Presidential Problems.* He also helped reorganize the Equitable Life Assurance Society after financial scandals had damaged its reputation. People believed so strongly in him that his name restored their confidence.

After a three-month illness, Cleveland died on June 24, 1908. His last words were: "I have tried so hard to do right." Cleveland was buried in Princeton.

Oscar Handlin

Related articles in *World Book* include:

Harrison, Benjamin
Haymarket Riot
Hendricks, Thomas A.

President of the United States
Stevenson, Adlai E. (1835-1914)

Outline

I. Early life
  A. Boyhood   B. Lawyer
II. Political career
  A. Minor offices
  B. Mayor of Buffalo
  C. Governor of New York
  D. Election of 1884
III. First Administration (1885-1889)
  A. Reforms
  B. Labor problems
  C. Veterans' affairs
  D. The currency and the tariff
  E. Other actions
  F. Cleveland's family
  G. Life in the White House
  H. Election of 1888
IV. Between terms
  A. New York attorney   B. Election of 1892
V. Second Administration (1893-1897)
  A. Labor unrest
  B. Tariff defeat
  C. Foreign affairs
  D. Saving the gold standard
VI. Later years

Questions

How was Cleveland's marriage unique?

Why did Cleveland pay a substitute to serve for him in the Civil War?

Why did Cleveland execute two criminals himself?

How many Presidents have been defeated for reelection and later won a second term?

Who were the *mugwumps*? How did they affect Cleveland's nomination in 1884?

Historians have criticized two actions of Cleveland's second term which were popular at the time. Why?

What actions made Cleveland an unpopular President?

Where was Cleveland's jaw operation performed? Why was it kept secret?

How did Cleveland feel about labor agitation? What did he do about it during his first term?

What words, spoken as he died, summed up his life?

Additional resources

Collins, David R. *Grover Cleveland: 22nd and 24th President of the United States.* Garrett Educational, 1988. Suitable for younger readers.

Kent, Zachary. *Grover Cleveland: Twenty-Second and Twenty-Fourth President of the United States.* Childrens Pr., 1988. For younger readers.

Nevins, Allan. *Grover Cleveland: A Study in Courage.* Dodd, 1932. Pulitzer Prize winner.

Welch, Richard E., Jr. *The Presidencies of Grover Cleveland.* Univ. Pr. of Kansas, 1988.

Cliburn, Van (1934-), is an American concert pianist. He performs works written primarily by romantic composers of the 1800's and 1900's. These composers include Johannes Brahms, Frédéric Chopin, Franz Liszt, Sergei Rachmaninoff, Robert Schumann, and Peter Ilich Tchaikovsky.

Cliburn was born in Shreveport, La. His full name is Harvey Lavan Cliburn, Jr. His mother began teaching him to play the piano when he was 3 years old. Cliburn studied piano at the Juilliard School in New York City. He made his concert debut in Houston in 1947 but did not begin an active concert career until 1954. Cliburn first gained worldwide fame in 1958, when he won the International Tchaikovsky Piano Competition in Moscow. In 1978, he stopped giving concerts. But he resumed performing in public in 1989.   F. E. Kirby

Click beetle is the name used for any one of a group of beetles that spring and snap. There are about 700 kinds of click beetles in the United States and Canada. Most of them have long brown bodies. But some are black, gray, or marked with bright colors.

The young of the click beetle are long, slender worms called *wireworms.* They bore into seeds of young corn, wheat, and other grains. They also feed on the roots of field and garden plants or live in decaying wood.

Some click beetles found in tropical regions and the Southern United States can glow in the dark. One kind has two glowing spots on each side of its body. See **Beetle** (Kinds of beetles).

Scientific classification. Click beetles are members of the order *Coleoptera.* They make up the click beetle family, *Elateridae.*   David J. Shetlar

See also **Wireworm** (with picture).

Cliff is a steep face of rock. Many processes of erosion form cliffs. Waves cut imposing and scenic cliffs along coastlines. Rivers create deep canyons with steep sides. Glaciers grind away the rock along valley walls and produce cliffs that appear after the glacier melts. Glaciers also pluck rock fragments away from high mountain slopes where snow collects to form walls around amphitheaterlike basins.   H. J. McPherson

Cliff dwellers were Indians who built their homes in canyon walls and under rock overhangs in what is now the Southwestern United States. Most cliff dwellings were built between A.D. 1000 and 1300. The most famous ones were developed by Indians called *Anasazi.* These Indians were the ancestors of the modern-day Pueblo Indians (see **Pueblo Indians**). The term *cliff dwellers* describes the dwelling practices of various

early Indian peoples, not one cultural group. Many cliff dwellers abandoned their homes about 1300, perhaps because of hostile Indian invaders, climate changes, loss of food supply, or severe drought.

Ruins of cliff dwellings lie in northern Arizona, northern New Mexico, southern Utah, and southern Colorado. Archaeologists have found bows and arrows, garments, sandals, wooden implements, and even mummies of the cliff dwellers in the ruins.

Way of life. The cliff dwellers farmed on the plains at the foot of their cliff homes or on the flat-topped hills, called *mesas,* above their dwellings. They grew beans, corn, cotton, squash, and tobacco and raised turkeys. They hunted deer and mountain sheep with arrows that had points of flaked stone. The people ate from pottery dishes and bowls that they painted with red or black designs. In summer, both men and women wore skirts woven from cotton, milkweed, and yucca fibers. In winter, the cliff dwellers wore fur robes and blankets made of cords wrapped with turkey feathers or rabbit skin.

Some cliff dwellers lived in caves that could provide shelter for several family groups, especially along river canyons. But most lived in two- or three-story cliff houses. The people built their homes on protected ledges or in spaces in cliff walls, using sandstone blocks and mud mortar. They built the small rooms one upon another and placed each story back a short distance from the edge of the one below. As many as 1,500 people could live in some of these dwellings.

The cliff homes had few doors on the ground level. The people used ladders to reach the first roof. In case of attack, they drew up the ladders. Other ladders, steps, or winding paths were cut into the stone. They led from the caves and homes up to the tops of the mesas and down to the valleys.

Most of the cliff dwellers' villages had underground chambers called *kivas,* which the people entered through a hatchway in the roof. Men held councils in the kivas and also used them for secret religious ceremonies. The people plastered the walls and painted many with symbolic paintings in red, white, green, and yellow. Eastern cliff dwellers had round kivas. Cliff dwellers in the South and West built rectangular ones.

History. The Anasazi gradually developed multilevel homes, called *pueblos.* These homes were made of stone, adobe, or timber. In the A.D. 900's, the Anasazi began to build their homes on the floors of canyons. About 1000, they began to live in caves and on mesa tops. During the next 300 years, the Anasazi culture reached its highest point. About 1200, some occupants of the mesas started building pueblo dwellings on the sheer sides of canyons. Some of the most spectacular of these cliff dwellings can still be seen at Mesa Verde National Park in southwestern Colorado (see **Mesa Verde National Park**).

Cliff dwellers in what are now northern New Mexico and southern Colorado completely abandoned their cliff cities by 1300 and moved to other pueblo villages to the south and east. Scholars do not know for sure why the cliff-dwelling Anasazi left their homes. Some of the cliff dwellings in southern New Mexico were occupied as late as 1450.   Alfonso Ortiz

See the *Places to visit* section of the **Arizona, Colorado, New Mexico,** and **Utah** articles for the national

Cliff Palace is the largest cliff dwelling in Mesa Verde National Park in southwestern Colorado. About 400 people lived there at one time. Some sections of the structure are four stories high.

James P. Rowan

monuments that include ruins of cliff dwellings.

Additional resources

Cordell, Linda S. *Prehistory of the Southwest.* Academic Pr., 1984.
Ferguson, William M., and Rohn, A. H. *Anasazi Ruins of the Southwest in Color.* Univ. of New Mexico Pr., 1986.
Matlock, Gary. *Enemy Ancestors: The Anasazi World, With a Guide to Sites.* Northland Pr., 1988.
Muench, David. *Anasazi: Ancient People of the Rock.* Crown, 1986. First published in 1974.

Clifford, Clark McAdams (1906-   ), served as United States secretary of defense under President Lyndon B. Johnson from March 1968 to January 1969. In that short time, Clifford became the leader of a group of officials who persuaded Johnson to de-escalate the Vietnam War. Clifford argued that the burden of fighting in the war should be transferred from United States troops to South Vietnamese forces as quickly as possible.

Clifford was born in Fort Scott, Kans. He received a law degree from Washington University in St. Louis in 1928, and practiced law in St. Louis until he entered the Navy in 1944. Clifford began his public career in 1946 as special counsel and speechwriter to President Harry S. Truman. Clifford has also practiced law in Washington, D.C.

In 1992, U.S. and New York state officials filed legal charges against Clifford. Federal officials charged that he, as chairman of First American Bankshares, Inc.—a Washington, D.C., bank—had helped hide the fact that the bank was illegally owned by another bank, Bank of Credit and Commerce International SA, also known as B.C.C.I. A huge international bank, B.C.C.I. had been closed in 1991 by banking regulators worldwide and charged with fraud, money laundering, and bribery. New York officials charged that Clifford had accepted bribes in return for helping B.C.C.I. officials influence First American Bankshares, Inc. Clifford declared he was innocent of the charges.   Charles Bartlett

Climate is the sum of all weather events in an area during a long period of time. *Climatologists* (scientists who study climate) often describe the climate in terms of an area's average monthly and yearly (1) temperatures and (2) amounts of *precipitation.* Precipitation consists of rain, snow, hail, and other forms of moisture that fall to earth. Climatologists also describe the year-to-year changes that produce major wet and dry spells.

Climate and weather are not the same. Weather is the condition of the atmosphere during a brief period. One day's weather may be stormy, wet, and cool. The next day's may be sunny, dry, and somewhat warmer. To determine the climate of an area, scientists study the daily weather conditions over many years.

Every place on the earth, no matter how small, has its own climate. Places that lie far apart may have a similar climate. Yet there may be important differences between the climate of a hill and a nearby valley, or of a city and the surrounding countryside.

The importance of climate

Climate affects the way of life of people no matter where they live. For example, it influences the kinds of clothing people wear and the kinds of foods they grow and eat. It also influences the types of homes they live in and the types of transportation they use. In addition, climate helps determine the kinds of plants and animals that can live in an area.

Clothing and climate. People wear clothing that protects them against the climate of their area. In warm regions, people wear clothes made of a lightweight material, such as cotton or linen. Much of the clothing in warm regions is white or light-colored because these colors reflect the sun's rays. In cold regions, people wear heavy clothing made of such materials as fur or wool. People of the Arabian deserts wear loose, flowing robes that protect them from both the hot days and the cold nights of the desert. In regions that have cold winters and warm summers, people wear heavy clothing in the winter and light clothing in summer.

Food and climate. Most food crops grow best in areas that have a certain climate. A mild, fairly dry climate is best for growing wheat. Rice thrives in a warm, rainy climate. Many orchards are planted on a hillside, rather than in a nearby valley. Frost, which may damage fruit, occurs more often in valleys than on hillsides.

Housing and climate. Homes provide protection against the climate. People who live in an area with a hot season and a cold season build sturdy, well-insulated housing that keeps out both heat and cold. In hot, dry regions, people build houses with extra-thick walls that keep out the heat. In rainy places, houses may have a steep, pointed roof so that rain can run off easily.

Transportation and climate. In many places, the climate helps determine the kind of transportation that people use. For example, the people who live near the equator in west-central Africa travel largely by boat along the rivers. This area has a hot, wet climate, and so plants and trees grow quickly. The heavy rains and thick forests hamper the construction and maintenance of roads and railroads. People who live in cold, snowy areas often use skis, sleds, or snowmobiles for transportation.

Animal life and climate. Certain animals have adapted to life in certain climates. For example, camels live in the hot, dry deserts of Africa and Asia. These animals can go without water for days or even months. Crocodiles are found in rivers, swamps, and marshes in hot regions, including parts of Central America. Polar bears live in the Arctic, and penguins live in Antarctica. Both the Arctic and Antarctica have an extremely cold climate.

Plant life and climate. Plant life also varies with climate. Cactuses grow chiefly in areas that are hot and dry. These plants differ greatly from the evergreens that are found in cold northern regions. The beech and maple forests that thrive in the climate of New England differ from the grasslands of the Midwestern United States. Tall trees grow in the warm, rainy climate of many regions near the equator. But only mosses and other small plants can live in the extremely cold areas near the North and South poles.

Describing and classifying climates

The scientific study of climate is called *climatology*. In describing the climate of a certain place, a climatologist considers a number of characteristics of the atmosphere. The most important of these characteristics are temperature, precipitation, humidity, sunshine and cloudiness, wind, and air pressure.

Climatologists begin by describing the climate in terms of average temperature and precipitation amounts. They also consider the variations that occur between the different seasons of the year. For example, the average yearly temperature in both St. Louis and San Francisco is about 55° F. (13° C). Yet these two cities have different climates. St. Louis has fairly cold winters and hot summers, with precipitation the year around. San Francisco, on the other hand, has mild, rainy winters, and cool, almost rainless, summers.

Climatologists have developed various systems of climatic classification. However, many of these experts recognize 12 major kinds of climate: (1) tropical wet, (2) tropical wet and dry, (3) highlands, (4) desert, (5) steppe, (6) subtropical dry summer, (7) subtropical moist, (8) oceanic moist, (9) continental moist, (10) subarctic, (11) polar, and (12) icecap. The world map with this article shows the locations of these climates. But the map does not indicate the differences within each major kind of climate. For example, New England and part of the Midwestern United States have the same general kind of climate—continental moist. That is, these areas generally have warm to cool summers and cold winters, with moderate precipitation in all seasons. However, there are a num-

How climate affects ways of life

Jeffrey Foxx, Woodfin Camp, Inc.

Cool autumns are part of New England's *continental moist* climate. A tightly built house keeps out the cool air. Many people frequently wear a lightweight coat for warmth outdoors.

Joe Rychetnik, Van Cleve Photography

Long, cold winters are common in areas of Alaska with a *polar* climate. Sturdy wooden homes provide protection from the cold, and people wear clothing of such materials as fur or wool.

ber of differences between the climate of New England and that of the Midwest.

Why climates differ

In addition to describing and classifying climates, climatologists try to learn why the climate of one place is different from that of another. They have determined that climates differ for a number of reasons, including (1) differences in latitude, (2) differences in the availability of moisture, (3) differences in land and water temperatures, and (4) differences in the land surface.

Differences in latitude affect climate in a number of ways. Most importantly, places at different distances from the equator get different amounts of energy from the sun. This energy difference occurs because the position of the sun in the sky varies with latitude. In *tropical* areas close to the equator—that is, areas between the Tropic of Cancer and the Tropic of Capricorn—the sun shines almost directly overhead throughout the entire year. These direct rays are an intense source of energy, and so they produce high temperatures. Most regions near the equator have a hot or warm climate. See **Tropic of Cancer; Tropic of Capricorn.**

The sun never rises far above the horizon in areas near the North and South poles—north of the Arctic Circle and south of the Antarctic Circle on the map. Because the sun is low in the sky, its rays are slanted. Slanted rays shine less intensely than direct rays do, and so they produce lower temperatures. Therefore, the regions near the poles generally have a cold climate. See **Antarctic Circle; Arctic Circle.**

Locations in the *middle latitudes* tend to have temperatures that average between those of equatorial and polar areas. The middle latitudes lie between the Arctic Circle and the Tropic of Cancer in the Northern Hemisphere, and between the Antarctic Circle and the Tropic of Capricorn in the Southern Hemisphere. Middle latitude locations receive more direct, higher intensity sunlight in the summer and less direct, lower intensity sunlight in the winter. Longer periods of sunlight during summer days and shorter periods during winter days increase the effects of these seasonal differences on temperatures. Thus, summers are warm, and winters are cold.

Places at different distances from the equator are also affected by different wind systems. Winds result from the uneven heating of the air around the earth. Air heated by the sun expands and rises, and cooler air flows to take its place, producing belts of prevailing winds. Prevailing winds in tropical areas blow from east to west. Winds in the middle latitudes tend to blow from west to east, but these winds and the winds near the poles are highly variable in direction. Because winds transport heat and moisture, they affect an area's temperature, humidity, precipitation, and cloudiness. As a result, areas with different prevailing wind directions may have different climates. See **Wind** (General circulation).

Differences in the availability of moisture also affect climate. The air absorbs the greatest amount of moisture from warm parts of the ocean near the equator. Wind systems carry this moisture to the land where it may fall to the ground as precipitation. As a result, most of the wettest places in the world are near the equator or in locations where the prevailing winds blow inland from the ocean. On the other hand, little precipitation occurs in polar regions, where water temperatures are cold. In addition, little precipitation occurs in areas that are long distances from an ocean.

Differences in land and water temperatures. In spite of the importance of latitude in determining climate, two places at the same latitude may have different climates. This situation may occur if one place is in the inland area of a continent and the other is in a coastal area. Water heats and cools more slowly than land does. In summer, bodies of water do not become so warm as

People of the Sahara, including these Tuareg women, wear loose, flowing garments. Such clothing protects them from the heat and the cold of a *desert* climate. Their tent provides shade.

In Vanuatu, many houses have a thatch roof to keep rain from dripping in. This southwest Pacific island nation has a *tropical wet* climate. Many of the people wear little clothing.

What the world's climate is like

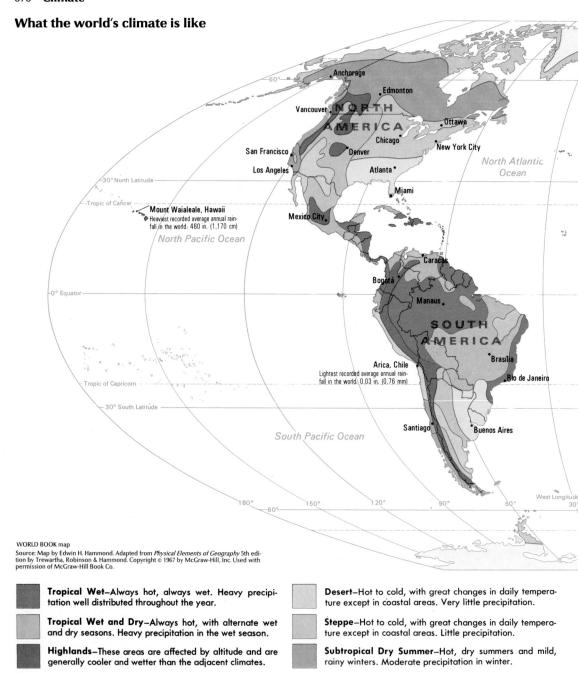

WORLD BOOK map

Source: Map by Edwin H. Hammond. Adapted from *Physical Elements of Geography* 5th edition by Trewartha, Robinson & Hammond. Copyright © 1967 by McGraw-Hill, Inc. Used with permission of McGraw-Hill Book Co.

Tropical Wet–Always hot, always wet. Heavy precipitation well distributed throughout the year.

Tropical Wet and Dry–Always hot, with alternate wet and dry seasons. Heavy precipitation in the wet season.

Highlands–These areas are affected by altitude and are generally cooler and wetter than the adjacent climates.

Desert–Hot to cold, with great changes in daily temperature except in coastal areas. Very little precipitation.

Steppe–Hot to cold, with great changes in daily temperature except in coastal areas. Little precipitation.

Subtropical Dry Summer–Hot, dry summers and mild, rainy winters. Moderate precipitation in winter.

the land, and in winter they do not become so cold. As a result, the inland area of a continent may be warmer in summer than the coast, which is cooled by the ocean air. In winter, the inland area of a continent may be colder than the coast, which is warmed by the ocean air. A large lake may have similar effects on nearby land.

Bergen, a city on the southwest coast of Norway, lies about 1,315 miles (2,116 kilometers) north of Omaha, Nebr. Because Bergen is farther from the equator than Omaha is, the Norwegian city might be expected to have

a colder, drier climate. But ocean air gives Bergen an average January temperature that is higher than the average January temperature in Omaha. Ocean air also keeps Bergen's average July temperature lower than Omaha's. Moist ocean winds bring a yearly average of 80 inches (203 centimeters) of precipitation to Bergen. Omaha receives a yearly average of 25 inches (64 centimeters).

Differences in the surface of the land result in many differences among climates. For example, as air

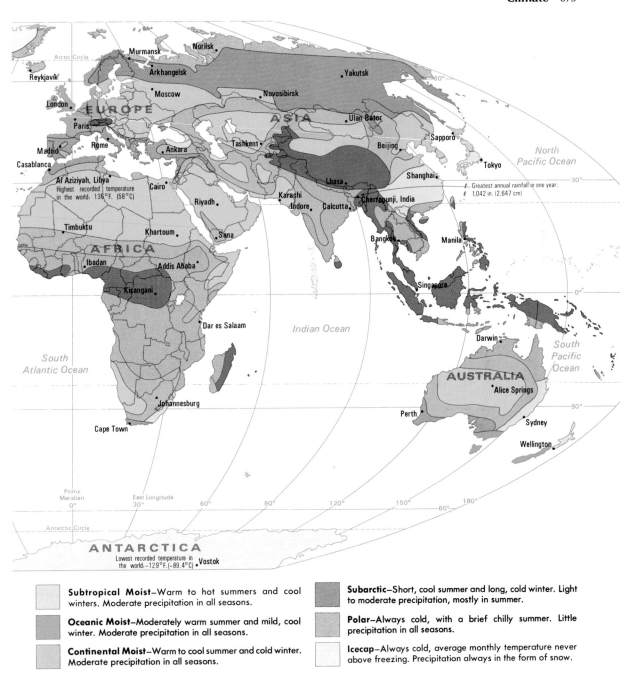

Subtropical Moist–Warm to hot summers and cool winters. Moderate precipitation in all seasons.

Oceanic Moist–Moderately warm summer and mild, cool winter. Moderate precipitation in all seasons.

Continental Moist–Warm to cool summer and cold winter. Moderate precipitation in all seasons.

Subarctic–Short, cool summer and long, cold winter. Light to moderate precipitation, mostly in summer.

Polar–Always cold, with a brief chilly summer. Little precipitation in all seasons.

Icecap–Always cold, average monthly temperature never above freezing. Precipitation always in the form of snow.

rises and expands, its temperature becomes colder. Cold air cannot hold so much moisture as warm air can. Therefore, air that rises to pass over a mountain becomes colder and may lose much of its moisture. As a result, a place located on a mountain generally has a cooler, wetter climate than does a place at a lower elevation. Mountain slopes that face moist ocean winds have especially heavy precipitation.

Places in hilly or mountainous regions have a *highlands* climate. This kind of climate cannot be defined ex-

actly. Nearby places in a highlands region may have somewhat different climates if they lie (1) at different elevations, or (2) in different positions relative to the prevailing winds.

Mountains may have major effects on the climate of nearby lowland areas. For example, the Cascade Mountains run through western Oregon and Washington. The lowland areas of Oregon and Washington west of the Cascades receive much precipitation from the prevailing winds, which blow in from the ocean. But by the

Scientists launch a balloon that will carry instruments into the earth's upper atmosphere. The instruments will measure air temperature, wind speed, and humidity.

Scientists work on a buoy whose instruments measure water temperature, flow rate, and other factors related to *El Niño,* a warm Pacific current that has widespread climatic effects.

time these winds have moved eastward over the Cascade Mountains, they have lost most of their moisture. As a result, some parts of eastern Oregon and Washington have a dry climate.

Differences in climate may occur even within a small, fairly level area. Such differences result from small differences in the surface of the land. In the Northern Hemisphere, gently sloping land that faces north has a somewhat cooler climate than does a slope that faces south, toward the equator. Also, the center of a large city is generally warmer than the surrounding region. Automobiles and the heating systems of buildings produce a large amount of heat in the city. In addition, such surfaces as pavements and the walls of buildings absorb much energy from the sun and thus heat the lower air in a city.

The changing climate

Changes in climate take place slowly through the years. For example, the climate of many areas of North America was somewhat colder in the 1960's and early 1970's than in the 1930's and 1940's. This change formed part of a worldwide cooling pattern that began in the late 1940's. Yet the climate of North America is much warmer today than it was about 15,000 years ago. At that time, glaciers covered much of what is now Canada and the northern United States.

Climatologists believe there may be a number of causes of climatic change. One cause might be a change in the amount of energy given off by the sun or in the earth's orbit around the sun. Such changes may produce a variation in the amount of heat received from the sun. Another cause of climatic change may be *volcanic dust.* When a volcano erupts, it throws huge amounts of this dust into the atmosphere. The dust may stay in the air for many years, scattering the sun's rays and reducing the amount of sunlight that reaches the ground. As a result, a volcanic eruption may have cooling effects on the climate.

Agricultural and industrial activity also causes large amounts of particles to be discharged into the air. These particles may have effects similar to those caused by volcanic dust.

Another cause of climatic change may be carbon dioxide, a gas that occurs naturally in the atmosphere. Carbon dioxide is also produced by burning. Since about 1900, the amount of carbon dioxide in the atmosphere has increased considerably because people have burned large amounts of fuel in their homes and in factories. Carbon dioxide allows sunlight to reach the earth and warm its surface, but it prevents some surface heat from escaping out of the atmosphere. This *greenhouse effect* may raise the temperatures near the ground.

Although a general cooling of the earth's climate has

occurred since the 1940's, some areas have become warmer. In addition, some areas have become wetter, and others have become drier. Climatologists do not know exactly why these changes have taken place. Neither do they know which changes form part of a natural pattern and which ones, if any, have been caused by people. Some climatologists believe temperature variations caused by increased carbon dioxide or particles in the air may have brought changes in the earth's wind systems. Such changes, in turn, may have caused various kinds of climatic changes.

Climatologists want to learn why climatic changes occur, chiefly because some of these changes could hurt food production. Knowledge of what is involved in such climatic changes may help scientists prepare for them. John A. Harrington, Jr.

Related articles. See the section on *Climate* in the various state, province, country, and continent articles, such as Alabama (Climate). See also **Weather** and its list of *Related articles.* Other related articles in *World Book* include:

Acclimatization	Meteorology
Animal (Where animals live)	Nuclear winter
Arctic (Climate)	Ocean (As an influence on climate)
Biome	
Clothing (Protection)	Phenology
Desert	Plant (Where plants live)
Drought	Races, Human (Climatic adaptations)
Food (Geographic reasons)	
Greenhouse effect	Rain
Gulf stream	Season
Ice Age	Shelter (Climate)
Icecap	Snow
Isotherm	Temperature
Lake (Climate)	Tropics
Latitude	Wind

Additional resources

Critchfield, Howard J. *General Climatology.* 4th ed. Prentice-Hall, 1983.
Gallant, Roy A. *Earth's Changing Climate.* Four Winds, 1979. For younger readers.
Gay, Kathlyn. *The Greenhouse Effect.* Watts, 1986. Suitable for younger readers.
Gedzelman, Stanley D. *The Science and Wonders of the Atmosphere.* Wiley, 1980.
Levenson, Thomas. *Ice Time: Climate, Science, and Life on Earth.* Harper, 1989.
Schotterer, Ulrich. *Climate: Our Future?* Rev. ed. Univ. of Minnesota Pr., 1992.

Climatology. See Climate.

Clingmans Dome is the highest peak in the Great Smoky Mountains and in Tennessee. The mountain rises 6,643 feet (2,025 meters) on the Tennessee-North Carolina boundary, about 35 miles (56 kilometers) southeast of Knoxville. For the location of Clingmans Dome, see **Tennessee** (physical map).

The Clingmans Dome area is a popular resort region. It has mountain woodlands with cool streams and a variety of plants. The road from Gatlinburg, Tenn., past Newfound Gap to near the top of Clingmans Dome is the most spectacular trip that can be taken by motor vehicle in Great Smoky Mountains National Park. Charles S. Aiken

Clinical psychology is the scientific study, diagnosis, and treatment of people who have psychological problems adjusting to themselves and the environment. Clinical psychologists deal with both normal and abnormal behavior. They administer and interpret psychological tests and diagnose and treat mental disorders. They study the structure and development of personality, and they work to prevent serious disturbances in mental health.

Clinical psychology is a scientific and *applied* field of psychology. That is, it puts into practice the theories developed in the different fields of psychology. For example, clinical psychologists apply many findings of abnormal psychology when they diagnose and treat mental disorders. They also draw knowledge from the fields of learning, motivation, perception, personality, developmental psychology, physiological psychology, and social psychology.

Clinical psychologists work in government agencies, hospitals, clinics, universities, and private practice. The chief activities of clinical psychologists are (1) testing and diagnosis, (2) psychotherapy and consultation, and (3) research.

Testing and diagnosis. Clinical psychologists develop, administer, and interpret tests that measure aptitude, intelligence, and personality. Through their interpretation of test results, they help determine proper school placement for students of all ages. Clinical psychologists also help employers determine people's aptitudes for certain jobs. In addition, clinical psychologists use personality tests in diagnosing mental disorders. See **Testing.**

Psychotherapy and consultation. Clinical psychologists treat mental disorders that result in disturbed human relationships or individual anxiety or unhappiness. They deal with brief, minor disturbances such as stress resulting from a school failure or grief due to the loss of a loved one. They also try to solve the prolonged problems of internal emotional conflicts often called *neuroses* and of *psychoses*. Psychoses are problems in which a person's thoughts, feelings, words, or perceptions are severely unrealistic.

Psychotherapy is the clinical psychologist's chief tool in treating mental disorders. In most kinds of psychotherapy, the psychologist talks with the patient in a series of informal interviews. In most cases, the psychologist tries to help the patient understand the cause of the patient's personality disturbance (see **Mental illness** [Methods of treatment]).

Understanding and preventing mental disorders is an important goal of clinical psychologists. They develop and take part in consultation programs to educate the public in methods of improving child care and family and school relationships and expanding mental health facilities. They also work with the clergy, teachers, and other people who deal with children to help identify and solve psychological problems that develop at an early stage.

Research. Clinical psychologists are trained to design and conduct scientific experiments. Through their knowledge and use of research techniques, they improve various methods of diagnosing and treating mental disorders. They propose and test new theories on the structure and development of personality. They also develop and evaluate new testing and treatment methods. Leah Blumberg Lapidus

Clinker. See Cement and concrete (How cement is made).

Clinker-built vessel. See Ship (Viking ships; illustrations).

42nd President of the United States 1993-

Bush
41st President
1989-1993
Republican

Clinton
42nd President
1993-
Democrat

Al Gore
Vice President
1993-

© Robert Kusel, Sipa Press

© Michael Evans, Sygma

Clinton, Bill (1946-   ), was elected President of the United States in 1992. Clinton, a Democrat, won the presidential election while serving his fifth term as governor of Arkansas. In the election, he defeated President George Bush, his Republican opponent, and Ross Perot, a Texas businessman who ran as an independent.

Clinton took office at a time when the nation's attention had shifted sharply from foreign affairs to domestic issues. The years before his election had seen a series of turbulent world events, including the end of the Cold War struggle between the United States and the Soviet Union, and—in 1991—the breakup of the Soviet Union itself. By 1992, Americans were troubled chiefly by fears about their country's economic health. The unemployment rate had climbed to the highest level since 1984. Many people were concerned about what they saw as a decline in U.S. productivity compared with that of other nations. Another concern involved the federal government's policy of *deficit spending,* or borrowing to finance expenditures, which over the years had resulted in a large national debt. In addition, Americans had become increasingly frustrated over signs of growing racial conflict, crime, and poverty, especially in the nation's cities.

During his campaign, Clinton argued that he was the best candidate to solve the country's economic and social problems. He promised to reduce the need for deficit spending and to expand the educational and economic opportunities of poor and middle-class Ameri-

cans. Clinton's positions included both traditionally liberal and traditionally conservative ideas. He once declared, "The change I seek . . . isn't liberal or conservative. It's different and it's both."

Clinton, who was 46 when he took office, was the third youngest person ever to serve as President, after Theodore Roosevelt and John F. Kennedy. In 1978, Clinton had become one of the youngest Americans ever elected as a governor, when he won that office in Arkansas at the age of 32. Clinton was a skillful public speaker known for his ability to seize the attention of a wide variety of audiences. His hobbies included reading, solving crossword puzzles, and playing the tenor saxophone. Clinton also enjoyed jogging and playing golf.

Early life

Boyhood. Clinton was born on Aug. 19, 1946, in Hope, Ark. His given and family name was William Jefferson Blythe IV. Clinton's parents were Virginia Cassidy Blythe (1923-   ) and William Jefferson Blythe III (1918-

Important dates in Clinton's life

1946 (Aug. 19) Born in Hope, Ark.
1968 Graduated from Georgetown University.
1968-1970 Attended Oxford University as Rhodes Scholar.
1973 Graduated from Yale Law School.
1975 (Oct. 11) Married Hillary Rodham.
1977-1978 Served as attorney general of Arkansas.
1979-1980 Served first term as governor of Arkansas.
1982 Again elected governor of Arkansas, and later reelected three more times. Held office until 1992.
1992 Elected President of the United States.

Ernest C. Dumas, the contributor of this article, is a political columnist for The Arkansas Times *and Journalist in Residence at the University of Central Arkansas.*

1946). His father, a traveling heavy-equipment salesman and former automobile dealer, was killed as a result of a car accident three months before Bill was born. Later, relatives and friends often told the boy how much he resembled his father, who was known for his good looks and lively personality.

During the first years of his life, young Bill—called Billy—lived with his mother and her parents in Hope. When the boy was about 2, his mother left him in the care of his grandparents for a year while she studied in New Orleans to become a nurse-anesthetist. When Billy was 4, his mother married Roger Clinton (1909-1967), a car dealer. The family lived for a time in Hope, then moved to Hot Springs, Ark., in 1953. There, Virginia and Roger Clinton had another son, Roger, Jr. (1956-   ). Billy began using his stepfather's last name while in elementary school. He formally changed his name to William Jefferson Clinton when he was 15.

Virginia Clinton had a strong influence on her older son. She cared deeply about the problems of people she met in her hospital work, and she and Bill often had long conversations about situations one or the other considered unfair. But Clinton's life at home was not easy. Roger Clinton, Sr., was an alcoholic who sometimes verbally or even physically abused his wife. At least once, Bill stood up to his stepfather to protect his mother. Clinton later said that his troubled family life made him skilled at solving disagreements and avoiding conflicts. Clinton grew close to his stepfather shortly before the older man died of cancer in 1967.

School life. In Hot Springs, Clinton attended a Roman Catholic school for two years before enrolling in public school. The Clintons, who were Baptists, sent their son to the smaller Catholic school to ease his move to the large public school system of Hot Springs. Young Bill enjoyed his schoolwork and earned good grades. In high school, he was active in a variety of clubs and held

Clinton Campaign Headquarters

Young Bill, shown at about the age of 5, spent his early childhood in the town of Hope, Ark. The boy resembled his father, who was killed in a car accident before Bill was born.

many offices. He also played tenor saxophone in the high school band, serving as band major during his senior year.

Clinton early showed an interest in—and a gift for—politics. As a schoolmate later recalled, Bill was always "running for something." Clinton became convinced he

WORLD BOOK photo by Brian Dickerson

The Clinton home in Hope, Ark., became young Bill's home after his mother's second marriage when the boy was 4. The family moved to Hot Springs, Ark., a few years later.

Clinton Campaign Headquarters

Seventeen-year-old Clinton shakes hands with President John F. Kennedy, *above*. Clinton's meeting with Kennedy helped persuade the youth to pursue a political career.

would pursue a political career in 1963, when, at the age of 17, he met President John F. Kennedy. Clinton met Kennedy while visiting Washington, D.C., as a delegate to the American Legion Boys Nation, a citizenship training program in which young people form a model of national government.

College education. After graduating from high school in 1964, Clinton attended Georgetown University in Washington, D.C. In college, Clinton majored in international affairs. He studied hard and remained active in school life, serving as class president during his freshman and sophomore years. Between 1966 and 1968, Clinton helped pay his college expenses through a job with the Senate Foreign Relations Committee, then headed by Senator J. William Fulbright, an Arkansas Democrat.

Clinton had been strongly influenced by black Americans' fight for social justice during the civil rights movement of the 1950's and 1960's. In April 1968, the assassination of civil rights leader Martin Luther King, Jr., led to widespread rioting in Washington. Clinton and a friend worked as Red Cross volunteers during the rioting, bringing food and clothing to people whose homes had been burned. Clinton graduated from college a few months later.

Following his graduation, Clinton entered Oxford University in Oxford, England, as a Rhodes Scholar. He had won the scholarship during his senior year at Georgetown. Clinton remained at Oxford for two years.

Law school. Clinton entered Yale Law School in 1970, after leaving Oxford. He helped pay his expenses through a scholarship and by holding part-time jobs, sometimes three at a time.

From August to November 1972, Clinton worked in Texas as a state coordinator for the presidential campaign of Democratic nominee George S. McGovern. Clinton showed skill in managing the campaign, though McGovern failed to win the state's electoral votes in the election.

Clinton's family. At Yale, Clinton met fellow law student Hillary Rodham (Oct. 26, 1947-   ) of Park Ridge, Ill. Hillary and Bill began to date in 1971 and were married on Oct. 11, 1975. The couple had one child—a daughter, Chelsea (1980-   ). After the marriage, Hillary continued to pursue her own career as an attorney, eventually becoming one of the nation's most prominent lawyers. She also played an active role in public affairs. She remained known as Hillary Rodham until 1982, when she adopted her husband's last name.

Entry into politics

After receiving his law degree in 1973, Clinton returned to Arkansas. There, he took a position on the faculty of the University of Arkansas Law School in Fayetteville. Soon afterward, Clinton announced his intention to run for a seat in the U.S. House of Representatives. In 1974, Clinton became the Democratic nominee to represent Arkansas's Third Congressional District, which includes Fayetteville. Representative John Paul Hammerschmidt, a popular Republican, narrowly defeated Clinton in the general election.

In 1976, Clinton won the Democratic primary for attorney general of Arkansas. He ran unopposed in the general election and took office in January 1977. As at-

Allan Tannenbaum, Sygma

Clinton's family includes his wife, Hillary Rodham Clinton, and their daughter, Chelsea. *Above,* the Clintons wave to supporters at the Democratic National Convention in 1992.

torney general, Clinton became known as a supporter of consumers' interests. For example, he opposed the construction by an Arkansas utility company of two large coal-burning power plants, demanding that the company promote efficiency and conservation instead. The plants were eventually built. Clinton also unsuccessfully fought several increases in utility rates.

Clinton became a candidate for governor of Arkansas in early 1978, midway through his two-year term as attorney general. In his campaign, Clinton focused on a number of issues important to Arkansans, including the need for economic development and improvements in the state's educational system. He also promised to upgrade the state's road and highway network.

Clinton overwhelmed his four Democratic opponents in the primary, winning 60 percent of the vote. He went on to easily defeat Republican Lynn Lowe in the general election. Clinton's impressive showing in the election,

Clinton Campaign Headquarters

Clinton entered politics in 1974, campaigning for a seat in the U.S. House of Representatives. Clinton won the Democratic primary, but he was narrowly defeated in the general election.

combined with his liberal policies and his youth, brought him his first national attention.

Governor of Arkansas, 1979-1980

Early difficulties. Clinton was inaugurated governor in January 1979. Once in office, he began efforts to establish a wide range of programs and policies. But he failed to gather broad support for these efforts, and most of them met with little success. To pay for a road improvement program, Clinton pushed through the legislature a measure increasing various fees and taxes, including motor vehicle license fees. Clinton had been elected partly on the basis of his campaign promise to upgrade the highways. But the increase in license fees was extremely unpopular, especially among poor, rural Arkansans. Clinton also came under attack by local leaders, who accused him of failing to attract industries to the state. In addition, the powerful wood-products industry—one of the state's largest employers—began working against Clinton because his administration had condemned the industry's timber-management practices, called *clearcutting.*

Reelection defeat. Clinton ran for reelection in 1980 against conservative Republican Frank D. White, a savings and loan executive. Despite the troubled nature of Clinton's first term, few political experts expected White to win. But White's campaign stressed Clinton's unpopular license fee increase. White also profited from a federal government decision to hold about 18,000 Cuban refugees temporarily at Fort Chaffee, then a military reserve training facility, near Fort Smith, Ark. In May and June 1980, discontent among the Cubans led to breakouts and rioting. White claimed that Clinton had not done enough to persuade President Jimmy Carter to hold the Cubans elsewhere. In the election, White gained 52 percent of the vote to Clinton's 48 percent.

Clinton was deeply affected by his defeat. He returned to private life, joining the law firm of Wright, Lindsey and Jennings in Little Rock, Ark. For the next year, he reviewed his actions as governor, trying to understand what personal and political weaknesses had caused him to lose the election. He also began planning to challenge White in the election of 1982.

Governor of Arkansas, 1983-1992

Return to office. In his 1982 campaign, Clinton worked to convince voters that he understood his mistakes, had matured, and had learned the importance of listening. He failed to win a majority of votes in the Democratic primary, but he won the nomination in a runoff against former Lieutenant Governor Joe Purcell. In the general election, Clinton defeated White by 55 percent to 45 percent of the vote.

Clinton returned to office in January 1983. During his second term, he worked to build a broad base of support for his policies. He abandoned some of the strongly liberal positions of his first term. In addition, Clinton decided to concentrate on two main problems—education and the economy—instead of a wide range of issues, as he had in his first term.

Clinton's opponents argued that his 1980 defeat had taught him to avoid taking stands or raising issues that might be unpopular. Nevertheless, Clinton was reelected in 1984 and again in 1986, each time by a wide

© *Arkansas Democrat-Gazette* from Sipa Press

Clinton's inauguration as governor of Arkansas in 1983 marked his return to office after two years in private life. Clinton had been elected governor in 1978 but lost a reelection bid in 1980. He was elected to a total of five terms as governor.

margin. In 1984, Arkansas passed a constitutional amendment changing the governor's term of office from two years to four, beginning with the 1986 election. Clinton was elected to a fifth term in 1990.

Reforms in education. Beginning in 1983, Clinton set as his main goal the improvement of the Arkansas public school system. Arkansas had long ranked near the bottom of the states in many measures of educational achievement. For example, a smaller percentage of the state's adults had a college education than in nearly any other state. During his first term, Clinton had taken preliminary steps toward improving education in Arkansas. In one such move, he proposed a measure—passed into law in 1979—that required new teachers to pass a certifying examination before being allowed to teach.

In 1983, at Clinton's urging, the legislature passed a series of educational reforms. These reforms included a measure—the first of its kind in the nation—requiring that teachers pass a basic skills test to keep their jobs. The legislature passed the measure despite strong opposition from the Arkansas Education Association, an organization of Arkansas teachers. Other reforms increased courses offered by Arkansas schools and imposed a test for entry into high school. To pay for the reforms—and to raise teachers' salaries—the legislature approved an increase in the state sales tax.

Clinton continued to promote educational reform after 1983. Under his leadership, Arkansas became the second state in the nation to establish a policy of open enrollment, allowing children to attend public schools outside their district. To raise college enrollment rates in Arkansas, the state offered scholarships to poor and middle-class students who showed academic achievement in high school.

Economic developments. Arkansas has traditionally been a state with few major resources and an underdeveloped economy. It has relied heavily on low-skill, low-paying manufacturing jobs. Since the 1940's, the movement of industries to the South has helped Arkansas' economy grow. But the state has had to struggle to compete for jobs with its more prosperous neighbors.

During his first term, Clinton had sought unsuccessfully to reduce the state's dependence on manufacturing jobs. After his reelection, he worked instead to broaden its industrial base. In 1985, at his urging, the legislature passed an economic package designed to attract businesses and capital to Arkansas. Clinton made special efforts to bring high-technology companies such as computer and electronics firms to the state. His actions helped Arkansas reduce unemployment and increase production in the late 1980's and early 1990's.

Steps to the presidency. Throughout his years as governor, Clinton played an active role in Democratic Party politics and in regional and national political life. For example, in 1985 and 1986, he served as chairman of the Southern Growth Policies Board. This organization, which then included 12 Southern states and Puerto Rico, works to help its members plan for rapid economic and population growth. Also in 1985, he was elected vice chairman of the National Governors' Association (NGA), made up of the governors of the 50 states and 5 U.S. territories. Clinton served as chairman of the NGA in 1986 and 1987. In 1990 and 1991, he headed the Democratic Leadership Council, an organization of moderate Democratic officeholders from all levels of government, as well as business and community members.

In 1987 and 1988, Clinton worked to obtain the support of Congress and President Ronald Reagan for the NGA's proposals on welfare reform. The proposals led to passage of the Family Support Act of 1988 (see **Welfare** [Recent developments in welfare programs]).

At the Democratic National Convention in 1988, Clinton gave the speech nominating Michael S. Dukakis as the party's candidate for President. Dukakis lost the election to Bush, then Vice President.

Election as President

The Democratic nomination. In October 1991, Clinton formally announced his candidacy for the Democratic nomination for President. His chief challengers for the nomination were Massachusetts Senator Paul E. Tsongas and former California Governor Edmund G. Brown, Jr., known as Jerry. Clinton also faced opposition from Texas businessman Ross Perot. Perot, running as an independent, began a presidential campaign without formally declaring his candidacy.

For a time, Clinton's campaign faltered over charges of marital infidelity. The Clintons acknowledged that they had encountered some difficulties in their relationship, but they said their marriage was strong. Clinton also came under attack for his actions during the early 1970's, which, his opponents charged, showed that he had sought to evade military service during the Vietnam War (1957-1975). Clinton denied that he had acted improperly, and his campaign rapidly regained ground. Tsongas, an early front-runner, suspended his campaign for lack of funds in March 1992. Clinton had already seized a commanding lead over Brown, and he soon had enough delegates to ensure the nomination.

During the spring and early summer, opinion polls showed strong voter support for Perot. Voters liked Perot largely because of his status as an "outsider," someone unconnected to the political life of Washington, D.C. Americans mistrusted Washington politicians because of their links to powerful interest groups. In addition, the capital had recently emerged from a series of scandals, including several involving misuse of official privileges. Clinton chose not to mount an active campaign against Perot. Instead, he worked to convince voters that, as a governor who had never served in Washington, he, too, was an "outsider." He also suggested that his Democratic Party ties would enable him—unlike Perot—to work with Congress and so achieve his goals as President.

At the Democratic National Convention in New York City in July 1992, Clinton was named the Democratic presidential nominee. At his request, Senator Al Gore of Tennessee was nominated for Vice President. The Republicans nominated President Bush and Vice President Dan Quayle to oppose Clinton and Gore.

The 1992 election. During the presidential campaign, Clinton took advantage of many Americans' perception of Bush as unconcerned about domestic issues. He also seized upon the widespread belief that the gap between rich and poor had grown under Bush and his predecessor, Ronald Reagan. Clinton promised to stimulate economic growth by encouraging business expansion in various ways, including tax breaks for new plants, new technology, and new small businesses. He also called for rebuilding the nation's transportation and communication networks and improving education. He proposed to raise the taxes of wealthy Americans to help reduce the federal budget *deficit* (shortage).

Bush charged that Clinton lacked experience in foreign affairs. He also argued that the only effective way to stimulate the economy and reduce the deficit was to cut spending and lower taxes. Bush defended his record on the economy and other domestic issues, claiming that Congress—which was made up largely of Democrats—had rejected most of his proposals.

Perot had dropped his undeclared candidacy in mid-July, explaining that he had determined he could not win. However, at the beginning of October, Perot reentered the race, formally announcing his candidacy. He chose as his running mate Vice Admiral James B. Stockdale, a retired Navy officer.

Perot proposed to eliminate the federal budget deficit through, in part, a wide range of measures to lessen

Clinton's election

Place of nominating convention	New York City
Ballot on which nominated	1st
Republican opponent	George Bush
Independent opponent	Ross Perot
Electoral vote*	370 (Clinton) to 168 (Bush) and 0 (Perot)
Popular vote	44,908,233 (Clinton) to 39,102,282 (Bush) and 19,721,433 (Perot)
Age at inauguration	46

*The *table* in the article on **Electoral College** gives the electoral vote by states.

Running mates Clinton and Senator Al Gore of Tennessee, *left,* accepted the Democratic nomination for President and Vice President at the party's national convention in New York City in July 1992.

© Ira Wyman, Sygma

government spending and increase tax revenues. He also called for reducing certain taxes to encourage investment. In the election, Clinton defeated Bush and Perot.

Clinton's Administration (1993-   )

Presidential appointments. Clinton appointed more women and minorities to his Cabinet than had any previous President. Clinton also named many women and minorities to other high-level government positions. In July, he nominated Ruth Bader Ginsburg to fill a vacancy on the Supreme Court of the United States. The Senate approved her in August, and she became the second woman to serve as an associate justice of the court. Associate Justice Sandra Day O'Connor, appointed by President Ronald Reagan in 1981, was the first.

National affairs. Early in his presidency, Clinton concentrated on the economy and other domestic issues. In February, he proposed an economic plan aimed at reducing the budget deficit through tax increases and spending reductions. Following narrow approval by the House, the Senate passed Clinton's budget in August by a vote of 51-50. The deciding vote was cast by Vice President Gore. Six Democrats joined all 44 Republicans in

the Senate in opposing the budget package. All the Republicans in the House also had voted against the plan. Opponents of the budget argued it raised taxes unnecessarily and did not include enough cuts in government spending.

Clinton also worked on plans to reform the U.S. health care system. He appointed his wife, Hillary, to head a committee to try to find ways of providing low-cost health care for all Americans.   Ernest C. Dumas

See also **Democratic Party; Gore, Al; President of the United States.**

Outline

I. **Early life**
   A. Boyhood
   B. School life
   C. College education
   D. Law school
   E. Clinton's family
II. **Entry into politics**
III. **Governor of Arkansas, 1979-1980**
   A. Early difficulties
   B. Reelection defeat
IV. **Governor of Arkansas, 1983-1992**
   A. Return to office
   B. Reforms in education
   C. Economic developments
   D. Steps to the presidency
V. **Election as President**
   A. The Democratic nomination
   B. The 1992 election
VI. **Clinton's Administration (1993-   )**
   A. Presidential appointments
   B. National affairs

Questions

What was Clinton's original name? How did he get the name Clinton?

What difficulties did Clinton encounter in his first term as governor? What issues were important in his reelection defeat?

What were Americans' main concerns when Clinton became President?

How did Clinton work to improve education in Arkansas?

Why did young Clinton become skilled at avoiding conflicts?

When did Clinton become convinced he would pursue a political career?

How did Clinton build support for his policies after he won election for a second term as governor in 1982?

What factors have traditionally affected the Arkansas economy?

How did Clinton campaign against President George Bush in the 1992 presidential race?

How did Clinton first gain national attention?

Vice President and Cabinet

Vice President	*Al Gore
Secretary of state	*Warren M. Christopher
Secretary of the treasury	*Lloyd M. Bentsen, Jr.
Secretary of defense	*Les Aspin
Attorney general	*Janet Reno
Secretary of the interior	Bruce E. Babbitt
Secretary of agriculture	Mike Espy
Secretary of commerce	*Ronald H. Brown
Secretary of labor	Robert B. Reich
Secretary of health and human services	Donna E. Shalala
Secretary of housing and urban development	*Henry G. Cisneros
Secretary of transportation	Federico F. Peña
Secretary of energy	Hazel R. O'Leary
Secretary of education	Richard W. Riley
Secretary of veterans affairs	Jesse Brown

*Has a separate biography in *World Book.*

Clinton, De Witt (1769-1828), an American statesman, promoted the building of the Erie Canal. As early as 1809, he advocated building the canal. Clinton served as a canal commissioner during the early years of its construction. The canal was completed in 1825, while Clinton was governor of New York. See **Erie Canal.**

Clinton was born in Little Britain, N.Y. He graduated from Columbia College and then studied law. He served as private secretary to his uncle, George Clinton, then governor of New York. He developed a strong interest in politics. In 1797, he was elected to the state assembly, and in the following year, he served in the state senate. In 1802, Clinton was sent to the United States Senate to fill a vacancy. The next year, he resigned his seat to become mayor of New York City. He was mayor from 1803 to 1815, except for two short intervals when he served in the New York Senate and was lieutenant governor of the state. In 1812, Clinton was an unsuccessful candidate for President of the United States. He served as governor of New York from 1817 to 1822 and again from 1825 to 1828. During the time Clinton was governor of New York, a school system was established.

Detail of an oil portrait (1826) by Samuel F. B. Morse; The Metropolitan Museum of Art, New York City, Rogers Fund, 1909

De Witt Clinton

Richard E. Ellis

Clinton, George (1739-1812), an American statesman and soldier, served as Vice President of the United States from 1805 until his death. He served under two different Presidents, Thomas Jefferson and James Madison. Only one other Vice President, John C. Calhoun, shares this record.

Clinton also served as the first governor of New York. He was elected in 1777 after New York's constitutional convention and won reelection six consecutive times, serving until 1795. He was reelected again in 1801 and served until 1804. Clinton strongly believed in states' rights and opposed New York's ratification of the United States Constitution. Under the name "Cato," he published several letters against adoption of the Constitution. The American statesman Alexander Hamilton started *The Federalist* papers largely to answer Clinton's objections.

Clinton was born in Little Britain, N.Y. He served as a brigadier general in the Continental Army in 1777. He also was elected to the New York Assembly in 1768 and the Continental Congress in 1775. A statue of Clinton represents New York in the U.S. Capitol.

Richard D. Brown

See also **Vice President of the U.S.** (picture).

Clinton, Sir Henry (1730-1795), served as commander in chief of the British Army from 1778 to 1781, during the Revolutionary War in America. He retreated from Philadelphia to New York, and stayed there about two years. Then in 1780 he invaded South Carolina and captured Charleston. He returned to New York, leaving Lord Cornwallis in command in the South. After Cornwallis surrendered in 1781 at Yorktown, Clinton resigned. He was unfairly blamed for Cornwallis' defeat. Clinton was born in Newfoundland. See also **Cornwallis, Charles.**   Paul David Nelson

Clipper ship was a fast, slender sailing vessel that was developed in the United States in the mid-1800's. To be classed a clipper, a ship needed a narrow *hull* (body) that was deeper in the back than at the front, and many large sails mounted on tall *masts* (sail poles). Clipper ships were modeled after the "Baltimore Clippers," small, swift sailing ships developed on Chesapeake Bay for sea use. The name *clipper* came from the way the ships "clipped off" the miles. Traders used clipper ships to bring tea and opium from China, and wool and gold from Australia. Clipper ships carried passengers across the Atlantic Ocean, and around Cape Horn to California during the gold rush of 1849-1857.

The *Rainbow,* designed by John W. Griffiths and launched in 1845, was the first true clipper ship. It was much larger and faster than the earlier "Baltimore Clippers." Other famous clipper ships included the *Sea Witch* and the *Cutty Sark.*

Perhaps the most famous builder of clipper ships was Donald McKay, a Canadian. McKay did most of his work in East Boston. His ships included the *Flying Cloud, Stag Hound, Lightning, Sovereign of the Seas,* and *Great Republic.* When it was launched in 1853, the *Great Republic* was the largest sailing ship in the world. It measured about 335 feet (100 meters) long.

Some typical, fast clipper trips included a voyage across the Atlantic Ocean in 12 days, 6 hours by the *James Baines;* an 89-day, 4-hour voyage from New York City around Cape Horn to San Francisco by the *Andrew Jackson;* and a run of 465 miles (748 kilometers) in 24 hours by the *Champion of the Seas* in 1854. More than 25 years passed before a steamship beat the *Champion of the Seas'* record. The opening of the Suez Canal between the Mediterranean and Red seas in 1869 did away with the need for clippers for the tea trade. Many clippers began carrying wool from Australia, but in this trade, speed was not essential. Thus, in the late 1800's, *square-riggers* (ships designed to carry larger cargoes

Oil painting on canvas (1869) by Frank Vining Smith; Mariner's Museum, Newport News, Va.

The *Cutty Sark,* above, was one of the most famous clipper ships. The slender hulls and many sails of the graceful clippers made the ships the fastest vessels of the mid-1800's.

The **Great Republic,** a clipper ship, was the largest sailing vessel in the world when it was launched in 1853. The ship measured about 335 feet (100 meters) long. The slender hulls and many sails of the graceful clippers made the ships the fastest vessels of the mid-1800's.

Color lithograph (1853) by Nathaniel Currier (Granger Collection)

at slower speeds) gradually replaced the clipper ships.

James C. Bradford

See also **Ship** (Clipper ships).

Clive, Robert (1725-1774), was the British administrator and military leader who brought India into the British Empire.

Clive was born in Shropshire (now Salop), England. He joined the English East India Company, Britain's trading company in India, in 1743. In 1747, he received a commission in the company's armed services. The British and French trading companies were struggling for control of India, and Clive won several important victories over the French and their Indian allies. In 1757, he led 3,200 troops to victory over 50,000 enemy troops at the Battle of Plassey. This victory enabled the English to gain control of Bengal, the richest province in India.

Clive returned to England in 1760 and entered Parliament. He was named Baron Clive of Plassey in 1762. In 1773, some of Clive's enemies persuaded Parliament to investigate his career in India. The investigation showed that Clive had made a fortune, but that he had also rendered "great and meritorious service to his country." Sickness during the last year of his life caused Clive to become an opium addict. He committed suicide in 1774.

Brijen K. Gupta

Clock is an instrument that shows the time. Clocks not only measure and tell time but also serve as decorations in homes and other buildings.

The first clocks were probably developed in the late 1200's. They had no hands or dial but told time by ringing a bell. The word *clock* probably comes from the French word *cloche* and the German word *Glocke,* both of which mean *bell.*

Kinds of clocks

Modern clocks range from small, inexpensive models to large, ornamental grandfather clocks with beautiful wood cases and complex chimes. Traditional clocks, called *dial clocks,* have hands that show the time by pointing to numbers on a dial. Other clocks, called *digi-*

tal clocks, show the time in digits on the clock face. Many clocks have chimes or sound an alarm. Others have mechanical birds or dancing figurines that mark the hours or other intervals of time.

Every clock has two main parts, the *case* and the *works,* or *movement,* inside the case. The works performs three functions. In addition to showing the time, it supplies power to run the clock and it keeps time. Clocks differ according to how their works carry out one or more of these three functions. This article classifies clocks into two groups, *mechanical clocks* and *electric clocks,* according to how they are powered.

Timekeeping in most clocks is based on the frequency of some regularly repeated action, such as the swing of a pendulum. Clocks with extremely stable frequencies keep time more accurately than those with less stable frequencies. For example, the operation of atomic clocks, the most accurate clocks ever made, is based on the vibrations of certain atoms and molecules. Each of these particles has a natural, characteristic frequency that is extremely stable. As a result, the best atomic clocks would not lose or gain more than a second in 1 million years.

Mechanical clocks are powered by various mechanical devices that must be wound at various intervals. Some have to be wound every day, but others can run for seven or eight days without rewinding. There are two main kinds of mechanical clocks, *weight driven* and *spring driven.* Almost all of them are dial clocks.

Weight-driven clocks are powered by a heavy weight that hangs from a cord or chain. When the clock is wound, the cord or chain gets wrapped around a drum and draws the weight up near the drum. As gravity pulls the weight down, the cord or chain slowly unwinds and turns the drum. This action of the drum turns a number of gear wheels that are connected in a series called the *train.* The hands of the clock are attached to individual wheels in the train. Each of these wheels turns at a specific speed. A pendulum and a mechanism called the *escapement* prevent the weight from being lowered too fast. The pendulum and the escapement also regulate the clock's speed.

The escapement includes an *escape wheel* and a *verge*. The escape wheel is connected to the train and turns when the clock runs. The pendulum, which is the timekeeping device of the clock, swings from side to side at a steady rate. As the pendulum swings, it tilts the verge from side to side. With each tilt, two hooks called *pallets*—one at each end of the verge—catch on the escape wheel and stop it. When the pendulum swings back, the pallets release the wheel, and the wheel turns slightly. This process regulates the speed of the escape wheel and of the wheels in the train. It also causes the tick-tock sound of the clock.

Spring-driven clocks contain a coiled spring called the *mainspring*. This spring gets wound up when the clock is wound. Then the mainspring unwinds slowly, turning the wheels in the train. Some spring-driven clocks also have a battery that automatically rewinds the mainspring before the spring runs down.

The escapement in a spring-driven clock resembles that of a weight-driven clock. However, many spring-driven clocks have a *balance wheel* instead of a pendulum as the timekeeping device. A coiled spring called the *balance spring,* or *hairspring,* is connected to the balance wheel. This spring coils and uncoils and makes the balance wheel swing back and forth at a fixed rate. The swinging motion causes the verge to tilt. The pallets alternately catch and release the escape wheel and regulate the speed of the train.

Electric clocks can be *battery powered* or *line powered.* A line-powered clock receives power from an electric outlet. Almost all digital clocks manufactured since the 1930's have been electric models.

Battery-powered clocks. Many battery-powered clocks have a balance wheel or a pendulum that regulates their speed. Others have a miniature tuning fork or

© Shafer, Bavaria Verlag

Human figures decorate a clock at the Church of Our Lady in Nuremberg, Germany. The figures are mechanical, and perform a pageant daily at noon. Nuremberg was a clockmaking center in the 1500's and 1600's.

a tiny bar of quartz crystal. The battery activates the tuning fork or crystal, which vibrates with high, steady frequencies. In clocks with a tuning fork, an *indexing mechanism* changes the number of vibrations into the correct speeds for the gear wheels. Quartz-based clocks contain a complex electric circuit that translates the number of vibrations into time information. The circuit

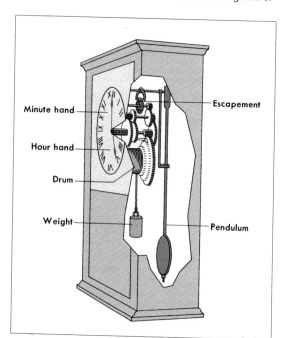

Minute hand

Hour hand

Drum

Weight

Escapement

Pendulum

A weight-driven clock, *left,* is powered by a weight that is lowered from a drum, *shown in green.* As the weight descends, the drum revolves and turns gear wheels, *pink,* that move the hands. The pendulum and escapement, *orange,* control the clock's speed.

A line-powered digital clock, *below,* is powered by an alternating electric current. The current flows through the transformer to the integrated circuit, which changes the current's frequency into timed electric impulses. The display driver makes these impulses strong enough to run the electronic display.

Westclox, a Talley Industries Co. (WORLD BOOK diagrams)

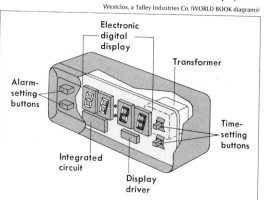

Electronic digital display

Transformer

Alarm-setting buttons

Time-setting buttons

Integrated circuit

Display driver

Some historical clocks

An Egyptian water clock from about 1400 B.C. is shown above. As water drains away, dots inside the pot measure the water level and tell how much time has passed.

A sundial uses the sun's motion across the sky to tell time. The sun casts a shadow that moves across the dial and points to the hours. This sundial is from the 1100's B.C.

Early mechanical clocks were weight driven and had only one hand. Some had a bell that struck the hours. This clock was made in Germany during the late 1400's.

Early portable clocks were powered by a coiled mainspring. Many such clocks had a separate cover, *above left.* This clock was made in France during the mid-1500's.

Time Museum, Rockford, Ill. (WORLD BOOK photos)

Pendulums for clocks were developed during the mid-1600's. These devices greatly improved timekeeping accuracy. This Dutch pendulum clock dates from the 1650's.

Marine chronometers are clocks designed especially for use in navigating the sea. This chronometer is one of the first ones built. It was made in England in 1777.

also controls the time display. Most quartz-based clocks are accurate to within 60 seconds a year.

Line-powered clocks. In line-powered clocks, the current from the electric outlet not only supplies power but also regulates the clock's speed. The flow of alternating current reverses its direction 120 times every second (see **Electric current** [Direct and alternating current]). A motor or an integrated circuit counts the changes in direction and uses that information to control the time display.

Most digital clocks are line powered. In some, the digits are printed on flip cards, rotating drums, or a moving tape. Other line-powered models and some quartz-based clocks have electronic digital displays, such as a *liquid crystal display* (*LCD*) and a *light-emitting diode display* (*LED*). A liquid crystal display uses digits that reflect the light around it. A light-emitting diode display has digits shaped from electronic devices called *diodes,* which give off light.

History

Prehistoric peoples probably told the time of day by watching shadows cast by the sun. As the sun moved, the lengths of the shadows changed. When the shadows were short, the watchers knew the time of day was near noon. When the shadows were long, they knew the day was either beginning or ending.

Sundials, which were developed more than 4,000 years ago, are the oldest known instruments designed for telling time. As the sun crosses the sky, it casts a shadow on the dial. A sundial tells time by measuring the length or the angle of the shadow. See **Sundial.**

Other early timekeeping devices included hourglasses and water clocks. In these devices, sand or water flowed from one container into another at a steady rate. By measuring the material in either container, people could tell how much time had passed. See **Hourglass; Water clock.**

The first mechanical clock was probably invented in China in the late 1000's. However, this invention was never developed further, and later Chinese clocks were based on European models.

Historians believe the first mechanical clocks in Western civilization were developed by a number of inventors during the late 1200's. These clocks were weight driven, but they had no pendulum or hands. They had a bell that rang to indicate the hour. By the mid-1300's, the dial and hour hand had been added. The first spring-driven clocks were probably developed in Italy during the late 1400's.

Most early clocks ran unevenly and inaccurately. The pendulum and the balance spring, which were developed during the mid-1600's, greatly improved timekeeping accuracy. Minute and second hands became common. By the mid-1700's, inventors had developed most of the mechanisms found in modern mechanical clocks.

Electric clocks, introduced in the mid-1800's, were in many homes by the 1920's. Quartz-based clocks appeared during the 1930's, and scientists developed the first atomic clock in the 1940's. Digital clocks became popular in the 1970's, particularly as wrist watches. In the 1980's, the *chip*—a complex electronic circuit etched onto a tiny piece of silicon—was incorporated into clock mechanisms. Besides displaying the time, watches with electronic chips can store information, and serve as electronic calculators and miniature game boards.

James Jespersen

Related articles in *World Book* include:

Atomic clock	Hour	Time
Banneker, Benjamin	Minute	Watch
Chronometer	Pendulum	

Cloister, *kloys tuhr,* in architecture, refers to a covered walk that encloses the courtyard of a monastery, convent, church, or college. Columns along one or more sides support the roof. The term *cloister* can also refer to the courtyard itself or to any place of religious seclusion. The word comes from a Latin word that means *a closed-off space.*

Both architecturally and symbolically the cloister unifies the monastery. An *oratory* (small chapel) or church usually opens off one side of the cloister. Common rooms and private rooms open off the other three sides. Many cloisters contain a garden and a fountain or well, and are used for work and recreation as well as for walkways. Cloisters are also sometimes used as graveyards for monks and notable associates of the monastery. See **Monasticism** (picture).

Beginning in the late 700's, the cloister became an important part of a monastery. Gradually, cloisters were added to other religious institutions and to colleges. In England, for example, Westminster Abbey, Oxford University, and Eton College have impressive cloisters.

The Roman Catholic Church established what is known as the *rule of cloister.* The current rule states that all houses of religious orders must have an enclosure appropriate to the order's character and ministry and reserved only for members. Religious orders whose ministry is primarily prayer and meditation require a stricter observance than do orders engaged in active ministry in the outside world.   David G. Schultenover

Clone is a group of genetically identical cells. For example, tumors are clones of cells inside an organism because they consist of many replicas of one mutated cell.

Another type of clone occurs inside a cell. Such a clone is made up of groups of identical structures that contain genetic material, such as *mitochondria* and *chloroplasts.* Some of these structures, called *plasmids,* are found in some bacteria and yeasts. Techniques of genetic engineering enable scientists to combine an animal or plant gene with a bacterial or yeast plasmid. By cloning such a plasmid, geneticists can produce many identical copies of the gene (see **Genetic engineering**).

The term clone also refers to a group of organisms that are genetically identical. Most such clones result from *asexual reproduction,* a process in which a new organism develops from only one parent (see **Reproduction**). Except for rare spontaneous mutations, asexually reproduced organisms have the same genetic composition as their parent. Thus, all the offspring of a single parent form a clone.

Single-celled organisms, such as bacteria, protozoa, and yeast, usually reproduce asexually. Clones of these organisms are useful in research. For example, various drugs and other compounds can be tested on bacterial clones. All the test bacteria have the same genetic makeup. Therefore, any differences in effectiveness among the different compounds result from the compounds themselves and not from the bacteria.

Algae, fungi, and such simple plants as club mosses can reproduce asexually as well as sexually and can be cloned. Higher plants usually reproduce sexually and form seeds. However, many—if not all—higher plants can also reproduce asexually through a process called *vegetative propagation,* and so they can form clones (see **Plant** [Vegetative propagation]). Plant clones are useful for measuring the effects of various environmental factors or chemical compounds on genetically identical plants. Breeders use cloning to collect plants with certain desired traits. Farmers and gardeners raise apples, potatoes, and roses by means of clones.

Hydras, flatworms, and other animals can be cloned through asexual reproduction or the process of *regen-*

Robert Frerck, Odyssey Productions

A cloister is a covered walk that encloses a courtyard. Most cloisters are part of a church, convent, monastery, or college. The cloister shown at the left was designed in the medieval Romanesque style for the Benedictine monastery of Santo Domingo de Silos in Spain.

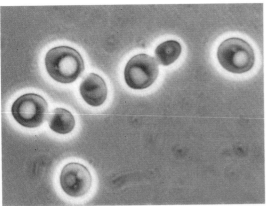
Yeast cells form clones when they reproduce. Each cell divides to create a genetically identical cell.

Anheuser-Busch, Inc.

eration (see **Regeneration**). But most higher animals form clones naturally only when identical twins or other genetically identical multiple births occur.

An experimental technique has been developed for cloning certain higher animals. This process involves destroying the nucleus of an egg cell of the species to be cloned. The nucleus is then removed from a body cell of an animal of the same species. This donor nucleus is injected into the egg cell. The egg, with its new nucleus, develops into an animal that has the same genetic makeup as the donor. If a number of eggs receive transplants from the same donor, the resulting offspring form a clone. Scientists used this technique to clone such amphibians as frogs and salamanders as early as the 1950's. But the procedure does not yet work with mammals, partly because of the tiny size of the eggs.

Daniel L. Hartl

Closed captioning is a system that provides *subtitles* (printed dialogue) on television broadcasts for hearing-impaired and deaf viewers. The subtitles, often called *captions,* are put into an electronic code and then broadcast with the TV signals. The captions appear only on TV sets that have a decoding device. Sets with screens measuring 13 inches (33 centimeters) or more that are manufactured after July 1993 and sold in the United States must have a decoder built into them. Closed captioning came into use in 1980 in the United States and in 1981 in Canada. By 1990, closed captions were viewed by over a million people.

The major United States television networks use closed captioning for all prime-time broadcasts, as well as for most major sports events, children's programs, newscasts, and special events. Almost all prime-time network broadcasts in Canada are closed captioned. Some local stations use closed captioning for news programs.

When programs are prerecorded for later broadcast, captions are typed into a computer and added to the videotape before broadcast. Captions are also typed in advance for programs broadcast *live* (as they happen) if a script is available. They are then added to the TV signal during broadcast. For live broadcasts with spontaneous dialogue, the dialogue is recorded on a shorthand machine linked to a computer. The computer instantly produces encoded subtitles.   Martin H. Block

Closed shop is a workshop or an industry in which only members of a labor union may be hired. In some closed shops, the union supplies all of the employees. When new employees must be hired, the employer obtains them through a union.

Closed shops differ from *union shops*. In a union shop, an employer may hire nonunion employees, but the new workers must join the union within a short period of time after they have been hired. The closed shop was declared illegal by the Taft-Hartley Act of 1947. However, the union shop is not illegal. See also **Taft-Hartley Act; Open shop; Union shop; National Labor Relations Act.**   Daniel Quinn Mills

Closure. See Cloture.

Cloth. See Textile.

WORLD BOOK photo

YOU SAID YOU HAD
SOME QUESTIONS.
GO AHEAD.

Closed captioning enables hearing-impaired and deaf people to understand dialogue on television. With the aid of a decoding device, a printed caption appears on the TV screen.

© R. Michael Stuckey, Comstock

Shopper in the United States

Design Photographers International

Eskimo in Alaska

Bruno Barbey, Magnum

Masai people in Kenya

D. Seymour, Magnum

Bullfighters in Spain

Women in Morocco

W. King, FPG

Clothing is one of people's most important needs. Most people wear some kind of garments, accessories, or ornaments. People in different parts of the world wear many different types of clothes. This variety occurs because individuals have different purposes for wearing clothes, use different materials and methods for making clothes, and follow different clothing customs.

Clothing

Clothing includes all the different garments, accessories, and ornaments worn by people throughout the world. An Eskimo may wear boots, warm pants, and a heavy coat. An African in a village may wear only a piece of cloth tied around the waist. A nurse may wear a white uniform, cap, and shoes. A London banker may wear a business suit and a hat.

Each of these persons dresses differently, but they all feel a need to wear some kind of clothing. Like food and shelter, clothing is one of people's most important needs.

Throughout history, many people have worn clothing more for decoration than for covering the body. Even in cold climates, some people seem more interested in

decorating their bodies than in protecting them. In the 1830's, for example, the famous British biologist Charles R. Darwin traveled to the islands of Tierra del Fuego, off the southern tip of South America. There he saw people who wore only a little paint and a small cloak made of animal skin, in spite of the cold rain and the sleet. Darwin gave the people scarlet cloth, which they took and wrapped around their necks. Even in the cold weather, these people wore clothing more for decoration than for protection.

No one knows exactly why or when people first wore clothes. But they probably began to wear clothing more than 100,000 years ago—and probably for much the same reasons we wear clothes today. Early people may have worn clothing to protect themselves, to improve their appearance, and to tell other people something about themselves. For example, a prehistoric hunter may have worn the skin of a bear or a reindeer in order to keep warm or as a sign of personal skill, bravery, and strength in hunting.

By the end of the Old Stone Age—about 25,000 years ago—people had invented the needle, which enabled

Richard Martin, the contributor of this article, is Executive Director and Dean of the Fashion Institute of Technology in New York.

Marilyn Silverstone, Magnum
Women in India

Van Bucher, Photo Researchers
Schoolchildren in Japan

Björn Bölstad, Photo Researchers
Colorado Indian in Ecuador

Camera Press, Pix
Ballet dancers in Russia

WORLD BOOK photo by Lee Balterman
Football players in the United States

them to sew skins together into clothing. They had also learned to make yarn from the threadlike parts of some plants or from the fur or hair of some animals. In addition, they had learned to weave yarn into cloth. By this time, people had begun to raise plants that gave them a steady supply of materials for making yarn. They had also started to herd sheep and other animals that gave them wool. These few advances took thousands of years. Most changes in the ways of making clothing and in the materials used for clothing have come only during the last few hundred years.

Until about 200 years ago, people had no machines for making clothes. Most families made their own clothing. Sometimes businesses paid groups of workers to make clothes, which the businesses then sold. But most of the people who made clothes worked at home. There were no clothing factories.

During the late 1700's and 1800's, the invention of several machines brought the clothing industry out of the home and into the factory. Machines that could spin thread, weave cloth, and sew clothes led to the growth of the clothing industry. Today, people in most parts of the world can buy ready-to-wear garments made in large clothing factories.

The clothing industry is a giant business in many countries. Clothes and clothing materials are important items of trade between nations. Shoppers in many lands buy Italian knitwear and shoes, Australian wool, and Japanese silk. Stores throughout the world sell clothes designed in London, Paris, and Milan. As a result, many people in different countries—especially people who live in cities—wear similar clothes. But there are still differences in dress among most regions of the world.

People in various regions dress differently for many reasons. They may need protection from different kinds of weather. They may have different materials and methods for making clothes, or they may have different habits of dress.

This article discusses why people wear clothes, describes clothing around the world, and traces the history of clothing. Then it describes the clothing industry and tells of career opportunities in the industry. For further descriptions of the clothing worn by various peoples, see the many country articles in *World Book*.

Most people, no matter where they live, wear some kind of clothing. Any person may wear certain clothing for a variety of individual reasons. But in general, people wear clothes for three main reasons: (1) protection, (2) communication, and (3) decoration. Most clothing serves all three purposes.

Protection. Clothing helps protect people's physical and emotional health.

Physical protection. People have probably worn clothing for physical protection since they first put on animal skins, leaves, or other clothing materials. In many areas of the world, people need clothing for protection from the weather. Clothing also protects people who work on dangerous jobs, take part in rough sports, or engage in other hazardous activities.

In cold climates, people wear warm garments made of wool, fur, or closely woven fabrics. They also wear warm shoes or boots.

In warm climates, people wear clothes made of such lightweight materials as cotton or linen, which have a fairly open weave. These materials absorb perspiration and allow air to flow around the body. People in these climates sometimes wear white or light-colored clothes because such colors reflect the sun's rays. They may also wear sandals, which are more comfortable than shoes or heavy boots in warm weather. Large hats made of straw serve as sunshades.

In many places, people must wear clothes for protection against several kinds of weather. For example, peo-

ple of the Arabian deserts wear loose, flowing garments that shield their bodies from the blazing sun. The same garments protect them against the cold night air. Even in less severe climates, people may require protective clothing during the hot and cold seasons.

Certain activities require special protective clothing. A soldier in combat wears a steel or plastic helmet and a nylon vest lined with plastic sheeting or fiber glass. Welders wear protective shields over their faces. Astronauts wear special suits and helmets for protection against changes of air pressure and temperature. Factory workers wear heavy shoes to protect their feet. Football players wear padded equipment to guard against injury.

In some societies, people may wear clothing for protection against unusual types of physical harm. For example, people in France wore plain clothes during the French Revolution in the late 1700's. Revolutionaries might have thought that people wearing fancy clothes belonged to the upper class, and they would probably have killed them. In some countries, people believe that evil spirits can cause bodily harm. These people may wear special clothes that they think have magic power to deal with such spirits.

Emotional protection. Clothing protects people's emotional health by helping satisfy some of their needs. For example, most people need to feel they are accepted as members of society or of some special group. Many persons also want to feel they are independent individuals—different in at least some small way from everyone else.

People who want to belong to a certain group usually dress in a style similar to that of people in the group. Through their choice of clothes, they tell members of the group that they share their attitudes, beliefs, and way of life. People who want to show their independence may wear different styles of clothing from that worn by others. By wearing such clothes, they seem to say, "Look at me. I am someone special."

Communication. People communicate by means of the clothes they wear. Their clothes may tell others who they are, what they are like, how they feel, and what they would like to be.

Who people are. People can identify some famous individuals, such as the President of the United States or a well-known actor, without looking at their clothes. However, few individuals are so well known. In most cases, a glance at a person's clothes helps people identify the person.

Clothing may reveal such facts as a person's occupation, approximate age, and sex. Bus drivers, mail carriers, nurses, police officers, and priests wear special clothing to help other people know what they do. People of different ages usually dress differently, and men and boys dress differently from women and girls. Some types of dress or uniforms show that a person belongs to a certain group. For example, Boy Scouts and Girl Scouts wear special uniforms.

What people are like. Clothes tell something about people's beliefs and feelings, their personality, and their general approach to life. Confident people often show more independence in choosing their style of dress

NASA

Astronauts wear protective clothing. The space suit worn by astronauts on the moon protected them from heat and cold. It also provided an artificial atmosphere in which they could live.

A uniform is the distinctive clothing that identifies a person as a member of a certain group or organization. For example, this boy's uniform shows that he is a Boy Scout.

than does someone who is shy or unsure of himself. The confident individual is likely to try new clothing styles. A shy person may seek security by following current styles. Others may be unconcerned about their dress and care little whether they dress in what others consider attractive clothing.

Some people wear plain clothes because of strong beliefs about personal behavior. These people believe it is wrong to care about wearing clothes as decoration. They believe that, instead, people should be concerned with other matters. Members of the Amish religious group have this kind of belief. Amish men wear plain, dark clothes, and Amish women wear long, plain dresses.

How people feel. Clothing often helps communicate the mood of a person. People who are sad or upset may show little concern for their appearance. Clothing with bright colors and bold designs may indicate happiness. Such clothing may even brighten the mood of others who see a person wearing it.

In many societies, clothing of certain colors has special meaning. For example, people in mourning may wear black clothes. But colors may have different meanings in various societies. A color worn for weddings in one country may be worn for funerals in another land.

Most brides in the United States wear white gowns. But the people in India wear white clothes to mourn the dead.

What people want to be. People often wear clothes that they think make them appear a certain way. People may dress to hide their feelings or their age, or they may dress like people in some occupation. A person who feels sad may wear bright clothes to hide this mood from others. Many children enjoy wearing the clothes of their mother or father to "play grown-up." A person entering show business may imitate the dress of some entertainer whose success is established. When applying for jobs, many people wear clothes that they think make them look older or younger than their real age. They may also dress as they think people holding a certain job should look.

Decoration. Most people want to wear clothing that makes them feel attractive—even if its chief purpose is protection or communication. Such protective clothes as raincoats, snow boots, and sweaters come in bright colors and bold patterns. Even military uniforms are designed to improve the appearance of servicemen and servicewomen.

Many people accept frequent changes in clothing styles because they want to appear attractive by wearing the latest fashions. A woman may stop wearing an old coat that is still in excellent condition. She does so because she feels it no longer makes her so attractive as does a new style of coat.

A ceremonial costume is probably worn more as decoration than as covering by this man in New Guinea. Decoration is one of the chief reasons most people wear clothing.

Clothing around the world

For thousands of years, people in different parts of the world have worn different types of clothes. Today, the Western style of clothing—common in the United States, Canada, and Europe—has spread throughout the world. But the clothing worn by different peoples still varies widely, especially among people who do not live in cities.

Why clothing varies. There are four main reasons for worldwide variety in clothing: (1) differences in the purposes for wearing clothes, (2) differences in the materials available for making clothes, (3) differences in ways of making clothes, and (4) differences in clothing customs. These differences result in clothing variety

from continent to continent, from country to country, and even from person to person.

Purpose. As we have seen, people wear clothes for three basic purposes—protection, communication, and decoration. But people in various regions of the world often need different kinds of protection, especially if they live in different climates. People may also wear clothes that have a special meaning not understood by people of other countries. For example, many Muslim women wear veils in public because their religion requires them to hide their faces from strangers. In addition, people have different ideas about what makes clothing attractive.

Different purposes for wearing clothes cause much of the worldwide variety in clothing styles. People wear clothes for various kinds of protection. They also wear clothes to communicate with other people and to decorate themselves. The pictures in the first row below show examples of clothing worn for protection in different climates. The pictures in the second row show examples of garments worn in various countries for communication and for decoration.

Clothing in hot climates   **Clothing in cold climates**

David Moore, Black Star

Boy in American Samoa

Berko, DPI

Old man in Mexico

Paolo Koch, Rapho Guillumette

Russian family in Moscow

George Holton, Photo Researchers

Lapp family in Finland

Clothing for communication   **Clothing for decoration**

Sabine Weiss, Rapho Guillumette

Chef in France

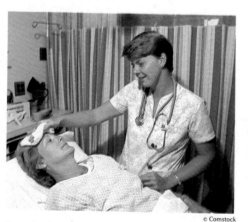

© Comstock

Nurse in the United States

Dennis Stock, Magnum

Geishas in Japan

Available materials. People in different countries may have different materials available for making clothes. For example, the people of France can wear clothes made from a much greater variety of materials than can the people of China. French stores sell garments made not only of such natural materials as cotton, fur, leather, silk, and wool, but also of such artificially made fibers as nylon and rayon. Most people in China must choose clothing made of cotton.

Ways of making clothes vary from country to country. Highly industrialized nations, such as Canada, Japan, and the United States, use many kinds of machines and a variety of processes to make clothes. For example, textile manufacturers in those countries can rapidly produce yards of cotton cloth woven many different ways. These textile manufacturers can also dye the cloth and rapidly sew it into different kinds of clothes.

People living in a village in India may have only hand-powered equipment for weaving cloth. They may create a variety of designs—maybe more than a machine can—but they need much more time than a machine to make the cloth. They would also have to sew their clothes by hand.

Clothing customs affect styles. These customs develop in a country as generation after generation of children learns what clothes to wear. For example, a Mexican farmer and a Chinese farmer may wear clothes made from similar materials and by the same basic methods. They also may need their clothes for the same purpose. But the custom in Mexico is to wear straw hats with brims that tilt up. In China, custom calls for straw hats with brims that slant down.

Different materials and methods for making clothes produce differences in clothing styles. Cotton clothes, for example, look much different than clothes made of plastics. The pictures below show some of the materials and methods used in various countries for making clothes.

Van Bucher, Photo Researchers
Spinning cotton in India

Frederick de Van from Nancy Palmer
Power loom in the U.S.

Bruno Barbey, Magnum
Leather clothing in Brazil

© Cary Wolinsky, Stock, Boston
Wool clothing in Australia

Differences in clothing customs result in differences in clothing styles. Such special clothing as uniforms and ceremonial garments clearly illustrate the influence of clothing customs. The pictures below show clothing worn by religious groups and police forces in various countries.

Religious clothing   **Police uniforms**

Marc Riboud, Magnum
Buddhist monks in Thailand

C. Knight, Photo Researchers
Catholic nuns in the U.S.

Dean Brown from Nancy Palmer
Royal Canadian Mountie

Marilyn Silverstone, Magnum
Policeman in India

Traditional costumes

Traditional costumes of many lands are shown on the following four pages. Such styles of clothing developed over hundreds of years. Many of the costumes shown are no longer worn, or are worn only as part of celebrations during festivals and holidays. This is especially true of the European costumes shown. Many of the costumes on the first two pages are still worn as everyday dress, particularly in rural areas. Traditional costumes are often called *national costumes*. But most such costumes do not represent all the people of a nation.

All illustrations in this section created for WORLD BOOK by Bill Randall and Carl Link.

Africa and the Middle East

Morocco   **Senegal**   **Ghana**

Kenya   **Somalia**   **Syria**   **Israel**   **South Africa**

Egypt   **Zaire**   **Ethiopia**   **Nigeria**   **Saudi Arabia**

Asia and the Pacific Islands

China

Mongolia

Burma

India

Indonesia

Tahiti   Philippines

Thailand

Korea

Malaysia

Vietnam

Afghanistan

Japan

Europe

Switzerland   Germany   Austria   Norway   Sweden

The Netherlands   Scotland   Wales   France   Greece

Spain

Czechoslovakia   Russia

Hungary

North and South America

United States Eskimos

Mexico

United States Cowboy

United States Indians

Guatemala

Brazil

Chile

Ecuador

Bolivia

Argentina

Peru

For thousands of years, people have worn some kind of clothing. They probably made their first clothes from the fur of animals they killed. Gradually, they learned to use other materials. They also invented tools and machines to weave cloth and sew clothing.

This section of the article covers chiefly the history of clothing in the Middle East, Europe, and North America. The people of these regions have made the greatest contribution to the development of the Western style of dress. Information about non-Western clothing appears in other *World Book* articles. For example, see the **Indian, American,** article to learn about the clothing of North and South American Indians. See the **Africa** and **Asia** articles for information about clothing worn on those continents. Also see such country articles as **Argentina** and **Japan** to learn about the clothing worn by the peoples of those countries.

Ancient times began more than 5,000 years ago and lasted until about the A.D. 400's. Most of our information about clothing worn in ancient times comes from vases, statues, and *frescoes* (wall paintings). A large amount of jewelry has survived from the period. However, few woven fabrics or leather items have lasted through the years. Some garments from ancient times have been preserved under special conditions, such as the dry climate of Egypt.

The colors of most ancient paintings and statues have worn away through the centuries. For that reason, clothing shown on such items appears white or light-colored. Some ancient peoples—such as the Egyptians—actually wore white clothes. But many other peoples probably wore colorful garments. For example, frescoes uncovered during the 1700's at the site of the ancient Roman city of Pompeii show people wearing brightly colored clothing.

The Egyptians used linen in making most of their clothes. Many slaves and children did not wear clothes, but high-ranking families wore them to indicate their status in society. The Egyptians wore garments made of rectangular pieces of fabric.

During the early years of the ancient Egyptian civilization, men wore a wide girdle, a diaperlike *loincloth,* or a short, wraparound skirt. Through the years, men began wearing longer skirts, and they often wore one skirt over another. Egyptian women at first wore sheathlike dresses. These tight-fitting garments had either one or two straps over the shoulders. Most of the dresses hung to the feet and left the breasts bare. The women often wore jewelry.

Later, both men and women often wore long, robe-like garments instead of skirts and dresses. They made these robes by folding rectangular pieces of cloth in

Wooden statue from Egypt (2300's B.C.); The Brooklyn Museum, Brooklyn, N.Y., Charles Edwin Wilbour Fund

Skirts were a common type of clothing worn by many Egyptian men. Men often wore one skirt over another. The Egyptians made most of their clothes from linen.

Stone statue from Sumer (about 2800 B.C.); (Raymond V. Schoder, S.J.)

The kaunakes was a type of skirt worn by the Sumerians. Historians believe that the kaunakes was made of sheepskin or of cloth covered with several rows of wool fringe.

Sculpture from Iraq (800's B.C.); The Brooklyn Museum, Gift of Hagop Kevorkian (Robert S. Crandall)

The Assyrians usually put fringe on their clothing. King Ashurnasirpal II, *above,* wore the style of beard and long, curled hair common among Assyrian men.

Wall painting from Knossos, Crete (about 1500 B.C.); (Raymond V. Schoder, S.J.)

The Cretans wore clothing different from that of any other ancient people. The men wore short skirts held up by a belt. Some of these belts may have been metal.

half lengthwise and cutting a hole on the fold for the head. People wore the robes draped in various ways. Sometimes they let the robes hang straight and full. Other times they tied the robes at the waist with a wide sash.

Egyptian men and women both wore wigs made of human hair, palm-leaf fibers, or wool. Many men shaved their heads, and so did some women. Men and women occasionally wore sandals, but most Egyptians went barefoot. See **Egypt, Ancient** (Food, clothing, and shelter; pictures).

The Sumerians, Babylonians, and Assyrians herded sheep and dressed in the wool their flocks provided. They lived in Mesopotamia, an area that extended through parts of what are now Iraq, Syria, and Turkey. The Sumerians lived in the southern part of this region. The Babylonians lived in the center, and the Assyrians in the north.

The Sumerians wore either a smooth-fitting skirt with fringe at the bottom or a skirt called a *kaunakes.* Some historians believe the kaunakes was made of cloth covered with rows of wool fringe. Others think it was made of shaggy sheepskin. Sumerian women wore a capelike garment in addition to the kaunakes. The Assyrians and Babylonians wore chiefly a large shawl or scarf wrapped around the waist and hips. They arranged this garment with one end draped over the left shoulder. The Assyrians and some Babylonians wore a short-sleeved tunic under the shawl.

The people of Mesopotamia usually had fringe on the edges of their clothing. During the early years of this period, they wore various types of headdresses and generally went barefoot. Later in the period, these people wore sandals, shoes, and boots. Assyrian men were noted for their long, heavy, curled hair and their black beards.

The Persians were among the first people to cut and fit garments, rather than simply drape themselves in pieces of fabric. Ancient Persia covered much of what is now Iran.

The Persians were hunters and horsemen. Historians believe they began to wear fitted animal skins because the fitted clothing was better suited to hunting and riding than were loose, flowing garments. Later, they made garments of woven cloth.

Persian men wore trousers that were tightly fitted at the ankles. Shoes or boots were worn with the trousers. The men also wore tunics and coats with sleeves. Persian women wore garments similar to those of the men, but they also wore long veils. Persian garments set a pattern for the fitted type of clothing that later developed in western Europe.

The Hebrews left little information about their clothing. The Old Testament provides some description of early Hebrew garments, and some paintings and carvings from the years of Assyrian and Egyptian rule show Hebrew people. These sources indicate that the Hebrews dressed much like their Middle Eastern neighbors, who wore wraparound shawls and tunics. According to the Bible, the Hebrews sewed tassels on their clothing. The men wore locks of hair called *sidelocks* on the side of the head. For religious reasons, the Hebrews

avoided wearing clothing made of a mixture of linen and wool.

The Cretans lived on Crete, an island about 80 miles (130 kilometers) south of Greece. They wore clothes unlike those of any other ancient people. Cretan women wore dresses that had the tight-waisted, corseted look of Western women's dress of the mid-1800's. Skirts on the dresses were long and bell-shaped with layers of wide ruffles. The women's blouses had sleeves but left the breasts bare. The women used hair ornaments, necklaces, and other jewelry.

Cretan men wore short skirts that dipped in front and back. The skirts were held at the waist by tight belts, some of which may have been metal. Men wore boots or sandals or went barefoot. Both men and women wore various types of headdresses.

The Greeks wore soft, flowing garments made of rectangular pieces of cloth. Men and women wore the same types of clothes. Common garments included the *chiton,* a straight, hanging garment fastened at the shoulders and tied at the waist, and the *himation,* a kind of large cloak. The *chlamys* was a shorter cloak for a man that left his fighting arm bare.

Greek jewelry included gold earrings, hair decorations, and brooches called *fibulae* for fastening garments at the shoulder. The people went barefoot at home and wore boots or sandals for hunting and traveling. Men wore a broad-brimmed hat called the *petasos* and a narrow-brimmed or brimless hat called the *pilos.* Greek women decorated their heads with a great variety of bands, caps, and scarves. See **Greece, Ancient** (pictures).

Archaeological Museum, Knossos, Crete (Bernard G. Silberstein from Rapho Guillumette)

Cretan women wore fancy dresses similar to that of the Cretan snake goddess shown above. The women also wore hair ornaments, necklaces, and other kinds of jewelry.

Sculpture from the Acropolis, Athens (about 460 B.C.) (Raymond V. Schoder, S.J.)

The chiton, *above,* was a straight, hanging garment commonly worn by the Greeks. They often used brooches called *fibulae* to fasten the chiton at the shoulder.

Statue, *Sosandra of Calomis* (about 460 B.C.) (Raymond V. Schoder, S.J.)

Statue (A.D. 100's); The Louvre, Paris

Greek men and women both wore soft, flowing garments. The Romans had similar styles of clothing because they based their garments chiefly on those of the Greeks.

Roman boys wore a good luck charm called a *bulla* around the neck. They wore it until manhood. The boy shown above has on a type of cloak called a *toga.*

The Romans wore clothing based chiefly on that of the Greeks. The Greek chiton and himation became the Roman *tunic* and *pallium* for men and the *stola* and *palla* for women. The tunic varied in length but was short for soldiers. The stola hung to the floor. It was worn over a long tunic called the *tunica talaris,* a short shirtlike garment called the *camisia,* and a tight, corsetlike band of cloth called the *strophium.* The pallium and palla were outdoor garments that the Romans could use as blankets if necessary.

Roman citizens wore a carefully draped cloak called a *toga.* The toga hung over the left shoulder and was wrapped around under the right arm. Only people who were citizens of Rome could wear it. Slaves and exiled citizens were forbidden to wear the toga. Freed slaves were required to have special permission to wear it. See **Toga.**

Later in the Roman period, both men and women wore a type of wide-sleeved tunic called the *dalmatica.* Boys and girls wore a locket called the *bulla* as a good luck charm. Boys wore the bulla until manhood. Girls wore it until they married. Men wore sandals, shoes, and boots. Women usually wore sandals, though they also wore shoes.

The Romans developed an enormous trade in textiles. They imported woolens from Britain and Gaul, linen from Egypt, cottons from India, and silks from China and Persia. See **Rome, Ancient** (pictures).

The Middle Ages began with the fall of the West Roman Empire in the late 400's and lasted until about the 1400's. During the Middle Ages, western Europe developed independently of what remained of the old Roman Empire, which was called the *Byzantine,* or *East Roman, Empire.*

The Byzantine Empire. The ruling classes of the empire wore highly decorated cloaks and tunics. These wealthy people used silk fabrics woven with threads of gold, and they decorated their clothes with pearls and precious stones. Poorer people wore plain tunics and blouses.

During early Byzantine times, the emperor and the men of his court wore a type of cloak called a *paludamentum* over their tunics. The empress also wore a paludamentum, and with it she wore a wide jeweled collar called a *maniakis.* Women of the court wore long stolas and pallas. In later Byzantine times, the emperor and empress wore a long, narrow scarf called a *lorum* instead of a paludamentum. Noblemen began to wear long, tight stockings called *hosa.*

Western Europe. The Celtic peoples of Britain and Gaul had adopted some ideas from Roman clothing during the time of the Roman Empire. During the Middle Ages, the styles of the Byzantine Empire gradually blended with those of western Europe. Through the years, Byzantine clothing increasingly influenced the style of dress in western Europe. Members of the ruling classes especially began to wear clothes that were fancier than the usual rough garments made of cloth, fur, and leather.

During the early Middle Ages, people made their

Detail of a mosaic (524-547); Church of San Vitale, Ravenna, Italy (Raymond V. Schoder, S.J.)

Clothing of early Byzantine times included garments like those worn by the emperor and the men of his court. The picture above shows Emperor Justinian and some of his attendants.

clothes at home as they had done for hundreds of years. Families raised sheep and grew flax. They spun thread and wove it into fabric for their clothes. As towns grew, specialized shops gradually appeared, run by weavers, tailors, cobblers, and other craftworkers who made clothes. During the 1100's, these craftworkers began to organize simple labor unions called *guilds* (see **Guild**). The quality of cloth improved as the craftworkers developed greater skills. They began to cut, fit, and decorate clothes in more elaborate ways.

Men and women of the early Middle Ages wore simple tunics and circular or rectangular cloaks. Later, fitted clothes began to replace the loose, flowing cloaks and tunics. The woman's tunic developed into a long dress that was laced to closely fit the upper part of her body. Men wore loose breeches under their tunics. They also wore various kinds of tight leg coverings. For example, they might wrap their legs in long pieces of cloth or wear long stockings of bright colors.

During the 1100's and 1200's, women wore metal hairnets, veils, and draped throat covers called *wimples*. Men wore hoods that had long tails called *liripipes*. Both men and women wore a type of outer tunic—adopted from the crusaders' garments—called a *surcoat*. Some surcoats were sleeveless and cut with low armholes. The woman's surcoat was long and worn over a long-sleeved gown. Men wore sleeveless surcoats of various lengths from the knee to the ankle.

During the 1300's, clothes of the upper classes became increasingly fancy, and accessories became popular. Dozens of buttons were used to trim men's outer garments. Many clothes had decorative edging called *dagging*. Men wore a close-fitting, low-waisted jacket called a *cote-hardie* with an expensive jeweled belt. A long, tight-fitting gown worn by women had the same name. In the late 1300's, both men and women wore fancy garments called *houppelandes*. At first, the man's houppelande was a long outer garment that hung to the floor. It was gradually shortened and became a jacket. The woman's houppelande was long and high-waisted with long, flaring sleeves.

In the later Middle Ages, the wealthy wore silks and other fine fabrics woven in Italy and Spain or brought to Europe from the East by traders. Lords and ladies of the courts trimmed their clothes with expensive ermine, marten, and sable fur. But most people wore linen and wool clothes. They dressed in much plainer styles than those worn by the ruling classes. The lesser nobility and the middle classes lined and trimmed their clothes with fox, otter, and rabbit fur. The common people wore garments made of the skins of goats, sheep, or wolves. See **Middle Ages** (pictures).

The surcoat was a tunic worn in Europe in the 1200's. These knights wear surcoats over chain-metal armor.

Detail of an illuminated Old Testament manuscript; The Pierpont Morgan Library, New York City

The wimple was a throat cover worn by western European women during the 1200's. The women wore it with various hoodlike head coverings.

Detail of an illuminated manuscript, *Le Roman de la Rose*; Bibliothèque Nationale, Paris (Hubert Josse)

Fur trim was worn on clothing during the 1400's and 1500's. Fox and rabbit fur were often used.

Detail of *Elderly Couple* by Jan Gossaert (about 1520); The National Gallery, London (Raymond V. Schoder, S.J.)

Italian clothing became more elaborate during the Renaissance than ever before. In this wedding scene, the two men at the far right wear a kind of draped turban called a *chaperon*.

Detail of a painted chest; Accademia di Firenze, Florence, Italy (Hubert Josse)

The Renaissance began in Italy about 1300 and spread throughout Europe during the 1400's and 1500's. Towns thrived during the Renaissance, and the number of merchants and craftworkers grew rapidly. The Byzantine Empire fell, and western Europe took the lead in clothing design. European dress of the 1400's shows the influence of ideas and attitudes that developed during the Renaissance.

Clothing was fancier and more complicated than ever before. Women wore many kinds of elaborate headdresses, including the high, cone-shaped *hennin.* The hennin—worn in many European countries during the late 1400's—rose 3 to 4 feet (0.9 to 1.2 meters) high and was draped with a veil. Jewelry and bright-colored fabrics with large, flowered designs were popular.

Men wore longer stockings as jackets became shorter. The stockings became close-fitting trousers that resembled tights. Men wore many kinds of hats, including a draped turban called the *chaperon.* They also wore pointed-toe shoes called *poulaines.* On some shoes, the points measured 6 inches (15 centimeters) or more.

Men of the early 1500's wore many layers of outer garments, and their clothing was heavily padded. They put on linen shirts under tight-fitting upper garments called *doublets.* Over the doublet, they wore a jacket called a *jerkin,* which had a skirt that hung to between the waist and the knee. A knee-length gown with large sleeves came over the jerkin. Men also wore short, puffed breeches called *upper stocks* that were sewn to tight stockings called *netherstocks.*

Women's clothing was cut and sewn to fit tightly above the waist. During the first half of the 1500's, women wore dresses with low, square necklines and with skirts propped out stiffly over petticoats. Many skirts were split in front to show elaborate underskirts. Both men's and women's garments were often slashed so that the fabric of garments worn underneath could be pulled through in small puffs.

The stiff and formal fashions of the Spanish court influenced styles throughout Europe during the late 1500's. Men wore stockings and either padded breeches called *trunkhose* or slimmer knee breeches. Padding in the doublet developed into the *peasecod belly* fashion, which had a pointed bulge over the abdomen. The wide skirts of women's dresses were supported by a device called a *farthingale.* One type of farthingale was an underskirt with a rigid frame made of whalebone, wire, or wood. The frame made the skirt stand out stiffly away from the body. Another kind of farthingale was a long, thick pillow that women tied around the waist under a dress. Both men and women wore fancy starched collars called *ruffs.* See **Renaissance** (pictures).

Detail from a manuscript of the 1400's; Bibliothèque Nationale, Paris

Renaissance clothing included men's hats with the brim pointed in front and turned up in back. King Louis IX of France wore such a hat when he started on a crusade, as shown above.

Lady with a Pink by Hans Memling; The Metropolitan Museum of Art, New York City, the Jules S. Bache Collection, 1949

The hennin was a style of high, cone-shaped headdress worn by European women during the Renaissance.

Detail of *Portrait of Lady Guilford* by Hans Holbein the Younger; The City Museum, St. Louis (Raymond V. Schoder, S.J.)

Puffs of fabric were often pulled through slashes in clothing in the Renaissance.

Earl of Leicester by an unknown artist; National Portrait Gallery, London

Stylish men of the 1500's wore a *peasecod belly,* which bulged over the abdomen.

Portrait of Marchesa Doria by Anton van Dyck; The Louvre, Paris (Raymond V. Schoder, S.J.)

The ruff was a large starched collar worn by men and women in the Renaissance.

The 1600's. Fancy, decorated clothing remained popular throughout most of Europe during the 1600's. Spain declined in importance, and France took the lead in setting clothing styles.

Men began to replace their doublets with waistcoats worn under knee-length coats. In the mid-1600's, loose, knee-length trousers took the place of tight, padded breeches. But knee breeches came back into style by the end of the century.

Except in Spain, women began to wear many petticoats instead of farthingales under their gowns. Women also started wearing three-quarter sleeves. This startling change bared female arms for the first time since the fall of the Roman Empire more than 1,000 years earlier. With the shorter sleeves, women wore muffs and longer gloves. By the late 1600's, they were wearing *bustle* gowns. A bustle was a cushion that made a skirt stick out in back. Women also wore a type of high headdress called a *fontange.*

Men often wore high boots, and they carried a sword on a long sash that hung over the shoulder. They also wore fancy plumed hats over their long hair. Both men and women began to wear heeled shoes, many of which were trimmed with bows and buckles. Flat collars made of lace and linen gradually replaced the stiff ruff. A scarflike neckcloth, in turn, succeeded the flat collar in the late 1600's. Men began wearing huge, curled wigs called *periwigs* by about 1660.

The Puritans in England and the Puritan colonists who came to America preferred plainer versions of the clothing of the day. The women wore plain, dark-colored dresses and simple white caps. The men cut their hair short and wore high, stiff hats. They dressed in dark-colored breeches, doublets, and jerkins. Both men and women wore white collars.

The 1700's brought many changes in the manufacture of cloth. About 1764, James Hargreaves, an English weaver, invented the *spinning jenny,* a machine that spun a number of threads at the same time. Then, between 1774 and 1779, an English weaver named Samuel Crompton developed the *spinning mule.* This machine produced as much thread as could 200 persons spinning by hand. In the mid-1780's, Edmund Cartwright, an English clergyman, developed a steam-powered loom. With such machines as these, English weavers produced large quantities of cloth at prices lower than those charged by guild craftworkers, who wove by hand. Large factories took over the production of cloth, and many people stopped making cloth at home. See **Industrial Revolution.**

Clothing styles changed rapidly. But only the nobility and the wealthy could afford the new fashions. Most people still wore comfortable, long-lasting woolen clothing. Many continued to make their own fabrics and clothes.

French fashions set the clothing standards in Europe during most of the century. But late in the 1700's, the French Revolution interrupted France's fashion leadership, and England took the lead. After the revolution, France regained leadership in the design of women's clothes, but English tailoring continued to influence men's fashions. Clothing styles in England and France

James Stuart, Duke of Richmond and Lennox by Anton Van Dyck; The Metropolitan Museum of Art, N.Y.C., Gift of H. G. Marquand

Clothing of the 1600's included fancy, heeled shoes for men and women. Many shoes were trimmed with bows. Lace and linen collars became popular in the 1620's.

Marie Thérèse of Spain, Queen of France, and the Grand Dauphin by Pierre Mignard; The Prado, Madrid (Hubert Josse)

Three-quarter sleeves were worn by women during the 1600's, as were long gloves or muffs. To make their dresses curve out from the waist, women wore many petticoats.

Detail of *Salon of Madame Geoffrin* by an unknown French artist; National Museum of Versailles and of the Trianons, Versailles, France (Hubert Josse)

Waistcoats worn under knee-length coats replaced the doublet as the fashion for men during the 1600's. Men wore knee breeches during much of the century.

Detail of *Portrait of the Artist with his Wife and Daughter* by Nicolas de Largillière; The Louvre, Paris (Bulloz)

Periwigs were huge, curled wigs worn by men during the late 1600's and the 1700's. Men began to wear a scarflike neckcloth instead of the flat collar in the late 1600's.

affected those in the United States. Many Parisian designers distributed dolls dressed in fashions to be copied in England, America, and other parts of the world.

Both men and women wore fancy hairstyles. Men covered their heads with large powdered wigs of various shapes. By the 1770's, women wore their hair in high, carefully arranged styles called *pompadours.* They made their hair stiff with grease and powder and decorated it with feathers, jewels, and ribbons. They also added hairpieces to their own hair and wore wigs. Sometimes women did not comb out or re-dress their hair for several weeks because the styles were so complicated.

Women wore tight corsets and great round skirts held out by a hoop. During the 1780's, a bustle replaced the hoop. The style included very large fancy hats. Men wore variations of the coats, waistcoats, and breeches introduced during the late 1600's.

The outbreak of the French Revolution in 1789 brought great changes in clothing style in France and throughout the rest of Europe as well. Men started to wear much plainer clothes, with less color and ornamentation. They adopted top hats and hats called *bicornes.* Bicornes had brims folded up to form two points. These hats had replaced the *tricorne.* The tricorne, which had the brim folded to make three points, had been popular for most of the 1700's. Women began wearing clothing that imitated the styles of ancient Greece. This clothing included sandals and lightweight cotton dresses. Women cut their hair short and curled it, and they wore wide-brimmed bonnets. Dresses had low necklines and high waistlines with drawstrings. This dress style became known first as *Directoire* and then, in the early 1800's, as *Empire.*

The 1800's. Much production of clothing by hand ended during the 1800's, and the clothing industry became firmly established in the United States. Two

Americans—the inventor Elias Howe and a machinist named Isaac Singer—developed improved sewing machines in the mid-1800's. These machines and other inventions made the manufacture of cloth and clothing easier. Manufacturers began to make inexpensive, ready-to-wear clothes. Production methods used by manufacturers gradually improved. But many people still preferred to have their clothes made by a tailor or dressmaker if they could afford it. Others continued to wear homemade garments.

The Empire style lasted until the 1820's. Tight-waisted, full-skirted gowns became popular during the 1830's and 1840's, and women wore many petticoats under them. By the 1850's, women wore stiff wire or whalebone petticoats called *crinolines* to support their skirts. Earlier types of crinolines were underskirts made partly of horsehair.

By the 1870's, full-skirted dresses gave way to bustle gowns. In the 1880's, a European designer introduced the first suits for women. A type of blouse called a *shirtwaist*—worn with a separate skirt—became fashionable in the Gay Nineties. Women wore costumes that were designed in an "hourglass" style. This style required a woman to lace in her waist tightly to make it as small as possible.

In the 1800's, men's clothes continued to become plainer. By about 1815, fashionable men in Europe and the United States were wearing trousers instead of knee breeches, which had been the style for more than 200 years. For general wear in the early part of the century, men wore the long *tail coat.* Later, the knee-length, full-skirted *frock coat* replaced the tail coat. Then the plain *sack coat,* which is still worn today, replaced the frock coat. Men kept the tail coat for formal wear only. A coat called the *tuxedo* was also worn for formal occasions in the late 1800's. Men also wore caps, round bowler hats, high top hats, and straw hats. *Knickers,* which resem-

Detail of *Gathering in a Park* by Louis Joseph Watteau; Cognacq-Jay Museum, Paris (Bulloz)

Large, fancy hats became stylish for women during the late 1700's. Women also wore tight corsets and round skirts.

Detail of *Portrait of Madame Seriziat* by Jacques Louis David; The Louvre, Paris (Hubert Josse)

Women's clothing became simpler in the early 1790's. Fashionable women wore lightweight cotton dresses.

Engraving; Library of the Carnavalet Museum, Paris (Lauros-Giraudon)

Tight-waisted dresses with full skirts were popular in the 1830's. Women wore many petticoats under their skirts.

Engraving; Carnavalet Museum, Paris (Lauros-Giraudon)

Fashionable men of the 1800's wore the frock coat, *left,* the tail coat, *center and right,* and top hats.

bled the old knee breeches, became popular for sports after 1870.

The 1900's. From 1890 to 1920, improved manufacturing methods brought rapid growth to United States companies that made ready-to-wear clothing. Both men and women began to wear mostly clothing that was *mass-produced* in factories (see **Mass production**). As a result of mass production, women's fashions could change more rapidly than ever before. But men's clothing styles changed little until the 1960's.

In the 1900's, women began to wear looser, lighter-weight clothing. The changing styles—especially in leisure and sports clothes—gradually uncovered different parts of women's bodies. Legs were bared in the 1920's, abdomens in the 1940's, and thighs in the 1960's. Today, women wear less clothing than in any other period since ancient times.

For a few years around 1910, women wore *hobble skirts.* These skirts were so tight at the bottom that a woman could hardly walk. Clothing became simpler and less formal during World War I (1914-1918). In the 1920's, women adopted the "boyish" look. Dresses were straight and unfitted, and they ended at, or a little above, the knee. In the 1930's, some women began wearing slacks. Skirts became longer during the 1930's and then shorter during the early 1940's. During World War II (1939-1945), women wore many tailored styles with padded shoulders. Slacks—worn by women working in war industries—also became popular.

Women's fashions changed greatly after World War II. Crinolines and long, full skirts returned. Nylon garments, including stockings and *lingerie* (underwear), became available in large quantities. During the 1950's, straight, tight-fitting *sheath dresses* and shorter hemlines gained popularity. *A-line dresses* and loose-fitting *shifts* came into style during the early 1960's. The very short *miniskirt* quickly spread to other countries after it

first appeared in England during the mid-1960's.

From 1900 to 1950, both single-breasted and double-breasted men's suits were popular. Shoulders were *natural* (unpadded) about 1910 but gradually became more padded. During the 1950's, many men switched to single-breasted *Ivy League* suits, which had narrow lapels and natural shoulders. They also began wearing colored shirts with business suits.

Both men and women developed great fondness for sportswear and wash-and-wear fabrics during the 1950's and 1960's. Leisure and sports clothes for women included knee-length Bermuda shorts, tapered slacks, and ski and stretch pants. Men wore Bermuda shorts, slacks, and colorful sport shirts. Improvements in sewing machines and in dress patterns brought an increased interest in sewing.

In the 1960's, many young men started to wear colorful fashions, many of which included fancy jewelry. They also grew beards and mustaches. During the early 1970's, men of all ages joined in the change to colorful clothes. They began wearing shirts in checks, stripes, and many colors with business suits. They also wore wide ties in fancy prints, stripes, or bright swirling colors. Men of all ages began growing beards and mustaches. They also began wearing their hair longer than in the 1960's. Women's fashions included skirts of every length—from the miniskirt to the *maxiskirt,* which fell to the ankle. Many people seemed to have an "anything goes" feeling toward clothing styles.

During the 1980's, men's and women's fashions "softened." In the early 1980's, men wore suits with padded shoulders but a loose fit. By the late 1980's, suits had natural shoulders and were less formal. Women's fashions included many options. Women wore slacks, skirts of every length, and sportswear that combined sweaters, jackets, skirts, and dresses. Exercise wear that fit tightly was popular, but so too was oversized, baggy clothing.

Bettmann Archive

The hourglass style was worn by women during the 1890's. This style called for waists laced in tightly to make them as small as possible.

Photo Researchers

The boyish look was fashionable during the 1920's. Women wore straight, unfitted dresses that hung to the knee, and long necklaces.

Photoworld

Pants outfits became stylish for women during the 1940's. Fashionable women generally wore tailored styles with padded shoulders.

M. A. Keller, The Stock Market

Tailored clothing with loose, casual styling became popular business wear for both men and women during the 1980's and early 1990's.

The clothing industry is one of the largest industries in the world. It includes the manufacture of women's, children's, and infants' clothes and men's and boys' wear. It also produces furs, including "fake furs"; embroidery; hats, jewelry, shoes, and other accessories; items called *findings* (buttons, hooks, snaps, zippers, and thread); underwear and sleepwear; foundation garments; and sportswear.

The main clothing centers of the world are London, New York City, Paris, and Milan. The United States leads all countries in the manufacture of clothing. The United States clothing industry is one of the nation's major industries. There are about 21,000 U.S. clothing manufacturers, and they employ about 1,100,000 people. About 8,000 of these companies make women's clothes. The Canadian clothing industry has more than 2,400 manufacturers.

The largest number of garment factories in the United States operate in the Middle Atlantic States—New York, New Jersey, and Pennsylvania. New York leads all the states, with about 5,100 clothing manufacturers. New York City ranks as the chief clothing manufacturing center of the United States, followed by Los Angeles-Long Beach, Philadelphia, Detroit, Jersey City, and Dallas-Fort Worth.

Most clothing manufacturers have small factories. These firms employ an average of fewer than 100 persons, though some have as many as 1,000 workers.

Clothing materials include many natural and artificially created substances. People have used some materials, such as animal furs, for clothes for thousands of years. Other materials, including plastic sheetings and artificially created fibers, came into practical use during the 1900's.

Natural materials include fur, leather, and cloth that is made of plant or animal fibers.

Fur and leather provide many of the warmest and longest-wearing clothes. They are also used in some of the most expensive, fragile, and luxurious garments. Fur comes only from warm-blooded animals. Leather comes from either warm-blooded or cold-blooded animals.

Fur is used mostly for coats and coat linings. Such furs as *mouton,* a fur made of sheepskin, make warm coats that wear well. Chinchilla fur is soft, fragile, and not so warm as other furs. Most furs are dyed, plucked, sheared, or treated in some other way before being made into clothes. See **Fur.**

Most leather is used to make shoes. Such items as gloves and handbags—and some jackets, pants, skirts, and suits—are also made of leather. Tanners manufacture leather by treating hides to make them soft and flexible and to prevent them from rotting. Most leather for clothing is made from cowhide. See **Leather.**

Cotton, flax, silk, and wool are the natural fibers most widely used in clothing. They are long and flexible and can easily be made into thread. Cloth made from each of these fibers has a special quality that makes it popular. Silk has great luster and softness, for example, and wool provides warmth.

Threads of cotton, flax, silk, and wool fibers are usually knitted or woven into fabric (see **Knitting; Weaving**). Such methods as braiding and lace making are occa-

sionally used to make clothing materials. Wool can be made into felt by pressing and rubbing together warm, damp wool fibers. Other kinds of fibers do not stick together when pressed unless they have been treated with an adhesive substance.

Cotton fibers come from the *boll* (seed pod) of the cotton plant. Fibers from the stem of the flax plant are woven into linen. Silk, the strongest of all natural fibers, comes from cocoons spun by silkworms. Sheep provide most of the wool that people use, though such animals as the alpaca and various breeds of goats also furnish wool. See **Cotton; Linen; Silk; Wool.**

Manufactured materials include paper, plastic sheetings, rubber, and artificially produced fibers. Clothing manufacturers are using more of these materials because they have certain advantages over natural ones. For example, many are stronger, more shrink-resistant, or less expensive than natural fibers.

In 1884, a French chemist and inventor named Hilaire Chardonnet patented the first successful artificial fiber. He called it *artificial silk.* Chardonnet's fiber was first manufactured in the United States in 1910. It was named *rayon* in 1924. Since then, scientists have developed many other artificial fibers, sometimes called *synthetics.* Chemists develop them from natural substances or by combining two or more chemical compounds. Other synthetics include nylon and polyester.

Today, many widely used fabrics are blends of natural and synthetic fibers. For example, such fabrics could be a mixture of cotton and polyester or wool and nylon. These fabrics have the characteristics of each fiber used in the blend. A fabric made of wool and nylon is warm because of the wool and is shrink-resistant because of the nylon. See **Synthetics** and its list of *Related articles.*

Paper, plastic sheetings, and rubber have been used less in clothes than have synthetic fibers, but their use is increasing. Some paperlike fabrics are made of fibers held together by adhesive substances. Others are made by combining synthetic fibers with natural fibers or rayon. The synthetics melt when heated and hold the network of fibers together as a fabric. Such fabrics are widely used in making disposable diapers, which are thrown away after being soiled once. Paperlike fabrics are also used for other disposable garments, including bibs, underwear, and rainwear. Manufacturers use plastic sheetings in making such products as handbags, raincoats, and shoes. Rubber is used chiefly to make such flexible, long-lasting, waterproof clothing as boots and gloves.

Ready-to-wear clothes. Most clothes worn today are ready-to-wear garments. Mass production of clothing saves customers both the time it would take to make clothes themselves and the money they would spend on clothes made by a dressmaker or tailor.

Designing is the first step in the manufacture of ready-to-wear clothing. Fashion designers in London, New York City, Paris, and Milan create most clothing styles. They work under great pressure to produce designs—especially of women's fashions—that people will want to buy.

In the United States, most large clothing manufacturers employ their own designers. These experts create styles in addition to those that come from Paris and the other fashion centers. Manufacturers try to sell the designs to buyers from clothing stores. Most smaller clothing manufacturers purchase designs from independent designers, as do firms that produce garments which change little in fashion.

After a designer has an idea for a style, he or she chooses the colors and types of fabrics in which to make the garment. The designer then makes samples of the garments, and buyers from stores come to see them. If the buyers see a style they think their customers will like and will buy, they order garments of that design. The final test for any style comes when the clothes appear in stores. If enough people buy a particular style, stores will reorder it from the manufacturer. If customers ignore a style, it soon disappears—and another style takes its place.

Manufacturing and selling. After receiving orders from stores for a certain design, the manufacturer cuts patterns of the garment in various sizes. Ready-to-wear clothes come in standard sizes for different ages and figure types.

Clothing manufacturers buy fabrics in large rolls called *bolts.* Expert examiners unroll the bolts of material and inspect them for rips or other flaws. *Spreaders* pile the bolts on large tables. Workers called *markers* outline each pattern in chalk on the material. In some companies, the markers transfer pattern markings to a large piece of paper that serves as a guide for cutting the material. Next, *cutters* use electric cutting machines or hand cutting tools to cut out the various parts of the garments. Then *sorters,* who also are called *assorters,* *assemblers,* or *bundlers,* number the pieces of material and put all the pieces that are alike in a bundle. The bundles, along with the necessary buttons and trimmings, are then sent to the sewing room.

Most sewers handle only one or two parts of a garment. For example, a sewer may stitch only shoulder seams and hems. Another sewer may make pockets and collars. On some elaborate, expensive coats, dresses, or suits, one person may do all or most of the sewing by hand. *Finishers* do all the outside stitching, such as making buttonholes. *Pressers* iron the completed garments.

Some clothing companies handle all the steps in the manufacture and distribution of their products. Others send their cut garments to clothing *contractors,* who sew them together and return them. Sometimes clothing *jobbers* buy cut garments and complete the manufacturing and distribution process. Manufacturers sell most garments directly to retail stores. They may also sell to wholesale dealers, who in turn sell to retailers.

Protecting the public. In the United States, federal laws protect the public in the purchase of clothing. Several of these laws require clothing manufacturers, wholesalers, and retailers to cooperate with textile manufacturers in placing accurate labels on all garments.

The Wool Products Labeling Act of 1939 requires labels on wool fabrics to tell the kind and amount of wool used. If wool fiber from a garment that has been worn is shredded up and made into yarn or fabric, manufacturers must label the new product *reused.* If the wool has been made into a fabric before but not used in a garment that was actually worn, manufacturers must say the wool has been *reprocessed.* The Textile Fiber Products Identification Act of 1958 calls for labels that show fiber content by percentage. This law applies to all fabrics except those made of wool. The Fur Products Labeling Act of 1952 requires labeling of fur garments and accessories. The label must identify the type of animal fur and tell if it has been bleached or dyed. The label must also indicate if the garment or the fur used in making the garment is imported, and if the garment is second-hand. The Flammable Fabrics Act of 1953 prohibits the sale of fabrics that burn easily.

WORLD BOOK photo by Ralph Brunke

Ready-to-wear clothes come in a wide variety of styles, colors, and fabrics. Most clothes bought today are of this type.

Leading clothing-producing states and provinces

Value added by manufacture	
New York	●●●●●●●●●●●●●●●●●●●●●● $5,005,400,000
California	●●●●●●●●●●●●●●●●● $3,988,200,000
Pennsylvania	●●●●●●●●●● $2,198,900,000
North Carolina	●●●●●●●●● $1,916,800,000
Georgia	●●●●●●●●● $1,900,700,000
Texas	●●●●●●●● $1,697,300,000
Tennessee	●●●●●●● $1,524,200,000
Quebec	●●●●●● $1,425,800,000
New Jersey	●●●●●● $1,392,200,000
Alabama	●●●●●● $1,328,000,000

Figures are for 1987. All figures are in U.S. dollars. Sources: U.S. Bureau of the Census; Statistics Canada.

Fashion designers hold important positions in the clothing industry. The sale of a garment depends largely on the popularity of its design. In turn, the jobs of many people and the profits of many companies depend on the work of designers. People who wish to become fashion designers may take fashion-designing courses in college or attend special design schools in New York City or some other large city.

A successful fashion designer may have special personal qualifications or talents. In addition, most designers know how to drape and sketch new styles, draw and cut patterns, and sew garments. Many designers start their careers as assistants in design departments, as sample makers, or as artists in pattern houses. In time, some designers establish their own firms or form partnerships with other designers.

Fashion coordinators perform a variety of jobs. For example, they may plan an entire fashion show or select the shoes that a model wears for an advertisement. Most large department stores employ fashion coordinators who select merchandise, plan displays, and promote sales. For such work, a person must have a thorough knowledge of current fashion trends.

Fashion writers and artists specialize in describing or illustrating clothes for advertisements and articles in magazines and newspapers and for direct-mail ads. They may work for advertising agencies, department stores, manufacturers, publications, or wholesalers. Experts called *copywriters* prepare the written material for clothing advertisements. They must have a talent for writing and a knowledge of clothing design and materials. Fashion editors decide what current fashions will appear in their publications. They may travel to Paris or other fashion centers to attend fashion shows. These ed-itors must know what types of displays will catch a reader's attention, and they should be able to forecast fashion trends.

Fashion illustrators need some knowledge of clothing construction in addition to a talent for drawing. Fashion photographers must know how to work with fashion models and arrange merchandise attractively as well as how to use camera equipment.

Garment manufacturing. Men and women who are interested in making clothes may become cutters, dressmakers, finishers, sewing-machine operators, or tailors. They must be able to work quickly and skillfully with their hands. Most garment makers start in training positions under experienced workers. People with training in business management or industrial engineering may find opportunities in garment-manufacturing plants as production managers or plant engineers.

Merchandising. Qualified people may find positions with stores as buyers, department heads, or salespeople. In time, they could become officers in a store or chain of stores. Many men and women open their own small retail clothing shops.

A number of colleges and business schools offer specialized management courses that provide training for merchandising positions. Most large department stores and specialty stores offer management-training programs to college graduates and occasionally to experienced members of their staffs.

Teaching. Men and women with enough college training may qualify to teach high school or college courses related to clothing. Teaching specialties include clothing design, the history of clothing, the merchandising of clothes, and the meaning and importance of clothing in society. Richard Martin

WORLD BOOK photo by Steinkamp/Ballogg

A fashion designer uses computer graphics to create original clothing designs. Printouts of various designs are hanging on the wall behind the computer.

WORLD BOOK photo by Steinkamp/Ballogg

Dressmakers learn their trade by working with plastic figures called *mannequins.* By using a mannequin, a dressmaker can adjust a garment to fit the shape of the human body.

Related articles in *World Book*. See the section of the many country articles in which clothing is discussed, such as **Japan** (Way of life). See also the following articles:

Articles of clothing

Derby	Moccasin
Glove	Necktie
Handkerchief	Shoe
Hat	Stockings
Helmet	Turban

Clothes making and care

Amalgamated Clothing and Tex- tile Workers Union	Knitting
	Sewing
Dry cleaning	Spinning
Dye	Textile
Fashion	Weaving
Garment Workers' Union, International Ladies'	

Clothing materials

Acrylic	Linen
Broadcloth	Mohair
Brocade	Muslin
Calico	Net
Camel's-hair cloth	Nylon
Canvas	Percale
Cashmere	Polyester
Chenille	Ramie
Corduroy	Rayon
Cotton	Satin
Damask	Silk
Denim	Swiss
Felt	Synthetics
Flannel	Taffeta
Fur	Tweed
Gabardine	Velvet
Gingham	Voile
Jersey	Wool
Lace	Worsted
Leather	

Clothing in history

Colonial life in America (Clothing; pictures)
Egypt, Ancient (Food, clothing, and shelter; pictures)
Gauntlet
Greece, Ancient (Food, clothing, and shelter; pictures)
Indian, American (Clothing; pictures)
Pioneer life in America (Clothing)
Renaissance (pictures)
Roaring Twenties (Changing attitudes; pictures)
Rome, Ancient (Food, clothing, and shelter; pictures)
Toga
Tunic
Western frontier life (Clothing)

Other related articles

Arabs (Clothing; pictures)	Home economics
Batik	(Clothing and textiles)
Button	Jewelry
Climate (Clothing and	Modeling
climate)	Needle
Doll (Costume dolls)	New York (Manufacturing)
Easter (Wearing new	Pin
clothes)	Sewing machine
Embroidery	Strauss, Levi
Eskimo (Clothing; pictures)	Tartan
Fiber	Thread
Fire department (Protective	Twill
clothing)	Uniform
Flax	Zipper
Hairdressing	

Outline

I. Why people wear clothes
  A. Protection
  B. Communication
  C. Decoration
II. Clothing around the world
  A. Why clothing varies   B. Traditional costumes
III. Clothing through the ages
IV. The clothing industry
  A. Clothing materials
  B. Ready-to-wear clothes
  C. Protecting the public
V. Career opportunities

Questions

What are the three main reasons for wearing clothes?
What improvements did the *spinning jenny* and the *spinning mule* bring to the manufacture of cloth?
What are some ways in which federal laws protect the U.S. public in the purchase of clothing?
What advantages do synthetic fibers have over natural ones?
When did people learn to make yarn and cloth?
How do customs influence clothing styles?
What cities rank as the world's chief clothing centers?
Who were among the first peoples to wear fitted clothes?
Why does clothing vary in different parts of the world?

Additional resources

Ewing, Elizabeth. *History of Children's Costume.* Scribner, 1978.
Franck, Irene M., and Brownstone, D. M. *Clothiers.* Facts on File, 1987. Also suitable for younger readers.
Govier, Heather. *Clothes.* Garrett Educational, 1991. For younger readers.
Jerde, Judith. *Encyclopedia of Textiles.* Facts on File, 1992.
Langner, Lawrence. *The Importance of Wearing Clothes.* Rev. ed. by Julian Robinson. Elysium Growth Pr., 1991.
Men and Women: Dressing the Part. Ed. by Claudia B. Kidwell and Valerie Steele. Smithsonian Institution, 1989.
O'Hara, Georgina. *The Encyclopedia of Fashion.* Abrams, 1986.
Racinet, Albert C. A. *The Historical Encyclopedia of Costumes.* Facts on File, 1988.
Robinson, Katherine. *The Clothing Care Handbook.* Fawcett, 1985.
Rowland-Warne, L. *Costume.* Knopf, 1992. For younger readers.
Schnurnberger, Lynn. *Let There Be Clothes: 40,000 Years of Fashion.* Workman, 1991.
Scott, Stephen. *Why Do They Dress that Way?* Good Bks., 1986.
Sichel, Marion. *History of Men's Costume.* Chelsea Hse., 1990. First published in 1984.
Wilcox, R. Turner. *Five Centuries of American Costume.* Scribner, 1976. First published in 1963. *Folk and Festival Costume of the World.* 1977. First published in 1965.

Clotho. See **Fates.**

Cloture, also called *closure,* shuts off debate in a legislative body. A legislature may vote to effect cloture. Free and open debate is necessary in a democracy in order to reach sound decisions and protect minority groups. But if debate is unlimited, a minority in a legislature may prevent any action simply by continuing to debate. This activity is known as *filibustering.*

In 1917, the United States Senate adopted a rule that provided for cloture upon the vote of two-thirds of the senators present. The Senate amended the rule in 1975 to require a vote of at least 60 senators, three-fifths of its members, to achieve cloture on most issues. On proposed changes in Senate rules, however, cloture requires a vote of two-thirds of the senators who are present.   Peter Woll

See also **Filibustering.**

Peter Black, Tom Stack and Associates

A towering cumulus cloud may rise to great heights and may develop into a cumulonimbus cloud that brings a thunderstorm.

Bernie Mendoza, Tom Stack and Associates

Some cumulonimbus clouds have rounded bumps on their undersides. Tornadoes sometimes come from these clouds.

Van Bucher, Photo Researchers

High cirrus clouds look like tufts of hair. They are so high and cold that the water they contain is frozen into ice crystals.

Van Bucher, Photo Researchers

Medium-high altocumulus clouds, *above,* may appear as small cloud patches arranged in bands or irregular groups.

Russ Kinne, Photo Researchers

Low stratus clouds cover the sky with a thick, even blanket. These clouds usually bring rain or snow.

Cloud is a mass of small water droplets or tiny ice crystals that floats in the air. Fluffy white clouds floating across a blue sky, or the colors of clouds at sunset, are part of the beauty of nature. Clouds also play an important part in the earth's weather. The water that they bring as rain and snow is necessary to all forms of life. Clouds can also bring destruction or even death, in the form of hail or tornadoes.

Some clouds are great fleecy masses, and others look like giant feathers. Still others are dull gray or black sheets that darken the earth. Most clouds change shape

continually. They do so because parts of the cloud evaporate when mixed with air that is drier than the cloud. Cloud shapes also change because of the action of winds and air movements.

Kinds of clouds

Scientists give names to clouds that describe their appearance. For example, the prefix *strato-* means *layerlike* or *sheetlike*. Clouds that appear as layers or sheets are called *stratus* clouds. The prefix *cumulo-* means *pile* or *heap,* and *cumulus* clouds are piled-up masses of white clouds. The prefix *cirro-* means *curl,* and *cirrus* clouds are curly white clouds. These terms and a few others are used to form the names of the most common clouds. The various types of clouds are grouped into different

Margaret A. LeMone, the contributor of this article, is a Scientist at the National Center for Atmospheric Research.

Cirrus fibratus and cirrus floccus clouds are thicker than the wispy cirrus clouds, and cover larger areas of the sky.

Josef Muench

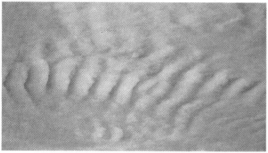

Altocumulus undulatus clouds, *above,* form bands across the sky. The gaps between the bands may be wide or narrow.

Ray Brod

Russ Kinne, Photo Researchers

Stratocumulus clouds cover the sky with large, rounded masses within a few thousand feet of the ground.

	Feet*	Meters*
		18
	55	
Cirrus	50	15
	45	
	40	12
Cirrocumulus	35	
	30	9
Cirrostratus	25	
Cumulonimbus		
	20	6
	15	
Altocumulus	10	3
Cumulus Congestus		
Stratocumulus	5	
Stratus		
Stratus	0	0

*Scale indicates altitude in thousands of feet or thousands of meters.

WORLD BOOK diagram by Herb Herrick

Different clouds are seen at various altitudes above the earth. This diagram shows examples of some common clouds and their approximate altitudes. Many clouds are found only within a certain range of altitudes. Other clouds, such as the cumulonimbus, extend from very low to very high altitudes.

classes according to their height above the ground.

Low clouds. Two kinds of clouds, *stratus* and *stratocumulus,* are usually seen near the earth. The *bases* (lower edges) of most of these clouds are less than 6,000 feet (1,800 meters) above sea level. A stratus cloud looks like a smooth, even sheet. Drizzle often falls from it. A stratocumulus cloud is not as even in thickness as a stratus cloud. It has light and dark areas on the bottom, indicating, as its name suggests, that there are piles of clouds in the layer.

Middle clouds, called *altostratus, altocumulus,* and *nimbostratus,* usually lie from 6,000 to 20,000 feet (1,800 to 6,100 meters) above the earth. Nimbostratus clouds sometimes may be closer to the ground. An altostratus cloud forms a smooth white or gray sheet across the sky. If the cloud is not too thick the sun may be seen through it. An altocumulus cloud appears in many shapes. It may be seen as unconnected piles or as a layer of clouds piled together. A nimbostratus cloud is a smooth layer of gray. Frequently, the cloud itself cannot be seen because of the rain or snow that is falling from it.

High clouds, called *cirrus, cirrostratus,* and *cirrocumulus,* are formed entirely of ice crystals. Other clouds are mainly water droplets. Cirrus clouds are the delicate wispy clouds that appear high in the sky, sometimes higher than 35,000 feet (10,700 meters). A cirrostratus cloud is a thin sheet of cloud. It often causes a halo to appear around the sun or moon. This halo is a good way to recognize a cirrostratus cloud. Cirrocumulus clouds

How clouds form

Clouds form when moist air rises and becomes cooler. The air usually rises by (1) convection, (2) lifting, or (3) frontal activity. Cool air cannot hold so much water vapor as warm air can, and the excess vapor changes into tiny drops of water or crystals of ice. These drops or crystals form clouds.

By convection. Solar radiation heats the ground and the air next to it, *right.* The warm air becomes lighter and *convection* (a flow of air) carries it upward. As the air rises, it becomes cooler. If the air is moist, some water vapor condenses and forms clouds, such as the cumulus clouds shown below.

Ray Atkeson

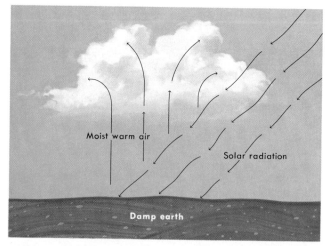

By lifting. Warm, moist air blowing over mountains or hills is lifted, *right.* When the air rises, it cools and cannot hold all its water vapor. This vapor *condenses* (changes to drops of liquid) and forms clouds over the high ground, *below.* Clouds formed in this way cover the tops of some mountains permanently.

WORLD BOOK photo by Val L. Mitchell

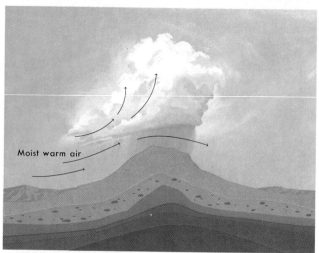

By frontal activity. A weather front occurs when two masses of air at different temperatures come together. The diagram, *right,* shows cool air moving under warm air along a cold front. The warm air is cooled as it rises above the cool air. Many clouds form, *below,* along the front at all altitudes.

Robert H. Glaze, Artstreet

WORLD BOOK diagram by Herb Herrick

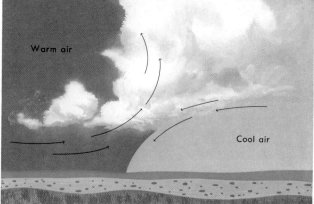

look like many small tufts of cotton hanging high in the sky. These clouds rarely form.

Clouds at more than one height. *Cumulus* and *cumulonimbus* clouds may rise to great heights while their bases are near the ground. Cumulus clouds are heaped-up piles of cloud. They may float lazily across the sky or change into the most spectacular of all clouds, the cumulonimbus. A cumulonimbus cloud may reach heights as great as 60,000 feet (18,000 meters) from its base. Its top, which contains ice crystals, spreads out in the shape of an anvil. This kind of cloud is often called a *thunderhead* because heavy rain, lightning, and thunder come from it. Sometimes hail or, on rare occasions, a deadly tornado comes from a cumulonimbus cloud.

How clouds form

Clouds form from water that has evaporated from lakes, oceans, and rivers, or from moist soil and plants. This evaporated water, called *water vapor,* expands and cools as it rises into the air. Air can hold only a certain amount of water vapor at any given temperature. Warm air can hold more water vapor than cool air can. When the temperature drops, some of the water vapor begins to *condense* (change to a liquid) into tiny water droplets.

For water vapor to condense, particles so small they can be seen only through a microscope must be present. These particles, called *condensation nuclei,* become the centers of the droplets. Many condensation nuclei are tiny salt particles or small particles present in smoke. Most droplets measure from $\frac{1}{2,500}$ to $\frac{1}{250}$ inch (0.01 to 0.1 millimeter) in diameter.

If the temperature is cold enough, and other conditions are right, water vapor does not condense and form a liquid droplet. Instead, the water vapor turns directly to ice through a process called *sublimation.* For sublimation to occur at temperatures above $-40°$ F. ($-40°$ C), small particles similar to condensation nuclei, with a shape somewhat like an ice crystal, must be present. These particles are called *freezing nuclei.*

A cloud often contains both water droplets and ice particles if the temperature is between 32° and $-40°$ F. (0° and $-40°$ C). Water droplets do not always freeze at the normal freezing temperature of water, 32° F. They may remain liquid down to a temperature of $-40°$ F.

Rain or snow forms when water evaporates from the liquid droplets and freezes on an ice crystal. The crystal grows larger until it falls out of the cloud. It falls to earth as a snowflake unless it enters a layer of air where the temperature is above freezing. Then the snowflake melts and becomes a raindrop.

Water vapor can rise to form clouds in several ways. When the sun warms the ground, the air next to the ground is heated. Because warm air is lighter than the same volume of cooler air, the warm air rises. This rise of warm air is called a *convection current,* and this method of cloud formation is called *convection.* As the air rises, it expands and becomes cooler. If enough water vapor is in the expanding air, the vapor will condense and form clouds.

Clouds also form by *lifting.* When warm, moist air moves up the side of a hill or over a mountain range, it is lifted and cools by expansion. This cooling causes the water vapor to condense and form clouds that hang over the mountains.

Weather fronts, which form where masses of warm and cool air meet, produce clouds by *frontal activity.* The water vapor in the rising warm air becomes cooler and condenses, creating the water droplets that form clouds.

Clouds and the weather

Storms. Weather forecasters study clouds carefully because certain types often appear before storms. In many cases, a warm front or a low pressure system may be identified by these clouds, which form in a definite order over several days. First, a few wispy cirrus clouds appear in the west. Soon more appear and gradually merge into cirrostratus clouds that cover the sky. The cirrostratus clouds are later hidden by a lower layer of altostratus clouds that becomes thicker and hides the sun. Light rain or snow may begin to fall from the altostratus layer. The base of the clouds becomes still lower as nimbostratus clouds move in with heavier rain or snow. Cumulus and cumulonimbus clouds often develop within the nimbostratus ones. As a result, the rain may include heavy showers.

As the storm moves past, the rain or snow ends but the sky remains overcast with stratocumulus clouds. These low clouds disappear when fair weather returns.

A cold front brings clouds in a different order. Often, both middle and high clouds come before the front. The most striking feature of most cold fronts is a wall of large cumulus or cumulonimbus clouds along the advancing edge of cold air. As this wall passes overhead, the temperature falls. Heavy showers may also occur, and in the Northern Hemisphere, the direction of the wind usually shifts from the south to the northwest. · After the line of clouds passes, many cumulus or stratocumulus clouds may remain for a short time. Clearing weather then occurs rapidly.

In summer, it is often possible to watch a thunderstorm form. The sky may be clear in the morning, or a few altocumulus clouds might be present. As the earth becomes warmer, small cumulus clouds appear and begin to grow. These clouds may become large, towering cumulus clouds that bring a little rain. As the towering cumulus clouds continue to grow, an anvil of clouds spreads out at the top and extends ahead of the main clouds. The clouds are now cumulonimbus, and a thunderstorm usually follows.

Heating and cooling of the earth are also influenced by clouds. Most cloudy days are cooler than clear days because the clouds reflect much sunlight back into space. This reflected sunlight does not heat the earth. On the other hand, clouds have an opposite influence on the earth's temperature at night. The earth gives off heat toward space, causing the ground to cool off. Clouds intercept much of this heat and send it back toward the ground. For this reason, most cloudy nights are warmer than clear nights. The heat is trapped in the lower layer of air between the cloud and the ground. Therefore, low clouds trap much more heat than do higher clouds.   Margaret A. LeMone

Related articles in *World Book* include:

Cloudburst	Rainmaking
Fog	Water (picture:
Lightning	The water cycle)
Rain	Weather

Cloud chamber, Wilson. See Wilson cloud chamber.

Cloud seeding. See Rainmaking.

Cloudburst is a sudden heavy rain falling for a short period of time in a small area. Cloudbursts are usually associated with thunderstorms. They occur most often in desert and mountain regions, and in the interiors of continents, such as the Great Plains of the United States. The uprushing air currents of a thunderstorm support a large amount of water in the form of raindrops. If the air currents are suddenly cut off, the mass of rain quickly falls out over a small area. Stream beds become torrents, and rivers form in valleys that are usually dry. During a cloudburst, more than 1 inch (2.5 centimeters) of rain may fall in 15 minutes. See also **Cloud; Rain; Weather.**   Margaret A. LeMone

Clove is the name given to the dried flower buds of a tropical tree. The dried buds are used as spices. The name comes from the French word for *nail* because of the shape of the flower bud. The clove tree grows wild in parts of Indonesia and the West Indies. It is grown as a crop in Indonesia, Madagascar, and Tanzania.

The clove tree, an evergreen, grows 15 to 30 feet (4.6 to 9 meters) tall. The large, smooth, oblong leaves taper to a point. The tree's purplish flowers grow on jointed stalks. The buds of these flowers, called *cloves,* are picked before they open. They are reddish when picked, but turn dark brown when dried. Cloves have a fragrant odor and a warm, sharp taste. They are used chiefly in cooking. An oil from the clove tree's buds and stem is used to flavor desserts and candies and to scent soaps.

Clover is a valuable crop used to feed farm animals and to enrich the soil. It contains large amounts of protein and minerals. Clover is used for pasture and to make hay and silage. In addition, clover enriches the soil by adding more nitrogen to the soil than the plant needs for growth (see **Nitrogen** [Nitrogen and life]). Bacteria

WORLD BOOK illustration by Lorraine Epstein

Varieties of clover differ chiefly in appearance and in the way they grow. The illustration above shows, *from left to right,* white clover, red clover, strawberry clover, and crimson clover.

that live in clover's roots take nitrogen from the air for the plant's growth and health. Clover uses only some of the nitrogen. After farmers plow clover into the soil, the rest of the nitrogen becomes part of the soil and can be used by other plants.

Clovers are *legumes* (members of the pea family). There are about 250 kinds of true clovers, including the *red, white, strawberry,* and *crimson* species. A type called *subterranean clover* has burrs that bury themselves underground. Sweet clover and certain other plants in the pea family are commonly called clovers. However, botanists do not classify them in that group.

The various clovers differ in the manner in which they grow. Some species are *annuals*—that is, they live for only one growing season. Others are *perennials* and can live for more than two growing seasons without being replanted. Species of clover also differ in appearance. They range from 6 inches to 3 feet (15 to 91 centimeters) in height, and have leaves that consist of three to six leaflets. Some people believe that four-leaf clovers bring luck. The plants produce clusters of tiny flowers that are white, yellow, or any of various shades of red. The number of flowers in each cluster ranges from 5 to 200.

Clover probably originated in southwestern Asia Minor and southeastern Europe. Today, both wild and cultivated species grow throughout the world.

Red clover has been used for centuries as a rotation crop. Today, it is used extensively as an animal food and soil-improving crop throughout Europe and northern and central North America. Red clover is generally planted with another crop, such as oats, barley, wheat, grasses, or certain legumes. It has purplish-red flowers and lives for two to three years.

There are three types of red clover—early flowering,

Clove trees grow in regions that have a warm, wet climate. The trees reach a height of 15 to 30 feet (4.6 to 9 meters).

© Peter Arnold

© W. H. Hodge from Peter Arnold

© George Whitely, Photo Researchers

Cloves, the flower buds of the clove tree, are reddish when picked. Dried cloves, which are used as a spice, are dark brown.

Grant Heilman

A field of red clover provides feed for farm animals. The crop is used for pasture or to make hay and silage. Red clover is also used extensively as a rotation crop.

late flowering, and wild. Early flowering red clover, which produces two to four hay crops a year, is the most commonly cultivated red clover in the United States.

White clover has white or pinkish-white flowers. Its stems spread along the ground and take root in the soil at each *node,* the place where a leaf joins the stem. The roots are short and so cannot reach water far underground. As a result, white clover is grown in regions that have an abundant supply of water. For example, the plant is cultivated in the Eastern United States and Canada, which have plentiful summer rain. Farmers also raise white clover on irrigated land in the western sections of those countries.

Strawberry clover is a valuable pasture crop in the Western United States, especially in areas that have extremely wet and salty soil. Other pasture crops cannot survive in such soil. Strawberry clover has pink flowers that grow in strawberrylike clusters.

Crimson clover is widely cultivated in the Southeast and Pacific Coast regions of the United States. Farmers plant it in the fall to provide protection against erosion during the winter. They use crimson clover for pasture and hay and to improve the soil. The flowers of this clover are dark red and grow in pointed clusters.

Subterranean clover provides winter and early spring pasture in regions that have mild winters. It is raised chiefly in Australia and Chile and in California and Oregon. The seeds of subterranean clover form in burrs that bury themselves in the soil. The plant got its name from this unusual method of growth.

Scientific classification. True clovers belong to the pea family, Leguminosae. Red clover is *Trifolium pratense;* white clover, *T. repens;* strawberry clover, *T. fragiferum;* crimson clover, *T. incarnatum;* and subterranean clover, *T. subterraneum.* Sweet clover is genus *Melilotus.*   Vern L. Marble

See also **Flower** (pictures: Flowers of prairies and dry plains; Flowers of summer-dry regions); **Lawn** (picture: Lawn enemies); **Legume; Lespedeza; Shamrock.**

Clovis I, *KLOH vihs* (466?-511), a Frankish king, became the first powerful ruler of the Merovingian dynasty, the founders of the French state. In 481, when Clovis inherited the royal title, he was only one of several Frankish kings. Then, in 486, he defeated the last great Roman army in Gaul. In one campaign after another, he defeated the Alamanni, the Visigoths, and the Burgundians. By 507 he ruled over most of Gaul, western Germany, and the Low Countries of northwestern Europe.

Clovis was the first Germanic king to become an orthodox Christian. Most Germanic rulers either became Arian heretics or remained pagans. By his conversion to Christianity, Clovis won the support of his Catholic subjects, including the clergy.   William C. Bark

See also **Fleur-de-lis; Franks; Goths; Merovingian dynasty; Salic law.**

Clown is a type of comic performer who usually works in a circus. To make audiences laugh, most clowns wear funny costumes and makeup and behave in a strange or silly manner. Many clowns develop humorous routines that emphasize playful antics and tricks.

There are two chief types of circus clowns—*auguste* and *whiteface.* Auguste clowns wear extravagant makeup and baggy suits and appear stupid and clumsy. Whiteface clowns are more elegant. They wear white makeup and clown suits and often perform opposite auguste clowns, especially in European circuses. Another type, known as *tramp* clowns, or *hobo* or *Charley* clowns, became popular in American circuses. They resemble tramps, with their tattered suits, unshaven faces, and red noses. They always look sad or lonely.

The first clowns date back to ancient times. They have

Ringling Bros. and Barnum & Bailey Combined Shows, Inc.

Clowns wear colorful, silly costumes and makeup. Most clowns provide comedy at the circus. They often work in groups, performing comic skits and routines. Many clowns are skillful acrobats, jugglers, and magicians.

been called by such names as jester, fool, and buffoon. The word *clown* was popularized in the early 1800's by Joseph Grimaldi, a famous British comic actor. To this day, circus clowns are often called *Joeys* after Grimaldi.

The American circus clown began in the late 1700's as a kind of comedian who stood in front of an audience and told jokes. Because the first circuses were small in size, a single clown could entertain the entire audience with jokes and songs. During that time, clowns ranked among the great stars of the circus. As circuses grew larger in the mid-1800's, individual clowns could no longer entertain audiences. Groups of frolicking clowns replaced the single performing clown. However, in the mid-1900's, such performers as the tramp clown Emmett Kelly continued the earlier tradition.   Don B. Wilmeth

See also **Circus** (pictures); **Jester.**

Club is a group of persons organized for some particular purpose, such as social enjoyment and entertainment. A club is usually confined to one community, but there are many state and national groups.

Modern clubs in England and the United States grew out of informal gatherings in the English taverns of the 1500's and 1600's. Groups of literary men and actors, along with the wealthy men who supported them, often met to talk and exchange views. One of the early London clubs met in the Mermaid Tavern in Cheapside. Among its members were Shakespeare, Ben Jonson, Beaumont, Fletcher, and Donne. Jonson established the Apollo Club at the Devil Tavern in 1624 and drew up bylaws for it. In 1764, Dr. Samuel Johnson and Sir Joshua Reynolds founded a club that still exists. It is called the Literary Club or simply The Club, and its first members included such distinguished figures from politics and the arts as David Garrick, Edmund Burke, and Oliver Goldsmith.

Related articles. Clubs and organizations are listed in *World Book* under the key word in the name of the group. Example: **Lions Clubs, International Association of.** See also **Parliamentary procedure.**

Club moss is any one of a group of plants that look somewhat like large mosses. Actually, club mosses are more closely related to ferns and horsetails than they are to mosses. They are also known as *ground pines* or by their scientific name *Lycopodium.* Club mosses were among the first land plants. They appeared on earth about 300 million years ago. Today, the plants are becoming scarce because of their overuse as Christmas greenery. The greatest variety of club mosses grow in tropical regions.

Club mosses have horizontal stems that spread across the soil. The stems produce roots that grow downward and leafy stems that grow upright. The erect stems may have many branches and are covered with small, needlelike green leaves. *Spores* (tiny reproductive cells) grow on enlarged leaves, which are usually tightly clustered at the tips of branches. Most species of club mosses grow only a few inches or centimeters high.

Scientific classification. Club mosses belong to the club moss family, Lycopodiaceae. They make up the genus *Lycopodium.*

See also **Fern; Horsetail; Plant** (picture: Lycophytes).

Clubfoot is an abnormal condition of the foot, usually present at birth. But it may develop later as the result of injury or poliomyelitis or other diseases. The condition is also called *talipes* (pronounced *TAL uh peez*). In the commonest form of clubfoot, the foot is bent downward and inward so that the person can walk only on the toes and on the outside of the foot. Sometimes the foot is bent in an upward and outward position so the person can use only the heel for walking. Doctors begin treatment early, sometimes when the baby is only a week old. They use massage, manipulate the foot into position, and use casts to hold the corrected position. In severe cases of clubfoot, surgery may be necessary to correct the condition.   William J. Kane

Clumber spaniel is a short, heavy hunting dog. It has a white coat with orange- or lemon-colored markings. Males stand about 20 inches (51 centimeters) high at the shoulder, and weigh as much as 85 pounds (39 kilo-

R. W. Meyer
The Clumber spaniel has a low, heavy body.

grams). Females weigh up to 70 pounds (32 kilograms). The Clumber spaniel was probably developed in the late 1700's in England. It is named for Clumber Park, the home of a nobleman who helped develop the breed. The dog is slow but thorough on a hunt. It is not widely used by hunters in the United States.

Critically reviewed by the Clumber Spaniel Club of America

Clutch. See **Transmission.**

Clyde, River, is the chief commercial waterway in Scotland. The River Clyde rises in the Southern Uplands

E. R. Degginger
Club mosses have erect green stems and tiny leaves. They are not true mosses, but rather are related to ferns and horsetails.

of Scotland and flows northward for 100 miles (160 kilometers). It empties into the Firth of Clyde, an inlet of the sea along the west coast. The Falls of Clyde near the town of Lanark once furnished the power for many mills in the Lowlands. Shipbuilding yards once lined the river's banks in Glasgow, Scotland's largest city. The *Queen Mary, Queen Elizabeth,* and other famous ships were built there. Below Glasgow, the river widens into the Firth of Clyde, which is over 50 miles (80 kilometers) long.   A. S. Mather

See also **Firth of Clyde.**

Clydesdale. See Horse (Draft horses; picture).

Clymer, George (1739-1813), a Philadelphia merchant and politician, was one of six people who signed both the Declaration of Independence and the Constitution of the United States. He represented Pennsylvania at the Constitutional Convention in Philadelphia in 1787. Clymer later helped win *ratification* (approval) of the Constitution in Pennsylvania.

Clymer was born in Philadelphia. By the early 1770's, he had become a successful merchant there. Clymer also became a leader among Pennsylvanians who supported a movement in the American Colonies for independence from Great Britain. After the Revolutionary War in America began in 1775, he helped finance and supply American armies. Clymer also served in the Second Continental Congress, which approved the Declaration of Independence in 1776.

From 1785 to 1788, Clymer served in the Pennsylvania legislature. He became a Pennsylvania member of the first U.S. House of Representatives, serving from 1789 to 1791. Clymer also was a founder and president of both the Philadelphia Bank and the Philadelphia Academy of Fine Arts.   Richard D. Brown

Clytemnestra, *KLY tuhm NEHS truh,* was a princess in Greek mythology. She married Agamemnon, king of Mycenae, and her sister Helen married his brother Menelaus. Clytemnestra bore a son, Orestes, and three daughters, Iphigenia, Electra, and Chrysothemis. Agamemnon sacrificed Iphigenia to obtain a favorable wind from the gods for the Greek fleet sailing to attack Troy (see **Trojan War**). Clytemnestra hated Agamemnon for sacrificing their daughter and waited for 10 years until the end of the war to take revenge.

While awaiting Agamemnon's return, Clytemnestra fell in love with his cousin Aegisthus. When her husband came back from Troy, Clytemnestra and Aegisthus killed him. Orestes avenged his father's death by killing Clytemnestra and Aegisthus.   Cynthia W. Shelmerdine

See also **Agamemnon; Orestes.**

CN Tower. See Toronto (Recent events).

Cnidarian, *ny DAIR ee uhn,* is the name of a group of soft-bodied water animals. The group includes the freshwater hydras, hydroids, jellyfish, sea fans, sea anemones, and corals. These animals make up the *phylum* (large group) called *Cnidaria.* There are approximately 9,000 species of cnidarians, and most of them live in the sea. Cnidarians are also called *coelenterates.*

The body of a cnidarian may be shaped like a cylinder, a bell, or an umbrella. The mouth opens at one end and leads to a digestive cavity. Every cnidarian has at least two layers of cells that form its body wall. An outer layer makes up the body covering, and an inner layer lines the digestive cavity. Many cnidarians have a third,

or middle, layer consisting of a stiff, jellylike material that helps support the animal.

A *medusa,* or jellyfish, is a cnidarian that has a bell- or umbrella-shaped body. Its mouth is at the underside of the body. Tentacles with special stinging cells hang downward from the body's ringlike edge. Medusas swim about freely in the sea.

A *polyp* is a cnidarian that has a body shaped like a hollow cylinder. A polyp lives with one end of its body attached to the sea bottom. The mouth and tentacles extend upward at the other end. Polyps may exist singly or may live together in colonies. Colonies are produced when polyps form buds that detach and become new polyps. Hydras and sea anemones are examples of single polyps, and hydroids and most corals are colony-forming polyps.

Some cnidarians have either medusa or polyp stages, or both, in their life cycles. The medusas are produced from special polyp buds that eventually break free and swim away. Then the medusas produce eggs and sperm that unite and develop into polyps.   L. Muscatine

Related articles in *World Book* include:
Coral	Portuguese
Hydra	man-of-war
Jellyfish	Sea anemone
	Sea fan

Cnossus. See Knossos.

Cnut. See Canute.

Coach is a four-wheeled vehicle drawn by animals. Coaches served as the main means of public travel before the development of railroads. They were usually pulled by horses, and carried passengers, mail, and express freight. The word *coach* comes from *Kocs,* a town in Hungary where an early coachlike vehicle was built in the 1450's. Emperor Frederick III of Germany built one of the first true coaches in 1474.

Coaches developed from the two-wheeled wagons and carts that people had used since the time of the ancient Egyptians over 5,000 years ago. Their use spread throughout Europe in the 1500's. But travel by horseback was more comfortable, because of the poor roads and riding qualities of coaches. For years, coaches were used mainly for state occasions. The first public coach line in England began about 1640.   John H. White, Jr.

See also **Stagecoach; Wagon; Colonial life in America** (Travel and communication [picture: Colonial stagecoaches]); **Transportation** (History [picture: Transportation in early modern times]).

Coach dog. See Dalmatian.

Coagulant, *koh AG yuh luhnt,* is any substance that causes a fluid to clot, or thicken. Milk curdles because *rennin,* an enzyme, causes clots to form. One of the most important coagulant actions is the clotting of blood. Scientists have found many blood-clotting factors. The combined action of all of them produces a blood clot. If any one factor is missing, the tendency for blood to clot is reduced. Doctors then try to supply the missing substance. For example, in the blood disease *hemophilia,* doctors use an antihemophilic globulin to help the blood to clot. In other diseases, they may give the patient vitamin K or fibrinogen to induce the blood to clot and control hemorrhages.   David Green

See also **Anticoagulant; Blood** (Controlling bleeding); **Fibrin; Hemophilia; Vitamin** (Vitamin K).

Fossil ferns and a lump of coal, *left,* were both formed from the remains of plants that died many millions of years ago. While the plants lived, they stored up energy from the sun. The plants that became fossils gave up their store of energy in the process. Only the outline of their appearance remains. But the energy of the coal-forming plants is preserved in the coal. When the coal is burned, it releases this energy in the form of heat.

WORLD BOOK photo

Coal

Coal is a black or brown rock that can be ignited and burned. As coal burns, it produces useful energy in the form of heat. People use this heat to warm buildings and to make or process various products. But the main use of the heat from coal is the production of electricity. Coal-burning power plants supply more than half the electricity used in the United States and nearly half that is used throughout the world. Another major use of coal is the production of *coke,* a raw material in the manufacture of iron and steel. In addition, the coke-making process provides raw materials used to make such products as drugs, dyes, and fertilizers.

Coal was once the main source of energy in all industrial countries. Coal-burning steam engines provided most of the power in these countries from the early 1800's to the early 1900's. Since the early 1900's, petroleum and natural gas have become the leading sources of energy in much of the world. Unlike coal, petroleum can be easily made into gasoline and the other fuels needed to run transportation equipment. Natural gas has replaced coal as a source of heat for some applications. However, people are rapidly using up the world's supplies of petroleum and natural gas that can be removed from the ground economically. If the present rates of use continue, little may remain of these supplies

by about 2050. By contrast, the world's supply of coal can last more than 250 years at the present rate of use. Increased use of coal, especially for producing electricity, could relieve a shortage of gas and oil.

Historically, the burning of coal has been a major cause of air pollution. But since the 1970's, air pollution from coal burning has declined despite increases in coal consumption. This is due partly to the use of air pollution control systems by utilities and industries, as required by the United States Clean Air Act of 1970. It is also due to better coal-cleaning procedures and the use of coals with low sulfur content.

In the past, few jobs were harder or more dangerous than that of an underground coal miner. During the 1800's, many miners had to work underground 10 or more hours a day, six days a week. Picks were almost the only equipment they had to break the coal loose. The miners shoveled the coal into wagons. In many cases, children as young as 10 years of age hauled the coal from the mines. Women worked as loaders and haulers. Over the years, thousands of men, women, and children were killed in mine accidents. Thousands more died of lung diseases from breathing coal dust.

Today, machines do most of the work in coal mines. Mine safety has been improved, work hours have been shortened, and child labor is prohibited. The death rate from U.S. mine accidents has dropped greatly since 1900. However, coal mining remains a hazardous job.

This article discusses how coal was formed, where it is found, its uses, and how it is mined. The article also discusses the cleaning and shipping of coal, the coal industry, and the history of the use of coal.

Joseph W. Leonard III, the contributor of this article, is Professor of Mining Engineering at the University of Kentucky. The article was critically reviewed by the National Coal Association.

Coal developed from the remains of plants that died 400 million to 1 million years ago. For this reason, it is often referred to as a *fossil fuel.* The coal-forming plants probably grew in swamps. As the plants died, they gradually formed a thick layer of matter on the swamp floor. Over the years, this matter hardened into a substance called *peat.* In time, the peat deposits became buried under sand or other mineral matter. As the mineral matter accumulated, some of it turned into such rocks as sandstone and shale. The increasing weight of the rock layers and of the other overlying materials began to change the peat into coal. Coal, sandstone, and other rocks formed from deposited materials are called *sedimentary rocks.*

The first stage in the formation of coal produces a dark brown type of coal called *lignite.* Lignite develops from buried peat deposits that have been under pressure. The pressure results from the weight of the overlying materials and from movements within the earth's crust. As the pressure increases, lignite turns into *subbituminous coal.* Under greater pressure, subbituminous coal turns into a harder coal called *bituminous coal.* Intense pressure changes bituminous coal into *anthracite,* the hardest of all coals. Bituminous coal is also known as *soft coal;* anthracite, as *hard coal.*

Anthracites are the oldest coals in most cases, and lignites are the youngest. Some anthracites began to form as long as 400 million years ago. Some lignites developed within the last 1 million years.

The greatest period of coal formation occurred during a time in the earth's history called the *Carboniferous Period,* from about 360 million to 290 million years ago. During the Carboniferous Period, swamps covered much of the earth. Tall ferns and other treelike plants grew in the swamps and produced huge amounts of peat-forming matter after they died.

Today's plentiful deposits of bituminous coal developed largely from the vast peat deposits formed during the Carboniferous Period. It took about 3 to 7 feet (0.9 to 2.1 meters) of compact plant matter to produce a bed of bituminous coal 1 foot (0.3 meter) thick.

Plant materials are still accumulating in some parts of Maine, the Okefenokee Swamp in Georgia and Florida, and other swampy locations. These materials could eventually develop into coal.

Coal beds are also called *coal seams* or *coal veins.* Present-day seams range in thickness from less than 1 inch (2.5 centimeters) to 400 feet (120 meters) or more. The thickest seams are subbituminous coals and lignites. Many coal deposits consist of two or more seams separated by layers of rocks. These formations were produced by new coal-forming swamps developing over buried ones. Each new swamp became buried and developed into a separate seam of coal.

Some coal beds lie nearly parallel to the earth's surface. Other beds have been tilted by earth movements and lie at an angle to the surface. Most of the deepest beds consist of anthracites or bituminous coals. In many cases, earth movements have uplifted deep anthracite and bituminous beds to a position nearer the surface. Such movements also account for coal seams in hills and mountains.

The development of coal

The formation of coal involved three main steps. (1) The remains of dead plants turned into a substance called *peat.* (2) The peat became buried. (3) The buried peat was subjected to great pressure. After thousands or millions of years under pressure, the peat turned into coal. Each of these steps is illustrated below.

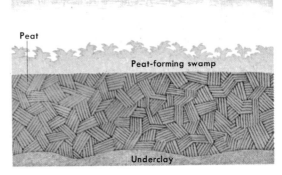

A thick layer of peat developed as plant matter accumulated and hardened on the floor of a swamp. The matter built up as plants that grew in the swamp died and sank to the bottom. Peat-forming swamps once covered much of the earth.

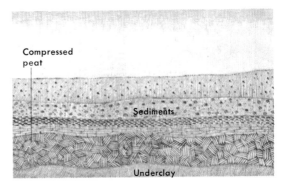

Deposits of loose mineral matter, called *sediments,* completely covered the peat bed. As these sediments continued to pile up over the bed, they compressed the peat.

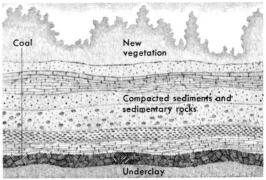

WORLD BOOK diagrams by Jean Helmer

Pressure on the peat increased as the sediments became more compact and heavier. Some sediments hardened into rock. The increasing pressure turned the peat into coal.

Where coal is found

Coal is found on every continent. Deposits occur as far north as the Arctic and as far south as Antarctica. Some coal deposits occur off ocean coastlines. However, deep underwater deposits have little value at this time because they are difficult to mine.

Coal deposits that can be mined profitably are called *coal reserves.* In most cases, a coal seam must be at least 24 inches (61 centimeters) thick for mining engineers to class it as a reserve. Some long-range estimates of coal reserves include beds 12 to 24 inches (30 to 61 centimeters) thick. But such thin beds would probably be mined only after more productive deposits were exhausted. Most estimates of coal reserves include only tested deposits. The reserves may actually be somewhat larger or smaller than the estimates.

To estimate coal reserves, mining engineers drill into the ground in suspected coal-bearing areas. A drill brings up samples of the rock formations in the order in which they occur. The depth and thickness of a coal seam can thus be estimated. By taking a number of such samples, engineers can estimate the extent of a particular deposit. A large area of tested reserves is called a *coal field.*

World coal reserves. No reliable estimates exist for the total amount of coal that lies beneath the earth's sur-face. The world's *proved recoverable reserves* of coal total over 1.1 trillion short tons (1 trillion metric tons). This figure represents the amount of coal that can be profitably recovered from known deposits with current technology. Most of the proved recoverable reserves are in Australia, China, Germany, India, Indonesia, Poland, Russia, South Africa, and the United States.

Location of U.S. and Canadian reserves. About half of all U.S. coal reserves lie in the eastern half of the nation, from the Appalachian Highlands to the eastern edge of the Great Plains. The rest of the reserves are in the western part of the country, especially the Rocky Mountain States, the northern Great Plains, and Alaska. The eastern reserves include nearly all the nation's anthracite deposits. They also include more than four-fifths of its bituminous deposits. The western reserves include almost all the subbituminous coal and lignite in the United States.

Canada's coal reserves consist chiefly of bituminous coal. The nation also possesses large fields of subbituminous coal and lignite. However, these deposits are smaller than the bituminous deposits. More than 95 percent of Canada's reserves are in the country's western provinces—British Columbia, Alberta, and Saskatchewan.

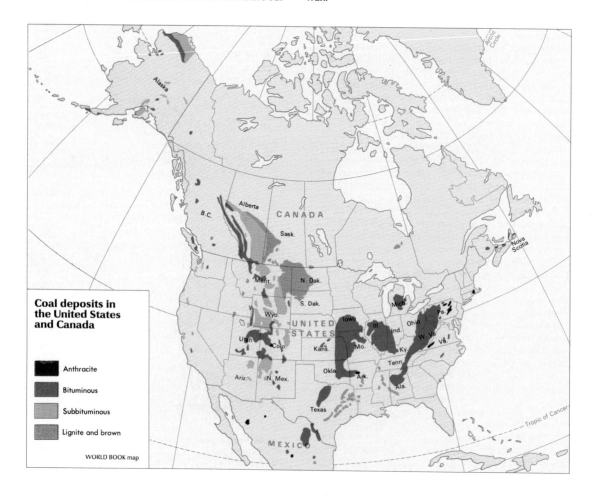

Coal deposits in the United States and Canada

■ Anthracite

■ Bituminous

░ Subbituminous

▒ Lignite and brown

WORLD BOOK map

The way in which coal is used depends on its chemical composition and moisture content. Coal is often referred to as a mineral. But unlike a true mineral, coal has no fixed chemical formula. All coal consists of certain solids and moisture. The solids are composed chiefly of the elements carbon, hydrogen, nitrogen, oxygen, and sulfur. However, coal varies widely in the amount of each element it contains as well as in the amount of moisture it contains. No two deposits of coal are exactly alike in their makeup.

Coal is usually classified according to how much carbon it contains. Coal can thus be grouped into four main classes, or *ranks:* (1) anthracites; (2) bituminous coals; (3) subbituminous coals; and (4) lignites, or brown coals. The carbon content of the coals decreases down through the ranks. The highest-ranking anthracites contain about 98 percent carbon. The lowest-ranking lignites have a carbon content of only about 30 percent. The amount of moisture in the coals can be as low as less than 1 percent, in anthracites and bituminous coal, and as high as 45 percent, in lignites. High-moisture subbituminous and lignite coals have a lower *heating value* than do anthracites and bituminous coals. Heating value refers to the amount of heat that is produced by a given amount of coal when it is burned.

Bituminous coals are by far the most plentiful. They are also the most widely used of the major ranks of coals. They have a slightly higher heating value than do anthracites and are the only coals suited to making coke. Anthracites are slow to ignite. They also burn too slowly to be suitable for industrial purposes such as the generation of electricity. Anthracites are also the least plentiful of the four ranks of coals. About 2 percent of the coal in the United States is anthracite.

Coal as a fuel

Coal is a useful fuel because it is abundant and has a relatively high heating value. However, coal has certain impurities that limit its usefulness as a fuel. These impurities include sulfur and various minerals. As coal is burned, most of the sulfur combines with oxygen and forms a poisonous gas called *sulfur dioxide.* Most of the minerals turn into ash. The coal industry refers to ash-producing substances in coal as ash even before the coal is burned.

Coal known as *low-sulfur coal* can be burned in fairly large quantities without adding harmful amounts of sulfur dioxide to the air. *Medium-* and *high-sulfur coals* can cause serious air pollution if burned in large quantities without proper safeguards.

The United States Department of Energy (DOE) classifies sulfur content according to the weight of the sulfur in a sample of coal that can produce 1 million British thermal units (Btu's) of heat. Such a sample is low-sulfur coal if it contains 0.60 pounds (0.272 kilograms) or less of sulfur, medium-sulfur coal if its sulfur content is 0.61 to 1.67 pounds (0.277 to 0.758 kilograms), and high-sulfur coal if it contains 1.68 pounds (0.763 kilograms) or more of sulfur.

Some of the ash produced by burning powdered coal may also escape into the air. Like sulfur dioxide, such *fly ash* can contribute to air pollution. However, devices

Uses of coal in the United States

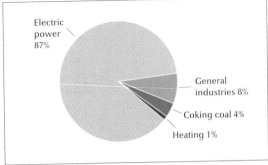

Electric power 87%

General industries 8%

Coking coal 4%

Heating 1%

Figures are for 1991. Source: U.S. Energy Information Administration.

have been developed to trap fly ash in smokestacks and so prevent it from polluting the air.

Coal is used as a fuel chiefly in the production of electricity. Electric power plants use more than three-fourths of the coal mined in the United States.

Electric power production. Most electric power plants are *steam-turbine plants.* All nuclear power plants and almost all plants fueled by coal, gas, or oil are steam-turbine plants. They use high-pressure steam to generate electricity. The steam spins the wheels of turbines, which drive the generators that produce electricity. Steam-turbine plants differ mainly in how they create heat to make steam. Nuclear plants create the heat by splitting uranium atoms. Other plants burn coal, gas, or fuel oil. Steam-turbine plants produce about 70 percent of the electricity used in the United States. Coal-burning

National Coal Association

A conveyor system at a power plant removes coal from a stockpile and carries it to the plant's boilers. Coal-burning power plants produce most of the electricity used in the world.

plants account for most of this output. See **Electric generator; Electric power; Turbine.**

Bituminous coals have long been the preferred coals for electric power production because they are the most plentiful coals and have the highest heating value. Subbituminous coals and lignites have the lowest heating value. However, nearly all the subbituminous coal and about 90 percent of the lignite in the United States have a low sulfur content. On the other hand, about 50 percent of the nation's bituminous coal has a medium- or high-sulfur content. To meet federal and state pollution standards, power plants are burning more subbituminous coal and lignite. However, these coals cause problems for industry because they quickly lose their moisture, break up, and become dusty. This dustiness makes them difficult to handle and transport.

Other uses of coal as a fuel. In parts of Asia and Europe, coal is widely used for heating homes and other buildings. In the United States, natural gas and fuel oil have almost entirely replaced coal as a domestic heating fuel. However, the rising cost of oil and natural gas has led some factories and other commercial buildings to switch back to coal. Anthracites are the cleanest-burning coals, and so they are the preferred coals for heating homes. However, anthracites are also the most expensive coals. For this reason, bituminous coals are often preferred to anthracites for heating factories and other commercial buildings. Subbituminous coals and lignites have such a low heating value that they must be burned in large amounts in order to heat effectively. As a result, they are seldom used for domestic heating.

In the past, coal also provided heat for the manufacture of a wide variety of products, from glass to canned foods. Since the early 1900's, manufacturers have come to use natural gas in making most of these products. Coal is used mainly by the cement and paper industries. However, some industries have switched back to coal to avoid paying higher prices for natural gas.

Coal as a raw material

Many substances made from coal serve as raw materials in manufacturing. Coke is the most widely used of these substances. Coke is made by heating bituminous coal to about 2000 °F (1100 °C) in an airtight oven. The lack of oxygen prevents the coal from burning. The heat changes some of the solids in the coal into gases. The remaining solid matter is coke—a hard, foamlike mass of nearly pure carbon. It takes about $1\frac{1}{2}$ short tons (1.4 metric tons) of bituminous coal to produce 1 short ton (0.9 metric ton) of coke. For an illustration of the coke-making process, see **Coke.**

The coal used to make coke is called *coking coal.* To be suitable for coking, the coal must have various characteristics, such as a low-sulfur content and a specified amount of ash. Only certain types of bituminous coals have all the necessary characteristics.

About 90 percent of the coke produced in the United States is used to make iron and steel. Most coking plants are a part of steel mills. The mills burn coke with iron ore and limestone to change the ore into the pig iron required to make steel. It takes about 900 pounds (410 kilograms) of coke to produce 1 short ton (0.9 met-

A coking plant heats coal in airtight ovens to make *coke,* an essential raw material in the manufacture of steel. This batch of red-hot coke is being released from an oven into a railcar. The car will carry it to another part of the plant to cool.

ric ton) of pig iron. For a description of the role of coke in the iron-making process, see the *World Book* article **Iron and steel** (Raw materials; illustration: How a blast furnace operates).

The coke-making process is called *carbonization.* Some of the gases produced during carbonization turn into liquid ammonia and coal tar as they cool. Through further processing, some of the remaining gases change into light oil. Manufacturers use the ammonia, coal tar, and light oil to make such products as drugs, dyes, and fertilizers. Coal tar is also used for roofing and for road surfacing.

Some of the gas produced during carbonization does not become liquid. This *coal gas,* or *coke oven gas,* burns like natural gas. But coal gas has a lower heating value and, unlike natural gas, gives off large amounts of soot as it burns. Coal gas is used chiefly at the plants where it is produced. Coal gas provides heat for the coke-making and steel-making processes.

Gas can be produced from coal directly, without carbonization, by various methods. Such methods are known as *gasification.* The simplest gasification method involves burning coal in the presence of forced air or steam. The resulting gas, like coke oven gas, has a low heating value and produces soot. It is used chiefly in some manufacturing processes. Coal can be used to make high-energy gas and such high-energy liquid fuels as gasoline and fuel oil. But the present methods of producing these fuels from coal are costly and complex. The section *The coal industry* discusses how researchers are working to develop cheaper and simpler methods.

Coal mines can be divided into two main groups: (1) surface mines and (2) underground mines. In most cases, surface mining involves stripping away the soil and rock that lie over a coal deposit. This material is known as *overburden.* After the overburden has been removed, the coal can easily be dug up and hauled away. Underground mining involves digging tunnels into a coal deposit. Miners must go into the tunnels to remove the coal.

Surface mining is usually limited to coal deposits within 100 to 200 feet (30 to 61 meters) of the earth's surface. The more overburden that must be removed, the more difficult and costly surface mining becomes. Most coal deposits deeper than 200 feet are mined underground. Surface mines produce about 60 percent of the coal mined in the United States. Underground mines produce the rest.

Surface mining

Nearly all surface mining is *strip mining*—that is, mining by first stripping away the overburden. Many coal seams are exposed on the sides of hills or mountains. In some cases, these seams are mined from the surface without removing any overburden. Miners use machines called *augers* to dig out the coal. This method of surface mining is known as *auger mining.*

Strip mining depends on powerful machines that dig up the overburden and pile it out of the line of work. The dug-up overburden is called *spoils.* In time, a strip mine and its spoils may cover an enormous area. The digging up of vast areas of land has caused serious environmental problems in the past. As a result, the U.S. government now requires that all new strip-mined land be *reclaimed*—that is, returned as closely as possible to its original condition. Strip mining thus involves methods of (1) mining the coal and (2) reclaiming the land.

Mining the coal. Most strip mines follow the same basic steps to produce coal. First, bulldozers or loaders clear and level the vegetation and soil above the mining area. Many small holes are then drilled through the rocky overburden to the coal bed. Each hole is loaded with explosives. The explosives are set off, shattering the rock in the overburden. Giant power shovels or other earthmoving machines then clear away the broken rock. Some of these earthmovers are as tall as a 20-story building and can remove more than 3,500 short tons (3,180 metric tons) of overburden per hour. After a fairly large area of coal is exposed, explosives may be used again. Coal-digging machines then scoop up the coal and load it into trucks. The trucks carry the coal from the mine.

Although most strip mines follow the same basic steps, strip-mining methods vary according to whether the land is flat or hilly. Strip mining can thus be classed as either (1) area mining or (2) contour mining. Area mining is practiced where the land is fairly level. Contour mining is practiced in hilly or mountainous country. It involves mining on the *contour*—that is, around slopes.

In area mining, an earthmover digs up all the broken overburden from a long, narrow strip of land along the edge of the coal field. The resulting deep ditch is referred to as a *cut.* As the earthmover digs the cut, it piles the spoils along the side of the cut that is away from the mining area. The piled spoils form a ridge called a *spoil bank.* After the cut is completed, the coal is dug, loaded into trucks, and hauled away. The earthmover then digs an identical cut alongside the first one. It piles the spoils from this cut into the first cut. This process is repeated over and over across the width of the coal field until all of the coal has been mined. The spoil banks form a series of long, parallel ridges on the land that can later be leveled.

Area mining is impractical where coal seams are embedded in hills. If a seam lies near the top of a hill, an earthmover may simply remove the hilltop and so expose the coal. If a seam lies near the base of a hill, it must be mined on the contour.

In contour mining, an earthmover removes the shattered overburden immediately above the point where a seam *outcrops* (is exposed) all around a hill. The resulting cut forms a wide ledge on the hillside. The spoils may be stored temporarily on the hillside or used to fill in the cuts. After the exposed coal has been mined and hauled away, the earthmover may advance up the slope and dig another cut immediately above the first one. However, the depth of the overburden increases sharply with the rise of the slope. After the first or second cut, the overburden may be too great for a coal company to

Strip mining depends on giant earthmoving machines like the one at the top of this picture. The earthmover strips away the soil and rock that lie over a coal deposit. A coal-digging machine, *center,* then scoops up the coal and loads it into a truck.

remove profitably. But if the seam is thick enough, a company may dig an underground mine to remove the rest of the coal.

Reclaiming the land. The chief environmental problems that strip mining can cause result from burying fertile soil under piles of rock. The rocks tend to give off acids when exposed to moisture. Rainwater runs down the bare slopes, carrying acids and mud with it. The runoff from the slopes may wash away fertile soil in surrounding areas and pollute streams and rivers with acids and mud.

The first step in reclaiming strip-mined land is to reduce the steep slopes formed by the spoils. The spoil banks created by area mining can be leveled by bulldozing. The spoils from contour mining can be used to fill in the cuts in the hillsides. As much topsoil as possible should then be returned to its original position so that the area can be replanted.

Mining companies now reclaim all strip-mined land, much of which has been turned into farms and recreation areas. In 1977, the U.S. Congress passed a law requiring mine owners to reclaim all the land they use for strip mining after 1978. In every case, the mine owners must restore the land as nearly as possible to its original condition. Many older strip-mined lands have not been reclaimed. But since 1977, the government has collected over $3 billion in fees from coal producers to reclaim these older mines.

Auger mining. A coal auger is a machine shaped like an enormous corkscrew. It bores into the side of a coal outcrop on a slope and twists out the coal in chunks. Contour mines often use augers when the overburden in a slope is too great to remove. An auger can penetrate the outcrop and recover coal that could not otherwise be mined. Some augers can bore 200 feet (61 meters) or more into a hillside.

Companies often employ auger mining to mine outcrops of high-quality coal that cannot be mined economically by other methods. However, auger mining

can recover only a small portion—as little as 15 percent—of the coal in a seam. The method is best used in combination with contour mining.

Underground mining

Underground mining is more hazardous to workers than surface mining. The miners may be injured or killed by cave-ins, falling rocks, explosions, and poisonous gases. To prevent such disasters, every step in underground coal mining must be designed to safeguard the workers.

Underground mining generally requires more human labor than surface mining. But even so, underground mines are highly mechanized. Machines do all the digging, loading, and hauling in nearly all the mines. Nonmechanized mines produce only about 1 percent of the coal mined underground in the United States.

In most cases, miners begin an underground mine by digging two access passages from the surface to the coal bed. One passage will serve as an entrance and exit for the miners and their equipment. The other passage will be used to haul out the coal. Both passages will also serve to circulate air in and out of the mine. As the mining progresses, the workers dig tunnels from the access passages into the coal seam.

Underground mines can be divided into three main groups according to the angle at which the access passages are dug into the ground. The three groups are (1) shaft mines, (2) slope mines, and (3) drift mines. Some mines have two or all three types of passages.

In a shaft mine, the access passages run straight down from the surface to the coal seam. The entrance and exit shaft must have a hoist. Most mines under more than 700 feet (210 meters) of cover are shaft mines. In a slope mine, the access passages are dug on a slant. They may follow a slanting seam or slant down through the cover to reach the seam. Drift mines are used to mine seams of coal that outcrop in hills or mountains. The access passages for these mines are dug into a

Kinds of underground mines

There are three main kinds of underground mines: (1) shaft mines, (2) slope mines, and (3) drift mines. In a shaft mine, the entrance and exit passages are vertical. In a slope mine, they are dug on a slant. In a drift mine, the passages are dug into the side of a coal bed exposed on a slope.

WORLD BOOK diagrams

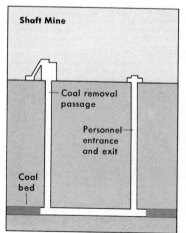

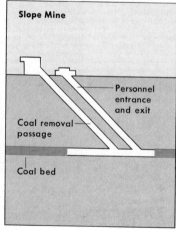

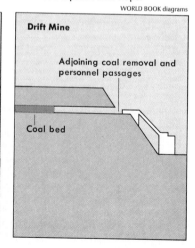

seam where the coal bed outcrops on a slope.

Two main systems of underground mining are used: (1) the room-and-pillar system and (2) the longwall system. Each system has its own set of mining techniques. Either system may be used in a shaft, slope, or drift mine. The room-and-pillar system is by far the more common system of underground mining in the United States. The longwall system is more widely used elsewhere, especially in European countries.

The room-and-pillar system involves initially leaving pillars of coal standing in a mine to support the overburden. Miners may begin a room-and-pillar mine by digging three or more long, parallel tunnels into the coal seam from the access passages. These tunnels are called *main entries*. In most cases, the walls, or ribs, of coal separating the main entries are 40 to 80 feet (12 to 24 meters) wide. Cuts are made through each wall every 40 to 80 feet. The cuts thus form square or rectangular pillars of coal that measure 40 to 80 feet on each side. The coal dug in building the entries is hauled to the surface.

The pillars help support the overburden in the main entries. But in addition, the entry roofs must be bolted to hold them in place. To bolt the roof, the miners first drill holes 3 to 6 feet (0.9 to 1.8 meters) or more into the roof. They then anchor a long metal bolt into each hole and fasten the free end of each bolt to the roof. The bolts bind together the separate layers of rock just above the roof to help prevent them from falling. The miners must also support the roof in all other parts of the mine as they are developed.

A conveyor belt or a railroad track is built in one of the main entries to carry the coal to the access passages. A railroad may also transport the miners along the main entries. At least two main entries serve chiefly to circulate air through the mine. The mine may also need such facilities as water drainage ditches, gas drainage pipes, compressed air pipes, water pipes, and electric power cables. These facilities are built into the main entries and later extended to other parts of the mine.

After the main entries have been constructed, the miners dig sets of *subentries* at right angles from the main entries into the coal seam. Each set of subentries consists of three or more parallel tunnels, which serve the same purposes as the main entries. Cuts are made through the walls separating these tunnels, forming pillars like those between the main entries. At various points along each set of subentries, the miners dig *room entries* at right angles into the seam. They then begin to dig *rooms* into the seam from the room entries.

As the miners enlarge a room, they leave pillars of coal to support the overburden. A room is mined only a certain distance into the seam. When this distance is reached, the miners may remove the pillars. The room roof collapses as the pillars are removed, and so they must be removed in *retreat*—that is, from the back of the room toward the front. The miners' exit from the room thus remains open as the roof falls. Pillars are also sometimes removed from entries. Like room pillars, they must be removed in retreat to protect the miners.

All room-and-pillar mining involves leaving some pillars in place. Room-and-pillar mines differ, however, in

their mining methods. Mechanized room-and-pillar mines use two main methods: (1) the conventional mechanized method and (2) continuous mining.

The conventional mechanized method produces about 10 percent of the coal mined underground in the United States. This method was more widely practiced during the 1930's and 1940's than it is today. During the 1930's, it largely replaced the earlier method of digging coal by hand. Since about 1950, continuous mining has increasingly replaced the conventional method.

The conventional method involves five main steps. (1)

The room-and-pillar system

Most underground mines in the United States use the *room-and-pillar system* of mining. First, the miners dig tunnels called *main entries* into the coal bed from the entrance and exit passages. They then dig sets of *subentries* into the bed from the main entries and sets of *room entries* into the bed from the subentries. Pillars of coal are left standing in all the entries to support the mine roof. As the room entries are extended, they create large *panels* of coal. The miners eventually dig *rooms* into the panels to recover as much coal as possible from the bed. This floor plan of a room-and-pillar mine shows how the entries are developed.

WORLD BOOK diagram by Linda Kinnaman

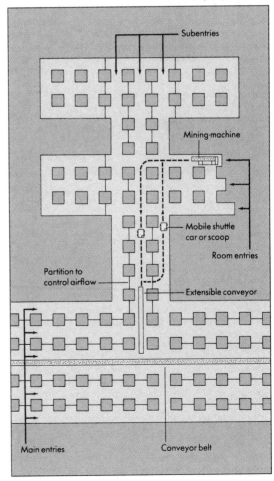

Types of underground-mining equipment

The type of equipment that an underground mine requires depends on the method of mining it uses. Mechanized mines use three main methods: (1) the conventional method, (2) continuous mining, and (3) longwall mining. Each of the three methods calls for a different type of equipment.

WORLD BOOK illustrations by Robert Addison

Conventional-mining equipment. The conventional method of mining involves a series of steps, three of which require special machinery. First, a cutting machine, *left,* cuts a deep slit along the base of the coal *face* (coal exposed on the surface of a mine wall). Another machine, *center,* drills holes into the face. Miners load the holes with explosives and then set the explosives off. The undercutting along the bottom of the face causes the shattered coal to fall to the floor. A loading machine, *right,* gathers the coal onto a conveyor belt.

Continuous-mining equipment eliminates the series of steps in mining a face. A continuous-mining machine, *right,* gouges out the coal and loads it onto a shuttle car in one operation.

Longwall-mining equipment. Longwall mining differs from the other methods of underground mining in its system of roof support. The other methods are used only in room-and-pillar mines, where pillars of coal are left to support the mine roof. In the longwall method, movable steel props support the roof over one long coal face. The miners move a cutting machine back and forth across the face, shearing off coal. The coal falls onto a conveyor. As the miners advance the cutter into the bed, the roof supports are moved forward. The roof behind the miners is allowed to fall.

Consolidation Coal Company

A worker operating a continuous miner can produce about 2 short tons (1.8 metric tons) of coal per hour. These machines dig about 60 percent of the U.S. coal mined underground.

A machine that resembles a chain saw cuts a long, deep slit, usually along the base of the coal face. (2) Another machine drills a number of holes into the face. (3) Each hole is loaded with explosives. The explosives are set off, shattering the coal. The undercutting along the bottom of the face causes the broken coal to fall to the floor. (4) A machine loads the coal onto shuttle cars, scoops, or a conveyor. (5) Miners bolt the roof that has been exposed by the blast.

A separate crew of miners carries out each of the five steps. After a crew has completed its job on a particular face, the next crew moves in. The miners can thus work five faces of coal at a time. But there are frequent pauses in production as the crews change places.

Continuous mining accounts for about 60 percent of the output of U.S. underground coal mines. The method uses machines called *continuous miners.* A continuous miner gouges the coal from the *coal face*—that is, the coal exposed on the surface of a wall. One worker operating a continuous miner can produce about 2 short tons (1.8 metric tons) of coal per hour. The machine automatically loads the coal onto shuttle cars or a conveyor belt, which carries it to the railroad or conveyor in the main entries.

A continuous miner can usually dig and load coal much faster than the coal can be hauled out of a mine. The machine can work faster than the haulage, roof-bolting, ventilation, construction, and drainage systems can be completed. As a result, a continuous miner must frequently be stopped to allow the other mine systems to catch up.

The longwall system of underground mining involves digging main tunnels or entries like those in a room-and-pillar mine. However, the coal is mined from one long face, called a *longwall,* rather than from many short faces in a number of rooms.

A longwall face is about 300 to 700 feet (91 to 210 meters) long. The miners move a powerful cutting machine back and forth across the face, plowing or shearing off the coal. The coal falls onto a conveyor belt. Movable

steel props support the roof over the length of the immediate work area. As the miners work the machine farther into the seam, the roof supporters are advanced. The roof behind the miners is allowed to fall. After a face has been dug out 4,000 to 6,000 feet (1,200 to 1,800 meters) into the seam, a new face is developed and mined. This process is repeated over and over until as much coal as possible has been removed from the seam.

The longwall system originated in Europe. Underground mines in Europe are much deeper, on the average, than U.S. underground mines. The pressure of the overburden becomes intense in an extremely deep mine. Longwall mining relieves the pressure by allowing the roof to cave in throughout most of a mine. In a European longwall mine, the roof remains in place only over the main entries, over the longwall face, and over two tunnels leading to the face. The mines can thus recover up to 90 percent of the coal in a seam.

Mine safety laws in the United States require longwall mines to have fully developed subentries as well as main entries. Thus U.S. longwall mining includes some of the main features of the room-and-pillar system. One kind of longwall mining is called the *retreating longwall system.* This type of mining uses the room-and-pillar system to reach and expose the long coal face. Longwall equipment then mines the coal. These mines are much more productive than room-and-pillar mines because less coal is left in place.

Longwall mines produce about 30 percent of the coal mined underground in the United States. However, more and more U.S. mines are adopting longwall techniques. A few American mines have adopted another variation of the longwall method called *shortwall mining.* A shortwall face is only about 150 to 200 feet (46 to 61 meters) long, and it is mined with continuous-mining machines rather than with longwall equipment. This system, which was developed in Australia, is suited to coal seams whose structure prevents them from being divided into long faces.

Some coal is shipped to buyers exactly as it comes from the mine without any processing. In the coal industry, such coal is called *run-of-mine coal.* It ranges in size from fine particles to large chunks. About 10 percent of the coal sold by U.S. companies is run-of-mine coal.

The two largest users of coal, the electric power industry and the coking industry, have definite quality requirements for the coal they buy. Much run-of-mine coal does not meet these requirements because it is the incorrect size or contains unacceptable amounts of impurities. As a result, mining companies sort their coal according to size and *clean* the coal to remove impurities. The companies sort about 50 percent of their coal without cleaning it, and both sort and clean 40 percent of the coal.

Companies sort coal by crushing large pieces and passing the coal through a screening device. The following section describes the cleaning process.

Cleaning coal. Mining companies clean coal in *preparation plants.* Most large coal mines have a preparation plant on the mine property. The plants use a variety of machines and other equipment to remove the impurities from coal.

Ash and sulfur are the chief impurities in coal. The ash consists chiefly of mineral compounds of aluminum, calcium, iron, and silicon. Some of the sulfur in coal is also in the form of minerals, especially *pyrite,* a compound of iron and sulfur. The rest is *organic sulfur,* which is closely combined with the carbon in coal. Run-of-mine coal may also contain pieces of rock or clay. These materials must be removed in addition to the other impurities.

Preparation plants rely on the principle of *specific gravity* to remove impurities. According to this principle, if two solid substances are placed in a solution, the heavier substance will settle to the bottom first. Most mineral impurities in coal are heavier than pure coal. As a result, these impurities can be separated from run-of-mine coal that is placed in a solution. The entire coal-cleaning process involves three main steps: (1) sorting, (2) washing, and (3) dewatering.

Sorting. Large pieces of pure coal may settle to the bottom of a solution faster than small pieces that have many impurities. Therefore, the pieces must first be sorted according to size. In many preparation plants, a screening device sorts the coal into three sizes—coarse,

How impurities are removed from coal

Mining companies remove mineral impurities from coal by a process called *cleaning.* The process involves three main steps. (1) A screening device sorts the coal into batches of three sizes. (2) Each batch is piped into a separate washing device and mixed with water. The impurities in coal are heavier than pure coal. As a result, the first pieces of coal to settle to the bottom of each solution are those that contain the most impurities. Any loose pieces of rock or clay mixed in with the coal also sink to the bottom. All the waste pieces are discarded. (3) The clean pieces are dewatered with vibrators, spinning devices, or hot-air blowers. The coal is then ready for shipment to buyers.

WORLD BOOK diagram

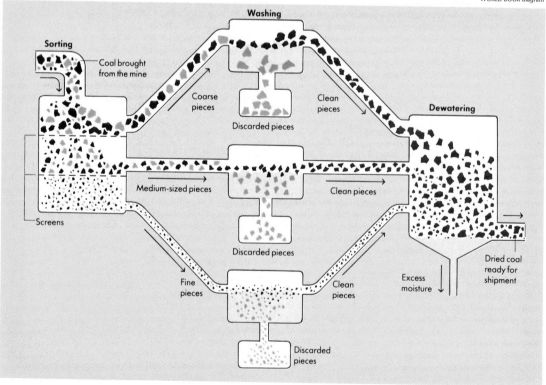

Unit trains carry most large overland shipments of coal in the United States. A unit train normally carries only one kind of freight and travels nonstop from its loading point to its destination.

medium, and fine. Large chunks are crushed and then sorted into the three main batches according to size.

Washing. The typical preparation plant uses water as the solution for separating the impurities from coal. Each batch of sorted coal is piped into a separate washing device, where it is mixed with water. The devices separate the impurities by means of specific gravity. The heaviest pieces—those containing the largest amounts of impurities—drop into a refuse bin. Washing removes much of the ash from coal. But the organic sulfur is so closely bound to the carbon that only small amounts can be removed.

Dewatering. The washing leaves the coal dripping wet. If this excess moisture is not removed, the heating value of the coal will be greatly reduced. Preparation plants use vibrators, spinning devices called *centrifuges,* and hot-air blowers to dewater coal after it is washed.

In most cases, the separate batches of coal are mixed together again either before or after dewatering. The resulting mixture of various sizes of coal is shipped chiefly to electric power companies and coking plants. All coking plants and many power companies grind coal to a powder before they use it. They therefore accept shipments of mixed sizes. Some coal users require coal of a uniform size. Preparation plants that supply these users leave the cleaned coal in separate batches.

Shipping coal. Most coal shipments within a country are carried by rail, barge, or truck. A particular shipment may travel by two or all three of these means. Huge cargo ships transport coal across oceans, between coastal ports, and on large inland waterways, such as the Great Lakes.

Barges provide the cheapest way of shipping coal within a country. But they can operate only between river or coastal ports. Trucks are the least costly means of moving small shipments of coal short distances by land. Much coal, however, must be shipped long distances over land to reach buyers. Railroads offer the most economical means of making such shipments. About two-thirds of the coal shipped from mines in the United States goes by rail.

Many large shipments of coal in the United States are delivered to electric power companies and coking plants by *unit trains.* A unit train normally carries only one kind of freight and travels nonstop from its loading point to its destination. A 100-car unit train may carry 10,000 short tons (9,100 metric tons) or more of coal. To meet the need for low-sulfur coal, more and more power plants east of the Mississippi River are importing subbituminous coal from the West. Unit trains help speed such long-distance shipments.

A 273-mile (439-kilometer) underground pipeline carries coal from a mine in Arizona to a power plant in Nevada. The coal is crushed and mixed with water to form a *slurry* (soupy substance) that can be pumped through the pipeline. The coal and power industries favor building other such pipelines in the United States.

In the past, nearly all coal shipments consisted of anthracite, bituminous coal, or subbituminous coal. It costs as much to ship a given amount of lignite as it costs to ship the same amount of a higher-ranking coal. But lignite has the lowest heating value of the four ranks. It therefore could not formerly compete with the higher-ranking coals in distant markets. Lignite was used chiefly by power plants built in the lignite fields. Conveyor belts or small railways carried the coal from the mines to the plants. But a growing need for low-sulfur coal and improvements in coal preparation technology have increased the amount of lignite shipped in the United States. Some is shipped by rail from mines in the Western United States to plants in the Midwest.

In most countries, the central government owns all or nearly all the coal mines. The major exceptions are Australia, Canada, Germany, South Africa, and the United States. In these countries, all or nearly all the coal mines are privately owned. In each of these countries, however, the central government regulates certain aspects of the coal industry.

The United States and Australia are the leading coal exporters in the world. About one-fourth of all coal exports come from mines in the United States. The other leading exporters include Canada, Poland, Russia, and South Africa. Japan purchases approximately 30 percent of the world's coal exports—far more than any other country.

This section of the article deals chiefly with the coal industry in the United States. However, much of the information in this section also applies to other countries.

Coal producers. The United States has about 3,500 active coal mines and about 3,000 coal-mining companies. Most of the companies are small, independent firms that own and operate one or two small mines. All the small companies together supply less than a third of the coal mined in the United States. The 30 largest coal companies in the United States produce about two-thirds of the nation's coal. Some of the companies are independently owned, but many are owned by corporations outside the coal industry. The chief outside owners include oil companies, railroads, and ore-mining firms.

Steel companies and electric utilities in the United States also own coal mines. These companies produce coal chiefly for their own use. Their mines are known as *captive mines.*

The National Coal Association (NCA) works to promote the interests of coal producers. The NCA is jointly sponsored by the producers and the firms that supply them with equipment, technical advice, and transporta-

tion. The association tries to increase efficiency within the industry, to encourage favorable legislation, and to inform the public about the industry. The National Independent Coal Operators Association represents the smaller coal producers.

Mineworkers. Most large coal-mining companies have a full-time staff of professional workers, including engineers, lawyers, and business experts. They also employ electricians, mechanics, and construction workers. Skilled miners, however, provide the labor on which the industry depends. Underground mining requires more miners than does surface mining. The United States has about 120,000 coal miners. About two-thirds of them work in underground mines.

Mechanization has helped miners become more productive. In 1950, each coal miner in the United States produced, on the average, about 7 short tons (6.4 metric tons) of coal daily. Today, the production rate averages about 32 short tons (29 metric tons) per miner per day. On the average, a strip miner produces more than twice as much coal as does an underground miner.

Increased mechanization has also made miners' jobs more specialized. The job of most miners is to operate a certain type of machine, such as a continuous miner or a power shovel. A beginning miner must work as an apprentice for a specified period to qualify for a particular job. Mine supervisors must have a license from the department of mining in their state. Generally, the licenses are granted to miners who have two to five years' experience and who pass a written examination.

Most mining engineering jobs call for a college degree in engineering. If the job is directly related to mine safety, it may also require a state engineering license called a *P.E. (professional engineer) certificate.* Some mining engineering jobs require a P.E. certificate only. The states grant P.E. certificates to applicants who meet certain educational requirements, have on-the-job experience, and pass a written examination. In some states, applicants must have an engineering degree. Other states require only a high school education.

Labor unions. About 45 percent of all coal miners in the United States belong to the United Mine Workers of America (UMW). The UMW was organized in 1890. At that time, the nation's coal miners lived and worked under miserable conditions. The mines were dangerously unsafe, and the miners earned barely enough to live on. Most miners and their families lived in *company towns,* which were owned and run by the mining companies. In many company towns, the housing and other facilities were far from adequate. Frequently, miners were not paid in cash. Instead, the mining companies gave them coupons that could be exchanged for goods at company-owned stores or used to pay rent on a company-owned house. The store prices and rents were unreasonably high in many cases, and some miners were always in debt to the mining companies.

During the first half of the 1900's, the UMW did much to improve the wages and working conditions of American coal miners. Through strikes and hard bargaining, the union forced the mining companies to grant the miners increasingly favorable work contracts. The UMW owed much of its success to the vigorous leadership of

National Coal Association

Coal miners provide the labor on which the coal industry depends. These miners have just finished their day's work in an underground mine. The train will carry them to the mine exit.

John L. Lewis, who headed the union from 1919 to 1960. During Lewis' long term as UMW president, the union had the overwhelming support of its members.

Although the UMW is still important, its influence has declined. This change partly reflects a steadily improving mine safety record. Also, increased mechanization and the closing of inefficient mines has reduced the total number of jobs.

This change is also due to the rapid growth of strip mining. Strip mining requires fewer miners than does underground mining. It also requires a different type of miner. Strip miners are chiefly heavy-machine operators. Unlike underground miners, they have little need for traditional mining skills. Some strip miners are members of the UMW. But many belong to various building trades unions or to no union.

The UMW has also lost influence among its members. Many UMW members feel that their contracts with the mining companies are still far from satisfactory. The miners want better health and retirement benefits and stricter mine safety measures. During the 1970's, small groups of miners frequently took matters into their own hands and went out on *wildcat strikes,* which did not have the approval of union leaders.

Mine safety. Since 1900, more than 100,000 workers have been killed in coal mine accidents in the United States. Many more have been injured or disabled. Because of this extremely high accident rate, more and more aspects of mine safety have been brought under government regulation.

The federal government and the governments of the coal-mining states set minimum health and safety standards that the coal companies and miners have to follow. To make sure that all miners know their responsibilities, the companies must give every new miner a course in mine safety. The improvements in mine safety have greatly reduced the death and injury rates from mine accidents. In the early 1900's, about 3.5 miners per 1,000 were killed in mine accidents annually. The annual death rate has dropped to about .5 today—an improvement of about 85 percent.

Mine safety involves four main types of problems. They are (1) accidents involving machinery, (2) roof and rib failures, (3) accumulations of gases, and (4) concentrations of coal dust.

Accidents involving machinery kill or injure more U.S. coal miners in a typical year than any other kind of mining accident. Most strip mine accidents involve machinery. The machines in underground mines must often operate in cramped, dimly lit spaces. Thus, the miners must be doubly alert to prevent accidents.

Roof and rib failures can be prevented in many cases if a mining company carries out a scientific roof support plan. The federal government requires all U.S. mining companies to draw up such a plan for any new mine. The government must then approve the plan before mining is begun. Mining engineers make a roof support plan after studying all the rock formations surrounding the coal bed. The plan deals with such matters as the number of pillars that must be left standing, entry widths, mine geometry, and the number of roof bolts that must be used.

Accumulations of gases. Certain gases that occur in underground coal mines can become a serious hazard if they accumulate. *Methane* and *carbon monoxide* are especially dangerous. Methane is an explosive gas that occurs naturally in coal seams. It is harmless in small amounts. However, a mixture of 5 to 15 percent methane in the air can cause a violent explosion. Carbon monoxide is a poisonous gas produced by the combustion of such fuels as coal and oil. Blasting in an underground mine may produce dangerous levels of carbon monoxide if the mine is improperly ventilated.

The air vents in a mine normally prevent harmful gases from accumulating. A powerful fan at the surface circulates fresh air through the mine. The circulating air forces polluted air to the surface. As an added precaution against methane, federal law requires all underground mines to have automatic methane detectors. A mine is required to shut down temporarily if a detector shows a methane accumulation of more than 2 percent.

Concentrations of coal dust. Anyone who breathes large amounts of coal dust over a period of years may develop a disease called *pneumoconiosis* or *black lung* (see **Black lung**). The disease interferes with breathing and may eventually cause death. Thousands of coal miners have been victims of the disease. In addition, high concentrations of coal dust are explosive. A mixture of coal dust and methane is especially dangerous.

Proper ventilation removes much of the coal dust from the air in a mine. However, mines must also use other dust control measures. In the United States, federal law requires that underground mines be *rock-dusted.* In this process, the miners spray powdered limestone on all exposed surfaces in the mine entries. The limestone dilutes and coats the coal dust and so lessens the chance of an explosion. Mines use water sprays to hold down the dust along a face that is being mined.

Government regulation. State departments of mining have traditionally set and enforced safety standards

Leo Touchet, The Photo Circle

Bolting the roof is an essential safety practice in an underground mine. Roof bolts are long metal rods that are inserted into the mine roof. After a bolt is fastened to the roof, *above,* it helps prevent the rock layers immediately overhead from falling.

How strip-mined land is reclaimed The law requires mine owners in the United States to reclaim all the land they use for strip mining. The first step is to level the piles of dug-up soil and rock, *left*. The area may then be reseeded, *center*. The project is finally completed when the new vegetation is fully grown, *right*.

Bucyrus-Erie Company

for American coal mines. In the past, the U.S. Bureau of Mines had this responsibility at the federal level. On occasion, Congress has made urgently needed standards a matter of law, as in the Federal Coal Mine Health and Safety Act of 1969. This act strengthened the safety standards for mine ventilation, coal dust concentrations, roof supports, and mining equipment. The regulation of coal dust has helped reduce the occurence of black lung among miners. In addition, the act established a federal black lung benefits program. This program provides financial and medical benefits to miners already disabled by black lung.

The Mine Safety and Health Administration enforces

federal mine safety standards. This agency routinely inspects the mines for safety. The United States Department of the Interior, the United States Environmental Protection Agency (EPA), and state environmental protection agencies regulate the environmental aspects of U.S. coal-mining activities.

Coal research is sponsored by the U.S. Department of Energy, the U.S. Department of the Interior, the EPA, and several coal and oil companies. The goals of most coal research are (1) to find ways to burn more coal without increasing air pollution and (2) to develop economical methods of converting coal into liquid fuels and synthetic natural gas.

Leading coal-producing countries

Tons of coal mined in a year

China	●●●●●●●●●●●●●●●●
	1,202,000,000 short tons (1,090,000,000 metric tons)
United States	●●●●●●●●●●●●◖
	994,000,000 short tons (902,000,000 metric tons)
Soviet Union	●●●●●●●●●◖
	754,000,000 short tons (684,000,000 metric tons)
Germany	●●●●◖
	387,000,000 short tons (351,000,000 metric tons)
India	●●●
	263,000,000 short tons (239,000,000 metric tons)
Australia	●●◖
	240,000,000 short tons (218,000,000 metric tons)
Poland	●●◖
	231,000,000 short tons (210,000,000 metric tons)
South Africa	●●◖
	196,000,000 short tons (178,000,000 metric tons)
Czechoslovakia	●◖
	113,000,000 short tons (103,000,000 metric tons)
United Kingdom	●◖
	102,000,000 short tons (93,000,000 metric tons)

Figures are for 1991, prior to the breakup of the Soviet Union and of Czechoslovakia. Source: U.S. Energy Information Administration.

Leading coal-producing states and provinces

Tons of coal mined in a year

Wyoming	●●●●●●●●●●●●●●●●
	193,854,000 short tons (175,861,000 metric tons)
West Virginia	●●●●●●●●●●●●●◖
	166,935,000 short tons (151,441,000 metric tons)
Kentucky	●●●●●●●●●●●●◖
	158,330,000 short tons (143,635,000 metric tons)
Pennsylvania	●●●●◖
	64,471,000 short tons (58,487,000 metric tons)
Illinois	●●●●◖
	60,253,000 short tons (54,661,000 metric tons)
Texas	●●●●
	53,825,000 short tons (48,829,000 metric tons)
Virginia	●●●
	41,811,000 short tons (37,930,000 metric tons)
Montana	●●◖
	38,277,000 short tons (34,724,000 metric tons)
Alberta	●●◖
	35,660,000 short tons (32,350,000 metric tons)
Indiana	●●◖
	31,456,000 short tons (28,536,000 metric tons)

Figures are for 1991.
Sources: U.S. Energy Information Administration; Statistics Canada.

Pollution control. In 1977, Congress passed a law requiring all U.S. electric power plants built since 1971 to meet federal pollution standards by 1982. These standards, which were further tightened in the Clean Air Act of 1990, prohibit the burning of medium- or high-sulfur coals without a means of controlling sulfur dioxide pollution. Medium- and high-sulfur coals make up more than a third of all U.S. coal reserves. These resources can be used for electric power production only after ways are found to control sulfur dioxide pollution.

Cleaning removes some of the sulfur from coal. But it does not remove enough from high-sulfur and some medium-sulfur coals to meet air quality standards. Sulfur dioxide can be controlled to some extent by devices called *scrubbers.* A scrubber absorbs sulfur dioxide fumes as they pass through a plant's smokestacks.

Researchers are now working to develop new processes for using coal to produce power. These processes will make coal use more efficient and safer for the environment. They include *fluidized-bed combustion.* In this process, crushed coal is burned in a bed of limestone. The limestone captures sulfur from the coal and so prevents sulfur dioxide from forming. The heat from the burning coal boils water that is circulated through the bed in metal coils. The boiling water produces steam, which may be used to produce electricity.

Coal conversion. To turn coal into a high-energy fuel, the hydrogen content of the coal must be increased. Bituminous coals have the highest hydrogen content of the four ranks of coal. On the average, they consist of about 5 percent hydrogen. The hydrogen must be increased to about 12 percent to produce a high-energy liquid fuel and to about 25 percent to produce synthetic natural gas.

The process of converting coal into a liquid fuel is called coal *hydrogenation* or *liquefaction.* Various methods of coal hydrogenation have been developed. In the typical method, a mixture of pulverized coal and oil is treated with hydrogen gas at high temperatures and under great pressure. The hydrogen gradually combines with the carbon molecules, forming a liquid fuel. This process can produce such high-energy fuels as gasoline and fuel oil.

Coal can easily be turned into low-energy gas by the carbonization and gasification methods described in the section *The uses of coal.* Low-energy gas can also be produced from unmined coal. This process, called *underground gasification,* involves digging two widely spaced wells from ground level to the base of a coal seam. The coal at the bottom of one well is ignited. Air is blown down the second well. The air seeps through pores in the seam, and the fire moves toward it. After a passage has been burned between the two wells, the air current forces the gases up the first well. Compared with natural gas, low-energy gas made from coal has limited uses. Low-energy gas must be enriched with hydrogen for its heating value to equal that of natural gas.

The present methods of obtaining high-energy fuels from coal cost too much for commercial use. Hydrogen is expensive to produce. In addition, most fuels made from coal contain unacceptable amounts of sulfur and ash. Researchers are trying to develop cheaper methods

of coal conversion. In 1980, Congress passed the Energy Security Act, which provides federal funding for coal conversion research and for the construction of synthetic fuel plants. In 1984, two commercial-sized coal gasification plants began operating in the United States. However, both plants rely heavily on the federal government for financial support.

History of coal use

No one knows where or when people discovered that coal can be burned to provide heat. The discovery may have been made independently in various parts of the world during prehistoric times. The Chinese were the first people to develop a coal industry. By the A.D. 300's, they were mining coal from surface deposits and using it to heat buildings and smelt metals. Coal had become the leading fuel in China by the 1000's.

Commercial coal mining developed more slowly in Europe. During the 1200's, a number of commercial mines were started in England and in what is now Belgium. The coal was dug from open pits and used mainly for smelting and forging metals. But most Europeans regarded coal as a dirty fuel and objected to its use.

Wood, and charcoal made from wood, were the preferred fuels in Europe until the 1600's. During the 1600's, a severe shortage of wood occurred in western Europe. Many western European countries, but especially England, then sharply increased their coal output to relieve the fuel shortage.

Developments in England. During the 1500's, English factories burned huge quantities of charcoal in making such products as bricks, glass, salt, and soap. By the early 1600's, wood had become so scarce in England that most factories had to switch to coal. By the late 1600's, England produced about 80 percent of the

A Pennsylvania mine of the late 1800's was like coal mines everywhere before mining became mechanized and child labor was abolished. Boys and mules provided much of the labor.

Coal production in the United States since 1800*

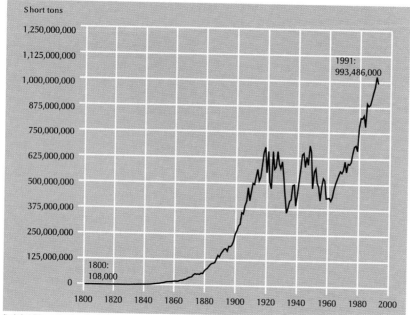

Year	Short tons	Metric tons
1800	108,000	97,980
1810	178,000	161,500
1820	334,000	303,000
1830	881,000	799,200
1840	2,474,000	2,244,400
1850	8,356,000	7,580,400
1860	20,041,000	18,180,900
1870	40,429,000	36,676,600
1880	79,407,000	72,036,800
1890	157,771,000	143,127,400
1900	269,684,000	244,653,200
1910	501,596,000	455,040,200
1920	658,265,000	597,167,900
1930	536,911,000	487,077,400
1940	512,256,000	464,710,800
1950	560,388,000	508,375,400
1960	434,330,000	394,017,500
1970	612,661,000	555,796,700
1980	825,673,000	749,038,000
1985	883,638,000	801,623,000
1990	1,026,307,000	931,050,000
1991	993,486,000	901,275,000

*Includes all types of coal—anthracite, bituminous and subbituminous coals, and lignite.
Sources: U.S. Bureau of Mines; U.S. Energy Information Administration.

world's total coal output. It remained the leading coal producer for the next 200 years.

Charcoal had also been widely used in England as a fuel for drying malt, the chief ingredient in beer. Brewers tried using coal for this process. But the gases it produced were absorbed by the malt and so spoiled the flavor of the beer. The brewers found, however, that the undesirable gases could be eliminated if they preheated the coal in an airtight oven. They thus developed the process for making coke. About 1710, an English ironmaker named Abraham Darby succeeded in using coke to smelt iron. Coke then gradually replaced charcoal as the preferred fuel for ironmaking.

The spread of the new ironmaking process became part of a much larger development in England—the Industrial Revolution. The revolution consisted chiefly of a huge increase in factory production. The increase was made possible by the development of the steam engine in England during the 1700's. Steam engines provided the power to run factory machinery. But they required a plentiful supply of energy. Coal was the only fuel available to meet this need.

During the 1800's, the Industrial Revolution spread from England to other parts of the world. It succeeded chiefly in countries that had an abundance of coal. Coal thus played a key role in the growth of industry in Europe and North America.

Developments in North America. The North American Indians used coal long before the first white settlers arrived. For example, the Pueblo Indians in what is now the Southwestern United States dug coal from hillsides and used it for baking pottery. European explorers and settlers discovered coal in eastern North America dur-

ing the last half of the 1600's. In the 1700's, a few small coal mines were opened in what are now Nova Scotia, Virginia, and Pennsylvania. The mines supplied coal chiefly to blacksmiths and ironmakers. Most settlers saw no advantage in using coal as long as wood was plentiful. Wood and charcoal remained the chief fuels in America throughout the 1700's.

The Industrial Revolution spread to the United States during the first half of the 1800's. By then, coal was essential not only to manufacturing but also to transportation. Steamships and steam-powered railroads were becoming the chief means of transportation, and they required huge amounts of coal to fire their boilers. As industry and transportation grew in the United States, so did the production and use of coal. By the late 1800's, the United States had replaced England as the world's leading coal producer.

The United States led in coal production until the mid-1900's. Its demand for coal then declined as the use of petroleum and natural gas increased. The Soviet Union surpassed the United States in coal production from the late 1950's through the late 1970's. During the 1980's, China usually ranked first, and the United States usually ranked second.

Recent developments. The growing scarcity of petroleum and natural gas has led to a sharp rise in the demand for coal. As a result, U.S. coal production increased greatly in the 1970's and 1980's. The increased output was used mainly to produce electricity. Today, electricity can be produced more cheaply from coal than from either natural gas or fuel oil.

Joseph W. Leonard III

Critically reviewed by the National Coal Association

Related articles in *World Book* include:

Basic coal products

Ammonia   Coke oven gas
Coal tar   Gas (fuel)
Coke

Other related articles

Black lung   Iron and steel
Child labor   Jet
Damp   Lewis, John L.
Diamond   Mining
Energy supply   Peat
Hanna, Mark   Safety lamp
Heating (Coal)   United Mine Workers of
Hydrogenation   America
Industrial Revolution   West Virginia (pictures)

Outline

I. How coal was formed
II. Where coal is found
  A. World coal reserves
  B. Location of U.S. and
    Canadian reserves
III. The uses of coal
  A. Coal as a fuel   B. Coal as a raw material
IV. How coal is mined
  A. Surface mining   B. Underground mining
V. Cleaning and shipping coal
  A. Cleaning coal
  B. Shipping coal
VI. The coal industry
  A. Coal producers
  B. Mineworkers
  C. Labor unions
  D. Mine safety
  E. Government regulation
  F. Coal research
VII. History of coal use

Questions

How was coal formed?
What is by far the chief system of underground coal mining in the United States?
What is the main use of coal?
Why are coal miners more productive today than they were in the past?
How is coal usually classified? What are the four main classes of coal?
What are *preparation plants*? Why are they needed?
Why did many countries in western Europe sharply increase their coal output during the 1600's?
What is *strip mining*? What environmental problems can it cause? How can these problems be prevented?
Why has coal mining become a less dangerous occupation than it was in the past?
Why have more and more power plants switched from bituminous coal to subbituminous coal or lignite?

Additional resources

Level I
Asimov, Isaac. *How Did We Find Out About Coal?* Walker, 1980.
Hansen, Michael C. *Coal: How It Is Found and Used.* Enslow, 1990.
Kraft, Betsy H. *Coal.* Rev. ed. Watts, 1982.

Level II
Davis, Bertha, and Whitfield, Susan. *The Coal Question.* Watts, 1982.
Gordon, Richard L. *World Coal: Economics, Policies, and Prospects.* Cambridge, 1987.
Schobert, Harold H. *Coal, The Energy Source of the Past and Future.* Am. Chemical Soc., 1987.

Coal gas. See Coke oven gas.
Coal oil. See Kerosene.
Coal tar is a thick, black, sticky liquid obtained as a by-product in the manufacture of coke and coke oven gas from soft coal. Various grades of tar are recovered by *condensing* (changing to liquid) hot vapors from a coke oven or a coal gas producer. Manufacturers heat coal tar and condense its vapors to produce light oils, such as *benzene* and *toluene.* Benzene is used as a solvent and in the production of perfumes and some gasolines, and toluene is used in the manufacture of dyes, paints, explosives, and antiseptics.

Tar acids, such as *carbolic acid,* and tar bases, such as *aniline,* are other coal tar products. Carbolic acid and aniline are used to make dyes. *Creosote* and *pitch* are heavy liquid coal tar products. Creosote preserves wood, and pitch is used in the manufacture of roofing materials and paint. Sir William H. Perkin, an English chemist, pioneered in coal tar chemistry by making mauve, the first synthetic dye. *Petrochemicals* (chemicals made from petroleum) are increasingly supplementing coal tar chemicals for use in industry and chemistry.

Joseph W. Leonard III

Related articles in *World Book* include:

Aniline   Dye
Benzene   Naphtha
Coal (Coal as a raw material)   Perfume
Coke   Pitch
Coke oven gas   Tar
Creosote   Toluene
Distillation (Destructive distilla-
tion)

Coalescence theory. See Rain (Formation of rain; diagram: The coalescence theory).

Coalition, кон uh LIHSH uhn, is a combination of political interest groups working toward a mutual goal. Coalitions often form in countries with parliamentary forms of government because these systems have a number of political parties. A single party may be unable to win a majority in the parliament, causing various parties to form coalitions that have a majority of seats.

In the United States, various conditions encourage interest groups to form coalitions to pressure legislators and executives. These conditions include the separation of powers among branches of the federal government and frequent disagreements among members of the same political party. In the U.S. Congress, for example, conservative Democrats and Republicans have formed a powerful coalition that often shapes legislation. Coalitions between Democrats and Republicans exist at all levels of government.   Peter Woll

See also **Political party** (Multiparty systems).

Coanda, kaw ahn DA, **Henri-Marie,** ahn REE ma REE (1885-1972), was a Romanian aviation pioneer, engineer, and inventor. He is best known for developing a disk-shaped craft based on what is now called the *Coanda effect,* the tendency of a fluid passing a curved surface to attach itself to the surface. This principle is used in a sensing and control technology called *fluidics.* Coanda also invented an airplane based on a jet-propulsion system and a device that uses the energy of the sun to convert salt water to fresh water. Coanda was born in Bucharest, Romania.   Tom D. Crouch

U.S. Coast Guard

The Coast Guard patrols United States waterways in such vessels as the patrol craft *Mustang, above*. The Coast Guard also protects U.S. ports and ships and enforces sea laws.

United States Coast Guard

Coast Guard, United States, is a branch of the armed services. It also serves as the chief agency for protecting life and property at sea and enforcing United States maritime laws. The Coast Guard fights smuggling, protects ships and ports, and rescues victims of sea disasters. In peacetime, it operates as a branch of the Department of Transportation. In time of war, it becomes an active part of the United States Navy. The Coast Guard's many duties give special meaning to its motto, *Semper Paratus*, which means *always ready.*

The Coast Guard is the nation's oldest continuous seagoing force. Since 1790, it has grown from a fleet of 10 small sailing vessels to a force of modern ships and airplanes. Its members have fought in every major war of the United States. They have rescued hundreds of thousands of people from disasters and have saved billions of dollars' worth of property from shipwrecks and floods. The many risks and dangers they face have led to the saying, "You have to go out, but you don't have to come back."

The Coast Guard has a peacetime strength of about 39,000 active and 12,000 reserve members. The Coast Guard emblem was adopted in 1927. "Semper Paratus" is the Coast Guard's famous marching song.

What the Coast Guard does

Protecting life and property. The Coast Guard has worldwide duties. Its ships, which are called *cutters,* pa-

trol oceans and inland waterways. Its lifesaving stations along the U.S. coast and Great Lakes stand ready for emergencies. When accidents occur, rescue boats and aircraft go into action immediately. They rescue shipwrecked people, people who have been in boating accidents and airplane crashes, and victims of hurricanes. They also tow damaged vessels to shore. The Coast Guard helps rescue any person or ship, regardless of nationality. It provides emergency medical aid to crews of all vessels at sea and takes injured or critically ill crew members to shore bases for treatment.

Ships at sea depend on Coast Guard aids to navigation. Such guides as beacons, buoys, fog signals, lighthouses, and radio stations reduce the dangers of navigation. Loran stations use radio signals to help ships determine their exact positions at sea (see **Loran**). Coast Guard units report weather information to the United States National Weather Service, which uses the data for forecasting.

Special Coast Guard cutters called *icebreakers* clear icebound harbors on the North Atlantic coast and on inland lakes, rivers, and canals. Icebreakers also support research scientists in the Arctic and Antarctic. The International Ice Patrol, operated by the Coast Guard, locates and tracks icebergs in shipping lanes in the North Atlantic and warns ships about them. Patrols along U.S. coasts protect valuable fishing grounds and prevent the importation of illegal drugs. The Coast Guard's port security program helps keep waterfronts safe by controlling traffic, regulating shipment of dangerous cargoes, and monitoring pollution.

Enforcing sea laws. The Coast Guard enforces all federal laws and treaties on the high seas and on the navigable waters of the United States. These include criminal laws, inspection laws, pollution laws, revenue and navigation laws, and nautical rules of the road. The Coast Guard enforces and helps establish safety regulations governing the construction and operation of merchant ships and passenger ships. It also establishes safety rules for passengers, and tests and licenses crew members. To help prevent boating accidents and deaths, the Coast Guard establishes safety standards for yachts, motorboats, and other noncommercial vessels.

The Coast Guard Auxiliary, a voluntary association of yacht and motorboat sailors and owners and aircraft owners, also promotes safety. It checks boats for safety equipment, helps with rescues, and conducts classes on boating safety. The Coast Guard also helps other federal agencies enforce their laws concerning customs, immigration, and quarantines.

Supporting the Navy. The Coast Guard and the United States Navy help each other in peacetime and in wartime. The Coast Guard participates in military exercises with the Navy and with forces of countries that are members of the North Atlantic Treaty Organization (NATO). As part of the Navy in wartime, the Coast Guard helps guard the nation's ports and shipping lanes, and provides air-sea rescue services. The Navy aids the Coast Guard in preventing the smuggling of illegal drugs into the United States.

Life in the Coast Guard

Careers in the Coast Guard include a variety of challenging positions. A member of the Coast Guard can become an expert in a specialized field. Coast Guard training also prepares members for civilian jobs when their enlistments end or they retire from service.

Applicants must be at least 17 years of age and not older than 26. They must meet Coast Guard physical standards and pass the Armed Forces Qualifications Test. They may have no more than two dependents.

Most Coast Guard officers receive their training at the U.S. Coast Guard Academy in New London, Conn. Applicants to the Coast Guard Academy must be high school graduates between 17 and 22 years old. They must be unmarried, meet rigid physical standards, and be of good moral character. Cadets are appointed on the basis of a nationwide competition each year. Appli-

Work of the Coast Guard

U.S. Coast Guard

A motor lifeboat battles rough water during a rescue.

U.S. Coast Guard

Coast Guard lifeboats pick up plane crash survivors.

U.S. Coast Guard

An icebreaker clears ice from a shipping lane.

Coast Guard patrols enforce fishing regulations that help maintain fish populations. This coastguardsman is inspecting a fishing net to ensure it is the proper size.

U.S. Coast Guard

cations to enter the competition should be sent to the Director of Admissions, U.S. Coast Guard Academy, New London, CT 06320.

Officers and enlisted men and women in the Coast Guard hold similar ranks and earn the same pay as those in the Navy. Enlisted men wear the same blue uniforms as male Coast Guard officers, and enlisted women wear the same blue dress uniforms as female officers. The only differences in the uniforms is in the rank insignia. See **Rank, Military.**

Training a recruit begins at "boot camp" at Cape May, N.J. Recruits receive eight weeks of basic training. They take courses in communications, fire fighting, first aid, gunnery, military drill, physical education, and seamanship. Specially trained petty officers teach the courses.

The Coast Guard tries to place men and women in positions for which they are best suited. It encourages them to take specialist courses. They can earn a rating as electronics technician, health services technician, photojournalist, marine science technician, machinery technician, radioman, and in other specialties. For further training, enlisted men and women can take correspondence courses offered by the Coast Guard or attend intensive Goast Guard schools.

Training an officer. A cadet at the Coast Guard Academy takes a four-year course and graduates with a Bachelor of Science degree and a commission as an ensign in the Coast Guard. Members of each new class enter the academy during the summer, usually in late June or early July. These cadets are called *swabs.* They spend their *swab summer* becoming adjusted to military life. Coast Guard cadets spend part of each summer at sea, training aboard the bark *Eagle* and on major cutters. See **United States Coast Guard Academy.**

Men and women between the ages of 17 and 26 with a bachelor's degree from an accredited college or university may take a special Coast Guard officer-candidate course. This 17-week course is conducted at the Coast Guard Reserve Training Center in Yorktown, Va. Enlisted men and women who qualify may also take the course. Graduates receive commissions as ensigns and serve at least three years of active duty. Other programs enable licensed merchant marine officers, graduates of maritime academies, former military pilots, engineers, and lawyers to become Coast Guard officers.

Ships, aircraft, and weapons of the Coast Guard

Ships and stations. The Coast Guard maintains a fleet of several hundred ships and boats that can perform various assignments. These vessels include buoy tenders, cutters, icebreakers, lifeboats, surfboats, and tugboats.

The service operates about 45 offices devoted to marine safety, port security, and shipping-inspection duties. The Coast Guard also maintains light towers, navigational aids, and about 250 law enforcement and search and rescue stations.

Aircraft play a major part in Coast Guard operations. The Coast Guard uses cargo planes, jets, and helicopters for patrol, law enforcement, and search and rescue missions. Helicopters are particularly important to the Coast Guard in air-sea rescues, in bringing help to flood victims, and in rescuing disaster victims in inland areas that could not otherwise be reached. During World War II (1939-1945), Coast Guard aircraft bombed enemy submarines. Aircraft of the Coast Guard were also used to rescue many survivors of torpedoed ships.

Weapons. All Coast Guard vessels are armed with at least small arms. Weapons used by the Coast Guard range from 9-millimeter pistols, M-16 rifles, and machine guns on small patrol vessels to 76-millimeter cannons and Harpoon missiles on large cutters. In addition, some Coast Guard vessels carry sonar and antisubmarine weapons. Coast Guard cadets and recruits receive small-arms training. The service also operates a special training program for crews of small armed vessels. The crews of larger Coast Guard vessels periodically train with the Navy.

Organization of the Coast Guard

Coast Guard headquarters are in Washington, D.C. The commandant of the Coast Guard—an admiral— heads the service, assisted by a vice commandant, a planning and control staff, and officers of Coast Guard departments. The United States and its possessions are divided into 10 Coast Guard districts. Each district is headed by a district commander.

Regulars and reserves. The *Regular Coast Guard* makes up the core of the service. It consists of officers and enlisted men and women who have chosen the Coast Guard as a full-time career. The *Coast Guard Reserve* is a group whose members may be called to active duty in time of emergency. Their training is similar to that of the regulars and includes port security and other wartime missions.

Women in the Coast Guard serve as enlisted or commissioned personnel in the Regular Coast Guard or Coast Guard Reserve. They are trained in all occupational specialties. The Coast Guard has women pilots and women serving as commanding officers of cutters.

Women first entered the Coast Guard in 1942 as a reserve group called the SPARS. The name SPAR comes from the first letters of the Coast Guard motto, *S*emper *Pa*ratus, and its English translation, *A*lways *R*eady. The SPARS filled administrative jobs to free Coast Guard men for sea duty during World War II. When the war ended in 1945, the SPARS had 10,000 enlisted women and 1,000 officers. All of them were discharged or placed on inactive duty by June 1946, and the group was dissolved. In November 1949, shortly before the Korean War, the SPARS was reactivated. It was disbanded again in 1974, when women became a part of the Regular Coast Guard.

History

The Coast Guard began its history as the Revenue Cutter Service. This service was created in 1790 at the recommendation of Alexander Hamilton, the first secretary of the treasury. Congress established this fleet of 10 small sailing vessels to stamp out smuggling and piracy along the coasts of the United States. Revenue Cutter

Service officers had permission to board all vessels that entered United States waters and to examine their cargoes.

From 1790 until 1798—when the Navy was reorganized—the Revenue Cutter Service served as the nation's only naval force. The service saw its first wartime activity from 1798 to 1800, when it cooperated with the Navy in fighting French privateers. The service also fought during the War of 1812.

New duties. For many years, private organizations such as the Massachusetts Humane Society operated the only lifesaving services on the Atlantic Coast. In 1831, the Revenue Cutter Service began its first winter cruising to aid seafarers and ships in distress. This activity may have lasted only on season, however. In 1837, Congress authorized the use of public vessels to cruise the coast in rough weather and help mariners in distress. In 1848, Congress funded the construction of lifesaving stations to be staffed by volunteers. In 1871, the government took over the stations and formed the U.S. Life-Saving Service, which was operated by the Revenue Cutter Service. In 1878, the Life-Saving Service became an independent bureau of the Department of the Treasury. The Revenue Cutter and Life-Saving services were combined as the United States Coast Guard in 1915. The Federal Lighthouse Service became a part of the Coast Guard in 1939. The Bureau of Marine Inspection and Navigation was transferred from the Department of Commerce to the Coast Guard in 1942.

World War I. On April 6, 1917, after the United States declared war on Germany, the Coast Guard's more than 200 officers and 5,000 men were ordered to go into action with the Navy. The Coast Guard served in the thick of the action, convoying cargo ships and screening transports from the enemy.

A great sea tragedy occurred on Sept. 26, 1918. The cutter *Tampa,* having escorted a convoy from Gibraltar to England, was returning to a port in Wales when it

U.S. Coast Guard

The *Eagle,* an old sailing ship, is used by the U.S. Coast Guard Academy to train cadets. The men and women of the Coast Guard also receive training on modern ships.

disappeared with a loud explosion. The entire crew of 111 coastguardsmen and 4 navy men was lost. Authorities believe that a German *U-boat* (submarine) torpedoed the cutter. In proportion to its strength, the Coast Guard suffered greater losses in World War I than any of the other United States armed forces.

World War II saw the United States Coast Guard serving as a specialized branch of the Navy. The service was responsible for handling and stowing explosives and other dangerous cargoes, and for protecting vessels and port facilities from fire, negligence, or damage. The Coast Guard also furnished weather reports, provided cutters for convoy duty, manned many Army and Navy vessels, took part in Pacific operations, and developed beach-landing methods for the Allied invasion of Europe in 1944.

The Coast Guard Auxiliary was formed in 1939. During World War II, its members offered their boats and their services to the Coast Guard without pay. They wore uniforms and served under military discipline while on active duty.

The Coast Guard Reserve was established in 1941. During the war, about 7,100 reserve officers and about 135,000 enlisted men were on active duty in the Coast Guard.

Recent developments. In 1957, three cutters, *Storis, Bramble,* and *Spar,* were the first U.S. ships to sail through the Northwest Passage, the deepwater passage across the top of North America. In 1967, the Coast Guard was transferred from the United States Treasury Department to the newly created Department of Transportation.

From 1965 to 1972, during the Vietnam War, Coast Guard squadrons patrolled the coastal waters of South Vietnam. The 56 cutters were assigned to prevent the flow of Communist troops and equipment from North Vietnam to South Vietnam.

In 1972, Congress passed the Ports and Waterways Safety Act. This legislation directed the Coast Guard to establish regulations governing the construction of oil tankers and other ships carrying polluting substances in United States waters. The legislation also authorized the

Helicopters are often used in rescue operations. The helicopter shown above is descending to pick up a stranded boater.

Coast Guard to develop vessel traffic control systems to help prevent accidents in crowded harbors and waterways.

In 1989, the Coast Guard headed the cleanup of nearly 11 million gallons (42 million liters) of crude oil that spilled into Prince William Sound in southeastern Alaska. The oil spill—the largest in North American

Navigational buoys serve as guides to vessels along coasts. The Coast Guard inspects and repairs these buoys regularly.

Important dates in Coast Guard history

1790	The U.S. Congress authorized the construction of 10 cutters for a Revenue Cutter Service.
1819	Congress authorized revenue cutters to protect United States merchant vessels against piracy.
1861	The cutter *Harriet Lane* fired the first shot from any vessel in the Civil War.
1898	The cutter *McCulloch* sent the first news of the victory over the Spanish fleet at Manila Bay.
1915	The Revenue Cutter Service and the Life-Saving Service combined to form the U.S. Coast Guard.
1917	During World War I, the Coast Guard served as part of the Navy.
1939	The Lighthouse Service of the Department of Commerce was transferred to the Coast Guard.
1945	The icebreaker *Mackinaw* made the first winter trip through the Soo locks on Lake Superior.
1957	The cutters *Storis, Bramble,* and *Spar* became the first U.S. ships to sail through the Northwest Passage.
1967	The Coast Guard was transferred from the Treasury Department to the Department of Transportation.
1976	The Coast Guard Academy admitted women students for the first time.
1979	Two Coast Guard women officers became the first women to command U.S. warships.
1989	The Coast Guard supervised the cleanup of a huge oil spill off the Coast of Alaska after the tanker *Exxon Valdez* ran aground in Prince William Sound.

Coast Guard airplanes, such as this medium-range aircraft, are used for search and rescue missions at sea. The planes are also used to patrol U.S. waters and enforce maritime laws.

U.S. Coast Guard

The cleanup of oil spills in U.S. waters is supervised by the Coast Guard. This Coastguardsman measures oil along the shore of Prince William Sound in Alaska after a 1989 spill.

U.S. Coast Guard

history—occurred after the U.S. tanker *Exxon Valdez* struck a reef in the sound.

Critically reviewed by the United States Coast Guard

Related articles in *World Book* include:

Beacon
Boating (Boating regulations)
Buoy
Flag (picture: Flags of the armed forces)
Flood

Icebreaker
Lighthouse
Loran
Navy, United States
United States Coast Guard Academy

Outline

I. **What the Coast Guard does**
  A. Protecting life and property
  B. Enforcing sea laws
  C. Supporting the Navy
II. **Life in the Coast Guard**
  A. Careers in the Coast Guard
  B. Training a recruit
  C. Training an officer
III. **Ships, aircraft, and weapons of the Coast Guard**
  A. Ships and stations   C. Weapons
  B. Aircraft
IV. **Organization of the Coast Guard**
  A. Coast Guard headquarters
  B. Regulars and reserves
  C. Women in the Coast Guard
V. **History**

Questions

What is the motto of the Coast Guard? What does it mean?
What are the Coast Guard's law-enforcement duties?
How is the Coast Guard related to the Navy?
What is the *Regular Coast Guard*?
How does the Coast Guard aid navigators?
What kind of training do most officers receive?
What is the International Ice Patrol?
What kinds of services did the Coast Guard perform during World War II?
Why was the Coast Guard's forerunner, the Revenue Cutter Service, established?
How are aircraft important to the Coast Guard?

Coast Guard Academy, United States. See United States Coast Guard Academy.

Coast Ranges are a system of mountain ranges that forms the western coast of North America for about 2,500 miles (4,020 kilometers). The ranges extend from Kodiak Island, Alaska, to southern California. Ten separate mountain ranges make up the Coast Ranges region. The Kodiak, Kenai, Chugach, and St. Elias ranges, and the Alexander Archipelago, a group of islands formed by the tops of sunken mountains, are in Alaska. The Queen Charlotte Islands and the Vancouver Range are in British Columbia. The Oregon Coast Range extends from southern Washington to central Oregon. The California Coast Range is in central California, and the Los Angeles Ranges rise along the coast of southern California. The Coast Ranges are interrupted by the Olympic Mountains in northwestern Washington and by the Klamath Mountains in southern Oregon.

The northern coast is sunk in great bays and straits from Shelikof Strait to Puget Sound. The southern coastline is high and regular, broken only by a few harbors.

Jois C. Child

See also **United States** (The Pacific Ranges and Lowlands).

Coastal plain. See Plain; United States (The Coastal Lowlands).

Coat of arms. See Heraldry.

Coati, *koh AH tee,* also called *coatimundi, koh AH tee MUHN dee,* is a member of the raccoon family. It has a long, flexible snout and often carries its long, ringed tail straight up. Coatis live in wooded areas from Arizona southward to northern Argentina. They measure from 16 to 26 inches (41 to 66 centimeters) long, not counting the tail, and weigh from 10 to 15 pounds (4.5 to 6.8 kilograms). Coatis of the dry hills of Arizona have sandy-blond fur. Chocolate-brown coatis live in the rain forest of Panama. South American coatis are reddish-brown.

Coatis eat almost anything they can easily find, including insects, land crabs, snails, spiders, and a variety of

The coati is related to the raccoon. It has a long flexible snout and a long ringed tail. The animal uses its claws to dig in the ground, and it will eat almost any food it can easily find.

A typical coaxial cable contains 22 tube-enclosed communications wires and many other wires for maintenance and control. The cable is about 3 inches (8 centimeters) in diameter.

fruits. They also eat birds' eggs, lizards, and mice.

Coatis move about mostly in the daytime and are at home both on the ground and in trees. They are curious, intelligent animals and continually sniff the air and dig into the ground with their claws as they wander through the woods. Females and young coatis travel in bands of 6 to 20 animals, but adult males live alone. The word *coatimundi* is an Indian term meaning "lone coati," and it actually refers only to the males.

Each year, one male joins each band for the mating season, which lasts about a month. About 10 or 11 weeks after mating, the pregnant females leave the group. They build tree nests of sticks and leaves and give birth to three or four young. About six weeks later, the mothers and their young rejoin the bands. See also **Animal** (picture: Animals of the tropical forests).

Scientific classification. Coatis form the genera *Nasua* and *Nasuella* in the raccoon family, Procyonidae. One species is *Nasua narica.*   Hugh H. Genoways

Coatimundi. See Coati.

Coatsworth, Elizabeth (1893-1986), was an American author best known for her children's books. Much of her work deals with rural New England, but she also wrote fantasies and stories with settings in early American history and the Far East. She won the 1931 Newbery Medal for *The Cat Who Went to Heaven* (1930), which resembles a Japanese Buddhist folk tale.

Coatsworth's other children's books include *Away Goes Sally* (1934), *Sword of the Wilderness* (1936), *Here I Stay* (1938), *Door to the North* (1950), *First Adventure* (1950), *The Enchanted* (1951), *Silky* (1953), *The White Room* (1958), *The Hand of Apollo* (1965), *They Walk in the Night* (1969), *Grandmother Cat and the Hermit* (1970), and *Under the Green Willow* (1971). Coatsworth also wrote novels, poetry, and stories for adults. She was born in Buffalo, N.Y.   Virginia L. Wolf

Coaxial cable is an electrical conductor that is used to transmit long-distance telephone calls, cable television programs, and other communications. Coaxial cables can carry more signals over a longer distance than ordinary twisted wire cables can. In addition, short coaxial cables are often used to connect electronic devices within a computer or aboard an aircraft.

A typical coaxial cable contains 22 *coaxials*. A coaxial consists of a copper tube with a copper wire held in the tube's center by plastic insulators. The tube is $\frac{3}{8}$ inch (9.5 millimeters) in diameter, and the insulators are spaced about 1 inch (2.5 centimeters) apart along the tube. The tube and wire have the same *axis* (center), and are therefore called *coaxial.* The tube shields the signal from outside electrical interference and prevents the signal from losing its strength. The coaxial is wrapped with steel tape for strength, protection, and electrical shielding.

A coaxial cable may contain several insulated wires, as well as the coaxials. The wires are used for control and maintenance. The cable is wrapped in a plastic-and-lead sheath. A 22-tube cable is about 3 inches (8 centimeters) in diameter. The smallest coaxial cables are about $\frac{1}{10}$ inch (2.5 millimeters) in diameter. Electric signals are sensitive to changing temperatures, so most cables are buried in the earth, which has a more constant temperature. Amplifiers that strengthen the signals may be placed as close as 2 miles (3.2 kilometers) apart.

Coaxials often work in pairs. One coaxial carries signals in one direction, while the other handles signals in the other direction. One pair of tubes in a cable is usually reserved for use in case of damage to another pair. A pair of coaxials can carry up to 13,200 separate signals at once. A fully equipped 22-tube cable, with a pair of tubes in reserve, can carry as many as 132,000 conversations simultaneously.   Richard W. Moss

See also **Cable; Telephone; Television.**

Cobalt is a silver-white metallic element used chiefly in alloys. Cobalt has many of the properties of iron and nickel. All three metals are hard and magnetic, and they react with common acids to produce hydrogen.

Cobalt has the chemical symbol Co. Its atomic number is 27, and its atomic weight is 58.9332. Cobalt has a density of 8.9 grams per cubic centimeter. It melts at 1495° C and boils at 2870° C. Cobalt was discovered in 1737 by a Swedish chemist named Georg Brandt.

Sources. The total amount of cobalt in the earth's crust is relatively small. Cobalt occurs in compounds with arsenic, oxygen, or sulfur; and in ores of nickel and other metals. Cobalt is also found in meteorites. Canada has large deposits of an arsenide ore that contains cobalt, nickel, and iron. These deposits lie in Ontario. Cobalt ore also occurs in Azerbaijan, Finland, Kazakhstan, Russia, Zaire, and Zambia. The United States has little cobalt. Small deposits lie in Idaho, Missouri, and Pennsylvania.

Uses. Most of the cobalt used in the United States is in the form of alloys. The rest is in the form of compounds or isotopes.

Cobalt is alloyed with aluminum and nickel, iron, or certain other metals to make magnets. The magnets are used in radios, TV sets, and many other kinds of devices. Cobalt is combined with carbon and tungsten or with chromium, iron, and some other metal to produce exceptionally hard alloys for such implements as drilling bits and cutting tools. Many cobalt alloys can withstand extremely high temperatures. For this reason, they are used in gas turbines, jet engines, and other equipment that operates at high temperatures.

Cobalt compounds include cobalt oxides and cobalt salts. Cobalt oxides are used as pigments to tint enamel, pottery, and glass. The paint industry uses cobalt salts as drying agents in paints and varnishes. An organic compound of cobalt, vitamin B_{12}, is essential for preventing a disease called *pernicious anemia* (see **Anemia**).

The most widely used isotope of cobalt is *cobalt 60.* Scientists prepare this radioactive isotope by bombarding ordinary cobalt, or *cobalt 59,* with neutrons in a nuclear reactor. Cobalt 60 has a *half-life* of about 5 years—that is, about half the atoms in a sample of cobalt 60 decay in 5 years. As cobalt 60 decays, it gives off two kinds of radiation—*beta particles* and *gamma rays.* Cobalt 60 is used to treat cancer because the radiation it emits kills cancer cells. It also is used in diagnosing certain diseases. For example, doctors test for pernicious anemia by feeding a patient vitamin B_{12} containing some cobalt 60. A radiation detector then measures the amount of cobalt 60—and the vitamin—in the patient's urine. Doctors thus determine if the body is absorbing the vitamin normally.   Kenneth Schug

Cobb, Ty (1886-1961), was one of the greatest and most exciting players in baseball history. He ranks as the all-time leading hitter in the major leagues with a .367 lifetime batting average. Cobb's career total of 4,191 hits also was a major league record until Pete Rose broke it in 1985. Cobb won 12 American League batting titles, including 9 in a row from 1907 to 1915. He also was an expert base runner, stealing 892 bases during his 24-year career.

Tyrus Raymond Cobb was born in Banks County, Georgia, near Homer. He was nicknamed "The Georgia Peach." Cobb, an outfielder, began his major league career with the Detroit Tigers in 1905 and played with the team until 1926. He also managed the Tigers from 1921 to 1926. He spent 1927 and 1928, the final years of his career, playing for the Philadelphia Athletics. Cobb was a fierce competitor who was unpopular with opponents because of his frequent rough play. In 1936, he became one of the first five players elected to the National Baseball Hall of Fame.   Dave Nightingale

Additional resources

Alexander, Charles C. *Ty Cobb: Baseball's Fierce Immortal.* Oxford, 1984.
McCallum, John D. *Ty Cobb.* Praeger, 1975.

Cobden, Richard (1804-1865), was an English manufacturer and statesman who vigorously urged free trade. He believed that eliminating tariffs and other restrictions on trade would improve relations between nations and lead to world peace.

Cobden was born near Midhurst, Sussex. He became a partner in a textile business in 1828. Cobden helped organize the Anti-Corn Law League in 1838. England's corn laws were designed to keep the price of small grains high (see **Corn laws**). He was elected to Parliament in 1841, and helped repeal the corn laws in 1846. He also championed free trade and world peace. Cobden opposed Britain's part in the Crimean War (1853-1856), and this stand contributed to his defeat in 1857. Cobden was reelected in 1859.   Vernon F. Snow

See also **Peel, Sir Robert** (Prime minister).

Cobra, *KOH bruh,* is any one of a group of poisonous "hooded" snakes. Cobras are highly active, and, when excited, flatten the neck by moving the ribs. This movement gives the appearance of a hood. In most snakes, the neck ribs are shorter than those farther back. But in cobras with large hoods, the neck ribs are the longest. These ribs are almost straight instead of curved like those of the body.

Cobras use their deadly poison in two ways. Some types bite their victims with poisonous fangs in the front of the upper jaw. Others also squirt the poison at the eyes of the victim. In these kinds, the fangs are shaped so that the poison is sent forward when the cobra tilts back its head. This "spitting" is most developed in two African cobras and one East Indian. The venom harms humans only when it gets in their eyes. It causes severe irritation and even blindness if not washed out immediately. The bite may cause death in a few hours.

A full-grown Indian cobra is nearly 6 feet (2 meters) long, and about 6 inches (15 centimeters) around. Its color ranges from yellowish to dark brown. On the back of its hood it has a mark like a pair of spectacles. It is sometimes called "spectacled cobra."

Most cobras eat many kinds of animals, such as frogs, fishes, birds, and various small mammals. A dangerous

Wide World

Ty Cobb was one of the first players elected to the National Baseball Hall of Fame. His lifetime batting average was .367.

WORLD BOOK illustration by Robert Lewington, The Garden Studio

An Indian cobra may grow to nearly 6 feet (2 meters) in length. The snake's color ranges from yellowish to dark brown. It has a mark like a pair of spectacles on the back of its hood.

enemy of the cobra is the tiny mongoose. This animal attacks and usually kills the snake. See **Mongoose.**

Cobras live in Africa, Southern Asia, and the East Indies, including the Philippine Islands. The *king cobra* of southeastern Asia is by far the largest of the group, and the longest poisonous snake known. It reaches a length of 18 feet (5.5 meters). It has a narrow hood. Most king cobras retreat from people and will attack only when they are surprised while guarding their eggs.

Cobras are found in various types of country, and may even enter houses. Cobras are not so dangerous as generally believed, because of the way they attack. Unlike rattlesnakes and other vipers, cobras prepare for battle by lifting up the front of the body without curving it like an S. Thus, an opponent can well judge how far a forward jab will reach. A person can easily knock down a rearing cobra by swinging a level stick. The cobra's fangs do not deliver the poison nearly so well as the viper's. The cobra's are shorter, and cannot be folded back. But cobras often chew an object after they have seized it. This habit helps inject the poison.

The jugglers and snake charmers of India usually use the cobra because of its unusual hood and its habit of rearing upright. They pretend to charm snakes with music, but the snakes can hear only a limited range of sounds and cannot hear the music. When they are being "charmed," they are only holding themselves on guard. They would do the same thing without music.

Scientific classification. Cobras belong to the terrestrial poisonous snake family, Elapidae. The Indian cobra is *Naja naja.* The king cobra is *N. hannah.*   Albert F. Bennett

See also **Asp; Snake charming; Snakebite.**

Coca, *KOH kuh,* is the name of a large group of tropical South American shrubs or small trees. Coca plants grow about 3 to 12 feet (0.9 to 3.7 meters) tall. Two species of coca shrubs are cultivated as drug plants—the *Huánuco* coca, also called *Bolivian coca;* and the *Colombian coca.* The Huánuco coca is a greenish-brown plant with shiny, thick stems. The leaves are about 1 to 3 inches (2.5 to 7.6 centimeters) long with smooth edges. The Colombian coca is pale green and has smaller leaves.

The leaves of both the Huánuco and Colombian coca plants contain several drugs used in medicine as *anesthetics* (painkillers). These drugs include cocaine, tropacocaine, and hygrine. Cocaine also is illegally used for nonmedical purposes. Such use of cocaine can be hazardous and addictive (see **Cocaine**). South American Indians chew coca leaves with lime to improve endurance. The drugs in the leaves act as a stimulant and keep them from feeling tired or hungry, but they do not nourish the body.

Scientific classification. Coca plants belong to the coca family, Erythroxylaceae. The scientific name for the Huánuco coca is *Erythroxylum coca.* The Colombian coca is *E. novogranatense.*   James E. Simon

Cocaine, *koh KAYN,* is a powerful drug made from leaves of the coca shrub of South America. United States laws forbid the importation, manufacture, and use of cocaine for nonmedical purposes. But many people obtain it illegally and use it for its pleasurable effects. Such use can be dangerous, with users developing a compulsive desire for and dependence on the drug.

Medical use of cocaine in the United States is extremely limited. A few surgeons prescribe cocaine as a local *anesthetic* (painkiller) during certain kinds of surgery. They prefer cocaine because, in addition to blocking pain sensations, it causes small arteries to tighten, thus reducing bleeding during surgery.

Illegal use of cocaine has increased rapidly since the 1970's. Most users of the drug seek the feeling of intense pleasure, known as a *high,* that occurs for a short period after taking cocaine. Many people take the drug in social settings, using it because their friends do.

Illegal cocaine is a white powder that consists of cocaine hydrochloride—the active ingredient—mixed with other compounds. It is most commonly taken by "snorting" a small amount into the nose, where it is absorbed through the nasal lining. Some cocaine users inject the drug into a vein to produce more rapid and powerful effects. Just as rapid and even stronger effects are obtained by smoking a type of cocaine called *free base.* Cocaine is also smoked in a potent pellet form called *crack.* The injecting and the smoking of cocaine account for most drug-related medical emergencies.

Physical and psychological effects. Cocaine is a *stimulant*—that is, it increases the activity of the nervous system. Cocaine causes sudden increases in heart rate and blood pressure. It also produces a feeling of *euphoria* (a sense of well-being). People feel alert and powerful, and their thinking seems better and clearer than usual. Occasionally, strong feelings of anxiety and fear occur instead of the expected high.

Cocaine use can be habit-forming. When the drug's effects wear off, usually after 20 to 40 minutes, people often feel depressed, and take another dose in an effort to regain the euphoria. Habitual users may eventually come to feel that nothing is enjoyable without cocaine.

The long-term use of cocaine may cause some people to suffer depression or *psychosis* (severe mental breakdown), which makes them unrealistically suspicious or fearful. These symptoms may continue for weeks or months, even after a person has stopped using the drug.

History. The Andean Indians of South America have chewed coca leaves for thousands of years. This practice does not produce a high, but it does reduce fatigue and hunger, and it helps the Indians work more effectively in the high altitude of the mountains.

A German scientist discovered how to extract cocaine from the coca leaves in the mid-1800's. Many physicians at first considered it a miracle drug. During the late

1800's, doctors prescribed cocaine for all sorts of physical and mental ailments, including exhaustion, depression, alcoholism, and morphine addiction. Many of the patent medicines of the day contained cocaine.

Unfortunately, overuse caused many people to become dependent on the drug, and complications surfaced. Enthusiasm over the drug gave way to disappointment. By the mid-1900's, medical and nonmedical use of cocaine had become far less common. During the 1970's, however, claims of the drug's harmlessness and exciting effects triggered renewed popularity for its illegal use. As use of the drug increased, the number of cocaine-related problems also increased. In the 1980's, concern over cocaine use helped trigger widespread antidrug movements in the United States.   Mark S. Gold

Cochise, *koh CHEES* or *koh CHEEZ* (1800?-1874), was an American Indian chief who fought white settlers in what are now Arizona and New Mexico. He led the Chiricahua band of the Apache Indians. The name *Cochise* means *firewood* in Apache.

During the 1850's, the Chiricahua were friendly with the whites. The peaceful relations ended in 1861, when Cochise was falsely accused of kidnapping a settler's child. The United States Army captured Cochise and several members of his tribe and ordered him to return the child. Cochise escaped, but the troops seized six Chiricahua and threatened to kill them if the child was not returned. Cochise then took several whites as hostages and offered to exchange them for the captured Apaches. The Army refused, and so Cochise hanged his hostages. He then went to war against the settlers.

In 1867, a frontiersman named Thomas J. Jeffords went to Cochise's camp and persuaded him to let mail carriers pass through the Indian land. In 1869, Jeffords led General Oliver O. Howard to Cochise to discuss peace. Cochise agreed to stop fighting and moved his band to a reservation in Arizona.   Edgar Perry

Additional resources

Carlson, Vada F. *Cochise: Chief of the Chiricahaus.* Harvey Hse., 1973. For younger readers.
Thrapp, Dan L. *The Conquest of Apacheria.* Univ. of Oklahoma Pr., 1967.

Cochran, *KAHK ruhn,* **Jacqueline** (1912-1980), was an American businesswoman and pioneer airplane pilot. She started flying in 1932, and was the only woman in the McRobertson London-Melbourne Race in 1934. Cochran also became the first woman to compete in the Bendix Trophy Race, which she won in 1938. During World War II (1939-1945), she organized and commanded the Women Airforce Service Pilots (WASPs). In 1945, she became the first civilian woman to receive the Distinguished Service Medal. Cochran owned a cosmetics firm from 1935 to 1963. In 1971, she was elected to the National Aviation Hall of Fame. She was born in Pensacola, Fla.   Richard P. Hallion

Cock-of-the-rock is the name of two species of South American birds. One species lives in rocky ravines near mountain streams in the Andes from Colombia to Bolivia. The other species lives in the mountains from Colombia to French Guiana and in northern Brazil. The male cock-of-the-rock has rich orange or red plumage and a large crest on the top of the head. The female is dull-colored. At the mating season, males gather to-

San Diego Zoo

Cocks-of-the-rock live in South America. The female, *left,* has dull colors. The male, *right,* has bright orange feathers.

gether in a cleared spot in the forest, where they dance and call to attract females. The female makes its nest of plant fibers that it glues together with resin and attaches to crevices on rocks. Cocks-of-the-rock feed on fruit.

Scientific classification. Cocks-of-the-rock make up the genus *Rupicola* in the family Cotingidae.   Stuart D. Strahl

Cockatiel, *KAHK uh TEEL,* also spelled *cockateel,* is a gray bird related to the cockatoo. It lives throughout Australia, except in coastal areas. The cockatiel is about $12\frac{1}{2}$ inches (32 centimeters) long and has a crown of feathers on its head and a long, tapered tail. Cockatiels are gray, and the males have bright orange and yellow patches on their faces. Females have duller face patches.

The cockatiel lives in open country and is often found in trees bordering rivers or streams. Its favorite foods are seeds, grain, fruit, and berries, so farmers consider it a nuisance. The cockatiel is a popular pet. It may learn to "speak" a few words.

Scientific classification. The cockatiel belongs to the family Cacatuidae. Its scientific name is *Nymphicus hollandicus.*   John W. Fitzpatrick

See also **Parrot.**

WORLD BOOK illustration by John F. Eggert
Male cockatiel

Cockatoo, *KAHK uh TOO,* is the name of several large birds that look like parrots. Cockatoos live in Australia, Indonesia, and neighboring islands. Unlike parrots, cockatoos have a crest of feathers that can be raised and lowered. A cockatoo's coloring may be combinations of white, black, red, rose, or gray. The common white cockatoo has a yellow or rose crest. The cockatoo has a powerful, curved bill and a thick tongue. It has strong feet with which it climbs about the branches of trees.

Cockatoos feed on seeds, nuts, and fruits. These birds are serious pests in regions where there are many orchards. They are often seen in large flocks that fly

WORLD BOOK illustration by Trevor Boyer, Linden Artists Ltd.

Cockatoos resemble parrots. The two species shown above are the black cockatoo, *left,* and the sulfur-crested cockatoo, *right.*

swiftly. Although they rarely learn to talk and often scream loudly, cockatoos make amusing pets because they can perform stunts and acrobatics.

    Scientific classification. Cockatoos belong to the family Ca-catuidae. The black cockatoo is *Probosciger aterrimus.*

John W. Fitzpatrick

See also **Parrot.**

Cockcroft, Sir John Douglas (1897-1967), a British nuclear physicist, won the 1951 Nobel Prize in physics with Ernest T. S. Walton for being first to disintegrate atomic nuclei with artificially accelerated particles. In 1932, Cockcroft and Walton bombarded lithium nuclei with high-speed protons, producing two helium nuclei in the reaction. During World War II (1939-1945), Cockcroft ran an atomic research laboratory near Montreal, Canada. After the war, he led the British Atomic Energy Research Establishment. In 1959, he became the first head of Churchill College of Cambridge University. In 1961, he won the Atoms for Peace Award. He was born in Todmorden, near Huddersfield.   Roger H. Stuewer

    See also **Particle accelerator; Walton, Ernest T. S.**

Cocker spaniel, sometimes called the *American cocker,* is one of the most popular dogs in the United States. Cockers are favorite pets and show dogs. They are named for their ability to hunt birds called wood-cock. However, few cockers are now used as hunting dogs. Most weigh 22 to 28 pounds (10 to 13 kilograms) and stand about 15 inches (38 centimeters) at the shoulder. Cockers have a soft, thick coat with *feathers* (long hairs) on the ears, chest, and legs. Many cockers have coats that are solid black or black with tan markings. Cockers with coats of *any solid color other than black*—and also nonblack cockers with tan markings—are called *ascobs.* Cockers with red and white, black and white, or three-colored combination coats are called *parti-colors.* See also **Dog** (picture: Sporting dogs).

    Critically reviewed by the American Spaniel Club

Cockfighting is a sport in which two *gamecocks* (fighting roosters) battle each other to the death. The sport is illegal in most of the United States, in Canada, and in many other countries. It is sometimes carried on secretly. Cockfighting is a popular public sport in Spain, Latin America, and part of the Orient.

    Gamecocks are specially bred to achieve physical power, speed of movement, courage, and the killer instinct. They usually are brightly colored and have long spurs on their legs. But breeders generally trim the spurs down, and attach artificial spurs to the gamecocks' legs. The spurs are usually steel, brass, or bone. The birds use them to rip and tear at their opponents.

    A cockfight takes place in an enclosed pit, usually outdoors. Spectators place bets on their favorite gamecocks. At the start of the fight, handlers hold their birds firmly and allow them to peck at each other. When the birds are angry, they are released and start to fight.

    Cockfighting probably began in Asia thousands of years ago. The sport came to ancient Greece and Rome by way of India and China. It spread throughout Europe. During the 1600's, the sport became popular in England, where the training and breeding of fighting cocks became an important industry.   Don B. Wilmeth

Cockle is a sea animal with a tough, protective shell. It is a kind of clam. It has a round, grooved shell divided into two equal parts. The cockle moves about by using a long, muscular organ called a *foot.* This foot is strong enough to flip the animal short distances. Cockles live in shallow water along ocean coastlines in many parts of the world. They may be from $\frac{1}{2}$ inch to 8 inches (1.3 to 20 centimeters) in diameter. The largest kinds of cockles are found on the Pacific coast of Central America.

    Scientific classification. Cockles are in the phylum Mollusca and the family Cardiidae.   M. Patricia Morse

Cocklebur is the name of certain species of annual weeds belonging to the composite family. They all have spiny burs, and there are usually two seeds in each bur. One seed begins to grow a season before the other seed. Hooked prickles that cover the burs stick to clothing and fur. Cocklebur seedlings are poisonous and can kill hogs and young cattle that graze on them.

    Cockleburs are native to North America. They are found in low areas in fields and by roadsides. Cockleburs grow from 1 to 3 feet (30 to 91 centimeters) tall, and their rough leaves are heart-shaped or irregular. Some

WORLD BOOK photo

The cocker spaniel is a popular American pet.

WORLD BOOK illustration by Robert Hynes

The cocklebur has spiny, prickly burs.

of the flowers of the cocklebur bear pollen, while others develop burs that bear seeds. The pollen-bearing flowers grow on the upper branches, and the seed-bearing ones grow on the lower. To get rid of cockleburs, the plants must be destroyed before the seeds ripen.

Scientific classification. Cockleburs make up the genus *Xanthium* in the composite family, Asteraceae or Compositae.

Margaret R. Bolick

Cockney is a nickname for a citizen of London, particularly one from the East End area. According to tradition, a cockney is anyone born within the sound of the bells of St. Mary-le-Bow Church. *Cockney* also applies to a dialect of English. Speakers change certain vowel sounds; for example, *lady* becomes *lydy* and *road, rowd*. They also drop the *h* at the start of words, and may add one in a word starting with a vowel; for example, *ard* for *hard* and *hanswered* for *answered*. The word *cockney* originally meant a misshapen egg. See also **London** (The people). Robert E. Dowse

Cockroach is an insect best known as a household pest. It is closely related to grasshoppers and crickets. Cockroaches have lived on the earth for about 250 million years. There are over 3,500 species found throughout the world. They live in a variety of places, from tropical rain forests to deserts. About 20 species live in human dwellings and are considered pests.

Cockroaches have flat, oval bodies and long legs covered with bristles that serve as a sense of touch. Many cockroaches fly, and all run fast. These insects have long *antennae* (feelers) that provide a sense of smell.

Cockroaches are scavengers. They eat all kinds of food and a variety of other substances, including paper, soap, plants, and dead animals. The pest species can live in almost any dwelling as long as the temperature is over 65 °F (18 °C) and water is available. They can be a serious problem in apartments, hospitals, and restaurants. Most cockroaches avoid light and are active chiefly at night. If they live in a dirty place, they carry germs.

Most species of cockroaches are found outdoors. In tropical rain forests, cockroaches may live on the forest floor or high in the trees. Some of these tropical cockroaches grow to 5 inches (13 centimeters) long, and many are brightly colored. Cockroaches frequently inhabit caves with bats.

Cockroaches found in United States homes include the *German cockroach, American cockroach, Australian cockroach, brown-banded cockroach,* and *Oriental cockroach.* The most common of these pest cockroaches is the German cockroach, also called the *Croton bug.* It got its name after it was found in large numbers in the Croton waterworks system in New York City in the mid-1800's. The adults are pale tan and about $\frac{1}{2}$ inch (1.3 centimeters) long. Every 25 days, the females lay egg cases containing about 32 young. The young become adults in about three months. This cockroach is highly adaptable and resistant to many pesticides.

WORLD BOOK illustration by Shirley Hooper, Oxford Illustrators Limited

Cockroach

Since the mid-1980's, a species called the *Asian cockroach* has become established as a pest in Florida and neighboring states. This cockroach, which is native to southeast Asia, is closely related to the German cockroach. Unlike most other species, the Asian cockroach is attracted to lights and bright surfaces. In addition, it is frequently found outdoors.

To keep cockroaches at a minimum in the home, keep the rooms clean and dry. Fix leaky faucets, do not overwater house plants, and do not leave out water or dried food for pets. Do the dishes before going to bed at night and store food in sealed containers. Throw away old paper bags and newspapers to avoid creating hiding places for cockroaches. Do not use any pesticide unless it has been approved for use in the home.

Scientific classification. Cockroaches make up the order Blattodea or Blattaria. The scientific name for the German cockroach is *Blattella germanica.* The Asian cockroach is *B. asahinai.*

Betty Lane Faber

Cockscomb is a flower with heads of red and yellow blossoms shaped like a rooster's comb or like an ostrich

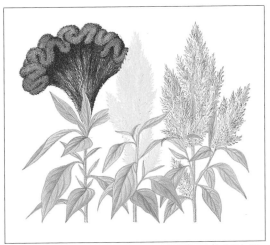

WORLD BOOK illustration by Christabel King

The cockscomb is a plant with crested or feathery clusters of red or yellow flowers. It is often grown in gardens.

plume. It comes from tropical America, Asia, and the East Indies, but it now grows in all parts of the United States. It will bloom from midsummer until the fall frost if planted in light, rich soil that is kept damp.

Scientific classification. Cockscombs belong to the amaranth family, Amaranthaceae. They are *Celosia argentea,* variety *cristata.*

Cocktail. See Alcoholic beverage (Distilled beverages).

Cocoa. See Chocolate.

Cocoa butter. See Chocolate (Manufacturing).

Coconut. See Coconut palm.

Coconut palm is the tall, graceful tree on which the coconut grows. It probably is native to Southeast Asia and the islands of Melanesia in the Pacific Ocean. But it has been introduced into all the tropical and subtropical parts of the world. It stands from 40 to 100 feet (12 to 30 meters) high. Large featherlike leaves spread from the top of its branchless trunk.

The coconut palm is one of the most useful trees. People in the tropics build houses and bridges from its wood. They use whole leaves to make thatch roofs, and strips of leaves to make hats, mats, and baskets. They also make a sweet drink called *toddy* or *tuba* from the sap of the tree's blossoms. They also use this sap to make sugar, vinegar, and an alcoholic beverage.

The coconut is the fruit of the coconut palm. Clusters of these large round fruits grow among the leaves of the tree. Each coconut has a smooth light-colored *rind.* Under the rind is a 1- to 2-inch (2.5- to 5-centimeter) *husk* of reddish-brown fibers. The husk and rind surround a brown, woody shell that has three soft spots called *eyes* at one end. The rind and husk are usually cut away before the coconuts are marketed.

The coconut seed lies inside the shell. It is a ball of crisp, white, sweet-tasting coconut *meat* covered by a

Leading coconut-growing countries

Tons of copra produced in a year

Philippines	●●●●●●●●●●
	2,030,000 short tons (1,842,000 metric tons)
Indonesia	●●●●●●●
	1,275,000 short tons (1,157,000 metric tons)
India	●●◖
	476,000 short tons (432,000 metric tons)
Mexico	●
	202,000 short tons (183,000 metric tons)
Vietnam	●
	166,000 short tons (151,000 metric tons)

Figures are based on a three-year average, 1988-1990. Source: *FAO Production Yearbook, 1990,* Food and Agriculture Organization of the United Nations.

tough brown skin. Its hollow center holds a sugary liquid called coconut *milk.* The coconut seed measures from 8 to 12 inches (20 to 30 centimeters) long and from 6 to 10 inches (15 to 25 centimeters) across.

 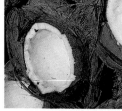

© Russ Kinne, Photo Researchers, Inc.   © Robert W. Mitchell, Earth Scenes

Coconuts grow in clusters among the leaves of the coconut palm, *left.* The coconut seed lies inside the shell, *right.* It is a ball of crisp, white, sweet-tasting coconut meat covered by a tough brown skin. The seed's hollow center holds a sugary liquid.

Eric Hosking

Coconut palms are tall trees that produce coconuts. Large leaves spread from the top of the branchless trunks.

A well-tended tree produces about a hundred coconuts a year. Each fruit takes about a year to ripen. Ripe coconuts fall from the tree. However, on plantations, the coconuts are usually cut from the trees every two or three months.

Solid, dried coconut meat is called *copra.* Copra contains a valuable oil that is used for cooking and to make margarine and soap. Tropical lands produce millions of tons of copra each year. About 6,000 medium-sized coconuts make 1 short ton (0.9 metric ton). To make copra, coconuts are split open and dried in the sun or in ovens. Some coconuts are dried by smoking.

Throughout the world, people enjoy eating crisp, juicy chunks of fresh coconut meat. Shredded and dried coconut meat adds a distinctive flavor and texture to candy bars and other foods. People in tropical lands also use the coconut husk. They weave the short, stiff fibers (called *coir*) of the husk into mats, ropes, and brooms.

Growing coconut palms. In the tropics, people can plant coconut palms all year. They half bury the coconut in a horizontal position. Within six months, a leaf sprouts from one of the eyes and pushes through the husk. The palm can be transplanted after one to four years. The palm will bear coconuts after seven or eight years. Coconut palms need much water and a temperature of at least 72 °F (22 °C) most of the year.

A disease called *lethal yellowing* has destroyed many coconut palms in Florida, Texas, Mexico, the Bahamas, and areas of the Caribbean. The disease is caused by microorganisms carried by insects called *planthoppers.*

Scientific classification. The coconut palm belongs to the palm family, Arecaceae or Palmae. Its scientific name is *Cocos nucifera.*   Alwyn H. Gentry

See also **Copra; Tree** (picture); **Palm** (Kinds of palms; pictures: Coconut palms).

Cocoon is a protective covering that encloses the pupa and sometimes the larva of many insects. The mature larva prepares the cocoon as a shelter around itself. Inside the cocoon, the larva changes to a pupa and eventually transforms into an adult insect. Among the insects that spend part of their lives in cocoons are wasps, bees, caddis flies, moths, and some ants. Many spiders spin silk cocoons around masses of their eggs and sometimes around their prey.

The chief substance of most cocoons is silk. But the larva often incorporates other substances, including soil, sand grains, plant materials, and hair or waste from its own body. Some cocoons contain very little silk at all.

Most moth larvae (caterpillars) form cocoons. But many species pass the pupal stage in soil or in parts of plants without forming a cocoon. A few butterfly caterpillars make flimsy cocoons, but most pupate as a hard-shelled *chrysalis.* Perhaps the best-known cocoon is that of the caterpillar of the *Bombyx mori* moth, which supplies most of the world's commercial silk.

Most moth caterpillars build their cocoons in protected places in fallen logs, openings in tree bark, or among debris and fallen leaves. Cocoons of some large species, such as *Cecropia, Promethea,* and *Polyphemus* moths, are fastened to twigs of trees and can easily be found during winter. The pupae spend the winter inside the cocoon and secrete a dissolving fluid to emerge from the cocoon in spring or summer.

Other moths, including certain species of *tiger moths,* spend the winter as larvae and form cocoons in spring or summer before pupating. Some species of *clothes moths* form an incomplete cocoon or pupal case early in larval life and carry it on their backs as they feed. Later, they complete the cocoon and use it for their pupal stage.   Charles V. Covell, Jr.

Related articles in *World Book* include:

Caterpillar	Moth
Chrysalis	Pupa
Larva	Silk (Raising silkworms)
Metamorphosis	

Cocteau, *kahk TOH* or *kawk TOH,* **Jean,** *zhahn* (1889-1963), a French writer, often used his many talents to shock the public. He had a great range of creativity and won fame as a poet, playwright, author of ballet plots, screenwriter, novelist, and artist. Cocteau defied the conventions of his time with an unorthodox private life, which included homosexuality and the use of opium. He also insisted that the artist occupies a central role in culture.

Cocteau frequently used the myths and dramatic plots of ancient Greece in his plays. *Orpheus* (1926) is a study of a poet's agonizing search for inspiration and his struggle to gain acceptance for his work. *The Infernal Machine* (1934) is an adaptation of Sophocles' *Oedipus Rex.* Its theme is that humanity's fate is controlled by dangerous powers that govern the universe. In Cocteau's fantastic style, these plays use unexpected colloquial phrases, events out of time sequence, and symbols explainable in terms of modern psychology.

Cocteau's best-known novel, *Les Enfants terribles* (1929), tells of four young people who create a sinister, unreal world of their own. He also created ballets, notably *Parade* (1917). He wrote and directed several films, including *The Blood of a Poet* (1932), *Beauty and the Beast* (1946), and *Orpheus* (1950). In his later years, he devoted his time to painting and to decorating chapels. Cocteau was born in Maisons-Laffitte. He was elected to the French Academy in 1955.   Dora E. Polachek

Cod is a major food fish. It lives in the northern waters of the Atlantic and Pacific oceans. Cod belong to the codfish family, which also includes the pollock and the haddock. The codfish family is second only to the herring family in the amount of fish caught each year. But unlike herring, which are used largely for agricultural and industrial purposes, most cod are eaten by people.

E. R. Degginger, Bruce Coleman Inc.   WORLD BOOK illustration by Shirley Hooper, Oxford Illustrators Limited

The cocoon of a Cecropia moth, *left,* is attached to a tree twig. The opened cocoon, *right,* reveals the pupa inside.

The Pacific cod lives in the waters of the northern Pacific Ocean and the Bering Sea. It is an excellent food fish and has long been important to the fishing industry.

Appearance and habits. Cod have three fins on the back and two fins on the underside near the tail. A fleshy growth called a *barbel* extends from the end of the chin. Cod may be any color from gray to red to brown or black, with the upper parts marked with many small, dark spots. Most adult *Atlantic cod* range from 2 to 3 feet (0.6 to 0.9 meter) in length and weigh from 5 to 25 pounds (2.3 to 11 kilograms). But cod of up to 6 feet (1.8 meters) and 212 pounds (96 kilograms) have been recorded. The *Pacific cod* rarely exceeds 3 feet (91 centimeters) in length and usually weighs from 3 to 20 pounds (1.4 to 9 kilograms).

Cod live near the ocean floor, but they often swim up to midwater and sometimes approach the surface while feeding. The fish swim at an average speed of 4 miles (6 kilometers) per hour.

Cod *spawn* (produce eggs) offshore during the late winter and the early spring. A cod may spawn from 3 to 8 million eggs at a time. But only a small percentage of the eggs develop into mature fish. The eggs of most species of cod rise to the surface and become part of the *plankton*—the mass of small, drifting aquatic organisms. The newly hatched fish feed on the plankton. When the cod are 1 to 2 inches (2.5 to 5 centimeters) long, they move to the ocean's bottom, where they feed on worms and small shrimp.

Some cod migrate in response to seasonal changes in water temperature. Cod also may migrate to spawn and to search for food. Mature cod eat small fish; squid; and shellfish, such as clams, crabs, and shrimp.

Cod fishing and marketing. There are 25 species of the codfish family found in North America, but not all of them are commonly called cod. The Atlantic cod ranks as the most important codfish, accounting for more than four-fifths of the annual catch of about $2\frac{4}{5}$ million short tons (2.5 million metric tons). The number of Atlantic cod in a given area varies because of seasonal migrations. In more southerly parts of its range, the fish is found only during the cold months. The best fishing grounds for Atlantic cod are the offshore banks of North America—especially the Grand Banks, which is off Newfoundland, and Georges Bank, which is off Boston. The most important cod fishing areas in the northeastern Atlantic are around Iceland and in the Barents, Norwegian, Baltic, and North seas.

The Pacific cod ranges from the waters off California north to the Bering Sea and west to Japan and Korea. The best fishing grounds for Pacific cod are in the southeast Bering Sea. Prior to its breakup, the Soviet Union was the leading country in catching Pacific cod. The United States ranked second and Japan was third.

When cod is split, salted, and dried, it can be kept for long periods without spoiling. In past centuries, ships could not carry perishable food on long voyages because there was no refrigeration. Cod became an important food on such voyages. As early as the 1500's, European fishing crews crossed the Atlantic to catch cod. At first, the fish were caught with lines and bait. But since the 1600's, cod have been caught mainly with nets.

In the United States, the demand for cod has increased sharply since the introduction of precooked codfish sticks in the 1950's. In addition, the fish-and-chips franchise business depends almost exclusively on cod. Cod is also a source of cod-liver oil, a food supplement rich in vitamins A and D.

Scientific classification. Cod belong to the codfish family, Gadidae. The scientific name for the Atlantic cod is *Gadus morhua.* The Pacific cod is *G. macrocephalus.*   Tomio Iwamoto

See also **Cod-liver oil.**

Cod-liver oil is a yellow, fishy smelling oil obtained from the livers of codfish. It contains large amounts of the vitamins A and D. At one time, many people took cod-liver oil to protect against vitamin A and D deficiencies. People who do not receive enough vitamin A may develop skin and eye problems. A lack of vitamin D can cause *rickets,* a disease that leads to deformed bones.

Today, cod-liver oil is rarely used. A balanced diet provides all the vitamins A and D a person normally requires. For example, fortified milk is high in both vitamins, and green and yellow vegetables are a good source of vitamin A. People who need extra amounts of these vitamins generally take them in capsules. Such vitamin capsules are cheaper and more convenient than cod-liver oil.   Eugene M. Johnson, Jr.

Code, in law, combines all the laws on a given subject in a single statute or ordinance. It is passed by a legislative body, such as a federal congress, a state legislature, a county board of supervisors, or a village board. It is purely *statutory law,* as distinguished from the *common law* that arises from court decisions.

In theory, it is possible for all the laws in a code to be *new* in the sense that no law has ever been passed dealing with the particular subject. But in practice, a code nearly always represents a systematic and comprehensive revision of all the laws that the legislative body has passed on a given subject.

Statutes usually develop only as problems arise that point out the need for rules and regulations on certain points. The development of laws concerning automobiles is an example. The first rules set speed limits and required drivers to keep to the right. Then vehicles, and later drivers, were licensed. Stop signs, traffic lights, and traffic regulations were established. Many cities passed regulations without regard to making them consistent with state laws.

Such piecemeal legislation left many gaps, uncertainties, and conflicts among the many separate regulations. As a result, most states revised their motor-vehicle laws, made them consistent, filled the gaps, and removed uncertainties. They enacted a single series of laws called a *Motor Vehicle Code.*

Other well-known codes include the federal criminal code, state commercial codes, and local or county building codes. Some villages combine all their laws into a *village code.* Sherman L. Cohn

Code Civil. See Code Napoléon.

Code Napoléon, *KAWD na paw lay AWN,* is the name often given to the code that contains the civil, as distinguished from the criminal, law of France. In 1800, Napoleon Bonaparte appointed a commission of jurists to combine all French civil laws into one code. The code went into effect in 1804. That same year, after Napoleon became emperor of France, the code became known as the *Code Napoléon.* But its official name is *Code Civil.*

The Code Napoléon represented a compromise between the customary law of northern France and the Roman law of the south. It also compromised between the ideas of the French Revolution and older ideas. It gave new liberty to the people, but kept such ideas as the system of inheritance. The Code Napoléon influenced law in Europe, South America, the state of Louisiana, and the province of Quebec. But its influence has declined. Even in France, the Code Napoléon has been changed by new laws and court decisions.

Edward W. Cleary

Code of Hammurabi. See Hammurabi.

Code of Justinian. See Justinian Code.

Codeine, *KOH deen,* is a drug that is usually manufactured from morphine, a drug made from opium. Codeine also can be obtained directly from opium. Its effects are similar to those of morphine, except it is much less potent and retains effectiveness when administered orally. Codeine is used primarily to relieve pain and to suppress coughing. A person who uses the drug for an extended period may develop an addiction.

Barbara M. Bayer

See also **Morphine; Opium.**

Codes and ciphers are forms of secret communication. In general, a code replaces words, phrases, or sentences with groups of letters or numbers. A cipher rearranges letters or uses substitutes for them to disguise a message.

The technology of secret communication is called *cryptology.* It has two opposing parts: *communications security* and *communications intelligence.*

People use communications security, also called *COMSEC,* to make messages secret. Children keep secrets by talking in a secret language known as *pig Latin.* A general puts orders into code. In baseball, a coach rubs his cheek as a sign for the batter to swing at the next pitch. The study and practice of the methods of COMSEC is called *cryptography.*

Communications intelligence, also called *COMINT,* consists of gaining information about or access to messages without the permission of the communicators. COMINT includes eavesdropping, bugging rooms, wiretapping telephone conversations, and cracking the codes or ciphers of enemy forces. Solving the secret communications of other people without their permission is called *cryptanalysis.* Success in COMINT has led to diplomatic advantages and military victories.

In cryptology, the original message is called the *plaintext.* Its secret form is the *ciphertext* or *cryptogram.* The method that changes one into the other is the *cryptosystem.* Within the cryptosystem, a *key* controls operations. The receiver of a ciphertext must have been given the cryptosystem and key to convert the ciphertext back

into plaintext. *Encrypting* is the process of converting plaintext into ciphertext. *Decrypting* is changing ciphertext into plaintext by the legitimate receiver.

This article explains only the encrypting procedures. From them, the decrypting procedures can be determined. In addition, the article deals only with communications using letters and numbers. The principles also apply to other forms, such as TV scramblers.

Communications security

The letters, numbers, words, punctuation marks, and other symbols that make up a plaintext can be turned into secret form in only two ways. One method, called *transposition,* shuffles them. The other, called *substitution,* replaces them with symbols. Transposition and substitution may be combined. Cryptograms are usually sent in groups of five letters or numbers to help detect dropped or added characters and to conceal clues to the cryptosystem and the plaintext.

Transposition. A simple transposition reverses consecutive pairs of letters. In such a cipher, the message DO NOT DEPART would become ODOND TPERA T. A more secure form of transposition is *columnar* transposition. In this method, shown below, the plaintext is written horizontally by lines under the key numbers and then taken out vertically by columns in the order of the key numbers.

```
4 1 2 5 3
a w a i t
m y o r d
e r s
```

For example, the message AWAIT MY ORDERS becomes WYRAO STDAM EIR (WYR from column 1; AOS, 2; TD, 3; AME, 4; and IR, 5).

Substitution. The simplest form of substitution is *monoalphabetic* substitution. It replaces each letter of the plaintext with a particular symbol. For example, if the substitute for *a* is *X,* all the *a*'s in the plaintext become *X*s in the ciphertext. The complete list of substitutes for the 26 letters may be set out in a *cipher alphabet:*

```
a b c d e f g h i j k l m n o p q r s t u v w x y z
X 7 + P D M 3 U A J 6 Z R C $ G 5 N E B W % 9 H S K
```

	a	b	c	d	e	f	g	h	i	j	k	l	m	n	o	p	q	r	s	t	u	v	w	x	y	z
1	G	B	O	Y	R	D	P	Z	E	F	Q	A	H	S	T	I	U	N	J	V	C	L	W	K	M	X
2	B	O	Y	R	D	P	Z	E	F	Q	A	H	S	T	I	U	N	J	V	C	L	W	K	M	X	G
3	O	Y	R	D	P	Z	E	F	Q	A	H	S	T	I	U	N	J	V	C	L	W	K	M	X	G	B
4	Y	R	D	P	Z	E	F	Q	A	H	S	T	I	U	N	J	V	C	L	W	K	M	X	G	B	O
5	R	D	P	Z	E	F	Q	A	H	S	T	I	U	N	J	V	C	L	W	K	M	X	G	B	O	Y
6	D	P	Z	E	F	Q	A	H	S	T	I	U	N	J	V	C	L	W	K	M	X	G	B	O	Y	R
7	P	Z	E	F	Q	A	H	S	T	I	U	N	J	V	C	L	W	K	M	X	G	B	O	Y	R	D
8	Z	E	F	Q	A	H	S	T	I	U	N	J	V	C	L	W	K	M	X	G	B	O	Y	R	D	P
9	E	F	Q	A	H	S	T	I	U	N	J	V	C	L	W	K	M	X	G	B	O	Y	R	D	P	Z
10	F	Q	A	H	S	T	I	U	N	J	V	C	L	W	K	M	X	G	B	O	Y	R	D	P	Z	E
11	Q	A	H	S	T	I	U	N	J	V	C	L	W	K	M	X	G	B	O	Y	R	D	P	Z	E	F
12	A	H	S	T	I	U	N	J	V	C	L	W	K	M	X	G	B	O	Y	R	D	P	Z	E	F	Q
13	H	S	T	I	U	N	J	V	C	L	W	K	M	X	G	B	O	Y	R	D	P	Z	E	F	Q	A
14	S	T	I	U	N	J	V	C	L	W	K	M	X	G	B	O	Y	R	D	P	Z	E	F	Q	A	H
15	T	I	U	N	J	V	C	L	W	K	M	X	G	B	O	Y	R	D	P	Z	E	F	Q	A	H	S
16	I	U	N	J	V	C	L	W	K	M	X	G	B	O	Y	R	D	P	Z	E	F	Q	A	H	S	T
17	U	N	J	V	C	L	W	K	M	X	G	B	O	Y	R	D	P	Z	E	F	Q	A	H	S	T	I
18	N	J	V	C	L	W	K	M	X	G	B	O	Y	R	D	P	Z	E	F	Q	A	H	S	T	I	U
19	J	V	C	L	W	K	M	X	G	B	O	Y	R	D	P	Z	E	F	Q	A	H	S	T	I	U	N
20	V	C	L	W	K	M	X	G	B	O	Y	R	D	P	Z	E	F	Q	A	H	S	T	I	U	N	J
21	C	L	W	K	M	X	G	B	O	Y	R	D	P	Z	E	F	Q	A	H	S	T	I	U	N	J	V
22	L	W	K	M	X	G	B	O	Y	R	D	P	Z	E	F	Q	A	H	S	T	I	U	N	J	V	C
23	W	K	M	X	G	B	O	Y	R	D	P	Z	E	F	Q	A	H	S	T	I	U	N	J	V	C	L
24	K	M	X	G	B	O	Y	R	D	P	Z	E	F	Q	A	H	S	T	I	U	N	J	V	C	L	W
25	M	X	G	B	O	Y	R	D	P	Z	E	F	Q	A	H	S	T	I	U	N	J	V	C	L	W	K
26	X	G	B	O	Y	R	D	P	Z	E	F	Q	A	H	S	T	I	U	N	J	V	C	L	W	K	M

The plaintext *attack* would become ciphertext XBBX+6. The ciphertext 3$ decrypts into *go*.

In *polyalphabetic* substitution, a plaintext letter is replaced by substitutes from several cipher alphabets rather than from a single one. A common method of this substitution uses a table like that on page 749. Correspondents may agree to use all 26 ciphertext alphabets of the table in turn, repeating them if the message is more than 26 letters long. In this method, the first letter of the plaintext is enciphered using the scrambled alphabet in line 1. The second letter uses that of line 2, and so on.

A more flexible method of polyalphabetic substitution employs a *keyword* to specify the ciphertext alphabets to be used. If the keyword is BOX, for example, the cipher alphabets beginning with the letters B, O, and X will be used in that order. To encipher, the keyword is written repeatedly above the plaintext. The substitute for each plaintext letter is found under that plaintext letter in the cipher alphabet that begins with its keyletter:

keyword	B O X B O X B O X B O X B O
plaintext	r e p o r t p o s i t i o n
ciphertext	J P T I V J U U N F L Z I I

Different keywords applied to the same plaintext will yield quite different ciphertexts. The great advantage of the use of a keyword is that it can be changed easily in case of overuse or actual or feared discovery. Its disadvantage is its regular repetition. One way of avoiding this repetition is to use a long phrase, perhaps taken from a book. Such a phrase is called a *running key:*

running key	T H E M O L E H A D B E E N
plaintext	r e p o r t p o s i t i o n
ciphertext	D U K H V T K G Y S C U W R

Polyalphabetic substitutions adapt easily to cipher machines and, in certain systems, strongly resist solution. As a result, they are among the most widely used ciphers in the world today.

Another type of substitution, called *polygraphic* substitution, puts two or more letters into cipher as a unit. As a result, a change in any one plaintext letter changes the encipherment of the whole. The *Playfair system,* used during World War I (1914-1918) and World War II (1939-1945), starts with a 25-letter scrambled alphabet arranged in a 5-letter by 5-letter square. The plaintext letters are enciphered in pairs according to their positions in relation to each other within the square. The *Hill cipher* converts plaintext letters into numbers and then plugs them into algebraic equations. To encipher the text, the cipher clerk solves the equations.

Public-key systems. In most cryptosystems, both sender and receiver must have the same cryptosystem and key. In *public-key cryptosystems,* however, the encrypting and decrypting keys differ. They are related mathematically through a number that is the product of two large primes (see **Factor**). The product is public and serves as the encrypting key. The primes are secret and serve as the decrypting key. The system depends for its security upon the difficulty of factoring large numbers. If the product is long enough, for example, 300 digits, finding the primes would take centuries.

Cipher machines. Mechanical and electromechanical machines, as well as computers, can generate complex cryptosystems that cannot be worked easily or accurately by hand. The most famous mechanical system was invented by Boris C. W. Hagelin, a Swedish engineer. It shifts a cipher alphabet to various positions in a key sequence more than 100 million letters long. The United States Army used Hagelin's system during World War II.

Electromechanical rotor machines are more powerful than mechanical machines. The "Enigma," used by the Germans during World War II, was the best known. This machine had an electric keyboard into which the plaintext was typed. The electric signal representing the plaintext letter passed through a succession of wired codewheels called rotors. This created an electric maze that changed as the rotors turned, thus constantly changing the encipherment.

Transistors and integrated circuits have enabled cryptographers to increase the complexity of cipher systems. For example, they can generate long, irregular keys. These keys are in the form of *bits,* or binary digits—0's and 1's. If the plaintext has been converted to the same form, the system enciphers the message by "adding" the key to the plaintext, using the $0+0=0$, $1+1=0$, $1+0=1$, and $0+1=1$.

Codes. In theory, codes cannot be distinguished from ciphers because there is no one point at which a cipher alphabet becomes a code. In practice, however, most codes fill a book, while a cipher can be written on a single piece of paper or embodied in a cipher machine. The cryptosystem is called a code if the plaintext elements consist not only of letters but also of hundreds of words, phrases, sentences, syllables, numbers, and punctuation marks. In the code, all these elements are replaced by groups of numbers or letters. For example, 77181 may mean *Wait for further instructions,* and POVR could stand for *aircraft carrier.* Even a dictionary can serve as a codebook if each plaintext word is replaced by numbers standing for its page, column, and word number.

Communications intelligence

Frequency analysis. Cryptanalysis is based on the fact that letters are used with varying frequency in English and other languages with alphabets. The proportion of their frequency is remarkably stable. In English, the letter *e* is used more than any other (12%), followed by *t* (9%), *a* and *o* (8% each), *i, n,* and *s* (7% each), *r* (6%), and *h* (5%). When a cryptanalyst counts the letters of a sufficiently long monoalphabetic substitution and finds that *X* is the most common, he or she assumes that X stands for *e.* The analyst replaces all the X's with the *e*'s and starts to guess at words. For example, *e?e?* might be *even* or *ever.* In short messages, the most frequent letter may not be *e.*

Individual letter frequency is not the only way letters can be identified beneath their ciphertext disguises. Clues are provided by contacts—that is, which letters stand to the right and to the left of a particular letter. For example, three high-frequency letters that rarely contact each other are *a, o,* and *i.* A high-frequency letter that follows vowels in 80% of its appearances is *n.* One that precedes vowels 100 times more often than it follows them is *h.* The five most common letter pairs are, in order, *th, he, in, er,* and *an.* The five most common words are *the, of, and, to,* and *a.*

Monoalphabetic substitution is the simplest form of substitution cipher. But the solution to more complicated systems often consists of reducing them to a form in which this method can be applied. One example is a cryptogram enciphered by polyalphabetic substitution using a keyword. Discovering the number of letters in the keyword will permit the cryptanalyst to assemble all the letters enciphered with a single ciphertext and then to apply frequency analysis.

Unbreakable ciphers. A basic assumption of practical cryptography is that outsiders know the general system. Secrecy must reside only in the keys. For example, possession of a cipher machine should not permit a cryptanalyst to solve messages encrypted with it if he or she does not know the key settings.

Many modern cryptosystems are considered unbreakable. A cryptanalyst may study volumes of ciphertext or in some cases may even know the plaintext for a given ciphertext. But he or she still may be unable to reconstruct the cryptosystem so that the next message can be read because too many solutions are possible, none of which can be determined to be the right one.

Only one cryptosystem is considered theoretically and practically unbreakable. This cipher, called the *onetime system,* requires a key—often in numbers—that is random and that never repeats. The cipher clerk first converts the letters of the plaintext to numbers. For example, *a* may become *01, b* may become *02,* and so on. The cipher clerk then adds the key to the numerical plaintext. The sum is an unbreakable cryptogram:

plaintext	C A L L G E O R G E
numerical equivalents	03 01 12 12 07 05 15 18 07 05
key	41 73 96 47 18 11 33 56 34 54
ciphertext	44 74 08 59 15 16 48 64 31 59

In adding, no numbers are carried and, in a two-digit sum, the first digit is dropped. The message is sent as 44740 85915 1648643 159. Cryptanalysts cannot solve this cryptogram using trial and error because the key, being patternless, cannot show whether one plaintext is more likely than another. Even knowing a portion of the key will not reveal what the next element of the key will be.

The one-time system can best serve in two-way communication. The system is seldom used in multiple-number communications networks because not enough keys can be distributed to users for all their needs. Also, if a particular key is used more than once, messages using that key may be breakable.

History

Documents indicate that secret writing arose independently in many civilizations as soon as writing became widely used. The Arabs first devised a science of cryptanalysis in the A.D. 700's, using letter frequencies.

Cryptology came into widespread use in the West during the 1300's, when ambassadors were first assigned residence in other countries. They frequently used codes to send confidential reports home and to get secret orders. In succeeding centuries, experts emerged who secretly unsealed diplomatic dispatches and solved the ciphers in which they were written.

During the mid-1800's, the widespread use of the telegraph led to the development of military field ciphers. In the early 1900's, many military messages were sent in cipher by radio. Because these transmissions could be easily intercepted, cryptanalysis became a powerful intelligence force.

What many cryptanalysts consider the most important single solution in history occurred during World War I. The British cryptanalyzed a message from the German foreign minister, Arthur Zimmermann, to the German ambassador in Mexico. It promised that if Mexico would fight the United States, Germany would see that it got back its "lost territories" of Texas, Arizona, and New Mexico. Its disclosure helped bring the United States into the war. See **World War I** (The United States enters the war).

The enormous wartime burden of encrypting radiograms stimulated inventors to mechanize the work. In 1917, Gilbert S. Vernam, an American engineer, automated cryptography by joining an electromagnetic ciphering device to a teletypewriter. Using a key of punched tape, the mechanism encrypted the plaintext and transmitted the cryptogram. A receiving cipher teletypewriter automatically decrypted the ciphertext and printed out the plaintext. In 1918, Joseph O. Mauborgne, a United States Army major, devised the one-time system. About the same time, the rotor was invented independently by Edward H. Hebern, an American businessman, and Arthur Scherbius, a German electrical engineer. Their machines were adopted by their countries during the 1920's.

Later developments. In 1932, Marian Rejewski, a Polish mathematician, aided by information from a spy, solved Scherbius' machine, the Enigma. During World War II, the British expanded this work massively, using thousands of people and forerunners of computers to solve German messages.

Codebreakers had a major impact on both the Atlantic and Pacific theaters of the conflict. U.S. and British codebreakers helped defeat German submarines in the Atlantic. In the Pacific, cryptanalysis played a crucial role in sinking Japan's merchant marine fleet. Codebreaking also enabled Allied forces to identify and shoot down the airplane carrying Admiral Isoroku Yamamoto, Japan's chief naval leader. Cryptanalysis led to many victories against German forces in North Africa and Europe. The code solutions hastened Germany's defeat and shortened the war by months. See **World War II** (The Ultra secret).

In 1971, Martin Hellman, an electrical engineer at Stanford University, and his student, Whitfield Diffie, published the concept of asymmetric, or public-key, ciphers. The first practical realization of this concept came in 1977 with the system now known as RSA. It is named for its inventors at the Massachusetts Institute of Technology, Ronald Rivest, Adi Shamir, and Leonard Adelman.

Since the 1970's, the use of cryptography in private business has grown rapidly. In 1976, the U.S. government approved a complicated electronic transposition-substitution cryptosystem called the Data Encryption

Standard. This system was designed to protect data stored in or transmitted between computers. It serves in the automated teller machines in banks and in subscription television.   David Kahn

Additional resources

Janeczko, Paul B. *Loads of Codes and Secret Ciphers.* Macmillan, 1984. For younger readers.
Kahn, David. *The Codebreakers: The Story of Secret Writing.* Macmillan, 1967. *Kahn on Codes.* 1983.

Codfish. See Cod.
Codicil. See Will (Codicil).
Codling moth is a small brown and bronze-colored moth. The caterpillars of this moth cause severe damage to apples. They also destroy such fruits as pears, quinces, and English walnuts. Originally a native of Europe, the codling moth now lives in all parts of the world.

In spring, the adult moths emerge from their cocoons under loose bark and trash. They lay their eggs on leaves and twigs. The *larvae* (caterpillars) bore into young apples. This usually causes the fruit to die and drop off. A second or, in some areas, even a third generation of larvae may bore into larger apples.

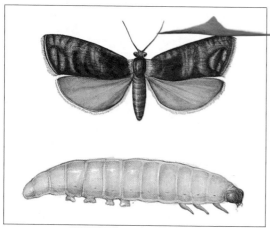

WORLD BOOK illustration by Shirley Hooper, Oxford Illustrators Limited
The codling moth is a small brown and bronze-colored moth. As a caterpillar, it can cause damage to apples and other fruit.

The chief method of controlling codling moths is by a series of four to seven sprayings with insecticide. Some growers use traps baited with a special *pheromone* (chemical substance) that attracts male moths. These traps help growers judge the best time to spray. Orchards and packing sheds should also be kept clean of all loose bark, fallen apples, and trash.

Scientific classification. The codling moth belongs to the family Tortricidae. Its scientific name is *Cydia pomonella.*

John R. Meyer

Cody, *KOH dee,* **John Patrick Cardinal** (1907-1982), was archbishop of Chicago from 1965 until his death in 1982. Pope Paul VI appointed him a cardinal of the Roman Catholic Church in 1967. Cardinal Cody won recognition as a church administrator while archbishop of New Orleans and Chicago, though his last years were marked by controversy.

Cardinal Cody was born in St. Louis. He was ordained a priest in Rome in 1931 where he received doctorates in philosophy and theology. Cardinal Cody served for five years on the staff of the Vatican secretary of state in the 1930's. He was appointed archbishop of New Orleans in 1964 and archbishop of Chicago in 1965.

Robert P. Imbelli

Cody, William Frederick. See Buffalo Bill.
Coeducation is the teaching of males and females together in the same class or school. In many countries, coeducation is uncommon, especially in high school. In the United States, however, most schools are coeducational. A few private schools admit students of only one sex. Most of these schools are operated by religious groups.

Most early schools in the United States enrolled only boys and men. Many people thought women had weaker minds than men and would be disturbed by too much education. During the 1800's, however, new educational opportunities opened up for girls and women. Oberlin College, founded in 1833 as Oberlin Collegiate Institute, became the first coeducational college in the United States. Several women's colleges also were established. Mount Holyoke Female Seminary (now Mount Holyoke College) opened as a school for women in 1837. By 1850, it offered a curriculum similar to that of men's colleges. Vassar College, another early women's college, was founded in 1861. By the mid-1800's, a number of high schools had become coeducational. By 1882, public elementary schools had begun to admit both boys and girls.

During the mid-1900's, most private men's and women's colleges became coeducational. They did so primarily to attract more students but also to meet demands made by the women's rights movement. In addition, government regulations cut off federal funds from schools that discriminated on the basis of sex. However, some women's colleges, including Mount Holyoke and Smith, chose to remain all-female schools. Officials of these colleges believed women could better develop leadership and other abilities if they did not have to compete with men.   Helen S. Astin

See also **Education** (Education for whom?).

Coelacanth, *SEE luh kanth,* is a primitive type of fish found in the western Indian Ocean. Scientists have found fossils of coelacanths that lived more than 300 million years ago. These fish were believed extinct until one was caught off the coast of South Africa in 1938. Since then, many more coelacanths have been caught. Coelacanths are members of an ancient group of fishes known as *sarcopterygians.* Lungfishes are the only other

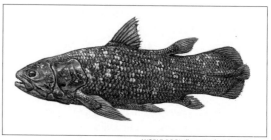

WORLD BOOK illustration by John D. Dawson
The coelacanth lives in the western Indian Ocean.

surviving members of this group. See **Fish** (The Age of Fishes).

Coelacanths are dark brown to blue-gray in color. They grow to more than 5 feet (1.5 meters) in length and weigh up to 160 pounds (73 kilograms). Coelacanths have muscular, limblike fins on the underside of their body. They apparently use these fins as a perch while resting on the ocean bottom. Coelacanths feed on other fishes. Unlike most fish, the female coelacanth does not lay eggs. She gives birth to live young.

Scientific classification. Coelacanths belong to the class of bony fish, Osteichthyes. They make up the coelacanth family, Coelacanthidae.   John E. McCosker

Coelenterate. See Cnidarian.

Coelom, *SEE luhm,* is the body cavity of vertebrates and higher invertebrates. The coelom is an important characteristic in distinguishing the lower animal phyla from the higher phyla. A number of internal organs, such as the liver and the kidneys, are contained within the coelom.

Animals that have a coelom are called *eucoelomates.* They have a body plan that can be described as a "tube within a tube." The digestive tract forms the inner tube, and the body wall forms the outer tube. The coelom is the space between the tubes. This arrangement results from the animal's development as an embryo.

In its early stages, the embryo consists of a hollow sphere of cells called the *blastula.* The cavity within the blastula is called the *blastocoele.* Eventually, the cells located at one point on the blastula begin to *invaginate—* that is, they start to fold inward into the blastocoele. This tubelike invagination forms a primitive gut, lined by a layer of cells called *endoderm.*

The cells on the outer wall of the blastula make up a layer called the *ectoderm.* A third layer of cells, the *mesoderm,* develops between the ectoderm and endoderm. The mesoderm completely fills what remained of the blastocoele. The coelom, a totally new cavity, develops within the mesoderm and, therefore, is lined entirely by mesodermal cells.

Certain lower invertebrates have a tube-within-a-tube body plan but lack a true coelom. These *pseudocoelomates,* including roundworms and rotifers, have a body cavity that serves some of the functions of a true coelom. In pseudocoelomate embryos, the mesodermal cells do not completely fill in the blastocoele. The blastocoele is retained and becomes the body cavity in the adult animal. Unlike a true coelom, this pseudocoelom is not lined completely by mesoderm.

Invertebrates called *acoelomates,* which are simpler than pseudocoelomates, have a solid mesodermal layer with no body cavity. Flatworms and ribbon worms are acoelomates.   G. J. Kenagy

Coercive Acts. See Intolerable Acts.

Coeur d'Alene Mountains, *KUR duh LAYN,* form the northern part of the Bitterroot Range of the Rocky Mountains. They are also called the Bitterroot Mountains. They extend for about 40 miles (64 kilometers) along the Idaho-Montana border. For location, see **Idaho** (physical map). The Coeur d'Alene Mountains look like a rolling upland cut by many streams, and have few prominent peaks. Ridge elevations vary from 5,200 to 6,800 feet (1,580 to 2,070 meters) above sea level.

Harley Johansen

Coffee is a drink made from the roasted and ground beans of the coffee plant. It is the favorite hot drink in almost every country in the world.

The United States ranks as the largest consumer of coffee. Americans drink about 400 million cups every day. The rich aroma of coffee adds much to the pleasure of drinking it. The *coffee break* has become an integral part of the business world. Each morning and afternoon, millions of workers pause for a few minutes of relaxation over a cup of coffee.

On the average, each person in the United States drinks the brew from about 10 pounds (4.5 kilograms) of coffee annually. Each year, the United States uses about 2,600,000,000 pounds (1,180,000,000 kilograms) or about one-fifth of all the coffee grown in the world. Other leading coffee-consuming countries include Brazil, France, Germany, Italy, Japan, and the United Kingdom. Brazil produces about a fourth of the world's coffee crop. Colombia ranks second in production. Coffee is vital to the economies of many Latin-American countries.

From bean to cup

The coffee plant. The scientific name of the common coffee plant is *Coffea arabica.* It originally grew wild in Ethiopia. It is now cultivated in Java, Sumatra, India, Arabia, equatorial Africa, Hawaii, Mexico, Central and South America, and the West Indies.

Coffea arabica is a shrub with glossy, evergreen leaves. It is 14 to 20 feet (4.3 to 6.1 meters) high when fully grown. As a rule, coffee growers prune it to under

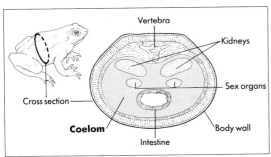

WORLD BOOK diagram by Marion Pahl

The coelom is the body cavity between the digestive tract and the body wall. All vertebrates and higher invertebrates have a coelom, in which various internal organs are located.

Giuseppe Mazza   Dave Cormier, DPI

Coffee comes from berries, *left,* that grow on a shrub. Each berry contains two beans. Roasted beans, *right,* are ground up and brewed with hot water to make coffee.

Leading coffee-growing countries

Amount of coffee beans produced in a year

Brazil	●●●●●●●●●●●●●●
	3,300,000,000 pounds (1,497,000,000 kilograms)
Colombia	●●●●●●●●
	1,748,000,000 pounds (793,000,000 kilograms)
Indonesia	●●●●
	897,000,000 pounds (407,000,000 kilograms)
Mexico	●●●◀
	795,000,000 pounds (361,000,000 kilograms)
Vietnam	●●◀
	561,000,000 pounds (254,000,000 kilograms)
Ivory Coast	●●◀
	561,000,000 pounds (254,000,000 kilograms)
Guatemala	●●
	434,000,000 pounds (197,000,000 kilograms)
Ethiopia	●●
	422,000,000 pounds (191,000,000 kilograms)
India	●◀
	372,000,000 pounds (169,000,000 kilograms)
Uganda	●◀
	355,000,000 pounds (161,000,000 kilograms)

Figures are for a three-year average, 1989-1991.
Source: Food and Agriculture Organization of the United Nations.

12 feet (3.7 meters). It has white flowers that are self-pollinating.

The coffee fruit is called a berry. It begins to grow while the plant is blossoming and ripens from green to yellow to red. The average plant produces enough berries each year to make about $1\frac{1}{2}$ pounds (0.7 kilogram) of roasted coffee.

A coffee plant is usually six to eight years old before it bears a full crop of berries. The common variety of coffee plant grows best at altitudes that range from 3,600 to 8,000 feet (1,100 to 2,400 meters) in a tropical climate. The majority of coffee plants grow from seeds that are first planted in nursery beds. After a year in the nursery, the seedlings are transplanted to prepared fields. Approximately 500 to 1,000 seedlings are planted per acre of land.

Preparation for market. Most berries are hand-picked. However, some are harvested by machines that vibrate the berries off the trees. After the berries are picked, they are put through a bath of running water called a *sluice*. Sticks, leaves, and the green and bad berries float on the top. The good berries sink to the bottom.

Pulping. The good berries then go to a pulping house, where machinery removes the pulp. Each berry contains two *beans* (seeds). Each bean has a thin parchmentlike skin, and a second covering called the *silver skin*. At first, the uncovered coffee beans appear soft and bluish-green, but later they become hard and pale yellow.

Following the pulping process, the beans are run through a series of fermenting and washing tanks. The coffee beans are then dried and left to cure for several weeks.

Hulling and peeling make up the next step in the preparation of coffee for the market. Milling machines remove the parchment and the silver skin. As the beans come from the machine, a fan blows off the loose skins.

The beans then go to a machine called the *separator,* which removes sand, dust, and small or broken beans. The beans are sorted until only the largest and best of the coffee beans remain.

Roasting. Most coffee is shipped in 132-pound (60-kilogram) burlap bags. At the roasting plant, the beans are emptied into chutes leading from an upper to a lower floor. An air-suction device removes dust and other materials from the coffee. The coffee then goes to the blending machine, a cylinder that mixes different types of coffee.

From the blender, the beans flow by gravity to storage bins, then to roaster ovens. There, they are roasted 900 °F (482 °C) for 16 to 17 minutes. The beans lose about a sixth of their weight during roasting. The beans are then cooled and cleaned, and carried to bins where they are stored until ground. After being ground to *drip, regular,* or *fine* requirements, the coffee is packed in vacuum tins or in paper bags.

Instant coffee can be either *powdered* or *freeze-dried.* Both require adding water to make coffee.

Powdered instant coffee is made by brewing coffee in huge containers and evaporating the water from the brew. The remaining powder crystals become coffee again when water is added.

Freeze-dried instant coffee is made by converting freshly brewed coffee into an extract and freezing it in

National Federation of Coffee Growers of Colombia
A worker picks coffee berries by hand, *above.* Most coffee berries are hand-picked. However, machines are sometimes used to vibrate the berries off the plants.

Preparing coffee for market. Workers spread and shake coffee beans to remove excess moisture, *left.* The beans are then dried in the sun, *center,* and left to cure for several weeks. After being shipped to a processing plant, the beans are roasted, *right,* to bring out their flavor.

slabs. The slabs are ground into chunks and put in pressurized chambers. Moisture in the form of ice is drawn off of the chunks, leaving dry coffee crystals. See **Freeze-drying.**

A good cup of coffee. Best brewing results are obtained by using one standard coffee measure, or two level tablespoons of coffee, to each cup. The water should be freshly drawn from the cold-water tap. Most coffee is made in *percolators, drip* pots, or *vacuum* coffeemakers, which strain boiling water through the coffee.

Kinds of coffee

More than a hundred kinds of coffee are sold in the United States. They may be divided into three general groups—*Brazils, Milds,* and *Robustas.* The Milds include all *Coffea arabica* grown outside of Brazil. *Coffee Robusta* is a different kind of coffee, most of which grows in Africa. Most coffee is named for the region where it grows or the port from which it is shipped. *Mocha* is named for the port of Mocha (Al Mukha) in Yemen. *Java* grows in and near Java.

American roasters place great importance on the taste of their blends. They pack different blends for different parts of the country. Coffee prepared for the South often has chicory added to it.

Coffee contains caffeine, a substance that acts as a stimulant on the nervous system (see **Caffeine**). Some persons find it more healthful to drink *decaffeinated coffee.* In most cases, the removal of caffeine is a cold-water extraction, which is done with the help of chemicals.

History

According to legend, coffee was discovered in Ethiopia when goatherds noticed that their flocks stayed awake all night after feeding on coffee leaves and berries. Coffee reached Arabia in the 1200's. *Coffee* comes from the Arabic word *qahwah.*

Before its use as a beverage 700 years ago, coffee was used as a food, then a wine, and then a medicine. Coffee moved from Arabia to Turkey during the 1500's, and to Italy in the early 1600's. Coffee houses sprang up throughout Europe in the 1600's and people met there for serious discussions. Coffee probably came to America in the 1660's. Coffee growing was introduced in Brazil in the 1700's.

Coffee-exporting countries have tried for many years to control coffee prices and surpluses. At first, they agreed to export quotas that limited each country's exports. They also tried to control prices by stockpiling some coffee instead of exporting it. But in 1963, the United Nations helped arrange an International Coffee Agreement that included both exporting and importing countries. Exporting countries accepted export quotas. Importing countries agreed to observe a floor on prices and to limit their coffee purchases from countries that did not sign the agreement.

Scientific classification. Coffee belongs to the madder family, Rubiaceae. The scientific name for the common coffee plant is *Coffea arabica.*   Jaime E. Lazarte

Related articles in *World Book* include:
Brazil (pictures)
Burundi (picture)
Chicory
Colombia (picture: The Andes Mountains)
Costa Rica (picture)
El Salvador (picture)
Ethiopia (picture)
Guatemala (picture)

Coffee house was a type of cafe that served as a center of business, cultural, and political life in London. Coffee houses thrived from about 1650 to 1850.

Many Londoners went to one or more coffee houses several times daily to learn the latest news. As newspapers developed, reporters also obtained information there. Many men kept regular hours at coffee houses, so that friends and clients knew when and where to find them. Eventually, each house developed a group of customers who had similar business, cultural, political, or religious interests. For example, actors, painters, writers, and politicians gathered at certain coffee houses.

In 1730, London had about 500 coffee houses. During the 1800's, they were gradually displaced by the home delivery of mail, the growth of daily newspapers, and the appearance of private clubs.   Thomas A. Erhard

Cofferdam is a temporary walled enclosure used in construction. It creates a space that protects workers and excavation sites from water and cave-ins. Cofferdams are used in building such structures as bridge piers, dams, and foundations. Simple cofferdams used in shallow water can be mounds of earth or sandbags. Cofferdams used in deeper water or deep excavations are usually made of interlocking steel sheets driven into the ground. Sometimes, they are made of closely spaced columns of wood, concrete, or metal. Such cofferdams must be braced to resist horizontal pressure from earth, water, and other sources. They may be made fairly watertight by packing clay behind the sheets or posts.   William E. Saul

Coffin. See Funeral customs; Sarcophagus.

Coffin, Robert Peter Tristram (1892-1955), was an American author best known for his poems about Maine, his native state. Coffin won the 1936 Pulitzer Prize for poetry for his collection *Strange Holiness* (1935).

Coffin was born in Brunswick, Me. Many of his writings describe the world of his childhood and youth in Maine. The central elements of his poetry are the sights and sounds of the Maine coast. In his later poetry, especially *People Behave Like Ballads* (1946), Coffin wrote about the rural people of Maine, whose endurance and good humor he valued highly. Coffin's verse is generally optimistic in tone.

Coffin also wrote novels, biographies, and criticism. His novel *Lost Paradise* (1934) re-creates his boyhood on a farm on the Maine seacoast. *Portrait of an American* (1931) is a biography of his father. Coffin's critical essays on poetry were published in *New Poetry of New England: Frost and Robinson* (1938) and *The Substance That Is Poetry* (1942).   Elmer W. Borklund

Cognac. See Alcoholic beverage (Brandy).

Cohan, *koh HAN,* **George M.** (1878-1942), was a leading figure in the American theater during the early 1900's. Cohan wrote more than 40 plays and musicals, and he produced, directed, and starred in most of them. His shows were noted for their high spirits and distinctive American flavor.

Cohan's plays include *Broadway Jones* (1912), *Seven Keys to Baldpate* (1913), and *The Song-and-Dance Man* (1923). He wrote such musicals as *Little Johnny Jones* (1904), *Forty-five Minutes from Broadway* (1906), and *George Washington, Jr.* (1906). Cohan's shows are seldom performed today, but several of his songs remain popular. They include "I'm a Yankee Doodle Dandy," "Give My Regards to Broadway," "You're a Grand Old Flag,"

UPI/Bettmann
George M. Cohan

"Mary's a Grand Old Name," and "Harrigan." Cohan also wrote "Over There," the most popular American patriotic song of World War I (1914-1918).

George Michael Cohan was born in Providence, R.I. As a child, he performed with his parents and sister in a popular vaudeville act called "The Four Cohans." Cohan began to write songs and vaudeville sketches while a teen-ager.   Thomas A. Erhard

Cohen, *KOH uhn,* **Leonard** (1934-   ), is a Canadian poet and novelist. He has also won international fame as a songwriter and folk singer, setting his own poems to music. He has recorded many albums.

Most of Cohen's poetry is romantic, but his romanticism is often mixed with irony and dark cynicism. He prefers metrically regular forms. His central subjects are love, death, and spiritual vision. Cohen's first book of poetry was *Let Us Compare Mythologies* (1956). Other important poetic works include *The Spice-Box of Earth* (1961), *Flowers for Hitler* (1964), *The Energy of Slaves* (1972), and *Book of Mercy* (1984). *Selected Poems 1956-1968* (1968) is a good introduction to Cohen's poetry. He has written two novels. *The Favorite Game* (1963) follows the adventures of a young poet in Montreal. *Beautiful Losers* (1966) is a lyrical dream of Montreal, combined with Canadian religious history and the nature of sainthood. Leonard Norman Cohen was born in Montreal.
    Laurie R. Ricou

Cohesion, *koh HEE zhuhn,* is the force that holds a material together. It results from the attraction that atoms and molecules have for one another. This attraction decreases as the distance between particles increases. Thus, with few exceptions, cohesion is highest in solids. Liquids are less cohesive than solids, and gases are practically noncohesive. Powders can also exhibit cohesion, especially if they consist of fine particles packed together. Packed dirt, for example, can be a solid driving surface because of its cohesive properties.

Because of cohesion, effort is required to separate a material into two parts. This effort is called the *work of cohesion.* The work required to separate the material is twice its surface tension because two new surfaces have been created (see **Surface tension**).

Scientists can calculate the theoretical maximum stress a solid can withstand before breaking if they know the work of cohesion. This maximum is known as the solid's *tensile strength.* These calculated strengths are usually much higher than measured values. Scientists believe this is so because small surface cracks and other imperfections develop in solids and make them easier to break. Glass fibers, for example, have great resistance to breakage when first manufactured, but they develop fine cracks and lose strength rapidly.   R. Hogg

See also **Adhesion; Molecule** (Molecules and matter).

Cohn, Ferdinand Julius (1828-1898), was a German botanist and pioneer in bacteriology. He became the first to show that bacteria are plantlike organisms. In 1872, he published the first systematic classification of bacteria into genera based upon their form. Cohn's discovery of heat-resistant *spores* (reproductive cells) in bacteria helped to finally disprove the theory of spontaneous generation (see **Spontaneous generation**). He was born in Breslau, Germany (now Wrocław, Poland).
    Keith R. Benson

Coin. See Coin collecting; Money.

WORLD BOOK photo

Many coin collectors mount their coins in albums. The collector above is using a magnifying glass to examine the details of a coin. She holds the coin by the edges to avoid staining it. Her coin catalog, *rear*, provides information about various coins.

Coin collecting is one of the most popular hobbies in the world. Most coin collectors simply enjoy trying to acquire a complete set of a nation's coins or of one or more particular coins. Some people collect coins as works of art. Others collect them as an investment, to be sold later at a profit. Through coins, a collector can also learn something about certain famous people and events in a country's history.

Imaginative coin collectors can build many types of collections. They can specialize in coins of one country or in various kinds of coins, such as cents or dollars. They can collect coins of unusual sizes or shapes. Many collectors concentrate on coins that illustrate a certain subject, such as animals, ships, or famous women.

The collecting or study of coins is called *numismatics,* and a coin collector is often called a *numismatist.* These words come from the Greek word *nomisma* and the Latin word *numisma,* both of which mean *a piece of money* or *a coin.* Numismatics includes paper money and also medals, tokens, and similar objects. This article tells how to begin and care for a coin collection.

Starting a coin collection. The best source of coins for a beginning collector is the change received when making various purchases. Friends also can help the beginning collector by letting him or her check the coins they may have—and swap money for any coins found that are not in the beginner's collection. Many beginning collectors go to a bank and exchange their money for rolls of coins. They then examine the rolls to find coins for their collection.

A coin's value depends on two factors—its condition and how easily it can be obtained. The most valuable coins are both *uncirculated* (unused) and scarce. A beginner should seek easily obtainable coins at first.

As collectors learn more and more about the hobby,

Edward C. Rochette, the contributor of this article, is Former Executive Vice President of the American Numismatic Association.

they can start to acquire coins of greater value from several sources. For example, coin dealers and many collectors sell, trade, and buy coins. Some collectors obtain coins through auctions held in various communities or conducted by mail. In many countries, a government agency sells uncirculated coins to collectors.

A person should have some basic information about coin collecting before starting to acquire coins. Several books for beginners can be obtained at bookstores, hobby shops, and libraries.

Many collectors subscribe to a specialized newspaper, such as *Coin World* or *Numismatic News,* both of which are published weekly. The American Numismatic Association, the largest organization of coin collectors, publishes a monthly magazine, *The Numismatist,* with a section for young collectors. The association sponsors a program through the magazine that awards ancient coins to young people who complete certain numismatic activities. The magazine provides the names of U.S. coin clubs. These coin clubs encourage new collectors to attend their meetings and exhibitions.

Collecting United States coins. Any person who collects U.S. coins should have *A Guide Book of United States Coins.* This book is called the Red Book because of its red cover. It gives the approximate price of any U.S. coin, depending on its condition and scarcity. A new edition is published annually.

The law requires U.S. coins to be dated with the year in which they are *struck* (made). The Department of the Treasury operates mints in Philadelphia; Denver; San Francisco; and West Point, N.Y. The Philadelphia and Denver mints make most coins for general circulation. The other two mints also make commemorative coins for special occasions. They also make gold and silver bullion coins that are purchased by people investing in the metal. At least some coins struck at each of these mints have a *mint mark.* All coins made at the Denver

The condition of coins

The condition of a coin plays an important part in determining its value. This table lists the grades used to describe a coin's condition, based on the amount of wear it has received. Coins are assigned numerical grades for greater accuracy in describing their condition.

Uncirculated coins are struck for general use but have never been circulated. The coins are graded for original luster, lack of scuff marks, and eye appeal. All values begin with the letters MS (Mint State). Grades range from MS-60 (low) to MS-70 (high).

About Uncirculated (AU) coins have been in circulation but show only traces of wear on the highest points of the design. Grades range from AU-50 to AU-59.

Extremely Fine (EF) coins show slight wear. Grades are either EF-40 or EF-45.

Very Fine (VF) coins show light to moderate wear on all parts of the design. Grades are either VF-20 or VF-30.

Fine (F) coins show moderate to considerable wear on all parts of the design. The grade given is F-12.

Very Good (VG) coins are well worn. The grade is VG-8.

Good (G) coins are heavily worn. Major features of the design are visible only in outline. The grade is G-4.

About Good (AG) coins are very heavily worn, with the date barely legible. These coins are seldom collected. The grade is AG-3.

Some rare and interesting coins

Coin collectors prize coins that are rare or have some interesting feature. The Brasher doubloon is one of the rarest early American coins. The American commemorative half dollar honors the black educator Booker T. Washington. The Macedonian coin portrays Alexander the Great.

Coins of the United States

Brasher doubloon (1787)

Pine-tree shilling (1652)

Indian-head cent (1902)

Booker T. Washington commemorative half dollar (1950)

Coins of other countries

Macedonian tetradrachm (336 to 323 B.C.)

Roman denarius (A.D. 41 to 54)

Phoenician shekel (126 B.C. to A.D. 66)

Persian drachm (A.D. 590 to 627)

Frankish denier (A.D. 888 to 898)

Indian anna (1943)

Canadian dollar (1935)

Vatican 20-lire coin (1959)

WORLD BOOK photos by James Simek

mint are stamped with a small *D,* and all coins except cents made at the Philadelphia mint receive a small *P.* Cents do not have mint marks. At the San Francisco and West Point mints, only commemorative coins and proof coins receive a mint mark. The San Francisco coins bear a small *S,* and those from West Point bear a small *W.* Bullion coins do not have mint marks.

Until 1965, dimes, quarters, and half dollars contained 90 per cent silver. Most collectors tried to assemble a complete set of these coins—as well as cents and nickels—by date and mint mark. In 1965, the government replaced silver dimes and quarters with coins made of nickel and copper. In 1971, the government made a simi-

lar change in the metal composition of half dollars. During the late 1960's, the price of silver rose rapidly. As a result, the value of the silver in a coin rose above the coin's face value. Millions of silver dimes, quarters, and half dollars were melted for their silver. Almost no silver coins remain in circulation.

Every year, the United States Mint strikes a limited number of cents, nickels, dimes, quarters, half dollars, and dollars for collectors. Many people buy a number of sets of these special *proof* coins as an investment. Information on proof sets and other numismatic items may be obtained from the Customer Service Center, United States Mint, 10001 Aerospace Drive, Lanham, MD 20706.

Collecting coins of other countries offers an almost endless variety of opportunities. Some collectors try to acquire one coin from every country in the world. Other people build a collection of one-cent pieces from every country that issues such coins.

A reference book, *Standard Catalogue of Modern World Coins,* edited by Colin R. Bruce II, provides annually updated information about coins from other lands. Several other books deal with coins of specific countries and regions, such as Canada and Latin America.

Many nations sell their coins in uncirculated and proof condition to collectors. A few countries have taken advantage of the interest in coin collecting. They have issued coins with designs featuring subjects that have little in common with the country. Although the coins can be used as money, they do not circulate because they cost much more than their face value. These coins are called *Non-Circulating Legal Tender.*

Many collectors specialize in coins from ancient Greece, Rome, or Palestine. Various ancient coins, especially those of Greece, are prized for their beauty and craftsmanship. Some collectors specialize in coins issued in Europe during the Middle Ages.

Caring for a coin collection. Coins should be protected from dust, fingerprints, and moisture, and from objects that could scratch them. A coin should be touched as little as possible. If one must be handled, it should be held by the edges and never put on the palm of the hand. Moisture from the skin can stain a coin.

Many stores sell albums in which to keep coins. Some collectors put their coins in metal cabinets that have trays lined with soft cloth. Others use small envelopes designed to hold coins.

Collectors should avoid cleaning their coins. Rubbing a coin to remove dirt or stains may increase the amount of wear on the metal and thus reduce the coin's value. A coin also may be scratched accidentally while being cleaned.   Edward C. Rochette

For more information about coins, see the *World Book* article on **Money** and its list of *Related articles.*

Additional resources

Breen, Walter H. *Walter Breen's Complete Encyclopedia of U.S. and Colonial Coins.* Doubleday, 1988.
Cribb, Joe, and others. *The Coin Atlas: The World of Coinage from Its Origins to the Present Day.* Facts on File, 1990.
Krause, Barry. *Collecting Coins for Pleasure & Profit: A Comprehensive Guide and Handbook for Collectors and Investors.* Betterway Pubns., 1991.
Krause, Chester L., and Mishler, Clifford. *Standard Catalog of World Coins.* Krause. Published annually.

Coke is a hard, grayish substance obtained when soft coal is heated in an airtight coke oven. It is hard and *porous* (full of tiny holes), and, in most cases, contains 87 to 89 per cent carbon. Coke produces intense, smokeless heat when it burns.

Coke is made by heating *pulverized coal* (coal ground to a powder) in an airtight oven. As the coal heats, it *decomposes* (decays). It cannot burn completely without air. Coal tar and coke oven gas evaporate from the decomposed coal and are drawn out of the oven. The escaping tar and gas form the pores in the coke. The hot coke is taken out of the oven and cooled with water at a *quenching tower* to keep it from burning in the air.

Coke is valuable in *smelting* (melting) iron ore. Coke used in smelting is called *metallurgical coke.* In the United States, over 95 per cent of such coke is made in giant coking plants with *by-product ovens* equipped to save coal tar and coke oven gas. These ovens hold from

From coal to coke

Coal is converted to coke in the ovens of huge coking plants, *top.* Coal is transferred from a *car dumper* to the *oven-charging bin,* which feeds it into containers called *hoppers.* A *larry car* dumps the coal from the hoppers through *charging holes* into each oven. In the ovens, *lower left,* the coal is heated, and gases and other substances are drawn off. After 12 to 18 hours, all of the coal has been converted to coke. The oven is then opened, and the *pusher ram* shoves the coke into a *quenching car, lower right.* This car brings the coke to the *quenching tower, top,* where it is cooled with water. The coke is then dumped onto a *coke wharf* before being screened for size and shipped.

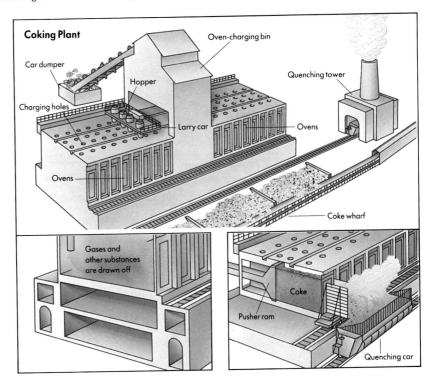

4 to 20 short tons (3.6 to 18 metric tons) or more of coal. If not properly sealed, by-product ovens can leak coal dust and harmful gases. Environmental concerns have led the coke industry to reduce leaks and to improve the operation and design of ovens.   Joseph W. Leonard

See also **Coal; Coke oven gas; Gas** (How gas is manufactured); **Iron and steel** (Raw materials); **Petroleum coke.**

Coke oven gas, also called *coal gas,* is the gas obtained when coal is heated in an airtight place. It consists mainly of hydrogen and methane. Coke oven gas is burned to produce heat in industrial plants and in homes. It was formerly used for illumination. Coke oven gas is made by heating coal in a *by-product coke oven* that heats to about 2000 °F (1100 °C). As the coal heats, coke oven gas and other by-products are given off. The gas leaves the oven through pipes and is stored in large tanks called *gas holders.* See **Gas** (How gas is manufactured).   Joseph W. Leonard

Cola nut. See **Kola nut.**

Colbert, *kawl BAIR,* **Jean Baptiste,** *zhahn bah TEEST* (1619-1683), a French statesman, served King Louis XIV as superintendent of finance from 1661 until his death. A believer in firm government control over the country's economy, Colbert worked to make France financially strong. He supported commerce, industries, and internal improvements such as canals and roads. He built a strong navy and sent explorers and colonists to America. Colbert's efforts to keep the budget balanced failed when his rival the Marquis de Louvois, the war minister, persuaded Louis XIV to begin a costly series of wars. Colbert was born in Reims. *Colbertism* became another word for *mercantilism,* the most common European economic system of Colbert's day.   Donald A. Bailey

Colchicum, *KAHL chuh kuhm,* is a poisonous plant which grows wild in the moist meadowlands of England, Ireland, and of middle and southern Europe. It is sometimes called the meadow saffron. Its flowers range in color from purple to white and bloom in the autumn. Florists call the flowers, which look much like those of the crocus, *autumn crocus.* Colchicum is easily grown when planted in light, moist, sandy loam.

WORLD BOOK illustration by Christabel King

The colchicum is a poisonous European plant. Its flowers range in color from purple to white and bloom in the autumn.

Colchicine, a bitter drug taken from the colchicum plant, is used in small quantities to treat gout and rheumatism. Botanists use the drug in experiments in plant breeding. Colchicine causes the number of chromosomes in a plant cell to double, a condition known as *polyploidy.* Polyploid plants may be larger than the plants from which they were produced.

Scientific classification. The colchicum plant belongs to the lily family, Liliaceae. Its scientific name is *Colchicum autumnale.*   Jerry M. Baskin

See also **Crocus.**

Cold. See **Climate; Heat.**

Cold, Common. The common cold results from any of a number of viral infections of the upper respiratory tract. It is the most widespread and common of all diseases. Although many people consider colds to be minor illnesses, colds are a major cause of absence from school and work. Every year in the United States, colds cost billions of dollars in lost working hours.

Common-cold infections vary in severity from a mild cold without fever to extensive, fatal pneumonia. Scientists have made great progress in identifying the more than 100 viruses that cause these illnesses. They have found that a reason people have so many colds is that different viruses can cause similar illnesses. Also, one cold virus does not give immunity against another.

People of all ages are susceptible to colds. But children—and adults living with children—seem to be most susceptible. Research has shown that colds cause about 100 million illnesses each year in Americans.

Symptoms. Colds are viral infections of the mucous membranes of the nose, throat, and, sometimes, of the air passages and lungs. A person with a cold usually has a stuffy nose and may have difficulty breathing. The infection may spread to the ears, sinuses, and eyes. In many cases, it spreads to the throat, causing soreness and hoarseness. When colds spread to the air passages and lungs, they may cause bronchitis and pneumonia.

The simplest kind of cold lasts a few days. More severe colds may last longer, often causing fever and aches and pains throughout the body. Occasionally, the patient also has chills and a loss of appetite.

Colds can be dangerous because they make people more susceptible to other infections, particularly bacterial infections of the ears, sinuses, and lungs. Colds are especially dangerous to the elderly and to people who have lung ailments or are weakened by poor health.

Treatment. There is no specific treatment for colds. But a doctor often prescribes drugs to relieve the discomfort caused by cold symptoms. For example, pain-relieving drugs may be given to lessen muscular aches and pains. Nasal sprays or drops shrink the mucous membranes and may help the patient to breathe easier. Vaporizers also may provide relief. A patient who has a fever should stay in bed. This provides rest and isolates the patient from other people.

People with colds should eat nourishing foods and drink plenty of fluids, such as fruit juices, tea, or water. If the cold persists or seems to get worse, a doctor should be called. If complications begin to develop, the doctor can treat them early. Often the doctor prescribes antibiotics to control bacterial complications.

Spread. Experts do not know all the ways in which cold germs spread. But doctors believe that a person can get a cold by breathing in the germs. Whenever a person with a cold coughs or sneezes, tiny droplets of moisture that contain cold germs spray out into the air. For this reason, colds seem to spread most rapidly in places where many people gather together, such as in schools, offices, theaters, or buses. A person should always cover the mouth and nose when coughing or sneezing. Then the germs cannot spray out into the air. Doctors also believe that cold germs can be spread by direct contact, especially by the hands.

Prevention. Colds are transmitted by people who have them. Therefore, isolating people who have colds is one of the best ways to prevent colds from spreading.

Although scientists have developed several vaccines for cold viruses, especially influenza virus, none has proved effective against all types of colds. However, influenza vaccines should be given to people who risk becoming seriously ill by getting a cold.

The cells of human beings produce chemical substances called *interferons* that help fight cold viruses. Scientists have found ways of obtaining interferons by laboratory processes. See **Interferon.**   Neil R. Blacklow

See also **Cold sore.**

Cold-blooded animal is an animal that has little physiological control over its body temperature. Many cold-blooded animals, including most water animals, are warm when their surroundings are warm and cool when their surroundings are cool. Almost all animals are cold-blooded except birds and mammals, which are warm-blooded. See **Warm-blooded animal.**

Some cold-blooded animals can control their body temperature to a certain extent by varying their activities. For example, the body of an active cecropia moth produces so much heat by muscular action that the animal becomes warmer than its surroundings. Most cold-blooded land animals adjust their body temperature by moving to different surroundings—into sunlight when they become too cool and into shade when they become too warm. Scientists refer to cold-blooded animals as *ectothermic* or *poikilothermic.*

James Edward Heath

Cold frame is a boxlike structure built or placed on the ground to protect plants during cold weather. Gardeners use cold frames in spring to shelter tender seedlings sprouted before the start of the growing season. Cold frames also extend the growing season of plants in fall by protecting them from frost.

A cold frame consists of a rectangular structure made of wood, concrete, or brick, with a cover of glass or transparent plastic. The cover lets in sunlight and retains heat. Most cold frames have a cover that slants downward toward the south, in order to let in as much sunlight as possible. On warm days, one side of the cover can be raised to cool the frame.

In most cases, gardeners plant seeds indoors in pots or in long boxes called *flats.* In the spring, they put the pots or flats containing the seedlings into cold frames. They may bury the pots to help the soil in the pots retain moisture. To prepare a growing area for seedlings planted directly inside a cold frame, a gardener replaces about 1 foot (30 centimeters) of soil with equal layers of gravel and richer soil.

In summer, plants that need shade can be protected from bright sunlight by replacing the transparent cover-

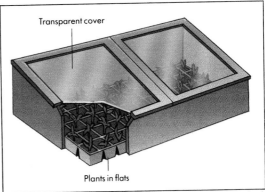

Transparent cover

Plants in flats

WORLD BOOK diagram by Paul D. Turnbaugh

A cold frame shelters plants outdoors. The transparent cover lets in sunlight and retains heat. The cold frame shown above holds *flats* (trays) of seedlings that were sprouted indoors.

ing with wooden slats or burlap. A structure similar to a cold frame but heated by electricity or other means is called a *hotbed* (see **Hotbed**).   William H. Carlson

Cold sore is a cluster of small blisters caused by a virus called *herpes simplex virus.* Cold sores can occur anywhere on the body. However, they appear mostly on the face, especially on or near the mouth. Cold sores are also called *fever blisters.* In many cases, they develop when a person has a cold or a fever.

In most cases, the herpes simplex virus that causes cold sores enters the body through the mouth or nose. The sores begin with itching, tingling, pain, and redness. Then the blisters appear. They soon break open, leaving yellowish crusts. The sores heal by themselves two to seven days after the blisters break open.

Many people suffer repeated attacks in which cold sores form in the same places. Most likely, these repeated attacks occur because the virus remains in the body after the sores heal. The dormant virus usually causes no symptoms, but certain conditions can reactivate it and produce new cold sores. These conditions include fever, overexposure to sunlight, emotional upset, and injury on the site of a previous sore.

Cold sores cannot be prevented. Doctors sometimes prescribe a drug called *acyclovir* for people who have frequent cold sores. This drug hinders outbreaks but does not cure the disorder.   Charles J. McDonald

See also **Herpesvirus.**

Cold storage is a method of storing foods and other perishable products by holding them at low temperatures above freezing and in moist air. Low temperatures prevent spoilage by checking the growth of most harmful bacteria and slowing undesirable chemical reactions. Household refrigerators and commercial walk-in refrigerators used by grocers, butchers, restaurants, and warehouses generally keep food at 32 °F to 41 °F (0 °C to 5 °C). However, even at these temperatures, most fresh foods can only be preserved about one to four weeks. Furs are also kept in cold storage during the summer. Florists use cold storage to store flowers, plants, and bulbs. Pharmacists, physicians, and scientists use it to preserve drugs, serums, medicines, and specimens for research. See also **Food, Frozen; Refrigeration; Cudahy, Michael.**   Theodore P. Labuza

Cold War is the term used to describe the intense rivalry that developed after World War II between groups of Communist and non-Communist nations. On one side were the Union of Soviet Socialist Republics (U.S.S.R.) and its Communist allies, often referred to as the *Eastern bloc.* On the other side were the United States and its democratic allies, usually referred to as the *Western bloc.* The struggle was called the *Cold War* because it did not actually lead to fighting, or "hot" war, on a wide scale.

The Cold War was characterized by mutual distrust, suspicion, and misunderstandings by both the United States and the Soviet Union, and their allies. At times, these conditions increased the likelihood of a third world war. The United States accused the U.S.S.R. of seeking to expand Communism throughout the world. The Soviets, meanwhile, charged the United States with practicing imperialism and with attempting to stop revolutionary activity in other countries. Each bloc's vision of the world also contributed to East-West tension. The United States wanted a world of independent nations based on democratic principles. The Soviet Union, however, tried to tightly control areas it considered vital to its national interest, including much of Eastern Europe.

Though the Cold War did not begin until the end of World War II, in 1945, U.S.-Soviet relations had been strained since 1917. In that year, a revolution in Russia established a Communist dictatorship there. During the 1920's and 1930's, the Soviets called for world revolution and the destruction of capitalism, the economic system of the United States. The United States did not grant diplomatic recognition to the Soviet Union until 1933.

In 1941, during World War II, Germany attacked the Soviet Union. The Soviet Union then joined the Western Allies in fighting Germany. For a time early in 1945, it seemed possible that a lasting friendship might develop between the United States and the Soviet Union based on their wartime cooperation. However, major differences continued to exist between the two, particularly with regard to Eastern Europe. As a result of these differences, the United States adopted a "get tough" policy toward the Soviet Union after the war ended. The Soviets responded by accusing the United States and the other *capitalist* allies of the West of seeking to encircle the Soviet Union so they could eventually overthrow its Communist form of government.

Two great blocs came into being. The United States led the Western bloc. By the early 1950's, this group included Canada, France, Great Britain, West Germany, Japan, the Philippines, and many other countries of Western Europe and Latin America. The Soviet Union led the Eastern bloc, which included Albania, Bulgaria, Czechoslovakia, East Germany, Hungary, Poland, and Romania. China joined the Eastern bloc following the Communist take-over of its government in 1949. The nonaligned or *neutral* nations—those in neither bloc—included India, Indonesia, Cambodia, and most African states.

During the late 1940's and the 1950's, the Cold War became increasingly tense. Each side accused the other

---

Burton I. Kaufman, the contributor of this article, is Professor of History at Virginia Polytechnic Institute and State University.

of wanting to rule the world. Each side believed its political and economic systems were better than the other's. Each strengthened its armed forces. Both sides viewed the Cold War as a dispute between right and wrong. They saw every revolt and every international incident as part of the Cold War. This situation made it difficult to settle any dispute peacefully through compromise, with each side giving up something. Fear grew among all peoples that a local conflict would touch off a third world war that might destroy humanity.

The nature of the Cold War began to change in the 1960's. Neither the East nor the West remained a *monolith* (united bloc). Communist China challenged Soviet leadership. China accused the Soviet Union of betraying Communism and being secretly allied with the United States. Some Communist countries followed China's leadership, and others remained loyal to the U.S.S.R.

Among the nations of the Western bloc, France harshly criticized many U.S. policies and demanded independent leadership in Europe. West Germany also acted independently of U.S. policies. It searched for new economic and political relationships with other European countries, including East Germany.

Economic developments caused major shifts in the world balance of power during the 1960's. The rapid industrialization of Japan and West Germany made them important nations in the struggle for power. Their emergence and the growing strength of China led to new relationships. In 1970, Soviet and West German leaders signed a treaty pledging peaceful relations between their nations. The long-disputed status of West Berlin was settled in 1971 when France, Great Britain, the Soviet Union, and the United States agreed that the city was not part of West Germany. But the four powers also provided for economic and political ties between West Berlin and West Germany. Also in 1971, China joined the United Nations (UN). The United States established diplomatic relations with China in 1979.

Cold War tensions rose again after the Soviet Union invaded Afghanistan in 1979. Soviet leaders said the invasion was designed to help defend Afghanistan's pro-Communist government from Afghan rebels. In the late 1980's, however, Cold War tensions began to ease sharply after the signing of a major U.S.-Soviet arms-control agreement and after the U.S.S.R. removed its troops from Afghanistan.

Tensions further decreased after major democratic reforms took place in Eastern Europe. In 1991, the Soviet Union broke up into a number of independent, non-Communist states. Many historians thought that these and other developments marked the end of the Cold War. But some believed the Cold War would continue as long as both Communism and democracy lasted. For a discussion of the principles of Communism and democracy, see **Communism** and **Democracy**.

The coming of the Cold War

Historians do not agree on exactly when the Cold War began. But most agree that the Yalta Conference, a meeting of Allied leaders in February 1945, marked the high point of wartime good will between the United States and the Soviet Union. Most historians also agree that relations between the two countries deteriorated noticeably within the first year after the conference.

The alliance breaks up. With Germany nearly defeated, the leaders of the Big Three nations met at the Yalta Conference to plan for the peace that would follow the war. These leaders were President Franklin D. Roosevelt of the United States, Prime Minister Winston Churchill of Great Britain, and Premier Joseph Stalin of the Soviet Union. At Yalta, the leaders agreed to set up *occupation zones* (areas controlled by the Allies) for postwar Germany and made plans to form the United Nations. In addition, Stalin promised that the U.S.S.R. would go to war against Japan within three months after Germany surrendered. See **Yalta Conference.**

The Allied leaders also developed the Declaration on Liberated Europe, in which they pledged to hold democratic elections in countries freed from the control of Germany and its allies. The Soviet Union failed, however, to keep this agreement. At the time it was made, Soviet forces had driven German troops out of most of Eastern Europe and had established a pro-Communist government in Poland. In spite of the Declaration on Liberated Europe, Stalin was determined to maintain tight control over Eastern Europe. He especially felt that control of Poland, which had been used as a route to invade the Soviet Union, was necessary to Soviet security. The United States felt betrayed by Stalin's refusal to carry out all of his promises and by his determination to establish a "sphere of influence" in Eastern Europe.

Roosevelt died in April 1945 and was succeeded as President by Harry S. Truman. Germany surrendered in May 1945. The main Allied leaders met for the final time at Potsdam, near Berlin, in July 1945. Just before the meeting, Churchill's Conservative Party was defeated in an election. Clement R. Attlee succeeded Churchill during the Potsdam Conference.

At Potsdam, the Allies agreed that the German people should be allowed to rebuild their lives "on a democratic and peaceful basis." However, serious disagreements arose. Great Britain and the United States charged that the U.S.S.R. was communizing the countries of Eastern Europe. Even before World War II ended, the U.S.S.R. had taken over the Baltic states of Latvia, Estonia, and Lithuania; parts of Poland, Finland, and Romania; and eastern Czechoslovakia. Soviet troops occupied a third of Germany and all of Bulgaria, Hungary, Poland, and Romania. Nevertheless, the Western nations reluctantly agreed to a Soviet-backed transfer of 40,000 square miles (100,000 square kilometers) of German territory to Polish control. See **Potsdam Conference.**

The Iron Curtain descends. During 1945 and early in 1946, the Soviet Union cut off nearly all contacts between the West and the occupied territories of Eastern Europe. In March 1946, Churchill warned that "an iron curtain has descended across the Continent" of Europe. He made popular the phrase *Iron Curtain* to refer to Soviet barriers against the West. Behind these barriers, the U.S.S.R. steadily expanded its power.

In 1946, the U.S.S.R. organized Communist governments in Bulgaria and Romania. In 1947, Communists took control of Hungary and Poland. Communists seized full power in Czechoslovakia early in 1948. These countries became Soviet *satellites* (nations controlled by the U.S.S.R.).

Albania already had turned to Communism. Enver Hoxha, who led the Communist National Liberation Army in an Albanian civil war during World War II, established a Communist government in 1944.

Yugoslavia also joined the Communist bloc. The Communist Party of Yugoslavia had helped drive out the Germans near the end of the war. Communists led by Josip Broz Tito then took over the government.

East and West opposed each other in the United Nations. In 1946, the U.S.S.R. rejected a U.S. proposal for an international agency to control nuclear energy production and research. The Soviet Union believed the United States had a lead in nuclear weapons and would have a monopoly if controls were approved. The Soviet Union pictured itself as a defender of peace and accused the United States of planning a third world war.

See the *History* section of the articles on each Communist country mentioned in this section.

The West holds the line

The *Containment Policy.* In the fall of 1946, Greek Communists revolted against the Greek government. Great Britain had been giving military and economic aid to Greece. But the British told the United States they could no longer give enough help to the Greeks. The British also warned that they could not help Turkey resist Communist pressure.

In March 1947, President Truman declared that the United States would help any free nation resist Communist *aggression* (attack). Congress granted his request for $400 million for aid to Greece and Turkey. With this aid, both Greece and Turkey successfully resisted Communism. The new American policy became known as the *Truman Doctrine.* Aimed at Soviet expansion in Europe, the Truman Doctrine developed into the *Containment Policy.* The Containment Policy was designed to *contain* (hold back) the expansion of Communism throughout the world.

The foreign ministers of the United States, Great Britain, France, and the Soviet Union met in Moscow in March and April 1947. They tried to draw up a German peace treaty. But the ministers could not agree on ways to end the occupation or on how to unify Germany.

The failure of the conference convinced U.S. Secretary of State George C. Marshall that the U.S.S.R. would not help Europe recover from World War II. In June 1947, Marshall proposed giving U.S. economic aid to all European nations that would cooperate in plans for their own recovery. This proposal grew into the European Recovery Program, or Marshall Plan, which began in 1948. The United States believed that a strong, stable Western Europe would block the spread of Communism. Meanwhile, in September 1947, the U.S.S.R. and eight other European Communist parties set up the *Cominform,* a new version of the Communist International. See **Marshall Plan.**

Czechoslovakia and Poland wanted to take part in the Marshall Plan, but the U.S.S.R. would not let them accept U.S. aid. Instead, the Soviet Union set up the Council for Mutual Economic Assistance (COMECON) in January 1949. This organization was designed to unite the East European satellites economically and politically.

In June 1948, the Western Allies announced plans to unify their German occupation zones and establish the West German Federal Republic (West Germany). West Germany was formally established in September 1949. It had independence in some of its internal affairs, and it joined the Marshall Plan.

Also in June 1948, the U.S.S.R. harshly criticized Tito, the Communist leader of Yugoslavia. Tito then declared his country's independence from Soviet control.

The Berlin blockade was the Soviet answer to the West's plans for West Germany. In June 1948, Soviet troops blocked all railroad, highway, and water traffic through East Germany to West Berlin. The city lay 110 miles (177 kilometers) inside the Soviet occupation zone. The Soviet leaders thought their blockade would force the West to leave Berlin. Instead of pulling out of West Berlin, the Americans, British, and French set up the *Berlin airlift.* For 11 months, West Berlin was supplied with food and fuel entirely by airplanes. The U.S.S.R. lifted the blockade in May 1949. The Allies ended the airlift in September.

The West rearms. Military strength became more and more important in the late 1940's. During the Berlin blockade, the United States pledged continuing military aid to Western Europe. The United States, Canada, and 10 Western European nations signed the North Atlantic Treaty in April 1949. This mutual defense treaty set up the North Atlantic Treaty Organization (NATO), a military alliance (see **North Atlantic Treaty Organization**). The goals of the alliance included the prevention of Soviet expansion and the defense of West Germany. In September 1951, the United States signed the ANZUS mutual defense treaty with Australia and New Zealand.

The nuclear arms race began on Aug. 29, 1949, when the Soviet Union tested an atomic bomb. Until then, the United States had been the only nation that knew how to make the atomic bomb.

Communist expansion in Asia. During the 1940's, Communist strength increased in the Far East. The U.S.S.R. had occupied Manchuria just before the end of World War II. After they left in 1946, the Chinese Communists took over most of northern Manchuria. The U.S.S.R. also set up a North Korean "people's republic."

In China, Mao Zedong's Communist troops fought the Nationalist armies of Chiang Kai-shek. The United States gave military aid to Chiang. Late in 1949, Chiang and his government fled to the island of Taiwan, near the mainland of China. The conquest of China by Mao's forces put China into the Communist bloc.

The Korean War. At the end of World War II, Soviet troops occupied North Korea and U.S. forces occupied South Korea. The North Koreans had a strong army. They got Soviet military aid even after Soviet troops withdrew from North Korea late in 1948. The United States withdrew its forces from South Korea in June 1949.

North Korean troops invaded South Korea on June 25, 1950, and the Korean War began. On June 27, President Truman sent U.S. forces to aid the South Koreans. At the request of the United States, the United Nations Security Council voted to send UN troops to help South Korea. The Soviet delegation was *boycotting* (not attending) the council, and missed a chance to veto the decision. Seventeen nations contributed men to the UN force, and Chinese Communist troops aided the North Koreans.

Peace talks began in July 1951. They went on for two years while bloody fighting continued. Finally, in July 1953, representatives of the UN and the Communists signed an armistice. In 1954, representatives of both sides met in Geneva, Switzerland, to discuss a political settlement. But they could not agree on a way to unite North and South Korea.

The Korean War was the first war in which troops of a world organization fought an aggressor nation. For the first time, Americans fought a "hot war" against Communism. Some historians believe the Korean War was a major turning point in the Cold War. It extended the Containment Policy to the Far East. It also introduced limited warfare to the East-West conflict as a substitute to all-out—and possibly nuclear—war. Each side avoided attacking targets that could have led to expansion of the war. And each side limited the weapons it used and the territory in which it would fight. See **Korean War.**

To the brink and back

The death of Stalin changed the character of the Cold War. The Soviet leader died in March 1953, two months after Dwight D. Eisenhower became President of the United States. The new Soviet rulers governed as a committee at first. Premier Georgi M. Malenkov and his associates adopted a softer policy toward the Soviet satellites and the West. For example, they allowed the Soviet wives of U.S. servicemen to follow their husbands to America. The U.S.S.R. also set up a cultural exchange program with the West. Soviet troops put down a revolt in East Germany in June 1953, but the Soviet Union's softer course of action was obvious.

The arms race continued. The United States tested its first hydrogen bomb in November 1952, and the U.S.S.R. set off its first H-bomb in November 1955. Military alliances were strengthened during this period. Also in 1955, West Germany joined NATO. In response, the U.S.S.R. and its Eastern European satellites signed the Warsaw Mutual Defense Pact, a military alliance. In 1955, the United States announced its support of the military alliance of the Baghdad Pact, which later became the Central Treaty Organization. See **Warsaw Pact.**

In January 1954, the new U.S. secretary of state, John Foster Dulles, had outlined a new American military policy. The United States, he warned, would meet Communist aggression by "massive retaliation" with nuclear weapons. The United States, Dulles said, would strike back "at places and with means of our own choosing."

Cold War tensions increased in eastern Asia during 1954 and 1955. The nationalist Vietnamese in Indochina were led by Communists and supported by China. In the spring of 1954, after years of fighting, they defeated the French at Dien Bien Phu. A cease-fire agreement was signed in Geneva in July 1954. It recognized the temporary division of Vietnam and gave North Vietnam to the Communists. Nationwide elections were to be held in 1956. However, neither the United States nor South Vietnam signed the agreement, and South Vietnam refused to hold the elections. The agreement also established the independence of Cambodia, Laos, and South Vietnam.

In September 1954, the United States and seven other nations signed the Southeast Asia Collective Defense Treaty (see **Southeast Asia Treaty Organization**). This treaty was designed to prevent further Communist expansion in Southeast Asia. After the defeat of France in Indochina, the United States increased its aid to South Vietnam. The United States believed that if one Southeast Asian nation fell to Communism, the others would also topple over, one after another. This was called the "domino theory." But even with U.S. support, South Vietnam could not defeat the Communist rebels. The rebels, called Viet Cong, were supported by North Vietnam. In 1955, the United States began sending military advisers to help the South Vietnamese government.

The United States also increased its support of the Chinese Nationalists on Taiwan. In September 1954, the Chinese Communists staged air and artillery attacks against the islands of Quemoy and Matsu. These islands, in the Formosa Strait, were held by the Nationalist Chinese. In 1955, Congress voted to let President Eisenhower use armed force if necessary to protect the Chinese Nationalists.

The spirit of Geneva. In Europe, a thaw in the Cold War became apparent in 1955. The Western Allies and the U.S.S.R. signed a peace treaty with Austria in May. Soviet troops left that country, and Austria became an independent, neutral nation. That same month, Nikita S. Khrushchev, the Soviet Communist Party chief, apologized to Tito and resumed trade with Yugoslavia.

Eisenhower and Khrushchev met in Geneva in July. Both leaders agreed that a nuclear war would be a disaster for both sides. Political observers began to write of a "big thaw" in East-West relations and called it the "spirit of Geneva." After the Geneva conference, the U.S.S.R. announced a cut of 640,000 men in its armed forces. The Soviet Union said it also had reduced the armies of its satellites.

Dulles still distrusted the Soviet Union in spite of its softer line. In January 1956, he told the American people that the United States had been on the brink of war several times. "If you are scared to go to the brink, you are lost," Dulles warned. The use of "brinkmanship" had become part of U.S. policy.

In February 1956, Khrushchev called for *peaceful coexistence* (competition without war) between East and West. He also began a campaign of *destalinization* (removal of Stalinist influences) in the U.S.S.R. and its satellites. In April 1956, the U.S.S.R. dissolved the Cominform.

Unrest in Eastern Europe. The new Soviet policy encouraged the peoples of Eastern Europe to expect more freedom from Soviet rule. In Poland, riots and strikes broke out in Poznań in June 1956, and spread to other cities. The rioters demanded a more liberal government and an end to Soviet rule. A few months later, the U.S.S.R. allowed Władysław Gomułka, a Polish Communist leader, to rejoin the Polish Communist Party. The U.S.S.R. had jailed Gomułka in 1951 for trying to set up an independent Communist government in Poland. Khrushchev and other Soviet leaders flew to Warsaw to confer with Gomułka in October 1956. Faced with further rebellion, the U.S.S.R. agreed to relax some controls in Poland. See **Poland** (Communist rule).

In Hungary, a revolt against Communism began in October 1956. A rebel government led by Imre Nagy demanded withdrawal of all Soviet troops. Early in November, Soviet tanks rolled into Budapest. The fighting spread to all parts of the country, and thousands of Hungarian "freedom fighters" were killed. The Soviet Union smashed the revolt in about two weeks. In spite of the new Soviet policy, the Soviet Union could not allow Hungary to break up the bloc of Eastern European satellites. See **Hungary** (Communist Hungary).

Trouble at Suez. During the period that the U.S.S.R. was putting down unrest in its Eastern European satellites, trouble was stirring in the Middle East. The United States feared Communist expansion in that area. Both the U.S.S.R. and the West sought Egypt's support by offering aid for its development plans. Each side offered to help build the Aswan High Dam. After Egypt courted Communist aid for the dam and bought Communist arms, the United States and Great Britain canceled offers to help with the project. President Gamal Abdel Nasser of Egypt struck back by seizing the Suez Canal from international control. He said Egypt would use profits from operating the canal to build the dam "without pressure from any nation." But he did accept Soviet aid.

In October 1956, while the U.S.S.R. was involved with the Hungarian revolt, Israel invaded Egypt. Britain and France immediately joined in the attack. They wanted to return the Suez Canal to international control. The United States and the U.S.S.R. supported a United Nations resolution demanding an immediate truce. In addition, the U.S.S.R. threatened to send troops to help Egypt. The UN arranged a truce after a few days of fighting. But the U.S.S.R., by backing Egypt against Israel, had won friends among the Arab nations of the Middle East.

New challenges

Khrushchev's power in the Soviet Union reached its peak in the late 1950's. Sometimes the U.S.S.R. followed a hard policy, mainly in response to China's challenge to Soviet leadership of the Communist bloc. At other times, the U.S.S.R. stressed peaceful coexistence, giving special attention to economic aid and scientific progress. But the Soviet Union continued to encourage "wars of liberation." As a result, the United States came to regard "peaceful coexistence" as the Communist effort to conquer countries without a major war.

The missile gap. The U.S.S.R. improved its ability to produce nuclear weapons, and the Western bloc feared a missile gap, or Soviet rocket superiority. In June 1957, the U.S.S.R. successfully tested an intercontinental ballistic missile (ICBM). That same year, the U.S.S.R. launched the first artificial earth satellite, *Sputnik 1.* In January 1958, the United States launched its first earth satellite. Soviet rocket power was more advanced, but the two powers had clearly established a nuclear "balance of terror." A brief thaw in the Cold War followed. The U.S.S.R. stopped testing nuclear weapons in March 1958, and the United States halted its tests in October.

The Eisenhower Doctrine was approved by Congress in March 1957 because the United States feared Communist penetration in the Middle East. This policy permitted the President to "use armed force to assist any . . . nation . . . [in the Middle East] requesting assistance against armed aggression from any country controlled by international Communism."

In July 1958, a revolution ended the rule of the pro-Western government of Iraq. Nearby Lebanon feared a Communist revolution and asked the United States for aid. Eisenhower quickly sent about 6,000 sailors and marines to help Lebanon. Great Britain sent paratroopers to protect Jordan against Iraqi pressure. In spite of Soviet protests, the American and British forces stayed in the Middle East for about three months.

The Far East. In 1958, the Chinese Communists again fired on Quemoy and Matsu, Taiwan's offshore islands. Dulles warned that any attack on these islands would be considered aggression against Nationalist China, a U.S. ally. But occasional firing continued during the 1960's.

Germany. During the late 1950's, Europe remained the most important Cold War battleground. The U.S.S.R. tried repeatedly to damage the reputation of the West in Germany. In November 1958, the U.S.S.R. demanded peace treaties for East and West Germany. Such treaties would have ended the military occupation, and Western troops would have had to leave. The United States refused to yield to the demand, and kept its forces in Berlin. As a result, the U.S.S.R. kept threatening to sign a separate peace treaty with East Germany.

The spirit of Camp David. Another temporary thaw in the Cold War began in the spring of 1959. The foreign ministers of the United States, Great Britain, France, and the U.S.S.R. met in May. In July, Vice President Richard M. Nixon visited the U.S.S.R. and met with Khrushchev. Two months later, Khrushchev visited the United States. He conferred with Eisenhower at Camp David in Maryland. Khrushchev was so friendly that observers spoke of the "spirit of Camp David," recalling the earlier "spirit of Geneva." Eisenhower and Khrushchev discussed a *summit* (top-level) conference to be held in Paris in 1960. The President accepted Khrushchev's invitation to visit the Soviet Union after the summit meeting.

The U-2 incident abruptly ended the thaw. An American U-2 spy plane was shot down in the U.S.S.R. in May 1960. The Soviet Union captured the pilot, Francis Gary Powers, who confessed he was a spy. Eisenhower accepted personal responsibility for the flight. He admitted that U-2 planes had been flying over the U.S.S.R. taking photographs for four years.

When the summit conference began on May 15, Khrushchev demanded that Eisenhower apologize for the U-2 incident. Eisenhower refused, and Khrushchev

angrily canceled his invitation for the President to visit the U.S.S.R.

Africa. The Cold War struggle moved to Africa in July 1960. Premier Patrice Lumumba of the Congo asked the UN to deal with a revolt in his newly independent nation. He charged that the Belgians were aiding the rebel Katangans. The U.S.S.R. sided with Lumumba against a group led by Congolese President Joseph Kasavubu. The UN intervened in the dispute, keeping the U.S.S.R. and the West from direct military action. The Soviet Union charged that the UN favored the West.

The troika proposal. In September 1960, Khrushchev went to New York City for the meeting of the UN General Assembly. He again criticized the United States for the U-2 flights. The Soviet leader showed his anger by taking off a shoe and pounding his desk with it.

Khrushchev tried to destroy the power of the UN to send troops into trouble spots. He called for three secretaries-general—a *troika* (a Russian term for a vehicle drawn by three horses)—to replace the UN secretary-general. One of the secretaries-general would be a Communist, one from a neutral nation, and one from the West. The General Assembly defeated the proposal.

The Bay of Pigs. John F. Kennedy became President of the United States in January 1961. Cold War tensions were high—in Europe, in Asia, and even on the doorstep of the United States, in Cuba.

The Cuban government of Fidel Castro had become openly Communist in 1960. Castro condemned the United States and began to receive military aid from the Soviet Union and other Communist countries. The Cuban government seized millions of dollars' worth of American property in Cuba. The United States ended diplomatic relations with Cuba in January 1961.

In April 1961, the United States sponsored an invasion of Cuba by anti-Castro Cubans at the Bay of Pigs. The attack was poorly planned and failed badly. The unsuccessful invasion strengthened Castro's control of Cuba,

Highlights of the Cold War

Winston Churchill warned in a famous 1946 speech that an "Iron Curtain" had come down across Europe. U.S. President Harry S. Truman introduced the former British prime minister to an audience at Westminster College in Fulton, Mo.

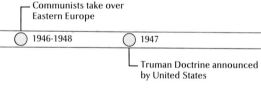

Communists take over
Eastern Europe

1946-1948   1947

Truman Doctrine announced
by United States

Winston Churchill Memorial
and Library in the U.S.

United Press Int.

The Greek Civil War ended in defeat for the Communist rebels. U.S. aid sent under the Truman Doctrine aided the victors.

and it caused the United States to lose face.

The Berlin Wall. Kennedy and Khrushchev met in Vienna, Austria, in June 1961. Khrushchev demanded a free Berlin and an end of the military occupation. The two leaders failed to reach agreement, and Khrushchev again threatened to sign a separate peace treaty with East Germany. In July 1961, the U.S.S.R. canceled cuts in its armed forces and increased military spending.

Growing numbers of East Germans were fleeing to West Germany. On Aug. 13, 1961, the East German Communists began to build a wall of cement and barbed wire between East and West Berlin. To confirm the West's right to stay in West Berlin, the United States sent troops to the city by highway. U.S. tanks enforced Western rights to enter East Berlin without showing papers to Communist border guards. Some East Germans escaped to West Berlin after the wall was built, but many were killed in the attempt. The wall remained, splitting Berlin in two. See **Berlin Wall.**

The space race begins. On April 12, 1961, a Soviet cosmonaut, Yuri Gagarin, made the first flight in space around the earth. Later that year, Alan B. Shepard, Jr., and Virgil I. Grissom piloted American spaceships. In 1962, astronaut John H. Glenn, Jr., became the first American to circle the earth in space.

In September 1961, the U.S.S.R. ignored an unofficial agreement against nuclear weapons tests, and resumed nuclear bomb testing in the atmosphere. The United States then resumed underground testing. American tests above ground were started again in April 1962.

The Cuban missile crisis. In October 1962, the United States learned that the U.S.S.R. had secretly installed missiles and missile bases in Cuba, about 90 miles (140 kilometers) from Florida. President Kennedy demanded that the U.S.S.R. remove them. He set up a naval "quarantine" of Cuba. The U.S.S.R. offered to remove the missiles if the United States would dismantle its military bases in Turkey. The United States refused.

After a week of extreme tension, Khrushchev agreed to remove the missiles. See **Cuba** (History).

Easing Cold War tensions

After the missile crisis in Cuba, Cold War tensions again eased. In July 1963, the United States, the U.S.S.R., and Britain approved a treaty to stop the testing of nuclear weapons in the atmosphere, in outer space, and under water. In August, the United States and the U.S.S.R. set up a *hot line* between the White House and the Kremlin. This direct communications link was installed to reduce the risk of accidental nuclear war.

In 1963, the U.S.S.R. faced a serious shortage of grain. Kennedy approved a plan to sell the U.S.S.R. $250 million worth of American wheat. That same year, the two nations agreed to cooperate in space projects using weather and communications satellites.

President Lyndon B. Johnson, who became Chief Executive after Kennedy was assassinated in November 1963, continued to work for peaceful coexistence. In 1964, the United States and the U.S.S.R. signed their first *bilateral* (two-nation) treaty. It provided that a *consul* (representative) of each nation would have an office in a city of the other country. It also provided protection for Americans traveling in the U.S.S.R. and for Soviet citizens traveling in the United States. The U.S. Senate approved the treaty in 1967, and the U.S.S.R. approved it in 1968. The two nations also extended an agreement for educational, scientific, and cultural exchanges.

The shifting Cold War battleground

The character of the Cold War changed again in the mid-1960's. The United States and the U.S.S.R. each had large numbers of nuclear weapons. Each had an antimissile defense system. But both powers realized that there would be no victor in an all-out nuclear war. Also, conflicts within both the Eastern and Western blocs changed the two-sided nature of the balance of power.

Berlin blockade set up by Soviet Union		Communists win control of China	
◯ 1948-1949	◯ 1949	◯ 1949	◯ 1950-1953
	NATO pact signed by 12 countries		Korean War—first use of UN troops in battle

---

The Berlin airlift of 1948-1949 defeated an attempt by the Soviet Union to force the Western Allies out of West Berlin.

The Korean War ended in 1953 with an armistice. Fighting had continued during two years of peace talks.

The great blocs split. Following the Soviet Union's destalinization campaign, the U.S.S.R. and Communist China began to move along different paths. In 1960, at the third Congress of the Romanian Communist Party, the U.S.S.R. and China quarreled bitterly and openly. The Soviet Union soon cut off technical aid to China. When China attacked India in 1962, the U.S.S.R. supported India. The Soviet Union again backed India when Pakistan and India fought in 1965. China threatened India and aided Pakistan.

Khrushchev fell from power in October 1964. The new Soviet leaders tried to heal the split with China. But Premier Aleksei N. Kosygin and General Secretary Leonid I. Brezhnev were unable to reunite the Communist bloc.

In 1966, China launched a "cultural revolution." One aim of this revolution was to eliminate all Soviet influence from China. The Chinese accused the Soviet Union of betraying world Communism and being secret allies of the United States. The Chinese threat to the Soviet Union became more real when China exploded its first hydrogen bomb in June 1967.

In March 1969, Soviet and Chinese troops began to fight each other on an island in the frozen Ussuri River. This river is the border between Chinese Manchuria and the Soviet Union's maritime territories. Both countries claimed they owned the island. The fighting soon ended, but the border controversy remained unsettled.

Some of the Soviet Union's satellites also shifted their loyalty. Albania had sided with China in 1961, and neither China nor Albania attended the 23rd Communist Party Congress in Moscow in 1965. Yugoslavia remained independent, with its own brand of "national Communism." Other Communist nations, including Romania, Poland, and Cuba, loosened their ties with the U.S.S.R.

Differences also sharpened among the Western nations. President Charles de Gaulle of France challenged the leadership of the United States and Great Britain. France established diplomatic relations with China in 1964, and sharply criticized U.S. policy in the Vietnam War. At de Gaulle's request, NATO moved its military headquarters from France in 1967, and the French withdrew their troops from the alliance. France also blocked Great Britain's entry into the European Economic Community (EEC). In 1967, de Gaulle further strengthened France's relations with the U.S.S.R. and Eastern Europe. In June of that year, France sided with the Arabs against Israel in the Arab-Israeli War. In 1968, France exploded a hydrogen bomb.

The growing strength of Europe was another factor in the changing nature of the Cold War. More than 20 years after the end of World War II, the nations of Western Europe were enjoying prosperity. The EEC, also called the European Common Market, had become a powerful economic force. Western European nations gradually increased trade with Communist countries. Many Western European leaders worried more about Germany's return to power than about the U.S.S.R.

Soviet-American relations in the 1960's reflected the changing nature of the Cold War. In 1966, the U.S.S.R. and the United States agreed to permit direct air service between Moscow and New York City. By January 1967, they and 60 other nations had signed the first international treaty providing for the peaceful exploration and use of outer space.

President Johnson and Premier Kosygin met for the first time in June 1967. Kosygin went to the United States to address the UN General Assembly. The two leaders met in Glassboro, N.J., and discussed the Vietnam War, the Arab-Israeli dispute, and disarmament.

In August 1967, the U.S.S.R. and the United States submitted proposals at the Geneva Disarmament Conference for a treaty to prevent the spread of nuclear weapons. In 1968, they agreed on an addition to the treaty providing for international inspection and controls. France refused to sign the treaty. The U.S. Senate approved it in 1969. The treaty, called the Treaty on the

---

Death of Stalin
alters Cold War

Soviet Union downs
U-2 spy plane

| 1953 | 1955 | 1960 | 1961 |

Summit conference
held in Geneva

German Communists
build Berlin Wall

United Press Int.

At Geneva, U.S. President Dwight D. Eisenhower, *second from left,* met with Soviet, French, and British leaders.

John Bryson, Rapho Guillumette

A U.S. spy plane was shot down over the U.S.S.R. in 1960, and the U.S.S.R. canceled a summit meeting with the United States.

Non-Proliferation of Nuclear Weapons, went into effect on March 5, 1970, after being *ratified* (formally approved) by the United States, the U.S.S.R., Britain, and more than 40 other nations. Since then, over 100 additional nations have ratified it.

In 1969, Soviet and U.S. representatives began a series of Strategic Arms Limitation Talks (SALT). The representatives worked toward an agreement to control the production of nuclear weapons.

The invasion of Czechoslovakia. Hopes for an easing of Cold War tensions in Europe were jolted in August 1968, when Soviet, Bulgarian, East German, Hungarian, and Polish troops invaded Czechoslovakia. The invasion halted a move by Czechoslovakia to give more individual freedom to the its people. In October, Czechoslovakia and the U.S.S.R. signed a treaty that allowed Soviet troops to remain and assured that Czechoslovakia would continue as a Soviet satellite.

The battle for the neutral nations continued in the 1960's. In Latin America, the United States still guarded against the threat of Communism. In April and May 1965, the United States, at the request of the Dominican Republic, sent troops to the Dominican Republic to prevent a Communist take-over during a revolt there. The crisis eased, and the United States troops left.

In the Middle East, a six-day war broke out between Israel and the Arab powers in June 1967. The United States backed the Israelis. The U.S.S.R. helped arm the Arabs before the war began, but this did not prevent their defeat. Scattered fighting continued in the area during the late 1960's. The United States and the U.S.S.R. increased aid to the opposing sides. In Africa, most of the newly independent nations remained neutral. They took aid from all the major Cold War powers.

The Vietnam War threatened to turn the Cold War into a general hot war. During the early 1960's, the United States stepped up its support of South Vietnam against the Communist Viet Cong forces. The United States blamed the struggle on Communist North Vietnam, viewing the war as "aggression from the north."

The United States gradually *escalated* (increased) its military effort. In 1965, it began large-scale bombing of North Vietnam. By 1968, over 500,000 U.S. troops were in Vietnam. The Viet Cong and North Vietnamese received war materials from the Soviet Union and China.

The fighting spread throughout Indochina. Cambodia and Laos, both of which bordered South Vietnam, tried to stay neutral. But Communist forces used both countries as bases for raids into South Vietnam, and the two nations were drawn into the war. Thailand backed the West in the struggle. The United States used bases there for bombing raids on North Vietnam.

Peace talks started in Paris in May 1968. But the talks stalled, and the fighting went on. In 1969, the United States established new training programs to help the South Vietnamese take over most of the fighting. This policy became known as *Vietnamization.* Also in 1969, President Richard M. Nixon began to gradually reduce the number of U.S. soldiers in Vietnam. In 1973, the United States completed its withdrawal of ground forces. The war ended in 1975, after Communist troops conquered South Vietnam. See **Vietnam War.**

The Cold War in the 1970's

The loosening of ties among members of both the Communist and Western blocs during the 1960's led to new international relationships in the 1970's. Several Communist and democratic nations developed friendlier relations with one another, helping ease tensions.

In 1970, West Germany and Poland signed a treaty to reject the use of force and to recognize the boundaries created in Europe after World War II. West Germany and the Soviet Union ratified a similar treaty in 1972.

The status of West Berlin, a major Cold War problem, was settled in the early 1970's. France, Britain, the U.S.S.R., and the United States signed an agreement in

---

Castro announces
he is a Communist

Communists win
Vietnam War

Communist rule comes to an end in
several Eastern European countries

1961   1964   1975   1979   1989

United States bombs
bases in North Vietnam

Soviet Union
invades Afghanistan

German Communists
open Berlin Wall

Wide World

Fidel Castro, *left,* declared Cuba was Communist, and was welcomed to the Soviet Union by Premier Nikita S. Khrushchev.

Francois Sully, *Newsweek*

U.S. Marines entered the Vietnam War in 1965, increasing the number of American troops in Vietnam at that time to 27,000.

1971 stating that West Berlin was not part of West Germany. The Berlin agreement also allowed free movement of traffic between West Germany and West Berlin. The pact took effect in 1972, after details were worked out. In 1973, East and West Germany joined the UN.

Also in 1973, Britain finally entered the European Economic Community (EEC), also known as the European Common Market. The increased economic ties among the EEC nations made Western Europe a powerful, independent force in world affairs. Japan also began acting more independently of U.S. policies.

China's relations with the West improved in the early 1970's. Canada and several other Western nations established diplomatic relations with Communist China for the first time. China was admitted to the UN in October 1971. In February 1972, Nixon visited China for seven days. During the visit, Nixon and Chinese Premier Zhou Enlai agreed to increase contacts between their two countries. In 1979, the United States and China established diplomatic relations. As part of the agreement, the United States ended diplomatic ties with Taiwan.

In 1972, Nixon and Soviet leader Leonid I. Brezhnev signed two agreements, together known as SALT I, to limit the production of U.S. and Soviet nuclear weapons. *SALT* stands for *Strategic Arms Limitation Talks*. In 1979, the two countries signed another pact, SALT II, limiting long-range bombers and missiles. But SALT II did not go into effect officially. The U.S. Senate stopped considering the treaty after Soviet troops invaded Afghanistan in late 1979 and early 1980.

The Cold War after 1980

Cold War tensions increased in the early 1980's. The renewed friction resulted chiefly from the Soviet intervention in Afghanistan and from continued American fear of Soviet and Cuban influence in the Middle East, Southeast Asia, Africa, and Central America. U.S. President Ronald Reagan and his Administration adopted a policy they called *linkage,* tying any U.S. arms agreement to consideration of Soviet expansion.

Meanwhile, the growing military power of the Soviet Union led the United States to increase its defense budget. Many observers thought the U.S. defense build-up would lead to a more dangerous nuclear arms race. But events in the late 1980's led to a sharp reduction in U.S.-Soviet tensions. In 1987, Reagan and Soviet leader Mikhail Gorbachev signed a treaty to eliminate many of the ground-launched, nuclear missiles of both nations. The treaty went into effect in 1988. In 1988 and 1989, the U.S.S.R. withdrew its troops from Afghanistan. Also in the late 1980's, the Soviet Union began to reduce its conventional military forces in Eastern Europe. In the U.S.S.R., Gorbachev worked for a more decentralized economic system and allowed more democracy and freedom of expression. He also encouraged similar actions in Eastern Europe.

Beginning in 1989, Communist rule came to an end in a number of Eastern European countries, including Poland, Hungary, East Germany, and Czechoslovakia. In addition, East Germany began to allow its people to pass freely to West Berlin through the Berlin Wall, and the East Germans soon began to tear the wall down. Germany was reunified in 1990, when East Germany united with West Germany. In 1991, the Soviet Communist Party

lost control of the Soviet government. Later that year, the Soviet Union was dissolved, and the republics that made up the nation became independent states. Russia was by far the largest of these states. In 1992, Russian President Boris Yeltsin and U.S. President George Bush formally declared that their countries did not regard each other as potential enemies. Many people believe that such events marked the end of the Cold War.

Burton I. Kaufman

Related articles in *World Book* include:

Conferences, organizations, and treaties

Conference on Security and Cooperation in Europe	Organization of American States	Strategic Arms Limitation Talks
	Potsdam Conference	United Nations
Helsinki Accords	San Francisco Conference	Warsaw Pact
North Atlantic Treaty Organization	Southeast Asia Treaty Organization	Yalta Conference

Programs, strategy, and weapons

Arms control	Iron Curtain	Point Four Program
Foreign aid	Marshall Plan	
Foreign policy	Nuclear weapon	Sputnik
Guided missile	(The Cold War)	Strategic Defense Initiative
Hot line		

Other related articles

Astronaut	Europe (History)	Neutrality	Space exploration
Communism		Peace	
Democracy	Korean War	Quemoy	Third World
Espionage			Vietnam War

Outline

I. The coming of the Cold War
  A. The alliance breaks up   B. The Iron Curtain descends
II. The West holds the line
  A. The *Containment Policy*   D. Communist expansion in Asia
  B. The Berlin blockade   E. The Korean War
  C. The West rearms
III. To the brink and back
  A. The death of Stalin   C. Unrest in Eastern Europe
  B. The spirit of Geneva   D. Trouble at Suez
IV. New challenges
  A. The missile gap   F. The U-2 incident
  B. The Eisenhower Doctrine   G. Africa
                            H. The troika proposal
  C. The Far East   I. The Bay of Pigs
  D. Germany   J. The Berlin Wall
  E. The spirit of Camp David   K. The space race begins
                            L. The Cuban missile crisis
V. Easing Cold War tensions
VI. The shifting Cold War battleground
  A. The great blocs split   D. The invasion of Czechoslovakia
  B. The growing strength of Europe   E. The battle for the neutral nations
  C. Soviet-American relations   F. The Vietnam War
VII. The Cold War in the 1970's
VIII. The Cold War after 1980

Questions

What made it difficult for the Communists and the democracies to settle disputes peacefully in the late 1940's and the 1950's?

Where did U.S. troops fight troops of a major Communist power for the first time?

How did the death of Stalin affect the Cold War?

What was the "spirit of Geneva"?

What is the *Containment Policy*?

Why did East German Communists build the Berlin Wall?

How did the U-2 incident affect the Cold War?

Why did the Cold War change during the mid-1960's?
What was the *Eisenhower Doctrine*?
What is the *hot line*? Why was it established?

Reading and Study Guide

See *Cold War* in the Research Guide/Index, Volume 22, for a *Reading and Study Guide.*

Additional resources

Gaddis, John L. *The Long Peace: Inquiries into the History of the Cold War.* Oxford, 1987.
Simons, Thomas W., Jr. *The End of the Cold War?* St. Martin's, 1990.
Woods, Randall B., and Jones, Howard. *Dawning of the Cold War.* Univ. of Georgia Pr., 1991.

Cole, Nat "King" (1917-1965), was an American singer and pianist. During the early 1940's, Cole was considered one of the leading jazz pianists of his day. His trio, with guitar and bass, inspired Ahmad Jamal, Oscar Peterson, Art Tatum, and other pianists to form groups with the same instruments. Cole's vocal recording of "Straighten Up and Fly Right" (1943) won him fame as a singer. He continued to perform as a jazz musician, but his image as a singer dominated the rest of his career. Cole's vocal hits include "It's Only a Paper Moon" (1943), "The Christmas Song" (1946), "Nature Boy" (1948), and "Mona Lisa" (1950).

AP/Wide World
Nat "King" Cole

Cole was born in Montgomery, Ala., and raised in Chicago. His given and family name was Nathaniel Adams Coles. In 1946, his trio became one of the first black music groups to have its own radio show. In 1958, he portrayed composer W. C. Handy in the film *St. Louis Blues.* His daughter, Natalie Cole, also became a successful singer.   Frank Tirro

Cole, Thomas (1801-1848), was a leader of the first group of American landscape painters. Cole helped de-

Oil painting on canvas; Museum of Art, Rhode Island School of Design, Walter H. Kimball Fund
A Thomas Cole painting called *Landscape* was completed about 1828. The artist's romantic style is reflected in his dramatic, panoramic treatment of the vast American wilderness.

velop a distinctly American style of landscape painting. He painted dramatic, panoramic scenes of the American wilderness in a romantic way.

Cole first gained fame in 1825 for his scenes along the Hudson River Valley in New York. His paintings stimulated other artists of his time to paint American landscapes. This group became known as the Hudson River School. Some of Cole's paintings illustrate symbolic stories with moral themes. These works include the five canvases of *The Course of Empire* (1836) and the four works that are entitled *The Voyage of Life* (1840).

Cole was born in Lancashire, England. He and his family moved to the United States in 1818. Cole studied painting at the Pennsylvania Academy of the Fine Arts from 1823 to 1825.   Sarah Burns

See also **Hudson River School.**

Coleman, William Thaddeus, Jr. (1920-   ), was United States secretary of transportation from 1975 to 1977. Coleman, appointed by President Gerald R. Ford, was the second black Cabinet member in U.S. history. The first black Cabinet member was Robert Weaver, who was secretary of housing and urban development from 1966 through 1968. As secretary of transportation, Coleman worked to help the bankrupt railroads in the Northeast solve their problems. He also worked to help cities improve their transportation systems.

Previously, Coleman had served as an attorney on transportation matters for the governments of Pennsylvania and Philadelphia. Coleman also is a civil rights leader. He helped write the legal argument that resulted in the 1954 decision by the Supreme Court of the United States banning segregation in public schools.

Coleman was born in Philadelphia. He graduated from the University of Pennsylvania and from Harvard Law School.   William J. Eaton

Coleridge, Samuel Taylor (1772-1834), was a poet, philosopher, and critic of the English romantic movement. His poem "The Rime of the Ancient Mariner" is one of the greatest in English literature, and all his major poems are among the most original. They embody ideals of romanticism, a literary movement that stressed imagination, passion, and the supernatural. His literary criticism has influenced most later critics.

His life. Coleridge was born in Devonshire. He studied at Cambridge University, where he met Robert Southey in 1794. The two young poets favored the principles of the French Revolution and planned to found a *pantisocracy* (a utopian society) in the United States. They also collaborated in 1794 on a drama opposing monarchy.

In 1795, Coleridge met William Wordsworth, and they became intimate friends. They published *Lyrical Ballads* (1798), which contains the first version of "The Rime of the Ancient Mariner." In 1798, Coleridge got an *annuity* (regular income) from Josiah and Thomas Wedgwood. It enabled him to abandon a plan to become a clergyman. Then he and Wordsworth traveled to Germany. Coleridge absorbed ideas from German philosophers, especially Immanuel Kant, who influenced his own literary theories. On his return to England, he translated two plays by German author Friedrich Schiller.

About 1800, Coleridge's health began to fail. He had begun taking opium to relieve the pain of rheumatism. His marriage, never happy, caused him increasing distress after he fell in love with Wordsworth's sister-in-law, Sara Hutchinson. He spent his last years under a doctor's care, largely to control his opium addiction.

His writing. Coleridge's other famous poems are "Kubla Khan" and "Christabel." Coleridge said, possibly incorrectly, that "Kubla Khan" was inspired by an opium dream. "Christabel" is an unfinished narrative of medieval times. Both poems deal with the visionary and the supernatural, combining vivid, dreamlike images with rich literary references and intricate symbolism.

Coleridge blended keen psychological insights with precise pictures of natural scenes in his meditative lyrics, notably "Dejection: An Ode" (1802). He called many of these works "conversation poems" and addressed them to friends, including Wordsworth and essayist Charles Lamb.

Coleridge was most influential in his literary criticism. He said that a good poem has an *organic* (natural), not a *mechanical* (artificial), unity. He used this idea, among other ways, to greatly elevate the reputation of English playwright William Shakespeare. Coleridge emphasized that poetry is creative or expressive, rather than imitative, and insisted that imagination, not reason, is the foundation of the fine arts. Coleridge's best-known critical work, *Biographia Literaria* (1817), contains valuable analyses of Wordsworth's poetry. Much of Coleridge's shrewdest criticism appears in notebooks, lectures, journalistic essays, and marginal comments on other writers. A devout man, Coleridge often discussed religion, morality, and theology.   Frederick W. Shilstone

See also **Ballad** (The ballad style); **Lake Poets.**

Additional resources

Bate, Walter J. *Coleridge.* Harvard Univ. Pr., 1987. First published in 1968.
Fruman, Norman. *Coleridge: The Damaged Archangel.* Braziller, 1971.

Colette, *koh LEHT* (1873-1954), was a French author. She was one of her country's few modern novelists who expressed a closeness to nature in her writing. Her mother had taught her tenderness for every plant and animal, and Colette expressed these feelings in her writing. Her style is sensitive and sensual and brings out the perfumes and colors of her native region of Burgundy. She also portrayed Parisian life.

Colette is especially noted for her insights into women's struggles for independence and identity. But her characters also reflect her broader interest in stages of female development, from adolescence through young womanhood, motherhood, and aging. Her novels include anecdotes from her life in the early 1900's.

Colette was born Sidonie-Gabrielle Colette in St.-Sauveur-en-Puisaye, near Auxerre. Her first works were four autobiographical novels (1900-1904) about a girl named Claudine. Colette's other novels include *The Vagabond* (1910), *Chéri* (1920), *The Ripening Seed* (1923), *Sido* (1929), *The Cat* (1933), and *Gigi* (1944).   Edith Kern

Coleus, *KOH lee uhs,* is the name for a group of plants native to tropical and nearly tropical areas of Asia, Africa, Australia, and the Pacific Islands. There are over 150 species of coleus.

One of the best-known species is the *common coleus.* It is a popular house plant, largely because its leaves show patterns of white, green, yellow, pink, red, bronze,

or purple in various combinations. The common coleus may grow 2 to 3 feet (61 to 91 centimeters) tall or more, but gardeners usually keep it shorter. It is a *perennial*—that is, it can live for more than two years. But the plant cannot survive outdoors in cold regions. Gardeners grow the common coleus in pots, hanging baskets, and window boxes.

© Robert P. Comport, Earth Scenes
Coleus

Coleus plants grow easily. Seeds may be planted indoors in late winter or spring and replanted outdoors in warm weather. Pieces cut from a coleus stem or root develop easily in most soils or sand in a humid place at room temperature.

Scientific classification. Coleus plants belong to the mint family, Lamiaceae or Labiatae. The scientific name for the common coleus is *Coleus hybridus.*   Kenneth A. Nicely

Colfax, Schuyler, *SKY lur* (1823-1885), served as Vice President of the United States from 1869 to 1873 during the first term of President Ulysses S. Grant. Colfax was an active leader of the Whig and Republican parties.

Colfax was elected to the U.S. House of Representatives in 1855 and was Speaker of the House from 1863 to 1869. He was an early supporter of voting rights for blacks. But his association in 1872 with the Liberal Republican Party, which opposed Grant, kept him out of the vice presidency during Grant's second term. Colfax was born in New York City.   Irving G. Williams

See also **Credit Mobilier of America; Vice President of the United States** (picture).

Colic, *KAHL ihk,* is a severe cramping pain resulting from the contraction of any of the hollow, muscular abdominal organs, such as the stomach and intestines. Many babies and some children and adults suffer from colic. Physicians do not fully understand the causes of such pains, especially in babies. The disease may occur if the baby's digestive system has not developed enough to handle its food properly. Indigestion or constipation may cause gas to form in the intestines, resulting in colic. Some people develop colic from emotional tension. It may also be caused by arsenic or lead poisoning, blood diseases, gallstones, kidney stones, narrowing of the intestine, intestinal worms, or appendicitis.

Treatment for colic depends on the cause. Giving a baby a pacifier may help reduce tension. Patting a baby's back gently may help the baby expel gas. In some cases, it may be necessary to change the kind or amount of a baby's food. In most cases, babies outgrow the disease. A physician should be notified if colic pain persists. Adults who suffer from colic may require psychiatric counseling.   Arnold Gerald Coran

Colitis, *koh LY tihs,* is a disease involving inflammation of the *colon* or other parts of the large intestine. There are three main types of colitis: (1) inflammatory colitis, (2) amebic colitis, and (3) mucous colitis.

Inflammatory colitis usually occurs in people from 20 to 40 years old. Physicians do not know what causes the disease, but many believe that nervous tension and other psychological factors may make the illness worse.

The patient suffers severe diarrhea, often accompanied by fever and rectal bleeding, particularly in a type of inflammatory colitis called ulcerative colitis. As ulcerative colitis progresses, ulcers develop in the lining of the colon and cause scarring. Drugs often help reduce the inflammation, but surgical removal of the colon may be required in extremely severe attacks. A prolonged case of ulcerative colitis greatly increases the possibility of getting cancer of the colon. Many doctors recommend surgery for patients who have had the disease for more than 10 years.

Amebic colitis results from consuming food or water contaminated by a certain type of parasitic ameba. Symptoms of amebic colitis include abdominal cramps, diarrhea, and fever. Deep ulcers may form in the colon and may even perforate it, causing *peritonitis* (see **Peritonitis**). Physicians treat amebic colitis with drugs, and surgery is not necessary in most cases unless perforation occurs.

Mucous colitis, also called *spastic colon,* is caused by spasms of the muscles in the wall of the colon. The patient may have severe cramps, and the feces may contain mucus—but no blood. Physicians use certain drugs and diets to relieve the symptoms.   Charles S. Lieber

See also **Colon; Diarrhea; Dysentery; Ileitis.**

Collage, *kuh LAHZH,* is a picture or design made by gluing pieces of paper or other materials onto a canvas or another surface. The term comes from the French word *coller,* meaning *to paste* or *to glue.*

Most artists use such common items as photographs and ticket stubs to make collages. The pasted materials may be combined with lines and colors painted by the

Merz Drawing (1924) by Kurt Schwitters; The Museum of Modern Art, New York City, Katherine S. Dreier Bequest

Collages broke down traditional differences between painting and sculpture and influenced many art styles of the mid-1900's.

artist. By arranging the materials in a certain way, an artist can create strange or witty effects not possible in traditional painting.

Some painters use collage to develop color compositions. For example, an artist can move a piece of colored paper over parts of a picture until the color is where the artist wants it. Art students use collage techniques to study proportion and color relationships. Many elementary schools include collage in their art courses.

Modern artists began experimenting with collage about 1912. Georges Braque, Juan Gris, and Pablo Picasso created paintings onto which they pasted pieces of paper, oilcloth, or wallpaper. In *The Bottle of Anis del Mono,* Gris used pieces of newspaper and a liqueur bottle label. This picture appears in the **Painting** article. Beginning about 1920, such painters as Max Ernst cut out book and magazine illustrations for collages. They pasted parts of one picture onto sections of another to create mysterious fantasies.   Rebecca Jeffrey Easby

Collagen, *KAHL uh juhn,* is a protein found throughout the bodies of human beings and animals. Collagen provides strength and gives shape to connective tissues, such as ligaments and tendons, and to bones. It also provides much of the strength and flexibility in skin and blood vessels.

There are many kinds of collagens in the body. All of them are made by cells and secreted into the *intercellular substance* (material outside the cells). Single collagen molecules can come together and form larger structures, a process important in the formation of tissues.

Collagen may be damaged by injuries, such as cuts and broken bones. A major part of the process by which wounds heal involves the removal of damaged collagen, the formation of new collagen, and the shaping of this new collagen into a tissue. Many of the problems of arthritis are caused by damage to the collagen in cartilage and bone. In certain inherited disorders, collagen is abnormal. Patients with these disorders may have fragile, rubberlike skin and very loose joints. In other diseases of collagen, the bones are easily broken or the skin blistered by minor injury.

Animal collagen has many uses. Gelatin is made from collagen and is used in foods and glues. Collagen is used in shampoos and other cosmetics. In medicine, collagen is used to make artificial heart valves and to repair scars and wrinkles.   George P. Stricklin

Collarbone is a long, slender, curved bone that connects the breastbone with a hooklike projection on the shoulder blade. The technical name for the collarbone is *clavicle.* The breastbone is properly called the *sternum,* the hooklike projection, *acromion,* and the shoulder blade, *scapula.*

Humans have two collarbones, one to support each shoulder. The bones are shaped somewhat like the italic letter *f.* They hold the arms in proper position at the sides of the body. When a person breaks a collarbone, the shoulder drops downward and forward toward the chest. Most broken collarbones are caused by falling on the shoulder. A hard blow on the shoulder also may break the collarbone. In addition, such a blow may tear ligaments at the joints between the clavicle, the acromion, and the sternum.

Animals that walk on four legs, such as dogs, have no collarbones. Those that hang from trees, such as

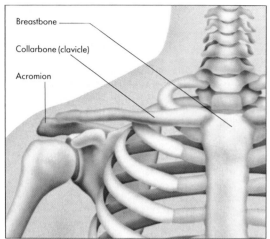

Breastbone

Collarbone (clavicle)

Acromion

WORLD BOOK illustration by Leonard Morgan

The collarbone, or *clavicle,* connects the breastbone with the *acromion,* a hooklike projection of the shoulder blade. The collarbone holds the arm in proper position at the side of the body.

apes, have large collarbones. Occasionally, humans are born without collarbones.   Bruce Reider

See also **Human body** (Trans-Vision picture).

Collards, *KAHL uhrdz,* are the leaves of the collard plant, a vegetable related to the cabbage. The collard resembles kale but can grow in warmer climates (see **Kale**). It is usually grown in the Southern United States. The plant may grow 2 to 4 feet (61 to 120 centimeters) tall. In warm climates, the seeds may be planted in September and the leaves picked the following spring and summer. Seeds may also be planted in summer and the leaves picked the following winter. Collards are cooked and eaten. They provide a rich source of vitamin A.

Scientific classification. Collards belong to the mustard family, Brassicaceae or Cruciferae. It is *Brassica oleracea.*

Hugh C. Price

Collection agency is an organization that collects the payment of past-due bills. Many physicians, dentists, hospitals, stores, and manufacturers hire a collection agency instead of spending their own time trying to collect such debts. The agency receives a fee ranging from a fourth to half of the amount it collects. There are more than 5,000 collection agencies in the United States.

A collection agency deals with a debtor chiefly through letters and telephone calls. At first, an agency may merely urge the payment of a bill so that the debtor's credit rating does not suffer. Each successive letter or call is firmer in its demand for payment. If the debtor does not pay, the agency may take legal action. It may obtain a court order requiring the debtor's employer to pay the agency part of the debtor's wages. But in many cases, the agency tells the *creditor* (the person to whom the money is owed) the money cannot be collected. The creditor then decides what legal action to take, if any. About 30 states license collection agencies, but only a few regulate collecting practices.   Joanna H. Frodin

Collective behavior is a term in sociology that refers to how people act in crowds and other large, relatively unorganized groups. The various types of collective behavior include fads, panics, and riots. Collective behav-

ior often arises in situations that stimulate people's emotions. These situations include sporting events, protest demonstrations, and disasters such as floods and fires.

Much collective behavior is impulsive, unplanned, and brief. Thus, it differs from the more predictable, longer-lasting actions of such organized groups as school classes, teams, and social clubs. However, some types of collective behavior fit into organized social frameworks. For example, an organized political party or social movement might use mass demonstrations as a device in seeking social change.

Before the 1900's, scientists knew little about the forces at work in collective behavior. During the 1890's, Gustave Le Bon, a French physician and social scientist, made one of the first psychological studies of crowds. The American sociologists Robert E. Park and Ernest W. Burgess introduced the term *collective behavior* in their book, *Introduction to the Science of Sociology* (1921).

Collective behavior occurs in so many forms that social scientists have reached few conclusions about its origins, development, and consequences. Some investigators believe the pace of modern life and the growth of mass communications have increased the amount of collective behavior.   Gary T. Marx

See also **Group dynamics; Riot; Vandalism.**

Collective farm is a farm operated by a group cooperatively. The farm may be owned jointly by the group, by individuals in the group, or by the government. On most collective farms, workers receive a share of the farm's profits, some of its products, and a small wage. In many countries, the workers also help manage the farm. Collective farms differ from *state farms,* which the government owns and runs. On state farms, the government pays the workers a wage and, in some cases, gives them a small portion of the farm's products.

Collective farms were introduced in Russia after Communists gained control there in 1917. Beginning in 1929, Soviet dictator Joseph Stalin forced millions of peasants to give up their land and join government-controlled collective farms. Later, he combined some of these farms to create state farms. Soviet leaders thought the collective and state farms would be more efficient and productive than the tiny family farms they replaced. After World War II ended in 1945, new Communist governments in China, North Korea, and most countries of Eastern Europe imitated the Soviet system.

But the collective and state farms in Communist countries proved to be inefficient and unpopular. Most farmers resented their low earnings and the government's tight control over production. As a result, production remained below government expectations, and food shortages became common.

In the late 1980's, non-Communist governments replaced Communist governments in many countries of Eastern Europe. In 1991, the Soviet Union broke up into a number of independent, non-Communist states. All Eastern European countries in which the government had owned most farms—and many of the former Soviet states—took steps to redistribute much state-owned land to private farmers.   Stuart D. Goldman

Collectivism is a political and economic system in which the government or the people as a group own the land, factories, and other means of production. Collectivism originated during the early 1800's as a revolt against *capitalism,* the most popular economic system of the time. Capitalism called for individual ownership of property and little government intervention in business. Collectivists claimed these ideas led to poverty, unemployment, and other hardships for workers. Such writers as Robert Owen of Great Britain and Charles Fourier of France called for a new economic system based on cooperation and collective ownership. Their ideas led to the establishment of cooperative communities in the United States, including Brook Farm, Mass., and New Harmony, Ind. (see **Communal society**).

Several forms of collectivism developed during the late 1800's. They included *syndicalism,* which called for workers to own and manage industries, and *cooperatives,* which are businesses owned by the people who use their services. Major modern forms of collectivism include *communism* and *socialism.*   Richard C. Wiles

See also **Cooperative; Socialism; Syndicalism.**

College. See Community college; Universities and colleges.

College degree. See Degree, College.

College entrance examination is a test or a series of tests that helps determine whether a person meets the admission requirements of a college or university. Most colleges throughout the world require applicants to take some kind of entrance examination. Colleges that require these tests also have other standards for admission, such as good high school grades and strong personal recommendations.

Many nations have established one examination that all students must pass to qualify for admission to a university. The United States has no such test. Instead, many U.S. universities and colleges require applicants to take examinations given by the College Entrance Examination Board (CEEB). Others require tests prepared by the American College Testing Program (ACT). Some schools accept scores from either of these agencies. The ACT and CEEB tests are given several times each year throughout the United States and other countries.

Most students who plan to attend college take a college entrance examination during their junior or senior year in high school. A student may take the test as many times as he or she wishes.

The College Entrance Examination Board gives two types of entrance examinations, the Scholastic Aptitude Test (SAT) and the Achievement Tests. Information about the CEEB tests is available from the College Entrance Examination Board, 45 Columbus Avenue, New York, NY 10023.

The Scholastic Aptitude Test consists of multiple-choice questions and has three sections: (1) verbal, (2) mathematical, and (3) standard written English. The verbal section of the test measures reading comprehension and the ability to understand word relationships. The mathematical section of the test measures the ability to understand mathematical concepts and to use them in solving problems. The standard written English test requires the student to answer questions about grammar and composition.

Students can prepare for the SAT by taking the CEEB's Preliminary Scholastic Aptitude Test (PSAT). Most high schools give the PSAT to 11th graders each October. The PSAT is also the qualifying test for the National Merit Scholarships.

The Achievement Tests measure a student's knowledge in specific subject areas. The CEEB gives 14 one-hour tests in such areas as foreign language, English composition, mathematics, and science. Many schools that require the Achievement Tests ask their applicants to take tests in three subjects.

Planned revisions. In 1990, the CEEB decided to make changes in its tests in the spring of 1994. The changes would include a new requirement that students write an essay as part of the Achievement Tests. The CEEB's plans also called for including nonmultiple-choice questions in the mathematics section of the SAT.

The American College Testing Program examination has two parts. The major part consists of four tests: (1) English, (2) mathematics, (3) science reasoning, and (4) reading. These tests also use multiple-choice questions. The second part of the examination is the Student Profile. Students complete this section by answering a series of questions about their achievements, goals, and special interests. Information about the ACT tests can be obtained from the American College Testing Program, Box 168, Iowa City, IA 52243.

Scores on the CEEB Achievement Tests and the verbal and mathematical sections of the SAT are reported on a scale ranging from 200 to 800 points. There is no "passing" grade, and each college has its own standards for interpreting the scores. The CEEB helps students interpret their test results by providing a *percentile rank* for each score. The percentile rank shows how a student's score compares with the scores of others who took the test. For example, a score of 500 on the verbal section might place a student at the 86th percentile compared with a national sample of high school juniors and seniors. In other words, the student scored higher than 86 per cent of the sample group.

The ACT tests are scored on a scale of 1 to 36. The ACT also provides a percentile rank for each score.

Both the ACT and the CEEB send score reports to the student's high school and to the colleges to which the student is applying. A student can request as part of his or her CEEB score report a listing of percentile ranks for three specific colleges. This listing shows how the student's scores compare with the scores of the members of the freshman class at those schools.

Some educators criticize the emphasis placed on test scores. They believe that the tests measure only a few of the many abilities necessary for success in college. They also claim that the tests may discriminate against disadvantaged and minority groups.

The Advanced Placement Program (AP) is a CEEB testing program that allows high school students to earn college credit for knowledge gained in high school. Each May, the AP offers college-level examinations in many high school subjects. A sufficiently high score on one of these tests may qualify a student to receive credit for college work in the subject. A student who scores well on several tests may be given sophomore instead of freshman status.   James Crouse

College of Cardinals. See Cardinal; Pope.

Collie is a breed of dog that originated in Scotland, probably during the 1600's. Scottish farmers used the dog to guard and control flocks of sheep. Like other sheepdogs, collies have a thick, weatherproof coat. Their intelligence, willingness to work, and good eye-

WORLD BOOK photo

A short-haired collie has a smooth, short coat.

sight suit these dogs for taking care of sheep. British colonists brought collies to America during the 1700's. The dogs became popular as pets after Queen Victoria of England brought several collies to the royal residence at Windsor Castle in the 1860's.

The most common variety of collie has a coarse, long-haired coat. Another variety has a smooth, short-haired coat. A collie may be brown and white; black, white, and tan; blue-gray; or all white. The dogs stand about 22 to 26 inches (56 to 66 centimeters) high and weigh from 50 to 75 pounds (23 to 34 kilograms).

Critically reviewed by the Collie Club of America

Collins, Michael (1930-), was an astronaut on the Apollo 11 mission, which made the first manned landing on the moon. Collins piloted the command module, *Columbia,* as it orbited the moon. His fellow astronauts, Neil A. Armstrong and Edwin E. Aldrin, Jr., landed on the moon on July 20, 1969.

Collins was born in Rome, Italy, while his father was stationed there with the United States Army. He graduated from the U.S. Military Academy in 1952 and became an Air Force officer. He became an astronaut in 1963. Collins piloted the Gemini 10 flight in 1966. He resigned from the astronaut program in 1969. From 1971 to 1978, Collins was director of the Smithsonian Institution's National Air and Space Museum. He later became an aerospace consultant. Lillian D. Kozloski

Collins, Wilkie (1824-1889), an English author, was one of the most successful writers of detective fiction in the 1800's. *The Woman in White* (1860) and *The Moonstone* (1868) rank as his best and most popular novels.

Some critics rank *The Moonstone* among the world's outstanding detective stories. Sergeant Cuff, a character in the novel, was one of the first detectives in English fiction. The book is about a diamond called the moonstone which is stolen from the forehead of an image of the moon god of India. A curse, and sometimes murder, follows the diamond until it is returned.

William Wilkie Collins was born in London. He became a lawyer in 1851 but never practiced law. However, he used his knowledge of law in writing his books. Collins gained his first literary success with *Antonina* (1850), a historical novel set in ancient Rome. In 1851, he

met Charles Dickens and the two became close friends. Collins' first important mystery novel, *The Dead Secret* (1857), appeared in Dickens' magazine *Household Words.* David Geherin

Collodi, *kuh LOH dih,* **Carlo** (1826-1890), an Italian author, wrote the famous children's story *The Adventures of Pinocchio* (1883). His real name was Carlo Lorenzini. He took the pen name *Collodi* from the village where he spent much of his youth. Collodi was born in Florence and worked as a journalist for many years. He also wrote humorous fiction for adults and many children's stories.

In Collodi's famous story, Pinocchio is a wooden puppet carved by a kindly old man named Geppetto. The puppet comes to life and has many unhappy adventures because he is lazy and selfish. At the end of the story, Pinocchio has learned to be generous and honest and to work hard. As a reward, a fairy grants his wish and turns him into a real boy. Richard H. Lansing

Colloid, *KAHL oyd,* is a material composed of tiny particles of one substance that are *dispersed* (distributed), but not dissolved, in another substance. The mixture of the two substances is a *colloidal system.* A colloidal system composed of solid or liquid particles dispersed in a gas is called an *aerosol* (see **Aerosol**). A system made up of solid or liquid particles in water is sometimes called a *sol* or a *hydrosol.* The word *colloid* is often used alone to mean *colloidal system.* The remainder of this article uses *colloid* in this way.

Colloids include such familiar products as milk, soap solutions, paint, and ink. Other common products, such as pottery and paper, are made from colloids. Blood and most other fluids in living things are colloids.

The solid particles of a colloid may be crystals, groups of molecules, or large, single molecules. At least one dimension of a typical colloidal particle measures between a few nanometers and a few thousand nanometers. One nanometer equals one billionth of a meter, or $\frac{1}{25,400,000}$ inch. Some individual particles are too small to see, even with an optical microscope. These particles scatter light, however, producing bright dots that are visible in an instrument called an *ultramicroscope* (see **Ultramicroscope**).

Liquid colloids can be divided into three groups: (1) lyophobic, (2) lyophilic, and (3) association.

In lyophobic colloids, the particles have little attraction for the liquid in which they are dispersed. As a result, the particles tend to *coagulate* (clump). Mixing a chemical called a *dispersant* with a lyophobic colloid can decrease this tendency, however. For example, dispersants minimize the coagulation of pigments that give certain inks their color.

In lyophilic colloids, there is an attraction between the particles and the liquid, so the particles have little tendency to coagulate. Many animal and plant fluids, such as blood and gums, are lyophilic colloids.

In association colloids, the colloidal particles are large molecules that are part lyophilic and part lyophobic. These molecules form clusters called *micelles* that turn their lyophobic parts away from the liquid molecules and expose only the lyophilic parts. Soaps and detergents are association colloids. Their micelles surround and hold oily pieces of dirt. R. Hogg

Colobus, *KAHL uh buhs,* is a type of monkey that lives in Africa south of the Sahara to the Zambezi River. Adult

© Mark Boulton, Photo Researchers

The colobus is a type of monkey that lives in Africa. The animal has a stocky build, and many have black-and-white fur. The monkeys live mainly in trees but often travel on the ground.

colobus monkeys weigh from $6\frac{1}{2}$ to 32 pounds (2.9 to 14.5 kilograms), depending on the species. They measure from 16 to $31\frac{1}{2}$ inches (41 to 80 centimeters) long, not including a $20\frac{1}{2}$- to $39\frac{1}{2}$-inch (52- to 100-centimeter) tail. Males are larger than females in most species. Colobus monkeys have a stocky build. Their fur may be black, black and white, red, or olive. Unlike most other monkeys, colobus monkeys have no thumbs. Many scientists recognize nine species of colobus monkeys.

Most colobus monkeys live in a variety of forested environments, including tropical rain forests, wooded mountain areas, and patches of forests along rivers. They live mainly in trees but frequently travel on the ground. Colobus monkeys are called "leaf-monkeys" because they eat chiefly leaves. They also eat fruit, flower buds, bark, and other plant parts.

Colobus monkeys live in groups that range from about 3 to 80 members. Most groups consist of a few adult males and several adult females and their young. Some groups have only one adult male. Black-and-white colobus monkeys aggressively defend their territory from other groups. Red colobus monkeys generally do not defend their home areas.

The number of colobus monkeys has declined significantly since the late 1800's. Both the hunting of the monkeys for their fur and the clearing of forests for settlements and agriculture have contributed to their decline. In some regions, entire populations of colobus monkeys have been eliminated.

Scientific classification. Colobus monkeys belong to the Old World monkey family, Cercopithecidae.

Randall L. Susman

See also **Monkey** (picture: Red colobus).

Cologne, a perfume. See **Cologne; Perfume.**

Cologne, *kuh LOHN* (pop. 916,153), is a city in western Germany. For location, see **Germany** (political map). Its German name is Köln. Cologne lies along the Rhine River. It is the largest city in the state of North Rhine-Westphalia and the chief industrial, commercial, and cultural center of the large region called the Rhineland.

The *Ringstrassen,* a network of semicircular roads, forms Cologne's boundary line. These roads replaced the city's medieval fortified walls. Most of Cologne's commercial and residential areas lie on the west bank of the Rhine River. Most of the industrial areas are on the east bank. The city has numerous museums, theaters, libraries, and schools of higher education.

Cologne Cathedral is the city's most famous landmark. A magnificent Gothic structure, the cathedral features two 515-foot (157-meter) towers, beautiful stained-glass windows, and lovely works of art. It was started in 1248, but was not completed until 1880. The cathedral is the largest Gothic church in northern Europe. Cologne's numerous other medieval buildings include the old City Hall, which dates from the 1300's. Cologne University, the city's largest school of higher education, was founded in 1388.

Cologne's major industries include metal processing and the production of automobiles, beer, chemicals, electric power, motors, pharmaceuticals, and petrochemicals. A world-famous perfume called *eau de Cologne* was originally made in Cologne and is now produced both there and elsewhere. Cologne has long been an important river port and railroad center, and it has a large, modern airport. It is also a center of the insurance business in Germany.

Roman soldiers established a settlement on the site of what is now Cologne not long before the birth of Jesus Christ. The Ubii, an ancient Germanic people, had lived there long before the Romans arrived. Roman officials made the settlement a colony in A.D. 50. Norman invaders destroyed Cologne during the late 800's. The city was rebuilt in the 900's. From then until the 1500's, it prospered as an important member of the Holy Roman Empire (see **Holy Roman Empire**). France occupied Cologne from 1794 to 1815, when Prussia took the city. In 1871, Cologne became part of the newly united nation of Germany.

During World War II (1939-1945), Allied bombing attacks destroyed many parts of Cologne and forced most of the residents to leave. However, most of the people returned after the war, and the destroyed and damaged areas were soon rebuilt. Melvin Croan

Heinz Herfort, Bruce Coleman Inc.

Majestic Cologne Cathedral rises along the west bank of the Rhine River in Germany. The city of Cologne is an important industrial, commercial, and cultural center.

Carl Purcell, Tom Stack & Assoc.

Bogotá, Colombia's capital and largest city, lies in a basin high in the Andes Mountains. Steep mountains rise east of the city. The cable car in the foreground carries sightseers to one of the mountaintops for a spectacular aerial view of Bogotá.

Colombia

Colombia, *kuh LUHM bee uh,* is a country in north-western South America. It is the only country on the continent with a coast along both the Atlantic Ocean and the Pacific Ocean. Colombia ranks second in population and fourth in area among the countries of South America. Only Brazil has more people, and only Brazil, Argentina, and Peru cover a larger area.

Colombia's landscape and climate offer striking contrasts, ranging from the snow-capped peaks of the Andes Mountains to hot lowland plains. The equator crosses southern Colombia. Yet parts of the country have a chilly climate because of their high elevation.

The population of Colombia is distributed extremely unevenly. Most of the people live in valleys and basins of the Andes Mountains. Bogotá, Colombia's capital and largest city, lies in a basin of the Andes.

The differences in climate throughout Colombia enable farmers to grow many kinds of crops, including coffee, rice, bananas, and potatoes. Colombia produces more coffee than any other country except Brazil.

Colombia's economy depends heavily on agriculture, though manufacturing is growing in importance. Colombia has huge supplies of many raw materials used in industry and enormous sources of energy. However, the country has not fully developed its vast resources.

During the early 1500's, Colombia's natural wealth, especially its gold, attracted Spanish explorers. The Spaniards conquered most of the Indians, the region's original inhabitants. Colombia remained a Spanish colony for nearly 300 years. After gaining independence in 1819, it suffered long periods of violence and civil war. But unlike a number of other Latin-American countries, Colombia has a tradition of democratic government.

Colombia was named after Christopher Columbus.

The nation's official name is República de Colombia (Republic of Colombia).

Government

Colombia is a republic. The country's Constitution was adopted in 1886 and has been revised numerous times. All citizens 18 years of age and older may vote.

National government. A president, elected by the people to a four-year term, heads Colombia's government. The president may be elected to any number of terms but not to two terms in a row. A presidential candidate must either hold a high government office or practice a profession that requires a university education. Colombia has no vice president. Congress, the nation's legislature, consists of a 114-member Senate and a

Facts in brief

Capital: Bogotá.

Official language: Spanish.

Area: 439,737 sq. mi. (1,138,914 km²). *Greatest distances*—northwest-southeast, 1,170 mi. (1,883 km); northeast-southwest, 850 mi. (1,368 km). *Coastline*—580 mi. (933 km) along the Pacific Ocean; 710 mi. (1,143 km) along the Caribbean Sea.

Elevation: *Highest*—Cristóbal Colon, 18,947 ft. (5,775 m) above sea level. *Lowest*—sea level, along the coasts.

Population: *Estimated 1994 population*—35,487,000; density, 81 persons per sq. mi. (32 per km²); distribution, 73 per cent urban, 27 per cent rural. *1985 census*—27,837,932. *Estimated 1999 population*—38,664,000.

Chief products: *Agriculture*—bananas, beef cattle, cassava, coffee, corn, cotton, milk, potatoes, rice, sugar cane. *Manufacturing*—cement, chemicals, metal products, processed foods and beverages, textiles and clothing. *Mining*—coal, emeralds, gold, iron ore, natural gas, petroleum, salt.

Money: *Basic unit*—peso. For the price of the peso in U.S. dollars, see **Money** (table: Exchange rates).

199-member House of Representatives. Voters elect senators and representatives to four-year terms.

Local government. Colombia is divided into 23 departments, 9 national territories, and the Special District, which consists of Bogotá. Each department has a governor appointed by the president and an assembly elected by the people. The territories are thinly settled areas, chiefly in eastern Colombia. The president appoints the head of each territory. A mayor appointed by the president governs the Special District.

Politics. Two parties have long dominated Colombian politics. They are the Conservative Party and the Liberal Party. Both parties follow moderate policies. But most Colombians strongly support one or the other.

Courts. The Supreme Court is Colombia's highest court. It has 28 justices, who serve life terms. Colombia is divided into 27 judicial districts. Each district has a superior court headed by a justice of the Supreme Court.

Armed forces. Colombia's army has about 57,000 members, its navy about 8,500, and its air force about 4,200. All men 18 years old must register for the draft.

People

Population. Colombia has about 35 million people. Nearly all of them live in western Colombia, mainly in valleys and basins of the Andes Mountains. Only about 2 per cent of the people live in the hot lowlands of eastern Colombia.

Bogotá, the capital, is Colombia's largest city. It has about 4 million people. Two other Colombian cities, Cali and Medellín, have more than a million people each. Rural Colombians, who are called *campesinos*, have poured into the nation's large cities since the 1940's in search of a better life. Many campesinos lack the education and skills needed for city jobs. As a result, Colombia's large cities have such problems as poverty, unemployment, slum housing, and high crime rates.

Ancestry. Many Indians lived in what is now Colombia when the first Spanish colonists arrived in the 1500's. The Spaniards conquered the Indians and later brought in black slaves from Africa. Over the years, many Indians, Spaniards, and blacks intermarried. Today, *mestizos* (people of mixed white and Indian ancestry) make up from 50 to 60 per cent of Colombia's population. *Mulattoes* (people of mixed black and white ancestry) account for 15 to 25 per cent. *Zambos* (people of black and Indian ancestry) make up about 3 per cent of all Colombians. About 20 per cent of the people are of unmixed European ancestry, chiefly Spanish. About 4 per cent are of unmixed black ancestry, and about 1 per cent are of unmixed Indian ancestry.

Language. Nearly all Colombians speak Spanish, the country's official language. Colombians closely guard their language to keep it from changing. They even passed a law to protect it from unnecessary change. Colombians consider their Spanish purer than that of other Latin-American countries. The traditional languages of Colombia's Indians have largely died out.

Way of life. In general, city dwellers in Colombia live better than country people. The cities have most of the nation's schools, medical facilities, and cultural activities. The majority of middle- and upper-class Colombians live in cities.

In Colombia's large cities, tall office and apartment

Chip and Rosa Peterson

Masked and costumed Colombians parade down the streets of Barranquilla during carnival. The colorful festival of carnival is celebrated just before Lent in many Roman Catholic countries.

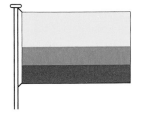

Colombia's flag, adopted in 1861, has a yellow stripe for the golden New World, a red stripe for the blood shed for independence, and a blue stripe for the Atlantic Ocean.

The coat of arms, adopted in 1834, is topped by a condor. It shows a pomegranate, horns of plenty, a liberty cap, and the Isthmus of Panama (once part of Colombia).

WORLD BOOK map

Colombia lies in northwestern South America. It borders five other countries, the Pacific Ocean, and the Caribbean Sea.

Colombia map index

Colombia

International boundary
Road
Railroad
⊛ National capital
• Other city or town
+ Elevation above
 sea level

WORLD BOOK map

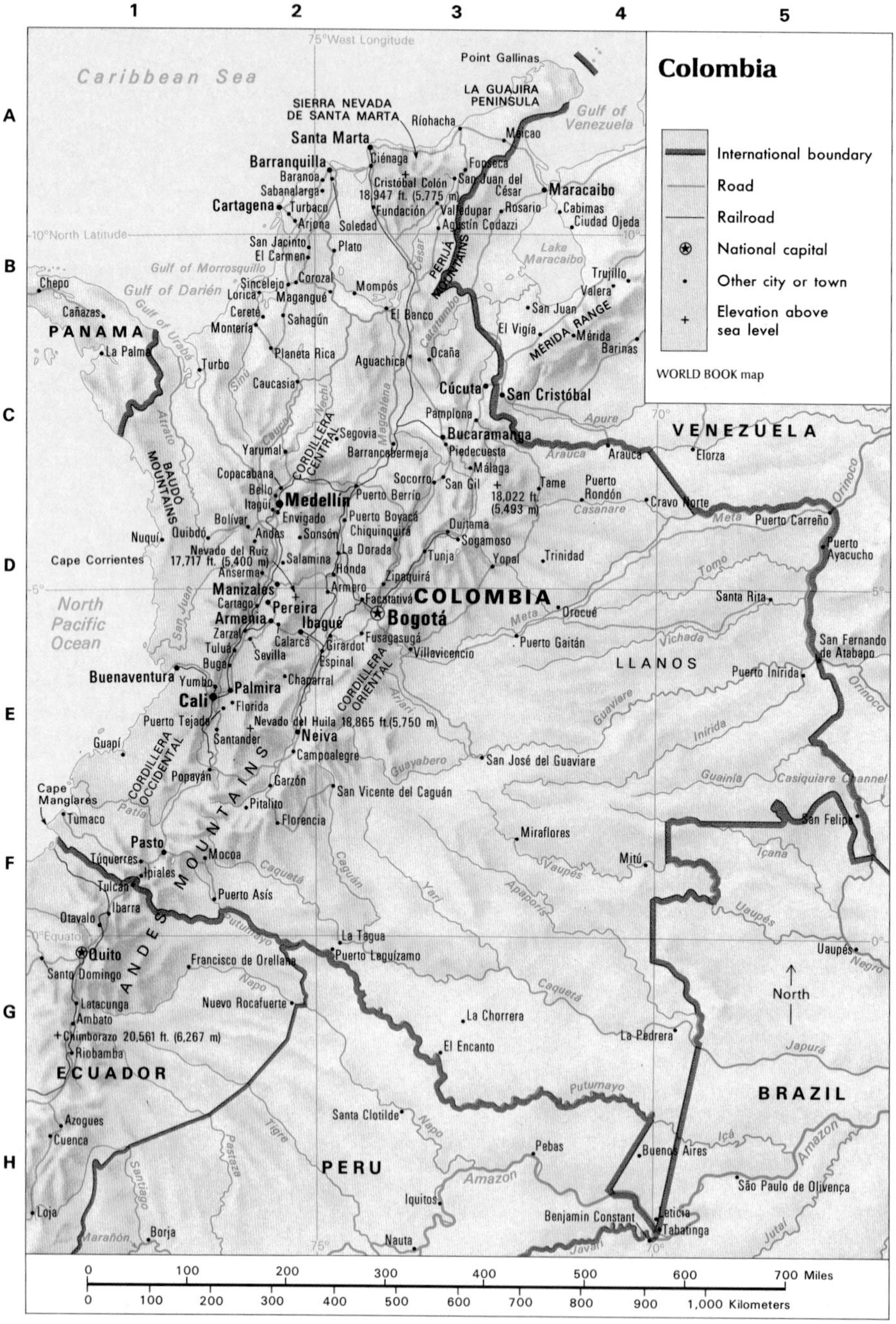

buildings are replacing the traditional Spanish-style architecture. Spanish-style buildings are low, sprawling adobe structures with red tile roofs and patios.

Many rural Colombians build simple houses from locally available materials. In the warm, wet coastal regions, for example, they use bamboo poles and palm leaves to build well-ventilated houses. But in the cooler mountain zones, many houses have thick adobe walls.

Many Colombian families are large. Rural families especially include numerous children. Family ties are strong. Several generations may live in the same household or as neighbors. In general, women have less freedom than men do, particularly among the upper class.

Most members of Colombia's small upper class are descended from the country's Spanish settlers. They form a tightly knit group and socialize mainly with other members of the upper class. Their wealth has traditionally come chiefly from large rural landholdings. But today, more and more upper-class Colombians make their money in business and industry.

In Colombia's cities, the size of the middle class and the working class is growing as developing industries provide many new jobs. The middle class includes business people, government officials, and such professionals as doctors, lawyers, and engineers. Middle-class Colombians live in comfortable houses or apartments in attractive neighborhoods. Working-class people include salesclerks, factory and construction workers, and other Colombians with low-paying jobs. Many of them live in run-down buildings in older neighborhoods.

Crowded slumlike squatter settlements stand at the edges of Colombia's large cities. They are called *tugurios* (pronounced *too GOO ree ohz*). Most tugurios have no running water, electricity, or sewers. Many newcomers from rural areas build shacks in the tugurios out of tin, cardboard, and other scrap materials. Some children in these areas run away or are abandoned by their parents, who cannot support them. These homeless children, called *gamines* (*gah MEE nays*), roam the streets and alleys. Most are boys.

Education. The Colombian government estimates that about 80 per cent of the nation's adults can read and write. The government requires all children from the ages of 7 through 11 to attend school. However, many rural children cannot meet this requirement because their schools have only two or three grades. Colombia has about 40 universities. The National University in Bogotá is the largest university.

Clothing. Most of Colombia's city dwellers dress much like people in the United States and Canada. Most rural people have few garments, and some of them wear shoes only on special occasions. In chilly mountain areas, many Colombians wear woolen *ruanas* (blankets with a slit in the middle for the head).

Food and drink. Different regions of Colombia have their own special dishes. In general, however, Colombians eat much starchy food, such as potatoes, rice, and noodles. They enjoy stews and thick soups. A favorite soup, called *ajiaco* (*ah hee AH koh*), contains potatoes, chicken, corn, and *cassava* (a root crop). Poor Colombians eat little meat and few fresh fruits or vegetables.

Both adults and children drink *agua de panela* (*AH gwah day pah NEHL ah*), a beverage consisting of brown sugar dissolved in water. Colombians also drink much

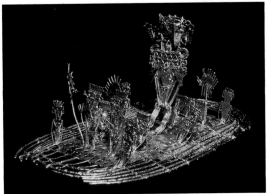

Loren McIntyre, Cher Agency

The Raft of El Dorado is an example of the elegant sculptures made by Indian goldsmiths hundreds of years ago. It represents the coronation of a new Chibcha ruler. The ruler was covered with gold dust to represent a god and then rowed out on a lake and washed free of the gold to represent a human ruler.

of the beer brewed in the country. Although Colombia is a leading coffee producer, most Colombians do not drink as much coffee as Americans do.

Recreation. Soccer is by far the most popular spectator sport in Colombia. Bullfights and auto races also draw large crowds. Swimmers and sunbathers enjoy the beaches along the Caribbean coast, and the snow-capped slopes of the Andes attract skiers. Folk songs and dances preserve the traditional music and dances of the Indians, Spanish colonists, and black African slaves.

Religion. Nearly all Colombians are Roman Catholics, and most of them actively practice their religion. The Catholic Church has a close relationship with the government. However, Colombia's Constitution guarantees freedom of worship.

The arts. Advanced Indian civilizations created Colombia's earliest works of art hundreds of years ago. Gigantic stone statues of Indian gods still stand high in the Andes Mountains in southern Colombia. Bogotá's Gold Museum displays elegant jewelry, small figures, and other beautiful objects crafted by Indian goldsmiths.

Indian artistic traditions were gradually forgotten after Spanish colonists arrived in Colombia. Until the 1900's, Colombia's arts largely reflected European styles. During the mid-1900's, several Colombian artists won international recognition for their original works. They include the painters Fernando Botero and Alejandro Obregón and the sculptor Edgar Negret.

Colombians greatly admire writers, especially poets. Many Colombian lawyers, teachers, and other professionals write poetry in their spare time. *María* (1867), a novel by Jorge Isaacs, became the first work of Colombian literature to win popularity throughout Latin America. It is a sentimental tale of love and death set in rural Colombia. Colombia's most outstanding writer today, Gabriel José García Márquez, won the Nobel Prize for literature in 1982. His tales about life in Latin America combine fantasy with realistic description.

The land

Colombia covers 439,737 square miles (1,138,914 square kilometers). It can be divided into three main

Loren McIntyre, Cher Agency

The Andes Mountains cover most of western Colombia. Many farmers in the Andes grow coffee, Colombia's leading crop. Coffee trees thrive in the mild climate on the steep slopes, *above*.

Victor Englebert, ZEFA

Colombia's Eastern Plains consist mainly of flat grassland, called *llanos*. Raising cattle is the chief economic activity in this sun-baked region. The cowboys above are rounding up cattle.

land regions: (1) the Coastal Lowlands, (2) the Andes Mountains, and (3) the Eastern Plains.

The Coastal Lowlands lie along the Caribbean Sea and the Pacific Ocean. The Caribbean is an arm of the Atlantic Ocean.

The Caribbean Lowlands have about 20 per cent of Colombia's people and about 12 per cent of its industry. The busy Caribbean ports of Barranquilla, Cartagena, and Santa Marta handle most of Colombia's foreign trade. Beyond these cities lie banana, cotton, and sugar cane plantations; cattle ranches; and many small farms. The narrow Guajira Peninsula forms the northernmost tip of Colombia. It is a dry area and has excellent coal deposits. The peninsula is the home of many Guajiro Indians.

The Pacific Lowlands consist mostly of swamps and dense forests. Heavy rains fall nearly every day. Few people live in the region.

The Andes Mountains cover about a third of Colombia. They fan out from the southwestern corner of the country into three ranges—Cordillera Central, Cordillera Oriental, and Cordillera Occidental. The ranges stretch northeast across western Colombia. They include the Nevado del Ruiz, an active volcano west of Bogotá. In 1985, the volcano erupted twice and caused 25,000 deaths. The eruptions triggered floods and mud slides that buried the city of Armero and damaged other areas. An isolated range of the Andes, the Sierra Nevada de Santa Marta, rises from the Caribbean coast. It includes Colombia's highest peak, Cristóbal Colón, which rises 18,947 feet (5,775 meters) above sea level.

About three-fourths of Colombia's people live in the Andes. Rich mines, fertile farms, and large factories in valleys and basins of the Andes produce most of Colombia's wealth. Coffee trees thrive on mountain slopes in areas of mild climate. Colombia's two most important rivers separate the three ranges. The Magdalena River separates the Cordillera Central and the Cordillera Oriental. The Cauca River separates the Cordillera Central and the Cordillera Occidental. Farmers grow various crops in the rich soil of the river valleys.

The Eastern Plains spread over nearly 60 per cent of Colombia. Only about 2 per cent of the people live in this hot, flat region. Tropical forests cover much of the south. In the north, farmers graze cattle on prairielike grassland called *llanos*. Several rivers cross the plains.

Climate

Colombia's climate varies with elevation. The highest temperatures occur at the lowest altitudes—in the Coastal Lowlands and the Eastern Plains. Temperatures are much lower in the Andes Mountains. A zone of mild climate lies between 3,000 and 6,000 feet (900 and 1,800 meters). Above 6,000 feet (1,800 meters), the climate is cool the year around. Few people live in the cold mountain areas above 10,000 feet (3,000 meters).

Temperatures within a region vary little from season to season. For example, Bogotá, which lies about 8,660 feet (2,640 meters) above sea level in the Andes, has an average temperature of 58° F. (14° C) in January and 57° F. (14° C) in July. Each year, most of Colombia has one or two wet seasons with heavy daily rainfall, and one or two dry seasons with little or no rainfall.

Economy

Colombia is a developing country. Its economy has long depended heavily on agriculture. Since the 1950's, however, manufacturing has steadily grown in importance. Most businesses are privately owned. But the government is active in guiding the economy.

Agriculture employs slightly more than a fifth of Colombia's workers and accounts for about half of all export earnings. The country's varied climate and terrain enable farmers to grow a variety of products.

Coffee is Colombia's leading export crop by far. About an eighth of the world's trade in coffee comes from Colombia. Coffee trees grow on more than 300,000 small Colombian farms. Other major crops include bananas, cassava, corn, cotton, potatoes, rice, and sugar cane. Cattle are raised for meat, milk, and leather exports. Flowers are also an important source of income.

A small number of wealthy landholders own most of the farmland in Colombia not used to grow coffee. They hire workers or rent land to tenant farmers. Tenant farmers and many landowners work very small farms and produce barely enough to feed their families.

Manufacturing employs about a fifth of Colombia's workers. Most factories are in or near Bogotá, Medellín, and Cali. Many of them are small, family-operated plants. Colombia's chief manufactured products include textiles and clothing, processed foods and beverages, chemicals, metal products, and cement.

Mining is a rapidly growing industry in Colombia. Petroleum and coal are major exports. Only coffee provides more income. Colombia also has large reserves of natural gas and iron ore. In addition, it supplies more than 90 per cent of the world's emeralds. It is also a leading producer of gold. Large underground salt deposits supply the raw material for Colombia's thriving chemical industry.

Service industries include stores, banks, insurance firms, transportation and communication companies, and institutions that provide community services, such as schools, hospitals, and government agencies. Service industries employ about two-fifths of all Colombian workers. Many of these workers, such as salespeople and office clerks, hold low-paying jobs that require few skills.

Energy sources. Hydroelectric plants supply about 70 per cent of Colombia's electricity. Oil, gas, and coal produce the rest. In spite of Colombia's vast energy resources, some rural areas lack electricity.

Trade. Coffee is Colombia's leading export. It accounts for about half of all export earnings. The government has tried to reduce Colombia's dependence on income from coffee. As a result, exports of other farm goods have become increasingly important. Colombia's chief imports include chemicals, machinery, and transportation equipment. Colombia trades mainly with the United States, Venezuela, Japan, and Germany.

Authorities estimate that the smuggling of illegal drugs, such as cocaine and marijuana, from Colombia into the United States and other countries produces nearly twice the income that coffee does. However, only a few Colombians control the drug traffic and benefit

Loren McIntyre, Cher Agency

Colorful textiles rank among Colombia's leading manufactured goods. The textile industry uses cotton grown in Colombia. The factory above is in Medellín.

from the huge sums of money brought into the country. See also the *Colombia today* section of this article.

Transportation and communication. The Magdalena River once served as Colombia's chief transportation route. A major railway and highway run along its valley. Less than 3 per cent of Colombians own an automobile. Bus travel is popular. Bus routes link most cities. Air travel is very important because of the rugged terrain. Airlines serve all parts of the country. Bogotá, Medellín, and Cali have major international airports.

Colombia has an average of about 1 radio for every 10 people and 1 television set for every 15 people. Colombians have great respect for the printed word. About 30 daily newspapers are published in the country. *El Espectador* and *El Tiempo* have the largest circulations. Both are independently owned and published in Bogotá, though they are sold throughout the country. Many of Colombia's political leaders, including several former presidents, have been journalists or newspaper editors.

History

Early days. Many Indian groups lived in what is now Colombia long before the first Europeans arrived. They included settled farming communities and nomadic hunting and fishing groups. The Chibcha, an advanced civilization in the Andes, traded emeralds and salt for gold and cotton with Indians along the coast.

By 1500, Spanish explorers had sailed along Colombia's Caribbean coast. The first permanent Spanish settlement in South America was founded at Santa Marta in 1525. A Spanish lawyer, Gonzalo Jiménez de Quesada, led an expedition into the Andes from 1536 to 1538 and conquered the Chibcha. In 1538, Jiménez de Quesada founded Bogotá, which he named after the Chibcha chief Bacatá. He called the surrounding area the New Kingdom of Granada because it reminded him of the region in Spain known as Granada.

Spanish rule gradually spread over the New Kingdom of Granada as Spanish colonists founded more and more towns. The colony lacked the mineral wealth of Mexico and Peru. But it produced emeralds, platinum, and some gold. Spanish settlers in the Andes forced the Indians to work in the mines and on large estates that raised cattle and grain. Many Indians died of mistreatment or of diseases brought by the Spaniards. Some Indians and Spaniards intermarried, producing the beginning of a mestizo population. Along the Caribbean coast, the Spaniards brought in black slaves from Africa to work on sugar cane and cacao plantations.

Most settlements in the New Kingdom of Granada were isolated by the rugged terrain, which made the colony difficult to unify and to govern. In 1564, the Spanish government appointed a president to govern the colony. In 1717, Spain combined the colony with neighboring territories into one large colony called the Viceroyalty of the New Kingdom of Granada. The viceroyalty consisted of what are now Colombia, Venezuela, Ecuador, and Panama. Bogotá was the capital.

Independence. Although the New Kingdom of Granada had some able presidents, many colonists disliked Spanish rule. In 1780 and 1781, many people violently protested against new taxes. Spain crushed the revolt. But a movement for independence had begun.

Most parts of the viceroyalty set up independent governments in 1810. The French army occupied Spain at that time, and Spain's South American colonies took advantage of the mother country's weakness to declare their freedom. Spain sent troops to South America after the defeat of France in 1814. Bitter fighting followed.

In 1819, the Venezuelan general Simón Bolívar defeated Spain in the Battle of Boyacá, north of Bogotá. Bolívar then became the first president of Gran Colombia, a republic made up of the territory of the former viceroyalty. The name Colombia was chosen in honor of Christopher Columbus. Gran Colombia lasted only a short time. By 1830, Venezuela and Ecuador had broken away and become separate nations.

Political disorder troubled Colombia from its start as a separate country. Conflicts arose over how strong the central government should be and how much influence the Roman Catholic Church should have on the government. These conflicts split the country into two groups. One group supported a strong central government and a powerful role for the church. It later became the Conservative Party. The other group favored a weak central government and strong regional governments. This group, which became the Liberal Party, also wanted to limit the role of the church.

Disputes between Colombia's Liberal and Conservative parties often erupted into violence and civil war. The country had nine Constitutions after independence, partly because each administration wanted to write a new Constitution after taking office. The Constitution of 1853 abolished slavery. The Constitution of 1886, which established the Republic of Colombia, represented a victory for the Conservatives. It provided for a strong central government. But it did not prevent a fierce civil war, called the War of the Thousand Days, which was fought from 1899 to 1902.

The 1900's. Colombia lost Panama in 1903. That year, the Colombian Senate refused to approve a treaty that allowed the United States to build a canal across Panama. Panama then revolted against Colombia with help from the United States and quickly agreed to the canal project. In 1922, the United States paid Colombia $25 million for the loss of Panama. During World War II (1939-1945), Colombia helped the United States keep the Panama Canal open.

Continuing disputes between Colombia's two major political parties reached a climax in 1948. That year, a popular Liberal Party leader, Jorge Eliécer Gaitán, was assassinated in Bogotá. Riots followed that left the center of Bogotá in ruins and many people dead. The fighting soon spread to the countryside, where warfare and banditry continued until the mid-1960's. Colombians call this period La Violencia (The Violence). About 200,000 Colombians were killed during La Violencia.

By 1957, conditions in Colombia had become so unbearable that the Liberal and Conservative parties agreed to form a coalition (joint) government. Between 1958 and 1974, they shared all political offices, and the leaders of each party alternated as the nation's president every four years. The coalition, known as the National Front, restored the people's confidence in their government and improved the economy.

Colombia today has many of the same social and economic problems that trouble other Latin-American nations. A major problem is the unequal distribution of wealth. A small number of Colombians hold most of the country's wealth and political power. But large numbers of people, especially in rural areas, suffer from malnutrition, poverty, and poor education. At times, unrest among students, city workers, and rural people flares up into violent antigovernment outbursts.

Unlike many other Latin-American countries, Colombia has had an elected government throughout most of its history. Today, a major government concern is to promote economic growth by curbing inflation, reducing Colombia's dependence on coffee, and developing the nation's mineral resources. Colombia maintains close ties with the United States.

In the mid-1980's, Colombia's government began a determined effort to stop the country's large drug traffic. Huge amounts of drugs were being smuggled into the United States. The Colombian government's efforts to stop the drug traffic have been met with violent resistance by the country's drug dealers. The dealers declared "total war" against everyone involved in the campaign against their drug trade. They killed large numbers of public officials, including judges, and placed bombs in the offices of newspapers that spoke out against drug traffic. Stopping the drug traffic is also difficult because the illegal drug trade provides jobs and income for many people in Colombia. In 1989, the United States supplied the Colombian government with military equipment and advisers to help it oppose the drug dealers. Also, Colombia agreed to *extradite* (surrender) citizens that the United States wanted to try in court for drug-related offenses.　William J. Smole

Related articles in *World Book* include:

Cities

Bogotá	Medellín	Santa Marta

Other related articles

Andes Mountains	García Márquez, Gabriel José	Panama (History)
Bolívar, Simón		Panama Canal
Chibcha Indians	Pan-American conferences	South America

Outline

I. **Government**
    A. National government   D. Courts
    B. Local government   E. Armed forces
    C. Politics
II. **People**
    A. Population   E. Education   H. Recreation
    B. Ancestry   F. Clothing   I. Religion
    C. Language   G. Food and drink   J. The arts
    D. Way of life
III. **The land**
    A. The Coastal Lowlands   C. The Eastern Plains
    B. The Andes Mountains
IV. **Climate**
V. **Economy**
    A. Agriculture   E. Energy sources
    B. Manufacturing   F. Trade
    C. Mining   G. Transportation and communication
    D. Service industries
VI. **History**

Questions

For whom was Colombia named?
What is Colombia's leading crop?
What parts of Colombia have a chilly climate?
What is unusual about Colombia's coastline?
What three countries were once part of Colombia?

Where do most of Colombia's people live?
What is the ancestry of most Colombians?
Why is air travel very important in Colombia?
What was *La Violencia*?
Why can Colombian farmers grow many kinds of crops?

Additional resources

American University. *Area Handbook for Colombia.* 3rd ed. U.S. Government Printing Office, 1977.

Jacobsen, Peter O., and Kristensen, P.S. *A Family in Colombia.* Watts, 1986. For younger readers.

Kline, Harvey F. *Colombia: Portrait of Unity and Diversity.* Westview, 1983.

Colombo, *kuh LUHM boh* (pop. 683,000), is the capital, major seaport, and largest city of Sri Lanka. It lies on the west coast (see **Sri Lanka** [map]). Most of the island's shipping passes through its harbor. Colombo is the center of Sri Lanka's tea, coconut, and cotton trade.

Colombo is an old city, founded before the mid-1300's. Scholars believe the city was originally known as *Kolamba,* a native term meaning both *port* and *leafy mango tree.* The name *Colombo* is the European version of this term. The Portuguese, who came in 1505, were the first Europeans to control Colombo. The Dutch occupied the city from 1656 to 1796 and erected a number of buildings that still stand. Perhaps the most impressive is the Wolfendhal Church, built in 1749. Colombo is also the home of the University of Sri Lanka. According to tradition, Buddha visited the temple of Kalaniya just outside Colombo. Commonwealth of Nations leaders set up the Colombo Plan there in 1950.   Robert LaPorte, Jr.

Colombo Plan, *kuh LUHM boh,* provides assistance for economic development to countries of south and Southeast Asia. The assistance includes training personnel, scientific research in agriculture and industry, consultative services, and financial aid.

The Consultative Committee, which directs the program, has headquarters in Colombo, Sri Lanka. It consists of representatives from the 26 member countries: Afghanistan, Australia, Bangladesh, Bhutan, Burma, Cambodia, Canada, Fiji, India, Indonesia, Iran, Japan, Laos, Malaysia, the Maldives, Nepal, New Zealand, Pakistan, Papua New Guinea, the Philippines, Singapore, South Korea, Sri Lanka, Thailand, the United Kingdom, and the United States.

Member countries within the region plan their own development programs with the advice of the committee. They pay most of the cost of these programs. Member countries outside the region contribute financial assistance and cooperate in other ways. The Colombo Plan Technical Cooperation Scheme is the chief means for technical cooperation.

Percy Spender, then foreign minister of Australia, proposed the idea of the Colombo Plan at a meeting of the Commonwealth Foreign Ministers at Colombo in January 1950. The Consultative Committee held its first meeting in May 1950 and published the principles of the plan in November. The Colombo Plan began operating in July 1951.   Norman D. Palmer

See also **Australia** (The postwar years).

Colón, *koh LOHN* (pop. 59,840), is the third largest city in Panama. Only Panama City and San Miguelito have more people. Colón is in central Panama, at the Atlantic Ocean end of the Panama Canal (see **Panama** [map]).

Colón is one of Latin America's busiest commercial centers. Since 1953, it has had a *free trade zone,* where merchants can import and export goods without paying *duties* (taxes). As a result, many trading vessels carry a variety of goods to and from Colón. Merchant ships from many nations also anchor at Cristóbal, just south of Colón, while waiting for passage through the canal. The main streets of Colón are often crowded with sailors, traders, and tourists. The city has many bars, nightclubs, and gambling establishments. Colón also has duty-free shops, which sell many products at low prices. Many Colón residents are descendants of people who came from Jamaica and other Caribbean islands to work on the Panama Canal, which opened in 1914.

Colón was founded as a result of the California gold rush. The city began in 1849 as the starting point of a railroad that carried people across the Isthmus of Panama. These people came by ship from the Eastern United States, crossed the isthmus, then continued by ship to California. The town was first named *Aspinwall* after one of the railroad's builders. In 1890, the name was changed to *Colón,* the Spanish word for *Columbus,* to honor Christopher Columbus. Columbus had landed nearby in 1502.   Nathan A. Haverstock

Colon, *KOH luhn,* is a mark of punctuation shown as :. Its primary function is to separate an introduction from what it introduces: a list, a long quotation, an illustration, or an explanation. A colon is most often used when the words preceding it form a complete sentence, as in the second sentence of this article. There are two exceptions. A colon ends the formal opening of a business letter, and it may be used after the main headings of an outline. See also **Punctuation.**   Susan M. Gass

Colon, *KOH luhn,* is a part of the large intestine. This muscular tube carries *chyme* (partially digested food) from the *cecum* (the first part of the large intestine) to the *rectum* (the last part). The colon is divided into four sections. The *ascending colon* extends upward on the right side of the abdominal cavity. It joins the *transverse colon,* which extends across the cavity to the opposite side. This section meets the *descending colon,* which passes down the left side and joins the S-shaped *sigmoid colon.* In human beings, the colon is about 5 feet (1.5 meters) long. It removes water and mineral salts from the chyme. Its strong muscles contract and relax and so push the residue toward the rectum. Mucus that covers the colon's inner surfaces lubricates them and eases the passage of chyme.   Arnold Gerald Coran

See also **Human body** (Trans-Vision); **Colitis; Diverticulitis; Dysentery; Intestine.**

Colonel. See **Rank, Military.**

Colonial architecture. See **Architecture** (Colonial architecture in America); **Colonial life in America** (The home; pictures); **Georgian architecture.**

Colonial Dames of America, National Society of the, is a society of women organized in 1891 to create an interest in American colonial history. Membership is by invitation and is based on descent from some ancestor who came to an American colony before 1750, and who, by distinguished services, contributed to the founding of the nation. The society was organized in Philadelphia. It has about 16,000 members. Headquarters are at Dumbarton House, 2715 Q Street NW, Washington, DC 20007.   Critically reviewed by the National Society of The Colonial Dames of America

Colonial life
in America

Many different kinds of people lived in the 13 English colonies that became the United
States. This picture shows just
a few of them, including, *left
to right,* an Indian, a Pilgrim, a
New England farmer, a house-
wife, a town crier, and a
Southern planter and his
daughter.

Colonial life in America. The story of the American
colonists is one of the great adventure tales of all time. It
is the story of determined men and women who sailed
across the Atlantic Ocean from Europe, conquered a
wilderness, fought the native Indian inhabitants, and
founded a new nation. The colonial period began with
the settlement of Jamestown in 1607, and ended with the
start of the Revolutionary War in 1775.

Most of the colonists were English. But America also
attracted thousands of Dutch, French, Germans, Scotch-
Irish, Scots, and Swedes. The colonists brought different
customs and religious beliefs but shared a common
dream. All were dissatisfied with life in the Old World
and wanted to make a better life in the New World.

The English were latecomers to the Americas, but
they were the first Europeans to live in the New World
in large numbers. England hoped to compete with other
European powers for the riches of the New World.
Spain had already developed a huge colonial empire in
Central and South America. France came to control Canada and much of the Mississippi Valley.

The Spanish and French were interested chiefly in

*James Kirby Martin, the contributor of this article, is Professor
of History at the University of Houston, and editor of* Interpreting Colonial America: Selected Readings. *The paintings and
drawings—unless otherwise noted—are by H. Charles McBarron, a special consultant to the Smithsonian Institution.*

sending furs, gold, and other riches back to Europe.
They also wanted to convert the Indians to Roman Catholicism. Their early settlements served as outposts for
soldiers and traders, or as missions conducted by
priests. On the other hand, the English colonies were
settled by people from almost every walk of life. These
people wanted to set up permanent homes in America.

In making America their homeland, the colonists occasionally received help from the Indians. But most
often, the Indians viewed them as invaders and fought
to keep their land. The colonists, however, drove the Indians west and took the land. They produced plenty of
food and other items on their farms and plantations. The
colonists carried on a thriving trade with England and
other countries. They built cabins, mansions, villages,
and cities. They established churches, schools, and local
institutions of government.

By the end of the colonial period, most colonists enjoyed living conditions equal to those of Europe's
wealthiest nations. They also had more freedom to govern themselves than did any other people at that time.

This article deals entirely with the 13 original English
colonies that became the United States. For the history
of each colony, from settlement to statehood, see the
separate *World Book* articles on the states, such as
Georgia (History). See also **United States, History of the**
(The colonial heritage). For the history of other colonies,
see **Canada, History of; Latin America** (History).

The Thirteen Colonies

Between 1607 and 1733, the English established 13 permanent colonies on the Atlantic coast of North America. Most of the early settlements developed through business projects operated by individuals or by companies that were organized by English merchants. These people obtained permits from the king to colonize lands in the New World that he claimed belonged to him.

The English colonizers had two main goals: (1) to make profits, and (2) to expand English trade and industry. They advertised America as a land of opportunity, and persuaded many Europeans to migrate to the colonies. Many merchants provided the settlers with transportation, land, and tools.

Why the colonists came to America

America gave thousands of Europeans a chance to make a new start. The settlers knew they faced serious problems and would suffer severe hardships. But they had important reasons for risking the dangerous voyage across about 3,000 miles (5,000 kilometers) of ocean.

Economic opportunities. The settlers included many people who could not find work in their European homelands. Everyone could find some sort of work in America. The New World had rich land to farm and much timber to cut. Its waters and woodlands provided plenty of fish and game. These offerings were strong attractions for people who could not make a decent living in Europe.

Freedom of worship. Some of the settlers, beginning with the Pilgrims, moved to America chiefly because they hoped to gain freedom of worship. Throughout the colonial period, other groups headed for the colonies to escape rulers who persecuted them because of their religious beliefs. Among these groups were Quakers, Roman Catholics, Huguenots, and Jews.

The Thirteen Colonies in 1763

This map shows the 13 British colonies that became the United States. Their population grew to nearly 2 million in a little more than 150 years after a small band of Englishmen established the first permanent settlement at Jamestown.

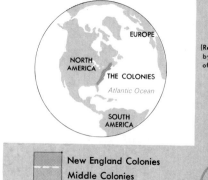

	New England Colonies
	Middle Colonies
	Southern Colonies
	Proclamation Line of 1763

Distance Scale
0 Miles   200   400
0 Kilometres   400   600

WORLD BOOK map-FHa

Land ownership. Many settlers came to America because they were offered land free or at low cost. In those days, owning land gave people a feeling of independence, and the promise of a good life for their children. Land ownership made a person a *freeholder.* A freeholder had certain rights in the community, generally including the right to vote.

Land was distributed in various ways in the colonies. Under English law, all the land belonged to the king. The king issued permits, called *charters,* which allowed individuals or companies to colonize a certain area. Then each *proprietor* (individual owner) or company distributed the land to settlers. In the early colonization of Virginia, the company gave each settler 100 acres (40 hectares) of free land to develop. Later, the king took back the company's charter and established direct royal control over the colony. Under royal control, each new settler in the colony received some free land, usually 50 acres (20 hectares). A person could purchase more land for about five shillings per 50 acres. A system of *headrights* also provided for free land. Under this system, anyone who paid for the transportation of a settler received 50 acres free.

In the Northern Colonies—a region that was called New England—land was assigned to groups of settlers who wanted to form a new community, or *town.* After space was left for public buildings, town proprietors divided the land among the settlers. Each settler got land for a house, garden, and cow shed. A settler also had a strip of farmland for raising crops.

In most of the other colonies, early settlers started as freeholders. Proprietors or companies gave the settlers some land, and sold them more at bargain prices. In some colonies, individuals got large tracts of land by promising to develop the property. The promoters

Bettmann Archive

Advertising helped sell shares of the stock companies that developed England's early settlements in the New World.

The colonies and the dates of their first permanent settlements

Virginia	1607	Delaware	1638
Massachusetts	1620	Pennsylvania	1643
New Hampshire	1623	North Carolina	c. 1653
New York	1624	New Jersey	1660
Connecticut	1633	South Carolina	1670
Maryland	1634	Georgia	1733
Rhode Island	1636		

brought settlers to the colony and gave them some land free. After the colony developed, the promoters could charge high prices for the remaining land.

Early settlements

The English made an unsuccessful attempt to establish a colony in North America in 1585. That year, a group sponsored by Sir Walter Raleigh started a settlement on Roanoke Island, off the coast of what is now North Carolina. The settlers soon returned to England, and another group landed in 1587. This group disappeared mysteriously (see **Lost Colony**).

In 1606, two trading firms, the Virginia Company of London and the Virginia Company of Plymouth, were granted a colonizing charter from King James I (see **London Company; Plymouth Company**). Two colonies were planned: one between present-day New York and the Carolinas and one between New York and Newfoundland. Although the Virginia Company of Plymouth soon failed, the charter led to the eventual establishment of Jamestown and Plymouth. Experiences in these colonies guided future English colonization in America.

Jamestown was the first permanent English colony in America. The first known Europeans to land on what is now Jamestown Island, in Virginia, were about 100 men and boys. They came ashore on May 24, 1607 (May 14, according to the calendar then in use). The group planned to explore Virginia and trade with the Indians.

Serious problems almost ruined the colony. The area was swampy and unhealthful. About two-thirds of the original adventurers soon died of disease or starvation. More people came to Jamestown, but food was still scarce. So many settlers died in the winter of 1609-1610 that the period became known as the "starving time."

The Europeans expected to find gold and other treasures in the wilderness, but they found none. There was nothing that they could send back to England for sale except lumber products. By 1614, they had learned how to raise tobacco. Exporting tobacco saved the colony by providing a way for the settlers to support themselves.

Hostile Indians added to the difficulties. At first, the Indians were friendly. But they soon realized that the Europeans intended to take their lands. The Indians began to attack the adventurers. Relations improved after Chief Powhatan's daughter, Pocahontas, married John Rolfe, a colonist, in 1614. Powhatan's death in 1618 ended the period of cooperative relations. The Indians killed many settlers in a massacre in 1622.

In spite of many hard times, Jamestown survived. Planters and their families replaced the explorers and traders. The Virginia Company of London also sent young women to Jamestown to marry bachelors. The Jamestown colony survived chiefly because the colonists learned how to produce their own food and supplies and because family life developed after women settled there. See **Jamestown; Virginia** (History).

Plymouth was the second permanent English settlement in America. A group of men, women, and children who had separated from the Church of England established the colony in 1620 on the southeastern shore of what is now Massachusetts. They became known as Pilgrims because of their wanderings in search of religious freedom. They were farmers and skilled workers who wanted to raise their families where they could live according to their religious beliefs. These beliefs required them to work hard and live simply.

Although the Pilgrims were quite different from the Jamestown adventurers, they had many similar prob-

New England village   Many New England settlers lived on the Atlantic Coast and earned their living chiefly as fishermen, shipbuilders, or seagoing traders. The rocky soil was not suitable for large farms, but New England had plenty of fine shipbuilding timber, and some of the best fishing waters in the world.

lems. The Pilgrims' poor diets helped diseases attack them during the winter, soon after they landed. Only about half the 99 Pilgrims survived the winter.

The Pilgrims had good relations with the local Indians, who had been suffering from deadly diseases for several years. Thus, the Indians wanted allies and soon signed a friendship treaty with the Pilgrims. The treaty lasted about 54 years. The Pilgrims also had the help of Squanto, an Indian who taught them how to raise corn and showed them the best fishing areas. See **Squanto.**

The story of how the Pilgrims established Plymouth Colony is one of the most famous chapters of American history. This story shows how courage and hard work can triumph over tremendous difficulties. The Pilgrims did not change their simple way of life as their colony developed. As a result, Plymouth never became prosperous. In 1691, it became part of the large colony of Massachusetts. For the story of how the Pilgrims developed their colony, see **Plymouth Colony.** See also **Pilgrims.**

Development of the colonies

After English colonists had settled Jamestown and Plymouth, large areas of the Atlantic seacoast were colonized. The later colonists suffered hardships, but there were no more "starving times" in colonial America.

The colonies are generally grouped according to location: (1) the Northern or New England Colonies, (2) the Middle Colonies, and (3) the Southern Colonies.

The Northern Colonies were Connecticut, Massachusetts, New Hampshire, and Rhode Island. Most New Englanders lived in villages and had small farms. The climate was too cool and the soil too rocky for large farms. However, New England Colonies had plenty of fine timber and some of the best fishing waters in the world.

The Middle Colonies were Delaware, New Jersey, New York, and Pennsylvania. Their climate favored large farms, where wheat and other grains were grown.

The Southern Colonies were Georgia, Maryland, North Carolina, South Carolina, and Virginia. The warm climate and rich soil of the South were fine for growing tobacco and rice. Life in the Southern Colonies developed chiefly on plantations.

Types of colonies. There were three major types of American colonies: (1) *royal,* (2) *proprietary,* and (3) *corporate.* A royal colony was under the direct control of the king. A proprietary colony was controlled by a prominent individual—the proprietor—under a grant from the king. A corporate colony was operated, as a rule, under a charter obtained from the king by a company's stockholders.

All the 13 English colonies were founded either as proprietary or corporate colonies. By the time the Revolutionary War began in 1775, eight of them had become royal colonies—Georgia, Massachusetts, New Hampshire, New Jersey, New York, North Carolina, South Carolina, and Virginia. Two colonies—Maryland and Pennsylvania—were proprietary, and Pennsylvania's governor also ruled the region that later became Delaware. Connecticut and Rhode Island could be considered corporate colonies. However, their charters had been obtained by groups of colonists in America, not by stockholders in England.

Population growth. The population of the colonies increased rapidly during the late 1600's and the 1700's because of both local births and a large number of immigrants. Most of the new immigrants made their homes in the Middle Colonies, though the other colo-

Philadelphia market   Certain days of each week were declared "market days" in every colonial city. On those days, the farmers of the surrounding countryside brought fresh meats, fruits, and vegetables to be sold in the city's special market areas. This painting was adapted from a print made in the late 1700's.

nies also had many new settlers. The immigrants included large groups of Germans and Scotch-Irish. Like many early settlers, they had fled hard times and religious persecution. The Germans became known as the best farmers among the colonists. The Scotch-Irish won fame as the most fearsome Indian fighters.

The birth rate in America during the 1700's was probably higher than that of any other country. The birth rate and increased immigration caused the population of the colonies to grow rapidly. It was about 250,000 in 1700, and increased to more than 1 million by 1750. The population doubled to over 2 million by 1770. In 1775, there were nearly $2\frac{1}{2}$ million people in the colonies.

Population estimates made for 1770 show that the Southern Colonies had almost as many people as New England and the Middle Colonies combined. The southern population was close to 1 million, New England's was about 571,000, and that of the Middle Colonies was about 556,000. Virginia was by far the largest colony, with over 447,000 people. Massachusetts had more than 266,000 people, and Pennsylvania was third, with over 240,000. Georgia, the youngest colony, had the smallest population, about 23,000.

As the population of the colonies increased, trade and manufacturing developed rapidly. These activities centered mainly in towns that had good harbors. Five towns became the most important American cities of the 1700's. They were, in order of size of population: Philadelphia (including suburbs), New York City, Boston, Charles Town, S.C. (renamed Charleston in 1783), and Newport, R.I.

Philadelphia was the busiest colonial port and the largest manufacturing center of the mid-1700's. In 1760, the Philadelphia area had over 23,000 people, and by 1775 its population had grown to about 40,000. New York City had a population of about 25,000; Boston, 16,000; Charles Town, 12,000; and Newport, 11,000.

Relations with the Indians

In a few places, the Indians were friendly and helped the settlers. But in most places, tribes tried to drive the colonists out of lands that had been their hunting grounds for thousands of years. Many terrible battles occurred. See **Indian wars.**

The fighting between the colonists and the Indians became worse as settlements pushed westward. Large-scale warfare between England and France deepened the conflict. In four wars from 1689 to 1763, English and French troops in America battled each other over land claims. Many English colonists fought French colonists who had settled in Canada and the Mississippi Valley. Each side had strong supporters among the Indian tribes. For that reason, these wars became known as the French and Indian wars. As a result of the last of the four wars, France lost almost all its possessions in North America to Great Britain. For the details of these wars, see **French and Indian wars.**

After their victory, the British recognized the claims of the Indians to the western lands that the tribes occupied. In 1763, the British issued a proclamation that prohibited colonists from settling west of the Appalachian Mountains. The British hoped to prevent additional fighting between the colonists and the Indians.

Settlers who were ready to move to lands beyond the mountains refused to obey the proclamation. Opposition by the colonists to the Proclamation of 1763 helped lead to the Revolutionary War (see **Revolutionary War in America** [Background and causes of the war]).

Southern plantation A colonial planter built his mansion to resemble a fine English country house. Behind the mansion were a kitchen, smokehouse, coach house, barns, and slaves' cabins. Most plantations were on a bay or river and had a wharf where their products could be loaded on ships.

An engraving from *A Popular History of the United States.* Library of Congress

America's first representative legislature, the House of Burgesses, met at Jamestown in 1619. Its elected members, with the governor and council, made the laws of Virginia.

Society and government

Colonial society consisted of several classes. At the top class were wealthy merchants and planters, and their families. They were called the "gentry" or the "better sort." They lived in mansions and most often traveled in comfortable carriages. The men used "Esquire" after their names, and their wives were addressed as "Madam." Some of the gentry were also well educated. They included ministers, lawyers, and doctors.

Below the gentry were members of the "middling sort." Most of them were farmers or shopkeepers who owned property but were not wealthy. This class also included craftworkers. The next lowest rank was called the "lower sort" or the "meaner sort." It consisted of poor people, such as unskilled laborers. At the bottom of society were people who lacked freedom, such as slaves and *indentured servants.* An indentured servant was a person who came to the colonies under a contract to work for a master without wages. Instead of paying wages, the master paid for the servant's passage from Europe. The servant also received food, clothing, and housing. Contracts usually covered four years.

The social structure of colonial America was more flexible than that of Europe. Members of the lower classes—except slaves—could rise to a higher class. A successful farmer could become the owner of a large estate. If his sons went to college, they became members of the gentry. Shopkeepers or craftworkers might become wealthy merchants. Indentured servants, after serving their contract, received "freedom dues," including land for a farm or tools to set up a trade. Skilled

workers, known as "artisans," earned good wages and could invest money in property or a business.

Only slaves were forced to spend their lives at the lowest level of society. Most slaves had no rights. Slaves were blacks, originally brought from Africa against their will and sold to planters. Most slaves lived in the Southern Colonies and worked as field hands, skilled plantation laborers, or house servants. In the other colonies, slaves usually worked in homes, fields, or shops. Slaves and their children could be freed by their owner. But freed blacks generally found it hard to make a living. They often had to accept jobs that paid low wages. If they left home, they might be arrested as runaway slaves and sold into slavery again. But some colonies forced newly freed slaves to leave.

Government. Each colony had a governor and a legislature. The king of England appointed the governor of royal colonies. In proprietary colonies, the proprietor named the governor. In Connecticut and Rhode Island, the people elected the governor. All the colonial legislatures except Pennsylvania's *unicameral* (one-house) system consisted of two houses, and resembled the English Parliament in structure. Today, most state legislatures still have that basic structure.

A colonial legislature was called an Assembly, except in New England, where it was known as a General Court. Male colonists elected the members of the lower house in all the colonies. Women did not have the right to vote. In Connecticut and Rhode Island, male citizens also elected the upper house. In Massachusetts, the

WORLD BOOK illustrations by Robert Addison

Public disgrace in the pillory or the ducking stool was a common punishment for colonists found guilty of such minor offenses as drunkenness, swearing, slander, or disturbing the peace.

upper house was elected by the lower house. In the other colonies, the king or the proprietor appointed the upper house, which was known as the Council.

The laws passed by a colonial legislature had to be approved by the English government. Governors appointed by the king had the responsibility of carrying out his orders. The king expected these governors to enforce the laws of England, especially acts of Parliament that regulated colonial trade.

Voting requirements differed in the various colonies, and changed from time to time. One of the most important requirements was property ownership. By 1750, most white adult male citizens who owned property could vote. Other possessions could be substituted for property. Also, a tenant farmer could vote in some colonies if his lease ran for a certain number of years. Requirements for voting often were poorly enforced. People who could not vote, besides women, were indentured servants, slaves, and the very poor.

Most of the colonies limited voting and other rights of citizenship to members of a certain church group, especially during early colonial times. In the royal colonies, citizens were expected to be members of the Church of England, often called the Anglican Church. In New England, all citizens were expected to attend the Congregational Church. As a result, Roman Catholics and Jews could not vote in most colonies.

The colonists based their laws on certain ideas that suited their social system, religious values, and business life. They believed that men who owned property had a strong interest in good government. The gentry had the time, talent, and experience for public service, and voters most often elected them to office. In most elections, only a small percentage of those qualified to vote went to the polls. This occurred partly because of poor roads and great distances to polling places.

Local government in the colonies was based on English county and town governments. In the Southern Colonies, the county court conducted most public business. This court consisted of justices of the peace, appointed by the governor. The justices tried certain civil and criminal cases. They also levied taxes, supervised road construction and ferry service, and organized the *militia* (citizen soldiers). In New England, the courts only dealt with matters of law. Citizens held town meetings at which they voted on local laws and on town officials. The town meeting still exists in some New England towns (see **Town meeting**). In the Middle Colonies, there were county and town units of local government.

Law enforcement in the colonies was the job of constables and sheriffs. Persons accused of a crime punishable by death were tried by certain high courts. Death by hanging was the customary penalty for armed robbery, counterfeiting, murder, piracy, or treason.

Local courts with juries tried persons accused of such minor offenses as drunkenness, slander, swearing, theft, disturbing the peace, or breaking the Sabbath. Punishments included fines, public whipping, and suffering disgrace with the pillory, stocks, or ducking stool (see **Pillory; Stocks; Ducking stool**).

Colonial households were large. Some of them included grandparents, aunts, uncles, and cousins living together in one home. Servants and slaves also belonged to the extended family group. All members of the group worked together to support the household.

By law and custom, the colonial father was responsible for the behavior and welfare of every member of the household. He decided on all important matters affecting the family. His wife, children, servants, and slaves obeyed him without question.

Houses. The first settlers built houses that closely resembled those they had known in Europe. The colonists later changed their housing styles so they could make the best use of local building materials. The first cottages of Jamestown and Plymouth had thatched roofs, like English cottages. After the colonists found wood more plentiful than reeds or straw, wood shingles replaced thatch.

All the colonies had plenty of wood, and frame houses could be seen everywhere. In the Northern Colonies, where winters were very cold, the colonists built brick or stone chimneys inside the framework to supply warmth. In some homes, one chimney served several fireplaces. In the Southern Colonies, which had a generally mild climate, chimneys stood outside the framework of most homes.

Most early southern houses had $1\frac{1}{2}$ stories. A typical New England house of the 1600's had two stories in front and one in back. Some New England homes were built of the fieldstone that the colonists found in many areas. In areas near the Appalachian valleys, limestone was used to build many houses. Bricks were made in every colony during the 1700's, but wood cost less and remained the most popular building material throughout the colonial period.

Many houses in the Delaware River Valley and the Hudson River Valley were of Scandinavian or Dutch design. The Swedish colonists who came to Delaware in 1638 built the first log cabins in America. The log cabin became the typical home of the pioneers who moved westward (see **Log cabin**). Most of the houses that were built by the Dutch settlers had $1\frac{1}{2}$ stories. Their doors were divided into upper and lower parts which opened separately. These doors became known as "Dutch doors."

Many wealthy colonial merchants and planters built homes in a style called Georgian architecture. Most Georgian houses were square or rectangular, with a central stair hall and many tall windows. The front door of the house was large and impressive, and the main rooms had fine wood paneling. See **Georgian architecture.**

The mansion of a typical southern plantation stood on a hill and overlooked a bay or river. It was surrounded by gardens, orchards, and shade trees, with a kitchen, laundry, and smokehouse nearby. Farther away were the stables and carriage house, and cabins where the slaves lived.

Some wealthy South Carolina colonists developed a type of town house that was especially suited for the climate of Charles Town. This town house was only one room wide, but had three or four stories and several porches. Cool sea breezes swept through every room of the tall, narrow house.

Furnishings of the first settlers were homemade, except for a few possessions brought from Europe. Many families made most of their own furniture and other household articles throughout the colonial period. Wealthy colonists imported their furnishings, generally from England. After colonial cabinetmakers developed their craft, the homes of the well-to-do had much fine American furniture.

The homemade furnishings of the settlers were plain and strong. Thick wooden planks, set on sturdy supports, served as a table. Blocks of wood, small barrels, or rough benches and stools were used as chairs. Mattresses consisted of canvas bags stuffed with straw and were placed on the floor or on bedsteads made of log slabs.

Life in most colonial homes centered around the fireplace. The women prepared food there, and cooking utensils hung nearby. The fireplace provided most of the family's heat and light, and everyone gathered in front of it to eat, work, relax, or entertain visitors. A spinning wheel stood on the hearth.

The homes of most wealthy colonists had finely designed tables, chairs, beds, chests, and sofas. Some of this furniture came from the shops of such great English furniture designers as Thomas Chippendale, George Hepplewhite, Thomas Sheraton, and the Adam brothers. After 1750, colonial craftworkers copied many favorite English designs. They used native cherry, maple, pine, or walnut, and also mahogany imported from the West Indies.

The chairs and sofas of a Georgian mansion were richly upholstered in leather, tapestry, silk damask, or embroidered linen. Benjamin Franklin attached rockers to the legs of a chair that had a straight back made of slats. The slat-back American rocking chair became popular in many parts of the world.

Tables were graceful, and many had special features that saved space. These features included folding legs, and tops fitted with drop leaves. The drop leaves were hinged parts that rested on the legs when the table was being used. At other times, the legs were folded and the drop leaves lowered.

The most popular chests of drawers were "highboys" and "lowboys." A highboy was large and tall, with many drawers and short legs. A lowboy was a small, low chest of a few drawers. A lowboy often served as a side table. Tall cupboards stood in the halls, bedrooms, kitchen, and dining room. Some, called dressers, were divided into an upper section of open shelves, and a lower section with doors. The open shelves were used to display dishes and pewterware.

Most fine colonial bedrooms had a four-poster—a bed with a tall post at each corner. The four posts supported a *canopy* (overhead covering). Curtains hung from the frame of the canopy, and could be drawn together to keep out cold air. The mattress, stuffed with feathers, rested on woven ropes fastened to the bedstead several feet above the floor. The space between the floor and the mattress generally was used to store a child's bed during the day. This movable bed, called a *trundle bed,* was pulled out at night.

Some well-furnished colonial homes had a handsome clock. The most famous colonial clock was called a grandfather clock. It had a tall wooden case and stood

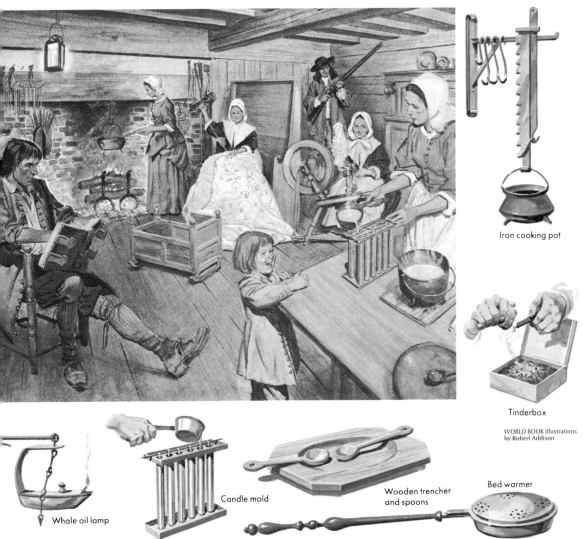

Iron cooking pot

Tinderbox

WORLD BOOK illustrations
by Robert Addison

Whale oil lamp

Candle mold

Wooden trencher
and spoons

Bed warmer

Farmhouse   Every member of the family shared in the tasks of a colonial household. The early settlers made most of their own clothing, furniture, and cooking utensils. In farmhouses throughout the colonies, the family gathered at nightfall to work in the light and warmth of the fireplace.

on the floor. Other furnishings included candlesticks, chandeliers, and mirrors. The windows had heavy curtains made of brocade, damask, or linen. Floors were covered with imported carpets or colorful rugs, hand made in the home.

Clothing in colonial times varied according to a person's occupation or position in the community. Members of a farming family wore rough, homemade garments. Wealthy merchants or planters and their families had expensive clothing, made of imported materials and designed in fashionable English styles. Male servants who worked in the fields sometimes wore only breechcloths in summer.

Making clothing was an important task in most colonial households. On small farms, the women planted and tended a patch of flax, harvested the crop, spun the yarn, and wove it into linen. They wove woolen cloth from yarn spun from the fleece of sheep. Linens and

woolens were colored with dyes made from certain barks, berries, roots, or walnut hulls. The colonists tanned cowhide and deerskin, and made the leather into shoes or leggings.

In summer, workingmen wore breeches and a long linen shirt. In winter, they wore woolen or leather breeches, knitted stockings, and heavy shoes. For outdoor wear in cold weather, a man had a loose-fitting overcoat, leather leggings, woolen mittens, and a fur cap. A woman wore a dress of linen or wool, a petticoat, and a single undergarment called a shift. A cape or hooded cloak was worn outdoors. Children wore the same kind of clothes as adults.

A wealthy colonist ordered fashionable clothing from London, or from a local tailor who copied the latest English styles. A typical style of the times called for close-fitting breeches of brocade, silk, or velvet, fastened at the knees with silver buckles. With the breeches, a gentle-

Fire screen

Spectacles

Writing implements

Foot stove

WORLD BOOK illustrations by Robert Addison

Living room   During the 1700's, many wealthy colonists built mansions in a style known as Georgian architecture. The living room had paneled walls and a large, richly decorated fireplace. Much of the furniture of a mansion was made by skilled craftworkers who copied fashionable English designs.

man wore a white linen shirt with lace ruffles at the neck and wrists. Over the shirt, he wore a long, brightly colored waistcoat and a knee-length coat. The coat had wide, flowing sides, and was decorated with gold braid and several rows of fancy buttons. Silk hose, and shoes with silver buckles completed a colonial gentleman's costume.

A fashionable gentleman wore a wig that he sometimes powdered white. Outdoors, he put a black *cocked hat* (a hat with the brim turned up) on top of the wig. During the late 1600's, wigs were large and expensive. A man who wore one was called a "bigwig." After 1750, many colonial men wore wigs. The most popular wig was small and resembled the wearer's natural hair. It was called a "tie" wig because a man pulled it back and tied it with a short ribbon.

Women of wealthy families wore a low-necked dress with a tight-fitting bodice, and ruffles at the elbows. It

had a full skirt, looped back to display a brightly colored embroidered petticoat. Under the dress, a hoop of steel or whalebone supported the skirt. A tightly laced corset pinched in the waist. A woman of fashion wore silk stockings and silk or leather shoes. She had several types of capes for outdoor wear.

During the 1600's, fashionable women generally wore simple hair styles. The hair was usually arranged so that a loose curl or two hung to the shoulder. Large, fancy hairdos became the fashion about 1760. Servants spent much time helping their mistress pile her hair high on a frame that she wore on her head.

Food was plentiful during most of the colonial period. After the first few years, the colonists kept themselves better supplied with food than any other people in the world. On their farms, they raised grain, cattle, hogs, sheep, chickens, fruits, and vegetables. In the fields and woodlands, they hunted deer, pigeons, squir-

Candelabrum

Candle snuffer
and wick trimmer

Wig powderer

Pannier, worn under hoop skirt

Snuffbox

Clay pipe and pipe-lighting tongs

WORLD BOOK illustrations by Robert Addison

Dining room Wealthy colonists entertained in the style of the gentry of England. They often held large dinner parties at which the guests enjoyed a wide variety of fine foods and wines. The chandelier, dishes, silverware, and table linen were all imported from London.

rels, wild turkeys, and other game. From the river and ocean waters, they took clams, oysters, lobsters, and many kinds of fish.

Corn was a basic food in almost every household. The people ate it in many forms, most commonly as corn bread. A woman mixed corn meal with water or milk, salt, and lard, and shaped it into buns. Then she baked or fried the buns on a hoe or on a griddle, or placed them in the ashes of the fireplace. Corn bread had different names in various parts of colonial America—ash-cake, hoecake, johnnycake, or corn pone. Cooks also made corn hominy. Sometimes they roasted ears of corn in the husks.

Rye or wheat bread was made with yeast. In many homes, the women baked these breads in a small oven that was built into the fireplace or outside the house, against the hot chimney. They also baked bread in an iron bake kettle, which had a tight-fitting lid. The kettle

stood on a bed of hot coals, with embers piled around it and on top of the lid.

Meat or game was usually cooked with vegetables into a stew. Women made the stew in a large iron pot that hung over the fire on a pothook, fastened to a crane or a chimney bar. The iron pot had short legs and sometimes was placed on a bed of coals. Whole fowl or large cuts of meat were often roasted on sharp-pointed rods called spits. Handles on the spits allowed the meat to be turned above the fire.

The colonists had difficulty storing food for the winter because they had no methods of canning or refrigeration. They salted or smoked some meats, and dried or pickled certain vegetables. Root vegetables, and such fruits as apples or pears, were kept in cool, dry cellars. As a rule, the colonists depended on bread and meat for their food during the winter.

Most families ate bread and cold meat for breakfast

and supper. Dinner was served at noon or early in the afternoon. The colonists drank large amounts of beer, cider, rum, or wine with all their meals. They did so because they believed their water was polluted. By the 1700's, tea, coffee, and hot chocolate had become popular.

Health of the colonists was poor by today's standards. Most of the people frequently suffered some type of illness, and they did not know how to treat or prevent many serious illnesses. But people in other places also lacked such knowledge. The medical care the colonists received was probably no worse than that of Europeans.

Contagious diseases sometimes spread rapidly and took many lives in the colonies. The settlers suffered ep-

Detail from the frontispiece to Dilworth's *New Guide to the English Tongue.* Folger Shakespeare Library, Washington, D.C.

Children's games in colonial times included many that are still popular. The youngsters shot marbles, flew kites, and played hopscotch, leapfrog, prisoners' base, and blindman's buff.

From *Alle de Wercken*, 1657-59, by Jacob Cats. Folger Shakespeare Library, Washington, D.C.

Shearing sheep and cutting bristles from hogs supplied materials for many colonial household items. The sheep's wool was spun into yarn, and the hog bristles were used to make brushes.

idemics of measles, smallpox, diphtheria, typhoid fever, scarlet fever, and yellow fever. Other widespread illnesses included dysentery, gout, influenza, pneumonia, rheumatism, scurvy, and tuberculosis.

Most colonists took medicines made of certain barks, herbs, or roots. These medicines, although believed to be powerful cures, usually failed. One helpful medicine was quinine, a bitter substance taken from the bark of the cinchona tree. The colonists used it for a common malarial fever called ague. Doctors still use quinine to treat certain types of malaria. Popular medicines were made from tobacco leaves and the roots of the ginseng plant and the sassafras tree.

There were few trained doctors and nurses during most of the colonial period. Most doctors studied medicine by helping experienced physicians. One of the first public hospitals in America was the Pennsylvania Hospital. It was chartered in Philadelphia in 1751, and still serves the community.

Recreation. The colonists combined work with play whenever they could. They often gathered to perform some task together and, at the same time, to enjoy games, contests, and other recreation. Neighbors got together to help a newcomer build a barn or a house. A barn or house raising was an opportunity for the men and boys to stage foot races, or shooting or wrestling contests. They also competed in plowing or corn husking. The women and girls held quilting bees, and everyone enjoyed spelling bees and singers. All these activities gave people a chance to share good things to eat and drink, and to exchange news and gossip.

Weddings and holidays were important occasions for feasting and amusement. Many wedding celebrations lasted several days, during which the guests feasted, danced, and played card games. Christmas was a joyful holiday season in most of the colonies. But Massachusetts followed the Puritan custom in England and outlawed the celebration of Christmas in 1659. In 1681, the colony repealed this law. Some colonies added Thanksgiving Day to the fall calendar as a harvest feast. Several colonies celebrated May Day as a spring festival.

Horse racing became popular in most of the colonies during the late 1600's. Virginians raised a special type of horse for their sport of *quarter racing,* a quarter-mile (0.4-kilometer) race along a straight path. Cockfighting was also popular in the Southern Colonies. Everywhere, fishing and hunting were favorite sports which kept colonial households well supplied with fresh foods.

The colonial tavern, sometimes called an "ordinary," developed as a favorite gathering place for men. The men gathered in the tavern to talk, smoke, eat and drink, play cards, or read a newspaper. Many taverns had a bowling green, a smooth, flat plot of grass where their customers could bowl.

Colonial children played many games that are still popular, including hopscotch, leapfrog, London Bridge, hide and seek, prisoners' base, and blindman's buff. Colonial toys included balls, dolls, marbles, kites, tops, rolling hoops, and jump ropes. Most toys were homemade, but children from rich families had doll tea sets or toy soldiers that were imported from England. Almost every household had several cats and dogs, and children who lived in the country made pets of young farm animals.

Travel. Most of the early colonists rarely traveled far from home. As a rule, long journeys were made only by traders, or wealthy merchants or planters. These people generally traveled for business or pleasure by boat on rivers, bays, and the coastal waters. Freight and passengers were carried in many types of sailing vessels, including brigantines, schooners, shallops, sloops, and yawls. Large ships that sailed across the ocean carried small boats which could be put over the side for travel on shallow inland waters.

Land transportation was slow and difficult. The first colonial roads were merely paths that followed ancient Indian trails through the woodlands. The colonists widened the paths for travel on horseback, and later for carts or wagons pulled by horses or oxen. Ferries carried travelers across rivers. Most of the wooden bridges built by the colonists could be used only by foot travelers, not by vehicles. By 1760, Philadelphia had two stone bridges.

The colonists put much effort into building roads. By 1760, a person could travel by road from New Hampshire to Georgia. At about the same time, stagecoach service linked Boston with Providence, and New York City with Philadelphia and Annapolis.

By the mid-1700's, comfortable passenger vehicles were being used in the towns by government officials and wealthy colonists. These vehicles included carriages, chariots, and coaches, drawn by four, six, or eight horses; two-horse chaises, curricles, and phaetons; and one-horse "riding chairs." Many carriages had richly carved wooden sides, and seats upholstered in leather or brightly colored cloth. Brass or silver ornaments decorated the harnesses.

A town crier read news to the townsfolk until newspapers came into general use in the mid-1700's.

Colonial stagecoaches began operating in the mid-1700's. Taverns provided food and lodging along the way.

Communication. During the 1600's, the colonists exchanged news chiefly by word of mouth. Someone would learn about an event from a peddler or a ship captain, and repeat the story to his neighbors. Friends exchanged news in letters that they often gave to travelers to deliver.

News was also spread by *postriders*, the first colonial mail deliverers. A postrider carried letters or messages, traveling on horseback along a certain route called a post road. On the way, the postrider picked up news and passed it on to individuals at such stopping places as post offices and taverns. In most towns, a town crier read news to the people.

Mail service operated irregularly in colonial times. Until 1700, it existed only in Massachusetts, New York, and Pennsylvania. In 1753, Benjamin Franklin of Pennsylvania and William Hunter of Virginia were appointed to manage the colonial postal service. Under their direction, post offices were established in all the colonies, and service improved greatly.

Newspapers came into general use after the mid-1700's. The first successful American newspaper, *The Boston News-Letter,* had started publication in 1704. During the next 60 years, newspapers were published in every colony except Delaware and New Jersey.

Etching of an old Pennsylvania inn by E. T. Scowcroft. Free Library of Philadelphia

The task of building homes and communities in a rugged land demanded great energy and effort. As a result, the early American colonists had little time for the arts or sciences. In 1743, Benjamin Franklin wrote that "the first drudgery of settling new colonies" was completed and there could be "leisure to cultivate the finer arts and improve the common stock of knowledge." By the end of the colonial period, some colonists had made important contributions to literature and painting. Other colonists were active in such scientific fields as astronomy and botany.

Literature. The earliest descriptions of colonial life were written to tell Europeans about the settlements in the New World. John Smith wrote about Jamestown and New England, William Bradford described the Plymouth Colony, and John Winthrop told of the Massachusetts Bay Colony.

Religious writings made up the bulk of colonial literature published in America during the 1600's. The first book printed in the colonies was a collection of psalms, published in 1640. Several ministers prepared this book, which became known as the *Bay Psalm Book.* Three religious leaders—Jonathan Edwards, Cotton Mather, and John Woolman—wrote many books and pamphlets during the 1700's. See **Bay Psalm Book.**

Colonial poets also dealt chiefly with religious subjects. Michael Wigglesworth, a New England poet, wrote *Day of Doom,* the most popular literary work of the time. Anne Dudley Bradstreet, another New Englander, became America's first woman poet. She is best known for her collected poems, *The Tenth Muse Lately Sprung Up in America.*

Writings on political subjects became important during the mid-1700's. Dozens of revolutionary pamphlets and poems were circulated after Great Britain passed the Stamp Act of 1765 (see **Stamp Act**). Benjamin Franklin was one of the most influential political writers, but he did not limit himself to politics. Franklin's witty proverbs helped make his *Poor Richard's Almanac* a favorite publication of the colonists. For a detailed account of colonial writers and their works, see the *World Book* article **American literature.**

Painting. During the mid-1700's, several young colonists were trained by visiting European artists. These American artists, who went to Europe for further study and became world famous, included John Singleton Copley, Charles Willson Peale, Gilbert Charles Stuart, and Benjamin West.

Earlier American artists, called *limners,* had little formal training. They traveled throughout the colonies and earned a living by painting portraits of wealthy colonists. Well-known colonial limners included Charles Bridges, Gustavus Hesselius, Henrietta Johnston, John Smibert, and Jeremiah Theüs.

Science. During most of the colonial period, educated people had broad scientific interests. Many of them worked to improve education and expand scientific study in the New World.

Benjamin Franklin won honors throughout the world for his scientific experiments and inventions. He led all the people of his day in the study of electricity. In 1752, Franklin flew a homemade kite during a thunderstorm and proved that lightning is electricity. Then he invented the lightning rod, a way to tame electricity. See **Franklin, Benjamin** (The scientist).

Franklin also encouraged other scientists. In 1727, he formed the Junto, a debating club. Most of the members were interested in science as well as politics. They met regularly in Philadelphia to exchange ideas. In 1743, Franklin founded the American Philosophical Society. This organization became the chief center of colonial science.

John Bartram was the most famous botanist of the period. In 1728, he planted America's first botanical garden. Other noted colonial botanists included John Banister, John Clayton, Cadwallader Colden, John Mitchell, and Alexander Garden, for whom the gardenia was named.

Colonial scientists of the 1700's were well informed about new discoveries in astronomy, chemistry, meteorology, and physics. They often exchanged ideas with European scientists. Many performed laboratory experiments or kept records of rainfall, temperature, and the appearance of comets.

Baptismal Certificate by Henrich Otto. Free Library of Philadelphia

Documentary script, surrounded by floral designs in color, was developed as an art by a number of German colonists.

Colonial Williamsburg

Colonial architecture has been preserved in the stately Governor's Palace reconstructed in Williamsburg, Va.

Mrs. Thomas Van Alstyne by an unknown
artist. New-York Historical Society

Woman's portrait, by a colonial artist with little training, has a glaring
error. The subject is shown with two
right hands.

Portrait of Isaac Royall and His Family by Robert Feke. Harvard Law School, Cambridge, Mass.

Painting of a distinguished New England family is a fine example of the work
of Robert Feke, a colonial artist whose portraits have become famous.

"**The Duke's Plan of 1661,**" one of the earliest maps of a colonial city, was made a
few years before the English captured New Amsterdam and named it New York.

British Museum, London

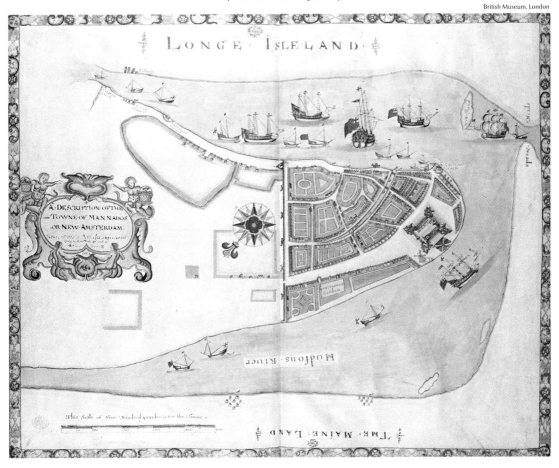

Planting corn for food, a skill learned from the Indians, saved many early settlers from starvation.

The homemade plow, *below left,* and the ancient mattock, *below right,* were important colonial farm tools.

The cradle scythe came into common use during the mid-1700's for harvesting grain on colonial farms.

The wedge-shaped iron froe, a basic colonial tool, was often used to split logs into the slabs that made a sturdy table.

WORLD BOOK illustrations
by Robert Addison

Throughout the colonial period, farming was the most important way of making a living. Farming meant survival for the first settlers. To stay alive, they had to produce food, along with materials for clothing and shelter. As their settlements grew, the colonists raised grains, tobacco, livestock, and other farm products for export.

The colonists also developed such industries as fishing and whaling, lumbering, shipbuilding, ironmaking, rum distilling, and flour milling. Colonial craftworkers made furniture, glassware, pottery, and metalware of pewter, iron, or silver.

Farming

Most colonial farmers were successful because they worked hard and land was plentiful. By today's standards, colonial farming methods were wasteful. The colonists usually planted the same kind of crop repeatedly, and the soil became exhausted after a few harvests. Then the farmers simply cleared more land. The most skillful farmers were the German settlers, who rotated their crops and added fertilizers to the soil. These methods kept their land highly productive.

Tools. The colonial farmer worked mostly with hand tools, including an ax, hoe, scythe, sickle, and spade. He also had a *mattock,* a kind of pickax with flat blades. The farmer used a mattock to break up soil or cut roots. These tools were not much better than the sharpened sticks used by the Indians. Some farmers had a homemade wooden plow. It was so heavy that four horses or oxen were required to pull it. Sometimes farmers used tools called harrows and drags, fitted with iron teeth, to break up the soil or prepare seedbeds.

Crops. In spite of wasteful methods and poor tools, the colonial farmer was as prosperous as any farmer of the day, anywhere in the world. Even in New England,

"Colonel Phillip Skene's sawmill and blockhouse, Fort Ann, N.Y." from a sketch by Thomas Anburey. Library of Congress

Great supplies of lumber were produced by all the colonies. The timber was used in building homes and ships, and in making millions of barrels for colonial trade and industry.

with its rocky land and short growing season, farmers were well-off. They produced enough vegetables, grain, and meat to feed their families, and usually had extra crops for sale.

Corn was the most important crop of early colonial times. The Indians showed the first settlers how to plant and cultivate it, and how to grind the kernels to make corn meal. Farmers in all the colonies raised corn. As colonial farming developed, wheat replaced corn as the chief grain. But farmers continued to raise large crops of corn to feed their livestock.

Wheat was the most valuable crop of the Middle Colonies. There, a farmer had the advantage of excellent soil and a highly favorable climate. The Middle Colonies exported so much wheat and wheat flour that they became known as the "bread colonies." These colonies also exported large quantities of beef and pork to Europe and the West Indies.

Many Maryland and Virginia planters specialized in growing tobacco. But by the 1700's, they also started raising food crops, including corn and wheat, for export. This was because most tobacco exported to England sold for prices that constantly rose and fell. Maryland and Virginia had mills that ground grain.

The farmers of Georgia and South Carolina developed two important crops—rice and indigo. About 1724, the South Carolina rice growers introduced irrigation systems, which increased the size of their crops. The indigo plant was the chief source of a blue dye. European textile industries used great amounts of the dye. Most of the Southern Colonies' exports went to England.

The Southern Colonies grew some cotton, but this crop did not become important until after the Revolutionary War. Some farmers in Pennsylvania and Virginia began to raise flax and hemp about 1750. These products were used in making clothing and rope. They

Huge barrels that could easily be rolled aboard a ship were used for exporting such products as rum, tobacco, or naval stores.

WORLD BOOK illustrations by Robert Addison

Making barrels and casks for colonial trade required the skills of men called coopers.

Processing tobacco in Virginia was illustrated by this picture which appeared in a London magazine of 1750. Most colonial tobacco was exported to English merchants.

"Tobacco Manufactory" from the
Universal Magazine, London. Huntington Library, San Marino, Calif.

became especially important during the war, when most manufactured goods could not be imported.

Timber from all the colonies was used to produce valuable lumber and *naval stores.* In colonial times, naval stores consisted mainly of pitch and tar. These products were vital in building or repairing wooden sailing ships.

Trade and industry

Colonial trade centered around the exchange of raw materials for European goods. English merchants were the chief customers of the colonists, and English manufactured goods were the settlers' main imports.

Trade of the colonists was strongly influenced by England's economic system, called *mercantilism.* Under this system, the English government protected the nation's industries against competition from the industries of other countries. A basic principle of mercantilism was governmental control of colonial trade. Parliament tried to strengthen that control by passing a series of laws called the *Navigation Acts.* Some of these laws required the colonists to trade almost entirely with merchants in England or in other English colonies, and to use English ships. Other laws tried to force the colonists to produce chiefly goods that would benefit English industries. The laws encouraged exports of iron, tobacco, and naval stores, which were greatly needed in England. The laws also prohibited the export of certain colonial farm products to England. The English feared these products would compete with English farm products. See **Mercantilism; Navigation Acts.**

The colonists got around the restrictions by developing trade routes that linked colonial ports with southern Europe, the West Indies, and Africa. These three-cornered routes became known as the "triangular trade routes." On one of the routes, the colonists shipped fish, grain, lumber, and meat to southern Europe. There, the products were exchanged for fruit and wine. These were carried to England and traded for manufactured goods that went back to the colonies. On another triangular route, American food products and lumber were traded in the West Indies for fruit, molasses, and sugar.

These materials were then taken to England and exchanged for manufactured goods, which went to America. Another route involved trading in rum and slaves. Rum, made in New England, was exchanged in Africa for slaves. The slaves were exchanged in the West Indies for molasses, which went to New England to be used in making rum.

Fishing and whaling became major industries in New England for two important reasons. First, the rocky New England land was not suitable for raising large crops. Second, New England ports were within easy sailing distance of the finest fishing and whaling waters of North America. These Atlantic coastal waters included the famous fishing area of the Grand Banks, off Newfoundland.

The principal colonial fishing centers were Boston, Gloucester, Marblehead, and Salem. The catches included cod, halibut, herring, and mackerel. Each year, huge amounts of fish were salted and dried for export. The chief markets for the better grades of fish were in southern Europe. The poorer grades were generally sold in the West Indies to be used as food for the slaves who worked on sugar plantations.

Nantucket, New Bedford, and Provincetown became important whaling centers. Whales were valuable for their oil, used as fuel in lamps; and for whalebone, used as a stiffening material in women's clothing. For details of the early whaling industry, see **Whale** (American whaling).

Lumbering and shipbuilding. From the time of the first settlements, lumbering was an important activity in all the colonies. Lumber products ranked among the chief exports of the colonists. The first export from Jamestown consisted of a cargo of clapboard and other building materials shipped to England in 1608.

The colonists used much lumber in building houses, seagoing vessels, and boats for rivers. Many wood products played an important part in other colonial industries. For example, millions of staves were used to make barrels, casks, and hogsheads for shipping fish, indigo, rice, tobacco, and whale oil.

New England was the center of the shipbuilding in-

Colonial trade routes   Manufactured goods from England accounted for most colonial imports. Exports consisted mostly of raw materials. The maps on these pages include the famous "triangular trade routes." The colonists used these routes to get around English laws that were designed to control colonial trade.

Ships sailing directly to England carried colonial products that were in great demand by English industries.

A major triangular route included the West Indies. Goods traded there for colonial products were then taken to England.

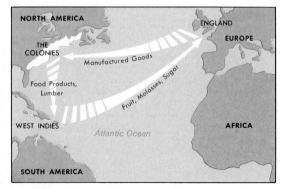

dustry, largely because of the demand there for fishing boats and merchant ships. The New England forests provided good shipbuilding timber, including cedar, maple, oak, and white pine. Virginia and the Carolinas also became important in the shipbuilding industry. Their live oak trees provided excellent ship timber.

The English encouraged colonial shipbuilding because their own best timber had been used up. By the end of the colonial period, about a third of England's merchant ships were being made in America.

Ironmaking. Iron ore, the most important metal found by the settlers, was mined in most of the colonies. The colonists obtained charcoal, the chief fuel used to smelt iron ore, from their large supplies of hardwoods. The ore deposits and fuel supplies made it fairly easy to develop ironmaking industries.

The first colonial blast furnace began operating about 1621 at Falling Creek, Virginia. The first successful ironworks was built 10 miles (16 kilometers) north of Boston in 1646. The site is now Saugus, Mass. By 1770, Hunter's ironworks at Falmouth, Virginia, was manufacturing $1\frac{1}{2}$ short tons (1.4 metric tons) of pig iron daily. Colonial ironworks were producing about a seventh of the world's iron by 1775.

The colonies exported much iron to England in the form of iron bars. But the colonists themselves provided the most important market of the ironmaking industry. Every colonial village or large farm had a blacksmith shop where smiths hammered out iron nails, axes, hoes, and other farm tools. Large ironworks also manufactured these products. Other iron products included cooking pots, kettles, wire, and materials used in making or repairing metal parts of carriages and wagons.

Other industries. Many industries developed because communities needed certain products or services. Almost as soon as a colonial village was established, someone set up a grist mill to grind grain into flour or meal. Next, perhaps, a blacksmith built a shop to make or repair farm tools. As the community grew, it needed coopers to make barrels. Other industries that developed included brewing, brickmaking, glassmaking, papermaking, ropemaking, and tanning.

From *A Collection of Voyages*, 1704, by Awnsham and Churchill. Folger Shakespeare Library, Washington, D.C.

Colonial whaling developed as an industry in the 1700's. But early New England settlers got valuable products, including oil for lamps, from stranded whales that they hauled ashore.

Charles Town, pictured about 1739, was the busiest seaport and richest city of the Southern Colonies. The city's wealth was based chiefly on large exports of rice, indigo, and deerskins.

New York Public Library, I. N. Phelps Stokes Collection

An important triangular route was sailed by ships carrying goods exchanged in southern Europe to ports in England.

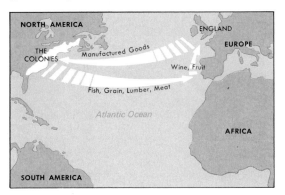

Ships of colonial slave traders sailed a route that linked West Africa, the West Indies, and home ports in the colonies.

WORLD BOOK maps-FHa

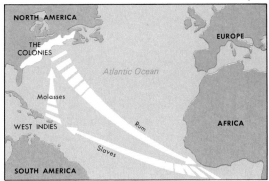

Money. The English government did not allow the colonists to mint coins. But Massachusetts built a mint anyway, and from 1652 to 1682 made various silver coins, including pine-tree shillings (see **Pine-tree shilling**). Massachusetts and the other colonies sometimes were permitted to issue paper money. Coins came to the colonies chiefly through trade with the West Indies. Most of the coins were Spanish money, made of gold or silver. Colonial merchants weighed the coins on special scales, because customers frequently clipped or shaved the edges to get the precious metal.

The early colonists generally traded goods with each other to get the items they wanted. Sometimes furs and Indian wampum were used as part of this system of *barter* (see **Barter; Wampum**). Certain crops often took the place of money. Southerners used tobacco, and northerners used grain or cattle. People in Maryland and Virginia sometimes used tobacco notes. These notes resembled paper money, and their value was established by tobacco stored in warehouses. See **Money** (History of United States currency).

Crafts

During the early colonial period, most of the settlers made their own furniture and household articles. Wealthy colonists generally imported their furnishings from England. Later, skilled colonial craftworkers made many products of wood, iron, silver, pewter, glass, or leather. Some workers copied European styles, but others developed a special American style. Examples of their work may be seen today in many museums.

Most craftworkers had shops in the cities or towns. In New England, some of them traveled from one community to another. Many customers supplied them with the raw materials needed for their work. In the Southern Colonies, many indentured servants were skilled craftworkers. After serving their period of indenture, some set up their own shops.

Furniture. Most early colonial chairs, tables, beds, and chests were bulky and heavy. But the cabinetmakers improved their designs, and the furniture became lighter and more graceful. The styles that were developed to please various colonial tastes are described in **Furniture** (Early American furniture).

Ironwork. Many articles made of iron by colonial blacksmiths are prized today as examples of fine craftsmanship. They include hinges, kettles, latches, locks, and weather vanes. Blacksmiths were important members of almost every community because they made and repaired tools and many other articles.

Silverware. The work of the silversmiths was almost as important as that of blacksmiths. Their customers considered silverware an investment because the metal itself had a high value. Valuable silver pieces included candlesticks, platters, bowls, coffee and tea pots, saltcellars, and sets of tableware.

Almost every colonial town had a silversmith, but the main silversmithing centers were Boston, Philadelphia, and New York City. Three noted silversmiths were Bostonians—John Coney, John Hull, and Paul Revere.

Pewter was used in most colonial households in some form because it was less expensive than silver. Pewter-ware resembles silverware, and pewterers made the same kind of articles as silversmiths. See **Pewter** (History).

Glass. The first successful American glass factory was established in Salem County, New Jersey, in 1739. Another began operating in Manheim, Pennsylvania, in 1765. These factories produced bottles, window panes, and much fine table glass that were sold throughout the colonies. See **Glass** (Early American glass).

Other crafts. Craftworkers who worked with leather used hides that had been tanned in the colonies. Most of these workers were saddlers and harness makers. They also made boots and shoes.

Gunsmiths developed their craft in all the colonies. The gunsmiths of Pennsylvania developed the "long rifle," which became known as the *Kentucky rifle* during the Revolutionary War. Some colonial rifles were beautifully carved and inlaid with silver.

Colonial Williamsburg

Needlework picture by Dorothy Cotton. Henry Francis du Pont Winterthur Museum, Winterthur, Del.
Colonial needlework is highly prized by collectors of antiques.

Spinning and weaving were important home industries throughout the colonies.

Colonial Williamsburg

Made by John Coney. Museum of Fine Arts, Boston, Gift of Mrs. J. R. Churchill

Silversmithing was a leading craft in the colonies. Most towns had a silversmith, *left*, who made beautiful silver pieces, such as the sugar bowl, *above*.

Corning Museum of Glass, Corning, N.Y.

Henry Francis du Pont Winterthur Museum, Winterthur, Del.

Walter H. Miller

Glassmaking began in the American Colonies during the mid-1700's. Some colonists who learned glassmaking techniques, *left*, established glass factories and manufactured various household items. The first successful glass factory opened in Salem County, New Jersey, in 1739. Most of the first American glassmakers were European immigrants, and they closely followed English, German, and other European models. Early American glassware included pieces that were beautifully colored and molded in patterns, like the blue sugar bowl pictured above left. A glass taper, or candlestick, *above right*, provided indoor lighting as well as elegant decoration.

Museum of Fine Arts, Boston, William E. Nickerson Fund

Furniture made by colonial cabinetmakers of the mid-1700's is noted for its graceful design. Some card tables, *left*, have needlepoint tops.

Pewter was used for many colonial household items because it was less expensive than silver. An engraved tankard, *right*, could be found in many homes.

Pewter tankard made by Simon Edgell. Henry Francis du Pont Winterthur Museum, Winterthur, Del.

Every year, millions of visitors tour the region that once was colonial America. Throughout the region, historic sites offer interesting glimpses of colonial life. Almost every town or city has churches or houses that date from the 1700's and a few from the 1600's. In some places, a visitor may walk through the streets of an entire colonial community that has been rebuilt. Many public buildings and museums display colonial relics in cities that were important during colonial times—Boston, Charleston, New York City, Newport, and Philadelphia. Newport has over 300 colonial buildings.

Places to visit

Following are brief descriptions of some especially interesting places to visit. See also the *Places to visit* section of the *World Book* article on each state.

Amstel House, in New Castle, Del., has exhibits of colonial arts, furnishings, and crafts. The house was built in the early 1700's.

Batsto is a partially restored colonial village in southeastern New Jersey. It includes an ironmaster's house, a blacksmith shop, a general store, and a glassware exhibit.

Charles Towne Landing, near Charleston, S.C., marks the area where South Carolina's first permanent English settlement was established. It has replicas of colonial buildings and a colonial trading ship.

Ephrata Cloisters, in Ephrata, Pa., is a restored religious community built by German Seventh-Day Baptists in 1732.

Farmers' Museum, near Cooperstown, N.Y., has many colonial farm tools. Nearby is the **Village Crossroads,** a typical colonial village.

Fort Niagara, near Youngstown, N.Y., was the scene of fighting during the French and Indian Wars and the Revolutionary War. It was built in 1726.

Harvard University, in Cambridge, Mass., is the oldest institute of higher learning in the United States. It was founded in 1636.

Henry Francis du Pont Winterthur Museum, near Wilmington, Del., has a magnificent collection of early American furniture. Visitors must write for permission to go through this museum.

Photri from Marilyn Gartman

Jamestown Festival Park on the James River in Virginia

Witch House in Salem, Mass.

Plimoth Plantation in Plymouth, Mass.

Dick Hanley, Photo Researchers

Plimoth Plantation

Jamestown Island, on the James River in Virginia, is the site of the first permanent English settlement in America. It is a national park. Nearby, **Jamestown Festival Park** has reproductions of old James Fort and of the three ships that brought the first settlers to Jamestown.

Ocracoke Island, a hideout of the pirate Blackbeard, lies southeast of Pamlico Sound off North Carolina's shore.

Old Gaol Museum, in York, Me., was built in 1653, and is one of America's oldest buildings. It served as a *gaol* (jail) until 1860.

Old Narragansett Church, in North Kingstown, R.I., is the oldest Episcopal church in the northern United States. It was built in 1707.

Old Salem is a restored colonial village in Winston-Salem, N.C. Moravians founded the village in 1766.

Old Sturbridge Village, in Sturbridge, Mass., is a recreation of a New England town in 1800.

Old Town Mill, in New London, Conn., is a colonial grain-grinding mill, built in 1650.

Plimoth Plantation, in Plymouth, Mass., is a re-creation of the first Pilgrim settlement.

St. Marys City, a village near Leonardtown, Md., was Maryland's first settlement, established in 1634.

Saugus Iron Works National Historic Site, in Saugus, Mass., is a reconstruction of America's first successful ironworks, built in the 1640's.

Shelburne Museum, in Shelburne, Vt., is a reconstruction of an early American village. The buildings house one of the world's most complete collections of articles used by the settlers.

Strawbery Banke, in Portsmouth, N.H., is a restoration of a colonial village, settled in 1630.

Whitehorse Tavern, in Newport, R.I., was built in 1673.

Whitfield House, in Guilford, Conn., is the oldest stone house in New England, begun in 1639.

Williamsburg is a Virginia city whose colonial buildings have been restored or rebuilt. Colonial Williamsburg provides a glimpse of the buildings, gardens, furnishings, crafts, and social life of the 1700's.

Witch House, in Salem, Mass., was the home of Judge Jonathan Corwin, a judge at the witchcraft trials of the early 1690's. James Kirby Martin

Farmers' Museum, Cooperstown, N.Y.

Blacksmith shop at Farmers' Museum in Cooperstown, N.Y.

DPI

Fort Niagara near Youngstown, N.Y.

Meeting house in Ephrata, Pa.

Saugus Iron Works in Saugus, Mass.

Bradley Smith, Photo Researchers

Scenic Art Color Slides

Related articles. For the history of each colony, from settlement to statehood, see the separate state articles in *World Book,* such as **Georgia** (History). See also:

Colonization

Dutch West India Company	New Netherland
Jamestown	New Sweden
London Company	Ohio Company
Lost Colony	Plymouth Colony
Massachusetts Bay Colony	Plymouth Company
New England, Dominion of	Williamsburg
New England Confederation	

Government and law enforcement

Blue laws	Money (History of United
Ducking stool	States currency)
Flag (pictures: Flags in United	Pillory
States history)	Stocks
House of Burgesses	Town meeting
Mayflower Compact	

Education and communication

American literature (Colonial	Freedom of the press
literature [1608-1764])	Hornbook
Bay Psalm Book	School (Colonial schools)
Education (The colonial period)	Town crier

Biographies
The New England Colonies

Alden, John and Priscilla	Mather, Cotton
Andros, Sir Edmund	Mather, Increase
Billings, William	Mather, Richard
Bradford, William (1590-1657)	Philip, King
Bradstreet, Anne D.	Randolph, Edward
Brewster, William	Samoset
Carver, John	Sewall, Samuel
Cotton, John	Shirley, William
Dudley, Thomas	Squanto
Dyer, Mary	Standish, Miles
Eaton, Theophilus	Uncas
Edwards, Jonathan	White, Peregrine
Endecott, John	Wigglesworth, Michael
Faneuil, Peter	Williams, Roger
Goddard, Mary K.	Winslow, Edward
Goddard, William	Winthrop, John
Hooker, Thomas	Winthrop, John, Jr.
Hutchinson, Anne M.	Wise, John
Massasoit	

The Middle Colonies

Bradford, William (1663-1752)	Penn, William
Bradford, William, III	Stuyvesant, Peter
Franklin, Benjamin	Tennent, Gilbert
Jemison, Mary	Tennent, William
Johnson, Sir William	Van Rensselaer, Kiliaen
Minuit, Peter	Woolman, John
Pastorius, Francis D.	Zenger, John Peter

The Southern Colonies

Bacon, Nathaniel	Oglethorpe, James E.
Berkeley, Sir William	Pinckney, Elizabeth L.
Byrd, William, II	Pocahontas
Calvert, Cecilius	Powhatan
Calvert, Charles	Rolfe, John
Dare, Virginia	Smith, John
De La Warr, Lord	Spotswood, Alexander
Dinwiddie, Robert	

Other related articles

Bacon's Rebellion	French and Indian wars
Black Americans (Colonial	Georgian architecture
times)	Great Awakening
Charter Oak	Indentured servant
Claiborne's Rebellion	Indian wars

Mayflower	Salem (Mass.)
Molasses Act	Salem witchcraft trials
Patroon system	Shot tower
Pennsylvania Dutch	Slavery (Slavery in the United
Pilgrims	States)
Pioneer life in America	Spinning
Plymouth Rock	Thanksgiving Day
Puritans	Witchcraft

Outline

I. The Thirteen Colonies
  A. Why the colonists came to America
  B. Early settlements
  C. Development of the colonies
  D. Relations with the Indians
II. Society and government
  A. Colonial society
  B. Government
  C. Voting requirements
  D. Local government
  E. Law enforcement
III. The home
  A. Houses
  B. Furnishings
  C. Clothing
  D. Food
  E. Health
  F. Recreation
IV. The church and the school
  A. The church   B. The school
V. Travel and communication
  A. Travel   B. Communication
VI. Arts and sciences
  A. Literature
  B. Painting
  C. Science
VII. Economy
  A. Farming
  B. Trade and industry
  C. Crafts
VIII. A visitor's guide to colonial America

Questions

How did the English settlers in the New World differ from the Spanish and French?
What were the three major types of English colonies?
How did many of the colonial boys learn a trade or profession?
What were two of the most important reasons for the survival of the Jamestown settlement?
Why were the Middle Colonies known as the "bread colonies"?
What were the five most important colonial cities of the 1700's?
How did the colonists get around the trade restrictions of the Navigation Acts?
What were the two most important crops of Georgia and South Carolina?
What were three chief reasons for discontented Europeans to migrate to the colonies?
What was the purpose of the Proclamation of 1763?

Additional resources

Level I
Alderman, Clifford L. *The Story of the Thirteen Colonies.* Random Hse., 1966.
Bosco, Peter I. *Roanoke: The Story of the Lost Colony.* Millbrook, 1992.
Bradford, William, and others. *Homes in the Wilderness: A Pilgrim's Journal of Plymouth Plantation in 1620.* Linnet, 1988. Reprint of 1939 edition also known as *Mourt's Relation.*
Carter, Alden R. *Colonies in Revolt.* Watts, 1988.
Fisher, Leonard E. *The Homemakers.* Watts, 1973. Other titles from the author's series on colonial period craftworkers include *The Glassmakers,* 1964; *The Printers,* 1965; *The Blacksmiths,* 1976.
Grant, Neil. *The New World Held Promise: Why England Colonized North America.* Messner, 1974.

Johnson, Gerald W. *America Is Born: A History for Peter.* Morrow, 1959. A standard work.

Kalman, Bobbie. *Historic Communities Series.* 8 vols. Crabtree, 1990-1992. Titles in this series include *The Gristmill* (1990), and *Tools and Gadgets* (1992).

Madison, Arnold. *How the Colonists Lived.* McKay, 1981.

Penner, Lucille R. *Eating the Plates: A Pilgrim Book of Food and Manners.* Macmillan, 1991.

Reische, Diana L. *Founding the American Colonies.* Watts, 1989.

Scott, John A. *Settlers on the Eastern Shore, 1607-1750.* Facts on File, 1991. First published in 1967.

Sewell, Marcia. *The Pilgrims of Plimoth.* Atheneum, 1986.

Siegel, Beatrice. *A New Look at the Pilgrims: Why They Came to America.* Walker, 1987. First published in 1977. *The Basket Maker and the Spinner.* 1987.

A Sourcebook on Colonial America. 6 vols. Ed. by Carter Smith. Millbrook, 1991. Titles in this series include *The Arts and Sciences, Daily Life,* and *Governing and Teaching.*

Level II

Bailyn, Bernard. *The People of British North America: An Introduction.* Vintage Bks., 1988. First published in 1986.

Bridenbaugh, Carl. *Cities in the Wilderness: The First Century of Urban Life in America, 1625-1742.* 2nd ed. Oxford, 1971. *Jamestown, 1544-1699.* 1980.

Colonial British America: Essays in the New History of the Early Modern Era. Ed. by Jack P. Greene and J. R. Pole. Johns Hopkins, 1983.

Deetz, James J. *In Small Things Forgotten: The Archaeology of Early American Life.* Doubleday, 1977.

The Encyclopedia of Colonial and Revolutionary America. Ed. by John M. Faragher. Facts on File, 1988.

Ferling, John E. *A Wilderness of Miseries: War and Warriors in Early America.* Greenwood, 1980.

Fischer, David H. *Albion's Seed: Four British Folkways in America.* Oxford, 1989.

Hawke, David F. *Everyday Life in Early America.* Harper, 1988.

Hoffer, Peter C. *Law and People in Colonial America.* Johns Hopkins, 1992.

Larkin, David, and others. *Colonial: Design in the New World.* Stewart, Tabori, 1988.

Morgan, Edmund S. *The Puritan Family: Religion and Domestic Relations in Seventeenth-Century New England.* Greenwood, 1980. Reprint of 1966 revised edition.

Nash, Gary B. *Red, White, and Black: The Peoples of Early North America.* 3rd ed. Prentice-Hall, 1992.

Reich, Jerome R. *Colonial America.* 2nd ed. Prentice-Hall, 1989.

Tunis, Edwin. *Colonial Living.* Crowell, 1976. First published in 1957. *Colonial Craftsmen and the Beginnings of American Industry.* 1976. First published in 1965.

Ward, Harry M. *Colonial America, 1607-1763.* Prentice-Hall, 1991.

Wilbur, C. Keith. *Homebuilding and Woodworking in Colonial America: An Illustrated Source Book of Practical Techniques Used by the Colonists.* Globe Pequot, 1992.

Work and Labor in Early America. Ed. by Stephen Innes. Univ. of North Carolina Pr., 1988.

Colonial National Historical Park. See National Park System (table: National historical parks).

Colonialism is a term that usually refers to the rule of a group of people by a foreign power. The people and their land make up a colony. Most colonies are separated by an ocean from the ruling nation. The foreign power sends people to live in the colony, to govern it, and to use it as a source of wealth. The rulers and the people of most colonies belong to different ethnic groups. The rulers also have a more advanced technology than do the people of most colonies.

Colonialism dates back to ancient times. The Romans ruled many colonies in Europe, the Middle East, and Africa. Beginning in the A.D. 1400's, European nations built vast colonial empires in Africa, Asia, North America, and South America. The major colonial powers of Europe were France, Great Britain, the Netherlands, Portugal, and Spain. By the 1970's, most colonial empires had broken up.

Nations have sought colonies chiefly to gain economic benefits. They have wanted land and such valuable products as diamonds, gold, and spices for themselves. They also have wanted to expand their industry and trade by gaining (1) sources of raw materials, (2) markets for their goods, (3) sources of goods that could be exported to other countries, and (4) opportunities for investment. In addition, nations have practiced colonialism to increase their reputation among other nations, to gain military advantages, and to spread their religion to other peoples.

Some people believe that widespread colonialism still exists. They define colonialism as any form of economic, political, or social *oppression* (unjust treatment) of one group by a group of different ancestry. However, this definition is not widely accepted. Other people use the term *neocolonialism* for the indirect control they believe is exercised by developed nations over developing nations. According to these people, many developing nations depend on investment capital from developed nations. Such dependence supposedly allows the developed nations to take advantage of the developing ones. This article discusses colonialism as it is generally defined.

History of colonialism

Ancient colonialism. The Roman Empire was the greatest colonial empire of ancient times. Rome began its overseas expansion about 264 B.C. At its height, the Roman empire extended from northern Britain to the Red Sea and Persian Gulf. The empire collapsed in A.D. 476.

Early European colonialism. In the 1400's, Portugal and Spain began to send explorers in search of sea routes to India and the Far East. Muslims controlled land routes across the Middle East and so controlled trade between Asia and Europe. Europeans hoped to take over this trade. Portugal gained control of what is now Brazil. It also established trading posts in West Africa, India, and Southeast Asia. Spain gained control of part of what is now the United States and most of Latin America.

During the 1600's, the Dutch and the English took control of the Asian trade from the Portuguese. The Dutch gained control of the islands that became the Dutch East Indies (now Indonesia), and the English became a strong influence in India. The Dutch, English, and French also took over parts of Latin America.

The English and French moved into parts of Canada as well. The Dutch, English, and French claimed sections of what became the United States. There, the English eventually established the Thirteen Colonies. In 1624, the Dutch settled New Netherland, which included parts of what are now Connecticut, Delaware, New Jersey, and New York. The English took over New Netherland in 1664.

The four French and Indian wars between the British and the French took place in North America from 1689 to 1763. The last of these wars ended in a British victory, and Great Britain took control of almost all of France's North American possessions. During the late 1600's and the 1700's, large numbers of English and other European settlers made their home in North America.

Later colonialism. The Thirteen Colonies gained independence from England in the Revolutionary War (1775-1783). Most colonies in Latin America fought for and won their independence in the 1700's and early 1800's.

European colonial expansion slowed somewhat during the early and mid-1800's, though Great Britain claimed several colonies in Australia. Many people had come to believe that colonies were not worth the trouble and expense involved in managing them. However, the Industrial Revolution and the rise of European nationalism contributed to great colonial expansion during the late 1800's and early 1900's in Africa and Asia. On those two continents, the industrial nations sought raw materials for their factories, markets for their manufactured goods, and opportunities for investment. They also sought territories that would improve their position against European rivals.

Belgium, France, Germany, Great Britain, Italy, Portugal, and Spain divided almost all Africa among themselves, leaving only Ethiopia and Liberia independent. Great Britain extended its control in India, Burma, and what is now Malaysia. The French took over Indochina. The Dutch expanded their control in the East Indies. The United States acquired the Philippines. France, Germany, Great Britain, Spain, and the United States competed for control of the Pacific Islands.

Also in the late 1800's and early 1900's, conquests gave Japan an empire that included Korea and Taiwan. During World War II (1939-1945), Japan added to its empire by conquering a number of colonies formerly held by Western nations. The empire collapsed after Japan was defeated in 1945. Most of the colonies were returned to the Western nations.

Three factors helped bring large-scale colonialism to an end during the 1950's and 1960's. First, the European nations had been weakened by the war. In addition, many people had come to oppose colonialism as unjust. Finally, nationalist feelings and demands for self-government had been growing among most colonies in Africa and Asia. Some of these colonies gained independence peacefully. Others became independent only after fighting a war against their ruler.

Colonialism today. France, Great Britain, Portugal, Spain, and other nations still govern a few overseas areas. However, most nations do not officially call such areas *colonies.* Great Britain, for example, calls them *dependencies.* The United States governs a number of overseas areas, including American Samoa, Guam, and various other Pacific islands; Puerto Rico; and the Virgin Islands.

Colonial policies

Many colonial rulers forced their way of life on the people of their colonies. These rulers did so partly because they considered the culture of the colonial people inferior to their own. Many rulers tried to convert the colonial people to their own religion. Many colonial rulers also made their own language the official language of the colonies.

Most colonial rulers helped make the colonies more modern by building railways, roads, and factories and by setting up schools and hospitals. However, the colonial powers were chiefly concerned with establishing economic and political policies that would be most beneficial to themselves.

Economic policies. Ruling nations sought economic benefits from their colonies. In ancient times, such nations increased their wealth by forcing conquered peoples to work for them and to make payments in return for protection from other nations. These payments were called *tribute.*

From the 1400's to the 1700's, an economic system called *mercantilism* existed in Europe. Under this system, the European powers molded the economy of their colonies to fit their own trading needs.

For example, England passed a series of laws during the 1600's and 1700's to strengthen its control over the economy of the Thirteen Colonies. Some of these laws required the American colonists to trade almost entirely with merchants in Great Britain or in other British colonies, and to use British ships. Other laws limited colonial manufacturing because the British wanted the colonists to depend largely on Great Britain for manufactured goods. To encourage the Americans to export goods needed by Great Britain, the British granted certain trading privileges to such exports. Other European nations handled trade with their colonies in a way similar to that used by the British.

Slavery was an important part of colonial economic policies during the mercantilist period. In the South American colonies, the Europeans first forced the native Indians to work on the plantations that produced cotton and other raw materials. Later, they imported slaves from Africa.

Most countries in North and South America abolished slavery during the 1800's. About the mid-1800's, the British decided that mercantilism had hurt some of their industries. As a result, Great Britain gradually adopted a system of *free trade,* which eventually ended controls on colonial trade. By 1870, most other colonial powers also had removed controls from their trading practices.

Free trade did not prevent the expansion of colonialism in Africa and Asia. Colonies still could provide raw materials and markets for European goods. Also, European bankers and industrialists made profits by investing in the factories, mines, plantations, and railroads being created in so-called "backward" regions. The European nations established colonies in these regions partly to protect such investments.

By the early 1900's, most colonial powers had again adopted a system of economic controls. However, these controls were not nearly so restrictive as those of the mercantilist period.

Political policies used in governing colonies varied widely. Some ruling nations made their colonies completely dependent. Others allowed them some self-government. The colonial rule of Belgium, France, and Great Britain in Africa and Asia shows how political policies differed.

Belgium's chief colony was the Belgian Congo (now Zaire) in Africa. Belgium gained control of the Congo in 1885 and ruled it entirely from Brussels, the Belgian capital. The Belgians gave the Congolese no share in the government. Uprisings occurred in the Congo in 1959, and Belgium granted independence in 1960.

Likewise, the French governed their colonies completely from Paris. The people of the upper class in the colonies were expected to become like the French—culturally, economically, and politically. Two colonial revolts showed the unwillingness of the French to accept the end of colonialism. A revolt against French rule began in Indochina in 1946 and did not end until 1954, when the French withdrew after suffering heavy losses. Also in 1954, a revolution broke out in Algeria, a French territory in Africa. The fighting there continued until 1962, when Algeria became independent. France has peacefully granted independence to most of its other possessions.

Britain at first governed its colonies largely through British officials. But through the years, the British gave colonials a growing role in local courts, legislative councils, and public service. For example, the people of India played an increasing part in their government from 1918 to 1939, the period between World War I and World War II. India gained independence from Britain in 1947. Its successful change from colony to nation led Britain to grant independence to other colonies.

Effects of colonialism

Colonialism has had both good and bad effects on colonies and ruling nations. Rulers did bring some economic development to their colonies by introducing Western agricultural, industrial, and medical techniques. At the same time, however, the colonial powers often *exploited* (took advantage of) their colonies economically. In many colonies, the ruling powers disrupted and transformed the traditional economic structure. They limited the colonies to producing mainly raw materials and to buying most of their manufactured goods from the ruling countries. In this way, they destroyed the colonies' commercial and manufacturing activities. Although there were advantages for the colonies in becoming part of a worldwide economic system, the people of the colonies lost control over their economic activities. In addition, higher living standards and peace led to great population increases that sometimes kept those standards from improving further—or even lowered them.

Colonial rule brought many people under the political control of European nations. But it also ended local wars in many areas and united those areas under one nation. Ruling powers set up modern educational systems and introduced democratic forms of government. Yet in many cases, the rulers gave the colonial people too little training to prepare them for independence. Many rulers also tried to force their culture on colonial people. Many historians believe that knowledge of Western culture benefited colonial peoples in various ways. However, after gaining independence, many former colonies have had to struggle to redefine their cultural identity.

Colonialism brought wealth and power to the ruling nations. But it also led to nationalist feelings and resistance movements among colonial peoples—and thus helped bring about its own end.

One unexpected result of the end of colonialism has been the migration of many people from former colonies to the countries that once ruled them. Large numbers of Indians, Pakistanis, and West Indians have gone to Britain. Many people from Indonesia and Suriname have moved to the Netherlands. A number of North Africans now live in France. This migration has created ethnic diversity in European nations that once had unmixed populations.   Allen J. Greenberger

Related articles in *World Book.* See the *History* section of the articles on countries mentioned in this article. See also:

Africa (History)	Imperialism
Asia (History)	Latin America (Colonial rule)
Canada, History of	Mandated territory
Colonial life in America	Mercantilism
Colony	Minority group (How a group
Commonwealth of Nations	becomes a minority)
East India Company	Nationalism
Enclave	Racism (History)
Europe (Colonial	Rome, Ancient
expansion)	Territory
Exploration	Trust territory
Governor general	United States, History of the
Immigration (Europe)	World, History of the

See also *Colonialism* in the Research Guide/Index, Volume 22, for a *Reading and Study Guide.*

Additional resources

Betts, Raymond F. *Uncertain Dimensions: Western Overseas Empires in the Twentieth Century.* Univ. of Minnesota Pr., 1985.
Chamberlain, Muriel E. *Decolonization: The Fall of the European Empires.* Basil Blackwell, 1985.
Fieldhouse, David K. *The Colonial Empires: A Comparative Survey from the Eighteenth Century.* Dial, 1966. *Colonialism, 1870-1945: An Introduction.* St. Martin's, 1981.
Ward, Barbara. *Five Ideas That Change the World.* Greenwood, 1984. First published in 1959. Includes a section on colonialism.

Colony. See Animal (Animal homes and communities).

Colony is a settlement established by people outside their native land, and ruled by the mother country. Nations establish colonies to find more room in which people can live, to increase trade by providing a market for manufactured goods, to gain sources of raw materials, to secure military advantages, and to increase the prestige of the mother country.

Climate has often decided how a colony develops. Temperate lands, such as the areas that are now the United States, Canada, and Australia, have attracted large numbers of colonists who have pushed out the inhabitants of the region. Elsewhere, especially in Latin America, the colonists created new multiracial societies. Outside of the Western Hemisphere, tropical colonies attracted few colonists. These few, instead of pushing out the inhabitants of the region, took control of the colonized territory, as the Belgians did in the Belgian Congo in Africa.

Colonies in time became independent of the mother country. For example, the American Colonies broke away from Great Britain and became the United States. Canada, Australia, New Zealand, and India were once British colonies. But they are now independent members of the Commonwealth of Nations, an association of nations that includes Britain and many of its former possessions. A number of former French colonies, such as Senegal, have joined France as members of the French Community. Almost half the members of the United Nations are former colonies that have become independent since World War II (1939-1945).   Allen J. Greenberger

See also **Colonialism** and its list of *Related articles.*

Colony, Penal. See Penal colony.

John Shaw, Tom Stack & Assoc.

H. Armstrong
Roberts

Dwight R. Kuhn,
Bruce Coleman Inc.

Zig Leszczynski,
Animals Animals

The great variety of colors in nature includes the dazzling colors of autumn leaves, *top,* and the appetizing colors of ripe fruits and vegetables, *above left.* A brightly colored flower, *above center,* attracts a honeybee to its pollen. The brilliant blue and yellow of a South American arrow poison frog, *above right,* serve as a vivid warning to the animal's enemies.

Color

Color fills our world with beauty. We delight in the colors of a magnificent sunset and in the bright red and golden-yellow leaves of autumn. We are charmed by gorgeous flowering plants and the brilliantly colored arch of a rainbow. We also use color in various ways to add pleasure and interest to our lives. For example, many people choose the colors of their clothes carefully and decorate their homes with colors that create beautiful, restful, or exciting effects. By their selection and arrangement of colors, artists try to make their paintings more realistic or expressive.

Color serves as a means of communication. In sports, different colored uniforms show which team the players are on. On streets and highways, a red traffic light tells

drivers to stop, and a green light tells them to go. On a map printed in color, blue may stand for rivers and other bodies of water, green for forests and parks, and black for highways and other roads.

We use the names of colors in many common expressions to describe moods and feelings. For example, we say a sad person *feels blue* and a jealous one is *green with envy.* We say an angry person *sees red.* A coward may be called *yellow.*

Color plays an important part in nature. The brilliant colors of many kinds of blossoms attract insects. The insects may pollinate the flowers, causing the plants to develop seeds and fruits. Colorful fruits attract many kinds of fruit-eating animals, which pass the seeds of the fruits in their droppings. The seeds may then sprout wherever the droppings fall. In this way, fruit-bearing plants may be spread naturally to new areas.

The colors of some animals help them attract mates. For example, a peacock spreads his brightly colored feathers when courting a female. The colors of many

Gunter Wyszecki, the contributor of this article, is Director of the Institute of Optics at the National Research Council of Canada. He is also Adjunct Professor at the School of Optometry at the University of Waterloo and coauthor of Color in Business, Science, and Industry *and* Color Science.

The Old Guitarist (1903), an oil painting on wood panel;
The Art Institute of Chicago, Helen Birch Bartlett Collection

D. P. Hershkowitz, Bruce Coleman Inc.

Focus on Sports

Communicating with color. Color is often used to express moods and to communicate information. The use of blues in Pablo Picasso's painting *The Old Guitarist, above left,* creates a sad and lonely feeling. The exciting colors of a neon sign, *upper right,* capture people's attention. The colors of football uniforms, *lower right,* help spectators tell which team the players are on.

other animals help them escape from enemies. For example, Arctic hares have brownish fur in summer. In winter, their fur turns white, making it difficult for enemies to see the hares in the snow.

Although we speak of seeing colors or objects, we do not actually see them. Instead, we see the light that objects reflect or give off. Our eyes absorb this light and change it into electrochemical signals. The signals travel through nerves to the brain, which interprets them as colored images. However, there is much that scientists still do not know about how our eyes and brain enable us to sense color.

The relation between color and light

To understand how we see color, we must first know something about the nature of light. Light is a form of energy that behaves in some ways like waves. Light waves have a range of *wavelengths.* A wavelength is the distance between any point on one wave and the corresponding point on the next wave. Different wavelengths of light appear to us as different colors. Light that con-

tains all wavelengths in the same proportions as sunlight appears white. See **Light.**

When a beam of sunlight passes through a specially shaped glass object called a *prism,* the rays of different wavelengths are bent at different angles. The bending breaks up the sunlight into a beautiful band of colors. This band contains all the colors of the rainbow and is called the *visible spectrum.* At one end of the spectrum, the light appears as violet. It consists of the shortest wavelengths of light that we can see. Farther along the spectrum, the light has increasingly longer wavelengths. It appears as blue, green, yellow, orange, and red, each shading into its neighboring colors in the spectrum. The longest wavelengths of light that we can see appear deep red in color.

Light waves are a form of *electromagnetic waves,* which consist of patterns of electric and magnetic energy. The visible spectrum is only a small part of the *electromagnetic spectrum*—the entire range of electromagnetic waves. Beyond the violet end of the visible spectrum are ultraviolet rays, X rays, and gamma rays.

The visible spectrum A band of colors called the *visible spectrum* forms when white light passes through a *prism* (a specially shaped glass object). The prism bends the shortest light waves most. They appear violet. It bends the longest waves least. They appear red. All other colors lie in between. Ultraviolet and infrared fall outside the spectrum and are invisible to people. The length of light waves is measured in *nanometers*. One nanometer is a billionth of a meter, or about $\frac{1}{25,000,000}$ of an inch.

WORLD BOOK illustration by Leonard Morgan

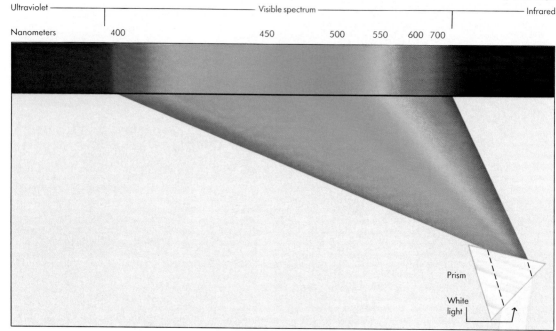

Ultraviolet ———————————————— Visible spectrum ———————————————— Infrared

Nanometers   400   450   500   550   600 700

Prism

White light

Beyond the red end of the visible spectrum are infrared rays and radio waves. See **Electromagnetic waves.**

Such objects as traffic lights and neon signs appear colored because the light that they give off contains a limited range of wavelengths. However, most objects appear colored because their chemical structure absorbs certain wavelengths of light and reflects others. When sunlight strikes a carrot, for example, molecules in the carrot absorb most of the light of short wavelengths. Most of the light of longer wavelengths is reflected. When these longer wavelengths of light reach our eyes, the carrot appears orange.

An object that reflects most of the light of all wavelengths in nearly equal amounts appears white. An object that absorbs most of the light of all wavelengths in nearly equal amounts appears black.

How we see color

The roles of the eyes and brain. Our ability to see color depends on many highly complicated workings of the eyes and brain. When we look at an object, light coming from the object enters our eyes. Each eye focuses the light, forming an image of the object on the *retina.* The retina is a thin layer of tissue covering the back and sides of the inside of the eyeball. It contains millions of light-sensitive cells. These cells absorb most of the light that falls on the retina and convert the light to electrical signals. These electrical signals then travel through nerves to the brain.

The retina has two main types of light-sensitive cells— *rods* and *cones.* The cells are named after their shapes.

Rods are extremely sensitive to dim light but cannot distinguish wavelengths. For this reason, we see only tones of gray in a dimly lit room. As the light becomes brighter, the cones begin to respond and the rods cease functioning. The retina of a person with normal color vision has three types of cones. One type responds most strongly to light of short wavelengths, which corresponds to the color blue. Another type reacts chiefly to light of middle wavelengths, or green. The third type is most sensitive to light of long wavelengths, or red.

The brain organizes nerve signals from the eye and interprets them as colored visual images. Exactly how

WORLD BOOK photos by Larry McCann

Color vision requires a certain level of lighting. In dim light, colored objects, such as marbles, *above left,* appear gray. In bright light, the same objects, *above right,* appear in color.

the brain makes us aware of colors is still much of a mystery. Scientists have developed several theories to explain color vision. Some of these theories are discussed in the section *History of color studies.*

Some people do not have full color vision. Such people are said to be color blind. There are different types and degrees of color blindness, depending on different abnormalities in the retina's cones. In severe cases, one type of cone may be absent or not functioning. People who have such an abnormality confuse certain colors with others. Very few people cannot see colors at all. Most color-vision problems are inherited and cannot be cured. See **Color blindness.**

Surprising color-vision effects. Many operations of the eyes and brain work automatically and almost instantly in providing us with color vision. We have learned unconsciously not to "see" certain visual effects of these operations, especially as our eyes adjust to changes of color. When we do become aware of such effects, they may seem dramatic or startling. Some of the color-vision effects that we normally do not notice can be easily demonstrated.

We can demonstrate one color-vision effect by covering half a sheet of brightly colored paper with plain white paper. If we stare at the colored area for about 30 seconds and then remove the white paper, the area that had not been covered will seem much lighter than the half that had been covered. It seems lighter because our eyes *adapt to* (become accustomed to) colors. Such a visual effect is called *chromatic adaptation.*

If we stare at a colored image for about 30 seconds and then look at a white surface, we see an *afterimage.* The afterimage has the same shape as the original image but different colors. Where the original image was red, the afterimage will be green. Where the image was green, the afterimage will be red. Blue areas become yellow, and yellow areas become blue. Black and white also reverse. The technical name for this amazing color-vision effect is *successive contrast.*

WORLD BOOK illustration

Phantom colors are colors that appear in areas that are only black and white. A faint area of phantom pink can be seen in the center of the triangle formed by the three circles above.

We can also demonstrate that the appearance of a color is influenced by surrounding colors. If we place the same color against different background colors, the color will look different in each case. In addition, a color appears lighter when surrounded by a dark background than when surrounded by a light background. This color-vision effect is called *chromatic induction* or *simultaneous contrast.*

Sometimes, we may see colors in areas that are only black and white. Such colors are called *phantom colors.* Phantom colors may be seen by staring at flashing black-and-white patterns, such as those produced by a rapidly rolling black-and-white television picture.

Color vision in animals

Apes, monkeys, many kinds of birds, and some species of fishes have color vision much like ours. However, numerous other animals see colors differently from the way we do. For example, research shows that crocodiles see colors as various shades of gray. The eyes of certain other animals are sensitive to light that we cannot see. For example, bees can see ultraviolet light, which is invisible to people. On the other hand, bees cannot see the color red.

Methods of color production

Manufacturers, artists, and craftworkers produce objects in a tremendous variety of colors. To create so many different colors, they use one of two basic methods. These methods are (1) mixing colorants and (2) mixing colored lights.

Mixing colorants. A great variety of colors can be created by mixing *colorants.* Colorants are chemical substances that give color to such materials as ink, paint, crayons, and chalk. Most colorants consist of fine powders that are mixed with liquids, wax, or other substances to make them easier to apply to objects. Colorants that dissolve in liquids are called *dyes.* Colorants

To see an afterimage, stare at the center of the flag for about 30 seconds. Then look at a sheet of white paper. You will see an image of the flag with its proper colors.

that do not dissolve but spread through liquids or other substances as tiny solid particles are called *pigments.*

When two different colorants are mixed, a third color is produced. For example, when paint with blue pigment is mixed with paint that has yellow pigment, the resulting paint appears green. When light strikes the surface of this paint, much of it penetrates the paint layer and hits pigment particles. The blue pigment absorbs most of the light of long wavelengths—light that appears red, orange, and yellow. The yellow pigment absorbs most of the light of short wavelengths—light that ap-

pears blue and violet. Most of the light of medium wavelengths is not absorbed but reflected through the surface of the paint. When this light reaches our eyes, we see the paint as green. In a colorant mixture, each colorant absorbs, or subtracts, some of the wavelengths of light that strike it. For this reason, colorant mixtures are sometimes referred to as *subtractive color mixtures* or *color by subtraction.*

Any three colorants that can be mixed in different combinations to produce nearly any other color are known as *primary colorants* or *primary colors in paint.*

The effects of neighboring colors   The appearance of a color is influenced by the other colors around it. The same color looks different when it is placed against different background colors. In addition, in certain two-color combinations, the colors seem to mix, forming a third color. In some other combinations, however, the colors seem to clash, creating a sense of visual vibration.

WORLD BOOK illustrations

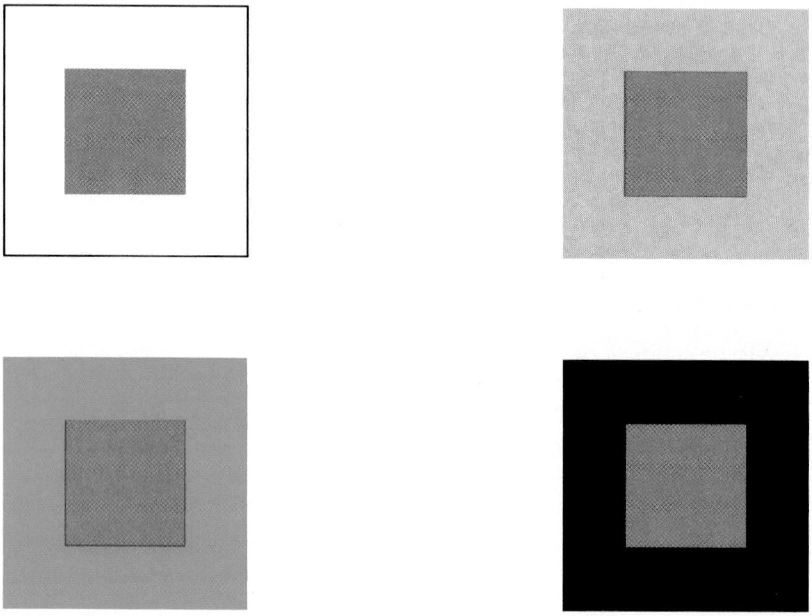

A color looks different against different background colors. The orange squares in the above illustrations are all the same color. But the orange seems lighter against the black background than against white or gray. It appears more yellow against green than against gray or white.

Visual mixing occurs when two colors seem to blend, forming a third color. Seen from a distance, the red and orange above seem to form a red-orange square.

Visual vibration occurs when two colors seem to clash and vibrate in our vision. In the diagram above, the purple and yellow stripes appear to flash, dazzling our eyes.

**How a mixture
of two pigments
produces a third color**

When light strikes *pigments* (coloring particles) in paint, the pigments absorb, or subtract, certain wavelengths of light and reflect others. In paint containing a mixture of different pigments, each pigment subtracts different wavelengths. Because the color we see depends on what wavelengths have been subtracted, producing colors by mixing pigments is called *color by subtraction.*

WORLD BOOK illustration

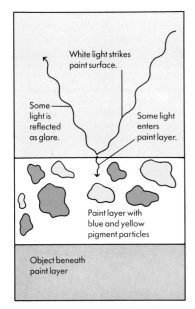 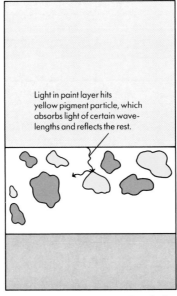 

Light strikes the surface of a paint layer containing blue and yellow pigment particles. Some light is reflected as glare, and the rest penetrates the paint.

Light strikes a yellow particle, which absorbs, or subtracts, the light of short wavelengths and reflects the light of longer wavelengths.

Light strikes a blue particle, which absorbs light of long wavelengths. Medium wavelengths are reflected from the paint and appear green to our eyes.

A common group of primary colorants consists of red, yellow, and blue. When primary colorants are mixed in pairs, the resulting colors are called *secondary colorants* or *secondary colors in paint.* Orange is formed by mixing red and yellow, green by mixing yellow and blue, and purple by mixing blue and red. Color experts have found that *magenta* (purplish-red), yellow, and *cyan* (blue-green) also make a good set of primary colorants. These three colorants can be mixed to produce an extremely wide range of colors.

Mixing equal amounts of three primary colorants results in a color that is almost black. However, special black colorants, such as a fine black powder called *carbon black,* provide better blacks. Mixing black with a color produces a *shade.* Primary colorants absorb much light, and so they cannot be mixed to produce very light colors. For such purposes, either a chemical compound called *titanium dioxide* or some other special white colorant must be added. Mixing white with a color produces a *tint.* The combination of black and white forms gray. Mixing gray with a color creates a *tone.*

Mixing colored lights. When lights of different colors are projected together onto a screen, they blend and form new colors. Mixing colored lights produces new colors differently from the way mixing colorants does. Mixing colorants results in new colors because each colorant subtracts some wavelengths of light. But mixing colored lights produces new colors by adding light of different wavelengths. For this reason, colored light mixtures are sometimes called *additive color mixtures* or *color by addition.*

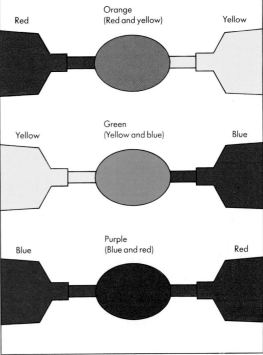

WORLD BOOK illustration by Zorica Dabich

Primary and secondary colors in paint. Red, yellow, and blue are common primary colors. They can be mixed to form the secondary colors orange, green, and purple, as shown above.

The color triangle

A color triangle has a color or white or black at each point. Adding white to a color produces a *tint*. Adding black forms a *shade*. Adding gray (a mixture of black and white) creates a *tone*.

WORLD BOOK illustration

[Color triangle diagram with circles labeled: Color, Shade, Tint, Tone, Black, Gray, White]

In an additive color mixture, the primary colors differ from those in paint. The *primary colors in light* are red, green, and blue. When red and green lights are mixed, the result is yellow light. A mixture of blue and green lights forms blue-green light, and blue and red lights form purple light. Combining all three primary colors in light in the proper proportions results in white light.

The colors of any two lights are *complementary* if they form white light when mixed. Therefore, the complementary color of any primary color in light is the color formed by combining the two other primary colors. The complement of blue is yellow (red light plus green light). The complement of red is blue-green (blue light plus green light). The complement of green is purple (red light plus blue light).

Color television pictures are created by additive mixtures of the three primary colors in light. A color TV screen has thousands of tiny areas that glow when struck by a beam of electrons. Some areas produce red light, others produce green light, and still others produce blue light. When we watch a color program, we do not see each red, green, or blue area. Instead, we see a range of many colors produced when the red, green, and blue lights blend in our vision. We see white light when certain amounts of red, green, and blue light are combined. The combining of the primary colors to pro-

Mixing colored lights

Lights of different colors are made up of different wavelengths. Projecting two different colored lights together onto a screen results in a new color because the wavelengths of one light are added to those of the other. For this reason, mixing colored lights is also called *color by addition*.

Primary colors in light

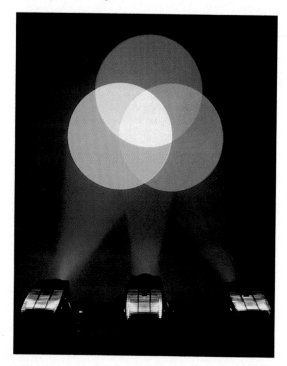

Complementary colors in light

A blend of red and blue lights creates purple, the complement of green.

A blend of blue and green lights creates blue-green, the complement of red.

A blend of green and red lights creates yellow, the complement of blue.

WORLD BOOK photos by Arnold Ryan Chalfant & Associates

Red, green, and blue are the primary colors in light. They can be combined in various ways to form different colors. Combining all three primary colors results in white light.

The complement of a primary color in light is produced by combining the two other primary colors. The colors that result from combining two primary colors in light are shown above.

duce white light makes it possible for a color TV to show black-and-white pictures. See **Television** (How television works).

Producing color harmony

When neighboring colors have a pleasing effect, we say that they produce color harmony. In selecting clothes or decorating homes, many people consider what colors look good together. Artists and scientists have developed guidelines for combining colors. But there are no fixed rules of color harmony because too many factors affect whether colors go well together.

A *color circle,* or *color wheel,* shows the relations among colors. It is a helpful tool for choosing harmonious color combinations. A color circle consists of a range of colors in the form of a circle. The colors run from red, through the other colors of the spectrum, and back to red again. Three colors an equal distance apart on the color circle are called a color *triad.* The colors in a triad often go well together. The primary colors on the color circle—red, yellow, and blue—form a triad. The *secondary colors*—green, orange, and purple—are mix-

WORLD BOOK illustration by Arnold Ryan Chalfant & Associates

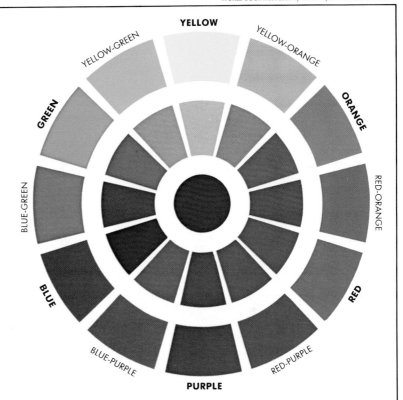

The color circle, also called the *color wheel,* indicates the relations among colors. The outer circle shows three primary colors (yellow, red, and blue) and three secondary colors (orange, purple, and green) labeled in boldface capital letters. They are separated by six intermediate colors labeled in lightface capitals. The inner circle shows darker colors obtained by mixing two colors that lie opposite each other in the outer circle.

Harmonious color combinations   Certain colors have a pleasing effect when used together. The diagrams below show how harmonious color combinations can be found by connecting various positions on the color circle.

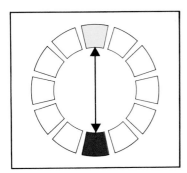

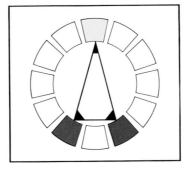

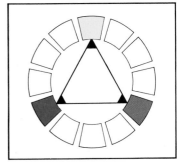

Complementary colors in paint, such as yellow and purple, lie directly opposite each other on the color circle.

Near-complementary colors, such as yellow and red-purple or yellow and blue-purple, lie nearly opposite.

A triad consists of three colors spaced an equal distance apart, such as the primary colors yellow, red, and blue.

tures of two primary colors. They lie at equal distances from the primary colors and also form a triad. *Intermediate colors* are mixtures of a primary and a secondary color. They lie between primary and secondary colors. A mixture of two secondary colors forms a *tertiary color.*

Any two colors that lie directly opposite each other on the color circle are called *complementary colors in paint.* Such pairs of complementary colors include red and green, orange and blue, and yellow and violet. Complementary colors often go well together. A color also may harmonize with colors that lie next to its complement, such as red with blue-green or yellow-green. Such colors are called *near-complementary colors* or *split complementary colors.* Colors that lie next to each other on the color circle, such as blue-green, blue, and blue-violet, also may form pleasing combinations. *Monochromatic* color schemes are made up of shades, tones, and tints of a single color. Such color combinations can create pleasant effects. For more information on producing color harmony, see **Interior decoration** (Using color; Color and light; pictures).

Characteristics of color

Every color has three basic characteristics. They are (1) hue, (2) lightness, and (3) chroma. Color experts describe an object's color in terms of these characteristics.

Hue is the property that gives a color its name—for example, red, orange, yellow, green, blue, or violet or a combination of such names. The dramatic differences that we see among the colors in the spectrum are produced by very slight differences in the wavelengths of light. For example, the wavelengths that appear as yellow are only slightly shorter than those that appear as orange. But there is a great visual difference between orange and yellow. This difference is a difference in hue.

Lightness is a measurement of the amount of light reflected from a colored object. The lightness of a color may be expressed by comparing the color's level of reflected light with that of samples on a lightness scale. A lightness scale runs from black, through shades of gray, to white. Black reflects very little light. A color that reflects about the same amount of light as black has a very low lightness level. Gray reflects more light than black. Thus, a color that reflects about the same amount of light as a shade of gray may have an intermediate level of lightness. White reflects nearly all the light that strikes it. Therefore, a color that reflects about the same amount of light as white has a very high lightness level. Color experts use the term *brightness* to describe the lightness level of a colored light source.

Chroma is a measurement of the *saturation* (concentration) of a color. For example, a teaspoon of red poster paint powder mixed with a teaspoon of water produces paint of a deep red color. The paint has a high concentration of red colorant, and so it has a high chroma. If we dilute the paint with a cup of water, the resulting mixture will have a low concentration of red colorant and, therefore, a low chroma.

How colors are classified

Experts estimate that we can distinguish perhaps as many as 10 million colors. Each color differs from all others in some degree of hue, lightness, or chroma. Our names for colors are far too inexact to describe accurately all the colors we see. As a result, people often have difficulty trying to describe or match a certain color. Matching colors is especially important in such industries as paint and textile manufacturing. Manufacturers of paints and textiles must minimize differences in the color of a particular paint or fabric from one batch of paint or bolt of fabric to another.

To overcome problems in describing and matching colors, color experts have developed various systems of classifying colors. Two widely used classification systems are (1) the Munsell Color System and (2) the CIE System of Color Specification.

The Munsell Color System is one of the most popular and useful means of classifying colors. It was developed in the early 1900's by Albert H. Munsell, an American portrait painter. The system classifies colors according to the three basic characteristics of hue, lightness, and chroma. However, Munsell used the term *value* for lightness.

The Munsell system may be displayed in many ways. A common display shows samples of different colors arranged around a vertical axis. Different hues are arranged around the axis like the spokes of a wheel, with each spoke consisting of a different hue. The axis serves as the value, or lightness, scale. It is divided into 10 sections. These sections correspond to 10 levels of value from black at the bottom, through shades of gray, to white at the top. All color samples at the same level have the same value. Colors close to the axis have low chroma. The farther from the axis a color is located, the higher is its chroma.

To match a particular color using the Munsell system or a similar system, one must find that color among the color samples provided. However, the number of samples in such systems cannot approach the number of colors we are able to distinguish. For this reason, it is sometimes impossible to find an exact color match.

The CIE System of Color Specification. Manufacturers of such products as foods, paints, paper, plastics, and textiles must often match colors precisely. Because color vision varies among people, two colors that match for one person may not match for another. For this reason, manufacturers do not rely on the human eye to match colors precisely. Instead, they use the CIE System of Color Specification. *CIE* stands for Commission Internationale de l'Éclairage (International Commission on Illumination), an international organization that establishes standards for measuring color.

A paint manufacturer who wants to produce the same color of green paint at two factories may use the CIE system to make sure that the two greens match. First, color experts analyze the color of the green paint made at one factory to determine the wavelengths of light that compose it. They make the analysis with a *spectrophotometer.* This instrument separates the light reflected from the paint into its various wavelengths and measures their *intensity* (strength). Then, tables of numbers are used to convert this information into three numerical values—one for each of the primary colors in light, which will match the original green when mixed. These tables of numbers, called *standard observers,* define the color-matching properties of a human eye having normal color vision.

The paint made at the second factory is also analyzed

The Munsell Color System

WORLD BOOK illustrations by Arnold Ryan Chalfant & Associates

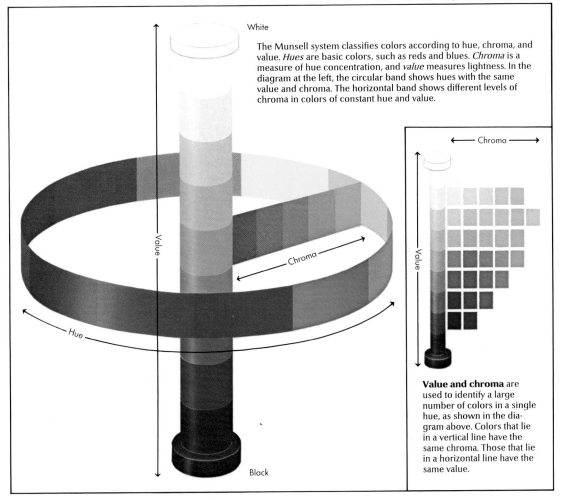

White

The Munsell system classifies colors according to hue, chroma, and value. *Hues* are basic colors, such as reds and blues. *Chroma* is a measure of hue concentration, and *value* measures lightness. In the diagram at the left, the circular band shows hues with the same value and chroma. The horizontal band shows different levels of chroma in colors of constant hue and value.

Chroma

Value

Chroma

Hue

Value

Black

Value and chroma are used to identify a large number of colors in a single hue, as shown in the diagram above. Colors that lie in a vertical line have the same chroma. Those that lie in a horizontal line have the same value.

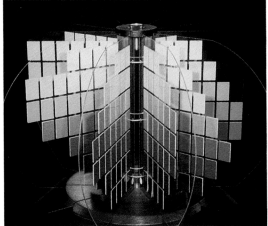

Munsell Color, Baltimore

A Munsell color tree displays many color samples arranged around a central axis. Such a color tree can be helpful when a person is trying to match a particular color.

using a spectrophotometer. Small amounts of pigment are then added to adjust the color of the paint. Pigment is added until the analysis results in the same three primary color values that were produced by the paint made at the first factory. When these three primary color values are reached, the two green paints will match, even though they may contain different mixtures of pigments.

History of color studies

Early theories of color vision. Many thinkers in ancient times developed theories about the nature of color. Since then, scientific experiments have confirmed some of their ideas and disproved others.

Empedocles, a Greek philosopher of the 400's B.C., believed that color vision was caused by tiny particles that were given off by objects and passed through the eyes. He thought that the eyes either produced a color reaction to the particles or recognized them as colored. In the early 300's B.C., the Greek philosopher Plato proposed that color vision was caused by rays that shot out from the eyes toward objects. Aristotle, a Greek philosopher of the later 300's B.C., may have been the first person to realize that there is a relation between color and light. However, he also thought that color was caused by something transparent between objects and the eyes. Galen, a Greek physician of the A.D. 100's, believed that color vision arose because rays from the eyes empowered the surrounding air to carry tiny images of objects to the eyes. He thought that these images then were analyzed by a visual spirit which moved between the eyes and the brain.

During the early 1000's, an Arab physicist, Ibn Al-Haytham, also known as Alhazen, recognized that vision is caused by the reflection of light from objects into our eyes. He stated that this reflected light forms optical images in the eyes. Alhazen believed that the colors we see in objects depend on the light striking the objects and on some property of the objects themselves.

Newton and Goethe. During the late 1600's and early 1700's, Sir Isaac Newton, an English scientist, performed many experiments to investigate the nature of color. Using a prism, Newton demonstrated that white light contains all the colors of the rainbow. He also was the first person to show that colored lights can be combined to form white light. Newton realized that light rays themselves are not colored but that the sensation of color is produced in the brain.

During the late 1700's and early 1800's, Johann Wolfgang von Goethe, a German poet, experimented with colored lights and shadows. He wrote a book on optics that seemed to contradict many of Newton's findings. Goethe did not believe that colored lights could be combined to form white light. He thought that all colored lights were actually mixtures of light and darkness. Goethe's experiments were useful in demonstrating many aspects of color vision. However, Goethe's theories of color vision based on these experiments are no longer accepted by scientists.

The three-component theory of color vision was proposed in 1801 by Thomas Young, an English physicist. It was further developed during the 1850's by a German physicist, Hermann von Helmholtz. The three-component theory is also known as the *Young-Helmholtz theory* or the *trichromatic theory*. The theory proposes that the eye has three types of fibers that are sensitive to different wavelengths of light. When light strikes the fibers, they generate electrical signals that travel directly to the brain. According to the three-component theory, the color sensations that arise in the brain correspond to the electrical signals in a simple and direct way. Scientific experiments have confirmed the existence of the three types of fibers, which are now called *cones.* Each type of cone is particularly sensitive to one of three general ranges of wavelengths of light—those corresponding to red, green, and blue.

The opponent color theory was proposed in 1874 by Ewald Hering, a German physiologist. Hering suggested that, somewhere in the nerves of the eyes and brain, there are two response mechanisms, each of which involves a pair of opposing colors. This means that the response mechanisms can signal only one of the two colors at a time. One response mechanism signals either red or green, and the other signals either yellow or blue. A third mechanism signals the level of lightness. The brain interprets these signals, producing our

sense of color. The opponent color theory explains many aspects of color vision better than the three-component theory does. For example, the opponent color theory provides an explanation for the fact that we see no such colors as reddish-green or yellowish-blue.

Recent theories combine ideas from the three-component and opponent color theories to describe the various stages of color vision. In the first stage of color vision, three types of cones in the retina absorb light and generate electrical signals, as proposed by the three-component theory. During the second stage of color vision, nerves in the eyes and brain create three new signals, which correspond to those described by the opponent color theory. The nerve signals may pass through further stages before the brain finally interprets them as the sensation of color.   Gunter Wyszecki

Related articles in *World Book* include:

Animal (How animals protect themselves; pictures)	Pigment
Color blindness	Printing (picture: Printing with process colors)
Dye	Prism
Electromagnetic waves	Protective coloration
Eye	Rainbow
Interior decoration	Spectrometer
Light	Technicolor
Newton, Sir Isaac	Television (How television works; illustration)
Paint	

Outline

I. The relation between color and light
II. How we see color
    A. The roles of the eyes and brain
    B. Surprising color-vision effects
III. Color vision in animals
IV. Methods of color production
    A. Mixing colorants   B. Mixing colored lights
  V. Producing color harmony
VI. Characteristics of color
    A. Hue   C. Chroma
    B. Lightness
VII. How colors are classified
    A. The Munsell Color System
    B. The CIE System of Color Specification
VIII. History of color studies

Questions

What are the three basic characteristics of every color?
Why does a carrot appear orange?
Who was the first person to show that colored lights can be combined to form white light?
What is the *visible spectrum?*
How is a *tint* produced? A *shade?* A *tone?*
What are the three *primary colors in light?*
Why do we see only tones of gray in a dimly lit room?
What is a color *triad?*
Why are colorant mixtures sometimes called *subtractive color mixtures?*
What are *phantom colors?*

Additional resources

Level I

Ardley, Neil. *The Science Book of Color.* Harcourt, 1991.
Branley, Franklyn M. *Color: From Rainbows to Lasers.* T. Y. Crowell, 1978.
Simon, Hilda. *The Magic of Color.* Lothrop, 1981. *Sight and Seeing: A World of Light and Color.* Philomel, 1983.

Level II

Birren, Faber. *Creative Color.* Schiffer, 1987. First published in 1961.
De Grandis, Luigina. *Theory and Use of Color.* Abrams, 1986.
Sloan, Annie, and Gwynn, Kate. *Color in Decoration.* Little, Brown, 1990.

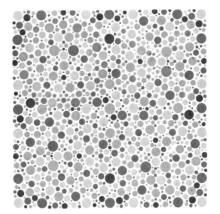

Testing color vision. These color patterns are examples of the figures used to find out whether people confuse certain colors with others.

At the left, people who confuse both blue and yellow may not see the ○ and ×.

At the right, people who confuse both red and green may not see the ○ and ▷.

These plates are copyrighted by American Optical Company and are reproduced here by permission. However, these reproductions do not present true testing conditions and cannot be used as a color vision deficiency test.

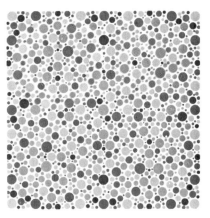

Color blindness, sometimes called daltonism, is the inability to tell all colors apart. The ability to see color originates in specific visual cells, called *cones*, in the retina of the eye. A person with normal color vision has three types of cones, and each type is sensitive to a different color. Color-blind people lack one, two, or all of these types of cones.

Most color-blind people have *dichromatic vision.* People with this kind of color blindness can see only yellows and blues. They confuse reds with greens, and some reds or greens with some yellows. Only a very few people are truly blind to all colors. They have *achromatic vision.* They see in shades of white, gray, and black—somewhat like a black-and-white photograph.

More men than women are color blind. About 8 of every 100 men are color blind, compared to about 1 of every 200 women. There is no cure for color blindness.

Many animals, including cats and horses, probably do not see colors as we do. But the condition is normal in their eyes, not defective.

Many color-blind people do not realize that their eyesight is defective. They have learned to use the color names that everyone else uses. These people may be hampered in their everyday activities, and their condition may place them in danger. If they confuse red and green, for example, they may only be able to tell traffic signals apart by their brightness. Many armed forces refuse to accept color-blind people for military service. In addition, color blindness can be a hindrance for airline pilots, fashion designers, and members of certain other professions.

Most people can be easily tested for color blindness. The *Hardy-Rand-Rittler (H-R-R)* and *Ishihara* tests indicate both the type and the degree of color blindness. In these and similar tests, colored triangles, squares, and other shapes lie in a jumble of dots. These dots vary in both color and intensity. As the person identifies the colored shapes, an examiner can determine the person's ability to see colors. Other tests, such as the *Holmgren* yarn-matching test and the *Farnsworth-Munsell 100-hue* disk-matching test, measure the ability to match colors.

Color blindness is inherited. If a color-blind man marries a woman who has no family history of color blindness, their children will have normal vision. Their daughters, however, will carry the gene for color blindness, and may pass it on to their children. If a woman whose father is color blind marries a man with normal vision, each of their sons has a 50-50 chance of inheriting the disorder. Injury to the retina or optic nerve and various diseases of the eye can also cause color blindness.   Ramesh C. Tripathi and Brenda J. Tripathi

See also **Eye** (Color blindness).

Arnold Ryan Chalfant & Associates (WORLD BOOK photos)

To a color-blind person, some colors look the same. A person who confuses red and green with other colors may say these pictures look the same or are equally colorful. Most people with normal color vision would say the photograph on the right is the more colorful of the two.

Rocky Mountain columbine, the state flower, and other wildflowers bloom in the San Isabel National Forest, *above.* The three mountain peaks in the background are called the Three Apostles.

Colorado *The Centennial State*

Colorado is a state of unusual natural beauty in the Rocky Mountain region of the United States. The scenic wonders of the Rockies and the cool, pleasant climate make the state a center for summer tourists. In winter, the deep, powdery snow of Colorado attracts skiers to world-famous resorts. Each year, millions of visitors travel to such tourist areas as Aspen, Estes Park, and Colorado Springs.

But not all of Colorado is mountainous, and only part of the state's income comes from tourists. Most Coloradans live and work on the dry, flat plains that make up the eastern two-fifths of the state. Tunnels bored through the mountains bring water to the plains for busy cities

The contributors of this article are John L. Dietz, Professor of Geography at the University of Northern Colorado, and Duane A. Smith, Professor of History at Fort Lewis College and coauthor of A Colorado History.

and prosperous farms. Colorado's location halfway between the major cities of California and the Midwest has helped make it the main transportation and distribution center for the Rocky Mountain region. The state's regional importance has led many large financial and manufacturing companies to set up branch offices there.

Herds of cattle and sheep graze on the mountains and plains of Colorado. Irrigated farms produce rich crops of potatoes and sugar beets. Wheat and corn fields spread across the plains.

Mining also has an important part in the state's economy. A series of mining booms has sparked Colorado's growth since the 1850's. The colorful story of Colorado gold and silver mining in the 1800's has become famous through music. The musical comedy *The Unsinkable Molly Brown* and the opera *The Ballad of Baby Doe* describe life during the great mining booms.

Colorado mines still produce gold and silver ores. But

Interesting facts about Colorado

WORLD BOOK illustrations by Kevin Chadwick

Colorado has the highest average altitude—about 6,800 feet (2,100 meters) above sea level—of any state in the United States.

The first *community chest,* a single fund drive to support a number of charitable causes, was established in Denver. It was organized by four clergymen—a priest, a rabbi, and two ministers—in 1887. They named it the Charity Organization Society.

The largest silver nugget ever found in North America, *right,* was discovered in Aspen in 1894. The nugget weighed 1,840 pounds (835 kilograms) and was 93 per cent pure sterling silver, the largest silver nugget of such purity ever found in the world.

Largest nugget

Colorado had three governors in one day. Alva Adams had been governor for two months when charges of election fraud forced him out of office on March 17, 1905. The state legislature named James H. Peabody governor. He resigned the same day and Jesse F. McDonald, Adams' lieutenant governor, took office.

Great Sand Dunes

Great Sand Dunes National Monument, *above,* has been called one of the United States' strangest natural wonders. This huge area of sand, lying at the base of the Sangre de Cristo Mountains in south-central Colorado, is constantly shifting. It sometimes forms dunes as high as 700 feet (210 meters).

Denver & Colorado Convention & Visitors Bureau

Denver, Colorado's capital and largest city, boasts a spectacular view of the Rocky Mountains, which lie just west of the city.

petroleum is the state's most important mineral product today. Colorado also leads the nation in the production of molybdenum, a metal that hardens steel.

The U.S. government owns more than a third of Colorado's land. The government controls grazing, logging, and mining on those lands. The U.S. Mint in Denver makes coins. One of the state's largest employers manufactures space vehicles for the government. The U.S. Air Force has its academy close to Colorado Springs, its defense headquarters in nearby Cheyenne Mountain, and its finance center in Denver.

The Spanish word *colorado* means *colored red.* The name was given first to the Colorado River, which flows through canyons of red stone. The state was named for the river. Colorado's nickname is the *Centennial State.* Colorado joined the Union in 1876, the *centennial* (100th anniversary) of the Declaration of Independence. Denver is the capital and largest city of Colorado.

© Nicholas Devore III, Photographers/Aspen

Raising beef cattle is Colorado's leading agricultural activity. Herds of cattle graze on the state's plains and mountains. The cattle also are fattened in feed lots.

Colorado in brief

Symbols of Colorado

On the state flag, adopted in 1911, the red *C* stands for *Colorado,* which is Spanish for *colored red.* The golden ball represents the state's gold production, and the blue and white bars symbolize blue skies and white mountain snows. On the seal, adopted in 1877, the triangular figure represents the "all-seeing" eye of God. The mountains stand for Colorado's rugged land, and the pick and hammer for the importance of mining.

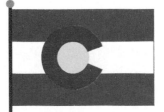

State flag

State seal

Colorado (brown) ranks eighth in size among all the states and third in size among the Rocky Mountain States (yellow).

General information

Statehood: Aug. 1, 1876, the 38th state.
State abbreviations: Colo. (traditional); CO (postal).
State motto: *Nil sine Numine* (Nothing Without Providence).
State song: "Where the Columbines Grow." Words and music by A. J. Fynn.

The State Capitol is in Denver, Colorado's capital since 1876. Territorial capitals were Colorado City (1862), Golden (1862-1867), and Denver (1867-1876).

Land and climate

Area: 104,100 sq. mi. (269,618 km²), including 371 sq. mi. (960 km²) of inland water.
Elevation: *Highest*—Mount Elbert, 14,433 ft. (4,399 m) above sea level. *Lowest*—3,350 ft. (1,021 m) above sea level along the Arkansas River in Prowers County.
Record high temperature: 118 °F (48 °C), at Bennett on July 11, 1888.
Record low temperature: −61 °F (−52 °C), at Maybell in Moffat County on Feb. 1, 1985.
Average July temperature: 74 °F (23 °C).
Average January temperature: 28 °F (−2 °C).
Average yearly precipitation: 15 in. (38 cm).

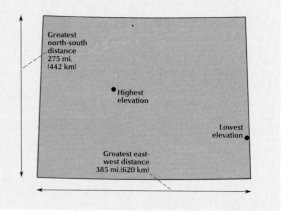

Greatest north-south distance 275 mi. (442 km)

Highest elevation

Lowest elevation

Greatest east-west distance 385 mi.(620 km)

Important dates

Zebulon M. Pike explored Colorado.

The Colorado gold rush attracted thousands of prospectors and settlers.

1803   1806   1848   1859   1876

The United States acquired eastern Colorado in the Louisiana Purchase.

The United States took western Colorado after the Mexican War.

Colorado became the 38th state on August 1.

State bird
Lark bunting

State flower
Rocky Mountain columbine

State tree
Blue spruce

People

Population: 3,307,912 (1990 census)
Rank among the states: 26th
Density: 32 persons per sq. mi. (12 per km²), U.S. average 69 per sq. mi. (27 per km²)
Distribution: 82 per cent urban, 18 per cent rural
Largest cities in Colorado

Denver	467,610
Colorado Springs	281,140
Aurora	222,103
Lakewood	126,481
Pueblo	98,640
Arvada	89,235

Source: U.S. Bureau of the Census.

Population trend

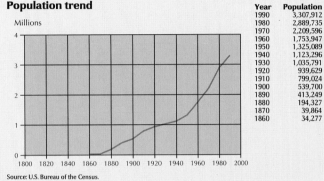

Millions

Source: U.S. Bureau of the Census.

Year	Population
1990	3,307,912
1980	2,889,735
1970	2,209,596
1960	1,753,947
1950	1,325,089
1940	1,123,296
1930	1,035,791
1920	939,629
1910	799,024
1900	539,700
1890	413,249
1880	194,327
1870	39,864
1860	34,277

Economy

Chief products

Agriculture: beef cattle, hay, wheat, milk, corn.
Manufacturing: scientific instruments, food products, machinery, fabricated metal products, electrical equipment, printed materials.
Mining: petroleum, coal, natural gas.

Gross state product

Value of goods and services produced in 1991: $74,307,000,000. *Services* include community, social, and personal services; finance; government; trade; and transportation, communication, and utilities. *Industry* includes construction, manufacturing, and mining. *Agriculture* includes agriculture, fishing, and forestry.

Source: U.S. Bureau of Economic Analysis.

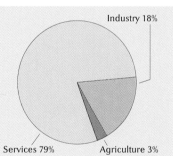

Industry 18%

Services 79%

Agriculture 3%

Government

State government

Governor: 4-year term
State senators: 35; 4-year terms
State representatives: 65; 2-year terms
Counties: 63

Federal government

United States senators: 2
United States representatives: 6
Electoral votes: 8

Sources of information

Tourism: Colorado Tourism Board, 1625 Broadway, Suite 1700, Denver, CO 80202
Economy: Office of Economic Development, 1625 Broadway, Suite 1710, Denver, CO 80202
Government: Legislative Council, State Capitol Building, Denver, CO 80203
History: Colorado Historical Society, 1300 Broadway, Denver, CO 80203

The U.S. Mint in Denver issued its first coins.

North American Air Defense Command completed its underground operations center in Cheyenne Mountain.

1906   **1958**   **1966**

The U.S. Air Force Academy's permanent campus opened near Colorado Springs.

People

Population. The 1990 United States census reported that Colorado had 3,307,912 people. The population had increased 14 per cent over the 1980 census figure, 2,889,735. According to the 1990 census, Colorado ranks 26th in population among the 50 states.

About four of every five Coloradans live in one of the state's six metropolitan areas—Denver, Colorado Springs, Boulder-Longmont, Fort Collins-Loveland, Greeley, and Pueblo (see **Metropolitan area**). For their populations, see the *Index* to the political map of Colorado.

The state has four cities with populations over 100,000. They are, in order of size, Denver, Colorado Springs, Aurora, and Lakewood.

Most of Colorado's cities grew up near the eastern edge of the mountains. Denver, the largest city in the state, is a business, financial, and manufacturing center. Colorado Springs attracts large numbers of tourists. Colorado Springs also serves several military bases, including the United States Air Force Academy. The largest city in western Colorado is Grand Junction. See the articles on the cities listed in the *Related articles* at the end of this article.

Population density

About 80 per cent of Colorado's people live in urban areas. About half of the people live in or near Denver, the state's largest city and capital.

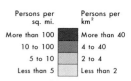

Persons per sq. mi.	Persons per km²
More than 100	More than 40
10 to 100	4 to 40
5 to 10	2 to 4
Less than 5	Less than 2

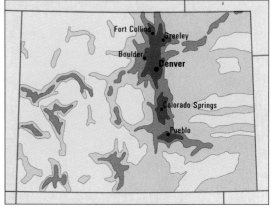

WORLD BOOK map; based on U.S. Bureau of the Census data.

Colorado map index

Metropolitan areas

Boulder-Longmont 225,339
Colorado Springs 397,014
Denver 1,622,980
Fort Collins-
  Loveland 186,136
Greeley 131,821
Pueblo 123,051

Counties

Adams ....265,038..D 13
Alamosa ....13,617..I 10
Arapahoe ....391,511..E 12
Archuleta ....5,345..J 8
Baca ....4,556..I 15
Bent ....5,048..H 15
Boulder ....225,339..D 11
Chaffee ....12,684..G 10
Cheyenne ....2,397..F 15
Clear Creek ......7,619..E 10
Conejos ....7,453..J 10
Costilla ....3,190..J 11
Crowley ....3,946..G 13
Custer ....1,926..H 11
Delta ....20,980..F 7
Denver ....467,610..D 11
Dolores ....1,504..I 6
Douglas ....60,391..E 12
Eagle ....21,928..D 9
Elbert ....9,646..E 13
El Paso ....397,014..F 12
Fremont ....32,273..G 11
Garfield ....29,974..E 6
Gilpin ....3,070..D 10
Grand ....7,966..D 10
Gunnison ....10,273..F 8
Hinsdale ....467..H 8
Huerfano ....6,009..I 11
Jackson ....1,605..C 9
Jefferson ......438,430..E 11
Kiowa ....1,688..G 15
Kit Carson ....7,140..E 15
Lake ....6,007..F 9
La Plata ....32,284..I 7
Larimer ....186,136..C 11
Las Animas ......13,765..I 13
Lincoln ....4,529..F 14
Logan ....17,567..B 15
Mesa ....93,145..F 6
Mineral ....558..I 8
Moffat ....11,357..C 6
Montezuma ....18,672..I 6
Montrose ....24,423..G 6
Morgan ....21,939..D 13
Otero ....20,185..H 13
Ouray ....2,295..H 7
Park ....7,174..F 10
Phillips ....4,189..C 16
Pitkin ....12,661..F 8
Prowers ....13,347..H 16
Pueblo ....123,051..H 12
Rio Blanco ....5,972..D 6
Rio Grande ......10,770..I 9
Routt ....14,088..C 8
Saguache ....4,619..H 9
San Juan ....745..I 7
San Miguel ....3,653..H 6
Sedgwick ....2,690..B 15

Cities and towns

Agate ....E 13
Aguilar ....520..I 12
Air Force Academy
  see United
  States Air
  Force Academy
Akron ....1,599.°D 14
Alamosa ....7,579.°I 10
Alamosa East*† ..1,389..I 10
Allenspark ....E 1
Allison ....J 7
Alma ....148..E 10
Anton ....D 14
Antonito ....875..J 10
Applewood*† ...11,069..D 11
Arapahoe ....F 16
Arboles ....I 7
Arriba ....220..E 14
Arvada ....89,235..G 3
Aspen ....5,049.°F 8
Aspen Park ....H 2
Ault ....1,107..D 12
Aurora ....222,103..G 3
Austin ....F 7
Avon ....1,798..E 9
Avondale ....H 13
Bailey ....I 1
Barr Lake ....F 3
Basalt ....1,128..E 8
Baxterville ....H 10
Bayfield ....1,090..J 7
Bellvue ....D 2
Bennett ....1,757..D 12
Berthoud ....2,990..E 3
Bethune ....173..E 16
Beulah ....H 11
Black Forest† ...8,143..J 4
Black Hawk ....227..G 1
Blanca ....272..I 11
Blue Mountain ....C 5
Blue River ....440..E 10
Bonanza City ......16..H 10
Boncarbo ....J 12
Boone ....341..H 13
Boulder ....83,312.°D 11
Bow Mar* ....854..E 11
Bowie ....F 7
Boyero ....F 14
Brandon ....G 15
Branson ....58..J 13
Breckenridge ...1,285.°E 10
Briggsdale ....C 12
Brighton ....14,203.°F 4
Bristol ....H 16
Broadmoor ....K 3
Brookside ....183..G 11
Brookvale ....H 2
Broomfield .....24,638..G 3
Brush ....4,165..C 14
Buckingham ....C 13
Buena Vista ....1,752..F 10
Buffalo Creek ....I 2
Buford ....D 7
Burlington .....2,941.°E 16
Burns ....E 8
Byers† ....1,065..D 13
Caddoa ....H 15
Cahone ....I 5
Calhan ....562..F 13
Cameo ....F 6
Camp Bird ....H 7
Campion† ....1,692..E 3
Campo ....121..J 16
Canfield ....F 3
Canon City ....12,687.°G 11
Capulin ....J 10
Carbondale .....3,004..E 8
Cardiff ....E 8
Cascade ....K 3
Castle Rock ....8,708.°I 3
Castlewood*† ..24,392..E 12
Cedaredge ......1,380..F 7
Cedarwood ....I 11
Center ....1,963..I 10
Central City .....335.°G 1
Chama ....I 11
Cheraw ....265..H 14
Cherry Hills
  Village ....5,245..H 3
Cheyenne Wells ..1,128.°F 16
Chimney Rock ....J 8
Chipita Park ....K 3
Chivington ....G 15
Chromo ....J 8
Cimarron ....G 7
Cimarron Hills*† .11,160..F 12
Clark ....B 8
Clifton† ....12,671..F 6
Climax ....E 9
Coal Creek ....157..G 11
Coaldale ....G 10
Coalmont ....C 9
Cokedale ....116..J 12
Collbran ....228..E 7
Colona ....G 7
Colorado City† ..1,149..H 12
Colorado
  Springs ....281,140.°F 12
Columbine† .....23,969..B 8
Columbine
  Valley ....1,071..H 3
Commerce
  City ....16,466..G 3
Como ....E 10
Conejos ....°I 10
Conifer ....H 2
Cope ....D 14
Cortez ....7,284.°I 6
Cotopaxi ....G 10
Cowdrey ....B 9
Craig ....8,091.°C 7
Crawford ....221..G 7
Creede ....362.°H 8
Crested Butte ....878..F 8
Crestone ....39..H 10
Cripple Creek ....584.°F 11
Crook ....148..B 15
Crowley ....225..H 13
Cuchara ....I 11
Dacono ....2,228..F 3
Dailey ....C 15
De Beque ....257..E 6
Deckers ....I 2
Deer Trail ....476..E 13
Delhi ....I 13
Del Norte ......1,674.°I 9
Delta ....3,789.°G 6
Denver ....467,610.°D 11
Deora ....I 15
Dillon ....553..E 10
Dinosaur ....324..C 5
Divide ....K 2
Dolores ....866..I 6
Dove Creek ....643.°H 5
Doyleville ....G 9
Drake ....D 2
Dupont ....G 3
Durango ....12,430.°J 7
Eads ....780.°G 15
Eagle ....1,580.°E 8
East Portal ....G 1
Eastlake ....F 3
Eaton ....1,959..D 4
Echo Lake ....H 1
Eckley ....211..D 15
Edgewater ......4,613..G 3
Edler ....J 15
Edwards ....E 9
Egnar ....H 5
Elbert ....F 12
Eldora ....F 1
Eldorado Springs ...D 3
Elizabeth ....818..I 4
Elk Springs ....C 6
Ellicott ....F 12
Empire ....401..G 1
Englewood .....29,387..H 3
Erie ....1,258..F 3
Estabrook ....I 2
Estes Park .....3,184..E 1
Evans ....5,877..E 4
Evergreen† .....7,582..H 2
Fairplay ....387.°F 10
Falcon ....F 12
Farisita ....I 11
Federal
  Heights* .....9,342..D 11
Firestone ......1,358..F 3
Flagler ....564..E 15
Fleming ....344..B 15
Florence ....2,990..G 11
Florissant ....K 2
Fort Carson*† ..11,309..G 12
Fort Collins ..87,758.°C 11
Fort Garland ....I 11
Fort Lupton ....5,159..F 4
Fort Lyon ....H 14
Fort Morgan ....9,068.°C 13
Fountain ....9,984..G 12
Fowler ....1,154..H 13
Franktown ....I 4
Fraser ....575..D 10
Frederick ....988..F 3
Frisco ....1,601..E 10
Fruita ....4,045..F 5
Fruitvale† .....5,222..F 6
Galeton ....D 4
Garcia ....J 11
Garden City ......199..E 4
Gardner ....I 11
Garfield ....G 9
Gateway† ....7,510..G 5
Gato ....J 8
Gem Village ....J 7
Genoa ....167..E 14
Georgetown ....891.°G 1
Gilcrest ....1,084..E 4
Gilman ....E 9
Glade Park ....F 5
Glen Haven ....D 2
Glendale* ......2,453..D 11
Glendevey ....B 10
Glenisle ....I 1
Glenwood
  Springs ......6,561.°E 8
Golden ....13,116.°G 2
Goodrich ....C 13
Gould ....C 10
Granada ....513..H 16
Granby ....966..D 10
Grand
  Junction ....29,034.°F 6
Grand Lake ....259..C 10
Granite ....F 9
Grant ....H 1
Greeley ....60,536.°C 12
Green Mountain
  Falls ....663..K 3
Greenwood
  Village ....7,589..H 3
Greystone ....C 6
Grover ....135..B 13
Guffey ....K 1
Gunbarrel*† .....9,388..E 11
Gunnison ....4,636.°G 8
Gypsum ....1,750..E 8
Hamilton ....C 7
Hartman ....108..H 16
Hartsel ....F 10
Hasty ....H 15
Haswell ....62..G 14
Haxtun ....952..C 15
Hayden ....1,444..C 8
Heeney ....D 9
Henderson ....G 3
Hereford ....B 12
Hesperus ....J 6
Hideaway Park ......D 10
Hillrose ....169..C 14
Hoehne ....I 13
Holly ....877..H 16
Holyoke ....1,931.°C 16
Hooper ....112..I 10
Hot Sulphur
  Springs ....347.°D 10
Hotchkiss ....744..F 7
Howard ....G 10
Hoyt ....D 13
Hudson ....918..F 4
Hugo ....660.°F 14
Hygiene ....E 2
Idaho Springs ..1,834..G 1
Idalia ....D 16
Ignacio ....720..J 7

Schools. O.J. Goldrick opened the first school in Colorado in 1859. The students at the school were the children of gold miners in the Cherry Creek area (now Denver).

Today, a seven-member board of education heads the state department of education. Board members are elected to six-year terms. They appoint a commissioner of education to direct the department. Elected school boards and appointed superintendents run the local districts.

Children must attend school from age 7 through 15. For the number of students and teachers in Colorado, see **Education** (table).

Libraries. Colorado's first public library was established in Denver in 1860. Today, Colorado has approximately 140 public libraries. Of these, about 30 are county libraries. The Colorado State Library is located in Denver.

Museums. The Denver Art Museum features an Indian and native arts collection. The Denver Museum of Natural History has displays about animals. The Colorado Heritage Center in Denver has exhibits on the early West. The State Historical Society operates museums in Denver, Fort Garland, Georgetown, Leadville, Montrose, Platteville, Pueblo, and Trinidad.

Universities and colleges

Colorado has 23 universities and colleges that grant bachelor's or advanced degrees and are accredited by the North Central Association of Colleges and Schools. For enrollments and further information, see **Universities and colleges** (table).

Name	Mailing address
Adams State College	Alamosa
Beth-El College of Nursing	Colorado Springs
Colorado, University of	*
Colorado Christian University	Lakewood
Colorado College	Colorado Springs
Colorado School of Mines	Golden
Colorado State University	Fort Collins
Colorado Tech	Colorado Springs
Denver, University of	Denver
Denver Conservative Baptist Seminary	Denver
Fort Lewis College	Durango
Iliff School of Theology	Denver
Mesa State College	Grand Junction
Metropolitan State College of Denver	Denver
Naropa Institute	Boulder
National Technological University	Fort Collins
National Theatre Conservatory	Denver
Northern Colorado, University of	Greeley
Regis University	Denver
St. Thomas Seminary	Denver
Southern Colorado, University of	Pueblo
United States Air Force Academy	U.S.A.F. Academy
Western State College	Gunnison

*For campuses, see **Universities and colleges** (table).

Place	Population	Map key
Iliff	174	B 14
Indian Agency		J 7
Ironton		H 7
Ivywild		K 4
Jamestown	251	F 2
Jansen		J 12
Jaroso		J 10
Jefferson		E 10
Joes		E 15
Johnstown	1,579	E 3
Juanita		J 8
Julesburg	1,295°	B 16
Karval		G 14
Keenesburg	570	D 12
Ken Caryl*†	24,391	E 11
Keota	5	C 13
Kersey	980	C 12
Kim	76	J 14
Kings Canyon		B 9
Kiowa	275°	E 12
Kirk		E 15
Kit Carson	305	F 15
Kittredge		H 2
Kremmling	1,166	D 9
Kutch		F 13
Lafayette	14,548	F 3
La Garita		H 9
Laird		D 16
La Jara	725	J 10
La Junta	7,637°	H 14
Lake City	223°	H 8
Lake George		J 2
Lakeside	11	G 3
Lakewood	126,481	G 3
Lamar	8,343°	H 15
Laporte		D 2
Larkspur	232	I 3
La Salle	1,783	E 4
Las Animas	2,481°	H 14
Lasauses		J 10
Las Mesitas		J 10
La Veta	726	I 11
Lawson		G 1
Leadville	2,629°	F 9
Leadville North*†	1,757	F 9
Lewis		I 5
Liberty Bell Village		H 7
Limon	1,831	E 14
Lincoln Park†	3,728	G 11
Lindon		D 14
Littleton	33,685°	H 3
Livermore		B 11
Lochbuie	1,168	D 12
Log Lane Village	667	C 13
Loma		F 5
Longmont	51,555	F 3
Longview		I 2
Louisville	12,361	F 3
Louviers		H 3
Loveland	37,352	E 3
Lucerne		D 4
Ludlow		I 12
Lycan		I 16
Lyons	1,227	E 2
Mack		E 5
Maher		G 7
Manassa	988	J 10
Mancos	842	I 6
Manitou Springs	4,535	K 3
Manzanola	437	H 13
Marble	64	F 8
Marvel		J 6
Masonville		D 2
Matheson		F 13
Maybell		C 7
Maysville		G 10
McClave		H 15
McCoy		D 9
Mead	456	E 3
Meeker	2,098°	D 7
Meeker Park		E 1
Meredith		E 9
Merino	238	C 14
Mesa		F 6
Mesita		J 11
Milliken	1,605	E 3
Milner		C 8
Minturn	1,066	E 9
Model		I 13
Moffat	99	H 10
Mogote		J 10
Molina		F 7
Monte Vista	4,324	I 10
Montezuma	60	E 10
Montrose	8,854°	G 7
Monument	1,020	J 3
Morrison*	465	E 11
Mosca		I 10
Mount Crested Butte	264	F 8
Mountain View	550	G 3
Nathrop		G 10
Naturita	434	H 6
Nederland	1,099	F 1
New Castle	679	E 7
Niwot†	2,666	F 2
Norfolk		B 11
North Avondale		G 12
North La Junta		H 14
Northglenn	27,195	G 3
Norwood	429	H 6
Nucla	656	H 6
Nunn	324	B 12
Oak Creek	673	C 8
Ohio		G 9
Olathe	1,263	G 7
Oliver		F 7
Olney Springs	340	H 13
Ophir*	69	H 7
Orchard		C 13
Orchard City	2,218	F 7
Orchard Mesa*†	5,977	F 6
Ordway	1,025°	H 13
Ortiz		J 10
Otis	451	D 15
Ouray	644°	H 7
Ovid	349	B 16
Padroni		B 14
Pagosa Springs	1,207°	J 8
Palisade	1,871	F 6
Palmer Lake	1,480	J 3
Pando		E 9
Pandora		H 7
Paoli	29	C 15
Paonia	1,403	F 7
Parachute	658	E 6
Paradox		G 5
Parker	5,450	H 4
Parlin		G 9
Parshall		D 10
Peetz	179	B 14
Penrose†	2,235	G 11
Peyton		F 12
Phippsburg		C 8
Pierce	823	D 4
Pine		I 2
Pinecliffe		G 2
Pitkin	53	G 9
Placerville		H 6
Plateau City		F 7
Platner		D 14
Platoro		I 9
Platteville	1,515	E 4
Pleasant View		I 5
Poncha Springs	244	G 10
Portland		G 11
Portland*		H 7
Powder Wash		B 6
Powderhorn		H 8
Pritchett	153	I 15
Proctor		B 15
Prospect Heights*	19	G 11
Pueblo	98,640°	H 12
Radium		D 9
Ramah	94	F 13
Rand		C 10
Range		D 8
Rangely	2,278	D 5
Raymer	98	C 13
Red Cliff	297	E 9
Red Feather Lakes		B 10
Redstone		E 8
Redvale		H 6
Rico	92	I 6
Ridgway	423	H 7
Rifle	4,636	E 7
Riverside		H 3
Rockvale	321	G 11
Rocky Ford	4,162	H 14
Roggen		D 12
Rollinsville		G 1
Romeo	341	J 10
Rosedale		E 4
Rush		F 13
Rye	168	H 12
Saguache	584°	H 10
Salida	4,737°	G 10
San Acacio		J 11
San Juan		J 12
San Luis	800°	J 11
San Pedro		J 11
Sanford	750	J 10
Sargents		G 9
Sawpit	36	H 7
Security [-Widefield]†	23,822	K 4
Sedalia		H 3
Sedgwick	183	B 15
Segundo		J 12
Seibert	181	E 15
Severance	106	D 3
Shamballah Ashrama		I 3
Shawnee		I 1
Sheridan	4,976	H 3
Sheridan Lake	95	G 16
Sherrelwood*†	16,636	D 12
Silt	1,095	E 7
Silver Cliff	322	H 11
Silver Plume	134	G 1
Silver Springs		H 2
Silverthorne	1,768	E 10
Silverton	716°	H 7
Simla	481	F 13
Slick Rock		H 5
Snowmass		E 8
Snowmass Village	1,449	F 8
Snyder		C 14
Somerset		F 7
South Fork		I 9
Southglenn*†	43,087	D 12
Springfield	1,475°	I 15
Starkville	104	J 12
Steamboat Springs	6,695°	C 8
Sterling	10,362°	C 14
Stoneham		C 13
Stonewall		J 11
Stonington		I 16
Strasburg		E 12
Stratmoor*†	5,854	F 12
Stratton	649	E 15
Stratton Meadows*		F 12
Stringtown		E 9
Sugar City	252	H 14
Summitville		I 9
Superior	255	F 2
Swink	584	H 14
Tabernash		D 10
Telluride	1,309°	H 7
Texas Creek		G 10
Thatcher		I 13
Thornton	55,031	G 3
Tiffany		J 7
Timnath	190	D 3
Timpas		H 13
Toponas		D 8
Towaoc†	700	J 5
Towner		G 16
Trinchera		J 13
Trinidad	8,580°	J 12
Twin Lakes		F 9
Two Buttes	63	I 16
Tyrone		I 13
United States Air Force Academy	9,062	J 4
Uravan		G 5
Utleyville		I 15
Vail	3,659	E 9
Vallecito		I 7
Vancorum		H 6
Vernon		D 16
Victor	258	G 11
Vilas	105	I 16
Villa Grove		H 10
Villegreen		I 14
Virginia Dale		B 11
Vona	104	E 15
Walden	890°	B 9
Walsenburg	3,300°	I 12
Walsh	692	I 16
Ward	159	F 1
Wattenberg		F 3
Welby*†	10,218	D 12
Weldona		C 13
Wellington	1,340	C 11
Westcliffe	312°	H 11
Westminster	74,625	G 3
Westminster East*†	5,197	D 12
Weston		J 12
Wetmore		H 11
Wheat Ridge	29,419	G 3
Whitewater		F 6
Widefield, see Security [-Widefield]		
Wiggins	499	C 13
Wild Horse		F 15
Wiley	406	H 15
Williamsburg	253	G 11
Windsor	5,062	D 3
Winter Park	528	G 1
Wolcott		E 9
Wondervu		F 2
Woodland Acres		H 12
Woodland Park	4,610	J 3
Woodmoor*†	3,858	F 12
Woodrow		D 14
Woody Creek		E 8
Wray	1,998°	D 16
Yampa	317	D 8
Yellow Jacket		I 5
Yoder		F 13
Yuma	2,719	D 15

*Does not appear on map; key shows general location.
†Census designated place—unincorporated, but recognized as a significant settled community by the U.S. Bureau of the Census.

°County seat.
Source: 1990 census. Places without population figures are unincorporated areas.

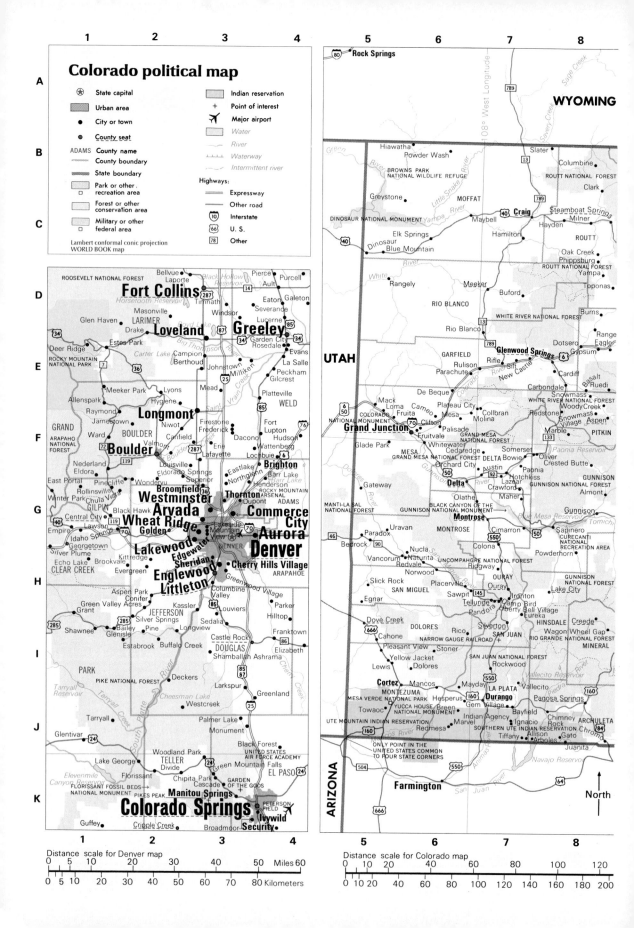

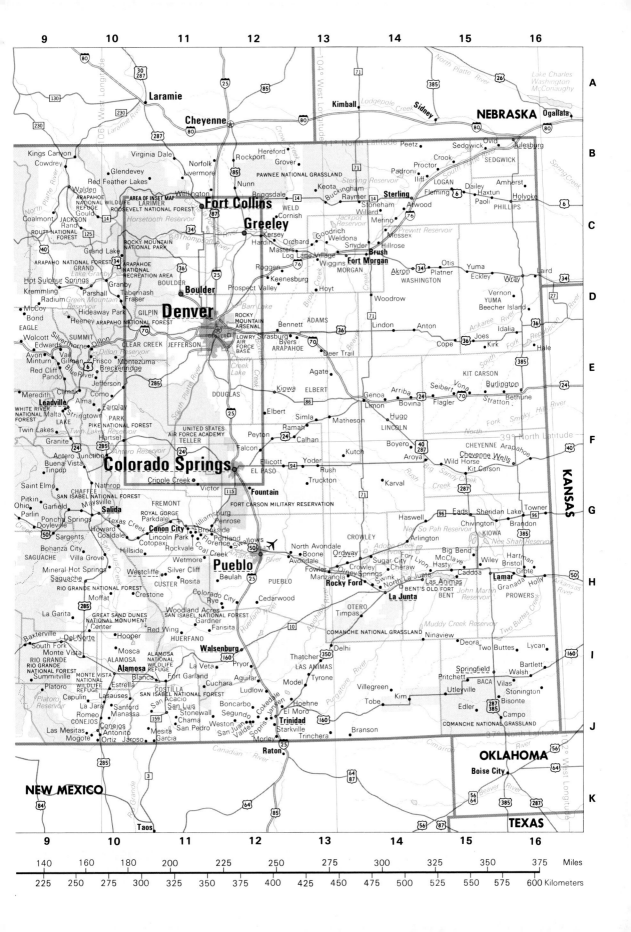

Beautiful Colorado attracts millions of tourists each year. In summer, visitors enjoy the state's cool climate. Campers pitch their tents on forested mountain slopes or near beautiful mountain streams. High peaks test the skill of mountain climbers. Old mining towns and Indian cliff dwellings lure tourists interested in history. People who like to fish cast for trout in the clear, swift streams. In autumn, hunters search for deer and other big game. In winter, skiers visit such famous Colorado resorts as

Aspen, Arapahoe Basin, Steamboat Springs, Vail, and Winter Park. The ski season in Colorado begins in late November and ends in April.

Many Colorado cities and towns hold fairs, festivals, races, and rodeos during the summer. In winter, the state hosts a variety of skiing and other winter sports events and competitions. In addition, many art, business, education, and religious groups hold conferences in Colorado.

Mesa Verde National Park, near Cortez

James P. Rowan

Places to visit

Following are brief descriptions of some of Colorado's many interesting places to visit:

Air Force Academy, north of Colorado Springs, trains the nation's air force officers. The Visitors Center, located at the south entrance, shows films about the academy.

Bent's Old Fort, east of La Junta, is a reconstructed trading post and a national historic site. The fort, originally built in 1833, was the first permanent American settlement in Colorado.

Buffalo Bill's Grave, on top of Lookout Mountain near Golden, honors the famous scout and showman William F. Cody (see Buffalo Bill).

Central City, once a rich gold camp, is now popular for its small stakes gambling clubs. A theater festival is held each summer in the opera house.

Cumbres & Toltec Scenic Railroad runs between Antonito and Osier and Osier and Chama, N. Mex. Steam-powered trains carry passengers through beautiful and historic areas, including Cumbres Pass, the Toltec Gorge, Tanglefoot Curve, and the Los Pinos River Valley.

Garden of the Gods, near Colorado Springs, is a breathtaking cluster of huge red sandstone rocks. Thousands of worshipers gather there on Easter Sunday for sunrise services. See Garden of the Gods.

Museum of Western Art, in Denver, houses paintings and sculptures by a number of Western artists, including Frederic Remington, Charles M. Russell, and Thomas Moran.

Narrow gauge railroad, between Durango and Silverton, is the last passenger railroad of its type in the country. The tracks of the railroad are set closer together than modern ones. Summer visitors can take a 90-mile (140-kilometer) round trip through beautiful canyons.

Pikes Peak, west of Colorado Springs, is probably the most famous mountain in the Rockies, even though 30 Colorado peaks are higher. Visitors can reach the top of the mountain by automobile toll road, cog railway, on horseback, or on

foot. For more information, see Pikes Peak.

Red Rocks Amphitheater, near Denver, is an open-air amphitheater that seats 9,000 people. It is surrounded by massive natural red rock formations that provide excellent acoustics. It hosts concerts and stage shows, as well as sunrise services on Easter Sunday.

Royal Gorge, near Canon City, is a massive canyon cut by the Arkansas River. The gorge, more than 1,000 feet (300 meters) deep, is crossed by the world's highest suspension bridge. See Royal Gorge.

United States Mint, in Denver, manufactures millions of coins each year. Tours of the mint are given. See Mint.

National parks, monuments, and forests. Colorado has two national parks—Rocky Mountain and Mesa Verde. Rocky Mountain National Park, in north-central Colorado, has more than 100 peaks that rise over 11,000 feet (3,350 meters). Mesa Verde National Park, near Cortez, preserves Indian cliff dwellings almost a thousand years old. See the separate articles in *World Book* on each national park.

Seven other areas of scenic beauty or historical interest have been designated as national monuments. These are the Black Canyon of the Gunnison, Colorado, Dinosaur, Florissant Fossil Beds, Great Sand Dunes, Hovenweep, and Curecanti National Recreation Area.

Twelve national forests cover about 13,774,000 acres (5,574,100 hectares) in Colorado. Completely within the state are Arapaho, Grand Mesa, Gunnison, Pike, Rio Grande, Roosevelt, Routt, San Isabel, San Juan, Uncompahgre, and White River national forests. Manti-La Sal forest lies partly in Utah.

Other parks. The city of Denver maintains many beautiful mountain parks that are outside its city limits. Since 1963, Colorado has created state parks on land administered by the state fish and game commission. For information about these parks, write to Colorado State Parks, 1313 Sherman, Denver, CO 80203.

Sky Pond in Rocky Mountain National Park

National Park Service

Annual events

January-June
National Western Stock Show in Denver (January); Breckenridge Ullrfest Winter Carnival (January); Steamboat Springs Winter Carnival (February); World Cup Ski Racing Competitions in Vail and Aspen (February and March); Winter Park Wingbreak (April); Iron Horse Bicycle Classic in Durango (May); Telluride Wine Festival (June); Telluride Bluegrass Festival (June); Frog Rodeo in Empire (June).

July-December
Denver Cherry Creek Arts Festival (July); Strings in the Mountains Chamber Music Festival in Steamboat Springs (July); Central City Opera Festival (July and August); Colorado Shakespeare Festival in Boulder (July and August); Festival of the Arts in Crested Butte (August); Colorado State Fair in Pueblo (August); Festival of Mountain and Plain in Denver (September); Rocky Mountain Colorfest, throughout southwestern Colorado (September and October); Larimer Square Oktoberfest in Denver (September); Parade of Lights in Denver (December).

U.S. Air Force

The U.S. Air Force Academy near Colorado Springs

Denver & Colorado Convention & Visitors Bureau

Narrow gauge railroad between Durango and Silverton

Aspen Skiing Company

World Cup skiing in Aspen

Land and climate

Land regions. Colorado has four main land regions: (1) the Colorado Plateau, (2) the Intermontane Basin, (3) the Rocky Mountains, and (4) the Great Plains.

The Colorado Plateau, along the western border, covers about a fifth of the state. It is an area of high hills, plateaus, deep valleys, and *mesas* (flat-topped hills with steep sides). Farmers raise a variety of crops in the valleys. During summer months, cattle and sheep graze on the grasslands of the mesas.

The Intermontane Basin, north of the plateau, is Colorado's smallest land region. It is a region of rolling hills and sagebrush plateaus wedged between mountain ranges near the northwest corner of the state. The word *intermontane* means *between mountains.* Herds of sheep graze on the plateaus, and forests cover the hills in this region.

The Rocky Mountains cover the middle two-fifths of Colorado. The Colorado Rockies have been called the *Roof of North America* because between 50 and 60 peaks reach 14,000 feet (4,270 meters) or more above sea level. These peaks are the tallest in the entire Rocky Mountain chain, which stretches from Alaska to New Mexico.

The Continental Divide runs through the Colorado Rockies. Streams east of the divide flow into the Atlantic Ocean. Those west of it flow into the Pacific. The Colorado Rockies are one of the country's most popular areas for mountain climbing, fishing, hunting, and skiing.

The Rocky Mountains of Colorado consist of five main mountain ranges: (1) the Front Range, (2) the Park Range, (3) the Sawatch Range, (4) the San Juan Mountains, and (5) the Sangre de Cristo Mountains. The easternmost group is the Front Range, which includes Mount Evans (14,264 feet, or 4,348 meters), Longs Peak (14,255 feet, or 4,345 meters), Pikes Peak (14,110 feet, or 4,301 meters), and other mountains that rise to the west of Denver and Colorado Springs. The *Sangre de Cristo* (Blood of Christ) Mountains are just south of the Front Range. Together, the Front Range and the Sangre de Cristo Mountains form a wall that faces the Great Plains to the east.

The Park Range, west of the Front Range, stretches from a point near the Wyoming border south to the beginning of the Arkansas River. South of the Park Range is the Sawatch Range, which includes Mount Elbert (14,433 feet, or 4,399 meters), the highest peak of the Rocky Mountains. The rugged San Juan Mountains occupy southwestern Colorado.

The mountains of Colorado surround many level, almost treeless areas called *parks.* The largest of these areas include North Park, Middle Park, South Park, and the San Luis Valley. See **Rocky Mountains.**

The Great Plains cover roughly the eastern two-fifths of Colorado. Colorado's Great Plains region is part of the vast Interior Plain of North America that stretches from Canada to Mexico. It slopes gently upward from east to west toward the base of the Rocky Mountains. Farmers once thought the area was too dry for farming. But irrigation projects in the valleys and dry farming on the higher lands have made large-scale agriculture possible (see **Dry farming; Irrigation**).

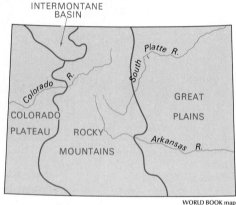

WORLD BOOK map

Land regions of Colorado

Map index

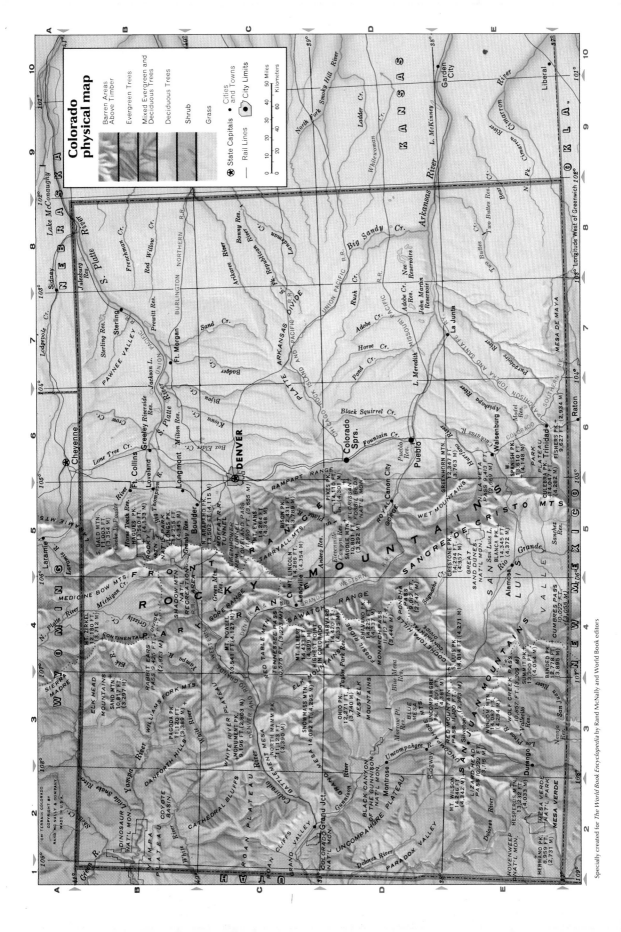

Colorado physical map

Barren Areas
Above Timber

Evergreen Trees

Mixed Evergreen and
Deciduous Trees

Deciduous Trees

Shrub

Grass

⊛ State Capitals
• Cities and Towns
◉ City Limits
— Rail Lines

Miles: 0 10 20 30 40 50
Kilometers: 0 20 40 60

Specially created for The World Book Encyclopedia by Rand McNally and World Book editors

Rivers and lakes. More important rivers begin in Colorado than in any other state. These rivers provide water for many states. Three major tributaries of the Mississippi-Missouri river system rise on the eastern slope of the Rocky Mountains. These are the Arkansas, South Platte, and Republican rivers. West of the Rockies, the Colorado River begins at Grand Lake, flows through Middle Park, and winds southwest into Utah. The Colorado drains a twelfth of all the land of the United States. Several of the chief tributaries of the Colorado, including the Uncompahgre, Gunnison, San Juan, and Dolores rivers, also rise in the state. The Rio Grande starts in the San Juan range, and flows east and south into New Mexico. The North Platte River flows north from North Park into Wyoming.

Rivers add much to Colorado's scenic beauty. Many have carved deep gorges, or tumble down mountains in lovely waterfalls and cascades. The Royal Gorge of the Arkansas River, west of Canon City, is more than 1,000 feet (300 meters) deep. A bridge that stands 1,053 feet

Tom Algire

Unusual rock formations stand in the Colorado National Monument. They make up part of the Colorado Plateau, a region of high hills and deep valleys in western Colorado.

(321 meters) above the floor of the Royal Gorge is the highest suspension bridge in the world. In some places, the Black Canyon of the Gunnison River in western Colorado is 2,400 feet (732 meters) below the surrounding land.

Many beautiful lakes lie in the mountains. Grand Lake, formed by glaciers, covers about 600 acres (240 hectares) near the town of Grand Lake. It is Colorado's largest natural lake. Summit Lake, 12,740 feet (3,883 meters) above sea level, is one of the highest lakes in the coun-

Average monthly weather

	Denver						Pueblo				
	Temperatures				Days of rain or snow		**Temperatures**				Days of rain or snow
	F°		C°				F°		C°		
	High	Low	High	Low			High	Low	High	Low	
Jan.	42	16	6	−9	6	Jan.	45	14	7	−10	5
Feb.	45	19	7	−7	6	Feb.	49	19	9	−7	4
Mar.	51	25	11	−4	8	Mar.	55	25	13	−4	6
Apr.	61	34	16	1	9	Apr.	65	35	18	2	7
May	69	43	21	6	11	May	73	45	23	7	10
June	81	52	27	11	9	June	84	54	29	2	7
July	87	58	31	14	9	July	90	60	32	16	9
Aug.	85	57	29	14	8	Aug.	88	59	31	15	9
Sept.	77	48	25	9	5	Sept.	81	49	27	9	4
Oct.	66	37	19	3	6	Oct.	69	37	21	3	4
Nov.	53	26	12	−3	5	Nov.	55	23	13	−5	4
Dec.	45	18	7	−8	4	Dec.	47	16	8	−9	3

Average January temperatures

Wintertime temperatures vary widely in Colorado, with the western half of the state being much colder than the east.

Average July temperatures

The plains and plateaus of Colorado are almost always warmer than the mountains in the summer.

Average yearly precipitation

Precipitation is distributed unevenly throughout the state. The western slopes receive the most rain and snow.

WORLD BOOK maps

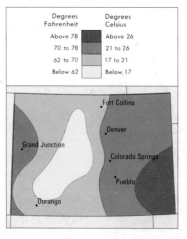

Degrees Fahrenheit	Degrees Celsius
Above 32	Above 0
24 to 32	-4 to 0
18 to 24	-8 to -4
Below 18	Below -8

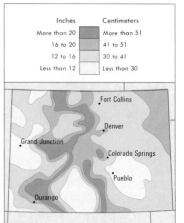

Degrees Fahrenheit	Degrees Celsius
Above 78	Above 26
70 to 78	21 to 26
62 to 70	17 to 21
Below 62	Below 17

Inches	Centimeters
More than 20	More than 51
16 to 20	41 to 51
12 to 16	30 to 41
Less than 12	Less than 30

Kent and Donna Dannen
Grasslands near La Junta in the Great Plains region of eastern Colorado are used for farming.

try. Many artificial lakes have been created by damming the rushing mountain streams. John Martin Reservoir, formed by a federal flood-control project on the Arkansas River, is the largest lake. It covers more than 29 square miles (75 square kilometers) when full. The water is used for irrigation.

Plant and animal life. Because of the large differences in altitude and moisture, Colorado's land has a wide variety of plant life. Plants include many kinds of cactus, greasewood, sagebrush, and yucca in the drier areas. The chief grasses are buffalo and grama grass. Spring wild flowers include buttercups, sand lilies, wild geraniums, and yarrows. Summer brings columbines, dogtooth violets, Indian paintbrushes, mountain lilies and daisies, and wild irises and roses. Forests cover about a third of the state. Common trees include ashes, aspens, cottonwoods, firs, maples, pines, and spruces.

About 850,000 deer, elk, and other big game animals roam Colorado. Pronghorns and prairie dogs live on the plains. Fur-bearing animals include bears, beavers, bobcats, foxes, marmots, martens, rabbits, and skunks. Game birds include several kinds of grouse, pheasants, and quail. Colorado game fish include bass, catfish, crappies, perch, and trout.

Climate. Colorado's climate is generally dry and sunny. But because of the great differences in altitude, temperatures vary widely in short distances. The mountains are almost always cooler than the plains and plateaus. Burlington, on the plains, has an average January temperature of 28° F. (−2° C). Leadville, in the mountains, has a January average of 18° F. (−8° C). Average July temperatures are 74° F. (23° C) in Burlington and 55° F. (13° C) in Leadville. Colorado's highest temperature, 118° F. (48° C), occurred at Bennett on July 11, 1888. Maybell in Moffat County had the lowest, −61° F. (−52° C), on Feb. 1, 1985.

Colorado's average yearly *precipitation* (rain, melted snow, and other forms of moisture) is about 15 inches (38 centimeters). This moisture is not distributed evenly. The western slopes get the most rain and snow. The San Luis Valley, in southern Colorado, is the driest area.

The dry air makes Colorado's climate comfortable. The sun warms the thin air quickly, especially at high altitudes. The *chinook,* a warm wind that occasionally blows down the eastern slopes in winter, can raise temperatures on the plains by 20 Fahrenheit degrees (11 Celsius degrees) or more in a short time.

Economy

Colorado's economy is divided roughly along the natural lines of its land. The Eastern Plains are the state's main farming region. Along the border between the Eastern Plains and Rocky Mountains lie Colorado's largest urban areas, where service industries and manufacturing are centered. The Rocky Mountains have many recreational areas, including some of the nation's favorite ski resorts. West of the Rockies lie the state's main petroleum and coal fields.

Service industries account for about four-fifths of Colorado's *gross state product*—the total annual value of goods and services produced in the state. The wholesale and retail trade industry employs more people in Colorado than any other industry. Colorado's popularity as a site for vacations and conventions contributes to the strength of the state's retail trade. Tourists spend about $4 billion a year in Colorado.

Natural resources. Mineral deposits, a pleasant climate, rich soils, and water are Colorado's greatest natural resources.

Soil. The soils of the eastern plains and the valleys of the western mountains are among the most fertile in the nation. These soils contain the minerals needed by plants. The eastern soils are brown. In years of rainfall, they produce excellent crops. In dry years, the soil must be irrigated. The high mountains and some western plateaus have thin, stony soils called *lithosols.*

Minerals. Vast deposits of coal, gold, molybdenum, natural gas, and petroleum help support Colorado's economy. Huge oil shale deposits offer promise of future mineral development. Supplies of building materials such as gravel, sand, and stone seem large enough for the state's future needs.

Water is precious in the dry West. The control of water sources is a continuing concern to the people. Six major rivers rise in Colorado. By agreement with other states, and with Mexico, Colorado cannot use more than a specified amount of the water in these streams.

Distribution of water within the state is uneven. The *Western Slope* (the land west of the Continental Divide) covers slightly more than a third of the land area. But it gets more than two-thirds of the *surface water* (runoff from rain and snow). The *Eastern Slope,* with almost two-thirds of the land area, gets less than a third of the surface water. There have been bitter legal and political fights over water rights within the state.

Many dams and tunnels have been built for *transmountain diversion* of water. Western Slope water is brought through tunnels in the mountains for use on the dry but heavily populated Eastern Slope. Some of this water goes to homes and factories. The rest is used to irrigate the fertile soil of the plains. These projects help solve eastern Colorado's water problems. The future growth of Colorado, both in manufacturing and agricul-

Production and workers by economic activities

Economic activities	Per cent of GSP* produced	Employed workers	
		Number of persons	Per cent of total
Community, social, & personal services	22	420,100	26
Wholesale and retail trade	17	374,700	24
Finance, insurance, & real estate	15	96,700	6
Government	14	282,300	18
Manufacturing	12	185,500	12
Transportation, communi- cation, & utilities	11	97,800	6
Construction	4	66,600	4
Agriculture	3	46,700	3
Mining	2	18,600	1
Total	100	1,589,000	100

*GSP = gross state product, the total value of goods and services produced in a year.
Figures are for 1991.
Sources: *World Book* estimates based on data from U.S. Bureau of Economic Analysis, U.S. Bureau of Labor Statistics, and U.S. Department of Agriculture.

ture, depends on the amount of water available.

Service industries account for 79 per cent of Colorado's gross state product. Most of the service industries in Colorado are concentrated in the Denver metropolitan area.

Community, social, and personal services are the leading service industry in Colorado in terms of the gross state product. The industry consists of a wide variety of businesses. They include doctors' offices and private hospitals; hotels and ski resorts; and data processing, engineering, and legal services. Colorado hotels benefit from the many conventions held in the state. Data processing and engineering companies receive much business from government agencies.

Wholesale and retail trade rank as Colorado's second most important service industry. Denver is the wholesale distribution center for the Rocky Mountain region of the United States. The wholesale trade of automobiles, groceries, and mineral products is especially important. Major types of retail establishments include automobile dealerships, food stores, and restaurants. Retail merchants receive much business from tourists.

Finance, insurance, and real estate form the third most important service industry in Colorado. Denver is an important regional banking and financial center. Several of the nation's leading insurance and investment firms have large branch offices in Denver.

Government is the fourth-ranking service industry in Colorado. Government services include public schools and hospitals, and the military. The federal government plays a larger role in Colorado's economy than it does in most other states. The U.S. Air Force has extensive facilities in the Colorado Springs area, including the Air Force Academy and the North American Aerospace Defense Command. The federal government owns much of Colorado's unpopulated land. It controls grazing, logging, mining, and recreation there. State government offices are based in Denver.

Transportation, communication, and utilities rank fifth among Colorado service industries. Denver is one of the nation's major hubs of the airline, railroad, and trucking industries. Englewood is the home of US West, one of the leading telecommunication companies in the United States. More information about transportation and communication appears later in this section.

Manufacturing accounts for 12 per cent of Colorado's gross state product. Goods manufactured in the state have a *value added by manufacture* of about $12 billion yearly. Value added by manufacture means the increase in value of raw materials after they become finished goods.

Scientific instruments are the leading type of manufactured product in Colorado in terms of value added by manufacture. Medical instruments and devices that measure electricity provide most of the income for this industry. A plant in Denver makes medical instruments. Plants in Loveland and in the Colorado Springs area make devices that measure electricity.

Food processing ranks second in value among Colorado's manufacturing activities. Beer brewing, soft drink bottling, meat packing, and the production of animal feed are major parts of Colorado's food-processing industry. Major breweries are located in Fort Collins and Golden.

Farm and mineral products

This map shows the areas where the state's leading farm and mineral products are produced. The major urban areas (shown in red) are the state's important manufacturing centers.

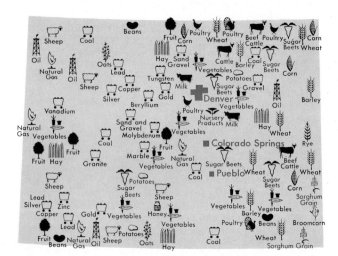

The state's other leading manufactured products, in order of value, include machinery, fabricated metal products, electrical equipment, and printed materials. Computers are the most important type of machinery made in Colorado. Factories in the Denver and Boulder areas manufacture metal doors and trim. Major kinds of electrical equipment made in the state include telephone equipment, television cameras, and electronic medical devices. The Denver area also produces a large volume of newspapers and business forms. Large factories in Colorado also make aircraft, luggage, primary metals, rubber and plastic products, sporting goods, and clothing.

Agriculture accounts for 3 per cent of Colorado's gross state product. Colorado has about 26,000 farms. They range in size from large ranches to small *truck* (vegetable) farms.

Livestock and livestock products account for about 70 per cent of the value of all Colorado farm products. Beef cattle are the leading farm product by far, and Colorado is an important state in beef cattle production. Grazing of cattle on ranches has been important for many years. Colorado farmers also *finish* (fatten) cattle in *feed lots*. Operators of feed lots put range cattle in relatively small pens. There, the cattle are fattened on special feed. They gain weight faster because they eat grain and other feed with high food value. These animals bring better prices in the market. The Greeley area has the most feed lots. Colorado is also a leading producer of sheep for both meat and wool. Milk ranks among the state's most valuable farm products.

The chief field crops, in order of importance, are hay, wheat, and corn. Hay, which is used for cattle feed, grows in most parts of the state. Northeastern Colorado produces the most wheat and corn. Crop farmers also raise large amounts of beans, grain sorghum, potatoes, and sugar beets. Apples are the leading fruit in Colorado. Greenhouse and nursery products are an important source of agricultural income. Greenhouses produce carnations prized for their size and beauty.

Mining provides 2 per cent of the gross state product. Petroleum, coal, and natural gas are Colorado's chief mineral products.

Rio Blanco County in northwestern Colorado has the most productive oil fields. These fields yield about half of the state's total petroleum production. The area east of Denver also has important oil fields.

Northwestern Colorado is also the leading area for coal production. About half the state's coal comes from surface and underground mines in Moffat County. Surface mines in Rio Blanco County and underground mines in Routt County also have major coal production.

Large natural gas fields lie near Denver and Durango. The field near Denver provides the most gas. The huge Hugoton field of the Great Plains extends into the southeast corner of Colorado.

Among Colorado's other mineral products, sand and gravel, gold, and molybdenum provide the most income. Sand and gravel are obtained from pits along the rivers of the state's northern Great Plains region. Gold and molybdenum come from mines in the Rocky Mountains. Molybdenum is used in making strong varieties of steel. Some of the ores that contain gold or molybdenum also contain copper, lead, silver, and zinc. Colo-

© Barry Staver

Meat packing is an important economic activity in Colorado. Food processing is one of the state's leading industries.

rado also produces granite and limestone.

Colorado also has large deposits of oil shale, a source of petroleum. The shale, a type of rock, is found in northwestern Colorado. Oil companies have been experimenting with this shale since the 1920's. The high cost of processing remains a major obstacle to rapid development.

Electric power. Plants that burn coal supply about 90 per cent of Colorado's electric power. Hydroelectric plants generate most of the rest of the electricity. Plants that burn natural gas and petroleum supply only a small amount of Colorado's power.

Transportation. Colorado has about 75,000 miles (121,000 kilometers) of roads, two-thirds of which are surfaced. In winter, highways that cross the mountains are kept open by snowplows. The 1.7-mile (2.7-kilometer) Eisenhower Memorial Tunnel carries motor traffic through the Rockies at about 11,000 feet (3,400 meters) above sea level. It is the world's highest road tunnel. The highest road in the United States climbs to the top of 14,264-foot (4,348-meter) Mount Evans near Denver.

Denver's Stapleton International Airport is the state's major air terminal. But a new terminal, Denver International Airport, was scheduled to open in 1993. It will replace Stapleton International Airport. Many passengers traveling to or from the West Coast change planes in Denver.

Eleven railroads operating within the state provide freight service. Passenger trains serve more than 10 Colorado cities. The 6.2-mile (10-kilometer) Moffat Tunnel, one of the longest U.S. railroad tunnels, goes through the Rockies in Colorado.

Communication. Colorado's oldest newspaper is Denver's *Rocky Mountain News,* first published in 1859. Today, Colorado has about 130 papers, including about 30 dailies. Leading papers include the *Colorado Springs Gazette-Telegraph, Denver Post, Pueblo Chieftain,* and *Rocky Mountain News.*

The state's first commercial radio station, KFKA in Greeley, began broadcasting in 1921. KFEL-TV (now KWGN-TV) in Denver, Colorado's first TV station, began operation in 1952. Today, the state has about 15 television stations and about 165 radio stations.

Constitution of Colorado was adopted in 1876. It has been *amended* (changed) about 100 times. All constitutional amendments must be approved by the people in an election. Amendments may be proposed by a two-thirds vote of the state legislature, by a petition of the voters, or by a constitutional convention. Such a convention requires the approval of two-thirds of the legislators and a majority of the people voting on the issue.

Executive. The governor and lieutenant governor of Colorado are elected as a team to four-year terms. Voters cast a single vote for both officials. Neither office may be held by one person for more than eight consecutive years.

Under a constitutional amendment approved in 1966, the state reorganized the executive branch. Over 100 agencies, boards, and other units were consolidated into 20 principal departments. Three principal departments are under the direction of elected officials. These officials—the secretary of state, attorney general, and treasurer—are elected for four-year terms and may serve up to eight consecutive years. The governor, with the consent of the Senate, appoints most of the heads of the remaining departments.

Legislature, called the *General Assembly,* consists of a 35-member Senate and a 65-member House of Representatives. Senators serve four-year terms, and representatives serve two-year terms. Both are limited to no more than eight consecutive years in office. The Assembly meets each year beginning on the Wednesday after the first Tuesday in January. The length of the legislative session is not limited by law. A special session may be called by a vote of two-thirds of the members of the Senate and the House of Representatives.

Courts. Colorado's highest court is the Supreme Court, composed of a chief justice and six associate justices. The governor appoints the justices to the court. After a justice serves for two years, he or she must win the approval of the voters in an election. If approved, the justice serves a 10-year term. The justice's later terms are also for 10 years, but he or she must be voted in each time.

Colorado's next highest court is the six-member Court of Appeals. Most major civil and criminal cases are tried in district courts in the state's 22 judicial districts. Appellate and district court judges are appointed and approved like justices. However, the appellate court judges serve full terms of eight years, and district court judges serve six years. District courts may act as probate or juvenile courts, except in Denver where those courts are separate. Each Colorado county has a county court, and larger towns have municipal courts.

Local government is carried on through 63 counties and about 260 cities and towns. The city and county of Denver operate as a single government, with the same borders and the same officials. Each of the other 62 counties is governed by either three or five commissioners. The commissioners are elected by the voters to four-year terms.

Communities with more than 2,000 persons are called *cities,* and those with smaller populations are *towns.* Cities and towns may adopt *home rule* charters, which give them greater control over their own affairs. Under certain conditions, home rule charters and laws passed under such charters may replace state laws. The governing body of a town is called a *board of trustees,* and the governing body of a city is called a *council.* Most of the cities and towns in Colorado have a chief administrative officer.

Revenue. State taxes provide more than half of the state government's *general revenue* (income). Income taxes, motor fuel and highway taxes, and a sales tax produce the largest amounts. About a fourth of the revenue comes from federal grants and programs.

Politics. Colorado voters have elected about as many Democrats as Republicans to Congress. Voters in Denver and Pueblo usually support Democrats. Voters in Denver's suburbs and in northeastern Colorado generally favor Republicans.

Colorado has favored Republicans more often than Democrats in presidential elections. For Colorado's voting record in presidential elections, see **Electoral College** (table).

The governors of Colorado

	Party	Term		Party	Term
John L. Routt	Republican	1876-1879	Julius C. Gunter	Democratic	1917-1919
Frederick W. Pitkin	Republican	1879-1883	Oliver H. Shoup	Republican	1919-1923
James B. Grant	Democratic	1883-1885	William E. Sweet	Democratic	1923-1925
Benjamin H. Eaton	Republican	1885-1887	Clarence J. Morley	Republican	1925-1927
Alva Adams	Democratic	1887-1889	William H. Adams	Democratic	1927-1933
Job A. Cooper	Republican	1889-1891	Edwin C. Johnson	Democratic	1933-1937
John L. Routt	Republican	1891-1893	Ray H. Talbot	Democratic	1937
Davis H. Waite	Populist	1893-1895	Teller Ammons	Democratic	1937-1939
Albert W. McIntire	Republican	1895-1897	Ralph L. Carr	Republican	1939-1943
Alva Adams	Democratic	1897-1899	John C. Vivian	Republican	1943-1947
Charles S. Thomas	Democratic	1899-1901	W. Lee Knous	Democratic	1947-1950
James B. Orman	Democratic	1901-1903	Walter W. Johnson	Democratic	1950-1951
James H. Peabody	Republican	1903-1905	Dan Thornton	Republican	1951-1955
Alva Adams	Democratic	1905	Edwin C. Johnson	Democratic	1955-1957
James H. Peabody	Republican	1905	Stephen L. R. McNichols	Democratic	1957-1963
Jesse F. McDonald	Republican	1905-1907	John A. Love	Republican	1963-1973
Henry A. Buchtel	Republican	1907-1909	John D. Vanderhoof	Republican	1973-1975
John F. Shafroth	Democratic	1909-1913	Richard D. Lamm	Democratic	1975-1987
Elias M. Ammons	Democratic	1913-1915	Roy Romer	Democratic	1987-
George A. Carlson	Republican	1915-1917			

Indian days. Indians roamed the plains of present-day Colorado before white explorers arrived. Early explorers found the Arapaho, Cheyenne, Comanche, Kiowa, and Pawnee tribes on the plains. The Utes lived in the mountain valleys.

Exploration and settlement. Spanish explorers who came in the 1600's were the first white people to visit the Colorado region. The Spaniards failed to find gold, and left without attempting to settle the area. In 1682, the explorer Robert Cavelier, Sieur de La Salle, claimed for France an area that included what is now eastern Colorado. In 1706, Juan de Ulibarri, a Spanish official, claimed the region for Spain.

In 1803, the United States bought present-day eastern and central Colorado as part of the Louisiana Purchase. During the next 20 years, Americans explored much of the region. Zebulon M. Pike, an Army officer, entered the Colorado area in 1806. Pike's record of the trip describes the mighty mountain that was named for him—Pikes Peak. Another officer, Major Stephen H. Long, led an exploring party in 1820. The first permanent American settlement was Bent's Fort, completed in 1833 near present-day La Junta. The fort, built by the trader William Bent, was used as a base by Kit Carson and other famous frontiersmen for trade in beaver pelts. Mexico won control of western Colorado from Spain in 1821. The United States took control during the Mexican War (1846-1848) and kept the land under the terms of the treaty that ended the war.

The gold rush. Colorado had few settlers until the late 1850's. Then, in 1858, prospectors found gold along Cherry Creek, near the site of present-day Denver. Gold hunters rushed into the area. "Pikes Peak or Bust" became the slogan of the prospectors as they traveled the long, hard trail to the Colorado gold fields. About 100,000 people had reached the area at the height of the rush, in 1859. However, more than half turned back, disappointed not to have found gold quickly or easily.

Governing the growing area became a major problem. The Indians claimed that the land had been given to them by various treaties. The miners ignored the Indian claims and set up what they called the Jefferson Territory. Congress refused to recognize the Jefferson Territory, and created the Colorado Territory in 1861. William Gilpin was appointed as the first territorial governor. See **Jefferson Territory.**

Territorial days. Indians and whites fought many small clashes and three important battles during the 1860's and 1870's. In 1864, troops of the Colorado militia attacked a Cheyenne and Arapaho village at Sand Creek and killed nearly 300 Indians. This battle became known as the Sand Creek Massacre. The U.S. government criticized the attack, and paid the Indians for their losses. In 1868, a large force of Indians attacked 50 army scouts on the Arikaree River in eastern Colorado. The scouts fought for several days on Beecher Island in the river. They finally were saved by other troops.

The last big Indian battle in Colorado was the Meeker Massacre in 1879. In this fight, the Ute Indians killed their reservation agent, Nathan C. Meeker, and ambushed a body of troops. After the battle, a respected Ute chief named Ouray helped calm the Indian warriors and settle their problems with the whites.

Many settlers started ranches and farms along the streams. Crude irrigation systems were developed along the eastern edge of the mountains, and in the San Luis Valley. Horace Greeley, a famous New York City editor who believed in developing the West, helped sponsor a farming colony in Colorado in 1870. Greeley made popular the expression "Go West, young man."

In 1870, the Denver Pacific Railroad linked Denver with the main line of the Union Pacific at Cheyenne, Wyo. This line connected Colorado and the East. The Kansas Pacific built its line to Denver later in 1870.

Statehood. Colorado was admitted to the Union on Aug. 1, 1876. Territorial governor John L. Routt was elected as the first state governor.

A new mining boom brought wealth to Colorado in the early years of statehood. This time silver caused the growth. Leadville and Aspen boomed as silver centers.

Horace A. W. Tabor became the symbol of this colorful era. He was called the *Silver King*. With his profits

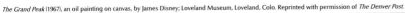

The Grand Peak (1967), an oil painting on canvas, by James Disney; Loveland Museum, Loveland, Colo. Reprinted with permission of *The Denver Post.*

American exploration of Colorado began during the early 1800's. Colorado's most famous land feature, Pikes Peak, *left,* was sighted in 1806 by American Army officer Zebulon Pike. The mountain is named for him.

Historic Colorado

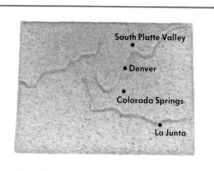

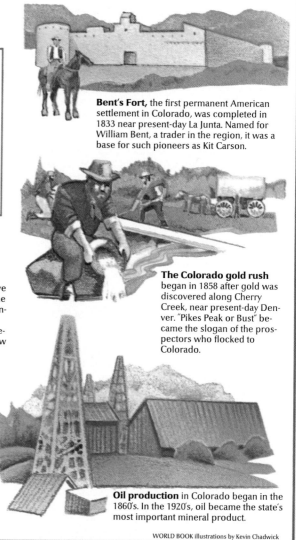

Bent's Fort, the first permanent American settlement in Colorado, was completed in 1833 near present-day La Junta. Named for William Bent, a trader in the region, it was a base for such pioneers as Kit Carson.

The Colorado gold rush began in 1858 after gold was discovered along Cherry Creek, near present-day Denver. "Pikes Peak or Bust" became the slogan of the prospectors who flocked to Colorado.

Union Colony, a cooperative agricultural community in the South Platte Valley, was sponsored by the famous New York City editor Horace Greeley in 1870. The colony is now the town of Greeley.

The U.S. Air Force Academy was founded at Colorado Springs in 1958.

Oil production in Colorado began in the 1860's. In the 1920's, oil became the state's most important mineral product.

WORLD BOOK illustrations by Kevin Chadwick

Important dates in Colorado

1706 Juan de Ulibarri claimed the Colorado region for Spain.

1803 The United States acquired eastern Colorado as part of the Louisiana Purchase.

1806 Zebulon M. Pike explored Colorado.

1848 The United States took western Colorado after the Mexican War.

1858 Gold was discovered at Cherry Creek, near the site of what is now Denver.

1859 The Colorado gold rush attracted thousands of prospectors and settlers.

1861 Congress created the Colorado Territory.

1870 The Denver Pacific Railroad was completed to Denver.

1876 Colorado became the 38th state on August 1.

1879 The Meeker Massacre marked the end of serious Indian fighting.

1899 The state's first beet-sugar factory began operating.

1906 The U.S. Mint in Denver issued its first coins. Congress established Mesa Verde National Park.

1915 Rocky Mountain National Park was established.

1927 The Moffat Tunnel, a railroad tunnel through the mountains, was completed.

1956 The Colorado River water storage project was approved by Congress.

1958 The U.S. Air Force Academy's permanent campus opened near Colorado Springs.

1959 The Colorado-Big Thompson irrigation system was completed.

1962 Ground was broken for the three-dam Curecanti water storage system (now the Wayne N. Aspinall Storage Unit). The system was completed in 1976.

1966 North American Air Defense Command—now North American Aerospace Defense Command—completed its operations center in Cheyenne Mountain.

1985 The Frying Pan-Arkansas Project, which transfers water across Colorado, was completed.

from several mines, Tabor built magnificent buildings in Leadville and Denver. His investments in Denver helped that frontier town become a business and financial center. Tabor became a U.S. senator. President Chester A. Arthur attended Tabor's wedding to the beautiful Elizabeth "Baby" Doe.

In 1893, business slumped all across the nation. For this reason, the U.S. government canceled its agreements to buy large amounts of silver. Silver prices dropped. In Colorado, many silver mines closed and the miners lost their jobs. Other businesses suffered because people who were unemployed could not afford to buy their products.

Progress as a state. Colorado's growth continued in spite of the state's troubles. A major gold discovery at Cripple Creek softened the blow of the silver crash. Farmers tried different crops, and expanded their irrigation systems. Sugar beets and potatoes became valuable Colorado crops. The state's first sugar refinery opened in Grand Junction in 1899. In 1902, construction started on a railroad over the Continental Divide. In 1906, the U.S. Mint in Denver produced its first coins.

By 1910, Colorado had almost 800,000 people. Agriculture had replaced mining as the state's most important industry. Colorado had more irrigated land than any other state. The food processing industry grew as canneries and more sugar refineries were built.

The 1910's and 1920's. The development of automobiles in the early 1900's caused rapid growth in two Colorado industries—oil and tourism. The family car made vacation travel easier, and Colorado's splendid scenery attracted thousands of tourists. Cars also increased the demand for petroleum products. Colorado's first oil wells were drilled in the Arkansas Valley during territorial days, but production was small. Later, new oil fields were discovered. By 1920, oil had become Colorado's most important mineral product.

The state government kept pace with the advances in industry. For example, a plan of workers' compensation was passed in 1915. In 1927, the famous Moffat railroad tunnel was completed with state funds.

The Great Depression. Colorado's economy suffered during the Great Depression of the 1930's. Farm prices dropped sharply, and stayed low. A long period of dry weather began on the eastern plains. Wind whipped the dry, powdery soil into huge dust clouds, and dust storms darkened the sky. The state and federal governments began programs to restore the wind-damaged land, and to help the unemployed. In 1935, the state adopted a 2 per cent sales tax to raise money for old age pensions. Highway construction and other programs helped put the unemployed back to work.

The mid-1900's. Colorado's economy boomed during World War II (1939-1945). The war brought a great demand for Colorado metals and oil. The government established several air bases in the state and several federal agencies in the Denver area. The army opened Fort Carson near Colorado Springs and a huge ordnance plant at Pueblo. Military payrolls in Colorado jumped from $3 million in 1940 to $152 million in 1945.

The population of the state increased after World War II, and Colorado has ranked among the nation's fastest growing areas since 1945. Many suburbs developed around major cities in central Colorado.

With the population growth, Colorado's need for flood control, irrigation, and water storage became severe. Central Colorado and the eastern plains have often suffered either long droughts or sudden floods. Cherry Creek Dam near Denver was completed in 1949. In 1947, the Alva B. Adams Tunnel was completed. This tunnel carries water through the Rocky Mountains from western Colorado to the area northeast of the mountains. It is part of the huge Colorado-Big Thompson Project, which was completed in 1959. This project is a series of dams, pumping stations, reservoirs, and tunnels that irrigates about 720,000 acres (291,000 hectares) of farmland. It also includes six hydroelectric power plants.

More federal offices and military installations were established in Colorado during the 1950's. The laboratory of the National Bureau of Standards (now the National Institute of Standards and Technology) moved from Washington, D.C., to Boulder in 1954. The Air Force set up its worldwide financial center in Denver. The United States Air Force Academy opened its Colorado Springs campus in 1958. The North American Air Defense Command (NORAD) combat operations center made its headquarters near Colorado Springs. The center, now called the North American Aerospace Defense Command, was completed in 1966. It is 1,200 feet (366 meters) underground in Cheyenne Mountain.

By 1954, manufacturing had replaced agriculture as the state's leading industry. The larger manufacturing plants produced atomic warheads, missiles, and other military items. The manufacture of electronic parts and the mining and milling of uranium became important industries in western Colorado.

Work on the Colorado River Storage Project began in 1956 and continued into the 1990's. A major part of this project, the Wayne N. Aspinall Storage Unit of three dams, was completed in 1976. The project includes power plants, reservoirs, and water purification systems. It was designed to bring water for irrigation, energy, and recreation to Colorado and five other states along the Colorado River and its tributaries.

In the early 1960's, work began on the Frying Pan-Arkansas Project. The project was designed to transfer

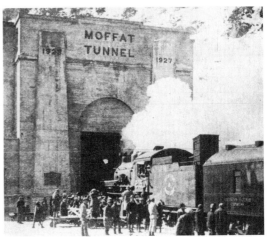

The Moffat Tunnel was completed in 1927. It greatly shortened the route between Denver and Salt Lake City.

water from western Colorado to the plains in the eastern part of the state. The project began operation in 1972 and was completed in 1985.

Recent developments. In 1976, floodwaters of the Big Thompson River swept through an area of homes, summer cabins, trailer camps, and vacation resorts in Big Thompson Canyon, near Loveland. The flood, which was caused by heavy rains, killed more than 135 people.

Colorado, particularly the Denver area, became a center for energy-related activities in response to the nationwide energy shortage that developed during the 1970's. Energy companies in Colorado expanded their operations. These firms planned to develop Colorado's vast deposits of coal, natural gas, oil shale, and petro-leum. The expansion in energy-related fields resulted in tremendous population growth during the late 1970's and early 1980's. This energy boom later collapsed, and by the mid-1980's, Colorado's economy had fallen into a statewide slump. However, signs of improvement began to appear by the end of the 1980's.

In addition to a sagging economy, Colorado faces the problems of air and water pollution, overcrowding along the eastern edge of the Rocky Mountains, and urban decay. Agriculture, mining, and population have declined in the state's rural areas. Future prosperity depends on improved economic and urban planning and the availability of an adequate supply of clean water.

John L. Dietz and Duane A. Smith

Study aids

Related articles in *World Book* include:

Biographies

Bonfils, Frederick G.	Hart, Gary W.
Carpenter, M. Scott	Pike, Zebulon M.
Dempsey, Jack	Sabin, Florence R.
Greeley, Horace	White, Byron R.
Guggenheim, Meyer	

Cities

Aspen	Leadville
Colorado Springs	Pueblo
Denver	

History

Arapaho Indians	Indian wars
Cheyenne Indians	Jefferson Territory
Cliff dwellers	Ute Indians
Comanche Indians	Westward movement
Dust Bowl	

Physical features

Arkansas River	Rio Grande
Colorado River	Rocky Mountains
Moffat Tunnel	Royal Gorge
Pikes Peak	

Other related articles

Easter (picture: Outdoor sunrise services)	United States Air Force Academy
Garden of the Gods	Western frontier life

Outline

I. People
  A. Population
  B. Schools
  C. Libraries
  D. Museums

II. Visitor's guide
  A. Places to visit
  B. Annual events

III. Land and climate
  A. Land regions
  B. Rivers and lakes
  C. Plant and animal life
  D. Climate

IV. Economy
  A. Natural resources
  B. Service industries
  C. Manufacturing
  D. Agriculture
  E. Mining
  F. Electric power
  G. Transportation
  H. Communication

V. Government
  A. Constitution
  B. Executive
  C. Legislature
  D. Courts
  E. Local government

  F. Revenue
  G. Politics

VI. History

Questions

How are eastern Colorado's water problems being solved?
What are two main mineral products of Colorado?
Where is the highest road in the United States?
Where are most of Colorado's cities?
Why is Colorado called the Centennial State?
Why was H. A. W. Tabor important to Denver?
How did the slogan "Pikes Peak or Bust" originate?
What is Colorado's chief agricultural activity?
What military defense center is located underground in Colorado? Where is it?
What mountains are called the Roof of North America?

Additional resources

Level I

Corning, Josie. *Denver, Colorado.* Crestwood, 1989.
Downey, Matthew T., and Metcalf, F. D. *Colorado: Crossroads of the West.* 2nd ed. Pruett, 1986.
Kent, Deborah. *Colorado.* Childrens Pr., 1989.
Metcalf, Fay D.; Noel, Thomas J.; and Smith, Duane A. *Colorado: Heritage of the Highest State.* Pruett, 1984.

Level II

Abbott, Carl, and others. *Colorado: A History of the Centennial State.* Rev. ed. Colorado Associated, 1982.
Athearn, Robert G. *The Coloradans.* Univ. of New Mexico Pr., 1976.
Cassells, E. Steve. *The Archaeology of Colorado.* Johnson Bks., 1983.
Caughey, Bruce, and Winstanley, Dean. *The Colorado Guide.* Rev. ed. Fulcrum, 1991.
Colorado Geographic Series. Falcon Pr. Pub. Co., 1985- . Multivolume work, publication in progress. Titles include *Colorado Mountain Ranges,* by Jeff Rennicke (1986); and *Colorado Parklands,* by Stewart M. Green (1988).
A Colorado Reader. Ed. by Carl A. Ubbelohde, Maxine Benson, and Duane A. Smith. 2nd ed. Pruett, 1982.
Ellis, Richard N., and Smith, Duane A. *Colorado: A History in Photographs.* Univ. Pr. of Colorado, 1991.
Lorch, Robert S. *Colorado's Government: Structure, Politics, Administration, and Policy.* 5th ed. Univ. Pr. of Colorado, 1991.
Smith, Duane A. *The Birth of Colorado: A Civil War Perspective.* Univ. of Oklahoma Pr., 1989.
Ubbelohde, Carl A.; Benson, Maxine; and Smith, Duane A. *A Colorado History.* 6th ed. Pruett, 1988.

Colorado, University of, is a state-supported coeducational university with campuses in Boulder, Colorado Springs, and Denver. It also has a health sciences center in Denver. The university offers courses in arts and sciences, business, education, engineering and applied sciences, environmental design, law, and other fields. The health sciences center includes schools of dentistry, medicine, nursing, and pharmacy. The university grants bachelor's, master's, and doctor's degrees.

The Boulder campus includes the Laboratory for Atmospheric and Space Physics, Sommers-Bausch Observatory, Nuclear Physics Laboratory, and several research institutes. In Boulder, the university holds a Conference on World Affairs every spring and several fine arts festivals during the summer. The university was founded in 1876. For enrollment, see **Universities and colleges** (table).

Critically reviewed by the University of Colorado

Colorado Desert occupies about 2,000 square miles (5,200 square kilometers) of southeastern California. It lies between the Santa Rosa and Coast ranges on the west and the Colorado River on the east (see **California** [physical map]). The desert also extends south into northwestern Mexico. The Mojave Desert lies north and northwest of the Colorado Desert. Parts of the Colorado Desert are 245 feet (75 meters) below sea level. The desert's Eagle Mountain is a valuable source of iron ore. The Imperial and Coachella valleys are rich farming regions. About 15 geothermal power plants in or near Imperial Valley turn heat from the earth into energy (see **Imperial Valley**).　　John Edwin Coffman

Colorado National Monument, in western Colorado, includes many strange rock formations, such as Devil's Kitchen, Window Rock, and Independence Monument. It also has prehistoric remains and a wildlife preserve. The monument was established in 1911. For its area, see **National Park System** (table: National monuments).　　Critically reviewed by the National Park System

Colorado potato beetle. See **Potato beetle.**

Colorado River, one of the major rivers in the United States, is 1,450 miles (2,334 kilometers) long. It flows across 1,360 miles (2,189 kilometers) of the United States and 90 miles (145 kilometers) of Mexico. It rises in the Rocky Mountains of Colorado, and flows southwest into Utah. It is joined by the Green River in eastern Utah and by the San Juan River in southern Utah. The Colorado then continues southwest into Arizona. After merging with the Little Colorado River in northern Arizona, the river swings west through the Grand Canyon. The Virgin River of Nevada joins its course beyond the Grand Canyon. The Colorado then turns south and forms the Arizona-California border. It then flows across the Mexican border to the Gulf of California. Arizona's Bill Williams and Gila rivers merge with the river north of the Mexican border. The Colorado drains an area of about 250,000 square miles (650,000 square kilometers).

The Grand Canyon of the Colorado River presents an outstanding example of the effects of wind, water, and weather on the earth's surface. For millions of years, the river worked its way into layer after layer of rock, gradually deepening and broadening its channel. Sand, pebbles, and boulders carried by the river produced a constant grinding action. The action of wind and temperature and the gradual elevation of the Colorado plateau added to the effect of the grinding. The Grand Canyon now consists of a great gash in the earth 1 mile (1.6 kilometers) deep and between 14 and 18 miles (23 and 29 kilometers) wide in some places.

Many rapids and waterfalls lie along the course of the

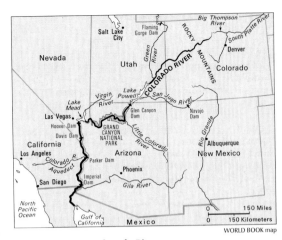

The route of the Colorado River

WORLD BOOK map

Colorado. The waters carry tons of silt and sand. Until Hoover Dam was built, the river deposited these materials in its lower river valley, forming a rich delta country in Mexico. The Hoover Dam, completed in 1936, helps check floods and erosion, and provides a dependable supply of water and electric power. Davis, Parker, and Imperial dams, which lie downstream from Hoover Dam, also help regulate the flow of water. In 1956, Congress passed a bill providing for the construction of four major power dams and a number of water-supply units on the Colorado and its branches. The Navajo Dam was completed in 1963, and the Flaming Gorge and Glen Canyon dams were completed in 1964. The Colorado-Big Thompson Project diverts water from the Colorado. The water is used to irrigate 720,000 acres (291,000 hectares) of land in northeastern Colorado.

In 1963, a plan was announced to develop wildlife preserves and recreation areas along the banks of the lower Colorado River. Since that time, two wildlife preserves were expanded, and a new preserve was established. Two state parks and other recreational areas were developed.　　Lay James Gibson

See also **Grand Canyon National Park; Hoover Dam.**

Colorado Springs, Colo. (pop. 281,140; met. area pop. 397,014), is a tourist and recreation center located in the Rocky Mountains. It lies 6,035 feet (1,839 meters) above sea level, east of Pikes Peak. For location, see **Colorado** (political map). Colorado Springs has a healthful year-round climate, with an average of more than 300 days of sunshine. It is the state's second largest city. Denver is the largest.

Colorado College, Colorado Tech (formerly Colorado Technical College), and the University of Colorado at Colorado Springs are located in the city. Points of interest include the Garden of the Gods, Pikes Peak, the Will Rogers Shrine of the Sun Memorial, and the Prorodeo Hall of Champions & Museum of the American Cowboy. The city is also the site of the United States Olympic Training Center.

The United States Air Force Academy is north of Colorado Springs. Other military installations include the headquarters of the North American Aerospace Defense Command (NORAD), with its command center located under Cheyenne Mountain; Fort Carson, home of the

U.S. Army's 4th Infantry Division; Peterson Air Force Base, home of the U.S. Space Command and 1st Space Wing; and Falcon Air Force Base, home of the Consolidated Space Operations Center.

Colorado Springs' industries include the research and development of space technology as well as other electronics research and assembly work, plastics and metals processing, and printing and publishing. The city was founded in 1871. It has a council-manager form of government and is the seat of El Paso County.　　Dru Wilson

Colosseum, *KAHL uh SEE uhm,* also called the Flavian Amphitheater, *FLAY vee uhn AM fuh thee uh tuhr,* was the largest outdoor theater of ancient Rome. The Colosseum still ranks among the finest examples of Roman architecture and engineering, even though it survives only as a ruin. It stands near the center of modern Rome.

Construction of the Colosseum started during the reign of the Emperor Vespasian, who ruled from A.D. 69 to 79. The building was dedicated in A.D. 80. Until 404, the Colosseum was the site of mock naval battles, combat between gladiators, battles between men and wild

D. and J. Heaton, Colorific Photo Library Ltd.

The Colosseum, or Flavian Amphitheater, in downtown Rome, is one of the most famous ruins in the world. The classical Roman structure rises to a height of four stories on one side.

animals, and other public entertainment. After that date, gladiatorial battles were no longer held, but fights with wild animals continued there until 523. During the Middle Ages, stones from the structure were used to construct new buildings.

The Colosseum has four stories and is oval in shape. It could seat about 50,000 spectators on marble and wooden benches. The Colosseum is 157 feet (48 meters) high, about 620 feet (189 meters) long, and about 510 feet (155 meters) wide. The arena on the floor of the Colosseum is about 285 feet (87 meters) long and 180 feet (55 meters) wide. A wall about 15 feet (4.6 meters) high separated spectators from the arena.

The Colosseum is made of brick and concrete with stone covering the exterior. The first three stories consist of arches decorated with half columns. The fourth story was added later and has plainer decoration. Large brackets in the fourth-story walls held poles that supported awnings to protect spectators from the sun and

rain. The Colosseum had about 80 entrances, 2 reserved for the emperor. A network of passages and chambers ran beneath the structure.　　William J. Hennessey

See also **City** (picture: Rome).

Colossians, *kuh LAHSH uhnz,* **Epistle to the,** is the 12th book of the New Testament. It is a letter from the apostle Paul to the Christians in Colossae (in what is now western Turkey). Some scholars doubt that Paul actually wrote the letter. They believe it was written in his name by one of his followers. If Paul wrote Colossians, he did so while in prison, possibly in Rome, in about A.D. 60. Colossians is mainly a warning against combining Christianity with a "philosophy" (Col. 2:8) that involved Jewish observances among other things. The author argued that faith in Jesus is completely sufficient, and that nothing need be added to it. See also **Paul, Saint; Bible** (Books of the New Testament).　　Terrance D. Callan

Colossus of Rhodes. See Seven Wonders of the Ancient World.

Colour. See Color.

Colt. See Horse.

Colt, Samuel (1814-1862), developed the first successful repeating pistol. The pistol, patented in England in 1835, had a cylinder of several chambers that could be discharged in succession by the same locking and firing mechanism (see **Handgun**).

Colt established a factory at Hartford, Conn., where he produced arms that were used in the Mexican War (1846-1848) and during the Civil War (1861-1865). After Colt's death, his company made the six-shooters that were used throughout the West. Colt was born in Hartford.

Merritt Roe Smith

Wood engraving (1856) by H. Wright Smith; The New York Public Library, New York City

Samuel Colt

Colter, John (1770?-1813), an American trapper, discovered and explored the Yellowstone region. He was born near Staunton, Va. In October 1803, he enlisted for the Lewis and Clark expedition near Maysville, Ky. He stayed with the expedition until 1806.

Colter left the expedition in 1806 to become a mountain man. He planned to join two companions and remain in the upper Missouri River area for at least two years in pursuit of his fortune. For a considerable period, Colter was lost to civilization. He probably spent his time in the West, wandering along the Missouri River and through the Rocky Mountains. The scene of his greatest activity was along the Yellowstone River. He associated closely with many Indian tribes.

In 1807, Colter was in the Yellowstone Basin on a fur-hunting expedition. During this period, he explored the wild countryside and discovered the great thermal springs area that is now Yellowstone National Park. He also discovered several passes through the Rocky Mountains. Colter's exploits in the mountains have been a basic source of information about frontier expansion in that region. He returned to St. Louis in 1810 and retired as a mountain man.　　Thomas D. Clark

Coltrane, John William (1926-1967), was a famous jazz saxophonist and composer. His sometimes violent style made him one of the most controversial and widely imitated jazz musicians of the 1960's. Coltrane was also one of the first jazz performers to reflect the influence of the music of India. His best-known compositions are "Giant Steps" (1959), "Equinox" (1960), and "Impressions" (1961).

Coltrane was born in Hamlet, N.C. He played in the bands of Dizzy Gillespie and Johnny Hodges during the early 1950's. He achieved greater recognition as a frequent soloist with the Miles Davis quintet between 1955 and 1960. Coltrane formed his own quartet in 1960, and scored a popular success with a recording of the song "My Favorite Things." Previously a tenor saxophonist, he played the soprano saxophone on this record. Coltrane did much to popularize the soprano saxophone among jazz musicians.   Frank Tirro

Coltsfoot is a wild plant native to Europe and Asia. It also grows in the north-eastern part of the United States and in Canada. The coltsfoot has light-yellow, daisylike flowers that bloom in March or April. The plant's large leaves grow after the flowers have withered. The leaves are downy on the underside. They are round at first but later become shaped like a heart or a colt's foot. The *false coltsfoot* and the *beetleweed* are not true coltsfoot plants.

WORLD BOOK illustration by Robert Hynes
Coltsfoot

Scientific classification. The coltsfoot is in the composite family, Asteraceae or Compositae. It forms the genus *Tussilago*.
      David J. Keil

Colugo. See Flying lemur.

Colum, *KAHL uhm,* **Padraic,** *PAW drihk* (1881-1972), was an Irish playwright, poet, biographer, short-story writer, essayist, folklorist, and children's author. He was an original member of the group of Irish writers who made Dublin's Abbey Theatre famous. Colum wrote three important plays for the Abbey—*Broken Soil* (1903), revised as *The Fiddler's House*), *The Land* (1905), and *Thomas Muskerry* (1910). Each is a realistic study of peasant or provincial life in Ireland.

Colum was born in County Longford, and moved to the United States in 1914. He then began writing young people's books based on myth and folklore. These books include *The Adventures of Odysseus* (1918) and *The Children of Odin* (1920). These works are important for bringing classical literature to children.

Colum's verse—from *Wild Earth* (1907) to *Collected Poems* (1953)—is a subtle rendering of simple speech and song patterns. Colum's verse is clear in style and nostalgic in feeling.   Edward Hirsch

Columbia. Long before the Revolutionary War in America (1775-1783), many people felt that America should have been named Columbia after the explorer Christopher Columbus. During the war, poets in the Thirteen Colonies used the name Columbia to describe the new nation that was to become the United States.

Chromolithograph (1893) after a painting by Rodolfo Morgari; Chicago Historical Society
Columbia is often pictured as a robed woman carrying an American flag. This picture shows her with U.S. statesmen, *upper left,* and figures representing the continents, *lower right.*

The word was first used by Phillis Wheatley, a black slave poet in Massachusetts, in a poem honoring George Washington. Philip Freneau popularized the term in several poems during and after the Revolutionary War. The name appeared first in law in 1784 when King's College in New York City became Columbia College. Towns, counties, and institutions throughout the United States have since adopted the name.

Many artists have symbolically pictured Columbia as a tall, stately woman dressed in flowing garments and holding an American flag. A blue drape with white stars is usually part of her costume. During the 1800's, Columbia appeared on the prows of ships, in patriotic paintings, and in pageants representing the spirit of the Revolutionary War. The *Statue of Freedom,* on top of the United States Capitol in Washington, D.C., is often incorrectly identified as a statue of Columbia.   Merrill Jensen

Columbia, Mo. (pop. 69,101; met. area pop. 112,379), is an important regional center of education and health care. Columbia is one of Missouri's largest cities. It lies in central Missouri, about midway between St. Louis and Kansas City (see **Missouri** [political map]).

Columbia is the home of the main campus of the University of Missouri, which was founded in 1839 as the first state university west of the Mississippi River. The university's school of journalism, which opened in 1908, is the oldest in the world. Stephens College and Columbia College are also in the city. Many of Columbia's workers are employed by the city's hospitals and clinics, which include the University of Missouri-Columbia Hospital & Clinics, Boone Hospital Center, and a veterans' hospital. Columbia serves as a major center of retail and agricultural trade for the surrounding region. MFA, Inc. (Missouri Farmer's Association), an agricultural cooperative that operates throughout the Midwest, has its headquarters in the city. Several insurance companies also have their home offices in Columbia.

The Smithton Land Company founded a village near what is now Columbia in 1819. Columbia was incorporated in 1826. It is the seat of Boone County and has a council-manager government.   George Kennedy

Columbia, S.C. (pop. 98,052; met. area pop. 453,331), is the state's capital and largest city. It lies on the Congaree River, near the junction of the Broad and Saluda rivers. For location, see **South Carolina** (political map).

In 1786, the South Carolina legislature voted to move the state capital from the coastal city of Charleston to the middle of the state. The legislators called the new capital *Columbia,* a name poets had used for the country. The legislature first met there in 1790.

Description. Columbia, the county seat of Richland County, covers about 108 square miles (280 square kilometers). The Columbia metropolitan area spreads across 1,529 square miles (3,960 square kilometers) and extends into Lexington County.

Almost a third of the workers in the Columbia area are employed by the federal, state, county, or local government. The city has over 300 factories. Chief industries include chemicals, concrete products, electronics equipment, lumber, processed foods, textiles, and metal products. Columbia is South Carolina's trading center. The State Farmers Market there is a leading farm products market of the Southeast.

Historic buildings in Columbia include the First Baptist Church, built in 1859, and the state capitol, called State House. In 1860, the Secession Convention met in the church to discuss the possibility of South Carolina's leaving the Union. In Charleston, a few days later, the convention voted to do so. In 1865, during the Civil War, Union troops under General William T. Sherman captured Columbia. State House still bears scars from shells fired by Sherman's army.

Other attractions in Columbia include the Governor's Mansion, the Museum of Art and Science, Riverbanks Park Zoo, and President Woodrow Wilson's boyhood home. The Town Theatre, established in 1919, is one of the oldest little theaters in the United States. Columbia has a symphony orchestra and is the home of Benedict College, Columbia College, the University of South Carolina, and other educational institutions.

Government and history. Columbia has a council-manager form of government. Six council members and a mayor are elected to four-year terms. The council appoints a city manager to supervise the business of the city.

Congaree Indians lived in what is now the Columbia area until the early 1700's. They then moved farther north. White settlers built farms and cotton plantations in the area, and in the 1800's, cotton milling became one of Columbia's most important industries.

Columbia grew until the Civil War began in 1861. It began to grow again by the 1880's. Many textile mills expanded, and new industries came to the area.

In the late 1960's, the city began a program to beautify Columbia and encourage more people to make use of the downtown area. Construction of several office buildings began during the mid-1970's. The Strom Thurmond Federal Office Building was completed in 1979, and the Richland County Judicial Center was opened in 1980.

Bonita S. Richardson

See also **South Carolina** (pictures).

Columbia Plateau. See Idaho (Land regions); **Oregon** (Land regions); **Washington** (Land regions); **United States** (The Western Plateaus).

Columbia River is one of the chief rivers of the Western United States and Canada. It is the second longest river in the Western Hemisphere that flows into the Pacific Ocean. Only the Yukon River is longer. The Columbia is 1,243 miles (1,995 kilometers) long. It drains an

Columbia River

The Columbia River rises in the Canadian Rockies and drains southeastern British Columbia and much of the Pacific Northwest. More than 50 dams make the river's drainage basin the greatest center of water power in the world.

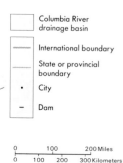

	Columbia River drainage basin
	International boundary
	State or provincial boundary
•	City
—	Dam

0   100   200 Miles
0   100   200   300 Kilometers

WORLD BOOK map

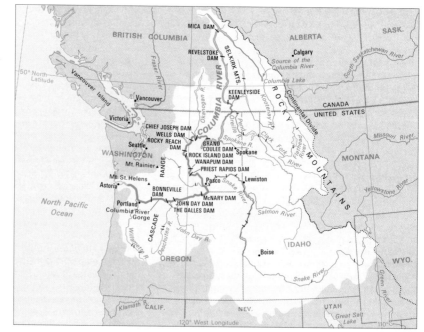

area of about 250,000 square miles (647,000 square kilometers), mostly in the United States.

Dams on the river generate about a third of the hydroelectric power produced in the United States. The Columbia is also a major source of water for irrigation.

The Columbia was named by Captain Robert Gray of Boston, who sailed into the mouth of the river in 1792. Gray named the river for his ship. In 1805, the American explorers Meriwether Lewis and William Clark traveled down the Columbia during their historic expedition to the Pacific Coast. In 1811, the Canadian explorer David Thompson became the first white person to navigate the entire length of the river.

The course of the Columbia. The Columbia River begins in Columbia Lake, which lies in the southeastern part of the Canadian province of British Columbia. From there, it flows northwest for about 200 miles (320 kilometers), bounded by the Canadian Rockies on the east and the Selkirk Mountains to the west. The river curves around the Selkirks and then flows south to the Canadian-United States border.

About 100 miles (160 kilometers) after entering the state of Washington, the Columbia begins a large curve westward. As the river continues to flow west to the Pacific Ocean, it forms the boundary between Washington and Oregon. The Columbia passes through the Cascade Range by way of the Columbia River Gorge.

The mouth of the Columbia forms a deep harbor on the Pacific Coast. Astoria, Ore., an important fishing port, lies at the mouth of the river.

Hydroelectric power and irrigation. Fourteen large dams on the Columbia—11 in the United States and 3 in Canada—provide water for hydroelectric power and irrigation. Grand Coulee Dam, about 90 miles (140 kilometers) northwest of Spokane, Wash., is the greatest single source of water power in the United States. Inexpensive electricity produced by the Columbia River dams has encouraged industrialization in the Pacific Northwest, including aluminum plants along the river and aircraft factories in Seattle and other cities in Washington. Irrigation water provided by the dams has turned millions of acres of arid land into a productive farm region. Also, reservoirs created by the dams are used for boating, fishing, swimming, and other activities. The dams also control flooding by the river.

Commerce. Large ocean vessels travel on the Columbia between the Pacific Ocean and Portland, Ore. Smaller vessels go from the ocean through the locks of Bonneville Dam and continue up the river to Pasco, Wash. Canals and lock systems also permit barges to use the lower part of the Columbia and sail up the Snake River as far as Lewiston, Ida. Cargoes transported on the Columbia include grain, forest products, iron and steel products, and petroleum products.

Wildlife of the Columbia River includes such fishes as perch, salmon, and trout. In the Canadian Rockies, forests of fir, larch, hemlock, and spruce trees grow along the river. These mountain areas are the home of bears, bighorn sheep, moose, and timber wolves. Bobcats, coyotes, and elk live in the grasslands that border the river in the United States.   John Edwin Coffman

See also **Bonneville Dam; British Columbia** (The mid-1900's); **Grand Coulee Dam; Gray, Robert; Oregon; Washington.**

Columbia University is a coeducational, privately endowed university in New York City. The university lies in upper Manhattan. Columbia is a leading university in liberal arts and professional studies.

Its divisions include 16 graduate and undergraduate schools. More than half of the students are enrolled in graduate schools. These schools include those of architecture and planning, arts and sciences, business, engineering, international affairs, journalism, law, library service, public health, and social work; and the college of physicians and surgeons. Columbia's undergraduate programs include courses in arts, engineering, and nursing. The university's undergraduate schools include Columbia College, which offers a core curriculum in contemporary civilization and the humanities. The university also has a School of General Studies. It provides undergraduate liberal arts courses for adults.

Affiliated institutions. Two colleges in New York City are affiliated with Columbia University. Barnard College was established by the trustees of Columbia University as an undergraduate school for women. It was founded in 1889 and awarded its first bachelor's degrees in 1893. Barnard students now attend classes at Columbia and receive degrees from the university.

Teachers College is a graduate school of education. Its programs lead to master's and doctor's degrees. Teachers College was established in 1887 and became part of Columbia in 1898. It granted its first degrees in 1901. See **Teachers College, Columbia University.**

Union Theological Seminary in New York City is affiliated with Columbia University. For musically gifted students, Columbia has joint programs with the Juilliard School, which is also in New York City.

Other facilities. Columbia University operates regional institutes, centers, and programs. These facilities offer graduate studies and conduct research in many fields. These fields include applied social research, cancer research, human nutrition, international change, urban and environmental affairs, and war and peace studies. The Lamont-Doherty Geological Observatory conducts research in oceanography and geological sciences. The Harriman Institute conducts research and offers studies on countries that were formerly part of the Soviet Union.

The university has cooperative programs with many museums, hospitals, libraries, and other institutions in New York City. Columbia's libraries have about $5\frac{3}{4}$ million volumes and 59,000 serials. The Butler Library has collections of rare books and historical documents.

History. Columbia was one of the earliest colleges founded in colonial America. King George II of England chartered it as King's College in 1754. It stood for many years near the present site of the city hall of New York City. A medical school was added in 1767, and the buildings were used as a hospital during the Revolutionary War. The school reopened as Columbia College after the war. Columbia moved to a temporary site in midtown New York City in 1857.

Columbia added schools of law and mines, and the faculties of political sciences, philosophy, and pure science. With the founding of the school of architecture in 1896, Columbia became a university. In 1897, the university moved to its present site. Columbia College was open only to men until 1983. For the enrollment of

Columbia University, see **Universities and colleges** (table).   Critically reviewed by Columbia University

See also **Barnard, Frederick A. P.; Butler, Nicholas Murray.**

Columbian Order. See Tammany, Society of.

Columbine, *KAHL uhm byn,* is the name of a group of flowering plants that occur naturally in Asia, Europe, and North America. These plants grow each year from underground rootstocks and flower from April to July. Bees and hummingbirds are attracted to columbines because the flower petals hold large amounts of nectar. Gardeners plant many kinds of columbines in rock gardens and flower beds.

The *wild columbine* bears red and yellow nodding flowers on the upper part of rigid, slender stems. Each flower has five long-spurred petals and many *stamens* (pollen-producing parts). The *Rocky Mountain columbine,* also called *blue and white columbine,* is the state flower of Colorado. Its large blue and white flowers have petals up to 2 inches (5 centimeters) long. The long spurs on the petals curve outward and are slightly swollen at the tip. The *short-spurred columbine* bears blue or purple flowers. Its short spurs bend inward and end in a hook.

Scientific classification. Columbines belong to the crowfoot family, Ranunculaceae. The scientific name for the wild columbine is *Aquilegia canadensis.* The Rocky Mountain columbine is *A. caerulea.* The short-spurred columbine is *A. brevistyla.*

Melinda F. Denton

See also **Flower** (picture: Flowers of woodlands and forests).

Columbite, *kuh LUHM byt,* is a mineral oxide composed of niobium, iron, and manganese. It has the chemical formula $(Fe,Mn)Nb_2O_6$. Columbite is the chief source of the element niobium. Its composition varies greatly, with the element tantalum (Ta) often taking the place of all or part of the niobium. When there is more tantalum than niobium, the mineral is called *tantalite.* Columbite is black, and occurs in blocklike crystals in coarse granite rocks called *pegmatites.* See also **Niobium; Tantalum.**   Robert B. Cook

Columbium. See Niobium.

Columbus, Ga. (pop. 179,278; met. area pop. 243,072), is the state's second-largest city. Only Atlanta has more people. Columbus is an industrial and military center. It lies on the Chattahoochee River, which forms Georgia's southwestern boundary with Alabama. For the location of Columbus, see **Georgia** (political map).

Production of cotton cloth and other textiles is the major industry in Columbus. Other leading industries produce candy, machinery, metals, peanut products, and soft drinks. Seven hydroelectric plants on the Chattahoochee River provide power for the city's factories. Water power helped make Columbus one of the South's first industrial centers. The city is the northernmost port on the river. Fort Benning, a large Army base, lies south of Columbus.

A National Historic District in downtown Columbus covers 28 blocks and includes many historic homes that rank among the oldest in Georgia. The homes include the Walker-Peters-Langdon house, built in 1828; and the Folly, a structure with more than 15 sides, erected in 1862. The city is the home of Columbus College. The state theater of Georgia, the Springer Opera House, was built in Columbus in 1871. The Columbus Museum of Arts and Sciences and the Confederate Naval Museum are in the city. The National Infantry Museum is at Fort Benning. Other cultural attractions include a symphony orchestra and a ballet company.

Creek, or Muskogee, Indians lived in what is now the Columbus area before white settlers arrived. The Georgia legislature founded Columbus in 1827 as an outpost for protection against the Indians. The city grew quickly after its first cotton mill opened in 1838. Union forces captured Columbus in April 1865 in one of the last battles of the Civil War.

In 1971, Columbus and Muscogee County were consolidated under a council-manager form of government. Columbus was the first Georgia city to adopt a consolidated city-county government.   James O. Wheeler

Columbus, Ohio, is the capital and largest city of the state. It is also a leading industrial center. Columbus lies near the center of Ohio, where the Olentangy and Scioto rivers meet. The city is the home of the main campus of Ohio State University, one of the nation's largest universities.

Almost all of Ohio lies within 150 miles (241 kilometers) of Columbus. In 1812, the state legislature chose the site for the capital because it could be reached easily from all major Ohio cities. Many state leaders wanted to name it Ohio City. But General Joseph Foos, a legislator from Franklin County, suggested *Columbus* to honor the explorer Christopher Columbus.

The city covers 190 square miles (492 square kilometers) and is the seat of Franklin County. Columbus has about 25 suburbs. The Columbus metropolitan area consists of 3,607 square miles (9,342 square kilometers) in Delaware, Fairfield, Franklin, Licking, Madison, Pickaway, and Union counties.

The limestone State Capitol stands in Capitol Square, a 10-acre (4-hectare) park at the intersection of the city's main avenues, High and Broad streets. For a picture of the Capitol, see **Ohio** (Government).

The Civic Center consists of a group of buildings that cover four blocks on both shores of the Scioto River. The buildings on the west shore include the Veterans Memorial Auditorium and Exhibition Hall. Columbus' tallest building, the State Office Tower, rises 624 feet (190 meters) on the east shore. Other east shore structures include federal and state office buildings, police headquarters, LeVeque Tower, and City Hall. A bronze statue of Christopher Columbus stands 20 feet (6 meters) high in City Hall Plaza. The city received the statue from the citizens of Genoa, Italy, the explorer's birthplace. The Avenue of Flags runs two blocks south from City Hall Plaza. It features a display of the 50 state flags.

Facts in brief

Population: *City*—632,910. *Metropolitan area*—1,377,419.
Area: *City*—190 sq. mi. (492 km²). *Metropolitan area*—3,607 sq. mi. (9,342 km²).
Altitude: 777 ft. (237 m) above sea level.
Climate: *Average temperature*—January, 30 °F (−1 °C); July, 75 °F (24 °C). *Average annual precipitation* (rainfall, melted snow, and other forms of moisture)—37 in. (94 cm).
Government: Mayor-council. *Terms*—4 years for the mayor and 4 years for the 7 council members.
Founded: 1812. Incorporated as a city in 1834.

Randy De Puy, Tom Stack & Assoc.

The Columbus City Hall stands in a plaza on the bank of the Scioto River. The statue of Christopher Columbus was given to the city by citizens of Genoa, Italy, the birthplace of the explorer.

The Ohio state fairgrounds and Ohio State University are on the north side of Columbus. German Village, a restored German settlement of the mid-1800's, covers 233 acres (94 hectares) just south of downtown.

People. About 97 per cent of Columbus' people were born in the United States. Blacks form the largest ethnic group, with about 23 per cent of the population. People of English, German, and Italian ancestry make up other large groups in the city.

Church groups, such as the Metropolitan Area Church Board (MACB), have helped the city fight against racial problems, juvenile delinquency, and poverty. More than 600 Christian congregations are represented in the MACB. Many non-Christian congregations also work in cooperation with the group. Another group, the Columbus Metropolitan Area Community Action Organization, helps manage federal, city, and state welfare programs.

In 1960, Columbus became the nation's first city to build apartment projects for the aged that included special recreational facilities. The city also maintains other recreation centers for elderly citizens.

Economy of Columbus is well balanced. About a fourth of the city's workers are employed in retail or wholesale stores. Government agencies and manufacturing firms each employ about a fifth of the labor force. Almost a fifth hold jobs in education, health, and other service industries.

Columbus is headquarters for several computer information services. The Chemical Abstracts Service is the world's largest computer-based chemical information service. The Online Computer Library Center provides computer information services for libraries and other institutions.

Research firms located in the city include the Battelle Memorial Institute, which conducts scientific research for private industry and the government (see **Battelle Memorial Institute**). The institute operates the largest independent, nonprofit research laboratories in the world.

Manufacturers in Columbus produce airplanes and automobile parts, cement mixers, coal-mining equipment, electric appliances, foundry and machine shop materials, and telephone equipment. Other industries in the city include printing and publishing.

Columbus has one daily newspaper, *The Columbus Dispatch.* The city also has five television stations and eight radio stations. Railroads provide freight service to Columbus. In addition, airlines use Port Columbus International Airport.

During the 1950's, new suburban shopping centers, restaurants, and theaters began to take business away from downtown Columbus. Construction of office buildings, motels, and an underground parking garage in the early 1960's attracted many people to the city during the day. But night life continued to suffer, and several theaters and restaurants closed. The reopening of two theaters and the opening of Ohio Center, a large convention center, brought more people back into the downtown area during the 1980's.

Education. Columbus pioneered in several areas of education. In 1837, the city began the nation's first state-operated school for the blind. The first junior high school in the United States opened in Columbus in 1909. And in 1922, Ohio State University founded radio station WOSU, the first educational radio station in North America.

Today, about 67,000 children attend about 130 public elementary and high schools and special schools in Columbus. About 45 per cent of the students are black. Almost 12,000 students attend the city's 43 private and church-supported schools.

The Columbus Board of Education has made special efforts to involve the community in its work. The board sponsors radio and television shows, holds neighborhood meetings, and publishes reports on the city's schools and their students and staff.

Ohio State University is the largest university in Ohio. Other institutions of higher learning in Columbus include Capital University, Columbus College of Art and Design, Franklin University, Ohio Dominican College, and Pontifical College Josephinum, the only seminary in the Western Hemisphere that is supervised directly by the Vatican. Three other seminaries, three colleges, two business schools, and a technical institute are also in the Columbus metropolitan area.

The Columbus Public Library has 20 branches. It owns more than a million volumes.

Cultural life. The Columbus Symphony Orchestra and the city's ballet company perform at the Ohio Theatre. Opera/Columbus and Broadway touring shows are presented at the Palace Theatre.

The Columbus Museum of Art has an outdoor sculpture park and garden featuring American and European sculpture of the 1800's and 1900's. The exhibit presents the works of such artists as Alexander Calder, Aristide Malliol, and Henry Moore. The city's Center of Science and Industry includes a planetarium. In addition, the Ohio Historical Center has exhibits of Indian life in early Ohio.

The Greater Columbus Arts Festival, held each June on the downtown riverfront, features displays of architecture and painting, and performances of dance and drama. The state fair is held annually in August. It includes agricultural exhibits and entertainment, and provides a showplace for Ohio artists.

Columbus has more than 150 parks and playgrounds, 5 public golf courses, and 3 city reservoirs for swimming and other water sports. The metropolitan Columbus park system consists of 11 parks that cover more than 11,000 acres (4,400 hectares). The Park of Roses displays about 36,000 rose plants. The Columbus Zoo features baby farm animals that youngsters may feed and pet. The zoo is known for its ape collection. The first gorilla born in captivity was born in the Columbus Zoo in 1956.

Government. Columbus has a mayor-council form of government. The voters elect the mayor and seven council members to four-year terms. A city income tax provides Columbus with about half its revenue.

During the 1960's, the lack of good public transportation became an important problem in the Columbus

City of Columbus

Columbus, Ohio's capital and largest city, lies in the central part of the state. It is also a major industrial center. The map shows important points of interest in the Columbus area.

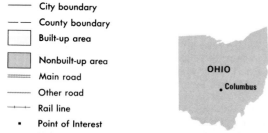

———	City boundary
— —	County boundary
☐	Built-up area
▨	Nonbuilt-up area
▤	Main road
———	Other road
+—+	Rail line
▪	Point of Interest

OHIO

▪ Columbus

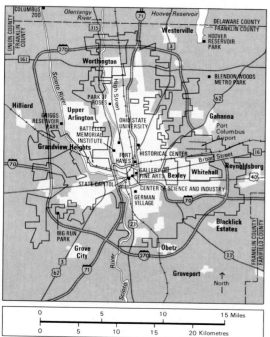

0	5	10	15 Miles
0	5	10	15	20 Kilometres

WORLD BOOK maps

area. Columbus and nearby cities established the Central Ohio Transit Authority in 1970 to deal with this problem. The agency purchased Columbus' privately owned bus company.

History. The Delaware and Wyandot Indians lived in what is now the Columbus area before white settlers first arrived. In 1797, settlers founded Franklinton, the first city in the area, on the west side of the Scioto River. The Ohio legislature established Columbus on the east bank, opposite Franklinton, in 1812. Within a year, Columbus had about 300 people. They included many Germans, and Germans continued to settle on the south side of the city throughout the 1800's. In 1816, the Ohio legislature moved to Columbus from Chillicothe, the temporary state capital. By that year, the city's population had grown to about 700.

During the 1830's, Columbus developed as a transportation and trade center. In 1831, a canal connecting Columbus with the Ohio and Erie Canal opened the way to increased trade with Eastern cities. The National Road, one of the principal pioneer routes to the West, reached Columbus in 1833. The city had about 3,500 people when it was incorporated in 1834.

The arrival of the railroad in the middle 1800's brought more commerce to Columbus. When the Civil War began in 1861, the city had a population of 18,629. During the war, Columbus became the assembly point for Ohio troops and the site of the largest Northern prison for Confederate soldiers. In 1871, Columbus extended its boundaries and annexed most of Franklinton across the river. By 1900, the city's population had grown to 125,500 and buggy manufacturing had made Columbus the industrial leader of central Ohio.

In 1913, nearly 100 people died when the Scioto River flooded Columbus. After this flood, the greatest disaster in the city's history, Columbus began a waterfront renewal project. The city built flood walls, bridges, and the beginning of the Civic Center.

Columbus continued growing during the 1900's. The city's population jumped from 290,500 in 1930 to about 565,000 in 1980. Maynard E. Sensenbrenner, who served as mayor of Columbus during most of the 1950's, 1960's, and early 1970's, developed a policy of annexing an average of $6\frac{1}{2}$ square miles (17 square kilometers) of unincorporated land around the city each year.

During the 1960's, an urban renewal program led to the rebuilding of the south side's German Village, which had been in poor condition since the early 1900's. Several old buildings also were rebuilt or replaced as part of downtown renewal projects. New construction included seven office buildings, two high-rise apartment buildings, and three motels. A 41-story state office building was completed in 1975.

Ohio Center, a downtown convention center, opened in 1980. An addition to the Ohio Center was completed in 1993. The center, with this addition, was renamed the Greater Columbus Convention Center. Construction of the Columbus City Center was completed in 1989. This shopping mall, which is located south of the State Capitol, includes more than 100 stores. It is connected to office buildings and a hotel. The 1990 U.S. census established Columbus as Ohio's largest city, with a population of about 633,000.   Mark A. Ellis

See also **Ohio** (picture: The State Capitol).

Christopher Columbus

1451-1506

Signature

SCALA/Art Resource
Coat of arms

Christopher Columbus has been depicted by many artists over the years. The woodcut at the right is based on a lost painting that dates from 1550. It is considered one of the most accurate likenesses of the explorer. Columbus had a distinctive signature, *above left,* and coat of arms, *above right.*

Woodcut (1575) by Tobias Stimmer; frontispiece in *The Columbus Gallery* by Néstor Ponce de León, 1893

Columbus, Christopher (1451-1506), was an outstanding navigator and organizer of expeditions. He achieved fame by sailing west across the Atlantic Ocean in search of a sea route to Asia. But he did not accomplish this goal. Instead, he encountered islands in the Caribbean Sea. At that time, the people of Europe and the Americas did not know of each other's existence. During his four voyages westward—between 1492 and 1504—Columbus explored what are now the West Indies and the coasts of Central and South America.

Columbus was not the first European to reach the Western Hemisphere. The Norse (also called the Vikings) had settled for a time on the coast of North America about A.D. 1000. But that contact did not last, and most Europeans of the 1400's did not know it had taken place. Columbus' voyages led to enduring links between the Eastern and Western hemispheres.

The world of Columbus

The Europe into which Columbus was born in 1451 was struggling against the growing power of the Ottoman Turks, who had conquered much of southeastern Europe. In 1453, the Ottomans took control of Constantinople (now Istanbul, Turkey), a major center of trade between Europe and Asia. The Ottomans made Constantinople the capital of their empire, cutting off easy European access to Asian goods. The only alternative to a difficult, dangerous land journey was a sea route—either around Africa or westward across the Atlantic.

Marvin Lunenfeld, the contributor of this article, is Distinguished Teaching Professor of History at the State University of New York College at Fredonia and the author of 1492: Discovery, Invasion, Encounter.

The desire for a sea route to Asia launched a remarkable wave of European exploration, despite the fact that Europe had limited resources. For example, the wealth of the countries of Europe could not match the wealth of China, which launched seven mammoth sea expeditions between 1405 and 1433, reaching as far as eastern Africa. However, European explorers combined the seafaring skill of the Italians with the resources of the Portuguese and the Spanish. Europe constantly improved its ships and navigational aids, as well as its arms and firepower. Europeans also had other qualities that encouraged overseas exploration, including a passion for trading and a desire to preach Christianity worldwide.

Early years

Boyhood. The exact date of Columbus' birth is not known. He was born sometime between Aug. 25 and Oct. 31, 1451, in Genoa, then capital of a self-governing area on the northwest coast of Italy. Genoa was an important seaport, and Genoese ships traded throughout the Mediterranean region.

Christopher's given and family name was *Cristoforo Colombo*. In English, he is known as *Christopher Columbus,* the Latinized forms of the name. He called himself *Cristóbal Colón* after he settled in Spain. His father, Domenico Colombo, was a wool weaver. To increase his income, Domenico also worked as a gatekeeper and wine merchant. Christopher's mother, Susanna Fontanarossa, was the daughter of a wool weaver.

Christopher was the oldest of five children. His brothers, Bartholomew and Diego, worked closely with him on many of his enterprises. Christopher and his brothers may have been tutored or sent to a monastery school to learn basic Latin and mathematics. Christopher's formal education ended at about age 14.

Young adulthood. Christopher's ambitious father pushed the boy into a business career, and Christopher began to sail on trading trips. He worked as an agent for the Spinola, Di Negro, and Centurione families of Genoa. In the mid-1470's, in his first documented voyage, Columbus took part in a trading expedition to the island of Chios, a Genoese possession in the Aegean Sea. In 1476, he settled in a Genoese colony in Lisbon, Portugal. There is a legend that he reached Portugal by swimming ashore clinging to an oar after being attacked by pirates. In Lisbon, Columbus joined with his brother Bartholomew to draw and sell maps.

Columbus frequently attended Mass at a chapel at the Convento dos Santos, a school for aristocratic young women. There, he met Felipa Perestrello Moniz, whom he married in 1479. Felipa's father was the first governor of Porto Santo, a Portuguese island in the Madeira group off the Atlantic coast of northern Africa. The young couple moved to Porto Santo, and then to the nearby island of Madeira. Their only child—a son, Diego—was born in 1480. Felipa died in 1484 or 1485.

Between 1480 and 1482, Columbus made voyages to the Canary Islands and the Azores, island groups in the Atlantic Ocean west of Africa. Columbus also visited Portugal's fortified trading posts in western Africa, where he observed the trade in gold and slaves. Some historians believe Columbus also went to England and Ireland, and even to Iceland, where he may have learned of early Norse explorations.

The plan to sail westward

The basis of the plan. By the 1480's, the Portuguese had invented the *caravel,* a sturdy ship that could sail against the wind. They were trying to reach the Indies— what are now India, China, the East Indies, and Japan— by sailing around Africa. By doing this, they hoped to gain direct access to gold, silk, gems, and spices. The cloves, nutmeg, and mace of the Spice Islands (now the Moluccas of Indonesia) served as medicines as well as seasonings. These valuable items had been transported to Europe by means of dangerous and costly overland caravans that were often hindered by Ottoman officials. While Portuguese sailors were trying to reach Asia by sailing around Africa, Columbus thought of what he believed to be the easy way—sailing due west.

Many people in the 1400's relied on a map of the world designed by Ptolemy, an astronomer and geographer in Alexandria, Egypt, during the A.D. 100's. Ptolemy's map showed most of the world as covered by land. Columbus found further confirmation for his idea of sailing west to Asia in the letters of Paolo Toscanelli, an influential scholar from the Italian city of Florence. Toscanelli believed that China lay only 5,000 nautical miles (9,300 kilometers) west of the Canary Islands. Columbus planned to sail 2,400 nautical miles (4,500 kilometers) west along the *latitude* (distance from the equator) of the Canaries until he reached islands near Japan. There, he hoped to establish a trading town.

Columbus' plan was based in part on two major miscalculations. First, he underestimated the circumference of the world by about 25 per cent. Columbus also mistakenly believed that most of the world consisted of land rather than water. This mistake led him to conclude that Asia extended much farther east than it actually did.

Presentation of the plan to Portugal. About 1483, Columbus gained audiences with King John II of Portugal. The king placed Columbus' proposal before his council, which rejected it. Columbus did not have to prove to the council that the world was round because educated people at that time knew it was. The council turned down his plan on the belief that he had greatly underestimated the length of the journey. The king's advisers thought that Portugal's resources should be invested in finding a route around Africa to Asia.

Years of waiting. In 1485, Columbus and his son went to Spain, a bitter rival of Portugal. At that time, Spain consisted of the united kingdoms of Castile and Aragon. Columbus arrived during Spain's war to drive the Muslims out of Granada, the only remaining Islamic kingdom on Spanish soil. Two wealthy Spanish aristocrats offered to give Columbus some ships. But to do so, they needed the permission of Spain's King Ferdinand and Queen Isabella. In 1486, Columbus gained an interview with the monarchs, but they were in no position to finance an expedition. They were also cautious about reopening conflict with Portugal. Spain and Portugal had recently settled their disputes over various islands off Africa. The Treaty of Alcaçovas, signed in 1479, had conceded the Canary Islands to Spain and the Madeira and Cape Verde islands and the Azores to Portugal.

However, the intensely religious monarchs were interested in how Columbus vowed to use the proceeds from his expedition. He promised to use the money to recapture Jerusalem from the Muslims. There, he said, he would rebuild the Jews' holy Temple and bring on a new "Age of the Holy Spirit." His eloquent arguments gained him support among Franciscan friars and Jews, including Jews who had converted to Christianity.

Queen Isabella was about the same age as Columbus, and she admired men of conviction. At her insistence, Columbus' plan was put before a commission of experts. They met in the Spanish cities of Salamanca and Córdoba during 1486 and 1487 under the leadership of Isabella's spiritual adviser, Hernando de Talavera. Although the committee's first report rejected Columbus' plan, Isabella granted him a small salary.

During this period, Columbus lived with a woman named Beatriz Enríquez de Harana. She gave birth to his second son, Ferdinand, in 1488.

For the next several years, Columbus followed the Spanish court as it traveled through the country. In 1490, the experts issued a final report. They scoffed at his plan—not because they thought that the world was flat or sea monsters would devour the ships, but because they still believed his estimates were wrong. The committee favored the belief that the world was large and covered mostly by water rather than small and composed mostly of land. In addition, Columbus' demands had increased. He wanted to become a titled aristocrat, to rule the lands he discovered, and to be able to pass these privileges on to his sons. He also wanted a percentage of the wealth he brought back to Spain.

Success in Spain. Columbus refused to give up. He sent his brother Bartholomew to seek support from the English and French courts, but the attempts were unsuccessful. Columbus' chance finally came when Spain conquered Granada in January 1492. In the aftermath of this victory, Luis de Santangel, a royal treasurer, convinced

Columbus' three ships from his first voyage westward were re-created to commemorate the 500th anniversary of his landing. Leading the procession is the reconstructed *Niña,* followed by the *Pinta* and the *Santa María.*

Spain '92 Foundation

Isabella that she was missing a great opportunity. Thus, in April 1492, Columbus' plan suddenly received royal approval. There is no truth to the story that Isabella offered to pawn her jewels to pay for the voyage. Columbus' supporters—including Santangel, who ran a government agency that had extra money in its treasury—provided the funds for the expedition.

First voyage westward

Ships and crews. Palos, a small port in southwestern Spain, was home to the Pinzón and Niño families. They provided two of the ships and selected the crews for Columbus' first voyage. Martín Alonso Pinzón, an experienced seafarer, captained the *Pinta,* a caravel with square-rigged sails that could carry about 60 short tons (54 metric tons). His brother, Vincente Yáñez Pinzón, captained the slightly smaller *Niña,* a caravel with *lateen* (triangular) sails. Columbus captained the third vessel, the *Santa María.* It was chartered from Juan de la Cosa, who came along as sailing master. It was slightly bigger than the other two ships. All three were made of wood, had no engines or motors, and provided few comforts.

Columbus' first voyage westward
On Aug. 3, 1492, Columbus sailed from Spain in search of a route to the Indies across the Atlantic Ocean. On October 12, he reached an island that he called San Salvador. For many years, historians believed that Columbus' first landing took place on present-day San Salvador, shown on the map below. But today, scholars do not agree on the exact site of this landing.

WORLD BOOK map

Detail of *Landing of Columbus* (1844) by John Vanderlyn; U.S. Capitol Rotunda (U.S. Capitol Historical Society)

Columbus first landed in the West Indies on Oct. 12, 1492. The painting above is how an artist of the 1800's imagined Columbus claimed the island for Spain. The woodcut at the right, which appeared in the first printed version of a letter Columbus sent to Spain in 1493, shows him trading with the Indians.

New York Public Library

A total of about 90 crew members sailed aboard the three ships. In addition to the officers and sailors, the expedition included a translator, three physicians, servants for each captain, a secretary, and an accountant.

Aboard ship, there was endless work to be done handling the sails and ropes and pumping out water that seeped or washed aboard. Cleaning and repair work filled the remaining hours. The crews cooked on portable wood-burning stoves. Their main meal consisted of a stew of salted meat or fish, hard biscuits, and watered wine. The sailors had no sleeping quarters, so they huddled on deck in good weather or found a spot below deck during storms. Only a few officers had bunks.

Sailing west. The fleet set out from Palos on Aug. 3, 1492, and sailed to the Canary Islands, a possession of Spain off the coast of Africa. Repairs were made on the island of Grand Canary, and the crews loaded provisions on the island of Gomera. The ships left Gomera on September 6. Because he had journeyed south before sailing west, Columbus could take advantage of the trade winds. At that latitude, these winds always blow from the northeast.

Columbus had few navigational instruments. He knew enough about celestial navigation to measure latitude by using the North Star. However, he had no instruments for determining the ship's position from the stars except a crude quadrant that was not accurate when the ship rolled. He used a compass to plot his course, estimated distances on a chart, relied on a half-hour glass to measure time, and guessed his speed. Together, these activities make up a method of navigation known as *dead reckoning.*

After a month of smooth sailing, the crews became anxious that they had not yet reached the islands Columbus had led them to expect. There was no full-fledged

mutiny, but only the authority of the Pinzón brothers enabled Columbus to quiet the crews' loudly expressed doubts. Then, signs of approaching land began to appear, such as coastal seaweed on the surface of the water and land-based birds flying overhead.

Between the evening of October 11 and the morning of October 12, a sailor on the *Pinta* named Juan Rodríguez Bermejo called out, "Land, land!" Isabella had offered a reward to the first person to sight land. However, Columbus said that he had seen a flickering light hours earlier, and he claimed the reward.

The first landing. Before noon on October 12, the ships landed on an island in the Caribbean Sea, in what are now called the West Indies. Columbus named the island *San Salvador* (Spanish for *Holy Savior*). He later learned that inhabitants of the area called the island Guanahaní. However, historians are not sure which island this is. In 1926, Watling Island in the Bahamas was officially renamed San Salvador Island because Columbus scholars considered it the most likely landing site. Other islands where he might have landed include Samana Cay and Conception in the Bahamas, and Grand Turk in the Turks Islands.

Columbus believed he had arrived at an island of the East Indies, near Japan or China. Because of this belief, he called the islanders *Indians*. People realized within 30 years that Columbus had not reached the Indies, but the name *Indian* continued to be used.

The islanders were probably the Taíno, a subgroup of the Arawak people. They were skilled farmers who made cotton cloth, grouped their dwellings into villages, and had well-developed social and governmental systems. Columbus described them as gentle, "primitive" natives living in an island paradise. This description set the pattern for European attitudes toward the Western

Hemisphere, despite later knowledge of the highly advanced Aztec of Mexico and Inca of Peru. In his writings, Columbus referred to the partial nudity of the Taíno. To the Europeans, this lack of clothing meant the Indians were not "civilized," even though it was appropriate to the warm climate.

On October 28, the fleet entered the Bay of Bariay off Cuba. Thinking they were near the Asian mainland, the captains explored harbor after harbor. They then sailed along the northern coast of the island of Hispaniola, now divided between the Dominican Republic and Haiti. Columbus called it *La Isla Española* (the Spanish Island).

The night of December 24, an exhausted Columbus gave the wheel of the *Santa María* to a sailor, who passed it to a cabin boy. The ship crashed and split apart on a reef near Cap-Haïtien, in present-day Haiti. Aided by a local chief, the crew built a makeshift fort. Columbus left about 40 men there to hunt for gold. He then started home on the *Niña,* sailing from Samaná Bay on the northeast coast of Hispaniola on Jan. 16, 1493. He brought several captured Taínos with him. Martín Pinzón captained the *Pinta.*

Return to Spain. The homeward voyage was rough and difficult. Some of the Taínos died. After about a month of travel, the *Niña* and the *Pinta* became separated during a storm. The *Niña* came ashore on the Portuguese island of Santa Maria in the Azores. Columbus and his crew were almost arrested by the governor, who assumed they had been trading illegally in Africa. Columbus set out again, but storms forced him to seek shelter in Lisbon. The *Niña* finally reached Palos on March 15, 1493.

Columbus had been concerned that Martín Pinzón would reach Spain first and claim the glory. Indeed, Pinzón had reached a small village in Spain a few days earlier and had notified the monarchs of his arrival. However, they refused to see him until they had heard from Columbus. The *Pinta* arrived at Palos a few hours after the *Niña.*

The Return of Christopher Columbus from the New World (1839), an oil painting on canvas by Eugène Delacroix; The Toledo Museum of Art, Toledo, Ohio, "Gift of Thomas A. DeVilbiss Bequest Fund"

Columbus returned to Spain on March 15, 1493. He later reported his findings to King Ferdinand and Queen Isabella, *above.* They gave him the titles *Admiral of the Ocean Sea* and *Viceroy of the Indies* and ordered a second voyage.

Columbus reported to Ferdinand and Isabella at Barcelona, Spain, where they gave him a grand reception. Columbus had little to show except some gold trinkets and the few Taínos who survived the harsh trip, but the monarchs determined to exploit his find. They quickly applied to Pope Alexander VI for control over the lands visited so far, and also of all lands west of a line 100 leagues (about 300 nautical miles, or 560 kilometers) from the Azores. The pope granted Ferdinand and Isabella the right to preach the Christian faith in the islands, and they used this right as the basis for sweeping claims over the lands. However, Portugal complained that these terms violated an earlier treaty.

In 1494, negotiations opened in the town of Tordesillas in Spain. Spain and Portugal eventually agreed to move the line to 370 leagues (about 1,100 nautical miles,

Columbus' voyages of exploration

Columbus made four voyages westward between 1492 and 1504. He explored the coasts of Cuba, Hispaniola, Jamaica, and Puerto Rico on the first and second voyages. Columbus reached the mainland of South America on the third and fourth voyages.

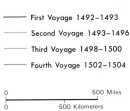

—— First Voyage 1492–1493
—— Second Voyage 1493–1496
—— Third Voyage 1498–1500
—— Fourth Voyage 1502–1504

0   500 Miles
0   500 Kilometers

WORLD BOOK map

Florida
Gulf of Mexico
Bahamas
San Salvador
To Palos, Spain
To Cádiz, Spain
North Atlantic Ocean
1492–1493
Conception
Samana Cay
To Cádiz, Spain
Isle of Pines
Cuba
Grand Turk
To Sanlúcar, Spain
Isabela
Cap-Haïtien
Hispaniola
Santo Domingo
Jamaica
St. Ann's Bay
Puerto Rico
Bay Islands
Marie-Galante
1493–1496
Central America
Caribbean Sea
Martinique
1502–1504
Mosquito Coast
Almirante Bay
Portobelo
Trinidad
1498–1500
Paria Peninsula
South America
North Pacific Ocean

or 2,060 kilometers) west of the Cape Verde Islands. This later enabled Portugal to claim Brazil and the Newfoundland Banks. See **Line of Demarcation.**

Second voyage westward

Return to the islands. Columbus was put in charge of 17 ships for a second voyage. The all-volunteer crew of about 1,200 to 1,500 men included colonists who intended to settle in the islands. Most dreamed of quick wealth and a rapid return home. Priests went along to try to convert the Indians to Christianity.

The fleet sailed from Cádiz, Spain, on Sept. 25, 1493. It took on supplies in the Canaries and completed the ocean crossing in a speedy 21 days. In another three weeks, the ships reached Hispaniola. They passed many islands. Columbus named one of them—present-day Marie-Galante in the French West Indies—after his flagship. Columbus also landed briefly at Puerto Rico, the only part of what is now the United States that he visited.

Trouble, settlement, and exploration. In Hispaniola, Columbus searched in vain for the sailors he had left at the fort. No one discovered exactly what had happened, but apparently the crew had fought among themselves about local women. The survivors had probably been killed by the Taínos, whom they had mistreated.

Columbus moved eastward along the north coast of Hispaniola and established Isabela, a fortified post. There, the Spanish colonists quickly saw that the riches promised by Columbus would not materialize. They resented being given orders by a Genoan rather than a Spaniard, and some fell ill from tropical fevers. Shortly after their arrival, 12 of the 17 ships returned to Spain with orders to bring more supplies to Isabela. The ships also carried discontented colonists back to Spain. To prevent rebellion, and also to make the voyage produce a quick profit, Columbus sent some men into the interior of Hispaniola to search for a gold mine.

Leaving his brother Diego in charge, Columbus left Isabela during the spring of 1494 to explore the southern coast of Cuba (which he called *Juana*). After traveling down its long coastline, Columbus declared that it was the Asian mainland. Although this was not so, he forced the crews to sign an affidavit saying they agreed with him. Columbus also landed at Jamaica.

When Columbus returned to Hispaniola, he found his brother Bartholomew waiting for him. Columbus immediately appointed Bartholomew provincial governor of Hispaniola. This appointment angered many of the Spanish settlers. In addition, they complained about having only *cassava* (tapioca), corn, fish, and yams to eat.

The brothers also had to quiet the Indians, who were no longer peaceful after the Europeans treated them harshly. In addition, the Taínos had begun to suffer and die from infectious diseases brought over unintentionally by the Europeans, and food had become scarce. Columbus forced all male Taínos over age 14 to pan rivers for gold. Those who failed to collect an assigned quota of gold were punished, sometimes by having their hands cut off. The quotas were almost impossible to meet. When the Indians threatened to rebel, Columbus used their rebellion to justify enslaving them.

In Spain, the priests and Spanish colonists who had left Isabela in the early months of 1494 complained to

Ferdinand and Isabella about conditions in Hispaniola. The priests criticized the maltreatment of the Taínos, and the colonists charged Columbus with misgovernment in the colony. Columbus decided to return to Spain to defend himself, arriving in June 1496. Again, Columbus' powerful oratory and impressive presence succeeded. The king and queen reconfirmed his titles and privileges, and they granted his request for additional men, supplies, and ships. But few men wanted to sail with him this time because the islands had failed to yield the expected profit. To assemble crews, Ferdinand and Isabella had to pardon prisoners. So low had Columbus' reputation sunk that his sons, who served as pages at court, were mocked by other boys. They jeered, "There go the sons of the Admiral of the Mosquitoes."

Third voyage westward

Third journey to the west. On May 30, 1498, Columbus departed from Sanlúcar, Spain, with six ships. He charted a southerly course. Ferdinand and Isabella wanted Columbus to investigate the possibility that a mainland lay south or southwest of the lands he had already explored. The possibility that such a mainland existed had been accepted by the king of Portugal, and Spain wanted to stake its claim.

The fleet ran into a windless region of the ocean and was becalmed in intense heat for eight days. It reached an island Columbus called *Trinidad* (meaning *Trinity*) on July 31 and then crossed the Gulf of Paria to the coast of Venezuela. Columbus observed an enormous outflow of fresh water—later found to come from the Orinoco River—that made him realize this land could not be an island. He wrote in his journal: "I believe that this is a very great continent which until today has been unknown." Columbus imagined that the great rush of fresh water must be a river flowing from the Garden of Eden.

Some scholars believe that while in Spain, Columbus had heard of English-sponsored landings in Nova Scotia and Newfoundland in 1497 by Italian explorer John Cabot. The news may have made Columbus think he might not have reached Asia. He did not mention his doubts, wanting to first explore and claim the land for Spain. For this reason, instead of being named for Columbus, the American continents were named after Amerigo Vespucci, an Italian navigator. A few years later, in a document backdated to 1497, the claim was made that Vespucci had been the first to explore the mainland, believing he had reached a "New World."

Problems in Hispaniola. Columbus found the Hispaniola colony seething with discontent. He tried to quiet the settlers by giving them land and letting them enslave the Indians to work it, but that failed to satisfy many. A rebellion had been led by the chief justice, Francisco Roldán. For a time, Roldán and the Taínos—with whom he had established an alliance—held part of the island. Columbus managed to subdue the rebellion through negotiation and a show of force.

Columbus in disgrace. By 1500, many complaints about Columbus had reached the Spanish court. Ferdinand and Isabella sent a commissioner named Francisco de Bobadilla to investigate. Upon arrival in Santo Domingo—the capital of Hispaniola—in August 1500, Bobadilla was shocked by the sight of several Spanish rebels swinging from gallows. He freed the remaining prisoners, arrested Columbus and his brothers, put them in chains, and sent them to Spain for trial. Once at sea, the captain of Columbus' ship offered to unchain him. But Columbus refused, saying he would only allow the chains to be removed by royal command.

In Spain, Columbus and his brothers were released by order of the king and queen. The rulers forgave Columbus, but with conditions. Columbus was allowed to keep his titles, but he would no longer be permitted to govern Hispaniola. Nicolás de Ovando was sent to serve as governor of Hispaniola, with about 30 ships carrying 2,500 colonists.

Fourth voyage westward

The final voyage. Columbus planned still another journey, which he called the "High Voyage." He saw it as his last chance to fulfill the promise of his earlier expeditions. His goal was to find a passage to the mainland of Asia. Columbus still believed that China lay close by. Ferdinand and Isabella granted his request for ships because they wanted to get him out of the way. But they instructed him not to stop at Hispaniola unless absolutely necessary to get supplies, and then only in preparation for his return to Spain.

On May 9, 1502, Columbus set sail from Cádiz, Spain, with four ships. Columbus' son Ferdinand, about 14 years old, sailed with his father. Ferdinand's account of the trip, though written many years later, remains the best record of the voyage. The fleet stopped briefly at the Canary Islands, then sailed to Martinique—in what is now the French West Indies—in just 21 days. It then headed toward Hispaniola.

A dangerous hurricane. Governor Ovando was sending 21 ships to Spain when he received a message from Columbus warning of an impending storm and asking permission to land. Feeling contempt for Columbus, and reminding him that he was forbidden to land at Hispaniola, Ovando ignored the warning and sent his ships to sea. Columbus' fleet weathered the storm. However, all but one of Ovando's ships sank in a hurricane. Columbus' enemies Bobadilla and Roldán drowned. The ship that reached Spain was the one carrying Columbus' share of the gold collected in Hispaniola, and the personal possessions he had left there.

Further explorations. At the end of July, Columbus and his fleet reached the coast of Honduras. For the rest of the year, they sailed east and south along the coasts of what are now Honduras, Nicaragua, Costa Rica, and Panama. The ships were battered by rough winds and driving rains.

At the narrowest part of the Isthmus of Panama, Columbus heard tales that a large body of water lay a few days' march across the mountains. But he did not follow up on this information, so he missed a chance to become the first European to see the Pacific Ocean. Columbus abandoned his search for a passage to Asia on April 16, 1503. He was exhausted and suffering from malaria, which made him delirious.

The hard journey home. Columbus' fleet had to move slowly, because his ships were leaking badly from holes eaten in the planking by shellfish. On June 25, the two remaining ships had to be beached at St. Ann's Bay, which Columbus had called Santa Gloria, on the northern coast of Jamaica.

Columbus realized that the chances were slim that another expedition would arrive to rescue him and his crew. Captain Diego Mendez volunteered to try to get help by paddling to Hispaniola in an Indian dugout canoe. Mendez reached Hispaniola, but Ovando refused to provide a ship until more vessels arrived from Spain.

The crews had no tools to repair the ships or to build new ones, and they made no effort to feed themselves. Instead, they relied on the islanders to provide food. The Jamaicans started avoiding them. Columbus later claimed that he used information from an almanac to predict a total eclipse of the moon, which so impressed the islanders that they resumed providing food.

At last, at the end of June in 1504—after being marooned for a year—Columbus and the 100 surviving crew members sailed from Jamaica on a ship chartered by Mendez. They reached Sanlúcar, Spain, on Nov. 7, 1504.

Final days

Queen Isabella died just a few weeks after Columbus returned to Spain. King Ferdinand granted Columbus an audience and listened to his requests. However, Ferdinand tried to persuade Columbus to trade in the rewards and privileges due him in exchange for an estate

Oil painting on canvas (about 1880) by Lorenzo Delleani; Galleria d'Arte Moderna, Genoa, Italy (SCALA/Art Resource)

A chained Columbus was sent back to Spain in 1500. The ship's captain offered to free him, but Columbus refused, saying he would only allow the chains to be removed by royal command.

in north-central Spain. Columbus, in turn, tried to persuade Ferdinand to restore his authority and increase his income, but these requests were not granted.

Columbus spent his last days in a modest house in Valladolid, Spain, suffering from a disease that may have been Reiter's syndrome. On May 20, 1506, at the age of 54, Columbus died. Many people believed Columbus was poor at the time of his death, but he actually died wealthy.

Columbus' remains were transported to Seville, Spain, and later to Santo Domingo, in what is now the Dominican Republic. Some historians believe that his bones were moved to Havana, Cuba, in 1795, and, finally, back to Seville in 1899. Other historians believe that the bones of one of Columbus' brothers or of his son Diego were removed from Santo Domingo instead, and that Columbus' final resting place is Santo Domingo.

Columbus' impact on history

Christopher Columbus had a strong will and stuck with his beliefs. His single-minded search for a westward route to Asia changed Europeans' commonly accepted views of the world and led to the establishment of contact between Europe and the Americas.

Many exchanges took place between the Eastern and Western hemispheres as a result of Columbus' voyages. The Europeans grew important cash crops—cotton, rubber, and sugar cane—in the Americas. They established vast plantations worked by Indians and by imported African slaves. They also obtained furs and precious metals. These valuable resources created fortunes for the Dutch, English, French, Portuguese, Russians, and Spanish. The wealth and human resources of the Western Hemisphere gave these countries a huge advantage over the rest of the world in later centuries.

Europeans brought many deadly diseases to America. The previous separation of the Native American peoples from those of Europe and Asia meant that the Native Americans had no resistance to these diseases. As a result, malaria, measles, smallpox, tetanus, typhus, and other infectious diseases swept through the newly exposed populations, killing vast numbers of people. In turn, some Europeans became infected by a form of syphilis unknown in Europe.

The love of freedom and the sharing of leadership among the Native American populations inspired a new belief in personal liberty among Europeans. This belief became a basis for democratic revolutions against European monarchies and greatly influenced the structure of government in the United States.

The Americas also provided many foods that became popular throughout the world. These foods included cassava, cayenne, chocolate, hot peppers, paprika, peanuts, sweet potatoes, tomatoes, and white potatoes. Europe and Asia, in exchange, supplied the Americas with cattle, goats, honey bees, horses, pigs, rice, sheep, wheat, and many trees and other plants.

Recent research into the life and times of Christopher Columbus has somewhat diminished his heroic image as an isolated visionary by placing him in the context of a broad wave of exploration. Historians continue to praise his persistence, courage, and maritime ability. Critics point to his cruelty to the Indians, his poor administration of Hispaniola, and his role in beginning the heedless exploitation of the natural resources of the Americas. Columbus' explorations ended centuries of mutual ignorance about what lay on either side of the Atlantic Ocean. To him belong both the glory of the encounter and a share of the blame for what followed.

Marvin Lunenfeld

Related articles in *World Book* include:

Caravel	Haiti (History)
Cattle (History)	Isabella I
Columbus Day	Latin America (European dis-
Exploration (The great	covery and exploration;
age of European discovery)	map)
Ferdinand V	Vespucci, Amerigo
Flag (pictures: Flags in	Virgin Islands (Exploration)
American history)	

Outline

Questions

On what two miscalculations did Columbus base his plan to sail westward?

What is the only part of the present-day United States that Columbus visited?

What is *dead reckoning*?

How did the Ottoman take-over of Constantinople in 1453 affect trade between Europe and Asia?

What exchanges took place between the Eastern and Western hemispheres as a result of Columbus' voyages?

What made Columbus realize he might not have reached Asia?

Did Spain restore Columbus' authority after the fourth voyage?

Where might Columbus' first landing in the Western Hemisphere have taken place?

Why did Columbus call the islanders he encountered *Indians*?

What happened to the first settlement at Hispaniola?

Additional resources

Level I

Fritz, Jean. *Where Do You Think You're Going, Christopher Columbus?* Putnam, 1980.

Levinson, Nancy S. *Christopher Columbus: Voyager to the Unknown.* Lodestar, 1990.

Soule, Gardner. *Christopher Columbus on the Green Sea of Darkness.* Watts, 1988.

Level II

Granzotto, Gianni. *Christopher Columbus.* Univ. of Oklahoma Pr., 1988. First published in 1985.

In the Wake of Columbus: Islands and Controversy. Ed. by Louis De Vorsey, Jr., and John Parker. Wayne State Univ. Pr., 1985. Articles discussing the location of Columbus' landfall.

Morison, Samuel E. *Admiral of the Ocean Sea: A Life of Christopher Columbus.* Little, Brown, 1942. Pulitzer Prize winner.

Columbus, Knights of. See Knights of Columbus.
Columbus Day honors Christopher Columbus' first
voyage to America in 1492. Columbus Day became a
legal federal holiday in the United States in 1971. It is
celebrated on the second Monday in October. Before
1971, a number of states celebrated Columbus Day on
October 12. Cities and organizations sponsor parades
and banquets on Columbus Day.

The first Columbus Day celebration was held in 1792,
when New York City celebrated the 300th anniversary of
the landing. In 1892, President Benjamin Harrison called
upon the people of the United States to celebrate Columbus Day on the 400th anniversary of the event. Columbus Day has been celebrated annually since 1920.

Although the land Columbus reached was not named
after him, many monuments honor him. The Republic of
Colombia in South America and the District of Columbia
in the United States bear his name. So do towns, rivers,
streets, and public buildings. The name *Columbia* has
also been used as a poetic personification of the United
States (see **Columbia**). The Columbus Memorial Library
in Washington, D.C., contains about 350,000 volumes on
the American republics.

Many Latin-American countries celebrate October 12
as the *Día de la Raza* (Day of the Race). It honors the
Spanish heritage of the peoples of Latin America. Celebration ceremonies feature speeches, parades, and colorful fiestas.   Jack Santino

Column is a freestanding vertical architectural element. When used for structural purposes, columns are
often arranged in rows to permit the thickness of walls
to be reduced by supporting weight from above. Some
columns, erected for decorative or memorial purposes,
stand alone. Columns are constructed of various materials, including wood, stone, brick, metal, and concrete.

A typical column consists of three parts: base, shaft,
and capital. The base is the lowest part of the column. It
supports the central upright shaft, which is usually cylin-
drical. The shaft is crowned by the capital. The horizontal area above the column and supported by it is called

the *entablature*. The base, column, and entablature together compose an *order* (see **Architecture** [Architec-
tural terms]). Through the centuries, architects have
used various kinds of columns. The ancient Egyptians favored heavy, massive columns. The Persian column was
generally tall and slender.

The Greek orders. The ancient Greeks refined the
column to a high degree. They developed three basic
classical orders—Doric, Ionic, and Corinthian. The shaft
diameter of each type of column decreases gradually as
the shaft rises, and each type has a subtle outward curve
called *entasis*.

The Doric column is the oldest and simplest of the
three types. It developed primarily on Greece's mainland
and in its western colonies. The Doric style has no base.
Usually, the shaft tapers upward to a height of 5 to 7
times its lower diameter. Along the shaft, 16 to 20 shallow vertical grooves called *flutes* meet in sharp ridges.
One or several horizontal grooves, called *necking,* mark
the meeting of the shaft and the capital. The capital has
two parts of almost equal thickness. The upper, a flat
square block called the *abacus,* rests on a round pillow-
like tablet called the *echinus.* A celebrated building
using the Doric order is the Parthenon, on the Acropolis
of Athens (see **Parthenon**).

The Ionic column is more slender and decorative
than the Doric. It was invented by the Greeks of the Aegean Islands and Asia Minor. The Ionic shaft stands on a
circular base, which sometimes includes a square block
at the bottom called a *plinth.* Its height is usually 9 to 10
times its lower diameter. Ordinarily, 24 flutes, divided by
narrow *fillets* (flat surfaces), run along the shaft. The capital consists of *volutes* (scrolls) that separate the echinus
from the abacus. Ionic columns stand on the Erech-
theum at Athens (see **Acropolis**).

The Corinthian column is the most ornamental of the
Greek orders. A variation of the Ionic, it has a similar
fluted shaft, but it has a more elaborate capital. The capital consists of a central core resembling an inverted bell.
The core is surrounded by carvings of acanthus leaves

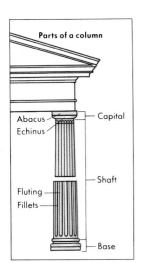

Parts of a column

Abacus
Echinus
Capital

Shaft

Fluting
Fillets

Base

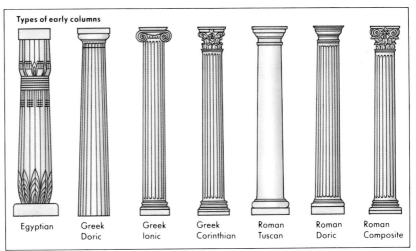

Types of early columns

Egyptian | Greek Doric | Greek Ionic | Greek Corinthian | Roman Tuscan | Roman Doric | Roman Composite

WORLD BOOK illustrations by Sarah Woodward

A column is a vertical support that consists of a shaft and a capital and often rests on a base. Columns created by the ancient Egyptians, Greeks, and Romans greatly influenced later architecture.

The Comanche Indians won fame as skilled horseback riders. The drawing at the left shows Comanches practicing battle maneuvers.

Detail of drawing (about 1836) by George Catlin; The Newberry Library, Chicago, Edward E. Ayer Collection

arranged in rows. From these leaves, four volutes project to meet the corners of the abacus. The monument of Lysikrates at Athens has Corinthian columns.

The Roman orders. The ancient Romans based their column designs on those of the Greeks. They also created two new orders—the Tuscan and the Composite. The Roman Doric order resembles the Greek but adds a simple molded base. The Tuscan order is an elementary version of the Doric without flutes. The Romans adopted the Greek Ionic with little change, but they elaborated and enriched the Corinthian. The Composite order combines features of both the Ionic and the Corinthian.

The Romans also erected independent, isolated columns as memorials to famous people and events. Sculptors decorated many of these massive, towerlike columns with carved or molded horizontal or spiraling bands called *friezes* that portray events related to the memorial. An example is Trajan's Column in Rome.

Columns of later periods. During early Christian and medieval times, architects freely adapted the classical orders for use in basilicas and cloisters. The Cathedral of Notre Dame in Paris has a combination of classical and medieval styles. The Renaissance and baroque periods revived the use of Roman-style columns, as in the colonnades of St. Peter's Square in Rome. In the 1800's and 1900's, all types of columns have been used, particularly on public buildings.   William J. Hennessey

See also pictures of columns with **Architecture; Pompeii; Rome; Washington, D.C.; World, History of the.**

Coma is a state of deep and complete loss of consciousness. The word comes from the Greek word *koma,* meaning *deep sleep.* People in this state ordinarily cannot be aroused by stimulants such as spirits of ammonia, light slapping, or a pinprick. Drug overdoses, seizures, head injuries, tumors, and strokes may cause coma. Patients with diabetes or diseases of the liver or kidneys also can fall into a coma. Doctors treat coma according to its cause. For example, if it is caused by a drug, the doctor gives an antidote.   James N. Davis

Comanche Indians, *kuh MAN chee,* were a southern Plains tribe that hunted buffalo from Nebraska to northern Mexico. They won fame as the most skilled Indian horseback riders of the Southwest. In battle, many Comanche eluded arrows and bullets by hanging against the side of—or even under—their horses.

The Comanche lived chiefly as hunters and followed wandering buffalo herds. They hunted on foot until the 1700's, when the Spaniards brought horses to the Great

Plains. Then the Comanche became master riders. For many years, the Comanche fiercely defended their land from other tribes and white ranchers.

In 1867, the Comanche agreed to move to a reservation in what is now Oklahoma. By 1900, whites had settled on parts of the reservation. In the early 1900's, the United States government transferred to each Comanche ownership of 160 acres (65 hectares) of land. Many disliked farming and sold or leased their land to whites.

Today, most of the approximately 2,500 Comanche living in tribal communities are in or near Comanche County, Okla. Many of them work as accountants, bookkeepers, farmers, nurses, ranchers, or teachers. The Comanche, Apache, and Kiowa Indian tribes jointly own about 4,500 acres (1,820 hectares) of land in and around Lawton, Okla. The tribes have developed two industrial parks there.   C. B. Clark

See also **Indian, American** (Family life [picture: A village scene]); **Quanah.**

Comaneci, *ков muh NEECH* or *kAW mah NEHCH,* **Nadia,** *NAH dee uh* (1961-   ), a Romanian gymnast, became the first gymnast to receive a perfect score of 10 in the Olympic Games. In the 1976 Olympic Games in Montreal, Canada, Comaneci earned scores of 10 seven

© Duomo

Nadia Comaneci, Romanian gymnast, won three gold medals in the 1976 Olympic Games and two in 1980. She is shown above during a gold-medal performance on the balance beam, in 1980.

times. She won gold medals in the uneven parallel bars, balance beam, and all-around competitions. In the 1980 Olympics in Moscow, Comaneci won gold medals in the balance beam and floor exercise events.

Comaneci was born in Gheorghe Gheorghiu-Dej, Romania. She began her gymnastics career at the age of 6, after Bela Karolyi, a famous gymnastics coach, discovered her. In 1989, Comaneci defected to the United States.   Dave Nightingale

Combine is a farm machine that cuts and threshes grain or other crops in one operation. The word *combine* stands for *combined harvester-thresher.* Some are large, self-powered machines. Others are smaller models pulled by tractors. Large combines cut paths wider than 20 feet (6 meters). Small ones cut paths about 6 feet (1.8 meters) wide. Those with special attachments can collect and shell corn, soybeans, and other crops.

As a combine crosses a field, a *cutting bar* on the front cuts the stalks of grain. Paddles on a long, rotating reel press the stalks against the cutting bar. The cut stalks fall onto a platform, and a *feeder* carries them to a *threshing drum.* In the drum, a revolving cylinder beats most of the grain off the stalks, creating straw. The grain falls through a grate into a *grain pan.* The straw moves to *straw racks,* which tumble it to remove any remaining grain. The straw then drops from the combine.

All the grain collects in the grain pan. From there, it passes to a series of sieves, where a fan blows the husks away from the kernels. The kernels fall through the sieves and are carried to temporary storage in a *grain tank.* Finally, an *unloading conveyor* empties the grain from the grain tank into trucks or wagons that transport the grain to storage bins.

One of the first successful combines was built in the 1830's by Hiram Moore and John Haskall, near Kalamazoo, Mich. It was pulled by 20 horses. A wheel that rolled along the ground drove the cutting and threshing machinery. In the 1880's, steam engines began to power combines. Internal-combustion engines were replacing steam engines by the early 1900's.

Most early combines were used west of the Rocky Mountains. Farmers elsewhere used reapers and threshing machines, which required more time and labor than did combines (see **Reaper; Threshing machine**). After World War I ended in 1918, new designs of combines, plus a labor shortage, caused more farmers to use combines. Since then, combines have replaced most reapers and threshing machines.   Gerald E. Rehkugler

Combustion is a chemical reaction that gives off heat and light. In most cases, combustion involves the rapid combination of oxygen with a fuel to produce burning. The fuel may be solid, liquid, or gaseous. Combustion occurs, for example, when oxygen in the air reacts with the charcoal in a barbecue grill or with the methane gas in a stove burner. In some cases, such chemicals as fluorine or chlorine take the place of oxygen in the combustion process. When oxygen combines slowly with another substance, the reaction is usually called *oxidation.* The rusting of iron is an example of oxidation. See **Oxidation; Oxygen.**

In most cases, combustion occurs between a gaseous fuel and the oxygen in the air. The fuel may begin as a solid or liquid, but it must be *vaporized* (changed to a gas) before it can burn. The lowest temperature at which a solid or liquid produces enough gas for combustion is called its *ignition temperature.* The energy given off by burning fuel is called the *heat of combustion.* It is usually measured in calories per gram (see **Calorie**). The ignition temperature and the heat of combustion differ from fuel to fuel, and they determine how different fuels are used.

Sometimes, a substance suddenly ignites and burns without having contact with a spark or flame. This is called *spontaneous combustion.* It occurs when chemical reactions within the substance produce heat that cannot escape. The substance slowly reaches its ignition temperature and begins to burn. Spontaneous combustion may occur when piles of oily rags, coal, and cotton are left unattended.   James G. Quintiere

See also **Dust explosion; Fire.**

Comedy is a form of drama that deals with humorous or ridiculous aspects of human behavior. Most comedies have a playful mood and end happily.

In *comedies of character,* the humor comes from the major traits of the characters. *Comedies of ideas* deal primarily with social issues. *Situation comedies* rely on comic actions and events. Most *comedies of manners* are humorous treatments of the social codes of the upper classes. Most *romantic comedies* concern people who are in love. An exaggerated kind of comedy called *farce* is sometimes considered a separate type. But farce may be treated as a form of situation comedy.

The first important comic playwright was Aristophanes, who lived in Greece from about 445 to 385 B.C. Most of his comedies deal with public issues. The ancient Roman playwrights Plautus and Terence wrote situation comedies based on events from everyday life.

During the Middle Ages, farce was the major type of comedy. In the late 1500's and early 1600's in England, William Shakespeare wrote plays with almost every type of comedy, while Ben Jonson specialized in satiric comedies of character, with each character dominated by a single trait, such as greed. In the mid-1600's, Molière became the most famous comic playwright in France, with plays similar to Jonson's. In the late 1600's, such English playwrights as William Wycherley and William Congreve raised the comedy of manners to a high level.

Many playwrights of the 1700's wrote sentimental comedies. These dramatists included Sir Richard Steele of England and Pierre Marivaux of France. Later in the 1700's, witty comedies were written by Oliver Goldsmith and Richard Brinsley Sheridan, both of England, and by Pierre de Beaumarchais of France.

In the early 1900's, the British dramatist George Bernard Shaw proved a master of the comedy of ideas, which discusses moral or philosophical issues without interrupting the humor. Noel Coward wrote comedies of manners about England's sophisticated society.

During the mid-1900's, the Irish-born playwright Samuel Beckett and Romanian-born Eugène Ionesco pioneered in the theater of the absurd, in which bizarre comic events mingled with serious action. The *dark comedies* of Harold Pinter in England and Edward Albee in the United States are an offshoot of this school. In the late 1900's, Alan Ayckbourn in England and Neil Simon in the United States have specialized in situation comedies about everyday life.   Gerald M. Berkowitz

See also **Drama; Humor; Burlesque.**

Comedy of manners. See Drama (European drama: 1660-1800); English literature (Restoration drama).

Comenius, *kuh MEE nee uhs,* **John Amos** (1592-1670), was a Czech educational reformer and religious leader. He criticized the educational conditions of his time and called for a reorganization of schooling.

Comenius described his educational system in a book called *Didactica Magna* (*The Great Didactic*), which he finished about 1635. He proposed that education be organized in graded stages, from easy to difficult. He also called for teachers to use kindness instead of harsh discipline and to teach certain classes in their students' native language rather than Latin.

Comenius, whose Czech name was Jan Amos Komenský, was born in Uhersky Brod, near Zlín, in what is now the Czech Republic. According to the custom of his time, he wrote in Latin and used a Latin name. About 1616, he was ordained a pastor in a Protestant group called the Brethren, now the Moravian Church. Comenius became a bishop in 1648.   Douglas Sloan

Comet, *KAHM iht,* is an object that resembles a fuzzy star and travels along a definite path through the solar system. Some of the brightest comets develop a long, shining tail when they come near the sun. The tail of a comet may stream across space as far as 100 million miles (160 million kilometers). A comet has a distinct center called a *nucleus* that measures less than 10 miles (16 kilometers) in diameter. A hazy cloud called a *coma* surrounds the nucleus. Its diameter may be as large as 1 million miles (1.6 million kilometers). The coma and nucleus make up the comet's head.

Most comets cannot be seen without a telescope. Some are visible to the unaided eye, but only for several weeks or months when they pass closest to the sun. Halley's Comet is probably the best-known comet. It was named for the English astronomer Edmond Halley, who recognized that it could be seen an average of every 77 years as it orbited the sun. Astronomers determined that the comet would complete two orbits during the 1900's—in 1910 and in 1986.

A number of other extremely bright comets have been seen since 1910. For example, Comet Arend-Roland and Comet Mrkos appeared in 1957 and Comet Ikeya-Seki in 1965. In 1973, Comet Kohoutek became the first comet to be studied by men in space. Astronauts in the Skylab space station photographed it and so provided much new information about comets.

For centuries, many people believed the coming of a comet would bring a disaster, such as a war or an epidemic. Halley's Comet revived these fears in 1910, but the earth passed through the edge of the comet's tail with no harm. However, a collision between the earth and a comet's nucleus could be very destructive.

The composition of comets. Scientists once believed the nucleus of a comet consisted of tiny solid particles held together loosely by gravitation. Today, most astronomers think the nucleus resembles a dirty snowball that was formed in the cold, distant regions of the solar system. The nucleus probably consists of frozen gases and ice mixed with dust. The gases include ammonia, carbon dioxide, carbon monoxide, and methane. The gases and water make up from 70 to 80 per cent of the total mass. The remaining 20 to 30 per cent may resemble meteoric particles. This portion consists of fine

European Southern Observatory

Halley's Comet becomes visible to the unaided eye an average of every 77 years when it nears the sun.

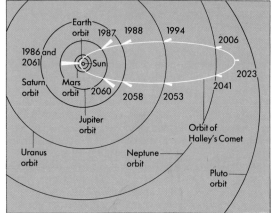

WORLD BOOK diagram by Linda Kinnaman

A comet travels through the solar system in a long, narrow orbit. The orbit of Halley's Comet, shown in the diagram above, crossed the orbit of the earth in 1986, and astronomers predict that it will do so again in 2061.

grains and larger chunks of metals and rocky material.

As a comet approaches the sun, the heat causes the outer layers of the icy nucleus to evaporate. The evaporation releases dust and gases, which form the coma around the nucleus. The pressure of the sun's light may push the smallest dust particles and gas molecules away from the coma, forming one or more tails. This pressure

Famous comets

Name	First recorded sighting	Period of orbit (years)
Halley's Comet	About 240 B.C.	76-79*
Tycho Brahe's Comet	1577	Unknown
Biela's Comet	1772	6.6-6.8*
Encke's Comet	1786	3.3
Comet Flaugergues	1811	3,000
Comet Pons-Winnecke	1819	5.6-6.3*
Great Comet of 1843	1843	513
Donati's Comet	1858	2,000
Great Comet of 1882	1882	760
Comet Morehouse	1908	Unknown
Comet Schwassmann-Wachmann 1	1927	16.1-16.4*
Comet Humason	1961	2,900
Comet Ikeya-Seki	1965	880
Comet Tago-Sato-Kosaka	1969	420,000
Comet Bennett	1969	1,680
Comet Kohoutek	1973	75,000
Comet West	1976	500,000

*Period changes

makes a comet's tail point away from the sun. When a comet approaches the sun, its tail brings up the rear. But when the comet moves away from the sun, its tail leads.

All of a comet's light comes from the sun. The brightness of a comet results partly from sunlight reflected by its nucleus and coma. In addition, when a comet is closest to the sun, gas molecules in the coma release energy absorbed from the sun's rays.

The paths of comets. Most comets travel around the sun in *elliptical* (oval-shaped) paths. The time it takes a comet to make a complete orbit is called its *period.* Some comets have short periods of less than seven years. Others travel in such huge orbits that they pass near the sun only once in thousands or even millions of years. No comet seems to have approached the sun from beyond the limits of the solar system. Therefore, all comets seen by astronomers are considered part of the solar system.   Elizabeth Roemer

See also **Halley's Comet; Moon** (The moon's surface); **Space Exploration** (Probes to comets).

Comic opera. See **Opera** (Baroque opera).

Comics are a series of related cartoons that tell a story. Most comic strips appear in newspapers. A comic may tell part of a continuing story, or it may be a complete story in itself. Some comics are published in magazine form as *comic books.* A majority of comics feature a continuing cast of characters. In most comics, conversation between the characters appears near their heads in white areas called *balloons.* A few comics, called *pantomime strips,* have no conversation at all.

The main purpose of comics is entertainment. Most early comics used humor and became known as *funnies.* Today, many comics are based on humor, but others tell exciting adventure and fantasy stories. Still others describe dramatic events in the lives of such people as doctors, police officers, reporters, and secretaries.

Surveys show that comic strips are the most popular feature in newspapers. Some strips, such as Charles Schulz's "Peanuts," appear in more than 2,000 newspapers. In addition, about 150 million comic books are sold annually in the United States and Canada.

The popularity of comics has made them a useful tool in advertising. Many companies use comics or characters from famous comics to promote their products. Comics are also used in educational publications.

Comics have inspired books, motion pictures, plays, songs, and radio and television programs. They have popularized such expressions as "hot dog" and "Good Grief!" Comics have even influenced a movement in the fine arts called pop art.

How comics are created. Most comic strips are the work of one person who does both the drawing and writing. But some strips are produced by two or more people. In many cases, a writer works out the story, and a cartoonist draws the *panels* (individual pictures). Comic books require a great amount of material, and many artists and writers may work to produce one comic book.

A cartoonist separates the events of a story so that they can be drawn in individual panels. The action must move smoothly from one panel to the next and, in some cases, from one installment to the next.

© 1939 King Features Syndicate, Inc.

"Krazy Kat," drawn by George Herriman from 1910 to 1944, portrayed the adventures of Krazy Kat, *center,* and the mouse Ignatz.

© 1986 Marvel Comics Group, Division of Cadence Industries Corp. Distributed by KFS.

Superheroes, such as Spider-Man, with their extraordinary powers, are popular in adventure comic strips.

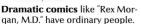

© 1979 Field Enterprises, Inc. By permission News America Syndicate

Dramatic comics like "Rex Morgan, M.D." have ordinary people.

© 1986 Washington Post Writers Group

Satiric comics poke fun at political issues and social problems and attitudes. In "Bloom County," Berke Breathed created human and animal characters to express his views.

The cartoonist finishes the comic strip about six weeks before it appears in print. Most cartoonists have a distributing company called a *syndicate* that acts as their business agent. The cartoonist sends the strip to the syndicate, which distributes it to newspapers in all parts of the world.

History. The first comic strip to become widely popular, "Hogan's Alley," appeared in 1895. Richard F. Outcault drew it for the Sunday edition of *The World* of New York City. The strip starred a mischievous little boy, Mickey Dugan, who became known as the Yellow Kid (see **Outcault, Richard Felton**). In 1896, the strip was renamed "The Yellow Kid." Soon, other newspapers began to feature comic strips in order to attract more readers. In 1897, Rudolph Dirks started "The Katzenjammer Kids" for the *New York Journal.* The first successful daily strip, Bud Fisher's "A. Mutt" (later retitled "Mutt and Jeff"), began in 1907 in the *San Francisco Chronicle.*

In the 1930's, adventure strips became popular. Chester Gould created the detective strip "Dick Tracy" in 1931. Such adventure strips as "Prince Valiant" (1937) by Harold Foster and "Superman" (1938) by Jerry Siegel and Joe Shuster became popular during this period.

Over the years, many comic strips have mixed entertainment with the artist's political views. Such political comic strips include "The Yellow Kid," Harold Gray's "Little Orphan Annie" (1924), Al Capp's "Li'l Abner" (1934), and Walt Kelly's "Pogo" (1949). Today, strips that contain humorous comments about political and social events include Johnny Hart's "B.C." (1958), Garry Trudeau's "Doonesbury" (1970), and Berke Breathed's "Bloom County" (1980).

The first comic book, a collection of reprinted "Yellow Kid" strips, appeared in 1897. In the 1920's, the first comic books made up of original material were published in Japan. Comic books began to appear in their present magazine form in the 1930's.

Comics lost some popularity after television became widespread in the late 1940's. Comic books especially suffered because a few publishers printed ones that contained obscenities and violence. In 1954, almost all U.S. comic book publishers adopted the Comics Code Authority, which prohibited such material.

By the 1960's, comics had regained some of their popularity. They once appealed mostly to children and uneducated adults. But today, such strips as "Peanuts" (1950), Mell Lazarus' "Miss Peach" (1957), and Mort Walker's "Beetle Bailey" (1950) can be enjoyed by both children and adults, and by the educated as well as the uneducated. These comics are simple and funny, but they are also sophisticated.   Charles P. Green

See also **Capp, Al; Schulz, Charles M.; Cartoon.**

Comma. See Punctuation (The comma).

Commager, *KAHM uh juhr,* **Henry Steele** (1902-   ), an American educator and historian, won high praise for his books *The Growth of the American Republic* (with Samuel E. Morison, 1931) and *America: the Story of a Free People* (with Allan Nevins, 1942). Commager and Nevins also wrote *The Heritage of America* (1939). Commager edited *Documents of American History* (1934) and often wrote for periodicals on historical and public issues.

Commager was born in Pittsburgh, Pa., and earned a Ph.D. degree from the University of Chicago in 1928. He has taught history at New York University, Columbia University, and Amherst College.   Gerald L. Gutek

Command. See **Air Force, United States** (Organization of the Air Force); **Army, United States** (Organization of the Army); **Navy, United States** (Organization of the Navy).

Commander. See **Rank, Military.**

Commander in chief has supreme command of a nation's armed services. In the United States, the President is the commander in chief of the Army, Navy, and Air Force, and Marine Corps. The title of *commander in chief* may also be given to an officer commanding a theater of operations, a major naval fleet, a unified command of units from two or more of the military services, or a specified command assigned to a specific function. See also **President of the United States; Constitution of the United States** (Article II, Section 2).   Allan R. Millett

Commandments, Ten. See **Ten Commandments.**

Commando is the British term for a soldier who is trained to take part in specialized hit-and-run or raiding operations. U.S. soldiers who qualify for difficult commandolike training can become members of the Army *Special Forces* or of Army *Ranger* units. Similar units in the U.S. Air Force are called *Special Operations* units (formerly *Air Commandos*). In the U.S. Navy, such units are known as *SEAL* (for *sea, air,* and *land*) teams.

The word *commando* was originally a Portuguese term. It was first used in South Africa during the 1830's to describe surprise attacks of the Dutch and Portuguese settlers against the African people. Prime Minister Winston Churchill suggested the name for the British *combined operations units* that used guerrilla warfare tactics during World War II (see **Guerrilla warfare**). Commando raids destroyed war plants and materials, rescued Allied agents, or tried out invasion tactics.

Famous commando operations during World War II included a raid on St.-Nazaire, France, in March 1942. Commandos destroyed the largest dock in western Europe. Canadian and British commandos staged the largest raid, on Dieppe, France, on Aug. 19, 1942. They fought for nine hours, but suffered heavy losses. The U.S. Marine Corps employed commandos known as *Raiders* in the difficult Pacific campaign during World War II. U.S. Special Forces, Special Operations, and Ranger units, as well as SEAL teams, were used during the Vietnam War (1957-1975). In 1976, Israeli commandos in a daring raid freed 103 hostages held by terrorists in Uganda's Entebbe airport.   John W. Gordon

See also **Army, United States** (Special units); **Rangers; Wingate's Raiders.**

Commedia dell' arte. See **Drama** (Italian Renaissance drama; picture).

Commerce. See **Business; Trade.**

Commerce, Chamber of. See **Chamber of Commerce; Chamber of Commerce of the United States.**

Commerce, Department of, is an executive department of the United States government. The department's chief responsibility is to promote the nation's economic development, international trade, and technological advancement. The department helps the President form national economic policy and provides economic data, studies, and advice to other federal agencies and to private enterprise. The secretary of commerce, a member of the President's Cabinet, heads the department.

Functions. The department is the chief government agency that operates foreign trade programs. It collects, analyzes, and distributes commercial statistics. It conducts population and agricultural censuses and coastal and geodetic surveys. It publishes nautical and aeronautical charts. It establishes weights, measures, and standards for commodities. The department issues patents, registers trademarks, and provides weather forecasts. It also promotes travel to the United States and advises the President on communications policy.

Organization. The secretary of commerce is appointed by the President with the approval of the Senate. The secretary administers the department and advises the President on matters that affect industry and commerce. The secretary serves as the President's chief contact with the business world. The deputy secretary is the secretary's chief assistant and serves as acting secretary in the secretary's absence. There are also 6 undersecretaries, plus several other high officials.

The undersecretary for international trade directs the International Trade Administration (ITA). The ITA works to promote trade growth and to strengthen the nation's international economic position. Assistant secretaries in the ITA handle economic policy, import administration, trade development, and U.S. and foreign commercial services. The undersecretary for travel and tourism heads the U.S. Travel and Tourism Administration.

The undersecretary for economic affairs provides economic policy advice to the secretary of commerce and directs the operation of the Bureau of the Census, the Bureau of Economic Analysis, and the chief economist. The assistant secretary for economic development administers the Economic Development Administration, which promotes programs to create jobs and increase incomes in economically weak areas of the nation. The assistant secretary and commissioner directs the Patent and Trademark Office.

The assistant secretary for communications and information heads the National Telecommunications and Information Administration. This agency advises the President on regulation of the telecommunications industry and other communications policies. The assistant secretary for congressional and intergovernmental affairs advises the secretary of commerce on legislation and other congressional activities. There is also an assistant secretary for administration.

The undersecretary for oceans and atmosphere directs the National Oceanic and Atmospheric Administration. This agency coordinates the work of federal agencies involved in conservation, development, educational activities, exploration, monitoring, and research relating to the oceans and the atmosphere.

The Minority Business Development Agency coordinates programs to help members of minority groups establish new businesses and expand existing businesses. The undersecretary for technology oversees the National Institute of Standards and Technology, the National Technical Information Service, and the Technology Administration.

History. Congress established the Department of Commerce and Labor on Feb. 14, 1903, at the request of President Theodore Roosevelt. The department included eight bureaus that handled matters concerning the census, corporations, fisheries, immigration, labor, navigation, standards, and statistics. On March 4, 1913, Congress set up a separate Department of Labor and a new Department of Commerce.

Since 1913, many bureaus and agencies have been transferred to or from the department. In 1925, for example, Congress switched the Patent Office (now the Patent and Trademark Office) from the Department of the Interior to the Department of Commerce. In 1966, Congress transferred several agencies from the Department of Commerce to the newly formed Department of Transportation.

The seal of the Department of Commerce

Critically reviewed by the Department of Commerce

Related articles in *World Book* include:

Census, Bureau of the
Flag (picture: Flags of the U.S. government)
National Institute of Standards and Technology
National Oceanic and Atmospheric Administration
Weather Service, National

Commercial. See Advertising (Television; Radio; Creating advertisements).

Secretaries of commerce

Name	Took office	Under President
George B. Cortelyou	1903	T. Roosevelt
Victor H. Metcalf	1904	T. Roosevelt
Oscar S. Straus	1906	T. Roosevelt
Charles Nagel	1909	Taft
William C. Redfield	1913	Wilson
Joshua W. Alexander	1919	Wilson
* Herbert C. Hoover	1921	Harding, Coolidge
William F. Whiting	1928	Coolidge
Robert P. Lamont	1929	Hoover
Roy D. Chapin	1932	Hoover
Daniel C. Roper	1933	F. D. Roosevelt
Harry L. Hopkins	1938	F. D. Roosevelt
Jesse H. Jones	1940	F. D. Roosevelt
* Henry A. Wallace	1945	F. D. Roosevelt, Truman
* W. Averell Harriman	1946	Truman
Charles Sawyer	1948	Truman
Sinclair Weeks	1953	Eisenhower
Lewis L. Strauss	1958	Eisenhower
Frederick H. Mueller	1959	Eisenhower
Luther H. Hodges	1961	Kennedy, L. B. Johnson
John T. Connor	1965	L. B. Johnson
Alexander B. Trowbridge	1967	L. B. Johnson
Cyrus R. Smith	1968	L. B. Johnson
Maurice H. Stans	1969	Nixon
Peter G. Peterson	1972	Nixon
Frederick B. Dent	1973	Nixon, Ford
Rogers C. B. Morton	1975	Ford
* Elliot L. Richardson	1976	Ford
* Juanita M. Kreps	1977	Carter
Philip M. Klutznick	1980	Carter
Malcolm Baldrige, Jr.	1981	Reagan
C. William Verity	1987	Reagan
Robert A. Mosbacher	1989	Bush
Barbara H. Franklin	1992	Bush
* Ronald H. Brown	1993	Clinton

*Has a separate biography in *World Book*.

Commercial art includes many types of art used for business purposes as well as illustration. It is often called *advertising art,* because much commercial art is used in the selling of products and services. Commercial art is different from *fine art,* such as painting and sculpture, because it must be reproduced by printing, by photographing, or by other methods.

Commercial artists work for advertising agencies, department stores, manufacturers, typographers, publishers, TV stations, and many other types of businesses. They create art for such things as advertisements, books, computer programs, filmstrips, logos, magazines, packages, and trademarks. The artwork in *World Book* is produced by commercial artists.

Commercial art studios range in size from only a few to more than 100 employees. More than half of all commercial artists work independently and are paid by assignment. They are called *free-lance artists.* More than 175,000 people work in phases of commercial art in the United States.

The early commercial artists were self-taught or had some training in fine art. These artists worked on design, drawing, lettering, and all steps in preparing a piece of artwork for reproduction.

In recent years, the field has expanded and developed greatly. Today, many commercial artists specialize in such specific parts of commercial art as design, calligraphy, illustration, photography, and photo retouching. Specialists within these areas include fashion illustrators, product illustrators, book illustrators, technical illustrators, cartoonists, computer graphic artists, film animators, and photographers.

Some commercial artists become art directors. Art directors plan and direct the work of other artists. They work for such businesses as advertising agencies, design studios, graphics studios, and television stations. Most commercial artists specialize in one such field.

Commercial art is a relatively new profession. Few people were employed in the field before 1900, and educational training for a professional career in commercial art was not available until about 1930. Today, there are many commercial art schools that offer four-year training programs, and many colleges and universities offer degrees in commercial art.   Charles P. Green

Related articles in *World Book* include:

Advertising	Graphic arts	Photography
Animation	Photoengraving	Poster
Cartoon	and photolithog-	Printing
Design	raphy	

Commercial paper is a term used broadly to describe business documents that are either orders or promises to pay money. There are two main kinds of commercial paper, the *draft* and the *promissory note.* A draft is a written order to a business or individual to pay a specified amount of money to another business or individual. The most common type of draft is a check. A promissory note is a written promise to pay a specified sum of money to a certain person on a future date.

When financial experts speak of *commercial paper,* they use the term in a narrow sense to mean short-term promissory notes issued by corporations. Many corporations borrow money by selling such notes to investors. On the date specified on the note, the corporation pays the investor the full amount of the note, plus interest. The interest rate on most commercial paper is less than the interest on a bank loan. However, only large corporations with good credit ratings can issue commercial paper. Most commercial paper *matures* (becomes due) in less than six months.

Many people believe commercial paper is a good investment, particularly during periods of inflation. The short maturity period enables investors to redeem their money quickly and reinvest it at higher interest rates. However, such notes are *unsecured*—that is, they do not give the lender legal claim to any property if the loan is not repaid.   William G. Dewald

See also **Check; Draft; Note.**

Commission, Military, is a written order and oath of service giving an officer rank in the armed services. In the United States, the President commissions officers with the approval of the Senate. An officer accepts the commission voluntarily, and it does not have to be renewed.

A commission may be resigned if existing law permits. The President may remove an officer from the commissioned list for cause. A board of officers handles dismissals. The term *in commission,* when referring to a ship or an aircraft, means that the vessel or airplane is available for active service. See also **Canada, Armed Forces of.**   Allan R. Millett

Commission form of government. See City government.

Commission on Civil Rights. See Civil Rights, Commission on.

Commission on Obscenity and Pornography. See Obscenity and pornography.

Commission on the Status of Women. See Women's movements (In Western societies).

Committee for State Security. See KGB.

Committee of Public Safety. See French Revolution (Terror and equality).

Committee of the whole is a committee composed of all the members present at a meeting of an organization. A group may form a committee of the whole when the members wish to consider a matter informally together, instead of having a committee of a few members discuss the matter and report back to the group. It is used chiefly by legislative bodies and large organizations.

The committee of the whole is a complicated, time-consuming device. The members of a group must first vote to *resolve* (change) themselves into such a committee. After the committee has been formed and has completed its discussion, the members must vote on the committee's proposal or report. They then vote to *rise from the committee,* or end the committee meeting, and report to the group. The chairman of the committee reads the report to the group. The group can then discuss and vote on the report.

Most organizations may consider a matter informally without forming a committee of the whole. This procedure is often a more practical means of dealing with group business.   Ned A. Shearer

Committees of correspondence were organized by towns, counties, and colonies before and during the Revolutionary War in America (1775-1783). The first committee of correspondence was appointed by the town of Boston in 1772 at the suggestion of Samuel Adams. The committee's purpose was to keep in touch with other Massachusetts towns in their struggle to uphold the rights of the colonists. The first colonial committee was appointed by Virginia in 1773. The committees played an important part in drawing the colonists together for their struggle with Great Britain. See also **Committees of safety.**   Richard D. Brown

Committees of safety sprang up in the colonies to carry on necessary functions of government during the Revolutionary War in America. The committees provided the transitional government after colonial governors had been overthrown and before the colonies could set up their first state governments. In Connecticut and New Hampshire, the committees of safety continued their work even after the state governments had begun operating.

On July 18, 1775, the Second Continental Congress urged the colonies to set up committees of safety. The new committees took over much of the work of the earlier committees of correspondence, which had carried on vigorous programs of propaganda against the British since 1772.   William Morgan Fowler, Jr.

See also **Committees of correspondence.**

Commodity Credit Corporation (CCC) is a corporation within the United States Department of Agriculture. It is wholly owned by the United States government. The CCC is managed by an eight-member board of directors appointed by the President. The board works under the general supervision of the secretary of agriculture. The CCC has capital stock of $100 million held by the United States, and is authorized to borrow up to $25 billion.

The main purposes of the CCC are to stabilize and protect farm income and prices, assist in maintaining balanced and adequate supplies of agricultural commodities and their products, and help in the orderly distribution of commodities. The CCC conducts price support, export, and storage programs. In carrying out these programs, it engages in buying, selling, lending, and other activities. The CCC also obtains agricultural commodities for sale to other government agencies, foreign governments, and relief agencies, and to meet domestic requirements.

In carrying out its operations, the CCC uses the facilities and personnel of various agencies of the Department of Agriculture. A commodities office in Kansas City, Mo., has specific responsibilities for the acquisition, handling, storage, and disposal of commodities and products held by the CCC. The Commodity Credit Corporation was created in 1933.

Critically reviewed by the Commodity Credit Corporation

Commodity exchange is an organized market for agricultural goods, especially grains. Commodity exchanges, also called *boards of trade* or *commodity markets,* provide a market for *commodities* (goods) in much the same way that stock exchanges do for stocks and bonds.

The chief commodities that are bought and sold on exchanges include barley, corn, cotton, oats, soybeans, soybean meal and oil, and wheat. Other goods that are traded on exchanges include beef cattle and hides, butter, coffee, eggs, pork products, sugar, and such metals as copper, gold, lead, and tin. The Chicago Board of Trade is the largest commodity exchange in the world.

Commodity exchanges are voluntary trade associations. They are called *organized markets* because all members must follow certain trading rules. All business, for example, must be conducted on the trading floor within certain hours. Rules set the *commission* (fee) that may be charged in a transaction, and the time within which payment must be made. Federal laws regulating commodity trading are administered by the Commodity Futures Trading Commission, an independent agency of the United States government.

Cash market. Most commodity markets deal only in *cash trading.* Cash trades involve buying and selling real commodities. The sale contract may call for immediate delivery or for delivery at a specified future date. The contract is fulfilled by actual delivery of the product. Buyers of commodities represent milling and processing companies, exporters, or owners of terminal storage facilities. Sellers represent farmers or owners of rural grain elevators. Government-certified samples of grain available for immediate delivery are kept on the trading floor for inspection by interested buyers.

Futures market. The largest commodity exchanges also have *futures,* or *contract,* markets. In these markets, traders buy and sell contracts to receive or deliver a certain quantity and grade of commodity at a specified future time. The contract's price is determined by a public auction held in a *pit* (circle) on the exchange floor.

Unlike cash trading, futures trading seldom results in the actual exchange of a commodity. At any time before the delivery month, a trader can cancel out a contract by buying or selling an offsetting contract of equal amount for the same delivery month. For example, suppose a trader buys a futures contract for 5,000 bushels of wheat at $3.75 a bushel, to be delivered in September. But in July, September wheat futures are selling for $3.80 a bushel. The trader decides to sell 5,000 bushels of wheat futures for September delivery. The two contracts offset one another, and the trader makes a profit of 5¢ a bushel, or $250.

Trading in futures contracts generally falls into two broad categories. These categories are *speculative trading* and *hedging.*

Speculative trading is buying or selling futures contracts in hopes of making a profit from future price changes. Such traders, called *speculators,* try to forecast prices months in advance, and they buy or sell on the basis of these estimates. A speculator who buys futures contracts in anticipation of rising prices is called a *long.* After prices go up, the speculator sells the contracts at a profit. Speculators are called *shorts* when they sell futures contracts for a commodity they do not actually have. They believe prices will go down. They will then buy the contract back at a lower price, making a profit on the two transactions. Traders who sell short are also called *bears,* and those who buy in anticipation of rising prices are called *bulls* (see **Bears and bulls**).

Hedging occurs when owners of a commodity buy or sell futures contracts to reduce risks caused by price changes. By hedging, the commodity owners shift that risk to speculators.

To understand how hedging reduces business risks, suppose that a miller buys 5,000 bushels of wheat at $3.75 a bushel on the cash market. He decides that he will receive a fair return for his work if he can sell flour made from the wheat at the equivalent of $3.80 a bushel. The selling price of flour is based partly on the cost of wheat at that time. But it takes the miller about a month to process the flour. The price of wheat might drop during that time, and he would not be able to sell his flour at $3.80. The miller wants to protect himself. He does so by selling 5,000 bushels of wheat futures at $3.75 a bushel at the same time he makes his cash purchase.

The miller might have to sell his flour at the equivalent of $3.65 a bushel. He would then lose 15¢ a bushel. But the futures price usually moves in step with the cash price. Therefore, the price for September wheat futures would also drop about 15¢ a bushel. The miller could then buy back his wheat futures at $3.60 a bushel. Thus, he would still receive the equivalent of 5¢ a bushel for his work. What he lost in selling the flour, he gained in buying back the wheat futures at a lower price. His profit was the same as if there had been no change in the price of wheat.   Robert Sobel

Commodity organization. See **Farm and farming** (Farm organizations).

Common carrier is a person or company that transports passengers and goods by water, land, or air for a fee. Common carriers include truck lines, express companies, bus lines, street railways, railroads, steamboat companies, air transport, and pipelines. Telephone and telegraph companies are also considered to be common carriers, though they do not transport goods. Stores that provide a delivery service solely for customers are not common carriers.

The common law has placed the carrier under two great obligations. First, its service is compulsory, for it must serve anyone who can pay. Second, the common carrier is liable for loss or injury to goods or passengers carried. These obligations are regulated by law. In the United States, trade between states is under federal control. States control common carrier operations within their borders.

It is generally stated that common carriers are responsible for any loss or accident except those due to an "act of God or of the public enemy." In this sense, an "act of God" means any unavoidable accident that occurs through no fault of a human being. A train being struck by lightning is an example of an "act of God." The term *public enemy* includes any government that is at war with the government of the common carrier. Robbers, bandits, and rebels are not regarded as public enemies in this sense.   John R. Lorenz

See also **Federal Communications Commission; Interstate Commerce Commission.**

Common Cause is a citizens' organization that works for political and social reform in the United States. The group calls for reform of congressional procedures. It backed the successful effort to give 18-year-olds the right to vote in national elections and helped bring about the 1974 law that provides for federal financing of presidential campaigns. The law also sets limits on private contributions to presidential and congressional candidates, as well as on spending by presidential candidates who accept federal funds. The organization supports legislation that would limit spending by congressional candidates and favors limiting the influence of political action committees (PAC's) and interest groups. Common Cause supports no political party.

The organization maintains that none of the nation's major problems can be solved unless the government becomes more responsive to the needs and desires of the general public. Therefore, Common Cause works to make Congress more representative and more responsible, especially in the operation of its committee system.

Common Cause was founded in 1970 by John W. Gardner, who was secretary of health, education, and welfare from 1965 to 1968. The headquarters of Common Cause are located at 2030 M Street NW, Washington, DC 20036.   Murray Clark Havens

Common law is a body of rulings made by judges on the basis of community customs and previous court decisions. It forms an essential part of the legal system of many English-speaking countries, including the United States and Canada. Common law covers such matters as contracts, ownership of property, and the payment of claims for personal injury.

Early in England's history, judges decided cases according to the way they interpreted the beliefs and unwritten laws of the community. If another judge had ruled in an earlier, similar case, that judge's decision was often used as a *precedent* (guide). After many judges decided the same question in a similar way, the ruling became law.

Common law is often contrasted with *civil law,* a body of rules passed by a legislature. Under civil law, a judge decides a case by following written rules, rather than previous court decisions.

Common law differs from *equity,* a set of standards developed to allow greater flexibility in court decisions. During the late Middle Ages, England created courts of equity to decide cases that courts of common law might treat too strictly. These courts decided cases by broad principles of justice and fairness, rather than by the rigid standards of common law. The monarch's chancellor presided over a court of equity called the *court of chancery.*

The legal system of the United States has developed from English common law and equity. Only one U.S. state, Louisiana, modeled its legal system on civil law. Louisiana used the civil law of France, called the *Code Napoléon.* During the late 1800's, many states combined their courts of common law and courts of equity. One group of judges administers the combined courts. In Canada, similarly, only the province of Quebec based its legal system on French law.   David M. O'Brien

See also **Civil law; Equity; Law** (Common-law systems; The Middle Ages; Beginnings of U.S. law); **Lien.**

Common market is an economic union of nations. Members of a common market work to eliminate tariffs and other trade barriers among themselves and to follow a uniform trade policy with nonmember countries. The members also work to achieve free movement of workers and financial capital from one member nation to another. Nations form common markets to stimulate industrial growth and efficiency, to increase employment, and to make more and cheaper goods and services available to consumers. The European Community is an example of a common market. For more information on how a common market operates, see **European Community.**

Some groups of countries have partially or completely removed trade barriers among themselves. However, they are not true common markets because each member maintains its own trade policies with nonmember countries, and workers and capital do not move freely among the members. The most important of these groups—or the agreements that have established them—include:

Association of Southeast Asian Nations (ASEAN). Founded: 1967. Members: Brunei, Indonesia, Malaysia, Philippines, Singapore, and Thailand. See **Association of Southeast Asian Nations.**

Australia-New Zealand Closer Economic Relations Trade Agreement. Went into effect: 1983. Parties: Australia and New Zealand.

European Free Trade Association (EFTA). Founded: 1960. Members: Austria, Finland, Iceland, Liechtenstein, Norway, Sweden, and Switzerland. See **European Free Trade Association.**

United States-Canada Free Trade Agreement. Went into effect: 1989. Parties: United States and Canada.

Robert M. Stern

Common Sense. See Paine, Thomas.

Common stock. See Stock, Capital (Kinds).

Commoner, Barry (1917-   ), is an American biologist and educator. Since the early 1950's, he has warned the public of the dangerous effects of modern technology on the environment.

Commoner has expressed concern over the widespread use of developments in modern technology without concern for their effect on the balance of nature. These technological developments include the use of chemical fertilizers, detergents, nuclear power, pesticides, and incinerators.

Commoner has worked to make biology a useful tool in the solution of various human problems. He has urged other scientists to make their special knowledge available to the public with that same goal.

Commoner was born in New York City and graduated from Columbia University in 1937. He received a Ph.D. from Harvard University in 1941. Commoner served on the faculty of Washington University in St. Louis, Mo., from 1947 to 1981.

In 1980, Commoner was the presidential candidate of the Citizens' Party, a liberal political party that he helped found. He and his party called for public control of the energy industry, an end to nuclear power development, and a switch to solar energy. Commoner's books include *Science and Survival* (1966), *The Closing Circle* (1971), and *The Politics of Energy* (1979). He joined the faculty of Queens College of the City University of New York in 1981. Sheldon M. Novick

Commons, House of. See House of Commons.

Commonwealth is a term sometimes used for a state, a country, or a group of states and countries. The term has no precise definition in international law. Any group of nations may sign a treaty pledging political or economic support to one another and call themselves a commonwealth. The term originally meant a group of people banded together for the common good or public welfare. The United States may be called a commonwealth. The U.S. states Pennsylvania, Massachusetts, Virginia, and Kentucky call themselves commonwealths. Puerto Rico and the Northern Mariana Islands are other U.S. commonwealths. Australia's official name is The Commonwealth of Australia. The Commonwealth of Nations includes such countries as the United Kingdom, Canada, and Australia. See **Commonwealth of Independent States; Commonwealth of Nations.**

Anthony D'Amato

Commonwealth Games are an amateur sports competition for members of the Commonwealth of Nations. Like the Olympic Games, these games are held every four years in a different country. The athletes compete in such events as boxing, cycling, swimming and diving, track and field, weightlifting, and wrestling.

In 1891, the Rev. Astley Cooper, an English sports fan, proposed a periodic "festival" to improve ties among the nations and colonies of the British Empire. The first games, called the British Empire Games, took place in 1930 in Hamilton, Canada. The name was changed to Commonwealth Games in 1974. Dave Nightingale

Commonwealth of Independent States is a loose association of independent nations that were formerly republics of the Soviet Union. These member nations are Armenia, Belarus, Kazakhstan, Kyrgyzstan, Moldova, Russia, Tajikistan, Turkmenistan, Ukraine, and Uzbekistan. The headquarters is in Minsk, in Belarus.

The Soviet Union was made up of 15 republics. In the early 1990's, two of the republics, Georgia and Lithuania, declared their independence. In August 1991, the Soviet Union began to break apart after an attempted coup. All the other republics except Russia declared their independence during the coup or soon after. Russia proclaimed itself the successor to the Soviet Union. Eleven republics formed the Commonwealth of Independent States (C.I.S.) in December 1991, shortly before the Soviet Union ceased to exist. In October 1992, Azerbaijan, one of the 11, announced that it was no longer a member. Moldova, another original member, left the C.I.S. in August 1993, when its Parliament failed to ratify the membership treaty. The four former republics that did not join the C.I.S. were Georgia, Estonia, Latvia, and Lithuania.

Members of the Commonwealth of Independent States

Name	Area		Population	Capital	Official language
	In sq. mi.	In km²			
Armenia	11,506	29,800	3,373,000	Yerevan	Armenian
Belarus	80,155	207,600	10,480,000	Minsk	Belarusian
Kazakhstan	1,049,156	2,717,300	16,992,000	Alma-Ata	Kazakh
Kyrgyzstan	76,641	198,500	4,409,000	Bishkek	Kyrgyz
Russia	6,592,850	17,075,400	151,436,000	Moscow	Russian
Tajikistan	55,251	143,100	5,252,000	Dushanbe	Tajik
Turkmenistan	188,456	488,100	3,631,000	Ashkhabad	Turkmen
Ukraine	233,090	603,700	53,125,000	Kiev	Ukrainian
Uzbekistan	172,742	447,400	20,453,000	Tashkent	Uzbek

The C.I.S. was created for several reasons. Many of the members wanted to keep some of the economic ties they had with one another as Soviet republics. Each of the members also wanted to guarantee its own territory and sovereignty. The C.I.S. members also sought to reassure the rest of the world that the nuclear weapons of the former Soviet Union were under reliable control (see **Arms control** [History of arms control]). Basically, the C.I.S. was intended to help the new countries continue to work together and thus make the breakup of the Soviet Union as peaceful as possible.

Despite the goals of the C.I.S., members soon began to dispute various matters. The C.I.S. originally aimed to have a single military for all its members. But most of the member countries have announced their intention of creating their own armed forces. Russia and Ukraine have disputed the ownership of the Crimea, a strategically important peninsula in the Black Sea. Many of the C.I.S. countries rejected the idea of a common economic market in which the ruble—the former Soviet monetary unit—would continue to be used. Some of them have already created their own currencies.

Experts believe many of the commonwealth's problems result from a lack of clear purpose or structure. Russia, for example, seemed to see the C.I.S. as permanent. But other members expressed fears that Russia—with its great size and power—might dominate the C.I.S. Some of the members, such as Ukraine, viewed the C.I.S. as just a temporary association to help the former republics become truly independent countries. The C.I.S. does not have a charter that sets forth its duties and powers. It also lacks a governing body to enforce decisions or settle conflicts.   Nancy Lubin

Commonwealth of Nations is an association of independent countries and other political units that have lived under British law and government. It includes the United Kingdom (Britain), about 50 independent nations that were once British colonies, and about 25 other political units, such as territories and dependencies.

Britain is involved in some way in the government of most of the units in the Commonwealth. In the rest, Australia or New Zealand has some involvement in the government. For a list of Commonwealth members and their status, see the table with this article. Members cover about a fourth of the earth's land surface and have about a fourth of the world's population.

The Commonwealth countries have a tradition of mutual cooperation that stems from their common history. The Commonwealth heads of government assemble from time to time to exchange views on important international issues. At these meetings, the leaders seek to identify common goals in economic and foreign affairs. They work to coordinate their national policies to pursue these goals. But the nations are not required to obey conclusions reached at the conferences.

The Commonwealth of Nations conducts various programs through Commonwealth agencies. For example, several jointly financed programs provide economic aid and technical assistance to developing nations in the group. The Commonwealth also supports agencies that promote cooperation in such activities as broadcasting, cable and satellite communication, education, health care, and scientific research. The Commonwealth Secretariat leads and coordinates Commonwealth activities.

The secretariat has its headquarters in London.

Independent members of the Commonwealth of Nations consist of former British colonial areas, dependencies, or dominions that have become self-governing but have retained their Commonwealth ties. Despite the Commonwealth's tradition of cooperation, each nation maintains its own foreign policy, which reflects its own interests. All of the independent members recognize the British monarch as head of the Commonwealth. But the monarch is mainly a symbol and has no real power to govern. Britain and about 15 other Commonwealth nations are monarchies that regard the British ruler as head of state. A few others have their own monarchs. Over half the Commonwealth nations are republics.

Dependencies are Commonwealth areas that do not have complete self-government. They are administered by independent Commonwealth members. Most dependencies are developing toward self-government.

A majority of the dependencies are areas that have been annexed to the British Crown. This means that persons living in them are British citizens. These dependencies were formerly called *colonies* or *crown colonies*. A governor appointed by the British government is the highest official in each such dependency. The governor holds all political power in some dependencies. Others have elected assemblies, and in them the governor's power is limited. Some of the dependencies have become practically self-governing. Most of these areas are ruled as though they were parts of Britain.

The term *dependency* may also refer to other kinds of political units. These include *crown dependencies, joint administrations, self-governing areas,* and *territories.*

Crown dependencies are self-governing territories annexed by the British Crown. They are not bound by acts of the British Parliament unless the crown dependencies are named.

Joint administrations are controlled by two nations that have interests there. Each of the nations is responsible for its own property and personnel in the area.

Self-governing areas control their own internal affairs. They have agreed to let a Commonwealth nation handle their defense and foreign relations. But these areas can declare full independence at any time.

Territories are dependencies of Australia or New Zealand. Each territory has an administrator chosen by the government of Australia or New Zealand. In some territories, this official holds all political power. In other territories, the administrator shares power with an elected assembly. Some territories have become nearly self-governing. Australia and New Zealand control defense and foreign policy for their territories.

History. The Commonwealth of Nations began to take form in the early 1900's. At that time, representatives of certain British colonies met with British representatives at Imperial Conferences. All these colonies had self-government in domestic affairs. But Britain managed their foreign policy and defense.

During the 1910's and 1920's, the self-governing colonies moved toward independence in foreign affairs. Representatives at a 1926 Imperial Conference declared all participating countries to be completely self-governing nations. They described these nations as equal in rank, "united by a common allegiance to the Crown and freely associated as members of the British Commonwealth of Nations." The Statute of Westminster, a British law of 1931, legalized the 1926 declaration. The original Commonwealth members were Australia, Britain, Canada, Ireland, New Zealand, Newfoundland, and South Africa.

In 1932, the Commonwealth nations established a system of trade called *Commonwealth Preference*. Under this system, Britain imported goods from other Commonwealth countries without imposing the usual tariffs. Other Commonwealth nations negotiated favorable trade agreements with each other.

Between 1947 and 1980, about 40 more British colonies became independent nations. Nearly all of these nations joined the Commonwealth. During the same period, Newfoundland became a province of Canada, and Ireland and South Africa gave up Commonwealth membership because of disagreements with other countries in the group. By the mid-1960's, nearly half the Commonwealth members were black African nations.

In 1977, Britain completed a plan to discontinue its special trade agreements with Commonwealth nations. It began this plan in 1973, when it joined the European Community, an organization of European nations that cooperate in economic and other matters. Individual Commonwealth members now participate in the European Community and its trade agreements. See **European Community**.   Anthony Sutcliffe

Related articles. All of the countries and most of the other political units in the accompanying table have separate articles in *World Book*. Other related articles include:

British America	Flag (pictures)
Colony	Governor general
Commonwealth Games	Territory

The Commonwealth of Nations

Independent members

Antigua and Barbuda	Nauru
Australia	New Zealand
Bahamas	Nigeria
Bangladesh	Pakistan
Barbados	Papua New Guinea
Belize	St. Christopher and Nevis
Botswana	St. Lucia
Brunei	St. Vincent and
Canada	the Grenadines
Cyprus	Seychelles
Dominica	Sierra Leone
Gambia	Singapore
Ghana	Solomon Islands
Grenada	Sri Lanka
Guyana	Swaziland
India	Tanzania
Jamaica	Tonga
Kenya	Trinidad and Tobago
Kiribati	Tuvalu
Lesotho	Uganda
Malawi	United Kingdom (Britain)
Malaysia	Vanuatu
Maldives	Western Samoa
Malta	Zambia
Mauritius	Zimbabwe
Namibia	

Dependencies of United Kingdom

Anguilla	Cayman Islands	Pitcairn Is. Group
Bermuda	Channel Islands	South Georgia
British Antarctic	Falkland Islands	and the South
Territory	Gibraltar	Sandwich Islands
British Indian Ocean	Hong Kong	St. Helena
Territory	Man, Isle of	Turks and Caicos
British Virgin Is.	Montserrat	Islands

Territories of Australia

Antarctica (Aust.)	Christmas Island	Heard and
Ashmore and	Cocos (Keeling) Is.	McDonald Islands
Cartier Islands	Coral Sea Island	Norfolk Island

Areas associated with New Zealand

Cook Island	Ross Dependency
Niue Island	Tokelau

Communal society, *KAHM yuh nuhl* or *kuh MYOO nuhl*, is a community formed by people who believe that they can make a better life together than any of them could make alone. Members of communal societies value *collective* (group) needs above personal needs. Most of these societies are based on a shared interest, such as religion or politics. For example, members of a religious group called *Hutterites* have established communal societies that follow the laws of the Bible (see **Hutterites**). Some communal societies, such as the *kibbutzim* in Israel, are cooperative farming settlements (see **Kibbutz**). A communal society created as an example of a better world is called a *utopia*.

Communal societies differ from traditional society mainly in the ways they favor collective needs. For example, no one owns private land in most communal societies. Some communal societies also may forbid marriage or single-family households. In addition, in nearly all successful communal societies, members do all their work for the community and restrict their contact with the rest of society.

In the 1800's, such European thinkers as the Comte de Saint-Simon, Robert Owen, Étienne Cabet, and Pierre Joseph Proudhon reacted against the uneven distribution of wealth in society. These people sought a cure for the evils in society through a communal society that would allow some private ownership, but not inherited wealth. These ideals inspired such well-known United States communal societies as Oneida, N.Y., and New Harmony, Ind. (see **Oneida Community** and **New Harmony**). Communal societies also appeared in many other countries, including France, Great Britain, Japan, and Tanzania.

A strong interest in communal living also developed in the United States in the 1960's and the 1970's. During this period, young people formed thousands of cooperative groups called *communes* in all parts of the country. Most of these communes had been disbanded by the early 1980's. Present-day communal societies include Twin Oaks, near Louisa, Va., and more than 100 Hutterite Bruderhofs (colonies) in South Dakota, Montana, and the Prairie Provinces of Canada.   Jennie Keith

See also **Amanites; Brook Farm; Shakers**.

Commune, *KAHM yoon,* is the smallest district of local government in France and some other countries. It resembles the *township* in the United States. The French commune has a mayor (*maire*) who governs the town with the help of deputies and a council. A commune may be a small village or a large city. Usually 12 communes make up a *canton,* the next largest political division.   William M. Reddy

See also **Austria** (Government); **Communal society**.

Communicable disease. See Disease (Infectious diseases; table).

WORLD BOOK photo

Newspapers and magazines

WORLD BOOK photo

Citizens band (CB) radio

NBC (WORLD BOOK photo)

Television news broadcast

WORLD BOOK photo

Letters

Illinois Bell (WORLD BOOK photo)

Operator-assisted telephone calls

WORLD BOOK photo

Classroom discussion

The many kinds of communication enable people to share information and provide entertainment in a variety of ways. The pictures on this page show some examples of how people communicate with other individuals, with small groups, and with a large audience.

Communication

Communication is sharing information or providing entertainment by speaking, writing, or other methods. Probably the most important type of communication is personal communication, which happens when people make their thoughts and wishes known to one another. People communicate in many ways, including by talking, by moving their hands, and even by making faces. People also use telephone calls and letters for personal communication. Without personal communication, parents would not know what their children need. Teachers could not help their students learn. Friends could not make plans with one another. People could not share knowledge. Each person would have to learn everything for himself or herself. In fact, human beings probably could not survive for long.

Another important type of communication happens when messages are sent to a large audience. That type of communication is called *mass communication*. Books are one of the oldest methods of mass communication. Television is one of the newest. Newspapers and radio are other ways that information can be sent to many people. Just as human beings probably could not survive without personal communication, modern nations

probably could not exist without mass communication. News of election results, earthquakes, or other important events can spread to huge numbers of people in minutes through mass communication.

This article deals with human communication. For information on animal communication, see specific articles such as **Ant** (Communication).

The importance of communication

Communication is all around us. Most large cities have at least one daily newspaper. We often see the letter carriers that deliver mail. The air around us contains invisible television signals that can be picked up and changed into sounds and pictures by a TV set. We use communication in many ways at home, in school, in business and industry, and in world affairs.

At home, we use many types of personal and mass communication. A clock radio may wake us up in the morning, tell us the time and what weather to expect, and report the day's news. A telephone allows us to talk privately to persons nearby or far away. A note from

George N. Gordon, the contributor of this article, is Professor of Communications and Chairman of the Department of Communications at Fordham University. He is the author of Communications and Media *and other books about communication.*

someone in the family may say that a friend has called or remind us of an appointment.

A newspaper provides many kinds of communication. Some articles, such as news stories and recipes, furnish information. Other features, such as comic strips and humorous articles, are mostly for fun.

Millions of people watch television for amusement during their free time. But TV provides more than just entertainment. Most people get about two-thirds of their news from TV news broadcasts. TV commercials also provide information on products and services.

In school, teachers use a variety of communication methods to help their students learn. Often, they lecture to an entire class or guide a group discussion. At other times, teachers help students individually.

Textbooks are probably the type of mass communication used most often in school. About one-fourth of the books sold in the United States are schoolbooks.

Teachers also use many other communication devices, including filmstrips, posters, tape recordings, and motion pictures. Educational films give students many experiences they could never have in real life. Actors and actresses re-create important events in history, such as the French Revolution or Christopher Columbus' landing in America. Motion pictures take students to distant worlds, such as the ocean bottom or the South Pole. Animated cartoons show processes that students could not otherwise see, such as the working of an automobile engine or how the human body fights germs.

Many classrooms have TV sets that receive specially prepared lessons by way of *closed-circuit television.* Such television is sent by wires to a limited number of viewers and not broadcast over the air. Teachers also have their students watch regular TV broadcasts of important events, such as the launching of a spacecraft or the swearing-in of a new President.

In business and industry. Nearly every large business has workers throughout the country, such as employees at branch offices and salespeople calling on customers. For this reason, businesses need fast, dependable communication. Much business communication takes place by telephone or by a device called a *teletypewriter,* which sends and receives written messages over wires. Using such communication, a chain of stores can change the price of an item in all its stores in a few minutes. Before the days of speedy communication, it would have taken weeks to inform every store.

Many businesses have a communication network consisting of two or more computers linked by private telephone lines. The computers exchange vast quantities of data at high speed. The machines then translate the information into written form by means of automatic typewriters, high-speed printers, or visual display screens called *cathode-ray tubes* (CRT's).

Most large corporations also print their own magazines or newspapers for their employees. These publications are called *house organs.* They provide information about the company's plans, new products, and other matters. A large business may also communicate with its employees by closed-circuit television and may produce its own training films and videotape recordings.

In world affairs. In the days before modern fast communication, news traveled slowly between nations. The long time needed to receive messages sometimes caused problems. For example, the War of 1812 might never have happened if there had been telegraphs or telephones then. The war began partly because Great Britain interfered with U.S. shipping. The United States declared war on Britain on June 18, 1812. Two days before the declaration, Britain had announced it would stop interfering with U.S. shipping. But the news had to cross the Atlantic Ocean by ship and did not reach the United States until the fighting had begun. Faster communication also would have prevented the chief battle of the war. Soldiers fought the battle at New Orleans in January 1815, 15 days after a peace treaty had been signed in Europe. About 315 people were killed and about 1,290 were wounded in that battle.

Even speedy communication can bring bad results if messages are not carefully expressed. In 1945, near the end of World War II, the United States and its allies sent radio messages to Japan warning that the Japanese faced "prompt and utter destruction" if they did not surrender. Japanese officials intended to answer that they would withhold comment until they had more time to think about the message. Instead, they replied with a word that meant they would ignore the warning. If a different reply had been chosen, the United States might not have dropped atomic bombs on the Japanese cities of Hiroshima and Nagasaki. About 132,000 men, women, and children were dead or missing after the blasts, which some people believe happened partly because of this failure of communication.

People often say that communication has made the world grow smaller. The world seemed huge when messages from Europe reached North America only after an ocean voyage of many weeks. Now, radio can transmit a human voice around the world in seconds. Almost as quickly, a person can telephone another person in nearly any country. Communications satellites have made worldwide TV broadcasting possible. Viewers at home can watch events on another continent, such as a Nobel Prize ceremony or the signing of a treaty.

The development of communication

Prehistoric times. Early people probably communicated with one another by sounds and gestures long before they developed actual words. No one knows how human speech began, but experts who study language and prehistoric ways of life have made a number of guesses. Many of these scholars think language began as an imitation of sounds in nature, such as the barking of certain animals and the howling of wind.

After language developed, people exchanged news chiefly by word of mouth. Runners carried spoken messages over long distances. People also used drumbeats, fires, and smoke signals to communicate with other people who understood the codes they used.

Paintings and drawings were the first steps toward a written language. Prehistoric artists began to use a series of pictures to tell a story, such as the history of a good hunting trip or a violent storm. Gradually, people developed a system of small pictures that stood for most common objects and ideas. Such a system is known as *pictographic writing.* Middle Eastern people called Sumerians developed the first pictographic writing about 3500 B.C.

Pictographic writing worked well for familiar things,

but people had difficulty writing new or unusual words. Gradually, they learned to make each symbol represent a sound instead of an object or idea. As a result, they could write any word in the spoken language.

Writing ranked second only to speech among the most important early inventions in communication. It enabled people to exchange messages over long distances without depending on a messenger's memory. Information also could be kept for later use. With the invention of writing, prehistoric times ended and the period of written history began.

During ancient times, the chief means of long-distance communication was writing. Businesses and wealthy individuals hired professional messengers, who carried letters on foot, on horseback, or by ship. Military leaders also used homing pigeons to carry messages.

About 500 B.C., the ancient Greeks developed a fast method of sending messages from city to city. The system was based on a series of brick walls. The walls were close enough together so that each could be seen from the one next to it. Indentations along the top of each wall represented the letters of the alphabet. To send a message, a person lit fires in the appropriate places on the wall. A watcher on the next wall saw the fires and relayed the message. This system of communication is called *visual telegraph.*

The ancient Romans got news from a handwritten sheet called *Acta Diurna* (*Daily Events*). A few copies of the paper were made each day and posted in public.

During the Middle Ages, which began about A.D. 400 and lasted about a thousand years, Christianity had an important influence on communication. Few people could read and write, and most of those who could were church leaders. As a result, most books and other written communication involved religious themes.

Artists called *scribes,* most of whom were monks, copied books by hand, letter by letter. No two books were exactly alike. The scribes decorated their work with pictures and designs in gold, silver, and colors.

Because scribes often toiled for months to produce a single volume, the number of books they produced was small. But the output was sufficient for the small number of people who could read. Many scribes themselves could not even read the books they copied.

Most news during the Middle Ages spread by word of mouth. Town criers walked the streets announcing births, deaths, and other events of public interest. Entertainers, peddlers, and other people who traveled from place to place also carried messages and news.

The start of printing in the Western world came during the Renaissance, a period of great intellectual activity that spread throughout Europe from the 1300's to the 1600's. The intellectual awakening of the Renaissance created a demand for books that hand copying could not satisfy. The problem was solved by the invention of printing, which had been known for centuries in Asia but was not learned by Europeans until the 1400's.

The first European printers did not make books. In-

Highlights in the history of communication

Prehistoric people used paintings and drawings to tell stories.

The Semites invented the use of the alphabet for writing.

| About 20,000 B.C. | About 3500 B.C. | About 1500 B.C. | 59 B.C. |

The Sumerians developed the first known system of writing.

The Romans began a handwritten newssheet that was a forerunner of today's newspapers.

WORLD BOOK illustration
by Richard Hook

Smoke signals were one of the earliest forms of long-distance communication. Such signals could send only limited information—a warning, for example.

Cuneiform writing consists of wedge-shaped characters stamped on clay. The clay cylinder above was inscribed during the 500's B.C. in Babylon.

Deutsches Museum, Munich,
Germany

Deutsches Museum, Munich,
Germany

Wax tablets were once a common writing surface. The early Greeks wrote on such tablets with a pointed tool called a *stylus* and laced the tablets together.

stead, they made playing cards, which were in great demand. An artist carved a raised image of a card on a block of wood. Then a printer inked the raised image and pressed a blank card against it. The picture was transferred to the card. Printers soon used this method, called *block printing,* to make books as well as cards. But it took a long time to carve every word on blocks.

The invention of movable type made printing much faster because the same carved letters could be used over and over again. After printing a page, the printer could separate the pieces of type and rearrange them.

Printing with movable type had existed in Asia since the 1000's, but the invention did not spread to Europe at that time. Most historians consider Johannes Gutenberg, a German metalsmith, to be the inventor of movable type in Europe. In the mid-1400's, Gutenberg brought together several inventions to create a whole new system of printing. He made separate pieces of metal type, both capitals and small letters, for each letter of the alphabet. He lined up the pieces of type in a frame to form pages. Gutenberg created his own ink from paint, dye, and other substances. Finally, he rebuilt a wine press to make the first printing press in Europe. Gutenberg had found it hard to produce evenly printed copies by hand, but the new printing press made it possible to put uniform pressure on the paper.

Printing quickly became the most important means of mass communication, and the art of hand copying died out. However, many people feared that the new art of printing was black magic that came from the Devil. They did not understand how books could be produced so quickly, or how all copies could look exactly alike. To soothe people's fears, early printers concentrated on producing Bibles and religious books rather than scientific works or other writings.

The large numbers of printed Bibles made it possible for many people to read the Scriptures for themselves. As a result, some people began to question certain practices of the Roman Catholic Church. In this way, printing helped give birth to the Protestant Reformation of the 1500's. This movement began as an effort to reform the Catholic Church and ended with the establishment of Protestant churches.

The 1600's and 1700's. By the 1600's, the art of printing was also used in business. Printed newssheets called *corantos,* which were somewhat like newspapers, appeared in the Netherlands, England, and other trading nations. The corantos reported mostly business news, such as which ships had landed and what goods they carried. The newssheets also printed advertising. The corantos soon added nonbusiness news and became the first true newspapers.

The spread of printing continued in the 1700's. Books, magazines, and newspapers made information available to more and more readers. People also exchanged news by letter, and many nations established postal systems. Before the 1700's, most letters were delivered by ship captains or other travelers.

The Chinese invented paper.		The German metalsmith Johannes Gutenberg reinvented movable type.		Printed newssheets called *corantos* appeared.
By A.D. 1	About 1045	Mid-1400's	Mid-1500's	1600's
	Pi Sheng, a Chinese printer, invented movable type.		The English made the first pencils of *graphite,* the substance used today.	

Detail of an Italian manuscript (about 1331) by Giovanni de' Nuxiglia; Bibliothèque Nationale, Paris (SCALA/EPA)

During the Middle Ages, artists copied books by hand, letter by letter. They covered their work with gold, silver, and colored decorations called *illumination.*

Bettmann Archive

Printing from movable type was invented in Asia during the 1000's and in Europe during the 1400's. A shop of the 1600's is shown above. At the left, typesetters assemble type to form pages. In the background, an assistant inks a page. At the right, a printer turns a huge screw on the printing press to push paper against the type.

Most communication, however, was no faster in the 1700's than it had been in ancient times. News traveled only as fast as people did, on foot, on horseback, or by ship. Then, in the late 1700's, a French engineer named Claude Chappe developed a means of rapid long-distance communication. Chappe devised a visual telegraph similar to that of the ancient Greeks. It consisted of a series of towers between Paris and other European cities. An operator in each tower moved a crossbar and two large, jointed arms on the roof to spell out messages. An observer on the next tower read the messages by telescope and passed them on.

In the early 1800's, many new inventions revolutionized communication. An important advance in printing came in 1811, when a German printer named Friedrich Koenig used a steam engine to power a press. Printers still had to set type by hand, but the actual printing went hundreds of times faster. *The Times* of London first used Koenig's press in 1814. The invention allowed *The Times* and other newspapers to print large numbers of copies cheaply, making mass circulation of newspapers possible. By the 1840's, major newspapers in the United States had circulations of 30,000 or more and sold for 1 or 2 cents a copy.

The invention of steamships and locomotives increased the speed at which people and news could travel. But rapid communication did not begin until the invention of the electric telegraph, which sent messages over wires in seconds. Inventors in Denmark, Germany,

Great Britain, and other countries built various telegraphs during the early 1800's. But the devices all had two weaknesses. They lacked a constant source of electricity, and they were difficult to use.

During the 1830's, the American painter and inventor Samuel F. B. Morse began work on an electric telegraph. After years of experimenting, Morse and his partner, Alfred Vail, developed a simple telegraph that had a stable current produced by batteries and electromagnets. The device sent messages in a code of dots and dashes known as *Morse code.* Morse patented his invention in 1840. For the first time, news traveled with the speed of electricity. Newspapers began to use the Morse telegraph almost at once. By the 1860's, telegraph lines linked most cities. The telegraph became the chief means of long-distance communication.

The telegraph could send messages only where wires were strung. In 1858, an underwater telegraph cable was laid across the Atlantic Ocean. But the cable failed after a few weeks. The first successful transatlantic cable was laid in 1866, largely due to the efforts of Cyrus W. Field, an American millionaire, and Lord Kelvin, a British physicist. This cable made it possible to send a message between Europe and North America in minutes.

Communication was further aided by the invention of photography. Many American, British, and French scientists contributed to its development, and no one person can be called the inventor of photography. In 1826, a French physicist named Joseph Nicéphore Niépce made

---

The French engineer Claude Chappe developed a visual telegraph.

Joseph Nicéphore Niépce, a French physicist, made the first permanent photograph.

| Late 1700's | 1811 | 1826 | 1830's |

Friedrich Koenig, a German printer, invented a steam-powered printing press.

The French painter Louis J. M. Daguerre developed an improved photograph.

American Antiquarian Society, Worcester, Mass.

Postal service was established in many nations during the 1700's. This postrider carried mail between Boston and other cities in the American Colonies.

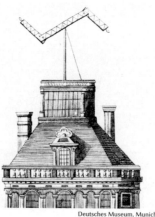

Deutsches Museum, Munich, Germany

The Chappe telegraph consisted of a series of towers. An operator in each tower moved a crossbar and two large, jointed arms to send coded messages.

Detail of *Intérieur d'un Cabinet de Curiosités;* Société Française de Photographie, Paris

A daguerreotype was an early type of photograph printed on a metal plate. Louis J. M. Daguerre took this picture of a collection of rare objects in 1837.

The beginning of speedy communication

This table shows how new means of communication steadily shortened the time needed to send a message from New York City to San Francisco during the mid-1800's.

Year	Fastest means of communication	Time, New York City to San Francisco
1845	Clipper ship around Cape Horn	About 4 months
1858	Overland stagecoach	About 25 days
1860	Telegraph to St. Joseph, Mo.; pony express to Sacramento, Calif.; steamer to San Francisco	About 10 days
1861	Transcontinental telegraph	A few seconds

the first permanent photograph. Niépce's technique, which he called *heliography,* involved exposing a metal plate to light for about eight hours. As a result, he could only photograph such immovable objects as houses.

The French painter Louis J. M. Daguerre worked as Niépce's partner for several years. In the 1830's, Daguerre developed an improved type of photograph called a *daguerreotype.* A daguerreotype took only a few minutes to be exposed. About the same time, the British inventor William Henry Fox Talbot invented a method of photography that used a paper negative instead of a metal plate. Fox Talbot's invention, which he called a *talbotype* or *calotype,* was not widely used because it produced less clear pictures than a daguerreotype. But the idea of using a flexible negative became

the key to modern photography. With other methods, the photographer used glass or metal plates that had to be changed after each exposure. With Fox Talbot's method, the film could be moved through the camera and used to take a series of pictures.

In the late 1800's, a large number of inventions improved communication. These included the typewriter, telephone, phonograph, and motion picture. In 1868, Carlos Glidden, Christopher Latham Sholes, and Samuel W. Soulé, three American partners, patented the first practical typewriter. E. Remington and Sons, the manufacturer of the famous Remington rifle, began to produce the typewriter in the mid-1870's.

Alexander Graham Bell, a Scottish-born teacher of the deaf, patented a kind of telephone in 1876. Bell's device made it possible to transmit the human voice over wires. Elisha Gray, an American inventor, patented a similar machine about the same time. But the first telephone network, which was built in New England in 1878, used Bell's design. By 1890, the Bell telephone had spread to most major U.S. cities.

In 1877, the American inventor Thomas A. Edison invented the first practical phonograph. It recorded sound on a cylinder covered with foil. About 10 years later, Emile Berliner, a German immigrant to the United States, invented a phonograph that used disks instead of cylinders. By the early 1900's, Berliner's disk phonograph had replaced Edison's model.

Until the 1880's, printers set type entirely by hand, just

The American painter Samuel F. B. Morse patented his electric telegraph.

The first successful transatlantic telegraph cable linked Europe and North America.

Alexander Graham Bell patented a type of telephone.

| 1840 | 1864 | 1866 | 1868 | 1876 |

The British physicist James Clerk Maxwell reported his theory of electromagnetism, which led to radio.

Three American inventors patented the first practical typewriter.

Bettmann Archive

Samuel F. B. Morse developed one of the first successful electric telegraphs. He also developed Morse code, a system of sending messages by dots and dashes.

Bettmann Archive

An early typewriter was patented in the 1860's by three American inventors—Carlos Glidden, Christopher Latham Sholes, and Samuel W. Soulé.

Bettmann Archive

Alexander Graham Bell designed one of the first successful telephones and demonstrated it at the 1876 Centennial Exposition in Philadelphia.

as Gutenberg had done. Then in 1884, Ottmar Mergenthaler, a German mechanic in the United States, patented the Linotype machine. The Linotype used a keyboard to set type mechanically, eliminating the need for hand setting. The invention sped the production of newspapers and other publications.

In 1887, an American clergyman named Hannibal W. Goodwin developed a Celluloid film that was tough but flexible. George Eastman, a manufacturer of photographic equipment, introduced the film in 1889. Using Eastman film, Edison and other inventors succeeded in making and projecting motion pictures during the 1890's. Edison probably bought his design for a motion-picture projector from the American inventors Thomas Armat and Charles Francis Jenkins.

The beginning of the electronic age, near the end of the 1800's, revolutionized communication once again. At that time, the only means of quick long-distance communication were the telegraph and the telephone, both of which could send messages only along wires. During the electronic age, inventors used a branch of science and engineering called electronics to send signals through space. The electronic age made possible the invention of radio, television, and other wonders of modern communication.

Electronic communication developed from the ideas and experiments of several scientists. In 1864, the British physicist James Clerk Maxwell theorized that electromagnetic waves traveled through space at the speed of

Famous first words

"What hath God wrought!" Samuel F. B. Morse sent this message from Washington, D.C., to Baltimore over the world's first commercially practical telegraph line on May 24, 1844.
"Glory to God in the highest, on earth peace, good will toward men." This message of Aug. 16, 1858, was the first official communication sent over a transatlantic cable.
"Mr. Watson, come here. I want you!" Alexander Graham Bell spoke these words, the first communication by telephone, on March 10, 1876. Bell had accidentally spilled a jar of acid and was calling for his assistant, Thomas A. Watson.
"Mary had a little lamb. . . ." Thomas A. Edison recited this verse, the first phonograph recording, in 1877.
"S." Guglielmo Marconi received this signal, the first transatlantic wireless message, on Dec. 12, 1901.
"Wait a minute, wait a minute. You ain't heard nothin' yet." Al Jolson spoke these words in the first partly talking motion picture, *The Jazz Singer* (1927).
"That's one small step for a man, one giant leap for mankind." United States astronaut Neil Armstrong spoke these words on July 20, 1969, as he became the first person to set foot on the moon.

light. In the late 1880's, the German physicist Heinrich Hertz proved the existence of these waves. Hertz could not see any practical application for his research. But in 1895, an Italian inventor named Guglielmo Marconi combined the ideas of Maxwell, Hertz, and others to send signals through space. Marconi called his device the *wireless telegraph.* We call it radio.

— Thomas A. Edison developed the first practical phonograph.

— Ottmar Mergenthaler, a German-born mechanic, patented the Linotype machine.

| 1877 | 1880's | 1884 | 1895 |

— The German physicist Heinrich Hertz discovered electromagnetic waves.

— The Italian inventor Guglielmo Marconi developed the *wireless telegraph* (radio).

Bettmann Archive

Thomas A. Edison's phonograph recorded sound on a cylinder covered with foil. This picture shows the inventor with an early version of his phonograph.

Historical Pictures Service

Linotype machines used a keyboard to set type mechanically. Their introduction sped the production of newspapers and other publications.

The Marconi Company

Guglielmo Marconi combined the ideas of several scientists to send signals through the air. His invention, the *wireless telegraph,* led to present-day radio.

At first, only Morse code signals were sent by Marconi's device. In 1906, Reginald A. Fessenden, a Canadian-born physicist, attached a telephone mouthpiece to a wireless telegraph and became one of the first persons to transmit speech. On Christmas Eve in 1906, several radio operators picked up Fessenden's first broadcast. They were shocked to hear Christmas music and a Bible reading instead of the *dit-dah-dit* of Morse code.

During the early 1900's, Lee De Forest of the United States and certain other electrical engineers developed various devices called *vacuum tubes,* which could detect and amplify radio signals. Vacuum tubes made possible the development of radio as we know it.

Experimental radio stations, many of which were connected with engineering schools or universities, appeared as early as 1908. By 1917, there were about 8,600 licensed broadcasters in the United States. Several of those early broadcasters claimed to have been the first commercial radio station. Two of the earliest stations were KDKA in Pittsburgh and WWJ in Detroit, both of which began regular broadcasts in 1920.

Radio stations soon sprang up throughout the United States. In 1922, station WEAF in New York City accepted a fee to allow a company selling apartments to advertise on the air. This advertisement was the first radio commercial. Until that time, radio programs were paid for with profits from the sale of radios. But advertising soon became the chief source of funds for broadcasting. The United States developed a system of commercial radio—and later television—in which most programs are paid for by advertisers. In most other countries, radio and TV networks get much of their funds from the government.

The development of modern communication. Television, like many other inventions, originated from the research and thinking of many people. Attempts to send pictures through space date back to the 1800's. A working system was developed in 1925, when John Logie Baird, a Scottish engineer, demonstrated the possibility of television transmission. In 1936, the British Broadcasting Corporation (BBC) transmitted the world's first open-circuit TV broadcasts. The Radio Corporation of America (now RCA Corporation) began regular telecasts in 1939. RCA used an improved TV camera and electronic picture tube perfected by Vladimir K. Zworykin, a Russian-born American physicist.

Television programs were suspended in the early 1940's, during World War II. But broadcasting resumed after the war. By the early 1950's, TV stations had sprung up throughout the United States.

In the late 1800's, a Danish engineer named Valdemar Poulsen had invented a machine that recorded sounds on steel wire. But Poulsen's invention gained little attention. During the 1930's, German engineers developed recorders that recorded sounds on magnetic tape. Unlike a phonograph recording, a tape recording could be played back immediately after being made.

Videotape recorders, developed during the 1950's, recorded pictures as well as sound on magnetic tape. At

---

Reginald A. Fessenden, a Canadian-born physicist, transmitted voice by radio.

Vladimir K. Zworykin, a Russian-born physicist, demonstrated the first all-electronic TV system.

| 1906 | 1907 | 1929 | 1936 |

The American inventor Lee De Forest patented the *triode,* an improved vacuum tube.

The British Broadcasting Corporation made the world's first TV broadcasts.

Bettmann Archive

A motion-picture camera of about 1915 was used to film silent movies. Several inventors developed movie cameras in the late 1800's and early 1900's.

Bettmann Archive

Radio became a major source of family entertainment during the 1920's. This photograph shows a singer making a broadcast during the early days of radio.

One of the first TV broadcasts was a demonstration of self-defense techniques. It appeared in 1936 on the British Broadcasting Corporation (BBC).

British Broadcasting Corporation

first, only TV stations used videotape recorders. But cassette videotape recorders, developed during the 1970's, made such recording cheap enough for home use. By plugging the cassette videotape recorder into their TV sets, people could automatically record programs for later viewing. In the early 1980's, several companies introduced *videodiscs*, which enable people to watch prerecorded programs. The pictures and sounds on the videodiscs are transmitted by a special player to an attached TV set.

Artificial earth satellites called *communications satellites* first relayed messages between ground stations in 1960. Before that time, TV signals could only be sent by cable or where there were relay towers to reinforce the signals. Satellites made it possible to relay TV signals across oceans. The satellites could also transmit radio, telephone, and other communication.

During the 1970's, many newspapers and other publications began to use computerized editing and typesetting systems. Instead of using typewriters, writers and editors type articles on keyboards linked with a computer. As they type, the words are simultaneously stored in the computer and displayed on a screen called a *video display terminal* (VDT). In turn, the computer is connected to a device called a *photocomposition machine*. At the touch of a button, the machine sets the article in type on photographic film.

In the early 1980's, several companies began marketing *cellular mobile telephones*. In a cellular telephone system, a city is divided into districts called *cells*, each of which has a low-powered radio transmitter and receiver. As a phone-equipped car travels from cell to cell, a computer transfers a call from one transmitter and receiver to another without interrupting the conversation.

By the late 1980's, many businesses had begun to use a process called *facsimile*, or *fax*, to speed communication. A fax machine sends and receives copies of documents over telephone lines. It can reproduce both text and pictures.

Communication of the future probably will involve many forms of light-wave energy and *lasers*, devices that produce a narrow beam of intense light. A branch of physics called *fiber optics* has made it possible to use light to send more messages faster than could be done with electricity or radio waves. With fiber-optic communication, a laser beam transforms the electric signals of a telephone call or TV picture into light impulses. The laser is aimed into one end of a thin, transparent glass strand called an *optical fiber*. The light can travel great distances through the fiber without losing strength or clarity. At the receiving end, a device changes the laser light back into the original sounds and pictures. A bundle of optical fibers, each about the thickness of a human hair, can transmit thousands of telephone calls or TV programs at the same time.

Lasers are also used in a method of three-dimensional photography called *holography*. A device called a *beam splitter* divides laser light into two beams, one of which

---

Bell Telephone Laboratories developed the transistor.	Television networks began to record programs on videotape.	Xerox Corporation perfected *xerography*, a copying process.
1947	Mid-1950's	1960
Dennis Gabor, a British engineer, invented *holography* (3-D photography).		*Echo 1* became the first satellite to receive radio signals from a ground station and reflect them back to earth.

Ampex Corporation

Tape recorders that recorded sounds on magnetic tape were developed in the 1930's. This 1948 recorder was the first one manufactured in the United States.

American Telephone & Telegraph Co.

Telstar I, a communications satellite launched in 1962, relayed telephone calls, TV shows, and other communications between the United States and Europe.

WORLD BOOK photo

Computers revolutionized communication in the 1960's and 1970's. A computer terminal at an airport, *above,* relays information about flights and reservations.

is aimed at the object to be photographed. Then, mirrors bring the beams of light back together again. Where the two beams come together, they form a three-dimensional pattern that corresponds to the shape of the object. Holography soon may be used to produce motion pictures, photographs, and TV programs consisting of three-dimensional images that float in space. Viewers will be able to walk around the images as if they were real scenes, seeing new angles as they move.

The study of communication

The study of communication is not a single branch of education. Instead, it involves many fields of study. The scholars who explore communication include educators, historians, linguists, mathematicians, neurologists, psychologists, and sociologists. Most of these scholars study only a few aspects of communication. Others devote themselves to an overall study of the field. For example, the Canadian educator Marshall McLuhan has become known for his studies of mass communication. McLuhan explored the effects of mass media on society in several books, including *The Gutenberg Galaxy* (1962) and *Understanding Media* (1964).

The major areas of communication study include (1) sociology and psychology, (2) linguistics, (3) cybernetics and information theory, and (4) the study of nonverbal communication.

Sociology and psychology produced the first academic studies of mass communication during the 1930's.

Two American sociologists, Paul F. Lazarsfeld and Frank Stanton, studied the audiences of various radio programs. Their work encouraged other U.S. researchers, including social psychologist Hadley Cantril and sociologist Robert K. Merton, to investigate the effects of radio and TV broadcasting on the public.

During World War II, the warring nations conducted widespread propaganda operations. As a result, many scholars began to study propaganda and public opinion. Carl I. Hovland, an American psychologist, investigated how persuasive communication causes people to modify their beliefs. After the war ended in 1945, the study of communication attracted many American educators, including Bernard R. Berelson, George Gerbner, Elihu Katz, Joseph T. Klapper, and Wilbur L. Schramm. Most of these scholars studied the effects of mass communication on individuals and society.

Linguistics is the scientific study of language. One of the most important developments in linguistics was the introduction of *transformational grammar* during the 1950's by the American linguist Noam Chomsky. Transformational grammar consists of rules that determine all the sentences that can possibly be formed in any language. Chomsky found that the languages of the world are similar in more ways than they are different and that certain principles are true of all languages. These discoveries led him to believe that every person has the potential for learning the general rules of language at birth.

Corning Glass Works produced the first optical fiber suitable for long-range communication.

The first mailgram was transmitted by satellite.

| 1970 | 1970's | 1974 | Early 1980's |

Several manufacturers developed cassette videotape recorders.

Several companies began marketing cellular mobile telephones.

WORLD BOOK photo

Fiber-optic communication uses a laser to send signals through glass strands called *optical fibers,* shown above.

WORLD BOOK photo

A home computer, *above,* helps a girl practice arithmetic problems. Small computers that perform a variety of jobs gained popularity in the late 1970's.

© Paul Robert Perry

A cellular mobile telephone enables a motorist to make and receive calls. These devices, introduced in the 1980's, greatly improved mobile phone communication.

Another important field of linguistics is *semantics,* which analyzes the meanings of words and the communication problems created by language. Scholars who contributed to the growth of semantics include Alfred Korzybski, a Polish-American scientist, and S. I. Hayakawa, an American educator.

Cybernetics and information theory. A science called *cybernetics* is the study of how information is transmitted by the nervous systems of living things and by the control mechanisms of machines. An important part of cybernetics is the study of *feedback,* the process by which devices and organisms regulate themselves. Cybernetics was developed by the American mathematician Norbert Wiener, whose book *Cybernetics* was published in 1948.

A related science called *information theory* was developed about the same time by two other American mathematicians, Claude E. Shannon and Warren Weaver. Information theory deals with the mathematical laws that govern communication, especially the factors that interfere with the transmission of a message. Cybernetics and information theory have played important roles in the development of computer science.

The study of nonverbal communication is probably the oldest area of investigation into human communication. It dates from at least the 1800's, when teachers of acting and pantomime analyzed how facial and body movements could be used to convey emotion.

The modern study of nonverbal communication, sometimes called *body language,* includes two sciences called *kinesics* and *proxemics.* Kinesics is the study of body and facial movements as an accompaniment to speech. Kinesics was developed by an American anthropologist named Ray L. Birdwhistell. Birdwhistell used slow-motion films of speakers to analyze their gestures and expressions.

The science of proxemics was developed by the American anthropologist Edward T. Hall. Hall studied how people in different cultures use gestures, posture, speaking distance, and other nonverbal signals to communicate their feelings and social status. People would feel uncomfortable putting most such information into words. However, proxemics allows people to send and receive messages without the use of words.

George N. Gordon

Related articles in *World Book.* See the *Communication* section in the state, province, and country articles. See also:

Communication devices and media

Alphabet	Pony express
Book	Post office
Cable	Printing
Citizens band radio	Publishing
Codes and ciphers	Radio
Daguerreotype	Satellite, Artificial
Facsimile	Talbotype
Fiber optics	Tape recorder
Holography	Telecommunication
Intercom	Telegraph
Language	Telephone
Laser	Teletypewriter
Linotype	Television
Magazine	Typewriter
Motion picture	Videodisc
Newspaper	Walkie-talkie
Phonograph	Word processing
Photography	Writing

Biographies

Armstrong, Edwin H.	Hertz, Heinrich R.
Baird, John L.	Kelvin, Lord
Bell, Alexander Graham	Land, Edwin H.
Berliner, Emile	Lumière brothers
Cornell, Ezra	Marconi, Guglielmo
Daguerre, Louis J. M.	Maxwell, James Clerk
De Forest, Lee	McLuhan, Marshall
Dolbear, Amos E.	Mergenthaler, Ottmar
Eastman, George	Morse, Samuel
Edison, Thomas A.	Finley Breese
Farnsworth, Philo T.	Niépce, Joseph N.
Gabor, Dennis	Pupin, Michael I.
Glidden, Carlos	Sholes, Christopher L.
Gray, Elisha	Siemens, Ernst Werner von
Gutenberg, Johannes	Wheatstone, Sir Charles
Hayakawa, S. I.	Zworykin, Vladimir K.

Organizations

American Telephone and Telegraph Company
Associated Press
British Broadcasting Corporation
Canadian Broadcasting Corporation
Communications Satellite Corporation
Federal Communications Commission
International Telecommunication Union
Reuters
Tass
United Press International
Western Union

Other related articles

Advertising	Kinesics
Anthropology (Linguistic anthropology)	Linguistics
	Propaganda
Careers (Communications and media)	Public opinion
	Public relations
Cybernetics	Semantics
Information theory	Speech
Journalism	Symbol

Outline

I. The importance of communication
  A. At home
  B. In school
  C. In business and industry
  D. In world affairs
II. The development of communication
III. The study of communication
  A. Sociology and psychology
  B. Linguistics
  C. Cybernetics and information theory
  D. The study of nonverbal communication

Questions

What were the words of the first phonograph recording? Who spoke them?

How did the invention of printing contribute to the religious movement called the Protestant Reformation?

When was movable type developed in Asia? When was it developed in Europe?

What means of long-distance communication was used both in ancient Greece and in France in the 1700's?

How are radio and TV broadcasting paid for in the United States?

What is the science of *cybernetics*?

What source provides about two-thirds of the news that people hear every day?

Why might the War of 1812 be called the War of Faulty Communication?

How did the Linotype machine speed the production of newspapers and other publications?

Why was the invention of writing one of the most important events in the history of communication?

What is the science of *proxemics*?

Additional resources

Level I

Hellman, Hal. *Communications in the World of the Future.* Rev. ed. Evans, 1975.
Kalman, Bobbie, and Hughes, Susan. *How We Communicate.* Crabtree (Toronto), 1987.
Stewig, John W. *Sending Messages.* Houghton, 1978.

Level II

Beniger, James R. *The Control Revolution: Technological and Economic Origins of the Information Society.* Harvard, 1986.
Ellis, Andrew W., and Beattie, Geoffrey. *The Psychology of Language and Communication.* Guilford, 1986.
Graber, Doris A. *Processing the News: How People Tame the Information Tide.* Longman, 1984.
Hayakawa, S. I. *Through the Communication Barrier: On Speaking, Listening, and Understanding.* Harper, 1979.
McLuhan, Marshall. *Understanding Media: The Extensions of Man.* McGraw, 1964.
Williams, Frederick. *The Communications Revolution.* Sage, 1982.

Communications satellite. See Satellite, Artificial.
Communications Satellite Corporation (COMSAT) is a leading provider of communications satellite services in the United States and overseas. It is the U.S. participant in INTELSAT, a global communications satellite system. Through INTELSAT, COMSAT enables telephone messages, television signals, and other forms of communication to be sent between the United States and other countries.

COMSAT also provides services to the shipping and offshore oil-drilling industries through INMARSAT, an international maritime satellite system. The Federal Communications Commission (FCC) regulates COMSAT's activities in INTELSAT and INMARSAT. COMSAT Video Enterprises, a division of the company, provides motion pictures and other services to 1,600 hotels in the United States.

In 1962, Congress authorized the establishment of COMSAT as a shareholder corporation. It now has 60,000 shareholders.

Critically reviewed by the Communications Satellite Corporation

See also **Satellite, Artificial.**

Communion, in Christian churches, is the *sacrament* (holy ceremony) of the Lord's Supper. The Gospels and I Corinthians report that at the Last Supper, Jesus told His disciples to eat, for this was His body, and to drink, for this was His blood. Most Protestants call the sacrament the *Lord's Supper.* Anglicans, Roman Catholics, and members of the Eastern Orthodox churches call the ceremony the *Eucharist* or *Holy Communion.* Some Protestant churches observe the ritual monthly or weekly. Others observe it four times a year. Roman Catholics must receive Communion during the Easter season, and often they receive weekly or daily Communion.

Some churches use individual wafers of unleavened bread and, especially among Protestant churches, individual glasses of wine. The modern liturgical movement has proposed celebrating the sacrament more frequently. It also proposes using a shared loaf of bread and a common cup of wine.   Frank C. Senn

Related articles in *World Book* include:
Christianity (Beliefs)
Eastern Orthodox Churches (Services; Sacraments)
Mass
Protestantism (Belief in sacraments)
Roman Catholic Church (The seven sacraments)
Transubstantiation

Communism is a political and economic system that became one of the most powerful forces in the world. It shaped much of history from the early 1900's to the 1990's. Some people have considered Communism the greatest threat to world peace. Others have looked on it as the world's greatest hope.

The term *Communism* has several meanings. Communism can be a form of government, an economic system, a revolutionary movement, a way of life, or a goal or ideal. Communism is also a set of ideas about how and why history moves, and in what direction it is headed. These ideas were developed mainly by V. I. Lenin from the writings of Karl Marx. Lenin was a Russian revolutionary leader of the early 1900's, and Marx was a German social philosopher in the 1800's.

According to Communists, their long-range goal is a society that provides equality and economic security for all. Communists traditionally have called for government ownership rather than private ownership of land, factories, and other economic resources, called the *means of production.* They also have called for government planning of economic activity, and for strict rule by the Communist Party.

During the 1900's, millions of people lived under Communist rule. In 1917, Russia became the first state to be controlled by a Communist Party. Russia joined with three other territories in 1922 to form the Union of Soviet Socialist Republics (U.S.S.R.), or Soviet Union. By 1940, 12 more republics were added, and the Soviet Union had become one of the most powerful countries in the world.

After World War II (1939-1945), Soviet troops occupied most of Eastern Europe. The Soviet Union was thus able to help Communist governments take power in that region. In 1949, the Chinese Communist Party won a civil war for control of China.

The rapid spread of Communism after World War II brought about a struggle for international power and influence between Communist countries and non-Communist countries. This struggle was known as the Cold War. Most people believe that events in the late 1980's and early 1990's marked the end of the Cold War. These events included the collapse of several Communist governments in Eastern Europe in 1989 and the fall of Communism in the Soviet Union in 1991. By 1992, Communist parties remained in power in only a small number of countries, including China, Cuba, Laos, North Korea, and Vietnam.

The terms *Communism* and *socialism* are frequently confused. Communists usually refer to their beliefs and goals as "socialist." But socialists do not consider themselves Communists. Communists and socialists both seek public ownership or regulation of the principal means of production. But most socialists favor peaceful and legal methods to achieve their goals, while Communists have often used force without regard to law. Socialism may or may not be based on the teachings of Marx. Communism is based on the teachings of both Marx and Lenin.

Joan Barth Urban, the contributor of this article, is Professor of Politics at Catholic University of America and author of Moscow and the Italian Communist Party.

This article presents a broad survey of Communism in theory and as it was practiced in most Communist countries until about 1990. For a detailed description of life under Communism in China and the U.S.S.R., read the *World Book* articles on those countries. For a more complete understanding of how Communism compares with other political or economic systems, see **Capitalism** (How other systems differ from capitalism); **Economics** (Kinds of economies); **Government** (Who governs?); and **Socialism**.

Communism in theory

Communism in the 1900's has been based on the theories of Marx as interpreted and modified by Lenin. These theories are often called *Marxism-Leninism.*

Early communism. The word *communism* comes from the Latin word *communis,* which means *common* or *belonging to all.* The idea of *communal* property dates at least from the time of the early Greeks. In the 300's B.C., the Greek philosopher Plato discussed communal ideas in his book *The Republic.* Plato proposed that a ruling class own everything in common, putting the welfare of the state above all personal desires. A number of early Christian groups had some form of community ownership of property.

Over the centuries, many philosophers and reformers supported such communist ideals as community ownership and equality of work and profit. Then, in the 1800's, Marx transformed Communism into a revolutionary movement.

The ideas of Marx. Marx's basic ideas were first expressed in the *Communist Manifesto* (1848), a pamphlet that he wrote with Friedrich Engels, a German economist. Marx believed the only way to ensure a happy, harmonious society was to put the workers in control. His ideas were partly a reaction against hardships suffered by workers in England, France, and Germany during the Industrial Revolution, a period of rapid industrial growth from the 1700's to the mid-1800's. Most factory workers and miners were poorly paid and worked long hours under unhealthful and even dangerous conditions.

Marx believed that the triumph of Communism was inevitable. He taught that history follows certain unchangeable laws as it advances from one stage to the next. Each stage is marked by struggles that lead to a higher stage of development. Communism, Marx declared, is the highest and final stage of development.

According to Marx, the key to understanding the stages of historical development is knowing the relationship between different classes of people in producing goods. He claimed that the owners of factories and other means of production—the *ruling class*—use their economic power to force their will on the people. Marx assumed that the ruling class would never willingly give up power, and so struggle and violence were inevitable. He saw such *class struggle* between the rulers and the ruled as the means by which history moves from one stage to the next.

Marx called for the abolition of *capitalism,* an economic system in which the chief means of production are privately owned. Under capitalism, Marx believed, a struggle takes place between the *bourgeoisie* (pronounced *BOOR zhwah ZEE*) and the *proletariat.* The bour-

geoisie are the owners and managers of the means of production, and the proletariat are the workers. Marx argued that workers do not receive full value for their labor under capitalism, because the owners keep the profits. He believed that, under capitalism, wealth would become concentrated in the hands of a few people, and most people of the middle class would be forced to become workers. The workers' living standards would continually grow worse.

Finally, the workers would turn away from capitalism and their nation's political system. They would then revolt and seize control of industry and the government.

The workers would first establish a socialist state. Its government would be a *dictatorship of the proletariat,* a government controlled by workers, that would work to establish a classless Communist society. After classes had been eliminated, everyone would live in peace, prosperity, and freedom. There would be no more need for governments, police, or armies, and all these institutions would gradually disappear.

European reality in the early 1900's. By the early 1900's, capitalism was more successful in Europe's industrialized nations than Marx had predicted. Economic modernization was causing the middle classes to grow larger rather than smaller. The formation of labor unions, increased production of consumer goods, and the growth of democracy had led to a rise in living standards. Most Europeans felt an increasing sense of national pride, and few had turned away from their political systems.

During this period, many Marxists began to believe that social justice could be achieved within a democratic system. These moderates, called *democratic socialists,* thought such justice could be brought about by evolutionary rather than revolutionary means.

Lenin's contributions. Lenin believed that capitalism in Europe had escaped failure because of *imperialism*— a policy in which one country extends influence over other countries. Capitalists from European imperialist countries underpaid workers they hired in African and Asian colonies. This helped the capitalists produce goods cheaply, which in turn kept prices in Europe low. Low prices contributed to a high standard of living for Europeans, which helped prevent unrest in Europe. But the exploitation of workers in nonindustrial societies created the possibility of a Communist revolution there, which Marx had not foreseen.

Lenin agreed with Marx's idea that only revolutionary violence could bring about political change. But Lenin believed a highly centralized, tightly disciplined *vanguard* (leading group) of professional revolutionaries would lead the revolution. This vanguard would make up the Communist Party. Marx's idea of the dictatorship of the proletariat became, in Lenin's thinking, the dictatorship of the Communist Party, which claimed to represent the proletariat.

Communism in practice

In practice, Communism has varied from one Communist country to another. But until the late 1980's, certain basic features of Communism were shared by all Communist countries.

One of these features was *totalitarianism.* In totalitarian countries, the government controls almost all aspects of people's lives. Communist countries also were *party states.* In a party state, the ruling party dominates all government bodies. The countries had *centrally planned economies,* also called *command economies,* economies in which the state owned the means of production and the government planned most economic activity. Finally, Communist countries valued cooperation and *collective* (group) needs over personal freedom. In other words, they considered the well-being of the state and society to be more important than that of the individual.

The role of the Communist Party. The Communist Party performed four important roles in Communist systems. (1) It carefully selected party members. (2) It maintained total control over public policies. (3) It supervised every branch of government. (4) It carefully screened people for key jobs throughout society.

In Communist countries, the Communist Party functioned according to an idea introduced by Lenin called *democratic centralism.* According to this idea, all party members were required to support all decisions made by the party. Dissent from the *party line* (the party's policies) was called *factionalism* and could result in dismissal from the Communist Party.

Communist Party structure has varied from country to country. But Communist parties have shared certain basic characteristics.

The traditional Communist Party is structured like a pyramid. At the bottom of the pyramid are numerous local party organizations, formerly called *cells.* In the middle are various regional and district organizations. At the top is a party congress, made up of delegates from party organizations throughout the country.

Party congresses meet periodically, usually every three to five years. During meetings, each congress votes on issues facing the country and the party. It also elects the party's Central Committee, an administrative body.

Party congresses have more power in theory than in practice. They almost always vote according to the wishes of the most important Communist Party leaders. In addition, members of the Central Committee are already chosen before each congress, which merely approves those choices.

The most powerful decision-making bodies are the Central Committee, the Politburo, and the Secretariat. The Central Committee carries out the work of the party between congresses. It also approves the elections of members to two other administrative bodies, the Politburo and the Secretariat. The Politburo sets all important government policies. The Secretariat manages the daily work of the party. The head of the Secretariat, called the general secretary, is the most powerful person in the party and in the country.

The party state. Marx believed that in a Communist society, the powers of the state—and eventually the state itself—would gradually disappear. But no Communist country ever eliminated the state. Communists believed that a state dominated by the Communist Party was necessary to defend Communist countries against capitalist influence from other countries. Therefore, secret police as well as regular police forces and a strong military establishment would be needed until Communism had been attained worldwide.

In Communist states, all power rested with the Communist Party. The people who led the party also headed the government. The individuals who made up the government *bureaucracy* (the system of officials who carry out governmental functions) were all party members.

Communist governments established policies that they claimed were democratic, and thus representative of Marx's ideals. But these policies were actually undemocratic. For example, governments held local and national elections but limited the choice to only one candidate or to candidates of a single party. Legislatures that supposedly represented the people passed without question all laws proposed by Communist Party leaders. Constitutions that, in theory, protected people's rights were repeatedly violated by Communist leaders.

The centrally planned economy. Marx predicted that central planning of industrial and agricultural production would guarantee economic efficiency, job security, and income equality. Communist countries therefore *nationalized* (put under government control) factories and farms and established procedures for planning economic activity.

Communist planners made decisions that in non-Communist countries are made by individuals and corporations. Government planners determined what raw materials would be produced, when and where they would be produced, and what products they would be used to manufacture. The planners also decided to whom and at what prices the finished products would be sold. The planners had to ensure that resources and skilled labor were in the right place at the right time.

Communist economies experienced some success. Centralization enabled governments to focus their energies and rapidly industrialize their countries. It also helped the Soviet Union build up its military forces. Literacy and employment rates soared in Communist countries. In addition, Communist countries distributed income fairly equally. Therefore, the difference between the lowest and the highest wages was much smaller in Communist countries than in capitalist countries.

The centrally planned economy created serious problems, however, because it was inefficient. State-set prices did not reflect the actual cost of production, leading to waste of resources. The planned economy also failed to provide high-quality goods and services and could not respond quickly to changes in consumer demand. In many cases, consumer goods and housing were in short supply, and state-run farms did not produce adequate supplies of food. The shortages occurred partly because worker productivity and creativity lagged. Workers had little motivation to be productive because their wages remained about the same regardless of how much they produced.

In addition, the economy was not as fair as it may have appeared. Communist Party leaders and members of the bureaucracy enjoyed privileges denied to other citizens. These people and their families had special access to government cars, well-stocked grocery stores, comfortable housing, and better health care. As a result, they achieved a significantly higher standard of living than the average citizen, despite similarities in monetary income.

Restrictions on personal freedom. Communist leaders traditionally considered the needs of society more important than individual rights and liberties. As a result, personal freedoms were severely restricted. The amount of police repression varied, however. For example, when Joseph Stalin was dictator of the Soviet Union from 1929 to 1953, millions of Soviet citizens were executed or sent to labor camps. The government also ordered people to spy on their neighbors and encouraged them to inform on their family members. Stalin adopted these measures to eliminate real and imagined opposition to his policies. Similar conditions existed in China under Mao Zedong, who ruled that country from 1949 to 1976.

After Stalin's death in 1953, most Communist governments shifted from open terror to more subtle forms of repression. For example, they threatened to fire people from their jobs or to deny them a new apartment if they opposed the government. Governments also used material rewards to encourage obedience from citizens. A similar transition occurred in China after the death of Mao.

In Communist countries, individuals generally were free to do and say what they wished among friends and family. But they were not allowed to publicly criticize Communist Party leaders or policies or to openly oppose the Communist system. Governments also did not permit people to establish organizations or publications that opposed Communism. In addition, writers who were critical of Communism were not allowed to publish their work. All these restrictions existed despite the fact that many Communist governments had constitutions claiming to guarantee the freedoms of speech, press, and assembly.

Communists in most countries discouraged religious worship because they considered religion a threat to Communism. Church members found it more difficult to advance in their jobs and were not allowed to join the Communist Party.

Communism in the Soviet Union

Before 1917. Marx had expected his theories to be tested in Germany, Great Britain, or some other highly industrialized country. But it was in relatively agricultural Russia that Communists first succeeded in setting up a Communist-controlled government.

During the late 1800's, Russia began to modernize. Although the country was still largely agricultural, its industry began to flourish. As industrialization increased, discontent grew among the rising middle class and workers in the cities. In addition, a series of bad harvests in the 1890's caused starvation among the peasants. During this period, revolutionary activity grew, and radical ideas—including Marxism—became popular.

In 1898, Marxists founded the Russian Social Democratic Labor Party. The party split into two groups in 1903. The Bolsheviks, led by Lenin, accepted his idea of a small Communist Party made up of professional revolutionaries. The Mensheviks wanted the party to have wider membership and to reach decisions through democratic methods.

In 1905, large numbers of Russians revolted against the czar and forced him to establish an elective assembly. During the next several years, the government enacted some reforms. But World War I (1914-1918) created more problems for Russia. The nation suffered

heavy troop losses on the front and food shortages at home. In 1917, the people overthrew the czar. A democratic *provisional* (temporary) government was set up.

In autumn 1917, the Bolsheviks, led by Lenin, seized power and established a Communist government. When the Bolsheviks took over, they had fewer than 300,000 members in a country of more than 160 million people. The coup succeeded partly because the provisional government leaders did not want to withdraw from the war, and they could not carry out reforms while the war continued. The Bolsheviks also succeeded because of their effective organization and their appealing slogans, such as "Bread, Peace, Land."

Under Lenin. Lenin led Russia from 1917 until his death in 1924. For a short time, Lenin let the peasants keep farmland they had seized. He permitted workers to control the factories and to play important roles in local government. But the government soon tightened control and forced the peasants to give the government most of their products. The government also took over Russian industries and set up central management bureaus to run them. In addition, the state created a secret police force called the Cheka.

Soon after Lenin came to power, Russia made peace with Germany, but from 1918 to 1920 Russia was torn by civil war between Communists and non-Communists. The Communists defeated their rivals, who were divided and poorly organized. From the start, Lenin used force and terror against his political opponents. By 1921, conditions had become disastrous throughout the country. Peasant and sailor revolts broke out, and famine threatened. The world war, revolution, and civil war had brought Russia near economic collapse.

In 1921, realizing the need for a change in policy, Lenin introduced the New Economic Policy (NEP). The NEP called for Communists to cooperate with certain groups who were considered enemies of Communism. These included shopkeepers, peasants, engineers, scholars, and army officers. Russia's economy recovered steadily under the NEP. In 1922, the country became known as the Union of Soviet Socialist Republics (U.S.S.R.), or the Soviet Union.

By the time Lenin died in 1924, the Soviet Union had become a one-party state. All non-Communist political parties had been banned, and all public organizations— such as professional associations and labor unions—had become tools of the Communists. See Lenin, V. I.

Under Stalin. After Lenin died, leading Communists in the Soviet Union struggled for power. Through plotting and trickery, and by shifting alliances, Joseph Stalin gained complete control of the Communist Party and the Soviet government by 1929. Until his death in 1953, he ruled with an iron hand. The Soviet Union's economy and influence abroad grew rapidly—but at a great cost in human life and personal freedom at home.

Stalin established a centrally planned economy in the Soviet Union and, in 1928, began the *five-year plans.* These were comprehensive economic plans for the country. The first plan included a program that combined small peasant farms into *collective farms,* large farms owned and controlled by the government. In the early 1930's, Stalin ordered millions of peasants murdered or exiled when they resisted giving their land to collective farms.

Many other people opposed Stalin's policies during the 1930's. To crush this opposition, Stalin began a program of terror called the Great Purge. Communists suspected of opposing Stalin or his policies were executed or imprisoned. Stalin ordered many of his earlier Communist associates arrested or put to death. Numerous party officials were labeled "enemies of the people" and forced to confess imaginary crimes. The secret police assisted in the purges, in which army officers and citizens from all walks of life were imprisoned, sent to labor camps, or killed. The peak of mass terror came between 1935 and 1938.

During World War II, such political repression eased somewhat. The Soviet people rallied to defend their country from invading armies of the German dictator Adolf Hitler. But after the war ended, Stalin's secret police returned to using terror to maintain strict control over the people. See **Stalin, Joseph.**

Under Stalin's successors. Shortly after Stalin died in 1953, Nikita S. Khrushchev became head of the Soviet Communist Party. In 1958, Khrushchev also became the head of the Soviet government. He strongly criticized Stalin for his rule by terror. Khrushchev relaxed political control over writers, artists, and scholars. He also introduced reforms designed to improve the productivity and efficiency of the economy. But the reforms resulted in only slow gains.

In 1964, Communist Party officials forced Khrushchev to retire. Leonid I. Brezhnev replaced Khrushchev as head of the Communist Party. Brezhnev reestablished many of Stalin's rigid cultural and economic policies but did not return to rule by terror.

After Brezhnev's death in 1982, two other leaders briefly headed the government and the party. But no major changes were enacted until Mikhail S. Gorbachev became head of the country in 1985. Gorbachev's reform policies and the eventual collapse of Soviet Communism are discussed later in this article, in the section *The decline of Communism.*

The spread of Communism

The Comintern. The Bolsheviks thought the Russian Revolution of 1917 would spark revolution in other countries. But Lenin soon realized that worldwide revolutions would require careful direction and organization. In 1919, he established the *Comintern* (Communist International). The Comintern united all Marxist groups throughout the world who accepted Lenin's ideas on revolutionary violence and Communist Party organization.

The only Communist government established with the help of the Comintern was in Outer Mongolia (now called Mongolia) in the early 1920's. The Comintern succeeded there partly because Mongolians feared domination by the Chinese more than by the Soviets. Stalin had little faith in the Comintern, and he dissolved it in 1943.

World War II. The international instability that resulted from World War II provided opportunities for Communist gains in many countries. In 1939, the Soviet Union and Germany signed a *nonaggression pact,* an agreement in which they promised not to attack each other. A secret provision of the pact declared that certain areas in Europe would be divided between the two countries. In 1939 and 1940, the Soviet Union took over the Baltic countries of Latvia, Lithuania, and Estonia, and parts of Poland, Finland, and Romania. All of this territory became part of the Communist Soviet Union.

Toward the end of the war, the Soviet Union helped free many countries from German and Japanese control. The presence of Soviet troops enabled the U.S.S.R. to set up Communist-controlled governments in several of these countries, including Bulgaria, East Germany, Hungary, Poland, Romania, and North Korea. Winston Churchill, the former British prime minister, warned in 1946 that an "iron curtain" had descended across Europe, dividing eastern Europe from western Europe. Although supposedly independent, the Iron Curtain

---

Karl Marx and Friedrich Engels write the *Communist Manifesto.*

Soviet Union is established.

1848

1917

1922

1929

Bolsheviks (Communists) seize control of Russia; V. I. Lenin becomes dictator.

Joseph Stalin becomes dictator of Soviet Union.

Brown Bros.

Karl Marx, a German social philosopher, was the main founder of Communism.

Novosti

V. I. Lenin founded the Communist Party in Russia in 1917 and set up the world's first Communist Party dictatorship. Lenin ruled the country until his death in 1924.

AP/Wide World

Joseph Stalin ruled the Soviet Union as a brutal dictator from 1929 until 1953.

countries were actually *Soviet satellites* (countries controlled by the Soviet Union). The satellites had to follow Soviet foreign policy and adopt Communist political and economic practices.

In some other countries, Communists who had led national resistance movements during World War II grew stronger. Local Communists took over the governments of Albania, Yugoslavia, and Vietnam near the end of the war with little or no help from the Soviets. A Soviet-supported Communist regime gained complete control in Czechoslovakia in 1948. Communists also became important political forces in France and Italy.

In China, the Communists and the ruling Nationalist Party both fought the Japanese, who had invaded the country during the 1930's. After World War II, a civil war broke out in China between the Communists and the Nationalists. The Communists, led by Mao Zedong, gradually gained control by winning widespread peasant support in the countryside. By 1949, they had taken over mainland China.

From the late 1940's to the 1960's, most other attempts by Communists to take power failed. For example, Communists in Greece, Malaya (now part of Malaysia), and the Philippines fought guerrilla wars but failed to gain power. Armed forces from Communist North Korea invaded non-Communist South Korea in 1950. The invasion resulted in a three-year war between the North Koreans backed by Communist countries and the South Koreans backed by non-Communist nations. Neither side won complete victory in the Korean War (1950-1953), and Korea remained divided between a Communist north and a non-Communist south.

The only major gain by Communists during this period occurred in Cuba. Fidel Castro became dictator of Cuba in 1959, and two years later, he declared his government to be Communist.

Expansion in Southeast Asia. In 1946, the Communist leader Ho Chi Minh led a nationalist uprising in the colony of French Indochina. By 1954, Indochina had been divided into Communist North Vietnam, non-Communist South Vietnam, and neutral Cambodia and Laos. Communists in Cambodia, Laos, and South Vietnam continued to fight the new non-Communist or neutral governments. North Vietnam sent troops and supplies to help the Communists, and China and the Soviet Union also sent equipment.

The struggle in South Vietnam developed into a major conflict, the Vietnam War (1957-1975). The United States sent troops to support South Vietnam. A cease-fire agreement ended U.S. participation in 1973, but the war continued until the Communists won full control of South Vietnam in 1975. In 1976, the Communists unified North and South Vietnam into the single nation of Vietnam. Communists also conquered Cambodia in 1975. In Laos, the government came under Communist control in 1975.

Communist influence in other areas. In Africa, a left wing military group controlled the government of Ethiopia from 1974 to 1991. The military government adopted socialist policies and developed close relations with the Soviet Union. In 1975, leftist guerrilla forces formed Marxist-Leninist governments in Angola and Mozambique. They controlled the governments of these countries until 1990. Other African nations had Marxist-Leninist governments for short periods in the 1970's and 1980's. In Central America, an alliance of Marxist-Leninist groups called the Sandinista National Liberation Front held power in Nicaragua from 1979 to 1990. In 1990, however, a candidate backed by 14 anti-Sandinista parties won Nicaragua's presidential election.

In southwestern Asia in 1978, a Marxist-Leninist party seized power in Afghanistan. However, many Afghans rebelled against the new government. In 1979, the Soviet Union sent troops into Afghanistan to prevent the overthrow of the government. The invasion resulted in a lengthy conflict between Soviet troops and Afghan rebels. The Soviet occupation of Afghanistan ended in 1989. The rebels overthrew the government in 1992.

Millions die in Stalin's Great Purge.	"Iron Curtain" separates Communist and Western nations; Cold War begins.		North Korean Communists invade South Korea; Korean War begins.	
1930's	1940's	Late 1940's	1949	1950	1953
	Soviet Union takes over Baltic countries. Communist governments established in Eastern Europe.		Chinese Communists, led by Mao Zedong, take over China.		Stalin dies.

Bettmann Archive

Soviet troops occupied many Eastern European countries in the mid-1940's. Their presence enabled the U.S.S.R. to set up Communist-controlled dictatorships in some of the countries.

Eastfoto

Chinese Communists, led by Mao Zedong, defeated China's Nationalist government in a war from 1946 to 1949. Mao is shown here on horseback, moving across central China in 1947.

The Cold War

Beginning after World War II, the United States and the Soviet Union competed with each other for international influence and allies in the Cold War. Both countries attempted to gain international power by influencing other governments in their favor, often with military or economic aid.

The Cold War was characterized by mutual distrust, suspicion, and misunderstandings between the two sides. These conditions led to occasional confrontations. For example, the two sides supplied military aid to opposing forces in the Korean War. Another confrontation came in 1962, when the United States learned that the Soviet Union had secretly installed missile stations in Cuba that could launch nuclear attacks on U.S. cities. After a week of extreme international tension, the Soviet Union agreed to United States demands that the missiles be removed. For more examples of Cold War events, see **Cold War.**

Alarmed by Communist expansion in Eastern Europe and in China, the United States and its allies began giving military and economic aid to non-Communist countries. They also pledged to help nations threatened by Communist take-overs. In 1949, Western nations formed the North Atlantic Treaty Organization (NATO). This alliance provided its members with mutual defense against a possible attack by the Soviet Union or any other aggressor. In 1955, the Soviet Union and its Eastern European allies signed the Warsaw Pact, a treaty to provide for their common defense. The signers claimed they drew up the pact in response to the creation of NATO. Each side invested in a massive arms race, a competition to acquire nuclear weapons and other arms.

In the 1950's, fear of Communism in the United States led to widespread accusations and investigations of suspected Communist activities. This pursuit of Communists came to be called *McCarthyism,* after Senator Joseph R. McCarthy, a Wisconsin Republican. McCarthy charged that many individuals were Communists or Communist sympathizers, usually with little evidence to support his charges. Nevertheless, many people lost their jobs or suffered lasting career damage as a result of such accusations. See **McCarthyism.**

The decline of Communism

By the late 1970's, Communism was in crisis in many parts of the world. The population of Communist China had almost doubled under Mao Zedong, and the Chinese government was barely able to provide adequate food for its people. Dissatisfaction with Communism in the Soviet-controlled countries of Eastern Europe was growing stronger.

The Soviet Union was confronted with serious economic problems, a dissatisfied middle class, and disappointment with the Communist political system among key members of the political elite. Hostility among the country's numerous ethnic groups had smoldered for years. Many non-Russians resented the power of ethnic Russians and began to demand more control over their own affairs. In addition, corruption was growing among members of the Communist Party bureaucracy. In Western Europe, Communist parties faced declining electoral support by the late 1970's.

By the late 1980's, most Communist countries had experienced long periods of little or no economic growth. Centralized planning proved to be inefficient, and it hindered the development of new technologies. As a result, most Communist countries could not compete economically with Japan and the industrial powers of the West.

The Soviet Union under Gorbachev. Mikhail S. Gorbachev became head of the Soviet Communist Party in March 1985. When he took power, the Soviet Union faced a declining economy burdened by heavy military expenses. These expenses included maintaining troops in Eastern Europe, supporting unpopular leftist regimes in developing countries, and competing in the arms

```
┌─ McCarthyism develops                    ┌─ Communists win
│  in the United States.                   │  Vietnam War.
│                                          │
●────────────────●──────────────────●──────────────────●────────
  1950's           1961               1975               1985
                  └─ Fidel Castro declares              └─ Mikhail Gorbachev
                     Cuba to be Communist.                 becomes leader
                                                           of Soviet Union.
```

UPI/Bettmann

Fidel Castro, *left,* declared Cuba to be Communist and began to receive Soviet support. Castro is shown above signing an agreement with Soviet leader Nikita Khrushchev.

AP/Wide World

Communist Viet Cong guerrillas from North Vietnam march in South Vietnam. In 1975, the Communist North defeated the non-Communist South in the Vietnam War.

race. In addition, Soviet technology lagged far behind that of the West, and aging industrial equipment contributed to economic inefficiency. Inefficiency, in turn, caused shortages of food and other consumer products for Soviet citizens.

Dissatisfaction with the Communist system attracted many people to the Western way of life. Gorbachev and members of the Communist Party elite observed the West while traveling there. Other people learned about non-Communist countries through foreign radio broadcasts, contemporary books and motion pictures, and professional journals. Citizens began to want the Soviet Union to become more like Western countries.

In response to the U.S.S.R.'s problems, Gorbachev began a program of reform. First, he introduced *perestroika,* or restructuring of the Soviet political and economic systems. Political reforms included the legalization of non-Communist parties and candidates and the creation of a functioning parliament. Economic reforms included lifting the ban on private businesses run by families and individuals, and modifications in the central planning system. To help win popular support for reform, Gorbachev increased freedom of expression in a policy called *glasnost* (openness).

Gorbachev also worked to improve Soviet relations with other countries. In 1987, he and U.S. President Ronald Reagan signed a treaty that called for the dismantling of all ground-launched Soviet and U.S. intermediate-range nuclear missiles. Relations with the United States also improved when the U.S.S.R. withdrew its troops from Afghanistan in 1989. Gorbachev's acceptance of the collapse of Communism in Eastern Europe further reduced tensions with the West.

Gorbachev was chosen for the new office of president of the U.S.S.R. in 1990. But his policies had begun to provoke the opposition of hard-line Communists in the party. His plans to give the 15 republics of the Soviet Union more control over their own affairs further angered the conservatives. In August 1991, leading hard-line Communist officials staged a coup against Gorbachev and removed him from power. However, the coup soon failed, and Gorbachev resumed his duties. Shortly after returning to power, Gorbachev resigned as the party's head but remained president of the national government. He also ordered the suspension of all Communist Party activities.

By late 1991, most of the republics that made up the Soviet Union had declared independence. In December, 11 republics joined to form a loose organization called the Commonwealth of Independent States. Gorbachev resigned as head of the Soviet government, and the Soviet Union formally ceased to exist.

China after Mao. The Chinese economy was highly inefficient by the time Mao died in 1976. This was largely because of the failure of centralized planning, begun in the 1950's, including the establishment of huge collective farms. After Mao's death, a group of economic reformers led by Deng Xiaoping took control of the Chinese Communist Party. The new leadership allowed a return to private farming and the formation of small private businesses, such as tailor shops and restaurants. The government also reversed its policy of refusing foreign investment. It designated many coastal areas as *special economic zones* where foreign investors could produce consumer goods for export. These reforms resulted in substantial economic growth and in an improvement in living standards for many people.

The Deng regime maintained Communist Party control over the political system, however. In the late 1980's, many Chinese university students began demanding political reforms. In 1989, hundreds of thousands of students and workers demonstrated in Beijing's Tiananmen Square and in several other cities. They called for increased democracy and an end to corruption in government. However, the Chinese military crushed the demonstrations, and many protesters were killed. Shortly afterward, Communist Party and secret police controls were tightened.

In Eastern Europe, many people had always opposed Communism. Over the years, some Communists there also began to resist Soviet domination. In Hungary, some of these Communist reformers joined non-Communists in an uprising against Soviet control in 1956. Soviet armed forces invaded Hungary, put down the rebellion, and installed a new Communist regime. Soviet armed forces also crushed strikes and riots in East Germany in 1953.

The Communist government of Czechoslovakia, led by Alexander Dubček, adopted a reform program in 1968. The program included some genuine political competition, less centralized planning of the economy, and an end to censorship. Soviet leaders, fearful of losing control over Czechoslovakia, ordered troops into the country. Under pressure from the U.S.S.R., the Czechoslovak Communist Party replaced Dubček with a rigid pro-Soviet government in 1969.

In 1980, workers in several cities in Poland went on strike. The strikers called for higher wages, better working conditions, and political reforms. They also formed a free labor-union organization called Solidarity. In 1981, the Polish government, under pressure from the Soviet Union, imposed martial law and suspended Solidarity's activities. The Polish government officially outlawed the

Chinese citizens protest for greater democracy; military crushes the protests.

Soviet Union breaks up.

1989   1989-1991   1991

Communist rule ends in most Eastern European countries and in the Soviet Union.

AP/Wide World

Mikhail Gorbachev liberalized Soviet Communism as leader of the U.S.S.R.

East News from Sipa Press

A statue of Lenin is dismantled during Communism's collapse in Lithuania in 1991.

organization the following year.

In 1989, Communist parties began to lose control over the governments in four Eastern European countries that had been dominated by the Soviet Union since the late 1940's. These countries were Poland, Hungary, East Germany, and Czechoslovakia. The rapid liberalization of these countries occurred because the people realized that the Soviet Union, under Gorbachev, would not use armed forces to prevent it.

The Polish government ended its ban on Solidarity in 1989. That year, negotiations between Solidarity and the government led to partially free elections in which pro-Solidarity and other non-Communist candidates won control of the legislature. A coalition government was set up in the summer of 1989. It was the first Polish government since World War II not controlled by Communists.

Also in 1989, thousands of East Germans who had traveled to Hungary went to West Germany by crossing over a newly opened border between Hungary and Austria. Anti-Communist demonstrations soon followed in East Germany, and its hard-line Communist leadership resigned. In November, the country opened its long-closed borders with the West.

The disintegration of Communist authority in East Germany sparked anti-Communist demonstrations in Czechoslovakia. These quickly brought about the downfall of the Communist government, and members of liberal opposition groups took power. In Romania, a bloody revolt led to the execution of Communist dictator Nicolae Ceausescu. A group of former Communist Party members and officials called the National Salvation Front took control of the country. Communists who favored reforms also took power in Bulgaria.

In 1990, free multiparty elections were held in Czechoslovakia, Hungary, East Germany, Romania, and Bulgaria. Non-Communist parties came to power in Czechoslovakia, Hungary, and East Germany. The new East German government agreed to the unification of East and West Germany. Unification took place on Oct. 3, 1990. In Romania, the winning group was the National Salvation Front, which ran candidates as a political party.

In Bulgaria, the former Communist Party, which had renamed itself the Socialist Party, won the election. In 1991, the Communist Party won multiparty elections in Albania. But protests by Albanians led the Communists to form a coalition government with other parties. In early 1992, non-Communists took control of the governments in both Albania and Bulgaria.

Communism today

By 1992, Communism was in retreat around the world as a system of government. It also was losing supporters in some non-Communist countries.

In Communist countries. By 1992, Communists held a monopoly on power in only a few countries, including China, Cuba, Laos, North Korea, and Vietnam. But the governments of China and Vietnam were introducing economic reforms. In addition, North Korea indicated a willingness to reduce tensions with non-Communist South Korea.

In non-Communist countries. Hard-line Communist parties continued to exist in France, Greece, and Portugal, though they had relatively minor representation in legislative bodies. The once powerful Italian Communist Party split, and the larger of the two parties that resulted dropped its Marxist policies. The Communist Party of the United States may have had as many as 100,000 members in the 1930's. By the 1990's, only about 3,000 people belonged. In Eastern European countries and former Soviet republics, most Communist parties had reidentified themselves as socialist parties and abandoned Communist principles.   Joan Barth Urban

Related articles in *World Book.* See **Union of Soviet Socialist Republics** and its list of *Related articles.* See also:

Biographies

Browder, Earl R.	Hu Yaobang	Luxemburg, Rosa
Castro, Fidel	Jaruzelski, Wojciech	Mao Zedong
Ceausescu, Nicolae	Jiang Qing	Marx, Karl
Deng Xiaoping	Jiang Zemin	Reed, John
Engels, Friedrich	Kadar, Janos	Soong, Ching-ling
Guevara, Ché	Kim Il Sung	Tito, Josip B.
Ho Chi Minh	Li Peng	Zhao Ziyang
Honecker, Erich	Li Xiannian	Zhou Enlai
Hoxha, Enver	Lin Biao	

Other related articles

Bolsheviks	Mensheviks
Brainwashing	Politburo
China	Propaganda (History)
Cold War	Radio Free
Collective farm	Europe/Radio Liberty
Collectivism	Russia
Dictatorship	Smith Act
Economic determinism	Socialism
Iron Curtain	Totalitarianism
Materialism	

Outline

I. **Communism in theory**
  A. Early communism
  B. The ideas of Marx
  C. European reality in the early 1900's
  D. Lenin's contributions
II. **Communism in practice**
  A. The role of the Communist Party
  B. Communist Party structure
  C. The party state
  D. The centrally planned economy
  E. Restrictions on personal freedom
III. **Communism in the Soviet Union**
  A. Before 1917
  B. Under Lenin
  C. Under Stalin
  D. Under Stalin's successors
IV. **The spread of Communism**
  A. The Comintern
  B. World War II
  C. Expansion in Southeast Asia
  D. Communist influence in other areas
V. **The Cold War**
VI. **The decline of Communism**
  A. The Soviet Union under Gorbachev
  B. China after Mao
  C. In Eastern Europe
VII. **Communism today**
  A. In Communist countries
  B. In non-Communist countries

Questions

What did the word *communism* mean originally?
Who were the Bolsheviks? The Mensheviks?
What was McCarthyism? What led to it?
Who planned the Bolshevik Revolution of 1917?
What basic characteristics did Communist countries share until the 1980's?
Who wrote the *Communist Manifesto*?

How does socialism differ from Communism?
What problems faced the Soviet Union in the 1980's?
What was the Great Purge?
How did Lenin's ideas about Communism differ from Marx's
thinking?

Reading and Study Guide

See *Communism* in the Research Guide/Index, Volume 22, for a
Reading and Study Guide.

Additional resources

Atlas of Communism. Ed. by Geoffrey Stern. Macmillan, 1991.
The Collapse of Communism. Rev. ed. Ed. by Bernard Gwertz-
man and M. T. Kaufman. Times Bks., 1991.
Communism: Opposing Viewpoints. Ed. by Bruno Leone. 2nd ed.
Greenhaven, 1986. Also suitable for younger readers.
Forman, James D. *Communism: From Marx's Manifesto to 20th-
Century Reality.* Rev. ed. Watts, 1979. Also suitable for younger
readers.
Holmes, Leslie. *Politics in the Communist World.* Oxford, 1986.
Ulam, Adam B. *The Communists: The Story of Power and Lost Il-
lusions, 1948-1991.* Scribner, 1992.

Communist Manifesto. See Communism (The
ideas of Marx); **Marx, Karl.**

Communist Party. See Communism.

Community, in the social sciences, is a group of people who share similar beliefs and customs and who may
live in the same area. The community ranks second only
to the family among the oldest and most basic human
institutions. Members of a community are linked by
emotional bonds. They share a sense of belonging and
feel an obligation toward other members of the group.

Since the earliest times, human beings have banded
together in groups for companionship, help, and protection. The first communities consisted of small groups
of people who inhabited a specific territory. Most of
these communities were isolated and self-sufficient.
Members of the community identified themselves
strongly with the values and attitudes of the group.
Membership in the community tended to be stable, and
many people lived in the same group throughout their
lifetime. Such traditional communities still exist in many
rural areas.

The history of society includes a decline in the importance of the community. Large numbers of other institutions have taken over its functions. These institutions include schools, corporations, and regional and national
governments. The community has not disappeared,
however. Members of modern communities may not
live in the same place. Instead, people from different
areas may form a community on the basis of ethnic or
racial origin, religious or political beliefs, occupation,
friendship, or shared interests.

The term *community* has a different meaning in biology. Biologists define a community as a group of plants
and animals living together in the same area and depending on one another. For example, scientists might
study a desert or a swamp community.   Joseph Bensman

Community college is an institution that offers additional training beyond high school. Community colleges, sometimes called junior colleges, offer a variety
of programs. Most of the programs take two years to
complete. Some students take the first two years of a
program leading to a bachelor's degree. Others take
technical education programs that prepare them for
semiprofessional jobs. Still others take courses in what
are usually called "adult education programs." Most

community colleges also offer courses for students who
need additional preparation in basic skills. Community
and junior colleges grant associate's degrees for completion of two-year programs, and certificates for some
specialized programs.

Most of the institutions called *community colleges*
get financial support from local or state governments.
Most of the institutions called *junior colleges* are privately supported.

The first junior colleges in the United States were established in the late 1800's. By 1900, eight private junior
colleges were operating. Joliet Junior College, established in 1901 in Joliet, Ill., is the oldest public junior college still in operation.

By 1950, there were about 600 community and junior
colleges in the United States. More than half of the colleges operated as part of the local public school system
and shared financial support with all other schools in
the system. Many of them used high school classrooms
and equipment and offered limited educational programs because they lacked sufficient funds. As businesses and industries began searching for better educated people in the 1950's, many states and local
communities increased their support of community and
junior colleges. In the 1960's, from 30 to 50 new community and junior colleges were established each year. In
the early 1990's, there were about 1,150 community and
junior colleges with about 6 million students in the
United States.

How community colleges operate

Control and financing. Most of the two-year colleges in the United States are public institutions. That is,
they receive funds from local or state governments, or
both. Some state universities operate two-year branch
campuses. A few community colleges operate as part of
county or district school systems.

Some two-year colleges are private institutions. Some
of these colleges receive financial support from church
denominations. The rest of these colleges receive most
of their funds from tuitions, fees, and contributions.

Community colleges began receiving federal aid in
the 1960's. Federal funds help colleges in many ways.
They may be used to build new buildings, or to set up
vocational education or special education programs.
Federal funds also provide loans and other financial aid
to students.

Curriculum. Community colleges offer two main
types of programs. In one program, students take
courses designed to fulfill the freshman and sophomore
requirements that lead to a bachelor's degree. These
students must transfer from the community college to a
college or university that grants bachelor's degrees to
complete their junior and senior years.

In the second main program, community colleges
offer specialized training for semiprofessional jobs in
such fields as industry and engineering, health services,
business, and public service. Students in industrial programs train for such jobs as drafting and laboratory
work. Health programs train students for careers as
nurses, X-ray technicians, or other medical workers.
Business programs may include training in data processing, computer technology, and office management.
Public service programs train students to become city

planners, police officers, or other public employees.

Accrediting. Most two-year colleges are accredited by one of the six regional accrediting agencies recognized by the U.S. Department of Education. These same agencies accredit four-year colleges and universities. State boards of education also evaluate two-year colleges. Students attending two-year colleges approved by the state can easily transfer their credits to other colleges and universities approved by that state.

Faculty. Community colleges usually require teachers to have at least a master's degree. They prefer to hire teachers who would rather teach students in classrooms than conduct research in laboratories. Many community college teachers have taught in high schools, or in four-year colleges or universities. Some persons who do not have master's degrees are hired as teachers because they have had special training and experience.

Why community college?

Importance to students. One of the most attractive features of many community colleges is their wide range of technical training programs. Less than a third of the community college graduates continue their studies for bachelor's degrees. Special occupational programs allow students to take only those courses that interest them or that qualify them for better jobs.

Many community colleges have an "open-door" admissions policy. This policy allows students who might not qualify for admission to other colleges to continue their education.

Community colleges are often called "commuter colleges." Students within commuting distance may live at home and work at part-time jobs while they attend classes. Many community colleges have set up special programs for students who work during the day. The students may have classes until 10 or 11 p.m., or later. Evening classes are so popular that some community colleges have a larger number of evening students than they do day students. Some community colleges have established "weekend colleges" so that students can earn associate's degrees by attending classes on the weekends.

The cost of attending most community colleges is relatively low. Tuition and fees at these colleges average about $1,300 a year for residents.

Importance to community. Many community colleges try to provide educational programs that will benefit local business, industry, and government. They may conduct surveys to determine what types of trained personnel the community needs most. They may also ask community leaders to help plan courses of study. For example, colleges located in resort areas may offer courses in restaurant and hotel management, and colleges in rural areas may emphasize agricultural training. Some community colleges in large cities have developed special social and educational programs for disadvantaged minority groups. Many community colleges emphasize programs for older adults, including job retraining and cultural development.

In many states, a large number of high school graduates who want to go to college enroll first in community colleges. Florida and some other states have established *upper-division universities,* which have classes for juniors and seniors. These universities are especially designed for community college graduates, though not limited to them.

Two-year colleges in Canada

Canada has about 200 two-year colleges and institutes. They are called regional colleges, institutes of technology, colleges for general academic and vocational education, or colleges of applied arts and technology. These colleges are organized much like U.S. community colleges. They offer job training and technical training programs, and academic programs like those that university students take during their first two years. Some programs take over two years to complete. The Canadian schools grant diplomas of technology or applied arts. They get funds from provincial or local governments, or both. Most of these colleges have been established since the early 1950's. Terry U. O'Banion

Community property is the property husbands and wives own together under the laws of eight states—Arizona, California, Idaho, Louisiana, Nevada, New Mexico, Texas, and Washington. The laws differ in detail, but they generally consider any property received through the efforts of a husband or his wife as the joint property of both. This property does not include gifts and legacies to only one or the other, or property that one of them owned before the marriage. When the husband or wife dies, half the property goes to the survivor. Only the other half of the property can be willed. In case of divorce, most states require the husband and wife to divide community property evenly. Carlfred B. Broderick

Como, Lake. See Lake Como.

Comoros, *KAHM uh ROHZ,* is an *archipelago* (group of islands) in the Indian Ocean between the mainland of Africa and the island country of Madagascar. The island group consists of four main islands—Anjouan, Grande Comore, Mayotte, and Moheli—and several smaller ones. All the islands belonged to France until 1975. Three of the four largest islands declared their independence that year, but Mayotte chose to remain a French possession. The Comoran government considers Mayotte part of the country, but the people of Mayotte have voted to stay under French rule.

The country's official name is the *Federal and Islamic Republic of the Comoros.* The islands, including Mayotte, have an area of 863 square miles (2,235 square kilometers). Mayotte has an area of 144 square miles (373 square kilometers). Comoros has a population of about 633,000. Most Comorans live in rural villages. Moroni, on Grande Comore, is the capital and largest city.

Government. A president heads the government of Comoros. The people elect the president to a six-year term. The president appoints a prime minister and a Cabinet. The prime minister and the members of the Cabinet carry out the operations of the government. A legislative body called the Federal Assembly has 38 members. The members are elected by the people to five-year terms. The Comoran Union for Progress is the only legal political party. But there are several opposition groups, most of which are based in France.

People. Most of the people of Comoros have mixed ancestry. They are descendants of Arabs, black Africans, and other groups. About 85 percent of the workers have jobs related to farming. But the country has a shortage of good farmland, and it must import much of its food.

M. Huet, Hoa-Qui

Moroni, the capital of Comoros, lies on the west coast of Grande Comore Island. Moroni is the country's largest city.

The chief food is rice. Most of the rice is imported. In addition, the people eat such foods as bananas, cassava, coconuts, corn, fish, and sweet potatoes.

Major problems in the islands include poverty, disease, and hunger. Illness and malnutrition occur frequently, and the nation has a shortage of physicians and hospitals. These problems contribute to a high death rate, especially among young children.

Most of the people of Comoros are Muslims. The country's official languages are Comorian and French, though most Comorans do not speak or write French.

Land and climate. Most of the Comoro Islands were formed by volcanoes. Mont Kartala, a volcano on

Comoros

✳	National capital
•	Settlement
+	Elevation above sea level
——	Road

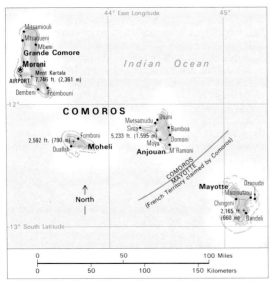

WORLD BOOK maps

Facts in brief

Capital: Moroni.
Official language: Comorian and French.
Total land area: 863 square miles (2,235 km²). *Coastline*—243 mi. (391 km). Area figures include Mayotte.
Elevation: *Highest*—Mont Kartala, 7,746 ft. (2,361 m). *Lowest*— sea level.
Population: *Estimated 1994 population*—633,000; density, 733 persons per sq. mi. (283 per km²), distribution, 69 percent rural, 31 percent urban. *1980 census*—385,890. *Estimated 1999 population*—755,000. Population figures include Mayotte.
Chief products: bananas, cassava, cloves, coconuts, corn, perfume oil, rice, sweet potatoes, vanilla.
Flag: A green field covers the flag. A crescent moon and four five-pointed stars are in the center. The green color and the crescent symbolize Islam. The four stars represent the four islands of the country. Adopted in 1978. See **Flag** (picture: Flags of Africa).
Money: *Basic unit*—franc.

Grande Comore, is still active. Plateaus and valleys lie below the volcanic peaks. Mangrove swamps form the shorelines of almost all the islands. Some of the islands have dense forests. However, much forestland has been cleared for farming. Such clearing has resulted in severe soil erosion on most of the islands.

Comoros has a cool, dry climate from May through October. A hot, rainy season lasts from November through April. Heavy rains during this period provide the islands with the only natural source of drinking water. The people store the water for year-round use.

Economy. Comoros is one of the world's poorest nations. It has no major industry, and no valuable minerals have been found there.

The economy of Comoros depends almost entirely on agriculture. The people raise such food crops as bananas, cassava, coconuts, and rice. They export cloves, *copra* (coconut meat), vanilla, and perfume oils from such plants as *ylang-ylang trees.* Money spent on imports has greatly exceeded earnings from exports. The country trades chiefly with France, Madagascar, Pakistan, and the United States. Comoros receives large amounts of financial aid from European and Arab nations. The country has an international airport—on Grande Comore—and several radio stations.

History. The first people who lived in the Comoro Islands came from mainland Africa, Madagascar, and Malaysia. Historians know little about them or when they came to the islands.

During the 1400's, Arabs landed on the Comoros and took over the islands. For the next 400 years, Arab sultans ruled each island as a separate kingdom.

France seized Mayotte in 1843 and by 1886 had gained control of the rest of the islands. The French granted the Comoros Islands self-rule in 1961.

In 1974, Anjouan, Grande Comore, and Moheli voted for complete independence, but Mayotte voted to remain under French control. France recognized the independence of the three islands but continued to rule Mayotte as a possession. In 1976, the people of Mayotte again voted for French rule.

Several Comoran governments held power for short periods after independence was declared. In 1978, voters in Comoros approved a new constitution. The constitution established a government that is headed by a president. Ahmed Abdallah Abderemane was elected president in 1978 and reelected in 1984. He was assassinated in November 1989. Said Mohamed Djohar was elected president in March 1990.   Leroy Vail

See also **Moroni.**

Compact disc, often called *CD,* is a round, flat platter on which information is stored in the form of *digital* (numerical) code. The main use of CD's is to store recorded stereophonic sound. Discs used for this purpose, called *audio CD's,* are played on a *CD player.* The other major type of CD is called *CD-ROM* (Compact *D*isc-*R*ead *O*nly *M*emory). CD-ROM's can store files of data, pictures, and sound as well as video game programs and other software. These discs are played on a computer's *CD-ROM drive* or on a *CD-ROM player.*

CD's are made of a hard plastic that is coated with a metal, usually aluminum. A protective plastic covers the metal. CD's have only one playing side. Most CD's measure about $4\frac{3}{4}$ inches (12 centimeters) across.

Audio CD's were the first commercially successful CD's. These were introduced in Japan and Europe in 1982, and in the United States in 1983.

Audio CD's have two major advantages over audio tapes and phonograph records—(1) they last longer, and (2) they enable the user to select any part of the recording quickly. To enable a given audio CD to be played on any CD player, manufacturers have established an industry standard known as the *Red Book.* One rule is that the CD be able to hold 74 minutes of sound.

Recording an audio CD. During recording, a microphone translates sound waves into electric signals. A device called an encoder divides these signals into 44,100 segments for each second of sound and then converts each segment into digital code. During disc manufacturing, a laser uses this code to cut a spiral track of microscopic pits into the surface of the disc. The pits represent the digital code. A disc may contain 3 billion pits.

Playing an audio CD. As the disc spins in a CD player, a laser beam shines on the pit spiral and is reflected by the metal coating. The intensity of the reflected light changes as the beam enters and leaves the pits. Differences in this intensity thus represent the digital code. The light strikes a device that translates these differences into an electric signal. Decoding circuits use this signal to reproduce the original sound in loudspeakers or headphones.

CD-ROM's are created and used in much the same way as audio CD's. In the CD-ROM drive, a light-sensitive device produces a digital electric signal. Special circuits process this signal and send it to a computer. The *Yellow Book* standard regulates CD-ROM. A standard CD-ROM can hold about 650 *megabytes* (million bytes) of data. One byte equals a letter or some other character.

Many CD-ROM's store mainly textual information. Other types of CD-ROM's include *multimedia CD's* and *Photo CD's.* Multimedia CD's hold text, sound, still pictures, and moving pictures. Some multimedia systems, such as Compact Disc Interactive (CD-I), work with a television set and stereo speakers.

A Photo CD can store 100 photographs taken with an ordinary 35-millimeter camera. Many photo shops can arrange for photographs to be transferred from negatives or slides to a CD. The consumer can use certain

WORLD BOOK photo

A compact disc, also called a CD, stores information in coded form. CD's are used chiefly to hold and play recorded music.

CD-ROM drives and multimedia drives to view the pictures on a television screen or computer monitor.

MiniDiscs measure only 2.5 inches (6.4 centimeters) across. The consumer can record sound on some MiniDiscs, then later erase the sound. A MiniDisc requires a special player.   Ken C. Pohlmann

See also **Phonograph** (Digital sound recording and reproduction); **High-fidelity system; Laser** (How lasers are used); **Multimedia; Optical disc.**

Comparative psychology is the study of differences and similarities in the behavior of animals of different species. Comparative psychologists may analyze a single activity as it occurs in many species. For example, they may examine the raising of young among birds, whales, tigers, and other animals. They also may study the complete behavioral pattern of two or more related species. For instance, they may compare the feeding, mating, and other activities of two desert rodents, the kangaroo rat of North America and the jerboa of Africa.

Some of the principal behavioral patterns of animals that comparative psychologists study include communication, learning, migration, orientation, reproductive behavior, and social behavior. *Communication* is the sharing of information among animals. *Learning* concerns the gaining of knowledge or skill. *Migration* is the travel of large groups of animals. *Orientation* consists of the ways that animals position themselves in relation to light, heat, and other forces. *Reproductive behavior* concerns the mating habits of animals and the ways they care for their young. *Social behavior* consists of group activities, such as the flocking of birds.

Comparative psychologists observe animals in their natural environment and in controlled conditions in laboratories and zoos. In both types of surroundings, researchers use methods that enable them to observe behavior while interfering as little as possible with the creatures' activities. For example, psychologists may attach electronic devices to the animals. The devices send signals pinpointing their location or relay information on blood pressure, temperature, and other body functions. In the laboratory, researchers may observe animal behavior from behind one-way mirrors. In the wild, they may watch from inside camouflaged enclosures.

Comparative psychologists may record animal behav-

WORLD BOOK photo by Kevin Walsh

A test of color recognition, *above,* requires a monkey to choose between different-colored objects to be given a reward, such as food. Comparative psychologists study the behavioral patterns of animals of different species.

ior on paper using code symbols for various types of behavior. They also film and tape-record certain activities. In addition, they may arrange for an animal to record data itself. For example, many experimenters use a device called a *Skinner box,* where an animal must operate a switch or other mechanism to obtain a reward. The switch also activates a recording device. Comparative psychologists, like other scientists, employ various statistical methods in their work. They often use computers to analyze large amounts of information.   Ethel Tobach

Comparison, in grammar, is the inflection of some adjectives and adverbs to express a greater or smaller degree of the quality the word denotes. *Inflection* means changing the form of a word. Possessive, demonstrative, and limiting adjectives cannot be compared.

The three degrees of comparison are the positive, comparative, and superlative. The *positive* is the simple degree, as in, "This book is *heavy*"; "This book is *interesting.*" The corresponding adverbs, *heavily* and *interestingly,* are also in the positive.

The *comparative* is used when two objects are being compared, as in, "This book is *heavier* (or *less heavy*) than the other," or, "*more interesting* (or *less interesting*) than the other." The corresponding adverbial forms, such as *more heavily* and *less interestingly,* are also in the comparative degree.

The *superlative* is used to point out the one among three or more objects that has the highest or lowest degree of the quality referred to: "This is the *heaviest* (or *least heavy*) book," or "the *most interesting* (or *least interesting*) book." The corresponding adverbial forms, such as *least heavily* and *most interestingly,* are also in the superlative degree. The superlative is also used in the intensive sense of *very,* without implying comparison, as in "That is *most attractive.*"

Regularly compared adjectives add the suffixes *-er* and *-est* to the positive form, as in *proud, prouder, proudest.* This change is described as *comparison by inflection.* If the adverbs *more, most, less,* or *least* are prefixed, the change is described as a *periphrastic comparison,* as in *proud, more proud, most proud.*

Irregularly compared adjectives include some of the most common adjectives in English—words that

have come down from Old English, or Anglo-Saxon, forms. The following list contains some irregularly compared adjectives.

Positive	Comparative	Superlative
bad	worse	worst
far	farther	farthest
good, well	better	best
little	less	least
old	older, elder	oldest, eldest

Some adjectives and adverbs, such as *perpendicular, square, eternal, unique,* and *perfect* may be considered absolute in meaning and therefore not subject to comparison. If *unique* means "having no equal," how can something be *more unique?* However, phrases like *more perfect, rounder,* and *yellowest* are commonly used. More precise phrases would be *more closely perfect, more nearly round,* and *most intensely yellow.*

The words *other* and *else* are often used to distinguish the elements that are being compared. For example, if Robert's height is being compared with that of the other boys in his class, a precise phrasing would read: "Robert is taller than *any other boy* (or *anybody else*) in his class," not "Robert is taller than *any boy* (or *anybody*) in his class."

Usage. When two objects are compared, the comparative form is used, not the superlative. "Helen is the *healthier* of the twins" is correct. "Helen is the *healthiest* of the twins" is wrong. When comparison is made by inflection, adding an adverb is unnecessary. *Happier* is an adequate comparison. *More happier* is not standard usage. The word *preferable* means "more desirable." *More preferable* is redundant.   Sara Garnes

See also **Adjective; Adverb; Inflection.**

Compass is a device for determining direction. The simplest form of the compass is a magnetized needle mounted on a pivot so that it can turn freely. The needle aligns itself with the earth's magnetic field and points toward magnetic north. Under the needle is a circular *compass card,* on which evenly spaced *points* and degrees are marked to indicate direction.

The four *cardinal points* of the compass are north, east, south, and west. The *intercardinal points* are northeast, southeast, southwest, and northwest. Large compasses are marked, clockwise, with the 360 degrees of a circle, in addition to cardinal and intercardinal points.

Listed below are the cardinal and intercardinal points and the position on the circle, in terms of degrees, to which each point corresponds.

North—0 or 360 degrees	**South**—180 degrees
Northeast—45 degrees	**Southwest**—225 degrees
East—90 degrees	**West**—270 degrees
Southeast—135 degrees	**Northwest**—315 degrees

A simple pocket compass helps people find their way when there are no landmarks to guide them. For example, if a person must walk west to reach the nearest town, he or she lines up the needle so that its ends are over the north and south marks on the compass card. The person then travels in the direction 90 degrees to the left of the north end of the needle.

The mariner's compass is a magnetic compass used aboard a boat or ship. In most cases, it has several magnets fastened on the underside of a compass card. The card rests on a pivot so it can turn freely inside the compass bowl and can always point toward magnetic north. The compass bowl has a transparent cover and is filled with a nonfreezable liquid mixture of alcohol and water or glycerin and water. This liquid mixture floats the card and at the same time *damps* (slows) the movement of the card so that it does not constantly swing from side to side with the motion of the ship.

Variation. The compass needle points in the general direction of the earth's *north magnetic pole*. The earth's magnetic field has a north pole and a south pole, just as the earth as a whole has poles known as the *true North and South poles*. The true poles are the "top" and "bottom" of the earth, where the earth's spin axis penetrates the earth's surface. The magnetic poles are not located at the true North and South poles. The north magnetic pole, for example, is a shifting point on the earth's surface, several hundred miles or kilometers from the true North Pole.

The direction in which the compass needle points is slightly different from the direction of the north magnetic pole at almost all places on earth. The difference arises because the earth's magnetic field is not aligned perfectly in the direction of magnetic north. Rather, the field veers slightly to the east or west at almost all places on earth. The angle between the direction of magnetic

A pocket compass has a magnetic needle that points north. A pocket compass helps people find their way when there are no landmarks to guide them.

north and the true North Pole at any location is called *variation* or *declination*. The variation of a compass is different at different places on the earth. The variation also changes slightly at different times of the year and in different years. Thus, to use a magnetic compass accurately, a person must know the amount of variation at his or her location and what variation correction must be made in reading the compass. This information appears on all mariners' charts and on many maps.

Deviation. If a magnetic compass is placed close to a metal object that contains iron, it will be drawn toward that object. The angle that is formed between magnetic north and the direction the compass points is known as *deviation*. When a magnetic compass is installed on a ship, it is mounted in *gimbals* (supporting rings that pivot) often in a stand called a *binnacle*. The binnacle has magnetic devices that correct major errors of deviation in the compass.

After these corrections have been made, the navigator *swings the ship*. That is, he or she heads the ship in different directions, checking the direction by various landmarks. The navigator notes how many degrees of deviation the compass shows from the exact direction of the ship. For instance, by sighting toward a lighthouse on the east, a navigator can tell that the ship is heading exactly east. However, after the navigator has corrected the compass reading for variation, the compass may indicate the ship is heading two degrees south of east. To head directly east when the ship is out of sight of land, the navigator will steer a course two degrees south of

east on the compass, after correcting for variation. The navigator may also check direction using a *gyrocompass*, which always points toward true north.

History. Chinese and Mediterranean navigators probably first used magnetic compasses to guide their ships in about the 1000's or 1100's. These compasses were simple pieces of magnetic iron, usually floated on straw or cork in a bowl of water. In about the 1300's, the compass card was marked off into 32 points of direction. During the following years, navigators learned more about deviation or variation of compasses in various parts of the world, and came to use magnetic compasses with greater accuracy.

When iron and steel vessels appeared in the late 1800's, it became more difficult to make accurate magnetic compass readings aboard a ship. The readings were affected by the metal of the ships. As a result, the gyrocompass was developed. It is not affected by magnetism and points toward true north.

Large ships today carry both magnetic compasses and gyrocompasses. Ordinary magnetic compasses are not satisfactory in aircraft, and so various gyroscopic and special magnetic compasses have been developed by scientists for use in aviation. Radio has also been used for compasses. In the 1940's and 1950's, scientists developed special gyroscopes for compass use in the polar regions.   Richard R. Hobbs

Related articles in *World Book* include:

Gyrocompass	Navigation
Invention (picture: The magnetic	North Pole
compass)	South Pole
Loadstone	Surveyor's compass
Magnetism	

Compass plant is a coarse plant that grows in the Midwestern United States. It reaches a height of 10 feet (3 meters), and is covered with short, rough hairs. The leaves are about $1\frac{1}{2}$ feet (46 centimeters) long and cut into several lobes. The lower leaves of the compass plant tend to line up edgewise in a north-south direc-

The yellow flower heads of the compass plant look like sunflowers. This coarse plant grows 10 feet (3 meters) tall.

tion. In this way, the leaves escape the strong midday sun, but get the full early morning and late afternoon sunlight. The compass plant is known as the *pilotweed* in some Midwestern States.

Scientific classification. The compass plant belongs to the composite family, Asteraceae or Compositae. The scientific name for the compass plant is *Silphium laciniatum.*

Robert A. Kennedy

Competency-based education refers to educational programs that require students to master certain skills or objectives. These skills or objectives are called *competencies.* In competency-based education, also known as CBE, groups of teachers, parents, and school administrators often work together to select the competencies. For example, they may decide to make the ability to distinguish fact from opinion one competency for a fourth-grade reading program.

Schools may use several kinds of CBE programs. One kind focuses on the basic skills of reading, writing, and arithmetic. Another kind involves basic skills and such practical skills as balancing a checkbook or completing an income tax form. In most CBE programs, students take *minimum competency tests* to determine how well they have learned the chosen skills. Some CBE programs require high school seniors to pass such tests before they may graduate.

Many educators believe CBE has several advantages over other programs. They say students work harder when given a clear set of goals. CBE programs can also ensure that students master certain skills during their school years. CBE tests can help teachers identify learning difficulties. As a result of CBE, some state governments have provided additional funds for *remedial programs.* These programs give special help to students who have difficulty mastering the competencies.

Critics of competency-based education fear that some students may not receive adequate preparation for the tests. These students may get discouraged and drop out of school. Some critics also believe that CBE remedial programs do not have a lasting effect.

CBE gained popularity in the United States during the 1970's. More than two-thirds of the states now require some CBE programs.   Ronald K. Hambleton

See also **Education** (What should be taught; How can performance be improved); **Curriculum** (Curriculum changes); **Teaching** (The effectiveness of teacher training).

Competition, in biology. See **Balance of nature** (Competition).

Competition, in economics. See **Monopoly and competition.**

Composer is a person who writes music. A composer creates a musical composition by arranging the elements of music in a meaningful order. These elements include harmony, melody, rhythm, tone, and *timbre* (tone color).

The role of the composer has varied greatly throughout history. For example, composers in the 1300's worked either for the church or for noble or royal patrons. By the 1600's, however, composers were also writing music for public concerts. Composers in the 1600's often performed their music as well. However, during the late 1700's and the 1800's, conductors and *virtuosos* (highly skilled performers) became important in present-

ing music to large audiences. Most composers mainly provided music for others to interpret in performance. Many composers of the 1900's have written music for motion pictures. Today, universities employ many composers to teach composition as well as to compose.

During the 1900's, the development of electronic music and *aleatory music* offered new possibilities for the performance of a composer's work. For a discussion of these types of music, see **Aleatory music** and **Electronic music.**   Thomas W. Tunks

See also **Classical music** and its list of *Related articles* on composers.

Composers, Authors and Publishers, American Society of. See **American Society of Composers, Authors and Publishers.**

Composite family, *kuhm PAHZ iht,* is the common name for a large family of flowering plants. The scientific name for this family is Asteraceae or Compositae. The family consists of more than 20,000 species of herbs and shrubs. These plants are found throughout the world and in most climates and habitats. The composite family includes such familiar plants as asters, daisies, goldenrods, lettuce, ragweeds, sagebrush, thistles, and zinnias.

In plants of the composite family, each flower head is a composite of many small flowers surrounded by a cuplike cluster of modified leaves called *bracts.* From a distance, the flower head resembles a single large flower. A daisy, for example, has an outer ring of long, white *ray flowers* that look like individual petals, and a yellow center of many tightly packed, tube-shaped *disk flowers.* A thistle head has only disk flowers, and all the flowers of a dandelion head are raylike.

Some plants of the composite family, including endive, chicory, lettuce, and artichoke, are used as food by human beings. The seeds of sunflowers and safflowers are important sources of vegetable oils. Calendula, camomile, wormwood, tansy, and arnica are used to make

WORLD BOOK illustration by Robert Hynes

Common dandelion

Shasta daisy

Bull thistle

Plants of the composite family include the common dandelion, the bull thistle, and the Shasta daisy. The flower heads of plants in this family are composites of many small flowers.

drugs. Chrysanthemums, asters, dahlias, and many others are grown for their beauty.   David J. Keil

See also **Flower** (Variations in flower structure).

Each plant mentioned in this article has a separate article in *World Book.*

Composite materials are solid substances that are produced by combining two or more separate ingredients. Manufacturers use composite materials to meet hard-to-achieve requirements for products—for instance, a boat hull that is both strong and light in weight, in addition to being waterproof.

A composite material retains *properties* (qualities) of each ingredient. Carbon-reinforced plastic, for example, consists of strong, lightweight carbon fibers set inside a *matrix* (a continuous solid body) of an artificial *polymer* (a substance composed of chainlike molecules). Carbon fibers, like other fibers, can be made into only threadlike or ropelike structures. But by combining carbon fibers with a polymer, manufacturers can produce strong, lightweight materials in almost any shape. Products made of this composite material include golf clubs and tennis racket bodies.

One of the most widely produced composite materials is fiberglass-reinforced polymer, which consists of glass fibers in a polymer matrix. Products made of this material include boats, sporting goods, automotive parts, and home appliances. Other common fiber materials include ceramics made of aluminum oxide or silicon carbide, and a polymer sold under the Du Pont Company trade name *Kevlar.*

Many other composite materials also consist of fibers set inside a matrix. One reason for this design is that some materials are extremely strong in fiber form. In this form, brittle materials such as glass can be produced free of cracks that would weaken them. Fibers of materials such as carbon and *polyethylene* (a kind of polymer) can be made with their strongest *chemical bonds* (forces that hold atoms together in molecules) lined up along the fiber axis. Such fibers are very strong and stiff along the axis. Another reason for the use of fibers in a matrix design is that many of these strong fibers cannot be used by themselves in a rope or fabric. They would rub against one another and break.

In most composite materials, the matrix is a polymer. Other matrix materials include metals and ceramics. A composite with a metal or ceramic matrix can withstand higher temperatures than can a polymer-matrix composite. Some automotive engines and racing bicycles have parts made of aluminum-matrix composites. Ceramic-matrix composites can be used for cutting tools.

Manufacturers produce composite materials in various ways. A polymer matrix is combined with fibers while it is a liquid. In *filament winding,* such fibers as glass and carbon are

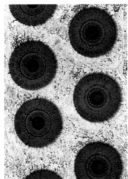

Specialty Materials

This composite material (shown in cross-section) is made of silicon carbide fiber and aluminum.

coated with a liquid polymer and wound around a thick rod. When the rod is removed, a tube of a *continuous fiber composite* remains. Another method of producing a continuous fiber composite is to press a polymer into layers of cross-woven fibers. *Short fiber composites* can be produced by spraying chopped fiber and polymer at the same time onto a surface that acts as a mold. Other composites are made with fiber mats or flakes.

Andreas Mortensen

See also **Materials.**

Composition, in writing, is putting together words to create thought. The word *composition* may refer either to the process of creating a piece of writing or to the piece itself. As a school assignment, a composition is sometimes called a *theme* or an *essay.* The process of composing involves gathering and arranging information and opinions to express a point of view. A composition is an expression of a writer's personality.

Preparing a composition may help you to think more clearly about a subject than simply talking about one. Preparing a composition can also help you present your thoughts so that others can understand them. The ability to write clearly and effectively is important to success in school and in many types of jobs.

Creating your subject is the first step in preparing your composition. Your teacher may assign you a topic or you may choose to create your own. If you are creating your own subject, begin by selecting a topic that interests you, or about which you have some knowledge. Reading about your topic will give you ideas you may not have encountered on your own. Avoid topics that are too broad or too general to be discussed fully in the limited space of your composition. On the other hand, avoid a topic that is too narrow to be discussed from several points of view. A composition that expresses only one point of view can seem dull or pointless.

Beginning your composition. To begin your composition, write down your most important thoughts on a topic. Some writers begin by jotting down a list, in no particular order, of things they might want to say about a subject. Other writers simply write pages of notes for a certain period of time. Most experienced writers revise and refine their notes over and over. As they revise, they add new information, eliminate unnecessary material, rearrange the order of presentation, and develop their most important ideas. Inexperienced writers often make a major mistake by skipping this step and starting to write the finished composition before they are ready.

During the beginning stage, do not worry about grammar, sentence•structure, or punctuation. Your goal during this stage is to create your basic ideas. As you revise your list or notes, you will be able to discover what you know about your subject and what you must learn.

Organizing your thinking. No writer can say everything possible about a subject. Therefore, you must assemble the most appropriate information into some sort of order before putting the sentences together. You can choose from many patterns of organization in planning your composition. You may find it desirable to combine two or more patterns. Your order will be determined by what you want to say.

You might begin your composition with a general statement, called a *thesis,* and proceed to examples or details that support or clarify that thesis. You can also begin with specific points and work toward a general principle that explains them. You may argue from the result of something to its causes, or from its causes to its result. If your composition deals with a process or is a narrative, you would probably do best with a chronological arrangement. You may decide to compare one idea with another and then develop an argument by first stating your own position and then answering opposing arguments. You can also reverse the order. If your composition describes something, you may lead up to your strongest impression or begin with that impression and make connections to other impressions or ideas.

The final stage of organizing your thoughts consists of developing an outline. An outline serves as the blueprint for your composition, identifying the principal ideas and how they should be organized.

To determine whether you have a workable plan of organization for your composition, try the following test. Attempt to construct from the outline a one-sentence statement of what you hope to accomplish in the composition. The sentence should state the purpose of the composition and how the ideas and examples in your outline meet that purpose. If you cannot get these two elements into one sentence, your plan of organization may be inadequate. For more information about outlines, see **Outline**.

Writing your composition. After making notes and revising them to develop an outline, you are ready to write your composition. Writing a composition should always be a process of rewriting. Your finished composition should go through several versions or drafts. For the first version, write your composition from beginning to end at a single sitting, if possible. In this initial draft, do not be concerned about sentence patterns, spelling, or correct grammatical usage. Write on every other line of the paper or double-space if you are typing so that you can easily revise this draft.

In a second session, review your draft, establishing the proper relationships between ideas, words, phrases, clauses, and sentences. Put yourself in the reader's place and ask yourself, do the ideas make sense? Are they illustrated with concrete and interesting examples? Make necessary corrections and revisions right on the draft. Pay particular attention to such linking words as *when, thus, but, so, for example,* and *on the other hand.* Such connecting words are signposts for your reader and are more important than filling a composition with colorful adjectives or long, impressive-sounding words. Plan to rewrite your draft as many times as you need to make the argument of your composition clear and forceful.

Your final editing. As the last step in the composing process, review your text to be sure it is correct. Check your spelling, punctuation, and capitalization, and make certain you are using acceptable grammar. A good method of checking your composition for mistakes is to read each sentence as a unit. Finally, type or write out your composition on white paper, exactly following directions on preparing the final copy.   Harold Patrick Brent

Related articles. See *A Student Guide to Better Writing, Speaking, and Research Skills* in the Research Guide/Index Volume 22. See also:

Capitalization	Punctuation	Spelling
Grammar	Sentence	Vocabulary
Outline		

Compost is a kind of fertilizer made from partly decayed plant material. Gardeners mix it with the soil to provide *nutrients* (nourishing substances) and to loosen the structure of the soil. It may also be used as a *mulch*—that is, spread on top of the soil to keep moisture in (see **Mulch**).

Compost is made by placing dead plant parts in a pile and allowing them to decay. Grass and garden clippings, leaves, and coffee grounds are the materials most commonly used, but any plant material is suitable. These materials are packed in layers about 6 inches (15 centimeters) deep. After each layer, a thin layer of manure or soil is usually added to speed decay. Watering the mixture also speeds decay. If a container is used for the compost pile, its walls should allow some air to enter. The compost should decay for five to seven months before it is used.   Taylor J. Johnston

See also **Gardening** (diagram: A compost pile).

Compound is a substance that contains more than one kind of atom. Every compound has a definite composition that can be described by a chemical formula. For example, water is a compound that contains two kinds of atoms, hydrogen (H) and oxygen (O). Water's chemical formula is written H_2O because there are exactly twice as many hydrogen atoms as oxygen atoms in any sample of water. Other familiar compounds include salt and sugar. These compounds and numerous others occur in nature. Many other compounds are artificially created.

There are more than 100 chemical elements. The atoms in one element are different from those in any other element. The atoms combine in many ways to form millions of compounds. In some cases, atoms of the same elements combine in different proportions to produce a large number of compounds. For example, atoms of carbon and hydrogen can combine to form methane (CH_4), which is the main component in natural gas. These same elements also form propane (C_3H_8), which is used as a fuel for torches and camping stoves. There are thousands of other compounds that contain only carbon and hydrogen.

Each compound has its own distinctive properties. Compounds may be solids, liquids, or gases. They also may have a variety of colors. Some compounds will readily undergo a chemical reaction, but others have little tendency to react.

Compounds can be divided into two groups. *Organic compounds* contain carbon atoms. Proteins, fats, carbohydrates, nucleic acids, and many other compounds in living things are organic compounds. All other compounds are called *inorganic compounds.*

Many substances that contain atoms from more than one element are *mixtures,* not compounds. A compound always has the same composition by weight. However, the composition of a mixture is not fixed and varies from sample to sample. For example, chocolate chip ice cream is a mixture. Its composition varies, and some samples contain more chocolate chips than others.

Chemists prepare compounds in several ways. Some compounds are formed by combining elements. The properties of a compound differ from those of the elements from which it was made. For example, the elements sodium and chlorine combine to form the compound sodium chloride, or table salt. Sodium is a soft metal that reacts violently with water and other substances. Chlorine is a yellowish gas that is poisonous. In contrast, sodium chloride is a hard, unreactive, white, crystalline solid.

Compounds can also be made from other compounds. Living things have the ability to add compounds together to form more complex compounds, and to break down compounds into simpler substances. In addition, many compounds break up into simpler compounds or elements when they are heated to high temperatures or exposed to electricity.   Ronald C. Johnson

Related articles. See **Chemistry** and its list of *Related articles* on specific chemical compounds. See also:

Acid	Chemical reaction	Molecule
Atom	Element, Chemical	Radical
Base	Isomers	Salt, Chemical

Compound eye is a type of eye that has many tiny lenses close together. Compound eyes differ from eyes that have only one lens, such as those of fish, birds, and mammals, including human beings. Two large groups of animals have compound eyes—insects and *crustaceans,* which include crabs and lobsters.

The number of lenses in a compound eye varies from fewer than 100 to more than 20,000 among different species of animals. Each lens is the top part of a structure called an *ommatidium.* Beneath the lens, an ommatidium consists of many light-sensitive cells called *photoreceptors,* each of which is connected to the brain by a nerve.

The surface of a compound eye is curved. As a result, no two ommatidia face exactly the same direction. Each ommatidium registers an impression of a small part of the animal's surroundings. A single ommatidium does not produce clear images of objects. Instead, the impressions from all the ommatidia form a "mosaic," from which the animal's brain distinguishes patterns of light and color. A compound eye has no mechanism for focusing, and so only nearby objects can be seen sharply. However, a compound eye is ideal for detecting motion because even the slightest movement causes a different image to fall on each ommatidium.

Many species of insects have compound eyes that

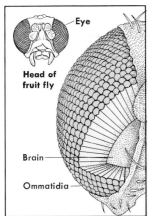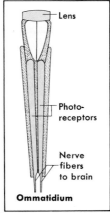

WORLD BOOK diagrams by Patricia J. Wynne

The compound eye of a fruit fly, *left,* is made up of structures called *ommatidia.* Each ommatidium, *right,* has a lens that lies on top of light-sensitive cells called *photoreceptors.*

can see ultraviolet light as a distinct color. The human eye cannot do this. Similarly, certain insects can detect the plane of polarization in polarized light, an ability that the human eye lacks (see **Polarized light**). The ability to detect the plane of polarization helps such insects as ants and bees to navigate by using the sun, because the polarization of sunlight varies according to the sun's position in the sky.   Timothy H. Goldsmith

See also **Insect** (Sight; picture); **Ant** (Sense organs).

Compression. See **Gasoline engine** (High and low compression); **Rotary engine.**

Compromise of 1850 was a series of acts passed in 1850, by which the United States Congress hoped to settle the strife between opponents of slavery in the North and slaveowners in the South. These laws helped delay civil war for about 10 years.

The main problem was whether the territory the United States received as a result of the Mexican War should have slavery. As part of the Compromise, California entered the Union without slavery. The territories of New Mexico and Utah were organized, but the slavery question was left to the settlers in each territory to decide. To satisfy the South, the Compromise gave Texas $10 million to abandon its claims to New Mexican territory and give up other claims. The Compromise also set up a stricter federal law for the return of runaway slaves. To please the North, the slave trade was abolished in the District of Columbia.

Daniel Webster, Henry Clay, and Stephen A. Douglas led in winning the passage of the Compromise laws. John C. Calhoun led Southern opposition to the laws. For a few years, the Compromise seemed to have ended the friction. Business people wanted peace so prosperity would continue. But many Northerners thought the Fugitive Slave Law was too harsh, and some states interfered with its enforcement. Slaves continued to escape to Canada by the *underground railroad.* However, slavery did not become a major issue again until the Kansas-Nebraska Act of 1854 made slavery legal in those territories where it had been prohibited by the Missouri Compromise in 1820.   Robert F. Dalzell, Jr.

Related articles in *World Book* include:

Fugitive slave laws	United States, History of
Kansas-Nebraska Act	the (picture: The Compro-
Omnibus bill	mise of 1850)
Underground railroad	

Compton-Burnett, Dame Ivy (1892-1969), an English novelist, ranks among the most accomplished literary stylists of her time. In achieving style, she largely ignored description, plot, and exciting action. Instead, she used highly polished dialogue to reveal the essential nature and inner thoughts of her characters. All her characters speak brilliantly—whether they are adults or children, masters or servants. Many of her books center around intricate family relationships. They are all set in the late Victorian upper-class atmosphere in which Compton-Burnett was raised. Her novels include *Bullivant and the Lambs* (1948), *Mother and Son* (1955), and *The Mighty and Their Fall* (1962).

Compton-Burnett was born in London. She was made a Dame Commander in the Order of the British Empire in 1967.   Jane Marcus

Comptroller of the currency. See **Treasury, Department of.**

© George Haling, Photo Researchers

Computers come in a wide range of sizes. A *mainframe* computer system may fill a large room, *above*. A *personal computer, left opposite page,* fits on a desk top. The tiniest computers consist of a *microprocessor,* a chip that fits through the eye of a needle, *right opposite page.*

Computer

Computer is a machine that performs calculations and processses information with astonishing speed and precision. A computer can handle vast amounts of information and solve complicated problems. It can take thousands of individual pieces of data and turn them into more usable information—with blinding speed and almost unfailing accuracy. The most powerful computers can perform billions of calculations per second.

Computers handle many tasks in business, education, manufacturing, transportation, and other fields. They provide scientists and other researchers with a clearer understanding of nature. They give people who work with words an effective way to create documents. They enable designers and artists to see things that have never been seen before. Computers produce new information so quickly and accurately that they are changing people's views of the world. For these and other reasons, the computer is one of the most interesting and important machines ever invented.

The most common type of computer, by far, is the *digital computer. Digital* means *having to do with numbers.* Digital computers perform tasks by changing one set of numbers into another set. All data—numerals, pictures, sounds, symbols, and words—are translated into numbers inside the computer. Everything a digital com-

puter can do is based on its ability to perform simple procedures on numbers—such as adding, subtracting, or comparing two numbers to see which is larger. Digital computers are so widespread that the word *computer* alone almost always refers to a digital computer. The largest digital computers are parts of computer systems that fill a large room. The smallest digital computers—some so tiny they can pass through the eye of a needle—are found inside wrist watches, pocket calculators, and other devices.

All digital computers have two basic parts—a *memory* and a *processor.* The memory receives data and holds them until needed. The memory is made up of a huge collection of switches. The processor changes data into useful information by converting numbers into other numbers. It reads numbers from the memory, performs basic arithmetic calculations such as addition or subtraction, and puts the answer back into the memory. The processor performs this activity over and over until the desired result is achieved. Both the memory and the processor are *electronic*—that is, they work by sending electrical signals through wires.

The smallest digital computers consist only of the memory and the processor. But larger digital computers are part of systems that also contain *input equipment* and *output equipment.* The operator uses an input device, such as a keyboard, to enter instructions and data into the computer. After processing is complete, an output device translates the processed data into a form

The contributors of this article are David Gelernter, Associate Professor of Computer Science at Yale University; and Keith Ferrell, Editorial Director, OMNI *and* COMPUTE *magazines.*

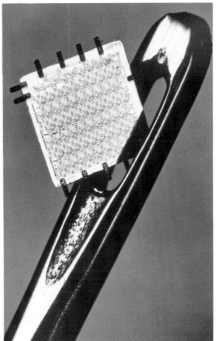

© Henley & Savage from The Stock Market

Bell Laboratories

understandable to the user—words or pictures, for example. Typical output devices include printers and visual displays that resemble television screens.

People can think about problems and figure out how to solve them. But computers cannot think. A person must tell the computer in very simple terms exactly what to do with the data it receives. A list of instructions for a computer to follow is called a *program.*

People have used calculating devices since ancient times. The first electronic digital computer, built in 1946, filled a huge room. Since then, rapid improvements in computer technology have led to the development of smaller, more powerful, and less expensive computers.

In addition to digital computers, there are two other general types of computers: *analog computers* and *hybrid computers.* Analog computers work directly with a physical quantity, such as weight or speed, rather than with digits that represent the quantity. Such computers solve problems by measuring a quantity, such as temperature, in terms of another quantity, such as the length of a thin line of liquid in a thermometer. *Hybrid computers* combine the features of analog and digital computers. They have many of the same kinds of parts as an analog computer. But like digital computers, they process data by manipulating numbers. This article focuses on digital computers. For information on analog computers, see **Analog computer.**

The importance of the computer

Computers are tremendously important in a variety of ways. For example, they simplify many difficult or time-consuming tasks to an extraordinary degree. They provide businesses, governments, individuals, and institutions with an efficient way to manage large amounts of information. Computers also help people to understand

things better by allowing them to make models and test theories.

The value of computers lies in their ability to perform certain basic tasks extremely quickly and accurately. These tasks include (1) solving numerical problems, (2) storing and retrieving information, and (3) creating and displaying documents and pictures.

Solving numerical problems. One of the most important and most difficult jobs performed by computers is the solution of complicated problems involving numbers. Computers can solve such problems amazingly quickly. In many cases, the solutions show how certain things work, behave, or happen.

In engineering and the sciences, the knowledge of how something works is often expressed in the form of an *equation.* An equation is a two-part mathematical sentence in which the parts are equal to each other. Engineers and scientists use equations or groups of equations to show how various things relate to one another. They use the solutions to these equations to predict what will happen if certain elements of a situation or an experiment are changed. Engineers and scientists rely on computers to solve the complicated sets of equations that they use to make predictions.

For example, with the help of a computer, an engineer can predict how well an airplane will fly. A large, complex set of equations expresses the relationships between the various parts of an airplane and what happens when the airplane flies. The engineer enters the numbers for the size and weight of a certain airplane's parts. The computer then solves the equations for this particular airplane. Based on the solutions, the engineer can predict how well the plane will fly. The engineer then might decide to change the size or weight of one of the airplane's parts to change the way it flies. Thus,

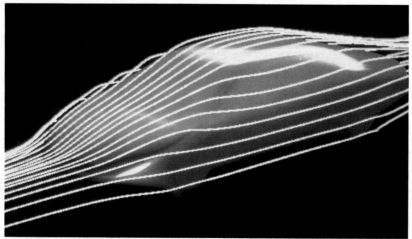

Computers enable engineers to predict how a machine will work. The photo at the left shows a computer image of a car being tested for wind resistance.

© Hank Morgan, Photo Researchers

the computer helps the engineer *simulate* (imitate) various conditions.

Computers help people develop and test scientific *theories.* A theory is a proposed explanation for how or why something happens. Theories, like known relationships, are often expressed as equations. Some equations are so complicated or time-consuming to solve that it would be impossible to develop the theory without the help of computers. Computers are particularly useful in developing and evaluating theories about things that are difficult to observe and measure.

For example, an astronomer can use the problem-solving ability of computers to develop theories about how galaxies are formed. First, the astronomer proposes a set of equations about a group of stars. A computer performs the calculations needed to solve the equations. The astronomer can then use the solutions to predict the shape of the galaxy that the stars should form if the theory is correct. To test the theory, the astronomer can observe a real galaxy to see if it has the predicted shape.

In economics and finance, computers solve equations to make predictions about money. Many of the equations that economists and business people use to make long-range predictions are extremely complicated. But some of the most widely used of all computer programs rely on fairly simple equations. Such programs help people and businesses figure out their taxes, create budgets, and calculate the value of their investments.

Storing and retrieving information. People use computers to store unbelievably large quantities of information. Information stored in a computer is sometimes called a *database.* Databases can be enormous—for example, a nation's entire census might be contained in a single database. A computer can search a huge database quickly to find a specific piece of information. In addition, the information can be changed easily and quickly—often in less than a second.

The efficiency with which computers store and retrieve information makes them valuable in a wide range of professions. For example, scientists use computers to store and quickly find results of experiments. Libraries use computer catalogs to hold information about their collections. Hospitals use computers to maintain records about their patients. Governments store election returns and census information on computers.

All kinds of businesses rely on computers to store large quantities of information about their employees, customers, and products. Computers also allow markets for stocks, bonds, currency, and other investments to keep track of current prices around the world. Banks maintain many kinds of records on computers, such as account balances and credit card information. Anyone who uses an *automatic teller machine* (ATM) is using a computer terminal. When an identification card and number are entered, the ATM can provide account information, dispense cash, and transfer funds between accounts.

John O. Hallquist © Discover Publications

A computer simulation can accurately represent an operation, situation, or system. The first three photos above show computer-generated images of a bomb's nose cone striking a steel plate. The fourth photo—which shows an actual nose cone after a test—reveals the great accuracy of the computer simulation.

Creating and displaying documents and pictures.
Computers can store a huge number of words in a way that makes it easy to manipulate them. For this reason, *word processing* is one of the most important and widespread uses of computers. A *word-processing program* allows people to type words into a computer to write articles, books, letters, reports, and other documents.

Word-processing programs make it easy for people to change text that has been typed into a computer. For example, they can quickly correct typing or spelling errors. Words, sentences, and entire sections of a document can be added, removed, or rearranged. If a computer is connected to a printer, the document may be printed at the touch of a key. Business people, journalists, scientists, secretaries, and students are among those who benefit from word-processing programs.

Computers are also important in the publishing industry. For example, most books, magazines, and newspapers are typeset by computers. In addition, a process known as *desktop publishing* enables people to design newsletters and other documents on personal computers. Documents that have been created in this manner look as good as or better than those produced in the traditional way.

Computer graphics—the use of computers to make pictures—make up one of the most fascinating and fastest-growing areas of computer use. Computers can produce pictures that look almost like photographs. First, the computer solves equations that predict how an object should look. It then uses these predictions to display a picture on a computer terminal screen or to print a picture on paper.

Computer programs that perform *computer-aided design* (CAD) are important in many fields, particularly engineering and architecture. CAD programs create pictures or diagrams of a new object. The programs then solve equations to predict how the object will work. Engineers and architects use CAD programs to design airplanes, bridges, buildings, cars, electronic machinery, in addition to many other types of machines and structures.

In addition, computers can produce pictures by converting information into pictorial form. The pictures can serve a variety of purposes. For example, computers enable business people, economists, and scientists to plot graphs from lists of numbers. In a technique called *computerized tomography,* or the *CT scan,* a computer uses X-ray data to construct an image of a body part on a screen. Doctors use these images to help diagnose diseases and disorders (see **Computerized tomography**).

Computer graphics also are used to create electronic video games. Terminal monitors or TV screens can display game boards and moving pictures. The player may use a keyboard or some other device, such as a *mouse* or a *joystick,* to play computer games.

Computer designers are experimenting with using computer graphics to create *virtual reality*—an artificial world in which the computer user can seemingly move about and handle objects. One virtual reality system has a headset with two tiny display screens, one screen for each eye. Images on the screens produce a three-dimensional view. Sensing devices contained in a special glove tell the computer when the user moves the fingers or hand. The computer then changes the images

to create the illusion of, for example, opening a door.

The images do not have nearly the detail of what is seen in the actual world. In addition, there is a delay between hand movements and the corresponding changes in the images. But virtual reality has a variety of applications. These applications range from simple game sets to sophisticated equipment used to control robots.

Other uses. Many complex machines need frequent adjustments to work efficiently. Small computers can be installed inside these machines and programmed to make these adjustments. In modern automobiles, such *embedded* (enclosed) computers control certain aspects of operation, such as the mixture of fuel and air entering the engine. Today's commercial airliners and military planes carry computers that help control the aircraft. Embedded computers also control the movements of industrial robots and guide modern weapons systems, such as missiles and field artillery, to their targets.

Computers can help solve many complicated problems that do not involve numerical equations. Doctors, for example, investigate illnesses, decide on diagnoses, and prescribe treatments. They solve such problems by applying their knowledge and experience, not by solving equations. A branch of computer science called *artificial intelligence* uses programs that help solve problems by applying human knowledge and experience.

© Brownie Harris, The Stock Market

© J. Wilson, Woodfin Camp, Inc.

Computer-aided design programs are important in many fields. An engineer, *top,* uses a light pen to modify the design of an airplane. A fashion designer, *above,* can consider her design in various colors and patterns on a computer screen.

Artificial intelligence systems called *expert systems* enable computers programmed with vast amounts of data to "think" about numerous possibilities—such as diseases that certain symptoms could indicate—and make a decision or diagnosis.

Computers also can be used to communicate information over long distances. They can send information to each other over telephone lines. As a result, computers keep banks, newspapers, and other institutions supplied with up-to-the-minute information. A *computer network* consists of many computers in separate rooms, buildings, cities, or countries, all connected together. Computer networks allow people to communicate by using *electronic mail*—a document typed into one computer and "delivered" to another. Such documents generally travel in only a few seconds, even if they are being sent over a long distance.

Computers also are used in teaching. Programs that perform *computer-aided instruction* (CAI) are designed to help students at all levels, from elementary school through the university level. The student sits at a computer terminal. The terminal's screen displays a question for the student to answer. If the answer is wrong or incomplete, the computer may ask the student to try again. It then may supply the correct answer and an explanation. CAI also is used in some adult education programs and as part of the employee-training programs of some corporations.

Basic principles of computers

A computer receives individual pieces of data, changes the data into more useful information, and then tells the operator what the information is. For example, a person who wants to find the sum of four numbers enters them into the computer. In only a fraction of a second, signals that represent these numbers are changed into signals that represent the sum. The computer then displays the sum for the user.

How a computer operates. People use input devices to enter data into computers. One of the most common input devices is the *computer terminal,* which looks like a typewriter keyboard combined with a television screen. Data that are typed on the keyboard appear on the screen. At the same time, the data go to the memory. The memory also stores a program—the step-by-

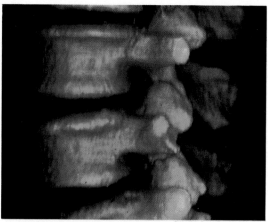

© CNRI/SPL from Photo Researchers

Computers use X-ray data to generate three-dimensional images of body parts such as the human spine, *above.* The images help doctors identify disorders without performing surgery.

step instructions for the computer to follow. The processor manipulates the data according to the program.

The processed information is sent to an output device, which presents it to the computer user. In many cases, the computer terminal that served as the input device also acts as the output device, and its screen displays the results. Printers are another important kind of output device. *File storage devices* are used to save information and programs for future use.

All data handled by computers, including words, enter the processor in the form of digits. Computers commonly use the digits of the *binary numeration system* (see **Numeration systems** [The binary system]). Unlike the familiar decimal system, which uses 10 digits, the binary system uses only two digits: 0 and 1. These digits are called *bits*. Different combinations of bits represent letters, symbols, and decimal numerals. Each such combination of bits is called a *byte*. For example, according to one standard code, the binary representation for the letter A is 100 0001, while the binary representation for the letter Z is 101 1010. Each symbol and decimal numeral also is represented by a specific combination of 0's and 1's.

© Brownie Harris, The Stock Market

Computers help meteorologists forecast the weather by solving equations that describe the behavior of the atmosphere.

© James Wilson, Woodfin Camp, Inc.

Computer games entertain children and adults. Many games display detailed moving pictures on monitors or TV screens.

© Lawrence Migdale, Photo Researchers

Schools use computers as a teaching aid. An elementary-school teacher and his students work at a computer, *above.*

Each of a computer's thousands or millions of tiny electronic circuits operates much like an ordinary light switch. When a circuit is off, it corresponds to the binary digit 0. When a circuit is on, it corresponds to the digit 1. Binary digits, like decimal numbers, can be added, subtracted, multiplied, and divided. Thus, a computer can perform all the basic arithmetic operations.

Computer hardware and software. The physical equipment that makes up a computer system is called *hardware.* Hardware includes input and output devices, file storage devices, the memory, and the processor. The input and output devices and the file storage devices also are known as *peripheral equipment.*

Computer *software* consists of the programs that a computer uses to perform a task. People can either create or purchase software. Computers have vast and varied capabilities because of the many different kinds of available software.

Kinds of computers

Computers vary widely in size, speed, and ability. The size of a computer partly determines the kinds and number of jobs it can do. But even a small computer can perform complicated tasks. For example, a modern desktop computer has more computing power than the huge, room-filling computers of the early 1960's.

The *microprocessor* plays an important role in almost all modern computers. A microprocessor is an electronic device consisting of thousands, or even millions, of transistors and related circuitry on a chip, usually of silicon. Microprocessors are as small as a fingernail, yet have the computing power of much larger computers built before microprocessors were developed. Moreover, a microprocessor generally costs much less than would comparable equipment made up of many components.

Digital computers may be grouped into three categories: (1) embedded computers, (2) personal computers

and workstations, and (3) mainframes. The borders between these categories change constantly as smaller, more powerful computers are developed.

Embedded computers control the operation of various types of machinery. Virtually all embedded computers are microprocessors. Such machines as automobiles, digital wrist watches, telephones, and videotape recorders contain embedded computers.

Personal computers and workstations are computers used by one person at a time. Such a computer usually fits on a desk top. Smaller, portable models are popular with people who often work away from their desks. Popular portables include *laptop computers,* which can be held on the lap; *notebook computers,* which are about the size of a looseleaf notebook; and *palmtop,* or *handheld, computers,* which can be operated while held in the hand. People commonly use personal computers for such activities as word processing, storing and updating information, performing simple calculations, and playing computer games. These computers also are valuable to business people, who use them to manage information about their inventories, customers, and employees.

Personal computers contain one or more microprocessors. By modern standards of computer speed and capacity, personal computers execute programs slowly and have limited memory and file storage capacity.

Workstations are more powerful than personal computers, and better suited to solving difficult engineering,

Computer terms

Binary code is used by computers to represent information. It consists of the 0's and 1's of the binary numeration system.

Bit, an abbreviation of the term *bi*nary digi*t,* may be either the digit 0 or 1.

Byte is a group of bits that act as a single unit of information, such as a letter or numeral.

Database is an organized collection of information stored on a magnetic disk or other direct-access storage device.

File storage device is any device used to save information until it is needed again.

Hardware refers to the physical parts of a computer system.

Input is any information that a user enters into a computer.

Mainframe is a large, powerful computer that many people can use at once. It can store large amounts of information.

Memory is the part of a computer that stores information.

Microprocessor is an electronic device consisting of thousands, or even millions, of transistors and related circuitry on a chip, usually of silicon, as small as a fingernail.

Modem is a device that allows computer users to communicate with one another over telephone lines.

Network is a system consisting of two or more computers connected by high-speed communication lines.

Operating system is a type of software that controls the operation of a computer system.

Output is any result provided by a computer.

Peripheral equipment consists of input devices, output devices, and file storage devices.

Personal computer is a desktop or handheld computer designed for general-purpose use.

Program is a set of instructions to be carried out by a computer, written in a computer language.

Simulation is the representation or imitation of a situation or system on a computer, usually with a mathematical model. The purpose is to predict and analyze what is likely to occur under various conditions.

Software refers to the programs used by a computer to perform desired tasks.

graphics, or scientific problems. Workstations are generally connected to form computer networks. These networks allow operators to exchange information very rapidly. They also enable printers and file storage devices to be shared by many workstations. One important type of computer network, the *local area network* (LAN), connects workstations located within the same building or in neighboring buildings. A *wide area network* (WAN) links workstations over large areas.

Mainframes are fast computers with large memories and file storage systems. These powerful computers solve very complicated problems and manage huge quantities of information. Most mainframes are housed in several large cabinets. Some mainframes do a single job, such as copying and storing the information generated by a laboratory experiment. Others perform many different tasks. *Minicomputers* and *superminis* have many of the capabilities of mainframes, but they are smaller and less expensive.

On a large mainframe, hundreds of people may be *logged on* (running programs) at one time. The use of a single powerful computer by many users at once is called *time-sharing*. The mainframe appears to run many programs at the same time. However, the computer actually switches rapidly from program to program, doing a bit of work on one and then hurrying on to another.

The fastest mainframes are called *supercomputers*. Supercomputers solve numerical problems as quickly as possible based on existing technology. They are used to model weather systems, to design cars and aircraft, and in many other ways. But supercomputers are rare, because they are extremely expensive. Individual supercomputer users—mostly scientists and engineers at large scientific installations—sometimes run programs by means of long-distance computer networks.

Mainframes known as *parallel computers* have provided great increases in speed over other computers. Most computers have a single processor. But a parallel computer has many processors that all operate at once. Each processor can work on a separate piece of a program. As a result, the program can be run much more quickly than on a computer with only one processor. The fastest supercomputers in the world are parallel computers. But parallel computers may even serve as especially fast workstations.

How a computer works

Computers can perform many different activities because they can store huge lists of numbers and do arithmetic very rapidly. All computers work essentially the same way. A computer *encodes* (translates) numbers, words, pictures, sounds, and other forms of data into the 0's and 1's of the binary numeration system. The computer's processor manipulates the binary numbers according to specified instructions. All changes of the data are accomplished by performing arithmetical calculations on these binary numbers. Thus, the binary numbers that represent the data are changed into binary numbers that represent the desired information. The results are *decoded* (translated back) from binary into decimal numbers, words, pictures, or some other form.

The operation of a computer can be broken down into three steps. They are (1) entering and encoding data and instructions, (2) processing data, and (3) decoding

the results and producing output. The storing of information occurs during all three steps of the process.

Entering and encoding data and instructions is performed using input equipment. This section explains how the computer encodes data entered through a terminal. It also describes a number of other input devices.

Terminals enable computer users to type *characters* (letters and numerals) directly into the computer. A terminal includes a keyboard unit and a *monitor*. The monitor usually consists of a *cathode-ray tube* (CRT). A CRT is a vacuum tube with a screen like that of a television (see **Vacuum tube**). The CRT display makes it possible for the user to check the data being entered into the computer and to make corrections if necessary.

As each character is typed, the circuitry inside the terminal puts the character's binary code into a temporary storage location called a *buffer*. As soon as a code appears in the buffer, the processor executes an instruction that moves it from the buffer to the computer's memory. The monitor also has a buffer. Whenever the processor sends a code into this buffer, the corresponding character appears on the screen.

Other input devices are also used with monitors. For example, some terminals enable users to communicate with the computer by drawing pictures or diagrams directly on the screen with a light pen. Such units encode drawings directly from the monitor. *Pen-based computers* recognize hand printing and other marks made on the computer screen with an electronic pen. These lightweight, portable machines can be used to record data in situations where typing would be difficult.

A device called a *mouse* can be used to give commands to a computer. When this handheld box is moved on a flat surface, it causes a pointer to point at a specific instruction or piece of data on the monitor. With many software programs, the instruction appears as an *icon* (picture) rather than words. Clicking a button on the mouse causes the instruction to be carried out or the data to be moved or changed. The ability to give commands to a computer by selecting icons rather than by typing words is known as *graphical user interface*.

Modems are devices that allow computers to communicate with other computers by using telephone lines. A modem translates sounds into tones that represent binary numbers. It can send the tones over the phone lines to other modems.

Modems and telecommunications software make it possible to communicate with computer users throughout the world. The communication may take place directly, from one computer to another, or by way of an *on-line service*. On-line services provide dozens of electronic "meeting rooms" where individuals can discuss shared interests. The services also offer many other features, including news and weather bulletins, financial advice, shop-at-home services, and computer games. Most on-line services charge a fee based on how much time customers spend using the service.

Less elaborate than on-line services are computer *bulletin board services*, known as BBS's. Computer users can call a BBS and "post" announcements or messages on the electronic "bulletin board," where they can be read by other computer users.

Disk drives and tape drives perform many functions in the operation of the computer. One of these functions

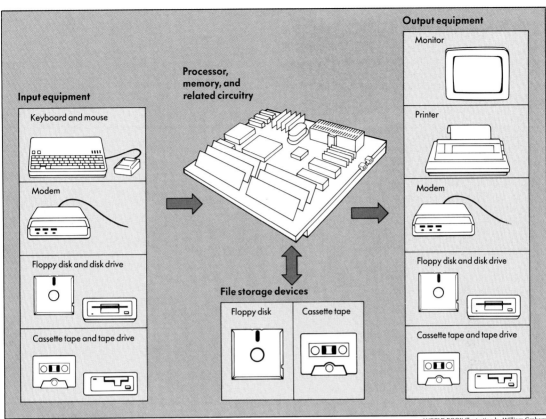

Input equipment

Keyboard and mouse

Modem

Floppy disk and disk drive

Cassette tape and tape drive

Processor,
memory, and
related circuitry

File storage devices

Floppy disk

Cassette tape

Output equipment

Monitor

Printer

Modem

Floppy disk and disk drive

Cassette tape and tape drive

WORLD BOOK illustration by William Graham

How a computer works

Computer systems come in a wide range of sizes and contain varying types of equipment. Nevertheless, all digital computers work essentially the same way. The diagram above illustrates the flow of information through a personal computer system. A human operator uses *input equipment* to provide data and instructions to the computer. The *processor* then performs calculations on the data, while the *memory* stores information during processing. The results then are sent to the *output equipment,* which presents them to the user. *File storage devices* enable information to be saved for future use.

is providing input in binary form. A disk drive is a machine that, among other things, reads 0's and 1's that are magnetically encoded onto disks. This information then goes to the buffer and the memory. A disk system provides quick and direct access to information anywhere on a disk. Flexible magnetic disks called *floppy disks* or *diskettes* are widely used to provide input to personal computers. *Hard disks* are used with larger computer systems, as well as with some personal computers.

Tape drives and magnetic tapes work in much the same way. However, a tape must be unwound or rewound to the location that contains the desired information. As a result, it takes longer to read information from a tape than from a disk.

Optical scanners also read data and instructions. Some scanners optically sense bar codes and other marks printed on identification and credit cards, grocery items, or documents. They then change these codes into electrical signals. Other scanners read information from *compact discs* or *optical disks.* Such disks contain digitally encoded data that can be read by a laser beam.

Other input devices include a *joystick* for moving figures about on a screen and a *graphic tablet* consisting of a pad and a special pen for producing illustrations.

Such devices are used with some personal computers. *Voice activators* enable computers to understand spoken words. Some mainframes obtain input by means of *card readers,* which take information from punched cards. The pattern of punches represents letters, numbers, and other symbols. Card readers once were popular, but today they are used less frequently.

Processing data. The processor, also called the *central processing unit* or *CPU,* is the heart of the computer. It manipulates the binary numbers that represent input according to a program, and converts them into binary numbers that represent the desired result.

Since the development of the *integrated circuit* in the 1960's, the processor in many computers is contained on a single microprocessor—a chip no larger than a fingernail (see **Integrated circuit**). All of the devices and wires that make up the processor are packed onto the surface of the chip. The chip is made of a *semiconductor* material, usually silicon (see **Semiconductor**). The circuitry on the chip contains many tiny devices called *transistors.* A transistor can either stop electric current or allow it to flow (see **Transistor**). The processor of a computer consists of two parts: (1) the *control unit* and (2) the *digital logic unit.*

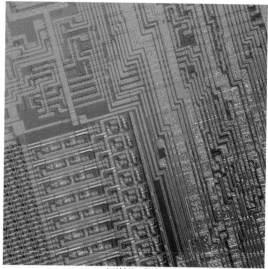

An integrated circuit contains all of the tiny devices that make up the processor on a single, tiny chip. This photo, taken through a microscope, shows a portion of such a chip.

The control unit directs and coordinates the operations of the entire computer according to instructions stored in the memory. The control unit must select the instructions in proper order because their sequence determines each step in the operations. Each set of instructions is expressed through a binary *operation code* that specifies exactly what must be done to complete a job. The operation code also provides information that tells where data for the processing operation are stored in the memory. The control unit interprets the instructions and relays commands to the logic unit. It also regulates the flow of data between the memory and the logic unit and routes processed information to output or file storage devices.

The digital logic unit, sometimes known as the *arithmetic/logic unit* or *ALU,* manipulates data received from the memory. It carries out all the functions and logic processes required to solve a problem. Computers use logic to perform arithmetical calculations—addition, subtraction, multiplication, and division.

In the digital logic unit, electronic circuits called *registers* temporarily store data from the memory. The data consist of electrical signals that represent binary digits. An electrical signal that has a low voltage level represents 0, and a signal that has a high voltage level represents 1.

To carry out an arithmetical calculation, the electrical signal for each input travels on a wire to another circuit. The answer comes out on a wire from the other end of the circuit. There are a number of basic circuits. Three such circuits are the *AND-gate,* the *OR-gate,* and the *NOT-gate* or *inverter.* The basic circuits are combined in different ways to perform arithmetic and logic operations with electrical signals that represent binary digits. For example, one combination of logic circuits performs addition. Another combination compares two numbers and then acts on the result of the comparison.

After an operation has been completed, the result

may be sent to the memory for storage until it is needed for another operation. In many cases, the result is sent to an output device or a file storage device.

Decoding the results and producing output. People use *output equipment* to get information from computers. Output equipment translates the electrical signals that represent binary numbers into a form that the user can understand. Often, the equipment also serves as input equipment. There are many types of output devices, such as terminals, printers, modems, and disk and tape drives.

Terminals, in addition to serving as input equipment, display output on the monitor. As information travels from the processor to the terminal, it moves through the buffer that was used in the input function. On a terminal, a user can receive data in the form of words, numbers, graphs, or pictures.

Printers produce output on paper. Like terminals, printers have buffers. To print a character, the processor puts the binary code for that character into the printer's buffer. The printer prints the character that corresponds to the code. Some printers operate much like typewriters. Others use heat, special chemicals, lasers, or combinations of these methods to place characters on paper.

Modems, which translate sounds into binary numbers during the input function, can also provide output by translating binary numbers into sounds. As a result, they enable users to receive information from distant computers.

Disk drives and tape drives also serve as both input and output equipment. Magnetic disks and tapes receive output in binary form. The drives interpret binary information from disks and tapes and present it to the user, often on a monitor. Output data presented on disks and tapes can easily be put back in the computer when needed.

Other output devices include *plotters, key punch machines,* and *audio devices.* Plotters use pens to create drawings, diagrams, and graphs on paper or clear plastic. Key punch machines record data by punching holes in cards or paper tape. Audio devices produce spoken words through a type of telephone or loudspeaker. Audio devices are becoming increasingly important.

Storing information. Computers can store information in two types of locations during the computing process—the memory and file storage devices. Memory, which is built into the computer, holds instructions and data during processing. File storage devices provide long-term storage of large amounts of information.

Memory, also called the *internal memory* or *main memory,* stores information and programs inside the computer. The memory receives data and instructions from an input device or a file storage device. It also receives information from the processor. The memory stores only the information that is currently needed by the processor. After the processor has finished with it, the information is transferred to file storage devices for permanent storage or sent directly to an output device for immediate use.

The devices and wires that make up the memory can be built from integrated circuits that fit onto one or more chips. The circuits, wires, and transistors form many *memory cells* capable of storing binary digits. These cells are arranged into groups. Each group is as-

BASIC language

```
10   SUM = 0

20   READ LENGTH

30   COUNTER = LENGTH

40   READ NEXT

50   SUM = SUM + NEXT

60   IF COUNTER = 1 GOTO 90

70   COUNTER = COUNTER − 1

80   GOTO 40

90   AVG = SUM/LENGTH

100  PRINT AVG

110  DATA 7, 35, 9000, 876, 29, 87, 90, 153

120  END
```

APL language

```
NUMBERS ← (35, 9000, 876, 29, 87, 90, 153)
LENGTH ← 7
SUM ← +/NUMBERS
ANSWER ← SUM ÷ LENGTH
```

Machine language

1. Load the first number on the list into a box called R1.
2. Load the length of the list into a box called R2.
3. If the number in R2 is 1, go to step 7.
4. Add the next number on the list to the number in box R1.
5. Subtract 1 from the number in box R2.
6. Go back to step 3.
7. Divide the number in box R1 by the length of the list.
8. The answer is now in box R1.

Programming languages enable people to write instructions that a computer can translate and execute. The languages allow the programmer to concentrate on the basic ideas of an operation, instead of on the details of what the machine must do. The BASIC and APL programs shown above both contain instructions for finding the average of a list of numbers. The steps in machine language show how a computer interprets and executes this type of program in any language.

signed an *address*—a number that makes it possible to locate specific pieces of information quickly.

File storage devices, also called *auxiliary storage units,* can store huge amounts of information for long periods of time. Such units are slower than the memory that is built into the computer. But they can hold much more information, and they are less expensive. For this reason, file storage devices are commonly used to store large quantities of data, programs, and processed information.

The most important file storage devices are magnetic disks and magnetic tapes. Disks and tapes are operated by disk drives and tape drives, which also serve as input and output equipment. These units encode data onto the surfaces of disks and tapes by turning the electrical signals that represent the 0's and 1's of binary code into magnetism. Every 0 is represented on the disk or tape by a little magnet pointing in a certain direction, and every 1 by a magnet pointing in the opposite direction. To read information from a disk or tape, the drive unit translates the magnetic signals into electrical signals and sends them to the memory. Magnetic disks and tapes are said to contain *random-access memory* (RAM) because the information on them can be searched or replaced with ease.

Some other types of file storage devices contain *read-only memory* (ROM)—information that the computer cannot change. ROM units may consist of a compact disc, a cartridge, or a silicon chip. They are used to store large databases and programs for computer games.

A popular method of storing large volumes of information is known as CD-ROM (*Compact Disc Read-Only Memory*). CD-ROM's store information for computers much as audio compact discs store music. The surface of the disc consists of small indentations and flat spaces that represent the 1's and 0's of binary code. CD-ROM's require special players to read them. A typical CD-ROM can store the equivalent of thousands of printed pages. Information on CD-ROM may include text, pictures, sound, and even moving pictures. Programs that combine several of these forms of information are called *multimedia programs.*

Programming a computer

Programming involves the preparation and writing of detailed instructions for a computer. These instructions tell the computer exactly what data to use and what sequence of operations to perform with the data. Without programs, a computer could not solve problems or deliver any other desired result.

Some people prepare their own computer programs. But in many cases, computer scientists and other computer specialists called *programmers* write instructions for computers. They use *programming languages* that consist of letters, words, and symbols, as well as rules for combining those elements.

A computer cannot work directly with a program written in a programming language. The instructions must be translated into a *machine language* composed of binary digits. These digits represent operation codes, memory addresses, and various symbols, such as plus and minus signs. Machine language is also known as *low-level language.*

Special programs called *compilers* and *assemblers* translate programming languages into machine language. Another special type of program called an *operating system* contains instructions for the operation of a computer. It controls the input and output devices, and it reads and responds to user commands. It also places programs and data into the memory and makes sure that the processor executes the right programs. Thus, the operating system combines the many separate parts of a computer into a single useful system.

Compilers, assemblers, and operating systems may be viewed as "smart programs" because they enable a computer to understand complicated instructions. The user communicates with the smart program, and the smart program communicates with the computer. A computer combined with a smart program acts like a different, smarter computer. This combination is called a *virtual machine.*

Preparing a program begins with a complete description of the job that the computer is to perform. This job description is obtained from the person for whom the program is being prepared, such as a business manager or an engineer. It explains what input data are needed, what computing must be done, and what the output should be. Computer programmers use the description to prepare diagrams and other pictorial aids that represent the steps needed to complete the task. The programmers may produce a diagram called a *systems flow chart* that shows how all the major parts of the job fit together systematically.

After a computer program is written, it is tested on the computer for mistakes. Computer experts refer to mistakes in programs as "bugs" and the testing of programs as "debugging."

A program generally is entered into a computer in what is known as an *interactive environment.* In such an environment, the programmer enters part of the program on a computer terminal. The computer's operating system responds immediately, telling the programmer how the computer will interpret each instruction. The programmer then can analyze each response. Programs that result from this interaction between the programmer and the computer generally are stored on some type of file storage device until needed.

Using programming languages. Computers appear to work directly with programming languages. But the smart program, not the computer, actually understands these languages. The smart program translates a program into machine language. The program then enters the translated version into the computer's memory. The processor reads and executes each translated instruction.

There are many different *high-level* programming languages. Some of them closely resemble the language of mathematics. Others enable programmers to use symbols and various everyday expressions, such as "READ," "PRINT," and "STOP." All high-level languages are designed to let the programmer concentrate on the basic ideas of a task rather than on the details.

The language that a programmer uses depends largely on the job to be done. If a task involves processing business data, the programmer would most likely use COBOL (*CO*mmon *B*usiness *O*riented *L*anguage). However, programming a computer to solve complicated scientific problems might require the use of a mathematically oriented language, such as FORTRAN (*FO*rmula *TRAN*slation).

Some high-level languages can be used for business, technical, or scientific programming. Such languages include APL (*A P*rogramming *L*anguage); C; and LISP (*LIS*t *P*rocessor).

Another commonly used programming language is BASIC (*B*eginner's *A*ll-purpose *S*ymbolic *I*nstruction *C*ode). This programming language is well suited for writing relatively simple programs for personal computers. Many elementary schools and high schools that offer a course in programming teach BASIC because it is easy to learn and to use. Pascal, named for the French mathematician and scientist Blaise Pascal, also is taught in many schools.

Some computer programs may be written in an *assembly language.* This kind of language is harder to use than a high-level language. The programmer must state

Computer firms manufacture hardware, software, and supplies. In this photo, quality control workers check computers on an assembly line.

each instruction very precisely, with much more detail than is needed when using a high-level language.

The computer industry

The manufacture, development, sales, and servicing of computer hardware and software make up one of the largest and most important industries in the world. Governments, institutions, and virtually all industries rely upon computers. By the year 2000, the computer industry is expected to be the second largest industry in the world in terms of annual revenue. Only agriculture will be larger.

The first commercial digital computers were manufactured in the 1950's. Throughout the 1950's, as the importance of computers increased, people's acceptance of them increased as well. More than 10,000 computers were in operation by 1961. Ten years later, the number of computers exceeded 100,000. By 1990, there were about 100 million data-processing computers—that is, computers that require input and output equipment—in operation worldwide.

The United States has the largest computer industry in the world, employing more than 1 million people. It also has more computers than any other country—more than 50 million, or about half the world's computers. Japan ranks second with more than 9 million computers, about 11 per cent of the world total. European countries account for nearly 25 per cent of all computers.

The economic growth of the computer industry has matched the increase in the number of computers. The United States produced about $1 billion worth of computers in 1958. Ten years later, the figure had reached $4.8 billion.

In the late 1970's, the computer industry's rate of growth increased dramatically. Advances in both computer technology and manufacturing technology enabled the United States to sell computers worth more than $30 billion in 1981. By 1990, the U.S. computer industry's annual revenues had topped $100 billion, and they continued to grow.

Manufacturing. From a few dozen companies in the early 1960's, the computer industry has grown to more than 10,000 firms around the world. These companies manufacture computers and such peripheral equipment as modems and printers. They also develop and publish software and provide various computer supplies, such as magnetic disks.

Some companies produce entire computer systems, ranging from personal computers to supercomputers. Many companies manufacture computer components, including processors. Some companies produce input and output equipment, such as terminals and printers. Other important products of the computer industry include equipment that increases a computer's abilities to provide visual and audio output, and the network boards and cables used to create computer networks.

The largest computer manufacturer in the United States—and the world—is International Business Machines Corporation (IBM). By the early 1990's, IBM's annual sales had reached nearly $65 billion. The Hewlett-Packard Company ranks second in the United States, followed closely by Digital Equipment Corporation (DEC). Both companies had more than $14 billion in annual sales in the early 1990's. Other leading U.S. computer

makers include Unisys, Apple Computer Incorporated, Compaq Computer Corporation, and Sun Microsystems Incorporated.

The largest computer manufacturer outside the United States is Japan's Fujitsu, followed closely by NEC Corporation, also of Japan. Each company had sales of more than $9 billion in 1988. The leading computer companies in Europe include Groupe Bull of France, Italy's Olivetti, and Siemens AG of Germany.

Research and development. The constant increase in computer power is a major reason for the computer industry's success. Such increases result from computer science research and development, which take place at businesses and universities throughout the world.

One area of great interest to computer researchers and manufacturers is memory speed and capacity. As software becomes more complex, it requires more computer memory in order to operate properly. At the same time, sophisticated software can manipulate increasingly large amounts of data, which occupy more space in the computer's memory.

The storage of information files is another important area of study. Researchers work to develop increasingly compact ways to store data, such as on magnetic disks, compact discs, or other devices.

Artificial intelligence is an exciting area of software research. Experts in this field design computer systems to perform tasks that appear to require intelligence, such as reasoning and learning. In this manner, artificial intelligence experts hope to increase the ability of computers to respond to problems in a "human" manner. See **Artificial intelligence.**

Sales. Computers are sold in a variety of ways. Large manufacturers of computers have teams of sales professionals. These teams call on corporations and institutions, analyze their needs, and provide the appropriate combination of hardware and software.

Another method of selling computers involves a *value-added reseller* (VAR). A VAR purchases computer

© Mark Sherman, Bruce Coleman Inc.

A repair specialist services a personal computer, *above.* Many computer makers and dealers provide repair services.

systems and components from a variety of sources. It then sells the finished products to computer users.

Retail outlets play an increasingly important role in the sale of personal computers. Computer stores, mail-order houses, and general merchandise stores also sell many computers.

Service and repair. Because people depend on their computers, it is important to have the machines serviced periodically and repaired promptly when necessary. Many computer manufacturers offer service contracts that provide for regular maintenance and prompt repairs. When a large computer system breaks down, service technicians must visit the computer itself. Some large businesses and institutions have their own computer maintenance staffs.

Careers. There are many career opportunities in the computer industry. Computer engineers are probably the most technically specialized computer experts. Hardware engineers design the circuits that are engraved on chips, and they develop and design the wiring that lets information flow smoothly through the computer. Engineers also design the technical aspects of memory, file storage, and peripheral equipment.

Computer programmers write the instructions that make computers operate properly. Systems analysts determine the most efficient use of computers for a particular situation. They study entire computer systems—hardware and software—and the purpose a computer is intended to serve.

Software publishers make up another career area. People in this field issue programs, write and edit instruction manuals, and provide technical services for customers.

Many career opportunities in computers exist outside the computer industry itself. For example, data processors enter information into computers. Workers in many industries oversee the computers that control machines.

Some of the industry's most successful individuals are self-taught. But most computer careers call for a college degree. College courses that help prepare students for careers in computers include programming, electrical engineering, systems analysis, and data processing.

The development of the computer

The ideas and inventions of many engineers, mathematicians, and scientists led to the development of the computer. The ancient abacus served as the earliest sort of calculating device. But its use was limited by the need to move each counter individually (see **Abacus**).

Early calculating devices. The first true calculating machines were developed in the 1600's. In 1642, the French mathematician, scientist, and philosopher Blaise Pascal invented the first automatic calculator. The device performed addition and subtraction by means of a set of wheels linked to each other by gears. The first wheel represented the numbers 1 to 10, the second wheel represented 10's, the third stood for 100's, and so on. When the first wheel was turned 10 notches, a gear moved the second wheel forward a single notch. The other wheels became engaged in a similar manner.

During the early 1670's, the German mathematician Gottfried Wilhelm von Leibniz extended the usefulness of the calculator that Pascal had invented. Leibniz's improvements included gear and wheel arrangements that made multiplication and division possible.

Leibniz also sought a counting system that would be easier for a machine to handle than the decimal system. He developed the binary system of mathematics in the late 1600's. Binary mathematics uses only the 0 and the 1, arranging them to represent all numbers.

An important contribution to the development of binary mathematics was made in the mid-1800's by George Boole, an English logician and mathematician. Boole used the binary system to invent a new type of mathematics. *Boolean algebra* and *Boolean logic* perform complex mathematical and logical operations on the symbols 0 and 1. Thus, a mechanical representation of binary mathematics would require the representation of only those two digits. This advance shaped the development of computer logic and computer languages.

Early punched-card computing devices. A French textile weaver named Joseph Marie Jacquard made the next great contribution to the development of the computer. In the weaving process, needles directed thread to produce patterns. In 1801, Jacquard invented the *Jacquard loom,* which used punched cards to automate this process for the first time. The cards had patterns of holes punched in them, and were placed between the rising needles and the thread. The presence or absence of a hole could be compared to the two digits of the binary system. Where there were holes, the needles rose and met the thread. Where there were no holes, the needles were blocked. By changing cards and alternating the patterns of punched holes, it became possible to mechanically create complex woven patterns.

The punched cards of the Jacquard loom inspired the English mathematician Charles Babbage. During the 1830's, Babbage developed the idea of a mechanical computer that he called an *analytical engine.* He worked on the machine for almost 40 years. When performing complex computations or a series of calculations, the analytical engine would store completed sets of punched cards for use in later operations. Babbage's analytical engine contained all of the basic elements of an automatic computer—storage, working memory, a system for moving between the two, and an input device. But the technology of Babbage's time was not advanced enough to provide the precision parts he needed to construct the machine, and he lacked funding for the project. Babbage, like others of his time, also lacked an understanding of the nature and use of electricity.

The first successful computer. In 1888, American inventor and businessman Herman Hollerith devised a punched card system, including the punching equipment, for tabulating the results of the United States census (see **Census**). Hollerith's machines used electrically charged nails that, when passed through a hole punched in a card, created a circuit. The circuits registered on another part of the machine, where they were read and recorded. Hollerith's machines tabulated the results of the 1890 census, making it the fastest and most economical census to date. In a single day, 56 of these machines could tabulate census information about more than 6 million people.

Hollerith's tabulator achieved widespread success. Governments, institutions, and industries found uses for the machine. In 1896, Hollerith founded the Tabulating Machine Company. He continued to improve his ma-

The punched-card tabulating machine invented by Herman Hollerith was the first successful computer. It was used to compute the results of the 1890 United States census, *above*.

chines during the following years. In 1911, he sold his share of the company. Its name was changed to the Computing-Tabulating-Recording Company (C-T-R). In 1924, the name was changed to International Business Machines Corporation (IBM).

The first analog computer. Vannevar Bush, an American electrical engineer, worked to develop a computer that would help scientists. In 1930, he built a device called a *differential analyzer* to solve differential equations. This machine was the first reliable analog computer. It derived measurements from the movements of its gears and shafts.

The first electronic computers. Some scientists and engineers saw greater computing potential in electronics. The first special-purpose electronic digital computer was constructed in 1939 by John V. Atanasoff, an American mathematician and physicist. In 1944, Howard Aiken, a Harvard University professor, built another

early form of digital computer, which he called the Mark I. The operations of this machine were controlled chiefly by electromechanical *relays* (switching devices).

In 1946, two engineers at the University of Pennsylvania, J. Presper Eckert, Jr., and John William Mauchly, built the first general-purpose electronic digital computer. They called it ENIAC (*E*lectronic *N*umerical *I*ntegrator *A*nd *C*omputer). ENIAC contained about 18,000 vacuum tubes, which replaced the relays that had controlled the operation of Mark I. The machine weighed more than 30 tons (27 metric tons), occupied more than 1,500 square feet (140 square meters) of floor space, and consumed 150 kilowatts of electricity during operation. ENIAC operated about 1,000 times as fast as the Mark I. It could perform about 5,000 additions and 1,000 multiplications per second. ENIAC also could store parts of its programming.

Although ENIAC performed its work rapidly, programming the huge machine took a great deal of time. Eckert and Mauchly next worked on developing a computer that could store even more of its programming. They worked with John von Neumann, a Hungarian-born American mathematician. Von Neumann helped assemble all available knowledge of how the logic of computers should operate. He also helped outline how stored programming would improve performance. In 1951, a computer based on the work of the three men became operational. It was called EDVAC (*E*lectronic *D*iscrete *V*ariable *A*utomatic *C*omputer). EDVAC strongly influenced the design of later computers.

Also in 1951, Eckert and Mauchly invented a more advanced computer called UNIVAC I (*UNI*Versal *A*utomatic *C*omputer). Within a few years, UNIVAC I became the first commercially available computer. Unlike earlier computers, UNIVAC I handled both numbers and alphabetical characters equally well. It also was the first computer system in which the operations of the input and output equipment were separated from those of the computing unit. UNIVAC I used vacuum tubes to perform arithmetic and memory-switching functions.

The first UNIVAC I was installed at the U.S. Bureau of the Census in June 1951. The following year, another UNIVAC I was used to tabulate the results of the United States presidential election. Based on available data,

ENIAC, completed in 1946, was the first general-purpose electronic digital computer. The enormous machine was invented by J. Presper Eckert, Jr., *front left*, and John W. Mauchly, *center.*

UNIVAC I accurately predicted the election of President Dwight D. Eisenhower less than 45 minutes after the polls closed.

The miniaturization of computer components.
The invention of the transistor in 1947 led to the production of faster and more reliable electronic computers. Transistors control the flow of electric current in electronic equipment. They soon replaced the bulkier, less reliable vacuum tubes. In 1958, Control Data Corporation introduced the first fully transistorized computer, designed by American engineer Seymour Cray. IBM introduced its first transistorized computers in 1959.

Miniaturization continued with the development of the integrated circuit in the early 1960's. An integrated circuit contains thousands of transistors and other tiny parts on a small chip. This device enabled engineers to design both minicomputers and high-speed mainframes with tremendous memory capacities.

Despite the shrinking size of their components, most computers remained relatively large and expensive. But dependence on computers increased dramatically. By the late 1960's, many large businesses relied on computers. Many companies linked their computers together into networks, making it possible for different offices to share information.

During the 1960's, computer technology improved rapidly. Different kinds of circuits were placed on silicon chips. Some of the circuits contained the computer's logic. Other chips held memory. By the early 1970's, the entire workings of a computer could be placed on a handful of chips. As a result, smaller computers became possible. The central chip that controlled the computer became known as a *microprocessor.*

The personal computer.
The first personal computer, the Altair, was introduced in 1975. Only electronics hobbyists bought these computers.

In 1977, two American students, Steven P. Jobs and Stephen G. Wozniak, founded the Apple Computer Company and introduced the Apple II personal computer. The Apple II was much less expensive than mainframes. As a result, computers became available to people other than computer specialists and technicians. Personal computers were purchased by small and medium-sized businesses that could not afford mainframes or did not need the immense computing power

Toshiba Corporation

A notebook computer is a portable computer that usually weighs less than 5 pounds (2.3 kilograms). A salesperson, *above,* uses a notebook computer to show products to a customer.

that mainframes provided. Millions of individuals, families, and schools also bought them.

In 1981, IBM entered the personal computer market with its PC. The machine was even more successful than the Apple II. Apple scored another success in 1984 with the introduction of its Macintosh, a powerful, easy-to-use desktop computer.

As computer power increased, so did computer speed. These increases were accompanied by a steady reduction in both size and cost. Modern personal computers are more powerful than UNIVAC I and can be purchased for less than $1,000.

Computers of the future.
Tomorrow's computers will be increasingly powerful. Computer researchers continue to seek ways to develop faster and more powerful machines and software. For example, experimental computers called *optical processors* use beams of laser light, rather than electric current, to process data. Many scientists believe that optical computers will someday work much faster than electronic ones. Much software research focuses on the development of new virtual-reality programs to provide increasingly realistic simulated experiences. Computer experts predict that virtual reality will play a large role in education and training as well as offer dramatic possibilities for entertainment. Much software research also focuses on the further development of artificial intelligence, which is intended to help computers make decisions rather than simply to manipulate data. One type of artificial intelligence, the expert system, translates patterns of experience into software. An expert system responds to input by asking questions and providing responses. In this manner, it constantly narrows the field of inquiry until a solution is achieved.

Much effort also is being devoted to making computers smaller. In the near future, most experts feel that computers will continue to be built from integrated circuits. But some scientists foresee the production of biological computers, which will be grown rather than manufactured. In addition, some experts believe that computer technology will develop methods of storing data on individual molecules. A molecular storage system could contain all of the knowledge of the human race in a space smaller than a paperback book.

Problems of the computer age

Because computers provide such convenient storage for large amounts of information, less and less information is stored on paper. Much of the convenience of computers stems from their ability to form networks by means of telephone lines. But a computer that makes up part of a network resembles a room with many doors. Intruders who slip through these "doors" are difficult to trace. For this reason, computer designers work to safeguard stored information from unauthorized access, as well as from system breakdown or failure.

Computers and privacy.
Many people fear that their right to privacy is threatened by the possible misuse or unauthorized disclosure of information in computer databases. Databases often contain private and personal information, such as medical, banking, or tax records. Other databases pertain to business plans or inventions that a company must conceal from competing companies. Still other databases store top-secret military infor-

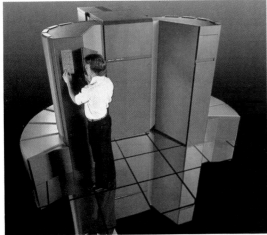

Cray Research, Inc.

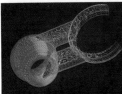

© Dale E. Boyer, Photo Researchers

A supercomputer can solve large, complicated numerical problems with amazing speed. The Cray supercomputer shown above generated a detailed image of part of the main engine of a space shuttle, *left*.

mation or other kinds of data important to a nation's security. Today, laws control the disclosure of data.

Computers and security. Computer operating systems are designed to prevent unauthorized entry into a computer, but computer crimes sometimes occur. Industrial spies and thieves often use telephone lines to gain access to computers. Some of these criminals steal or change the information in a computer database. Others steal money by using the capability of computers to transfer funds electronically from one account to another. Major problems can result if someone obtains illegal access to secret information in government or corporate databases. Sometimes, people within an organization commit computer crimes. Other crimes are committed by outsiders who create chaos by breaking into computer systems.

In the late 1980's, computer experts became aware of a dangerous type of program called a *computer virus.* A computer virus is designed to do mischief, sometimes by deleting or changing information and sometimes by simply inserting a message. A virus eventually enters a computer's operating system. It spreads by rapidly making copies of itself, thus "infecting" the other computer systems in a network. This process can quickly overload huge computer networks.

Various methods help safeguard computer systems and databases. Protective measures are built into many computer operating systems to prevent access by invaders. Many computers require a user to enter a secret password. Some systems automatically scramble information so that it can only be decoded by authorized personnel. Careful protection of these passwords and codes helps decrease the likelihood of illegal access. Antivirus programs are available to prevent computer viruses from doing mischief.

Other problems. Computers are valuable in many ways. But if a computer breaks or is damaged, the people who rely on it face great difficulties. Until the computer is fixed, these people may be worse off than if they never had a computer at all. For example, information may be lost if a computer system suffers damage in a natural disaster, such as a fire or flood. Computer breakdowns and faulty programming in business organizations delay transactions, disrupt work, and create inconveniences for consumers. An undetected computer malfunction that occurs at an air traffic control center could cause a collision. A computer failure at a national defense installation could have even more serious consequences.

Computers, together with their programs, are the most complicated machines in history—and, arguably, the most useful. As computers become more powerful and widespread, computer education must continue to increase as well.   David Gelernter and Keith Ferrell

Related articles in *World Book* include:

Animation (Computer animation)
Artificial intelligence
Automation
Babbage, Charles
Bar coding
Bush, Vannevar
Calculator
Computer chip
Copyright
Database
Desktop publishing
Electronics
Guided missile (Kinds of guidance systems)
Hopper, Grace M.
Information retrieval
Information science
Management information system
Multimedia
Photocomposition
Railroad (At interchanges)
Simon, Herbert A.
Spreadsheet
Systems analysis
Telephone (Routing the call; Computer services)
Turing, Alan M.
Virtual reality
Word processing

Outline

I. **The importance of the computer**
  A. Solving numerical problems
  B. Storing and retrieving information
  C. Creating and displaying documents and pictures
  D. Other uses
II. **Basic principles of computers**
  A. How a computer operates
  B. Computer hardware and software
III. **Kinds of computers**
  A. Embedded computers
  B. Personal computers and workstations
  C. Mainframes
IV. **How a computer works**
  A. Entering and encoding data and instructions
  B. Processing data
  C. Decoding the results and producing output
  D. Storing information
V. **Programming a computer**
  A. Preparing a program
  B. Using programming languages
VI. **The computer industry**
  A. Manufacturing   C. Sales
  B. Research and   D. Service and repair
     development   E. Careers
VII. **The development of the computer**
VIII. **Problems of the computer age**
  A. Computers and privacy   C. Other problems
  B. Computers and security

Questions

What is an expert system?
How does the binary system differ from the decimal system?
What role does the digital logic unit play in processing?
How do scientists use computers to develop theories?

What is an operating system?
How has the transistor affected computer technology?
What is a computer virus?
How does a modem work?
Why can mainframes satisfy the needs of many users at once?
Why did the computer industry's rate of growth increase dramatically during the late 1970's?

Reading and Study Guide

See *Computer* in the Research Guide/Index, Volume 22, for a *Reading and Study Guide.*

Additional resources

Level I

D'Ignazio, Fred. *Messner's Introduction to the Computer.* Messner, 1983.
White, Jack R. *How Computers Really Work.* Dodd, 1986.
Wicks, Keith. *Working with Computers.* Facts on File, 1986.

Level II

Freedman, Alan. *The Computer Glossary.* 5th ed. AMACOM, 1991.
Parker, R. Wayne. *The Computer Buyer's Handbook.* Fast Forward, 1991.
Trainor, Timothy N. *Computer Concepts and Applications.* Rev. ed. Mitchell Pub., 1987. Originally titled *Computer Literacy— Concepts and Applications.*

Computer chip is a tiny piece of material, usually silicon, that contains a complex electronic circuit. These chips are essential in modern computers and a variety of other electronic devices. The circuit on a computer chip, sometimes called an *integrated circuit,* is made up of electronic components built into the chip. Most chips are no larger than a fingernail.

There are two main kinds of computer chips: (1) *microprocessors,* which carry out the instructions that make up computer programs, and (2) *memory chips,* which hold computer programs and other data. Memory chips are used primarily in computers. Microprocessors are used in computers and hundreds of other products. A microprocessor serves as the "heart" of every personal computer. Larger computers have more than one such chip. Other products controlled by microprocessors include video games, digital watches, microwave ovens, and some telephones.

Structure. The body of most chips is made of silicon. This material is used because it is a *semiconductor.* In its pure form, silicon does not conduct electricity at room temperature. But if certain impurities are added to silicon, it can carry an electric current. Manufacturers "dope" silicon chips with such impurities as boron and phosphorus. The doped regions form the chip's electronic components, which control the electric signals carried on the chip. The kind and arrangement of the impurities determine how each component controls signals. Most components serve as switches called *transistors.* Others serve mainly as *capacitors,* which store an electric charge; *diodes,* which prevent current from flowing in one direction but not the other; and *resistors,* which control voltage.

Some chips contain millions of components. Certain parts of these components measure less than 1 *micrometer* (0.001 millimeter) across. Manufacturers create thin lines of metal—usually aluminum—on the chip to connect these tiny components.

External connections. Most chips connect with other devices by means of a container called a *package.* One common type of container is a *dual in-line package*

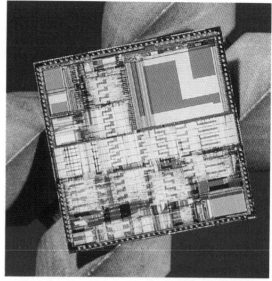

Tom Way, International Business Machines Corporation

A microprocessor is a chip that performs computer operations and holds some memory. This microprocessor measures 12.7 millimeters ($\frac{1}{2}$ inch) on a side.

(DIP), an oblong box about 2 inches (5 centimeters) in length. Two rows of metal pins extend downward from the box, one from each long side. Each pin is connected by a wire to an electric terminal on the chip.

In a computer, the packaged chip is mounted on a circuit board. Printed circuits on the board connect the package—and thus the chip—with other devices.

Characteristics of microprocessors. Microprocessors perform essential computer operations. A microprocessor obtains instructions and data from an external memory device; performs arithmetic and logic operations with these data and data contained in its own memory circuits; and, after obtaining a result, moves the calculated data back to the external memory device.

Tom Way, International Business Machines Corporation

Chips for the main control board of a personal computer are mounted inside square and oblong packages. Each chip is wired to metal pins that electrically connect its package to the main control board.

Word length. Instructions and other data handled by computers are in the form of "words." A word is a group of *bits.* A bit is a *binary digit*—a 0 or a 1. Computers operate on the basis of bits. For example, the presence of an electric charge in a capacitor can represent a "1" and the absence of a charge can represent a "0."

The maximum word length that a microprocessor can handle helps determine how rapidly it can operate. The earliest microprocessors used 4-bit words. As microprocessors advanced, they were able to handle longer words—usually made up of 8, 16, 32, or 64 bits.

Clock speed is another important characteristic of a microprocessor. Bits travel through a computer in pulses of electric current that occur at regular intervals called *clock cycles.* Today's microprocessors run at speeds of more than one million cycles per second, or 1 megahertz (MHz).

Instruction sets. There are two basic types of microprocessors: (1) complex instruction set computer (CISC), and (2) reduced instruction set computer (RISC). The microprocessors used in the first computers were the kind now known as CISC. Since about 1986, RISC chips have appeared in certain computers called workstations.

A CISC chip has a very large instruction set—that is, it has many ways to carry out each instruction. For example, it may be able to add two numbers by following any one of 10 procedures. These procedures take various numbers of clock cycles. The number of cycles depends on such factors as the size of the numbers to be added and the location of the numbers in the computer system. A RISC chip uses instructions that are always the same length and can be executed in one clock cycle. By using its special circuits, a RISC chip can execute many times more instructions per second than can a comparable CISC chip.

Memory chips. Most computers use two types of memory chips: (1) read-only memory (ROM), and (2) random access memory (RAM). A ROM chip retains its stored memory even when the computer is turned off, but the computer user cannot change the stored memory. In contrast, the user can change the memory stored in a RAM chip, but the chip holds its memory only as long as power is on.

There are two main kinds of RAM: static RAM (SRAM) and dynamic RAM (DRAM). SRAM holds its memory until the microprocessor changes it, but DRAM can only hold its memory for a few thousandths of a second. Therefore, a DRAM chip must be *refreshed* at least 100 times per second, or it will lose its data. To refresh a DRAM, the computer removes the information from each group of *cells* (memory storage units) in the chip, then puts the same information back. This may seem wasteful. But the time and expense involved are more than made up for by the amount of memory that can be fit into a small space on a DRAM and the cost of these devices. Most personal computers use DRAM's because they are inexpensive to make and can store much memory.

Researchers have developed memory chips with useful features of both ROM and RAM chips. These *erasable ROM* chips can be erased and reprogrammed, yet they do not lose their memory when the computer is turned off.

One successful design is the electrically, selectively erasable, programmable ROM (EEPROM) chip. A pulse of electric current can erase all the memory in a selected area of the chip. The user can then reprogram this area as if it were part of a RAM chip.

Chip manufacture. The manufacture of a computer chip begins with a wafer of doped silicon. The wafer measures from 1 to 8 inches (2.5 to 20 centimeters) in diameter. A photographic process reduces a large master design for the integrated circuit to microscopic size. Technicians use these microscopic designs, called *masks,* as stencils to make hundreds of chips on one wafer. After the wafer has been processed, it is divided into individual chips.

History. The first chips were patented in 1959 by two Americans—Jack Kilby, an engineer, and Robert Noyce, a physicist—who worked independently. During the 1960's, scientists developed chips for guided missiles and satellites. Engineers soon began to build smaller and faster computers by using chips in place of conventional circuits. The first microprocessors were produced in 1971 for use in desktop calculators.   Charles Melear

See also **Capacitor; Computer; Electronics; Transistor.**

Computer graphics are images created by a computer. These images include diagrams, cartoon animations, and even highly realistic pictures. The process by which computers draw, color, shade, and manipulate images is also known as computer graphics. Computer graphics enable us to gather, display, and understand information quickly and effectively. Computer graphics can even produce images of objects and processes that we have no other way of seeing, such as the inside of a molecule or the operation of a black hole.

Computer graphics have numerous uses in a wide variety of fields. Businesses follow sales from charts and graphs made by computers. Computer graphics help engineers create and test designs for such products as automobiles and aircraft. Through computer graphics, architects can view building designs drawn in three dimensions from any angle. Scientists use computer graphics to design new drug molecules, track weather systems, and test theories that describe how galaxies develop. Physicians use computer images of the inside

Thomas J. Watson Research Center

Using complex geometric shapes called *fractals,* a computer graphics program can create forms—like these mountains—that resemble the irregular shapes found in nature.

of the body to locate tumors and other disorders and plan treatment. Computer graphics are also used in art, in the production of cartoons and special effects in motion pictures, and in video games.

Computer graphics are created on a computer display screen. The screen consists of thousands of tiny dots called *picture elements,* or *pixels.* You can see individual pixels by looking closely at the letters that appear on a computer screen. A computer can turn each pixel on and off like a light bulb to make a pattern.

All computers need a *program* that tells them what to do. A computer graphics program directs the drawing on a computer's screen. The program may generate the image itself or it may copy an image from another source. For example, a program that draws molecules might start by solving equations that describe molecular structure. It can then use the solutions to display the shape of a molecule. But a program that copies a photograph might first convert points on the image into a list of numbers. The numbers can then instruct the computer which pixels to turn on and off.   A. K. Dewdney

See also **Computer** (Creating and displaying documents and pictures); **Virtual reality.**

Computerized tomography (CT), *tuh MAHG ruh fee,* is an X-ray system used to produce images of various parts of the body, such as the head, chest, and abdomen. Doctors use CT images to help diagnose and treat diseases. The technique is also called *computed tomography* or *computerized axial tomography* (*CAT*).

To produce a CT image, the patient lies on a table that passes through a circular scanning machine called a *gantry.* The table is positioned so that the organ to be scanned lies in the center of the gantry. A tube on the gantry beams X rays through the patient's body and into special detectors that analyze the image produced. The gantry rotates around the patient to obtain many images from different angles. A computer then processes the information from the detectors to produce a cross-sectional image on a video screen. By moving the table

in the gantry, doctors can obtain scans at different levels of the same organ or even the entire body.

Sometimes an iodine solution, called a *contrast agent,* is injected into the body to make certain organs or disease processes show up clearly in the CT scan. For example, the patient drinks a barium mixture to outline the inner surfaces of the stomach and bowel.

Doctors use CT scans to diagnose many conditions, such as tumors, infections, blood clots, and broken bones. CT also may be used to guide a biopsy needle into diseased tissue. In addition, it assists in treating some diseases that might otherwise require surgery. For example, doctors can use a CT scan to guide *catheters* (small tubes) to an abscess in the body and drain pus from the infected area.   P. Andrea Lum

See also **Radiology; X rays.**

COMSAT. See **Communications Satellite Corporation.**

Comstock Law is a United States law that prohibits the mailing of indecent materials or of information about birth control or abortion. The law, passed in 1873, is named for Anthony Comstock, a controversial reformer who crusaded for its passage.

The legislators who enacted the Comstock Law probably intended that it be used to prosecute pornography distributors in criminal court. Instead, the law was used to support a system of administrative censorship by postal officials, without going to court. For about 85 years, postal officials used the Comstock Law, sometimes very loosely, to censor mail. If post office inspectors decided a book, picture, or other mail was indecent, they seized all copies and refused to deliver them.

Since the mid-1900's, the Supreme Court of the United States has narrowed the legal definition of pornography in the process of interpreting the First Amendment to the Constitution. The court also has placed constitutional limits on censorship. Although the Comstock Law is still in force, most legal experts think the Supreme Court would find the system of postal censorship unconstitutional if it were challenged. As a result, the U.S. Postal Service almost never uses the law to seize mail, and the Department of Justice rarely tries to enforce the act in criminal court.   James C. N. Paul

See also **Obscenity and pornography.**

Comstock Lode was the greatest silver-mining center in the United States during the 1800's. Its rich deposits, which included valuable supplies of gold, lay in west-central Nevada. Mines on the Comstock Lode flourished from 1859 to 1865 and again from 1873 to 1882. During this second period, a body of ore known as the Big Bonanza produced silver and gold ore worth more than $100 million. The mining area was named for Henry T. P. Comstock, a prospector who took credit for its discovery. But other miners really found the ore first.

The immense wealth of the Comstock Lode drew thousands of people to western Nevada. Virginia City developed near the mines and quickly became one of the most prosperous cities in the West. The American author Mark Twain wrote about this bustling mining center in his book *Roughing It* (1872).   Duane A. Smith

See also **Nevada** (History); **Virginia City.**

Comte, *kawnt,* **Auguste,** *oh GOOST* (1798-1857), was a French social thinker and philosopher. He founded the philosophy of *positivism,* and originated a concept of social science known as *sociology.*

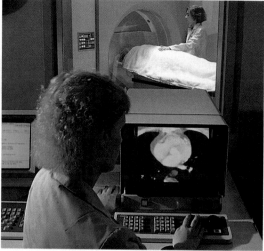

WORLD BOOK photo by Robert Frerck

A CT scanner makes a cross-sectional view of body parts. A scanning machine, *background,* shoots X-rays through the body from many angles. A computer forms an image on a screen.

Comte sought to discover the laws that he believed governed the evolution of the mind. In his six-volume work, *The Course of Positive Philosophy* (1830-1842), he framed his "law of the three states." This law advanced the idea that people try to understand phenomena in three ways. Comte believed that people first seek a *theological* (supernatural) explanation; then a *metaphysical* (abstract) explanation; and finally a *positive* explanation. The positive explanation is derived from an objective examination of the phenomena. Comte believed that students should concern themselves only with phenomena that have an objective, "positive," existence. This belief forms a basis of positivism.

Comte regarded all social thought as an interrelated whole, the laws of which can be found by assembling what he considered the facts. His ideas have influenced students of historical and social theory, and of criminology, and such authors as Herbert Spencer and John Stuart Mill, who were seeking a "science of society." Comte was born at Montpellier. Stephen A. Erickson

See also **Positivism; Sociology** (History).

Conakry, *KAHN uh kree* (pop. 705,280), is the capital, largest city, and chief port of Guinea. For location, see **Guinea** (map). The oldest part of Conakry lies on the island of Tombo at the tip of the Camayenne (Kaloum) Peninsula. This area features low, whitewashed buildings with red-tiled roofs. The newer part of Conakry is on the mainland. It has modern office buildings and extensive areas of inexpensive housing. Conakry is a shipping and government administration center. Its products include beverages and processed foods.

Conakry began as a small trading village in the mid-1400's. France took control of Guinea in the late 1800's. France made Conakry a major port and administration center. Guinea gained independence from France in 1958. Since then, Conakry has grown rapidly, and overcrowding has become a problem. A. G. Hopkins

Conant, *KOH nuhnt,* **James Bryant** (1893-1978), was an American chemist, educator, and government official. He was a pioneer in the development of organic chemistry theory. As a professor at Harvard University, Conant conducted research that led to an understanding of the structure and function of chlorophyll and hemoglobin molecules.

From 1933 to 1953, Conant served as president of Harvard University, where he introduced various educational and institutional reforms. He promoted a program of common core general education for all students at Harvard. During World War II (1939-1945), he chaired the National Defense Research Committee and worked as a scientific adviser on the project that developed the atomic bomb.

From 1953 to 1957, Conant was United States ambassador to West Germany. He later returned to the United States and conducted a study of the country's high schools. His recommendations brought changes in the administration of secondary education and in the teaching of mathematics, science, and foreign languages.

Conant was born in Dorchester, Mass. His autobiography, *My Several Lives: Memoirs of a Social Inventor,* was published in 1970. Martin D. Saltzman

Concentration camp is a place where people are imprisoned, and in some cases even tortured and killed, without legal proceedings. People are placed in concentration camps because of their political views, religious convictions, ethnic background, or social attitudes. The term *concentration camp* was first used by British authorities in 1900 to describe open-air prison camps Britain had set up in southern Africa during the Boer War (1899-1902). But the best-known concentration camps were those established by the Nazis, first in Germany and then, during World War II, throughout Nazi-occupied Europe. The Nazis built dozens of camps to terrorize, enslave, torture, and murder people, most of whom were Jews.

The first Nazi concentration camps were organized within weeks after Hitler came to power in January 1933. The first permanent camp was set up at Dachau near Munich, Germany, in March 1933. All other Nazi camps were modeled after the one at Dachau.

Before World War II began in 1939, the Nazis used concentration camps to terrorize and intimidate people. But after 1940, they used the camps to exploit and murder their prisoners. In 1941, the Nazis decided to murder all Jews under their control in Europe. A number of camps in Germany and eastern Europe served as killing factories, or extermination camps.

The most notorious extermination camp was at Auschwitz in Poland. About $2\frac{1}{2}$ million people were killed at Auschwitz. There, the Nazis used special gas chambers to kill as many as 2,000 people at a time. The bodies of the victims were burned in crematoriums. Thousands of other prisoners in Nazi camps died of starvation and disease. Still others died from experiments performed on them by Nazi physicians.

Allied forces liberated the Nazi camps in 1945. The remains of thousands of victims were discovered. No one knows the total number murdered in the camps, but the victims included about 4 million Jews. Altogether, Hitler's forces murdered at least 11 million people, including about 6 million Jews. Charles W. Sydnor, Jr.

See also **Auschwitz; Belsen; Buchenwald; Dachau; Holocaust.**

Concertina, *KAHN suhr TEE nuh,* is a musical instrument in which metal reeds are made to vibrate by air pressure produced by opening and closing a bellows. Small keys or plugs in the end plates of the instrument open valves that control the reeds. The treble concertina used the most is a small, six-sided instrument with a range of about $3\frac{1}{2}$ octaves. There are also tenor, bass,

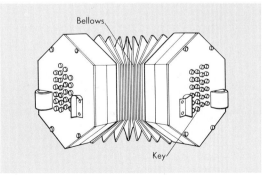

A concertina consists of metal reeds inside a bellows. Keys or plugs in the end plates open valves that control the reeds.

and contrabass concertinas. The British inventor Sir Charles Wheatstone patented the concertina in 1829.

Valerie Woodring Goertzen

See also **Wheatstone, Sir Charles**.

Concerto, *kuhn CHEHR toh,* is a musical composition played by one or more solo instruments and an orchestra. A concerto resembles a symphony in form. But most concertos have only three *movements* (sections), and most symphonies have four.

The concerto developed from the *concerto grosso* of the late 1600's and early 1700's. The concerto grosso featured a small group of soloists playing with an orchestra. The most famous of these are Johann Sebastian Bach's six *Brandenburg Concertos* (completed 1721).

During the late 1700's, Wolfgang Amadeus Mozart wrote concertos in three movements. In the first movement, the orchestra states many of the work's themes before the soloist begins. Near the end of the movement is the *cadenza,* in which the soloist plays alone and displays his or her technical skill. In the second and third movements, the soloist and orchestra play together. The second movement is slow, and the third is fast.

During the 1800's, two types of concertos became popular. One was the *symphonic concerto,* in which the soloist and orchestra participate equally. Ludwig van Beethoven and Johannes Brahms composed this type. The other type was the *virtuoso concerto,* in which the orchestra accompanies the soloist. Niccolò Paganini, Franz Liszt, and Frédéric Chopin wrote virtuoso concertos. Composers of the 1900's generally have followed Mozart's form. These composers include Béla Bartók, Sergei Prokofiev, and Igor Stravinsky.   R. M. Longyear

Conch, *kahngk* or *kahnch,* is any large sea snail with a heavy, spiral shell. Conchs live mainly on the floor of tropical seas. There are many kinds of conchs. But in North America, the word *conch* most commonly means the *queen conch,* also called the *pink conch.* This conch ranges from Bermuda, the Bahamas, and the Florida Keys to the West Indies. It grows to a length of about 1 foot (30 centimeters).

Jane Burton, Bruce Coleman Ltd.

A conch is a large sea snail with a spiral shell. The *queen conch, above,* lives on the floor of the Atlantic Ocean from Bermuda to the West Indies.

The queen conch has a soft body with a long, muscular organ called a *foot.* It uses its *operculum*—a pointed, hornlike part at the back end of the foot—to pull itself along. The shell varies widely in color—from white through pink, yellow, and orange—and has hornlike knobs. The queen conch feeds on seaweed and plant fragments on the sea floor. After mating, the female lays a string of about 500,000 eggs. The eggs hatch after a few days. The tiny young float in the sea for several weeks before they settle on the bottom.

The flesh of the queen conch is valued as food and as fish bait. For thousands of years, people have used conch shells as trumpets. The shells also can be burned to make lime or ground up to make porcelain. They are prized by shell collectors. The overfishing of conchs has sharply reduced their numbers in many areas.

Scientific classification. Conchs are in the phylum Mollusca, the class Gastropoda, and the subclass Prosobranchia. The scientific name for the queen conch is *Strombus gigas.*

Robert Robertson

See also **Mollusk; Shell** (picture); **Snail**.

Concord, Mass. (pop. 17,076), is an attractive residential town noted for its historic and literary attractions. It lies 19 miles (31 kilometers) northwest of Boston. For location, see **Massachusetts** (political map). Concord's largest industries make electronic test equipment and do metallurgical research. The Concord grape originated in Concord. Welch Foods Incorporated, a maker of fruit products, has its headquarters there.

A group of English Protestants called Puritans founded Concord in 1635. Concord became a center of revolutionary activity and a storage area for military supplies. Volunteers from the surrounding countryside called *minutemen* rallied to oppose British forces searching for these supplies. The patriots exchanged shots with British troops in a brief battle at Concord's North Bridge on April 19, 1775. The fight, which the poet Ralph Waldo Emerson called "the shot heard round the world," was one of the opening battles of the Revolutionary War in America. Today, a replica of the bridge and a statue called *The Minute Man* by Daniel Chester French mark the battleground. See **Concord, Battle of; Minutemen** (picture).

Concord was a center of American writing in the 1800's. Emerson, Louisa May Alcott, Nathaniel Hawthorne, and Henry Thoreau lived there. People may visit the Emerson House; Orchard House, where Alcott wrote most of *Little Women;* the Old Manse of Hawthorne; and the Wayside, where he lived. The Concord Museum displays period rooms of the 1600's to the 1800's. Nearby are Thoreau's Walden Pond, and Sleepy Hollow Cemetery, where most of the writers who lived in Concord are buried. Concord is governed by an open town meeting, a board of selectmen, and a town manager.

Renee Garrelick

Concord, N.H. (pop. 36,006), is the capital and one of the largest cities of the state. It is located on the Merrimack River in south-central New Hampshire (see **New Hampshire** [political map]). Called Penacook when it was founded in 1727, it took the name Rumford in 1733, and assumed its present name in 1765. Concord became the state capital in 1808.

Concord is the seat of Merrimack County. Government is the city's chief employer. The state, county, and city governments provide about 30 percent of the city's jobs. Other major employers are in the fields of medicine, law, electronics, printing, and insurance. The city is home to the New Hampshire Technical Institute, the Franklin Pierce Law Center, the Christa McAuliffe Planetarium, the state library and historical society, and most state offices. A home and the burial place of President Franklin Pierce are also in Concord. Concord has a council-mayor government.   Mike Pride

See also **New Hampshire** (Land and climate; picture: State Capitol).

Concord, Battle of, took place at Concord, Mass., on April 19, 1775, and marked the second clash between the patriots and the British in the Revolutionary War in America. The opening battle of the war was fought earlier the same day at nearby Lexington, Mass. During the previous winter, the Americans had gathered military supplies in case of war. The British government ordered its commander in chief in America, Lieutenant General Thomas Gage, to take military action against Massachusetts patriots. On the night of April 18, Gage sent 700 troops from Boston under Lieutenant Colonel Francis Smith to capture or destroy the supplies at Concord. But Paul Revere and William Dawes warned the countryside that the British were coming.

After a clash at Lexington early the next morning, the British continued on to Concord, 6 miles (10 kilometers) beyond Lexington. The Americans retreated across North Bridge, outside Concord. The main force of British troops searched for the patriots' supplies in the town, while others guarded the bridge. Several hundred colonists marched on the bridge and exchanged shots with the British troops. Three British soldiers and two Americans were killed. A few hours later, Smith's men headed back toward Boston. Fighting continued along the way, with about 250 British and about 90 Americans killed or wounded. The British casualties were the first suffered by Britain in the war.   Donna J. Spindel

See also **Revolutionary War in America** (picture).

Concorde. See Airplane (Supersonic airplanes).

Concrete. See Cement and concrete.

Concussion is a temporary disturbance of brain function caused by a sudden blow to the head. A concussion typically results in a temporary loss of consciousness, followed by a memory loss for the events just before and after the injury. More extensive memory loss occurs if the injury is severe. A mild concussion may or may not involve unconsciousness and memory loss. It causes a momentary state of confusion.

In a concussion, the blow causes the brain to bounce against the inside of the skull, injuring the brain's outer surface. Injury to the inner parts of the brain may also occur. The reason unconsciousness occurs is not well understood. One theory is that the blow disturbs function of the *cerebral cortex* (outermost part of the brain). Another is that the blow injures the deeper parts of the brain that control sleep cycles and alertness.

The victim of a concussion may stop breathing for a few seconds after the blow. In addition, the victim's pulse slows, the muscles relax, the pupils widen, and certain reflex actions disappear. As a result, a victim who is standing may fall down. Usually, the injured person regains consciousness within a few seconds and is soon alert and functioning normally. In more severe injuries,

the person may not regain full alertness for several days. After a concussion, some people develop dizziness, headaches, ringing in the ears, or changes in behavior. They also may have difficulty concentrating. Such problems may affect the person for months. For information on how to treat the victim of a concussion, see **First aid** (Concussion).   Richard D. Penn

Condensation. See Dew; Distillation (with diagram).

Condensed-matter physics. See Solid-state physics.

Condensed milk is a pasteurized, concentrated form of milk. It is made by evaporating water from whole milk to reduce the milk's volume by about half. It is not sterilized and must be refrigerated to prevent spoilage. Condensed milk, also called *concentrated milk,* is a good source of protein, calcium, and vitamin B_2. The partial evaporation of water from sweetened milk results in *sweetened condensed milk.* This product contains nearly 45 percent sugar. When sealed in a can, sweetened condensed milk requires no refrigeration. Both condensed milk and sweetened condensed milk are used primarily in ice cream, candy, and baked goods.   Robert T. Marshall

Condom. See Birth control (Methods of birth control).

Condominium, *KAHN duh MIHN ee uhm,* is a type of multifamily housing in which each dwelling is a separate piece of real estate. The owners of the dwellings—in almost all cases, the people who live in them—own in common the halls, stairways, grounds, and other areas used by all the residents.

Condominiums attempt to combine the advantages of owning a single-family home with those of renting an apartment. For example, condominium owners receive the same tax advantages as homeowners. They also share expenses for services used by all the residents.

Condominiums can benefit communities by increasing property taxes, which provide funds for public services. However, people who cannot afford to buy their dwellings are forced out of their homes by the conversion of such units to condominiums. The conversion of rental apartments to condominiums also reduces the number of available rental units. This reduction leads to an increased demand for the remaining rental housing and therefore to higher rents.

During the 1970's, condominiums became increasingly popular in the United States. In the 1980's, the large supply led to a reduced demand for them and a lower increase in their value. As a result, construction of condominiums decreased.   Albert Hunter

See also **Housing** (Condominium housing).

Condor is either of two large vultures found in the Western Hemisphere. The *California condor,* which once lived wild in southern California, is nearly extinct. Only about 60 California condors survive, most of them in captivity. The *Andean condor* of South America is more common, but it also is in danger of extinction. Andean condors live in the Andes Mountains and along the coast of Peru and Argentina.

Appearance. California condors are the largest flying land birds in North America, with a wingspan of 8 to $9\frac{1}{2}$ feet (2.4 to 2.9 meters). They weigh up to 31 pounds (14.1 kilograms). The Andean condor has a wingspread of about 10 feet (3 meters) and weighs up to 26 pounds (12 kilograms). Black feathers cover most of an adult condor's body. California condors have white on the underside of the wings. The upper wing surface of Andean condors is white. A collar of feathers circles the base of the neck—black feathers on California condors and white feathers on Andean condors. The featherless neck and head are red-orange in California condors and dark blue in Andean condors. Male Andean condors have a fleshy crest on the head.

Habits. In the wild, condors spend much of the day resting on high perches. Condors do not build nests. Instead, their eggs are laid in caves, in holes, or among boulders. A female California condor lays just one egg every two years. A female Andean condor also reproduces only every second year, laying one or two eggs.

Condors are powerful, graceful fliers. They can soar and glide for long distances, flapping their wings an average of only once an hour. They may search the ground for food as they fly. Like other vultures, condors eat the remains of dead animals.

Outlook for the California condor. By the 1980's, only a small number of California condors survived. Many California condors had been shot. Others died from lead poisoning after eating the remains of animals that had been shot with bullets containing lead. Still others may have died from eating poisoned animal bodies set out to kill coyotes. Increasingly, the growth of urban areas posed a major threat to condor survival. The condor's way of life requires vast areas of open, hilly country, and urban growth destroys such habitat.

In 1982, biologists began a program to capture all wild California condors. The last wild California condor was captured in 1987. Since then, more than 35 condors have been born and raised in captivity. In 1992, biologists began to release some of these condors into the wild.

Scientific classification. Condors belong to the New World vulture family, Cathartidae. The California condor is classified as *Gymnogyps californianus*. The Andean condor is *Vultur gryphus*.   Richard D. Brown

See also **Bird** (picture: Protecting species); **Vulture**.

Condorcet, *kawn dawr SEH,* **Marquis de** (1743-1794), was a French philosopher. His major work was *Sketch for a Historical Picture of the Progress of the Human Mind* (1793-1794). He believed that human nature could be perfected and that history showed humanity's progress toward an enlightened civilization. He opposed monarchy and religion. He felt that evils resulted from inadequate institutions and laws created by rulers and priests. Condorcet believed that history up to his time consisted of nine *epochs* (periods). In the 10th epoch, which he projected for the future, equality would develop among nations and classes, and people would improve physically, intellectually, and morally.

Condorcet was born in Picardy. His given and family name was Marie Jean Antoine Nicolas de Caritat. He was a brilliant mathematician and was elected to the French Academy. He supported the French Revolution and served in the revolutionary Legislative Assembly and

WORLD BOOK illustrations by Albert E. Gilbert

California condor
Gymnogyps californianus
Found mainly in captivity
Body length 50 inches
(127 centimeters)

Andean condor
Vultur gryphus
Found in the Andes, from
Venezuela and Colombia to
the Strait of Magellan
Body length 52 inches
(132 centimeters)

Convention. But he was arrested as an enemy of the revolution. He committed suicide in prison.   James Creech

Conduction. See Heat (How heat travels).

Conductor, Electrical. See Electric current.

Cone, in geometry, is a solid figure whose base lies on a plane and is bounded by a closed curve called the *directrix.* The *lateral surface* (side) of the cone consists of all the line segments connecting points of the directrix to the cone's *vertex,* a fixed point not on the plane of the base. When the directrix is a circle, the cone is a *circular cone.* If the line segment from the vertex to the center of the circle is perpendicular to the plane of the base, the cone is a *right circular cone.* When a right circular cone is intersected by a plane that does not contain the vertex, a curve called a *conic section* is formed. Circles, ellipses, hyperbolas, and parabolas are conic sections.

The *altitude* of a cone is the perpendicular line segment from the vertex to the plane of the base. The length of the altitude is the *height* of the cone. The *volume* (V) of a cone can be found by using the formula: $V = \frac{1}{3}Bh$. In the formula, B stands for the area of the base and h for the height of the cone. If the base of the cone is a circle, then $B = \pi r^2$, where r is the radius of the circle. The formula for volume can then be written: $V = \frac{1}{3}\pi r^2 h$. An approximate value for π (pi) is 3.1416.

In a right circular cone, all the line segments from the vertex to the directrix have the same length, called the *slant height.* The *lateral surface area* (L) of a right circular cone can be calculated with the formula: $L = \pi rs$. In this formula, r stands for the radius of the base and s stands for the slant height. The *total surface area* of the cone equals the lateral surface area plus the base area.

If a plane parallel to the base of a cone passes between the vertex and the base, the cone is divided into a smaller cone and a solid figure called a *frustum.* The volume of the frustum equals the volume of the original cone minus the volume of the smaller cone.

John K. Beem

See also **Circle; Ellipse; Hyperbola; Parabola.**

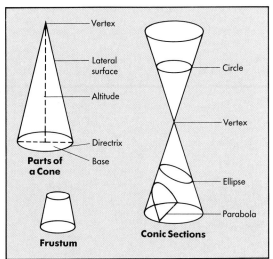

Vertex
Lateral surface
Altitude
Directrix
Base
Parts of a Cone

Circle
Vertex
Ellipse
Parabola
Conic Sections

Frustum

WORLD BOOK diagram by Hans W. Bobzien

A cone is a solid figure. If the top of a cone is cut off by a plane parallel to the base, a solid called a *frustum* remains. *Conic sections* are curves formed by planes intersecting cones.

Conestoga wagon was a sturdy, colorful wagon used by American pioneers. The wagon was named for the Conestoga Valley in Pennsylvania, where it was first built during the early 1700's. Conestoga wagons carried most of the freight and people that moved westward over the Allegheny Mountains from the 1770's until about 1850. These wagons were sometimes called the *camels of the prairies.*

Both ends of the wagon were built higher than the middle. A high, rounded, white canvas roof could be put on the vehicle, making it a *covered wagon.* Wheels with broad rims prevented bogging down in mud. The wheels could be removed and the wagon could be used as a boat. Conestoga wagons were drawn by teams of from four to six horses.   Odie B. Faulk

See also **Pennsylvania Dutch; Western frontier life** (picture); **Westward movement** (picture).

Coney. See Hyrax.

Confederate States of America was the name taken by six southern states when they organized their own government at Montgomery, Ala., in February 1861. The states *seceded* (withdrew) from the government of the United States in 1860 and 1861 because they feared that the election of Abraham Lincoln, a Republican President, might lead to restrictions on their right to do as they chose about the question of slavery. The first state to leave the Union was South Carolina on Dec. 20, 1860. Mississippi, Florida, Alabama, Georgia, and Louisiana followed South Carolina's lead in January 1861. In March 1861, Texas also seceded, and later in that year Virginia, Arkansas, North Carolina, and Tennessee joined the ranks to make 11 Confederate States in all.

The idea of a state leaving the Union was not new, and the South did not invent it. Throughout the United States, people who believed in the doctrine of states' rights had long argued that any state had the right to withdraw from the Union whenever it chose. They argued that individual states had formed the Union and therefore could also dissolve it. Some people in the New England states wanted to leave the Union during the War of 1812, because the war was unpopular there.

Government. Organization of a government for the Confederacy began on Feb. 4, 1861, when delegates from the six states that had seceded by that time met at Montgomery, Ala., and set up a temporary government. Jefferson Davis of Mississippi was elected president of the Confederacy, and Alexander H. Stephens of Georgia was chosen vice president. Both were to serve for one year. After the adoption of a permanent constitution, they were elected to six-year terms. Six prominent Southerners became members of the first Cabinet, and Montgomery was named the temporary capital. After Virginia seceded, the Confederate Congress voted on May 21, 1861, to move its capital to Richmond. The move was accomplished on May 29.

The Constitution of the Confederacy, adopted in March 1861, was modeled after the United States Constitution. But it contained six important differences:

1. The president's and vice president's terms were six years. The president could not serve successive terms.

2. Cabinet members received seats in Congress and had the privilege of debate. But they could not vote.

3. Foreign slave trade was ended, but not slavery.

4. Congress was forbidden to make appropriations

Confederate Cabinet

Secretary of state	Robert Toombs (1861)
	Robert M. T. Hunter (1861)
	Judah P. Benjamin (1862)
Secretary of the treasury	Christopher Memminger (1861)
	George A. Trenholm (1864)
Secretary of war	Leroy P. Walker (1861)
	Judah P. Benjamin (1861)
	George W. Randolph (1862)
	Gustavus Smith (Acting) (1862)
	James A. Seddon (1862)
	John C. Breckinridge (1865)
Secretary of the navy	Stephen R. Mallory (1861)
Postmaster general	John H. Reagan (1861)
Attorney general	Judah P. Benjamin (1861)
	Thomas Bragg (1861)
	Thomas Watts (1862)
	George Davis (1864)

for internal improvements, to levy a protective tariff, or to give bounties.

5. A two-thirds vote of both houses of Congress was necessary to admit a new state into the Confederacy or to make appropriations not requested by the heads of departments through the president.

6. The president could veto single items in appropriation bills.

The Confederate States hoped for a peaceful withdrawal from the Union. A number of persons in the Confederacy and in the Union worked hard to avoid war. But their efforts failed, and war began with the attack on Fort Sumter on April 12, 1861.

The border states were the slave states that lay between the North and the Deep South. When the war began, both the Union and the Confederacy made strong efforts to gain their support. North Carolina, Virginia, Arkansas, and Tennessee joined the Confederacy. Delaware, Maryland, Kentucky, and Missouri stayed in the Union. But the western counties of Virginia seceded from the South later in the war, and formed the state of West Virginia. And secessionist groups set up separate state governments in both Kentucky and Missouri, even though these states stayed in the Union. These groups also sent delegates to the Confederate Congress. This

accounts for the 13 stars in the Confederate flag even though only 11 states actually joined the Confederacy.

Foreign relations. Britain, France, the Netherlands, Spain, and Brazil were among the countries that recognized the Confederate States as a belligerent, but not as a nation. This meant that Confederate ships received the same privileges granted to vessels of the United States in foreign ports or on the high seas.

The Confederacy suffered great financial disadvantages. The wealth of the nation, before secession, lay mainly in the North, and the South lacked adequate resources for taxation. The Confederate government had to issue paper money early in the war. This money soon became almost valueless. The people of the Confederate States gave generously to their government and willingly bought government bonds. But their loyal financial support could not create resources that did not exist within the boundaries of the Confederacy.

Progress of the war favored the Confederacy in the first months. The defeat of the Union forces at Fredericksburg, in December 1862, led the emperor of France, Napoleon III, to offer his services as peacemaker between the Union and the Confederacy. The Union rejected this offer.

In 1863, the tide began to turn against the Confederacy. The Union armies could get more materials and supplies from the industrial North than the Confederate armies could obtain from the agricultural South. The North kept its army supplied with ammunition, food, and clothing, while the army of the South often lacked these supplies. Union ships blockaded Southern ports. The only way the South could bring in necessary supplies from overseas was to run the blockade. But Southern soldiers fought bravely until there was no longer any hope of victory.

The Confederate Congress met often during the war, mainly to follow the bidding of President Davis, who freely used his war powers. Union forces took Richmond on April 3, 1865. Danville, Va., then became the capital of the Davis government. The main Confederate army, the Army of Northern Virginia, surrendered on April 9, 1865. The people of the Confederacy had defended a way of living that to them seemed right. But

The Confederate States of America

	Confederate states
	Border states in the Union
	Union states and territories
★	Confederate capitals
✳	Union capital

0 — 400 Miles
0 — 400 Kilometers

WORLD BOOK map

they yielded to superior force. The road to reunion in spirit between the North and the South was long, but by the beginning of the 1900's resentment had been largely forgotten.   Thomas L. Connelly

Related articles. See the *History* section of the articles on the states of the Confederacy. See also:

Benjamin, Judah P.
Breckinridge, John C.
Civil War
Davis, Jefferson
Emancipation Proclamation
Flag (picture: Flags in United States history)
Fort Sumter
Johnston, Joseph Eggleston
Lee, Robert E.
Mallory, Stephen R.
Nullification
Seddon, James A.
Semmes, Raphael
States' rights
Stephens, Alexander H.
Walker, Leroy P.

Additional resources

Chesnut, Mary B. M. *Mary Chesnut's Civil War.* Ed. by C. Vann Woodward. Yale, 1981. An annotated and expanded version of the book first published in 1905 as *A Diary from Dixie.*
Coulter, E. Merton. *The Confederate States of America, 1861-1865.* Louisiana State Univ. Pr., 1950.
Eaton, Clement. *A History of the Southern Confederacy.* Macmillan, 1965. First published in 1954.
Patterson, Gerard A. *Rebels from West Point.* Doubleday, 1987.
Roland, Charles P. *The Confederacy.* Univ. of Chicago Pr., 1962. First published in 1960.

Confederation, Articles of. See Articles of Confederation.

Confederation Congress. See Congress of the Confederation.

Confederation of Canada was the union of British colonies that formed the Dominion of Canada in 1867. The dominion was established by the British Parliament under terms of the British North America Act. At first, it consisted of four provinces—New Brunswick, Nova Scotia, Ontario, and Quebec. It expanded across North America and developed into present-day Canada.

Early colonies of Canada. After the Revolutionary War in America ended in 1783, Britain still had four colonies in North America. These colonies, which spread across what is now eastern Canada, were Newfoundland, Nova Scotia, St. John's Island, and Quebec. New Brunswick was established in 1784, and St. John's Island was renamed Prince Edward Island in 1799.

Most of the people outside of Quebec were of English descent. The majority of them had come directly to Canada from England. Others were people loyal to the British government who had left the United States after the Revolutionary War in America. In Quebec, however, most of the people were of French descent. Quebec had been a French colony from 1608 until 1763, when Britain acquired it as a result of its victory in the French and Indian War.

In 1791, Britain divided Quebec into the colonies of Upper Canada and Lower Canada. Upper Canada occupied the region along the Great Lakes and the upper part of the St. Lawrence River. Most of its people were of British descent. Lower Canada lay to the northeast of Upper Canada and consisted primarily of French Canadians.

In 1837, minor rebellions broke out in both Upper and Lower Canada. The leaders of the revolts, William Lyon Mackenzie in Upper Canada and Louis Joseph Papineau in Lower Canada, both sought more authority over local affairs for their colonial legislatures. Conflicts between the French-speaking majority and the English-speaking minority contributed to the revolt in Lower Canada. Neither rebellion gained broad support, and British troops easily put them down. However, the events moved the British government to send a representative to examine the causes of the rebellions. The representative, the Earl of Durham, arrived in Canada in 1838. See **Rebellions of 1837.**

Lord Durham's Report was submitted in 1839. It took the position that the Canadian colonies would wish to remain in the British Empire if Britain allowed them to govern their local affairs. Lord Durham also recommended the eventual union of all the Canadian colonies under a central government. As a step toward this goal, he suggested combining Upper and Lower Canada. These proposals had been suggested earlier, and the British Parliament largely disregarded his report.

In 1840, however, Parliament passed the Act of Union. This act, which took effect in 1841, joined Upper and Lower Canada into a new colony called the Province of Canada. In 1848, Britain allowed a new form of government, called *responsible government,* in the Province of Canada. Under this system, an elected Legislative Assembly—rather than the British government's representatives in the colony—had the chief authority over local affairs. By 1855, similar governments had been set up in nearly all the Canadian colonies.

Continuing problems. During the 1850's, the political balance between the English- and French-speaking groups in the Province of Canada broke down. The colony's Legislative Assembly consisted of an equal number of members from each of the former colonies of Upper Canada and Lower Canada. But the united colony had more English-speaking than French-speaking people, and the English began to resent the equal political strength of the French minority. Because the two groups were almost evenly represented, it became more and more difficult for a government formed by either group to win broad support and stay in power.

Other conflicts arose because some people in the colony wanted to expand westward into the vast areas north and west of the Great Lakes. The British government had entrusted these areas to the Hudson's Bay Company, a large English fur-trading firm. Still other people pushed for construction of a railroad to link the Province of Canada with the Atlantic Coast colonies. Also, by the 1860's, all the Canadian colonies had become worried about military defense. The Civil War had begun in the United States in 1861, and many Canadians feared an invasion by American forces if Britain openly supported the rebelling Southern States. In addition, the colonies feared U.S. expansion into the territory north and west of the Great Lakes.

Moves toward confederation. During the mid-1860's, a group of political leaders in the Province of Canada finally decided that a strong union of all the colonies offered the best solution to their problems. The leaders of this group were John A. Macdonald, a conservative from the old area of Upper Canada; George Étienne Cartier, a conservative from Lower Canada; and George Brown, a liberal journalist and member of the colonial assembly. In September 1864, they met with political leaders from New Brunswick, Nova Scotia, and Prince Edward Island in Charlottetown, P. E. I. At this meeting, called the *Charlottetown Conference,* the delegates from the Province of Canada convinced the leaders of the other colonies that a confederation of the North American colonies should be created.

The details of the confederation were worked out the following month in Quebec City. This meeting, which included representatives from Newfoundland, became known as the *Quebec Conference.* The *Fathers of Confederation,* as the delegates to Charlottetown and Quebec came to be called, planned a new nation. They outlined their plan in 72 points called the *Quebec Resolutions.* The new nation would have two levels of government—provincial and national—and, like the United States, would be a federation. But it would follow the British system of parliamentary government. It would be a self-governing community within the British Empire, not an independent country. The plan also called for the creation of a province that the French-speaking Canadians would control. See **Quebec Conference.**

The plan for confederation did not easily win acceptance. Many people in the Atlantic Coast colonies were satisfied with their existing status. They feared they would lose control over their affairs in any union with the larger Province of Canada. Voters in New Brunswick and Prince Edward Island rejected confederation. Strong opposition blocked the plan in Newfoundland and Nova Scotia. The Province of Canada approved confederation. But many French Canadians there worried that their rights might be diminished in the new nation.

Approval of confederation. Resistance to the plan weakened as it became clear that Britain strongly favored the union. The British government hoped it would cost less to defend and assist a united colony than it would a group of separate colonies. The plan for confederation attracted additional support in 1865, when the United States decided to end an agreement that had helped increase trade with the British colonies. The col-

Fathers of Confederation

Public Archives of Canada, Ottawa

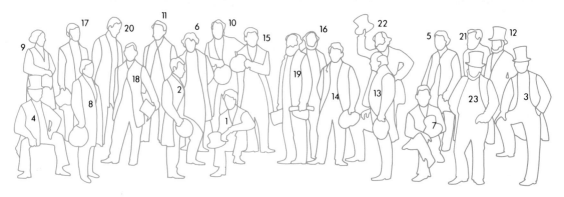

WORLD BOOK illustration by Bill and Judie Anderson

Plans for confederation began to take shape at a meeting of Canadian leaders in Charlottetown, P.E.I., in September 1864. The Charlottetown delegates, *above,* may be identified by comparing the numbers on the illustration with those in the table on the next page.

onies then realized they would have to cooperate, either to get a new trade agreement with the United States or to stimulate trade among themselves.

Confederation became even more appealing when the Fenian Brotherhood began to launch attacks on Canada in April 1866. The brotherhood, an organization of Irish-Americans, planned to capture Canada and hold it until Britain agreed to free Ireland. American and Canadian forces stopped the Fenian raiders, but the attacks persuaded many people in the colonies that a united Canada offered them the most effective defense.

During the height of the Fenian scare, the Nova Scotia legislature approved confederation. New Brunswick voters defeated the anticonfederation government in the colonial elections of June 1866. Samuel L. Tilley, the new premier, quickly succeeded in getting the legislature to approve the proposal for union.

Later in 1866, leaders of the Province of Canada, New Brunswick, and Nova Scotia met in London to prepare the final details. They adopted the Quebec Resolutions with only minor changes. The British Parliament readily approved the necessary legislation in March 1867. The legislation, which consisted chiefly of the Quebec Resolutions, was called the British North America Act. It provided for the formation of the Dominion of Canada and served as the new dominion's constitution.

The British North America Act took effect on July 1, 1867. The dominion it created consisted of four provinces—New Brunswick, Nova Scotia, Ontario, and Quebec. Ontario and Quebec had been formed by dividing the Province of Canada. The British North America Act also provided that other provinces could be added to the Dominion of Canada. The dominion's population totaled about $3\frac{1}{2}$ million. John A. Macdonald, one of the leading confederation supporters in the Province of Canada, became the first prime minister of the newly

Fathers of Confederation

Name	Position	Life dates	Occupation
Canada			
* **Sir Étienne-Paschal Taché** (Conservative)	Prime Minister, Chairman of the Quebec Conference	1795-1865	Doctor
1. **John Alexander Macdonald** (Conservative)	Attorney General for Upper Canada	1815-1891	Lawyer
2. **George Étienne Cartier** (Conservative)	Attorney General for Lower Canada	1814-1873	Lawyer
3. **George Brown** (Reform)	President of the Executive Council	1818-1880	Journalist
* **Oliver Mowat** (Reform)	Postmaster General	1820-1903	Lawyer
4. **Alexander Tilloch Galt** (Independent Conservative)	Minister of Finance	1817-1893	Financier
5. **William McDougall** (Reform)	Provincial Secretary	1822-1905	Lawyer
6. **Thomas D'Arcy McGee** (Reform, then Conservative)	Minister of Agriculture	1825-1868	Journalist
7. **Alexander Campbell** (Conservative)	Commissioner of Crown Lands	1822-1892	Lawyer
* **Jean-Charles Chapais** (Conservative)	Commissioner of Public Works	1811-1885	Merchant
8. **Hector-Louis Langevin** (Conservative)	Solicitor General for Lower Canada	1826-1906	Lawyer
* **James Cockburn** (Conservative)	Solicitor General for Upper Canada	1819-1883	Lawyer
Nova Scotia			
9. **Charles Tupper** (Conservative)	Premier and Provincial Secretary	1821-1915	Doctor
10. **William Alexander Henry** (Conservative)	Attorney General	1816-1888	Lawyer
11. **Robert Barry Dickey** (Independent Conservative)	Member of the Legislative Council	1811-1903	Lawyer
12. **Jonathan McCully** (Liberal)	Member of the Legislative Council	1809-1877	Editor
13. **Adams George Archibald** (Liberal)	Leader of the Opposition	1814-1892	Lawyer
New Brunswick			
14. **Samuel Leonard Tilley** (Liberal)	Premier and Provincial Secretary	1818-1896	Druggist
15. **William Henry Steeves** (Liberal)	Delegate without Portfolio	1814-1873	Politician
16. **John Mercer Johnson** (Liberal)	Attorney General	1818-1868	Lawyer
* **Peter Mitchell** (Independent Liberal)	Member of the Legislative Council	1824-1899	Lawyer
17. **Edward Barron Chandler** (Conservative)	Member of the Legislative Council	1800-1880	Lawyer
18. **John Hamilton Gray** (Conservative)	Leader of the Opposition	1814-1889	Lawyer
* **Charles Fisher** (Liberal)	Member of the Legislative Assembly	1808-1880	Lawyer
Newfoundland			
* **Frederic Bowker Terrington Carter** (Conservative)	Speaker of the Legislative Assembly	1819-1900	Lawyer
* **Ambrose Shea** (Liberal)	Leader of the Opposition	1815-1905	Merchant
Prince Edward Island			
19. **Colonel John Hamilton Gray** (Conservative)	Premier, Chairman of the Charlottetown Conference	1812-1887	Army officer
20. **Edward Palmer** (Conservative)	Attorney General	1809-1889	Lawyer
21. **William Henry Pope** (Conservative)	Provincial Secretary	1825-1879	Lawyer
22. **Andrew Archibald Macdonald** (Liberal)	Member of the Legislative Council	1829-1912	Merchant
23. **George Coles** (Liberal)	Member of the Legislative Assembly	1810-1875	Brewer, distiller
* **Thomas Heath Haviland** (Conservative)	Member of the Legislative Assembly	1822-1895	Lawyer
* **Edward Whelan** (Liberal)	Member of the Legislative Assembly	1824-1867	Journalist

* Members who attended only the Quebec Conference

formed nation. See **Macdonald, Sir John Alexander**.

Confederation set the stage for the development of a great country. Through the years, other provinces joined the Dominion of Canada. In 1931, Canada formally became an independent nation.   Michael Bliss

See also **British North America Act; Canada, History of** (The struggle for responsible government; map); **Hudson's Bay Company**.

Additional resources

Bliss, Michael. *Confederation 1867: The Creation of the Dominion of Canada.* Watts (New York City), 1975. *Confederation: A New Nationality.* Grolier (Toronto), 1981. Both suitable for younger readers.
Creighton, Donald. *The Road to Confederation: The Emergence of Canada, 1863-1867.* Macmillan (Toronto), 1964.
Garrod, Stan. *Confederation.* Fitzhenry & Whiteside (Markham, Ont.), 1981.

Conference on Security and Cooperation in Europe (CSCE) is any of a series of conferences designed to increase cooperation between certain Eastern and Western nations. Over 50 countries officially participate in the conferences. Until 1991, the participants were the Soviet Union and all the other countries in Europe, plus the United States and Canada. In late 1991, the Soviet Union broke up into a number of independent states. As a result, Russia assumed the Soviet Union's seat, and many of the other states that had been part of the Soviet Union joined the CSCE. A number of these states are in central Asia.

The first of many CSCE conferences met in 1975 in Helsinki, Finland. The conferences eased international tensions. They also stimulated the formation of human rights groups that helped overthrow many Communist governments in Eastern Europe and the Soviet Union. In 1990, a CSCE conference in Paris officially declared an end to the Cold War, a period of great hostility between the Communist and non-Communist nations. The Paris conference established a CSCE secretariat in Prague, in what is now the Czech Republic; a conflict-resolution center in Vienna, Austria; and in Warsaw, Poland, an office to monitor elections in European countries.

In 1992, the CSCE acquired the authority to send peacekeeping forces to its member nations. These forces would come from individual countries and such security organizations as the North Atlantic Treaty Organization (NATO). The CSCE also agreed to oversee the negotiation of arms-control agreements between its Eastern and Western members.   Joseph Preston Baratta

See also **Helsinki Accords**.

Confession, in religion. See **Eastern Orthodox Churches** (Sacraments); **Roman Catholic Church** (The seven sacraments).

Confession, in law, is a voluntary statement in which a person admits being guilty of a crime and describes how the crime occurred. Confessions form part of criminal law, which involves actions harmful to society.

In the United States, courts classify confessions into two basic groups. *Judicial confessions* are made during court proceedings. *Extrajudicial confessions* are made outside of court to officers of the law or to people who are not officials. Judges do not allow involuntary confessions to serve as evidence or proof in court. These confessions are obtained improperly by such methods as injuring, threatening, or making promises to a suspect.

In 1966, in the case of *Miranda v. Arizona,* the Supreme Court of the United States established the chief safeguards for the rights of suspects. The court ruled that before police officers question a person who is being held in custody, they must inform that person of certain rights. For example, the person has the right to remain silent and to have a lawyer present when being questioned by the police. If the police do not observe a suspect's rights, the court will not accept as evidence the statements that the suspect made to them.

In cases involving civil law, rather than criminal law, statements made by a party to a lawsuit are called *admissions* if the statements are against the party's own interest. Civil law covers such matters as contracts, personal injuries, and property ownership. Admissions may serve as evidence.   Paul C. Giannelli

See also **Escobedo v. Illinois; Miranda v. Arizona**.

Confirmation is a religious ceremony practiced by several faiths. In the Roman Catholic, Eastern Orthodox, and Lutheran churches, and in the Church of England, it is associated with baptism. Roman Catholics believe that it confers the grace of the Holy Spirit on baptized people. In Protestant churches, the baptized renew or affirm the promises made for them at baptism. In Judaism, boys are confirmed at the age of 13 in a ceremony called *bar mitzvah.* Some temples have similar ceremonies for girls called *bat mitzvah.* See also **Baptism; Bar mitzvah; Bat mitzvah**.   Frank C. Senn

Conflict of interest occurs if an individual has a financial or other interest in a company doing business with his or her employer. For example, a person working for a government agency that awards contracts to private industry may have a financial interest in a company bidding for these contracts. A conflict of interest occurs if the government employee favors the company in which he or she has an interest. The conflict-of-interest issue often arises when business executives take positions in government. Full-time government employees must give up all outside financial interests that might conflict with their duties. In 1977, Congress enacted a strict code of ethics, which included provisions to discourage conflicts of interest.   Charles O. Jones

Confucianism is a philosophy based on the ideas of the Chinese philosopher Confucius. It originated about 500 B.C. From the 100's B.C. to the A.D. 1900's, Confucianism was the most important single force in Chinese life. It influenced Chinese education, government, and personal behavior and the individual's duty to society.

Many people consider Confucianism a religion. But Confucianism has no clergy and does not teach the worship of a God or gods or the existence of a life after death. Confucianism can more accurately be considered a guide to morality and good government.

Early Confucianism. Confucius was born about 551 B.C. At that time, constant warfare raged among the many states that made up China. Rapid political change altered the structure of Chinese society, and many people no longer respected the established standards of behavior. Confucius feared that this threat to orderly social life would lead to the destruction of civilization.

Confucius believed his society could be saved if it emphasized sincerity in personal and public conduct. The key to orderly social life was the gentleman. Confucius defined a gentleman not as a person of noble birth, but as one of good moral character. A gentleman was truly reverent in worship and sincerely respected his father and his ruler. He was expected to think for himself, guided by definite rules of conduct. Confucius included many of these rules in sayings. For example, Confucius taught a version of the golden rule—"What you do not wish for yourself, do not do to others" (see **Golden rule**). A gentleman also studied constantly and practiced self-examination. He took, as Confucius said, "as much trouble to discover what was right as lesser men take to discover what will pay."

Confucius believed that when gentlemen were rulers, their moral example would inspire those beneath them to lead good lives. Virtuous behavior by rulers, he declared, had a greater effect in governing than did laws and codes of punishment.

When Confucius died about 479 B.C., he was largely unknown. His followers spread his ideas. The most important early Confucian philosophers were Mencius (390?-305? B.C.) and Xunzi (mid-200's B.C.). Mencius believed people were born good. He stressed the need to preserve "the natural compassion of the heart" that makes people human. Mencius emphasized the past as an ideal age and a model for examining present problems. In contrast, Xunzi believed people could be good and live together peacefully only if their minds were shaped by education and clear rules of conduct.

By about 200 B.C., the first large, unified Chinese empire had begun. The rulers approved of Confucianism's emphasis on public service and respect for authority. In 124 B.C., the government established the Imperial University to educate future government officials in Confucian ideals. The university based its teachings on five books of Confucian thought called the *Five Classics.* Mastery of the *Classics* became proof of moral fitness and the chief sign of a gentleman.

Later Confucianism. The early Confucianists concerned themselves primarily with the needs of society. However, ideas from Taoism and other philosophies helped shift the emphasis to additional areas of human experience. For example, a person's ability to live in harmony with nature was a minor issue to Confucius. But it became an important theme in Confucian thought during the 200's and 100's B.C.

From about A.D. 200 to 600, interest in Confucianism declined in China. Many Chinese turned instead to Buddhism and Taoism. These religions dealt with problems that the teachings of Confucianism largely ignored, such as the meaning of suffering and death.

A revival of interest in Confucius' philosophy began in the 600's. By the 700's, candidates for government jobs had to take a civil service examination based on Confucian ideas. The examination carried out Confucius' belief that an enduring state must be built on the merit of its rulers' advisers.

Zhu Xi (1130-1200) became a leader of a movement called *Neo-Confucianism.* Zhu developed a branch of Neo-Confucianism called the *rational wing.* It emphasized study and investigation of *Li,* the pattern behind human and natural relationships. Scholars led by Wang Yangming (1472-1529) developed the *intuitional wing* of Neo-Confucianism. They sought enlightenment by a combination of meditation and moral action.

Confucianism continued to actively influence Chinese life until it came into conflict with European ideas, especially Communism, in the 1900's. For many years, the Chinese Communist government opposed Confucianism because the philosophy encouraged people to look to the past rather than to the future. However, official opposition ended in 1977.   N. Sivin

See also **Confucius; I Ching; Mencius; Religion** (Confucianism; picture: Confucius' birthday); **Xunzi.**

Additional resources

Confucius. *The Analects of Confucius.* Trans. by Arthur Waley. Vintage Bks., 1989. First published in 1938.
Mencius. *Mencius.* Trans. by Dim C. Lau. Penguin, 1970.

Confucius, *kuhn FYOO shuhs* (551?-479? B.C.), was the most influential and respected philosopher in Chinese history. From about 100 B.C. to the revolution of 1911, the ideas of Confucius served as the single strongest influence on Chinese society. These ideas, which are called *Confucianism,* stress the need to develop moral character and responsibility.

Chinese governments made Confucius' teachings the official state philosophy. Millions of people in China—and in such nearby countries as Japan, Korea, and Vietnam—honored Confucius in much the same way as other peoples honor founders of religions. For details of the philosophy of Confucius, see **Confucianism.**

Confucius was born in the duchy of Lu, in what is now Shandong Province, China. His real name was Kong Qiu. The name *Confucius* is a Latin form of the title *Kongfuzi,* which means *Great Master Kong.* Confucius' parents died when he was a child. He failed in an attempt to become an adviser to a wise ruler. Confucius had wanted the position so he could put into practice his ideas for reforming society. Confucius received some minor official appointments, but at his death he was largely unknown in China. His disciples spread his teachings.

No book definitely written by Confucius exists. His disciples recorded his conversations and sayings in a book called *The Analects.*
                N. Sivin

See also **Religion** (picture: Confucius' birthday).

© Peter Gonzales

The conga drum is popular in Latin-American music. Musicians strike the drum with their fingers and hands. They usually play sitting down, holding one or two drums between their knees.

Conga drum is a percussion instrument chiefly used in Latin-American music. Jazz bands and combos sometimes use it as a rhythm instrument.

A conga drum is shaped like a slightly rounded cylinder and is made of wood or fiberglass. An animal skin covering called a *head* is stretched tightly across the top of the cylinder. Musicians strike the head with the fingers and the entire hand. They usually play a conga drum sitting down, with the drum held between the knees. They may also play the drum while standing, with the instrument mounted on a stand or suspended by a strap from the shoulder. There are three types of conga drum. They are, from highest to lowest pitch, the quinto, the conga, and the tumbadora.

The conga drum developed from an ancient African drum. This drum consisted of a section of a hollow tree trunk with an animal skin stretched across one end.

John H. Beck

Congenital defect. See Birth defect.

Conglomerate. See Rock (Clastic sediments; picture).

Conglomerate, in business, is a large corporation that controls or owns a number of companies that generally operate in unrelated markets. A corporation becomes a conglomerate through various types of *mergers* (combinations of two or more companies). Ordinarily, conglomerates tend to maintain the separate identity and management of their different companies.

There are three types of conglomerate mergers: (1) market extension mergers, (2) product extension mergers, and (3) pure conglomerate mergers. Market extension mergers combine companies that sell similar products or services in separate geographic markets, such as an international air carrier acquiring a regional airline. Product extension mergers bring together firms in related markets, such as an air carrier buying a bus company that serves several states. Pure conglomerate mergers combine firms in unrelated markets, such as an air carrier purchasing a fast-food chain.

Since the mid-1960's, conglomerates have made up three-fourths of all business mergers. Corporations often form conglomerates to avoid a disastrous loss. A conglomerate can usually offset temporary losses in some of its companies with the gains of others. Conglomerates also may obtain some savings by joining or coordinating production, marketing, financial, and management activities. Critics claim some conglomerates hurt competition by obtaining a strong position in a market without adding to the number of firms in that market. Critics fear that the financial power of some conglomerates can help them dominate markets previously composed of many small, single-industry firms.

However, supporters of conglomerates have argued that the financial power of a conglomerate does not guarantee it can control any market in which the firm sells. Supporters have also argued that conglomerates maintain competition by restoring some weak companies that otherwise might go bankrupt.   Robert B. Carson

Congo is a hot, humid country in west-central Africa. The equator runs through the country. Thick forests of trees and tangled bushes and vines cover the northern half of Congo. Much of this part of the country is inhabited chiefly by wild animals. The few people who live there travel by dugout canoe.

Congo was once a territory in French Equatorial Africa. It became independent in 1960. Its name in French, the official language, is République du Congo (Republic of Congo). Brazzaville is Congo's capital and largest city.

Most of Congo's soil is poor, but the country has several mineral resources. Congo is a transportation center. Pointe-Noire, on the Atlantic coast, is an important port.

Government. The president, Congo's most powerful official, is elected by the people to a five-year term. The president appoints a prime minister and Cabinet ministers to carry out day-to-day government operations.

Congo

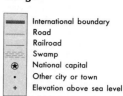

	International boundary
	Road
	Railroad
	Swamp
⊛	National capital
•	Other city or town
+	Elevation above sea level

WORLD BOOK maps

Congo's laws are made by a parliament consisting of a National Assembly and a Senate. The 125 members of the National Assembly are elected by the people to five-year terms. The Senate's 60 members are elected to six-year terms by local government councils.

People. Congo has about $2\frac{1}{2}$ million people. Most of the people live either on the southern border near Braz-

Facts in brief

Capital: Brazzaville.

Official language: French.

Area: 132,047 sq. mi. (342,000 km²). *Greatest distances*—north-south, 590 mi. (950 km); east-west, 515 mi. (829 km). *Coastline*—100 mi. (160 km).

Population: *Estimated 1994 population*—2,586,000; density, 20 persons per sq. mi. (8 persons per km²); distribution, 57 per cent rural, 43 per cent urban. *1985 census*—1,843,421. *Estimated 1999 population*—3,047,000.

Chief products: *Agriculture*—bananas, cassava, coffee, palm kernels and oil, peanuts, plantains, rice, rubber, sugar cane, sweet potatoes, yams. *Forestry*—limba, mahogany, okoumé. *Mining*—lead, natural gas, petroleum, potash, zinc.

Flag: A large green triangle is in the upper left corner, and a large red triangle is in the lower right corner. The triangles are separated by a yellow diagonal stripe. Adopted 1991. See Flag (picture: Flags of Africa).

Money: *Basic unit*—franc.

Brazzaville, the capital and largest city of Congo, is also a commercial center. The city lies on the Congo River.

zaville or on the coast in and around Pointe-Noire.

The people belong to four main groups: (1) the Kongo, (2) the Batéké, (3) the M'Bochi, and (4) the Sangha. Each group includes several subgroups. About 45 per cent of the people belong to the Kongo group, farmers who live west and southwest of Brazzaville. About 20 per cent are Batéké. They live north of Brazzaville and hunt and fish for a living. About 10 per cent are M'Bochi. Fishing was once the chief means of support for the M'Bochi. Today, many work as clerks and technicians. The Sangha live in the northern forests.

About half the people practice *fetish* religions. They believe that all things, even lifeless objects such as stones, have spirits. About 4,500 people are Muslims and most of the rest are Christians.

Most of the older Congolese cannot read or write, but about 75 per cent of the children now receive some elementary education. The Center of Administrative and Advanced Technical Studies in Brazzaville offers higher education to Congolese and to students from the Central African Republic, Chad, and Gabon.

Land. Congo covers 132,047 square miles (342,000 square kilometers) and includes the following six geographical regions:

The Coastal Plain extends about 40 miles (64 kilometers) inland from the Atlantic Ocean. The region is generally dry and treeless. Lagoons are near the coast.

The Mayombé Escarpment, and a series of plateaus rising from 1,600 to 2,600 feet (490 to 790 meters) above sea level, lie inland, behind the coastal plain. River valleys are cut into these forested ridges.

The Niari Valley, a richer farming region, lies beyond the Mayombé Escarpment. It is covered by wooded land and *savannas* (grassy plains).

The Stanley Pool Region, east of the Niari Valley, consists of a series of bare hills. Most of the land there has been cleared for farming. Stanley Pool is a lake formed by the widening of the Congo River.

The Batéké Plateau is a grass-covered elevated plain in central Congo. Deep, forested valleys containing tributaries of the Congo River divide the plateau.

The Congo River Basin in the north includes large swampy areas. The Ubangi, the main Congo tributary, forms the country's northeastern border.

Most of Congo is hot and humid, with rainfall throughout the year. Parts of the Congo River Basin have about 100 inches (250 centimeters) of rainfall a year, and temperatures average from 75 °F to 78 °F (24 °C to 26 °C). The Batéké Plateau averages less than 60 inches (150

centimeters) of rain a year. Temperatures there vary from 70 °F to 80 °F (21 °C to 27 °C). The coastal area is cooler and drier than the rest of the country because the cold Benguela ocean current flows along the coast.

Economy. Except for its forests and some minerals, Congo has few natural resources. The country also has few industries and a high rate of unemployment.

Most of the Congolese raise bananas, corn, rice, and other crops to feed their own families. Petroleum is the country's most valuable mineral. Other minerals include lead, natural gas, potash, and zinc. Lumber and petroleum are the chief exports.

Congo has one of the longest transportation systems in Africa. The Congo-Ocean railroad, a 320-mile (515-kilometer) line linking Brazzaville and Pointe-Noire, and its branch line form the only railroad. Barges use the Congo and Ubangi rivers north of Stanley Pool at Brazzaville, but rapids below Stanley Pool prevent barges from getting to or from the ocean. The Congo-Ubangi river system carries goods and passengers as far as Bangui, capital of the Central African Republic, a distance of 700 miles (1,100 kilometers). Most of the exports and imports of the Central African Republic and Chad move over the river system and the Congo-Ocean railroad. Gabon's manganese ore moves over the branch of the railroad. This shipping trade is important to the Congo economy. Building and maintaining roads is difficult because of heavy rains and thick forests.

History. A small part of what is now Congo probably was part of the Kongo kingdom, which flourished during the 1400's and 1500's (see **Kongo**). Portuguese explorers reached the Congo coast in the 1400's. Portuguese and other European traders bought slaves and ivory along the coast from the late 1400's to the 1800's. But Europeans did not explore the interior of what is now Congo until the late 1800's. Pierre Savorgnan de Brazza, a French explorer, reached the area in 1875. Henry M. Stanley, the famed British explorer, sailed down the Congo River from its source to the ocean in 1876 and 1877 (see **Stanley and Livingstone**).

In 1880, Brazza and Makoko, the Batéké king, signed a treaty that placed the area north of the Congo River under French protection. This area, then called Middle Congo, became a territory in French Equatorial Africa in 1903. In 1910, it was linked with the territories of Gabon, Chad, and Ubangi-Shari (now the Central African Republic). Middle Congo gained internal self-government in 1958. It became independent on Aug. 15, 1960.

Fulbert Youlou became the first president, but the

army and trade unions forced him to resign in 1963. A socialist government then took control, and Alphonse Massamba-Débat became president. In 1964, the government made Congo a one-party state. It took control of industries and recognized such Communist governments as those of China, North Korea, and North Vietnam. In 1968, military officers led by Major Marien Ngouabi removed Massamba-Débat from office and set up a temporary government. In 1970, a new constitution was adopted. Ngouabi became president of the country.

In 1977, Ngouabi was assassinated. An 11-member military council took control of the government. The council named Colonel Joachim Yhombi Opango president. It accused former President Massamba-Débat of plotting Ngouabi's assassination. Massamba-Débat was convicted and executed. In 1979, the military council was abolished and Colonel Denis Sassou-Nguesso replaced Opango as president.

In 1989, the government began to reduce state ownership of industries. In 1991, opposition political parties were legalized. In 1992, voters approved a new constitution. Elections were held in 1992. The Pan-African Union for Social Democracy (UPADS) won the most seats in both houses of parliament. Pascal Lissouba, of the UPADS, was elected president.   Samuel Decalo

See also **Brazzaville; Congo River.**

Congo (Kinshasa). See Zaire.

Congo River is the fifth longest river in the world. It flows 2,900 miles (4,667 kilometers) through west-central Africa. It carries more water than any river except the Amazon. The Congo River drains an area of about 1,400,000 square miles (3,630,000 square kilometers).

The Congo River begins south of Kabalo, Zaire, where the Lualaba and the Luvua rivers meet. From this point until Stanley Falls, the river is often called the Lualaba. After it passes over Stanley Falls near Kisangani, Zaire, the river is called the Congo. It is also known as the Zaire River.

Near Stanley Falls, the river turns westward and flows across northern Zaire. Several major rivers, including the Aruwimi, Lomami, and Ubangi, empty into the Congo. Near Mbandaka, Zaire, the Congo turns southwestward. It then forms the border between Zaire and the country Congo for about 500 miles (800 kilometers).

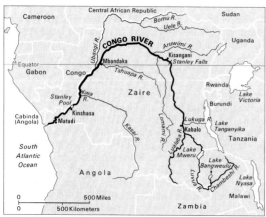

Location of the Congo River

WORLD BOOK map

The Kasai River joins the Congo about 300 miles (480 kilometers) southwest of Mbandaka. Near Kinshasa, Zaire, the Congo widens, creating a lake called Stanley Pool. The river then drops about 800 feet (240 meters) as it forms a series of 30 waterfalls between Kinshasa and Matadi, Zaire. The Congo empties into the Atlantic Ocean about 90 miles (140 kilometers) west of Matadi.

Unlike the Mississippi and the Nile, the Congo River has no delta. The Congo's muddy waters flow into a deep trench that extends far into the Atlantic Ocean.

The Congo is the main waterway of Zaire. Commercial ships use the river between the Atlantic and Matadi and between Kinshasa and Kisangani. The river serves as a major transportation route for Zairians, especially in areas that have few good roads. Rapids prevent navigation in some parts of the upper Congo.

In 1483, the Portuguese navigator Diogo Cão became the first European to reach the mouth of the Congo. Portuguese settlers established an outpost on the southern shore of the river near the Atlantic Ocean in the 1490's. But Europeans knew little about the rest of the river until after the British explorer Sir Henry M. Stanley completed an expedition from its source to its mouth in 1877.   Robert I. Rotberg

See also **Stanley and Livingstone; Zaire** (picture: The Congo River).

Congregationalists are members of a Protestant religious group. From 1620 to about 1800, the Congregationalists were the dominant religious tradition in New England. Unlike many other Christian denominations, Congregationalists rejected outside control by bishops and councils. They believed that each congregation should control its own affairs, including the selection of ministers. This principle strongly influenced the development of democratic government in the United States.

Congregational practices developed in England during the early 1600's as a branch of Puritanism. Puritanism was a movement that attempted to "purify" the Church of England of Roman Catholic beliefs and practices. The Puritans were influenced by the teachings of John Calvin, a leader of the Protestant Reformation.

Some Puritans, called *Separatists,* broke away completely from the Church of England because they believed they could not reform it. The Pilgrims, a Separatist group, settled Plymouth Colony in 1620 in what is now Massachusetts. These Separatists later became known as Congregationalists because of their insistence on the rights of local congregations. They interacted with and finally merged with non-Separatist Puritans who settled in New England.

From the mid-1600's to the early 1800's, the Congregationalist doctrines of the Puritans dominated religious and cultural life in most of New England. Congregationalists later became known for their liberal social goals, their willingness to cooperate with other religious groups, and their emphasis on education. Several of the oldest colleges in the United States, including Harvard and Yale universities, were founded in part as schools for training Congregationalist ministers.

Congregationalism's strong emphasis on local control in local religious matters contributed to the development of American beliefs in democratic civil government. During the early 1700's, for example, John Wise and other Congregationalist ministers opposed efforts by some religious and political leaders to deprive people of the right to direct their own affairs. Later, many Congregationalist ministers supported the cause of American independence.

During the 1800's, Congregationalism spread into the Midwestern and Western United States. However, Congregationalist churches in these areas later became Presbyterian. Also in the early 1800's, serious differences developed within the church between orthodox Congregationalists and a more liberal group called *Unitarians.* During the 1820's, many Congregationalist churches voted to become Unitarian and established their own association (see **Unitarians**). As a result, Congregationalism lost much of its influence in New England. Congregationalist churches formed a national council in 1871, but local congregations remained independent.

In 1931, Congregationalist churches merged with a union of three smaller groups to form the Congregational Christian Churches. These churches merged with the Evangelical and Reformed Church in 1957 to form the United Church of Christ. Several local churches in both groups did not join the merger.   John F. Wilson

See also **Edwards, Jonathan; Great Awakening; Wise, John; United Church of Christ; Calvin, John.**

Congress comes from a Latin word that means *a meeting.* Any group of people who represent organizations, regions, or nations, and who meet together to discuss their problems, may be called a congress. In the United States, the word *congress* usually refers to the Congress of the United States. An *international congress* is a conference attended by representatives of various nations. The name *congress* was given to several important international conferences that took place in the 1800's to determine boundaries and arrange political settlements in Europe. The most important were as follows:

Congress of Vienna (1814-1815), which divided up Napoleon's empire after the Napoleonic Wars.

Congress of Paris (1856), which settled the problems that grew out of the Crimean War. This congress also was an important step in the growing unity of Italy.

Congress of Berlin (1878), which took away from Russia Balkan land it had won from Turkey during the Russo-Turkish Wars.   Payson S. Wild

See also **Berlin, Congress of; Continental Congress; Vienna, Congress of.**

Congress of Industrial Organizations (CIO) was an association of labor unions active from 1938 to 1955. In 1955, it merged with the American Federation of Labor (see **American Federation of Labor and Congress of Industrial Organizations**). Most of the CIO unions had members only in the United States, but a few international unions also had chapters, or locals, in Canada. Most of the CIO unions were *industrial unions,* rather than *craft unions.* The CIO organized all workers in a plant into one union rather than just the workers in one particular craft.

The CIO was originally a group called the *Committee for Industrial Organization.* In 1935, eight presidents of AFL unions formed the CIO to carry on an organizing drive in mass-production industries. The CIO signed up unskilled as well as skilled workers. It placed skilled workers in the industrial unions rather than assigning them to separate crafts unions. Some AFL leaders opposed the idea of industrial unions. But the CIO set up

organizing committees and organized industrial unions in steel, automobile, rubber, and other major industries. The AFL did not accept these unions, and expelled unions that had taken part in the CIO. In 1938, the CIO formed its own federation and changed its name to the *Congress of Industrial Organizations.*

In its 1938 constitution, the CIO stated its main purposes: (1) to organize the unorganized; (2) to improve wages, hours, and working conditions; (3) to establish peaceful labor relations by forming unions strong enough to bargain with large industries; (4) to maintain collective bargaining and wage contracts; and (5) to secure legislation for the welfare of workers.

The Political Action Committee (PAC) of the CIO worked in national politics. State and city industrial councils were active in state and local politics. The CIO supported pro-labor political candidates and legislation in line with its main purposes.

CIO membership grew from about 4 million in 1938 to about 6 million in 1945. In 1949 and 1950, the CIO expelled 11 affiliated unions that it found to be dominated by Communists or by Communist sympathizers.

After many attempts at a merger, the CIO and AFL finally united in 1955. By then, the craft vs. industrial union conflict had become less important. More than half of the AFL's members were in industrial unions. Rivalry among labor leaders lessened after the deaths in 1952 of William Green, president of the AFL, and Philip Murray, president of the CIO. When the two organizations merged, the CIO had about 5,800,000 members, the AFL about 10,200,000.   Daniel Quinn Mills

See also **Dubinsky, David; Hillman, Sidney; Lewis, John L.; Murray, Philip; Reuther, Walter Philip.**

Congress of Racial Equality (CORE) is a civil rights organization in the United States. Its goals include equal rights, quality education, and economic and political opportunities for blacks.

When CORE was founded in 1942, it favored integration as a means of achieving its goals. In 1968, it changed its focus from integration to community control. CORE sought ways to enable the black community to control its schools and other institutions in order to provide quality goods and services for blacks.

Since the late 1970's, CORE has been involved in a number of lawsuits. A case in New Jersey ended in 1979 with a settlement in which CORE agreed to change its fund-raising methods. In 1981, CORE was found guilty of violating consumer rights in Alaska. In 1982, a New York lawsuit against CORE was settled out of court. The state attorney general had charged that CORE had collected funds for services to the poor that it did not provide. CORE headquarters are at 1916-38 Park Avenue, New York, NY 10037.   Jacob Cohen

Congress of the Confederation is the name sometimes used for the national legislature established by the Articles of Confederation. Also known as the Confederation Congress, the body operated the U.S. government from March 1, 1781, to March 4, 1789. The group's official title was the United States in Congress Assembled. But it replaced the Continental Congress, and many people continued to call it that. The Congress of the Confederation was replaced by the Congress established by the U.S. Constitution. See also **Articles of Confederation; Continental Congress.**   William Morgan Fowler, Jr.

Congress, the lawmaking branch of the United States government, consists of the Senate and the House of Representatives. During joint sessions, *above,* all members meet in the House chamber.

Congress of the United States

Congress of the United States makes the nation's laws. Congress consists of two bodies, the *Senate* and the *House of Representatives*. Both bodies have about equal power. The people elect the members of Congress.

Although Congress's most important task is making laws, it also has other major duties. For example, the Senate approves or rejects the U.S. President's choices for the heads of government departments, Supreme Court justices, and certain other high-ranking jobs. The Senate also approves or rejects treaties that the President makes.

Each member of Congress represents many citizens. Therefore, members must know the views of the voters and be guided by those views when considering proposed laws. Being a member of Congress also means answering citizens' letters, appearing at local events, and having local offices to handle people's problems with the government.

This article provides a broad description of Congress. For more information, see the separate *World Book* articles **House of Representatives** and **Senate**.

How Congress is organized

Congress is a *bicameral* (two-chamber) legislature. The 100-member Senate consists of 2 senators from each of the 50 states. The House of Representatives, usually called simply the *House,* has 435 members. House members, or *representatives,* are elected from *congres-*

Roger H. Davidson, the contributor of this article, is Professor of Government and Politics at the University of Maryland and co-author of Congress and Its Members.

sional districts of about equal population into which the states are divided. Every state must have at least one House seat. Representatives are often called *congressmen* or *congresswomen,* though technically the titles also apply to senators.

The Democratic and Republican parties have long been the only major political parties in Congress. In each house of Congress, the party with more members is the *majority party.* The other one is the *minority party.* Before every new session of Congress, Republicans and Democrats in each house meet in what is called a *caucus* or *conference* to choose party leaders and to consider legislative issues and plans.

Committees form an important feature of each chamber's organization. They prepare the bills to be voted on. The committee system divides the work of processing legislation and enables members to specialize in particular types of issues. The majority party in each chamber elects the head of each committee and holds a majority of the seats on most committees.

The Senate. According to Article I, Section 3 of the Constitution, the Vice President of the United States serves as head of the Senate with the title *president of the Senate.* However, the Vice President is not considered a member of that body and rarely appears there, except on ceremonial occasions or to break a tie vote. The Senate elects a *president pro tempore* (temporary president) to serve in the Vice President's absence. The Senate usually elects the majority party senator with the longest continuous service. The president pro tempore signs official papers for the Senate but presides infrequently. Most of the time, the president pro tempore appoints a junior senator as temporary president.

Democrats and Republicans each elect a chief officer

called a *floor leader*. A floor leader is also known as the *majority leader* or the *minority leader,* depending on the senator's party. Each party elects an officer called a *whip* to assist the floor leaders. Floor leaders or whips are typically at their desks at the front of the chamber. They arrange the Senate's schedule, work for passage of their party's legislative program, and look after the interests of absent senators.

Senators treasure their right to be consulted on bills, to offer amendments, and to speak at length in debate. Just one senator can slow down or halt the work of the Senate. Thus, Senate leaders spend much time considering fellow senators' needs and arranging compromises that will enable the work of the chamber to go on.

Sixteen permanent *standing committees* and several temporary *special* or *select committees* help the Senate make laws. Most committees have *subcommittees* to handle particular topics. Typically, a senator sits on about four committees and six subcommittees.

The House of Representatives. The *Speaker of the House,* mentioned in Article I, Section 2 of the Constitution, serves as presiding officer and party leader. The majority party nominates the Speaker, who is then elected by a party-line vote of the entire House. The Speaker is the most important member of Congress because of the office's broad powers. The Speaker refers bills to committees, names members of special committees, and nominates the majority party's members of the powerful Rules Committee. The Speaker votes in case of ties and grants representatives the right to speak during debates. With the help of assistants, the Speaker also influences committee assignments, arranges committee handling of bills, and schedules bills for House debate. As in the Senate, the House majority and minority parties each choose a floor leader and a whip.

The House has 22 standing committees and several special or select committees. Typically, a representative serves on about 2 committees and 5 subcommittees.

When Congress meets. A new Congress is organized every two years, after congressional elections in November of even-numbered years. Voters elect all the representatives, resulting in a new House of Representatives. About a third of the senators come up for election every two years. The Senate is a *continuing body* because it is never completely new. Beginning with the First Congress (1789-1791), each Congress has been numbered in order. The lawmakers elected in 1992 made up the 103rd Congress.

Congress holds one regular session a year. The session begins on January 3 unless Congress sets a different date. During the year, Congress recesses often so members can visit their home states or districts. Congress adjourns in early fall in election years and in late fall in other years. After Congress adjourns, the President may call a *special session*. The President may adjourn Congress only if the two houses disagree on an adjournment date.

The Senate and the House meet in separate chambers in the Capitol in Washington, D.C. The building stands on Capitol Hill, often called simply *the Hill*. Senators and representatives occasionally meet in a *joint session* in the larger House of Representatives chamber, mainly to hear an address by the President or a foreign official. The Constitution requires Congress to meet jointly to count the electoral votes after a presidential election. Legislation is never acted on in a joint session.

Congress's power to make laws

Origin of power. The Constitution gives Congress "all legislative powers" of the federal government. At the heart of Congress's lawmaking powers is its "power of the purse"—its control over government taxing and spending. Article I, Section 8 of the Constitution lists a wide range of powers granted to Congress. These *delegated,* or *expressed, powers* include the authority to coin money, regulate trade, declare war, and raise and equip military forces.

Article I, Section 8 also contains an *elastic clause* that gives Congress authority to "make all laws which shall be necessary and proper" to carry out the delegated powers. The elastic clause grants Congress *implied powers* to deal with many matters not specifically mentioned in the Constitution. For example, Congress has the expressed power to coin money. It has the implied power to create a treasury department to print money.

Limitations of power. Congress is limited in the use of its powers. The Constitution prohibits some types of laws outright. For example, Congress may not pass trade laws that favor one state of the United States over another state. The Bill of Rights, the first 10 amendments to the Constitution, forbids certain other laws. For instance, the First Amendment bars Congress from establishing a national religion; preventing religious freedom; or limiting freedom of speech, press, assembly, or petition.

The executive and judicial branches of government also limit Congress's powers. The President may veto any bill Congress passes. Congress can *override* (reverse) a veto only by a two-thirds vote in each chamber, which is usually difficult to obtain. The President's power to propose legislation acts as another check on

Facts in brief about members of Congress

Number: The Senate has 100 members, and the House of Representatives has 435.

Qualifications: Senate: (1) at least 30 years old, (2) a U.S. citizen for at least 9 years, and (3) a resident of the state from which the candidate seeks election. House: (1) at least 25 years old, (2) a U.S. citizen for at least 7 years, and (3) a resident of the state from which the candidate seeks election.

Nomination: Nearly all candidates for Congress are nominated in primary elections. A few are chosen by party conventions.

Election: A senator is elected by the voters from all parts of the state. A representative may (1) be elected by the voters of one congressional district of the state or (2) be elected *at large* (by voters throughout the state).

Term: Senators are elected to six-year terms, and representatives to two-year terms. In most states, there is no legal limit to the amount of time a member of Congress can serve. In the early 1990's, some states passed laws limiting the number of terms or years their senators and representatives could serve. In a few of these states, however, opponents of term limitations have challenged the laws, claiming they are unconstitutional.

Income: The Speaker of the House receives $171,500 a year. Majority and minority leaders of the House earn $148,400 a year. All other members of the House receive $133,600. In the Senate, the president pro tempore and the majority and minority leaders earn $148,400 a year. All other senators receive $133,600. All members of Congress receive allowances for office expenses, staff salaries, travel, and similar expenses.

Removal from office: Members of Congress may be expelled by a two-thirds vote of their particular chamber.

Congress. By its implied power of *judicial review,* the Supreme Court may declare a law passed by Congress to be unconstitutional. The courts also shape laws through their interpretations of them.

Finally, the power of public opinion limits what Congress can do. Lawmakers know that their actions must, in general, reflect the will of the people.

How Congress makes laws

Congress passes and the President signs about 650 laws during every two-year Congress. During that period, senators and representatives introduce about 10,000 bills. The legislative process sifts the proposals at every stage in the development of a bill to a law. To be enacted, a bill must survive committee and floor debates in both houses. It often must win the support of *special-interest groups,* or *lobbies.* A lobby represents a particular group, such as farmers or labor unions, and tries to influence legislators to pass laws favorable to that group. A bill must also gain a majority of votes in Congress and the President's signature. If the President vetoes the bill, it needs overwhelming support in Congress to override the veto.

Proposing new laws. Laws can be proposed by anyone, including lawmakers or their staffs, executive officials, or special-interest groups. The President can propose laws in speeches or public appearances. At a national convention, a political party may suggest laws to reflect the party's position on major issues. But to become a law, a bill must be sponsored and formally introduced in Congress by a member. Any number of senators or representatives may co-sponsor a bill.

A bill may be *public* or *private.* A public bill deals with matters of concern to people in general. Such matters include taxation, national defense, and foreign affairs. A private bill applies only to specific individuals, as in an immigration case or a claim against the government. To become a law, either kind of bill must be passed in exactly the same form by both houses of Congress and then signed by the President. Each proposed bill is printed and assigned a number, such as S. 1 in the Senate and H.R. 1 in the House of Representatives. Bills are also often known by popular names or by the names of their sponsors or authors.

Working in committees. After being introduced, a bill goes to a committee that deals with the matters the bill covers. Some bills involve various subjects and may be handled by several committees. For example, a trade bill may include sections on taxes, commerce, and banking. The bill may thus interest congressional tax, commerce, and banking committees.

The chief congressional committees are the 16 Senate and the 22 House standing committees. They handle most major fields of legislation, such as agriculture, banking, foreign policy, and transportation. Most standing committees have subcommittees, which hold hearings and work on bills on specialized matters.

The select and special committees of Congress propose laws on particular subjects or conduct investigations. In 1987, for example, each house appointed a select committee to examine the Iran-contra affair. The affair involved the sale of U.S. weapons to Iran in exchange for hostages, and the use of profits from the weapons sale to help the contra rebel forces in Nicaragua. *Joint committees* have members from both the House and the Senate. Such committees handle mainly research and administrative matters.

A proposed law reaches a critical stage after being referred to a committee. Committees *report* (return) only about 15 per cent of all bills they receive to the full Senate or House for consideration. Most bills are *tabled,* or *pigeonholed*—that is, never acted on. A committee's failure to act on a bill almost always spells death for the measure.

If committee leaders decide to proceed with a bill, they usually hold public hearings to receive testimony for and against the proposal. Testimony may be heard from a range of people, such as members of the President's Cabinet, scholars, representatives of special-interest groups, or lawmakers themselves.

Some bills go from committee to the full House or Senate without change. But most bills must be revised in committee *markup* sessions. In a markup session, members debate the sections of a measure and write amendments, thereby "marking up" the bill. When a majority of the committee's members vote for the revised bill, they report it to the full chamber with the recommendation that it be passed.

Legislative bargaining. To gain passage of a congressional bill, its sponsors must bargain for their fellow lawmakers' support. They need to give other legislators good reason to vote for the measure. To win a majority vote, the bill must be attractive to members with widely differing interests. Skillful legislators know how to draft a bill with broad appeal.

In a bargaining technique called *compromise,* legislators agree to take a position between two viewpoints. For example, lawmakers who want a major new government program and those who oppose any program at all might agree on a small trial project to test the idea.

In another form of legislative bargaining, called *pork barrel,* a bill is written so that many lawmakers benefit.

Standing committees of Congress

Senate	House of Representatives
Agriculture, Nutrition, and Forestry	Agriculture
Appropriations	Appropriations
Armed Services	Armed Services
Banking, Housing, and Urban Affairs	Banking, Finance, and Urban Affairs
Budget	Budget
Commerce, Science, and Transportation	District of Columbia
Energy and Natural Resources	Education and Labor
Environment and Public Works	Energy and Commerce
Finance	Foreign Affairs
Foreign Relations	Government Operations
Governmental Affairs	House Administration
Judiciary	Interior and Insular Affairs
Labor and Human Resources	Judiciary
Rules and Administration	Merchant Marine and Fisheries
Small Business	Post Office and Civil Service
Veterans' Affairs	Public Works and Transportation
	Rules
	Science, Space, and Technology
	Small Business
	Standards of Official Conduct
	Veterans' Affairs
	Ways and Means

The buildings where Congress works include the United States Capitol (1), the House office buildings (2), and the Senate office buildings (3). The floor plan shows the layout of the Capitol. The House of Representatives wing, *left,* includes the House Chamber, where the House holds its sessions. Senators meet in the Senate Chamber, located in the Senate wing, *right.*

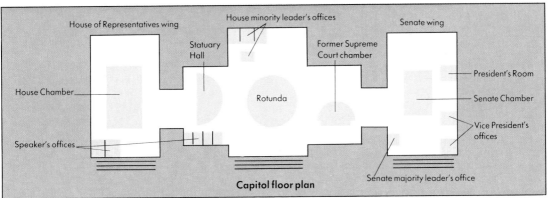

Capitol floor plan

WORLD BOOK diagram

For instance, a 1987 highway bill in the House included projects in so many members' districts that few representatives dared vote against it.

Some congressional bargaining involves an exchange of support over time. Lawmakers may vote for a fellow member's bill expecting that they will need that person's support later on another measure. This mutual help in passing bills is called *logrolling.*

In other instances, a member who is ill-informed on a bill may follow the lead of a lawmaker who is an expert on the subject. Some other time, the influence may flow the other way. This technique is called *cue giving* and *cue taking.* Lawmakers cannot be experts on every bill. They rely on associates who have worked on the bill.

Passing a bill. After a committee reports a bill, it is placed on a *calendar* (list of business) of whichever house of Congress is considering it. The Senate assigns all public and private bills to one calendar. It has a separate calendar for matters originating in the executive branch, such as treaties and presidential appointments. The House has five calendars. They involve (1) bills that raise or spend money, (2) all other major public bills, (3) private bills, (4) noncontroversial bills, and (5) motions to remove a bill from committee.

Committees screen out bills that lack broad support. Therefore, most measures that reach the House or Senate floor for debate and voting eventually pass. The Senate usually considers a bill by a simple motion or by *unanimous consent*—that is, without anyone's objection. The objection of one senator can block unanimous consent, and so Senate leaders work to make sure the bill is acceptable to their associates. Senators, however, cherish their tradition of free and sometimes lengthy debate. Senators opposed to a bill may make *filibusters*—long speeches designed to kill the bill or force its sponsors to compromise. To halt a filibuster, the Senate can vote *cloture*—that is, to limit the debate.

The House considers most bills by unanimous consent, like the Senate, or by the *suspension-of-rules procedure.* Both methods speed up legislation on largely noncontroversial bills. Representatives consider controversial bills under rules made by the Rules Committee. The rules control debate on a bill by setting time limits, restricting amendments, and, occasionally, barring objections to sections of the bill. Debate time is divided between the bill's supporters and opponents.

Legislators use various methods to vote on a bill. In a *voice vote,* all in favor say aye together, and those opposed say no. In *division,* the members stand as a group to indicate if they are for or against a bill. In a *roll-call vote,* the lawmakers each vote yes or no after their name is called. The House usually records and counts votes electronically. Members vote by pushing a button.

Senators and representatives tend to vote according to their party's position on a bill. If legislators know the views of their *constituents*—that is, of the people who elected them—they may vote accordingly. The President and powerful lobbies also influence how members vote.

From bill to law. After a bill passes one house of Congress, it goes to the other. The second house approves many bills without change. Some bills go back to the first house for further action. At times, the second house asks for a meeting with the first house to settle differences. Such a *conference committee* brings together committee leaders from both chambers to decide on the final bill. The two chambers then approve the bill, and it is sent to the President.

The President has 10 days—not including Sundays—to sign or veto a bill after receiving it. The veto is most powerful when used as a threat—lawmakers working on a bill want to know if the President is likely to approve it. If the President fails to sign or return the bill within 10 days and Congress is in session, the bill becomes law. But if Congress adjourns during that time, the bill does not become law. Such action is called a *pocket veto.*

Presidents veto about 3 per cent of the bills they receive. Only about 4 per cent of all vetoes are overridden by Congress. Presidents may veto a bill because it differs from their legislative program, or because they feel it is unconstitutional, costs too much, or is too hard to enforce.

Other duties of Congress

Passing laws lies at the heart of Congress's duties. But Congress also has nonlegislative tasks that influence national government and shape public policies.

Approving federal appointments. The Constitution requires the President to submit nominations of Cabinet members, federal judges, ambassadors, and certain other officials to the Senate for approval. A majority vote of the senators present confirms a presidential appointment. Senators approve almost all nominations to the executive branch because they believe that the President deserves loyal people in top jobs. The Senate examines judicial appointments more critically. About a fourth of all Supreme Court nominees have failed to win Senate confirmation. Some were rejected by a vote, but more commonly the Senate delayed acting on the nomination, often leading the President to withdraw it.

Approving treaties. According to Article II, Section 2 of the Constitution, the President has the power to make treaties "by and with the advice and consent of the Senate." A treaty requires the approval of two-thirds of the senators voting on it. The Senate has rejected outright very few treaties since the First Congress met in 1789. More often, the Senate amends the treaty or simply fails to act.

The most famous treaty rejection was the Senate's refusal to approve the Treaty of Versailles, which established peace with Germany at the end of World War I (1914-1918). The treaty included President Woodrow Wilson's proposal for the League of Nations, an international association to maintain peace. Senators proposed reservations to the treaty—particularly the League—but Wilson rejected them, leading to the treaty's downfall.

Presidents today try to keep the Senate informed as they arrange treaties. For example, President Ronald Reagan invited senators to follow negotiations for the Intermediate-Range Nuclear Forces (INF) Treaty, which called for the destruction of certain nuclear weapons in the United States and the Soviet Union. Objections from the senators sent U.S. diplomats back to the bargaining table to revise the treaty. Signed in December 1987, the treaty won Senate approval by the following May.

Conducting investigations. Congress has the implied power to investigate executive actions and public

and private wrongdoing because such inquiries may lead to new laws. Congressional committees conduct the investigations. Congress has launched investigations to uncover scandals, spotlight certain issues, embarrass the President, or advance the reputations of the lawmakers themselves. Televised congressional investigations have aroused great public interest and highlighted Congress's role in keeping the people informed. An early televised investigation took place in 1954, when millions of TV viewers watched Senator Joseph R. McCarthy charge the U.S. Army with "coddling Communists."

Proposing constitutional amendments. Congress can propose amendments to the U.S. Constitution by a two-thirds vote in both houses. Congress can also call a constitutional convention to propose amendments if at least two-thirds of the states formally request it. In addition, Congress determines whether the states vote on an amendment by means of state legislatures or special state conventions. Congress also decides how long the states have to consider an amendment. It allows seven years in most cases.

Handling presidential election results. Congress counts and checks the votes cast by the Electoral College, the group of electors that chooses the U.S. President and Vice President. Congress then announces the results of the election. In most cases, the public knows the winners from the outcome of the popular election. If no candidate has a majority of Electoral College votes, Congress selects the winners. The House chooses the President, and the Senate elects the Vice President.

Impeaching and trying federal officials. An impeachment is a charge of serious misconduct in office. The House of Representatives has the power to draw up charges of impeachment against officials of the national government. If a majority of representatives vote for impeachment, the Senate then sits as a court to hear the charges against the accused official. Impeachments rarely occur. The House voted to impeach President Andrew Johnson in 1868, but the Senate narrowly acquitted him. President Richard M. Nixon resigned in 1974 before representatives voted on impeachment charges recommended by the House Judiciary Committee.

Reviewing its own members. Congress can review the election and judge the qualifications of its own members. It can also *censure* (officially condemn) or expel members for improper conduct as well as apply a milder form of discipline, such as a fine or reprimand. Congress has censured members for such reasons as the conviction of crimes, *unethical* (morally wrong) conduct, or disgracing Congress.

Members of Congress at work

A typical day. The daily schedule of members of Congress reflects their jobs both as lawmakers and as representatives for their districts and states. Most members work at least 11 hours a day. Mornings involve office work and committee meetings, often with two or three meetings scheduled at the same time. Members choose which meeting to attend. They make brief appearances at other meetings or send aides to take notes. During the afternoon, and many mornings and evenings, the Senate and House are in session. Most legislators, busy with other work, do not stay in their particular chamber for debates. Instead, they follow them on

Representation in Congress

The Constitution of the United States provides for a *bicameral* (two-chamber) legislature. In the Senate, each state has equal representation—two senators per state. In the House of Representatives, population determines the number of representatives sent from each state.

State	Senate	House	State	Senate	House	State	Senate	House
Alabama	2	7	Louisiana	2	7	Ohio	2	19
Alaska	2	1	Maine	2	2	Oklahoma	2	6
Arizona	2	6	Maryland	2	8	Oregon	2	5
Arkansas	2	4	Massachusetts	2	10	Pennsylvania	2	21
California	2	52	Michigan	2	16	Rhode Island	2	2
Colorado	2	6	Minnesota	2	8	South Carolina	2	6
Connecticut	2	6	Mississippi	2	5	South Dakota	2	1
Delaware	2	1	Missouri	2	9	Tennessee	2	9
Florida	2	23	Montana	2	1	Texas	2	30
Georgia	2	11	Nebraska	2	3	Utah	2	3
Hawaii	2	2	Nevada	2	2	Vermont	2	1
Idaho	2	2	New Hampshire	2	2	Virginia	2	11
Illinois	2	20	New Jersey	2	13	Washington	2	9
Indiana	2	10	New Mexico	2	3	West Virginia	2	3
Iowa	2	5	New York	2	31	Wisconsin	2	9
Kansas	2	4	North Carolina	2	12	Wyoming	2	1
Kentucky	2	6	North Dakota	2	1			

closed-circuit TV. Members must be ready to go to their chamber for a vote or a *quorum call*—that is, a count taken to determine if the minimum number of lawmakers needed to hold a vote is present.

Telephone calls, letters, and visits from constituents take up much of a legislator's time. Many people contact members of Congress to give their views on bills. Other people seek help with jobs, immigration problems, social security payments, or appointments to military academies.

Senators and representatives have assistants in their Washington, D.C., offices and in their state or district offices. The size of a senator's staff depends on the population of the senator's state—the larger the population, the larger the staff. The average staff consists of about 40 to 50 people. By law, representatives may employ up to 18 aides. Party and committee leaders in Congress have additional aides. Most members also accept students who work without pay to gain political experience. The students work either in Washington or in local offices on legislation and relations with constituents.

Congressional travel. Members of Congress travel often to their home states or districts to appear at public events, study area problems, and talk with voters or local officials. In fact, about a third of all representatives return to their districts nearly every weekend. Sessions of the Senate and House are scheduled to accommodate the members' need to appear frequently before their constituents, and legislators receive allowances to cover their expenses. If members fail to visit their home states or districts fairly often, they are apt to be criticized for forgetting their constituents.

Fact-finding missions at home or abroad—sometimes called *junkets*—also crowd the schedules of senators and representatives. Critics charge that legislators enjoy foreign travel at public expense. Legislators argue that experience gained by travel abroad helps them understand world developments and legislate wisely.

Social responsibilities. Membership in Congress carries many social obligations. Both at home and in

Washington, individuals and groups interview legislators and expect them to attend social events.

History of Congress

The founding of Congress grew out of a tradition of representative assemblies that was brought from Great Britain and took root in the American Colonies in the early 1600's. Colonial assemblies had a wide range of powers, including authority to collect taxes, issue money, and provide for defense. In time, the assemblies increasingly voiced the colonists' interests against those of the British-appointed colonial governors.

As tensions worsened between Britain and the American Colonies in the 1760's, the colonial assemblies took up the colonists' cause. The First Continental Congress met in Philadelphia in 1774. It drew lawmakers from every colony but Georgia and could be considered the colonists' first "national" assembly. In 1776, the Second Continental Congress declared the colonies' independence from Britain. It served as a temporary national government until 1781, when the states adopted the Articles of Confederation and set up a national legislature called the Congress of the Confederation. This body functioned without an independent executive or judicial branch and soon showed its weakness.

In 1787, the Constitutional Convention met to strengthen the Articles of Confederation. But the delegates drew up a new plan of government instead—the Constitution of the United States. The power of the legislature remained important, but it was balanced by executive and judicial branches. The Constitution called for two chambers for the new Congress—earlier Congresses had one house—with equal representation in one chamber and representation by population in the other. The establishment of a two-house legislature became known as the *Great Compromise*. It solved a bitter dispute between delegates from small states, who favored equal representation for every state, and those from large states, who wanted representation based on state population.

Growth and conflict. When the new Congress met for the first time in New York City in 1789, the two chambers were small and informal. At the end of the First Congress, the Senate had only 26 members, and the House of Representatives 65. As new states joined the Union, the House grew faster than the Senate and developed strong leaders. Such House Speakers as Henry Clay in the early 1800's and Thomas B. Reed in the late 1800's brought power and high honor to their office. They also increased the House's power. The Senate enjoyed a golden age from about the 1830's to the 1860's, when it had such great speechmakers as Clay, Daniel Webster, and John C. Calhoun. Those men and their fellow senators debated the existence of slavery in the United States and other burning issues of the day.

Relations between Congress and the President shifted wildly throughout the 1800's. Most Presidents yielded to Congress and initiated few policies. During the early and middle 1800's, however, several strong Presidents sought to deal with Congress as an equal. Thomas Jefferson worked with congressional supporters to enact legislation drafted by the executive branch. Andrew Jackson promoted his policies through *patronage*—that is, his authority to make federal job appointments—and through his use of the veto. Abraham Lincoln used emergency authority to force Congress to accept his policies during the Civil War (1861-1865).

Congress recaptured power after each of the strong Presidents. Following the Civil War, the House ruled supreme, with the Speaker almost as important as the President. The Speaker became so strong that House members revolted in 1910 to limit the office's power.

Continued struggle for power. During the early to middle 1900's, voters elected several strong-willed individuals who established the President as a leader in the legislative process. These men included Presidents Theodore Roosevelt, Woodrow Wilson, and especially Franklin D. Roosevelt. Each proposed a package of new laws and worked to persuade or pressure Congress to enact that package. Congress began to rely increasingly on its committees to process legislation.

Relations between Congress and the presidency changed markedly in the late 1960's and early 1970's. Such events as the Vietnam War (1957-1975) and the Watergate scandal led Congress to limit the President's authority. The Vietnam War had never been officially declared by Congress. But Presidents Lyndon B. Johnson and Nixon, as commanders in chief of the nation's armed forces, had sent hundreds of thousands of U.S. troops into the conflict. Public opposition to the war spurred Congress to pass the War Powers Resolution in 1973 over Nixon's veto. The resolution restricts the President's authority to keep U.S. troops in a hostile area without Congress's consent. The law reasserted Congress's role in foreign affairs, but has had mixed success in curbing the President's warmaking authority.

In 1973, a Senate select committee began hearings on the Watergate scandal. The scandal involved illegal campaign activities during the 1972 presidential race. The investigation led the House to begin impeachment proceedings against President Nixon. Nixon was charged with obstructing justice, abusing presidential powers, and illegally withholding evidence. He resigned before an impeachment vote was held. Congress further declared its authority in 1974, when it passed an act that restricts the President's freedom to *impound* (refuse to spend) funds for projects approved by Congress.

Recent developments. In the 1980's and 1990's, conflict arose again between Congress and the President as a shortage of funds in the federal budget increased. President Ronald Reagan and his successor, George Bush, waged fierce battles with Congress over spending and tax policies. Disputes also erupted over such issues as civil rights policy, judicial appointments, and aid to foreign anti-Communist movements.

In the late 1980's and early 1990's, conflict over defense spending decreased after Communists lost control of many Eastern European countries and the Soviet Union. Attention turned to the sluggish U.S. economy and other domestic problems. But many of these issues, including reform of the nation's health care, banking, and educational systems, were left unresolved. Many critics blamed the inaction on competing special-interest groups and on *divided government,* in which opposing parties control Congress and the presidency. After 1986, Republican Presidents Reagan and Bush faced a Democratic-controlled Congress.

Numerous other problems have involved congressional ethics. In 1989, for example, House Speaker James C. Wright, Jr., resigned his seat after being accused of accepting improper gifts and of earning more income from outside sources than House rules permitted. Members of Congress also have been accused of doing special favors for wealthy individuals who give them large campaign contributions. Public criticism of the House increased in 1991, when it was discovered that many House members had regularly overdrawn their accounts at the House payroll office (often called the House "bank"). The practice involved no public funds, but the issue drew criticism of privileges enjoyed by Congress. In 1992, the U.S. Justice Department began an investigation to determine whether any of the members had broken the law by overdrawing their accounts.

Many people have also objected to Congress's ability to vote itself pay raises. In 1992, to limit this ability, the last of the required number of states ratified the 27th Amendment to the U.S. Constitution. This amendment requires that whenever a raise is authorized, it may not take effect until after the next congressional election.

The soaring cost of congressional campaigns has led to public concern about the campaign financing system. Critics fear that members of Congress spend too much time raising money and that large donors have too much influence on policy decisions. Big donors include *political action committees* (PAC's). A PAC obtains voluntary contributions from members or employees of a special-interest group and gives the funds to candidates it favors.   Roger H. Davidson

Related articles. See the articles **House of Representatives** and **Senate** and their *Related articles.* See also:

Articles of Confederation	Electoral College
Botanic Garden, United States	General Accounting Office
Capitol, United States	Government Printing Office
Congressional Budget Office	Impeachment
Congressional page	Library of Congress
Congressional Record	Lobbying
Constitution of the	President of the United States
United States	United States,
Continental Congress	Government of the

Outline

Questions

Why are there two houses of Congress?
In what ways is the power of Congress limited?
What powers does the Speaker of the House have?
What are *delegated powers* of Congress? *Implied powers?*
How does Congress influence the President's treaty-making power?
What techniques are used in legislative bargaining?
How did relations between Congress and the presidency change markedly in the late 1960's and early 1970's?
Why does Congress conduct investigations?
What is a *standing committee?* A *conference committee?*
Why do members of Congress travel often to their home states or districts?

Reading and Study Guide

See *Congress of the United States* in the Research Guide/Index, Volume 22, for a *Reading and Study Guide.*

Additional resources

Level I

Bernstein, Richard B., and Agel, Jerome. *The Congress.* Walker, 1989.
Oleszek, Walter J. *Congressional Procedures and the Policy Process.* 3rd ed. Congressional Quarterly, 1989.

Level II

Congress A to Z: CQ's Ready Reference Encyclopedia. Congressional Quarterly, 1988.
Congress and the Nation. 7 vols. Congressional Quarterly, 1965-1990.
How Congress Works. 2nd ed. Congressional Quarterly, 1991.
Mikva, Abner J., and Saris, P. B. *The American Congress: The First Branch.* Watts, 1983.

Congressional Budget Office is an agency of the United States Congress. It provides members of Congress with information on the nation's economy, the federal budget, and federal programs. The office, often called the CBO, does not recommend policies. It presents optional plans and programs, and studies their possible impact on the budget.

Each year the CBO reviews and analyzes the President's budget proposals. It prepares a forecast of the cost of continuing for five years the existing federal policies affecting taxation and spending. Staff members of the CBO regularly testify before congressional committees on budget matters. The CBO helps budget committees in the Senate and the House of Representatives prepare biannual budget proposals. It keeps track of how closely congressional spending and revenue actions match budgeted goals. The office issues an annual report on major budgetary options.

The CBO was created by the Congressional Budget and Impoundment Control Act of 1974. Congress passed the act to affirm its constitutional authority over the U.S. budget.   Critically reviewed by the Congressional Budget Office

See also **Budget** (Preparation of the U.S. budget).

Congressional page works as a messenger in the United States Senate or House of Representatives. Pages carry messages between the Capitol and the Senate and House office buildings, and run errands for the senators and representatives. Members of Congress appoint a limited number of young people from their home districts to work as pages. Pages range in age from 14 to 18 years. They are paid only for the periods the Senate or House is in session. Pages attend a special high school from 6:30 a.m. to 9:45 a.m.   Kenneth Janda

Congressional Record is a printed account of what is done and said in the United States Congress daily. Each member of Congress finds on his or her desk in the morning a copy of the *Record* for the day before. The *Congressional Record* prints everything said in Congress, except during executive sessions of the Senate. Members of Congress may make changes in their speeches before they are printed in the *Record,* and so the *Record* is not a completely accurate account of what was said in Congress. They also can have material other than speeches before Congress printed in the *Record.*

The *Congressional Record* began in 1873. Three other publications record earlier events in Congress. *Annals of Congress* describes proceedings from 1789 to 1824. *Congressional Debates* covers 1824 to 1837, and the *Congressional Globe* records events from 1833 to 1873.

Today, anyone may subscribe to the *Congressional Record* or buy separate parts of it from the Superintendent of Documents, Government Printing Office, Washington, DC 20402.   Kenneth Janda

Congressman or congresswoman is a member of the U.S. Congress. The term generally refers to a member of the House of Representatives. See also **Address, Forms of; Congress of the United States.**

Congresswoman. See **Congressman.**

Congreve, *KAHN greev,* **William** (1670-1729), was an English dramatist who wrote witty, sophisticated comedies. The best of his five plays are *Love for Love* (1695) and *The Way of the World* (1700). They contain lively and clever speeches as well as memorable characters and comic situations. They have a polished prose style and a civilized, realistic view of life. *The Way of the World* presents a satirical picture of a cultured, worldly, high society. The play laughs at hypocrites, boors, would-be wits, fools, and aging coquettes. Congreve's most popular play during his lifetime was *The Mourning Bride* (1697), his only tragedy. It contains the famous line "Music has charms to soothe a savage breast."

Congreve was born in Yorkshire, and grew up in Ireland. He entered law school in London in 1691, but preferred writing and the leisurely life of a man about town. He wrote little after 1700.   Jack D. Durant

Congreve, *KAHN greev,* **Sir William** (1772-1828), a British inventor, developed rockets that could carry explosives. His work, which included a book on rocketry, promoted the use of rockets as a major military weapon. The British used Congreve rockets against French troops during the Napoleonic Wars (1793-1815). British forces also bombarded Fort McHenry in Baltimore, Md., with such rockets during the War of 1812. See **Rocket** (Early rockets).

Congreve was born in Woolwich, England, and received a master's degree from Cambridge University in 1795. He succeeded to his father's baronet title in 1814. Congreve received 18 patents. He devised new methods of mounting naval guns and manufacturing gunpowder. He also invented a steam engine, a sprinkler system, and various other devices. ＿＿＿＿Romualdas Sviedrys

Conic projection. See **Map.**

Conifer, *KOH nuh fuhr* or *KAHN uh fuhr,* is any one of a large group of trees or shrubs that bears its seeds in cones. Most conifers have tall, straight trunks and narrow branches and grow in cold or cool climates. Common conifers include cedars, cypresses, firs, hemlocks, junipers, larches, pines, redwoods, sequoias, and yews. The cycad plant also bears cones, but it is not considered to be a conifer (see **Cycad**).

Conifers are one of the oldest groups of woody plants. Conifer fossils have been found in rocks that are about 300 million years old. Conifers include the largest, tallest, and oldest living things. The largest giant sequoia is about 275 feet (83.8 meters) high, and the base of its trunk has a circumference of 103 feet (31.4 meters). Redwoods, the tallest living trees, may tower more than 360 feet (110 meters) high. Some bristlecone pines are more than 4,600 years old.

Conifers form about 30 per cent of the world's forests. In North America, most of the wood used in houses and other buildings comes from conifers, especially Douglas-fir and loblolly pine. Conifers also provide much wood pulp for making paper and cardboard. In addition, millions of conifers are used every year as Christmas trees.

Most conifers are evergreen and have small, needle-like leaves. Other conifers, including redcedars and cypresses, have tiny, scalelike leaves that cling to the stem.

WORLD BOOK illustrations by John F. Eggert

The leaves of conifers may be scalelike or needlelike. The scalelike leaves of the *northern white-cedar, left,* cling to the stem. The needlelike leaves of the *red spruce, right,* grow out from the stem. The cones also differ in appearance.

These trees are also evergreen. Larches and baldcypresses are conifers but they lose their leaves every year.

Conifer cones range from less than $\frac{1}{2}$ inch (1.3 centimeters) long to more than 2 feet (61 centimeters) long. Conifers have two types of cones—male and female. In most conifers, both types grow on the same plant. The soft male cones produce and release pollen, then shrivel and die. The female cones are larger and become woody with age. Each of their scales has two structures called *ovules,* which contain *eggs* (female reproductive cells). Wind carries pollen from the male cones to the female cones, where the pollen fertilizes the egg. The ovules then develop into seeds. After the seeds become fully formed, they fall from the cones.

A few conifers have unusual, fleshy cones. Juniper seed cones resemble blueberries. Yew seed cones look like red berries with a single, large seed.

Scientific classification. Conifers make up the division Coniferophyta in the plant kingdom, Plantae. There are several families and many genera in this division. ＿＿＿＿Douglas G. Sprugel

Related articles in *World Book* include:

Arborvitae	Evergreen	Piñon
Baldcypress	Fir	Plant (pictures)
Balsam fir	Ginkgo	Redwood
Bristlecone pine	Gymnosperm	Sequoia
Cedar	Hemlock	Spruce
Cycad	Juniper	Tree (Needleleaf
Cypress	Larch	trees; pictures)
Douglas-fir	Pine	Yew

Conjoined twins. See Siamese twins.
Conjugation, in biology. See Paramecium.
Conjugation, *KAHN juh GAY shuhn,* is a complete list of the forms of a verb by mood, number, person, tense, and voice. A *synopsis* is a summary of these forms in only one person, as shown below for the verb *show.*

Each verb form expresses a different shade of meaning. Progressive forms indicate an action in progress at any particular time ("The first film *was showing* when we

Indicative mood

Simple forms

Tense	Active voice	Passive voice
Present	it shows	it is shown
Past	it showed	it was shown
Future	it will show	it will be shown
Present perfect	it has shown	it has been shown
Past perfect	it had shown	it had been shown
Future perfect	it will have shown	it will have been shown

Progressive forms

Tense	Active voice	Passive voice
Present	it is showing	it is being shown
Past	it was showing	it was being shown
Future	it will be showing	*
Present perfect	it has been showing	*
Past perfect	it had been showing	*
Future perfect	it will have been showing	*

*No commonly accepted usage in this voice

Emphatic forms

Tense	Active voice only
Present	it does show
Past	it did show

Imperative mood

Used only in the second person, present tense

Active voice	Passive voice
[you] show	[you] be shown

Subjunctive mood

Tense	Active voice	Passive voice
Present	[if] it show	[if] it be shown
Past	[if] it showed	[if] it were shown
Future	[if] it will show	[if] it will be shown
Present perfect	[if] it has shown	[if] it has been shown
Past perfect	[if] it had shown	[if] it had been shown
Future perfect	[if] it will have shown	[if] it will have been shown

arrived"). Emphatic forms may add a degree of emphasis, but they are used primarily to form questions ("*Does* it *show?*") and negative statements ("It *does* not *show*"). The imperative mood gives commands ("*Show* what it is like"). The subjunctive mood expresses urgency ("The people insisted that the film *be shown*"); wishing ("I wish it *were being shown* now"); or reflects a condition contrary to fact ("If the film *were shown,* we would be in trouble").   William F. Irmscher

See also **Mood; Number; Person; Tense; Voice; Verb.**

Conjunction, *kuhn JUHNGK shuhn,* is a word used to connect words, phrases, clauses, and sentences. The term comes from two Latin words that mean *joined with.* There are two kinds of conjunctions, *coordinating* and *subordinating.*

Coordinating conjunctions connect grammatically equal words, phrases, clauses, or sentences as in the following examples. Words—"He ate bread *and* butter." Phrases—"In red coats *and* with loud drums, the soldiers came marching." Clauses or sentences—"He reads well, *but* his sister reads better."

The principal coordinating conjunctions are:
Expressing addition: and, also, both, as well as, further, likewise.
Expressing separation or choice: either, or, neither, nor, else, whether, otherwise.
Expressing opposition: but, yet, still, only, whereas.

Conjunctions in pairs, as in the following examples, are called *correlative conjunctions.*

Both . . . and: *Both* John *and* Mary attend school.
Not only . . . but also: He *not only* reads *but also* writes.
Either . . . or: *Either* I must go now *or* I can never go.
Neither . . . nor: *Neither* the child *nor* the man went.
Whether . . . or: *Whether* it rains *or* shines, I will go.

Subordinating conjunctions join a subordinate clause to the principal clause of a sentence—elements that are not grammatically equal. "He can read better *than* I can." *Than* is a subordinating conjunction connecting the subordinate clause *I can* (*read* is understood) with the principal clause.

The commonest subordinating conjunctions are:
Expressing time and place: when, as, since, while, before, ere, after, until, where.
Expressing cause or reason: because, since, as, whereas, inasmuch as, for.
Expressing condition or supposition: if, unless, though, although, provided, in case, even if.
Expressing purpose or result: that, so that, lest, in order that, so . . . as.
Expressing comparison: than (after comparative), as . . . as, so . . . as.   Marianne Cooley

Conjunctivitis, *kuhn JUHNGK tuh VY tihs,* is an inflammation of the membrane that covers the white part of the eyeball and the inner lining of the eyelid. This membrane is called the *conjunctiva.* Conjunctivitis may be caused by infections of bacteria, viruses, or other microorganisms. It also may result from allergies or chemical burns. Most types of conjunctivitis caused by infection are contagious.

Symptoms of conjunctivitis include burning, itching, watering and redness of the eye, and the sensation that an object is lodged on the eyeball. In addition, pus may form and the eyelids may stick together.

Acute conjunctivitis, or *pinkeye,* is often caused by bacteria. In most cases, doctors can cure bacterial conjunctivitis within a few days by applying antibiotics. Most cases of viral conjunctivitis usually do not respond to drugs, but many types rapidly clear up by themselves. However, some types of viral conjunctivitis may last a long time and infect the *cornea,* the clear tissue at the front of the eye. When this occurs, the person's vision may decrease. Allergic conjunctivitis is frequently associated with hay fever. Cold compresses and medicated eyedrops help relieve the symptoms of allergic conjunctivitis. Conjunctivitis caused by exposure to chemicals can result in serious eye damage. In many cases, such damage can be minimized by immediately flushing the eye with water.   Ronald Klein

Conjuring. See Magician.

Conly, Robert Leslie. See O'Brien, Robert C.

Connally, John Bowden (1917-1993), was United States secretary of the treasury in 1971 and 1972. He was the first Democrat appointed to the Cabinet by President Richard M. Nixon, a Republican. Connally served as governor of Texas from 1963 to 1969. In 1973, he became a Republican. He was an unsuccessful candidate for the 1980 Republican presidential nomination.

Connally was born in Floresville, Tex., and graduated from the University of Texas School of Law. After serving as a Navy lieutenant commander during World War II, he became the manager of a radio station in Austin, Tex., in 1946. During the 1950's, Connally was attorney for a Texas oil company.

In 1961, President John F. Kennedy named Connally secretary of the Navy. Connally resigned after 11 months to seek the Texas governorship. In 1963, he was seriously wounded while riding in Kennedy's car in Dallas when the President was assassinated.   William J. Eaton

Connaught and Strathearn, Duke of (1850-1942), served as governor general of Canada from 1911 to 1916. He was the third son of Queen Victoria of Britain. Connaught's presence in Canada as governor general helped inspire patriotism there during the early years of World War I (1914-1918). During the war, Connaught helped reestablish the Canadian Patriotic Fund, which aided dependents of people serving in the Canadian armed forces.

Connaught was born in London. His full given name was Arthur William Patrick Albert, and he was known as Prince Arthur. In 1868, the prince became an army officer. During the late 1800's, he fought in Canada and Egypt and served with British troops in India and Ireland. In 1874, Prince Arthur became the Duke of Connaught and Strathearn. In the army, he became a general in 1893 and a field marshal in 1902. From 1907 to 1909, he served as commander in chief of British forces in and around the Mediterranean Sea.   Jacques Monet

©Steve Dunwell

A Connecticut village in autumn is ablaze with the brilliant colors of turning leaves. Every year, many vacationers visit the state to enjoy its scenic countryside and to explore its many picturesque villages and historic sites.

Connecticut　*The Constitution State*

Connecticut, *kuh NEHT ih kuht,* is the third smallest state of the United States. Only Delaware and Rhode Island have smaller areas. In spite of its small size, Connecticut is an important industrial state and a favorite vacationland. Hartford, the capital of Connecticut, is known as the Insurance City. About 50 insurance companies have headquarters in Hartford. Bridgeport and Hartford are Connecticut's two largest cities.

Connecticut is one of the nation's leading producers of helicopters, jet aircraft engines, propellers, and submarines. It also ranks high among the states in the processing of copper, and in the production of ball and roller bearings, cutlery, electric conductors, machine tools, and optical instruments.

The mighty Connecticut River cuts through the center of the state. The river flows into Long Island Sound,

The contributors of this article are John L. Allen, Professor of Geography at the University of Connecticut, and Richard Buel, Jr., Professor of History at Wesleyan University.

Connecticut's outlet to the Atlantic Ocean. The word *Connecticut* comes from an Algonquian Indian word meaning *on the long tidal river.* The state's biggest industrial cities are west of the Connecticut River. They stretch from Hartford in central Connecticut to Stamford near the southwestern border of the state. New York City lies south of Connecticut. Thousands of Connecticut residents commute to work there.

Connecticut's rural areas and small towns contrast sharply with its industrial cities. Many towns in Connecticut center around a *green* (public park). Near the green may stand a small white church, a town meeting hall, a tavern, and several colonial houses. Forests, rivers, lakes, waterfalls, and a sandy shore add to the beauty of Connecticut.

The people of Connecticut played an important role in the history of the United States. For many years, colonial Connecticut was governed under the *Fundamental Orders,* sometimes regarded as the first written constitution. The Fundamental Orders later served as one of the models for the U.S. Constitution. At the Constitu-

City Place in Hartford, Connecticut's capital, is the state's tall-est building. The 38-story office complex overlooks Bushnell Park and the Soldiers and Sailors Memorial Arch, *foreground.*

©Ray Hillstrom

Interesting facts about Connecticut

WORLD BOOK illustrations by Kevin Chadwick

The first telephone exchange in the world, *right,* opened in New Haven on Jan. 28, 1878. The exchange, which had 21 subscribers, was developed by George W. Coy. Its customers placed their calls through an operator.

The Hartford Courant, one of Connecticut's chief news-papers, has been published continuously longer than any other newspaper in the United States. The *Courant* began publication in 1764.

First telephone exchange

The first cookbook written by an American was published in Hartford in 1796. The book was *American Cookery* by Amelia Simmons.

First accident insurance policy

The first accident insurance policy sold in the United States, *above,* was issued on April 1, 1864, by James Goodwin Batterson of the Travelers Insurance Company of Hartford. Batterson sold the policy to James Bolter of Hartford as the two of them walked out of the Hartford post office. The policy covered only Bolter's two-block walk that day from the post office to his home on Buckingham Street. The $1,000 coverage provided by the policy cost Bolter 2 cents.

The football tackling dummy was invented at Yale University in New Haven in 1889. Amos Alonzo Stagg, its inventor, was a di-vinity student and a football player at Yale. He later became one of the most successful coaches in the history of college football.

tional Convention of 1787, Connecticut delegates helped work out the *Great Compromise* or *Connecticut Compromise.* It broke a deadlock over how many represent-atives each state should elect to Congress. This compromise and the Fundamental Orders earned Connecticut the nickname of the Constitution State.

Connecticut's people also made important contributions to the nation's industrial development. Eli Whitney helped make Connecticut the birthplace of mass-production manufacturing. Working in Hamden, he showed the advantages of using interchangeable parts in gunmaking. Whitney's methods led to the high-speed industrial production of today.

Steel manufacturing in the United States began in Hartford County. Connecticut workers were also the first Americans to make bicycles, dyed silk, friction matches, printing type, repeating pistols, rubber shoes, and vul-canized rubber. The first insurance policies providing coverage for accidents, automobiles, and aircraft were written in Hartford. The *Nautilus,* launched in Groton in 1954, was the world's first nuclear-powered submarine.

©Stuart Cohen, Stock, Boston

Yale University's Memorial Quadrangle features beautiful Gothic architecture. The university, located in New Haven, is the third oldest institution of higher learning in the United States.

Connecticut in brief

Symbols of Connecticut

On the state flag, adopted in 1897, the three grapevines on the shield symbolize the colony brought from Europe and transplanted in the wilderness. The state motto beneath the shield, *Qui Transtulit Sustinet,* means *He Who Transplanted Still Sustains.* The present version of the state seal first appeared in 1784. The seal also bears three grapevines and the state motto.

State flag

State seal

Connecticut (brown) ranks 48th in size among all the states and 5th in size among the New England states (yellow).

General information

Statehood: Jan. 9, 1788, the fifth state.
State abbreviations: Conn. (traditional); CT (postal).
State motto: *Qui Transtulit Sustinet* (He Who Transplanted Still Sustains).
State song: "Yankee Doodle." Composer unknown.

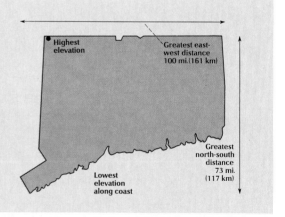

The State Capitol is in Hartford. New Haven and Hartford were twin capitals from 1701 to 1875, when Hartford became the only capital.

Land and climate

Area: 5,006 sq. mi. (12,966 km²), including 161 sq. mi. (416 km²) of inland water but excluding 538 sq. mi. (1,392 km²) of coastal water.
Elevation: *Highest*—2,380 ft. (725 m) above sea level, on the south slope of Mount Frissell. *Lowest*—sea level along the Long Island Sound shore.
Record high temperature: 105 °F (41 °C) at Waterbury on July 22, 1926.
Record low temperature: −32 °F (−36 °C) at Falls Village on Feb. 16, 1943.
Average July temperature: 71 °F (22 °C).
Average January temperature: 26 °F (−3 °C).
Average yearly precipitation: 47 in. (119 cm).

Highest elevation

Greatest east-west distance 100 mi.(161 km)

Greatest north-south distance 73 mi. (117 km)

Lowest elevation along coast

Important dates

Connecticut received a charter from England that served as a constitution until 1818.

Connecticut became the 5th state when it ratified the U.S. Constitution on January 9.

| 1633 | 1662 | 1776 | 1788 |

The first English settlement in Connecticut was made in Windsor.

Connecticut passed a resolution in favor of independence from Britain on June 14.

State bird
Robin

State flower
Mountain laurel

State tree
White oak

People

Population: 3,295,669 (1990 census)

Rank among the states: 27th

Density: 658 persons per sq. mi. (254 per km²), U.S. average 69 per sq. mi. (27 per km²)

Distribution: 79 per cent urban, 21 per cent rural

Largest cities in Connecticut

Bridgeport	141,686
Hartford	139,739
New Haven	130,474
Waterbury	108,961
Stamford	108,056
Norwalk	78,331

Source: U.S. Bureau of the Census.

Population trend

Millions

Year	Population
1990	3,295,669
1980	3,107,576
1970	3,032,217
1960	2,535,234
1950	2,007,280
1940	1,709,242
1930	1,606,903
1920	1,380,631
1910	1,114,756
1900	908,420
1890	746,258
1880	622,700
1870	537,454
1860	460,147
1850	370,792
1840	309,978
1830	297,675
1820	275,248
1810	261,942
1800	251,002
1790	237,946

Source: U.S. Bureau of the Census.

Economy

Chief products

Agriculture: greenhouse and nursery products, eggs, milk.

Manufacturing: transportation equipment, machinery, fabricated metal products, scientific instruments, chemicals, electrical equipment, printed materials.

Mining: crushed stone.

Gross state product

Value of goods and services produced in 1991: $93,640,000,000. *Services* include community, social, and personal services; finance; government; trade; and transportation, communication, and utilities. *Industry* includes construction, manufacturing, and mining. *Agriculture* includes agriculture, fishing, and forestry.

Source: U.S. Bureau of Economic Analysis.

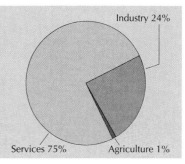

Industry 24%

Services 75%

Agriculture 1%

Government

State government

Governor: 4-year term
State senators: 36; 2-year term
State representatives: 151; 2-year term
Towns: 169 (no county governments)

Federal government

United States senators: 2
United States representatives: 6
Electoral votes: 8

Sources of information

Tourism: State Department of Economic Development, Tourism Division, 865 Brook Street, Rocky Hill, CT 06067-3405

Economy: State Department of Economic Development, Locational Services, 865 Brook Street, Rocky Hill, CT 06067-3405

Government: Office of the Secretary of State, Administrative Legislative Division, 30 Trinity Street, Hartford, CT 06106

History: Connecticut State Library, History and Genealogy Unit, 231 Capitol Avenue, Hartford, CT 06106

New London became the home of the U.S. Coast Guard Academy.

Connecticut passed a law banning construction of new nuclear power plants.

1910   **1954**   **1979**

The first atomic submarine was launched in Groton.

Population. The 1990 United States census reported that Connecticut had 3,295,669 people. The population had increased 6 percent over the 1980 figure, 3,107,576. According to the 1990 census, Connecticut ranks 27th in population among the 50 states.

About 96 percent of the people of Connecticut live in eight Metropolitan Statistical Areas (see **Metropolitan area**). These areas are Bridgeport, Danbury, Hartford, New Haven-Meriden, New London-Norwich, Stamford-Norwalk, Waterbury, and Worcester. For the populations of these metropolitan areas, see the Index to the political map of Connecticut.

Bridgeport is Connecticut's largest city. Other large cities, in order of population, include Hartford, New Haven, Waterbury, and Stamford.

Connecticut's largest population groups include people of Italian, Irish, English, German, and Polish descent. About 8 per cent of the state's people are blacks.

Schools. Connecticut's Yale University, founded in 1701, is the third oldest institution of higher learning in the United States. Only Harvard University and the College of William and Mary are older. The Litchfield Law School (later called Tapping Reeve Law School) was the first institution in the United States devoted entirely to teaching law. Tapping Reeve, a judge, founded the school in his home in 1774. In 1784, he moved the school to a building next to his home. The school operated until 1833. In 1817, Thomas H. Gallaudet founded the first free American school for the deaf, in Hartford. The school now operates in West Hartford as the American School for the Deaf.

Before 1650, schools in Connecticut were voluntary. A law passed in 1650 required Connecticut towns with at least 50 families to hire someone from the town to teach the children to read and write. Towns with at least 100 families were required to establish a school for more advanced study.

A commissioner of education and a 9-member board of education supervise Connecticut's public school sys-

---

Universities and colleges

Connecticut has 24 universities and colleges that grant bachelor's or advanced degrees and are accredited by the New England Association of Schools and Colleges. For enrollments and further information, see **Universities and colleges** (table).

Name	Mailing address
Albertus Magnus College	New Haven
Bridgeport, University of	Bridgeport
Bridgeport Engineering Institute	Fairfield
Central Connecticut State University	New Britain
Charter Oak State College	Farmington
Connecticut, University of	*
Connecticut College	New London
Eastern Connecticut State University	Willimantic
Fairfield University	Fairfield
Hartford, University of	West Hartford
Hartford Graduate Center	Hartford
Hartford Seminary	Hartford
Holy Apostles College and Seminary	Cromwell
New Haven, University of	West Haven
Quinnipiac College	Hamden
Sacred Heart University	Fairfield
St. Joseph College	West Hartford
Southern Connecticut State University	New Haven
Teikyo Post University	Waterbury
Trinity College	Hartford
United States Coast Guard Academy	New London
Wesleyan University	Middletown
Western Connecticut State University	Danbury
Yale University	New Haven

*For campuses, see **Universities and colleges** (table).

---

tem. The governor appoints the board members to four-year terms, and the board members elect the commissioner to the same term.

Connecticut law requires children to attend school from age 7 through 15. For the number of students and teachers in Connecticut, see **Education** (table).

Libraries. The Yale University Library, founded in 1701, is the oldest library still operating in Connecticut. It is one of the largest libraries in the world. The Scoville Memorial Library in Salisbury was founded in 1803 as the Bingham Library for Youth. In 1810, Salisbury began using taxes to support the library. It may have been the first free, tax-supported public library in the United States.

Today, Connecticut has about 200 public libraries and many school and special libraries. The state's largest public libraries are in Bridgeport, Hartford, and New Haven. The State Library in Hartford houses the state archives, many books about Connecticut, and a special law collection. Hartford also has law libraries and insurance libraries.

Museums. Yale's Peabody Museum has world-famous natural history exhibits. The Yale University Art Gallery is the oldest university art museum in the United States. The university also operates the Yale Center for British Art. Other fine art museums are in Farmington, Hartford, Middletown, New Britain, New London, Norwich, and at the University of Connecticut in Storrs. Children's museums are in Manchester, New Britain, New Haven, Stamford, and West Hartford. The American Clock and Watch Museum in Bristol displays timepieces made in the 1700's and 1800's. The New Haven Colony Historical Society exhibits the original model of Eli Whitney's cotton gin. It also owns valuable prints and early American portraits.

Population density

Connecticut's most densely populated areas lie chiefly along Long Island Sound and in the center of the state. Eastern and northwestern areas are less heavily populated.

	Persons per sq. mi.	Persons per km²
	More than 1,000	More than 400
	500 to 1,000	200 to 400
	100 to 500	40 to 200
	Less than 100	Less than 40

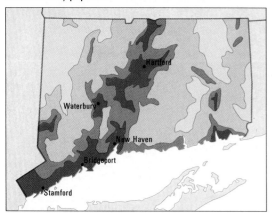

WORLD BOOK map; based on U.S. Bureau of the Census data.

Connecticut map index

Metropolitan areas

Bridgeport 443,722
Danbury 193,597
Hartford 1,157,585
New Haven-Meriden 530,180
New London-Norwich 290,734 (262,256 in Conn.; 28,476 in R.I.)
Stamford-Norwalk 329,935
Waterbury 221,629
Worcester 478,384 (469,716 in Mass.; 8,668 in Conn.)

Counties

Fairfield 827,645 H 5
Hartford 851,783 C 9
Litchfield 174,092 C 5
Middlesex 143,196 G 10
New Haven 804,219 G 7
New London 254,957 F 13
Tolland 128,699 C 11
Windham 102,525 C 13

Cities, towns, and boroughs

Abington C 13
Almyville D 14
Amesville B 5
Amston E 11
Andover 2,540▲D 11
Ansonia 18,403 G 6
Ashford 3,765▲C 13
Aspetuck I 5
Attawaugan C 14
Atwoodville D 12
Avon 13,937▲C 8
Bakersville C 7
Ballouville C 14
Baltic E 13
Bantam 757 D 5
Barkhamsted 3,369▲B 7
Bashan F 11
Beacon Falls 5,083▲G 7
Berlin 16,787▲E 9
Bethany 4,608▲G 7
Bethel† 8,835 17,541▲G 4
Bethlehem† 1,976 3,071▲E 6
Black Point H 12
Bloomfield 19,483▲C 9
Boardman Bridge E 4
Bolton 4,575▲D 11
Botsford G 5
Bozrah* 2,297▲F 12
Branchville H 4
Branford† 5,688 27,603▲H 8
Bridgeport 141,686 I 6
Bridgewater 1,654▲F 5
Bristol 60,640 D 7
Broad Brook† 3,585 B 10
Brookfield 14,113▲F 4
Brooklawn, see Stratfield-Brooklawn
Brooklyn 6,681▲C 14
Bulls Bridge E 4
Burlington 7,026▲D 7
Burnetts Corner G 14
Burnside D 9
Campville D 6
Canaan† 1,194 1,057▲A 5
Canaan Valley A 5
Candlewood Knolls F 4
Cannondale I 4
Canterbury 4,467▲D 14
Canton 8,268▲C 8
Canton Center C 7
Centerbrook G 11
Central Village D 14
Chaplin 2,048▲C 13
Cheshire† 5,759 25,684▲F 8
Chester† 1,563 3,417▲G 11
Chesterfield G 12
Chestnut Hill E 12
Clarks Corner D 13
Clarks Falls F 15
Clinton† 3,439 12,767▲H 10
Cobalt E 10
Colchester 3,212 10,980▲E 12
Colebrook 1,365▲B 6
Collinsville† 2,591 C 7
Columbia 4,510▲D 11
Conning Towers-Nautilus Park*† 10,013 G 13
Cornwall 1,414▲C 5
Cornwall Bridge C 4
Coventry 10,063▲C 11
Cromwell 12,286▲E 9
Crystal Lake† 1,175 B 11
Danbury 65,585 G 4
Danielson 4,441 C 14
Darien 18,196▲J 4
Dayville C 14
Deep River† 2,520 4,332▲G 11
Derby 12,199 H 6
Dodgingtown G 5
Drakeville C 6
Durham† 2,650 5,732▲F 9
Durham Center F 9
Eagleville D 12
East Berlin E 9
East Brooklyn† 1,481 C 14
East Canaan B 5
East Glastonbury D 10
East Granby 4,302▲B 9
East Haddam 6,676▲F 11
East Hampton† 2,167 10,428▲E 10
East Hartford 50,452▲D 9
East Hartland B 8
East Haven 26,144▲H 8
East Killingly C 15
East Litchfield D 6
East Lyme 15,340▲G 12
East Plymouth D 7
East River H 9
East Thompson B 15
East Village G 6
East Willington C 12
East Windsor* 10,081▲B 10
East Windsor Hill C 10
East Woodstock B 14
Eastford 1,314▲B 13
Easton 6,303▲H 5
Ekonk E 14
Ellington 11,197▲C 10
Ellsworth C 4
Elmville C 14
Enfield 45,532▲B 10
Essex† 2,500 5,904▲G 11
Fabyan B 14
Fairfield 53,418▲I 5
Falls Village B 5
Farmington 20,608▲D 8
Fenwick 89 H 11
Fitchville E 13
Flanders D 4
Franklin 1,810▲E 13
Gales Ferry G 13
Gaylordsville E 4
Georgetown† 1,694 H 4
Germantown G 4
Gilead E 11
Gilman E 12
Glasgo F 14
Glastonbury† 7,082 27,901▲D 10
Glenville J 3
Goshen 2,329▲C 5
Goshen Hill E 12
Granby 9,369▲B 8
Green Farms I 5
Greenwich 58,441▲J 3
Greystone E 7
Griswold* 10,384▲E 14
Grosvenor Dale B 14
Groton 9,837 45,144▲G 13
Grove Beach H 10
Guilford† 2,588 19,848▲H 9
Gurleyville C 12
Haddam 6,769▲F 10
Hadlyme G 11
Hallville F 13
Hamburg G 11
Hamden 52,434▲G 8
Hampton 1,578▲D 13
Hanover E 13
Harrisville B 14
Hartford 139,739 D 9
Hartland 1,866▲B 7
Harwinton 5,228▲D 7
Hawleyville G 5
Hayden G 9
Hazardville B 10
Hebron 7,079▲E 11
Higganum† 1,692 F 10
Hopeville E 14
Hoskins C 8
Hotchkissville E 6
Huntingtown G 5
Huntsville B 5
Hydeville B 12
Indian Neck H 8
Ivoryton G 11
Jewett City 3,349 E 14
Kensington† 8,306 E 8
Kent 2,918▲D 4
Kent Furnace D 4
Killingly* 15,889▲C 14
Killingly Center C 14
Killingworth 4,814▲G 10
Lake Pocotopaug*† 3,029 E 10
Lakeside D 5
Lakeville B 4
Laysville G 12
Lebanon 6,041▲E 12
Ledyard 14,913▲G 13
Leesville F 10
Leetes Island H 9
Leffingwell F 13
Liberty Hill E 12
Lime Rock B 4
Lisbon 3,790▲E 13
Litchfield 1,378 8,365▲D 6
Long Ridge I 3
Long Society F 13
Lords Point G 14
Lyme* 1,949▲G 11
Lyons Plain I 5
Macedonia D 4
Madison† 2,139 15,485▲H 10
Manchester 51,618▲D 10
Mansfield 21,103▲C 12
Mansfield Center D 12
Mansfield Depot C 11
Marble Dale E 5
Marion E 7
Marlborough 5,535▲E 10
Mashapaug A 13
Mechanicsville B 14
Melrose B 10
Meriden 59,479 F 8
Merrow C 11
Middle Haddam F 10
Middlebury 6,145▲F 6
Middlefield 3,925▲F 9
Middletown 42,762 F 9
Milford 48,168 49,938▲I 7
Mill Plain I 5
Milldale E 8
Millington F 11
Millstone H 12
Milton D 5
Minortown E 6
Mixville F 7
Mohegan F 13
Monroe 16,896▲H 6
Montville 16,673▲F 13
Moodus† 1,170 F 11
Moosup† 3,289 D 14
Morningside Park G 13
Morris 2,039▲D 6
Mystic† 2,618 G 14
Naugatuck 30,625 F 7
Nautilus Park, see Conning Towers-Nautilus Park
Nepaug C 7
New Britain 75,491 E 8
New Canaan 17,864▲I 4
New Fairfield 12,911▲F 4
New Hartford† 1,269 5,769▲C 7
New Haven 130,474 H 7
New London 28,540 G 13
New Milford† 5,775 23,629▲E 4
New Preston† 1,217 E 5
Newfield C 6
Newfield F 9
Newington 29,208▲D 9
Newtown 1,800 20,779▲G 5
Niantic† 3,048 H 12
Noank H 14
Norfolk 2,060▲B 6
Noroton J 4
Noroton Heights J 4
North Branford 12,996▲H 8
North Canaan* 3,284▲A 5
North Franklin E 12
North Granby† 1,455 B 8
North Grosvenor Dale† 1,705 B 14
North Haven 22,249▲G 8
North Plain G 11
North Somers A 11
North Stamford I 3
North Stonington 4,884▲G 14
North Westchester E 11
North Windham D 13
North Woodbury F 6
North Woodstock B 13
Northfield D 6
Northford G 8
Northville E 4
Norwalk 78,331 I 4
Norwich 37,391 F 13
Oakdale F 12
Oakville† 8,741 E 6
Occum E 13
Old Lyme 6,535▲H 11
Old Mystic G 14
Old Saybrook† 1,820 9,552▲H 11
Oneco D 15
Orange† 12,830▲H 7
Orcutts B 11
Oxford 8,685▲G 6
Packerville E 14
Palmers Hill J 3
Park Lane E 4
Pawcatuck† 5,289 G 15
Pequabuck E 7
Phoenixville C 13
Pine Meadow C 7
Pine Orchard H 8
Plainfield† 2,856 14,363▲D 14
Plainville 17,392▲E 8
Plantsville E 8
Plattsville H 5
Pleasant Valley B 7
Pleasure Beach H 13
Plymouth 11,822▲E 7
Pomfret 3,102▲B 14
Pomfret Center C 14
Pond Meadow H 10
Ponset F 10
Poquetanuck F 13
Poquonock C 9
Poquonock Bridge† 2,770 G 13
Portland† 5,645 8,418▲E 9
Preston* 5,006▲F 14
Preston City F 14
Prospect 7,775▲F 7
Putnam† 6,835 9,031▲B 14
Putnam Heights C 14
Quaddick B 15
Quaker Farms G 6
Quaker Hill G 13
Quinebaug† 1,031 A 14
Redding 7,927▲H 4
Redding Ridge H 5
Reynolds Bridge E 6
Ridgebury G 3
Ridgefield† 6,363 20,919▲H 4
Riversville J 2
Riverton B 7
Robertsville B 7
Rockfall F 9
Rockland G 9
Rockville C 11
Rocky Hill 16,554▲E 9
Rogers C 14
Round Hill J 3
Rowayton J 4
Roxbury 1,825▲F 5
Roxbury Falls F 5
Sachem Head H 9
Salem 3,310▲F 12
Salisbury 4,090▲B 4
Sandy Hook G 5
Saugatuck I 4
Saybrook Manor† 1,073 H 11
Saybrook Point H 11
Scantic C 10
Scotland 1,215▲D 13
Seymour 14,288▲G 6
Shailerville F 10
Sharon 2,928▲C 4
Sharon Valley C 4
Shelton 35,418 H 6
Sherman 2,809▲E 4
Sherwood Manor*† 6,357 B 10
Short Beach H 8
Simsbury† 5,577 22,023▲C 8
Somers 9,108▲B 11
Somersville B 10
Sound View H 12
South Britain F 5
South Canaan B 5
South Chaplin D 13
South Coventry*† 1,257 D 12
South Glastonbury E 10
South Kent D 4
South Killingly C 15
South Lyme H 12
South Willington C 11
South Windham† 1,644 D 12
South Windsor 22,090▲C 9
South Woodstock† 1,112 B 14
Southbury 15,818▲F 6
Southington 38,518▲E 8
Southport I 5
Southwood Acres*† 8,963 B 10
Sprague* 3,008▲E 13
Spring Hill D 12
Stafford 11,091▲B 12
Stafford Springs 4,100 B 11
Staffordville B 12
Stamford 108,056 J 3
Stanwich I 3
Sterling 2,357▲D 15
Stevenson G 6
Stonington 1,100 16,919▲G 14
Stony Creek H 9
Storrs† 12,198 C 12
Stratfield-Brooklawn* I 5
Stratford 49,389▲I 6
Suffield 11,427▲B 9
Taconic A 4
Taftville E 13
Talcottville C 10
Tariffville† 1,477 B 8
Terryville† 5,426 D 7
Thomaston 6,947▲E 6
Thompson 8,668▲B 14
Thompsonville† 8,458 B 10
Titicus H 4
Tolland 11,001▲C 11
Torrington 33,687 C 6
Trumbull 32,016▲H 6
Twin Lakes B 4
Uncasville G 13
Union 612▲B 12
Unionville D 8
Vernon 29,841▲C 10
Vernon Center C 10
Versailles E 13
Voluntown 2,113▲E 14
Wallingford† 17,827 40,822▲F 8
Wapping C 10
Warren 1,226▲D 5
Warrenville C 12
Washington 3,905▲E 5
Washington Depot E 5
Waterbury 108,961 F 7
Waterford 17,930▲G 13
Watertown 20,456▲E 6
Wauregan† 1,079 D 14
Weatogue† 2,521 C 8
Wequetequock G 14
West Cornwall C 5
West Goshen C 5
West Granby B 8
West Hartford 60,110▲D 8
West Hartland B 7
West Haven 54,021 H 7
West Mystic† 3,595 G 14
West Redding H 4
West Simsbury† 2,149 C 8
West Stafford B 11
West Suffield B 9
West Willington C 12
West Woodstock B 13
Westbrook† 2,060 5,414▲H 11
Westchester F 11
Westfield E 9
Westford B 12
Weston 8,648▲I 4
Westport 24,407▲I 5
Wethersfield 25,651▲D 9
Whigville D 7
White Oaks F 6
Willimantic† 14,746 D 12
Willington* 5,979▲C 12
Willington Hill C 12
Wilson C 9
Wilsonville A 14
Wilton 15,989▲I 4
Winchester Center 11,524▲C 6
Windermere C 10
Windham 22,039▲D 12
Windsor 27,817▲C 9
Windsor Locks 12,358▲B 9
Windsorville C 10
Winsted† 8,254 B 7
Winthrop G 10
Wolcott 13,700▲E 7
Woodbridge 7,924▲G 7
Woodbury† 1,212 8,131▲F 6
Woodmont 1,770 H 7
Woodstock 6,008▲B 14
Woodstock Valley B 13
Woodtick E 7
Woodville D 5

*Does not appear on map; key shows general location.
†Census designated place—unincorporated, but recognized as a significant settled community by the U.S. Bureau of the Census.

▲Entire town (township), including rural area.
Source: 1990 census. Places without population figures are unincorporated areas.

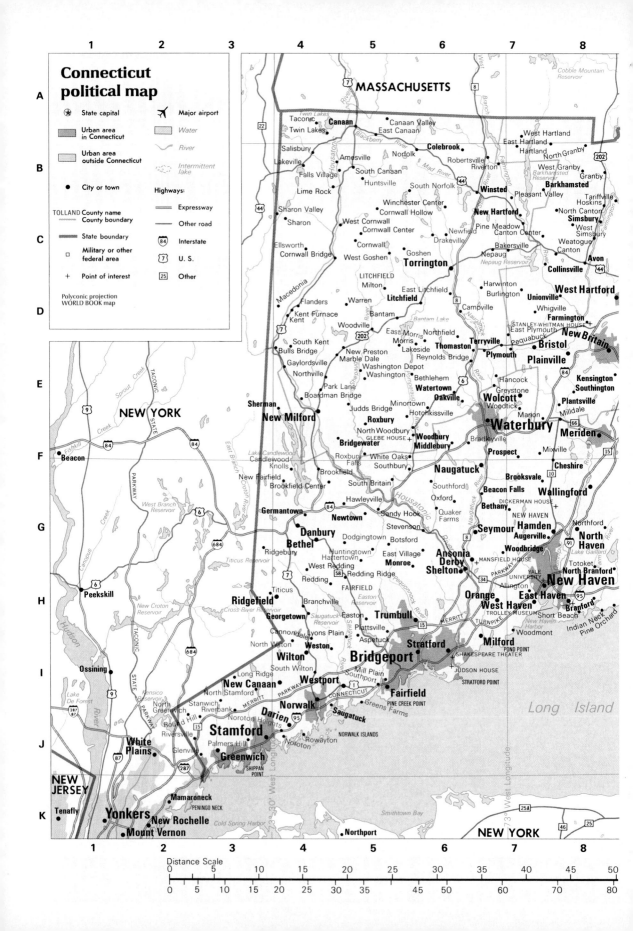

Connecticut political map

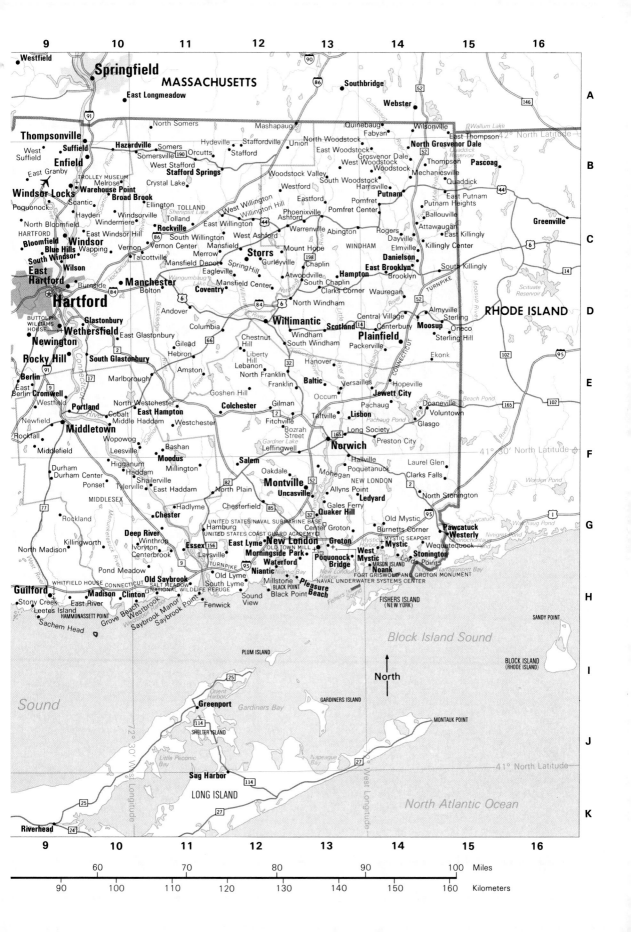

Southern Connecticut's seashore offers vacationers swimming, fishing, boating, and beautiful scenery. Inland, many summertime visitors hike and ride horseback across the state's wooded hills and valleys. Many people fish in Connecticut's rivers, streams, and lakes. Camping is a popular activity in both private campgrounds and state parks and forests. During winter, the state's snow-covered hills provide skiing and other winter sports. Tourists and students of American history also may visit many historic sites, museums, and colo-

nial buildings in cities and towns throughout the state.

One of the best-known annual events in Connecticut is the Dogwood Festival held in Fairfield in May. Visitors to the festival enjoy the beautiful dogwood trees that bloom in the city and tours of scenic gardens and historic houses. Country fairs are held in various Connecticut towns from early August to mid-October. During the winter, Connecticut's history is brought to life by sleigh rides through the countryside, antique shows and craft shows, and special holiday festivities.

Roy Gumpel, De Wys, Inc.

Roy Gumpel, De Wys, Inc.

Gillette Castle, *above,* was designed by the American playwright and actor William Gillette as his retirement home. The mansion, in Hadlyme, was completed in 1919.

The blessing of the fleet, *left,* is a colorful ceremony held each year in Stonington. It arose from an old Portuguese Catholic tradition of blessing fishing fleets before they set sail.

Places to visit

Following are brief descriptions of some of Connecticut's many interesting places to visit:

Colonial buildings are among Connecticut's most famous landmarks. Almost every Connecticut town has at least one example of Colonial architecture. *Whitfield House,* in Guilford, is the oldest house in the state. It was begun in 1639, and is the oldest stone house in New England. Three buildings stand as shrines to Nathan Hale, the famous Connecticut patriot. *Nathan Hale Homestead* in South Coventry was the home of Hale's parents. In East Haddam and New London are the *Nathan Hale Schoolhouses,* where Hale taught school from 1773 to 1775. Other Connecticut colonial buildings, with the location and original completion date of each, include *Putnam Cottage* (Greenwich, about 1690); *Buttolph-Williams House* (Wethersfield, 1692); *Noah Webster House* (West Hartford, 1748); *Glebe House* (Woodbury, 1750?); *Webb House* (Wethersfield, 1752); *Cheney Homestead* (Manchester, 1785?); and *Old State House* (Hartford, 1796).

Essex Steam Train, at Essex Junction, offers a scenic 16-mile (26-kilometer) round trip through the lower Connecticut River Valley. Passenger cars are drawn by a steam locomotive dating from the early 1900's.

Gillette Castle, in Hadlyme, is a Rhenish hilltop mansion created in 1919 by actor William Gillette. It contains many hand-carved fixtures created by Gillette.

Marinelife Aquarium in Mystic contains more than 6,000 specimens of marine life. Exhibits include an indoor theater that features demonstrations with dolphins, sea lions, and whales, and an outdoor exhibit of seals and sea lions.

Mark Twain Mansion, in Hartford, was the home of the famous American author during the late 1800's. The residence has many original furnishings and other personal belongings of Twain's family. A cottage near the Twain mansion was the home of American author Harriet Beecher Stowe during the late 1800's.

Mystic Seaport, in Mystic, recalls Connecticut's seafaring tradition. The seaport has been rebuilt to look like a whaling village of the 1800's. The *Charles W. Morgan,* New England's last wooden whaling ship, is in the harbor.

The Maritime Center at Norwalk explores the maritime culture and marine life of Long Island Sound. The center's features include more than 20 aquariums, a maritime history hall with exhibits, and boat-building demonstrations and workshops.

Trolley museums exhibit trolleys that date from the late 1800's and early 1900's. Visitors may ride on some of the trolleys. The museums are the Shore Line Trolley Museum in East Haven, and the Connecticut Electric Railway Association Museum in Warehouse Point.

U.S.S. *Nautilus* Memorial, in Groton, honors the *Nautilus,* the world's first nuclear-powered submarine and the first submarine to reach the North Pole. Visitors can explore the submarine's control room, handle working periscopes, and view films on naval history.

State parks and forests. Connecticut has 92 state parks and 30 state forests. For information, write to State Department of Environmental Protection, State Office Building, Hartford, CT 06106.

Annual events

January-June

U.S. Eastern Ski Jumping Championships in Salisbury (February); Spring Blossom Celebration throughout the state (mid-April to June); Dogwood Festival in Fairfield (May); Children's Services Horse Show in Farmington (May); Lobster Weekend in Mystic (May); Barnum Festival in Bridgeport (June-July).

July-December

Blessing of the fleet in Stonington (early July); Jazz Festival in New Haven (July); Greater Hartford Open Golf Tournament in Cromwell (July); Riverfest in Hartford and East Hartford (July); Ancient Fife and Drum Corps Muster and Parade in Deep River (July); Connecticut Traditional Jazz Festival in Essex (August); Mystic Outdoor Arts Festival (August); Native American Festival in Haddam (August); Norwalk Oyster Festival (September); Fall New Haven Antiques Show (September); Stamford Classic Marathon (October); Christmas Torchlight Parade in Old Saybrook (December).

Connecticut Department of Economic Development

The Branford Trolley Museum in East Haven

©Tom Algire

Mystic Seaport in Mystic

Connecticut Department of Economic Development

Mark Twain's house in Hartford

©Steve Dunwell

Ancient Fife and Drum Corps Parade in Deep River

Land regions. Connecticut has five main land regions: (1) the Taconic Section, (2) the Western New England Upland, (3) the Connecticut Valley Lowland, (4) the Eastern New England Upland, and (5) the Coastal Lowlands.

The Taconic Section covers the northwestern corner of Connecticut between the Housatonic River and the New York border. This region also extends north into Massachusetts. The Taconic Section includes the highest point in Connecticut, on the south slope of Mount Frissell.

The Western New England Upland occupies most of western Connecticut, and parts of Massachusetts and Vermont. In Connecticut, it lies from 1,000 to 1,400 feet (300 to 427 meters) above sea level. The land slopes from northwest to southeast. Many rivers flow between the region's ridges and steep hills.

The Connecticut Valley Lowland extends through the center of Connecticut and north into Massachusetts. It averages 20 miles (32 kilometers) in width. Basalt ridges, including Hanging Hills, Mount Lamentation, and Talcott Mountain, rise from 300 to 600 feet (91 to 180 meters) above the rivers of the region.

The Eastern New England Upland covers most of eastern Connecticut. The entire upland stretches from Connecticut to Maine. In Connecticut, it is heavily forested, and has narrow river valleys and low hills. Few of the hills rise as high as 1,200 feet (366 meters). The land slopes gradually from northwest to southeast.

The Coastal Lowlands are part of a larger region of the same name that covers the New England coast. In Connecticut, the region is a narrow belt, from 6 to 16 miles (10 to 26 kilometers) wide, along the southern shore. The coastal lowlands are somewhat lower and smoother than the rest of the state's regions. The lowlands are broken by low ridges, and beaches and harbors along the coast.

Coastline. Connecticut's 618-mile (995-kilometer) shoreline includes bays and mouths of many rivers. The Connecticut shore has many fine harbors, including Greenwich, Stamford, Norwalk, Bridgeport, New Haven, and New London. Long Island, a part of New York south of Connecticut, helps protect Connecticut's shore from Atlantic storms.

Several small islands lie off the Connecticut coast. The largest, Mason Island, covers about $1\frac{1}{2}$ square miles (3.9 square kilometers) near Mystic. Other islands include the Norwalk Islands off Norwalk, and The Thimbles near Branford.

Mountains. Connecticut's highest mountains are all in northwestern Litchfield County. The highest point in the state, on the south slope of Mount Frissell, has an altitude of 2,380 feet (725 meters). The top of Mount Frissell is in Massachusetts. Other mountains include Bear Mountain (2,355 feet, or 718 meters), Mount Gridley (2,200 feet, or 671 meters), Mount Riga (2,000 feet, or 610 meters), and Bradford Mountain (1,962 feet, or 598 meters).

Peter Vandermark, Stock, Boston

The Connecticut River flows through the center of the state and empties into Long Island Sound. Some ocean ships can sail on the Connecticut as far as Hartford.

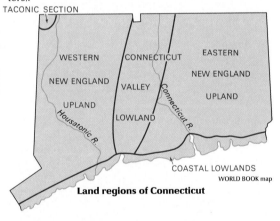

WORLD BOOK map

Land regions of Connecticut

Map index

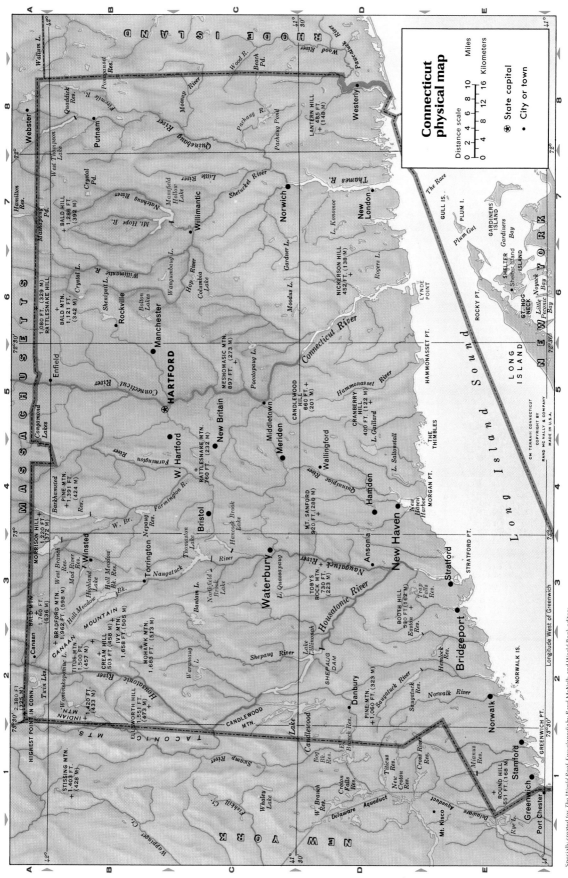

Connecticut physical map

⊛ State capital
• City or town

Distance scale

Miles
0 4 8 10
0 4 8 12 16
Kilometers

Specially created for *The World Book Encyclopedia* by Rand McNally and World Book editors

Rivers, waterfalls, and lakes. The Connecticut River flows south through the center of the state. It is Connecticut's chief river. Some oceangoing ships can sail on the Connecticut as far north as Hartford, 50 miles (80 kilometers) inland. The Housatonic River and its chief tributaries, the Naugatuck and Shepaug rivers, drain the Western New England Upland. The Thames and the Quinebaug are the chief rivers of eastern Connecticut. Connecticut has many small waterfalls. Kent Falls, the largest, plunges about 200 feet (61 meters) along a distance of about $\frac{1}{4}$ mile (0.4 kilometer) near Kent.

Over 1,000 lakes dot the landscape. Most are small lakes that were formed by glaciers thousands of years ago. Several of the largest ones are used as reservoirs. Others provide recreation activities. The largest lake, Lake Candlewood, was created artificially to store water for generating power. Other lakes include Bantam, Pachaug, Shenipsit, Twin Lakes, and Waramaug.

Plant and animal life. Forests cover more than 60 per cent of Connecticut. Trees include ash, beech, birch, elm, hemlock, hickory, maple, oak, and pine.

The mountain laurel, Connecticut's state flower, grows throughout the woodlands and along roads. Many people in western Connecticut call this evergreen flowering shrub *ivy.* Dogwood grows throughout the state. Bayberry, sheep laurel, and sweet fern cover many fields in the state.

Connecticut's animal life consists chiefly of small creatures, though the population of white-tailed deer has increased significantly since 1970. Animals prized by hunters and trappers include foxes, hares, minks, muskrats, otters, and rabbits. Freshwater ducks are the most common game birds. Partridges, ring-necked pheasants, and ruffed grouse are also hunted. Orioles, sparrows, thrushes, and warblers live in the state.

Connecticut waters in Long Island Sound have many clams, menhaden, lobsters, and oysters. Shad is the leading fish of the state's inland waterways. Trout and other game fish are plentiful in the lakes and streams.

Climate. Connecticut's weather is rarely very cold or very hot. January temperatures average 26° F. (−3° C), and July temperatures average 71° F. (22° C). The state's record low, −32° F. (−36° C), was set in Falls Village on Feb. 16, 1943. The record high in Connecticut, 105° F. (41° C), was set in Waterbury on July 22, 1926.

Although Connecticut is a small state, its climate and weather can vary greatly from one area to another. For example, the same storms that deposit large amounts of snow in the hills of northern Connecticut may produce only light rain along the coast, less than 50 miles (80 kilometers) away.

Yearly *precipitation* (rain, melted snow, and other forms of moisture) in Connecticut averages about 47 inches (119 centimeters). The average amount of yearly rainfall is distributed fairly evenly throughout the state.

Snowfall averages from about 25 inches (64 centimeters) yearly in the southeast part of Connecticut to about 35 inches (89 centimeters) in the western and central parts. The highest places in the northwest sometimes receive 80 inches (200 centimeters) of snow annually.

Average monthly weather

	Hartford						Bridgeport				
	Temperatures F°		C°		Days of rain or snow		Temperatures F°		C°		Days of rain or snow
	High	Low	High	Low			High	Low	High	Low	
Jan.	36	18	2	−8	13	Jan.	37	22	3	−6	12
Feb.	38	18	3	−8	11	Feb.	37	21	3	−6	10
Mar.	47	27	8	−3	12	Mar.	45	29	7	−2	12
Apr.	60	36	16	2	12	Apr.	55	37	13	3	13
May	72	47	22	8	12	May	67	48	19	9	11
June	81	57	27	14	10	June	76	58	24	14	7
July	86	62	30	17	10	July	82	64	28	18	9
Aug.	83	60	28	16	10	Aug.	80	63	27	17	10
Sept.	76	52	24	11	9	Sept.	74	56	23	13	9
Oct.	65	41	18	5	8	Oct.	64	45	18	7	7
Nov.	51	31	11	−1	10	Nov.	52	35	11	2	9
Dec.	39	20	4	−7	11	Dec.	40	25	4	−4	10

Average January temperatures

In winter, the state's temperatures are coldest throughout the northwest. The mildest areas lie along the Atlantic coast.

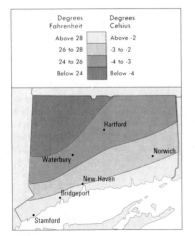

Degrees Fahrenheit	Degrees Celsius
Above 28	Above -2
26 to 28	-3 to -2
24 to 26	-4 to -3
Below 24	Below -4

Average July temperatures

In summer, temperatures are generally even throughout the state. The warmest area is the southwestern coast.

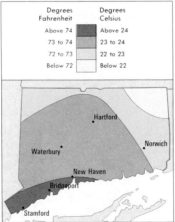

Degrees Fahrenheit	Degrees Celsius
Above 74	Above 24
73 to 74	23 to 24
72 to 73	22 to 23
Below 72	Below 22

Average yearly precipitation

The state gets a fairly even amount of rainfall. The heaviest snow falls in the western and central sections.

WORLD BOOK maps

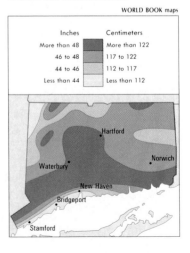

Inches	Centimeters
More than 48	More than 122
46 to 48	117 to 122
44 to 46	112 to 117
Less than 44	Less than 112

Service industries, taken together, make up about three-fourths of Connecticut's *gross state product*—the total value of all goods and services produced in a state in a year. However, manufacturing is also an important economic activity. It accounts for about a fifth of the gross state product. Manufacturing is centered in Fairfield, Hartford, and New Haven counties. Military vehicles and machine tools are among the state's most valuable manufactured products.

Finance, insurance, and real estate combined make up Connecticut's leading service industry. The Hartford area has a number of the nation's largest insurance companies. Many corporations have headquarters in the state, particularly in the urban areas near New York City. Trade and tourism are also important to Connecticut's economy. They each thrive in many parts of the state. Tourism brings in about $3½ billion a year.

Natural resources. Unlike many other states, Connecticut does not depend chiefly on its own natural resources for the raw materials of its industries. The state has many forests, but they are not commercially important. Connecticut lacks large deposits of valuable minerals, and much of its soil is unsuitable for farming.

Soil. Some of the soils at low elevations are dry. But they produce good vegetable and tobacco crops, especially along the Connecticut River. Much of the soil in the uplands is stony. It is best suited for growing grass that can be made into hay or used as cattle feed.

Minerals. Stone—especially a kind of basalt called traprock—and sand and gravel are Connecticut's leading minerals. Clays, feldspar, and mica are also found there.

Service industries account for 75 per cent of Connecticut's gross state product. Connecticut's service industries are concentrated in the 11 metropolitan areas.

The finance, insurance, and real estate industry accounts for 22 per cent of the gross state product. This is a much higher percentage than in most states. The Hartford area is the home of about 50 insurance companies, including 3 of the nation's largest. Some of the corpora-

Sikorsky Aircraft

Commercial helicopters are produced on an assembly line at a factory in Bridgeport. Connecticut is a leading state in the production of helicopters, jet aircraft engines, and propellers.

tions that operate insurance firms also operate investment and real estate companies.

Next in importance among Connecticut service industries are community, social, and personal services. Such services consist of a wide variety of economic activities. These include the operation of doctors' offices and private hospitals, engineering and law firms, and computer and data processing services.

Wholesale and retail trade are third among Connecticut's service industries in the amount they contribute to the gross state product. New Haven is an important center for the wholesale trade of fuels, lumber, and farm products. Major types of retail trade establishments include automobile dealerships, department stores, food stores, and restaurants.

Government ranks fourth in importance among the state's service industries. Government services include public schools and hospitals, and military activities. State government offices are centered in Hartford.

Transportation, communication, and utilities rank fifth in importance. United Parcel Service, a leading transportation company, and GTE, a major utility company, are both based in Connecticut. More information about transportation, communication, and utilities appears later in this section.

Manufacturing accounts for 20 per cent of Connecticut's gross state product. Goods manufactured there have a *value added by manufacture* of about $22 billion a year. Value added by manufacture is the increase in value of raw materials after they become finished goods.

The production of transportation equipment is Connecticut's most important manufacturing activity by far. Most of the transportation equipment made in the state is for military uses. Connecticut is a leading producer of aircraft parts, helicopters, and submarines. Large factories that make aircraft parts are in East Hartford, Middletown, North Haven, Stratford, and Windsor Locks.

Production and workers by economic activities

Economic activities	Per cent of GSP* produced	Employed workers	
		Number of persons	Per cent of total
Finance, insurance, & real estate	22	147,600	9
Community, social, & personal services	21	415,200	26
Manufacturing	20	323,400	21
Wholesale and retail trade	15	339,900	22
Government	9	209,300	13
Transportation, communication, & utilities	8	70,200	5
Construction	4	51,400	3
Agriculture	1	22,100	1
Mining	†	800	†
Total	100	1,579,900	100

*GSP = gross state product, the total value of goods and services produced in a year.
†Less than one-half of 1 per cent
Figures are for 1991.
Sources: *World Book* estimates based on data from U.S. Bureau of Economic Analysis, U.S. Bureau of Labor Statistics, and U.S. Department of Agriculture.

Farm and mineral products

This map shows where the state's leading farm and mineral products are produced. The major urban areas (shown in red) are the important manufacturing centers.

0 5 10 15 20 25 Miles
0 10 20 30 40 Kilometers

WORLD BOOK map

Bridgeport produces commercial helicopters, and Stratford makes military helicopters. Groton is a major national center for submarine production.

Machinery ranks second among Connecticut's manufactured products. Leading types of machinery made in the state include bearings, computers, machine tools, and printing machinery. The Bridgeport and Hartford areas manufacture most of Connecticut's machinery.

Fabricated metal products rank third in importance. Connecticut ranks high among the states in the production of cutlery and hardware. Other metal products include bolts, nuts, rivets, washers, and valve and pipe fittings. New Britain and New Haven are important hardware centers.

Scientific equipment is fourth in importance among Connecticut's manufactured products. Factories in the Danbury area make scientific measuring devices. The New Haven and Meriden area is a center for the production of medical and surgical instruments. Other products manufactured in Connecticut, in order of value, include chemicals, electrical equipment, printed materials, and food products. Pharmaceuticals and toiletries are the leading types of chemicals made in Connecticut. The state is a leading producer of electrical conductors, outlets, and switches.

Agriculture provides 1 per cent of the gross state product. Connecticut's 4,000 farms average about 120 acres (49 hectares) in size.

Greenhouse and nursery products are Connecticut's leading source of agricultural income. These products include ornamental shrubs, flowers, and young plants. Eggs and milk are the next most important farm products. Most egg farms are in the eastern part of the state. Dairy cattle can be found in Connecticut's rural areas.

Tobacco and hay are the state's leading field crops. Connecticut farmers raise an expensive variety of tobacco that is used to make cigar wrappers. The state's farmers also raise beef cattle, apples, and mushrooms.

Mining contributes less than 1 per cent of Connecticut's gross state product. Crushed stone is the state's chief mineral product. Sand and gravel provide most of the remaining income. These mineral products are used

mainly to make roadbeds and concrete. Most of the crushed stone is obtained from traprock quarries in New Haven and Hartford counties. Connecticut also mines small amounts of clays, feldspar, and granite.

Fishing industry. The annual fish catch in Connecticut is valued at about $43 million. Shellfish, which include clams, lobsters, oysters, and scallops, provide most of the income. Flounder and shad also provide some of the fishing income.

Electric power. Nuclear power plants provide about 60 per cent of Connecticut's electricity. Plants that burn petroleum provide most of the remaining electric power. Hydroelectric plants and plants that burn gas or coal provide small amounts of power.

Transportation. Connecticut has about 19,000 miles (30,600 kilometers) of roads and highways, most of which are surfaced. The Connecticut Turnpike crosses the state from the New York border, near Greenwich, to the Rhode Island border, in Killingly.

The Hartford and New Haven, Connecticut's first important railroad, began service between New Haven and Meriden in 1838. Today, four railroads in the state provide freight service. Passenger trains serve more than 45 cities and towns in Connecticut. Some of these trains carry thousands of Connecticut commuters to and from their jobs in New York City.

Bradley International Airport in Windsor Locks is Connecticut's major airport. The state's busiest seaports are Bridgeport and New Haven.

Communication. About 85 newspapers, including about 25 dailies, are published in Connecticut. The *Connecticut Courant* (now *The Hartford Courant*) began publication in 1764. It is the oldest continuously published newspaper in the nation. The *Courant* and the *Bridgeport Post, New Haven Register,* and *Waterbury Republican and American* are among Connecticut's chief newspapers.

Connecticut has about 70 radio stations and 11 television stations. The state's first radio station, WDRC, opened in Hartford in 1922. The first television station, WNHC (now WTNH-TV), began operating in New Haven in 1948.

Constitution of Connecticut was adopted in 1965. It replaced an earlier Constitution adopted in 1818. Colonial Connecticut's first constitution was the Fundamental Orders of 1639. Connecticut governed itself under the Fundamental Orders until it received a royal charter in 1662. The charter was the constitution until 1818.

An *amendment* (change) to the Constitution may be proposed by the legislature or by a constitutional convention. An amendment proposed by the legislature must be approved by a majority of the members of each house, and by a majority of electors voting on the amendment in a general election. If the amendment is approved by a three-fourths majority of each house, electors vote on it in the next general election. If it is approved by a majority of less than three-fourths of each house, it must be approved again by a majority in a regular session of the legislature after the next general election held in an even-numbered year. Then it is voted on in a general election.

A constitutional convention may be called by a two-thirds vote in each house of the legislature, or by a majority of electors voting on the question. An amendment proposed by a convention must be approved by a majority of the electors.

Executive. The governor of Connecticut is elected to a four-year term and may be reelected any number of times. The voters also elect the lieutenant governor, attorney general, comptroller, secretary of state, and state treasurer. All of these offices have four-year terms. The governor, with the approval of either house of the legislature, appoints most other top executive officials.

Legislature, called the *General Assembly,* consists of a 36-member Senate and a 151-member House of Representatives. Voters in each of Connecticut's 36 senatorial districts elect one senator. Voters in each of the state's 151 assembly districts elect one representative. Senators and representatives serve two-year terms.

The Connecticut legislature meets every year. Regular sessions begin on the Wednesday after the first Monday in January in odd-numbered years and on the Wednesday after the first Monday of February in even-numbered years. Legislative sessions must end by the Wednesday after the first Monday in June in odd-numbered years and by the Wednesday after the first Monday in May in even-numbered years. Special sessions of the legislature have no time limits. Special sessions may be called by the governor or by a majority of each house of the legislature.

In 1965, Connecticut *reapportioned* (redivided) its legislature to provide equal representation based on population. It also provided for reapportionment after each federal census. For a discussion of reapportionment, in

The state governors of Connecticut

	Party	Term		Party	Term
Jonathan Trumbull	None	1776-1784	**Charles B. Andrews**	Republican	1879-1881
Matthew Griswold	Federalist	1784-1786	**Hobart B. Bigelow**	Republican	1881-1883
Samuel Huntington	Federalist	1786-1796	**Thomas M. Waller**	Democratic	1883-1885
Oliver Wolcott	Federalist	1796-1797	**Henry B. Harrison**	Republican	1885-1887
Jonathan Trumbull II	Federalist	1797-1809	**Phineas C. Lounsbury**	Republican	1887-1889
John Treadwell	Federalist	1809-1811	**Morgan G. Bulkeley**	Republican	1889-1893
Roger Griswold	Federalist	1811-1812	**Luzon B. Morris**	Democratic	1893-1895
John Cotton Smith	Federalist	1812-1817	**O. Vincent Coffin**	Republican	1895-1897
Oliver Wolcott, Jr.	Jeffersonian		**Lorrin A. Cooke**	Republican	1897-1899
	Republican	1817-1827	**George E. Lounsbury**	Republican	1899-1901
Gideon Tomlinson	Jeffersonian		**George P. McLean**	Republican	1901-1903
	Republican	1827-1831	**Abiram Chamberlain**	Republican	1903-1905
John S. Peters	National		**Henry Roberts**	Republican	1905-1907
	Republican	1831-1833	**Rollin S. Woodruff**	Republican	1907-1909
Henry W. Edwards	Democratic	1833-1834	**George L. Lilley**	Republican	1909
Samuel A. Foot	Whig	1834-1835	**Frank B. Weeks**	Republican	1909-1911
Henry W. Edwards	Democratic	1835-1838	**Simeon E. Baldwin**	Democratic	1911-1915
William W. Ellsworth	Whig	1838-1842	**Marcus H. Holcomb**	Republican	1915-1921
Chauncey F. Cleveland	Democratic	1842-1844	**Everett J. Lake**	Republican	1921-1923
Roger S. Baldwin	Whig	1844-1846	**Charles A. Templeton**	Republican	1923-1925
Isaac Toucey	Democratic	1846-1847	**Hiram Bingham**	Republican	1925
Clark Bissell	Whig	1847-1849	**John H. Trumbull**	Republican	1925-1931
Joseph Trumbull	Whig	1849-1850	**Wilbur L. Cross**	Democratic	1931-1939
Thomas H. Seymour	Democratic	1850-1853	**Raymond E. Baldwin**	Republican	1939-1941
Charles H. Pond	Democratic	1853-1854	**Robert A. Hurley**	Democratic	1941-1943
Henry Dutton	Whig	1854-1855	**Raymond E. Baldwin**	Republican	1943-1946
William T. Minor	American*	1855-1857	**Wilbert Snow**	Democratic	1946-1947
Alexander H. Holley	American and		**James L. McConaughy**	Republican	1947-1948
	Republican†	1857-1858	**James C. Shannon**	Republican	1948-1949
William A. Buckingham	Republican	1858-1866	**Chester Bowles**	Democratic	1949-1951
Joseph R. Hawley	Republican	1866-1867	**John Lodge**	Republican	1951-1955
James E. English	Democratic	1867-1869	**Abraham A. Ribicoff**	Democratic	1955-1961
Marshall Jewell	Republican	1869-1870	**John N. Dempsey**	Democratic	1961-1971
James E. English	Democratic	1870-1871	**Thomas J. Meskill**	Republican	1971-1975
Marshall Jewell	Republican	1871-1873	**Ella T. Grasso**	Democratic	1975-1980
Charles R. Ingersoll	Democratic	1873-1877	**William A. O'Neill**	Democratic	1980-1991
Richard D. Hubbard	Democratic	1877-1879	**Lowell P. Weicker, Jr.**	Independent	1991-

*Sometimes called Know-Nothing
†Sometimes called Know-Nothing Republican

the state, see *The mid-1900's* section of this article.

Courts. Connecticut's judicial system consists of the Supreme Court, the highest court in the state; the appellate court; the superior court; and probate courts. The superior court is the only general trial court. There are 7 Supreme Court justices, 9 appellate court judges, and 150 superior court judges. At times, all 166 judges meet together and are considered superior court judges. The justices and judges of the higher courts are nominated by the governor and appointed by the General Assembly to eight-year terms. Connecticut's voters elect the state's 133 probate court judges to four-year terms.

Local government in Connecticut is centered in 169 *towns.* Connecticut towns are similar to *townships* in other states. The towns may include several communities and large rural areas under one government.

Many small Connecticut towns use the town meeting form of government. This pure form of democracy allows citizens to take a direct part in their local government. Each year, town voters meet to elect officials, approve budgets, and decide other business. See **Town meeting.**

Some towns have heavily populated areas called *boroughs* and *cities.* Most of the 11 boroughs have a government that is independent of the town government. In most of the 20 cities, the city and town governments operate as a unit—called a *city government.* The most common city government is the mayor-council type. Some cities use the council-manager form. Connecticut cities operate under state charters. All chartered cities have *home rule*—they are free to amend their own charters. Connecticut and Rhode Island are the only states that do not have county governments. The two states do have geographical areas called counties, however.

Revenue. Taxation provides about 55 per cent of the state government's *general revenue* (income). Most of the rest comes from federal grants and programs. General sales and use tax and personal income tax bring in the largest percentage of the state's revenue. Other sources of revenue include a public utility tax, a motor fuel tax, a cigarette tax, an insurance premium tax, inheritance taxes, the sale of licenses and permits, and legalized gambling.

Politics. Connecticut gave early support to the Republican Party after the party was formed in 1854. In presidential elections between 1856 and 1932, Connecticut voted for 15 Republicans and only 5 Democrats. The voters chose about three times as many Republicans as Democrats for governor during the same period. The Democrats gained strength during the 1930's. Since 1960, registered Democratic voters have outnumbered registered Republicans in Connecticut. For Connecticut's electoral votes and voting record in presidential elections, see **Electoral College** (table).

History

Indian days. Between 6,000 and 7,000 Indians lived in what is now Connecticut before the Europeans came. The Indians belonged to several tribes of the Algonquian Indian family. The Pequot, the most powerful tribe, lived in the south near the Thames River. The Mohegan, a branch of the Pequot tribe, lived near present-day Norwich. Uncas, the Mohegan chief, was characterized as an ideal Indian in James Fenimore Cooper's novel *The Last of the Mohicans.* Other Connecticut tribes included the Niantic, Paugusset, Quinnipiac, Saukiog, Siwanog, Tunxis, and Wangunk.

Dutch exploration. Adriaen Block, a Dutch explorer, sailed up the Connecticut River in 1614. Block claimed Connecticut for the Dutch as part of their colony of New Netherland. The Dutch did not act on this claim until 1633 when they built a small fort—called the *House of Hope*—on the present site of Hartford. But the Dutch never settled permanently in Connecticut. They claimed parts of Connecticut off and on until 1674, when the English finally drove them out of the area.

English settlement. English colonists from Massachusetts established Connecticut's first permanent settlements. Windsor, the first one, was founded in 1633. Other early settlements included Hartford, New London, Saybrook, and Wethersfield. Hartford, Wethersfield, and Windsor united in 1636 to form the *Connecticut Colony* (also called the *River Colony*). In 1638, New Haven was founded as an independent colony. It was originally a Puritan *theocracy* (church-ruled state). Beginning in 1643, other towns—including Branford, Guilford, Milford, Stamford, and Southold, on Long Island—joined the New Haven Colony.

Many early Connecticut settlers left Massachusetts in search of political and religious freedom. The most famous of these settlers was Thomas Hooker, a Congregational minister and the chief founder of Hartford. In 1638, Hooker preached a sermon calling for government based on the will of the people. The Connecticut Colony put his principle into practice in 1639, by adopting the *Fundamental Orders* as its law. The Fundamental Orders gave voters the right to elect government officials. The Fundamental Orders are regarded by some people as the first written constitution.

The Pequot War. Connecticut colonists feared the Pequot Indians because the tribe had attacked their settlements. The Pequot feared the colonists as a threat to Pequot supremacy in the region. Captain John Mason, aided by Mohegan and Narragansett warriors, led a small army against the Pequot in Mystic in 1637. The soldiers burned a Pequot fort, killing hundreds of Indians. Also in 1637, colonists defeated the remaining Pequot near Fairfield. See **Indian wars** (The Pequot War).

Expanding the colony. By 1660, many new towns had joined the Connecticut Colony, including Fairfield, Farmington, Middletown, New London, Norwalk, Saybrook, and Stratford. In 1662, John Winthrop, Jr., of the Connecticut Colony got a charter from the king of England. The charter gave the colony a strip of land 73 miles (117 kilometers) wide from Narragansett Bay to the Pacific Ocean. People of the time did not know that the distance to the Pacific Ocean was so great. This strip included the New Haven Colony. At first, New Haven objected to being part of the Connecticut Colony. But the two colonies united in 1665.

Colonial life. The earliest Connecticut colonists were farmers. Most of them raised only enough food for their

Historic Connecticut

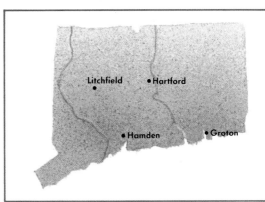

The Fundamental Orders were adopted by the Connecticut Colony in 1639. They set forth the idea of government by the consent of the people.

Samuel Colt invented the first successful repeating pistol, patented in the United States in 1836. Colt made firearms in his Hartford factory.

Litchfield Law School, founded in 1774, was the nation's first institution devoted entirely to teaching law.

Eli Whitney helped develop mass production in the early 1800's. Working in Hamden, he showed the advantages of using standard parts in gunmaking.

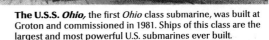

The U.S.S. *Ohio,* the first *Ohio* class submarine, was built at Groton and commissioned in 1981. Ships of this class are the largest and most powerful U.S. submarines ever built.

WORLD BOOK illustrations by Kevin Chadwick

Important dates in Connecticut

1614	Adriaen Block claimed Connecticut for the Dutch.
1633	The first English settlement in Connecticut was made in Windsor.
1636	The towns of Hartford, Wethersfield, and Windsor united to form the Connecticut Colony.
1637	Connecticut and other colonies defeated the Pequot Indians in the Pequot War.
1638	A group of wealthy Puritans founded New Haven.
1639	The Connecticut Colony adopted the Fundamental Orders.
1662	The Connecticut Colony received a charter from England. This charter served as Connecticut's constitution until 1818.
1665	The Connecticut and New Haven colonies united.
1687	Colonists preserved the Connecticut charter by hiding it, presumably in the Charter Oak in Hartford.

1776	Connecticut passed a resolution in favor of independence from Great Britain on June 14.
1788	Connecticut became the 5th state when it ratified the U.S. Constitution on January 9.
1910	New London became the home of the U.S. Coast Guard Academy.
1954	The *Nautilus,* the first nuclear-powered submarine, was built and launched in Groton.
1965	Connecticut apportioned its legislative districts on the basis of population. Connecticut adopted a new constitution.
1979	Connecticut passed a law banning the construction of nuclear power plants. Existing plants were allowed to continue operating.
1991	Connecticut established an individual income tax to raise additional state revenue.

own needs. Each family made most of its own clothing, household utensils, and farm tools.

During the late 1600's, Connecticut began exporting farm products to other lands, especially to the West Indies. Manufacturing started in Connecticut during the early 1700's. Clockmaking, shipbuilding, and silversmithing were the first important industries. Two brothers, Edward and William Pattison, made the first tinware in North America in the 1740's. The Pattison brothers became the first of Connecticut's famous *Yankee peddlers.* These house-to-house salesmen traveled in small carts selling a variety of Connecticut products. They were such shrewd businessmen that stories arose accusing them of selling wooden nutmegs. The stories gave Connecticut the nickname of the *Nutmeg State.*

Defending the colony. Sir Edmund Andros, named by the English king as governor of several other New England colonies, twice tried to gain control of Connecticut. In 1675, he sent troops to seize a fort in Saybrook. But his forces withdrew because Connecticut resisted strongly and the soldiers wanted to avoid a bloody battle. In 1687, Andros arrived in Hartford and demanded Connecticut's charter. But the people refused to give it to him. They supposedly hid the charter in a large oak tree, later called the Charter Oak.

The Revolutionary War. During the 1760's, Great Britain passed a series of laws that caused unrest in Connecticut and the other American Colonies. Some of these laws set up heavy taxes and restricted colonial trade. A few Connecticut colonists urged loyalty to Britain. But the great majority supported independence, and on June 14, 1776, Connecticut passed a resolution favoring it. About three weeks later, on July 4, the colonies adopted the Declaration of Independence. On July 9, 1778, Connecticut *ratified* (approved) the Articles of Confederation, the forerunner of the U.S. Constitution.

After the Revolutionary War began in Massachusetts in 1775, hundreds of Connecticut men joined the patriot forces. Governor Jonathan Trumbull and Nathan Hale rank among the most famous Connecticut patriots. Trumbull was the only colonial governor to hold office throughout the Revolution. He was a close friend and trusted adviser of General George Washington, who called him *Brother Jonathan* (see **Brother Jonathan**). Nathan Hale was hanged by the British as a spy. His dying words won him lasting fame: "I only regret that I have but one life to lose for my country."

During the Revolutionary War, Connecticut's long coastline lay open to attack from British-controlled Long Island, only a few hours away by boat. The British launched five major assaults and countless minor raids against the state. Although Connecticut lacked sufficient forces to protect its own coast, the state was asked to supply large detachments to the Continental Army to help defend the Hudson River in New York. The conflict over whether state or national defense should be more important created serious disputes among Connecticut's political leaders throughout the war.

At the Constitutional Convention of 1787, Connecticut's delegates supported the establishment of a strong national government. They played an important role in bringing about the *Great Compromise* (sometimes called the *Connecticut Compromise*). Convention delegates from large states wanted a state's representation

in Congress to be based on population. Delegates from small states wanted all states to have equal representation in Congress. The compromise provided for representation in proportion to population in the House of Representatives and equal representation in the Senate. It enabled the large and small states to join in supporting a central government that had substantial powers. Connecticut ratified the U.S. Constitution on Jan. 9, 1788, becoming the fifth state to join the Union.

During the 1780's, Connecticut gave up claims to most of the western land that the colony had been granted in the 1662 charter. Connecticut kept only its claim to the Western Reserve. Most of this land in northeastern Ohio was sold to the Connecticut Land Company in 1795. The money from the sale was used for education.

The 1800's. Until the 1850's, most of Connecticut's people continued to work on farms. But before 1900, Connecticut had become a thriving industrial state.

Connecticut owes much of its industrial importance to the inventors who worked there. Perhaps the most important of these inventors was Eli Whitney. Whitney is best known for his cotton gin. But he also helped develop the modern system of mass production. While working in Hamden in the early 1800's, Whitney built machine tools that made interchangeable gun parts. Until that time, all gun parts were made by hand and part of one gun usually would not fit another gun.

In 1808, Eli Terry of East Hartford became the first person to make clocks by mass production. In 1810, Rodney Hanks and his nephew, Horatio Hanks, built the nation's first silk mill in Mansfield. Samuel Colt of Hartford invented the first successful repeating pistol, and obtained a U.S. patent for it in 1836. Colt made pistols and other firearms in his Hartford factory. In 1839, Charles Goodyear of Connecticut found a way to *vulcanize* (strengthen) rubber. Goodyear patented his vulcanization method in 1844. People from Connecticut also pioneered in making bicycles, cigars, copper coins, nuts and bolts, pins and needles, silk thread, and rubber shoes.

Improved transportation helped Connecticut grow industrially. Fifteen railroad companies were organized in the state between the 1830's and 1850's. Steamships began serving Connecticut ports in the early 1800's. With these facilities, industries could import large quantities of raw materials inexpensively. Connecticut's industrial growth also was aided by thousands of Canadian and European immigrants. These workers provided relatively inexpensive factory labor.

Connecticut strongly supported the Union during the Civil War (1861-1865). Over 50,000 men joined the Union forces, and the state's industries helped produce arms, munitions, and other military needs.

The early 1900's. Many immigrants settled in Connecticut during the late 1800's and early 1900's. By 1910, about 30 per cent of the state's population was made up of people who were born outside the United States. Most of these people settled in cities. By 1910, almost 90 per cent of Connecticut's people lived in urban areas.

In 1910, the U.S. Coast Guard Academy was moved to New London from headquarters in Maryland and Massachusetts. The U.S. Navy opened a submarine base in nearby Groton in 1917. After the United States entered World War I in 1917, many of the nation's largest muni-

Electric Boat Division

The *Nautilus,* the world's first nuclear-powered submarine, was launched at Groton in 1954. On its maiden voyage, it broke all submarine records for underwater speed and endurance.

tions factories operated in Connecticut. About 67,600 people from Connecticut served in the armed forces during the war.

Connecticut industry continued to grow during the 1920's. At the same time, the Republican party controlled Connecticut politics. The Great Depression of the 1930's slowed industry and caused widespread unemployment in Connecticut. The depression swung many Connecticut voters over to the Democratic party. Democrat Wilbur Cross won election as governor four times during the 1930's. Economic conditions improved when the depression eased in the late 1930's.

The mid-1900's. During World War II (1939-1945), Connecticut was an important supplier of war materials. The state's factories made airplane engines, propellers, shell cases, and submarines.

Connecticut industry kept pace with the nuclear age and space age during the 1950's and 1960's. In 1954, the *Nautilus,* the world's first nuclear-powered submarine, was built and launched at Groton. In the late 1960's, the Groton shipyard began to build nuclear submarines that were armed with more powerful missile weapons. A nuclear energy plant for the production of electric power began to operate at Haddam Neck in 1968.

Also in the 1960's, Stratford plants produced reentry vehicles for spacecraft, and Middletown factories made small tape recorders to send signals into outer space. In 1969, when U.S. astronauts became the first people to walk on the moon, they carried oxygen and other supplies in backpacks made in Connecticut.

The 1950's and 1960's brought changes in the state government. In 1955, the Connecticut legislature approved new laws that gave voters a direct voice in choosing candidates for state elections. In 1964, Connecticut redrew the boundaries of its congressional districts. Six new districts with more equal populations were created for congressional elections.

Also in 1964, a federal court ruled against Connecticut's 327-year-old system for electing state legislators. Under this system, each town, regardless of its population, could elect at least one legislator. As a result, 10 per cent of the voters could elect a majority of the legis-

lators. This was possible because many thinly populated areas elected as many legislators as did heavily populated areas. In 1965, Connecticut *reapportioned* (redivided) its legislative districts to provide representation based on population. The Democrats, who were stronger in the large population centers, gained power.

Connecticut adopted its present constitution in 1965. The constitution requires that the legislature be reapportioned after each federal census.

During the 1950's and 1960's, many communities tore down slum sections and replaced them with new buildings. The construction of Hartford's Constitution Plaza turned a slum into an attractive business district. State spending for education, welfare, and other citizen services also rose rapidly during this period.

Recent developments. Protecting Connecticut against pollution has become a major challenge. In the late 1960's and early 1970's, the state legislature passed laws to reduce air and water pollution. Efforts also were made to halt the development of nuclear power plants in the state. Connecticut has three such plants. In 1979, the legislature passed a law prohibiting the erection of additional nuclear power plants.

Connecticut today ranks among the top states in *per capita* (per person) income. But population growth and rapid industrial growth have brought many problems. Cities and highways are crowded. Costs for education and housing are soaring. In 1979, the legislature developed a system that provided increased state aid for needy school districts. During the 1980's, Connecticut used part of its revenues to rebuild bridges and expand educational services.

The state government adopted the state's first individual income tax in 1971. But after public protests, the state government repealed the tax and raised taxes on cigarettes, gasoline, and general sales. The government established a lottery in 1971 to raise additional revenue. The government later developed more sources of revenue by permitting betting on greyhound racing and by legalizing other forms of gambling. In 1991, the government again adopted an individual income tax.

John L. Allen and Richard Buel, Jr.

Study aids

Related articles in *World Book* include:

Biographies

Andros, Sir Edmund	Putnam, Israel
Arnold, Benedict	Ribicoff, Abraham A.
Colt, Samuel	Sherman, Roger
Crandall, Prudence	Trumbull, Jonathan
Deane, Silas	Uncas
Eaton, Theophilus	Warner, Seth
Ellsworth, Oliver	Welles, Gideon
Gallaudet (Thomas H.)	Whitney, Eli
Gibbs, Josiah W.	Williams, William
Grasso, Ella T.	Winthrop, John, Jr.
Hale, Nathan	Wolcott, Oliver
Hooker, Thomas	Woolley, Mary Emma
Huntington, Samuel	Yale, Elihu
Johnson, William S.	

Cities

Bridgeport	New Haven	Stamford
Hartford	New London	

Questions

Why is Connecticut called the *Constitution State?*
What is Connecticut's chief economic activity?
What problems are some Connecticut towns attempting to solve on a regional basis?
What were the *Fundamental Orders?*
How did Connecticut provide its first school fund?
What technique first used in Connecticut led to modern manufacturing methods?
Who was *Brother Jonathan?*
Which city in Connecticut is called the *Insurance City?*
What defense products are made in Connecticut?
In what way are Connecticut counties unusual?

Additional resources

Level I
Fradin, Dennis B. *The Connecticut Colony.* Childrens Pr., 1990.
Gelman, Amy. *Connecticut.* Lerner, 1991.
Kent, Deborah. *Connecticut.* Childrens Pr., 1990.

Level II
Lewis, Thomas R., and Harmon, J. E. *Connecticut: A Geography.* Westview, 1986.
Roth, David M. *Connecticut: A Bicentennial History.* Norton, 1979.
Series in Connecticut History. Pequot, 1975. 5 vols: A. E. Van Dusen, *Puritans Against the Wilderness, to 1763;* D. M. Roth and F. Meyer, *From Revolution to Constitution, 1763-1818;* J. L. Trecker, *Preachers, Rebels, and Traders, 1818-1865;* R. O. M. Andersen, *From Yankee to American, 1865-1914;* H. F. Janick, Jr., *A Diverse People, 1914 to the Present.*
Taylor, Robert J. *Colonial Connecticut: A History.* KTO Pr., 1979.

Connecticut, University of, is a state-supported coeducational university in Storrs, Conn. Schools and colleges at the university include agriculture, allied health professions, business administration, education, engineering, family studies, fine arts, liberal arts and sciences, nursing, and pharmacy. The university has branches in Groton, Hartford, Stamford, and Waterbury, and it offers courses at the Litchfield County Center for higher education in Torrington. It has schools of law and social work in Greater Hartford. The schools of medicine and dental medicine are in Farmington. Courses at the university lead to bachelor's, master's, and doctor's degrees. The university was founded in 1881. For enrollment, see **Universities and colleges** (table).

Critically reviewed by the University of Connecticut

Connecticut River rises in northern New Hampshire, and forms the boundary between that state and Vermont. It then cuts across Massachusetts and Connecticut to empty into Long Island Sound. The river is 407 miles (655 kilometers) long. Industrial towns grew up along its middle course to take advantage of the power from its falls and rapids. Industries along the river include paper mills and hydroelectric power plants.   John L. Allen

Connective tissue holds together and gives shape to body organs and tissues. It also holds organs in place and supports the body. Compared with other types of tissue, connective tissue has relatively few cells and much *intercellular substance* (material outside the cells). Scientists divide connective tissue into three groups, according to the hardness of the intercellular substance. These groups are (1) soft *connective tissue proper,* (2) firm *cartilage,* and (3) hard *bone.* This article discusses connective tissue proper. For information on the other kinds of connective tissue, see **Bone; Cartilage.**

There are two chief types of connective tissue proper —*loose* and *dense.* Loose connective tissue forms the networks of thin fibers that surround such organs as the heart and lungs. It is also found under the skin and over the muscles. Dense connective tissue has more fibers and greater strength than does loose connective tissue. It forms tough capsulelike coverings that keep such organs as the kidneys in place. Dense connective tissue also forms the *ligaments,* which hold the bones and joints in place, and the *tendons,* which connect the muscles to the bones (see **Ligament; Tendon**).

In addition, connective tissue proper stores fat cells. Specialized kinds of this tissue, called *reticular tissue,* manufacture red and white blood cells.

The intercellular substance of connective tissue proper consists of long fibers mixed with a jellylike material. The fibers are mostly made up of a protein called *collagen* (see **Collagen**). Most collagen fibers resemble strong cords, but some form strands of delicate reticular tissue. Other fibers consist of a protein called *elastin,* which stretches easily.   George P. Stricklin

See also **Marfan syndrome.**

Connelly, Marc (1890-1980), wrote *The Green Pastures* (1930), perhaps America's most popular religious drama. The play has an all-black cast and is written in the dialect of Southern blacks. It takes place in heaven, and God (called "De Lawd") is the chief character. "De Lawd" changes from the Old Testament God of wrath to a God of mercy. The play is filled with humor and the recognition of human dignity. It won a Pulitzer Prize in 1930.

Connelly and George S. Kaufman earlier collaborated to write several lively, satirical comedies. *Dulcy* (1921), the best of their comedies, brought stardom to actress Lynn Fontanne. But their most significant collaboration was *Beggar on Horseback* (1924), an expressionistic dream play adapted from a German script. The play shows the forces in everyday life that oppose the creative person. Marcus Cook Connelly was born in McKeesport, Pa.   Frederick C. Wilkins

Connor, Ralph. See Gordon, Charles William.

Connors, Jimmy (1952-   ), is an American tennis champion and one of the best singles players in the world. In 1974, Connors won the men's singles title at three major tennis tournaments—the All-England (Wimbledon) Championships, the United States Open, and the Australian Open. Connors also won the U.S. Open in 1976, 1978, 1982, and 1983. In addition, he won Wimbledon in 1982. Connors has won a record 109 professional singles titles.

Connors, a left-hander, is known for an aggressive, hard-hitting style of play that puts constant pressure on his opponents. He is particularly noted for his return-of-service and for his two-handed backhand.

James Scott Connors was born in East St. Louis, Ill., and grew up in Belleville, Ill. He attended the University of California at Los Angeles (UCLA). In 1971, he won the National Collegiate Athletic Association singles championship. Connors became a professional tennis player in 1972.   Arthur Ashe

Conquistadors, *kahn KEES tuh dawrz,* were Spaniards who conquered Indian peoples in parts of Latin America mainly during the first half of the 1500's. *Conquistador* is a Spanish word meaning *conqueror.* Most conquistadors had little interest in exploration. Nevertheless, they were often the first Europeans to enter the regions they conquered, and some settled in those areas. The most famous conquistadors were Hernando Cortés, who defeated the Aztec Indians in Mexico, and Francisco Pizarro, who conquered the Inca empire in Peru. See also **Cortés, Hernando; Pizarro, Francisco.**

Helen Delpar

Conrad, Charles, Jr. (1930-   ), a United States astronaut, commanded the Apollo 12 mission that made the second manned moon landing. On Nov. 19, 1969, Conrad and astronaut Alan L. Bean landed in their lunar module, *Intrepid,* and stayed for about 31 hours. Conrad and Bean set up scientific instruments and collected rock and soil samples. They also removed parts from *Surveyor 3* for scientific examination. *Surveyor 3* was an unmanned spacecraft that had landed on the moon in April 1967. In 1973, Conrad was commander of the initial mission of the first manned U.S. space station, *Skylab.* Working in space, he helped repair the station's solar panel wing. This work made the station safe.

Conrad was born in Philadelphia. In 1953, he graduated from Princeton University and entered the Navy. Conrad completed Navy Test Pilot School and then served as a flight instructor. He became an astronaut in 1962. In 1965, Conrad piloted the Gemini 5 mission. He commanded the Gemini 11 mission in 1966.

In 1974, Conrad retired from the astronaut program and the Navy. Today, he is staff vice president for the New Business Space Systems Division of the McDonnell Douglas Corporation.   Lillian D. Kozloski

Conrad, Joseph (1857-1924), was a Polish-born author who wrote in English. He became famous for the novels and short stories that he wrote about the sea.

Conrad was born Józef Teodor Konrad Nalecz Korzeniowski near Kiev, in what was then Russian Poland. He left Poland at the age of 16 and arrived in England at the age of 20, unable to speak English. During the next 16 years, he worked his way up from deck hand to captain in the British Merchant Navy. He mastered English so completely that he was able to write some of its greatest novels. Conrad's rich prose style is noted for its gripping intensity, which can be precise in its realism or filled with metaphor.

Conrad used experiences of his life in many of his works. From his voyages in the Indian Ocean and Malay Archipelago came some of his best-known novels. He began with *Almayer's Folly* (1895) and *An Outcast of the Islands* (1896), both set in Borneo.

Such later masterpieces as *The Nigger of the "Narcissus"* (1897), *Lord Jim* (1900), *Typhoon* (1903), and *The Shadow Line* (1917) are also set in the eastern seas. Several of his short stories, including "The Secret Sharer" and "Youth," are set there, too. "Heart of Darkness" is based on his voyage up the Congo River, and his novel *Nostromo* (1904) uses memories of his early voyages in the Caribbean.

His sea stories were not superficial adventure tales, though they were sometimes dismissed as such in his day. Later critics hailed Conrad for his experiments with fictional point of view and multiple narrators. Conrad's work is also exceptional for its probing psychological analysis of the isolated self torn between such conflicting influences as sympathy and greed, heroism and cowardice, and idealism and cynicism. In *Nostromo,* for example, Conrad presented an epic picture of the clash between capitalism and revolution in South America. Conrad also wrote two absorbing novels about revolutionaries in Europe, *The Secret Agent* (1907) and *Under Western Eyes* (1911), and the autobiographical pieces collected in *The Mirror of the Sea* (1906) and *A Personal Record* (1912). After years of praise from critics but little public attention, Conrad only began to achieve popular success with the more melodramatic material of his novels *Chance* (1914) and *Victory* (1915).   Garrett Stewart

Additional resources

Jones, Michael P. *Conrad's Heroism: A Paradise Lost.* Univ. Microfilms, 1989. First published in 1985.
Najder, Zdzisław. *Joseph Conrad: A Chronicle.* Rutgers, 1983.
Page, Norman. *A Conrad Companion.* St. Martin's, 1986.
Watt, Ian P. *Conrad in the Nineteenth Century.* Univ. of California Pr., 1979.

Conrail, a United States railroad, is one of the largest freight carriers in the nation. It operates about 13,000 miles (21,000 kilometers) of rail routes in 14 Eastern and Midwestern states, the District of Columbia, and the Canadian province of Quebec. The name *Conrail* stands for *Consolidated Rail Corporation.*

Congress provided for the organization of Conrail through the Regional Rail Reorganization Act of 1973. The Railroad Revitalization and Regulatory Reform Act of 1976 authorized Conrail to take over the operations of the bankrupt Penn Central Transportation Company and five other bankrupt Northeastern railroads. These railroads included the Erie Lackawanna, Reading, and Lehigh Valley. The Penn Central had been formed in 1968 by the merger of the Pennsylvania and New York Central railroads. Conrail was technically a private corporation. But the U.S. government provided loans and loan guarantees to Conrail and named a majority of its directors.

Conrail seemed to flounder during its first five years. The Northeast Rail Service Act of 1981 gave it greater flexibility to eliminate unprofitable routes and improve worker productivity. Under the act, the federal government acquired nearly all the company's stock. Conrail's fortunes rose sharply, and it was profitable almost every year from 1981 through the mid-1980's. In 1987, the U.S. government sold all its Conrail stock to private investors.   Richard Saunders, Jr.

Conscientious objector is a person who claims that his beliefs prevent him from bearing arms in his country's armed forces. A conscientious objector may be willing to serve in the military, but only as a noncombatant, such as a medical corpsman. Or he may claim that his principles do not allow him to take part in any effort associated with war. Of the major countries, the United States and the United Kingdom were the first to consistently accept conscientious objection in exempting people from military service or combat training.

The history of conscientious objection in the United States dates back to colonial times, when men had to serve in their colony's militia. The first conscientious objectors in America were members of pacifist religious groups, such as the Quakers.

In 1661, Massachusetts became the first colony to exempt conscientious objectors from service in its militia. Congress passed the first federal draft law during the Civil War (1861-1865). This law recognized conscientious objectors, and they received special consideration in both the North and the South. To be classified as a conscientious objector, a man had to belong to a pacifist religious group. This requirement was also followed during World War I (1914-1918). Men classified as conscientious objectors were excused from combat, but were expected to perform some sort of military service.

The 1940 draft law required "religious training and belief," but not necessarily membership in a pacifist religious group, for conscientious objection. The 1948 draft law defined religious belief as belief in a "Supreme Being." But Congress removed the term "Supreme Being" in the 1967 law because the U.S. Supreme Court interpreted the term to include vaguely religious philosophies. Between 1967 and 1970, exemptions were granted chiefly to people whose "religious training and belief" led them to believe all war is wrong.

The religious requirement was strongly questioned during the 1960's. Many men sought exemptions on the basis of their personal philosophy or their belief that the Vietnam War (1957-1975) was immoral. Major churches came to support selective objection—the refusal to serve in a particular war. In 1970, the Supreme Court exempted from military service "all those whose consciences, spurred by deeply held moral, ethical, or religious beliefs, would give them no rest or peace if they allowed themselves to become part of an instrument of war." In western Europe, alternative forms of national service for objectors are often provided in an effort to reconcile the claims of national security and individual conscience.   Charles Chatfield

See also **Draft, Military** (Criticism of the draft); **Pacifism**.

Additional resources

Conscience in America: A Documentary History of Conscientious Objection in America, 1757-1967. Ed. by Lillian Schlissel. Dutton, 1968.

Drescher, John M. *Why I Am a Conscientious Objector.* Herald Pr. 1982.

Conscription. See Draft, Military.

TreePeople

Conservation includes the efforts of individual citizens to maintain or improve the quality of the environment. These volunteers plant trees in an urban area.

Conservation

Conservation is the management, protection, and wise use of natural resources. Natural resources include all the things that help support life, such as sunlight, water, soil, and minerals. Plants and animals are also natural resources.

The earth has limited supplies of many natural resources. However, our use of these resources keeps increasing as the population grows and our standard of living rises. Conservationists work to ensure that the environment can continue to provide for human needs. Without conservation, most of the earth's resources would be wasted, degraded, or destroyed.

Conservation includes a wide variety of activities. Conservationists work to keep farmlands productive. They manage forests to supply timber, to shelter wildlife, and to provide people with recreational opportunities. They work to save wilderness areas and wildlife from human destruction. They try to find ways to develop and use mineral resources without damaging the environment. Conservationists also seek safe, dependable ways to help meet the world's energy needs. In addition, they work to improve city life by seeking solutions to air pollution, waste disposal, and urban decay.

Conservationists sometimes divide natural resources into four groups: (1) inexhaustible resources, (2) renewable resources, (3) nonrenewable resources, and (4) recyclable resources.

Inexhaustible resources, such as sunlight, cannot be used up. Water is considered inexhaustible because the earth will always have the same amount of water. But

Eric G. Bolen, the contributor of this article, is Professor of Biology and Dean of the Graduate School at the University of North Carolina, Wilmington. The article was critically reviewed by Laurence R. Jahn, Consultant for Natural Resource Management.

water supplies vary from one area to another, and some areas have shortages of clean, fresh water. The supplies of salt and some other minerals are so abundant that they are not likely to be used up.

Renewable resources can be used and replaced. They include plants and animals, which reproduce and so replace themselves. Most renewable resources cannot be stored for future use. For example, old trees must be cut down, or they will rot and become useless for timber. In addition, because most renewable resources are living things, they interact with one another. Thus, the use of one such resource affects others. For example, the cutting down of trees affects many plants and animals, as well as soil and water resources. Soil may be considered a renewable resource because crops can be grown on the same land for years if the soil is cared for properly. But if the soil is allowed to wash or blow away, it can only be replaced over hundreds of years.

Nonrenewable resources, such as coal, iron, and petroleum, cannot be replaced. These resources take thousands or millions of years to form. Their supplies are being depleted faster than new supplies can form. Most nonrenewable resources can be stored for future use. Minerals are sometimes left in the ground to save them for the years ahead. Little interaction occurs among most nonrenewable resources, and so the use of one nonrenewable resource has little effect on another.

Recyclable resources, such as aluminum and copper, can be used more than once. For example, aluminum can be used to make containers and then be reprocessed and reused.

Some kinds of conservation have been practiced for hundreds of years. However, as a popular movement, conservation began in the United States during the early 1900's. The word *conservation* was probably first used by Gifford Pinchot, head of the U.S. Forest Service during President Theodore Roosevelt's Administration. The term comes from two Latin words—*servare,* which means *to keep* or *to guard,* and *con,* which means *together.* During the early 1900's, American conservationists worked chiefly to preserve the nation's forests and wildlife. Today, conservationists work in many fields, including forestry, geology, range ecology, soil science, wildlife biology, and urban planning. Conservationists are also called *environmentalists* and *ecologists.*

One of the most difficult challenges of conservation is to reconcile two, sometimes conflicting, goals—(1) to protect the environment and (2) to maintain or increase agricultural and industrial production. For example, the agricultural use of some chemical fertilizers and pesticides pollutes the environment but also greatly increases crop yields. Thus, most farmers do not want to stop using these chemicals, even though it would be best for the health of the environment. Such problems can be solved only through the combined efforts of many people. Business leaders, government officials, scientists, and individual citizens must all work together to conserve natural resources.

The importance of conservation

Conservation is important to many people for a wide variety of reasons. Farmers may practice conservation to prevent erosion and to maintain the quality of the soil. City dwellers may be chiefly concerned about air pollution, inadequate parks, and decaying neighborhoods. Nature lovers appreciate the beauty and other values of wildlife and landscapes. Business executives may promote conservation to help ensure continuous supplies of minerals and other resources on which their industries depend. But in general, conservation is important for two basic reasons: (1) to meet demands for natural resources and (2) to maintain the quality of life.

To meet demands for resources. The demand for natural resources has steadily increased as a result of the growth of the world population and the rise in standards of living in many countries. While the demand for resources has increased, the supply has not, and some resources are being used up rapidly.

From 1650 to 1850, the world population doubled. Since 1850, it has more than quadrupled. Today, the world has about $5\frac{2}{3}$ billion people. If the present rate of population growth continues, the number of people on earth will double every 41 years. Such a large increase in the population will result in even greater demands for natural resources. More land will be needed for living space and for growing food. More fuel and fresh water will be required. No one knows how many people the earth can support. But most conservationists believe the rate of population growth must be reduced to keep from depleting many of our natural resources.

Wildlife conservation requires setting aside areas where animal habitats are not disturbed. Mallards and other birds nest in Lower Klamath National Wildlife Refuge in California, *above.*

The rise in the standard of living in industrialized nations has created further demands for natural resources. Such industrialized nations as the United States, Canada, Australia, and Great Britain have high living standards, and they use a large share of the world's natural resources. In addition, many developing nations are working to raise their living standards and are increasing their demands for resources.

The high living standards in the United States and many other nations are supported largely by the growth of industry. Industry uses huge amounts of fuel and other resources, and it depends on continuous supplies of these resources. However, unless conservation is practiced, shortages of some resources may develop within the next 100 years.

In many cases, meeting demands for one resource makes it difficult to conserve another. The same land that is needed to produce food, wood, or fuel is often valued for its wildlife, recreational opportunities, or beautiful scenery. For example, the construction of a dam may provide water to irrigate farmland or to produce electric power. But it may also destroy scenic lands and wildlife habitats.

To maintain the quality of life. Conservationists use the term *quality of life* to refer to the health of the environment. Such factors as clean air and water, uncluttered living areas, and unspoiled scenic lands contribute to the quality of life.

Industrial development has created a high standard of living for many people. But it has also damaged the environment in ways that impair the quality of life. For example, many factories release smoke and other pollutants into the air and empty waste products into lakes and streams. As a result, the air in many cities is unhealthy to breathe, and the water in many lakes and streams is unsafe to drink or to swim in. Some methods of mining also cause pollution and may leave the land barren. In addition, the use of certain industrial products contributes to pollution. For example, the exhaust fumes from automobiles are a major source of air pollution.

To maintain or improve the quality of life, natural resources must be developed and used in ways that cause the least possible damage to the environment. In addition, some places need to be preserved in their natural state and protected from any form of development. Prairies, wetlands, forests, and other natural environments provide homes for many kinds of wildlife. They thus contribute to the *ecological diversity* of the earth. If such environments are not preserved, large areas of the earth will consist of *monocultures,* environments that support only a few species of plants and animals.

Monocultures have already replaced ecologically diverse environments in many parts of the world. For example, most of the prairies of North America have been replaced by corn and wheat fields. As a result, such wildlife as pronghorns and prairie chickens, which once were plentiful on the prairies, are no longer abundant throughout their former ranges. Conservationists are working to protect the few remaining prairies and to preserve other environments.

Kinds of conservation

This section divides the broad field of conservation into eight main categories. These categories are (1) soil conservation, (2) water conservation, (3) forest conservation, (4) conservation of grazing lands, (5) wildlife conservation, (6) mineral conservation, (7) energy conservation, and (8) urban conservation.

Each kind of conservation has different problems and solutions. In many cases, however, the management of one resource affects several other resources. For example, the conservation of forests helps conserve water, soil, and wildlife resources. Forests absorb rain water and so keep it from running off the land too rapidly. They thus help prevent rain water from washing away the soil. Forests also provide homes for wildlife. In the same way, every living thing depends on and interacts with other living and nonliving things. Living things and their physical environment form an *ecosystem.*

This section deals mainly with conservation problems and practices in the United States. But much of the information applies to other countries as well. The section *Conservation around the world* discusses specific conservation concerns in other countries.

Soil conservation. Soil is essential for the growth of plants, which in turn provide food for animals and human beings. Soil consists chiefly of minerals mixed with *organic* (plant and animal) matter. Soil forms from rocks and similar materials that are broken up into smaller particles by physical and chemical processes called *weathering.* The particles become mixed with *humus,* a substance formed from plant and animal remains. Bacteria in the soil break down the humus into nutrients needed by plants. See **Soil.**

The thin layer of fertile soil that covers much of the earth's land was formed by natural processes over thousands of years. But in many areas, careless human practices have destroyed the soil in just a few years.

Rain water, wind, and other natural forces gradually wear away the soil. This process, called *erosion,* normally occurs very slowly. But people have greatly increased the rate of soil erosion by removing natural *vegetation* (plant life) to clear land for construction projects, mining operations, or farmland. Plants protect the soil from the direct force of raindrops and wind. Their roots form an underground network that holds the soil in place. Plants also absorb some rain water so that less runs off the land. Thus, fewer soil particles are washed away.

Soil erosion has long been a major conservation problem, particularly on farmlands. In the United States, soil erosion has severely damaged about 175 million acres (71 million hectares) of land. Much of the eroded soil is deposited in lakes, streams, and rivers.

Farmers can reduce soil erosion by planting trees and leaving patches of natural vegetation between their fields and on other unplowed areas. The trees serve as windbreaks, and the plant cover slows the runoff of rain water. Many farmers also practice such soil conservation methods as *contour plowing, strip cropping, terracing,* and *minimum tillage.*

Contour plowing is practiced on sloping land. Farmers plow across a slope, instead of up and down. The plowed soil forms ridges across the slope. The ridges help slow the flow of rain water.

Strip cropping also helps slow the flow of rain water down a slope. Farmers plant grass, clover, or other close-growing plants in strips between bands of corn, times a field must be tilled. Normally, farmers till their fields three or more times a year. One form of minimum tillage is called *zero-tillage* or *no-till.* After harvesting a crop, farmers leave the *residues* (remains) from the crop on the field as a covering for the soil, instead of plowing them under. During the next planting, the farmer prepares the seedbed with a device that leaves the residues between the crop rows. Zero-tillage not only provides cover for the soil but also conserves tractor fuel. See **Farm and farming** (Preparing the soil).

Another major conservation problem on farmlands is declining soil fertility, which is caused partly by planting the same crop in a field year after year. Corn, wheat, and other grain crops drain the soil of an essential chemical called *nitrogen* if they are grown on the same field for several years. Farmers can maintain the fertility of the soil by practicing *crop rotation,* in which crops are alternated from year to year. The rotation crop is usually a *legume,* such as alfalfa or soybeans. Unlike corn and wheat, legumes restore nitrogen to the soil. See **Cropping system; Nitrogen.**

Some farmers add plant remains or *manure* (animal wastes) to their fields to enrich the soil. Many use chemical fertilizers for this purpose. However, excessive use of some chemical fertilizers may decrease the ability of bacteria to decay humus and produce nutrients naturally. As a result, the soil may gradually harden and lose much of its ability to absorb rain water. The soil then erodes more easily. In addition, the chemicals from fertilizers may wash out of the soil and enter lakes, streams, and even wells, polluting the water. Excessive use of pesticides causes similar problems.

A common problem on irrigated farmland is the build-up of various chemical salts in the soil. Most irrigation water contains small amounts of these salts. In time, the salts accumulate in the soil and may reduce plant growth and ruin cropland. See **Irrigation** (Providing artificial drainage).

Farmers can obtain advice on conservation problems

Grant Heilman

Soil conservation techniques include *contour plowing,* in which farmers plow across a slope, and *strip cropping,* in which farmers alternate strips of close-growing plants and grain crops.

wheat, or other grain crops. Grass and clover hold water and protect the soil better than grain crops do.

Terracing helps prevent soil erosion on hillsides. Farmers build wide, flat rows called *terraces* on the hillsides. A terraced hillside resembles a large staircase. The terraces hold rain water and so prevent it from washing down the hillside and forming gullies.

Minimum tillage, also called *conservation tillage,* consists of several methods of reducing the number of

© Jean-Claude Lejeune, Black Star

Terracing helps check soil erosion on hillsides. The terraces hold rain water and prevent it from washing down a hillside and forming gullies.

from the Soil Conservation Service, an agency of the U.S. Department of Agriculture. The agency works through local soil-conservation districts to help farmers and ranchers prevent soil erosion.

Water conservation. People require clean, fresh drinking water. People also use water for bathing, cooking, and cleaning. Farmers need water to irrigate dry croplands. Industries use water to produce electric power and in the manufacture of many products. Water is also important in recreation and transportation.

The demand for water is constantly increasing as a result of population growth and the expansion of agriculture and industry. The earth has an abundant supply of water, but the water is unevenly distributed. Some areas do not receive enough rainfall, while others receive more than they need.

Many dry regions of the United States, such as parts of the West and Midwest, face serious water shortages. In some areas, people obtain water by drilling wells to tap underground supplies. But in parts of the West and Midwest, farmers have drilled so many wells to provide water for irrigation that the level of the ground water has been greatly lowered. Many cities have also used up much of their ground water. In some cases, underground reservoirs can be refilled by pumping in water during periods of heavy rainfall.

Some rural areas and cities obtain water by damming rivers to create reservoirs. Dams are also built to control flooding. But in many cases, the construction of new dams to meet ever-increasing demands for water or to reduce flooding threatens wildlife. For example, during the late 1970's, conservationists opposed the construction of the Tellico Dam on the Little Tennessee River because of its possible harmful effect on a rare species of fish called the snail darter. However, the dam was completed in 1979, and some snail darters were transferred to the Hiwassee River in Tennessee in an attempt to ensure their survival.

A dam may harm certain fish because it changes the flow of a river and causes less water to travel downstream. As the land behind a dam becomes flooded, some wildlife habitats are destroyed. Certain streams should not be dammed because they carry too much silt. On such streams, the reservoirs would quickly fill up with silt and become useless for storing water.

Water supplies for cities and farms can be increased partly through *watershed management* (the management of vegetation to prevent rapid runoff of rain water and melting snow). Trees and other plants play an important part in the natural cycle of water. They keep water from running off the land and so allow it to filter into the ground. Underground supplies are thus refilled, and the water flows through underground channels into lakes and streams. When the plant cover is destroyed, this natural cycle is disturbed. Rain water runs off the land rapidly instead of filtering into the ground. Watershed management also helps reduce flooding and soil erosion.

Some cities near seacoasts meet a small part of their water needs by desalting seawater. This process, which is called *desalination,* requires large amounts of fuel for energy and is therefore expensive. For this reason, desalination is not practical on a large scale. But some scientists believe that solar energy will one day provide the cheap power needed for desalination.

Many communities have problems with water pollution. The disposal of sewage, industrial chemicals, and other wastes into lakes and streams makes the water unhealthy for wildlife and human beings. Even bodies of water as large as Lake Erie have become seriously polluted. Cities and industries can reduce pollution by removing harmful substances from wastes before emptying the wastes into lakes and streams. But waste treatment is expensive, and the job of cleaning up all the nation's lakes and streams will take many years. The U.S. Environmental Protection Agency enforces federal regulations that limit the amount and kinds of pollutants that can be dumped in lakes and streams. It makes surveys of pollution levels in water and locates the sources of pollutants. See **Water; Water pollution.**

Forest conservation. Forests serve as sources of timber and as homes for wildlife. They also provide recreational areas for campers, hikers, and hunters. In addition, forests are important as watersheds. They absorb large amounts of rain water and so prevent the rapid runoff of water that causes erosion and flooding.

Many forests in the United States are owned by the federal government. These national forests are managed by the U.S. Forest Service under the principle of *multiple use,* which means that they provide several benefits at once. For example, the forests are managed to furnish timber, to shelter wildlife, to provide recreational space, and to conserve water. However, the production of timber sometimes conflicts with the need to conserve other forest resources, such as wildlife and water.

The conservation of forests that are used to produce timber depends on replacing trees that are cut down so that the forest has a *sustained yield.* Sustained yield is an approximate balance between the annual harvest and the annual growth of wood. The **Forestry** article in *World Book* describes methods of harvesting trees to achieve sustained yield. It also describes how forest resources other than trees are managed and how forests are protected from fires, diseases, and insect pests.

Since the first European settlers came to North America, many forests have been cut down to clear land for farms and cities. Further forest destruction in the United States has been slowed. However, in many other countries, especially those in tropical areas, forest destruction continues at a rapid pace.

Conservation of grazing lands. Grazing lands, also called *ranges,* are grass-covered areas that are too dry to support farms or forests. These lands support a wide variety of wildlife, including pronghorns and mule deer. Ranges also provide pasture for cattle, horses, and sheep. Large areas of the Western United States are covered by ranges and are used to graze livestock.

The chief conservation problem on ranges is overgrazing, which results when too many animals graze an area or when the animals stay in one place too long. The grasses then die and are replaced by weeds and poisonous plants, which do not provide good pasture for livestock.

Overgrazing also results in increased runoff of water, which causes soil erosion. It also ruins wildlife habitats. For example, overgrazing often occurs on the fertile areas that border a stream. Livestock trample on stream banks and kill plant life. This results in increased erosion

© Jonathan Blair, Woodfin Camp, Inc.

Water pollution can make lakes and streams unfit for most uses. This waterway is contaminated by wastes from a paper mill. A pollution control worker collects samples for testing.

along the stream bank and may cause the stream to become too muddy to support fish.

Grazing lands must be carefully managed to ensure a continuous supply of *forage* (plant food) for wildlife and for livestock. To prevent overgrazing, range conservationists must determine the *carrying capacity* of the land. The carrying capacity is the largest number of animals that an area of land can support without destruction of plant life. Range conservationists limit the number of livestock on a range so that the carrying capacity is not exceeded. The livestock must also be moved from time to time so that the grasses can regrow.

To improve the vegetation on overgrazed lands, range managers sometimes practice *prescribed burning*. That is, they set fires to help control brush and poisonous plants. When properly controlled, such burning will not harm grasses. Herbicides can also be used to kill undesirable plants. But many conservationists oppose the use of herbicides because the chemicals in them harm wildlife.

Another problem on grazing lands is the control of such animals as bobcats, coyotes, and mountain lions, which sometimes prey on livestock. Many ranchers want these predators killed or removed. But most conservationists want to protect the animals.

Much of the grazing land in the Western part of the United States is owned by the federal government and managed by the U.S. Bureau of Land Management or the U.S. Forest Service. Both agencies issue permits to ranchers to use public grazing lands. The ranchers must agree to graze only a certain number of livestock on a range and to move the animals at set intervals. Some conservationists argue that the fee ranchers pay for grazing on public lands should be increased.

Wildlife conservation. Wild animals and plants make up an essential part of nature and contribute to the beauty and wonder of life. Wildlife also is important in scientific research.

Through the ages, human activities have contributed to the extinction of many wild animals. Extinct animals of North America include the passenger pigeon and Carolina parakeet. Today, human activities threaten the survival of many other animals.

In the past, uncontrolled hunting was one of the major causes of the extinction or near-extinction of many kinds of North American wildlife. But today, wild

George H. Harrison, Grant Heilman

Forest conservation is important partly to provide recreational areas for hikers and other outdoor enthusiasts. Forests are also sources of timber and provide homes for many kinds of wild animals.

Georgia Pacific (Designer Photo)

A tree nursery supplies seedlings for replanting forests that have been cut down for timber. Seedlings grow in a nursery for one to four years before being transplanted in a forest.

animals in the United States are protected by laws that regulate hunting and fishing. The destruction of habitats is the major threat to wildlife today. The development of land for homes, farms, industries, and transportation leaves fewer areas where wild animals can nest, breed, and feed, and where wild plants can grow. Pollution also damages wildlife habitats. Chemicals from sewage, industrial wastes, and fertilizers and pesticides build up in lakes and streams and in the soil. Some pollutants collect in the tissues of plants and animals. Animals that eat these poisoned plants and animals are also affected by the pollutants.

A chief goal of conservationists is to ensure the sur-

vival of wildlife. Wildlife conservation includes the enforcement of hunting and fishing laws. But in many cases, an entire habitat requires protection and management. Some areas must then be set aside as national parks, nature reserves, or wildlife refuges.

Farmers can help conserve such wildlife as rabbits and quail by leaving strips of natural vegetation along the edges of their fields. They can also reduce the use of harmful pesticides and fertilizers.

The populations of some species of animals have been reduced to the point that the animals may not survive in their natural environments. In some cases, such animals can be raised in captivity and then released into a protected area.

The U.S. Fish and Wildlife Service, an agency of the Department of the Interior, maintains wildlife refuges and fish hatcheries and conducts wildlife research. The agency has a special interest in wild animals, but it also works to conserve plants, soil, and water because these resources are essential to the survival of animals. The National Park Service protects wildlife in areas within the national park system. In addition, state agencies and many private organizations work to protect wildlife. See **Wildlife conservation.**

Mineral conservation. Minerals include such substances as copper, gold, iron, lead, and salt. Industries use minerals to manufacture countless products.

The use of many minerals has increased greatly throughout the world. The use of aluminum, for example, has tripled since 1960. The use of nickel has more than doubled during this time. Some minerals, such as *bauxite* (the mineral from which aluminum is obtained) and salt, are plentiful. But the proved reserves of such minerals as copper, lead, nickel, and zinc may be depleted within 100 years.

Most minerals can be profitably mined only where they occur in large deposits. Industries first develop the highest-grade and most easily minable ores. When these are depleted, lower-grade and harder-to-mine ores are developed. Many deposits can only be mined

Oxford Scientific Films

Grazing lands provide pasture for livestock. But improper management may result in overgrazing, which destroys the vegetation on the land. In this picture, the land on the left has been overgrazed, and the land on the right has been properly grazed.

Prescribed burning is one way to improve the vegetation on overgrazed land. The fire destroys weeds and other undesirable plants, and grasses can then regrow.

Steve Bunting

with advanced technology and large amounts of energy. Some require so much energy to mine and refine that they cannot be profitably developed.

Deposits of minerals are unevenly distributed throughout the world. This uneven distribution of minerals has played an important role in history. For example, the ancient Romans battled the Celts for the tin mines of southern England. A desire for gold was largely responsible for the Spanish explorations and conquests of lands in many parts of the New World.

The need for minerals continues to influence international relations today. Many countries must import large amounts of various minerals. The United States, for example, imports almost all of the sheet mica and strontium it uses and more than half of its chromium, cobalt, fluorine, manganese, nickel, platinum, and tin.

The mining and refining of minerals often results in destruction of scenic lands and wildlife habitats and in air and water pollution. One method of copper mining, for example, leaves large open pits on the surface of the land. Fumes from copper smelters, iron and steel mills, and other refineries pollute the air. Some refineries discharge wastes into lakes and streams.

Minerals can be conserved in a number of ways. Industries can reduce waste by using more efficient mining and processing methods. In some cases, industries can substitute plentiful materials for scarce ones. Some mineral products can be *recycled.* Aluminum cans are commonly recycled. Although bauxite is plentiful, it can be expensive to refine. Recycling aluminum products does not require the large amounts of electricity needed to refine bauxite. Products made from many other minerals, such as nickel, chromium, lead, copper, and zinc, can also be recycled.

The Bureau of Mines of the U.S. Department of the Interior works to ensure efficient mining, processing, use, and recycling of minerals. It also works to reduce the harmful environmental effects of mining.

Energy conservation. All industries require energy to operate. Energy is also used in transportation and recreation. In addition, we use energy to warm and cool our homes, to cook food, to provide lighting, and to operate many appliances.

About 95 per cent of the energy used throughout the world comes from oil, coal, and natural gas. These substances are called *fossil fuels* because they developed from fossilized remains of prehistoric plants and animals. Large deposits of fossil fuels take millions of years to form. The earth has a limited supply of fossil fuels. But the worldwide use of fossil fuels has nearly doubled

© Jerry Cooke, Animals Animals

Strips of natural vegetation along the edges of plowed fields can provide homes for such wildlife as deer and quail. Farmers can conserve wildlife by leaving such areas undisturbed.

© Steve Elmore, Tom Stack & Assoc.

Recycling is an important conservation activity in many communities. Sanitation workers make a curbside pickup of newspapers, aluminum cans, and other recyclable items, *above*.

Materials recycled in the United States

These graphs show the leading types of recycled items in the United States. The pie graph shows that paper products are the nation's chief source of recycled material. The bar graph shows that most lead-acid batteries and aluminum cans are recycled.

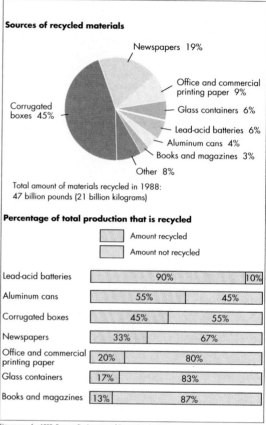

Sources of recycled materials

Newspapers 19%
Office and commercial printing paper 9%
Glass containers 6%
Corrugated boxes 45%
Lead-acid batteries 6%
Aluminum cans 4%
Books and magazines 3%
Other 8%

Total amount of materials recycled in 1988:
47 billion pounds (21 billion kilograms)

Percentage of total production that is recycled

☐ Amount recycled
☐ Amount not recycled

	Amount recycled	Amount not recycled
Lead-acid batteries	90%	10%
Aluminum cans	55%	45%
Corrugated boxes	45%	55%
Newspapers	33%	67%
Office and commercial printing paper	20%	80%
Glass containers	17%	83%
Books and magazines	13%	87%

Figures are for 1988. Source: Environmental Protection Agency data prepared by Franklin Associates.

every 20 years since 1900. As the supply dwindles, the cost of fossil fuels keeps rising.

Many nations are working to develop other sources of energy to reduce their dependence on fossil fuels. But every source of energy has some disadvantages that make its development difficult. The **Energy supply** article describes such sources of energy as nuclear energy, solar energy, and geothermal energy.

Until other sources of energy are further developed, nations must conserve fossil fuels to make the supply last as long as possible. Most of the responsibility for

WORLD BOOK diagram

Lifetimes of some important minerals*

This graph shows how long the reserve bases of certain minerals will last if they continue to be mined at the present rates. New discoveries and changes in technology will probably increase these lifetimes.

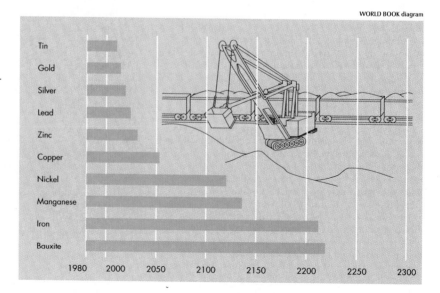

Tin
Gold
Silver
Lead
Zinc
Copper
Nickel
Manganese
Iron
Bauxite

1980   2000   2050   2100   2150   2200   2250   2300

*At 1989 production rates.
Source: U.S. Bureau of Mines.

conservation rests with industrialized nations because they consume the majority of the world's energy. The United States alone uses about 25 per cent of the world's energy, and it produces only about 20 per cent. Higher fuel prices and periodic fuel shortages have forced the United States and many other industrialized nations to develop better conservation programs.

Industries and individuals can conserve energy in many ways. Improved mining and manufacturing techniques can make the industrial use of fuel more efficient. Individuals can save fuel in their homes by installing insulation, which reduces the amount of fuel used for heating and air conditioning. People can set their thermostats at or below 65 °F (18 °C) in winter and at or above 78 °F (26 °C) in summer. These thermostat settings are required in most public buildings by the federal government. People can also conserve energy by using less hot water and turning off unnecessary lights. Motorists can save gasoline by driving smaller cars and by forming car pools. Much gasoline would be saved if more people used public transportation.

The development and use of energy causes many environmental problems. For example, strip mining of coal destroys plant life and exposes the land to erosion. Blowouts of offshore oil wells and leaks from tankers produce oil spills that pollute the oceans. The burning of fossil fuels pollutes the air and results in the formation of *acid rain,* which can kill fish in lakes and streams. Sound conservation practices, such as restoring strip-mined land as closely as possible to its original condition, can help reduce environmental damage.

The U.S. Department of Energy develops national energy programs and promotes energy conservation. It also conducts research to develop new energy sources.

Urban conservation. About three-fourths of the people in the United States live in or near cities. Since the 1800's, many U.S. cities have grown so rapidly that public services have not kept up with population increases. Cities thus have such problems as overcrowding, traffic jams, and inadequate public transportation

Lifetimes of fossil fuels*

This graph shows how long the proved reserves of fossil fuels will last if the present rates of production continue. New technologies, discoveries of new deposits, and changes in market conditions will probably lengthen these lifetimes.

WORLD BOOK diagram

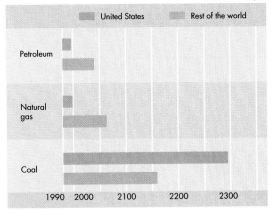

*At 1988 production rates.
Source: U.S. Energy Information Administration.

systems. Most large cities are also noisy and suffer from air pollution, partly because of the large number of motor vehicles in use. In addition, many cities lack sufficient parks and recreational facilities. The urban landscape consists largely of pavement and buildings.

Because of the drawbacks of city life, many people and businesses have moved to the suburbs. As suburbs nearest the city become crowded, people move farther and farther out, creating a condition known as *urban sprawl.* Much prime farmland in the United States has been lost to urban sprawl. When businesses and upper- and middle-class people move to the suburbs, the cities lose tax money needed to maintain city services and neighborhoods. Many cities are left with a large population of poor people living in crowded, run-down hous-

© Bruce M. Wellman, Tom Stack & Associates

Solar collectors can be used to help heat houses and many other buildings. The development of new energy sources reduces our dependence on the dwindling supplies of fossil fuels.

Steve Hale

Urban conservation includes efforts to restore houses and so maintain the attractiveness of old neighborhoods in cities.

ing. The heart of many cities consists of large slum areas, a condition known as *urban blight.*

The goal of urban conservation is to improve the quality of life in cities and to make them more attractive and pleasant places to live. Many cities have *urban renewal projects,* in which run-down buildings are torn down and replaced by public housing or other new developments. In some cities, old houses and apartment buildings are being restored instead of being torn down and replaced. Many cities try to enhance their environments by developing strips of grass or trees called *greenbelts.* Some cities are trying to reduce traffic problems and air pollution by improving public transportation systems and encouraging their use. Most cities also need to develop more parks and recreational facilities. See **Urban renewal.**

Many federal agencies, including the Department of Housing and Urban Development (HUD) and the Environmental Protection Agency, deal with the problems of the nation's cities. Most of the responsibility for living conditions in cities, however, rests with city governments. HUD helps cities finance housing and community development programs. The Environmental Protection Agency works to reduce air and water pollution. See **City** (City problems); **City planning.**

Early history of conservation

Prehistoric times. During early prehistoric times, there were not enough people on earth to use a large

amount of natural resources or to significantly damage the environment. Early prehistoric people thus had little need to practice conservation.

About $1\frac{1}{2}$ million years ago, people learned how to make fire. They built fires to cook food and to keep warm. They also set fires to kill animals. The fires drove the animals over cliffs or into traps. The fires also destroyed forests. Some scientists believe Africa's *savannas* (grasslands with widely scattered trees and shrubs) resulted from burning of forests.

The rise of civilization. A number of civilizations arose in the region surrounding the Mediterranean Sea during ancient times, between about 3000 B.C. and the A.D. 400's. Many people of the region tended large flocks of sheep and goats, which severely overgrazed the land. In time, the shallow soils of the region eroded. The grassy pastures turned to wastelands, and large areas became desertlike. Much of the land in the Mediterranean region remains in poor condition today.

Although ancient civilizations in the Mediterranean region damaged the land, they also developed some conservation practices to keep farmlands productive. For example, the Phoenicians, whose culture peaked about 1000 B.C., developed techniques of terracing hillsides to prevent soil erosion. The Greeks introduced the practice of crop rotation sometime before the 300's B.C. The Romans, whose empire reached its greatest size in the A.D. 100's, brought knowledge about irrigation practices to the lands they conquered. Many conservation techniques later spread to northern Europe and formed the basis for wise land management there.

The Industrial Revolution was a period during the 1700's and early 1800's when industrialization developed in Western Europe and the Northeastern United States. During this period, power-driven machines were invented and factories were organized. Machine-made goods produced in factories replaced handmade goods produced at home. Manufacturing, mining, and construction industries expanded rapidly. The Industrial Revolution resulted in increased production of many kinds of goods. It changed most Western nations from rural, agricultural societies to urban, industrial societies. It also brought many environmental problems.

During the Industrial Revolution, coal was burned to provide power for factories and to heat homes. As a result, smoke and soot polluted the air over London and other industrial cities. Wastes from iron smelting and other industries were dumped into lakes and rivers. The crowded cities also discharged large amounts of raw sewage into the water. Power-driven machines and improved tools increased people's ability to change the environment. They dammed rivers, cleared thick forests, turned vast prairies into cropland, and drained marshes.

During and after the Industrial Revolution, wildlife populations decreased at a rapid rate. With improved guns and traps, commercial hunters killed many animals. As people traveled to new lands, they brought animals that harmed native wildlife, especially on islands. Rats escaped from ships and preyed on birds and their eggs. Goats and sheep overgrazed land, destroying the food supply of wild animals. Wildlife habitats were destroyed as people cleared forests and drained marshes. Habitat destruction dramatically reduced wildlife populations, and it continues to be the major threat to wildlife. Since 1600, about 200 species of animals have become extinct, and many more have dwindled in number.

Conservation in the United States

Early conservation problems. When the European settlers came to North America, they found a vast land rich in natural resources. But they had to struggle to provide food and shelter for themselves. They regarded nature as a force that they had to fight and conquer. They cleared forests to provide logs for cabins and to establish farms. But most settlers did not follow sound agricultural practices. When the soil eroded or lost its fertility, they moved on to new lands. The settlers had little concern for conservation because they thought the frontier extended so far that it would last forever. Although many colonies passed hunting laws to conserve game animals, the laws were not well enforced.

A "frontier attitude" persisted among most Americans during the late 1700's and early 1800's. This attitude was reinforced by the explorations of Meriwether Lewis and William Clark. The two men were commissioned by President Thomas Jefferson to explore the Pacific Northwest. In 1804, Lewis and Clark embarked on a long trek up the Missouri River, across the Rocky Mountains, and down the Columbia River to the Pacific Ocean. After they returned in 1806, they described the bountiful supplies of wildlife and timber they had seen. Many people believed that an unlimited supply of natural resources awaited use by the young nation.

After Lewis and Clark opened up the West, trappers came to hunt animals for their furs. Beaver skins were especially valuable during the 1800's because men's hats were made from the fur. Trappers believed the supply of beavers was inexhaustible, and they trapped too many of the animals. They then had to travel farther and farther west to find more beavers.

The millions of *bison* (American buffalo) that roamed the plains represented another valuable resource. Their hides made warm robes, and their bones were used in fertilizer. During the late 1800's, commercial hunters slaughtered millions of bison. By 1889, only about 550 bison could be found alive in the United States. Only the enforcement of game laws and other protective measures saved the bison from extinction.

Such careless misuse of many of the country's natural resources aroused some people to the need for conservation. The first national park in the world—Yellowstone National Park—was established in 1872 to preserve the area's unusual natural features and scenic beauty. Conservation measures were promoted by a number of American naturalists, including John James Audubon, Henry David Thoreau, George Perkins Marsh, and John Muir. Audubon's paintings of birds and other animals of North America aroused public interest in the nation's wildlife. In his book *Walden* (1854), Thoreau discussed his belief that people should live in harmony with nature. Marsh wrote *Man and Nature* (1864), one of the first textbooks to discuss ecology and conservation. It was later retitled *The Earth as Modified by Human Nature*. Muir influenced Congress to establish Sequoia National Park and Yosemite National Park.

The rise of the conservation movement. During the early 1900's, conservation began to develop as a national movement. More people became interested in conservation, and the federal government took many steps to preserve the nation's natural resources.

Congress passed a conservation law called the Lacey Act in 1900. The act made it a federal crime to transport illegally killed animals across state borders. It also set controls on the trade in bird feathers, the importation of animals, and the commercial killing of game.

President Theodore Roosevelt made many important contributions to the conservation movement. In 1903, he established the first federal wildlife refuge at Pelican Island, Fla. At the urging of Gifford Pinchot, the head of the U.S. Forest Service, and other conservation leaders, Roosevelt added more than 140 million acres (57 million hectares) to the nation's forest reserves.

In 1908, President Roosevelt brought together governors, federal officials, scientists, business executives, and conservation leaders for a White House conference to adopt national policies for the use of natural re-

Bettmann Archive

Serious pollution problems accompanied the development and spread of the Industrial Revolution during the 1700's and early 1800's. The air in Sheffield, England, *left*, and many other cities became clouded with smoke and soot from coal-burning factories.

The slaughter of buffaloes for their hides almost resulted in the extinction of the animal in the United States in the late 1800's. Buffalo hides awaiting shipment east were piled high at Dodge City, Kans., *left.* Strict conservation measures were required to save the buffalo from extinction.

Kansas State Historical Society, Topeka

sources. The conference approved the principle of multiple use in the management of national forests and parks. The principle of multiple use provided that public lands be managed to serve many benefits. It thus protected these lands from being used solely or primarily for commercial development.

The 1908 conference had far-reaching effects. Within a few years, 41 governors established conservation commissions in their states. The National Conservation Commission was formed, and Gifford Pinchot became its chairman. The commission made the first inventory of the nation's natural resources. Based on the commission's recommendations, President Roosevelt later set aside some public lands as natural resource reserves to be used for scientific studies. In 1911, Congress passed the Weeks Law, which formally established the policy of multiple use in the management of national forests and other public lands.

Many conservation projects were begun during the Great Depression of the 1930's, partly to provide jobs for the unemployed. In 1933, President Franklin Roosevelt formed the Civilian Conservation Corps (CCC). Workers in the CCC planted trees, fought forest fires, made paths in national forests and parks, and built dams to control floods. Also in 1933, Congress established the Tennessee Valley Authority (TVA) to conserve the resources of the Tennessee Valley. The region suffered from serious soil erosion and from flooding. The TVA planted trees to restore the region's forests. It built several large dams to control flooding and to provide cheap electricity to rural areas.

The tragedy of the *Dust Bowl* in the early 1930's dramatized the need for soil conservation in the United States. The Dust Bowl was the name given to parts of the Great Plains where windstorms carried away the topsoil. The land had been damaged by a severe drought and by poor farming and ranching practices. The Dust Bowl covered about 50 million acres (20 million hectares). Many farm families suffered great hardships and had to leave the area. In 1935, President Franklin Roosevelt established the Soil Conservation Service to promote soil conservation practices among farmers and ranchers. See **Dust Bowl**.

In 1937, Congress passed the Federal Aid in Wildlife Restoration Act, which levied a federal tax on sporting arms and ammunition. The tax money is distributed to the states for use in wildlife management and research.

Aldo Leopold, an American naturalist, was one of the most influential leaders in the conservation movement during the mid-1900's. He wrote *Game Management* (1933), the first textbook on wildlife management. Leopold promoted the active management of wildlife.

Recent developments. Scientific discoveries about various forms of pollution had a major impact on the conservation movement during the 1970's. Rachel Car-

Bettmann Archive

Vast areas were set aside as national parks during the late 1800's and early 1900's. Yosemite National Park, *above,* was created largely through the efforts of the American naturalist John Muir, *right,* shown standing with President Theodore Roosevelt, an avid conservationist.

The Civilian Conservation
Corps employed workers to
plant trees in national forests,
left, and to perform various
other conservation tasks. President Franklin D. Roosevelt
formed the Civilian Conservation Corps in 1933.

Bettmann Archive

son, a marine biologist, wrote about the destructive effects of DDT and other pesticides in her book *Silent
Spring* (1962). She pointed out that pesticides poison the
food supply of wild animals and could also contaminate
the food supply of human beings. Most uses of DDT
were banned in 1972.

Publicity about DDT and other pollutants led to increased public concern about environmental health.
Membership in conservation organizations rose, and
people urged Congress to pass laws to protect the
health of the environment.

Congress passed the National Environmental Policy
Act in 1969. The National Environmental Policy Act requires that an *environmental assessment* be prepared
for all federally funded construction projects or other
activities that might affect the environment.

The act also requires preparation of an *environmental
impact statement* if, after the assessment has been reviewed, the project or activity is found to have environmental significance. Environmental impact statements
are reports that describe how proposed highways,
dams, power plants, or other construction projects
would affect the environment. Environmental impact
statements can be used in court to challenge projects
that may be environmentally harmful. In some cases, a
court may order that projects be stopped or redesigned
to minimize environmental damage. See **Environmental
impact statement**.

In 1970, the Environmental Protection Agency (EPA)
was established. The EPA sets and enforces pollution
control standards and assists state and local governments in pollution control.

In 1973, Congress passed the Endangered Species
Act, which provided more comprehensive protection
for threatened and endangered species of wildlife than
earlier laws had. The act prohibits federal projects that
would destroy the habitat of an endangered species. In
1978, Congress amended the act to allow exemption of
certain projects that serve the best interests of a region
or of the nation.

During the 1970's, the United States experienced peri-

odic fuel shortages, which led to higher prices for gasoline and home heating fuel. The fuel shortages helped
dramatize the need for energy conservation. In 1977,
Congress created the Department of Energy, which was
given responsibility to develop and promote new
sources of energy and ways to save existing supplies.

One project called for the production of synthetic
fuels, or fuels that can be substituted for crude oil and
natural gas. Synthetic fuels, also called *synfuels,* are
gases or liquids produced from coal, oil shale, bituminous sands, and biomass. Synfuels are expensive to
make and therefore not widely used. But if oil prices rise
greatly, synfuels may become an important energy alternative. See **Synthetic fuel**.

© Curt Gunther, Camera 5

Fuel shortages in the 1970's forced automobile drivers to wait
in long lines at the few stations that had gasoline. The shortages
dramatize the need for energy conservation.

In 1993, the Office on Environmental Policy was established. The office coordinates environmental policy within the federal government.

Conservation around the world

Many countries have conservation problems similar to those of the United States. Almost all industrialized nations, for example, face such problems as air and water pollution, urban crowding, and shortages of fossil fuels. This section chiefly deals with land management and wildlife conservation in Canada, Latin America, Europe, Asia, Australia, and Africa. It also discusses international conservation problems.

Canada has a large land area and a fairly small population. Most of the people live in the southern part of the country. Canada's interior is only sparsely settled. The country has bountiful supplies of natural resources. Evergreen forests, prairies, and tundra cover much of the country. Canada has many rivers and lakes, most of which are not seriously polluted. The country has rich deposits of copper, sulfur, uranium, zinc, and other minerals, many of which lie in remote areas of the interior.

Large areas of Canada have not been developed. Thus, many kinds of wildlife are as abundant as they were before the country was settled by Europeans. However, Canada has plans to develop some of the mineral resources of its interior. Unless such development is carefully planned and managed, the growth of the mining industry may result in destruction of wildlife habitats and a decrease in animal populations.

The drainage of wetlands in agricultural areas of Alberta, Saskatchewan, and western Manitoba has destroyed many wildlife habitats. The prairies of these provinces have fertile soil and are intensively farmed to produce cereal grains. Some people want to drain the remaining prairie wetlands, called *prairie potholes,* to increase crop production. But conservationists do not want the wetlands drained because they are important breeding places for ducks and other migratory birds. The wetlands also store runoff water and so help prevent flooding.

Canada and the United States have long worked together to protect waterfowl and other wild animals that cross their border. The two countries have treaties that protect migratory birds and other wildlife.

However, other issues are not settled. Canadians have called for action to prevent the production of harmful chemicals that cross the border in the smoke and other exhausts from factories in the United States. The chemicals mix with water vapor in the atmosphere to form sulfuric and nitric acids. These acids pollute rain, sleet, and snow. The polluted precipitation, commonly called *acid rain,* kills fish and other aquatic life in many Canadian ponds and lakes. Some conservationists also believe that northern forests may be dying because of acid rain. They argue that acid rain stops leaves from producing food for trees. Acid rain is thus a major conservation issue in Canada because of its destruction to the environment and the economic hardships it may cause. See **Acid rain.**

Latin America has vast tropical rain forests, where many unique species of plants and animals live. It also has valuable mineral deposits. Mexico, for example, has large deposits of petroleum and natural gas.

Most of Latin America was colonized by the Spanish, who were primarily interested in obtaining gold and other raw materials from the New World. The Spanish generally restricted their settlements to mining centers and areas that had a favorable climate. Thus, until recently, much of Latin America consisted of wilderness areas that were largely undisturbed, though the land around most cities was severely damaged. However, parts of Mexico and Central America were more extensively settled and suffered from widespread forest destruction, overgrazing, and soil erosion.

Many nations of Latin America have a rapidly growing population, and most of the people are poor. To raise living standards, a number of countries have begun programs to expand industry and agriculture. The tropical rain forests have commercially valuable trees, and timber production has increased. Many countries have cut through forests to build roads to reach remote areas where mineral deposits lie. In addition, farmers have cleared forests to provide land for growing crops. The soil of the tropical rain forests, however, does not generally make good farmland. Most tropical soils are not fertile, and few Latin American farmers can afford the large amounts of fertilizers needed to enrich the soil. In addition, tropical soils may harden when they are exposed to direct sunlight. They then become useless for growing crops. As a result, the farmers remove more trees each year to provide new cropland.

The expansion of industry and agriculture in Latin America has thus resulted in destruction of forests and wildlife habitats. Many countries have established national parks to conserve forests and wildlife. But in many cases, the parks are not well protected.

Europe. Much of the land in southern Europe has been severely damaged by the destruction of forests and by overgrazing of livestock. The soil has eroded from hillsides, and the vegetation on grasslands is sparse and of poor quality. Many countries of southern Europe have begun programs to replant trees on hill-

© Toby Molenaar, Woodfin Camp, Inc.

Forest destruction in Brazil and other South American countries continues at a rapid pace. These nations face the challenge of balancing economic development with conservation.

sides and to improve vegetation on grasslands.

In northern Europe, forests still cover much of the land, and environmental damage is not as great as it is in southern Europe. Northern Europeans were among the first people to recognize the environmental value of trees, and they developed the science of forestry. They also have practiced wildlife conservation for many years. In some countries, much of the land is privately owned, and the landowners take responsibility for protecting wildlife. Most of the countries have also established nature reserves.

Prior to its breakup in 1991, the Soviet Union, part of which was in Europe and part in Asia, had the world's largest forest reserves and had excellent forestry programs. The country also worked to conserve its polar bears and other wildlife resources. In addition, the Soviet Union made considerable commercial use of its wildlife. For example, the Soviets managed large herds of antelopelike animals called *saigas* and killed a certain number each year for their meat and hides.

Asia has about $3\frac{1}{4}$ billion people, more than any other continent. Many Asian countries have difficulty conserving their natural resources because the land must support so many people.

In Southeast Asia, many forests have been cut down to produce timber and to clear land for farms and industries. The destruction of forests has reduced the living space of wildlife. Much of Asia's wildlife is also threatened by overhunting. Many people kill animals for food or hunt them to sell to zoos, medical researchers, and pet traders. Because of habitat destruction and overhunting, many large animals of Asia, including elephants, lions, rhinoceroses, and tigers, have become endangered.

In China, people have cut down most of the forests for wood, which has caused serious soil erosion. The soil is deposited in rivers and streams, which lowers the quality of the water. The Huang He, or Yellow River, is so named because the light-colored soil gives the water

a yellowish color. The soil has also raised the riverbed. As a result, the Huang He often floods, causing great property damage and loss of life.

In the Middle East, deserts cover much of the land. However, with irrigation, some areas have been turned into productive farmlands. Israel is especially well known for its irrigation efforts. However, some farmland in Israel and a number of other countries of the region has been seriously damaged by the build-up of salts in the soil, a common problem on irrigated land.

Australia. Much of Australia is covered by ranges, and sheep ranching is widespread. In many dry regions, overgrazing has seriously damaged the vegetation.

Australia's wildlife includes many species of pouched animals called *marsupials.* Kangaroos and some other marsupials are grazing animals. They thus compete for food, water, and living space with the sheep that graze on the ranges. Ranchers have killed many kangaroos because they believe the animals reduce the grass supply for sheep. Hunters have also killed many kangaroos for their hides and to sell their meat for use in pet food. Because the government feared kangaroos might become extinct, it banned the sale of live kangaroos and kangaroo hides and meat to other countries in 1973.

The control of predators on ranges is a major problem in Australia, as it is in the United States. Wild dogs called *dingoes* prey on the sheep. Some ranchers have tried to kill the dingoes with poisons. But many conservationists oppose poisoning because they believe it also kills other species of wild animals.

The introduction of European rabbits in Australia in the 1850's created a major conservation problem for more than a century. In Australia, these rabbits had no natural predators or diseases to limit their population, and their numbers soared. The rabbits consumed so much forage that many sheep ranchers were forced to reduce the size of their flocks. After other control measures failed, Australian scientists succeeded in reducing the rabbit population in the 1950's by exposing the ani-

WORLD BOOK photo by Werner Braun

Farming in arid regions requires special techniques to conserve water. The almond tree being hoed by these farmers in Israel is surrounded by a bank of soil that helps retain rain water.

© Fred Ward, Black Star

The conservation of African wildlife is achieved partly through the establishment of reserves where wild animals are protected. These gnus roam a game reserve in Kenya.

mals to a disease called *myxomatosis*. This disease affects only rabbits. Although rabbits are still a problem in Australia, their numbers remain lower than they formerly were.

Africa. In northern Africa, many people live by tending herds of sheep and goats. Along the southern edge of the Sahara, much of the land has been severely damaged by overgrazing. In these arid areas, the sandy soil quickly erodes after the protective covering of vegetation has been removed. The land then becomes desertlike. Overgrazing and droughts have contributed to the expansion of the Sahara, which advances along parts of its southern border by as much as 30 miles (48 kilometers) a year.

In central and southern Africa, wildlife populations have been reduced by the destruction of habitats and by overhunting. Many species of African wildlife have been overhunted because they are prized as trophies and as sources of valuable products. Elephant tusks are valued as sources of ivory. Much of the ivory has been used to make beads and bracelets. Leopards are prized for their hides, which are used to make expensive fur coats. Many African nations have passed strict hunting laws, but the laws are difficult to enforce in remote areas. The commercial value of elephant tusks, leopard hides, and other animal products on the world market makes *poaching* (illegal hunting) extremely profitable. In 1989, many nations agreed to end the sale of ivory. But some conservationists believe that poaching will continue as long as people buy ivory. To help protect their wildlife, many African nations have established large national parks and nature preserves.

International problems. Many international conservation problems involve marine animals and other resources of the oceans. The commercial hunting of whales, for example, has been an international problem. Because of overhunting, several species of whales are threatened with extinction. Some countries tried to regulate the harvest of whales through participation in the International Whaling Commission, which set limits on the number of whales that can be killed each year. But the commission finally decided that a complete halt to commercial hunting was needed to conserve the whales. The conservation of animals, minerals, and other resources of the oceans may become even more important in future years.

The United Nations, the International Union for the Conservation of Nature and Natural Resources (IUCN), and other organizations support worldwide conservation programs. The IUCN gathers information on the world's endangered wildlife and publishes the data in its *Red Data Book.*

Conservationists throughout the world are concerned about the growing level of carbon dioxide in the atmosphere. Carbon dioxide helps warm the earth in a process called the *greenhouse effect.* The amount of carbon dioxide in the atmosphere is increasing chiefly because of the burning of the fossil fuels, such as coal, oil, and natural gas. The destruction of forests, which absorb carbon dioxide from the atmosphere, is also contributing to an increase in this gas. Some scientists believe that significant global warming may alter the earth's ecological balance and cause great changes in rainfall patterns and ocean levels. Conservationists are working to replant forests and decrease the use of fossil fuels. See **Greenhouse effect.**

Careers in conservation

Most careers in conservation require a college degree. Many people with an interest in the outdoors pursue a career in forestry, wildlife ecology, or soil conservation. Others work in conservation education, urban planning, or various other fields.

Forestry is one of the oldest conservation professions. Foresters are employed by the U.S. Forest Service, the National Park Service, state forest agencies, and logging companies. Some foresters specialize in *silviculture,* the science of growing trees. Others work in such areas as watershed management, fire protection, insect and disease control, or timber harvesting.

Wildlife biologists work for many federal agencies, including the U.S. Fish and Wildlife Service, the U.S. Forest Service, and the National Park Service. They may work in national wildlife refuges, nature reserves, rangelands, forest reserves, or fish hatcheries. Each state also has an agency responsible for wildlife management. In addition, private consulting firms employ wildlife biologists to prepare environmental impact statements. Many land development companies employ people with wildlife management training.

Soil conservationists are employed by the U.S. Soil Conservation Service, the U.S. Forest Service, the U.S. Bureau of Land Management, and various other federal and state agencies. State governments employ soil conservationists to promote the wise management of plant, soil, and water resources. Many agricultural specialties, including *agronomy, range ecology,* and *soil physics,* deal with resource management.

Urban planners and urban geographers work with regional or city planning agencies. These agencies work to improve city services. They also plan urban renewal projects and other city development programs.

Geologists, civil engineers, and scientists in many fields contribute to conservation. They conduct research and seek solutions to many conservation problems, including pollution control and the development of new energy sources.   Eric G. Bolen

Critically reviewed by Laurence R. Jahn

Related articles in *World Book* include:

Soil and water conservation

Coal (Strip mining)	Reclamation, Bureau of
Cropping system	Sewage
Dam (What does a dam do?)	Shelterbelt
Drainage	Soil
Erosion	Soil Conservation Service
Flood	Tennessee Valley Authority
Food supply	Water
Ground water	Water pollution
Irrigation	Wetland
Land Management, Bureau of	World Health Organization

Forest and wildlife conservation

Animal (The future of animals)	Forestry
Arbor Day	Fur (Trapping)
Bird (Bird study and protection)	National forest
Endangered species	National Park Service
Fish and Wildlife Service	National Park System
Fishing industry (Fishery conservation)	Salmon (Salmon conservation)

| Trapping (Trapping and wildlife conservation) | Tree farming
Wildlife conservation |

Mineral and energy conservation

| Energy supply
Mineral
Mines, Bureau of | Petroleum (Petroleum conservation) |

Urban conservation

| Air pollution
City (City problems)
City planning
Housing | Housing and Urban Development, Department of
Park
Urban renewal
Waste disposal |

Conservation organizations

| Audubon Society, National
Greenpeace
Izaak Walton League of America | National Wildlife Federation
Nature Conservancy
Sierra Club |

Conservation leaders

| Adamson, Joy
Audubon, John
James
Carson, Rachel
Commoner, Barry | Darling, Ding
Fossey, Dian
Leopold, Aldo
Miner, Jack
Mowat, Farley | Muir, John
Pinchot, Gifford
Roosevelt, Theodore |

Other related articles

| Agriculture, Department of
Balance of nature
Ecology
Environmental impact statement
Environmental pollution | Environmental Protection Agency
Interior, Department of the
Natural resources
Recycling |

Outline

I. **The importance of conservation**
  A. To meet demands for resources
  B. To maintain the quality of life
II. **Kinds of conservation**
  A. Soil conservation
  B. Water conservation
  C. Forest conservation
  D. Conservation of grazing lands
  E. Wildlife conservation
  F. Mineral conservation
  G. Energy conservation
  H. Urban conservation
III. **Early history of conservation**
  A. Prehistoric times
  B. The rise of civilization
  C. The Industrial Revolution
IV. **Conservation in the United States**
  A. Early conservation problems
  B. The rise of the conservation movement
  C. Recent developments
V. **Conservation around the world**
  A. Canada
  B. Latin America
  C. Europe
  D. Asia
  E. Australia
  F. Africa
  G. International problems
VI. **Careers in conservation**

Questions

What per cent of the world's energy does the United States consume? What per cent does it produce?
Why is conservation important?
Why did the settlers of North America have little concern for conservation?
What is *wastershed management?*
How can individuals conserve energy in their homes?
What are *environmental impact statements?*
How can farmers reduce soil erosion?
What is the goal of urban conservation?
What is the major threat to wildlife today?

Additional resources

Level I
Cutchins, Judy, and Johnston, Ginny. *The Crocodile and the*

Crane: Surviving in a Crowded World. Morrow, 1986. Discusses various endangered species.
Fogel, Barbara R. *Energy: Choices for the Future.* Watts, 1985.
McClung, Robert M. *Whitetail.* Morrow, 1987. Environmental problems of deer.
Whipple, Jane B. *Forest Resources.* Watts, 1985. History of American forest use and protection.

Level II
Berger, John J. *Restoring the Earth: How Americans Are Working to Renew Our Damaged Environment.* Knopf, 1985.
Huxley, Anthony J. *Green Inheritance: The World Wildlife Fund Book of Plants.* Doubleday, 1985.
Norton, Bryan G. *Why Preserve Natural Variety?* Princeton, 1988.

Conservation of energy. See Energy (The conservation of energy).
Conservation of mass, Law of. See Mass.
Conservation of matter, Law of. See Matter (Conservation of matter).
Conservation of momentum. See Momentum.
Conservation of parity. See Parity (in physics).
Conservatism is an attitude or philosophy that places great emphasis on tradition. Conservatives want to *conserve* (save) traditional institutions, values, and ideas, and they rely on them as a guide to wisdom and goodness. Therefore, they seek progress in line with proven values of the past. But the word *conservatism* is confusing because its meaning varies with time, place, and circumstance.

Political conservatism. Political conservatives take a limited view of what politics can achieve. They believe that the aim of politics, or government, is to help promote a good life for people in society. However, most conservatives doubt that the good life can be brought about mainly by political means. They believe that all political problems are basically moral problems, and that legislation cannot significantly change human attitudes. Conservatives believe that the human potential for evil is as great as the potential for good. They doubt that evil will disappear with social reform or education.

Conservatives emphasize the performance of duties as the price of rights. They also believe in the desirability of maintaining social classes. Conservatives believe that all people have equal protection under the law, but they deny that all are born with equal advantages and influence in society. Conservatives maintain that only a few are natural leaders, and that the leadership provided by these few is essential to social order. For these reasons, conservatives consider political and economic leveling foolish and bound to fail.

Conservatives see a connection between freedom and private ownership of factories and other means of economic production. They maintain that abolishing such private ownership would destroy individual liberty. Therefore, many conservatives believe that socialism and communism are the greatest threats to modern society.

History. The name *Conservative* was first used around 1830. It was applied to the descendants of the old British Tory Party, and the words *Tory* and *Conservative* are used interchangeably in Britain today. However, conservative ideas were expressed as early as the 1700's in the writings and speeches of the British statesman Edmund Burke. Early U.S. conservatives included John Adams and Alexander Hamilton. Conservatism arose partly as a reaction to the excesses of the French Revolution and to the belief that human nature could become perfect through social change and political revolution. Conservatives argued that social change must be brought about within the framework of traditional ideas and institutions.

A true conservative should also be distinguished from a *reactionary*. Reactionaries want to revolutionize existing society according to a model in past history. True conservatives are never revolutionary. They want to preserve the best in the past and continue it into the future.

The word *conservative* as used in the United States today is often confusing. Many Americans who call themselves conservatives advocate a return to the principles and theories of liberalism of the 1800's. They oppose almost all government regulation of the economy, and are economic liberals in the tradition of Adam Smith. Traditionally, however, conservatives have opposed both economic liberalism and socialism. They have tried to steer a middle course between the extremes of individualism and collective ownership, and have generally favored a strong central government.

Today, many U.S. conservatives believe that economic and social problems are solved best when government interference in the economy is kept to a minimum. They also believe that the need to protect society justifies some restriction of the rights of people accused of crime. Some conservatives oppose abortion, and some support state-sponsored prayer in public schools. In foreign policy, U.S. conservatives tend to regard military power as the basis of world peace.   Carl L. Davis

See also **Conservative Party; Judaism** (Conservative Judaism); **Liberalism; Right wing.**

Conservative Party is one of the two main political parties in Great Britain. The second is the Labour Party. A smaller third party in Great Britain is the Social and Liberal Democratic Party.

Historically, the Conservative Party took the place of the Tory Party that appeared in England during the late 1600's and flourished until the middle 1800's (see **Tory Party**). Benjamin Disraeli, a founder of the Conservative Party, worked for a new program for the Conservatives. He wanted the working class given the right to vote. Disraeli also sought to pass social legislation in favor of the workers and worked for stronger bonds between Great Britain and its empire.

Disraeli succeeded in "educating" his party. Conservatives passed the Reform Bill of 1867, which increased the number of working-class voters. After World War I (1914-1918), Conservatives helped reorganize the British Empire to achieve equality between Great Britain and the dominions. Winston Churchill, a Conservative, led a coalition government during most of World War II (1939-1945). In July 1945—near the end of the war—the coalition ended, and the Labour Party was elected to power.

The Conservative Party governed again from 1951 to 1964, and from 1970 to 1974. In 1975, the Conservatives elected Margaret Thatcher as leader of the party. Thatcher became the first woman to head a British political party. In 1979, the Conservative Party won control of the British government, and Thatcher became the first woman prime minister in British history. Under her leadership, the Conservatives won the 1983 and 1987 elec-

tions. John Major succeeded Thatcher as prime minister and Conservative Party leader in 1990. The Conservatives retained control of the government by winning national elections in 1992.   Robert E. Dowse

See also **Disraeli, Benjamin; Peel, Sir Robert.**

Consolidated school is the result of joining two or more school districts and combining their school populations. This term is generally used in rural or suburban areas. The need for more adequate school facilities in areas where the population is scattered led to the consolidation of independent school districts in many parts of the United States. Often, as many as six districts with inadequate schools have been combined to make two or three larger districts. Such consolidation ensures a more varied curriculum, and better libraries and teaching staffs.   Donald H. Eichhorn

Consonant is a letter or sound which in speech requires hindering of the breath by the tongue, teeth, or lips. There are two kinds of sounds. The open sounds with free breath are called *vowels*. The closed sounds, called *consonants,* are made with the breath wholly or partly checked. *Stopped consonants* require complete stoppage of the breath. They are *b, d, g, k, p, t.* Other consonants require only partial stoppage of breath. They are *l, m, n, r, w, y.* The *Spirants* are open consonants that require friction in the oral passages. They are *f, s, v, z. H* is an *aspirant,* or *breathed,* consonant. See also **Pronunciation; Vowel.**   Susan M. Gass

Consort. See **Prince consort; Queen.**

Conspiracy, *kuhn SPIHR uh see,* is an agreement between two or more people to do something that is against the law. One person cannot conspire with himself or herself. It is usually not necessary that the planned act actually be committed or that any person be defrauded or injured. The act of conspiring constitutes a crime. Each person involved in the conspiracy is criminally responsible for everything that results, whether it was intended or not. Conspiracy is punishable by fines or imprisonment. If loss of human life results from a conspiracy, murder may be charged.   George T. Felkenes

See also **Coup d'état.**

Constable, *KAHN stuh buhl,* is a police officer in a rural community of the United States. Constables may arrest people suspected of crime. But their main job is to carry out court orders. The word *constable* comes from the title of an official of the East Roman Empire called the *comes stabuli,* or count of the stable. In France, the constable was once a member of the monarch's household, or a commander of the monarch's armies. In England, all police officers are called constables.   Park Dixon Goist

Constable, John (1776-1837), ranks with J. M. W. Turner as the leading English landscape painter of the 1800's. Constable is known mainly for his paintings of the rural areas near his birthplace and in other parts of southern England. Constable sketched outdoors during the warmer months. During the winter, he worked in his studio and developed the sketches into paintings. Constable emphasized such environmental features as the appearance of the sky and clouds, and the effects of light and shadow on the landscape. He believed such features in a painting reflected nature accurately. Constable's fresh style influenced the impressionist painters of the late 1800's.

Constable's best-known paintings include *The White Horse* (1819), *The Hay Wain* (1821), and *Stoke-by-Nayland* (1836). Constable used vivid colors in many earlier paintings. After his wife died in 1828, he painted many dark, moody pictures that reflected his depression.

Constable was born in East Bergholt, near Ipswich. In his youth, he began to draw the countryside near his home. A love of his native environment is apparent in all his work. Constable studied at the Royal Academy of Arts, beginning in 1799. He was elected a full member of the academy in 1829. However, during his lifetime he received only limited recognition.   Douglas K. S. Hyland

See also **Painting** (The 1800's [picture]).

Constance, Lake. See Lake Constance.

Constantine, *KAHN stuhn TEEN* or *kawn stan TEEN* (pop. 448,578), is a trading center in Algeria about 50 miles (80 kilometers) from the Mediterranean Sea. See **Algeria** (map). It lies on a cliff above the Rhumel River. Railroads link Constantine, a grain shipping point, with the nearby ports of Skikda and Annaba. It was named for the Roman emperor Constantine the Great. He rebuilt it in A.D. 313 on the site of Cirta, a city that was destroyed by war. After hundreds of years of Arab, Berber, and Turkish rule, Constantine was captured by France in 1837. France held it until 1962, when Algeria gained independence.   Kenneth J. Perkins

Constantine I, *KAHN stuhn TEEN* or *KAHN stuhn TYN* (1868-1923), of Greece was king from 1913 to 1917 and 1920 to 1922. He succeeded his father, George I, who was assassinated. During World War I (1914-1918), Constantine pursued a policy of Greek neutrality. This activity brought him in conflict with the Greek prime minister, Eleutherios Venizelos, who favored the Allies. In 1916, Venizelos began a revolutionary movement that was supported by the Allies. Constantine was forced to leave Greece, which entered the war on the Allies' side. His second son, Alexander I, became king. Alexander died in 1920, and the people voted to restore Constantine to the throne. In 1921, Greece went to war against the Ottoman Empire. Greece was defeated, and in 1922, the Greek military forced Constantine to give up the throne. His oldest son, George II, became king. Constantine was born in Athens. See also **Greece** (History).

John A. Koumoulides

Constantine II, *KAHN stuhn TEEN* or *KAHN stuhn TYN* (1940-   ), of Greece was king from 1964 to 1973. He succeeded his father, Paul I. Constantine began his reign with much support from the Greek people. But conflict soon arose between him and prime minister George Papandreou over the extent of royal power, including control of the military. The king manipulated Papandreou into resigning in 1965. During the next two years, Greece experienced increasing social and political unrest. In 1967, the military seized power. Later that year, after trying to overthrow the military, Constantine fled Greece with his family. He went first to Rome and then settled in London. In 1973, Greece's military government declared him deposed. The next year, the Greek people voted to end the monarchy and make Greece a republic. Constantine was born in Psychico, near Athens. See also **Greece** (History).   John A. Koumoulides

Constantine the Great, *KAHN stuhn TEEN* or *KAHN stuhn TYN*, was the first emperor of Rome to become a Christian. He is also known as Constantine I. He was born about A.D. 275 and died in 337. During his reign, Christians regained freedom of worship, and the Christian church became legal. The Eastern Orthodox Churches regard Constantine as a saint. He rebuilt Byzantium (now Istanbul, Turkey), renamed it Constantinople, and made it his capital. He shifted the Roman Empire's strength from Rome to the eastern provinces and thus laid the foundations of the Byzantine Empire.

Constantine made many gifts to the Christian church. He built the first great Christian cathedral, the Lateran Basilica in Rome. He built other famous churches in and near Rome; and in Antioch, Syria (now Antioch, Turkey); Constantinople; and Jerusalem.

Constantine's official name was Flavius Valerius Aurelius Constantinus. He was born in Naissa (now Niš, Yugoslavia). His father, Constantius, became emperor of the western provinces in 305. Constantius died in 306, and his army proclaimed Constantine as successor. The system of shared rule between two senior and two junior emperors, started by Emperor Diocletian in 293, broke down completely. Seven claimants struggled for power. In 312, Constantine attacked Maxentius, his major rival in the west. Constantine later told how a vision before the battle had promised him victory if he fought under the sign of the cross. In another story, he ordered the first two letters of Christ's name in Greek to be marked on his soldiers' shields. With these marks, Constantine's forces defeated Maxentius at the Milvian Bridge on the Tiber River. As a result of his victory, Constantine became a strong supporter of Christianity. But the Arch of Constantine, a pagan monument constructed in Rome about 315, also honors his victory.

In 313, Constantine arranged a partnership with Emperor Licinius, ruler of the eastern provinces. They met in Milan and gave freedom of worship and equal rights to all religious groups. Constantine recognized the Christian church as a legal body with rights to hold property, and returned property that had been seized to Christians. For more than 10 years, Constantine and Licinius divided the empire. In 324, their rivalry resulted in warfare and a victory by Constantine, who then became sole ruler. Constantine made Constantinople his capital and the center of Roman government.

In 325, Constantine presided over the first great *ecumenical* (general) council of the Christian church. The council met in Nicaea, in what is now northwest Turkey, to deal with disputes among Christians, especially with the Arian heresy which considered Christ to have been of a different substance from God. More than 300 bishops from all parts of the empire attended. The council condemned Arianism and drew up a statement of essential beliefs, called the *Nicene Creed* (see **Nicene Councils**). Constantine was baptized a Christian on his deathbed. The empire was passed to his sons, Constantius, Constans, and Constantine II.   Erich S. Gruen

See also **Byzantine Empire** (Beginnings).

Constantinople. See Istanbul.

Constellation, *KAHN stuh LAY shuhn,* is a group of stars visible within a particular region of the night sky. The word *constellation* also refers to the region in which a specific group of stars appears. Astronomers have divided the sky into 88 areas, or constellations.

The ancient Greeks, Romans, and people of various other early civilizations observed groups of stars in the

| Big and Little | Cassiopeia | Orion |
| Dippers | Hercules | |

Additional resources

Berger, Melvin. *Star Gazing, Comet Tracking, and Sky Mapping*. Putnam, 1985.
Motz, Lloyd, and Nathanson, Carol. *The Constellations*. Double-day, 1988. For older readers.

WORLD BOOK illustration by Rob Wood

Constellations are groups of stars in a specific area of the sky. Each constellation has a Latin name. This map shows 7 of the 88 constellations, all in the Northern Hemisphere.

northern two-thirds of the sky. They named these groups of stars after animals and mythological characters. For example, the constellation Leo was named for a lion, Pisces for two fish, and Taurus for a bull. The constellations Andromeda, Cassiopeia, Orion, and Perseus are named for heroines and heroes in Greek mythology.

Between the early 1400's and the mid-1700's, European navigators explored the Southern Hemisphere and observed many constellations in the southernmost third of the sky. Mapmakers and explorers named these star groups for scientific instruments and other things as well as for animals. For example, the constellation Telescopium was named for the telescope. Musca was named for the fly, and Tucana for the *toucan*, a large-billed bird of Central and South America.

Some well-known groups of stars form only part of a constellation. Such smaller groups are called *asterisms*. The Big and Little Dippers are examples of asterisms. The Big Dipper lies in the constellation Ursa Major (Great Bear), and the Little Dipper is part of the constellation Ursa Minor (Little Bear).

Some constellations can be seen only during certain seasons due to the earth's annual revolution around the sun. The part of the sky visible at night at a particular place gradually changes as the earth moves around the sun. Also, observers at different latitudes see different parts of the sky. An observer at the equator can view all the constellations during the course of a year, but an observer at the North or the South Pole can see only a single hemisphere of constellations.   Raymond E. White

Related articles in *World Book* include:

Andromeda	Astronomy (Why the stars
Astrology	seem to move; The sky
	at different latitudes; maps)

Constellation, *KAHN stuh LAY shuhn,* a 36-gun frigate built in 1797, was the first United States Navy ship to capture a foreign warship. It captured the French frigate *L'Insurgente* on Feb. 9, 1799, during the undeclared war between France and the United States (1798-1800). Thomas Truxtun, who had supervised the construction of the *Constellation,* commanded the ship. His naval vic-

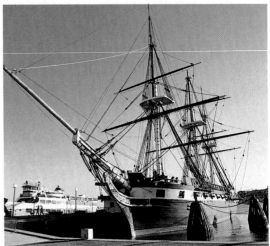

Kevin L. Martin

The *Constellation,* one of the first warships of the U.S. Navy and a national historic landmark, is docked at Baltimore.

tories made him a national hero. In the early 1960's, the *Constellation* was restored in Baltimore, Md., where it was originally launched. It was designated a national historic landmark in 1964.   Merrill Jensen

See also **Adams, John** (picture: Naval battles); **Navy, United States** (Undeclared war with France).

Constipation, *KAHN stuh PAY shuhn,* is a condition in which the bowel does not rid itself of waste materials in a normal manner. Constipated people do not have regular bowel movements and may have pain or tenderness over the colon. They may suffer from headaches and backaches.

Constipation can be caused by weakness of the bowel muscles or by strong, irregular contractions of these muscles. It may also occur when a person uses laxatives too frequently or does not eat enough of certain kinds of foods, especially those that contain fiber. In addition, constipation may accompany an illness that affects tissues or nerves of the bowel, such as the growth of a tumor that partially blocks the intestines.

When constipation results from a faulty diet, the patient should eat more green vegetables, fruits, whole grain bread and cereals, and other foods with fiber. The patient also should drink ample quantities of water. Constipation may be a symptom of a serious disease. If it persists, or is accompanied by rectal bleeding, it should be investigated by a physician.   André Dubois

See also **Laxative.**

Constitution is a statement outlining the agreed basic principles of formal organizations ranging from national governments to private clubs. It establishes the structure and purposes of the organization and the rights of its citizens or members. It also defines the powers of officers, how they are selected, and how long they can stay in office. Constitutions may also be called *articles of union* or *charters* (see **Charter**).

In Western political philosophy, the principles of constitutional government often have been based on a belief in a *higher law*—a body of universal principles of right and justice that is superior to detailed, everyday law. In modern democracies, a constitution's function is to put everyone—including the rulers—under law.

Government constitutions may be *written* or *unwritten.* The United States has a written constitution. The British constitution is unwritten. It consists of tradition and custom concerning the powers of the monarch, Parliament, and the courts. Many parts of the British constitution were taken from written documents such as the Magna Carta. However, the constitution itself has never been written out in a single document. The British constitution can be modified by Parliament.

Most modern governments have constitutions based on a single document. In most democracies, the written constitution can be changed only by a special process, such as a special election. Such amending procedures reflect the belief that a constitution should deal with basic principles, and that special deliberation should be required to modify or replace these principles.

Many countries now have nondemocratic or military governments. In these governments, a constitution can be changed by *fiat* (a command or decree) of the ruling group. In such countries, a constitution is more a statement of purpose than a statement defining powers.

In actual operation, constitutions in most democratic countries are unwritten in the sense that the formal document is not the only vital element. Custom and how various governmental bodies interpret the constitution are equally important and sometimes dominant. Under power called *judicial review,* U.S. courts may declare acts of government *unconstitutional* if the acts are considered to conflict with the basic law of the constitution. Most countries have important *nonlegal* rules which do not come from the written constitution or court interpretation. If these nonlegal rules are an essential part of the system of government, they are part of the "constitution" in the broad sense of the term. For example, most aspects of the political party system and the rules for nominating the President in the United States are not specified in the written constitution or subject to court action.   Robert G. Dixon, Jr.

See also **British North America Act; United Kingdom** (Government); **Constitution of the United States; Government; Bill of Rights.**

Constitution is a famous frigate of the United States Navy. Its popular name is *Old Ironsides.* The frigate was built at a Boston shipyard between 1794 and 1797. It was 204 feet (62 meters) long. The hull was made of oak from Massachusetts, Maine, and Georgia, and the masts of white pine. It could carry provisions for a crew of 475.

Calvin D. Campbell, Pictorial Parade

The *Constitution,* better known as *Old Ironsides,* one of the most famous vessels in the United States Navy, is docked at the Charlestown Navy Yard in Boston.

The *Constitution* was launched on Oct. 21, 1797. It was unharmed in battles with the Barbary powers in 1803 and 1804. In the War of 1812, it won a battle near Cape Race against the *Guerrière,* an English warship. During this battle, the ship earned its nickname. A sailor is said to have seen shot from the British guns bouncing off the *Constitution's* sturdy sides, and exclaimed that the ship had sides of iron. Isaac Hull, an American naval officer, commanded the frigate. Following a number of other battles, the *Constitution* was condemned in 1830 as unseaworthy and was ordered destroyed.

The poem "Old Ironsides," by Oliver Wendell Holmes, in which he wrote:

Oh, better that her shattered hulk
Should sink beneath the wave,

aroused public sentiment, and the vessel was rebuilt and restored to service in 1833. In 1855, it was put out of commission at Portsmouth Navy Yard and used as a training ship, but was again rebuilt in 1877. In 1897, a hundred years after its launching, the *Constitution* was turned into a barrack ship in Boston.

Between 1927 and 1931, American children raised money to help repair and restore the vessel so it could be preserved as a memorial. In 1930 Congress appropriated $300,000 to complete the work. On July 31, 1931, *Old Ironsides* was commissioned into active service. After sailing 22,000 miles (35,400 kilometers), it returned to the Boston Naval Shipyard on May 7, 1934. The *Constitution,* still in commission, is docked at the Charlestown Navy Yard in Boston. It is the oldest warship afloat in any of the world's navies.   James C. Bradford

Constitution Act of 1982. See **Canada, Government of** (The Constitution).

Constitution of the United States

Constitution of the United States sets forth the nation's fundamental laws. It establishes the form of the national government and defines the rights and liberties of the American people. It also lists the aims of the government and the methods of achieving them.

The Constitution was written to organize a strong na-

Bruce Allen Murphy, the contributor of this article, is Professor of History and Politics, and Fellow, Institute for the Arts and Humanistic Studies, at Pennsylvania State University.

tional government for the American states. Previously, the nation's leaders had established a national government under the Articles of Confederation (see **Articles of Confederation**). But the Articles granted independence to each state. They lacked the authority to make the states work together to solve national problems.

After the states won independence in the Revolutionary War (1775-1783), they faced the problems of peacetime government. The states had to enforce law and order, collect taxes, pay a large public debt, and regulate trade among themselves. They also had to deal with Indian tribes and negotiate with other governments.

The signing of the Constitution took place on Sept. 17, 1787, at the Pennsylvania State House (now called Independence Hall) in Philadelphia. American artist Howard Chandler Christy painted this picture in 1940. The painting hangs in the United States Capitol in Washington, D.C.

Scene at the Signing of the Constitution of the United States, an oil painting on canvas; U.S. Capitol Historical Society (National Geographic Society)

Signers of the Constitution included
William Jackson, who was the secretary
of the convention but not a delegate.
John Dickinson of Delaware was absent
but had another delegate sign for him.

1. George Washington
2. Benjamin Franklin
3. James Madison, Jr.
4. Alexander Hamilton
5. Gouverneur Morris
6. Robert Morris
7. James Wilson
8. Charles C. Pinckney
9. Charles Pinckney
10. John Rutledge
11. Pierce Butler
12. Roger Sherman
13. William S. Johnson
14. James McHenry
15. George Read
16. Richard Bassett

17. Richard D. Spaight
18. William Blount
19. Hugh Williamson
20. Daniel of St. Thomas Jenifer
21. Rufus King
22. Nathaniel Gorham
23. Jonathan Dayton
24. Daniel Carroll
25. William Few
26. Abraham Baldwin

27. John Langdon
28. Nicholas Gilman
29. William Livingston
30. William Paterson
31. Thomas Mifflin
32. George Clymer
33. Thomas FitzSimons

34. Jared Ingersoll
35. Gunning Bedford, Jr.
36. Jacob Broom
37. John Dickinson
38. John Blair
39. David Brearley
40. William Jackson

Ratification of the Constitution

Article VII of the U.S. Constitution required the approval of 9 states to put the Constitution into effect. This table gives the dates on which each of the 13 states ratified the Constitution.

Delaware	Dec. 7, 1787
Pennsylvania	Dec. 12, 1787
New Jersey	Dec. 18, 1787
Georgia	Jan. 2, 1788
Connecticut	Jan. 9, 1788
Massachusetts	Feb. 6, 1788
Maryland	April 28, 1788
South Carolina	May 23, 1788
New Hampshire	June 21, 1788
Virginia	June 25, 1788
New York	July 26, 1788
North Carolina	Nov. 21, 1789
Rhode Island	May 29, 1790

Leading statesmen, such as George Washington and Alexander Hamilton, began to discuss the creation of a strong national government under a new constitution.

Hamilton helped bring about a national convention that met in Philadelphia in 1787 to revise the Articles of Confederation. But a majority of the delegates at the convention decided instead to write a new plan of government—the Constitution of the United States. The Constitution established not merely a league of states but a government that exercised its authority directly over all citizens. The Constitution also defined clearly the powers of the national government. In addition, it established protection for the rights of the states and of every individual.

The supreme law of the land

The Constitution consists of a preamble, 7 articles, and 27 amendments. It sets up a *federal system* by dividing powers between the national and state governments. It also establishes a balanced national government by dividing authority among three independent

branches—the executive, the legislative, and the judicial. The executive branch enforces the law, the legislative branch makes the law, and the judicial branch interprets the law. The executive branch of the national government is usually represented by the President, the legislative branch by Congress, and the judicial branch by the Supreme Court. This division of the government into three branches is known as the *separation of powers.* Each branch can use its powers to *check and balance* (exercise control over) the other two. See **United States, Government of the** (Separation of powers).

Federal powers listed in the Constitution include the right to collect taxes, declare war, and regulate trade. In addition to these *delegated, or expressed, powers* (those listed in the Constitution), the national government has *implied powers* (those reasonably suggested by the Constitution). The implied powers enable the government to respond to the changing needs of the nation. For example, Congress had no delegated power to print paper money. But such a power is implied in the delegated powers of borrowing and coining money.

There are some powers that the Constitution does not give to the national government or forbid to the states. These *reserved powers* belong to the people or to the states. State powers include the right to legislate on divorce, marriage, and public schools. Powers reserved for the people include the right to own property and to be tried by a jury. In some cases, the national and state governments have *concurrent powers*—that is, both levels of government may act. The national government has supreme authority in case of a conflict.

The Supreme Court has the final authority to explain the Constitution. It can set aside any law—federal, state, or local—that conflicts with any part of the Constitution.

The need for the Constitution

The government established by the Articles of Confederation was not strong enough to govern the new nation. For example, it lacked an executive branch and a system of national courts. It could not regulate trade between the states or tax the states or their citizens. In

From *The National Archives of the United States* by Herman J. Viola, Publisher Harry N. Abrams, Inc., photographed by Jonathan Wallen

The United States Constitution is on display at the National Archives Building in Washington, D.C. A bronze and glass storage case filled with helium helps preserve the document. The case is lowered into a vault in the floor each night for safekeeping. More than 1 million people view the Constitution each year.

addition, it could not maintain its own army. The government was little more than an assembly of the representatives of 13 independent states. Before almost any measure could be adopted, it had to be approved by at least 9 of the states.

In 1783, after the Revolutionary War, the nation entered a period of unstable commercial and political conditions. Alexander Hamilton and his supporters would have had little success in their campaign for a new constitution if conditions had been better. Some historians have painted the troubles of the new republic in much too gloomy colors. But little doubt remains that the situation became steadily worse after 1783. Each state acted almost like an independent country. Each ran its own affairs exactly as it saw fit, with little concern for the needs of the republic. The states circulated a dozen different currencies, most of which had little value. Neighboring states taxed each other's goods. Britain refused to reopen the channels of trade that the colonies had depended on for their economic well-being. The state legislatures refused to pay the debts they had assumed during the Revolutionary War. Many states passed laws that enabled debtors to escape paying their obligations.

Worst of all, some people began to think once again of taking up arms in order to solve their problems. In western Massachusetts in 1786, hundreds of farmers under Captain Daniel Shays rebelled against the state

government in Boston. State troops finally put down Shays' Rebellion (see **Shays' Rebellion**). George Washington and other leaders wondered whether the colonies had rebelled against Britain in vain. They felt it was time to end these troubles and bring peace and order by forming a new national government. This new government would have to be strong enough to gain obedience at home and respect abroad.

Representatives from five states met in Annapolis, Md., in 1786. They proposed that the states appoint commissioners to meet in Philadelphia and consider revising the Articles of Confederation (see **Annapolis Convention**). Congress agreed to the proposal and suggested that each state select delegates to a constitutional convention.

The Constitutional Convention

The convention was supposed to open on May 14, 1787. But few of the 55 delegates had arrived in Philadelphia by that date. Finally, on May 25, the convention formally opened in Independence Hall. Twelve states had responded to the call for the convention. Rhode Island refused to send delegates because it did not want the national government to interfere with its affairs.

Of the 55 delegates, 39 signed the United States Constitution on Sept. 17, 1787. One of the signers was John Dickinson of Delaware, who left the convention but

Photri

The Assembly Room of the Pennsylvania State House, where regular sessions of the Constitutional Convention of 1787 were held, is shown as it looks today. The Declaration of Independence was adopted in this room in 1776, and the Articles of Confederation were ratified there in 1781.

asked another delegate, George Read, to sign for him. William Jackson of Philadelphia, a former major in the Revolutionary War who was chosen to serve as the convention secretary, witnessed the signatures. The delegates included some of the most experienced and patriotic men in the new republic. George Washington served as president of the convention. Benjamin Franklin, at the age of 81, attended as a representative of Pennsylvania. The brilliant Alexander Hamilton represented New York. James Madison of Virginia received the title of "Father of the Constitution" with his speeches, negotiations, and attempts at compromise. Madison told the delegates they were considering a plan that "would decide forever the fate of republican government." He kept a record of the delegates' debates and decisions.

Other men who had much to do with writing the new Constitution included John Dickinson, Gouverneur Morris, Edmund Randolph, Roger Sherman, James Wilson, and George Wythe. Morris was given the task of putting all the convention's resolutions and decisions into polished form. Morris actually "wrote" the Constitution. The original copy of the document is preserved in the National Archives Building in Washington, D.C.

Several important figures of the time did not attend the convention. John Adams and Thomas Jefferson were absent on other government duties. Samuel Adams and John Jay failed to be appointed delegates from their states. Patrick Henry refused to serve after his appointment because he opposed granting any more power to the national government. Three leading members of the convention—Elbridge Gerry, George Mason, and Edmund Randolph—refused to sign the Constitution because they disagreed with parts of it.

The background of the Constitution. The delegates to the Constitutional Convention relied greatly on past experience as they worked to create a new government. They recalled many important events in the development of constitutional government. These included the granting of Magna Carta, an English constitutional document, in 1215 and the meeting of the Jamestown

representative assembly in 1619 (see **Magna Carta**). Some of the American Colonies also served as examples of constitutional forms of government. While colonial governments had weaknesses, they had progressed beyond other governments of their time in achieving liberty under law.

All American states established constitutional governments after they declared their independence from Britain in 1776. In 1777, John Jay of New York had helped write a constitution for his state. John Adams of Massachusetts had helped write the Massachusetts Constitution of 1780. Delegates to the convention in Philadelphia used many ideas and words from the constitutions of these and other states.

The delegates also drew on their own experiences. Franklin had proposed a plan at the Albany Congress of 1754 to unify the colonies under a central government (see **Albany Congress**). Washington remembered his own problems during the war when, as commander in chief, he had to work with the frequently divided Continental Congress. Almost every delegate to the convention had served as a soldier or administrator of the government. They often disagreed on details but were united in wanting the new government to be strong enough to rule the nation. They also wanted it to respect the liberties of the states and of the people.

The compromises. The task of creating a new government was not easily accomplished. Disputes among the delegates nearly ended the convention on several occasions. For example, delegates from the large states disagreed with those from the small states about representation in the national legislature. The larger states favored the *Virginia Plan,* under which population would determine the number of representatives a state could send to the legislature. The small states supported the *New Jersey Plan,* which proposed that all the states would have an equal number of representatives. The Connecticut delegates suggested a compromise that settled the problem. Their plan provided for equal representation in the Senate, along with representation in

Photri

The chair used by George Washington during the Constitutional Convention had a carving of a half sun, *above.* On the day the Constitution was signed, Benjamin Franklin expressed a feeling of confidence in the nation's future by declaring that the carving was a "rising and not a setting sun."

Independence National Historical Park Collection

The silver inkstand shown above is one of the most historic items in the nation. It was used by the signers of the Constitution of the United States in 1787 and by the signers of the Declaration of Independence in 1776.

proportion to population in the House of Representatives. This proposal became known as the *Connecticut Compromise* or the *Great Compromise.*

Compromises also settled conflicts over the issue of slavery. The delegates from the Northern states wanted Congress to have the power to forbid the foreign slave trade. Most Southern delegates did not wish Congress to have this power. A compromise decided that Congress would not be allowed to regulate the foreign slave trade until 1808. Another compromise involved the question of how to count slaves in determining how many members of Congress a state could have. Slaves were not considered citizens, and so the convention agreed that only three-fifths of a state's slaves could be counted.

The delegates agreed that each state should hold a special convention to discuss and vote on the Constitution. They also decided that as soon as nine states had *ratified* (approved) the Constitution, the Constitution would take effect and they could begin to organize the new government.

Ratifying the Constitution

Less than three months after the Constitution was signed, Delaware became the first state to ratify it, on Dec. 7, 1787. New Hampshire was the ninth state, putting the Constitution into effect on June 21, 1788. But the Founding Fathers could not be sure that the Constitution would be generally accepted until the important states of New York and Virginia had ratified it. Powerful organized opposition to the Constitution had developed in these two states and in others. Such people as Elbridge Gerry, Patrick Henry, Richard Henry Lee, and George Mason spoke out against ratification.

Critics objected that a bill of rights had not been included, that the President had too much independence, and that the Senate was too aristocratic. They also thought Congress had too many powers and the national government had too much authority. Friends of the Constitution rallied support for ratification. They became known as *Federalists.* Their opponents were called *Anti-Federalists.* The two groups promoted their causes in newspapers, in pamphlets, and in debates in the ratifying conventions (see **Anti-Federalists; Federalist, The; Federalist Party**). The groups developed into the first American political parties.

Virginia ratified the Constitution on June 25, 1788, and New York did so on July 26. Early in January 1789, all the ratifying states except New York selected presidential electors in their legislatures or by a direct vote of the people. On February 4, the electors named George Washington as the first President of the United States. The first Congress under the Constitution met in New York City on March 4. Washington was inaugurated on April 30. North Carolina and Rhode Island refused to approve the Constitution and take part in the new government until Congress agreed to add a bill of rights.

The Bill of Rights

The Federalists might never have obtained ratification in several important states if they had not promised to support amendments to the Constitution. These amendments were written to protect individual liberties against possible unjust rule by the national government.

Interesting facts about the Constitution

Which two signers of the Constitution later became U.S. Presidents? George Washington and James Madison.

Which signers of the Declaration of Independence also signed the Constitution? George Clymer, Benjamin Franklin, Robert Morris, George Read, Roger Sherman, and James Wilson.

Who were the youngest and oldest signers of the Constitution? Youngest: Jonathan Dayton, 26 years old. Oldest: Benjamin Franklin, 81 years old.

Who was the first delegate to sign the Constitution? George Washington.

Who was called the "Father of the Constitution"? James Madison earned this title because he was a leading member of the convention and wrote a record of the delegates' debates.

Who actually "wrote" the Constitution? Gouverneur Morris.

When was the Constitution signed? Sept. 17, 1787.

What state did not send representatives to the Constitutional Convention? Rhode Island refused to send representatives because it did not want the federal government to interfere with Rhode Island's affairs.

In what order did the delegates sign the Constitution? In geographical order from north to south: New Hampshire, Massachusetts, Connecticut, New York, New Jersey, Pennsylvania, Delaware, Maryland, Virginia, North Carolina, South Carolina, and Georgia.

Which three leading delegates refused to sign the Constitution? Elbridge Gerry, George Mason, and Edmund Randolph refused because they objected to the powers that the Constitution gave the federal government.

How many delegates signed the Constitution? 39.

Where is the original Constitution displayed? In the National Archives Building in Washington, D.C.

Most state constitutions that were adopted during the Revolution had included a clear declaration of the rights of all people. Most Americans believed that no constitution could be considered complete without such a declaration. George Mason of Virginia was responsible for the first and most famous American bill of rights, the Virginia Declaration of Rights of 1776. He and Patrick Henry might have prevented ratification of the Constitution in Virginia if the Federalists had not agreed to their demands for amendments.

James Madison led the new Congress in proposing amendments. He suggested 15 amendments, and the Congress accepted 12 of them to be submitted for approval by the states under the amending process outlined in the Fifth Article of the Constitution. By Dec. 15, 1791, enough states had approved 10 of the 12 amendments to make them a permanent addition to the Constitution. These amendments are known as the *Bill of Rights.*

One of the two unapproved amendments dealt with the size of the House of Representatives. It would have changed representation from no more than one representative for every 30,000 people to one for every 50,000 people. The other unapproved amendment provided that whenever Congress changed the salaries of its members, the change could not take effect until after the next election of representatives had been held. This amendment was ratified in 1992. See **Bill of rights**.

The development of the Constitution

Through the years, the Constitution has developed to meet changing needs. James Madison declared, "In framing a system which we wish to last for ages, we should not lose sight of the changes which ages will produce." The Constitution was designed to serve the interests of the people—rich and poor, Northerners and Southerners, farmers, workers, and business people.

The Anti-Federalists accepted defeat when the Constitution was adopted and set about to win power under its rules. Their action set a style for American politics that has never changed. Americans sometimes feel dissatisfied with the policies of those who govern. But few Americans have condemned the constitutional system or demanded a second constitutional convention.

Delegates to the Constitutional Convention believed strongly in the rule of the majority, but they wanted to protect minorities against any unjustness by the major-

ity. They achieved this goal by separating and balancing the powers of government. Other basic constitutional aims included respect for the rights of individuals and states, rule by the people, separation of church and state, and supremacy of the national government.

Amendments are additions to the Constitution. Today, there are 27 amendments.

An amendment may be proposed by two-thirds of each house of Congress, or by a national convention called by Congress in response to requests by two-thirds of the state legislatures. It becomes part of the Constitution after being ratified either by the legislatures of three-fourths of the states or by conventions in three-fourths of the states. Congress decides which form of ratification should be used and how much time

Index to the Constitution

This index lists some important subjects discussed in the Constitution and the specific article or amendment that deals with each one. The index also gives the page in this article on which the information appears.

the states have to consider each amendment. In many cases, Congress has chosen a seven-year period for such consideration. The process of amending the Constitution was designed to be difficult, so that the nation would have to think carefully about any proposed changes before adopting them.

Laws have added to the meaning of the Constitution. The delegates to the Constitutional Convention knew they could not write laws for every possible situation. Therefore, they gave Congress the right to pass all laws that were "necessary and proper" to carry out powers granted by the Constitution to the President, Congress, and federal courts. Congress has passed laws to establish such administrative organizations as the Federal Aviation Administration and the Postal Service. Congress has also passed laws to regulate interstate commerce, thereby controlling many aspects of the economy.

Court decisions. Federal and state judges apply the Constitution in many court cases. The Supreme Court has the final authority in interpreting the meaning of the Constitution in any specific case. The court has the power of *judicial review*—that is, it can declare a law unconstitutional. The court has this power largely because of the decision of Chief Justice John Marshall in the case of *Marbury v. Madison* in 1803 (see **Marbury v. Madison**). Since that time, the court has ruled that all or parts of more than 125 federal laws and over 1,000 state laws were unconstitutional. The court can also overrule itself, and it has done so about 200 times.

Presidential actions. Strong Presidents have used their authority to expand the simple words of the Second Article of the Constitution into a source of great presidential power. Such Presidents include George Washington, Thomas Jefferson, Andrew Jackson, Abraham Lincoln, Theodore Roosevelt, Woodrow Wilson, and Franklin D. Roosevelt. Washington, for example, made the President the leading figure in foreign affairs. Lincoln used the powers set forth in the article to free slaves during the Civil War (1861-1865).

Customs have made the Constitution flexible and have added to the powers of the national government. For example, the President's Cabinet developed from the words in the Second Article that permit the chief executive to "require the opinion, in writing, of the principal officer in each of the executive departments, upon any subject relating to the duties of their respective offices. . . ."

State and party actions. The Constitution provides for a general method of electing a President. It does not mention political parties. But state laws and political-party practices have changed the constitutional system of voting into the exciting campaigns and elections that take place today.

The Constitution has continued to develop in response to the demands of an ever-growing society through all these methods. Yet the spirit and wording of the Constitution have remained constant. People of each generation have applied its provisions to their own problems in ways that seem reasonable to them.

The British statesman William E. Gladstone described the Constitution as "the most wonderful work ever struck off at a given time by the brain and purpose of man." In a world of change and struggle, the American people have no more precious possession than this great document. The complete text of the Constitution of the United States, with explanatory notes, begins on the next page.   Bruce Allen Murphy

Related articles in *World Book* include:

Biographies

There is a biography in *World Book* on each delegate who signed the Constitution of the United States as listed after the Seventh Article. See also the biographies on the following notable Americans:

Adams, John	Jay, John	Mason, George
Adams, Samuel	Jefferson, Thomas	Randolph,
Gerry, Elbridge	Marshall, John	Edmund
Henry, Patrick		

History

Albany Congress	Federalist Party
Annapolis Convention	Founding Fathers
Anti-Federalists	Shays' Rebellion
Articles of Confederation	United States, History of the
Continental Congress	(Forming a new nation)
Federalist, The	

Other related articles

Bill of rights	President of the United States
Congress of the United States	States' rights
Court	Supreme Court of the United
Fifteenth Amendment	States
Fifth Amendment	United States, Government of
Fourteenth Amendment	the
Government	Vice President of the United
Law	States
Political party	Voting

Outline

I. **The supreme law of the land**
II. **The need for the Constitution**
III. **The Constitutional Convention**
  A. The background of the Constitution
  B. The compromises
IV. **Ratifying the Constitution**
V. **The Bill of Rights**
VI. **The development of the Constitution**

Questions

Why were the Articles of Confederation of 1781 inadequate for governing the United States?

What compromises were made in forming the Constitution?

What were some major objections against the newly formed Constitution?

How did controversy over the Constitution result in creating the first American political parties?

In what two states was there especially powerful organized opposition to ratifying the Constitution?

What government body has the final authority in interpreting the Constitution?

What were some of the reasons for including a bill of rights in the Constitution?

What are *delegated powers*? *Implied powers*? *Reserved powers*? *Concurrent powers*?

Reading and Study Guide

See *Constitution of the United States* in the Research Guide/Index, Volume 22, for a *Reading and Study Guide*.

Additional resources

Barbash, Fred. *The Founding: A Dramatic Account of the Writing of the Constitution.* Simon & Schuster, 1987.

Bernstein, Richard B., and Rice, K. S. *Are We to Be a Nation? The Making of the Constitution.* Harvard, 1987.

Faber, Doris and Harold. *We the People: The Story of the United States Constitution Since 1787.* Scribner, 1987.

Fritz, Jean. *Shh! We're Writing the Constitution.* Putnam, 1987. For younger readers.

Ritchie, Donald A. *The U.S. Constitution.* Chelsea Hse., 1989.

(Text of the U.S. Constitution begins on the next page.)

This copy of the Constitution shows the Preamble and part of the first article.

The Constitution of the United States

The text of the Constitution is printed here in boldface type. All words are given their modern spelling and capitalization. Brackets [   ] indicate parts that have been changed or set aside by amendments. The paragraphs printed in lightface type are not part of the Constitution. They explain the meaning of certain passages or describe how certain passages have worked in practice.

Preamble

We the people of the United States, in order to form a more perfect Union, establish justice, insure domestic tranquility, provide for the common defense, promote the general welfare, and secure the blessings of liberty to ourselves and our posterity, do ordain and establish this Constitution for the United States of America.

Article I

The legislative branch

Section 1. All legislative powers herein granted shall be vested in a Congress of the United States, which shall consist of a Senate and House of Representatives.

The first three articles of the Constitution divide the powers of the United States government among three separate branches: (1) the legislative branch, represented by Congress; (2) the executive branch, represented by the President; and (3) the judicial branch, represented by the Supreme Court. This division, called the *separation of powers,* is designed to prevent any branch of the government from becoming too powerful.

Article I says that only Congress has the power to make laws. Congress cannot give these powers to any other body. Through the years, however, Congress has created various federal agencies to make regulations and put its policies into practice. Such agencies include the Federal Trade Commission, the Federal Power Commission and the Interstate Commerce Commission.

The two-house Congress was one of the most important compromises of the Constitutional Convention. The small states at the convention supported the *New Jersey plan,* under which each state would have had the same number of representatives. The large states at the convention wanted the *Virginia plan,* which provided representation based on population. As a compromise, one house was chosen according to each plan.

The House of Representatives

Section 2. (1) The House of Representatives shall be composed of members chosen every second year by the people of the several states, and the electors in each state shall have the qualifications requisite for electors of the most numerous branch of the state legislature.

Members of the House of Representatives are elected to two-year terms. If a person is eligible to vote for the "most numerous branch" of his or her state legislature, he or she is also eligible to vote for members of Congress. The "most numerous branch" is the house that has the most members. All states except Nebraska have a two-house state legislature. The question of who can vote for state legislators is entirely up to the state, subject to the restrictions of the Constitution and federal law. The 15th, 19th, 24th, and 26th amendments forbid the states to deny or restrict a citizen's right to vote because of race, sex, or failure to pay a tax; or age if the person is at least 18 years old.

(2) No person shall be a representative who shall not have attained to the age of twenty-five years, and been seven years a citizen of the United States, and who shall not, when elected, be an inhabitant of that state in which he shall be chosen.

Each state decides for itself the requirements for legal residence, subject to constitutional limits. Most representatives live not only in the state but also in the district from which they are chosen.

(3) Representatives and direct taxes shall be apportioned among the several states which may be included within this Union, according to their respective numbers, [which shall be determined by adding to the whole number of free persons, including those bound to service for a term of years, and excluding Indians not taxed, three-fifths of all other persons].

The actual enumeration shall be made within three years after the first meeting of the Congress of the United States, and within every subsequent term of ten years, in such manner as they shall by law direct. The number of representatives shall not exceed one for every thirty thousand, but each state shall have at least one representative; [and until such enumeration shall be made, the state of New Hampshire shall be entitled to choose 3, Massachusetts 8, Rhode Island and Providence Plantations 1, Connecticut 5, New York 6, New Jersey 4, Pennsylvania 8, Delaware 1, Maryland 6, Virginia 10, North Carolina 5, South Carolina 5, and Georgia 3].

The effect of this paragraph has been greatly changed, both by amendments and by new conditions. It now provides only three things: (1) the number of representatives given to each state shall be based on its population; (2) Congress must see that the people of the United States are counted every 10 years; and (3) each state gets at least one representative.

The Founding Fathers probably considered the words "and direct taxes" to apply to poll and property taxes. The 16th Amendment gives Congress the right to tax a person according to the size of his or her income, rather than to tax a person according to the population of the state in which the person happens to live.

In the reference to "three-fifths of all other persons," the "other persons" meant black slaves. Since there are no longer any slaves, this part of the paragraph no longer has any meaning.

The average House district has well over half a million people, so the requirement that there shall be no more than one representative for every 30,000 people no longer has any practical force. In 1929, Congress fixed the total number of representatives at 435.

(4) When vacancies happen in the representation from any state, the executive authority thereof shall issue writs of election to fill such vacancies.

If a vacancy occurs in a House seat, the state governor must call a special election to fill it. However, if the next regularly scheduled election is to be held soon, the governor may allow the seat to remain empty rather than call a special election.

(5) The House of Representatives shall choose their Speaker and other officers; and shall have the sole power of impeachment.

The House chooses an officer called the *Speaker* to lead meetings (see **Speaker**). The House alone has the power to bring impeachment charges against an official. The Senate tries impeachment cases. See **Impeachment.**

The Senate

Section 3. **(1) The Senate of the United States shall be composed of two senators from each state, [chosen by the legislature thereof,] for six years; and each senator shall have one vote.**

The Constitution at first provided that each state legislature should pick two senators. The 17th Amendment changed this rule by allowing the voters of each state to choose their own senators.

(2) Immediately after they shall be assembled in consequence of the first election, they shall be divided as equally as may be into three classes. The seats of the senators of the first class shall be vacated at the expiration of the second year, of the second class at the expiration of the fourth year, and of the third class at the expiration of the sixth year, so that one-third may be chosen every second year; [and if vacancies happen by resignation, or otherwise, during the recess of the legislature of any state, the executive thereof may make temporary appointments until the next meeting of the legislature, which shall then fill such vacancies].

Senators are elected to six-year terms. Every two years, one-third of the senators are elected and two-thirds are holdovers. This arrangement makes the Senate a continuing body, unlike the House, whose entire membership is elected every two

years. The 17th Amendment changed the method of filling vacancies. The governor chooses a senator until the people elect one.

(3) No person shall be a senator who shall not have attained to the age of thirty years, and been nine years a citizen of the United States, and who shall not, when elected, be an inhabitant of that state for which he shall be chosen.

In 1806, Henry Clay of Kentucky was appointed to fill an unexpired term in the Senate. He was only 29, a few months younger than the minimum age, but no one challenged the appointment. In 1793, Albert Gallatin was elected to the Senate from Pennsylvania. He was removed from office when the Senate ruled that he had not yet been a citizen for nine years.

(4) The Vice President of the United States shall be president of the Senate, but shall have no vote, unless they be equally divided.

The Vice President serves as president of the Senate, but votes only when a tie vote occurs. The Vice President's power to break ties can be important. In 1789, for example, Vice President John Adams cast the vote that decided the President could remove Cabinet members without Senate approval.

(5) The Senate shall choose their other officers, and also a president *pro tempore,* in the absence of the Vice President, or when he shall exercise the office of President of the United States.

The Senate elects an officer called the *president pro tempore* to lead meetings when the Vice President is absent.

(6) The Senate shall have the sole power to try all impeachments. When sitting for that purpose, they shall be on oath or affirmation. When the President of the United States is tried, the Chief Justice shall preside: and no person shall be convicted without the concurrence of two-thirds of the members present.

The provision that the Chief Justice, rather than the Vice President, shall preside over the Senate when a President is on trial probably grows out of the fact that a conviction would make the Vice President the President. The phrase "on oath or affirmation" means that senators are placed under oath when trying impeachment cases, just as jurors are in a regular court trial.

(7) Judgment in cases of impeachment shall not extend further than to removal from office, and disqualification to hold and enjoy any office of honor, trust or profit under the United States: but the party convicted shall nevertheless be liable and subject to indictment, trial, judgment and punishment, according to law.

If an impeached person is found guilty, he or she can be removed from office and forbidden to hold federal office again. The Senate cannot impose any other punishment, but the person may also be tried in regular courts. The Senate has convicted only five people, all of them judges. These men were removed from office, but none was tried in another court.

Organization of Congress

Section 4. **(1) The times, places and manner of holding elections for senators and representatives, shall be prescribed in each state by the legislature thereof; but the Congress may at any time by law make or alter such regulations, [except as to the places of choosing senators].**

As long as state legislatures chose the senators, it would not do to let Congress fix the place of choosing. This would have amounted to giving Congress the power to tell each state where to locate its capital. The words of the Constitution "except as to the places of choosing senators" were set aside by the 17th Amendment.

(2) The Congress shall assemble at least once in every year, [and such meeting shall be on the first Monday in December,] unless they shall by law appoint a different day.

In Europe, monarchs could keep parliaments from meeting, sometimes for many years, simply by not calling them together. This is the reason for the requirement that the Congress of the United States must meet at least once a year. The 20th Amendment changed the date of the opening day of the session to January 3, unless Congress sets another date by law.

Section 5. (1) Each house shall be the judge of the elections, returns and qualifications of its own members, and a majority of each shall constitute a quorum to do business; but a smaller number may adjourn from day to day, and may be authorized to compel the attendance of absent members, in such manner, and under such penalties as each house may provide.

Each house determines if its members are legally qualified and have been elected fairly. In judging the qualifications of its members, each house may consider only the age, citizenship, and residence requirements set forth in the Constitution. In acting on motions to expel a member, however, either house of Congress may consider other matters bearing on that member's fitness for office. A *quorum* is a group large enough to carry on business. Discussion and debate can go on whether a quorum is present or not, as long as a quorum comes in to vote.

(2) Each house may determine the rules of its proceedings, punish its members for disorderly behavior, and, with the concurrence of two-thirds, expel a member.

Either house can expel one of its members by a two-thirds vote. Each house makes its own rules. For example, the House of Representatives puts strict time limits on debate to speed up business. It is much more difficult to end debate in the Senate. A senator may speak as long as he or she wishes. Senators use this privilege to make long speeches called *filibusters* to delay Senate action. The Senate, however, may vote for *cloture,* a motion to end debate. On most matters, cloture requires a vote of 60 senators, or three-fifths of the total Senate membership. See Cloture.

(3) Each house shall keep a journal of its proceedings, and from time to time publish the same, excepting such parts as may in their judgment require secrecy; and the yeas and nays of the members of either house on any question shall, at the desire of one-fifth of those present, be entered on the journal.

The House *Journal* and the Senate *Journal* are published at the end of each session of Congress. They list all the bills and resolutions considered during the session, as well as every vote. All messages from the President to Congress also are included. The journals are considered the official documents for the proceedings of Congress.

(4) Neither house, during the session of Congress, shall, without the consent of the other, adjourn for more than three days, nor to any other place than that in which the two houses shall be sitting.

Section 6. (1) The senators and representatives shall receive a compensation for their services, to be ascertained by law, and paid out of the treasury of the United States. They shall in all cases, except treason, felony and breach of the peace, be privileged from arrest during their attendance at the session of their respective houses, and in going to and returning from the same; and for any speech or debate in either house, they shall not be questioned in any other place.

The privilege of *immunity* (freedom from arrest) while going to and from congressional business has little importance today. Members of Congress, like anyone else, may be arrested, tried, convicted, and sent to prison.

Congressional immunity from charges of *libel* and *slander* remains important. Libel is an untrue written statement that damages a person's reputation. Slander is a spoken statement that does so. Immunity under the speech and debate clause means that members of Congress may say whatever they wish in connection with congressional business without fear of being sued. This immunity extends to anything said by members during debate, in an official report, or while voting.

(2) No senator or representative shall, during the time for which he was elected, be appointed to any civil office under the authority of the United States, which shall have been created, or the emoluments whereof shall have been increased during such time; and no person holding any office under the United States, shall be a member of either house during his continuance in office.

These provisions keep members of Congress from creating jobs to which they can later be appointed, from raising salaries of jobs they hope to hold in the future, or from holding office in the other branches of government while they are serving in Congress.

In 1909, Senator Philander C. Knox resigned from the Senate to become secretary of state. But the salary of the secretary of state had been increased during Knox's term as senator. In order that Knox might accept the post, Congress withdrew the salary increase for the period of Knox's unfinished term.

Section 7. (1) All bills for raising revenue shall originate in the House of Representatives; but the Senate may propose or concur with amendments as on other bills.

Tax bills must originate in the House. The tradition that tax laws should originate in the lower house of the legislature came from England. There, the lower house—the House of Commons—is more likely to reflect the people's wishes because the people elect its members. They do not elect the upper house, the House of Lords. In the United States, this rule has little importance because the people elect both the Senate and the House. In addition, the Senate can amend a tax bill to such an extent that it rewrites the whole measure.

(2) Every bill which shall have passed the House of Representatives and the Senate, shall, before it become a law, be presented to the President of the United States; if he approve he shall sign it, but if not he shall return it, with his objections to that house in which it shall have originated, who shall enter the objections at large on their journal, and proceed to reconsider it. If after such reconsideration two-thirds of that house shall agree to pass the bill, it shall be sent, together with the objections, to the other house, by which it shall likewise be reconsidered, and if approved by two-thirds of that house, it shall become a law. But in all such cases the votes of both houses shall be determined by yeas and nays, and the names of the persons voting for and against the bill shall be entered on the journal of each house respectively. If any bill shall not be returned by the President within ten days (Sundays excepted) after it shall have been presented to him, the same shall be a law, in like manner as if he had signed it, unless the Congress by their adjournment prevent its return, in which case it shall not be a law.

A bill passed by Congress goes to the President for the President's signature. If the President disapproves the bill, it must be returned to Congress with a statement of the objections within 10 days, not including Sundays. This action is called a *veto*. Congress can pass a law over the President's veto by a two-thirds vote of each house of those members present. The President can also let a bill become law without signing it merely by letting 10 days pass. But a bill sent to the President during the last 10 days of a session of Congress cannot become law unless it is signed. If a bill the President dislikes reaches the President near the end of a session, the bill may simply be held unsigned. When Congress adjourns, the bill is killed. This practice is known as a *pocket veto*. The pocket veto is used by Presidents who find a bill unsatisfactory but do not want to veto it openly. See Veto.

(3) Every order, resolution, or vote to which the concurrence of the Senate and House of Representatives may be necessary (except on a question of adjournment) shall be presented to the President of the United States; and before the same shall take effect, shall be approved by him, or being disapproved by him, shall be repassed by two-thirds of the Senate and House of Representatives, according to the rules and limitations prescribed in the case of a bill.

Powers granted to Congress

Section 8. The Congress shall have power:

(1) To lay and collect taxes, duties, imposts and excises, to pay the debts and provide for the common defense and general welfare of the United States; but all duties, imposts and excises shall be uniform throughout the United States;

Duties are taxes on goods coming into the United States. *Excises* are taxes on sales, use, or production, and sometimes on business procedures or privileges. For example, corporation taxes, cigarette taxes, and amusement taxes are excises. *Imposts* is a general tax term that includes both duties and excises.

(2) To borrow money on the credit of the United States;

(3) To regulate commerce with foreign nations, and among the several states, and with the Indian tribes;

This section, called the *commerce clause,* gives Congress some of its most important powers. The Supreme Court has interpreted *commerce* to mean not only trade but also all kinds of commercial activity. Commerce "among the several states" is usually called *interstate commerce.* The Supreme Court has ruled that interstate commerce includes not only transactions across state boundaries but also any activity that affects commerce in more than one state. The court has interpreted the word *regulate* to mean *encourage, promote, protect, prohibit,* or *restrain.* As a result, Congress can pass laws and provide funds to improve waterways, to enforce air safety measures, and to forbid interstate shipment of certain goods. It can regulate the movement of people, of trains, of stocks and bonds, and even of television signals. Congress has made it a federal crime to flee across state lines from state or local police. It also has forbidden people who operate interstate facilities or who serve interstate passengers to treat customers unfairly because of race. See **Interstate commerce.**

(4) To establish an uniform rule of naturalization, and uniform laws on the subject of bankruptcies throughout the United States;

(5) To coin money, regulate the value thereof, and of foreign coin, and fix the standard of weights and measures;

From this section, along with the section that allows the Congress to regulate commerce and to borrow money, Congress gets its right to charter national banks and to establish the Federal Reserve System. See **Federal Reserve System.**

(6) To provide for the punishment of counterfeiting the securities and current coin of the United States;

Securities are government bonds.

(7) To establish post offices and post roads;

(8) To promote the progress of science and useful arts, by securing for limited times to authors and inventors the exclusive right to their respective writings and discoveries;

Photographs and films may also be copyrighted under this rule (see **Copyright; Patent**).

(9) To constitute tribunals inferior to the Supreme Court;

Examples of federal courts "inferior to the Supreme Court" include the U.S. district courts and the U.S. courts of appeals.

(10) To define and punish piracies and felonies committed on the high seas, and offenses against the law of nations;

Congress, rather than the states, has jurisdiction over crimes committed at sea.

(11) To declare war, grant letters of marque and reprisal, and make rules concerning captures on land and water;

Only Congress can declare war. However, the President, as commander in chief, has engaged the United States in wars without a declaration by Congress. Undeclared wars include the Korean War (1950-1953), the Vietnam War (1957-1975), and the Persian Gulf War (1991). *Letters of marque and reprisal* are documents that authorize private vessels to attack enemy shipping.

(12) To raise and support armies, but no appropriation of money to that use shall be for a longer term than two years;

(13) To provide and maintain a navy;

(14) To make rules for the government and regulation of the land and naval forces;

(15) To provide for calling forth the militia to execute the laws of the Union, suppress insurrections and repel invasions;

Congress has given the President power to decide when a state of invasion or *insurrection* (uprising) exists. At such times, the President can call out the National Guard.

(16) To provide for organizing, arming, and disciplining, the militia, and for governing such part of them as may be employed in the service of the United States, reserving to the states respectively, the appointment of the officers, and the authority of training the militia according to the discipline prescribed by Congress;

The federal government helps the states maintain the militia, also known as the National Guard. Until 1916, the states controlled the militia entirely. That year, the National Defense Act provided for federal funding of the guard and for drafting the guard into national service under certain circumstances.

(17) To exercise exclusive legislation in all cases whatsoever, over such district (not exceeding ten miles square) as may, by cession of particular states, and the acceptance of Congress, become the seat of the government of the United States, and to exercise like authority over all places purchased by the consent of the legislature of the state in which the same shall be for the erection of forts, magazines, arsenals, dockyards, and other needful buildings;—And

This section makes Congress the legislative body not only for the District of Columbia, but also for federal property on which forts and other federal works or buildings are located.

(18) To make all laws which shall be necessary and proper for carrying into execution the foregoing powers, and all other powers vested by this Constitution in the government of the United States, or in any department or officer thereof.

This section is known as the "necessary and proper" clause or the *elastic clause.* It allows Congress to deal with many matters that are not specifically mentioned in the Constitution but are suggested by powers granted to Congress in Article I. As times have changed, Congress has been able to pass needed laws with few amendments to the Constitution. This flexibility helps explain why the Constitution is one of the oldest written constitutions.

Powers forbidden to Congress

Section 9. (1) The migration or importation of such persons as any of the states now existing shall think proper to admit, shall not be prohibited by the Congress prior to the year one thousand eight hundred and eight, but a tax or duty may be imposed on such importation, not exceeding ten dollars for each person.

This paragraph refers to the slave trade. Dealers in slaves, as well as some slaveholders, wanted to make sure that Congress could not stop anyone from bringing African slaves into the country before the year 1808. That year, Congress did ban the importing of slaves into the United States.

(2) The privilege of the writ of *habeas corpus* shall not be suspended, unless when in cases of rebellion or invasion the public safety may require it.

A *writ of habeas corpus* is a legal order that commands people who have a person in custody to bring the person into court.

They must explain in court why the person is being restrained. If their explanation is unsatisfactory, the judge can order the prisoner released. See **Habeas corpus**.

(3) No bill of attainder or *ex post facto* **law shall be passed.**

A *bill of attainder* is an act passed by a legislature to punish a person without trial. An *ex post facto law* is one that provides punishment for an act that was not illegal when the act was committed. See **Attainder; Ex post facto**.

(4) No capitation, [or other direct,] tax shall be laid, unless in proportion to the census or enumeration herein before directed to be taken.

A *capitation* is a tax that is collected equally from everyone. A capitation is also called a *head tax* or a *poll tax*. The Supreme Court held that this section of the Constitution prohibits an income tax. The 16th Amendment set aside the court's decision.

(5) No tax or duty shall be laid on articles exported from any state.

In this sentence, *exported* means sent to other states or to foreign countries. The Southern States feared that the new government would tax their exports and that their economies would suffer as a result. This sentence forbids such a tax. However, Congress can prohibit shipment of certain items or regulate the conditions of their shipment.

(6) No preference shall be given by any regulation of commerce or revenue to the ports of one state over those of another: nor shall vessels bound to, or from, one state, be obliged to enter, clear, or pay duties in another.

Congress cannot make laws concerning trade that favor one state over another. Ships going from one state to another need not pay taxes to do so.

(7) No money shall be drawn from the treasury, but in consequence of appropriations made by law; and a regular statement and account of the receipts and expenditures of all public money shall be published from time to time.

Government money cannot be spent without the consent of Congress. Congress must issue a financial statement from time to time. Congress authorizes money for most government programs in lump sums because too much time would be needed to authorize each item separately.

(8) No title of nobility shall be granted by the United States: And no person holding any office of profit or trust under them, shall, without the consent of the Congress, accept of any present, emolument, office, or title, of any kind whatsoever, from any king, prince, or foreign state.

Congress cannot give anyone a title of nobility, such as countess or duke. Federal officials may not accept a gift, office, payment, or title from a foreign country without the consent of Congress.

Powers forbidden to the states

Section 10. **(1) No state shall enter into any treaty, alliance, or confederation; grant letters of marque and reprisal; coin money; emit bills of credit; make anything but gold and silver coin a tender in payment of debts; pass any bill of attainder,** *ex post facto* **law, or law impairing the obligation of contracts, or grant any title of nobility.**

(2) No state shall, without the consent of the Congress, lay any imposts or duties on imports or exports, except what may be absolutely necessary for executing its inspection laws: and the net produce of all duties and imposts, laid by any state on imports or exports, shall be for the use of the treasury of the United States, and all such laws shall be subject to the revision and control of the Congress.

Without the consent of Congress, a state cannot tax goods entering or leaving the state except for small fees to cover the cost of inspection. Profits from a tax on interstate commerce go to the federal government.

(3) No state shall, without the consent of Congress, lay any duty of tonnage, keep troops, or ships of war in time of peace, enter into any agreement or compact with another state, or with a foreign power, or engage in war, unless actually invaded, or in such imminent danger as will not admit of delay.

Only the federal government has the power to make treaties and to carry out measures for national defense.

Article II

The executive branch

Section 1. **(1) The executive power shall be vested in a President of the United States of America. He shall hold his office during the term of four years, and, together with the Vice President, chosen for the same term, be elected, as follows:**

(2) Each state shall appoint, in such manner as the legislature thereof may direct, a number of electors, equal to the whole number of senators and representatives to which the state may be entitled in the Congress: but no senator or representative, or person holding an office of trust or profit under the United States, shall be appointed an elector.

This section establishes the Electoral College, a group of people chosen by the voters of each state to elect the President and Vice President (see **Electoral College**).

(3) [The electors shall meet in their respective states, and vote by ballot for two persons, of whom one at least shall not be an inhabitant of the same state with themselves. And they shall make a list of all the persons voted for, and of the number of votes for each; which list they shall sign and certify, and transmit sealed to the seat of the government of the United States, directed to the president of the Senate. The president of the Senate shall, in the presence of the Senate and House of Representatives, open all the certificates, and the votes shall then be counted. The person having the greatest number of votes shall be the President, if such number be a majority of the whole number of electors appointed; and if there be more than one who have such majority, and have an equal number of votes, then the House of Representatives shall immediately choose by ballot one of them for President; and if no person have a majority, then from the five highest on the list the said House shall in like manner choose the President. But in choosing the President, the votes shall be taken by states, the representation from each state having one vote; a quorum for this purpose shall consist of a member or members from two-thirds of the states, and a majority of all the states shall be necessary to a choice. In every case, after the choice of the President, the person having the greatest number of votes of the electors shall be the Vice President. But if there should remain two or more who have equal votes, the Senate shall choose from them by ballot the Vice President.]

The 12th Amendment changed this procedure for electing the President and Vice President.

(4) The Congress may determine the time of choosing the electors, and the day on which they shall give their votes; which day shall be the same throughout the United States.

(5) No person except a natural-born citizen, or a citizen of the United States at the time of the adoption of this Constitution, shall be eligible to the office of President; neither shall any person be eligible to that office who shall not have attained to the age of thirty-five years, and been fourteen years a resident within the United States.

(6) In case of the removal of the President from office, or of his death, resignation, or inability to discharge the powers and duties of the said office, the same shall devolve on the Vice President, and the Congress may by law provide for the case of removal, death, resignation or inability, both of the President and Vice President, declaring what officer shall then act as President, and such officer shall act accordingly, until the disability be removed, or a President shall be elected.

On Aug. 9, 1974, President Richard M. Nixon resigned as chief executive and was succeeded by Vice President Gerald R. Ford. Until then, only death had ever cut short the term of a President of the United States. The 25th Amendment provides that the Vice President succeed to the presidency if the President becomes disabled, and specifies the conditions applying to that succession. See **Presidential succession**.

(7) The President shall, at stated times, receive for his services, a compensation, which shall neither be increased nor diminished during the period for which he shall have been elected, and he shall not receive within that period any other emolument from the United States, or any of them.

The Constitution made it possible for a poor person to become President by providing a salary for that office. The President's salary cannot be raised or lowered during his or her term of office. The chief executive may not receive any other pay from the federal government or the states.

(8) Before he enter on the execution of his office, he shall take the following oath or affirmation:—"I do solemnly swear (or affirm) that I will faithfully execute the office of President of the United States, and will to the best of my ability, preserve, protect and defend the Constitution of the United States."

The Constitution does not say who shall administer the oath to the newly elected President. President George Washington was sworn in by Robert R. Livingston, then a state official in New York. After that, it became customary for the chief justice of the United States to administer the oath. Calvin Coolidge was sworn in by his father, a justice of the peace, at his home in Vermont. Coolidge took the oath again before Justice Adolph A. Hoehling of the Supreme Court of the District of Columbia.

Section 2. **(1) The President shall be commander in chief of the Army and Navy of the United States, and of the militia of the several states, when called into the actual service of the United States; he may require the opinion, in writing, of the principal officer in each of the executive departments, upon any subject relating to the duties of their respective offices, and he shall have power to grant reprieves and pardons for offenses against the United States, except in cases of impeachment.**

The President's powers as commander in chief are far-reaching. But even in wartime, the President must obey the law.

(2) He shall have power, by and with the advice and consent of the Senate, to make treaties, provided two-thirds of the senators present concur; and he shall nominate, and by and with the advice and consent of the Senate, shall appoint ambassadors, other public ministers and consuls, judges of the Supreme Court, and all other officers of the United States, whose appointments are not herein otherwise provided for, and which shall be established by law: but the Congress may by law vest the appointment of such inferior officers, as they think proper, in the President alone, in the courts of law, or in the heads of departments.

The framers of the Constitution intended that in some matters the Senate should serve as an advisory body for the President.

The President can make treaties and appoint various government officials. But two-thirds of the senators present must approve before a treaty is confirmed. Also, high appointments require approval of more than half the senators present.

(3) The President shall have power to fill up all vacancies that may happen during the recess of the Senate, by granting commissions which shall expire at the end of their next session.

This means that when the Senate is not in session, the President can make temporary appointments to offices which require Senate confirmation.

Section 3. **He shall from time to time give to the Congress information of the state of the Union, and recommend to their consideration such measures as he shall judge necessary and** expedient; he may, on extraordinary occasions, convene both houses, or either of them, and in case of disagreement between them, with respect to the time of adjournment, he may adjourn them to such time as he shall think proper; he shall receive ambassadors and other public ministers; he shall take care that the laws be faithfully executed, and shall commission all the officers of the United States.

The President gives a State of the Union message to Congress each year. Presidents George Washington and John Adams delivered their messages in person. For more than 100 years after that, most Presidents sent a written message, which was read in Congress. President Woodrow Wilson delivered his State of the Union messages in person, as did President Franklin D. Roosevelt and all Presidents after Roosevelt. The President's messages often have great influence on public opinion, and thus on Congress. Famous messages to Congress include the Monroe Doctrine and President Wilson's "Fourteen Points."

During the 1800's, Presidents often called Congress into session. Today, Congress is in session most of the time. No President has ever had to adjourn a session of Congress.

The responsibility to "take care that the laws be faithfully executed" puts the President at the head of law enforcement for the national government. Every federal official, civilian or military, gets his or her authority from the President.

Section 4. **The President, Vice President and all civil officers of the United States, shall be removed from office on impeachment for, and conviction of, treason, bribery, or other high crimes and misdemeanors.**

Article III

The judicial branch

Section 1. **The judicial power of the United States, shall be vested in one Supreme Court, and in such inferior courts as the Congress may from time to time ordain and establish. The judges, both of the Supreme and inferior courts, shall hold their offices during good behavior, and shall, at stated times, receive for their services, a compensation, which shall not be diminished during their continuance in office.**

The Constitution makes every effort to keep the courts independent of both the legislature and the President. The guarantee that judges shall hold office during "good behavior" means that, unless they are impeached and convicted, they can hold office for life. This protects judges from any threat of dismissal by the President. The rule that a judge's salary may not be reduced protects the judge against pressure from Congress, which could otherwise threaten to fix the salary so low that the judge could be forced to resign. See **Court; Supreme Court of the United States**.

Section 2. **(1) The judicial power shall extend to all cases, in law and equity, arising under this Constitution, the laws of the United States, and treaties made, or which shall be made, under their authority;—to all cases affecting ambassadors, other public ministers and consuls;—to all cases of admiralty and maritime jurisdiction;—to controversies to which the United States shall be a party;—to controversies between two or more states; [between a state and citizens of another state;] between citizens of different states;—between citizens of the same state claiming lands under grants of different states, and between a state, or the citizens thereof, and foreign states, [citizens or subjects].**

The right of the federal courts to handle "cases arising under this Constitution" is the basis of the Supreme Court's right to declare laws of Congress unconstitutional. This right of "judicial review" was established by Chief Justice John Marshall's historic decision in the case of *Marbury v. Madison* (1803). See **Marbury v. Madison**.

The 11th Amendment to the Constitution set aside the phrase *between a state and citizens of another state*. A citizen of one state cannot sue another state in a federal court.

(2) In all cases affecting ambassadors, other public ministers

and consuls, and those in which a state shall be party, the Supreme Court shall have original jurisdiction. In all the other cases before mentioned, the Supreme Court shall have appellate jurisdiction, both as to law and fact, with such exceptions, and under such regulations as the Congress shall make.

The statement that the Supreme Court has *original jurisdiction* in cases affecting the representatives of foreign countries and in cases to which a state is one of the parties means that cases of this kind go directly to the Supreme Court. In other kinds of cases, the Supreme Court has *appellate jurisdiction*. This means that the cases are tried first in a lower court and may come up to the Supreme Court for review if Congress authorizes an appeal. Congress cannot take away or modify the original jurisdiction of the Supreme Court. However, it can take away the right to appeal to the Supreme Court, or it can fix the conditions one must meet to present an appeal.

(3) The trial of all crimes, except in cases of impeachment, shall be by jury; and such trial shall be held in the state where the said crimes shall have been committed; but when not committed within any state, the trial shall be at such place or places as the Congress may by law have directed.

Section 3. (1) Treason against the United States, shall consist only in levying war against them, or in adhering to their enemies, giving them aid and comfort. No person shall be convicted of treason unless on the testimony of two witnesses to the same overt act, or on confession in open court.

No person can be convicted of treason against the United States unless he or she confesses in open court, or unless two witnesses testify that he or she has committed a treasonable act. Talking or thinking about committing a treasonable act is not treason. See **Treason**.

(2) The Congress shall have power to declare the punishment of treason, but no attainder of treason shall work corruption of blood, or forfeiture except during the life of the person attainted.

The phrase *no attainder of treason shall work corruption of blood* means that the family of a traitor does not share the guilt. Formerly, an offender's family could also be punished.

Article IV

Relation of the states to each other

Much of this article was taken word for word from the old Articles of Confederation.

Section 1. Full faith and credit shall be given in each state to the public acts, records, and judicial proceedings of every other state. And the Congress may by general laws prescribe the manner in which such acts, records and proceedings shall be proved, and the effect thereof.

This section requires the states to honor one another's laws, records, and court rulings. The rule prevents a person from avoiding justice by leaving a state.

Section 2. (1) The citizens of each state shall be entitled to all privileges and immunities of citizens in the several states.

This means that citizens traveling from state to state are entitled to all the privileges and immunities that automatically go to citizens of those states. Some privileges, such as the right to vote, do not automatically go with citizenship, but require a period of residence and perhaps other qualifications. The word *citizen* in this provision does not include corporations.

(2) A person charged in any state with treason, felony, or other crime, who shall flee from justice, and be found in another state, shall on demand of the executive authority of the state from which he fled, be delivered up, to be removed to the state having jurisdiction of the crime.

If a person commits a crime in one state and flees to another, the governor of the state in which the crime was committed can demand that the fugitive be handed over. Returning an accused person is called *extradition*. A few governors have refused to extradite, perhaps because the crime was committed many years ago, or because they believed the accused would not get a fair trial. It is not clear how the federal government could enforce this section. See **Extradition**.

(3) [No person held to service or labor in one state, under the laws thereof, escaping into another, shall, in consequence of any law or regulation therein, be discharged from such service or labor, but shall be delivered up on claim of the party to whom such service or labor may be due.]

A "person held to service or labor" was a slave or an *indentured servant* (a person bound by contract to serve someone for several years). No one is now bound to servitude in the United States, so this part of the Constitution no longer has any force, being overruled by the 13th Amendment.

Federal-state relations

Section 3. (1) New states may be admitted by the Congress into this Union; but no new state shall be formed or erected within the jurisdiction of any other state; nor any state be formed by the junction of two or more states, or parts of states, without the consent of the legislatures of the states concerned as well as of the Congress.

New states cannot be formed by dividing or joining existing states without the consent of the state legislatures and Congress. During the Civil War (1861-1865), Virginia fought for the Confederacy, but people in the state's western part supported the Union. After West Virginia split from Virginia, Congress accepted the new state on the ground that Virginia had rebelled.

(2) The Congress shall have power to dispose of and make all needful rules and regulations respecting the territory or other property belonging to the United States; and nothing in this Constitution shall be so construed as to prejudice any claims of the United States, or of any particular state.

Section 4. The United States shall guarantee to every state in this Union a republican form of government, and shall protect each of them against invasion; and on application of the legislature, or of the executive (when the legislature cannot be convened) against domestic violence.

This section requires the federal government to make sure that every state has a "republican form of government." A republican government is one in which the people elect representatives to govern. The Supreme Court ruled that Congress, not the courts, must decide whether a state government is republican. According to the court, if Congress admits a state's senators and representatives, that action indicates that Congress considers the state's government republican.

The legislature or governor of a state can request federal aid in dealing with riots or other violence. During the Pullman strike of 1894, federal troops were sent to Illinois even though the governor said he did not want them (see **Pullman strike**).

Article V

Amending the Constitution

The Congress, whenever two-thirds of both houses shall deem it necessary, shall propose amendments to this Constitution, or, on the application of the legislatures of two-thirds of the several states, shall call a convention for proposing amendments, which, in either case, shall be valid to all intents and purposes, as part of this Constitution, when ratified by the legislatures of three-fourths of the several states, or by conventions in three-fourths thereof, as the one or the other mode of ratification may be proposed by the Congress; provided [that no amendment which may be made prior to the year one thousand eight hundred and eight shall in any manner affect the first and fourth clauses in the ninth section of the first article; and] that no state, without its consent, shall be deprived of its equal suffrage in the Senate.

Amendments may be proposed by a two-thirds vote of each house of Congress or by a national convention called by Congress at the request of two-thirds of the states. A national convention has never been called, in part because there are no established procedures for operating such a meeting and because of fear that such a convention could result in vast and possibly dangerous changes. To become part of the Constitution, amendments must be *ratified* (approved) by the legislatures of three-fourths of the states or by conventions in three-fourths of the states.

The framers of the Constitution purposely made it hard to put through an amendment. Congress has considered more than 9,000 amendments, but it has passed only 29 and submitted them to the states. Of these, 27 have been ratified. Only one amendment, the 21st, was ratified by state conventions. All the others were ratified by state legislatures.

The Constitution sets no time limit during which the states must ratify a proposed amendment. Ratification of the 27th Amendment took 203 years, longer by far than that of any other amendment. The amendment was first proposed in 1789 and did not become part of the Constitution until 1992. Nevertheless, the courts have held that amendments must be ratified within a "reasonable time" and that Congress decides what is reasonable. Since the early 1900's, most amendments have included a requirement that ratification be obtained within seven years.

Article VI

National debts

(1) **All debts contracted and engagements entered into, before the adoption of this Constitution, shall be as valid against the United States under this Constitution, as under the Confederation.**

This section promises that all debts and obligations made by the United States before the adoption of the Constitution will be honored.

Supremacy of the national government

(2) **This Constitution, and the laws of the United States which shall be made in pursuance thereof; and all treaties made, or which shall be made, under the authority of the United States, shall be the supreme law of the land; and the judges in every state shall be bound thereby, anything in the constitution or laws of any state to the contrary notwithstanding.**

This section, known as the *supremacy clause,* has been called *the linchpin of the Constitution*—that is, the part that keeps the entire structure from falling apart. It means simply that when state laws conflict with national laws, the national laws are superior. It also means that, to be valid, a national law must follow the Constitution.

(3) **The senators and representatives before mentioned, and the members of the several state legislatures, and all executive and judicial officers, both of the United States and of the several states, shall be bound by oath or affirmation, to support this Constitution; but no religious test shall ever be required as a qualification to any office or public trust under the United States.**

This section requires both federal and state officials to give supreme allegiance to the Constitution of the United States rather than to any state constitution. The section also forbids any religious test for holding federal office. The 14th Amendment applies the same rule to state and local governments.

Article VII

Ratifying the Constitution

The ratification of the conventions of nine states, shall be sufficient for the establishment of this Constitution between the states so ratifying the same.

Done in convention by the unanimous consent of the states present the seventeenth day of September in the year of our

Lord one thousand seven hundred and eighty-seven and of the independence of the United States of America the twelfth. In witness whereof we have hereunto subscribed our names,

George Washington—President and deputy from Virginia

Delaware	New Hampshire
George Read	John Langdon
Gunning Bedford, Jr.	Nicholas Gilman
John Dickinson	
Richard Bassett	**Massachusetts**
Jacob Broom	Nathaniel Gorham
	Rufus King
Maryland	
James McHenry	**Connecticut**
Daniel of St. Thomas Jenifer	William Samuel Johnson
Daniel Carroll	Roger Sherman
Virginia	**New York**
John Blair	Alexander Hamilton
James Madison, Jr.	
	New Jersey
North Carolina	William Livingston
William Blount	David Brearley
Richard Dobbs Spaight	William Paterson
Hugh Williamson	Jonathan Dayton
South Carolina	**Pennsylvania**
John Rutledge	Benjamin Franklin
Charles Cotesworth Pinckney	Thomas Mifflin
Charles Pinckney	Robert Morris
Pierce Butler	George Clymer
	Thomas FitzSimons
Georgia	Jared Ingersoll
William Few	James Wilson
Abraham Baldwin	Gouverneur Morris

Amendments to the Constitution

The Bill of Rights

The first 10 amendments, known as the Bill of Rights, *were proposed on Sept. 25, 1789. They were ratified on Dec. 15, 1791. They were adopted because some states refused to approve the Constitution unless a bill of rights was added.*

The amendments protect individuals from various unjust acts of government. Originally, the amendments applied only to the federal government. But the 14th Amendment declares that no state can deprive any person of life, liberty, or property without "due process of law." The Supreme Court has interpreted those words to mean that most of the Bill of Rights applies to the states as well. See **Bill of rights.**

Amendment 1

Freedom of religion, speech, and the press; rights of assembly and petition

Congress shall make no law respecting an establishment of religion, or prohibiting the free exercise thereof; or abridging the freedom of speech, or of the press; or the right of the people peaceably to assemble, and to petition the government for a redress of grievances.

Many countries have made one religion the *established* (official) church and supported it with government funds. This amendment forbids Congress to set up or in any way provide for an established church. It has been interpreted to forbid government endorsement of, or aid to, religious doctrines. In addition, Congress may not pass laws limiting worship, speech, or the press, or preventing people from meeting peacefully. Congress also may not keep people from asking the government for relief from unfair treatment.

All the rights protected by this amendment have limits. For example, the guarantee of freedom of religion does not mean that the government must allow all religious practices. In the 1800's, some Mormons believed it was a man's religious duty to have more than one wife. The Supreme Court ruled that Mormons had to obey the laws forbidding that practice. See **Freedom of religion; Freedom of speech; Freedom of the press.**

Amendment 2

Right to bear arms

A well-regulated militia, being necessary to the security of a free state, the right of the people to keep and bear arms shall not be infringed.

This amendment prohibits only the national government from limiting the right to carry weapons. The amendment was adopted so that Congress could not disarm a state militia.

Amendment 3

Housing of soldiers

No soldier shall, in time of peace be quartered in any house, without the consent of the owner, nor in time of war, but in a manner to be prescribed by law.

This amendment grew out of an old complaint against the British, who had forced people to take soldiers into their homes.

Amendment 4

Search and arrest warrants

The right of the people to be secure in their persons, houses, papers, and effects, against unreasonable searches and seizures, shall not be violated, and no warrants shall issue, but upon probable cause, supported by oath or affirmation, and particularly describing the place to be searched, and the persons or things to be seized.

This measure does not forbid legal authorities to search, to seize goods, or to arrest people. It simply requires that in most cases the authorities obtain a search or arrest warrant from a judge by showing the need for it. If a warrant cannot be obtained, the search or arrest is permitted only if the state's need for evidence outweighs the individual's right to privacy. In addition, the search or arrest may not be carried out in an unreasonable manner. See **Search warrant.**

Amendment 5

Rights in criminal cases

No person shall be held to answer for a capital, or otherwise infamous crime, unless on a presentment or indictment of a grand jury, except in cases arising in the land or naval forces, or in the militia, when in actual service in time of war or public danger; nor shall any person be subject for the same offense to be twice put in jeopardy of life or limb; nor shall be compelled in any criminal case to be a witness against himself, nor be deprived of life, liberty, or property, without due process of law; nor shall private property be taken for public use, without just compensation.

A *capital crime* is one punishable by death. An *infamous crime* is one punishable by death or imprisonment. This amendment guarantees that no one has to stand trial for such a federal crime unless he or she has been *indicted* (accused) by a *grand jury.* A grand jury is a special group of people selected to decide whether there is enough evidence against a person to hold a trial. A person cannot be *put in double jeopardy* (tried twice) for the same offense by the same government. But a person may be tried a second time if a jury cannot agree on a verdict, if a mistrial is declared for some other reason, or if the person requests a new trial. The amendment also guarantees that people cannot be forced to testify against themselves.

The statement that no person shall be deprived of life, liberty, or property "without due process of law" expresses one of the most important rules of the Constitution. The same words are in the 14th Amendment as restrictions on the power of the states. The phrase expresses the idea that a person's life, liberty, and property are not subject to the uncontrolled power of the government. This idea can be traced to Magna Carta, which provided that the king could not imprison or harm a person "except by the lawful judgment of his peers or by the law of the land." Due process is a vague rule, and the Supreme Court has applied it to widely different cases. At one time, the court used the due-process rule to strike down laws that prevented people from using their property as they wished. In 1857, for example, the court overturned the Missouri Compromise, which prohibited slavery in certain U.S. territories. The court said the compromise unjustly prevented slave owners from taking slaves—their property—into the territories. Today, the courts use the rule to strike down laws that interfere with personal liberty. See **Due process of law.**

The amendment also forbids the government to take a person's property for public use without fair payment. The government's right to take property for public use is called *eminent domain.* Governments use it to acquire land for highways, schools, and other public facilities. See **Fifth Amendment.**

Amendment 6

Rights to a fair trial

In all criminal prosecutions, the accused shall enjoy the right to a speedy and public trial, by an impartial jury of the state and district wherein the crime shall have been committed, which district shall have been previously ascertained by law, and to be informed of the nature and cause of the accusation; to be confronted with the witnesses against him; to have compulsory process for obtaining witnesses in his favor, and to have the assistance of counsel for his defense.

A person accused of crime must have a prompt, public trial by an open-minded jury. The requirement for a speedy and public trial grew out of the fact that some political trials in England had been delayed for years and then were held in secret. Accused persons must be informed of the charges against them and must be allowed to meet the witnesses against them face to face. Otherwise, innocent individuals may be punished if a court allows the testimony of unknown witnesses to be used as evidence. This amendment guarantees that persons on trial can face and cross-examine those who have accused them. They may be able to show that their accusers lied or made a mistake. Finally, accused individuals must have a lawyer to defend them if they want one.

Amendment 7

Rights in civil cases

In suits at common law, where the value in controversy shall exceed twenty dollars, the right of a trial by jury shall be preserved, and no fact tried by a jury, shall be otherwise reexamined in any court of the United States, than according to the rules of the common law.

The framers of the Constitution considered the right to jury trial extremely important. In the Sixth Amendment, they provided for jury trials in criminal cases. In the Seventh Amendment, they provided for such trials in civil suits where the amount contested exceeds $20. The amendment applies only to civil cases in federal courts. But because of a great decline in the value of the dollar over the years, it now applies to almost all such cases. Most state constitutions also call for jury trials in civil cases.

Amendment 8

Bails, fines, and punishments

Excessive bail shall not be required, nor excessive fines imposed, nor cruel and unusual punishments inflicted.

Bails, fines, and punishments must be fair and humane. In the case of *Furman v. Georgia,* the Supreme Court ruled in 1972 that capital punishment, as it was then imposed, violated this amendment. The court held that the death penalty was cruel and unusual punishment because it was not applied fairly and uniformly. Many states then adopted new laws designed to meet the court's objections. The court has ruled that the death penalty may be imposed if certain standards are applied to guard against its arbitrary use. See **Capital punishment**.

Amendment 9

Rights retained by the people

The enumeration in the Constitution, of certain rights, shall not be construed to deny or disparage others retained by the people.

Some people feared that the listing of some rights in the Bill of Rights would be interpreted to mean that other rights not listed were not protected. This amendment was adopted to prevent such an interpretation.

Amendment 10

Powers retained by the states and the people

The powers not delegated to the United States by the Constitution, nor prohibited by it to the states, are reserved to the states respectively, or to the people.

This amendment was adopted to reassure people that the national government would not swallow up the states. It confirms that the states or the people retain all powers not given to the national government. For example, the states have authority over such matters as marriage and divorce. But the Constitution says the federal government can make any laws "necessary and proper" to carry out its specific powers. This rule makes it hard to determine the exact rights of states.

Amendment 11

Lawsuits against states

This amendment was proposed on March 4, 1794, and ratified on Feb. 7, 1795. However, the amendment was not proclaimed until 1798 because of delays that occurred in certifying the ratification.

The judicial power of the United States shall not be construed to extend to any suit in law or equity, commenced or prosecuted against one of the United States by citizens of another state, or by citizens or subjects of any foreign state.

This amendment makes it impossible for a citizen of one state to sue another state in federal court. The amendment resulted from the 1793 case of *Chisholm v. Georgia,* in which a man from South Carolina sued the state of Georgia over an inheritance. Georgia argued that it could not be sued in federal court, but the Supreme Court ruled that the state could be. Georgia then led a movement to adopt this amendment. However, individuals can still sue state authorities in federal court for depriving them of their constitutional rights.

Amendment 12

Election of the President and Vice President

This amendment was proposed on Dec. 9, 1803, and ratified on July 27, 1804.

The electors shall meet in their respective states and vote by ballot for President and Vice President, one of whom, at least, shall not be an inhabitant of the same state with themselves; they shall name in their ballots the person voted for as President, and in distinct ballots the person voted for as Vice President, and they shall make distinct lists of all persons voted for as President, and of all persons voted for as Vice President, and of the number of votes for each, which lists they shall sign and certify, and transmit sealed to the seat of the government of the United States, directed to the president of the Senate;——the president of the Senate shall, in the pres-

ence of the Senate and House of Representatives, open all the certificates and the votes shall then be counted;——the person having the greatest number of votes for President, shall be the President, if such number be a majority of the whole number of electors appointed; and if no person have such majority, then from the persons having the highest numbers not exceeding three on the list of those voted for as President, the House of Representatives shall choose immediately, by ballot, the President. But in choosing the President, the votes shall be taken by states, the representation from each state having one vote; a quorum for this purpose shall consist of a member or members from two-thirds of the states, and a majority of all the states shall be necessary to a choice. And if the House of Representatives shall not choose a President whenever the right of choice shall devolve upon them, [before the fourth day of March next following,] then the Vice President shall act as President, as in the case of the death or other constitutional disability of the President.——The person having the greatest number of votes as Vice President, shall be the Vice President, if such number be a majority of the whole number of electors appointed, and if no person have a majority, then from the two highest numbers on the list, the Senate shall choose the Vice President; a quorum for the purpose shall consist of two-thirds of the whole number of senators, and a majority of the whole number shall be necessary to a choice. But no person constitutionally ineligible to the office of President shall be eligible to that of Vice President of the United States.

This amendment provides that members of the Electoral College, called *electors,* vote for one person as President and for another as Vice President. The amendment resulted from the election of 1800. At that time, each elector voted for two men, not saying which he wanted for President. The man who received the most votes became President, and the runner-up became Vice President. Thomas Jefferson, the presidential candidate, and Aaron Burr, the vice presidential candidate, received the same number of votes. The tie threw the election into the House of Representatives. The House chose Jefferson but took so long that people feared it would fail to choose before Inauguration Day. The House has chosen one other president—John Quincy Adams in 1825.

Amendment 13

Abolition of slavery

This amendment was proposed on Jan. 31, 1865, and ratified on Dec. 6, 1865.

Section 1. Neither slavery nor involuntary servitude, except as a punishment for crime whereof the party shall have been duly convicted, shall exist within the United States, or any place subject to their jurisdiction.

President Abraham Lincoln's Emancipation Proclamation of 1863 had declared slaves free in the Confederate States still in rebellion. This amendment completed the abolition of slavery in the United States.

Section 2. Congress shall have power to enforce this article by appropriate legislation.

Amendment 14

Civil rights

This amendment was proposed on June 13, 1866, and ratified on July 9, 1868.

Section 1. All persons born or naturalized in the United States, and subject to the jurisdiction thereof, are citizens of the United States and of the state wherein they reside. No state shall make or enforce any law which shall abridge the privileges or immunities of citizens of the United States; nor shall any state deprive any person of life, liberty, or property, without due process of law; nor deny to any person within its jurisdiction the equal protection of the laws.

The principal purpose of this amendment was to make former slaves citizens of both the United States and the state in which they lived. The amendment also forbids the states to deny equal rights to any person. The terms of the amendment clarify how citizenship is acquired. State citizenship is a by-product of national citizenship. By living in a state, every U.S. citizen automatically becomes a citizen of that state as well. All persons *naturalized* (granted citizenship) according to law are U.S. citizens. People born in the United States are also citizens regardless of the nationality of their parents, unless they are diplomatic representatives of another country or enemies during a wartime occupation. Such cases are exceptions because the parents are not "subject to the jurisdiction" of the United States. The amendment does not grant citizenship to Indians on reservations, but Congress passed a law that did so.

The phrase "due process of law" has been ruled to forbid the states to violate most rights protected by the Bill of Rights. The statement that a state cannot deny anyone "equal protection of the laws" has provided the basis for many Supreme Court rulings on civil rights. For example, the court has outlawed segregation in public schools. The judges declared that "equal protection" means a state must make sure all children, regardless of race, have an equal opportunity for education.

Section 2. Representatives shall be apportioned among the several states according to their respective numbers, counting the whole number of persons in each state, [excluding Indians not taxed]. But when the right to vote at any election for the choice of electors for President and Vice President of the United States, representatives in Congress, the executive and judicial officers of a state, or the members of the legislature thereof, is denied to any of the male inhabitants of such state, being twenty-one years of age, and citizens of the United States, or in any way abridged, except for participation in rebellion, or other crime, the basis of representation therein shall be reduced in the proportion which the number of such male citizens shall bear to the whole number of male citizens twenty-one years of age in such state.

This section proposes a penalty for states which refuse to give the vote in federal elections to all adult male citizens. States which restrict voting can have their representation in Congress cut down. This penalty has never been used. The section has been set aside by the 19th and 26th amendments.

Section 3. No person shall be a senator or representative in Congress, or elector of President and Vice President, or hold any office, civil or military, under the United States, or under any state, who, having previously taken an oath, as a member of Congress, or as an officer of the United States, or as a member of any state legislature, or as an executive or judicial officer of any state, to support the Constitution of the United States, shall have engaged in insurrection or rebellion against the same, or given aid or comfort to the enemies thereof. But Congress may by a vote of two-thirds of each House, remove such disability.

This section's purpose was to keep federal officers who joined the Confederacy from becoming federal officers again. Congress could vote to overlook such a record.

Section 4. The validity of the public debt of the United States, authorized by law, including debts incurred for payment of pensions and bounties for services in suppressing insurrection or rebellion, shall not be questioned. But neither the United States nor any state shall assume or pay any debt or obligation incurred in aid of insurrection or rebellion against the United States, or any claim for the loss of emancipation of any slave; but all such debts, obligations and claims shall be held illegal and void.

This section ensured that the Union's Civil War debt would be paid, but voided all war debts run up by the Confederacy. The section also said that former slaveowners would not be paid for slaves who were freed.

Section 5. The Congress shall have power to enforce, by appropriate legislation, the provisions of this article.

Amendment 15

Black suffrage

This amendment was proposed on Feb. 26, 1869, and ratified on Feb. 3, 1870.

Section 1. The right of citizens of the United States to vote shall not be denied or abridged by the United States or by any state on account of race, color, or previous condition of servitude.

Blacks who had been slaves became citizens under the terms of the 14th Amendment. The 15th Amendment does not specifically say that all blacks must be allowed to vote. The states are free to set qualifications for voters. But a voter cannot be denied the ballot because of race. Attempts by some states to do this indirectly have been struck down by Supreme Court decisions, federal and state laws, and the 24th Amendment. See **Fifteenth Amendment; Grandfather clause; Voting.**

Section 2. The Congress shall have power to enforce this article by appropriate legislation.

Amendment 16

Income taxes

This amendment was proposed on July 12, 1909, and ratified on Feb. 3, 1913.

The Congress shall have power to lay and collect taxes on incomes, from whatever source derived, without apportionment among the several states, and without regard to any census or enumeration.

In 1894, Congress passed an income tax law, but the Supreme Court declared it unconstitutional. This amendment authorized Congress to levy such a tax.

Amendment 17

Direct election of senators

This amendment was proposed on May 13, 1912, and ratified on April 8, 1913.

(1) The Senate of the United States shall be composed of two senators from each state, elected by the people thereof for six years; and each senator shall have one vote. The electors in each state shall have the qualifications requisite for electors of the most numerous branch of the state legislatures.

(2) When vacancies happen in the representation of any state in the Senate, the executive authority of such state shall issue writs of election to fill such vacancies: *Provided,* That the legislature of any state may empower the executive thereof to make temporary appointments until the people fill the vacancies by election as the legislature may direct.

(3) This amendment shall not be so construed as to affect the election or term of any senator chosen before it becomes valid as part of the Constitution.

This amendment takes the power of electing senators from the state legislatures and gives it to the people of the states.

Amendment 18

Prohibition of liquor

This amendment was proposed on Dec. 18, 1917, and ratified on Jan. 16, 1919.

Section 1. After one year from the ratification of this article the manufacture, sale, or transportation of intoxicating liquors within, the importation thereof into, or the exportation thereof from the United States and all territory subject to the jurisdiction thereof for beverage purposes is hereby prohibited.

Section 2. The Congress and the several states shall have concurrent power to enforce this article by appropriate legislation.

Section 3. This article shall be inoperative unless it shall have been ratified as an amendment to the Constitution by the legislatures of the several states, as provided in the Constitution, within seven years from the date of the submission hereof to the states by the Congress.

This is the prohibition amendment, which forbade people to make, sell, or transport liquor. It was widely ignored by the people and was repealed by the 21st Amendment in 1933.

Amendment 19

Woman suffrage

This amendment was proposed on June 4, 1919, and ratified on Aug. 18, 1920.

Section 1. The right of citizens of the United States to vote shall not be denied or abridged by the United States or by any state on account of sex.

Section 2. Congress shall have power to enforce this article by appropriate legislation.

Amendments giving women the right to vote were introduced in Congress one after another for more than 40 years before this one was finally passed.

Amendment 20

Terms of the President and Congress

This amendment was proposed on March 2, 1932, and ratified on Jan. 23, 1933.

Section 1. The terms of the President and Vice President shall end at noon on the 20th day of January, and the terms of senators and representatives at noon on the third day of January, of the year in which such terms would have ended if this article had not been ratified; and the terms of their successors shall then begin.

Section 2. The Congress shall assemble at least once in every year, and such meeting shall begin at noon on the third day of January, unless they shall by law appoint a different day.

Section 3. If, at the time fixed for the beginning of the term of the President, the President elect shall have died, the Vice President elect shall become President. If a President shall not have been chosen before the time fixed for the beginning of his term, or if the President elect shall have failed to qualify, then the Vice President elect shall act as President until a President shall have qualified; and the Congress may by law provide for the case wherein neither a President elect nor a Vice President elect shall have qualified, declaring who shall then act as President, or the manner in which one who is to act shall be selected, and such person shall act accordingly until a President or Vice President shall have qualified.

Section 4. The Congress may by law provide for the case of the death of any of the persons from whom the House of Representatives may choose a President whenever the right of choice shall have devolved upon them, and for the case of the death of any of the persons from whom the Senate may choose a Vice President whenever the right of choice shall have devolved upon them.

Section 5. Sections 1 and 2 shall take effect on the 15th day of October following the ratification of this article.

Section 6. This article shall be inoperative unless it shall

have been ratified as an amendment to the Constitution by the legislatures of three-fourths of the several states within seven years from the date of its submission.

This *lame duck amendment* moves the date that newly elected Presidents and members of Congress take office closer to election time. A *lame duck* is an official who continues to serve though not reelected. Before the amendment came into force, defeated members of Congress continued to hold office for four months. See **Lame duck amendment**.

Amendment 21

Repeal of prohibition

This amendment was proposed on Feb. 20, 1933, and ratified on Dec. 5, 1933.

Section 1. The eighteenth article of amendment to the Constitution of the United States is hereby repealed.

Section 2. The transportation or importation into any state, territory, or possession of the United States for delivery or use therein of intoxicating liquors, in violation of the laws thereof, is hereby prohibited.

Section 3. This article shall be inoperative unless it shall have been ratified as an amendment to the Constitution by conventions in the several states, as provided in the Constitution, within seven years from the date of the submission hereof to the states by the Congress.

This amendment repeals the 18th Amendment. Section 2 promises federal help to "dry" states in enforcing their own laws.

Amendment 22

Limitation of Presidents to two terms

This amendment was proposed on March 24, 1947, and ratified on Feb. 27, 1951.

Section 1. No person shall be elected to the office of the President more than twice, and no person who has held the office of President, or acted as President, for more than two years of a term to which some other person was elected President shall be elected to the office of the President more than once. But this article shall not apply to any person holding the office of President when this article was proposed by the Congress, and shall not prevent any person who may be holding the office of President, or acting as President, during the term within which this article becomes operative from holding the office of President or acting as President during the remainder of such term.

Section 2. This article shall be inoperative unless it shall have been ratified as an amendment to the Constitution by the legislatures of three-fourths of the several states within seven years from the day of its submission to the states by the Congress.

This amendment provides that no person can be elected President more than twice. Nobody who has served for more than two years of someone else's term can be elected more than once. A President can hold office for no more than 10 years. The amendment was supported by those who thought Franklin D. Roosevelt should not serve four terms. No other President had run for election to more than two consecutive terms.

Amendment 23

Suffrage in the District of Columbia

This amendment was proposed on June 16, 1960, and ratified on March 29, 1961.

Section 1. The district constituting the seat of government of the United States shall appoint in such manner as the Congress may direct: A number of electors of President and Vice

President equal to the whole number of senators and representatives in Congress to which the district would be entitled if it were a state, but in no event more than the least populous state; they shall be in addition to those appointed by the states, but they shall be considered, for the purposes of the election of President and Vice President, to be electors appointed by a state; and they shall meet in the district and perform such duties as provided by the twelfth article of amendment.

Section 2. The Congress shall have power to enforce this article by appropriate legislation.

This amendment allows citizens of the District of Columbia to vote in presidential elections. However, they cannot vote for members of Congress.

Amendment 24

Poll taxes

This amendment was proposed on Aug. 27, 1962, and ratified on Jan. 23, 1964.

Section 1. The right of citizens of the United States to vote in any primary or other election for President or Vice President, for electors for President or Vice President, or for senator or representative in Congress, shall not be denied or abridged by the United States or any state by reason of failure to pay any poll tax or other tax.

Section 2. The Congress shall have power to enforce this article by appropriate legislation.

This amendment forbids making voters pay a *poll tax* before they can vote in a national election. A poll tax, also called a *head tax*, is a tax collected equally from everyone. Some states once used such taxes to keep poor people and blacks from voting. The term *poll tax* does not mean a tax on voting. It comes from the old English word *poll*, meaning *head*. See Poll tax.

Amendment 25

Presidential disability and succession

This amendment was proposed on July 6, 1965, and ratified on Feb. 10, 1967.

Section 1. In case of the removal of the President from office or of his death or resignation, the Vice President shall become President.

Section 2. Whenever there is a vacancy in the office of the Vice President, the President shall nominate a Vice President who shall take office upon confirmation by a majority vote of both houses of Congress.

This section provides for filling a vacancy in the vice presidency. In 1973, Gerald R. Ford became the first person chosen Vice President under this provision. He was nominated by President Richard M. Nixon after Vice President Spiro T. Agnew resigned. In 1974, Nixon resigned and Ford became President. Nelson A. Rockefeller then became Vice President under the new procedure. For the first time, the nation had both a President and Vice President who had not been elected to their office. Before this amendment came into force, vacancies in the vice presidency remained unfilled until the next election.

Section 3. Whenever the President transmits to the president pro tempore of the Senate and the Speaker of the House of Representatives his written declaration that he is unable to discharge the powers and duties of his office, and until he transmits to them a written declaration to the contrary, such powers and duties shall be discharged by the Vice President as acting President.

This section provides that the Vice President succeeds to the presidency if the President becomes disabled. Vice President George Bush became the first acting President. He officially held

the position eight hours on July 13, 1985, when President Ronald Reagan had cancer surgery.

Section 4. Whenever the Vice President and majority of either the principal officers of the executive departments or of such other body as Congress may by law provide, transmit to the president pro tempore of the Senate and the Speaker of the House of Representatives their written declaration that the President is unable to discharge the powers and duties of his office, the Vice President shall immediately assume the powers and duties of the office as acting President.

Thereafter, when the President transmits to the president pro tempore of the Senate and the Speaker of the House of Representatives his written declaration that no inability exists, he shall resume the powers and duties of his office unless the Vice President and a majority of either the principal officers of the executive department or of such other body as Congress may by law provide, transmit within four days to the president pro tempore of the Senate and the Speaker of the House of Representatives their written declaration that the President is unable to discharge the powers and duties of his office. Thereupon Congress shall decide the issue, assembling within forty-eight hours for that purpose if not in session. If the Congress, within twenty-one days after receipt of the latter written declaration, or, if Congress is not in session, within twenty-one days after Congress is required to assemble, determines by two-thirds vote of both houses that the President is unable to discharge the powers and duties of his office, the Vice President shall continue to discharge the same as acting President; otherwise, the President shall resume the powers and duties of his office.

Amendment 26

Suffrage for 18-year-olds

This amendment was proposed on March 23, 1971, and ratified on July 1, 1971.

Section 1. The right of citizens of the United States, who are eighteen years of age or older, to vote shall not be denied or abridged by the United States or by any state on account of age.

Section 2. The Congress shall have power to enforce this article by appropriate legislation.

This amendment grants the vote to citizens 18 years of age or older. Passed during the Vietnam War, it reflected the opinion of many people of the time that young men who are old enough to be drafted into the armed forces should be able to vote for or against officials who lead the nation into war.

Amendment 27

Congressional salaries

This amendment was proposed on Sept. 25, 1789, and ratified on May 7, 1992.

No law varying the compensation for the services of the senators and representatives shall take effect, until an election of representatives shall have intervened.

This amendment prevents Congress from passing immediate salary increases for itself. It requires that salary changes passed by Congress cannot take effect until after the next congressional election. It had been passed in 1789 and sent to the states for ratification. The amendment had no time limit for ratification. It became part of the Constitution in 1992, after Michigan became the 38th state to ratify it.   Annotations by Bruce Allen Murphy

Constitutional Convention. See Constitution of the United States (The Constitutional Convention).

Constitutional Union Party was an American political party formed in 1859 by former members of the Whig and Know-Nothing parties. At a convention in Baltimore in 1860, the party nominated John Bell and Edward Everett for President and Vice President. The candidates lost, and the party died out. See also **Whig Party; Bell, John.**   David Herbert Donald

Construction, Building. See Building construction.

Construction Battalion. See Seabees.

Consul, *KAHN suhl,* is an official appointed by the government of one country to look after its commercial and cultural interests in a city of another country. A consul differs from a diplomatic representative. A consul attends primarily to business and cultural matters, while a diplomat is interested primarily in political relations (see **Ambassador**).

United States consuls issue birth, death, and marriage certificates to Americans temporarily within their jurisdiction, regulate shipping, and aid U.S. citizens who are traveling abroad. For example, they assist American tourists who are arrested or robbed in a foreign country. They may also issue visas to foreigners traveling to the United States.

The consular service of any leading country is divided into three ranks: consuls-general, consuls, and commercial agents. The consuls-general have charge of all consuls in a district. The commercial agents, although they have the same duties and powers as consuls, are not officially recognized by the government. The powers and duties of consuls are often determined by treaty.

The title *consul* was given to the two highest magistrates of the Roman republic during ancient times. The insignia were the purple-bordered toga, a staff of ivory, and an ornamental chair. The title, without the function, was retained under the empire. During the French Republic, from 1799 to 1804, the three chief magistrates were consuls. Napoleon Bonaparte, the first consul, held all the real power.   Robert J. Pranger

See also Foreign Service.

Consumer Affairs, United States Office of, is an agency of the U.S. government. It analyzes and coordinates all government activities in the field of consumer protection. The office serves chiefly in an advisory and informational role. It does not have the authority to enforce specific laws that protect consumers.

President Richard M. Nixon created the office in 1971. It succeeded the President's Committee on Consumer Interests, which President Lyndon B. Johnson had created in 1964. In 1973, the administrative functions of the office were transferred from the Executive Office of the President to the Department of Health, Education, and Welfare (now the Department of Health and Human Services). The director of the agency serves the President as Special Adviser for Consumer Affairs.

Consumer Federation of America (CFA) is an organization that promotes the interests of consumers in the United States. It is a federation of about 250 church, consumer, farm, and labor groups. These national, state, and local organizations have joined together to influence public policy as it is formulated by Congress, regulatory agencies, and the courts.

The federation operates a foundation that sponsors research and educates the public on such consumer concerns as product safety and inflation. CFA publications include *CFAnews* and *Indoor Air News.* The federation was established in 1968. The headquarters of the Consumer Federation of America are at 1424 16th Street NW, Suite 604, Washington, DC 20036.

Consumer Price Index is a statistical measurement of changes in the prices of goods and services bought by most people in the United States. The index, also called the CPI, is prepared by the Bureau of Labor Statistics, a government agency. The CPI compares the present cost of certain goods and services with their cost at an earlier time. Current prices are expressed as a percentage of average prices during the period from 1982 to 1984. For example, an index of 115 means that the average price level was 15 per cent higher than the average price level in the 1982 to 1984 period.

The Bureau of Labor Statistics compiles two versions of the CPI. One reflects spending by urban wage earners and clerical workers. The other shows expenditures by all consumers except those living in rural areas, those in the military, and those in institutions. The bureau also publishes separate CPI's for 27 large metropolitan areas, 4 regions of the United States, and 4 groups of cities classified by size. It gathers information on costs of food, clothing, housing, medical care, transportation, entertainment, and other goods and services from about 80,000 sources in 91 urban areas.

The Consumer Price Index is the chief measurement of inflation in the United States and the main method of evaluating government efforts to fight inflation. Many government and private organizations use the CPI as a yardstick for revising salaries, wages, welfare benefits, and other payments to keep pace with changing prices. As a result, the CPI affects the income of about half the people of the United States. For a chart showing changes in the CPI, see **Cost of living.**

Consumer Product Safety Commission is an independent agency of the United States government. It works to protect consumers from unsafe products that can cause illness, injury, or even death.

The commission promotes the development of voluntary safety standards by manufacturers. It also establishes and enforces uniform federal safety standards for the content, construction, and performance of consumer products. The commission has authority over more than 15,000 manufactured goods, including appliances, baby clothes, gardening tools, sports equipment, and toys. Cars, cosmetics, drugs, and food are regulated by other agencies. But the commission regulates the packaging of some of these products to ensure that children cannot open them easily.

The commission can order the recall, repair, or replacement of products that it considers hazardous. It has the authority to seize especially dangerous products or to forbid their sale. The agency conducts research on the causes and prevention of accidents associated with consumer products. It also conducts programs to help educate the public about product safety.

Congress created the commission in 1972. The President appoints the five members to seven-year terms, subject to the approval of the Senate.

Consumerism is a movement that promotes the interests of buyers of goods and services. It works to protect consumers from unsafe products; fraudulent advertising, labeling, or packaging; and business practices that limit competition. Consumerism, also known as *consumer protection* or the *consumer movement,* is active in many countries. This article discusses the movement in the United States.

Consumerism includes activities by consumers themselves, as well as government action on the federal, state, and local level. The movement seeks to provide adequate information about products so that consumers can make wise decisions in purchasing goods and services. Consumerism also tries to inform consumers of effective means of obtaining compensation for damage or injury caused by defective products.

The rise of the consumer movement has had major effects on business and industry. Many companies have become more responsive to the needs, wants, and safety of consumers. Other firms have not been responsive to these concerns. Some of them have experienced financial losses and unfavorable publicity resulting from lawsuits by dissatisfied consumers and government-ordered recalls of defective products.

The consumer's rights

Consumer groups and many other people believe consumers have several basic rights. For example, they believe consumers are entitled to (1) products whose quality is consistent with their prices and the claims of manufacturers; (2) protection against unsafe goods; (3) truthful, adequate information about goods or services; and (4) a choice among a variety of products. Buyers also have certain responsibilities. For example, they must use a product for the purpose intended by the manufacturer, and they should follow the instructions provided with the product.

The right to quality. Warranties and money-back guarantees provide assurances that a product will live up to the claims of the manufacturer. Most warranties are written statements that promise repair, replacement, or a refund if a product fails to perform as the manufacturer said it would for a certain period of time. A money-back guarantee promises a refund of the purchase price if the buyer is not completely satisfied.

The Magnuson-Moss Warranty Act of 1975 helps regulate warranties. This law requires that warranties be written clearly so they can be easily understood by the public. The act also gives the consumer the right to an *implied warranty* if the manufacturer does not provide a written warranty. An implied warranty is an unwritten guarantee that a product is suitable for the purpose for which it has been sold. For example, a hairdrier should dry hair. Only a product sold "as is" has no implied warranty. Such goods include damaged and second-hand items.

The right to safety. A number of agencies of the federal government play an important role in ensuring the safety of goods. For example, the Food and Drug Administration (FDA) enforces laws concerning the safety of food, drugs, and cosmetics. The Consumer Product Safety Commission sets safety standards for many household products. The National Highway Traffic Safety Administration sets and enforces safety requirements for automobiles and related products. All such agencies test products and inspect factories. They also investigate consumer complaints and furnish information about product safety. In addition, the agencies can order manufacturers to recall hazardous products.

Certification programs give consumers further information about product safety. For example, Underwriters Laboratories, Inc., a nonprofit organization, sets safety standards for building materials, electric appliances, and other products. It tests products submitted by manufacturers and awards a certifying seal to items that meet its standards.

Consumers can seek compensation in several ways for a loss or injury. For example, a person can sue by means of a *product liability suit* or a *malpractice suit.* A product liability suit is brought against a manufacturer or seller for damage or injury that is caused by a product. A malpractice suit is filed against an individual or a company in a service field, such as medicine or dentistry.

Consumers can file individual lawsuits in a regular court, or they can bring their claims to a *small-claims court.* Most small-claims courts handle consumer complaints involving up to $5,000. If many consumers have the same complaint, they may file their claims in a single lawsuit called a *class action suit.*

People can also bring their complaints to consumer and business organizations. For example, many business companies finance organizations known as *better business bureaus.* The bureaus bring consumer complaints to the attention of business firms. Large numbers of companies have special departments that handle consumer problems. In addition, newspapers publish special columns and radio and television stations broadcast programs that tell consumers how to make complaints.

The right to information. Advertising provides a major method by which manufacturers and sellers give information to consumers. The Federal Trade Commission (FTC) regulates advertising and administers several programs that handle deceptive claims. For example, the FTC may order a manufacturer to provide *corrective advertising* if misleading claims have been made.

The FTC and the state governments fight *bait-and-switch selling* and other deceptive sales methods. A bait-and-switch advertisement uses a special sale on a product as "bait" to attract customers to the advertiser's place of business. Salespeople then try to "switch" the customers to a more expensive product.

Various laws protect the consumer's right to adequate, truthful information. One of these laws is the Consumer Credit Protection Act of 1968, often called the Truth in Lending Act. It requires sellers to state clearly the charge made for loans and installment purchases and to express the interest rate as an annual rate. Another law affecting information given consumers is the Fair Packaging and Labeling Act of 1966, also known as the Truth in Packaging and Labeling Act. It requires that the package used for a product provide certain information. This information includes the identity of the product, the manufacturer's name and address, and the net quantity of the contents.

The United States Department of Agriculture requires that the grade of meat and dairy products appear on those items for the benefit of consumers. Many food stores use *unit pricing,* such as the price per ounce or per gram. This system helps consumers determine the best buy among several products in different sizes of packages. Food manufacturers also inform consumers by *freshness labeling,* also called *open dating.* A product is stamped with a date, which is the last day that it should be sold or used to assure quality or freshness.

Consumer organizations contribute much information about products. For example, Consumers' Research, Inc., and Consumers Union test a wide variety of products and publish the results. Consumers' Research is financed entirely by consumers who subscribe to its publications, and Consumers Union is supported chiefly by the sale of subscriptions, plus some contributions. Consumer groups also encourage the development of consumer education programs. Such programs emphasize the rights of consumers and provide information about managing money and making wise purchases.

The right to choose. The government regulates business in order to promote free and fair competition. The Sherman Antitrust Act of 1890 forbids monopolies. The act also prohibits *price fixing,* a stated or implied agreement by several manufacturers to charge a noncompetitive price for a product they all make. The U.S. Department of Justice and the FTC enforce the Sherman Act. The FTC also enforces the Clayton Antitrust Act of 1914 and the Celler-Kefauver Act of 1950. These laws are designed to prohibit businesses from forming combinations that would reduce competition.

Some supporters of consumerism favor regulation by the FTC of the amount of money that businesses spend for advertising. They argue that small or new companies cannot spend large sums for advertising and thus cannot compete with large or older firms. As a result, businesses with larger budgets have considerable control over the market and the prices that consumers pay.

History of the consumer movement

Early buyer-seller relationships. Some of the first attempts to protect consumers occurred during the Middle Ages. Guilds established by craftworkers set standards for products sold by their members. Another form of early consumer protection consisted of laws against *usury,* the lending of money at an excessive rate of interest. These laws regulated the rate of interest that moneylenders could charge borrowers.

Beginnings of consumerism. During the late 1800's and early 1900's, the sale of many impure and unsafe products led to increased consumer interest in legislation that established standards of quality. A number of writers called *muckrakers* exposed abuses by various companies. For example, the novelist Upton Sinclair wrote *The Jungle* (1906), which described filthy conditions in the meat-packing industry. This book helped lead to the Federal Food and Drugs Act of 1906.

The growth of large corporations and monopolies also contributed to an increased interest in consumerism. These giant business companies lacked competition from other firms, and so they regulated the supply of products and charged high prices for them. They also marketed many low-quality products. In the late 1800's, Congress passed the first antitrust and antimonopoly laws to protect consumers from these powerful companies.

As business and industry expanded, changes in technology resulted in new and increasingly complex products. Businesses also began to advertise extensively to distinguish their products from those of other compa-

nies. As a result, the consumer movement began to emphasize the customer's right to have adequate information about products. In 1929, Consumers' Research, Inc., was established to provide testing and rating services for consumers. A group of employees from that organization formed Consumers Union in 1936.

Growth of the movement. During the 1950's and 1960's, consumer awareness increased as a result of efforts by various crusaders. The author Vance Packard, in his books *The Hidden Persuaders* (1957) and *The Wastemakers* (1960), discussed sales promotion methods and certain techniques designed to increase the use of products. One of these techniques was the use of advertising to encourage people to desire various items. Ralph Nader, a leading consumer crusader, maintained in *Unsafe at Any Speed* (1965) that many kinds of automobiles were unsafe. His book led to the National Traffic and Motor Vehicle Safety Act of 1966. This law established safety standards for motor vehicles. Nader and his group of investigators, often called Nader's Raiders, also increased consumer interest in the safety of other products.

During the 1970's, a period of inflation, consumers became increasingly effective in exercising their rights. Inflation helped the growth of consumerism because of greater public concern about the cost and quality of products when prices go up continually. Consumer boycotts of beef, coffee, and sugar succeeded in temporarily lowering the prices of those products in the mid-1970's. During the 1980's, increased concern for health led consumers to demand more nutritional information on food packaging.

Today, consumer groups play a larger role than ever before in supporting the rights of consumers. For example, the Consumer Federation of America (CFA) presents the viewpoints of consumers to federal agencies. Public Citizen, an organization founded by Ralph Nader, conducts research on products, works to influence Congress and state legislatures, and develops educational programs for consumers. The Conference of Consumer Organizations provides assistance in organizing consumer groups. *Barbara B. Murray*

Related articles. Most of the federal agencies discussed in this article have separate articles in *World Book.* See also:

Better business bureau	Monopoly and competition
Clothing (Protecting the public)	Nader, Ralph
Consumer Affairs, United States Office of	National Consumers League
Consumer Federation of America	Packaging
	Pure food and drug laws
Consumers Union	Securities and Exchange Commission
Interstate Commerce Commission	Sinclair, Upton
Meat packing (U.S. government inspection)	Tarbell, Ida M.
	Textile (The textile industry)

See also *Consumerism* in the Research Guide/Index, Volume 22, for a *Reading and Study Guide.*

Additional resources

Consumer Adviser: An Action Guide to Your Rights. Rev. ed. Reader's Digest, 1989.
Mayer, Robert N. *The Consumer Movement: Guardians of the Marketplace.* Twayne, 1989.
Schmitt, Lois. *Smart Spending: A Young Consumer's Guide.* Scribner, 1989. Also suitable for younger readers.

Consumers League, National. See National Consumers League.

Consumers Union is an independent, nonprofit organization that tests and rates products and consumer services. Its full name is Consumers Union of United States. Consumers Union evaluates such things as appliances, machinery, food products, and insurance policies. It also calls attention to what it considers unsafe products, failures by government regulatory agencies, and weaknesses in consumer protection laws. Consumers Union sometimes files lawsuits on behalf of consumer interests.

The organization reports on its tests in *Consumer Reports,* its monthly magazine. Each issue of the magazine includes articles designed to help consumers spend money wisely and to inform them about consumer issues. In addition, Consumers Union publishes books on subjects of interest to consumers and provides information to the public through newspapers, newsletters, radio, and television.

To maintain its reputation for fairness, Consumers Union does not accept advertising in any of its publications and does not accept samples or other gifts from any business interest. Consumers Union was established in 1936. It has offices in Mount Vernon, N.Y.

Critically reviewed by the Consumers Union of United States

Consumption, a disease. See Tuberculosis.

Consumption, *kuhn SUHMP shuhn,* in economics, is the use of goods and services to satisfy needs and desires. Most business activity is aimed at providing goods and services for consumption. Examples of consumption include eating food, wearing clothing, and using soap. People who use goods and services are *consumers.*

The value of goods and services that a family consumes depends almost entirely on its income and wealth. Americans spend more than 95 per cent of their *after-tax income* on consumer goods and services. After-tax income is the amount of yearly income that remains after income taxes and other taxes have been paid.

Families with low incomes tend to spend a larger part of their earnings for essentials such as food and housing than do families with higher incomes. Those with the lowest incomes spend more than they earn and are forced into debt. As incomes rise, families tend to spend a larger part of their earnings for such items as clothing, education, and entertainment. John Maynard Keynes, a noted British economist, was one of the first to emphasize that the general level of consumption in an economy helps determine the general level of income (see **Keynes, John Maynard**).

About two-thirds of all the goods and services produced in the United States each year are used by consumers. The remaining third is used by the government or invested in buildings, manufacturing machinery, and other forms of capital in the United States or other countries. In the United Kingdom, consumers also use about two-thirds of the goods and services produced.

Henry J. Aaron

Related articles in *World Book* include:

Consumerism	Production
Economics (Consumers)	Standard of living
Income	Trade (Trade in the United
Marketing	States)

Contact lens is a device used to correct an eye's nearsightedness or farsightedness. Contact lenses can be made of hard or soft plastic. They float on a thin layer of

Michael Philip Manheim, West Stock   WORLD BOOK photo by Dan Miller

Contact lenses float on the eye's natural tear layer, *above right.* Balanced on the tip of a finger, *above left,* the lenses can be placed on the eye.

tears on the surface of the *cornea* (clear front surface of the eyeball). Contact lenses are curved to focus light rays on the retina. When the light rays are properly focused, a person sees clear images of normal size. Contact lenses provide more natural vision than glasses because they also allow normal side vision.

Most people wear contact lenses instead of glasses to look better and to feel more confident. Athletes and other active people like contact lenses because the lenses are less obstructive than glasses.

Hard contact lenses came into use in the early 1950's. They are made of rigid plastic and are relatively easy to clean and sterilize. Hard contact lenses that allow oxygen to pass through to the eye are called *gas permeable contact lenses.* These lenses are produced from special plastic. For many wearers, gas permeable contact lenses are more comfortable than normal hard contact lenses. Hard contact lenses are useful in correcting such eye disorders as *keratoconus* and *astigmatism.* These are conditions caused by a misshapen cornea.

Soft contact lenses originated in the early 1970's. They are softer and larger than hard contact lenses. Soft contact lenses absorb moisture and contain water. This composition enables the lenses to bend easily and makes them more comfortable than hard contact lenses. Originally it was necessary to remove soft contact lenses from the eye once a day. Now a type of soft contact lenses called *extended-wear contact lenses* can be worn on the eye without removal for up to seven days.

Soft contact lenses are more likely to cause infection than other types of contact lenses because impurities or bacteria may get into the water in the lenses. To avoid infection, wearers of soft contact lenses must regularly and thoroughly clean them in a special solution and sterilize them. A type of extended-wear contact lenses called *disposable contact lenses* can be worn for a week and then discarded and replaced with new ones. These lenses do not require cleaning or sterilizing.

Special types of contact lenses have been developed for unique needs. People with normal vision who want to change the color of their eyes may buy contact lenses that come in different colors and that do not alter vision. Some soft contact lenses are used to treat diseases. They contain medicine that is gradually released to the eye.

Both hard and soft contact lenses have been developed for use as bifocal contact lenses. These lenses are designed to help people who have trouble seeing both at a distance and close up. They are made to replace bi-focal glasses. Wearers look through one part of the lenses to see in the distance and through another part to see close up. The success rate of bifocal contact lenses remains limited for various reasons.

Monovision contact lenses offer another way to correct a problem with near and distant vision. A wearer uses a lens in one eye for close vision and one in the other eye for distant vision. Monovision lenses allow only one eye to be used at a time, and wearers sacrifice some depth perception.   Robert O. Graham

Containerization is a method of transporting cargo by packing it into large containers. This cargo then can be moved as a unit by ship, truck, airplane, or railroad, and from one type of transportation to another. Containerization reduces the time and cost required to load and unload cargo.

Most shipping containers are made of steel. They can carry *general cargo*—that is, anything that can be packaged or that forms a package in itself. Containers also handle hazardous goods and cargo requiring refrigeration or tanks. Most major ports have special cranes that lift containers on and off ships. A container's size de-

Cameramann International, Ltd. from Marilyn Gartman

Containers of products are removed from storage, *above,* and taken to ships or railroad cars for loading and shipment.

pends on its cargo. But most containers measure from 20 to 40 feet (6.1 to 12.2 meters) long and 8 to $9\frac{1}{2}$ feet (2.4 to 2.9 meters) high. Containers transported by air may be smaller. Containerization was first used in 1956. Ships built especially to handle containers are called *cellular vessels* or *container ships.* Today, about 90 per cent of the world's general cargo moves by containerization.

Barbara Yeninas

See also **Freight; Ship** (Container ships); **Railroad** (Freight service); **Transportation** (picture: Intermodal transport).

Contempt, in law, is willful disregard or disobedience of public authority, such as a court or legislative assembly. Contempt is usually shown by failure to obey specific demands, or by insults. Such acts are intended to challenge or reduce public authority and dignity. There are two kinds of contempt of court: those committed in a court, which disturb or interrupt its proceedings, and those that result from a refusal to comply with an order of the court. Both are punishable by fine or imprisonment. See also **Attachment.**   James O. Finckenauer

Continent is a part of the earth's surface that forms one of the great dry-land masses of the world. It usually has extensive plains or plateaus and one or more mountain ranges, and is surrounded or nearly surrounded by water. The continents of the world are Asia (16,992,000 square miles, or 44,009,000 square kilometers); Africa (11,680,000 square miles, or 30,251,000 square kilometers); North America (9,515,000 square miles, or 24,644,000 square kilometers); South America (6,885,000 square miles, or 17,832,000 square kilometers); Antarctica (5,400,000 square miles, or 14,000,000 square kilometers); Europe (4,033,000 square miles, or 10,445,000 square kilometers); and Australia (2,978,000 square miles, or 7,713,000 square kilometers). Technically, Europe is not a continent, but a peninsula of Asia. It is part of what may be called the Eurasian continent, which has a total area of 21,025,000 square miles (about 54 million square kilometers).   Frederick A. Cook

See the articles in *World Book* for each continent. See also **World** (graphs: Facts about the continents).

Continental. See **Money** (The first United States currency).

Continental Association was an agreement adopted by the First Continental Congress of the American Colonies on Oct. 20, 1774. It was designed to defend American rights. The chief provisions were that each colony would (1) stop importing all British and Irish goods and some foreign and West Indian products by Dec. 1, 1774; (2) halt participation in the slave trade effective Dec. 1, 1774; (3) stop consumption of all British and Irish goods and some foreign and West Indian products by March 1, 1775; (4) stop all exports to Britain, Ireland, and the West Indies beginning Sept. 10, 1775; and (5) appoint committees to report violations.

William Morgan Fowler, Jr.

Continental Congress was a convention of delegates from the American Colonies that first met in Philadelphia on Sept. 5, 1774. The meeting grew out of a desire for unity that had spread through the colonies. All the colonies had seen danger to themselves in certain acts of the British Parliament aimed against Massachusetts, especially the Boston Port Act and the Massachusetts Government Act. See **Intolerable Acts.**

The First Continental Congress was attended by 56 delegates representing 12 colonies. Georgia sent no delegates but agreed to support any plans made at the meeting. Leaders of the Congress included Samuel Adams, George Washington, Peyton Randolph, Patrick Henry, Richard Henry Lee, John Adams, John Jay, Joseph Galloway, and John Dickinson. Peyton Randolph of Virginia was chosen president of the Congress, and each of the 12 colonies had equal voting power.

The first Congress sought fair treatment from Great Britain rather than independence. It set forth the position of the colonies toward taxation and trade in a Declaration of Rights, adopted on Oct. 14, 1774. The Congress declared that Parliament had no right to pass laws that affected America, except possibly in the area of foreign

The Second Continental Congress adopted the Declaration of Independence on July 4, 1776. This painting shows members of the Congress voting in Independence Hall in Philadelphia.

Oil painting on canvas (begun late 1700's) by Robert E. Pine and Edward Savage; Historical Society of Pennsylvania, Philadelphia

trade. It claimed the right of each colonial assembly to regulate its own internal affairs.

Probably the boldest act of the Congress was to set up the Continental Association, which bound the colonists not to trade with Great Britain or use British goods until British trade and taxation policies had been changed. The delegates made plans to hold another Congress the following May, if necessary.

Second Continental Congress. The British government ignored the Congress, and fighting broke out between Massachusetts farmers and British troops at Lexington and Concord in April 1775. The Second Continental Congress met in Philadelphia on May 10, 1775. New delegates of note were Benjamin Franklin, Thomas Jefferson, and John Hancock. The Congress took on many governmental duties, uniting the colonies for a fight. An army was organized, and George Washington was appointed commander in chief. On July 8, 1775, the Congress issued a declaration setting forth the need to take up arms and the reasons for doing so. On July 10, it made a final, futile appeal to the king in an effort to right matters without additional fighting.

With the outbreak of war, the Second Continental Congress encouraged the colonies to adopt new republican governments. On July 4, 1776, the Congress approved the Declaration of Independence. Then it drew up an outline for a permanent union of states that resulted in the Articles of Confederation, the first federal constitution of the United States. The second Congress operated under great difficulties, because it depended on the states to carry out many of its decisions. On March 1, 1781, Maryland became the last of the states to ratify the Articles of Confederation. After ratification, the Congress was known as the *Congress of the Confederation,* but many people continued to call it the Continental Congress.

In addition to Peyton Randolph, the presidents of the Congress were Henry Middleton, John Hancock, Henry Laurens, John Jay, Samuel Huntington, Thomas McKean, John Hanson, Elias Boudinot, Thomas Mifflin, Richard Henry Lee, Nathaniel Gorham, Arthur St. Clair, and Cyrus Griffin.   Jack N. Rakove

See also **Articles of Confederation; Congress of the Confederation; Continental Association; Declaration of Independence.**

Additional resources

Burnett, Edmund C. *The Continental Congress.* Greenwood, 1975. First published in 1941.
Marston, Jerrilyn G. *King and Congress: The Transfer of Political Legitimacy, 1774-1776.* Princeton, 1987.
Rakove, Jack N. *The Beginnings of National Politics: An Interpretive History of the Continental Congress.* Johns Hopkins, 1982. First published in 1979.

Continental divide is the term used to designate the line of elevated land that separates areas drained to opposite sides of a continent. In North America it is also called the *Great Divide,* and separates westward-flowing and eastward-flowing waters. In South America, the continental divide follows the western portion of the Andes Mountains. In Europe, the divide separates streams flowing to the Atlantic and Arctic oceans on the north and to the Mediterranean and Black seas on the south. In Asia, the divide separates drainage into the Arctic and Pacific oceans on the north and east from drainage into the Indian Ocean on the south. The African divide separates drainage into the Atlantic Ocean from drainage into the Indian Ocean. See also **Divide** (diagram); **Great Divide.**   Frederick A. Cook

Continental drift. See Plate tectonics.

Continental shelf. See Ocean (The land at the bottom of the sea); **Earth** (map: Where oceans overflow the land).

Continental System was France's attempt to choke off Great Britain's trade with the rest of Europe in the early 1800's. Emperor Napoleon I adopted it as a means of destroying Britain financially. Napoleon began the system with his Berlin Decree of Nov. 21, 1806, which declared Britain to be in a state of blockade. His Milan

Decree of 1807 extended the blockade to neutral ships that stopped in Britain. Between 1808 and 1814, Napoleon tried to enforce the system by fighting the Peninsular War in Spain and Portugal and by invading Russia. The efforts failed and helped cause Napoleon's final defeat in 1815.   Eric A. Arnold, Jr.

See also **Napoleon I** (Fall from power).

Continuing education. See Adult education; American Association for Adult and Continuing Education.

Contour map. See Map (pictures).

Contour plowing. See Conservation (Soil conservation; pictures); **Farm and farming** (Preparing the soil).

Contraband, *KAHN truh band,* in commerce, means *trade forbidden by law.* The word *contraband* most often refers to goods useful in war, such as arms or ammunition. The warships of a country at war may search for, seize, and destroy contraband goods that are being shipped to its enemy in neutral ships. In modern total warfare, almost anything is "useful for military purposes" and may be declared contraband. During World War I (1914-1918), Great Britain declared cotton to be contraband, because Germany used it to manufacture explosives. During World War II (1939-1945), Germany and Great Britain published contraband lists of many items. See also **Blockade.**   Edwin B. Firmage

Contraception. See Birth control.

Contract is an agreement between two or more parties that is enforceable by law. A contract consists of voluntary promises to do or not do certain things. Promises in a contract are legal obligations. In the United States, Canada, and other countries that encourage private enterprise, much business activity depends on contracts. Contracts include promises to deliver or pay for goods, to perform or pay for labor or services, and to buy or rent land or other property.

In general, people or companies may include in their contracts any promises or terms they think fit. However, certain contracts are unenforceable. For example, the courts would not enforce an agreement to bribe a public official. They also may not require parties to obey a contract if one of the parties has clearly taken unfair advantage of another. The courts do not enforce contract obligations undertaken by minors or people who are mentally incompetent.

Most contracts are formed by an offer followed by an acceptance of the offer. In most cases, the offer and acceptance may be communicated either orally or in writing. However, the law requires that some contracts be in writing. These contracts include agreements to sell real estate and agreements that are to be performed over an extended period of time. Such contracts must name all the contracting parties, specify the price and all important terms, and be signed by any party who is to be legally obligated to perform the contract.

Most contracts are enforceable only if each party gets *consideration* (something of value) from the agreement. Consideration can be money, property, a promise, or some right. For example, when an owner sells his or her house, the promised home is the consideration for the buyer. The seller's consideration is the money the buyer promises to pay for the house. Promises that do not involve consideration generally do not create a contract. The promise of the owner to give the house to a friend

for nothing cannot be enforced as a contract.

Before a contract is formed, the parties usually discuss or negotiate its terms. If the parties intend to draw up a written contract, they may shake hands on a general deal before all the specific terms have been defined. In some cases, legal obligations are created by the handshake or by other actions performed prior to the signing of a formal document. After the contract has been formed, the parties may continue to negotiate the details of how it should be carried out, especially if the contract is complex. In many such cases, the parties prefer to work out disagreements on their own rather than ask a court to resolve them. In these cases, the contract may serve only as general guidelines governing the future relationship between the parties.

A contract is said to be *discharged* when the obligations in the agreement have been fulfilled. If either party violates the terms of the contract, a *breach of contract* occurs. A court may award money damages to the other party, or order the breaching party to perform properly.   James L. Winokur

See also **Bond; Lease.**

Contract bridge. See Bridge (card game).

Contractor. See Building trade.

Contrail, *KAHN trayl,* is a thin line of cloud that forms behind aircraft at high altitudes. Contrails consist of tiny water droplets or ice crystals. They form when water vapor in the air *condenses* (becomes liquid) or freezes.

Cameramann International, Ltd. from Marilyn Gartman

Contrails form behind aircraft at high altitudes. Ice crystals from a contrail may cause precipitation to fall from clouds.

Contrails are also called *condensation trails, exhaust trails,* or *vapor trails.*

A contrail may form in two ways. (1) The exhaust from an aircraft engine contains water vapor. This vapor may condense when it mixes with cold air around the plane. Contrails last longest in very cold air, and so they are rarely seen when an aircraft takes off or lands. This way is by far the most common. (2) When a plane moves through the air, water vapor may condense in thin clouds over the wings and behind the wing tips and the tips of the propellers. The condensation occurs because the air temperature drops as the pressure drops.

Contrails may have some effect on the weather. For example, ice crystals from a contrail may cause rain or snow to fall from certain clouds. The crystals act like the chemicals used to "seed" clouds in rainmaking operations. See **Rainmaking.**   Margaret A. LeMone

Contralto, *kuhn TRAL toh,* is the lowest voice a woman can sing, and falls in the lower register of an alto voice. Some parts in music are written either for a woman singing contralto or for a man singing the same part. He is called a *countertenor.*

Control rod. See Nuclear reactor (The control rods; illustration: Parts of a nuclear reactor).

Convection. See Heat (How heat travels); Cloud (How clouds form).

Convector. See Heating (Steam and hot-water heating systems; diagrams).

Convent is a religious community, usually of women, who have taken religious vows and live under religious rule. The term is commonly applied to an order or society of female Christian nuns, and especially to the building in which they live. The head of a convent is usually called a *mother superior,* but may have a different title, such as *abbess* or *prioress.*

The word *convent* comes from the Latin word *conventus,* which means *assembly* or *gathering.* Originally, the word meant any religious house. During the Middle Ages, the Franciscan order used it to distinguish its new form of life from the older abbey or monastery forms.

In a *cloistered* convent, the sisters and novices are isolated from the outside world. In their cloistered life, they seek their own salvation and that of others through a program of worship, prayer, and contemplation. The Carmelites and the Poor Clares are contemplative orders. *Uncloistered* convents include orders, societies, and institutes that conduct schools, maintain hospitals, and provide other types of social services. Examples are the Little Sisters of the Poor and the Daughters of Charity. To some degree, almost all orders seek to combine the two ways of life.

Buddhist and Taoist nuns also live in convents. They devote themselves to contemplative lives, but they are not as fully isolated from society as the Christian contemplative orders.   Anne E. Carr

See also **Nun; Religious life; Monasticism; Cloister.**

Convention. See Political convention.

Conversion. See Coal (Coal research); Petroleum (Refining petroleum).

Converter is a device used to convert electrical energy from alternating current to direct current. An *inverted converter* changes direct current to alternating current. See also **Electric current.**

Convertibility, *kuhn vur tuh BIHL uh tee,* is the absence of restrictions on exchanging the currency of one nation for that of another. Convertibility plays an important role in international trade. For example, an importer from nation A buying goods from nation B must find a way to pay for them. This is much easier if the two currencies are convertible, because all the importer needs to do is go to the bank and purchase a check for an equivalent amount in B's currency. Otherwise, the importer may not be able to buy B's goods if B restricts the availability of its currency. Convertibility exists for the world's major currencies. However, the currencies of China and other Communist nations and of some less developed countries are inconvertible.

Robert M. Stern

See also **Exchange rate; Money** (International finance; table: Exchange rates); **International trade** (Financing international trade).

Conveyor belt is a device that *conveys* (carries) large quantities of material from place to place. It consists of an endless belt that is looped over two pulleys. One of the pulleys is called the *drive pulley,* and supplies the power that keeps the belt moving. Most conveyor belts are powered by an electric motor.

The belt travels over a series of rollers that reduce friction and support the belt. The material moves along the belt at a moderate speed in a straight line. A conveyor belt can carry material at a much steeper grade, or slant, than can a truck or a railroad train. The steepness of the grade is limited only by the slant at which the material will slide down the belt. Conveyor belts such as those used in mines and quarries may be 1 mile (1.6 kilometers) or more in length.

Types of conveyor belts. The belt of a conveyor may be flat and wide, and the materials simply placed on the belt to be carried away. But for moving bulk material, such as sugar or salt, the belt forms a trough so the material can be moved without spilling. Other conveyor belts consist of chains that have buckets hanging from the chain. Some chain belts have either hooks or scoops that pick up the material and carry it from one place to another.

Many times, a conveyor belt makes up only a part of a

Conveyor belt

© John McGrail, Wheeler Pictures

Trough conveyor belts are used to move bulk material.

Eric Carle, Shostal

A moving sidewalk is actually a flat conveyor belt.

Bob Peterson, West Stock

A conveyor belt carries cheese along an assembly line.

much larger conveyor system. If the conveyor system must change directions or turn a corner, the material is dropped from one belt to another belt that moves in the desired direction. In such a system, each belt is called a *flight.* Different flights are needed for each change of direction required.

Uses. Conveyor belts play an important part in mass production. Automobiles, for example, move along the assembly line on a conveyor system (see **Assembly line**). Workers stand in one place, and the materials to be worked on move past them.

In airports, conveyor belts carry luggage from the ticket counter to the baggage room. Many buildings now use moving sidewalks, which consist of a ramplike conveyor belt with handrails. An escalator is a conveyor belt designed to form stairs as it moves around as an endless belt. In meat-packing plants, conveyor belts carry the carcasses of the animals from one station to another to be processed.

Conveyor belts are widely used to load and unload ships, trucks, and railroad cars. One such system moves over 6,000 short tons (5,400 metric tons) of coal an hour in a steady stream from railroad cars to the belt. The belt carries the coal to a loading tower that distributes the coal to the various parts of a ship. Mines transport their ores to ships or factories in much the same way.

Many industries use special types of conveyor belts to make their products. Large bakeries, for example, use conveyor belts to speed up the baking of bread. The mixed dough is placed in pans and put on an endless belt that passes through a walled oven over 100 feet (30 meters) long. It takes about 30 minutes to carry the pans through the oven. The continuous movement of a number of these belts allows large bakeries to bake over 30,000 loaves of bread an hour.   Marvin F. DeVries

See also **Escalator.**

Convoy is a group of merchant ships traveling together for defense against attack. Generally, one or more warships protect the convoy. During World War I (1914-1918) and World War II (1939-1945), most United States and British merchant ships crossing the Atlantic Ocean traveled in convoys. The convoys protected the ships chiefly from attacks by German submarines. The United States built many specialized ships for convoy duty and antisubmarine operations. The largest were warships known as *destroyer escorts* and aircraft carriers called *escort carriers* (see **Destroyer**). Britain and Canada used warships called *frigates* and *corvettes* (see **Warship** [Frigates]).   Norman Polmar

See also **World War II** (The Battle of the Atlantic).

Convulsions are involuntary contractions of groups of muscles often accompanied by loss of consciousness. Convulsions originate in the brain and may indicate damage to brain tissue, such as might result from injury, infections, or tumors. Convulsions may also occur during many illnesses. In young children, convulsions often accompany fever. Multiple convulsions of unknown causes occur in epilepsy.

Convulsions vary in form and degree. Sometimes the victim's whole body becomes rigid. At other times, the victim's body may twist and turn, and the muscles of the face, legs, and arms may twitch. In some types of epilepsy, only one limb, or even just a part of it, may be involved.

A person who has convulsions should be placed on his or her side to prevent choking if vomiting occurs. If the teeth are not tightly clenched, a handkerchief or another soft object may be placed between them to prevent injury to the tongue. A doctor should always be called for a patient with convulsions. Treatment depends on the cause.   Marianne Schuelein

See also **Epilepsy; First aid** (Convulsion and epileptic seizure).

Conway, Thomas. See Cabal; Washington, George (The army).

Cony. See Hyrax; Pika.

Cook, Frederick Albert (1865-1940), an American explorer, claimed he discovered the North Pole in April 1908. His story was questioned when Robert E. Peary returned from a polar expedition in September 1909. Danish scientists investigated and found that Cook could not prove his claims. His claim that he reached the summit of Mount McKinley, Alaska, also was disputed. Cook was imprisoned in 1923 for mail fraud. He was born in Callicoon Depot, N.Y.   John Edwards Caswell

Cook, James (1728-1779), was a British navigator and one of the world's greatest explorers. He commanded three voyages to the Pacific Ocean and sailed around the world twice. Cook became the first European to visit Hawaii and Australia's east coast. His voyages led to the establishment of colonies throughout the Pacific region by several European nations.

Cook had great ambition and curiosity. He declared that his goal was "not only to go farther than anyone had done before but as far as possible for man to go."

Early life. Cook was born in Marton, England, near York. He became an apprentice with a shipping company when he was 18 years old. On his earliest voyages, Cook worked aboard ships that carried coal to English ports.

Cook joined the British Navy in 1755, during the French and Indian War. He carried out a dangerous wartime mission in 1759, when he entered French territory in Canada to survey the St. Lawrence River for the navy. His charts contributed to the British capture of the French city of Quebec later that year.

First voyage to the Pacific. In 1768, the navy appointed Cook to lead a scientific expedition to Tahiti, a Pacific island. His ship, the *Endeavour,* sailed from England in August and reached Tahiti in April 1769. There, the scientists on the expedition watched the planet Venus pass between the earth and the sun. This observation was the main goal of the voyage. However, Cook also had secret orders to seek an unknown continent in the South Pacific. Geographers had long believed that a southern continent kept the world in balance. But Cook did not find it.

In October, Cook became the first European to visit New Zealand. In April 1770, the *Endeavour* sailed into Botany Bay on the east coast of Australia. Cook claimed the entire coast for Great Britain (see **Australia** [History; map]). He returned to England in July 1771. During the voyage, Cook became the first ship commander to prevent an outbreak of scurvy, a disease that had long plagued sailors. Cook had heard reports that scurvy was caused by a lack of fresh fruits and vegetables. He served his sailors fruit and sauerkraut to help prevent the disease.

Detail of an oil portrait by John Webber; National Portrait Gallery, London

James Cook, *above,* a British navigator, explored many islands in the Pacific Ocean. He landed on the Hawaiian Islands in 1778 and was killed by the Hawaiians during a fight in 1779. The British artist John Webber painted *Death of Cook, left,* in the late 1700's.

Detail of an oil painting on canvas; Dixson Galleries, Sydney, Australia

Second Pacific voyage. In July 1772, Cook left England on the *Resolution* in another attempt to find the southern continent. This expedition included a second ship, the *Adventure.*

Cook sailed farther south than any European had ever gone. He faced many hazards in the cold Antarctic waters. Jagged mountains of ice as high as 60 feet (18 meters) often blocked the way. Powerful winds blew icebergs toward the ships, and blinding fog increased the danger, especially at night.

Cook circled Antarctica, but ice surrounded it and prevented him from sighting land. The existence of the continent remained unproven until 1840. See **Antarctica** (Exploration).

In 1773 and 1774, Cook became the first European to visit a number of Pacific islands, including the Cook Islands and New Caledonia. He arrived back in England in July 1775 and was promoted to captain.

The final voyage. In July 1776, Cook set out with two ships, the *Resolution* and the *Discovery,* to look for the *Northwest Passage,* a possible northern sea route between Europe and Asia. Cook first sailed to New Zealand and other Pacific islands. In January 1778, he became the first known European to reach the Hawaiian Islands. Cook named them the Sandwich Islands for the Earl of Sandwich, Britain's chief naval minister.

Later in 1778, Cook sailed to the northwest coast of North America. He was the first European to land on Vancouver Island in British Columbia (see **British Columbia** [Discovery]). Cook then continued up the coast, sailed through Bering Strait, and entered the Arctic Ocean. But walls of ice blocked the expedition, and so

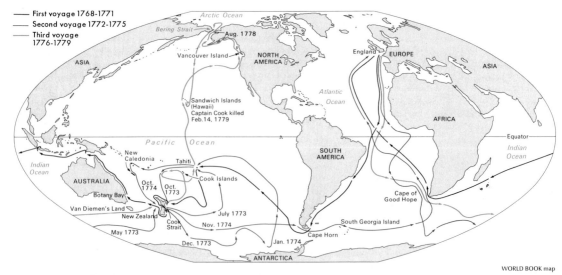

— First voyage 1768-1771
— Second voyage 1772-1775
— Third voyage 1776-1779

WORLD BOOK map

James Cook's explorations included three voyages to the Pacific Ocean. He reached New Zealand in 1769 and sailed to Australia in 1770. From 1772 to 1775, Cook sailed to New Zealand again and crossed the Antarctic Circle. In 1778, he reached the Sandwich Islands (now Hawaii).

Cook headed back to the Sandwich Islands in August.

In February 1779, an islander stole a boat from the *Discovery* at Kealakekua Bay. Cook tried to investigate the theft but was stabbed to death in a fight with islanders on February 14. The expedition returned to England in October 1780.   Vernon F. Snow

See also **Hawaii** (Visitor's guide; European exploration).

Additional resources

Beaglehole, John C. *The Life of Captain James Cook.* Stanford, 1974.

Hoobler, Dorothy and Thomas. *The Voyages of Captain Cook.* Putnam, 1983. For younger readers.

Withey, Lynne. *Voyages of Discovery: Captain Cook and the Exploration of the Pacific.* Morrow, 1987.

Cook, Mount. See Mount Cook.

Cook Islands lie in the South Pacific Ocean, about 1,800 miles (2,900 kilometers) northeast of New Zealand. For location, see **Pacific Islands** (map). The 15 islands of the Cook group are spread out over 850,000 square miles (2.2 million square kilometers) of ocean. They have a total land area of 93 square miles (240 square kilometers) and a total coastline of 90 miles (145 kilometers). The main islands include Rarotonga, Mangaia, Atiu, Aitutaki, and Mauke. The capital, Avarua, is on the northern shore of Rarotonga. The southern islands have fertile soil and a mild climate, Their chief exports include copra, fruits, and tomatoes. Most of the 17,000 people are Polynesians.

In 1773, Captain James Cook became the first known European to reach the islands. Great Britain took control of the islands in 1888, and gave administrative control to New Zealand in 1891. A new constitution gave the islanders control of their internal affairs in 1965. Today, the islands have an arrangement with New Zealand called *free association.* Under free association, the islands are self-governing, the people are citizens of New Zealand, and New Zealand offers the islands military support for defense.   W. B. Johnston

Cooke, Jay (1821-1905), an American financier, was the chief financial agent for the United States during the Civil War. He sold war loans, which totaled well over $1 billion. Cooke was born in Sandusky, Ohio. He worked his way up from a clerkship in a Philadelphia bank to the establishment of his own banking firm in 1861. In 1873, the failure of his company helped bring on a general financial panic. In 1878 and 1879, Cooke made another fortune in Western silver mines.   Kenneth Wiggins Porter

Cooke, Terence James Cardinal (1921-1983), archbishop of New York, was appointed a cardinal of the Roman Catholic Church in 1969 by Pope Paul VI. Cooke, at 48, was the youngest American ever to become a cardinal. Cardinal Cooke was born and raised in New York City. He was ordained in 1945 after graduating from St. Joseph's Seminary in Yonkers, N.Y. He earned a master's degree in social work at the Catholic University of America in Washington, D.C., and taught at Fordham University in New York City. He became archbishop of New York in 1968, and guided the archdiocese during the transition years after Vatican Council II (1962-1965).

Robert P. Imbelli

Cooke, William F. See Telegraph (Development).

Cooking is the preparation of food for eating. Cooking makes food more appetizing and easier to digest. In most cooking, the food is heated. But some cooking, such as the preparation of cold sandwiches and salads, involves no heating. Many people enjoy cooking as a pastime. Skillful cooks take great care in preparing delicious, attractive, and nutritious meals.

Most people can prepare such simple foods as hard-cooked eggs or a lettuce salad without written directions. But many foods, including breads, casseroles, and sauces, turn out best if they are prepared according to a recipe. Numerous cookbooks with a wide variety of recipes are available. Recipes also appear on some food packages and in many magazines and newspapers.

This article discusses basic principles of planning meals and preparing food. Some cookbooks give general tips on both techniques in addition to providing recipes. A beginner should first try simple meals and recipes and then go on to more difficult ones.

Planning meals

Meal planning involves several factors. The food should be nutritious and appealing, and its cost must be within a person's budget. The person also must consider the time required to prepare certain meals.

Planning nutritious meals requires a basic knowledge of the body's nutritional requirements and the nutrients in different foods. Nutritionists divide foods into basic groups and recommend a certain number of daily servings from each group. The **Nutrition** article describes these food groups and lists the recommended number of servings. Meals planned according to these guidelines provide the nutrients a person needs without adding extra calories.

Planning appealing meals. An appealing meal includes foods that have contrasting colors, textures, flavors, and temperatures. The selection of vegetables and fruits can be especially important in adding color to a meal. For example, a meal consisting of sliced turkey, cauliflower, mashed potatoes, white bread, and milk would look unappetizing. A green vegetable and an orange one, instead of cauliflower and potatoes, would make the meal more colorful and appealing. The textures of solid foods range from soft to crunchy, and a meal should include foods that vary in chewiness. Most meals also should include at least one hot food and one cold food. In addition, a person should serve foods that differ in flavor. But a food with a strong flavor should be served with weaker-flavored ones.

Planning economical meals. There are many ways to save money on food and still provide nutritious, tasty meals. Shoppers can watch for reduced prices on food, buy fresh produce only when it is in season, and select less expensive brands of food. In many cases, lower-priced foods can be substituted for higher-priced ones. For example, nonfat milk and nonfat dry milk solids are less expensive than whole milk. Some kinds of fish and poultry cost less than red meat. A person also can serve smaller portions of meat and larger portions of foods such as breads, cereals, and *legumes,* such as peas and dry beans.

Planning time-saving meals. Because of a lack of time, a person sometimes must plan meals that do not require much preparation. *Convenience foods,* which include canned foods, frozen dinners, and precooked meats, require little or no preparation. However, some

WORLD BOOK photos

Cooking is a basic household activity that can also be an enjoyable pastime. Skillful cooks take great care and pleasure in planning and preparing good meals, *left.* They serve foods that are attractive, tasty, and nutritious. An appealing, nourishing meal, *right,* includes a variety of foods that have contrasting colors, textures, flavors, and temperatures.

convenience foods cost more than the basic ingredients that would be used to prepare the same dishes. Time can also be saved by serving uncooked fruits and vegetables. Some main dishes can be prepared and frozen days ahead of time. Then they need only be thawed and heated before being served.

Methods of cooking

The basic methods of cooking include (1) baking, (2) roasting, (3) broiling, (4) frying, (5) boiling, (6) simmering, and (7) steaming. While a food is cooking, salt, pepper, and other seasonings may be added to improve its flavor. Certain foods, called *garnishes,* may be used to make a dish more attractive. They usually are arranged around the food after it has been cooked and before it is served. Common garnishes include parsley, tomato slices, and lemon wedges.

Baking. Food is baked by placing it in a pan in an oven. In most cases, the temperature of the oven ranges from 300 °F to 425 °F (149 °C to 218 °C). The word *baking* usually refers to the cooking of foods that are made from a batter or dough. Such foods include breads, cakes, cookies, and pastries. However, casseroles, a few vegetables and fruits, and some cuts of meats can also be baked.

Roasting is the same as baking. But the word *roasting* is used to describe the baking of certain kinds of meat. For example, a turkey or a leg of lamb is roasted, but a ham is baked. In baking and roasting, the meat is placed on a rack in a shallow pan and usually cooked uncovered in an oven. The temperature usually ranges from 300 °F to 325 °F (149 °C to 163 °C).

Broiling is used mainly to cook meats, but a few kinds of vegetables and fruits are sometimes broiled. The food is placed on a rack directly below or above a continuous source of heat.

Meat can be broiled in an oven by placing it in a *broiler pan,* a shallow pan with a rack inside. The pan lies 3 to 5 inches (8 to 13 centimeters) under the gas flames or electric heating unit. In *barbecuing,* a form of broiling, the meat is cooked on a grill over hot coals. In *panbroiling,* the meat is cooked in a lightly greased skillet over a burner. The fat that melts from the meat is poured out of the pan as it accumulates. In all these methods of broiling, the meat must be turned to cook both sides.

Frying involves heating food in fat, such as butter or vegetable oil, at a temperature of about 375 °F (191 °C). Frying adds calories to food because the food absorbs some of the fat in the pan.

There are three main methods of frying. These methods are: (1) deep-fat frying, (2) shallow frying, and (3) stir-frying. In deep-fat frying, a large amount of fat is heated in a heavy saucepan or a deep-fat fryer, and the food is immersed in the fat. Deep-fat frying is a popular way of cooking chicken, French fried potatoes, and shrimp. In shallow frying, the food is cooked in a small amount of fat in a skillet. Chicken, eggs, fish, and red meat are often shallow-fried. Stir-frying is an Oriental method of cooking meats and vegetables in a skillet or a *wok,* a large, thin metal pan with a round bottom. The meat and vegetables are cut into small pieces and cooked in an extremely small amount of fat. The food is fried at a high temperature for only a few minutes and must be stirred constantly.

Boiling is the heating of foods in boiling water, which has a temperature of about 212 °F (100 °C). It is a common method of cooking vegetables. The vegetables are boiled in a saucepan over a burner.

Simmering is the heating of foods in water that is kept just below the boiling point. Such foods as eggs, legumes, and meats should be simmered rather than boiled. Covered saucepans or *slow cookers* can be used to simmer foods. Slow cookers are electric appliances that simmer foods at low temperatures for up to 10 hours. A person simply puts the food and some water in a slow cooker and sets the temperature.

Steaming is used mostly to cook vegetables. The vegetables are placed on a rack in a saucepan, and water is added. The water should reach below the level of the rack. The saucepan is covered and heated on a burner so that the water boils and forms steam, which surrounds and cooks the vegetables. Steaming takes longer than boiling. However, steamed vegetables retain a greater amount of certain nutrients than boiled vegetables do.

Other methods. Some foods that require a long time to cook, such as stews and dried beans, may be prepared more quickly in a *pressure saucepan*. This utensil cooks foods at high temperatures by means of steam under pressure. Pressure saucepans are also called *pressure cookers.*

Another fast method of cooking uses *microwaves* (short radio waves). Microwave ovens heat foods much faster than gas or electric ovens do. They are especially useful for thawing frozen foods and heating soups, vegetables, and leftovers.

History

No one knows when or how people began to cook. Prehistoric people learned to make fire about $1\frac{1}{2}$ million years ago and probably cooked some food over small, open fires. But even before they made fire, prehistoric

Terms used in cooking

Baste —to brush or pour melted butter, drippings from cooked meat, or another liquid over a food.
Beat —to mix one or more ingredients vigorously with a spoon, an eggbeater, or an electric mixer.
Blanch —to boil a food for a short time.
Braise —to brown a piece of meat and then simmer it in a small amount of liquid in a tightly covered pan.
Bread —to coat a food with breadcrumbs, cracker crumbs, or cereal crumbs.
Brown —to cook a food quickly in a small amount of fat until the food turns golden-brown.
Coddle —to cook a food in water just below the boiling point; to simmer.
Cream —to mix one or more ingredients with a spoon or an electric mixer until the mixture becomes creamy.
Devil —to add hot or tangy seasonings to a food.
Dice —to cut a food into small cubes.
Fold —to add an ingredient to a mixture and gently stir with a spoon or spatula. The utensil is moved across the bottom of the mixing bowl, up one side, and across the top. The motion is repeated until the ingredients are well mixed.
Glaze —to cover a food with a sauce, syrup, or another liquid coating.
Grate —to shred a food by rubbing it against a grater.
Grease —to lightly coat a utensil with fat.
Marinate —to soak a food in a liquid mixture to improve its flavor and texture.
Pare —to peel the skin from a food.
Poach —to simmer a food in water or another liquid.
Purée —to form a paste from a food, usually by cooking the food until it is soft and then pressing it through a sieve.
Sauté —to fry a food until it turns golden-brown.
Skewer —to fasten a food onto a pointed metal or wooden stick.
Skim —to remove the top layer from a liquid food, such as soup or gravy.
Whip —to beat food rapidly so that it becomes foamy.

people may have broiled meat over burning wood taken from fires that had started naturally.

The ancient Egyptians cooked their food mostly over open fires. They also baked bread in clay ovens heated with burning wood or charcoal.

In ancient Rome, people cooked on raised brick hearths. They set large kettles on iron tripods over the fire. The Romans used two kinds of ovens. In one kind of oven, the fire was built inside the oven and allowed to burn until the oven was hot enough for baking. The other type had double walls with a space between them, and a fire was built underneath the oven. The flames and heat circulated in the space between the walls, thus heating the oven.

During the Middle Ages, a period that lasted from the A.D. 400's to the 1500's, people in Europe used fireplaces for cooking. They heated food in a kettle and broiled meat on a rod called a *spit.* Many towns had public ovens because large numbers of people did not have an oven in their home. During the 1600's and 1700's, most people in North America cooked their food in kettles or on spits in their fireplace, as Europeans did. Many fireplaces had built-in ovens. Iron cookstoves, most of which burned wood, became popular during the early 1800's. The first practical coal-burning stove was patented in 1833. See **Range** (History).

Today, most people in developed countries use gas or electric ranges or microwave ovens for cooking. As a result of improvements in these and other appliances, cooking today is much easier and faster than ever. Cooking also has been made easier by the introduction of convenience foods.   Margaret McWilliams

Related articles in *World Book* include:

Barbecue	Indian, American (Food)
Beef (chart: Beef	Kosher
cuts and how to	Meat
cook them)	Microwave oven
Blanching	Nutrition (Store and cook
Boiling point	foods properly)
Camping (Food and water)	Pastry
Colonial life in	Pioneer life in
America (Food; picture:	America (Food)
Farmhouse)	Range
Dutch oven	Solar energy
Food	(Solar cooking)
Food, Frozen	Western frontier
Food preservation	life (Food)

Additional resources

Level I
Better Homes and Gardens After-School Cooking. Meredith, 1987. *Better Homes and Gardens New Junior Cook Book.* Rev. ed. 1989.
Jacobson, Michael, and Hill, Laura. *Kitchen Fun for Kids: Healthy Recipes and Nutrition Facts for 7- to 12-Year-Old Cooks.* Holt, Rinehart, 1991.
Krementz, Jill. *The Fun of Cooking.* Knopf, 1985.
Moore, Carolyn E., and others. *Young Chef's Nutrition Guide and Cookbook.* Barron's, 1990.

Level II
Betty Crocker's Smartcook: The Essential Everyday Cookbook. Prentice-Hall, 1988. *Betty Crocker's Microwave Cookbook.* Rev. ed. 1990.
Child, Julia. *The Way to Cook.* Knopf, 1989.
Delmar, Charles. *The Essential Cook: Everything You Really Need to Know About Foods and Cooking.* Hill Hse. Pub. Co., 1989.
Rombauer, Irma S., and Becker, M. R. *The Joy of Cooking.* Rev. ed. Macmillan, 1985.

Cooley's anemia. See Thalassemia.

**30th President of
the United States 1923-1929**

Harding
29th President
1921-1923
Republican

Coolidge
30th President
1923-1929
Republican

Hoover
31st President
1929-1933
Republican

**Charles G.
Dawes**
Vice President
1925-1929

Keystone

Coolidge, Calvin (1872-1933), was a shy, silent New England Republican who led the United States during the boisterous Jazz Age of the 1920's. He was the sixth Vice President to become President upon the death of a chief executive. Coolidge was vacationing on his father's farm in Vermont when President Warren G. Harding died in 1923. The elder Coolidge, a notary public, administered the oath of office in the dining room. Never before had this ceremony been performed by such a minor official or by a President's father.

In 1924, Coolidge was elected to a full four-year term. He enjoyed great popularity and probably could have been reelected. But he decided to retire. His terse announcement became his most famous statement: "I do not choose to run for President in 1928." Herbert Hoover succeeded him.

Americans respected the views of the closemouthed Coolidge. His reputation for wisdom was based on his common sense and dry wit. He issued few unnecessary public statements and rarely wasted a word.

Coolidge, who had risen to fame as governor of Massachusetts, served as President during the Roaring 20's. Prosperity stimulated carefree behavior and a craving for entertainment. The nation's "flaming youth," featured in the novels of F. Scott Fitzgerald, set the pace. Sports figures became national heroes as Babe Ruth hit 60 home runs in one season and Gene Tunney defeated Jack Dempsey in the famous "long-count" bout. Charles A. Lindbergh made the first solo flight across the Atlantic Ocean. Motion pictures began to talk, with Al Jolson starring in *The Jazz Singer*. George Gershwin brought jazz into the concert hall with his *Rhapsody in Blue*. Americans defied Prohibition, and Al Capone and other gangsters grew rich by bootlegging liquor. A popular song summed up the spirit of the whole era: "Ain't We Got Fun?"

The solemn, frugal Coolidge seemed to be a misfit from another era. But people voted for him even if they did not imitate his conduct. They cherished him for having the virtues of their pioneer ancestors.

Early life

Childhood. Calvin Coolidge was born on July 4, 1872, in Plymouth Notch, a village near Woodstock in central Vermont. He was named for his father, John Calvin Coolidge, but his parents called him *Calvin,* or *Cal.* He dropped the name *John* after leaving college.

Calvin's parents had been childhood playmates in Plymouth Notch. His father was descended from an English family that came to America about 1630. When Calvin was 4 and his sister, Abigail, was 1, his father bought a small farm across the road from the family store. Cal helped with the farm chores and studied in a small stone schoolhouse nearby.

The elder Coolidge served three terms in the Vermont House of Representatives and one term in the state Senate, and held many local public offices. He passed his political shrewdness on to his son.

Education. Coolidge's mother, Victoria Josephine Moor Coolidge, died when he was 12 years old. The next year he entered Black River Academy at nearby Ludlow. He graduated in 1890. His sister, who also attended the school, had died of an intestinal ailment a short time before. He took a short course at St. Johnsbury Academy, and entered Amherst College in 1891.

As a college student, Coolidge showed great interest in political campaigns. He earned only fair grades during his first two years, but graduated *cum laude* in 1895.

Coolidge then read law with the firm of Hammond and Field in Northampton, Mass. He passed the Massachusetts bar examination in 1897, and about seven months later opened his own office in Northampton.

Political and public activities

Entry into politics. Coolidge became an active worker for the Republican Party in 1896. He was elected

The Roaring Twenties were an era of fads and heroes. The women above are doing the Charleston, a dance craze of the period. The American aviator Charles A. Lindbergh, *left,* became a world hero in 1927, when he made the first solo flight across the Atlantic Ocean. This picture was taken just before Lindbergh took off on his flight from New York City to Paris.

The world of President Coolidge

The Immigration Act of 1924 limited the number of immigrants admitted to the United States. It also established a quota system to prevent major changes in the racial or ethnic makeup of the nation's population.

The Golden Age of radio broadcasting began about 1925. Nationwide audiences listened to such programs as "The A & P Gypsies" and "The Voice of Firestone."

The Scopes Trial, in 1925, upheld the right of a state to ban the teaching of evolution in public schools.

The first successful liquid-fuel rocket was launched in 1926 by Robert H. Goddard, the American rocket pioneer.

Jazz was the leading form of popular music. Jazz musicians who became stars during the mid-1920's included Louis Armstrong, Duke Ellington, and Fletcher Henderson.

Babe Ruth of the New York Yankees hit 60 home runs during the 1927 baseball season, a record that stood until 1961.

The Kellogg-Briand Peace Pact was signed by 15 nations in 1928 and eventually by nearly all the nations of the world. The signers of the treaty, also called the Pact of Paris, agreed not to use war to solve international problems.

***Penicillium* mold,** which produces the antibiotic drug *penicillin,* was discovered in 1928 by Sir Alexander Fleming, a British bacteriologist.

Brown Bros.; Library of Congress

to the Northampton city council in 1898, and became city solicitor in 1900. He won reelection in 1901, but lost in 1902.

In 1904, Coolidge met his future wife, Grace Anna Goodhue (Jan. 3, 1879-July 8, 1957), a teacher at the Clarke School for the Deaf in Northampton. She was gay, talkative, and fun-loving—just the opposite of the quiet Coolidge. Shortly after their marriage on Oct. 4, 1905, he arrived home from his office with a bag containing 52 pairs of socks, all with holes. When his bride asked if he had married her to darn his socks, Coolidge, with characteristic bluntness, replied: "No, but I find it mighty handy." The Coolidges had two sons, John (1906-   ), who became a business executive, and Calvin, Jr. (1908-1924).

Coolidge was elected to the Massachusetts house of representatives in 1906, and was reelected the next year. He won election as mayor of Northampton in 1909, and was returned to office in 1910. From 1912 to 1915 Coolidge served in the state senate, with two terms as president of that body. He was elected lieutenant governor in 1915, and twice won reelection. He was elected governor in 1918.

As governor, Coolidge became nationally famous during the Boston police strike of 1919. In defiance of

police department rules, a group of Boston police officers had obtained a union charter from the American Federation of Labor. Police Commissioner Edwin U. Curtis suspended 19 of the union's leaders, and the next day almost three-fourths of Boston's more than 1,500 police officers went on strike.

Bands of hoodlums roamed Boston for two nights, smashing windows and looting stores. Coolidge mobilized the state guard, and order was restored. When Curtis fired the 19 suspended police officers, Samuel Gompers, president of the AFL, protested to Coolidge. In reply, Coolidge made his famous declaration: "There is no right to strike against the public safety by anybody, anywhere, any time."

Coolidge won reelection in 1919 by a record vote. In

Important dates in Coolidge's life

1872 (July 4) Born in Plymouth Notch, Vt.
1905 (Oct. 4) Married Grace Anna Goodhue.
1906 Elected to Massachusetts House of Representatives.
1909 Elected mayor of Northampton, Mass.
1911 Elected to Massachusetts Senate.
1915 Elected lieutenant governor of Massachusetts.
1918 Elected governor of Massachusetts.
1920 Elected Vice President.
1923 (Aug. 3) Sworn in as President.
1924 Elected to full term as President.
1933 (Jan. 5) Died in Northampton, Mass.

Calvin Coolidge Memorial Foundation

Coolidge's birthplace was this house in Plymouth Notch, Vt., near Woodstock. Coolidge spent most of his childhood there.

1920, he received some votes for the presidential nomination at the Republican national convention that chose Senator Warren G. Harding of Ohio. The delegates gave Coolidge the vice presidential nomination on the first ballot. Harding, friendly and easy-going, and Coolidge, silent and unsmiling, won an overwhelming victory over their Democratic opponents, Governor James M. Cox of Ohio and Assistant Secretary of the Navy Franklin D. Roosevelt.

Vice President. At Harding's invitation, Coolidge regularly attended meetings of the Cabinet. He was the first Vice President to do so.

Even in the social whirl of Washington, Coolidge remained unchanged. He rarely smiled, almost never laughed, and sat silently through official dinners. At one affair, a woman told him she had bet that she could get more than two words out of him. Replied Coolidge: "You lose."

Early on the morning of Aug. 3, 1923, while vacationing on his father's farm, Coolidge was awakened with the startling news of Harding's death. He dressed and knelt in prayer, then walked downstairs to the dining room. There, by the light of a kerosene lamp, his father administered the presidential oath at 2:45 a.m. After that, Coolidge went back to bed—and slept. Years afterward, when asked to recall his first thought upon becoming President, he replied: "I thought I could swing it."

Eighteen days later, Coolidge had a second oath of office administered by a justice of the Supreme Court of the District of Columbia. Attorney General Harry M. Daugherty had questioned the validity of the first oath, because Coolidge's father had authority to swear in only state officials of Vermont.

Coolidge's Administration (1923-1929)

Cabinet. Only three members of Harding's Cabinet remained in office throughout the Coolidge Administration. They were Secretary of the Treasury Andrew W. Mellon, Postmaster General Harry S. New, and Secretary of Labor James J. Davis. Herbert Hoover, secretary of commerce under Harding, served until he resigned in 1928 to run for President.

Corruption in government. Coolidge entered the White House just as the Teapot Dome and other scandals of the Harding Administration became public. Coolidge made no effort to shield the guilty, and his personal honesty was never questioned. In 1924, he forced the resignation of Attorney General Daugherty and other high officials who had been connected with the scandals. See **Harding, Warren Gamaliel** (Government scandals); **Teapot Dome.**

"Constructive economy." Coolidge continued Harding's policy of supporting American business at home and abroad. He favored a program of what he called "constructive economy," and declared that "the chief business of the American people is business." The government continued high tariffs on imports in an effort to help American manufacturers. Although Congress reduced income taxes, revenue from taxes increased and the administration reduced the national debt by about a billion dollars a year. Congress also restricted immigration beyond what it had done in 1921. Coolidge vetoed the World War I veteran's bonus bill, but Congress passed it over his veto.

Detail of an oil painting on canvas; © White House Historical Association

Grace Coolidge, Coolidge's wife, was a teacher of the deaf before their marriage. She posed for this portrait by the American artist Howard Chandler Christy in 1924.

Coolidge's election

Place of nominating convention ..... Cleveland
Ballot on which nominated 1st
Democratic opponent .... John W. Davis
Electoral vote* .... 382 (Coolidge) to
                                          136 (Davis)
Popular Vote .... 15,717,553 (Coolidge)
                                          to 8,386,169 (Davis)
Age at second inauguration 52

*For votes by states, see **Electoral College** (table).

Vice President and Cabinet

Vice President .... *Charles G. Dawes
Secretary of state .... *Charles Evans Hughes
                                       *Frank B. Kellogg (1925)
Secretary of the treasury .... *Andrew W. Mellon
Secretary of war .... John W. Weeks
                                       Dwight F. Davis (1925)
Attorney general .... Harry M. Daugherty
                                       *Harlan F. Stone (1924)
                                       John G. Sargent (1925)
Postmaster general .... Harry S. New
Secretary of the Navy .... Edwin Denby
                                       Curtis D. Wilbur (1924)
Secretary of the interior .... Hubert Work
                                       Roy O. West (1928)
Secretary of agriculture .... Henry C. Wallace
                                       Howard M. Gore (1924)
                                       William M. Jardine (1925)
Secretary of commerce .... *Herbert Hoover
                                       William F. Whiting (1928)
Secretary of labor .... James J. Davis

*Has a separate biography in *World Book.*

A paradox of the Coolidge era was that the President stood for economy and a simple way of life, and yet enjoyed great popularity with a public that largely had thrown thrift to the winds. Some economists warned that this period of prosperity would end in a dreadful depression. But most Americans believed that good times had come to stay. Coolidge did not try to stop the speculation which contributed to the stock-market crash of 1929 seven months after he left office.

Farmers did not share in the general prosperity. Farm prices had fallen, and the purchase of farm products by other nations had declined because of a worldwide surplus of agricultural products. Coolidge twice vetoed a bill to permit the government to buy surplus crops and sell them abroad. Coolidge also pocket-vetoed a bill that would have let the government operate the Muscle Shoals power facilities as an electric power project (see **Muscle Shoals; Veto**).

"Keep Cool with Coolidge." Coolidge had no important rivals for the Republican presidential nomination in 1924. After naming him on the first ballot, the party's national convention chose Charles G. Dawes, Director of the Bureau of the Budget, for Vice President. The Democrats nominated John W. Davis, former ambassador to Great Britain, for President, and Governor Charles W. Bryan of Nebraska for Vice President. Dissatisfied members of both parties formed the Progressive party. They nominated Senator Robert M. La Follette of Wisconsin for President and Senator Burton K. Wheeler of Montana for Vice President.

Both Democrats and Progressives urged defeat of the Republicans because of the Harding scandals. Republicans replied with the slogan "Keep Cool with Coolidge." Coolidge and Dawes received more than half of the popular votes cast in the election. On March 4, 1925, Chief Justice William Howard Taft became the first former President to administer the presidential oath of office. Coolidge's inaugural address was the first to be broadcast by radio.

Foreign affairs were marked by two main achievements: the improvement of relations with Mexico and the negotiation of the multilateral Kellogg-Briand Peace Pact to outlaw war (see **Kellogg-Briand Peace Pact**). Coolidge appointed Dwight W. Morrow as ambassador to Mexico. Morrow settled some old disputes and also obtained valuable concessions from Mexico for American and British owners of oil property.

Although Coolidge opposed joining the League of Nations, he favored membership in the World Court. But the Senate placed what he called "unworthy" conditions on membership, and the President let the matter drop. Earlier, in 1923 and 1924, Dawes had directed an international committee that worked out a plan by which Germany could pay its World War I *reparations* (compensation for damages). See **Dawes Plan**.

Life in the White House offered an interesting contrast between the taciturn Coolidge and his lively, charming wife. The difference was particularly noticeable at official receptions.

The President had an interest in many behind-the-scenes details of running the White House. He enjoyed appearing unexpectedly in the kitchen to inspect the iceboxes and to comment on future menus. He once protested mildly because he thought 6 hams were too

---

Quotations from Coolidge

The following quotations come from some of Calvin Coolidge's speeches and writings.

Do the day's work. If it be to protect the rights of the weak, whoever objects, do it.
Speech to the Massachusetts Senate, 1913

And be brief; above all things, Be Brief.
Speech to the Massachusetts Senate, January 1915

There is no right to strike against the public safety by anybody, anywhere, any time.
Telegram to the American labor leader Samuel Gompers during a strike by police in Boston, Sept. 14, 1919

. . . the chief business of the American people is business.
Speech to the American Society of Newspaper Editors, Washington, D.C., Jan. 17, 1925

This Nation believes thoroughly in an honorable peace. . . . It has never found that such a peace could be maintained only by a great and threatening array of arms.
Inaugural Address, March 4, 1925

. . . no Nation ever had an army large enough to guarantee it against attack in time of peace or insure its victory in time of war.
Speech, Oct. 6, 1925

I do not choose to run for President in 1928.
Statement to reporters, Aug. 2, 1927

Prosperity is only an instrument to be used, not a deity to be worshiped.
Speech in Boston, June 11, 1928

---

many for 60 dinner guests. Coolidge also liked to play practical jokes on the staff. He would ring for the elevator, then stride quickly down the stairs, or push all the buttons on his desk just to see all his aides run in at once.

Tragedy struck the Coolidges shortly after his nomination in 1924. Their son Calvin developed a blister on a toe while playing tennis with his brother on the White House courts. The resulting infection spread, and the 16-year-old youth died of blood poisoning. "When he went," Coolidge wrote in his autobiography, "the power and the glory of the presidency went with him." In 1926, the President's father died.

"I do not choose to run . . ." The Coolidges traveled to the Black Hills of South Dakota for a summer vacation in 1927. On August 2, the day before the fourth anniversary of his presidency, Coolidge called newsmen to his office in the Rapid City high school. He handed each reporter a slip of paper on which appeared the words: "I do not choose to run for President in 1928."

Coolidge's announcement caught the nation by surprise, because he had given no clue as to his plans. Coolidge wrote in his autobiography that "The chances of having wise and faithful public service are increased by a change in the presidential office after a moderate length of time." He also mentioned the "heavy strain" of the presidency, and expressed doubt that Mrs. Coolidge could serve four more years as First Lady "without some danger of impairment of her strength."

Coolidge had a typical response when reporters asked him to comment upon leaving the capital: "Goodby, I have had a very enjoyable time in Washington."

Later years

The Coolidges returned to Northampton, but the stream of tourists past their home made it impossible to enjoy a quiet life. In 1930, Coolidge bought an estate in Northampton called The Beeches, which had iron gates to keep curious visitors at a distance.

Coolidge published his autobiography in 1929, first in magazine installments, then in book form. The next year, he began writing a series of daily newspaper articles called "Thinking Things Over with Calvin Coolidge." He wrote chiefly about government, economics, and politics. He had become a life trustee of Amherst College in 1921, and was named a director of the New York Life Insurance Company in 1929.

The stock market crash in October 1929, and the resulting nationwide depression distressed Coolidge, who felt that he might have done more to prevent it. But following the renomination of Herbert Hoover in 1932, he said that the depression would have occurred regardless of which party had been in power.

Coolidge became increasingly unhappy as the depression deepened during the fall and winter of 1932. On Jan. 5, 1933, Mrs. Coolidge found him lying on the floor of his bedroom, where he had died of a heart attack. He was buried beside his son and father in the Plymouth Notch cemetery.

Mrs. Coolidge sold The Beeches and built another home in Northampton, where she lived until her death on July 8, 1957. Coolidge had written: "For almost a quarter of a century she has borne with my infirmities, and I have rejoiced in her graces." George H. Mayer

Related articles in *World Book* include:

Dawes, Charles G.
Harding, Warren G.
Hoover, Herbert
Mellon, Andrew W.

President of the United States
Roaring Twenties
Vice President of the United
States

Outline

I. **Early life**
  A. Childhood   B. Education
II. **Political and public activities**
  A. Entry into politics   C. Vice President
  B. As governor
III. **Coolidge's Administration (1923-1929)**
  A. Cabinet   D. "Keep Cool with Cool-
  B. Corruption in govern-   idge"
    ment   E. Foreign affairs
  C. "Constructive economy" F. Life in the White House
            G. "I do not choose to run . . ."
IV. **Later years**

Questions

What were some unusual features about Coolidge's inaugurations as President?
What made Governor Coolidge nationally famous?
Why did Coolidge abandon the idea of trying to get the United States into the World Court?
When was the slogan "Keep Cool with Coolidge" used?
Why was Coolidge so popular with the people?
How did the investigations of corruption in government affect Coolidge?
In what ways did Coolidge's outlook on life differ from that of the American people as a whole?
What was Coolidge's most famous statement?
How did Coolidge squelch a woman who had bet that she could get him to chat with her?
What tragedy struck Coolidge during his presidency?

Additional resources

Coolidge, Calvin. *The Autobiography of Calvin Coolidge.* Coolidge Memorial, 1989. First published in 1929.
Curtis, Jane, and others. *Return to These Hills: The Vermont Years of Calvin Coolidge.* Curtis-Lieberman, 1985.

Fuess, Claude M. *Calvin Coolidge: The Man from Vermont.* Greenwood, 1977. First published in 1940.
Kent, Zachary. *Calvin Coolidge: Thirtieth President of the United States.* Childrens Press, 1988. For younger readers.
McCoy, Donald R. *Calvin Coolidge: The Quiet President.* Univ. Pr. of Kansas, 1988. First published in 1967.

Cooling system. See **Air conditioning.**
Coon. See **Raccoon.**
Coonhound. See **Black and tan coonhound.**
Cooper. See **Barrel.**
Cooper, Gary (1901-1961), was an American motion-picture actor who appeared in more than 90 films. His cowboy roles in such movies as *The Virginian* (1929) and *The Westerner* (1940) made him a symbol of the courageous pioneer of the American West. In these and other films, including *Meet John Doe* (1941) and *Friendly Persuasion* (1956), Cooper came to represent the common person fighting evil. Cooper won Academy Awards for his performances in *Sergeant York* (1941) and *High Noon* (1952).

Cooper's real name was Frank James Cooper. He was born in Helena, Mont. He first gained fame as a romantic leading man in such films as *A Farewell to Arms* (1932). He first won critical praise in Frank Capra's sentimental comedy *Mr. Deeds Goes to Town* (1936).

Rachel Gallagher

United Press Int.
Gary Cooper

Cooper, James Fenimore (1789-1851), was an American novelist and social critic. He is best known for *The Leather-Stocking Tales,* five novels about Natty Bumppo, a frontiersman. The character has other names in the series, including Leatherstocking. In *The Leather-Stocking Tales,* Cooper became the first author to seriously portray American frontier scenes and characters.

In *The Leather-Stocking Tales,* Cooper described Natty Bumppo's retreat from the advancing settlement of the forest. The novels introduce Natty Bumppo as a young man and follow him to old age and death. *The Leather-Stocking Tales,* in the order of the hero's life, are *The Deerslayer* (1841), *The Last of the Mohicans* (1826), *The Pathfinder* (1840), *The Pioneers* (1823), and *The Prairie* (1827). These action-filled stories contrast two ways of life. Natty Bumppo and his brave, noble Indian friends live a life of freedom close to nature. The settlers bring civilization and social order, but they also selfishly or thoughtlessly misuse the wilderness.

Cooper's conservative ideas about society are reflected in many of his writings. His works show his concern for the freedom of individuals and the rights of property owners. Cooper declared that he believed in democracy. However, he said he feared that majority rule would bring disorder and injustice. Although he was deeply patriotic, Cooper thought that the United States should be governed by a small aristocracy of cultured and public-spirited landowners.

Cooper wrote several nonfiction works criticizing American life. The best known include the essays *A Let-*

ter to his Countrymen (1834) and *The American Democrat* (1838). He also wrote fiction about his ideals on civic leadership, including *Homeward Bound* (1838) and *Home as Found* (1838). Cooper defends property rights in three novels called *The Little-page Manuscripts.* They are *Satanstoe* (1845), *The Chainbearer* (1845), and *The Redskins* (1846).

Detail of an oil portrait by Asa Weston Twitchell; The New-York Historical Society, New York City

James Fenimore Cooper

Cooper wrote the first American novel about the sea, *The Pilot* (1823). This romance has a memorable character, Long Tom Coffin, who, like Natty Bumppo, is a daring figure who lives close to nature. Cooper also wrote other historical tales of exciting sea chases.

Cooper was born in Burlington, N.J. He was raised in the scenic lakeside community of Cooperstown, N.Y., which was named for his father, William Cooper. *The Pioneers* and *The Deerslayer* are set in this lake region. Cooper served in the U.S. Navy from 1808 to 1811. He settled in upstate New York, intending to become a gentleman farmer.

Cooper wrote his first novel, *Precaution,* in 1820, but it received little critical praise. His next novel was *The Spy* (1821), a story about families during the Revolutionary War. Its immediate success encouraged Cooper to devote himself to writing.   Alan Gribben

Additional resources

Grossman, James. *James Fenimore Cooper.* Stanford, 1967. First published in 1949.
James Fenimore Cooper: A Collection of Critical Essays. Ed. by Wayne Fields. Prentice-Hall, 1979.
Ringe, Donald A. *James Fenimore Cooper.* 2nd ed. Twayne, 1988.

Cooper, Leroy Gordon, Jr. (1927-   ), a United States astronaut, was the first person to make two orbital space flights. Virgil I. Grissom made two space flights before Cooper did, but Grissom did not orbit the earth during his first flight.

On May 15-16, 1963, Cooper circled the earth 22 times in the Mercury spacecraft *Faith 7.* He and Charles Conrad, Jr., orbited the earth 120 times on Aug. 21-29, 1965, in the Gemini 5 spacecraft. Gemini 5 was the first spacecraft to use *fuel cells,* devices that produce electricity from the chemical reaction between a fuel and oxygen. The flight lasted 190 hours 56 minutes and proved that people could live in a weightless state for the length of a trip to the moon.

Cooper was born in Shawnee, Okla. He attended the University of Hawaii from 1946 to 1949. Cooper received an Army commission through the university's ROTC program but transferred the commission to the Air Force. He graduated from the Air Force Institute of Technology in 1956 and became a test pilot in 1957. Cooper was selected as one of the seven original astronauts in 1959. He resigned from the astronaut program in 1970 and entered private business.   Lillian D. Kozloski

Cooper, Peter (1791-1883), was an American inventor, manufacturer, and philanthropist. He built a locomotive to demonstrate the use of steam power. He also helped

develop the American iron industry. Cooper helped Cyrus Field lay the underseas Atlantic Cable, and founded the Cooper Union. The Cooper Union provided free instruction in art, science, and engineering.

Cooper began earning a fortune in the 1820's, when he successfully manufactured glue and gelatin. He stayed in this business all his life. He also invested in real estate. In 1830, he completed his famous locomotive, *Tom Thumb,* which was especially designed for sharp curves and hills. With his son, Edward, and his son-in-law, Abram Hewitt, Cooper pioneered in the manufacture and sale of iron rails and structural iron beams. During the 1850's and 1860's, he helped promote telegraph and cable companies.

Throughout his life, Cooper took an active interest in civic affairs. He worked effectively for public education, improved water supplies, and better police and fire protection. After the Civil War, he supported political and

Baltimore & Ohio Railroad

The *Tom Thumb* was a steam locomotive built by American inventor and manufacturer Peter Cooper. The locomotive, completed in 1830, demonstrated the ability of steam engines to pull railroad cars. A replica of the original is shown here.

social reforms. He ran for President on the Greenback ticket when he was 85. Cooper published the book *Ideas for a Science of Good Government* (1883).

Cooper was born in New York City, but spent his youth in Peekskill, N.Y. He soon showed a talent for mechanics and invention. Although he had only a limited education, he received a practical training in hatmaking, brewing, and other trades. At 17, he was apprenticed to a coachbuilder, and he later worked as a machine builder.   W. Bernard Carlson

See also **Railroad** (History).

Cooper, Susan (1935-   ), an English author, won the 1976 Newbery Medal for her novel *The Grey King* (1975). This book was the fourth in her series of mystery stories called *The Dark Is Rising.* The stories tell about several British children and their roles in the struggle between the forces of good and evil. The earlier works in the series were *Over Sea, Under Stone* (1966), *The Dark Is Rising* (1973), and *Greenwitch* (1974). The fifth book, *Silver on the Tree* (1977), ended the series.

Cooper was born in Buckinghamshire. She moved to the United States in 1963.   Kathryn Pierson Jennings

Cooperative, *koh AHP ruh tihv,* is a business owned by the people who use its services. Some cooperatives sell goods or services produced by their members. In other cooperatives, farmers or other consumers buy as a group directly from suppliers. By reducing expenses, these organizations often provide lower costs for consumers and higher earnings for producers. About a third of the people in the United States belong to one or more cooperatives.

How cooperatives work

Members of the cooperative share equally in controlling the organization. They purchase or earn shares in the cooperative, providing the capital necessary to operate the business. Profits are used to improve the business or are returned to members. The members hold meetings annually to elect directors from among themselves. The directors hire managers to run the day-to-day activities of the cooperative.

Most cooperatives operate under six principles adopted by the International Cooperative Alliance in 1966. These principles are: (1) The cooperative is open to any person who will use its services and accept the responsibilities of membership. (2) Each member has one vote, regardless of how many shares the member holds. A few cooperatives assign the number of votes according to use of the cooperative. (3) The cooperative pays limited interest on its shares. The laws of most states set a maximum of 8 per cent interest or less. (4) All profits are returned to members according to how much they use the business. The cooperative usually pays the returns both in cash and in cooperative dividends. (5) The cooperative educates members to help them in making business decisions. It also helps the public understand how cooperatives operate. (6) Cooperatives work together at local, regional, national, and international levels to promote the cooperative movement.

Kinds of cooperatives

The chief kinds of cooperatives include (1) supply, or purchasing, cooperatives, (2) marketing cooperatives, (3) housing cooperatives, (4) credit unions, and (5) service cooperatives.

Supply, or purchasing, cooperatives are retail stores owned and operated by some or all of their customers. These cooperatives buy goods from farmers, private manufacturers, or wholesalers. By buying in large quantities, they pay reduced prices. They then sell the goods, usually at regular prices, to the public as well as to members. Members later receive refund payments based on the amount of their purchases.

The main types of supply cooperatives are *consumer cooperatives* and *farm supply cooperatives.* Consumer cooperatives sell food, household supplies, and other goods. Farm supply cooperatives specialize in farm supplies, such as feed, fertilizer, and seed.

Marketing cooperatives are groups of farmers who join together to get higher prices for their products. The cooperatives collect, process, sell, and ship the products of their members. Most of these groups have their own canneries, warehouses, and other facilities. Such cooperatives handle many well-known brands of food. For example, Sunkist is the trademark of a California citrus growers' cooperative. Other well-known cooperative brands include Land O Lakes dairy products, Ocean Spray cranberries, and Sun-Maid raisins.

Housing cooperatives are owned by people who form a corporation to buy the buildings in which they live. The individuals buy shares in the corporation. The shares entitle them to occupy an apartment or house in the cooperative, but they do not actually own their units. The members share maintenance costs.

Credit unions are the most numerous type of cooperative in the United States. They are formed by people with a common bond. For example, the members may work for the same company or belong to the same church or labor union. The members pool their savings. When one of them has to borrow money, he or she may borrow from the union at a low rate of interest.

Service cooperatives provide many services. Electrical cooperatives generate and sell electrical power in rural areas where private power companies cannot make enough profit. Service cooperatives also supply irrigation and telephone service in such areas. Members of a group health cooperative receive medical care for a monthly or yearly fee paid in advance.

Some mutual insurance companies are cooperatives jointly owned and controlled by the people who are insured by them. Cooperatives called *funeral societies* or *memorial associations* arrange contracts with funeral directors to provide simple, reasonably priced funerals for members. Other cooperatives provide automobile repair, legal help, and many other services.

Cooperatives around the world

Cooperatives are most common in the industrial nations, including Canada, Japan, the United States, and many countries of Western Europe. The developing nations of Africa, Asia, and Latin America have far fewer such organizations.

In Canada, about a third of the people belong to cooperatives. These enterprises provide farm supplies, health care, housing, loans, and many other goods and services. Most Canadian wheat farmers market their crops through large cooperatives called *wheat pools.* One of them, the Saskatchewan Wheat Pool, is the world's largest marketing cooperative.

In other countries, cooperatives are most widespread in the Scandinavian nations—Denmark, Norway, and Sweden. Consumer cooperatives do about 15 per cent of the retail business there. Most of the farmers belong to marketing cooperatives, and all three countries have much cooperative housing. Many Swedes regard cooperatives as halfway between capitalism, in which individuals own industry, and socialism, in which the government owns it. In Sweden, which has both private industry and government-owned industry, cooperatives are often called the *middle way.* Other nations with many cooperatives include Finland, France, Iceland, Italy, Switzerland, and the United Kingdom.

Israel has two types of cooperative farming settlements, *moshavim* and *kibbutzim.* The farmers in a moshav have their own plots of land, but those in a kibbutz work on a communal farm. Both types of settlements buy supplies and market crops cooperatively.

In North Korea, most farms are cooperatives known as *collective farms.* These farms are controlled by the country's Communist government. Workers on the collective farms receive cash payments and a share of the farms' products. They also may help manage the farms.

History

Most historians trace the beginnings of the modern cooperative movement to the early 1800's. Farmers who wanted more control over the prices they received for their products formed marketing cooperatives. One of the first of these organizations in the United States was a cooperative creamery established in 1810 by dairy farmers in Goshen, Conn. Farmers also formed purchasing cooperatives, in which they pooled their orders for coal, seed, and other products so they could buy in large quantities. A farmers' organization called the National Grange, founded in 1867, promoted both types of cooperatives. The Knights of Labor and other labor unions of the 1800's established consumer cooperatives to provide cheaper goods for low-paid workers.

In the early 1900's, the U.S. government began to support farmer cooperatives. The Capper-Volstead Act of 1922 recognized the right of farmers to form such organizations. It stated that organizing a cooperative did not violate antitrust laws. The Cooperative Marketing Act of 1926 established what is now the Agricultural Cooperative Service. This agency of the U.S. Department of Agriculture helps organize farmer cooperatives and improve their effectiveness.

During the 1960's and 1970's, rising prices created an increased interest in consumer cooperatives. Many people formed small neighborhood cooperatives called *buying clubs* to save money on groceries. The members took turns buying fruits, vegetables, and other foods from farms or wholesale markets and distributed the items among themselves.

Critically reviewed by the National Cooperative Business Association

Related articles in *World Book* include:

Credit union	Kibbutz
Farm and farming (Farming as a business)	Mutual company
	National Farmers Union
Farm Credit System	Owen, Robert
Housing (Cooperative housing)	Truck farming

Cooperative education is a method of education that combines classroom studies with practical work experience. Cooperative education programs typically involve formal written agreements between the school and employers. These agreements allow students to hold jobs, usually for pay, that are related to the students' fields of study or career goals. For example, a student in journalism may work for a local newspaper.

A faculty member, frequently called a *cooperative education coordinator,* finds jobs that fit the goals of students and of the cooperative program. The "coop" coordinator and the employer judge the performance of the student, and the student usually receives some form of graduation credit for satisfactory work. Such programs got their name because businesses, industries, and organizations cooperate with schools in employing students. The programs are also called *internships, cooperative work experience, work-study, career exploration, diversified occupations,* and *off-campus experience.*

Cooperative education operates in both colleges and high schools. In the United States, over 200,000 students at about 1,000 community colleges and 4-year colleges and universities are enrolled in cooperative education programs. About 1 million high school students take part in such programs. Schools in Canada, China, the United Kingdom, and other countries have similar programs.

Cooperative education began in the United States in the early 1900's. Herman Schneider, an engineering professor, developed the first cooperative education program in 1906 for engineering students at the University of Cincinnati. Other schools adopted similar programs during later years. Since 1960, cooperative education has expanded rapidly into all fields of study.

Kinds of programs. Cooperative education programs operate in various ways at different schools. There are four basic kinds of programs: (1) alternating, (2) parallel, (3) field experience, and (4) extended-day.

In alternating programs, the students are divided into two groups. One group attends classes while the members of the other group work at their jobs. After a certain length of time, usually a semester, the two groups exchange places. Therefore, a position is filled continuously.

In parallel programs, each student attends school part of the day and works part of the day. Many high schools and two-year colleges offer such a program.

In field experience programs, all participating students leave school for an extended work assignment. The length of the period spent on the assignment varies from 4 to 10 weeks.

In extended-day programs, students work full-time at a regular paying job and attend school part-time. The students request faculty approval of their job as a cooperative assignment. With approval, a student receives academic credit for successful performance at work.

Advantages of cooperative education. Cooperative education programs enable students to immediately determine how the information they learn in school is applied at work. Students learn that a job has many requirements, including subject knowledge, good work habits, judgment, and skills in communication and human relations. Students also gain practical experience and develop contacts with employers, which may help them obtain a job after graduation. Some students use the money earned from their cooperative education jobs to pay their school expenses.   Edwin L. Herr

See also **Career education.**

Cooperative Extension System is a nationwide educational network in the United States. It is funded by federal, state, and county governments and by private contributions. The system gives instruction and information to individuals and local communities about agriculture, natural resources, nutrition, child care, the development of community resources, and related topics. It also includes such youth programs as 4-H and provides problem-solving assistance to local communities.

The Cooperative Extension System includes the Extension Service of the U.S. Department of Agriculture (USDA), more than 3,000 county extension offices, and one or more land-grant universities in each of the 50 states (see **Land-grant university**). The Extension Service of the USDA distributes information gathered by the land-grant universities and by the USDA, and encourages the application of agricultural and other research. The Extension Service also coordinates the programs of the Cooperative Extension System.

Almost every county and many major cities in the United States have at least one county extension office. Each office is staffed by one or more county extension agents. Volunteers work with the agents. Specialists and researchers at the land-grant universities support the efforts of the county extension offices.

What is now the Cooperative Extension System was established in 1914 by the Smith-Lever Act. The first land-grant universities had been endowed under the Morrill Act of 1862.   Raymond J. Miller

See also **Agricultural education** (Colleges and universities); **County agricultural extension agent; County extension home economist; 4-H.**

Cooperstown (pop. 2,180) is a resort village on Otsego Lake, in the east-central part of New York state. For location, see **New York** (political map). William Cooper, a judge, purchased land and surveyed the wilderness site in 1785 and settled there in 1790. His son James Fenimore Cooper set two of his famous *Leather-Stocking Tales* in the region. Cooperstown was incorporated in 1807.

Cooperstown is the home of the National Baseball

The coot is a dark gray water bird that resembles a duck. The American coot, *above,* lives in the Western Hemisphere.

a white or yellow bill shaped like a chicken's bill. Fleshy, paddlelike flaps on their toes help them swim.

Coots live all over the world except the polar regions. The American coot is found from southern Canada to South America. The European coot, a species common in Europe and Asia, occasionally strays to Newfoundland and Labrador.

Most coots live in freshwater marshes. They build floating nests from dead plants. The female usually lays 9 or 10 eggs. Coots feed chiefly on algae and the seeds, leaves, and roots of other water plants. They also eat snails, worms, water insects, small fish, and tadpoles. Coots find their food on the surface of the water and on the ground, or they dive underwater to obtain it. Other birds often steal food that coots have obtained by diving.

Scientific classification. Coots belong to the rail family, Rallidae. The scientific name for the American coot is *Fulica americana.* The European coot is *F. atra.*   James J. Dinsmore

See also **Rail.**

Cop. See **Police** (introduction).

Copenhagen, *кон puhn HAY guhn* or *кон puhn HAH guhn* (pop. 472,729; met. area pop. 1,358,540), is the capital and largest city of Denmark. Its name in Danish is *København.* The city is Denmark's major port and chief economic, political, and cultural center. About a fourth of the Danish people live in the Copenhagen area. Some parts of Copenhagen lie on the east coast of the island of Sjælland. Other sections are on Amager, an island just east of Sjælland. For location, see **Denmark** (map).

The city. Town Hall Square lies in the heart of Copenhagen. The city's main streets and highways extend outward from the square, and a number of bus and train routes run through the area. Many office buildings and hotels are near the square, as is the Tivoli Gardens amusement park. Tivoli offers various forms of entertainment, including rides, ballet, and concerts.

A mall called Strøget extends between Town Hall Square and the King's New Market, another major square. Strøget, which is closed to motor traffic, has de-

Cooperstown is the home of the National Baseball Hall of Fame and Museum. The Hall of Fame and Museum honors great baseball players and features historic displays of the game.

Hall of Fame and Museum, which was established in 1939. Many people then believed that baseball had been invented in Cooperstown by Abner Doubleday in 1839 (see **Baseball** [The Abner Doubleday Theory]; **Doubleday, Abner**). Fenimore House and the Farmers' Museum also attract many visitors. Fenimore House is a museum of American folk art. The Farmers' Museum re-creates early American farm life.   John Kenneth White

Coot is the name of nine kinds of marsh birds in the rail family. Coots are sometimes called *mud hens* or *marsh hens.*

Coots have slate-gray feathers and resemble ducks. They range in size from about 13 to 23 inches (33 to 58 centimeters) long. Coots have short, rounded wings and

J. Messerschmidt, Bruce Coleman Inc.

Copenhagen is the capital and largest city of Denmark. The city is the nation's major port and serves as the center of Denmark's economic, political, and cultural activity.

partment stores, small shops, and sidewalk cafes. East of Town Hall Square is Christiansborg Castle, which houses Parliament and the Supreme Court. The National Archives and Royal Library are near the castle.

A world-famous statue called *The Little Mermaid* is in Copenhagen's harbor. It represents a character from a fairy tale by the Danish author Hans Christian Andersen. Other attractions include the Amalienborg Palace, the Stock Exchange, and the New Carlsberg and Thorvaldsen museums. Copenhagen is the home of the Royal Danish Ballet. The University of Copenhagen, Denmark's oldest university, was founded in 1479.

Economy. Copenhagen is the commercial and industrial center of Denmark. The city's products include beer, diesel engines, furniture, and porcelain. Trade is also important to the economy of Copenhagen.

Buses and commuter trains provide most public transportation in Copenhagen. Many people ride bicycles, and most of the major streets have special bicycle paths. An international airport lies near the city.

History. In the mid-1000's, Copenhagen was a small fishing village. It became a trade center because of its harbor and, by the 1100's, had developed into a town. It was chartered in 1254 and grew increasingly important economically during the next few centuries. Copenhagen became the capital of Denmark in 1443.

During various periods from about 1250 to 1810, fires and wars destroyed much of Copenhagen, and epidemics killed many of the city's people. Copenhagen recovered each time, however, and continued to grow as an economic, military, and political center.

Copenhagen expanded to the north and west in the 1850's. During the late 1800's, the city experienced rapid economic growth and began to industrialize. A *free port* was established in the city in 1894 (see **Free trade zone**). German troops occupied Copenhagen from 1940 to 1945, during World War II, but the city suffered little damage.   M. Donald Hancock

See also **Denmark** (pictures).

Copepod, *KOH puh pahd,* is the name of a large group of tiny animals that live either in the ocean or in fresh water. There are more than 7,500 species of copepods. They form part of the *plankton,* the mass of small organisms usually found at or near the water surface (see **Plankton**). Copepods can swim, but many of the smaller species cannot swim strongly enough to avoid being carried about by water currents. They feed on floating microscopic organisms and plant life. Copepods are an important source of food for many fish, especially herring.

Scientific classification. Copepods make up the class Copepoda in the subphylum Crustacea, phylum Arthropoda.

Jonathan Green

See also **Crustacean; Animal** (picture: Animals of the oceans); **Microscope** (picture).

Copernicus, *koh PUR nuh kuhs,* **Nicolaus,** *NIHK uh LAY uhs* (1473-1543), was a Polish astronomer who developed the theory that the earth is a moving planet. He is considered the founder of modern astronomy.

In Copernicus' time, most astronomers accepted the theory the Greek astronomer Ptolemy had formulated nearly 1,400 years earlier. Ptolemy had said that the earth was at the center of the universe and was motionless. He had also stated that all the observed motions of the heavenly bodies were real and that those bodies moved in complicated patterns around the earth.

Some astronomers before Ptolemy had suggested that the earth did in fact move. The Greek astronomer Aristarchus had even suggested that the earth and all the other planets moved around the sun. By Ptolemy's time, however, these theories had been rejected. Copernicus knew about some of these early theories. He also believed that Ptolemy's theory was too complicated. He decided that the simplest and most systematic explanation of heavenly motion required that every planet, including the earth, revolve around the sun. The earth also had to spin around its axis once every day. The earth's motion affects what people see in the heavens, so real motions must be separated from apparent ones.

Copernicus skillfully applied this idea in his masterpiece, *On the Revolutions of the Heavenly Spheres* (1543). In this book, he demonstrated how the earth's motion could be used to explain the movements of other heavenly bodies. Copernicus could not prove his theory, but his explanation of heavenly motion was mathematically strong and was less complicated than Ptolemy's theory. By the early 1600's, such astronomers as Galileo in Italy and Johannes Kepler in Germany began to develop the physics that would prove Copernicus' theory correct.

Copernicus was born in Thorn (now Toruń, Poland). He attended the University of Kraków. Through the influence of his uncle, he was appointed a *canon* (church official) of the cathedral chapter of Frauenburg (now Frombork, Poland). He used the income from this position to study law and medicine at the universities of Bologna, Padua, and Ferrara in Italy from 1496 to 1506. When he returned to Poland in 1506, he served as canon.   A. Mark Smith

See also **Astronomy** (The beginnings of modern astronomy; picture); **Galileo**; **Kepler, Johannes**; **Planet** (Explaining the motion of the planets); **Ptolemy.**

Additional resources

Armitage, Angus. *The World of Copernicus.* Beckman Pubs., 1972. First published in 1947 as *Sun, Stand Thou Still.*
Kuhn, Thomas S. *Copernican Revolution.* Harvard, 1957.
Rosen, Edward. *Copernicus and the Scientific Revolution.* Krieger, 1984.

Copland, *KOHP luhnd,* **Aaron,** *AIR uhn* (1900-1990), was an American composer who wrote in many styles and forms. He won the 1945 Pulitzer Prize for music for the ballet *Appalachian Spring* (1944). In 1949, he received an Academy Award for his music for the motion picture *The Heiress* (1948).

Several of Copland's early works show the influence of French and middle European music of the early 1900's. He also emphasized jazz in such early works as *Music for the Theater* (1925), for small orchestra, and his *Piano Concerto* (1926). From the mid-1930's to the mid-1940's, Copland incorporated folk music into his compositions. *El Salón Mexico* (1937), an orchestral work, uses traditional Mexican themes. His music for the ballets *Billy the Kid* (1938) and *Rodeo* (1942) includes folk songs of the American West. He blended elements of his earlier styles in *Symphony No. 3* (1946). Beginning in the early 1950's, he revived the lean, severe style of some of his earlier works. His work during this period includes *Piano Fantasy* (1957).

Copland was born in Brooklyn, N.Y. His parents were Russian Jews, and he used Jewish themes in such compositions as *Vitebsk* (1929) for cello, piano, and violin. Copland wrote several books in an effort to promote wider acceptance of modern music. These books include *What to Listen for in Music* (rev. ed. 1957) and *The New Music, 1900-1960* (rev. ed. 1968). Copland also wrote two volumes of autobiography, *Copland 1900 Through 1942* (1984) and *Copland Since 1943* (1990).

Richard Jackson

Copley, *KAHP lee,* **John Singleton** (1738-1815), is generally considered the greatest portrait painter in colonial America. His many superb portraits capture the character of Americans in settings of everyday life. He painted with remarkable directness and vitality, making rich use of color, texture, and light and shade.

Copley was born in Boston. In 1766, he sent *Boy with a Squirrel* to a London exhibition. The painters Sir Joshua Reynolds and Benjamin West praised this charming portrait and recommended that Copley study in Europe. Copley was having great success in America, so he put off going to London until 1774. He settled there permanently, and his portraits soon took on the brilliant looser brushwork and atmospheric quality characteristic of British painting.

In 1778, Copley began a career as a painter of historical subjects, fulfilling a lifelong ambition. He painted many historical works, the most successful being *Watson and the Shark* (1778) and *The Death of Lord Chatham* (1781). After 1790, Copley's work gradually declined.

In the past, critics praised Copley's straightforward, vivid American portraits and were critical of the lavish portraits and large historical paintings he did in England. Today critics still praise his American works, but they view his English works with less disfavor than in the past.

Elizabeth Garrity Ellis

See also **Hancock, John** (picture); **United States** (The arts [picture]).

Copper (chemical symbol, Cu) has been one of the most useful metals for over 5,000 years. Today, the uses of this reddish-orange metal range from house gutters to electronic guidance systems for space rockets.

Copper is the best low-cost conductor of electricity. As a result, the electrical industry uses about six-tenths

Copley's family portrait was painted in 1776. The picture shows Copley, his wife and their four children, and the artist's father-in-law. Copley's careful composition and his delicate handling of color make this one of his finest paintings.

How copper metal is produced

Milling begins when a crusher reduces copper ore to small pieces. Water is added to form a mixture called *slurry.* A ball mill grinds the crushed ore in the slurry into fine particles. The particles become concentrated in a flotation cell.

Smelting removes many impurities from the copper concentrate. A reverberatory furnace eliminates impurities in the form of gases and *slag* (solid waste), producing copper matte. A converter further purifies the molten copper.

Electrolytic refining uses slabs cast from the molten copper supplied by the converter. During this refining process, an electric current produces chemical reactions, which yield copper metal that is over 99.9 per cent pure.

Final processing consists of melting and casting the copper metal into cakes, billets, bars, and ingots. Such forms are used to manufacture various copper products, including kitchen utensils, pipes, wires, and brass hinges.

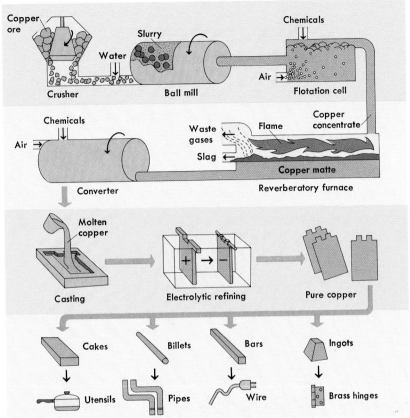

WORLD BOOK diagram

of the copper produced, chiefly in the form of wire. Copper wire carries most of the electric current inside homes, factories, and offices. Large amounts of copper wire are used in telephone and telegraph systems, as well as in television sets, motors, and generators.

Combined with other metals, copper forms such alloys as brass and bronze (see **Brass; Bronze**). Copper and its alloys can be made into thousands of useful and ornamental articles. In the home, copper serves as the basic material for lighting fixtures, locks, pipe, plumbing fixtures, doorknobs, drawer pulls, candlesticks, and clocks. Other commonly used copper products include lamps, mailboxes, pots, pans, and jewelry.

Chemical compounds of copper help improve soil and destroy harmful insects. Copper compounds in paint serve as pigments and help protect materials against corrosion. Also, copper in small amounts is vital to all plant and animal life.

In ancient times, the chief source of copper for the peoples near the Mediterranean Sea was the island of Cyprus. As a result, the metal became known as *Cyprian metal.* Both the word *copper* and the chemical symbol for the element, *Cu,* come from *cuprum,* the Roman name for Cyprian metal.

Properties of copper

The physical properties of copper make the metal valuable to industry. These properties include (1) con-

ductivity, (2) malleability, (3) ductility, and (4) resistance to corrosion.

Conductivity. Copper is perhaps best known for its ability to conduct electricity. Silver is the only better conductor, but silver is too expensive for common use. Copper alloys do not conduct electricity nearly as well as pure copper. Impurities in refined copper also greatly reduce electrical conductivity. For example, as little as $\frac{5}{100}$ per cent arsenic cuts the conductivity of copper by 15 per cent. Copper is also an excellent conductor of heat. This property makes it useful in cooking utensils, radiators, and refrigerators.

Malleability. Pure copper is highly *malleable* (easy to shape). It does not crack when hammered, stamped, forged, die-pressed, or spun into unusual shapes. Copper can be *worked* (shaped) either hot or cold. It can be rolled into sheets less than $\frac{1}{500}$ inch (0.05 millimeter) thick. Cold rolling changes the physical properties of copper and increases its strength.

Ductility. Copper possesses great *ductility,* the ability to be drawn into thin wires without breaking. For example, a copper bar 4 inches (10 centimeters) square can be heated, rolled, and drawn into a round wire that is thinner than a human hair. Such a wire would be more than 20 million times longer than the bar that was used to make it.

Resistance to corrosion. Copper is quite resistant to corrosion. It will not rust. In damp air, it turns from

Leading copper-mining countries

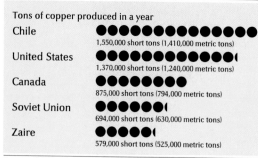

Tons of copper produced in a year

Chile	●●●●●●●●●●●
	1,550,000 short tons (1,410,000 metric tons)
United States	●●●●●●●●●● ◖
	1,370,000 short tons (1,240,000 metric tons)
Canada	●●●●●●●
	875,000 short tons (794,000 metric tons)
Soviet Union	●●●●●◖
	694,000 short tons (630,000 metric tons)
Zaire	●●●●◖
	579,000 short tons (525,000 metric tons)

Figures are for 1987, prior to the breakup of the Soviet Union.
Source: *Minerals Yearbook, 1988,* U.S. Bureau of Mines.

Leading copper-mining states and provinces

Tons of copper produced in a year

Arizona	●●●●●●●●●●●
	931,000 short tons (845,000 metric tons)
British Columbia	●●●●●
	389,000 short tons (353,000 metric tons)
New Mexico	●●● ◖
	285,000 short tons (259,000 metric tons)
Ontario	●●● ◖
	283,000 short tons (257,000 metric tons)
Utah	●● ◖
	198,000 short tons (180,000 metric tons)

Figures are for 1988. Sources: *Minerals Yearbook, 1988,* U.S. Bureau of Mines, except for Utah, which has a *World Book* estimate; *Canada's Mineral Production, 1988,* Statistics Canada.

reddish-orange to reddish-brown. After long exposure, copper becomes coated with a green film called *patina,* which protects it against further corrosion.

Other properties. Copper has an atomic number of 29, and an atomic weight of 63.546. It melts at 1083.4 °C and boils at 2567 °C. Copper has a density of 8.96 grams per cubic centimeter at 20 °C (see **Density**). It is about 14 per cent heavier than iron. Cold-rolled copper has a tensile strength from 50,000 to 70,000 pounds per square inch (3,500 to 4,900 kilograms per square centimeter). Copper keeps its strength and toughness up to about 400 °F (204 °C).

Copper ores

Most copper comes from about seven kinds of ores. These ores also may contain other metals, such as lead, zinc, gold, cobalt, platinum, and nickel. Copper ores usually contain less than 4 per cent copper. Some ores may yield as little as 0.2 per cent of copper.

The chief copper ores are *sulfides* (sulfur compounds). They include bornite; chalcocite, or copper glance; and chalcopyrite, or copper pyrites. *Oxidized ores,* such as azurite, cuprite, and malachite, also yield valuable amounts of copper. Almost pure copper, called *native* copper, rarely occurs in nature. Native copper supplies only a small percentage of the world's total copper production.

Sources of copper

About 9 million short tons (8.3 million metric tons) of copper are mined each year throughout the world.

Every continent has copper deposits. Much of the world's copper comes from the mountain ranges extending from Alaska to the tip of South America.

In some places, miners dig copper ore from mines far below the earth's surface. Elsewhere, they remove it from great open pits at the surface. In *open-pit* mining, large power shovels or other machines remove the ore from wide "steps" 40 to 70 feet (12 to 21 meters) high. Most of the copper mined in the United States comes from open pits. See **Mining** (picture: In an open-pit copper mine).

The United States mines about a seventh of the world's copper. But it uses more copper than it mines, and it imports large amounts from such countries as Canada, Chile, and Peru. About two-thirds of the copper mined in the United States comes from Arizona. The Keweenaw Peninsula in Michigan is one of the few remaining sources of native copper.

Canada mines about a tenth of the world's copper. Most of it comes from British Columbia and Ontario. Sudbury District in Ontario has the largest copper deposits in Canada. Manitoba, New Brunswick, Quebec, and Saskatchewan also produce important amounts.

Other areas. Chile is the world's leading copper-producing nation. Large mines near Santiago and in the Atacama Desert provide most of Chile's copper. Zaire is also a leading producer of copper. A huge copper mine operates in the southeastern part of the country. Large copper deposits also occur in Zambia, China, Australia, Peru, and Mexico.

Obtaining copper from the ore

At the mine, large power shovels load the copper ore, frequently in the form of big boulders, into trucks or railroad cars. These vehicles carry the ore to mills and smelters.

All ores do not go through exactly the same processes. There are variations, depending on the type of ore. However, all the processes are designed to separate valuable minerals from the ore and waste rock, to extract copper and any other metals that may be in the resulting mixture, and to purify the metals that are produced.

In a typical process, the ore is sent to the mill, where it is crushed and the waste rock removed. The resulting material is then sent to the smelter, where the metallic copper is removed. This copper may contain other metals, such as gold, silver, and nickel, that must be removed by refining.

Milling starts in a *crusher,* where the ore is ground into small pieces. Then water is added to the crushed ore to form a souplike mixture called *slurry.* The slurry passes into *ball mills,* which are rotating, drum-shaped cylinders half-filled with iron balls. As the cylinders rotate, the balls grind the ore into particles small enough to pass through a screen with 10,000 openings per square inch (1,600 openings per square centimeter).

The slurry next goes through a *flotation process* that concentrates the mineral-bearing particles. The slurry first passes into containers called *flotation cells.* There, chemicals and oil are added, and the entire mixture is agitated by paddles or air jets to make it bubble. One chemical makes the bubbles stable. Another coats the mineral particles so that they stick to the bubbles. The

Kennecott

A copper anode is a large, rectangular cake of blister copper used in the electrolytic refining process to produce copper that is more than 99.9 per cent pure.

bubbles rise to the top of the cell with the particles and form a froth. This froth is scraped off and dried. The product, called *copper concentrate,* may contain from 15 to 33 per cent copper. The waste material, called *tailings,* does not become attached to the bubbles. It is emptied from the lower part of the flotation cell.

Leaching is used to recover copper from ores that do not react to the chemicals used in the flotation process. In leaching, water containing sulfuric acid or other chemicals circulates through the ore and dissolves the copper. The copper-bearing solution then passes through troughs containing pieces of iron. Some of the iron dissolves and replaces the copper in the solution. The copper is deposited on the remaining pieces of iron. From time to time, the pieces of iron are agitated and washed to remove the copper, and more iron is added as needed. Copper obtained by leaching is called *precipitate copper.* It is from 60 to 90 per cent pure. Such copper is usually smelted and refined. But it is sometimes sold for use without further refining.

Smelting removes most of the remaining impurities from the copper. In smelting, copper concentrate (sometimes precipitate copper is added) first goes through a *reverberatory furnace.* Such a furnace may process as much as 350 short tons (318 metric tons) of copper concentrate at one time. A firebox at one end of the furnace shoots flames over the concentrate, changing it into a bubbling mass. The heat helps drive off some impurities in the form of gas. Other impurities rise to the top of the molten mass to form *slag,* which consists mostly of iron, lime, and silica. The slag is skimmed off and discarded. The new mixture, called *copper matte,* contains from 25 to 50 per cent copper. It still has impurities in the form of iron sulfide and other metals.

The copper matte next goes through a *converter.* In the converter, blowers force air through the molten copper matte, and silica is added. The silica combines with the impurities, forming slag. The slag is again skimmed from the top. The new mixture is called *blister copper,* because the surface blisters as the copper cools. Blister copper is from 97 to 99.5 per cent pure.

When blister copper does not contain significant amounts of gold or silver, it may be refined in a *fire-refining furnace.* This furnace removes most of the remaining impurities, mainly oxygen. In a process called *poling,* workers force green pine logs into the *melt* (furnace load) of molten copper. The logs create a blazing, bubbling turmoil in the hot copper. As the logs burn, oxygen and other gases are removed from the copper. The resulting copper is 99.9 per cent pure.

Electrolytic refining. Copper to be used in electrical conductors must be electrolytically refined to a purity of more than 99.9 per cent. To do this, blister copper is cast into cakes about 3 feet (91 centimeters) square and 3 inches (8 centimeters) thick. The cakes serve as *anodes* (positive poles) in the electrolytic process. For a discussion of this process, see **Electrolysis.**

The copper anodes are put into tanks containing a solution of copper sulfate and sulfuric acid. They are suspended alternately with *cathodes* (negative poles), which are thin sheets of pure copper called *starter sheets.* When an electric current passes through the tank, the anode bars gradually dissolve, depositing copper more than 99.9 per cent pure on the cathodes. Most of the remaining impurities in the anodes settle to the bottom of the tank and form a *sludge.* Processors use various methods to recover small amounts of gold, silver, platinum, and other metals from the sludge. After electrolysis, the copper cathodes are usually melted in an electric furnace and cast into various shapes and sizes, such as bars, cakes, ingots, and billets.

Making copper products

Fabricating plants, such as brass and wire mills, make semifinished forms including sheets, tubes, wires, and rods. They make these forms from copper bars, cakes, ingots, and billets. Manufacturers of copper products buy the semifinished forms from these plants.

Copper sheets are rolled from copper cakes that measure about 25 inches (64 centimeters) wide, 8 inches (20 centimeters) thick, and up to 72 inches (183 centimeters) long. The cakes are heated in a furnace to about 1700 °F (926 °C), then rolled on a hot mill into sheets about ½ inch (13 millimeters) thick. Other mills finish the sheets by rolling them to exact thicknesses. The sheets are then cut into pieces of the required size to make such products as roofing sheets and cooking utensils.

Copper tubes are made from copper billets that vary in diameter from 3 to 9 inches (8 to 23 centimeters) and are up to 52 inches (132 centimeters) long. Workers heat the billets in a furnace, then pierce them to produce a rough pipe. The pipe shells thus formed are forced through dies and over other devices to produce tubes of the required size. The tubes are used to make plumbing pipes, household gas lines, and electrical conduits.

Copper wire is made from copper bars that measure about 54 inches (137 centimeters) long and 4 inches (10 centimeters) square. After being heated in a furnace, the bars are rolled on a mill to form rods about $\frac{1}{4}$ inch (6 millimeters) thick. The rods are then pulled through the dies of wire-drawing machines. These dies reduce the rods to the desired wire sizes. Most copper wire is used to carry electric current.

Extruded copper. Some copper is *extruded* (squeezed) through a hole in a die to form the desired shape. Copper can be extruded into rods, tubes, and other special shapes. These are made into hinges, door pulls, and other pieces of hardware.

History

Copper was one of the first metals known to human beings. It came into use because early peoples found it in native condition and could easily beat it into tools, weapons, and ornaments.

Early civilizations. Copper was probably first used about 8000 B.C. by people living along the Tigris and Euphrates rivers, where Iraq lies today. As early as 6000 B.C., the Egyptians knew how to hammer native copper into sheets to make tools and ornaments. Copper was later used by many peoples, including the Chinese, the Inca of Peru, and the American Indians.

By about 3500 B.C., people had discovered how to melt and alloy copper with tin to make bronze. At about that same time, they learned to smelt copper from ore. From about 3000 B.C. to about 1100 B.C., bronze became important (see **Bronze Age**). Much later, the Romans used bronze swords. The process of combining zinc with copper to make brass was probably discovered sometime after 1000 B.C. The Romans started making brass coins in the 100's B.C.

Industrial developments. From early times until the A.D. 1800's, ample high-grade ore was available, and methods for processing and using copper changed only slightly. By the late 1800's, the rapid growth of electric lighting and telephone and telegraph systems had greatly increased the demand for copper, which dwindling deposits of high-grade ore could not meet. Also, most native copper deposits had been used up.

Geologists had located large ore deposits in the United States and Chile. But the copper content of the ore was so low that the ore could not be processed at a profit. About 1900, a young American mining engineer, Daniel C. Jackling, realized that low-grade ores could be processed cheaply by using mass-production methods. His process involved the use of steam shovels to strip off surface rock. Other special mass-production equipment was used for smelting and refining. New techniques for separating copper from the ore also increased the supply of available copper.

The Phelps-Dodge Company is the leading company among U.S. copper producers. The leading firm in Canada is Inco Limited (formerly the International Nickel Company of Canada, Limited). Robert J. Doedens

Related articles in *World Book* include:

Copper products

Brass	Monel metal	Wire
Bronze	Nickel silver	

Other related articles

Alloy	Chalcocite	Malachite
Arizona (Mining)	Chalcopyrite	Mineral (picture)
Azurite	Chile (picture)	Zaire (picture)

Additional resources

Fodor, R. V. *Gold, Copper, Iron: How Metals Are Formed, Found, and Used.* Enslow, 1989.
Herbert, Eugenia W. *Red Gold of Africa: Copper in Precolonial History and Culture.* Univ. of Wisconsin Pr., 1984.
U.S. Bureau of Mines. *Mineral Facts and Problems.* U.S. Government Printing Office, 1985. *Minerals Yearbook: Volume I: Metals and Minerals.* An annual publication.

Copperhead is a poisonous American snake, one of the pit vipers. Its body has broad chestnut-red bands. Most copperheads are about $2\frac{1}{2}$ feet (76 centimeters) long. The largest grow to about 4 feet (1.2 meters).

The copperhead bites people more often than most rattlesnakes, partly because it is silent and smaller, and

WORLD BOOK illustration by Richard Lewington, The Garden Studio

The copperhead is a poisonous American snake. It can be recognized by the broad chestnut-colored bands along its body.

is not so quickly noticed. The bite is seldom fatal to adults, but can seriously poison children who weigh less than 75 pounds (34 kilograms). This reptile usually eats rodents and other small mammals. The prey are killed with the poison and swallowed whole. Sometimes the snake eats insects and frogs. It gives birth to from three to seven young in August or September.

The copperhead lives south of a line from the northeastern tip of Massachusetts through Pittsburgh to the southeastern corner of Nebraska. From there the line passes southwest to the upper Rio Grande in Texas. In this area any snake is likely to be called a copperhead if its markings resemble one. But the copperhead can be told from nonpoisonous snakes by the presence of a pit in front of and below each eye. The snake's nostril is in front of the pit. The copperhead has no rattle on the end of its tail and therefore differs from rattlesnakes.

Scientific classification. The copperhead belongs to the viper family, Viperidae. Its scientific name is *Agkistrodon contortrix.* Laurie J. Vitt

See also **Snake** (pictures); **Viper.**

Copperheads was a name given to a group of Democrats who criticized President Abraham Lincoln's Administration during the Civil War. Loyal Unionists claimed the Copperheads were pro-Southern and reminded them of the poisonous snakes with the copper-colored heads. Copperheads cut the head of Liberty from the copper cent and wore it as a badge.

Copperheads opposed Lincoln's attempts to free the slaves in the South. They spoke out against political arrests and the military draft and favored compromise with the Confederate States to end the war. The movement reached its peak early in 1863. But Union military victories and Republican election victories in 1864 helped to end the movement.   Frank L. Klement

See also **Sons of Liberty; Seymour, Horatio; Vallandigham, Clement L.**

Coppola, *KAHP uh luh,* **Francis Ford** (1939-   ), is an American motion-picture director, producer, and writer. Many of his major films present a grim picture of modern society. His most important movies include *The Godfather* (1972), *The Godfather, Part II* (1974), and *The Godfather, Part III* (1990), which cover almost 100 years in the life of an American family involved in organized crime. His *Apocalypse Now* (1979) was the first major American motion picture to deal with the Vietnam War. Coppola won Academy Awards for cowriting the screenplays for *Patton* (1970) and both *Godfather* movies, and for directing *The Godfather, Part II.*

Coppola was born in Detroit. He received a Master of Cinema degree from UCLA in 1968. He submitted his first important film, *You're a Big Boy Now* (1966), as his master's thesis. He became the first

© Tom Zimberoff, Gamma/Liaison
Francis Ford Coppola

major American director to begin his career from a university degree program in filmmaking. His success created opportunities for other college-trained filmmakers. Coppola's other films include *The Conversation* (1974), *The Outsiders* (1983), *Peggy Sue Got Married* (1986), and *Tucker: The Man and His Dream* (1988).   Gene D. Phillips

Copra, *KAHP ruh* or *KOH pruh,* is the dried meat of the coconut. Copra is valuable for its oil, which is used in the manufacture of soap, candles, margarine, detergents, cosmetics, and other products. Copra is one of the main exports of islands in the Pacific Ocean.

Coconut meat is dried in the sun or in ovens called *kilns,* or by using hot air. Drying removes water from the meat, allowing the meat to keep for a longer time.

The oil in copra is pressed out. The remaining cake, called *coconut-stearin* or *poonau,* is used for fodder and poultry feed. Copra yields from 50 to 65 per cent of its weight in oil. Thirty average coconuts produce about 1 gallon (3.8 liters) of oil.   Michael J. Tanabe

See also **Coconut palm; Pacific Islands** (picture: Producing copra).

Copts, *kahpts,* is a term first used to refer to certain native residents of ancient Egypt. The Copts spoke a version of the ancient Egyptian language enriched by many Greek words and written with a modified Greek alphabet. The name Copts also refers to members of the Coptic Orthodox Church in modern Egypt, who use the Coptic language in their church service. However, like other Egyptians today, Copts speak Arabic.

The Copts played a leading role in the development of the early Christian church. They made their most important contribution to Christianity from the late A.D. 200's to the mid-300's, when a Copt, Anthony of Thebes, founded the early Christian monastic move-

ment. The Copts were interested in the lives and sayings of the saints. Most surviving Coptic literature concerns this subject. The Copts stressed the unity of the human and divine in Christ's nature, a belief known as the *Monophysite doctrine.* At the Council of Chalcedon in 451, however, church leaders from Rome and Constantinople declared Christ had two separate natures and condemned the powerful Coptic *patriarchate* (ruling division) in Alexandria. Some Copts submitted to the Council's decisions, but most chose to establish an independent church with its own patriarch and clergy.

In 642, Muslim Arabs conquered Egypt, and many Copts converted to Islam. Today, only a few million Copts live in Egypt, while other small Coptic communities are scattered throughout the world. In the 1970's, Coptic church leaders met with various Eastern Orthodox Churches and the Roman Catholic Church to explore the possibility of reunion.   Patrick T. R. Gray

Copying machine is any of several types of devices that copy documents or illustrations. Other devices, called *duplicators,* also produce copies. But duplicators use a special form called a *master,* while copying machines do not require a master (see **Duplicator**). The chief methods of copying are (1) electrostatic copying, (2) projection copying, and (3) contact copying. Most copying machines use the electrostatic method.

Electrostatic copying was invented in 1938 by Chester F. Carlson, an American physicist. Unlike earlier methods, which require liquid developers, Carlson's process is completely dry. It became known as *xerography,* a term that comes from two Greek words meaning *dry* and *writing.*

In xerography, a drum, belt, or plate coated with the element selenium or some other light-sensitive material is charged with static electricity. Light reflected from the *original* (the document or illustration to be copied) then passes through a lens. The light strikes the light-sensitive surface, forming on that surface a positively charged image corresponding to the dark areas of the original. The remainder of the surface loses its charge. Next, negatively charged *toner* (powdered ink) is dusted onto the surface. Because oppositely charged materials attract each other, toner sticks to the image. The inked image is then transferred to positively charged paper and heated for an instant. The toner melts, creating a permanent copy. Some electrostatic copiers project the image from the original directly onto specially coated paper, rather than onto a drum, belt, or plate.

Manufacturers produce a wide variety of electrostatic copiers, from personal copiers that make 5 to 8 copies a minute to units that can generate 135 copies a minute. Special features include automatic document feeding and sorting, image reduction and enlargement, *duplexing* (two-sided copying), color copying, and stapling. Some color copiers produce copies in black and one other color. Others produce full-color copies.

The newest type of electrostatic copier is a digital machine. A digital copier scans a document, converting the document into digital code, which is stored in the copier's memory. The user can then edit the document. The copier can even merge different parts of documents or transmit documents to other digital devices, such as facsimile (fax) machines and personal computers (see **Computer** [How a computer operates]). Some copiers also

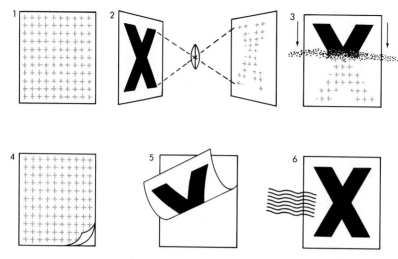

Electrostatic copying of a document involves six basic steps. (1) A light-sensitive surface receives a positive electric charge. (2) Light reflected from the document passes through a lens and strikes the light-sensitive surface. This step leaves a positive charge only in the area that corresponds to the image on the document. (3) Negatively charged, powdered ink is then dusted on. Because oppositely charged materials attract each other, the ink sticks to the image area. (4) A piece of paper is placed over the surface and given a positive charge. (5) The ink is attracted to the paper. (6) Heat fuses the ink to the paper, creating the copy.

WORLD BOOK illustration by Linda Kinnaman. Source material from Xerox Corporation.

perform other functions, such as sending and receiving fax messages.

Projection copying was developed in the mid-1800's. Common projection copiers include the copy camera and the photostat machine. A copy camera performs the steps used to develop and print ordinary photographs. First, the copy camera takes a photograph of the original. The film is then developed by a chemical solution, producing a negative. To make a positive copy, the image on the negative is projected onto positive paper. Finally, the paper is developed to create the copy. Copy cameras are used today to create the negatives used in making *lithographic plates* for printing (see **Photoengraving and photolithography**).

A *photostat machine* does not use photographic film to make a negative. Instead, it projects light reflected from the original directly onto light-sensitive paper. Developing the paper produces the copy. The photostat machine, like any other projection copier, can enlarge or reduce the size of the copy made from the original. One type of photostat machine enlarges and copies images from microfilm onto paper. See **Microfilm**.

Contact copying was first used in the mid-1800's. In this method, the original is placed in contact with light-sensitive negative paper and exposed to light. Next, the negative paper is held against positive paper, and the two papers are fed into a contact-copying machine. There, they pass through a developer, such as ammonia vapor or water. The developer brings out the image on the negative and transfers it to the positive paper (the copy). Blueprints and similar types of duplicates are made using the contact copying method (see **Blueprint**).

Eileen Feretic

See also **Library** (Photocopying); **Xerox Corporation**.

Copyright refers to a body of exclusive rights that protect the works of authors and other creative people against copying or unauthorized public performance. Copyright generally extends to original works of literary, dramatic, musical, or artistic expression.

The first modern copyright law was adopted in Great Britain in 1709. Today, most nations have copyright laws that cover works originally produced at home or abroad. In the United States, the Copyright Office of the Library of Congress is primarily responsible for administering copyright law.

Patents and trademarks are distinct from copyrights. A patent mainly prevents inventions and discoveries or improvements of useful processes from being copied. A trademark is a word, name, or symbol that is designed to distinguish the products or services of one company from those of another. See **Patent; Trademark.**

Works protected. Copyright law covers numerous types of original work. Such work may be literary, musical, dramatic, pantomime, *choreographic* (dance), pictorial, graphic, or sculptural. Other categories are motion pictures and other audio-visual works, sound recordings, computer programs, and architectural works.

Literary works consist of novels, poems, and all works that do not fall into any other category. Such other works include computer programs, catalogs, directories, and collections of data.

Musical works include original compositions and arrangements, and any accompanying words. New versions of earlier compositions may also be copyrighted.

Dramatic works mainly include plays intended for live performance, and screenplays. The copyright covers music for dramatic productions, such as operas, musical comedies, and musical plays for television.

Pantomimes and choreographic works can be copyrighted if they are filmed or taped, or are written. Choreographic works do not include social dance steps.

Pictorial, graphic, and sculptural works include photographs, holograms, greeting cards, picture postcards, cartoons, comic strips, posters, ceramic figurines, glassware, and decals. Lithographs, etchings, and other art reproductions by the original author are also covered, as are maps, globes, charts, jewelry, toys, various designs and patterns, and other examples of visual arts.

Motion pictures include all works consisting of a series of related images, regardless of whether the images are displayed on film, tape, or disc. Audio-visual works include motion pictures, as well as filmstrips and other works that consist of sequences of images but do not give the impression of motion when shown. Sounds accompanying audio-visual works are also protected.

Two main elements in a sound recording are covered by copyright protection. These elements are the contribution of the performer and the contribution of the people responsible for capturing and processing the sounds in the final recording. Copyright laws also forbid the unauthorized commercial distribution and rental of sound recordings.

Architectural works include buildings and architectural plans and drawings. Copyright law covers the overall form of an architectural work and the unique arrangement of elements and spaces in its design.

Copyright protection applies only to the extent of a person's expression. No protection is available for ideas, concepts, names, titles, short phrases, general themes, familiar symbols, or diaries, bank checks, and other types of blank forms. Works of the United States government—that is, works authored by a federal employee within the scope of his or her employment—may not be copyrighted.

Owners' rights. A copyright carries with it the exclusive right to reproduce and distribute copies or phonorecords of the copyrighted work. However, except for sound recordings and computer programs, once a copy has been sold, the purchaser may resell or rent the copy without permission of the copyright owner.

A copyright also gives the owner the sole right to prepare works based upon the copyrighted work, such as translations, condensations, and motion-picture versions. In addition, the owner has the exclusive right to perform the work publicly if it is a literary, musical, dramatic, or choreographic work; a pantomime; or a motion picture or other audio-visual creation. The copyright owner has the sole right to display the work publicly if it is a pictorial, graphic, sculptural, literary, musical, dramatic, or choreographic work; a pantomime; or individual images from a motion picture or other audio-visual work. The creators of certain works of visual art have the rights to be identified as the work's creator and to protect the integrity of the work.

Owners of copyrighted material may transfer their copyright to someone else through a written contract. Under the "works made for hire" doctrine, people who create a copyrighted work within the scope of their employment relinquish the copyright to their employer.

Authors of copyrighted works may terminate a copyright transfer, but they must wait at least 35 years to do so. After 35 years from the date of the transfer, the author may serve a notice of termination and record the notice in the Copyright Office. If an author is dead, the beneficiaries named in the copyright statute may terminate the transfer.

Copyrights secured before 1978 are good for 28 years. During the 28th year, the copyright may be renewed for an additional 47 years. Works created before 1978 that were neither published nor registered with the Copyright Office before that year are protected until 50 years after the author's death, or until Dec. 31, 2002, whichever is longer. Copyrights secured after Jan. 1, 1978, are good until 50 years after the author's death.

The copyrights of anonymous works, pseudonymous works, and works created within the scope of employment are good for 75 years from publication or 100 years from creation, whichever is shorter.

A copyright owner whose copyright is violated may file a court injunction to stop further infringements. Copyright infringers may be liable for actual damages and profits or for statutory damages. Unintentional infringement is also illegal but may be treated less harshly by the court than intentional infringement. Willfully violating a copyright is a criminal offense.

Users' rights. Copyright law includes a section on "fair use" that allows limited reproduction of copyrighted material for such purposes as critical commentary, news reporting, and educational use. For example, teachers may make a limited number of copies of a copyrighted work for classroom use. Archives and libraries may make one copy of a copyrighted work, but they may not regularly reproduce single or multiple copies of such a work. For more information on the clearance of photocopying rights, write to Copyright Clearance Center, 27 Congress Street, Salem, MA 01970.

Some taping of off-air broadcast material in the home and for home use only is considered fair use. The U.S. Supreme Court approved such use in the case of *Sony Corp. v. Universal City Studios, Inc.,* in 1984.

In some cases, copyrighted works may be used without permission if the user pays a set fee. Such use is covered in copyright law sections dealing with five types of licensing systems. These systems provide for (1) retransmission of broadcast signals by cable television companies, (2) use of musical compositions by record companies, (3) use of recorded music in jukeboxes, (4) noncommercial broadcasting of published musical, pictorial, graphic, and sculptural works, and (5) secondary transmissions of television superstations and network stations for home viewing.

How to obtain a copyright. The Copyright Office does not grant copyrights. It merely registers claims.

Registration is available for all forms of unpublished and published copyright claims. The Copyright Office recommends that registration be requested within three months after publication of the work.

Registration is obtained by sending the Copyright Office a completed application form, a fee of $20, and one or two copies of the work to be registered. Upon registration, the Copyright Office will issue the applicant a certificate of registration, which may be submitted in federal court as evidence of copyright ownership. Forms, instructions, and general information about copyright can be obtained from the United States Copyright Office, Library of Congress, Washington, DC 20559.

The Copyright Office recommends that a notice of copyright appear on each copy of any published work. This should consist of either the word "Copyright," the abbreviation "Copr.," or the symbol ©, accompanied by the name of the copyright owner or an abbreviation or other designation by which the owner can be recognized. If the work is a printed literary, musical, or dramatic work, the notice should include the year in which the work was first published. For example, "© Jane Doe 1994." If the work is a sound recording, the notice should contain the symbol ℗, the year of first publication of the recording, and the name of the copyright owner. For example, "℗ 1990 XYZ Records."

International copyright. The United States has participated in many international conventions and bilateral agreements covering copyright. These agreements provide U.S. citizens with copyright protection abroad.

The United States was a founder of the Universal Copyright Convention, signed in 1952. A person may obtain copyright protection in every country that has agreed to the convention by publishing his or her work first in one of the countries (or anywhere in the world if the person is a citizen of one of the countries) with the prescribed notice. Each country must then protect the work according to its own laws.

The Brussels Satellite Convention went into effect in the United States in 1985, and the Berne Convention did so in 1989. The Brussels Satellite Convention prohibits the unauthorized retransmission of satellite signals that carry TV programs. The Berne Convention establishes minimum standards of copyright protection that member states must give to literary and artisitic works.

The United States has also joined with several American republics in copyright conventions to protect literary property in the Western Hemisphere. The most important of these conventions is the Buenos Aires Convention, signed in 1910. In 1974, the United States joined the Geneva Phonogram Convention. This convention protects sound recordings.

History. The first modern copyright law was the Statute of Anne, passed by the British Parliament in 1709. This law made copyrights available to anyone for 14 years. Britain's Universities Copyright Act of 1775 helped explain the conditions under which an infringement suit could be brought.

The Constitution of the United States authorized Congress to establish copyright legislation. In 1790, Congress passed the first federal copyright act. In the landmark case of *Wheaton v. Peters* (1834), the U.S. Supreme Court ruled that all published works had to comply with the federal statute to be protected. Unpublished works could be protected under state copyright law.

In 1909, Congress passed a copyright law that allowed copyright registration for certain unpublished works, such as dramas, lectures, musical works, and works of art. In 1978, the Copyright Revision Bill took effect. This law recognized federal copyright for all types of unpublished material. It also preempted state common law copyright, which meant that copyright protection of both published and unpublished material had to be secured under federal law. The Computer Software Act of 1980 confirmed the ability to copyright computer programs. In 1984, the Record Rental Amendment gave copyright owners of sound recordings the right to control commercial lending of sound recordings. In 1990, a similar right was extended to owners of computer programs. Also in 1990, architectural works became copyrightable after Congress passed amendments bringing the United States into conformity with the Berne Convention.

In 1992, Congress passed legislation requiring manufacturers of digital audio recording machines, blank compact discs, and blank digital tapes to pay *royalties* (shares of profit) to recording companies, music publishers, and song writers. The machines can be used to copy recordings onto the discs and tapes. Because the manufacturers pay royalties, the law allows buyers of the machines, discs, and tapes to use them in making copies. However, the law also requires that blank discs and tapes be manufactured in such a way that further copies cannot be made from them.   Kent Dunlap

See also **Plagiarism.**

Coral, *KAWR uhl,* is a limestone formation formed in the sea by millions of tiny animals. Coral formations may look like branching trees, large domes, small irregular crusts, or tiny organ pipes. The living coral-forming animals color the formation in beautiful shades of tan, orange, yellow, purple, and green. When the animals die, they leave limestone "skeletons" that form the foundations of barriers and ridges called *coral reefs.* Coral reefs look like lovely sea gardens because of the many colorful sea animals that live among the corals. These animals include fishes, starfish, and sea anemones.

Sometimes coral masses build up until they rise above the water to form *coral islands.* The grinding, battering sea helps to build coral islands. It breaks up the coral growths and piles them up. Other creatures, such as calcifying algae, cement the pieces together and a rigid structure is formed. Often, soil lodges on the coral and vegetation begins to grow. Many Pacific islands were formed this way.

Coral reefs are found mostly in warm, shallow, and tropical seas, because the reef-forming corals cannot live in water colder than 65 °F (18 °C). Reefs abound throughout the South Pacific, in the East Indies and the Indian Ocean to Sri Lanka, and around Madagascar on the southeastern African coast. They also form along the tropical eastern coast of Brazil, through the West Indies,

Sea fan corals

Dwarf corals

Reef-building corals

Mushroom corals

Soft corals

Douglas Faulkner

Lettuce corals

along the Florida coast, and at Bermuda. There are three types of coral reefs: (1) fringing reefs; (2) barrier reefs; and (3) atolls.

Fringing reefs are submerged platforms of living coral animals that extend from the shore into the sea.

Barrier reefs follow the shoreline, but are separated from it by water. They form a barrier between the water near the shore and the open sea. A barrier reef may consist of a long series of reefs separated by channels of open water. Such reefs usually surround volcanic islands of the South Pacific. The Great Barrier Reef of Australia, about 1,250 miles (2,010 kilometers) long, is the largest coral reef in the world.

An *atoll* is a ring-shaped coral island in the open sea. It forms when coral builds up on a submerged mudbank or on the rim of the crater of a sunken volcano. The atoll surrounds a body of water called a *lagoon*. One or more channels connnect the lagoon to the open sea. Many coral islands of the South Pacific Ocean are atolls.

Coral reefs do not develop on the east coast of North America north of Florida and Bermuda. But small patches of coral grow as far north as New England. Certain kinds of coral grow as far north as the Arctic Circle.

How coral is formed. The animals that form coral belong to the same animal group as the hydras, jellyfish, and sea anemones. Most individual coral animals, called *polyps,* are less than 1 inch (2.5 centimeters) in diameter, but a small percentage measure as much as 1 foot (30 centimeters). A coral polyp has a cylinder-shaped body. At one end is a mouth surrounded by tiny *tentacles.* The other end attaches to hard surfaces on the sea bottom.

Most coral polyps live together in colonies. The *stony corals* attach themselves to each other with a flat sheet of tissue that connects to the middle of each body. Half of the coral polyp extends above the sheet and half below. Coral polyps build their limestone skeletons by taking calcium out of the seawater. Then they deposit *calcium carbonate* (limestone) around the lower half of the body. As new polyps grow, the limestone formation becomes larger and larger.

Coral polyps feed mainly on tiny swimming animals, such as the *larvae* (young) of many kinds of shellfish. Reef corals cannot live without algae. They use some food manufactured by algae that live in the polyps' own tissues. These algae produce chemicals that help the coral animals secrete their limestone skeletons. Coral reefs grow only in water with enough light for photosynthesis to occur in the algae.

Coral polyps reproduce either from eggs or by *budding.* Small, knoblike growths called *buds* appear on the body of an adult polyp, or on the connecting sheet, from time to time. These buds grow larger, separate from the parent, and begin to deposit their own limestone in the colony. Budding helps the colony increase its size.

New colonies of coral polyps form when the adult polyps of an old colony produce eggs. The eggs grow into tiny forms that swim away. Then the developing animals settle to the sea bottom and begin to form new colonies by budding.

Various marine animals eat living coral-forming animals. The loss of coral to such animals is usually balanced by the development of new coral colonies and the growth of old ones. But beginning in the 1960's, large numbers of crown-of-thorns starfish destroyed stony coral colonies on many reefs of the southwest Pacific Ocean. Scientists are trying to determine what has caused this starfish to become so numerous.

Precious and gorgonian corals. Other kinds of coral, in addition to stony corals, are found in the world's oceans. These corals are also colonies of polyps, but the skeletons they form are internal rather than external. *Precious* coral is a *species* (kind) valued for jewelry. It has a hard *core* (internal skeleton) that can be polished. Polishing brings out beautiful red, rose, or pink colors. Craftworkers carve it into beads and other ornaments. Precious coral grows in bushlike formations in the Mediterranean Sea and Sea of Japan.

Gorgonian corals have internal skeletons of a flexible, horny substance. These corals look like bushes, fans, or whips. They may be soft yellow, rose, purple, brown, tan, or black. In clear West Indian waters, gorgonian corals look like sea gardens as they wave on the reefs.

Scientific classification. Corals are in the phylum Cnidaria and the class Anthozoa. L. Muscatine

Related articles in *World Book* include:

Atoll	Great Barrier Reef	Sea fan
Australia (picture)	Limestone	Seashore
Gem (picture)	Petoskey stone	

Coral Sea, *KAWR uhl,* is the part of the Pacific Ocean between the northeast coast of Australia, the Solomon Islands, and the Vanuatu island group. It has an unusually large number of coral atolls and bank reefs. The boundaries of this sea are so indefinite that the name could be applied to large parts of the Southern Pacific. The reefs along the western shores of the Coral Sea have the finest specimens of coral (see **Coral**).

United States and Japanese naval forces fought a key World War II battle in the Coral Sea. Neither side won a clear-cut victory, but the Japanese offensive was checked for the first time in the war. D. N. Jeans

See also Pacific Islands (map).

Coral Sea, Battle of the. See Air Force (table: Famous air battles; World War II).

Coral snake is the name given to several closely related poisonous snakes of the Western Hemisphere. They are found in the Southern United States, Mexico, Central America, and tropical South America. They have small, blunt heads and brightly colored bodies.

Coral snakes are extremely poisonous. They do not strike as effectively as other venomous snakes, but they bite. They are dangerous if stepped on or handled. They are snake eaters.

The *eastern* coral snake generally ranges from 20 to 40 inches (51 to 100 centimeters) in length. It lives in the Southeastern United States and in extreme northeastern Mexico. Its body is encircled by broad black and red bands separated by narrow yellow ones. Just behind the snake's black snout is a wide yellow band followed by a black band. Some of these coral snakes are covered with black pigment that hides much of the red color. Some nonpoisonous snakes look like these coral snakes because they have similar coloring. But the coral snakes have red bands next to yellow ones. The harmless snakes have red bands next to black ones.

The *western,* or *Arizona,* coral snake is about 18 inches (46 centimeters) long. It lives in the lower parts of southern Arizona, in southwestern New Mexico, and in northern Mexico. It also has a black snout. Behind the

WORLD BOOK illustration by John F. Eggert

A South American coral snake grows about 4 feet (1.2 meters) long. The individual shown in this illustration has black, red, and white bands. Coral snakes are extremely poisonous.

snout is a white or yellow band followed by a red band.

The *South American coral snake* is about 4 feet (1.2 meters) long. It is common in tropical South America. Its body is encircled by bands of bright red separated by broad bands of black. Within each black band are two narrow bands of white or yellow. The white or yellow bands do not touch the red bands, a characteristic that distinguishes this snake from North American coral snakes. The scales of the snake are shiny and polished.

Scientific classification. Coral snakes belong to the family, Elapidae. The scientific name for the eastern coral snake is *Micrurus fulvius.* The western, or Arizona, is *Micruroides euryxanthus,* and the South American coral snake is *Micrurus lemniscatus.*   D. Bruce Means

See also **Snake** (picture: Some poisonous snakes of North America).

Coral tree, also known as *coralbean,* is the name of more than 100 species of trees and shrubs that grow in tropical and nearly tropical regions throughout the world. They are widely cultivated as shade trees and as ornamentals. Most coral trees are *deciduous*—that is, they lose their leaves and grow new ones each year.

Field Museum of Natural History

A coral tree bears large, brightly colored flowers.

Coral trees have compound leaves made up of three leaflets. Many species have thorns along the branches and even on the *petioles* (stems) of the leaves. Most coral trees bear large, showy flowers that are red or orange. Birds pollinate the flowers. In the Americas, coral trees are chiefly pollinated by hummingbirds.

The red and black seeds of many species of coral trees are used for necklaces and other jewelry. However, the seeds commonly contain substances that are poisonous if eaten. Local peoples extract some of these substances for use in medicines.

Scientific classification. Coral trees make up the genus *Erythrina* in the pea family, Fabaceae or Leguminosae.

Philip W. Rundel

Corbett, James John (1866-1933), became the world heavyweight boxing champion in 1892. He was regarded as one of the first scientific boxers. A bank teller, Corbett had his first professional bout in 1884, and won the heavyweight title from John L. Sullivan in 1892. He lost it to Bob Fitzsimmons in 1897. After trying twice to regain the championship, he retired from the ring and pursued a career as an actor. Corbett was born in San Francisco. He became known as "Gentleman Jim" for his fancy style of dress.   Bert Randolph Sugar

Corbin, Margaret Cochran (1751-1800), became a heroine at the Battle of Fort Washington in 1776, during the Revolutionary War in America (1775-1783). She was born in Franklin County, Pennsylvania. In 1756, Indians killed her father and captured her mother. An uncle raised her.

In 1775, Margaret's husband, John Corbin, enlisted in the Continental Army, and he served as a gunner in the Revolutionary War. Like many other soldiers' wives at the time, Margaret joined her husband in camp to cook, wash, and do other chores for the troops. At Fort Washington, on the site of present-day New York City, John Corbin was killed. Margaret replaced him at his cannon and fought until she was seriously wounded.

Corbin's wounds left her disabled. In 1779, the Continental Congress awarded her a military pension, making her one of the first women in the United States to receive such aid. Corbin is buried in the military cemetery at West Point, N.Y.   William Morgan Fowler, Jr.

Corbusier. See Le Corbusier.

Corcoran Gallery of Art, in Washington, D.C., has collections of paintings, sculpture, drawings, tapestries, photographs, and ceramics. It houses one of the world's most important collections of American art and displays works by Josef Albers, Thomas Cole, Mark Rothko, Gilbert Stuart, John Singer Sargent, Winslow Homer, and Thomas Sully, among others. The W. A. Clark Collection is devoted to masterpieces from Europe. The gallery also organizes exhibitions, one of the most important being the Biennial Exhibition of Contemporary American Painting. An art school operated by the gallery offers a Bachelor of Fine Arts degree as well as an open program of nondegree courses.

William Wilson Corcoran, a banker and philanthropist, founded the gallery in 1869. The Corcoran Gallery of Art is a self-supporting institution.

Critically reviewed by the Corcoran Gallery of Art

Cord is a unit for measuring firewood. A cord has a volume of 128 cubic feet (3.6 cubic meters). Any set of numbers totaling 128 cubic feet would be a cord. For exam-

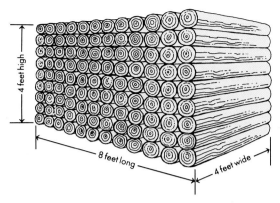

A cord of wood is 128 cubic feet (3.6 cubic meters).

ple, a pile of wood 4 feet (1.22 meters) wide, 4 feet high, and 8 feet (2.44 meters) long would represent a cord (4 feet × 4 feet × 8 feet = 128 cubic feet). The cord is not recognized as a legal measure by the United States government. Leland F. Webb

See also **Weights and measures** (table: Wood measurement [Inch-pound]).

Corday, *kawr DAY,* **Charlotte** (1768-1793), a French patriot, killed Jean Paul Marat, a radical leader of the French Revolution, during the Reign of Terror in 1793. She was tried in a Revolutionary court, and, four days later, she was guillotined. She sympathized with the Girondists,

Culver

Charlotte Corday

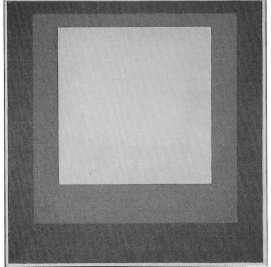

Casein painting on Masonite (1956); Corcoran Gallery of Art, William A. Clark Fund

The Corcoran Gallery collection includes works by Josef Albers and other major American artists. One of the Albers paintings on display is his abstract work *Homage to the Square: Yes.*

a group of representatives in the French legislature (see **Girondists**). When the Girondist leaders were arrested, Corday resolved to kill Marat, an opponent in the legislature. She obtained an interview with him. While he was in his bath, where he spent several hours each day seeking relief from a skin disease, she stabbed him to death. Charlotte Corday was born in Normandy, France.
Richard M. Brace

See also **Marat, Jean Paul.**

Cordial. See Alcoholic beverage (Liqueurs).

Cordillera, *KAWR duhl YAIR uh* or *kawr DIHL uhr uh,* is a group of mountain ranges, usually the principal mountain group of a continent. The word *cordillera* comes from a Spanish word meaning *cord* or *chain.* Spaniards use the word to mean any mountain chain. The term *cordillera* once was used in America to mean only the Andes Mountains. American geographers now use the term to mean any group of mountain systems, such as the western cordillera of North America, which includes the Sierra Madre, the Rockies, the Sierra Nevada, the Cascade Range, the Coast Ranges, and the Great Basin ranges. South America, Asia, and Europe also have cordilleras. Richard G. Reider

Cordite, *KAWR dyt,* was one of the original smokeless powders used to propel projectiles from guns. The name *cordite* refers to the cordlike lengths in which it was made. Cordite is composed of 30 per cent nitroglycerin, 65 per cent nitrocellulose, and 5 per cent petrolatum. The British government patented the cordite formula in 1889. This cordite burned with so much heat it damaged gun barrels. James E. Kennedy

Córdoba, *KAWR duh buh* (pop. 1,166,932), is the second largest city in Argentina. Only Buenos Aires, the capital, has more people. Córdoba is a major industrial center and the capital of the Argentine province of Córdoba. The city lies in northern Argentina, at the base of a mountain range called the Sierra de Córdoba. For the location of Córdoba, see **Argentina** (political map).

Córdoba ranks as Argentina's top producer of automobiles and tractors. The city is also a leading manufacturer of textiles and of glass and leather products. Despite its industrialization, Córdoba has preserved many traditional features, including old churches, public squares, and promenades. The oldest university in Argentina, the National University of Córdoba, was established in 1613.

Córdoba was founded in 1573 by Spaniards who had come to the area from Chile. Its location on early trade routes to Chile and Peru, along with rich agricultural land surrounding the city, helped Córdoba grow and prosper. Richard W. Wilkie

Córdoba, *KAWR duh buh* (pop. 304,826), is an ancient Moorish city in Spain, and the capital of Córdoba province. It lies 86 miles (138 kilometers) northeast of Seville. For location, see **Spain** (political map).

Romans occupied Córdoba in 206 B.C. The city reached its peak of importance in the A.D. 900's as a famous center of Moorish art and culture. The cathedral in Córdoba is the city's chief landmark. It was built as a *mosque* (Muslim house of worship) in the 700's and was made into a Roman Catholic cathedral in 1238. More than 1,000 pillars of granite, onyx, marble, and jasper support its arches.

Córdoba is the home of soft, fine-grained cordovan

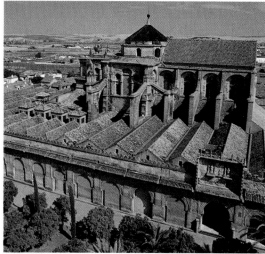

© Gian Berto Vanni, Art Resource

The cathedral in Córdoba, Spain, *above,* is the city's chief landmark. It was built as a Muslim house of worship in the 700's, and became a Roman Catholic cathedral in 1238.

WORLD BOOK illustration by Lorraine Epstein

Flowers of the coreopsis plant look like daisies and grow on slender stems. Coreopsis plants grow as high as 4 feet (120 centimeters). They are commonly called *tickseeds.*

leather. Nearby farms produce cereals, grapes, olives, and vegetables.   Stanley G. Payne

Corduroy, *KAWR duh roy,* is a cotton or cotton blend fabric with raised ribs of the cloth running lengthwise. The name probably comes from the French phrase *cord du roi,* meaning *king's cord.* Corduroy with wide ribs is called *wide-wale corduroy.* The type with narrow ribs is called *pin-wale corduroy.* Corduroy is made 54 inches (137 centimeters) wide for clothing, draperies, and upholstery. It may be in one color or a variety of printed patterns.   Christine W. Jarvis

Core, in geology. See Earth (Inside the earth).

CORE. See Congress of Racial Equality.

Corelli, *koh REHL ee,* **Arcangelo,** *ahr KAHN jeh LAW* (1653-1713), was one of the earliest major violinists and composers of violin music. Corelli's compositions became models for both solo and ensemble music for the violin. He developed the *concerto grosso,* which combines a large instrumental group with a trio that usually consists of two violins and a cello. Corelli also wrote violin sonatas in four *movements* (sections), which became a standard form for later sonata compositions. Corelli's works have been grouped into six collections. Each of the first five collections consists of 12 sonatas. The sixth is a collection of 12 concerti grossi.

Corelli was born in Fusignano, near Imola, in Italy. He studied violin as a teen-ager at the Accadèmia Filarmonia in Bologna, but spent most of his adult life in Rome. He gained a reputation as an excellent musician and conductor and was popular in Roman social circles. For many years, he directed an important series of concerts at the palace of his friend and patron, Cardinal Pietro Ottoboni.   Miriam Wagoner Barndt-Webb

Coreopsis, *KAWR ee AHP sihs,* is a large group of plants related to the sunflower. They are commonly called *tickseeds.* The plants may be from $1\frac{1}{2}$ to 4 feet (46 to 120 centimeters) high. Their yellow, red, or maroon flowers look like daisies and grow on slender stems. The flat fruits are small and dry and look like bugs. *Core-*

opsis is the Greek word for *bug.* Most coreopsis plants are perennials and live for several years. But some are annuals and live only one season. A common annual coreopsis is often called *calliopsis.* Gardeners cultivate both perennial and annual coreopsis plants.

Scientific classification. Coreopsis plants form the genus *Coreopsis* in the composite family, Compositae. The scientific name for the calliopsis is *C. calliopsidea.*   David E. Zimmer

See also **Flower** (picture: Flowers of prairies and dry plains [Tickseed]).

Corgi. See Cardigan Welsh corgi; Pembroke Welsh corgi.

Coriander, *KAWR ee AN duhr,* is an herb that grows in the countries around the Mediterranean Sea. The plant is about 3 feet (91 centimeters) high and has small white flowers. Its seeds have a pleasant odor when ripe, and they taste sweet after they have been dried out. The seeds are used as a spice in curries, sauces, and liqueurs, and to make small round candies. They are used

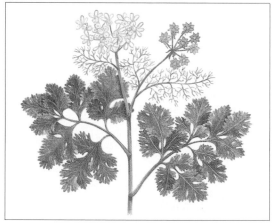

WORLD BOOK illustration by Lorraine Epstein

Coriander is an herb that grows in the Mediterranean region. People use the plant's sweet-tasting seeds as a spice in curries, sauces, and other foods.

in Europe more than in the United States or Canada. But the United States usually imports about 1,400,000 pounds (635,000 kilograms) of coriander seeds a year. Coriander-seed oil is used to flavor food, and as a medicine. About 500 pounds (230 kilograms) of seeds yield 5 pounds (2.3 kilograms) of oil.

Scientific classification. Coriander belongs to the parsley family, Apiaceae or Umbelliferae. Its scientific name is *Coriandrum sativum.*   Lyle E. Craker

Corinth, *KAWR ihnth,* was one of the most important cities of ancient Greece. It was founded in prehistoric times on the isthmus that connects the Peloponnesus with the rest of Europe. For the location of Corinth, see **Greece, Ancient** (map). According to Homer, it was the home of the legendary characters Bellerophon, Medea, and Sisyphus.

Corinth was favorably situated for trade by land. It

© Gian Berto Vanni, Art Resource

Corinth was an important city of ancient Greece. The Romans destroyed the city in 146 B.C., but they later rebuilt it. Some Roman ruins may be seen, *above.*

also had good harbors at Cenchreae and Lechaeum, on either side of the isthmus. By 750 B.C., Corinth had become the wealthiest city of ancient Greece. Except for two periods (454-404 B.C. and 146-44 B.C.), it maintained economic supremacy for about 1,300 years.

In 734 B.C., Corinthians founded colonies at Corcyra (now Corfu), an Ionian island west of Greece, and at Syracuse in Sicily. In 581 B.C., they instituted the Isthmian Games, a national festival held every second year in honor of their principal god, Poseidon. Corinth was famous for its skilled workers in bronze and clay and for its naval architects. Because of commercial and political rivalry with Athens, Corinth was chief instigator of the Peloponnesian War (see **Peloponnesian War**).

The Romans destroyed the city in 146 B.C., but later rebuilt it by order of Julius Caesar. Emperor Augustus made it capital of the Roman province of Achaea. Saint Paul visited Corinth in A.D. 51 and founded a church there (see **Corinthians, Epistles to the**).

In the Middle Ages, the city was largely confined to its citadel, Acrocorinth. American archaeologists began excavations in Corinth in 1896.   Ronald P. Legon

Corinth Canal, *KAW rihnth,* provides a waterway between the Gulf of Corinth and the Saronic Gulf in east-

central Greece. The canal is 4 miles (6 kilometers) long. It cuts through the narrow strip of land that connects the peninsula of Peloponnesus with the rest of the Greek mainland. A French company began building the canal in 1881, and Greece finished it in 1893. An attempt to build such a canal had been made by the Roman Emperor Nero in A.D. 67.   John J. Baxevanis

Corinthians, *kuh RIHN thee uhnz,* **Epistles to the,** are the seventh and eighth books of the New Testament. They are letters from the apostle Paul to members of the Christian church he had established in Corinth, Greece.

Paul wrote the first letter from Ephesus, in what is now Turkey, about A.D. 54. In the first half of the letter, he discussed problems that were reported to him orally, especially the problem of divisions within the church. In the rest of the letter, Paul discussed questions that the Corinthians raised in a letter they wrote to Paul.

Many scholars doubt that Paul wrote second Corinthians in the form in which we know it. They think that it consists of several shorter letters from Paul to the Corinthians that a later editor combined. Whether or not this is so, second Corinthians is mainly intended to repair the relationship between Paul and the Corinthians. Soon after Paul wrote his first letter, the Corinthians began to transfer loyalty to other apostles who had arrived in Corinth and seemed superior to Paul. The Corinthians questioned Paul's authority and sincerity. Paul wrote second Corinthians to persuade the Corinthians to accept him as they had done in the past.   Terrance D. Callan

See also **Paul, Saint; Bible** (Books of the New Testament).

Coriolanus, *KAWR ee uh LAY nuhs,* **Gaius Marcius,** *GAY uhs MAHR shee uhs,* was a general of the early Roman Republic. He was given his last name as a reward for his skill and bravery in capturing the town of Corioli from the Volscians, who were bitter enemies of Rome.

During a famine in 491 B.C., Coriolanus suggested that no grain be given to the poor unless they gave up their right to elect *tribunes* (representatives). The people became indignant over this, and exiled Coriolanus. He joined the Volscians to get revenge, and led their army to the gates of Rome. He was about to capture the city when his mother and wife persuaded him to spare Rome. The angry Volscians then killed Coriolanus. William Shakespeare told the story of this warrior in his tragedy *Coriolanus.*   Arther Ferrill

See also **Shakespeare, William** (*Coriolanus*).

Coriolis force, *KAWR ee OH lihs,* is the apparent effect of the earth's rotation on the motion of anything traveling across the face of the globe. The Coriolis force is too small to be noticeable when a person walks or drives. But it greatly affects the paths of objects flying over the earth. For example, a missile traveling above the earth tends to move in a straight line. But, to an observer rotating along with the earth, the path of the missile appears to curve, as if it were pushed. This apparent push is the Coriolis force. The Coriolis force prevents winds from the North and South poles and the equator from moving directly north or south. Winds that blow toward the equator seem to curve toward the west. Winds that move away from the equator seem to curve to the east. The Coriolis force also influences the direction of ocean currents. See also **Air** (Air movement); **Weather** (General circulation of the atmosphere).   James C. G. Walker

Cork (pop. 133,271) is the second largest city of the Republic of Ireland. Only Dublin, the capital, has more people. Cork is also the Irish Republic's second most important city—after Dublin—in such activities as manufacturing and trade and in education, medicine, and other services. Cork lies in southern Ireland, at the northwest end of Cork Harbour. For location, see **Ireland** (map). The central part of the city is on an island between two branches of the River Lee. The rest of Cork spreads over hilly land north and south of the river.

Cork's location on an island and hills gives the city a picturesque appearance. Cork has several beautiful churches, including St. Mary's Cathedral and St. Finbar's Cathedral. University College is in the city.

Cork is an exporting and importing center. Goods manufactured in the Cork area include alcoholic beverages and processed foods, chemicals, electronics products, petroleum products, steel, and textiles.

Vikings established Cork in the 800's, though a small settlement had previously been on the site. Cork grew rapidly during the 1700's, when its merchants established industries that processed agricultural products and handled goods being exported and imported. At that time, the originally swampy island was drained and became the core of the city. Cork later grew to include higher land north and south of the island. Cobh, a town near Cork, became the main port of departure for Irish emigrants sailing to North America in the 1800's.

Desmond A. Gillmor

Cork is a lightweight, spongy substance obtained from the bark of the cork oak tree. It does not absorb water readily and can be compressed a great deal, but it springs back when released. People used cork as early as 400 B.C. The Romans wore cork sandals and used cork to float anchors and fishing nets. Cork bottle stoppers have been made since the 1600's.

The tree. The cork tree is a live oak. This means that it is green the year round. It grows abundantly in Portugal and Spain, where most of the world's cork is produced. Italy is the third most important country in cork production. The cork oak has been planted in parts of California, and in some of the southeastern states, but the total yield of cork there is small. The outer layer of the bark is dead and is separated from the live inner bark by a layer of water-resistant cells called the *phello-*

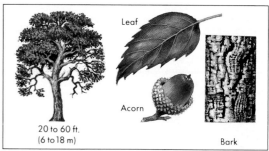

WORLD BOOK illustration by Chris Skilton

The cork oak tree provides most of the world's supply of cork. The cork is made from the tree's bark. The bark is stripped away every 8 to 10 years without damaging the tree.

derm. These cells have thin walls that become thickened and waxy. The cork tree lives from 300 to 400 years, but it seldom grows more than 50 feet (15 meters) high.

Gathering cork. A cork tree must be about 20 years old before its bark is thick enough to be stripped. The first layer removed is called *virgin bark.* Workers strip the bark in June, July, and August. Each tree can be stripped about once every 8 to 10 years. The best cork comes after the tree has been stripped twice.

A cork stripper uses a long-handled hatchet to cut long, oblong sections of bark from the top of the lowest branches to the bottom of the tree. The sections of bark are pried off carefully with the wedge-shaped handle of the hatchet. New phelloderms continue to form so that more cork is produced after each stripping. Cork will

Some uses of cork

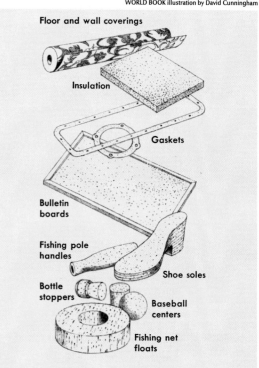

WORLD BOOK illustration by David Cunningham

© Odyssey Productions

Cork comes from the bark of the cork oak tree. Workers remove the bark and let it dry in the sun. Cork is used for wall coverings, bulletin boards, and many other products.

never grow again on a spot where the stripper's hatchet has damaged the live inner layer of bark down to the *cambium*. Cells in this tissue divide to form new layers of wood and bark cells.

Preparation for market. The slabs of stripped cork are boiled, and a rough, gritty outer layer is scraped off. The boiling dissolves tannic acid from cork, and softens the material so that the slabs can be straightened out. The slabs are then dried and packed in bundles. Before being loaded on ships, cork is sorted according to quality and thickness.

Uses. Most cork is used for insulation. For this purpose, it is ground and pressed into boards and pipe coverings. In this form, cork covers the walls and freezing pipes of thousands of cold-storage plants, meat-packing factories, ice cream plants, and oil refineries. Cork floats in water and is used in making buoys and floats for fishing nets. Linoleum is made by mixing cork powder with linseed oil and spreading this paste over canvas or burlap. Floors, walls, and ceilings are made soundproof with corkboard. One of its principal uses is for "corks," or bottle stoppers. Thin cork gaskets seal metal bottle caps. In addition, cork is used in waterproof coatings, in balloon fabric, and as wadding for shotgun cartridges. Cork shavings are burned to make *Spanish black*, or *cork black*, which is a paint used by artists.

Scientific classification. The cork oak tree is in the beech family, Fagaceae. It is *Quercus suber*.   Peter S. Ashton

See also **Bark; Insulation; Oak; Tree** (The parts of a tree).

Corliss, George Henry (1817-1888), an American engineer, helped improve the steam engine. His refinements included a more reliable *governor,* a device that held the engine's speed steady by controlling the supply of steam. His improved engine helped the textile industry. The speed was so steady that machines driven by the engine had less of a tendency to break fine threads. For the Philadelphia Exposition of 1876, Corliss designed a larger engine than any that had ever been built. Corliss was born in Easton, N.Y.   David F. Channell

Corm is a short, thick underground stem. The main function of a corm is food storage. During the growing season, the corm stores food made by the plant's leaves. At the end of the growing season, the aboveground parts of the plant usually die, but the corm stays alive. The next spring, new aboveground stems and leaves are formed, using the food that the corm has stored all winter. A new corm then develops above the old one, and the old corm dies. The new corm continues to grow as it, in turn, stores food.

Tiny corms, called *cormels,* grow out of the main corm. Gardeners separate the cormels from the corm and plant them. The cormels then grow into new plants.

Corms resemble bulbs in size and shape, but their internal structure is different. Bulbs consist mainly of fleshy leaves, but a corm is mostly stem tissue, covered by thin leaves. Gladiolus and crocus are well-known plants with corms.   Richard C. Keating

See also **Bulb; Stem.**

Cormorant, *KAWR muhr uhnt,* is a large, web-footed bird that catches fish by diving underwater. Cormorants are found throughout the world. Most of them live on seacoasts, but they are often seen on large rivers and lakes. Cormorants are related to pelicans. There are about 30 species of cormorants. The large species measure more than 30 inches (76 centimeters) long. Cormorants have long, powerful, hooked bills. Most species are strong fliers, and all are excellent swimmers.

A common cormorant of North America, the *double-crested cormorant,* perches in trees, on rocks, and on the ledges of sea cliffs. Hundreds of these birds live around the Bay of Fundy in Nova Scotia and New Brunswick. With their feathered bodies, long necks, and flat heads, they look like rows of bottles sitting on the cliffs. The double-crested cormorant has greenish-black, bronze-tinted feathers. During the nesting season, it has a crest of curved white feathers behind each eye. It has an orange throat. The *great cormorant* is larger than the double-crested cormorant and has white feathers bordering the throat. It lives along the Atlantic Coast of North America and coastal areas throughout Europe.

Cormorants look for fish while swimming on the water's surface. When they spot a fish, the birds dive below the surface and swim underwater with powerful kicks of their webbed feet. Cormorants usually return to the surface to eat their catch.

Scientific classification. Cormorants belong to the cormorant family, Phalacrocoracidae. The scientific name for the double-crested cormorant is *Phalacrocorax auritus*. The great cormorant is *P. carbo.*   James J. Dinsmore

See also **Pelican.**

WORLD BOOK illustration by John Rignall, Linden Artists, Ltd.

Double-crested cormorant

© Stan Osolinski, The Stock Market

The cormorant dives into the water to catch fish and returns to the surface to eat them. This photo shows a double-crested cormorant about to swallow a gar in the Florida Everglades.

Rows of corn cover much of the farmland in a region of the Midwestern United States called the Corn Belt. Corn is one of the world's most important crops. It is a leading source of energy in the human diet, serves as a major livestock feed, and has many industrial applications.

Corn

Corn, also called *maize,* is a plant whose food value and wide variety of uses make it the most important crop grown in the United States. It is also one of the most important crops in the world. In order of world grain production, corn ranks second, after wheat. Rice is a close third. Those three grains are the chief sources of energy in the human diet.

Corn has an amazing number of uses. The *kernels*—that is, the corn grain, or seeds—can simply be cooked and eaten. The kernels can also be used in making breakfast cereals, baked goods, salad dressing, and many other foods. Large quantities of corn grain, as well as cornstalks and other parts of corn plants, are fed to livestock. People eat this corn indirectly in the form of meat, eggs, and dairy products. Corn is also used in making many kinds of nonfood products, including ceramics, drugs, paints, paper goods, and textiles.

Corn is a cereal grass related to wheat, rice, oats, and barley. Corn was first used for food about 10,000 years ago by Indians living in what is now Mexico. For hundreds of years, the Indians gathered corn from wild plants. About 5000 B.C., they had learned how to grow corn themselves. Thus, corn came to be called *Indian corn.* But today the term generally refers only to varieties of corn that produce ears with multicolored kernels.

Lyndon W. Kannenberg, the contributor of this article, is Professor of Corn Breeding at the University of Guelph.

Depending on the variety, corn can be grown in most mild and tropical regions of the world. The United States is the world's leading producer and exporter of corn. It produces about two-fifths of the world's supply, chiefly in a region of the Midwest called the Corn Belt. Other major corn producers include Brazil, China, Mexico, Romania, Ukraine, and Yugoslavia. This article deals mainly with U.S. corn production.

Uses of corn

Food for people. Corn grain is especially rich in starch. Starch is a *carbohydrate,* a nourishing substance in food that provides the body with energy. Corn also supplies fats and protein. But corn protein lacks some of the important chemical units called *amino acids* that the body needs. In many developing countries in Latin America, Africa, and Asia, corn forms a major part of the human diet. Therefore, a large number of people in those countries can suffer from protein malnutrition if an alternative protein source is not available.

Corn can be eaten in several ways. Many people enjoy eating sweet corn on the cob after the ears have been boiled or roasted. Sweet corn kernels that have been removed from the cob are sold canned or frozen for easy preparation. Popcorn is a favorite snack food. People eat it plain or flavored with such foods and seasonings as salt, butter, caramel, or cheese.

Corn also serves as an important ingredient in many processed foods. A typical supermarket in the United States or Canada might carry more than 1,000 foods that contain corn or corn products. Such foods include breakfast cereals, salad dressing, margarine, syrup, cornstarch, and snack items. Corn meal, a flourlike substance made from ground corn grain, is used to make such foods as corn bread, tamales, and tortillas. Corn is also an ingredient in beer and whiskey.

Livestock feed. Corn is a major livestock feed in most Western countries. In the United States, about half the corn grain harvested each year is fed to hogs, cattle, sheep, and poultry. About 10 per cent of the U.S. corn crop is made into livestock feed called *silage.* Silage is made from entire corn plants, except for the roots, or from the parts that remain after the ears have been removed. Livestock also eat feed made from ground ears, whole shelled corn, or ground shelled corn.

Industrial uses. Corn is used in the manufacture of many industrial products. Such products include ceramics, explosives, construction materials, metal molds, paints, paper goods, and textiles. Manufacturers also use corn in making industrial alcohols, such as ethanol and butyl alcohol. Alcohol made from corn and other plants is mixed with gasoline to produce such motor fuels as gasohol and premium unleaded gasoline with ethanol. Corn is also used in producing penicillin and other antibiotics, vitamins, and industrial enzymes.

The corn plant

There are several thousand varieties of corn. Originally, varieties arose naturally. Today, nearly all new varieties are developed by scientists. Varieties grown in the same region may have many characteristics in common but differ greatly from varieties in other regions. For example, most Corn Belt varieties grow about 9 feet (2.7 meters) tall. Varieties in other regions may range from as little as 3 feet (0.9 meter) to as much as 20 feet (6 meters) tall. If the similarities among varieties are great enough, the varieties are considered to belong to the same *race.* Scientists have identified about 250 corn races. However, all varieties develop in the same manner and can breed with one another.

Food value of whole-grain field corn

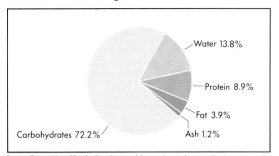

Source: *Composition of Foods—Raw, Processed, Prepared,* Agriculture Handbook No. 8, Agricultural Research Service, U.S. Department of Agriculture, 1975.

Appearance. A mature corn plant consists of the roots, stalk, leaves, and flowering parts. The typical Corn Belt plant has a single sturdy stalk supported by a root system with many branches. About 15 long, broad leaves grow along the stalk. The flowering parts of a corn plant are the *tassel,* the male reproductive structure at the top of the stalk, and the *ear,* the female reproductive structure about in the middle of the stalk. An ear consists of a cob covered by rows of kernels. The ear is enclosed and protected by special leaves called *husks.* A plant may have one or several ears. Most Corn Belt varieties bear one ear about 9 inches (23 centimeters) long per plant. Each ear has about 18 rows of kernels.

How the plant develops. A corn plant begins life as a seed. Mature corn seeds have three main parts: (1) the embryo, or germ; (2) the endosperm; and (3) the seed coat. The embryo is the part of the seed that develops into a new plant. The endosperm is a storehouse of food energy, mostly in the form of starch. The corn seedling uses that energy in its early development. The seed coat is a thin, tough outer covering around the endosperm and embryo that protects them from damage.

Physical development of the new corn plant begins

Grant Heilman · WORLD BOOK photo · WORLD BOOK photo

Uses of corn. Corn is made into many forms of nutritious feed, including flaked corn, *left.* People eat corn by itself or as an ingredient in a wide variety of foods, *center.* Manufacturers use corn in making such products as cosmetics, paper goods, and textiles, *right.*

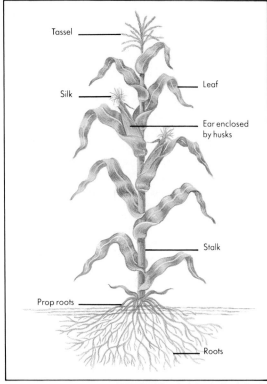

Tassel

Silk

Leaf

Ear enclosed
by husks

Stalk

Prop roots

Roots

WORLD BOOK illustration by Lorraine Moseley Epstein

A mature corn plant consists of the roots, stalk, leaves, ears, and tassel. Special leaves called *husks* enclose the ears. Long, threadlike *silks* extend beyond the tips of the husks.

two or three days after the seed is planted. Moisture absorbed by the seed causes it to swell. The lower part of the embryo, called the *primary root,* breaks through the seed coat and pushes down into the soil. One or two days later, several *seminal roots* start to form. Those roots are usually temporary. They anchor the seedling and absorb water and nourishment from the soil. About three to five days later, the upper part of the embryo breaks through, and the first leaves emerge.

Additional leaves appear during the next three or four weeks as the cornstalk grows taller. After all the leaves have started growing, the tassel, which is not yet visible, begins to form at the top of the plant. About the same time, buds start to form where the stalk and lower leaves meet. The lowest buds may form *tillers* (shoots). Higher buds will develop into one or more ears. The plant then enters a period of rapid growth. During that time, which lasts about five or six weeks, a permanent root system develops and the leaves grow to their largest size. The flowering parts continue to develop. *Prop roots,* also called *brace roots,* extend into the ground from the lower part of the stalk and provide additional support to the plant. The plant reaches its full size about 9 to 11 weeks after sprouting.

How the plant reproduces. A corn plant reproduces sexually. *Sperm* (male sex cells) from the pollen released by the tassel unite with *eggs* (female sex cells) in the ear in a process called *fertilization.* The fertilized eggs develop into kernels on the cob.

A tassel consists of small male flowers that grow in clusters. Each flower has three baglike structures called *anthers,* which produce pollen. An anther may contain as many as 2,500 pollen grains.

An unfertilized ear of corn consists of female flowers arranged in pairs on a cob. In most varieties, only one flower of each pair develops and is able to reproduce. Each developing flower sends out a long, threadlike *silk* from its *ovary,* an egg-bearing structure at the base of the flower. At blossoming time, a mass of silks extends beyond the tip of the husks.

When the corn plant has nearly reached its maximum height, its anthers split open and shed their pollen. The pollen shed usually lasts five to eight days. The wind blows the pollen about like dust. Most of the pollen falls on other corn plants, though some self-pollination will occur. When a pollen grain lands on a silk, it germinates and sends a *pollen tube* down through the silk. Two *sperm nuclei,* male structures that fertilize, travel down the tube. One nucleus fertilizes the egg inside the ovary, forming the embryo of the new seed. The other unites with two female structures called the *polar nuclei,* forming the endosperm. In a Corn Belt plant, the kernels reach maturity about eight weeks after fertilization. The rest of the plant dies at that time or soon after.

Kinds of corn

The many varieties of corn can be grouped into seven major kinds. They are (1) dent corn, (2) flint corn, (3) flour corn, (4) sweet corn, (5) popcorn, (6) waxy corn, and (7) pod corn. The classifications are based chiefly on different characteristics of the kernels.

Dent corn gets its name from the dent on the top of mature kernels. The dent forms when the soft, floury starch in the kernel dries and shrinks as the seed matures. Most kernels are yellow or white. Dent corn is the most widely grown kind of corn in North America. It is used chiefly for livestock feed. It is also used in making many processed foods and industrial products.

Flint corn has hard, round kernels with a smooth coat. The kernels range from white to deep red. Flint corn grows well in cool climates and reaches maturity early. It resists insect pests that attack kernels better than corn with softer kernels, such as dent corn. The

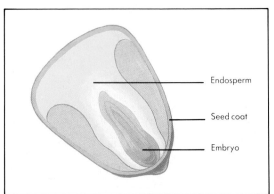

Endosperm

Seed coat

Embryo

WORLD BOOK illustration by Lorraine Moseley Epstein

A mature corn seed has three main parts. (1) The *embryo* develops into a new plant. (2) The *endosperm* stores starch and other food energy. (3) The *seed coat* protects the parts.

American colonists found that breeding flint corn with dent corn produced a superior dent variety. Like dent corn, flint corn is used as food for people and livestock. In the fall, many people decorate their homes with ears of flint corn or other colorful corn. Such corn is often called Indian corn. Flint corn is widely grown in Asia, Europe, and Central and South America.

Flour corn is one of the oldest kinds of corn. The Inca Indians of South America and the Aztec of Mexico grew flour corn perhaps more than 5,000 years ago. The kernels on most ears are white, blue, or a variety of colors. The kernels contain mainly soft starch and can be easily crushed into a flour. Flour corn is cultivated mostly in the Southwestern United States, western South America, and South Africa. It is used mainly for food by the people who grow it.

Sweet corn is the sweetest corn. People eat the cooked kernels directly from the cob or after they have been removed. Sweet corn is harvested before the kernels mature so it has the sweetest flavor. The kernels are soft and may be white or yellow. Sweet corn is grown chiefly in the Northern United States and the southern part of the Canadian province of Ontario.

Popcorn is a highly popular snack food. Like flour corn, it is one of the oldest kinds of corn and was grown by American Indians thousands of years ago. There are two main types of popcorn—*pearl popcorn* and *rice popcorn.* Pearl popcorn has rounded kernels that are usually yellow or orange. Rice popcorn, also called *hullless popcorn,* has pointed, white kernels. Popcorn kernels have a very hard endosperm with a small amount of soft, moist starch in the center. Steam created inside the kernels during heating causes them to explode, or pop. They turn inside out and produce a light, fluffy mass. The United States produces almost all the world's popcorn. See **Popcorn.**

Waxy corn gets its name from the waxlike appearance of its endosperm. The endosperm consists almost entirely of a starch called *amylopectin.* Such starch is especially useful as a thickener in manufacturing instant pudding mixes, gravies and sauces, and glues. Most waxy corn is grown in the United States and China.

Pod corn is the most primitive—and perhaps the oldest—form of corn. Each kernel is enclosed in a pod, or husk. The whole ear is also surrounded by husks. Pod corn has no commercial value and is raised almost entirely for scientific research.

Hybrid corn

In the United States and most other developed countries where corn is grown, farmers grow *hybrid corn* almost exclusively. Such corn is developed through breeding. It has exceptional vigor and produces high yields.

Hybrid corn is developed through *hybridization.* In that process, corn breeders select varieties of corn that have the characteristics they wish to be inherited by future generations. For example, one variety of dent corn may resist diseases better than another variety. However, the second variety may produce larger ears than the first variety. The plant breeders *inbreed* (self-pollinate) plants of each selected variety for several generations until pure hereditary lines have been established. They then cross the two inbred lines to obtain seed of a *single-cross hybrid.* Such seed will produce vigorous, uniform plants that combine the hereditary traits of the two parental inbred lines.

If farmers bred a crop of single-cross hybrids to get seeds for another season, the plants would be of varying quality and lower yield. As a result, corn farmers must purchase new single-cross hybrid seeds for planting the crop each year. Most breeding of hybrid corn has been done with dent corn. See **Hybrid.**

Where corn is grown

There are so many varieties of corn with such different growing needs that one variety or another can be raised in most *temperate* (mild) and tropical areas of the world. Each year, about 500 million short tons (460 million metric tons) of corn are produced worldwide on about 320 million acres (130 million hectares) of land. The annual harvest amounts to about 20 billion bushels.

Corn production in the United States accounts for about two-fifths of the world's grain corn supply. About three-fourths of the U.S. crop is grown in the Corn Belt, which covers parts of Illinois, Indiana, Iowa, Michigan, Minnesota, Missouri, Nebraska, Ohio, South Dakota, and Wisconsin. Iowa and Illinois are the leading states

Dent corn has a dent on the top of its yellow or white kernels. It is the most widely grown corn in North America and is chiefly used for livestock feed or silage.

Indian corn refers to types of corn with multicolored kernels, such as flour and flint corn. People often decorate their homes with Indian corn in the fall.

Pod corn is the most primitive kind of corn. Each of its kernels is enclosed in a separate pod, or husk. It is grown almost entirely for scientific research.

Leading corn-growing states

Bushels of corn grown in a year*

State		Bushels
Iowa	●●●●●●●●●●●●●●●●●●●●●●●	1,302,233,000 bushels
Illinois	●●●●●●●●●●●●●●●●●●◖	1,114,617,000 bushels
Nebraska	●●●●●●●●●●●●◖	866,600,000 bushels
Minnesota	●●●●●●●●◖	603,466,000 bushels
Indiana	●●●●●●●●◖	603,217,000 bushels
Ohio	●●●●●	338,217,000 bushels
Wisconsin	●●●◖	265,150,000 bushels
Missouri	●●◖	193,053,000 bushels
Michigan	●●◖	190,887,000 bushels
South Dakota	●●◖	185,600,000 bushels

*One bushel equals 56 pounds (25 kilograms). Does not include corn used for forage, grazing, or silage. Excludes sweet corn.
Figures are for a three-year average, 1988-1990. Source: U.S. Department of Agriculture.

in grain corn production. The United States is also the world's top producer of corn for silage. About a fourth of the yearly grain corn harvest in the United States is exported, and it makes up about half the world's total corn exports.

Corn production in other countries. China ranks as the second largest producer of corn. It accounts for about a seventh of the world's supply. Other countries that are leading producers of corn include Argentina, Brazil, France, India, Mexico, Romania, and Ukraine. In Canada, the leading corn-producing provinces are Ontario, Quebec, and Manitoba. Argentina, South Africa, and Thailand are among the leading corn-exporting

countries. Japan ranks as the largest importer of corn in the world.

How corn is grown

Most types of corn have a growing season of four to six months, usually beginning in April or early May. Much of the world's corn is grown on large farms that use modern machinery to perform nearly all the operations involved in producing corn.

Growing conditions. Most kinds of corn grow best in loamy, well-drained soils that range from slightly acid to neutral. Corn also needs such *nutrients* (nourishing substances) as nitrogen, phosphorus, and potassium. Those and other nutrients are generally added to the soil in the form of chemical fertilizers or manure. Many corn farmers also rotate their corn crop each year with such crops as alfalfa, clover, soybeans, or wheat. Crop rotation returns some nutrients to the soil and helps control soil erosion, weeds, insects, and diseases.

Most types of corn produce the highest yields at daytime temperatures of about 86 °F (30 °C) and average nighttime temperatures above 50 °F (10 °C) around flowering time. Ideal rainfall for growing is 18 to 25 inches (46 to 64 centimeters) in temperate regions and 25 to 36 inches (64 to 91 centimeters) in the tropics.

Preparing the soil. Most corn farmers use a *moldboard plow* to prepare the soil for planting. Such a plow turns over about the top 8 inches (20 centimeters) of soil in rows about 14 to 22 inches (36 to 56 centimeters) wide. The plowing buries weeds and the remains of the previous year's crop. Chemical fertilizers or manure may be added to the soil before plowing, at planting time, or as the plants grow. Immediately before planting, the ground may be tilled one or more times to break up clods of earth and produce an even, firm seedbed.

Planting begins when the soil temperature reaches about 55 °F (13 °C). Farmers generally begin planting during April to early May, though planting can start as early as February in such areas as southern Texas. Seeds are usually planted about 2 inches (5 centimeters) deep in rows about 30 to 40 inches (76 to 102 centimeters)

Corn-producing areas in the United States

About three-fourths of the U.S. corn crop comes from the Corn Belt, where the climate and soil are ideal for growing corn. The Corn Belt extends from Nebraska to Ohio and from Minnesota to Missouri. Smaller amounts of corn are grown in Washington, California, and many Eastern and Southern states.

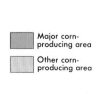

Major corn-producing area

Other corn-producing area

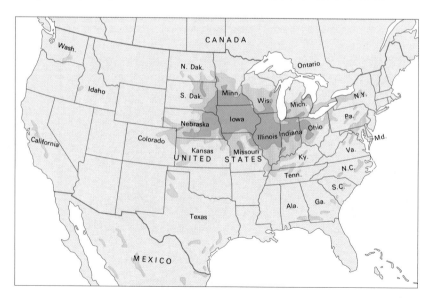

WORLD BOOK map

Corn-producing areas of the world

The United States produces about two-fifths of the world's grain corn supply. Other major corn-producing countries include China, Argentina, Brazil, France, India, Mexico, Romania, Ukraine, and Yugoslavia.

Major corn-producing area

Other corn-producing area

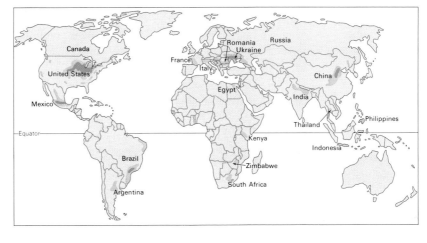

WORLD BOOK map

apart. But they may be planted at shallower or deeper levels, depending on the type of soil and its temperature and moisture content. The most commonly used corn-planting machines are called row planters. They can plant from 2 to 24 rows of seeds at a time. In the Corn Belt, farmers usually plant 4 or 6 rows at a time. Farmers may grow from 12,000 to 28,000 plants per acre (29,000 to 69,000 per hectare), depending on soil fertility, rainfall, and the availability of irrigation water.

Controlling pests and diseases. The major threats to corn crops are weeds, insects, birds, and fungi that cause such diseases as ear rot, stalk rot, and root rot. One way farmers protect their crops is by growing hybrids that resist insects and diseases. Chemicals also help protect corn from pests. Farmers use herbicides to control weeds, insecticides to control certain seed- and root-eating insects, and fungicides to control fungi that rot seeds. In addition, farmers use certain chemicals and noisemaking devices to discourage birds from feeding on their crops.

Harvesting. The harvesting of corn for grain begins when the moisture content of the mature kernels has dropped to about 28 per cent. However, many farmers will delay the harvest until the grain is drier to reduce artificial drying costs. Harvesting may take place as early as August in states that border the Gulf of Mexico or as late as October in the Northern United States and Canada. Almost all harvesting is done with a *corn combine,* a machine that picks the ears from the stalks, removes the husks, shells the corn, and cleans it in one operation (see **Combine**). The shelled grain is then dried with heated air and stored in bins for later sale or for use on the farm as livestock feed. Some corn is harvested by a machine that picks the ears from the stalks, removes the husks, and deposits the ears in an accompanying wagon. The ears are then usually stored in long, narrow corncribs that allow enough natural air movement to dry the corn to a safe storage moisture. The ears are removed from the cribs as they are needed.

Harvesting corn for silage begins when the kernel moisture has dropped to about 50 per cent and the overall moisture of the plant is about 65 per cent. A machine called a *forage harvester* cuts one or two rows of plants at a time near ground level. It then chops the plants into small pieces and blows the pieces into a wagon. The chopped corn is packed into a silo, where chemical changes called *fermentation* occur in the silage. Fermentation preserves the silage until it is used.

Corn in industry

Grain corn that is not used on producing farms to feed livestock is sold for export or to industry for processing. Four main industries process corn. They are, in order of the quantity of corn used: (1) the mixed-feed industry, (2) the wet-milling industry, (3) the dry-milling industry, and (4) the fermentation and distilling industry.

The mixed-feed industry uses whole grain corn and by-products of the other industries to make livestock and pet feeds. Manufacturers usually grind or crack the whole grain and then add other ingredients to produce a tasty, nutritious feed. They often shape the feed into pellets, which keep the ingredients from separating.

The wet-milling industry chiefly produces cornstarch. Manufacturers use cornstarch in making bakery items, corn syrup, drugs, laundry starch, paper goods, textiles, and many other products. By-products of wet milling include corn oil and animal feed, such as corn germ meal and corn gluten meal. Corn oil is used in such foods as salad dressing and margarine.

In the wet-milling process, cleaned and shelled corn is soaked in warm water for 24 to 48 hours to soften the kernels. The processors then coarsely grind the kernels, which frees the germ, or embryo, from each kernel. The germ is removed for use in corn oil and corn germ meal. The remaining material is finely ground and passed through screens to remove the seed coat and larger fragments. The material that passes through the screens consists of starch and a protein substance called *gluten.* The gluten is removed for use in corn gluten meal. The starch that remains is pure cornstarch.

The dry-milling industry separates the kernel parts and processes them into corn meal, corn flour, grits, or corn oil. Manufacturers use those products to make such items as cornflakes, explosives, and snack foods. There are two systems of dry milling: (1) the new process system and (2) the old process system.

The new process system, or *degerming system,* is used to process about 80 per cent of the corn used by the dry-milling industry. In this system, processors first clean the kernels and then increase their moisture con-

Grant Heilman

Row planters can plant from 2 to 24 rows of corn at a time. The planter shown above applies a weedkiller as it deposits the corn seeds. Fertilizers may also be added at planting time.

tent by treating them with water or steam. The grain is then fed into a machine called a *degermer.* The degermer separates the germ and the seed coat from the endosperm by coarse grinding. It also breaks up the endosperm and passes the particles through screens that sift out the large pieces. Processors use the germ to make corn oil and corn germ meal. They use the seed coats and bits of the kernel stuck to them to make an animal feed known as *hominy feed.* The largest endosperm pieces are called *flaking grits* and are used to make cornflakes. The remaining endosperm pieces are ground to produce such products as brewers' grits, corn meal, and corn flour.

The old process system, or *nondegerming system,* involves grinding whole corn kernels into corn meal called *old process meal* or *whole corn meal.* The meal generally has all parts of the kernel, though some meal is made without the seed coat. Old process meal has a

high oil content from the germ and cannot be stored long. It is used to make tortillas and snack foods.

The fermentation and distilling industry uses corn grain to produce alcohol. To produce alcohol from corn, many processors first remove the germ through coarse grinding. They then grind the remaining material into a meal and cook it to produce a *mash.* Barley malt and water are also cooked into a mash. The two mashes are combined, and enzymes in the barley malt convert the starch in the combined mash to sugar. The processors next add yeast or bacteria to the mash, which cause the sugar to ferment, or convert to alcohol. Manufacturers can then remove and purify the alcohol from the fermented mash by *distillation.* Distillation involves turning the alcohol into vapor by heating the mash and then cooling the vapor back into a liquid. Products and by-products of the fermentation and distilling industry include beer and whiskey, antibiotics, industrial enzymes, vitamins, and distillers' feeds.

History

Scientists cannot trace the ancestry of modern corn directly to a wild plant, as they can such other grains as rice and wheat. However, they do know that Indians living in what is now central or southern Mexico gathered and ate corn from wild plants about 10,000 years ago. The ancestry of corn probably involves *teosinte,* a wild grass that is closely related to corn. Some scientists believe that corn is descended directly from teosinte. Others think that corn is a product of natural hybridization between teosinte and a primitive popcorn.

The oldest known fossil corncobs are about 7,000 years old. They measure about 1 inch (2.5 centimeters) long and had 50 to 60 kernels.

Expansion of corn production. The cultivation of corn gradually spread to much of the Americas. Corn was most widely cultivated by the Aztec Indians of central Mexico, the Maya of southern Mexico and northern Central America, and the Inca of western South America. By the late 1400's, Indians grew corn as far south as Argentina and Chile and as far north as Canada.

Europeans knew nothing of corn until Christopher Columbus landed in Cuba in 1492. Columbus brought some corn seeds from the island back to Spain. Later ex-

J. C. Allen and Son

Corn harvesting is done almost entirely with a *combine, left.* The combine picks the ears from the stalks, removes the husks, and shells and cleans the corn. The shelled grain is then deposited in wagons and carried away for drying and storage.

plorers introduced corn from other parts of the Americas into many areas of the world. By the late 1500's, corn had become a well-established crop in Africa, Asia, southern Europe, and the Middle East.

Corn was a basic food in the American Colonies during the 1600's and 1700's. The colonists learned how to grow corn from the Indians. During the 1800's, the demand for corn increased rapidly in the United States, and corn became a major commercial crop. Production soared as farmers competed for the growing market.

Mechanization of corn farming. Before the 1800's, farmers used wooden or cast-iron plows. The heavy, gummy soil of the Midwestern prairies stuck to the surface of such plows, making it difficult to turn the soil. The problem was solved in 1837, when an American inventor named John Deere introduced the steel plow (see **Deere, John**). The sticky soil slid off Deere's smooth steel plow, enabling farmers to work the rich land of the Corn Belt far more easily.

Mechanical corn planters were developed in the early 1800's. Mechanical corn pickers came into common use during the 1930's and 1940's. By the mid-1950's, nearly 80 per cent of the U.S. grain corn crop was mechanically harvested. Today, almost all grain corn is harvested by combines that pick, husk, shell, and clean the corn in one operation.

Development of hybrids. During the early 1900's, an American geneticist named George H. Shull began experiments to produce vigorous, high-yielding hybrid corn. Shull established pure hereditary lines by inbreeding plants of the same variety. He then crossed two inbred lines to develop the first *single-cross hybrids,* which displayed vigor. But because the inbred parents produced very low hybrid seed yields, seed production was costly. About 1918, another American geneticist, Donald F. Jones, bred two single-cross hybrids and developed the first *double-cross hybrids.* The single-cross female parent produced enough double-cross hybrid

Corn Refiners Association

The wet-milling process is used mainly to produce cornstarch. The equipment shown above removes the embryos from water-softened corn kernels in the beginning of the process.

seeds to lower production costs and so make hybrids commercially important. Producers began selling double-cross hybrid corn seed in the 1920's.

By the 1960's, producers had begun marketing single-cross hybrids that produced more uniform, vigorous plants with higher grain yields than double-cross hybrids. Today, most corn seed comes from single-cross hybrids. The development of hybrid corn and better farming practices have helped increase U.S. corn yields over 300 per cent per acre since the early 1930's.

Scientific classification. Corn belongs to the grass family, Poaceae or Gramineae. All corn is *Zea mays.*

Lyndon W. Kannenberg

Related articles in *World Book* include:

Alcohol	Cornstarch	Iowa (picture)
Alcoholic beverage	Farm and farming	Plant
Chinch bug	Grain	Popcorn
Corn borer	Grass	South Dakota
Corn earworm	Hominy	(Places to visit)
Corn syrup	Hybrid	Starch

Outline

I. Uses of corn
   A. Food for people   C. Industrial uses
   B. Livestock feed
II. The corn plant
   A. Appearance   C. How the plant reproduces
   B. How the plant develops
III. Kinds of corn
   A. Dent corn   D. Sweet corn   F. Waxy corn
   B. Flint corn   E. Popcorn   G. Pod corn
   C. Flour corn
IV. Hybrid corn
V. Where corn is grown
   A. Corn production in the United States
   B. Corn production in other countries
VI. How corn is grown
   A. Growing conditions   D. Controlling pests and dis-
   B. Preparing the soil   eases
   C. Planting   E. Harvesting
VII. Corn in industry
   A. The mixed-feed industry
   B. The wet-milling industry
   C. The dry-milling industry
   D. The fermentation and distilling industry
VIII. History

Questions

Where and by whom was corn first used for food?
Why does popcorn pop?
How many races of corn are there?
How was corn introduced into many areas of the world?
What are single-cross hybrids?
Why do many farmers rotate their corn crop each year with other crops?
Why is pod corn raised?
What are the three main parts of mature corn seeds?
What is the chief product of wet milling?
Why did the steel plow enable farmers to work the rich land of the Corn Belt far more easily?

Additional resources

Elting, Mary, and Folsom, Michael. *The Mysterious Grain: Science in Search of the Origin of Corn.* Dutton, 1967. For younger readers.
Hardeman, Nicholas P. *Shucks, Shocks, and Hominy Blocks: Corn as a Way of Life in Pioneer America.* Louisiana State Univ. Press, 1981.
Mangelsdorf, Paul C. *Corn: Its Origin, Evolution, and Improvement.* Harvard, 1974.
Walden, Howard T. *Native Inheritance: The Story of Corn in America.* Harper, 1966.

Corn is a small, hard, shiny thickening of the *epidermis* (outer layer of the skin). This thick growth presses on the *dermis* (deeper skin layer) and causes it to become thin and tender. Pressure and friction cause corns. Therefore, corns often develop over the joints of the toes of persons who wear shoes that do not fit properly. But corns may form anywhere on the body where pressure and friction injure the skin. A *soft corn* is one located between the toes. Here the thickened skin remains soft because it is constantly bathed with sweat.

Corn plasters remove the thickened epidermis and are used to relieve the pain of corns. Most plasters contain chemicals that soften the outer horny accumulation. To cure a corn, the things that caused it to form must be removed. Because of the danger of infection, paring corns with sharp instruments should be done only by a doctor.   Paul R. Bergstresser

See also **Callus**.

Corn Belt. See Corn (introduction; Corn production in the United States).

Corn borer, also called the *European corn borer,* is a serious insect menace to corn crops. The borer is the larva of a night-flying moth. It is pinkish with small brown spots. The female moths begin to lay eggs on corn leaves in early June. The tiny borers feed on the young leaves and tassels. As they grow larger, they feed on the stems and ears. One or more generations of borers appear each year, depending on the length of the growing season. In winter, the larvae live in old corncobs, stems, and stubble. The corn borer eats chiefly corn and sorghum. But it attacks other plants, including celery, potatoes, beans, flowers, and weeds.

WORLD BOOK map

The corn borer came to the United States from Europe about 1910. It spread through the Eastern and Midwestern states, causing damage to the corn crop in the orange areas on the map.

Farmers destroy corn borers during the winter by feeding cornstalks to livestock, or by shredding or burning the stalks. They plant late in the season to avoid the first flight of the moths, and use hybrid corn plants that are not affected by the corn borer. In some cases, farmers use insecticides.

Scientific classification. The European corn borer belongs to the snout moth family, Pyralidae. It is *Ostrinia nubilalis.*

John R. Meyer

Corn earworm, also called *bollworm,* ranks among the worst insect pests in the United States. Most corn earworms are greenish-brown with dark stripes. They measure about $1\frac{1}{2}$ inches (4 centimeters) long. The adult is a grayish-brown moth.

On corn, the moths usually lay their eggs on the silk. The eggs hatch in two to eight days. As far north as Kentucky, three broods of the insects appear each year—in June, July, and August. Farther north, two broods are normal. To the south, as many as five broods may occur. Corn earworms also attack cotton, tomatoes, alfalfa, beans, and other crops. The corn earworm is called the *bollworm* when it attacks cotton bolls. Farmers plow under all crop remains and use crop varieties resistant to corn earworms to control the insects. Insecticides also may be needed to protect some crops.

Scientific classification. The corn earworm belongs to the owlet moth family, Noctuidae. Its scientific name is *Helicoverpa zea.*   John R. Meyer

Corn flour. See Corn (The dry-milling industry).

Corn Laws were measures passed in England between the 1400's and mid-1800's to control the price of small grains, called *corn* in England. The first Corn Laws prevented grain exports. By the 1500's, landowners could export grain if English prices fell too low. As the population grew in the 1700's, grain imports were permitted if prices rose too high.

By the 1830's, industry was developing in Britain, and support grew for the free trade proposals of economist Adam Smith. Landowners had lost support in Parliament. The Anti-Corn Law League, a group of factory owners and workers, wanted the laws repealed so bread would be cheaper. Parliament repealed the Corn Laws in 1846. Food imports then increased, and British agriculture declined.   Lacey Baldwin Smith

See also **Peel, Sir Robert.**

Corn oil is a vegetable oil made from the kernel of the corn plant. It is used mainly as a cooking and salad oil and in such food products as margarine and potato chips. Refined corn oil has a pale, yellow color.

The United States produces most of the world's corn oil. During processing, machines separate the *germ* (embryo) from the rest of the kernel. The germ contains about 20 per cent oil. The oil can be squeezed from the germ, or it can be obtained by *solvent extraction.* This method involves treating the germs with a liquid solvent, which separates the oil from the germ. Corn oil consists of about 55 per cent polyunsaturated fat, a substance many nutritionists consider essential to a healthy diet (see **Fat**).   Daniel R. Sullivan

See also **Corn** (Uses of corn; Corn in industry).

Corn snake. See Snake (pictures: How a snake swallows its prey; Some harmless snakes).

Corn State. See Iowa.

Corn syrup is a thick, sweet liquid made from cornstarch. Food processors use it to sweeten baked goods, candies, canned fruits, ice cream, and soft drinks. It also flavors ketchup, peanut butter, salad dressings, processed meats, and many other foods. Corn syrup gives creams and candies a smooth texture. It also attracts and holds moisture, and so it helps prevent baked goods from becoming stale.

Manufacturers make corn syrup from a mixture of cornstarch and water. To this mixture they add a weak acid solution or certain *enzymes* (protein molecules). This converts the starch to sugar. The resulting corn syrup consists mainly of two sugars, *glucose* and *maltose,* plus a sticky substance called *dextrin.* To make a sweeter syrup, manufacturers add another enzyme, which changes some of the glucose in the syrup to a sweeter sugar called *fructose.* Further treatment of the syrup produces *high-fructose corn syrup* (HFCS). Many food processors use HFCS because it costs less and is much sweeter, but not higher in calories, than other sweeteners.   Roger E. Wyse

See also **Sugar** (Cornstarch and other starches).

Corncrake. See Rail.

Cornea. See Eye (The sclera and the cornea).

Corneal transplantation. See Eye bank.

Corneille, *kawr NAY,* **Pierre** (1606-1684), was a French playwright. He is often called the father of French tragedy, but he is more truly the founder of French heroic comedy. Corneille favored tragicomedy and melodrama over conventional tragedy.

Corneille is best known for his tragicomedy *The Cid* (1636 or 1637). The French Academy condemned the play for breaking several "classical" rules. These rules held that a play should consist of a single plot in a single location within a day's time. Violence was also prohibited on stage. Although *The Cid* broke these rules, it enjoyed great popularity. The play was the first French drama to center on the characters' inner psychological conflict rather than on external changes alone. In addition, *The Cid* brought to the French stage a new lyrical language in keeping with the passionate nature of Corneille's heroes.

The subjects of most of Corneille's plays are taken from Roman history. Most of his leading characters, like their ancient models, show great pride, patriotism, honor, and stern courage. They are fearless, remorseless, and subject to violent emotions such as hatred, revenge, and superhuman ambition. Many of Corneille's plays show the effect of Spanish drama, especially in the passionate, boastful, and violent nature of their heroes. This influence pleased his audience, a status-conscious society often at war.

Corneille's other famous plays include *Horace* (1640), *Cinna* (1640), *Polyeucte* (1642), and *Rodogune* (1644). He described his drama theories in the prefaces to his plays and especially in his *Discourses on Tragedy* (1660). Corneille was born in Rouen.   Carol L. Sherman

Cornell, Ezra (1807-1874), was an American businessman and philanthropist. He rose with the rapidly growing telegraphic communications industry, and helped organize the Western Union Telegraph Company. He became wealthy, and in his later years devoted his energies and fortunes to educational projects. He is particularly remembered for helping found Cornell University (see **Cornell University**).

Cornell was born in New Britain, N.Y. His father was a poor potter, and he received little education. After several false starts in various fields, Cornell invented a machine that solved Samuel F. B. Morse's problem of laying cable for his first telegraph line. Cornell then became one of the leading builders of telegraph systems.
          Richard D. Humphrey

Cornell, Katharine (1893-1974), was an American stage actress. She won fame for the quality of her acting, primarily in romantic and character roles, and for her fine choice of plays. She became famous in *A Bill of Divorcement* (1921). Beginning with *The Green Hat* (1925), Guthrie McGlintic, her husband, directed her performances. Her greatest success came in *The Barretts of Wimpole Street* (1931). She also won praise for her acting in *Romeo and Juliet, Saint Joan, Candida, The Wingless Victory, No Time for Comedy, The Doctor's Dilemma, The Three Sisters,* and *Dear Liar.* She wrote an autobiography, *I Wanted to Be an Actress* (1941).

Cornell was born in Berlin, Germany, of American parents. She began acting with the Washington Square Players in New York City in 1916.   Don B. Wilmeth

Cornell University is a coeducational institution and the *land-grant university* of the state of New York. A land-grant university is partly endowed by the United States government under the Morrill, or Land-Grant, Act of 1862 (see **Land-grant university**). Cornell has 13 schools and colleges. Eleven of them are on the main campus in Ithaca. The other two, the medical college and the graduate school of medical sciences, are in New York City. Seven of the schools in Ithaca are private and four receive state support.

Cornell offers a wide range of courses in both the liberal arts and professional fields. The undergraduate units are the colleges of agriculture and life sciences; architecture, art, and planning; arts and sciences; engineering; and human ecology; and the schools of industrial and labor relations and hotel administration. Graduate study takes place in the schools of law and management, the college of veterinary medicine, and the graduate school. Programs of study lead to bachelor's, master's, and doctor's degrees.

Cornell University was founded in 1865. It was named for its founder, Ezra Cornell, an American businessman and philanthropist. Cornell students come from throughout the United States and from more than 90 other countries. For the enrollment of Cornell University, see **Universities and colleges** (table).
          Critically reviewed by Cornell University

See also **Cornell, Ezra; New York** (picture).

Corner Brook, Newfoundland (pop. 22,410), is an important newsprint manufacturing center. Corner Brook lies on the western coast of Newfoundland, on the Bay of Islands. For location, see **Newfoundland** (political map).

Corner Brook has a large paper mill that produces about 375,000 short tons (340,200 metric tons) of newsprint annually. Plants in the city also process fish and manufacture cement, plasterboard, and other building materials. Corner Brook's excellent port facilities and roads make it the major distribution center for western Newfoundland and southern Labrador.

Beothuk Indians lived in what is now the Corner Brook area before Europeans arrived there. Captain James Cook, a British explorer, visited the area in 1767. He probably gave the name Corner Brook to a stream that runs through the city. The community was later named after the stream. In the early 1800's, white settlers came to the area because of its rich fishing grounds. The town's economy centered on fishing until the paper mill began operating in 1923.

A junior college, the Sir Wilfred Grenfell College, opened in Corner Brook in 1975. It is affiliated with Memorial University of Newfoundland. Corner Brook has a mayor-council form of government.   C. M. Holloway

Cornering the market was a technique used to accumulate all or most of the available supply of a stock or commodity. The buyer did this to raise the price of the stock or commodity at will. Cornering affected speculators who *sold short,* or sold stock they did not yet own but planned to buy at lower prices. The market corner forced those who needed a stock to pay high prices to the controlling group. Various stock exchanges and the Securities and Exchange Commission have outlawed cornering. They limit the prices at which a speculator may sell short, because these practices have caused serious fluctuations in the stock market. See also **Fisk, James; Gould, Jay.**   Robert Sobel

Cornet is a brass musical instrument that resembles a shortened trumpet. Cornets and trumpets have the same range, but the cornet has a mellower tone quality. The main part of a cornet is a coiled tube about $4\frac{1}{2}$ feet (1.4 meters) long. The tube has three valves. Different pitches are produced by vibrating the lips in a cup-shaped mouthpiece. Notes are played by changing the tension of the lips and by pressing the valves.

The cornet developed from a valveless brass instrument called a posthorn. The modern cornet appeared after valves were invented in the early 1800's. The instrument soon became the main melodic brass instrument in bands. Some composers also wrote cornet parts for symphony orchestras, often in combination with trumpets. Because of its brilliant tone and carrying power, the trumpet has almost completely replaced the cornet in jazz groups, concert bands, and marching bands.

Stewart L. Ross

See also **Trumpet; Jazz** (The brass).

Cornflower. See Bachelor's-button.

Corning (pop. 11,938), is a glassmaking center on the Chemung River in south-central New York (see **New York** [political map]). Corning was named for Albany businessman Erastus Corning, who developed the area in the 1830's. The Flint Glass Company of Brooklyn, N.Y., moved to Corning in 1868 and became the Corning Glass Works. It produces glass products, including cookware, light bulbs, Steuben crystal, and huge telescopic lenses. It operates the Corning Glass Center, which offers exhibits and demonstrations on the history, uses, and making of glass. The Rockwell Museum has a collection of art of the American West. Corning was incorporated as a village in 1848, and as a city in 1890. It has a mayor-council government.   John Kenneth White

Cornplanter (1750?-1836) was a Seneca Indian leader. He supported Britain during the Revolutionary War in America (1775-1783). But in the 1780's and 1790's, Cornplanter helped prevent the Seneca from fighting in wars between Midwestern Indians and the United States government. In 1791, the Pennsylvania legislature rewarded his efforts to keep the Seneca out of the wars by granting him a large area of land on the Allegheny River. The *Cornplanter Grant* became a major Seneca settlement in 1796. In 1798, Pennsylvania Quakers began teaching Cornplanter and his people how to live like white frontier farmers and herders.   Michael D. Green

Cornstalk (1720?-1777), a Shawnee Indian chief, became a central figure in Indian wars in Ohio during the late 1700's. He became alarmed when a conflict between other Ohio Indians and Virginians led to an invasion by two armies of Virginians in 1774. Cornstalk feared the Virginians would overrun Ohio, and so he led a Shawnee army against one of the Virginian forces. His warriors were defeated at the Battle of Point Pleasant in October 1774. The battle ended what was called Lord Dunmore's War, named after Virginia's governor. In 1777, Cornstalk was visiting Point Pleasant when other Indians killed a settler. A mob took revenge by killing Cornstalk, his son, and three other Shawnee. These murders led to years of warfare in Ohio. Cornstalk was probably born in Pennsylvania.   Michael D. Green

Cornstarch is a fine white flour made by grinding and refining grains of corn. It is made of corn from which the seed-bearing part, called the *germ,* has been removed. The corn is ground in a process called *wet milling.* After removal of the corn proteins, the remaining cornstarch is dried in ovens. Since only 10 per cent of moisture remains in the cornstarch after drying, it is often mixed with other foods to protect them from moisture. Manufacturers use cornstarch in bakery products, baking powder, candies, and salad dressing. Cooks use it to thicken gravies and puddings. Manufacturers also use cornstarch in explosives, paints, and textiles. See also **Corn** (The wet-milling industry).   Mary E. Zabik

Cornucopia, *kawr nuh KOH pee uh,* is a horn of plenty, a symbol of nature's productivity. According to Greek mythology, it was one of the horns of Amalthaea, the goat who nursed the god Zeus when he was a baby. The horn produced ambrosia and nectar, the food and drink of the gods. In Roman mythology, the cornucopia was the horn of the river god Achelous. The hero Hercules broke off the horn in combat with Achelous, who was fighting in the form of a bull. Water nymphs filled the horn with flowers and fruit and offered it to Copia, the goddess of plenty.   Mary R. Lefkowitz

Cornwallis, Charles (1738-1805), the first Marquis Cornwallis, was a British general in the Revolutionary War in America. The surrender of his troops at Yorktown, Va., in 1781 was critical to the American triumph.

Cornwallis helped capture New York in 1776, then pursued General George Washington across New Jersey. He became second in command to Sir Henry Clinton in 1778. In 1780, he took charge of the Southern campaign. Invading North Carolina, he won a costly victory in 1781 at Guilford Courthouse against forces of General Nathanael Greene. Then, against Clinton's wishes, he moved into Virginia. A French fleet and French and American troops surrounded him at Yorktown. He surrendered there on Oct. 19, 1781.

Cornwallis was commander in chief and viceroy of India from 1786 to 1793 and again in 1805. He was lord lieutenant and commander in chief of Ireland from 1798 to 1801. He was born in London.   James Kirby Martin

Cornwallis, Edward (1713-1776), a British soldier and colonial official, led 2,500 settlers to Nova Scotia in 1749 and founded Halifax. After overseeing the initial settlement and establishing civil government, he served as governor and captain-general of Nova Scotia from 1749 to 1752. Cornwallis served in the British army from 1731 to 1748. He was governor of Gibraltar from 1762 until his death. Cornwallis was born in London.   Judith Fingard

Corona, *kuh ROH nuh,* is the outermost layer of the sun's atmosphere. It is visible to the unaided eye only during a total solar eclipse, when the rest of the sun is hidden by the moon. At such times, the corona appears as an irregularly shaped halo of light.

The corona consists chiefly of electrons, hydrogen ions, and ions of heavier elements that have lost many of their electrons. Such highly ionized atoms result because of the corona's high temperature, estimated at about 4,000,000° F., or approximately 2,200,000° C. The corona has an extremely low density. At its densest, near the solar surface, the corona has only about 16 billion particles per cubic inch (1 billion particles per cubic centimeter). The density rapidly decreases outward.

The corona is continually expanding into space, forming the *solar wind*. This stream of charged particles extends to the earth's orbit and beyond. Astronomers believe the solar wind flows primarily from *coronal holes,* which are regions of relatively low temperature and density in the corona. These coronal holes occur mainly around the sun's poles, but they sometimes appear at the lower solar latitudes.

The corona has a very irregular shape. Streaks of coronal gas called *polar tufts* spread outward from the sun's poles, and long, gaseous rays known as *coronal streamers* radiate from areas closer to its equator. The gas is guided by the sun's magnetic field, and so the corona takes on different shapes as the field changes.

Between eclipses, astronomers rely on instruments called *coronagraphs* to study the corona in a limited way. Coronagraphs on certain mountains enable them to observe the inner corona. During the 1970's and early

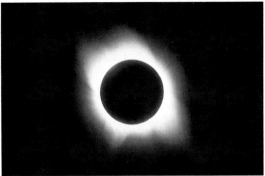

© Jay M. Pasachoff

The corona, as seen during a total solar eclipse

1980's, the United States launched spacecraft equipped with coronagraphs that provided observations of the outer corona. Data from the space station *Skylab* revealed that the corona is far more active than was previously believed. Violent coronal eruptions occur frequently during the maximum phases of the *sunspot cycle* (see **Sunspot**). Data from the *Solar Maximum Mission* satellite confirmed this condition. X-ray telescopes on orbiting satellites also showed the sun's corona. X-ray observations from other satellites indicated that most stars besides the sun have coronas too.   Jay M. Pasachoff

Coronado, Francisco Vásquez de (1510-1554), was a Spanish explorer. Coronado led an expedition

The Surrender of Lord Cornwallis at Yorktown (1817-1824), an oil painting by John Trumbull; Yale University Art Gallery

Lord Cornwallis surrendered his army to George Washington at Yorktown. This painting shows French and American officers, including Washington, lined up to receive the surrender.

into the American Southwest in search of the legendary Seven Cities of Cibola. Indians and earlier Spanish explorers had reported these cities to be rich in gold. Coronado found Indian villages but did not discover any golden cities.

Coronado was born in Salamanca, Spain. He left home after his wealthy parents promised the family fortune to his older brother. In 1535, Coronado sailed to Mexico with Antonio de Mendoza, the viceroy of Mexico. Coronado became governor of New Galicia province, northwest of Mexico City, in 1538.

In 1536 and 1539, Spanish explorers told Mendoza about the Seven Cities of Cibola. Mendoza named Coronado to command an expedition to find the golden cities and claim their wealth for Spain.

In 1540, Coronado set out from Compostela, the capital of New Galicia, with about 300 Spanish soldiers and a large number of Indian troops. He led his army into the area that became Arizona and New Mexico. He found a group of Zuni Indian settlements, which he identified as Cibola, in the area of what is now Gallup, N. Mex. Coronado captured the Zuni villages, but he found no sign of gold or other riches.

While Coronado's army camped in the villages of Cibola, some of his men made separate trips in search of

Bettmann Archive

Francisco Coronado, shown in a painting by N. C. Wyeth, set out in 1540 to search for seven cities that were said to be stocked with gold and gems. Instead, he reached parts of the Rio Grande and central Kansas.

golden cities. One group visited the Pueblo Indian villages of Acoma, Pecos, and Taos in what is now New Mexico. They also were the first Europeans to travel up the Rio Grande Valley. Another group of men found Indian settlements in Arizona, and the members of a third band became the first Europeans to reach the Grand Canyon.

Coronado and his army spent the winter of 1540 in Tiguex, a Pueblo village on the Rio Grande. In the spring, he led his army south across what is now Texas. He then went into present-day Kansas in search of Gran Quivira, a land reported to be rich in gold and silver. He was the first European to reach Palo Duro Canyon near what became Amarillo, Tex. North of the Arkansas River in Kansas, Coronado found settlements of Quivira Indians, but no gold. Discouraged, he finally returned to Tiguex during the winter of 1541 and later went home to New Galicia. In 1546, Coronado was accused of committing cruel acts against Indians in his army, but he was found innocent of the charges.   Charles Gibson

See also **Cibola, Seven Cities of; Pueblo Indians; Zuni Indians.**

Additional resources

Bolton, Herbert E. *Coronado: Knight of Pueblos and Plains.* Univ. of New Mexico Pr., 1990. First published in 1949.
Chavez, Angelico. *Coronado's Friars.* Academy of Am. Franciscan History, 1968.
Udall, Stewart L. *To the Inland Empire: Coronado and Our Spanish Legacy.* Doubleday, 1987.

Coronary bypass surgery. See Heart (Coronary artery disease).

Coronary thrombosis, also called *coronary occlusion*, is a condition in which a clot blocks the passage of blood in an artery of the heart. The portion of the heart muscle supplied by the blocked artery then dies. The death of the muscle is called a *heart attack* or a *myocardial infarction.*

Symptoms of a coronary thrombosis include severe chest pain, shortness of breath, vomiting, and a weak and rapid pulse. A coronary thrombosis can cause death. If the patient survives, the condition leaves scar tissue in the area of the heart muscle supplied by the artery where the clot developed.   Bruce A. Reitz

Coronado's expedition 1540-1542

The map below shows the explorations of Francisco Coronado in the American Southwest. Coronado searched in vain for the legendary cities of Cibola and Gran Quivira. The present-day state boundaries are also shown.

——— Route of main expedition

------ Route of secondary expedition

o   Indian pueblo

•   Spanish settlement

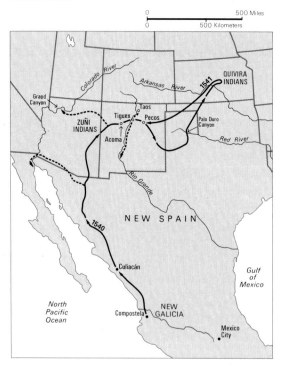

WORLD BOOK map

Coronation is a ceremony at which a king, queen, or pope publicly receives a crown as a symbol of rule. The ceremony is usually rich in color and tradition. Most coronations have religious as well as political features, and a religious official often performs the ceremony. During the proceedings, the new ruler also receives other official marks of royalty. When accepting this power, he or she usually makes a pledge to rule wisely.

The British coronation includes many features common to coronation ceremonies in other countries. The British ceremony takes place in Westminster Abbey. The new monarch is conducted from the west door of the Abbey along the nave to the crossing, where the ceremony is performed. First, the monarch sits in a Chair of Estate. The *regalia*—the crown, orb, scepter, rod, swords of state, spurs, ring, and bracelets that are used in the ceremony—are placed on the altar. The Archbishop of Canterbury then presents the monarch to the people in the abbey as the true ruler of the realm. The monarch takes the coronation oath, swearing to rule justly and to support the Church of England. The monarch receives a Bible, which is placed on the altar. The celebration of the communion service of the Church of England then begins.

The service is interrupted after the Creed, the cloak is removed, and the monarch moves to King Edward's Chair, also called the Coronation Chair. Here the monarch is anointed and clothed in a cloak of gold cloth. The spurs of St. George, a symbol of knighthood, are presented. The Sword of State is taken from its scabbard and carried before the monarch during the rest of the ceremony. *Armills* (bracelets) are put on the wrists of the monarch. While sitting in King Edward's Chair, the monarch receives the *orb*, a globe of gold surmounted by a cross signifying the rule of Christ over the world. The Coronation Ring, symbolizing the marriage of the ruler and the kingdom, is placed on the monarch's right hand. The monarch receives a rod with a dove to hold in the left hand. The dove symbolizes the Holy Ghost. The monarch holds a scepter with a cross in the right hand. On top of the scepter is the *Star of Africa,* the largest cut diamond in the world. After the monarch receives these symbols of authority, the Archbishop of Canterbury places the crown of St. Edward on the monarch's head.

The guns of the Tower of London fire a salute in honor of the coronation. The peers and peeresses, who were bareheaded until this moment, place their coronets and caps on their heads. The monarch moves to the throne after receiving a blessing from the archbishop. Nobles, carrying the Jewelled Sword of State, the Sword of Temporal Justice, the Sword of Spiritual Justice, and the Sword of Mercy, which has a blunted point, surround the throne. The monarch gives the rod and scepter to an attendant, then receives homage and fealty from representatives of the clergy and the public.

The monarch then leaves the throne, removes the crown, and offers the archbishop the bread and wine for Holy Communion. An altar cloth and an ingot of gold are placed on the altar. The monarch takes Holy Communion and returns to the throne. Then the monarch receives the crown, the scepter, and the orb, and leaves the throne. After walking in procession down the nave, the monarch leaves the Abbey through the west door. A banquet follows the coronation. In earlier times a fully armed knight, the King's Champion, rode into the banquet hall to challenge anyone who questioned the monarch's right to the throne.

The British coronation ceremony is quite ancient. The earliest record of the ceremony used in the coronation of an English king dates from about the A.D. 750's. King Edward I (1272-1307) made the Coronation Chair to contain the *Stone of Scone* (or *Stone of Destiny*), the Coronation Stone of kings of Scotland.

Development. Ancient Germanic tribes elected their rulers. The newly elected king received a spear, and a diadem of silk or linen was placed on his forehead. As the king sat upon a shield, his warriors lifted him to receive the acclamation of his followers.

Religious pageantry, taken from the Bible, influenced coronation ceremonies after the birth of Christianity. According to a custom mentioned in the Bible, kings were anointed with *chrism,* a mixture of oil and balm. People thought that chrism gave the anointed ruler special miraculous powers. In England, popular belief held that a person who even touched the king's clothes could be cured of illness. In some coronation ceremonies, the ruler was ordained as one of the lower ranks of the clergy. The Holy Roman emperor became a subdeacon and canon of St. Peter's Church and St. John Lateran in Rome.   I. J. Sanders

Related articles in *World Book* include:

Charlemagne (Military conquests)	Napoleon I (Crowned emperor)
Crown	Scone, Stone of
Elizabeth II (picture)	Westminster Abbey

Coroner is an official of a county or other local government who investigates any death not clearly due to natural causes. Coroners also have a legal responsibility to protect the personal property of any person who has died until the property can be turned over to the person's rightful heirs. In a case of suspicious death, the coroner conducts an inquiry called an *inquest.* A coroner's jury may hear the evidence and decide whether the death resulted from a criminal act. The jury's verdict is not conclusive, but it may become the basis of a murder indictment.

Most coroners are elected, a system many people oppose because elected officials may lack the necessary medical and legal training. Many states have replaced elected coroners with appointed officials called *medical examiners,* who must be physicians. In states with medical examiners, public prosecutors handle the legal aspects of the investigations.

The office of coroner originated in England and France. Early coroners guarded the fines collected by the king, or crown, and were called *crowners.* The word *coroner* comes from that title.   John I. Thornton

See also **Autopsy; Inquest; Jury** (Coroner's juries).

Corot, *kaw ROH,* **Camille,** *ka MEE yuh* (1796-1875), was a French landscape and figure painter. His work formed an artistic bridge between the tradition of classical composition of the early 1800's and the romantic movement's concern with nature which led to impressionism.

Corot began to study painting against his parents' wishes. In 1825, he went to Italy, where he became concerned with the play of light and color values. He began painting in solid masses in order to produce light and dark patterns of color. Corot's early work shows the influence of the French landscape painters, Claude (Lorrain) and Nicolas Poussin, and of the Dutch landscape painters of the 1600's.

Corot returned to France in 1828 and traveled a great deal, because a small income left him free from economic worries. He came under the influence of a group of nature painters in the village of Barbizon. Corot was called "the lyric poet" of this group. He changed his style, and began painting everything as if seen through a delicate gray veil, accented by a few details of bright color. Corot's style underwent a final change in 1871. He again painted in the style of his youth, but his works were now drenched in impressionist light and color. His painting, *A View near Volterra,* appears in the **Painting** article.

Corot painted portraits for his own pleasure throughout his career. He also painted religious pictures. His portraits, along with his early and last paintings, are considered his best works. Corot was born Jean Baptiste Camille Corot in Paris.   Ann Friedman

Corporation is a person or group of people who obtain a charter giving them certain legal rights and privileges. A corporation can own property, buy and sell, manufacture products, and bring lawsuits as if its members were one person. Business corporations are the most common type of corporation. Other types are municipal, government-owned, quasi-public, nonprofit, and single-person corporations. Business corporations make up only about 15 per cent of all business enterprises in the United States. Partnerships and individual proprietorships form the rest. But business corporations account for more than 75 per cent of all business assets.

Corporations are formed under *general incorporation laws.* People wishing to form a corporation file *Articles of Incorporation,* stating the purpose and makeup of the organization. A government official then issues a certificate that permits the corporation to exist. Investors in a corporation have *limited liability.* If the corporation fails, they can lose no more than their investment, because the corporation's debts are not their debts.

In the United States, state or federal government permission is required to form a corporation. State governments charter most corporations. National banks need federal approval. A corporation set up in one state can do business in other states if it files certain forms and pays required fees in those states.

Business corporations may be public or private. The most common type is the public corporation, which obtains funds by selling ownership shares, called *capital stock,* to large numbers of investors. There are two varieties of stock, *preferred* and *common.* Preferred stock does not extend voting rights in the corporation to stockholders but gives holders first claim on the company's assets after debts are paid. Common stock gives stockholders voting rights. Corporations reward stockholders for their investments by giving them part of the profits. These payments are called *dividends.*

When stock is first issued, the people forming the corporation determine the type of stock, the number of shares to be issued, and the price per share. Afterward, the stock value depends on the corporation's financial status. A corporation may raise funds by issuing new stock or by selling bonds. Bondholders do not have voting rights, but they have first claim on the corporation's assets. Stockholders and bondholders may sell their holdings. Most previously issued stocks and bonds are bought and sold on stock exchanges.

A public corporation is governed by a board of directors elected by common stockholders at regular meetings. The directors establish the policies of the corporation. The policies are carried out by officers chosen by the directors or by stockholders.

Most stockholders receive one vote for each share of common stock they own. The stock in most large corporations is widely distributed, and so a person or group owning much less than 51 per cent can usually obtain effective control.

Private corporations, unlike public corporations, have a limited number of owners. Some private corporations are large firms. But most are small companies in which all or most stock is held by family members. In such corporations, owners usually manage the company, rather than appoint others to do so. There is no open market for the sale of stock of private corporations.

Other corporations. Cities and towns may form *municipal corporations* to operate certain government enterprises, such as sewer, water, and school districts. Federal, state, or local governments may establish *government-owned corporations* to provide certain public welfare functions. *Quasi-public corporations* join private and government investors in high-risk investment situations, such as the development of space satellites. In these ventures, the government usually subsidizes or insures the private investor. *Nonprofit corporations,* such as the Red Cross, provide community services. They consist of members instead of stockholders and provide no dividends. Certain highly paid individuals, such as motion-picture stars or professional athletes, form *single-person corporations* to take advantage of corporate tax benefits.   Robert B. Carson

Related articles in *World Book* include:

Bond	Franchise	Multinational
Business	Holding company	corporation
Cartel	Joint-stock	Mutual company
Charter	company	Proxy
Conglomerate	Limited company	Stock, Capital

Corporation for Public Broadcasting is a private, nonprofit organization that promotes public television and radio in the United States. It is financed mainly by grants from the federal government.

The corporation, often called the CPB, uses about two-thirds of its funds to support the nation's approximately 700 public TV and radio stations. These stations broadcast primarily educational and cultural programs, with no commercials. The CPB finances the production and distribution of programs and conducts audience research.

The CPB was created by Congress in 1967 and began operating in 1968. The 10 members of its board of directors are appointed by the President, subject to the approval of the Senate. The CPB has headquarters at 901 E Street NW, Washington, DC 20004.

Critically reviewed by the Corporation for Public Broadcasting

See also **Television** (Public stations).

Corporative state. See Fascism (Economic life).

Corps, *kawr,* is an army unit consisting of two or more divisions. The term *corps* comes from a Latin word meaning *body*. A corps is normally composed of about 50,000 to 100,000 soldiers. Most corps are commanded by a lieutenant general. A corps can conduct major military operations. The word *corps* also refers to the U.S. Marine Corps and to such branches of the U.S. Army as the Corps of Engineers and the Signal Corps. See also **Army, United States** (table: Army levels of command).

Joel D. Meyerson

Corps of Engineers. See **Engineers, Corps of.**

Corpus Christi, *KAWR puhs KRIHS tee,* Tex. (pop. 257,453; met. area pop. 349,894), is a major United States seaport and a center of industry and tourism. It lies on Corpus Christi Bay, near the Gulf of Mexico (see **Texas** [political map]). The city was named for the bay. Corpus Christi has a council-manager government.

Description. Corpus Christi, the county seat of Nueces County, covers 392 square miles (1,015 square kilometers). This area includes 276 square miles (715 square kilometers) of inland water. About half the people of Corpus Christi are of Hispanic ancestry.

Corpus Christi has a mild climate and attracts many tourists and conventions. Temperatures in the city average 57 °F (14 °C) in January and 84 °F (29 °C) in July. For the monthly weather in Corpus Christi, see **Texas** (Climate). The city has fine facilities for fishing, sailing, and swimming, and crowds of tourists visit nearby Padre Island National Seashore. Cultural attractions in Corpus Christi include the Texas State Aquarium, the Art Museum of South Texas, the Corpus Christi Museum, and the Museum of Oriental Cultures. The city also has a symphony orchestra and Corpus Christi State University.

Oceangoing ships reach the Port of Corpus Christi via a 21-mile (34-kilometer) channel that links the city with the Gulf of Mexico. The port serves barges that use the Gulf Intracoastal Waterway, which runs along the coastline between Brownsville, Tex., and Carrabelle, Fla. Naval Station Ingleside, on northern Corpus Christi Bay, is home to U.S. Navy minehunters and minesweepers. Airlines use Corpus Christi International Airport.

Corpus Christi lies near natural gas and petroleum fields, cattle ranches, and fertile farmland. The city's chief manufactured products, in order of value, are chemicals, petroleum products, and processed foods. The Corpus Christi Army Depot is the largest employer.

History. Karankawa Indians lived in what is now the Corpus Christi area before white settlers arrived. About 1839, a trading post opened at the site to serve nearby ranchers. The settlement was named Corpus Christi probably in 1847 or 1848 and was incorporated as a city in 1852. In 1923, the city developed its first natural gas well. The city's deepwater port opened in 1926. Oil was discovered nearby in 1930. From 1920 to 1940, the city's population rose from 10,552 to 57,301.

The Corpus Christi Naval Air Station opened in 1941 and trained 40,000 naval fliers during World War II. Today, it is headquarters for the Naval Air Training Command and provides primary flight training for more than 300 pilots a year. The area's large supplies of natural gas and petroleum have attracted many industries to Corpus Christi. The population of the city grew to 167,690 by 1960 and to 257,453 by 1990. A project that dug the city's port to a uniform depth of 45 feet (13.7 meters) was completed in 1989. It improved the port's capability to handle larger ships.   Terry G. Jordan

Corpuscle, *KAWR puh suhl,* in physiology, is a term used for a small mass or body. It is often used to mean *cell,* especially in referring to the red cells and white cells of the blood. Certain parts of the nervous system, such as the nerve endings in the skin that respond to pressure, are called *corpuscles.*   Edward J. Shahady

Corral. See **Ranching** (Life on a cattle ranch).

Correggio, *kuh REHJ oh* (1489?-1534), was one of the greatest painters of the Italian Renaissance. His most important works are *frescoes* (paintings on damp plaster) on two church domes in Parma, Italy. In these paintings, Correggio created the illusion that the ceilings open into the sky and many divine figures inhabit the clouds above the viewer's head. This dramatic illusion influenced the paintings of the baroque period of the late 1500's and the 1600's.

Correggio's early paintings of religious and mythological subjects show a delicate, graceful style. Correggio worked primarily in Parma, though his paintings suggest that he may have visited Rome during the mid-

Oil painting of the late 1520's; The Louvre, Paris

Correggio's *The Mystic Marriage of Saint Catherine* shows the artist's soft treatment of flesh, his command of gentle light, and his delicate handling of shading. Correggio influenced painters of the baroque style in the 1600's.

dle or late 1500's to become more familiar with the paintings of Leonardo da Vinci and Raphael. Correggio's works show a more spirited emotional quality and dramatic handling of light than the paintings of those two masters.

Correggio's real name was Antonio Allegri. He took his name from the Italian town of his birth.

Eric M. Zafran

Corregidor, *kuh REHG ih DAWR,* a rocky fortified island, covers about 2 square miles (5 square kilometers) at the entrance to Manila Bay on the island of Luzon. It is sometimes called the *Gibraltar of the Pacific.* The island has a population of about 320. During the early days of World War II, United States and Filipino troops made a determined stand on Corregidor against overwhelming

Japanese forces. Their surrender to enemy troops on May 6, 1942, marked the end of organized U.S. resistance in the Philippines.

The Japanese held Corregidor until U.S. troops freed Luzon in February 1945. The United States ceded Corregidor to the Republic of the Philippines in 1947. In 1954, Corregidor became a Philippine national shrine dedicated to the American and Filipino troops who died there during World War II. The island has a war museum and a marble war memorial.   David J. Steinberg

Correspondence. See Letter writing.

Correspondence school is an educational institution that furnishes home-study material through the mail. Nearly 5 million persons are enrolled in more than 700 home-study schools in the United States. About 75 per cent of the courses are of the vocational type.

Colleges and universities provide correspondence courses for nearly 400,000 people. They coordinate their programs through the National University Continuing Education Association (NUCEA). Government agencies, the armed forces, religious institutions, and business and industry provide courses for over 1,700,000 people.

Nearly 1,500,000 people are enrolled in private home-study schools. The National Home Study Council was organized in 1926 by a group of home-study schools. It works with the National Commission on Accrediting and the Federal Trade Commission to maintain sound educational standards and business practices. The 110 accredited schools in the council have an enrollment of about 1,200,000 people.

The University Extension movement in England first used the correspondence plan in 1868. The earliest U.S. practical courses were developed in the early 1890's by President William Rainey Harper of the University of Chicago. The Blackstone School of Law in Chicago, and the International Correspondence Schools in Scranton, Pa., founded in 1891, are pioneer correspondence schools still in existence.   Douglas Clifford Smith

See also **Extension programs.**

Correspondent. See Foreign correspondent; War correspondent.

Corrosion, *kuh ROH zhuhn,* is the destruction of a material caused by the chemical action of a gas or liquid. Corrosion occurs chiefly in metals, but it may also affect ceramics. Rust is the most familiar form of corrosion. This reddish-brown substance forms on iron and steel that are exposed to moist air or to water containing impurities. See **Rust.**

In most cases, corrosion involves two related chemical reactions—*oxidation* and *reduction.* In oxidation, the atoms of a metal give up electrons to a liquid or a gas. In reduction, part of the same metal or an adjoining metal captures these electrons from the liquid or gas. The electrons that flow from one metal to the other form an electric current. In this sense, corrosion is an *electrochemical process* (see **Electrochemistry**).

There are many types of corrosion. One kind, called *localized attack,* occurs on small areas of bare metal and produces holes or cracks. Another type, *uniform corrosion,* attacks much larger areas, such as the surface of an aluminum pot or a copper roof. It can be beneficial. On copper roofs, for example, such corrosion produces a thin, greenish film called *patina* that protects the surface against further rapid corrosion.

© Guy Gillette, Photo Researchers, Inc.

Uniform corrosion is a common type of corrosion that attacks large areas. It produces a greenish film known as *patina* when it occurs on such a surface as a copper roof, *above.*

The type of corrosion and its severity depend on the chemical makeup of the metal and of the corrosive agent. Other major factors include stresses in the metal, the temperature of the corrosive agent, and the speed at which the agent moves against the metal. Corrosion tends to be more severe if the corrosive agent hits the metal at a high speed. If the agent contains solid particles, the corrosion is even worse and is called *erosion-corrosion.*   Cathleen J. Hapeman

See also **Oxidation; Reduction.**

Corrupt practices are unethical techniques used by politicians to gain a political advantage in an election. The term is most commonly used in referring to federal and state legislation, called *corrupt practices acts,* that govern campaigns and elections. These laws prohibit such activities as bribery, ballot-box stuffing, tampering with voting machines, and threatening or impersonating voters. Many of these laws also govern party campaign finances. For example, many states have laws that limit the amount spent by candidates and parties in state and local elections.

Congress established the Federal Election Commission in 1974 following campaign finance irregularities in the 1972 presidential election. The commission enforces federal laws regulating contributions and spending for presidential and congressional campaigns.
Charles O. Jones

See also **Election campaign** (Legal changes).

Corsair. See Pirate.

Corsica, *KAWR sih kuh* (pop. 240,178), is a French island in the Mediterranean Sea. It lies 9 miles (14 kilometers) north of the island of Sardinia, between southeast-

WORLD BOOK maps

Corsica is a French island in the Mediterranean Sea.

ern France and northwestern Italy. Corsica's name in French, the official language, is Corse. The island makes up two of the *departments* (main administrative districts) of France. It is the birthplace of Napoleon.

Size and description. Corsica has an area of 3,352 square miles (8,680 square kilometers). Its 275-mile (443-kilometer) coastline is high and craggy and has few natural harbors. The rocky interior is covered with scrub and cut by narrow, fertile valleys. Ajaccio, Corsica's capital and largest city, is on the western side of the island beside the Gulf of Ajaccio. Bastia, the second largest city, lies on the eastern side.

Economy. Corsica has a mild climate, and crops flourish in the rich soils of the valleys. Farmers raise olives, grapes and other fruits, grains, vegetables, and tobacco. Cork, pine, oak, and chestnut trees cling to the steep slopes of the mountains. Corsicans grind chestnuts into meal to make bread. Wool for clothing comes from sheep that graze in the mountains. Along the coast, the people fish for sardines and hunt for coral. Miners quarry granite and marble in the mountains. Some iron, lead, and copper are also mined.

The principal exports of Corsica are wool and cheese. The island's fastest-growing source of income is the tourist trade. Tourists enjoy the climate, the rugged scenery, and the colorful villages of Corsica.

History. Corsica was first settled about 560 B.C. by Phoenicians, who called the island *Cyrnos.* It was conquered in turn by Etruscans, Carthaginians, and Romans. The Romans renamed the island Corsica. Vandals captured Corsica in A.D. 469, but the island was recaptured by Rome, under Justinian I, in 534. Later, Corsica was ruled by Charlemagne.

Pope Gregory VII assumed sovereignty of Corsica in 1077, and granted it to the Bishop of Pisa to control. About 300 years later, Corsica came under the control of the Italian city of Genoa. In 1768, the Genoese sold the island to the French, who lost it to the British in 1794. In 1796, Napoleon sent an expedition to Corsica to reestablish French control. France has held the island since then, except for a brief occupation by British soldiers in 1814, and the occupation by Italians and Germans during World War II. Allied forces freed the island in 1943, and it again became part of France.

During the 1970's, protests against French rule arose in Corsica. Since then, some Corsicans have called for independence from France. Others have favored greater local control over the island's government. In 1982, the French Parliament created a Corsican regional assembly. Corsican voters elect the assembly, which controls local spending and the development of the island's economy, education, and culture.   William M. Reddy

Cortés, *kawr TEHZ,* **Hernando** (1485-1547), was a Spanish adventurer who conquered what is now central and southern Mexico. His daring schemes to seize land, power, and wealth made him the greatest Spanish conqueror in the Americas. Cortés' military triumphs led to 300 years of Spanish domination of Mexico and Central America. His name is also spelled *Cortez.*

Early life. Cortés was born in the Spanish town of Medellín, near Don Benito. When he was 14 years old, his parents sent him to Salamanca to study law. But he soon left school to seek adventure and wealth.

In 1504, Cortés sailed to Hispaniola (now the Domini-

can Republic and Haiti) in the West Indies. In Hispaniola, he fought in several Indian battles and engaged in a number of commercial operations.

Cortés took part in the Spanish conquest of Cuba by Diego Velázquez in 1511. Velázquez, who became governor of Cuba, later learned of a rich Indian empire in Mexico. In 1518, Velázquez chose Cortés to lead an expedition there to seek gold, claim land, and develop trade with the Indians. After Cortés began to organize the expedition, Velázquez became suspicious of Cortés' ambition and removed him from command. Cortés ignored the governor's order and set sail for Mexico with about 600 Spaniards in February 1519.

Cortés' fleet of 11 ships landed near what is now Veracruz on the east coast of Mexico. The Spaniards soon learned that the Aztec Indians ruled the empire and, in August 1519, began to march inland to Tenochtitlan (now Mexico City), the Aztec capital. Along the way, Cortés persuaded thousands of Indians to join his forces. Many Indians joined Cortés willingly because they hated the powerful Aztec.

Detail of an oil portrait (1525) by an unknown artist; Instituto Nacional de Anthropologia e Historia, Mexico City

Hernando Cortés

Conquest. Cortés and his army marched into Tenochtitlan in November 1519. The Aztec emperor, Montezuma, greeted him with gifts in a colorful ceremony. Many Indians believed that Cortés was Quetzalcóatl, the Aztec's most honored god. But Cortés soon imprisoned Montezuma and ruled the Aztec empire through him. The Spaniards seized large amounts of gold, destroyed a number of Aztec temples, and began to convert Indians to Christianity.

Several months after Cortés' conquest, Velázquez sent Spanish forces to arrest him for disobedience. Cortés and some of his men hurried to the coast to deal with them. Cortés persuaded Velázquez's troops to join his forces. But by the time Cortés returned to Tenochtitlan,

WORLD BOOK map

Hernando Cortés sailed from Cuba to Mexico in 1519 and conquered the Aztec Indians there in 1521. He led an expedition to Honduras from 1524 to 1526 and one to Lower California in 1535.

the Aztec had rebelled. After bloody fighting, they forced the Spaniards to retreat from the city in June 1520. Many of Cortés' men died in the battle, and most of the survivors were wounded.

Cortés then began to reorganize his forces and to obtain reinforcements from various Spanish settlements in the West Indies. In May 1521, Cortés' army of thousands of Indians and 1,000 Spaniards attacked Tenochtitlan. By August, his troops had destroyed the city and forced the Aztec to surrender. Within a few months, Cortés controlled all central Mexico.

Later life. For several years, Cortés controlled much of present-day Mexico. He also explored Central America as far south as Honduras. In 1528, he sailed to Spain. King Charles I gave him the title of *marquis* and the service of 23,000 Indians in Mexico. Cortés returned to Mexico in 1530 and engaged in exploring, farming, and mining. He traveled to Lower California in 1535. He became probably the wealthiest person in all Spanish America. He sailed back to Spain in 1540 and lived there the rest of his life.   Charles Gibson

See also **Alvarado, Pedro de; Aztec** (History); **Cuauhtémoc; Mexico** (The Spanish conquest); **Montezuma.**

Additional resources

Johnson, William W. *Cortés: Conquering the New World.* Paragon Hse., 1987. First published in 1975.
Madariaga, Salvador de. *Hernán Cortés: Conqueror of Mexico.* Greenwood, 1979. First published in 1942.
Marrin, Albert. *Aztecs and Spaniards: Cortes and the Conquest of Mexico.* Atheneum, 1986. Also suitable for younger readers.

Drawing with colored ink on parchment by an unknown artist; Biblioteca Apostolica Vaticana (Vatican Library)

Hernando Cortés conquered Mexico for Spain in the early 1500's. The manuscript in picture writing, *above,* shows Cortés meeting the Aztec ruler Montezuma in 1519. An Aztec artist created the manuscript at Montezuma's request.

Cortex. See Adrenal gland; Kidney; Root.
Cortex, Cerebral. See Brain (The cerebrum).
Corticosteroid. See Cortisone.
Cortina, *kawr TEE nah,* **Juan Nepomuceno,** *hwahn NAY poh moo SAY noh* (1824-1894), was an early leader of the civil rights struggle of Mexican Americans. He fought the unfair treatment received by Mexican Americans in Texas following the Mexican War (1846-1848). Cortina became a Mexican folk hero and was called the "Robin Hood of South Texas."

Cortina was born near Brownsville, Tex., when Texas still formed part of Mexico. As a young man, he became angry at the attempts of English-speaking Americans to deprive Mexican Americans of their property. Many Mexican Americans did not understand U.S. property laws. Those who did not register their land with the state or pay property taxes lost their land. Most courts did not protect the rights of Spanish-speaking people.

In September 1859, Cortina led about 100 men in a raid on Brownsville. His band killed three men who had abused Mexican Americans. Cortina led other raids in Texas until U.S. troops chased him into Mexico in 1860. From 1869 to 1876, Cortina served as governor of the Mexican state of Tamaulipas. He also became a brigadier general in the Mexican Army.   Feliciano M. Ribera

Cortisone, *KAWR tuh zohn,* is one of an important group of hormones made in the *cortex* (outer part) of the adrenal glands. These compounds, called *corticosteroids,* are essential for life. They play an important part in regulating salt and sugar balances in the body. These compounds also help the body adjust to environmental changes and other kinds of stress.

Scientists synthetically produce cortisone and other corticosteroids for use as drugs. Corticosteroids effectively reduce inflammation. Physicians use the drugs in treating arthritis, some kinds of cancer, disorders of the eyes and skin, and many other diseases. Patients who undergo a transplant operation may receive corticosteroids. The drugs lower the natural immune defenses of the body and help it accept the transplanted organ. Doctors also prescribe corticosteroids for people whose glands produce too little of the natural compounds.

Cortisone and other corticosteroids can cause serious—even fatal—side effects and thus must be used carefully. The side effects include swelling of body tissues, changes in behavior, ulcers, weakness of the bones and muscles, and an increased probability of developing infections. In addition, prolonged treatment with the drugs may cause the adrenal glands to temporarily stop producing natural corticosteroids. In such cases, withdrawal from the drugs must take place gradually to allow the glands to recover.

Biochemists isolated and determined the chemical structure of cortisone and many other corticosteroids during the 1930's and 1940's. In 1948, cortisone became the first of these compounds to be used as a drug on human patients.   Eugene M. Johnson, Jr.

See also **ACTH; Gland; Hormone; Julian, Percy L.**
Corundum, *kuh RUHN duhm* (chemical formula, Al_2O_3), is the second hardest pure mineral. Only diamond is harder. Corundum occurs as transparent nuggets in gravel, and as nontransparent grains and rare transparent crystals in rocks.

Varieties of transparent corundum are polished and

used as gemstones. Gemstones from corundum include the ruby, sapphire, Oriental amethyst, Oriental emerald, and Oriental topaz. The colors of the gemstones are caused by impurities in the corundum. For example, the red of the ruby is caused by the presence of traces of chromium, and the blue of the sapphire by iron and titanium. Gemstone corundum comes mainly from Australia, southeast Africa, Sri Lanka, Burma, and India.

Nontransparent corundum is used as an *abrasive* (grinding, smoothing, and polishing material). Emery, a common abrasive, is a natural mixture of corundum and other minerals. Abrasive quality corundum and emery are mined in Turkey and Greece.   David F. Hess

Related articles in *World Book* include:

Amethyst	Emery	Hardness	Sapphire
Emerald	Gem	Ruby	Topaz

Cosby, Bill (1937-   ), is a leading American entertainer, author, and TV producer. He is noted for his warm, gentle humor, which centers on the family and the trials and troubles of childhood. His television series, *The Cosby Show,* ran from 1984 to 1992. It ranked as one of the most popular television shows in the United States.

William Henry Cosby, Jr., was born in Philadelphia. He began his show business career as a nightclub comedian and has since recorded over 20 comedy albums. He starred in several motion pictures, including *Hickey and Boggs* (1972) and *Uptown Saturday Night* (1974). Cosby was the

© Michael Virden, Shooting Star
Bill Cosby

first black actor to co-star in a prime-time TV dramatic series. This series, *I Spy,* ran from 1965 to 1968. Another success came in 1972 when he became executive producer and host of the TV cartoon series *Fat Albert and the Cosby Kids,* based on one of his most famous comic characters.

Cosby is also an author. He has written *Fatherhood* (1986), a book of humorous essays; *Time Flies* (1987), a book about aging; and *Love and Marriage* (1989), which deals with romantic relationships.   Joe Robinowitz

Cosimo de' Medici. See Medici.

Cosine. See Trigonometry.

Cosmetic surgery. See Plastic surgery.

Cosmetics are substances applied to a person's body to cleanse, promote attractiveness, or alter the appearance. Cosmetics include underarm deodorants, face powder, lipstick, nail polish, perfume, skin creams, most shampoos, and some toothpastes.

More than 5,000 ingredients are used in the manufacturing of cosmetics. These ingredients include alcohols, alkalis, detergents, dyes, glycerol, oils, talc, and waxes. A person who manufactures or sells cosmetics, or who applies them to others, is called a *cosmetician.* The study of cosmetics and their uses is called *cosmetology.*

Kinds of cosmetics. Most cosmetics can be classified into four main groups, according to the part of the body for which they are used: (1) skin, (2) hair, (3) nails, and (4) mouth.

Skin cosmetics include such makeup as blushes, rouge, face powder, foundations, and lipstick. Also in this group are eyeliners, eye shadow, and mascara, as well as bubble baths, cold cream, underarm deodorants, foot powder, hair-removal substances, perfume, shaving cream, moisturizers, and suntan lotion.

Hair cosmetics include hair conditioners, mousses, sprays, styling lotions, straighteners, and permanent waves. Such hair-coloring products as dyes and bleaches are also hair cosmetics, as are shampoos that do not contain antidandruff ingredients.

Nail cosmetics. Nail polish and cuticle softeners are the chief products in this group.

Mouth cosmetics, also called *oral cosmetics,* include toothpastes and other substances that clean the teeth and gums but do not have cavity-fighting ingredients. Mouthwashes and sprays are also oral cosmetics.

Other cosmetics. Performers in motion pictures, television, theater, and circuses wear special cosmetics that must withstand the heat from powerful lights without melting or running. They also must be visible to the audience. Many people use special medicinal cosmetics to conceal birthmarks, scars, or other skin blemishes.

Cosmetics regulations. The Food and Drug Administration (FDA), an agency of the federal government, regulates cosmetics in the United States. The agency requires that cosmetics be safe and properly labeled. It tests products to determine if unsafe ingredients are present, and it inspects cosmetics factories. The FDA requires cosmetics manufacturers to list on each package the names of the ingredients used in the product, in order of descending concentration.

The FDA classifies as a cosmetic any product whose sole purpose is to improve a person's appearance. If a product also is intended to prevent disease or to affect any body structure or function, the FDA considers it a drug. For example, the FDA regards many *dentifrices* (products intended to clean the teeth and gums) as cosmetics. But those dentifrices that contain fluoride or other cavity-fighting ingredients are classified as nonprescription drugs. Similarly, cleaning and conditioning shampoos are considered to be cosmetics. However, antidandruff shampoos are regarded as drugs because they are intended to help prevent dandruff.

Soaps form a unique category. Most people consider all bar products used for cleansing to be soaps. However, the FDA defines soap as salts formed from fatty acids and alkalis. The agency has ruled that soap containing these ingredients is neither a cosmetic nor a drug. Such soap is the primary ingredient of most bar cleanser products, so these products are not considered cosmetics by the FDA. But the FDA regards as cosmetics some bar cleansers whose main ingredients are synthetic detergents. See **Detergent and soap.**

History. Men and women have used cosmetics for thousands of years. The ancient Egyptians applied perfumes and anointing oils to the body as early as 4000 B.C. They used these cosmetics for decoration, for protection against the hot, dry climate, and for religious reasons. The Egyptians, Greeks, and Romans made cosmetics from plants. They also used powdered minerals to make face and eye makeup and hair dyes.

By the A.D. 1100's, the use of cosmetics had spread to Western Europe. Africans of about the same period painted their bodies for war and for magical ceremonies. In North America, the first cosmetics were animal fats used by Indians long before Europeans arrived. The Indians applied these substances as a base for body paint and as protection against insects and the cold.

By the early 1900's, most people used only such basic cosmetics as face powder, rouge, and shampoos. Demand for a wider variety of cosmetics grew tremendously after the 1930's, as did widespread advertising and promotion of these products.   Clarence R. Robbins

Cosmic rays are high-energy particles that originate in outer space. Scientists believe these rays fill the Milky Way and other galaxies as well. Cosmic rays consist of subatomic particles that carry an electric charge, such as protons, electrons, and the nuclei of atoms. In outer space, they travel at nearly the speed of light, which is 186,282 miles (299,792 kilometers) per second.

Physicists measure the energy of cosmic rays in units called *electronvolts* (eV). Most cosmic rays have energies that range from a few million electronvolts (MeV) to a few billion electronvolts (GeV). A billion electronvolts would light a flashlight bulb for only about one ten-billionth of a second. However, when a cosmic ray proton carries that amount of energy, it can travel through an iron plate nearly 2 feet (60 centimeters) thick.

Cosmic rays originate from many sources in space. Scientists believe that exploding stars called *supernovae* and very dense stars known as *pulsars* produce great quantities of cosmic rays. Some cosmic rays come from the sun. Only cosmic rays with very high energies can penetrate the earth's atmosphere. Fewer than one in a million of those reach the earth's surface without colliding with an atom in the air. These collisions destroy both the cosmic ray and the atom, producing showers of high-energy subatomic particles. Some of these particles do reach the surface and even penetrate deep underground. The cosmic rays in outer space are called *primary cosmic rays*. The showers produced in the atmosphere are *secondary cosmic rays*.

Scientists study cosmic rays because these particles provide samples of matter that has traveled through millions of *light-years* of space. A light-year is the distance light travels in one year—about 5.88 trillion miles (9.46 trillion kilometers). Cosmic-ray research has enabled scientists to learn much about the physical conditions in regions far from the solar system.

Primary cosmic rays

Primary cosmic rays, also called *primaries,* are cosmic-ray particles that originate in space. There are two main types of primaries—*galactic* and *solar.*

Galactic cosmic rays come from outside the solar system. They make up most of the primaries. During periods of low activity on the sun, an average of about six galactic cosmic rays strike each square inch (6 square centimeters) of the top of the atmosphere each second.

About 98 per cent of galactic cosmic rays are atomic nuclei. The other 2 per cent consist of electrons and *positrons* (electrons with a positive charge). Of the nuclei, about 87 per cent are *protons* (hydrogen nuclei) and 12 per cent are helium nuclei. The rest of the nuclei include those of all the elements heavier than helium.

Physicists believe that most galactic cosmic rays are accelerated to their high energies by shock waves from supernovae or by strong magnetic fields around pulsars. Galactic cosmic rays can also gain energy from collisions with moving kinks in the weak magnetic fields in *interstellar space* (space between the stars). A magnetic field can be thought of as a set of imaginary lines of magnetic force extending through space. Like beads on a string, the particles move easily along these *field lines* but have difficulty cutting across the lines. When a field line moves, some of the energy of its motion is transferred to the particles traveling along it.

Once accelerated, the galactic cosmic rays in the earth's galaxy travel randomly in the galaxy's magnetic fields for an average of about 10 million years. They eventually either escape from the galaxy or are slowed down by collisions with interstellar matter.

Some galactic cosmic rays are kept out of the solar system by the *solar wind.* The solar wind consists of electrically charged atoms that flow outward from the sun throughout the solar system. The solar wind carries a magnetic field, which excludes many galactic cosmic rays from the solar system, especially during periods of high activity on the sun's surface. Thus, the concentration of galactic cosmic rays near the earth decreases as solar activity increases in an 11-year cycle called the *sunspot cycle* (see **Sunspot**).

Solar cosmic rays are produced by the sun during *solar flares.* Solar flares are spectacular eruptions at the sun's surface that occur mainly during periods of high activity in the sunspot cycle. The particles released in these flares typically have energies of only a few MeV, but particles with energies of up to a few GeV may be produced in large flares. Most solar cosmic rays are protons. Others consist of heavier nuclei or electrons.

Other high-energy particles in space. Some particles are accelerated to energies of many MeV in the earth's *magnetosphere.* A magnetosphere is the region of space filled by a planet's magnetic field. Jupiter, Saturn, Uranus, and Neptune also have magnetospheres in which particles are accelerated to energies of many MeV. Most particles stay trapped in the magnetospheres and form belts of radiation around the planets.

In addition, particles are accelerated to energies of a few MeV by shock waves in the solar wind. These shock waves are produced by solar flares or by fast streams in the solar wind that behave like gusts or jets.

Secondary cosmic rays

Secondary cosmic rays, or *secondaries,* are produced when primary cosmic rays collide with atomic nuclei high in the earth's atmosphere. In these collisions, the primaries break up, and some of their energy takes the form of subatomic particles. A number of the new particles collide with other nuclei in the atmosphere, producing even more particles. Such successive collisions produce a shower of secondaries that includes all types of subatomic particles. Secondaries occur from the upper atmosphere to the deepest mines in the earth.

Secondaries slow down in the atmosphere, and so only a small fraction of them reach the earth. Every minute, an average of about six particles strike each square inch of the earth's surface. Most of these particles are subatomic particles called *muons.*

The concentration of secondaries in the atmosphere is affected by the earth's magnetic field. The lines of this

How cosmic rays penetrate the earth's magnetic field

Primary cosmic-ray particles, even those with low energies, can enter the earth's atmosphere near the poles by traveling along the field lines of the magnetic field. Only particles with extremely high energies can cut across the field lines and reach the atmosphere near the equator. The magnetic field there reflects most particles, including many with high energies. Secondary cosmic rays are created in the atmosphere by collisions between the primary rays and atomic nuclei.

WORLD BOOK diagram

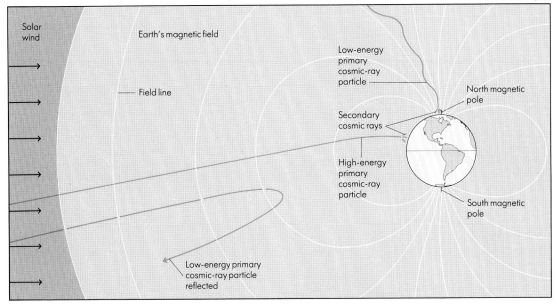

field curve from the earth's north magnetic pole to the south magnetic pole. Only primaries with extremely high energies can penetrate the magnetic field near the equator because they must cut across the field lines. Near the poles, even primaries with low energies can travel along the field lines and strike the atmosphere. Thus, the concentration of secondaries is lowest at the equator and increases toward the poles.

Effects of cosmic rays

The level of radiation produced on the earth by cosmic rays is far too low to harm living things. Scientists measure radiation in units called *rads.* Long-term exposure to more than a few rads a year is considered unsafe. At sea level, the dose from secondary cosmic rays is less than 0.04 rad per year. Even beyond the atmosphere, the dose from galactic cosmic rays is less than 10 rads per year. However, the level of radiation in the earth's radiation belts can endanger astronauts and damage instruments, as can radiation anywhere above the atmosphere after large solar flares. As a result, spacecraft that may encounter such radiation must carry shielding against it. Manned space missions try to avoid the radiation belts and large solar-flare events.

Problems have resulted on some spacecraft from the effects of galactic cosmic rays on the crafts' electronic circuits. A single cosmic ray that penetrates a tiny circuit chip can change the information stored on the chip. The high energy of galactic cosmic rays makes it almost impossible to shield against them. Therefore, scientists and engineers have had to develop circuit components that are less sensitive to cosmic-ray effects.

One useful effect of cosmic rays comes from a reaction of secondaries with nitrogen nuclei in the earth's at-

mosphere. This reaction produces a radioactive form of carbon, called *radiocarbon.* Living things continuously incorporate carbon—including radiocarbon—into their cells. Because radiocarbon breaks down at a constant rate, the amount of it left in once-living material can tell scientists the material's age (see **Radiocarbon**).

Cosmic-ray research

Early studies. During the late 1800's, physicists used instruments called *electroscopes* in the study of radioactivity. Even when shielded from the most powerful radioactive rays, the instruments continued to react as if an unknown form of penetrating radiation were present. In 1912, the Austrian physicist Victor F. Hess took electroscopes along on a balloon flight. They indicated that radiation increases with altitude, and so Hess concluded that the radiation must originate in the atmosphere or beyond. In 1936, Hess received the Nobel Prize for physics for discovering cosmic rays.

Physicists originally thought that cosmic rays were gamma rays (see **Gamma rays**). In the late 1920's, scientists discovered that cosmic rays, unlike gamma rays, are affected by magnetic fields. This effect indicated that the rays must be charged particles. In the late 1940's, the photographic study of cosmic rays revealed that primaries consist mainly of hydrogen nuclei and helium nuclei. In the 1950's, physicists studied the effects of the sun on cosmic rays. In 1961, they first observed electrons among primaries. Since the 1960's, spacecraft have enabled scientists to study primaries outside the earth's atmosphere and magnetic field.

Research today. Much cosmic-ray research today involves the physical nature of the stars and other objects that make up galaxies. If, as scientists believe, cosmic rays are accelerated by supernovae and pulsars, the particles provide samples of matter from places near these objects. Studying such cosmic rays helps scientists learn about the nuclear processes that occur when a star explodes as a supernova and about conditions near a pulsar. Cosmic-ray research also uncovers clues about the structure and distribution of the matter and magnetic fields that primaries encounter in interstellar space.

New instruments are being designed that will provide more detailed information about the origin, acceleration, and travel of the most energetic cosmic rays. These devices also will permit closer examination of the nuclear composition of lower-energy primaries.

Secondary cosmic rays were once the main source of subatomic particles used in research. From the 1930's through the 1950's, physicists discovered many new subatomic particles among secondaries. Today, physicists use machines called *particle accelerators* for most particle research. However, the study of cosmic rays may reveal new kinds of subatomic particles that exist only at energies much higher than accelerators can produce.   R. B. McKibben

See also **Radiocarbon.**

Cosmology. See Philosophy (Metaphysics).

Cosmology, *kahz MAHL uh jee,* in astronomy and astrophysics, is the study of the structure, dynamics, and development of the universe. It tries to explain how the universe was formed, what happened to it in the past, and what might happen to it in the future.

Astronomers interpreted three chief observations of the universe to develop the theories that make up modern physical cosmology. They noted that the sky's being dark at night contradicted a simple explanation of the universe. Astronomers also observed that distant galaxies move away from one another, and that the entire sky gives off radio waves.

During the 1700's and 1800's, several astronomers thought about the sky's being dark at night. In the simplest universe they could imagine, the universe extended forever with stars distributed evenly throughout it. But in such a universe, a person would be able to look anywhere in the sky, and the person's line of sight would eventually reach a star. The entire night sky would therefore appear to be a solid mass of stars as bright as the sun. But the sky is dark—and so the universe must have a more complex structure.

In the early 1900's, astronomers observed that the light from stars in distant galaxies was shifted toward the longer, or red, wavelengths of the *spectrum* (color pattern). This phenomenon, called *red shift,* is interpreted as resulting from the rapid motion of the galaxies away from one another. Astronomers can calculate the speed of a galaxy from its red shift (see **Red shift**). By studying the speed of the galaxies' motion at various distances from the earth, they found that all galaxies began moving away from one another 10 billion to 20 billion years ago.

In 1965, astronomers detected faint radio waves regardless of where they pointed their radio telescopes. This observation showed that the entire universe is a source of weak radio waves. It also reinforced the idea that the universe is expanding because the faint radio waves are similar to those that would be emitted by an extremely hot object that is moving away from the earth.

The big bang theory provides the best explanation of the three basic cosmological observations. According to this theory, the universe began as the result of an explosion—called the big bang—10 billion to 20 billion years ago. Immediately after the explosion, the universe consisted chiefly of strong radiation. This radiation formed a rapidly expanding region called the *primordial fireball.* After a few hundred years, the main part of the fireball was matter, chiefly hydrogen. It also included a small amount of helium and other light elements. Today, faint radio waves are all that remain of the radiation from the original fireball. Like the radiation, the matter continued to decrease in density after the explosion. In time, the matter broke apart in huge clumps. The clumps became galaxies. Smaller clumps within the galaxies formed stars. Part of at least one clump became a group of planets—the solar system.

The galaxies are still moving away from one another, and the best current evidence indicates that they will move apart forever. But astronomers do not rule out the possibility that all the galaxies will come together again in about 70 billion years. If this happens, all the material in the universe will explode again, resulting in a new phase of the universe resembling the present one.

The steady state theory offers another explanation of the cosmological observations. According to this theory, the universe has always existed in its present state. As the galaxies move apart, new matter appears between them and forms new galaxies. The theory does not say where this matter comes from. Today's astronomical observations do not support the steady state theory.   Kenneth Brecher

See also **Universe** (Cosmological theories).

Cosmonaut. See Astronaut.

Cosmos, *KAHZ muhs,* are tall, late-summer flowers native to Mexico and the American tropics. Their flowers range from white and pink to red and orange, and may be double or single. Seeds may be planted outdoors after the ground warms, or they may be planted indoors in early spring and then transplanted a few weeks before summer. Cosmos are well adapted to full sun, and to light soil that is not too rich. Most varieties need protection from wind because they are so tall. They make good background plants or fillers among shrubs. Cosmos also provide excellent cut flowers.

Scientific classification. Cosmos belong to the composite family, Asteraceae or Compositae. They make up the genus *Cosmos.* The scientific name for the familiar garden plants is *C. bipinnatus.*   Michael J. Tanabe

See also **Flower** (picture: Garden annuals).

Cosmos, *KAHZ muhs,* in physics and astronomy, is a term used to refer to everything that exists, from the smallest atoms to the most distant celestial bodies. It comes from an ancient Greek word meaning order, the universe, or the world. To the ancient Greeks, the cosmos was a well-ordered, harmonious system consisting of the earth, the sun, the stars, the moon, and the visible planets. Today, we know that the sun is only one of hundreds of billions of stars that form the Milky Way galaxy. This galaxy is one of billions of galaxies that make up the observable universe. See also **Cosmology; Galaxy; Universe.**   Kenneth Brecher

Cossacks, *KAHS aks,* were originally peasant soldiers who lived chiefly in the areas of the Dnepr and Don rivers, in what are now eastern Ukraine and western Russia. Beginning in the 1400's, Poland and Russia organized the Cossacks into military units to help fight Tatar invaders. Both Poland and Russia granted the Cossacks many privileges as a reward for their services. The Cossacks formed self-governing communities that were based on democratic principles. The word *Cossack* means *free person* in Turkic.

During the 1500's and 1600's, Poland and Russia tried to abolish the Cossack privileges, and the Cossacks often revolted. During the 1800's, some Cossack groups formed special units in the Russian Army.

In 1917, the Bolshevik Revolution led to the establishment of a Communist government in Russia. The revolution started a civil war, in which many Cossacks fought the Communists. The Communists broke up Cossack communities after winning the war in 1920.

Vojtech Mastny

See also **Ukraine** (History).

Cost. See Price.

Cost-benefit analysis, also called *benefit-cost analysis*, is a type of economic study that measures the costs and benefits to society of existing or proposed programs. Government and industry planners use cost-benefit analyses to help them make decisions.

Cost-benefit analysts focus on a clearly stated proposal, such as plans to create a park or to extend a highway system. They try to determine the effects of the proposal on as large a number of people as possible. Analysts formulate their estimates of costs and benefits in terms of dollars or other currencies. If the program produces economic benefits that exceed the cost of putting it into action, the program is judged to be worthwhile. Projects that produce such economic benefit are called *cost-effective.*

Stating costs and benefits in monetary terms poses a problem for analysts. Some factors, such as labor and materials, have measurable market prices. But other factors, such as the beautification of an area or increasing safety, have no market price. Cost-benefit analysts therefore must estimate a value called a *shadow price* for these factors.

Analysts also have the problem of studying policies that affect people for many years. A delay in receiving something generally lowers its current value. Analysts calculate this lower value through a procedure called *discounting.* Analysts often calculate the ratio between the discounted value of benefits and the discounted value of costs. If this ratio is greater than one, the project is considered to be economically worthwhile.

Robert H. Haveman

Cost of living is the amount of money needed to buy a standard amount of consumer goods and services. Needs of individual persons and families vary. Everyone needs food, clothing, and shelter, but wants go beyond these bare necessities. The cost of living includes the cost of transportation, reading, recreation, rent, electricity, gas, fuel, home furnishings, medical and personal care, taxes, and many other things.

When salaries and wages keep step with the prices of consumer goods and services, the worker's buying power remains stable. When prices rise, people with fixed incomes, such as pensions, fall behind in buying power. Changes in the cost of living have many causes.

Cost of living in the United States

The Consumer Price Index measures the cost of living. Current prices of goods and services are expressed as a percentage of average prices during the period from 1982 to 1984. An index of 140.3 means the average price level was 40.3 per cent higher than the average price level in the 1982 to 1984 period.

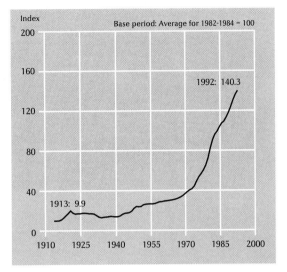

Year	Index	Year	Index
1915	10.1	1960	29.6
1920	20.0	1965	31.5
1925	17.5	1970	38.8
1930	16.7	1975	53.8
1935	13.7	1980	82.4
1940	14.0	1985	107.6
1945	18.0	1990	130.7
1950	24.1	1991	136.2
1955	26.8	1992	140.3

Source: U.S. Bureau of Labor Statistics.

For example, when spending on consumer goods rises faster than the nation's ability to produce them, prices tend to go up. But when more goods than money are available, prices go down.

The Bureau of Labor Statistics is the fact-finding agency of the United States government in the field of labor economics. It collects and analyzes data on employment, wages, and productivity. The bureau also collects data to measure changes in the prices of consumer goods and services, and reports its findings through its publications. It publishes a Consumer Price Index that summarizes this information. In preparing the Consumer Price Index, the Bureau of Labor Statistics regularly collects information on prices and costs from thousands of food stores, homeowners and tenants, and other sources.

A system called *indexing* or *indexation* is being increasingly used to tie prices, wages, and taxes to the rate of inflation. Indexing provides for automatic increases and decreases in prices, wages, and taxes as the official cost-of-living index rises and falls. For example, many U.S. labor contracts have an *escalator clause,* which automatically lifts wages as the Consumer Price Index rises. Henry J. Aaron

See also **Consumer Price Index; Inflation.**

San José, Costa Rica's capital and largest city, lies on a plateau in the agricultural center of the country. Modern stores and office buildings stand among Spanish-style churches and houses.

Costa Rica

Costa Rica is a small, mountainous country in Central America. It is bordered by Nicaragua on the north, the Caribbean Sea and Panama on the east, and the Pacific Ocean on the south and west. A chain of rugged mountains stretches across central Costa Rica from northwest to southeast. A few of the highest peaks in this chain are active volcanoes. Tropical forests grow on the country's coastal lowlands.

Spanish explorers arrived in what is now Costa Rica in the early 1500's. The Indians who lived there told them stories about deposits of gold and other precious metals supposedly mined in the region. The Spaniards named the land *Costa Rica*, which means *rich coast.* But the explorers found that the area has little mineral wealth.

Today, almost all Costa Ricans are of mixed Spanish and Indian ancestry. About three-fourths of the people live on a fertile plateau in the mountains of central Costa Rica. San José, the capital and largest city, lies in this region. Hillsides covered with coffee trees surround San José. Coffee ranks as the country's chief export. Bananas, another major export, grow on large plantations near the coasts.

Government

Costa Rica is a democratic republic. Its Constitution was adopted in 1949. A president serves as the nation's chief executive and head of state. The people elect the president to a four-year term. The president and the

Nathan A. Haverstock, the contributor of this article, is Affiliate Scholar at Oberlin College, and the author of The Organization of American States: The Challenge of the Americas.

members of the Cabinet make up the Council of Government. The council conducts foreign affairs and enforces federal laws. It may also veto bills passed by the Legislative Assembly, Costa Rica's legislature.

The Legislative Assembly has 57 deputies elected by the people to four-year terms. Neither the president nor the deputies may be elected to two terms in a row. The Supreme Court of Justice, the nation's highest court, has 17 justices appointed by the legislature. The army was abolished in 1948, but military forces may be organized for national defense if necessary.

Costa Rica has seven provinces. The provinces are divided into 80 *cantons* (counties). Each province has a governor who is appointed by the president. A council

---

Facts in brief

Capital: San José.

Official language: Spanish.

Official name: República de Costa Rica (Republic of Costa Rica).

Area: 19,730 sq. mi. (51,100 km²). *Greatest distances*— north-south, 220 mi. (354 km); east-west, 237 mi. (381 km). *Coastline*—380 mi. (612 km) on the Pacific; 133 mi. (214 km) on the Caribbean.

Elevation: *Highest*—Chirripó Grande, 12,530 ft. (3,819 m) above sea level. *Lowest*—sea level along the coasts.

Population: *Estimated 1994 population*—3,296,000; density, 167 persons per sq. mi. (65 per km²); distribution, 53 per cent rural, 47 per cent urban. *1984 census*—2,416,809. *Estimated 1999 population*—3,634,000.

Chief products: *Agriculture*—bananas, beef cattle, cacao, coffee, corn, rice, sugar cane. *Manufacturing*—cement, clothing, furniture, machinery, processed foods, textiles.

National anthem: "Noble Patria, Tu Hermosa Bandera" ("Noble Homeland, Your Beautiful Flag").

Money: *Basic unit*—colón. See **Money** (table: Exchange rates).

elected by the people governs each canton. The cantons provide fire protection, sanitation, water, and other local services.

All citizens 18 years or older are required to vote in national elections. The country has two major political parties, the National Liberation Party and the Social Christian Unity Party, and several minor ones.

People

Population and ancestry. In 1994, the population of Costa Rica totaled about $3\frac{1}{4}$ million and was increasing at a rate of about $2\frac{1}{4}$ per cent a year. If this rate continues, the population will double in about 30 years.

Many Spanish colonists who settled in Costa Rica in the 1500's and 1600's married native Indians. Their descendants are called *mestizos.* Today, mestizos and whites of unmixed ancestry make up more than 97 per cent of the population. Costa Rica also has two small minority groups—about 70,000 blacks and about 10,000 Indians. The blacks live along the Caribbean coast. Their ancestors came to Costa Rica from the island of Jamaica in the late 1800's to build railroads and to work on the banana plantations. The Indians live in isolated communities in the highlands and along the Caribbean and Pacific shores. They keep their tribes' traditional ways of life.

Costa Ricans take great pride in their country's heritage of democratic government and social equality. They also value their own personal dignity and strong family ties. Nearly all Costa Ricans speak Spanish, but many blacks still speak a Jamaican *dialect* (local form) of English. About 90 per cent of the people belong to the Roman Catholic Church.

Housing. About half of all Costa Ricans live on farms or in rural towns. Many farmers live in adobe cottages with thick, white stucco walls and red- or pink-tiled roofs. Other farmers live in brightly painted wooden houses. Most city people live in *row houses.* Such houses look much alike and are attached to one another in a row. Many Costa Ricans decorate their homes with plants and flowers. Wealthy families own spacious

R. Lyon, Alpha Photo Assoc.

An open-air market in Cartago is jammed on Sundays with shoppers who buy produce from farmers. The woman in the foreground is selling tickets for Costa Rica's national lottery.

ranch-style or Spanish-style homes surrounded by gardens.

Food. The diet of most Costa Ricans includes beans, coffee, corn, eggs, rice, and such tropical fruits as bananas, guavas, mangoes, oranges, and pineapples. Most families also serve beef, fish, poultry, and many kinds of soups. They often prepare *tamales* (ground pork and corn meal steamed in corn husks) and *tortillas* (thin flat bread made from corn or wheat flour).

Education. About 93 per cent of Costa Rica's people can read and write, a higher percentage than in any other Central American country. Costa Rican law requires all children to complete elementary school. Students who graduate may attend secondary school and then enter a university. The country has several universities, including the National University in Heredia and the University of Costa Rica near San José.

Recreation. Costa Ricans enjoy spending their leisure time outdoors. Many of them play soccer, the national sport, in neighborhood fields. Basketball, tennis, and swimming are also popular. Many Costa Ricans take

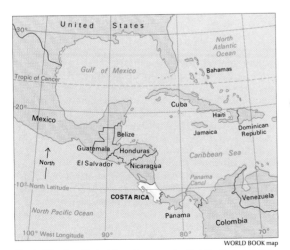

WORLD BOOK map

Costa Rica is a Central American country that lies between the Caribbean Sea and the North Pacific Ocean.

Costa Rica's state flag, used by the government, was adopted in 1848. The national flag has no coat of arms.

The coat of arms shows volcanoes, the Caribbean Sea, and the Pacific Ocean. Each star represents a province.

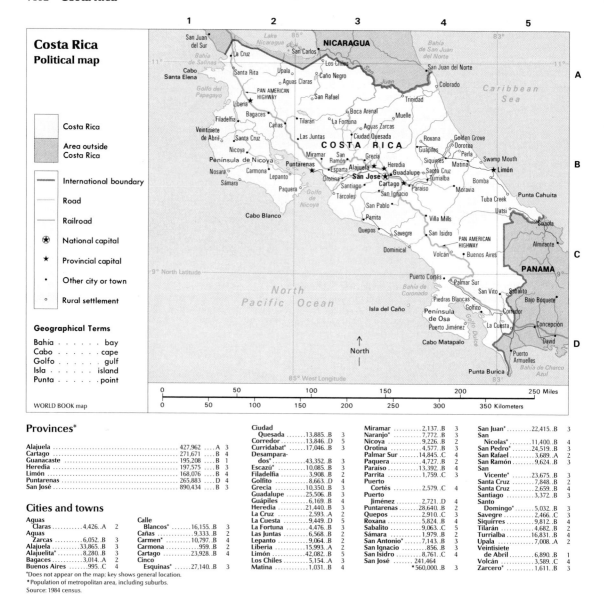

Costa Rica
Political map

Costa Rica

Area outside
Costa Rica

International boundary

Road

Railroad

⊛ National capital

★ Provincial capital

• Other city or town

○ Rural settlement

Geographical Terms

Bahía . . . . . . bay
Cabo . . . . . . cape
Golfo . . . . . . gulf
Isla . . . . . . island
Punta . . . . . . point

WORLD BOOK map

Provinces*

Alajuela	427,962	....A 3
Cartago	271,671	....B 4
Guanacaste	195,208	...B 1
Heredia	197,575	...B 3
Limón	168,076	...B 4
Puntarenas	265,883	...D 4
San José	890,434	...B 3

Cities and towns

Aguas Claras	4,426.	.A 2
Aguas Zarcas	6,052.	.B 3
Alajuela	33,865.	.B 3
Alajuelita*	8,280.	.B 3
Bagaces	3,014.	.A 2
Buenos Aires	995.	.C 4
Calle Blancos*	16,155.	.B 3
Cañas	9,333.	.B 2
Carmen*	10,797.	.B 4
Carmona	959.	.B 2
Cartago	23,928.	.B 4
Cinco Esquinas*	27,140.	.B 3
Ciudad Quesada	13,885.	.B 3
Corredor	13,846.	.D 5
Curridabat*	17,046.	.B 3
Desamparados*	43,352.	.B 3
Escazú*	10,085.	.B 3
Filadelfia	3,908.	.B 2
Golfito	8,663.	.D 4
Grecia	10,350.	.B 3
Guadalupe	25,506.	.B 3
Guápiles	6,169.	.B 4
Heredia	21,440.	.B 3
La Cruz	2,593.	.A 2
La Cuesta	9,449.	.D 5
La Fortuna	4,476.	.B 3
Las Juntas	6,568.	.B 2
Lepanto	9,064.	.B 2
Liberia	15,993.	.A 2
Limón	42,082.	.B 5
Los Chiles	5,154.	.A 3
Matina	1,031.	.B 4
Miramar	2,137.	.B 3
Naranjo*	7,772.	.B 3
Nicoya	9,226.	.B 2
Orotina	4,577.	.B 3
Palmar Sur	14,845.	.C 4
Paquera	4,727.	.B 2
Paraíso	13,392.	.B 4
Parrita	1,759.	.C 3
Puerto Cortés	2,579.	.C 4
Puerto Jiménez	2,721.	.D 4
Puntarenas	28,640.	.B 2
Quepos	2,910.	.C 3
Roxana	5,824.	.B 4
Sabalito	9,063.	.C 5
Sámara	1,979.	.B 2
San Antonio*	7,143.	.B 3
San Ignacio	856.	.B 3
San Isidro	8,761.	.C 4
San José	241,464	
	*560,000.	.B 3
San Juan*	22,415.	.B 3
San Nicolas*	11,400.	.B 4
San Pedro*	24,519.	.B 3
San Rafael	3,689.	.A 2
San Ramón	9,624.	.B 3
San Vicente*	23,675.	.B 3
Santa Cruz	7,848.	.B 2
Santa Cruz	2,659.	.B 4
Santiago	3,372.	.B 3
Santo Domingo*	5,032.	.B 3
Savegre	2,466.	.C 3
Siquirres	9,812.	.B 4
Tilarán	4,682.	.B 2
Turrialba	16,831.	.B 4
Upala	7,008.	.A 2
Veintisiete de Abril	6,890.	.B 1
Volcán	3,589.	.C 4
Zarcero*	1,611.	.B 3

*Does not appear on the map; key shows general location.
*Population of metropolitan area, including suburbs.
Source: 1984 census.

---

part in colorful festivals on religious holidays. Bullfights, fireworks, and masked parades attract thousands of Costa Ricans and foreign tourists to San José during the annual Christmas festivals.

Many Costa Ricans and tourists from other countries enjoy visiting Costa Rica's national parks. The national park system includes sandy beaches where sea turtles come to lay their eggs, tropical rain forests that are the homes of monkeys and colorful birds, and several active volcanoes.

The land and climate

A chain of high mountain ranges, which are called *cordilleras*, crosses central Costa Rica from northwest to southeast. The cordilleras divide the country into three land regions: (1) the Central Highlands; (2) the Caribbean Lowlands; and (3) the Pacific Coastal Strip.

The Central Highlands consist of two large areas of fertile farmland—the *Meseta Central* (Central Plateau) and the *Valle del General* (Valley of the General). The steep cordilleras surround each area. The Meseta Central is the country's heartland. About 75 per cent of the people live there. The Meseta's rich volcanic soil and favorable climate also make it the country's chief coffee-growing region. Daytime temperatures range from 75° to 80° F. (24° to 27° C) the year around. The area receives about 70 inches (180 centimeters) of rainfall a year. The Valle del General lies to the southeast. It is an agricultural region of hills and plains. Daytime temperatures range from 80° to 90° F. (27° to 32° C). Yearly rainfall averages about 110 inches (279 centimeters).

The Caribbean Lowlands, a wide band of swampy tropical jungles, lie along the east coast. The daytime high temperature averages about 100° F. (38° C). Yearly rainfall ranges from 150 to 200 inches (381 to 510 centi-meters).

The Pacific Coastal Strip is largely an area of low-lands along the west coast. Low mountains rise along most of the shore. This region has an ideal climate for growing bananas. Daytime temperatures range from 77 to 100 °F (25 to 38 °C). The annual rainfall totals about 130 inches (330 centimeters).

Economy

Costa Rica's most valuable natural resource is its fer-tile volcanic soil. Forests of oaks, pines, and such tropi-cal hardwoods as cedrelas and mahoganies cover about a third of the land. Costa Rica also has small deposits of bauxite and manganese.

About a fourth of Costa Rica's workers are engaged in farming or ranching. Bananas, beef cattle, *cacao* (seeds used to make chocolate), coffee, corn, rice, and sugar cane rank as the chief agricultural products. Farmers also grow oranges, beans, potatoes, and other fruits and vegetables. Manufacturing employs about a fifth of the labor force and is growing rapidly. The leading manu-factured products include cement, clothing, cosmetics, fertilizer, furniture, machinery, medicines, processed foods, and textiles.

Costa Rica's economy depends heavily on foreign trade. Its leading exports include bananas, beef, coffee, and sugar. Its chief imports include petroleum, chemi-cals, and manufactured goods. The United States is Costa Rica's major trading partner. Germany ranks sec-ond. Costa Rica belongs to the Central American Com-mon Market, an economic union that was formed to stimulate trade among its members.

The Pan American Highway links all of Costa Rica's provincial capitals except Limón and Puntarenas (see **Pan American Highway**). Railroads connect the port cit-ies of Limón and Puntarenas to San José. Costa Rica has an average of about 1 automobile for every 27 people. Costa Rican Airlines has flights from San José to other

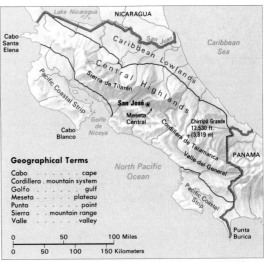

Geographical Terms

Cabo . . . . cape
Cordillera . mountain system
Golfo . . . . . . gulf
Meseta . . . . . plateau
Punta . . . . . . point
Sierra . . . mountain range
Valle . . . . valley

WORLD BOOK map

Costa Rica has three land regions. Most people live in the Cen-tral Highlands, where the temperatures are more comfortable than in the Caribbean Lowlands and the Pacific Coastal Strip.

Central American cities and to Mexico and the United States.

Most Costa Rican families own a radio. The country has about one television set for every six people. Costa Rica's four daily newspapers are all published in San José.

History

Indians were the first people to live in what is now Costa Rica. By 1000, the Corobicí tribe had settled in the northern valleys, and the Boruca had migrated to lands in the south. The Carib, Chorotega, and Nahau Indians arrived in the 1400's. Most of the Indians raised crops near their villages and hunted small game.

Reinhold A. Eckelhoefer

The Central Plateau is the agricultural heartland of Costa Rica. Coffee, corn, rice, and sugar grow on the rolling hill-sides. The city of San José lies in the distance.

Ann Hagen Griffiths, DPI

Coffee beans drying in the sun are raked by workers at a *beneficio* (processing plant) in the Central Plateau. Coffee ranks as Costa Rica's chief export.

Colonial period. Christopher Columbus arrived in Costa Rica in 1502. Rumors of gold deposits in the area soon lured hundreds of Spaniards to the new land. The Spaniards found little mineral wealth. But many of them stayed to become farmers in the Central Highlands. Governor Juan Vásquez de Coronado founded the first permanent settlement at Cartago in 1564. Many Spaniards tried to enslave the Indians, but most of the tribes fought fiercely to stay free.

Independence. Costa Rica remained a Spanish colony until 1821. That year, Costa Rica and Spain's other Central American colonies broke away from Spanish rule. They joined the Mexican Empire the next year. In 1823, the Central American states withdrew from Mexico and formed the United Provinces of Central America. The union began to collapse in 1838, and Costa Rica declared its independence.

In 1842, Francisco Morazán overthrew the dictatorship of President Braulio Carrillo and became president. Morazán attempted to revive the union, but his enemies killed him five months after he took office. Weak leaders governed the country until 1849, when Juan Rafael Mora began a 10-year term as president. Mora established Costa Rica's first national bank, its first street-lighting system, and many public schools.

Revolutions and reforms. Since the late 1800's, Costa Rica has had several revolutions. General Tomás Guardia overthrew the government in 1870 and ruled as a dictator for 12 years. He encouraged large-scale cultivation and heavy exports of coffee. His government improved the public school system and built a railroad from San José to Limón. In 1917, Federico Tinoco seized the presidency. Political turmoil forced him to resign in 1919, and Julio Acosta became the new leader. Under Acosta and his successors, Costa Rica became a model of democracy and social reform.

In 1948, Otilio Ulate won the presidential election, but the National Assembly declared the results illegal. Colonel José Figueres then led a revolt in support of Ulate to prevent what he said was a threatened Communist takeover. Figueres took office as interim president, reorganized the government, and placed banks under federal control. He also replaced Costa Rica's army with a 4,000-member Civil Guard with officers loyal to him. In 1949, Ulate was inaugurated as president.

Costa Ricans elected Figueres to the presidency in 1953. He raised the minimum wage, expanded the public school system, and increased the tax on imports. In 1955, a band of exiled Costa Ricans staged an air and land invasion of the country from Nicaragua. The revolutionaries tried to overthrow the Figueres government, but were quickly defeated. President Mario Echandi, who served from 1958 to 1962, tried to reduce the government's control over the economy. But the Legislative Assembly blocked many of his proposals. Francisco J. Orlich was elected president in 1962.

From 1963 to 1965, the volcano Irazú erupted and showered tons of ash over San José and the surrounding countryside. The volcanic eruptions damaged the coffee crop and forced thousands of people to abandon their homes.

Recent developments. Figueres won the presidency again in 1970, succeeding José Joaquín Trejos-Fernández. Figueres retired in 1974. Since 1974, Costa Rica has had an orderly succession of democratic governments. Costa Rican presidents have worked to maintain traditional neutrality in international affairs while maintaining good relations with the United States.

During the early 1980's, Costa Rica's economy began to decline. The country's economic problems included a high unemployment rate, low earnings from exports, and a large foreign debt. The United States increased its financial aid to Costa Rica in response to the problems.

Oscar Arias Sánchez, who served as Costa Rica's president from 1986 to 1990, played a leading role in creating a regional peace plan for Central America. He won the 1987 Nobel Peace Prize for his efforts.

Nathan A. Haverstock

Related articles in *World Book* include:

Outline

Questions

How did Costa Rica get its name?

What percentage of the people can read and write?

What is the national sport of Costa Rica?

How fast is Costa Rica's population growing?

Why did the ancestors of Costa Rica's blacks come to Costa Rica from the island of Jamaica in the late 1800's?

What are the *cordilleras*?

In which land region do most Costa Ricans live?

What are Costa Rica's leading exports?

What is Costa Rica's chief natural resource?

What was the United Provinces of Central America?

Costello, *kah STEHL oh* or *KAHS tuh LOH,* **John Aloysius,** *AL oh IHSH uhs* (1891-1976), served as prime minister of Ireland from 1948 to 1951 and from 1954 to 1957. In 1948, Costello, then head of the Fine Gael party, took control of the Irish Free State from Eamon de Valera, who had led the state for 16 years. Costello declared the state an independent republic in 1949. De Valera was prime minister between Costello's terms, and, in 1957, his victory ended Costello's second term. Costello was born in Dublin and received a law degree. He served as attorney general of the Irish Free State from 1926 to 1932. See also **De Valera, Eamon; Ireland** (The Republic of Ireland).   Thomas E. Hachey

Costume. See **Clothing; Theater** (Costume design).

Côte d'Azur, *koht da ZHOOR,* is the eastern end of the Mediterranean coast of France. This area includes part of the French Riviera, a famous vacation resort (see **Riviera**). The name *Côte d'Azur,* meaning *azure coast,* was given to this region because of its beautiful blue sea and sky. Groves of palm and orange trees and gardens of tropical flowers line the shore. The Côte d'Azur is a health resort area and playground for travelers from all parts of the world. Its chief cities include Cannes, Antibes, and Nice in France; and Monte Carlo in Monaco.
       Hugh D. Clout

Côte d'Ivoire. See **Ivory Coast.**

Cotillion, *koh TIHL yuhn,* is one of a family of ballroom dances for four couples in a square formation. These dances were popular from the late 1600's through the 1800's. About 1827, a new style of cotillion became popular as the final event of a ball. The couples sat around the edge of the room while a "gentleman leader" set up gamelike situations called *figures.* Figures included exchanging party favors or forfeiting places, as in musical chairs. There was always an element of surprise. A formal ball, especially at which debutantes are presented, is often called a cotillion.   Patricia W. Rader

Cotopaxi, *KOH toh PAK see,* in the Andes Mountains of Ecuador, is one of the world's highest active volcanoes.

It is 40 miles (64 kilometers) south of Quito, Ecuador (see **Ecuador** [map]). Its nearly perfect cone, with slopes of about 30 degrees, rises 19,347 feet (5,897 meters) above sea level, and is covered with glaciers and snow fields. Its crater is about 2,600 feet (792 meters) across. The volcano is in Cotopaxi National Park. Lava and hot ash rapidly melt snow on the flanks of the cone, sending big flows of mud down the mountainside. In 1877, a violent eruption caused ashfalls and mudflows that killed about 1,000 people.   Gregory Knapp

See also **Mountain** (diagram: Major mountains).

Cottage industry was a home-based system of manufacturing widely used during the 1700's and 1800's. The term *cottage industry* also refers to any present-day industry in which goods or services are made at home.

Cottage industry basically involved rural families adding to their agricultural income by making products in the home. A merchant provided the raw materials, collected and marketed the finished item, and paid the family a percentage of the price he received. The most important products made by cottage industry were cloth and clothing. Other products included shoes, cigars, and hand-decorated items.

In the United States, the cottage industry system developed in cities about 1870. The practice resulted in the harsh *tenement house system* and lasted until about 1920. Tenements were crowded, unsafe apartment buildings in which immigrant families both lived and worked. The immigrants worked for extremely low wages, usually making garments. This system declined partly because better management of factories made home-produced goods less competitive.

Today, some hand-decorating, sewing, and other highly specialized activities still operate as cottage industries. In addition, some economists point to the rise of a new cottage industry as office paperwork is increasingly handled by people using computers in their homes.   Warren Van Tine

See also **Industrial Revolution** (The textile industry).

E. Nagele, FPG

Attractive villages line the Côte d'Azur along the eastern Mediterranean coast of France. Visitors enjoy this popular resort area because of its balmy climate and natural beauty.

© Anthony Cassidy, Tony Stone Images   Webb AgPhotos

A field of cotton produces fluffy white bolls at harvesttime. A woman in India picks cotton by hand, *left.* The photo at the right shows a ripened boll that has split open.

Cotton

Cotton is the most widely used of all plant fibers. Cotton fibers are woven into soft, strong, absorbent fabrics to make clothing, bedsheets, carpeting, tablecloths, and other items. Other parts of the plant provide raw materials for a wide variety of useful products.

People have cultivated the cotton plant and woven its fibers into cloth for thousands of years. Today, cotton is a part of almost every person's life. Most people use cotton products daily, and many people have jobs in the cotton industry.

The leading cotton-growing countries are China and the United States. India, Pakistan, and Uzbekistan also produce large cotton crops. Together, these five countries grow about three-fourths of the world's cotton.

Uses of cotton

All parts of the cotton plant are useful. The most important part is the fiber, also called the *lint,* which grows out of the seeds that are inside the cotton *boll* (seed

C. Wayne Smith, the contributor of this article, is Professor of Cotton Breeding at Texas A&M University.

pod). Textile mills spin the fibers into yarn and weave the yarn into fabric. The *linters* (very short fibers on the seeds) are used in making padding, paper, explosives, and other products. Oil from cotton seeds forms the base of many food products. Farmers plow under the stalks and leaves to fertilize the soil. Even the hulls of cotton seeds are useful, serving as livestock feed and as a soil conditioner to improve the texture of the soil.

Cotton fibers are used mostly to make clothing. There are various types of cotton fibers that can be woven into fabrics for different kinds of garments, from rugged work clothing to delicate dresses. Unlike other fibers, the cotton fiber can absorb moisture in its center. This makes cotton clothing feel cooler in summer and warmer in winter than other clothing does because it moves moisture away from the wearer's skin. Clothing made of cotton also is durable because the fibers are strong.

Cotton seeds are used in a wide variety of goods. Manufacturers use the linters from the seeds as raw materials for rayon, paper, photographic film, and other products. Linters also are used to stuff mattresses, cushions, and pads. Bleached, sterilized linters are made into medical cotton pads.

Refined cottonseed oil is a popular cooking oil. It also is a main ingredient of such foods as salad dressing and

© David Austen, Tony Stone Images

A mechanical cotton picker pulls cotton from the bolls and blows it into a large steel basket at the back of the machine.

Cotton terms

Bale is a bundle of raw cotton. In the United States, a bale weighs about 500 pounds (227 kilograms).

Boll is the rounded mature seed pod of the cotton plant.

Boll weevil is a beetle whose young feed on cotton *squares* (buds), making them fall off.

Bur is the opened seed case of the cotton plant.

Carding is a process of cleaning and straightening cotton fibers.

Drawing is a process that further straightens the cotton fibers after carding and forms them into a loose rope called a *drawn sliver* (pronounced *SLY vuhr*).

Ginning is the process of separating the cotton fibers from the seeds.

Gray-state cloth, also called *gray goods* or *greige* (pronounced *gray*), is cotton fabric in its natural, grayish-white color before bleaching or dyeing.

Lint is raw ginned cotton that is ready for baling.

Linters are the short fibers that remain on the cotton seed after ginning.

Mercerization is the application of an alkaline solution to cotton cloth or thread to strengthen the cotton, make it hold dye better, and give it luster.

Picker is a machine that separates and cleans the fibers of cotton.

Pima cotton is a type of cotton with strong, silky fibers used to make fine, smooth fabrics.

Roving is a thin strand of cotton fibers ready for spinning.

Sizing is a mixture of starch, gum, and resins that strengthens cotton yarn to better withstand weaving or other finishing.

Sliver (*SLY vuhr*) is a loose rope of cotton fibers. A *card sliver* is thicker and has more tangled fibers than a drawn sliver.

Squares are the buds of cotton blossoms.

Staple is the average length of cotton fibers.

Trash is a term for leaves, stems, and other unwanted plant material in harvested cotton.

Upland cotton is the most common type of cotton.

margarine. Unrefined cottonseed oil is used to make soap, cosmetics, and drugs.

The cottonseed meal that remains after oil extraction serves as livestock feed and plant fertilizer. The cotton seed's protective covering, called the *hull* or *seed coat,* is used for animal feed and as a soil conditioner. Manufacturers also use the hulls to make plastics and synthetic rubber.

The cotton plant

In most parts of the world, the cotton plant is grown as an *annual*—that is, as a plant that grows and dies within one growing season. This section describes the upland cotton plant, from which about 90 percent of the world's cotton crop is produced.

Appearance. The mature upland cotton plant ranges from 2 to 5 feet (0.6 to 1.5 meters) in height and has spreading branches. Depending on growing conditions, each branch may produce from one to several bolls. The plant's leaves are 3 to 6 inches (7.5 to 15 centimeters) wide, some with three or five lobes in them and others with no lobes. The plant's *taproot* (long main root) may grow as deep as 4 feet (1.2 meters) into the ground.

How the plant develops. Farmers in most countries plant cotton seeds in the spring. Cotton seedlings emerge from the soil about a week after planting. Ap-

proximately three weeks later, *squares* (flower buds) begin to emerge on the plants. New squares continue to appear for about eight weeks. Each square grows for about three weeks and then opens into a creamy-white flower. The flower has five petals, which are surrounded by leaflike structures called *bracts* and specialized leaves known as *sepals.* The open flower measures about 2 inches (5 centimeters) across.

Within three days after opening, the petals turn pink and then reddish-purple as they dry and fall off. The flower must be pollinated during the first day it is open. Each flower usually pollinates itself.

After the petals fall, the seed pod develops into a boll. Inside the seed pod are about 20 to 40 seeds with fibers and linters growing from them. The seed pod matures into a green, walnut-sized boll in about six to nine weeks. Then the boll begins to dry and split open. The open dried boll, called a *bur,* curves back and exposes the fibers and seeds for harvest.

Kinds of cotton

Scientists have identified 39 *species* (kinds) of cotton plants. Only 4 of the 39 are cultivated. They are (1) *upland;* (2) *Pima,* also called *Egyptian* and *American-Egyptian;* (3) *tree;* and (4) *Levant.* The different species resemble each other in most ways. But they differ in such characteristics as height, type of fibers, and blooming time and color of flowers. Each species has varieties with different qualities. For example, some varieties grow best on irrigated land, and some have stronger fibers than others.

The four main species fall into two groups: (1) *New World cotton* and (2) *Old World cotton.*

New World cotton includes upland and Pima cotton. These types of cotton were first cultivated thousands of years ago by Indians in Central and South America and probably are native to these regions.

Upland cotton is cultivated in many parts of the world. The species may have gotten its name in the American Colonies. There, it was cultivated inland or, as the colonists said, "up land" from the Atlantic Coast. Upland fibers measure from about $\frac{3}{4}$ to $1\frac{1}{4}$ inches (1.9 to 3.2 centimeters) long. They can be made into many kinds of fabrics, including heavy canvas and fine, expensive cloth.

Pima cotton is one name for a species that developed along the coasts of what are now Peru and Ecuador. American colonists cultivated the species as *Sea Island cotton* along the southeast Atlantic Coast of what is now the United States. Scholars believe that growers in the early 1800's crossed Sea Island cotton with a variety of the same species in Egypt. Varieties developed from this cross were brought to the United States in the early 1900's and became known as *American-Egyptian cotton.* Cotton marketed in the United States today as Pima is descended from the original Pima (or Sea Island) cotton and American-Egyptian cotton.

About 8 percent of the world's cotton is Pima, Egyptian, and American-Egyptian. The fibers, which in most cases range from $1\frac{1}{4}$ to $1\frac{1}{2}$ inches (3.4 to 3.8 centimeters) in length, are much stronger than upland cotton fibers. Cotton from this species is used primarily to make high-

Leading cotton-growing countries

Tons of cotton grown in a year

China	●●●●●●●●●●●●●●●● 6,242,000 short tons (5,663,000 metric tons)
United States	●●●●●●●●●● 4,210,000 short tons (3,819,000 metric tons)
Pakistan	●●●●●◖ 2,328,000 short tons (2,112,000 metric tons)
India	●●●●◖ 1,874,000 short tons (1,700,000 metric tons)
Uzbekistan	●●●◖ 1,460,000 short tons (1,324,000 metric tons)
Brazil	●◖ 772,000 short tons (700,000 metric tons)
Turkey	●◖ 623,000 short tons (565,000 metric tons)
Australia	●◖ 477,000 short tons (433,000 metric tons)
Turkmeni-stan	● 392,000 short tons (356,000 metric tons)
Egypt	◖ 324,000 short tons (294,000 metric tons)

Figures are for 1991.
Sources: Food and Agriculture Organization of the United Nations; United States Department of Agriculture.

quality blouses and shirts. It also is used to make sewing thread.

Old World cotton includes *tree cotton* and *Levant cotton.* These species are native to northern Africa and parts of Asia and are also called *Asiatic species.* Levant cotton was an important source of lint for centuries in the Old World until other species were introduced and became more profitable. Old World species are relatively unprofitable because they have short, coarse fibers and low crop yields. Today, most of the Old World

How cotton develops   An upland cotton plant produces one to several flowers on each branch. After the petals fall, the seed pod develops into a boll. The boll then matures and opens.

WORLD BOOK illustrations by Lorraine Epstein

An open flower has creamy-white petals and measures about 2 inches (5 centimeters) across. The flower remains on the plant for about three days before the petals fall.

A cross-section of an un-opened boll shows the silky white fibers and brownish seeds inside. An unopened boll is approximately the size of a walnut.

Cotton fibers are exposed when the boll dries and splits open. The fibers, which have seeds within them, are called *seedcotton.* Farmers harvest cotton at this stage.

Cotton-producing areas of the world Cotton grows in many regions of the world. The leading cotton-producing countries are China and the United States. Pakistan, India, and Uzbekistan also produce large cotton crops. In the United States, Texas is the leading cotton producer.

WORLD BOOK map

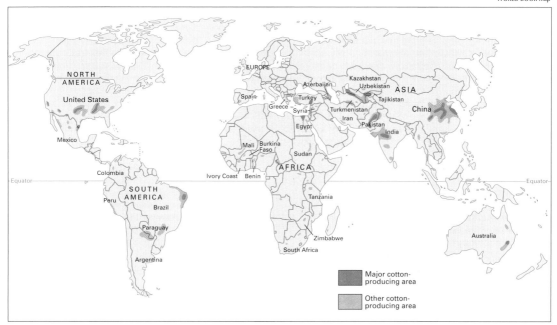

cotton that is cultivated is used in the communities where it is grown.

Where cotton is grown

The cotton plant originated in the tropics, which have warm to hot temperatures the year around, and it is considered a tropical plant species. Today, however, more than 50 percent of the world's cotton grows in temperate regions—that is, regions north of 30° latitude that have hot summers and cold winters. Farmers plant cotton mostly in areas that have 200 or more days a year in which temperatures do not drop below freezing.

Leading cotton-producing countries. The world's two largest producers of cotton are China and the United States. China produces about one-fourth of the world's cotton, and cotton textiles are a leading Chinese export. Cotton in China grows mainly in the east-central part of the country, near Beijing and Shanghai.

The United States grows about one-fifth of the world's cotton, mostly in the South and Southwest. Texas, California, and Mississippi produce almost two-thirds of the country's cotton.

Other countries. In addition to China, other leading cotton-producing countries of Asia include India, Iran, Kazakhstan, Pakistan, Syria, Turkey, Turkmenistan, and Uzbekistan. Important South and Central American producers include Argentina, Brazil, Colombia, Mexico, Paraguay, and Peru. Egypt, Ivory Coast, Mali, Sudan, and Zimbabwe are the main cotton-producing countries in Africa. In Europe, cotton grows mainly in Greece and Spain. Australia also produces a large cotton crop.

How cotton is grown

Cotton requires a warm to hot climate and a growing season that has many sunny days. The plant grows best in fertile, well-drained soil that gets adequate moisture during the growing season. Sunny weather after the bolls open helps dry the fibers for harvest.

Soil must be rich in nitrogen, potassium, phosphorus, and certain other nutrients to produce a good cotton crop. In industrialized nations, most farmers apply these

Leading cotton-growing states

Tons of cotton grown in a year

Texas	●●●●●●●●●●●●●●●●●●●
	1,076,000 short tons (949,000 metric tons)
California	●●●●●●●●●●(
	639,000 short tons (579,000 metric tons)
Mississippi	●●●●●●●(
	506,000 short tons (459,000 metric tons)
Arkansas	●●●●●
	341,000 short tons (309,000 metric tons)
Louisiana	●●●●(
	311,000 short tons (282,000 metric tons)
Arizona	●●(
	195,000 short tons (177,000 metric tons)
Tennessee	●●(
	160,000 short tons (145,000 metric tons)
Georgia	●●(
	149,000 short tons (135,000 metric tons)
Alabama	●(
	122,000 short tons (110,000 metric tons)
North Carolina	●(
	113,000 short tons (103,000 metric tons)

Figures are for a three-year average, 1990-1992.
Source: United States Department of Agriculture.

elements to the soil in the form of chemical fertilizer. In developing nations, the nutrients may come from the addition of animal manure.

Preparing the soil. Farmers in the United States plant cotton seeds between February and June, depending on the region. Growers *till* (plow) the soil sometime between the last harvest and the new planting season. Tilling loosens the soil so that each seed comes in contact with soil on all sides and thus can absorb moisture for sprouting. Tilling also plows under remains from the previous season's crop. This material decays in the soil and fertilizes the new crop. In the United States and many other countries, farmers till the land mainly by machine. In less industrialized countries, people or animals pull the plows. In areas with severe erosion or little topsoil, farmers do little or no tilling.

Planting is done by machines in most industrialized nations, and by hand in developing nations. After tilling, most farmers prepare *beds* (low ridges) in which they plant the cotton seeds. Planting in beds rather than on a flat field warms the seeds and drains excess moisture away from the seedlings. *Furrows* (narrow grooves) between the beds carry irrigation water. In hot, dry areas, farmers may plant the seeds on a flat field or between extremely low beds to capture rainfall for sprouting and growth.

Care during growth is important in producing a successful cotton crop. Cotton farmers must control diseases, insects, and weeds.

Diseases of cotton fall into four categories: (1) seedling diseases, (2) wilt, (3) blight, and (4) rot. Seedling diseases are caused by fungi. Cold, wet soils that slow or stop seedling growth help bring on these diseases. To kill fungi, farmers treat cotton seeds with chemicals before planting or add chemicals to the soil along with the seeds at planting.

Wilts, blights, and rots are symptoms of plant diseases caused by specific bacteria and fungi. The infections stunt growth or cause plants to wilt or rot. Farmers can best prevent these diseases by planting cotton varieties that are resistant to the disease-causing organisms and by using proper growing techniques. One such technique is to alternate the planting of cotton with crops that do not support disease-causing organisms.

Insects destroy an estimated 15 percent of the world cotton crop each year. Various types of bollworms and boll weevils do most of the damage. Whiteflies leave a sticky film on the fibers that makes them difficult to process and causes an unsightly mold to grow on them. Cotton growers control insects mainly with chemical insecticides. They also use special growing methods and cultivate cotton varieties that have some resistance to insects. In some areas, farmers destroy cotton stalks after harvest so insects cannot live on the stalks. Some farmers try to keep areas near cotton fields free of vegetation that could provide food for harmful insects.

Weeds reduce cotton crop yields by robbing the plants of moisture and nourishment. There are several ways to control weeds. In many developing countries, farmers remove weeds by hand. Nearly all farmers grow cotton in rows to make weed removal easier. Growers in some countries plow weeds under the soil to serve as fertilizer. Most cotton farmers in the United States use weedkillers called *herbicides* to control weeds. These chemicals prevent weeds from sprouting or kill them after they appear.

Harvesting of cotton usually occurs about 150 to 200 days after planting. Many developing nations harvest by hand. Producers in most industrialized nations use machine harvesters. Some countries use both methods. The following section describes machine harvesting.

Before harvest, many farmers apply a chemical called a *defoliant* to the crop. Defoliants cause the leaves to fall off, thus reducing the amount of *trash* (unwanted plant material) in the harvested cotton. Trash lowers the value of cotton by causing flaws in yarn and cloth.

Growers use either a *spindle picker* or a *stripper machine* to harvest cotton. The spindle picker has a series of barbed *spindles* (rods) that revolve as the machine moves along a row of cotton. The *seedcotton* (lint and seeds) catches in the spindles and is pulled from the bur. The machine then removes the seedcotton from the spindles and blows it into the picker.

Like spindle pickers, stripper machines pick seedcotton. But strippers also pull the burs and, in many cases, some leaves and stems off the plants. As a result, seedcotton harvested by a stripper machine contains much more trash than that harvested by a spindle picker.

After harvest, many farmers use a large machine to press the seedcotton into *modules* (compressed stacks) that weigh about 20,000 pounds (9,000 kilograms). Farmers store the modules on or near the cotton field until they are transported to a cotton gin. Other farmers load the seedcotton from the picker or stripper into large trailers and take the cotton immediately to the gin.

Processing and marketing

The processing and marketing of cotton varies somewhat from country to country. This section describes these activities in the United States.

Ginning and baling. The term *cotton gin* applies to the entire mechanical system that performs a process called *ginning*. Ginning separates the fibers from the seeds, dries and cleans the fibers, and then bales the

Edward S. Ross

A bollworm is a caterpillar that eats the buds and bolls of cotton plants. Bollworms are among the most destructive insect pests in the United States.

Cameramann International, Ltd.
Bales of cotton are stacked and moved by a fork-lift truck. Cotton is compressed, wrapped, and tied into rectangular-shaped bales after the ginning process is completed.

cotton. The machines that separate the fibers from the seeds are also called *gins*.

Upland cotton is ginned on a *saw gin* that grabs the fibers and breaks them away from the seeds. Pima cotton fibers are not as firmly attached to the seeds as upland fibers and so can be removed with a *roller gin*. This type of gin passes the seedcotton between two rollers that squeeze the seeds out from the fibers.

After separation, special machines clean and dry the fibers. The fibers are then compressed, wrapped, and tied into rectangular bales at the gin or at factories called *compress warehouses*. In the United States, most bales weigh about 500 pounds (227 kilograms) each. Many of the seeds removed during ginning are transported to oil mills or sold to ranchers and dairy farmers as cattle feed. Some seed may be returned to the farmer for planting the next season's crop.

Classing. Before American farmers sell their cotton on the market, a government agency called the United States Classing Office evaluates fiber samples from each bale. Until 1991, inspectors known as *classers* graded the bales on the basis of three characteristics: (1) the whiteness of the lint, (2) the amount of trash in the bale, and (3) how well the cotton was ginned. The classers also estimated how long the longest fibers were and called this estimated length the cotton's *staple*.

Today, the Classing Office also uses devices called *High Volume Instruments (HVI's)* to test and classify samples. HVI's measure fiber length (or staple), strength, and diameter. They also determine the amount of trash in the sample and measure the whiteness.

Selling. After classing, many U.S. farmers sell their cotton to a *broker*, also called a *cotton buyer*. Brokers, in turn, sell the cotton to shippers or textile mills. Some farmers sell directly to shippers or mills. Other producers pool their cotton to sell it in large blocks at competitive prices to shippers or mills.

Sales to textile mills usually take the form of *forward contracting*. In such a transaction, a mill agrees with a broker or farmer to buy a specific amount of a certain quality of fiber at a given price at a specified future time. This transaction, called a *forward contract*, may occur before planting or during the growing season.

In the United States, cotton of average quality can also be bought and sold on the New York Cotton Exchange in the *futures market*. In this system, traders buy or sell contracts to receive or deliver a certain quantity of cotton at a specified future time. The price they pay is based on their own estimate of what the future price will be. Buyers seldom actually receive the product for which they buy a contract. Instead, they sell the contract before delivery of the goods. If the price of cotton goes up after they buy the contract, they make a profit when they sell the contract. If the price goes down, they sell the contract at a loss. Cotton of higher-than-average or lower-than-average quality is traded in the United States in a spot market, where it is bought and sold for immediate delivery.

Making cotton into cloth

After cotton is harvested, ginned, and sold to textile manufacturers, spinning mills make it into yarn. The yarn is then made into cloth.

Cleaning and blending. At the mill, workers remove the wrapping and ties from the bales. They then peel layers of cotton from the bales and place them on conveyor belts. The belts move past spikes that fluff the cotton. The cotton then goes to machines that blend the fibers from different bales into a more even mixture. Once the cotton is blended, machines further clean and fluff the fibers and remove leaves, stems, and hulls.

In most mills, the fibers then move through a series of air ducts to a *carding machine,* which straightens the fibers into a thin, filmy sheet. A machine then forms the sheet into a loose rope called a *card sliver* (pronounced *SLY vuhr*), which is coiled into large cans. In some mills, the carding operation includes additional combing to further clean the fibers.

Spinning accomplishes three tasks: (1) it reduces the card sliver from a thick rope to slender yarn, (2) it straightens the fibers, and (3) it twists the fibers into yarn. First, the card sliver is pulled into a series of rollers. In a process called *drawing,* the rollers make the sliver thinner and the fibers more parallel. Drawing turns the card sliver into a more slender rope called a *drawn sliver.* Machines then pull the drawn sliver into a still thinner strand called a *roving.* The roving goes through additional drawing and is then twisted into yarn.

Lengths of yarn are tied end to end and wound on bobbins. In a process called *warping,* the yarn is wound onto a large spool called a *beam. A slashing machine* unwinds the yarn from the beam and dips it into a vat of *sizing.* Sizing is a mixture of starch, gum, and resins that strengthens the fibers so they can better withstand weaving. After drying, the yarn is made into cloth by weaving, knitting, or other processes. Newly woven cotton fabric is grayish-white and is called *gray-state cloth, gray goods,* or *greige* (pronounced *gray*).

Finishing is the final step in the production of woven goods. This process removes contaminants from the cloth and produces white fabrics that easily absorb dyes. Finishing consists of desizing, scouring, bleaching, and a process called *mercerization.*

Desizing soaks the fabric to remove the sizing. Machines then *scour* (wash) the fabric with a special solution to remove naturally occurring waxes from the fibers. *Bleaching* makes the fabric uniformly white so it

How cotton cloth is made At a textile mill, *carding machines* form cotton fibers into ropes called *slivers*. The slivers are drawn into a strand known as a *roving*, which is spun into yarn. In *warping*, the yarn is wound onto a huge spool. A *slashing machine* feeds the yarn through a mixture that strengthens it for weaving.

S. L. Craig, Jr., Bruce Coleman Inc.
Carding the fibers

S. L. Craig, Jr., Bruce Coleman Inc.
Forming the roving

S. L. Craig, Jr., Bruce Coleman Inc.
Spinning the yarn

Bill Barley, Shostal
Warping

Bill Barley, Shostal
Slashing

Bill Barley, Shostal
Weaving

can be sold as white fabric or evenly dyed. *Mercerization* is the application of a sodium hydroxide solution or other strong alkaline solution to the cloth. This process improves the luster of the fabric and makes it absorb dye more evenly.

After finishing, cotton that has not already been dyed before spinning or as yarn is dyed as fabric. Some cotton fabrics are preshrunk so that they do not become too small after they have been sold as garments.

History

Early days. Cotton plant species developed in both the Eastern and Western hemispheres. The oldest remains of cotton in the New World are fossilized plants dating from about 2900 B.C. found in present-day Mexico. In what is now Peru, Indians twined cotton to make fishing nets and other items as early as 2500 B.C. The earliest woven cotton dates from about 1900 B.C. in that same area. Indians in present-day Mexico and Peru used cotton extensively by about A.D. 1000.

The oldest evidence of cultivated Old World species, from about 2700 B.C., is cotton thread and fabric from the Indus River Valley region in what are now Pakistan and western India. The region first exported cotton textiles to Mesopotamia, an area that included most of modern-day Iraq and parts of Syria and Turkey, about 1500 B.C. Residents of Mesopotamia and nearby areas began cultivating their own cotton plants about 700 B.C. Europeans first grew and wove cotton in present-day Spain and Italy in the A.D. 700's. During the next several hundred years, cotton cultivation and weaving spread throughout much of Europe.

England. By the 1500's, imported cotton textiles had become common in England. The English began to weave cotton in the 1600's. They imported raw cotton from countries bordering the Mediterranean Sea, and later from America's Southern Colonies. In a system of production called the *cottage industry*, people spun and wove cotton at home and sold the cloth to merchants.

In the cottage industry system, the supply of woven cotton textiles could not keep up with the demand from merchants. This spurred the development of machines that could process cotton in large quantities. These machines, invented in England in the 1700's, were crucial in bringing about the Industrial Revolution, a period of rapid industrialization. They also made England one of the largest producers of woven cotton goods.

The first significant improvement in machinery for cotton processing was the *fly shuttle*, developed in 1733 by John Kay, an English inventor. The shuttle increased weaving speed by weaving the yarn mechanically rather than by hand. As a result, weavers needed more cotton yarn than before.

The *spinning jenny*, invented about 1764 by a weaver named James Hargreaves, enabled spinners to provide more yarn more quickly to weavers. It was the first machine to spin more than one yarn at a time. The *water frame*, invented by Richard Arkwright in 1769, spun yarn even more quickly by running on water power. Ten years later, a weaver named Samuel Crompton invented the *spinning mule*. This machine combined features of the spinning jenny and the water frame and gradually replaced both.

American colonists began growing cotton in the early 1600's. They wove cotton into coarse cloth for their own use. In the United States, large-scale cotton growing began in the South in the late 1700's. The colonists exported raw cotton to England, where it was made into textiles.

English manufacturers tried to keep the new spinning and weaving machines out of the United States. They wanted the United States to continue to sell its raw cotton to England and to buy back finished cloth. But Americans wanted to manufacture their own textiles. Finally, in the 1790's, the first American cotton mills were built in New England. Other mills soon sprang up.

In 1793, Eli Whitney developed a cotton gin that provided a fast, economical way to separate the cottonseeds from the fibers. This gin could do the work of 50 people and made it possible to send more cotton to the mills. Cotton textile manufacturing in New England grew rapidly.

With the invention of Whitney's cotton gin, the cotton industry in the Southern United States also expanded. The slave population grew in the early 1800's because planters needed more people to pick and gin cotton. Many Southern farmers felt they could not make money growing cotton without the slave labor. Many Northerners opposed slavery, and this conflict became one cause of the American Civil War (1861-1865).

In the 1830's, some cotton mills began to process cotton seeds in an attempt to extract cottonseed oil. But oil extraction was unsuccessful until just after the Civil War, when more efficient machines came into general use. Selling cottonseed oil then became profitable, and the number of mills processing cotton seeds grew. Also after the war, Southerners built large numbers of mills to make cotton cloth. These mills prospered in part because land was cheaper and taxes lower than in the North. In addition, Southern laborers worked for lower wages than Northern workers did.

The boll weevil began to seriously damage U.S. cotton crops in the 1890's. This beetle, native to Mexico and Central America, had spread into Texas early in that decade. By the early 1900's, it had multiplied across much of the South. Boll weevils cause the young squares to drop off the plant, thus decreasing the number of bolls that produce cotton fibers.

American cotton growers successfully fought off the boll weevil by modifying their growing methods. They picked and burned infested squares and bolls. They also planted cotton rows farther away from each other than usual so that heat from additional sunlight would kill developing weevils. The cotton industry recovered in the 1920's but then faltered again in the 1930's during the Great Depression, a severe worldwide economic slump.

Synthetic fibers. By 1960, the cotton industry was again thriving, and cotton accounted for about three-fourths of all fibers used in the United States. But this fraction began to shrink as synthetic fibers became increasingly popular. By 1977, only about one-third of all fibers used were cotton.

Decreased demand for cotton, as well as rising production costs, caused economic problems for United States cotton farmers. In response, the U.S. government enacted measures in the 1960's and 1970's to make it easier for farmers to obtain loans to support their farms. It also gave money to farmers who met certain requirements. In 1971, cotton farmers formed an organization now called Cotton Incorporated. It supports cotton research, works to develop new cotton products, and promotes the sale of cotton products.

Government assistance helped keep many farmers in business during this period. Then, at the end of the 1970's, demand for cotton clothing began to increase. Demand grew partly because people wanted softer, more comfortable clothing than synthetics could provide. The increase also resulted from a drop in the price of cotton goods, and the availability of a wider variety of high-quality blends of cotton and synthetics. By 1990, cotton had rebounded to make up about half of the total fibers used.

Technical advances. Farmers, researchers, and manufacturers are working to solve the problems that still face the cotton industry. Scientists have identified what makes some types of cotton plants resistant to certain pests. They are attempting to develop varieties that are naturally resistant to insects and diseases. Manufacturers also are developing ways of improving trash removal and methods of detecting and removing fibers damaged during manufacturing.

Scientific classification. Cotton makes up the genus *Gossypium* in the mallow family, Malvaceae. There are about 40 species, but only 4 of them are cultivated. Upland cotton is *G. hirsutum.* Pima cotton, Sea Island cotton, and American-Egyptian cotton are common names for *G. barbadense.* Tree cotton is *G. arboreum.* Levant cotton is *G. herbaceum.* Each of these four species includes several varieties.   C. Wayne Smith

Related articles in *World Book* include:

Cotton cloths

Broadcloth	Chenille	Gabardine	Percale
Brocade	Corduroy	Gingham	Swiss
Calico	Denim	Jersey	Twill
Canvas	Flannel	Muslin	Voile

Other related articles

Black Americans (The growth of slavery; pictures)	Pink bollworm
	Rayon
Boll weevil	Spinning
Brown lung	Textile
Cotton gin	Thread
Cottonseed oil	Weaving
Guncotton	Whitney, Eli

Outline

I. **Uses of cotton**
    A. Cotton fibers   B. Cotton seeds
II. **The cotton plant**
    A. Appearance
    B. How the plant develops
III. **Kinds of cotton**
    A. New World cotton   B. Old World cotton
IV. **Where cotton is grown**
    A. Leading cotton-producing countries
    B. Other countries
V. **How cotton is grown**
    A. Preparing the soil   C. Care during growth
    B. Planting   D. Harvesting
VI. **Processing and marketing**
    A. Ginning and baling   C. Selling
    B. Classing
VII. **Making cotton into cloth**
    A. Cleaning and blending   C. Finishing
    B. Spinning
VIII. **History**

Questions

Which parts of the cotton plant are made into manufactured products?

Which species of cotton produces about 90 percent of the world's annual cotton harvest?

What are the four main kinds of cotton diseases?

How do cotton farmers control weeds?

Who invented the cotton gin that stimulated the U.S. cotton industry in the early 1800's?

What tasks does spinning accomplish?

Why did the demand for cotton fabrics increase in the 1980's?

What is *mercerization?* What does it do?

When did American Indians first weave cotton textiles, according to archaeological evidence?

Why did English manufacturers want to keep new cotton spinning and weaving machines out of the United States in the late 1700's?

Cotton, John (1584-1652), was a Puritan minister and author. He was born in Derby, England. While serving as vicar of St. Botolph's Church in Lincolnshire from 1612 to 1633, Cotton became widely known as a pastor and preacher. In 1633, he fled to America to escape persecution as a Puritan. While serving with a church in Boston, Cotton became one of the most respected leaders of New England. Many New England children memorized his catechism, *Milk for Babes* (1646).

Cotton believed that church and state should be close partners, and he often advised both about proper government. He opposed unrestrained democracy, in which people ruled themselves. Cotton believed the people should choose their rulers, who should govern according to certain unchanging principles. Cotton became New England's spokesman against the extreme Calvinist political and religious views of Roger Williams, founder of the Rhode Island colony.   Mark A. Noll

See also **Williams, Roger** (In Rhode Island).

Cotton gin is a machine for removing the seeds from cotton fibers. It is widely believed that the American inventor Eli Whitney produced the first cotton gin. However, simple cotton gins were first used in India during ancient times. A version of these gins, the *roller gin,* had reached the American Colonies by the 1740's. In 1793, Whitney invented a faster, more economical way of separating cottonseeds from the fibers. His cotton gin helped make the United States the world's leading cotton grower.

Roller gins consisted of a pair of grooved wooden rollers that pressed the seeds from the cotton. These gins could remove the seeds from a variety of cotton called *long-staple.* But they could not remove the tightly clinging seeds from *short-staple* cotton. Short-staple cotton was raised only on small plots because it took one person a full day to separate the seeds from a pound (0.45 kilogram) of fiber.

Whitney's cotton gin could remove the seeds from short-staple cotton. As the crank on the gin turned, a cylinder covered with rows of wire teeth revolved. The teeth drew the cotton through slots so tightly spaced that the seeds could not enter. A roller with brushes removed the fibers from the teeth and deposited them in a hopper. Whitney's larger gins could process 50 times as much cotton in a day as could 50 people working by hand. Short-staple cotton quickly became a cash crop.

Today, the term *cotton gin* refers to the entire mechanical system that dries, cleans, removes the seeds, and bales the cotton. The machine that removes the seeds from cotton fiber is called a *gin stand.*

R. Douglas Hurt

See also **Agriculture** (picture: The cotton gin); **Cotton** (Ginning and baling); **Whitney, Eli.**

Additional resources

Green, Constance M. *Eli Whitney and the Birth of American Technology.* Little, Brown, 1965. First published in 1956.
Hays, Wilma P. *Eli Whitney and the Machine Age.* Watts, 1959. For younger readers.
Mirsky, Jeannette, and Nevins, Allan. *The World of Eli Whitney.* Macmillan, 1952.

Cottonmouth. See **Water moccasin.**

Cottonseed oil is an edible oil made from the seeds of cotton plants. It is used primarily to make shortening and margarine and as a cooking and salad oil. The southern and southeastern regions of the United States produce much of the world's cottonseed oil.

Cottonseeds consist of 15 to 24 per cent oil. Manufacturers remove the *hull* (outer covering) of the seed and then extract the oil. Most producers obtain the oil by *solvent extraction.* This method involves soaking the seeds in a solvent, which draws the oil from the seed. Crude cottonseed oil has a reddish-brown color and unpleasant flavor. Further refining and deodorizing removes the impurities from the oil and produces a colorless, mild-tasting product.   Daniel R. Sullivan

See also **Cotton** (Cottonseeds).

Cottontail. See **Rabbit.**

Cottonwood is a group of large, spreading poplar trees that grow in the United States. These trees grow quickly and make good shade trees, but they are short

National Museum of History and Technology

The cotton gin above is a model of the one Eli Whitney developed in 1793 to separate cotton fiber from the seed.

Alice K. Taylor, Photo Researchers

A cottonwood has a spreading, leafy crown, which makes it a good shade tree. Cottonwoods thrive in moist soils in many parts of the United States. They grow rapidly.

lived. Early in spring, their small, greenish flowers droop in long clusters called *catkins,* and form masses of cottony seeds. The shiny green leaves are shaped like a triangle, and have wavy, toothed edges. The thick, dull gray bark of the cottonwood tree splits into ridges and long furrows. Cottonwood trees grow in moist soils, especially along rivers.

The *eastern cottonwood* grows throughout the eastern regions of the United States. *Black cottonwood,* the tallest western broadleaf tree, grows along the Pacific Coast. The whitish or light brown wood of these trees is soft and weak. Manufacturers use it for boxes and crates, woodenware, luggage interiors, furniture, pulpwood, and *excelsior* (wood shavings used as packing material). Several other types of cottonwoods are used as windbreaks or ornamental trees, but they are not commercially important. Cottonwood is the state tree of Kansas, Nebraska, and Wyoming.

Scientific classification. Cottonwoods belong to the willow family, Salicaceae. The eastern cottonwood is *Populus deltoides.* The black cottonwood is *P. trichocarpa.*　　Richard C. Schlesinger

See also **Catkin; Poplar; Tree** (Familiar broadleaf and needleleaf trees [picture]).

Cotyledon, *KAHT uh LEE duhn,* is the leafy portion of a plant's *embryo.* The embryo is the part of the seed from which a mature plant develops. It consists of a *radicle* (short root) and a *plumule* (short bud), connected by a *hypocotyl* (short shoot) that bears one or more cotyledons. Because they form within seeds, cotyledons also are known as *seed leaves.* If a peanut is split apart, the two halves are the cotyledons. The remaining parts of the peanut embryo can be seen where the cotyledons are attached to the embryonic stem.

Flowering plants, called *angiosperms,* have embryos with one or two cotyledons. Those with one cotyledon are known as *monocotyledons* or *monocots.* Monocots include bananas, pineapples, and corn. Most bear leaves with parallel veins and flower parts in multiples of three. Angiosperms with two cotyledons are called *dicotyledons* or *dicots.* They produce leaves with a netlike pattern of veins and flower parts in multiples of four or five. Beans, squashes, and tomatoes are common dicots. *Gymnosperms* (nonflowering, woody plants) have embryos with two or more cotyledons, depending on the type of plant. Such needleleaf, cone-bearing trees as pines and hemlocks are gymnosperms.

Cotyledons have various functions. In some seeds, such as those of cereal grains, the cotyledon absorbs stored food from the *endosperm* (food storage tissue) of the seed. In other seeds, including those of peas and beans, the stored food is first absorbed by the developing embryo and then deposited in the fleshy cotyledons. When the seed of a pea sprouts, the cotyledons remain underground. In beans, however, the cotyledons appear above the ground and function briefly in *photosynthesis* (see **Photosynthesis**). Other cotyledons, such as those of morning-glories, resemble regular leaves in appearance and function.　　Joseph E. Armstrong

See also **Dicotyledon; Germination; Monocotyledon; Plant** (illustration: How a seed develops into a plant); **Seed** (illustration: The parts of a seed).

Cougar. See **Mountain lion.**

Cough is a strong, sudden expelling of air from the lungs. Coughing serves as a body defense that helps rid the lungs of harmful substances, such as pus or blood. But coughing also spreads germs that cause disease.

A person coughs if the lining of the respiratory tract becomes irritated. Certain nerves respond to this irritation, causing the individual to take a deep breath. These nerves also cause the *trachea* (windpipe) to close partially. The *diaphragm,* a large muscle that lies under the lungs, contracts rapidly, pushing air out of the lungs. The trachea then opens and the air rushes through the breathing passages and out of the mouth. The air carries along any substance in its path.

Irritants that produce coughing include smoking, air pollution, and respiratory infections. The irritation may lead to inflammation and cause the layer of mucus in the throat to thicken. Some cough medicines help reduce inflammation and loosen mucus so it can be coughed up easily. Others lessen the activity of certain nerves that produce coughing.

Mucus coughed up from the lungs helps physicians diagnose certain diseases. Doctors examine mucus under a microscope for evidence of bacteria, cancer cells, or other indication of disease.　　Barry L. Wenig

Coughlin, *KAWG lihn,* **Charles Edward** (1891-1979), was a Canadian-born Roman Catholic priest known for his political activities during the 1930's. Millions of Americans heard his weekly radio broadcasts and read his newspaper, *Social Justice.* Coughlin supported anti-Communism, anti-Semitism, isolation in foreign relations, and inflationary economic policies. His admiration for German dictator Adolf Hitler led his bishop to stop Coughlin's political activities after 1940. Coughlin was a parish priest in Royal Oak, Mich., from 1926 to 1966. He was born in Hamilton, Canada.　　David E. Kyvig

Coulee Dam. See **Grand Coulee Dam.**

Coulomb, *koo LAHM,* is a unit of electric charge in the metric system. Its symbol is C. The coulomb measures the amount of electricity flowing past a cross section of an electric circuit in one second when the current is one ampere. An electric current carrying one coulomb per second is called a current of one *ampere.* Ampere is the unit of rate or strength of flow. The name *coulomb* was given to the unit to honor the French physicist Charles Augustin de Coulomb. See also **Ampere; Farad.**
　　Leland F. Webb

Coulomb, *koo LAHM,* **Charles Augustin de,** *sharl oh goos TAN duh* (1736-1806), a French scientist, inventor, and army engineer, made fundamental contributions in the fields of friction, electricity, and magnetism. He formulated *Coulomb's law,* which states that the force between two electric or magnetic charges varies inversely as the square of the distance between them. He invented a number of instruments for measuring magnetic and electric forces. He also published papers on friction in machinery. The unit for the quantity of electricity, the coulomb, was named in his honor.

Coulomb was born in Angoulême. He was educated in Paris and entered the French Army. After nine years of army service in the West Indies, he devoted himself to scientific research.　　Richard G. Olson

Council, City. See **City government.**

Council of . . . See articles on councils listed under their key word, as in **Europe, Council of.**

Council on Foreign Relations is a private organization that studies problems in United States foreign policy. The council aims to develop new approaches to, and an understanding of, international relations. It does not, however, support or oppose any course of action.

The council encourages the publication of books on foreign affairs. The authors, who need not be council members, receive advice from study groups made up of experts who are members. Since 1922, the council has published a quarterly magazine called *Foreign Affairs.*

The Council on Foreign Relations sponsors about 150 meetings yearly for members. Leading government officials and experts in foreign affairs address the meetings. The council offers fellowships to selected individuals to broaden their knowledge of foreign affairs.

The council was established in 1921 and has over 2,500 members. It selects members for their experience and interest in foreign affairs. More than 35 committees on foreign relations in cities throughout the United States are associated with the council. The council has headquarters at 58 E. 68th Street, New York, NY 10021.

Critically reviewed by the Council on Foreign Relations

Counseling. See Guidance; Mental illness (Psychotherapy); Teaching (Other duties).

Counselor. See Lawyer.

Count is a title of honor going back to the days of the Roman Empire. The Latin word *comes* means *companion* or *follower,* and was used to indicate the companions of the Roman proconsuls. From this came the Spanish title *conde,* and the French *comte.* Count came into the English language as a translation of foreign titles equal to the English *earl.*

Counter Reformation, also known as the Catholic Reformation, generally refers to a period of Roman Catholic Church history in the 1500's and 1600's. The Counter Reformation consisted of two related movements: (1) a defensive reaction against the *Reformation,* a movement begun by Martin Luther in 1517 that gave birth to Protestantism, and (2) a Catholic reform.

Counteracting Protestantism. The Roman Catholic Church called the Council of Trent partly as a defense against Protestantism. The council met in sessions between 1545 and 1563 in Trent, Italy. It defined Catholic doctrine on questions disputed by Protestant theologians. The questions included original sin, grace, free will, the seven sacraments, the Mass, and the relation between Scripture and tradition. The council arranged for the pope to issue a catechism and books on *liturgy* (acts of worship), so there would be greater uniformity in church teachings. The church also published a list of books Catholics were forbidden to read because the books were considered harmful to faith or morals. In 1542, the church reorganized the Inquisition in Italy to help the courts fight Protestantism more effectively.

A number of wars resulting from religious conflicts broke out as Catholic governments tried to stop the spread of Protestantism in their countries. Such attempts led to civil war in France from 1562 to 1598 and rebellion in the Netherlands between 1565 and 1648. Religion was an issue in the fighting between Spain and England from 1585 to 1604. It was also a cause of the Thirty Years' War (1618-1648), which centered in Germany, but eventually involved most of the nations of Europe.

Catholic reform. The movement to reform the Roman Catholic Church started even before the Reformation. In Spain during the late 1400's and early 1500's,

Cardinal Francisco Ximénes de Cisneros made efforts to end abuses that had developed in the church. The Council of Trent tried to stamp out abuses by the clergy. It ordered bishops to live in their dioceses, visit their parishes, and set up seminaries to train priests.

During the Counter Reformation, many religious orders experienced reform and considerable growth. The Capuchins played a major role in the renewal movement through their preaching. The Jesuits and the Dominicans led a revival of philosophy and theology at Catholic universities. Jesuit colleges trained many members of upper-class Catholic families in Europe. Prayer and religious devotion intensified. Books teaching meditation and personal reform, such as those by Saint Ignatius Loyola and Saint Francis de Sales, became popular. Schools were set up to teach catechism.

Missionaries brought new peoples to Catholicism. Dominicans, Franciscans, Jesuits, and members of other orders worked among the inhabitants of Africa, Asia, and the Americas.

The Counter Reformation also affected art and literature. It inspired an enthusiasm and emotionalism that is represented, for example, in the works of the English poet Richard Crashaw in the mid-1600's. The Jesuits staged elaborate dramas at their colleges and influenced such artists as the Flemish painter Peter Paul Rubens and the Italian sculptor Gian Lorenzo Bernini.

John Patrick Donnelly

See also **Reformation; Roman Catholic Church** (The Reformation and Counter Reformation); **Pope** (Renaissance and Reformation); **Trent, Council of; Baroque;** Jesuits.

Additional resources

Catholicism in Early Modern History, 1500-1700: A Guide to Research. Ed. by John W. O'Malley. Ctr. for Reformation Research, 1988.
Dickens, Arthur G. *The Counter Reformation.* Norton, 1979. First published in 1969.
Evennett, Henry O. *The Spirit of the Counter-Reformation.* Notre Dame, 1970. First published in 1968.
O'Connell, Marvin R. *The Counter Reformation, 1559-1610.* Harper, 1974.

Counterfeiting is the unauthorized duplication of any object, especially money, with the intent to *defraud* (cheat someone). The printing and coining of money is the responsibility of national governments. In the United States, the Secret Service works to prevent the counterfeiting of U.S. currency. The manufacture of imitation brand-name goods, including clothes, computers, and automobile parts, is called *trademark counterfeiting* or *pirating.* Counterfeit products are almost always inferior to genuine ones. Consumers are defrauded when they buy them, believing they are getting the real ones. The Trademark Counterfeiting Act of 1984 made it illegal to make or sell counterfeit goods. George T. Felkenes

Counterpoint is a musical term for two or more independent melodies performed at the same time. Counterpoint is also called *polyphony.*

There are two basic types of counterpoint, *imitative* and *free.* In imitative counterpoint, a fragment of a theme called a *motive* is performed in different parts successively, often overlapping. The song "Three Blind Mice" is an example of imitative counterpoint called a *round.* Other examples include the *canon* and the *fugue* (see **Canon; Fugue**). Free counterpoint combines two different melodies. In one type, melodies are performed over a repeated pattern in the bass part. Compositions of this type include the *chaconne* and the *passacaglia*. In another type, one melody is performed against a countermelody. The German composer Johann Sebastian Bach treated hymns in his chorale preludes in this style.

Counterpoint developed in Europe about A.D. 850. One peak in the use of counterpoint occurred in the 1500's in the works of William Byrd of England, Giovanni Palestrina of Italy, and the northern European composer Josquin Desprez. Another high point occurred in the 1700's in the compositions of Bach.   R. M. Longyear

See also **Music** (Harmony).

Counting. See Arithmetic.

Country is a defined geographic territory under the authority of an independent government. The term may also be used to refer to the government of such a territory. A country may also be called a *nation* or a *state*. In 1993, there were 189 countries in the world, more than ever before. The number of countries has increased since the mid-1900's as more colonies have gained independence and large countries, such as the Soviet Union and Yugoslavia, have split up. In size, the countries of the world range from the Vatican City, which covers $\frac{1}{6}$ square mile (0.4 square kilometer), to Russia, which covers 6,592,850 square miles (17,075,400 square kilometers).

There are 9 huge countries, each with an area of more than 1 million square miles (2.6 million square kilometers), and 65 large countries with areas from 100,000 to 1 million square miles (260,000 to 2.6 million square kilometers). There are 30 countries with areas from 40,000 to 100,000 square miles (100,000 to 260,000 square kilometers), and 56 countries with areas from 3,000 to 40,000 square miles (7,800 to 260,000 square kilometers). Twenty-nine small countries cover less than 3,000 square miles (7,800 square kilometers) each. For lists of the countries of the world, see **World** (table: Independent countries of the world) and the various continent articles such as **Africa** (table: Independent countries).   Kevin R. Cox

See also **Nation**.

Country music is a type of American popular music associated with rural culture and the Southern region of the United States. It developed in the 1800's, combining elements of folk music from Britain, the blues of Southern rural blacks, popular songs of the late 1800's, and religious music. Country music, sometimes called *country and western music,* has been popular throughout the world since the 1940's.

During the 1920's, most country singers and instrumentalists came from such states as Georgia, Kentucky, North and South Carolina, Tennessee, and West Virginia. In the 1930's and 1940's, many artists from Alabama, Mississippi, Oklahoma, and Texas came to prominence. These performers created a wide variety of country music styles that today include bluegrass, Cajun, cowboy music, honky tonk, rockabilly, and western swing.

Characteristics. The musical instruments vary with each type of country music, but some are common to nearly all country groups. Instruments from many areas of the world combined in the New World to form the core of country music's instrumental sound. These instruments include the fiddle from Britain, the banjo from West Africa, the guitar from Spain, and the mandolin from Italy. As country music came under the influence of other kinds of music, other instruments were added and altered the basic sound. The piano, Hawaiian steel guitar, double bass, horns, and reed instruments have all been used in country music. Instruments that were electronically amplified first appeared in country music in the 1930's.

The story told in songs is an important part of country music. Many country songs today use direct language and realistic situations to describe the real concerns of adults. Most country songs are about love and romantic

Country Music Foundation Library   Richard Pasley, LGI   © Jay Blakesberg, Retna

Stars of country music include Hank Williams, *left,* Loretta Lynn, *center,* and Garth Brooks, *right.* Williams was a leading country performer of the 1940's and early 1950's. Lynn first became popular in the 1960's. Brooks was one of the most popular country performers of the early 1990's.

feelings. Many are happy songs, but some explain the feelings of loneliness, loss, and separation that result when love or romance ends, or when married couples are unfaithful. Some country songs are about work. Others express sacred themes, reflecting the importance of religion in Southern life. Some country songs are about events in the news, and some are humorous. Many old folk tunes are still sung in country music.

Styles vary from one style of country music to another. For example, bluegrass and other "mountain music" styles feature a high-pitched, nasal singing tone. Other singers sound like pop music vocalists.

Early years. Country music developed from the folk and religious music of the rural South. Beginning in the 1600's, immigrants from the British Isles brought their folk music to North America. This music included fiddling and singing. Solo fiddlers played dance music at social events, such as country dances, weddings, and wakes. Ballads and other folk tunes were often sung by one person, alone or accompanied by a fiddle. The religious music of the South included hymns and, beginning in the late 1800's, gospel songs and spirituals.

Folk music in the South changed through contact with other cultures. Between the mid-1800's and about 1920, the banjo, guitar, mandolin, and Hawaiian steel guitar were borrowed from many folk music traditions. Various combinations of these instruments were used both with and without vocalists. By about 1920, the *string band,* consisting of a fiddle, banjo, and guitar, was the standard instrumental group. String bands played dance music and folk tunes in homes, at parties, and at country fairs.

Commercial success. During the early 1920's, country music became available on records and on the radio. Record companies set up temporary recording studios in such Southern cities as Atlanta, Ga.; Charlotte, N.C.; Dallas; and Memphis. The music they recorded was often called *hillbilly music,* partly because of a popular band called the "Hill Billies." Sometimes, country entertainers were brought to New York City to record.

Early country radio shows were broadcast from cities as far north as Des Moines, Iowa, and Chicago, but the music was still concentrated in the South. There, it was broadcast from such cities as Atlanta; Dallas; Fort Worth, Tex.; Shreveport, La.; and Wheeling, W. Va. The most important radio show to feature country music—the "Grand Ole Opry"—was first broadcast from Nashville in 1925 as the "Barn Dance." It is still broadcast from Opryland, an entertainment park near the city.

Country music continued to change in the 1930's. Many groups added drums, pianos, and electric instruments to their sound. The singing style became smoother, and the accompaniments began to contain chords that sounded more like those found in other popular music of the day. In the late 1920's and early 1930's, the famous country singer Jimmie Rodgers performed in a style that combined country yodeling with black blues.

During the 1930's, radio stations broadcast country music to many regions of the United States. At the same time, Southerners moved to other parts of the country, taking their music with them. As a result, country music began to gain national popularity. During World War II (1939-1945), country music gained an international audience when members of the United States armed forces brought records to other countries. The most popular performers of the 1930's and 1940's included Roy Acuff, Gene Autry, the Carter family, Jimmie Davis, Red Foley, Tex Ritter, Jimmie Rodgers, Ernest Tubb, and Bob Wills.

After World War II. During the 1950's, mainstream pop singers recorded hits written by country composer and singer Hank Williams. These songs include "Cold, Cold Heart" and "Your Cheatin' Heart." Kitty Wells was the most popular solo female country singer from the mid-1950's to the mid-1960's.

During the late 1950's and the 1960's, the country music industry produced many records that blended characteristics of country and pop music. Vocal and string background ensembles became common, and much of the music was electronically amplified. This new style of country music was called the *Nashville Sound.* Its leading performers included Eddy Arnold, Patsy Cline, and Jim Reeves.

Country music today. In the 1970's, many country singers became national celebrities, and several became film and television performers. Such singers as Crystal Gayle, Loretta Lynn, Ronnie Milsap, Dolly Parton, and Kenny Rogers had hit records in both the country and popular markets.

Emmylou Harris, Waylon Jennings, Willie Nelson, and other singers have supported a return to a more basic, authentic country style. Many country entertainers who began careers in the 1980's drew inspiration from the roots of country music. Randy Travis, the Judds, Reba McEntire, and George Strait performed in styles associated with the 1950's and 1960's. Other stars, such as Alabama, Hank Williams, Jr., and Restless Heart, combined country music and rock. Garth Brooks, Lee Greenwood, Barbara Mandrell, and K. T. Oslin have explored the boundary between country music and pop.

Lydia Dixon Harden

Related articles in *World Book* include:

Acuff, Roy	Popular music	United States (The
Arnold, Eddy	Ritter, Tex	arts [picture:
Autry, Gene	Rodgers, Jimmie	Popular music])
		Williams, Hank

Additional resources

Country: The Music and the Musicians. Abbeville, 1988.
Dellar, Fred, and others. *The Harmony Illustrated Encyclopedia of Country Music.* Rev. ed. Crown, 1987. Also suitable for younger readers.
Malone, Bill C. *Country Music, U.S.A.* Rev. ed. Univ. of Texas Pr., 1985.
Stambler, Irwin, and Landon, Grelun. *The Encyclopedia of Folk, Country, & Western Music.* 2nd ed. St. Martin's, 1983.

County is usually a division of local government. Almost all the states of the United States are divided into counties. Louisiana has divisions called *parishes,* which correspond to counties. Alaska has similar divisions called *boroughs.* Connecticut is divided into eight counties used only for the election of sheriffs, and Rhode Island is divided into five counties that serve only as divisions of the state court system. All other U.S. states have county governments. The form of county organization and the number and powers of county officers vary from state to state. State legislatures determine the county boundaries.

Importance. The county is an important part of local government in all regions of the United States except

New England. In New England, the *town* is the center of local influence (see **Town**). In the Midwest and in the Middle Atlantic States, most counties share authority with *townships* (see **Township**). County revenues are raised chiefly by taxes on personal property and on real estate. State governments contribute some state-collected taxes to counties.

The number and size of counties vary from state to state and from region to region. The United States has 3,042 organized counties. Texas, with 254, has more counties than any other U.S. state.

Forms of county governments. Most county governments have a *decentralized* administration, with no executive head. The main county institution is an elective board that, in most cases, is called a *board of commissioners* or *board of supervisors.* It consists of from 1 to more than 100 members. The members of some boards are elected at large. The members of other boards are elected from districts, wards, or townships. Most county officers serve terms of from 2 to 4 years. They may include county commissioners or supervisors, sheriff, district attorney, coroner, registrar of wills, recorder of deeds, clerk of courts, jury commissioner, controller or auditor, treasurer, assessor, and others.

Some counties, especially urban counties, have an executive office that controls all other county offices. The executive office is headed by an elected county executive or by an administrator or manager appointed by the elective board.

Duties. County governments may administer justice, assess and collect taxes, record official documents, and register voters. They may also administer roads, public education, zoning, and licensing. Some counties manage such functions as sewage disposal, jails, and relief systems. Some maintain parks, airports, hospitals, libraries, electric service, and water service.

In counties where large cities occupy the entire county area, city and county governments may form a single unit. Denver, Honolulu, and San Francisco, for example, have combined city and county governments. In counties that are only partly covered by a city, the city and county may share responsibility for providing services to county residents. In Dade County, Florida, for example, the city of Miami provides police and fire protection to its own residents. But Dade County furnishes such protection to many county residents who live outside Miami. Such cities as Baltimore and Roanoke, Va., are not part of any county and do not form a part of county government. In these cities, municipal officials perform many of the duties that are ordinarily handled by county officials.

History. The word *county* comes from a French word that means *domain of a count.* The English, influenced by the French, began to call their *shires* counties about 1400. The English colonists brought the county system with them to America.   Susan H. Ambler

See also **Coroner; County agricultural extension agent; County extension home economist; District attorney; Sheriff.**

County agricultural extension agent is a public official who helps farmers and homemakers solve agricultural and family-living problems. Nearly every county in the United States has at least one agent. Agents are part of the Cooperative Extension System, a partnership of the federal, state, and county governments, and they receive funds from all levels.

County agricultural extension agents work to help farmers improve their farming and financial management practices. They advise all farmers, regardless of the size of their farms. In both rural and urban areas, agents advise 4-H leaders and provide information about gardening and insect control.

The agents also work with local leaders to improve rural communities. For example, they help develop plans to control pollution and try to make more jobs available for local people. Many county agricultural extension agents have a bachelor's degree in some field of agriculture.   Critically reviewed by the Department of Agriculture

See also **Agricultural education; County extension home economist; Farm and farming** (Obtaining management assistance); **4-H; Gardening** (Planning the garden).

County extension home economist is a public official who helps families and homemakers of all ages solve problems related to homemaking and the community. Extension home economists work in about two-thirds of the counties of the United States. They are part of the Cooperative Extension System, which is funded by federal, state, and county governments.

The home economics program of the Cooperative Extension System emphasizes consumer education and instruction about nutrition and the selection and preparation of food for a healthful diet. The program also teaches people how to improve their clothing, family relationships, health and sanitation, housing, and money management. Home economists extend their teaching further by training and advising homemaker group leaders, 4-H leaders, community leaders, and other volunteers.

County extension home economists spend much of their time helping families, especially in the field of nutrition education. In addition, home economists train and supervise assistants called program aides. More than 4,000 aides teach their low-income neighbors how to improve their diet.

Most county extension home economists have a bachelor's degree in home economics. They must also be able to use extension teaching methods.
        Critically reviewed by the Department of Agriculture

See also **County agricultural extension agent; 4-H.**

County government. See County.

Coup d'état, κoo day TAH, is a sudden take-over of a country's government by a group of conspirators. Usually, the conspirators are public officials who infiltrate and then use their country's armed forces, police, and communications to seize power. A coup d'état may lead to few or many changes in the government. Famous coups in history include those carried out by Napoleon Bonaparte in France in 1799, by the Bolsheviks in Russia in 1917, and by the Communists in Czechoslovakia in 1948. In the 1900's, most coups have occurred in politically unstable countries in Africa, Asia, Latin America, and the Middle East. *Coup d'état* is a French term meaning *stroke of state.*   Stephen Goode

See also **Junta.**

Couperin, koo PRAN, **François** (1668-1733), called "Le Grand" (The Great), was a French composer during the baroque period. Much of his work was written for the *harpsichord,* a keyboard instrument resembling a piano, in which the strings are plucked. For this instrument, Couperin wrote 27 *ordres* (suites) containing more than 200 highly imaginative, picturesque, and elegant pieces. Johann Sebastian Bach studied and sometimes imitated Couperin's style. Couperin also wrote chamber music and church music. In 1716, he published a harpsichord instruction book that is still used by students of the instrument.

Couperin was born in Paris. Many members of his family were also musicians. He became organist at the church of St. Gervais in 1688 and at the royal chapel in 1693. He often performed on the harpsichord before the royal court at Versailles, and he was music teacher to the children of King Louis XIV.   Joscelyn Godwin

Couplet, *KUHP liht,* is a rhyme of two lines. The *heroic couplet* is an English metrical form in iambic pentameter, used in sequence.

A *closed* couplet emphasizes the rhyme, and completes a thought within two lines. For example:

> A perfect Judge will read each work of Wit
> With the same spirit that its author writ:
> Survey the Whole, nor seek slight faults to find
> Where nature moves, and rapture warms the mind . . .

In an *open* couplet, clauses and sentences end anywhere, and the rhyme is not emphasized. For example:

> A thing of beauty is a joy forever:
> Its loveliness increases; it will never
> Pass into nothingness; but still will keep
> A bower quiet for us, and a sleep
> Full of sweet dreams, and health, and quiet breathing.

John Dryden and Alexander Pope used the closed couplet brilliantly. Other poets used open couplets with great skill. They include Geoffrey Chaucer, George Chapman, and John Keats. The word *couplet* also refers to any two lines of poetry that stand alone to form a stanza.   Paul B. Diehl

See also **Meter; Poetry; Rhyme.**

Coupon. See Rationing.

Courbet, *koor BEH,* **Gustave** (1819-1877), a French painter, helped found the realist movement in art. When Courbet began his career, the dominant art styles in France were neoclassicism and romanticism. Neoclassical artists chiefly portrayed historical subjects in a classical style. Romantic artists stressed dramatic and exotic themes. Courbet believed art should show the people and events of the time realistically and honestly.

In 1850, Courbet created great controversy when he exhibited two of his most important paintings, *The Funeral at Ornans* and *The Stone Breakers.* These paintings portray rural society in its native setting. Many urban viewers objected to Courbet's perceptive treatment of rural people. Painters of the time had been portraying these people sentimentally or as inferior to the urban middle and upper classes. In *The Funeral at Ornans,* Courbet painted the peasants and clergy life-sized. During this period, the peasants had become an important political force. Courbet's portrayal of this new force disturbed conservative critics.

Jean Désiré Gustave Courbet was born in Ornans, near Besançon. In 1840, he moved to Paris. Courbet sympathized with revolutionary movements devoted to ending the French monarchy. He became a member of the Commune, which governed the city briefly in 1871. After the Commune fell, Courbet was imprisoned and fined for his political activities. In 1873, he went into exile in Switzerland. Courbet's paintings later influenced such major art movements as naturalism and impressionism.
          Albert Boime

See also **Painting** (Realism; picture: *The Artist's Studio*).

Coureurs de bois, *koo RUR duh BWAH,* were French-Canadian frontiersmen of the late 1600's and the early 1700's who made their living by trading for furs with the Indians. At that time, Canada was a colony of France, and private fur traders were required to get a license from the government at Quebec. The government issued very few licenses, and most coureurs de bois traded illegally. *Coureurs de bois* means *vagabonds of the forest.* The adventurous life attracted many young men who had become bored with farming.

The coureurs de bois sold brandy to the Indians, and the missionaries frowned on their activities. But these adventurers learned Indian languages and customs. As a result, the coureurs de bois provided a link between the Indians and the French that helped to cement the alliance against the English during the French and Indian wars.   P. B. Waite

Courser is the name for a group of desert birds found in Africa, India, and Australia. Most coursers have long legs and short wings. They are normally seen running swiftly over the sand. They seldom fly unless disturbed

Oil painting on canvas (1850); the Louvre, Paris (Art Resource)

A Courbet painting called *The Funeral at Ornans* shows about 40 life-sized figures attending a burial in rural France. The painting caused great controversy when it was first exhibited. Critics objected to the sympathetic portrayal of common villagers. Most people believed only important individuals deserved such dignified and realistic treatment.

J. Robert, Jacana

Coursers are swift-running desert birds found in Africa, India, and Australia. The Egyptian plover, *above,* is a courser that lives along the Nile River in Egypt.

and then usually fly only a short distance. Coursers feed chiefly on insects.

There are nine species of coursers, most of which are brown and white. One species, the Egyptian plover, has bright gray, white, and black markings. The Egyptian plover is common along the Nile River. It is also called the *crocodile bird* because in folk tales the bird is described picking bits of food out from between a crocodile's teeth. The female Egyptian plover incubates her eggs at night and often buries them in the sand during the day to be heated by the sun. In southern Africa, coursers are noted for eating large numbers of locusts and are sometimes called *locust birds.*

Scientific classification. Coursers belong to the family Glareolidae. The Egyptian plover is *Pluvianus aegyptius.*

Donald F. Bruning

Court is a government institution that settles legal disputes and administers justice. Courts resolve conflicts involving individuals, organizations, and governments. Courts also decide the legal guilt or innocence of persons accused of crimes and sentence the guilty.

All courts are presided over by judges. These officials decide all questions of law, including what evidence is fair to use. In many cases, the judge also decides the truth or falsity of each side's claims. In other cases, a jury decides any questions of fact. The word *court* may refer to a judge alone or to a judge and jury acting together. It also may refer to the place where legal disputes are settled.

Some court rulings affect only the persons involved in a case. Other decisions deal with broad public issues, such as freedom of the press, racial discrimination, and the rights of persons accused of a crime. In this way, courts serve as a powerful means of social and political change.

Types of courts

Courts differ in their *jurisdiction* (authority to decide a case). Generally, courts are classified as *trial courts* or *appellate courts,* and as *criminal courts* or *civil courts.*

Trial and appellate courts. Nearly all legal cases begin in trial courts, also called *courts of original jurisdiction.* These courts may have general jurisdiction or limited, also called *special,* jurisdiction. Courts of gen-

eral jurisdiction hear many types of cases. The major trial court of any county, state, or other political unit is a court of general jurisdiction. Courts of limited or special jurisdiction specialize in one or more types of cases, such as those involving juvenile offenders or traffic violations.

The losing side often has the right to *appeal*—that is, to ask that aspects of the case be reconsidered by a higher court called an appellate or *appeals court.* Appellate courts review cases decided by trial courts if the losing side questions the ruling of the lower court on a matter of law. Appellate courts cannot review a trial court's decision on the facts.

Criminal and civil courts. Criminal courts deal with actions considered harmful to society, such as murder and robbery. In criminal cases, the government takes legal action against an individual. The sentences handed down by criminal courts range from probation and fines to imprisonment and, in some states, death.

Civil courts settle disputes involving people's private relations with one another. Civil suits involve such noncriminal matters as contracts, family relationships, and accidental injuries. In most civil cases, an individual or organization sues another individual or organization. Most civil decisions do not involve a prison sentence, though the party at fault may be ordered to pay damages.

How courts work

How criminal courts work. Most persons arrested on suspicion of a crime appear before a judge called a *magistrate* within 24 hours after the arrest. In cases involving minor offenses, the magistrate conducts a trial and sentences the guilty. In more serious cases, the magistrate decides whether to keep the *defendant* (accused person) in jail or to release him or her on bail. The magistrate also may appoint a state-paid defense attorney, called a *public defender,* to represent a defendant who cannot afford a lawyer.

Pretrial proceedings. In a case involving a serious crime, the police give their evidence of the suspect's guilt to a government attorney called a *prosecutor.* In some states, the prosecutor formally charges the defendant in a document called an *information.* The prosecutor presents the information and other evidence to a magistrate at a *preliminary hearing.* If the magistrate decides that there is *probable cause* (good reason for assuming) that the defendant committed the crime, the magistrate orders the defendant held for trial. In other states and in federal courts, the prosecutor presents the evidence to a *grand jury,* a group of citizens who decide whether the evidence justifies bringing the case to trial. If the grand jury finds sufficient evidence for a trial, it issues a formal accusation called an *indictment* against the suspect.

The defendant then appears in a court of general jurisdiction to answer the charges. This hearing is called an *arraignment.* If the defendant pleads guilty, the judge pronounces sentence. Many defendants plead guilty, rather than go to trial, in return for a reduced charge or a shorter sentence. This practice is called *plea bargaining.* Most criminal cases in the United States are settled in this way. But if the accused pleads not guilty, the case goes to trial.

Trial. The defendant may request a jury trial or a *bench trial,* which is a trial before a judge. The jury or judge must decide if the evidence presented by the prosecutor proves the defendant guilty "beyond a reasonable doubt." If not, the defendant must be *acquitted* (found not guilty).

If the defendant is found guilty, the judge pronounces sentence. Convicted defendants may take their case to an appellate court. However, prosecutors may not appeal an acquittal because the United States Constitution forbids the government to *put a person in double jeopardy* (try a person twice) for the same crime.

How civil courts work. A civil lawsuit begins when an individual or organization, called the *plaintiff,* files a complaint against another individual or organization, called the *defendant.* The complaint formally states the injuries or losses the plaintiff believes were caused by the defendant's actions. The complaint also asks for a certain amount of money in damages.

The defendant receives a *summons,* a notice that a complaint has been filed. It directs the defendant to appear in court on a certain date. The defendant then files a document called an *answer.* The answer contains the defendant's version of the facts of the case and asks the court to dismiss the suit. The defendant also may file a *counterclaim* against the plaintiff.

In most cases, the complaint and the answer are the first of a series of documents called the *pleadings.* In the pleadings, the plaintiff and defendant state their own claims and challenge the claims of their opponents. Most civil cases are settled out of court on the basis of the pleadings. However, if serious questions of fact remain, a formal *discovery* takes place. This procedure forces each *litigant* (party involved in the case) to reveal the testimony or records that would be introduced as evidence in court. If the case still remains in dispute after the discovery, it goes to trial.

Civil cases may be decided by a judge or by a jury. The judge or jury determines who is at fault and how much must be paid in damages. Both sides may appeal.

Courts in the United States

The United States has a dual system of federal and state courts. Federal courts receive their authority from the U.S. Constitution and federal laws. State courts receive their powers from state constitutions and laws.

Federal courts handle both criminal and civil cases involving the Constitution or federal laws, and cases in which the U.S. government is one of the sides. They also try cases between individuals or groups from different states, and cases involving other countries or their citizens. They handle *maritime* (sea) cases, bankruptcy actions, and cases of patent and copyright violation.

The federal court system includes district courts, courts of appeals, and the Supreme Court of the United States. District courts are federal courts of *original jurisdiction*—that is, they are the first courts to hear most cases involving a violation of federal law. The United States and its possessions have about 95 district courts. Each state has at least one such court.

Courts of appeals try federal cases on appeal from district courts. They also review the decisions made by such federal agencies as the Securities and Exchange Commission and the National Labor Relations Board.

The United States is divided into 12 *circuits* (districts), each of which has a court of appeals. An additional federal court of appeals, the United States Court of Appeals for the Federal Circuit, has nationwide jurisdiction.

The Supreme Court of the United States is the highest court in the nation. A person who loses a case either in a federal court of appeals or in the highest state court may appeal to the Supreme Court, but it may refuse to review many cases. In addition to its appellate jurisdiction, the court has original jurisdiction over cases involving two states or representatives of other countries.

The federal court system also includes several specialized courts. The United States Claims Court hears cases involving claims against the federal government. The Court of International Trade settles disputes over import duties. Taxpayers ordered to pay additional federal income taxes may appeal to the Tax Court of the United States. Military courts, called *courts-martial,* have jurisdiction over offenses committed by members of the armed forces. The Court of Military Appeals reviews court-martial rulings.

State courts. The lowest state courts are courts of limited or special jurisdiction. Some of these courts handle a variety of minor criminal and civil cases. Such courts include *police courts, magistrate's courts,* or *county courts,* and *justices of the peace.* Other lower courts specialize in only one type of case. For example, *small-claims courts* try cases that involve small amounts of money. *Probate* or *surrogate courts* handle wills and disputes over inheritances. Other specialized courts include *courts of domestic relations, juvenile courts,* and *traffic courts.*

Courts of general jurisdiction rank above courts of limited jurisdiction. These higher courts are known as *circuit courts, superior courts,* or *courts of common pleas.* About half the states have intermediate appeals courts, which hear appeals from courts of general jurisdiction. In some states, courts of general jurisdiction and appellate courts handle both criminal and civil cases. Other states have separate divisions on both levels. The highest court in most states is its supreme court.

Courts around the world

Courts in other countries. The judicial systems of most countries are based on either *common law* or *civil law.* Some combine the features of both systems. This use of the term *civil law* refers to a legal system. It should not be confused with the branch of law dealing with people's private relations with one another.

In common-law systems, judges base their decisions primarily on *precedents,* earlier court decisions in similar cases. Most English-speaking countries, including the United States, the United Kingdom, Canada, and Australia, have common-law systems.

Civil-law systems rely more strictly on written *statutes* (legislative acts). Judges may refer to precedents, but they must base every ruling on a particular statute and not on precedent alone. Most European, Latin-American, and Asian countries, and some African nations, have civil-law systems.

International courts deal only with disputes between nations. The International Court of Justice, the highest judicial body of the United Nations (UN), meets at The Hague in the Netherlands. Its decisions are not

United States court system

The U.S. court system has two levels—state and federal. State courts handle cases that affect state constitutions and laws. Federal courts hear cases that involve the U.S. Constitution and federal laws, plus cases in which the U.S. government is one of the sides.

WORLD BOOK illustrations by Bill and Judie Anderson

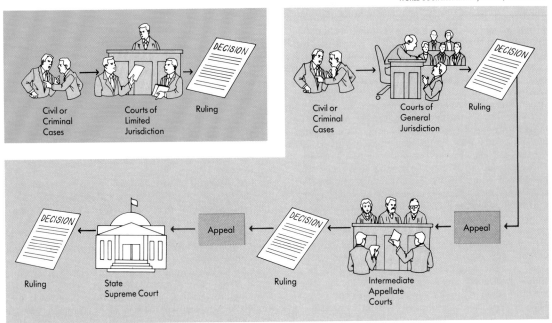

State courts vary according to their authority. Courts of limited jurisdiction decide minor cases. Courts of general jurisdiction hear more serious cases. These cases may be appealed to intermediate appellate courts, if the state has them, or go directly to the supreme court of the state.

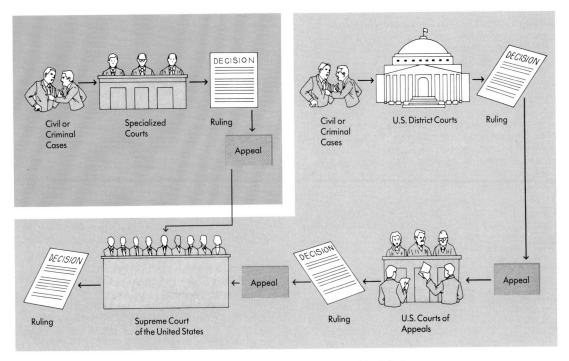

Federal courts include district courts, courts of appeals, and the Supreme Court of the United States. The federal system also has several specialized courts. The Supreme Court of the United States may review cases from state supreme courts if a question of federal law is involved.

binding unless the nations involved in the dispute agree to accept its rulings.

History

Early courts. Tribal councils or groups of elders served as the first courts. They settled disputes on the basis of local custom. Later civilizations developed written legal codes. The need to interpret these codes and to apply them to specific situations resulted in the development of formal courts. For example, the ancient Hebrews had a supreme council, called the *Sanhedrin,* which interpreted Hebrew law.

The ancient Romans developed the first complete legal code as well as an advanced court system. After the collapse of the West Roman Empire in the A.D. 400's, the Roman judicial system gradually died out in western Europe. It was replaced by *feudal* courts, which were conducted by local lords. These courts had limited jurisdiction and decided cases on the basis of local customs.

Development of civil-law and common-law courts. During the early 1100's, universities in Italy began to train lawyers according to the principles of ancient Roman law. Roman law, which relied strictly on written codes, gradually replaced much of the feudal court system throughout mainland Europe. In the early 1800's, the French ruler Napoleon I used Roman law as the foundation of the *Code Napoléon.* This code, a type of civil law, became the basis of the court system in most European and Latin-American countries.

By the 1200's, England had established a nationwide system of courts. These courts developed a body of law that was called *common law* because it applied uniformly to people everywhere in the country. Common-law courts followed traditional legal principles and based their decisions chiefly on precedents. English common law became the basis of the court system for most countries colonized by England, including the United States and Canada.

Development of U.S. courts. The American Colonies based their courts on the English common-law system. These colonial courts became state courts after the United States became an independent nation in 1776. Only Louisiana modeled its court system on civil law. In 1789, Congress passed the Judiciary Act, which created the federal court system.   Jack M. Kress

Related articles in *World Book.* For information on the courts of various states, provinces, and countries, see the *Government* section of those articles. See also:

Courts

Court-martial	District court
Court of appeals	International Court of Justice
Court of claims	Juvenile court
Court of International Trade,	Small-claims court
United States	Supreme Court of the U.S.
Court of Military Appeals	

Officials

Chief justice	Judge	Lawyer
Clerk of court	Jury	Marshal
District attorney	Justice of the	Public defender
Grand jury	peace	

Procedures and documents

Affidavit	Bail	Deposition	Fine
Appeal	Brief	Equity	Forfeiture
Attachment	Class action	Evidence	Garnishment

Habeas corpus	Oath	Sentence	Trial
Indictment	Petition	Subpoena	Warrant
Injunction	Plea bargain-	Suit	Witness
Inquest	ing	Summons	Writ
Mandamus	Quo warranto		

Other related articles

Civil law	Kangaroo court
Code Napoléon	Law
Common law	Law enforcement
Criminal justice system	Old Bailey
Judicial Conference of the	Star Chamber
United States	

Additional resources

Lee, Katherine J. *Courts & Judges: How They Work.* HALT, 1987.
Legal Breakdown: 40 Ways to Fix Our Legal System. Ed. by Stephen Elias and others. Nolo, 1990.
Warner, Ralph. *Everybody's Guide to Small Claims Court.* 4th ed. Nolo, 1990.

Court, Margaret Smith (1942-   ), an Australian tennis star, was one of the best female tennis players in history. She was rated among the world's top 10 female tennis players from 1961 to 1975, ranking number one seven times. Court was noted for her endurance and control, as well as her skill at blending power and delicacy in her shots.

In 1970, Court won the *grand slam* of tennis in singles competition—the Australian Open, the French Open, Wimbledon, and the United States Open. Maureen Connolly and Steffi Graf are the only other women to win the grand slam in singles. Court also won the grand slam in mixed doubles in 1963. Her career record of 64 titles in the four grand slam tournaments consisted of 24 in singles, 21 in women's doubles, and 19 in mixed doubles.

Margaret Smith was born in Albury, New South Wales. She married Barry Court in 1967. In 1977, she retired from tennis competition.   Arthur Ashe

See also **Tennis** (Tables).

Court-martial is a military court that tries people who belong to a country's armed forces and are accused of committing certain crimes. In the United States, these crimes are set forth in the Uniform Code of Military Justice. The crimes range from murder, robbery, and drug abuse to offenses specific to the military, such as absence without leave or disrespect to a superior officer. The code provides for three types of courts-martial: (1) general, (2) special, and (3) summary.

A *general court-martial* almost always consists of a military judge and a jury of at least five members of the military. Such a court may try a person for any crime in the Uniform Code. Usually, general courts-martial try only the most serious offenses, such as murder or spying. Punishments imposed by general courts-martial may include dishonorable discharge from the military and death.

A *special court-martial* almost always consists of a military judge and a jury of at least three members of the military. It may try any offense in the Uniform Code except those punishable by death. However, special courts-martial may not impose a punishment harsher than a bad-conduct discharge and six months in prison.

A *summary court-martial* consists of only one officer. It can try enlisted people, but not officers. Summary courts-martial usually try only minor offenses, such as short absences without leave. They may sentence the accused to no more than 30 days in prison and may not impose a discharge from the military.

In general and special courts-martial, defendants receive free counsel from defense attorneys who are also military officers. In addition, a defendant may hire a civilian lawyer. If a defendant is convicted by a general or special court-martial, the commanding officer who referred the case to the court reviews the court's decision. The officer may then approve the conviction and the sentence or make them less severe. A court of military review examines all cases that result in a military discharge or in sentences harsher than a year or more in prison. Certain cases may also be reviewed by the U.S. Court of Military Appeals and the Supreme Court of the United States.   Robert C. Mueller

See also **Court of Military Appeals; Uniform Code of Military Justice.**

Court of appeals is a high federal or state court. The United States Courts of Appeals rank next to the Supreme Court of the United States as a reviewing authority. Several of the states also have courts of appeals.

The U.S. Courts of Appeals hear most appeals from district courts and federal administrative agencies. They also review the decisions of some agencies. In some cases, the party who feels wronged has a right to appeal directly to the Supreme Court of the United States. In a few cases, the parties have a right to ask the Supreme Court to review a decision of a court of appeals. But in most cases, the Supreme Court only reviews cases that it decides present an important question of law.

In the early days of the United States, federal judges traveled from place to place to try cases and to hear appeals. The route which was assigned to the court was called the *circuit.* Today the circuits are geographical areas. Each circuit has one court of appeals.

The circuits are numbered 1 through 11. A twelfth, unnumbered circuit covers only the District of Columbia. The First Circuit includes Puerto Rico, the Third includes the Virgin Islands, and the Ninth includes Alaska and Hawaii. The judges of the First, Third, and Ninth Circuits travel to these places to hear cases. A special U.S. Court of Appeals for the Federal Circuit has nationwide jurisdiction. It specializes in cases involving patents and claims against the federal government.

Only three judges ordinarily sit to decide each case,

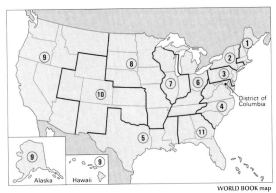

U.S. Courts of Appeals are federal courts that retry cases appealed from district courts. The United States is divided into 12 areas called *circuits,* each of which has a court of appeals.

though more than three judges are assigned to each circuit. A justice of the Supreme Court is assigned to each circuit as the *Circuit Justice.* In early times, the justice often helped decide cases at the court of appeals level, but now this rarely occurs. The chief judge has a position on the court of appeals like that of the chief justice of the Supreme Court. The chief judge assigns tasks to the other judges.   Jack M. Kress

See also **Appeal; Circuit rider; Court** (Federal courts); **District court; Supreme Court of the United States.**

Court of claims is a special federal or state court that settles claims against the government. The United States Claims Court hears lawsuits against the federal government. This court has 16 judges, including a chief judge. The President appoints them, with the approval of the United States Senate, to 15-year terms.

In 1855, Congress agreed that the United States government could be sued on certain claims and created the U.S. Court of Claims to handle such cases. The Federal Courts Improvement Act of 1982 replaced the U.S. Court of Claims with the U.S. Claims Court. The act expanded the power of the new Claims Court by widening its jurisdiction over contract claims against the government. Congress provides money to pay for judgments of the Claims Court. Judgments of the Claims Court may be appealed to the U.S. Court of Appeals for the Federal Circuit.   Jack M. Kress

Court of International Trade, United States, is a federal court that handles cases involving imports and other international business. The court hears both civil suits against the United States government and certain civil cases begun by the government. The court is in New York City, but it has nationwide authority and may conduct trials anywhere in the United States. The court was established in 1980 to replace the U.S. Customs Court. It consists of nine judges, who are appointed by the President subject to Senate approval. The President names one of the nine to serve as chief judge.

Critically reviewed by the United States Court of International Trade

Court of Military Appeals is the highest appeals court of the U.S. armed forces. It consists of three civilian judges appointed by the President. The court reviews all court-martial cases that provide for the death sentence, confinement for one year or more, or dismissal from the service. Military personnel may appeal to the court after a board of military review has examined the court-martial findings. The *Judge Advocate General* (chief legal officer) of the Army, Navy, Air Force, or Coast Guard may ask the court to review other court-martial cases. In some instances, the Supreme Court of the United States may review proceedings of the court. See also **Court-martial.**   Jack M. Kress

Courtship of Miles Standish, The. See Longfellow, Henry Wadsworth.

Cousin is a person outside your immediate family related to you by blood and descended from the same ancestor. The chart with this article shows how cousins are related.

First cousins are children of brothers and sisters, and so Frank, Julia, and Peter are first cousins. *Second cousins* are children of first cousins, and so Joan, Susan, and Agnes are second cousins, and so on. A *first cousin once removed* is the child of your first cousin, so Susan and Agnes are Frank's first cousins once removed. Helen

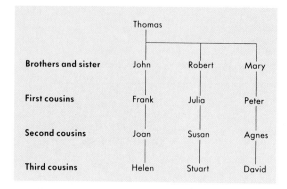

		Thomas		
Brothers and sister	John	Robert		Mary
First cousins	Frank	Julia		Peter
Second cousins	Joan	Susan		Agnes
Third cousins	Helen	Stuart		David

and Stuart are Peter's first cousins twice removed, and so on. See also **Family** (Family relationships).

Cousteau, *koo stoh,* **Jacques-Yves,** *zhahk eev* (1910-   ), is a French oceanographer, author, and motion-picture producer. He developed many techniques for undersea exploration. In 1943, Cousteau helped invent the *aqualung.* This breathing device enables a diver to move about freely under water for long periods. Cousteau also developed the first underwater diving station and an underwater observation vehicle called the *diving saucer.*

Since 1951, Cousteau has explored the oceans with his research ship *Calypso.* He has written books about sea life that have been translated into many languages. These books include *The Silent World* (1953), *The Living Sea* (1962), and *World Without Sun* (1964). He has produced many films about sea life, three of which won Academy Awards.

Courtesy of Doubleday

Jacques-Yves Cousteau

In 1960, Cousteau and Prince Rainier III of Monaco opposed France's plan to dump radioactive wastes into the Mediterranean Sea. France abandoned the plan that year. During the 1960's and 1970's, Cousteau's television series, "The Undersea World of Jacques Cousteau," dramatized underwater exploration and the need for conservation of ocean life. Cousteau was born in St.-André-de-Cubzac, near Bordeaux.   Carolyn Merchant

Cousy, *KOO zee,* **Bob** (1928-   ), ranks among the outstanding playmakers in the history of basketball. Cousy played guard for the Boston Celtics of the National Basketball Association (NBA) from the 1950-1951 season through the 1962-1963 season. He helped lead the Celtics to six NBA championships. Cousy won fame for his skillful dribbling and his accurate passing. He led the National Basketball Association in *assists* (passes to teammates that result in baskets) every season from the 1952-1953 season through the 1959-1960 season.

Robert Joseph Cousy was born in New York City. He won All-America honors at College of the Holy Cross in 1950. From 1963 to 1969, he was basketball coach at Boston College. From 1969 to 1973, he coached the Cincinnati Royals in the NBA.   Bob Logan

Couture, Thomas. See Painting (Realism; picture); Manet, Edouard.

Covenant, Ark of the. See Ark of the Covenant.

Covenanters, *KUHV uh nuhn tuhrz,* were members of a series of religious movements in Scotland during the last half of the 1500's and the 1600's. The Covenanters entered into *covenants* (agreements) with one another to defend their Presbyterian Church. They resisted opponents who tried to force them to accept other forms of worship and church government. In 1581, the first important covenant opposed efforts to restore Roman Catholicism to Scotland. When King Charles I tried to impose the Episcopalian prayer book and the English clergy on the Scots, they drew up the National Covenant of 1638 to resist him.

In 1643, the Church of Scotland and the English Parliament signed The Solemn League and Covenant, establishing Presbyterianism in Scotland, England, and Ireland. However, the English rulers ignored this agreement and persecuted the Presbyterians. The Covenanters continued to fight for their beliefs until finally, in 1690, King William III permitted the free expression of the Presbyterian faith in Scotland.   Peter W. Williams

See also **Scotland** (History).

Coventry, *KUHV uhn tree* (pop. 292,600), is a city in central England. For the location of Coventry, see **England** (political map). Coventry is an important industrial center, and also the site of the Lady Godiva legend and of one of the world's most strikingly modern cathedrals. Products made in Coventry include airplane parts, automobiles, bicycles, textiles, and electrical and engineering goods.

Coventry probably originated as a Saxon settlement in the A.D. 400's. Lady Godiva, who lived in the 1000's, rode naked through Coventry to get her husband—the city's ruler—to reduce heavy taxes (see **Godiva, Lady**). By the late 1300's, Coventry had become a center of textile manufacturing and watchmaking, and of *trade guilds* (organizations that protected and regulated trade).

In 1940, during World War II, German bombers destroyed most of downtown Coventry, including a 600-

Aerofilms, Ltd.

Coventry is the site of two of England's best-known cathedrals. The medieval cathedral at the left was destroyed in 1940, during World War II. A striking modern cathedral was built to its right. The ruins of the original structure have been preserved as a memorial.

year-old Gothic cathedral. The area was rebuilt after the war. The rebuilding project included the construction of the city's famous modern cathedral. The new cathedral, which was completed in 1962, stands next to the ruins of the old one, now kept as a memorial.   Peter R. Mounfield

See also **Cathedral** (picture: Cathedral interiors).

Covered wagon. See **Conestoga wagon; Pioneer life in America** (Crossing the plains); **Westward movement** (picture).

Covington, *KUHV ihng tuhn* (pop. 43,264), is a city in northern Kentucky. It lies at the junction of the Ohio and Licking rivers, across the Ohio River from Cincinnati, Ohio. For location, see **Kentucky** (political map).

Covington's industries include cherry processing and the manufacture of greeting cards, life preservers, and paper bags. An Internal Revenue Service tax-processing office is the city's largest employer.

The Roman Catholic Cathedral Basilica of the Assumption (formerly St. Mary's Cathedral) is a major landmark of Covington. Begun in 1895, it was modeled after the Cathedral of Notre Dame in Paris. It has one of the world's largest stained-glass windows. Another landmark is the John A. Roebling Suspension Bridge, which connects Covington and Cincinnati. Named after the man who built it, it was opened to traffic in 1866. Roebling and his son later built the Brooklyn Bridge.

Covington was settled in the early 1800's and was incorporated in 1834. The city was named after General Leonard Covington, a hero of the War of 1812. Covington has a council-manager form of government and is the seat of Kenton County.   Michael Farrell

Cow is a female adult animal of the bovine group. The term *cow* is also used for the female of other mammals, including moose and seals. Cows, bulls, and steers are called *cattle* (see **Cattle**).

Cow parsnip is a large, coarse plant which belongs to the parsley family. It grows from 4 to 8 feet (1.2 to 2.4 meters) high and has large, hairy leaves. Its small white flowers grow in huge clusters. The plant becomes a troublesome weed when allowed to grow in damp soil near water. The cow parsnip may be eaten in place of celery, but it has usually been used as fodder.

Scientific classification. The cow parsnip belongs to the parsley family, Apiaceae or Umbelliferae. Its scientific name is *Heracleum maximum.*   Albert Liptay

Coward, Sir Noel (1899-1973), a British playwright, actor, and composer, became famous for his witty, sophisticated comedies. Many of his plays deal with romantic conflicts between upper-class men and women.

Coward's first successful play was *The Vortex* (1924), a serious look at the moral decline of the idle upper class. But such witty romantic comedies as *Hay Fever* (1925), *Private Lives* (1930), *Design for Living* (1933), and *Blithe Spirit* (1941) are more typical. He also wrote *Tonight at 8:30* (1936), a collection of nine one-act plays to be performed in groups of three. Coward composed a number of musicals. The best-known musical is the operetta *Bitter Sweet* (1929).

Coward wrote two autobiographical books, *Present Indicative* (1937) and *Future Indefinite* (1954). *The Noel Coward Diaries* were published in 1982. He also wrote a novel, *Pomp and Circumstance* (1960), and short stories, many published in *The Collected Stories of Noel Coward* (1983). Coward also wrote, codirected, and starred in

the film *In Which We Serve* (1942).

Noel Pierce Coward was born in Teddington, near London. His first major success came in 1923 as part author and star of the musical revue *London Calling.* Coward starred in many of his own plays and sang his songs as a cabaret performer. Queen Elizabeth II knighted Coward in 1970.   Gerald M. Berkowitz

Larry Fried, Pix

Sir Noel Coward

Cowbird is the name of a group of birds found in North America and South America. The best-known species is the *brown-headed cowbird,* which lives from southern Canada to Mexico. The male brown-headed cowbird measures about 8 inches (20 centimeters) long. It has a brown head and a shiny black body. The smaller female is brownish-gray in color.

Brown-headed cowbirds lay their eggs in the nests of other birds, leaving the young for the foster parents to raise. The female cowbird chooses a nest that belongs to some smaller birds and lays an egg in it while the owners are away. She then flies off and does not return. The young cowbird is much larger than the other young birds in the nest and usually gets most of the food. As a result, the other nestlings sometimes starve. The foster parents do not seem to realize that they are raising an outsider. But if the egg is discovered, the nest owner may not allow it to hatch. For example, a yellow warbler may cover the egg and build another nest on top of the old one. The eggs of the brown-headed cowbird are white with brown specks.

Several other species of cowbirds are found in the Americas. Almost all of them, like the brown-headed cowbird, lay their eggs in the nests of other birds. Cowbirds feed on insects, worms, seeds, and berries.

Scientific classification. Cowbirds belong to the emberizid family, Emberizidae. The scientific name for the brown-headed cowbird is *Molothrus ater.*   Martha Hatch Balph

See also **Bird** (picture: Birds of grasslands).

WORLD BOOK illustration by Trevor Boyer, Linden Artists Ltd.

Brown-headed cowbirds range from Canada to Mexico. The female, *right,* is smaller than the male, *left.*

Detail from *Trail Herd to Wyoming* (1923), an oil painting on canvas by W. H. D. Koerner; Buffalo Bill Historical Center, Cody, Wyo.

The trail drive moved large herds of cattle great distances from Western ranches to a railroad station for shipment to Eastern markets. Cowboys rode ahead, behind, and at each side of the plodding herd. A trail drive lasted from two to three months.

Cowboy

Cowboy is a person who helps take care of a large herd of cattle for a ranch owner. In the United States, cowboys won fame in the days of the Western frontier. Their reputation for bravely facing danger and hardship made them heroes to many Americans. Exciting tales of cowboy life, sad cowboy songs, and colorful cowboy language have all become part of American folklore. Many of the most popular novels, motion pictures, and television shows have been about cowboys.

The height of the cowboy period lasted only about 20 years, from the mid-1860's to the mid-1880's. During that time, cowboys riding on horseback tended great herds of cattle on vast stretches of unfenced land called the *open range*. They also took cattle on long *trail drives*. Trail drives were the cheapest way to move cattle from Western ranches to railway stations for shipment to Eastern markets. But by 1890, far fewer cowboys were needed. The use of fences and the spread of farms had put an end to the open range, and expansion of the railroads had done away with the long trail drives.

There have probably never been more than 100,000 cowboys in the United States. But cowboys achieved an importance far beyond their numbers. Hard-working cowboys helped make the West a productive part of the United States. In the process, they came to stand for the frontier spirit of courage, independence, and self-

reliance. Today, the life of a cowboy on the old frontier might seem glamorous and exciting. But cowboys found it difficult, dangerous, and—at times—even dull.

Cowboys were sometimes called *cowpokes* or *cowpunchers* because they used sticks to poke cattle onto loading ramps. Today, most cowboys prefer to be called *cowhands* because they are hired *hands*, or workers, who tend cows. Cowboys call all cattle *cows*, even bulls and calves.

Most countries with cattle ranches have cowboys. This article deals chiefly with the height of the cowboy period in the United States. For a description of the life of a modern American cowboy, see **Ranching**.

A cowboy's equipment

American cowboys copied much of the equipment used by Mexican cowboys, who are called *vaqueros* (pronounced *vah KAIR ohz*). The big sombrero worn by vaqueros became an American cowboy hat. *La reata* (*lah ray AH tuh*), *the rope* in Spanish, became the *lariat* used by cowboys to rope cattle. Even the word *vaquero* became *buckaroo*, another English word for *cowboy*.

His clothing served a useful purpose. A cowboy hat, for example, had a wide brim to keep rain, snow, and sun off the cowboy's face. The air space in the hat's deep crown kept the cowboy's head cool. A cowboy also used his hat to fan a fire, to signal to other cowboys, and to scoop up water from a stream.

A coat got in a cowboy's way, and so he wore one only in bitter cold weather. Most cowboys wore a vest over their shirt instead of a coat. The vest had pockets to hold such items as a watch, tobacco, and a few coins.

A cowboy wore seatless leather trousers called *chaps* over his regular trousers. Chaps protected his legs from

Odie B. Faulk, the contributor of this article, is former Professor of History at Northeastern State University in Tahlequah, Okla., and the author of many books, including A Short History of the American West.

thorny brush and from rubbing during long hours in the saddle. Chaps were adapted from the trousers, called *chaparajos* (*chah pah RAH hohs*), worn by vaqueros.

Cowboy boots had high, tapered heels. The heels kept a horseback rider's feet from slipping through the stirrups. Their tapered shape prevented a cowboy's foot from catching in a stirrup if he fell from his horse. A cowboy who fell or got thrown would be dragged along the ground if he could not get free of the stirrup.

The spurs that cowboys fastened to the heels of their boots helped them control a horse. Each spur had a small spiked wheel at the back called a *rowel*. When a horse did something wrong, the cowboy pressed the rowel against the horse's side.

The bandanna, or neckerchief, a cowboy tied around his neck could be pulled over his nose on a dry, dusty trail or during a dust storm. Leather gloves protected a cowboy's hands from rope burns.

His horse. Cowboys spent most of their working hours in the saddle. Horses not only enabled cowboys to cover great distances but also helped them control the cattle. Few cowboys owned their own horse. Most cowboys rode horses that belonged to the ranch owner. Each cowboy had a string of horses assigned to him. Because a cowboy changed mounts frequently, he did not have a favorite horse that he loved above all others.

Cowboys rode horses called *mustangs* or *broncos.* Mustangs were descended from horses that Spanish explorers brought to North America in the 1500's. Some of the Spanish horses escaped, ran loose, and multiplied. By the mid-1800's, bands of mustangs roamed the Great Plains and Rocky Mountains. These small, swift horses made excellent "cow ponies." They had great strength, and they seemed to sense what a cow would do next.

Mustangs had to be tamed before cowboys could ride them. A wild horse would leap, kick, and twist to remove anything on its back. To *break* (tame) a mustang, a cowboy had to get on its back and whip the animal each time it bucked. Most mustangs soon learned that disobedience meant pain and thus began to obey the cowboy. But a few horses could never be broken. Cowboys who cured mustangs of bucking were often called *broncobusters.* In time, mustangs were bred with other horses to produce a larger and less wild animal.

His rope, or lariat, was a cowboy's most important tool. One end of the lariat was knotted to form a small eye, called a *honda.* The other end of the rope slipped through the honda to form a large, adjustable loop. A cowboy kept a coiled lariat hanging from his saddle. Every cowboy had to know how to rope cattle. Cowboys also used a lariat to pull cattle out of the mud, to tie up horses, and to drag wood to a campfire.

Cowboys adopted the roping techniques of the Mexican vaqueros. A skilled roper knew exactly when and how far to toss a lariat to catch the neck, horns, or legs of a running cow. He could then throw a 1,000-pound (450-kilogram) animal to the ground. To rope a cow, a cowboy on horseback wrapped the end of his lariat around his saddle horn. He whirled the loop overhead and then tossed it in front of the cow's onrushing feet or over its head. The cowboy's horse then stopped dead, the loop tightened, and the cow fell to the ground.

His saddle was a cowboy's most prized possession. Every cowboy owned a saddle, even though few cow-

Through the Alkali (1904), an oil painting on canvas by C. M. Russell; The Thomas Gilcrease Institute of American History and Art, Tulsa, Okla.

A cowboy on horseback used equipment and skills borrowed from Mexican cowboys, called *vaqueros.* Cowboys copied the hat, chaps, saddle, lariat, and roping techniques of the vaqueros.

boys owned a horse. A saddle had to be well made to hold up under constant use, and a cowboy selected his saddle carefully. A cowboy who had to sell his saddle was totally broke and down on his luck.

The saddle used by cowboys was adapted from that of the vaqueros. It had a large horn in front, to which the cowboy attached his lariat when roping cattle. The high *cantle* (back of the saddle) supported the cowboy's lower back and made all-day rides more comfortable.

His gun, in most cases, was a revolver with six chambers known as a *six-shooter.* Most of the time, however, a cowboy did not carry his gun. A gun was a nuisance to a man on horseback. It added extra weight and got in the way. Besides, few cowboys had much money to spend on bullets for practice, and a cowboy needed practice to become a good shot. But most cowboys liked to put on a gun to look impressive when they went into town. On a trail drive, a cowboy kept a gun tucked in his bedroll. A gun was useful for killing rattlesnakes, shooting a horse with a broken leg, and turning back stampeding cattle.

The life of a cowboy

A cowboy's life was filled with hard work, danger, and loneliness. Tending cattle was hard because the animals got into trouble so often. Cowboys had to pull cattle from quicksand, ease them out of barbed wire fences, and drag them from mud. They also had to nurse sick and injured cattle and help cows as they gave birth.

Each day, a cowboy faced the risk of broken bones, crippling accidents, and even death. Very few ranches were near a town with a doctor, and so cowboys doctored themselves most of the time. Untamed horses often threw riders, and a bad fall could easily break a man's leg. A broken bone that was improperly set could leave a cowboy crippled for life. Even roping could mean the loss of a finger or two if the cowboy's hand got caught between the rope and the saddle horn. A kick from a horse could kill a cowboy. And a mean horse might kill a rider by racing under a low branch. A cowboy could be trampled to death in a stampede.

In general, cowboys led a lonely life. Most ranches lay far from even the smallest town. A cowboy could go for weeks without seeing anyone but the few hands he worked with. Two events broke the monotony of a cowboy's life on the ranch—the roundup and the trail drive.

On the ranch, a cowboy's main job was to watch and protect the cattle as they grazed on the range. Cowboys also had to repair bridles, harnesses, and other equipment. The cattle the cowboys first tended were *Texas longhorns*. The cattle were named after their long horns, which had an average spread of about 4 feet (1.2 meters). Like mustangs, Texas longhorns were descended from

UPI/Bettmann Archive

Roping cattle was a skill every cowboy needed. A cowboy kept a coiled lariat hanging from his saddle. He knew exactly how to toss the lariat to catch a running animal's legs, head, or horns.

Spanish animals that had gotten loose and multiplied. When early settlers from the East moved to the West, they found longhorn meat to be tough and stringy. They eventually bred longhorns with their Eastern stock to produce more tender meat.

On large ranches, cowboys slept in a bunkhouse apart from the ranch owner's house. A bunkhouse had few comforts. Rows of bunks stood along the walls. Pegs on the wall held clothing and other equipment. Most cowboys went to bed early, exhausted from the day's work.

Before barbed wire fences came into use, cattle roamed freely on the open range. They could wander long distances in any direction. For this reason, small outposts called *line camps* stood near the boundaries of a ranch. Cowboys called *line riders* worked out of the camps. Each rider patrolled a certain area, watching for sick or stray cattle and for signs of cattle rustlers.

Barbed wire came into use in the mid-1870's. Cowboys then had the tough job of building fences. They had to dig the postholes by hand and tightly string the wire with its many sharp points from post to post. The line riders became *fence riders*. A fence rider had to spot tears in the barbed wire and mend them. On many ranches, windmills pumped water for the cattle. When the windmills broke down, cowboys had to fix them.

Cowboys worked almost every day, from sunup to sundown. Few cowboys got to town more than once a month, usually on payday. In town, a cowboy might drink and gamble away his pay in a saloon or gambling hall. Sometimes, a cowboy drank too much and walked down the street shooting his gun into the air. As a result, he landed in jail for the night and had to pay a fine the next morning. But most towns were not too hard on cowboys. They did not want to lose their business.

The roundup took place each spring and fall. A roundup was necessary to identify and brand newborn calves. A calf received the brand of its mother. Each ranch had its own brand, which it placed in a certain position on all its cattle. For example, a brand might be de-

UPI/Bettmann Archive

Branding took place during the roundup. After cowboys had rounded up the cattle, they gave each calf the brand of its mother. Branding served to identify cattle in the days of the open range, when animals could wander great distances over unfenced land.

A **chuck wagon** carried food, cooking utensils, drinking water, and the cowboys' bedrolls during the trail drive. Chuck wagons were also used on the range during roundups.

UPI/Bettmann Archive

scribed as a *cloverleaf* placed *right side, flank;* or the letter *R* placed *left side, jaw.* Cattle owners registered their brands with local officials.

Branding showed who owned an animal. It made recovering lost or stolen cattle easier. In the days of the open range, a cow could wander all the way from Texas to Montana. Anyone who found the stray could check to see whose brand it bore and then arrange to return the cow to its owner. Sometimes, a rancher would try to alter the brands on stray animals so that the strays appeared to bear his brand. In most cases, people caught changing a brand met with swift and stern justice.

In the days of the open range, cattle from several ranches in a region grazed together and so became mixed. At roundup time, cowboys from all the ranches worked together to bring in the cattle. Crews of cowboys scattered over the range. They searched for cattle and drove them to a central point.

After the cowboys had rounded up all the cattle, men from each ranch sorted out their cattle according to brand. They then separated the newborn calves from their mothers for branding. At the fall roundup, they also selected the cattle to be sold for beef. Cowboys rode well-trained *cutting horses* among the cattle to edge out, or *cut,* an animal from the herd.

After a cowboy cut a calf out, he drove it to a fire, where branding irons were kept red hot. The cowboy pressed an iron against the calf. The burn that resulted left a permanent scar. Another cowboy kept count of all the calves that were branded so the cattle owner would know how many cattle remained after those to be marketed had been cut out. Cowboys might also make a knife cut in a cow's ear for extra identification. When cattle were bunched together, it was hard to read their brands. But a cowboy could easily see an earmark.

After work each day at roundup time, cowboys from all the ranches got together to sing, tell tall tales, and trade gossip. At the end of most roundups, cowboys competed against one another to determine the best rider, roper, and broncobuster. The competition became known as a *rodeo,* the Spanish word for *roundup.*

The trail drive was a major event in a cowboy's life. A trail drive usually lasted about two or three months and covered as much as 1,000 miles (1,600 kilometers). During the long drive, cowboys moved from two thousand to three thousand cattle to a railroad station for shipment to Eastern markets. They worked long days and sometimes through part of the night.

Before the trail drive began, cowboys collected cattle from several ranches and turned them over to a *trail boss* employed by the ranch owners. The trail boss hired 10 to 12 cowboys to handle the herd during the drive. He also hired a *wrangler* and a cook. The wrangler looked after the 50 or more horses needed on the drive. Most wranglers were young and inexperienced.

The cook got the *chuck wagon* ready for the trail drive while the cowboys were busy during the roundup. This large covered wagon had to carry enough food for the cowboys during the long drive. It also carried cooking utensils, drinking water, and the cowboys' bedrolls.

The tough, hardy longhorns were ideal for trail driving. They ate almost any kind of plant, and their long legs and big hoofs enabled them to travel great distances. Heat and hunger did not seem to affect them. Above all, longhorns could travel as long as three or four days between drinks of water.

During the trail drive, the cowboys had to keep the cattle together and headed in the right direction. They rode ahead, behind, and on each side of the herd. Cattle sometimes panicked when crossing a river and began swimming in circles. Thunderstorms or any other sudden noise could frighten jittery cattle into stampeding. To stop a stampede, the cowboys would race in front of the herd. They would then wave their hats and fire their guns in the air to turn back the lead cattle.

The drive stopped each day just before sunset, and the cattle grazed for a while. The cowboys then herded them into a tighter group that was easier to control at night. Cowboys took turns watching the herd through the night. They often sang as they circled the herd because they thought their singing kept the cattle calm.

The cowboys ate after the cattle had settled down for the night. Their meals on the drive consisted mainly of beans, bacon, and biscuits. A cowboy slept next to a saddled horse so that he could jump into the saddle if the cattle stampeded during the night.

At the end of the trail drive, the cowboys arrived in a *cow town,* where the cattle were sold and loaded on a train. A cowboy usually wanted a shave and a haircut first and then a bath and clean clothes. Next, he wanted a good meal. After that, he was ready to celebrate in the nearest saloon. Cowboys received their wages at the end of the trail drive. Most of them spent their pay in a few days and then headed back to the ranch.

History

The growth of the cattle industry made cowboys necessary. Raising cattle became an important business in Texas after the Civil War ended in 1865. A cow cost from $4 to $5 in Texas, and millions of them roamed the open range. At the same time, Easterners wanted beef and were willing to pay from $40 to $50 a head. Texas cattle owners, seeing the big profits to be made, hired cowboys to drive cattle northward to the nearest railroad station for shipment to the East.

In 1866, cowboys drove thousands of cattle to the railroad station in Sedalia, Mo., in the first major trail drive. But farmers along the way objected to having cattle trample their fields. A few angry farmers with shotguns convinced cattle ranchers to find another route.

In 1867, the Union Pacific Railroad reached Abilene, Kans., which lay west of farming country. That year, the Chisholm Trail opened. It ran about 1,000 miles (1,600 kilometers) from southern Texas to Abilene. The Western Trail opened in 1876, after farmers settled beyond Abilene. It ended west of Abilene, in Dodge City, Kans. Abilene and Dodge City boomed as cow towns.

Cowboys got their start in Texas. By 1870, ranchers had discovered that cattle could survive the cold winters in the northern Great Plains. Ranches sprang up in what are now Montana, Wyoming, Colorado, and the Dakotas, which had almost no settlers at that time. Trail drives were used to stock northern ranches with cattle. Cowboys moved north with the cattle.

By the late 1880's, the open range was nearly gone. The invention of barbed wire made it possible to fence off individual ranches. Railroads extended all the way to the West Coast. Thus, the roundup and the long trail drive were no longer needed. Towns grew quieter as churches and schools began to outnumber saloons and gambling halls. The Wild West had been tamed.

The early cowboys. Frontiersmen who had moved to the West became the first cowboys. Probably nearly a fourth of all cowboys were blacks, and another fourth were Mexicans. Many of the black cowboys moved to the Western frontier after the Civil War. Others had been slaves on Texas ranches before the war. Many of the Mexican cowboys had remained in Texas after Texas declared its independence from Mexico in 1836. A sense of equality developed among cowboys because of the hard work and danger they shared. But black cowhands had difficulty finding jobs after the open range ended and jobs on ranches became scarce.

Most Westerners looked down on cowboys. They viewed cowboys as rough, rude, and uncivilized. But writers in the East made cowboys seem like heroes. Books, magazines, and newspapers told of the unlimited open prairie in the West and of brave young cowboys who performed difficult and daring feats. Soon, many young men in the East wanted to sleep under the Western stars. They headed west to become cowboys.

Cowhands today continue to work on ranches and tend cattle. They still must know how to rope and ride and be able to work long hours in any kind of weather. But they use machines for many jobs, such as digging holes for fence posts. Modern cowboys transport cattle by trucks and use helicopters to search for stray cattle.

Cowboy Hall of Fame. The National Cowboy Hall of Fame and Western Heritage Center opened in Oklahoma City, Okla., in 1965. It honors outstanding Americans who helped develop the West. The institution is sponsored by 17 Western states. It includes an art gallery of Western photographs, paintings, and sculptures; a reconstructed Western town; the Rodeo Hall of Fame;

and a library of Western history. Odie B. Faulk

Related articles in *World Book* include:

Bronco	Love, Nat
Chile (picture: Ranching and fishing)	Oklahoma (Places to visit; picture)
Chisholm Trail	Ranching
Chuck wagon	Rodeo
Clothing (picture: Traditional costumes)	Saddle
Gaucho	Texas (picture)
Horse	Western frontier life
Indian wars	Westward movement

Outline

I. A cowboy's equipment
- A. His clothing
- B. His horse
- C. His rope
- D. His saddle
- E. His gun

II. The life of a cowboy
- A. On the ranch
- B. The roundup
- C. The trail drive

III. History

Questions

How did cowboys brand cattle?

Where did the Chisholm Trail run?

What was a line rider's job?

Why did the cattle industry become important in Texas?

What are some items of cowboy clothing? How were they useful to a cowboy?

What purpose did a trail drive serve?

Why were cowboys also called *cowpokes* or *cowpunchers*?

What did it mean when a cowboy had to sell his saddle?

Why were roundups necessary?

What put an end to the open range?

Additional resources

Freedman, Russell. *Cowboys of the Wild West.* Clarion, 1985.

Landau, Elaine. *Cowboys.* Watts, 1990.

Slatta, Richard W. *Cowboys of the Americas.* Yale, 1990. For older readers.

Cowell, *KOW uhl,* **Henry** (1897-1965), was an American composer. His works and theories greatly influenced the development of experimental music in the United States. Cowell developed the technique of *tone clusters.* He created these dissonant effects by having a pianist strike groups of adjacent keys with the fingers, fist, or forearm. Such European composers as Béla Bartók used tone clusters in their works.

Cowell composed an enormous amount of music, including 19 symphonies. Perhaps his greatest symphony is Symphony No. 11 (*Seven Rituals of Music,* 1953). Cowell based several compositions on the music of India, Japan, and other Asian nations. Such works as *Tales of the Countryside* (1941) show the influence of his lifelong interest in folk music. Cowell followed the form of earlier American hymns in a series of 18 pieces for various combinations of instruments, which he called *Hymn and Fuguing Tune* (1944-1964).

Cowell discussed his theories in the book *New Musical Resources* (1930). He and his wife, Sydney, wrote *Charles Ives and His Music* (1955). This book helped establish Ives's reputation as a major American composer. Cowell was born in Menlo Park, Calif. Richard Jackson

Cowley, Abraham (1618-1667), was an English poet and essayist whose first volume of verse was published when he was 15. His major publications include *Poetical Blossoms* (1633), *The Mistress* (1647), and his unfinished epic, *Davideis* (1656). Cowley began as a rather derivative, mechanical love poet, strongly influenced by poet

John Donne and his followers. Later, Cowley began to write *Odes* in the manner of the Greek poet Pindar. This new style produced his best poem, "Ode to the Royal Society." Samuel Johnson published a famous attack on the metaphysical poets in his *Life of Cowley* (1779).

Cowley was born in London. As a follower of Charles II, he served the royalist cause in exile during the Puritan revolution. He returned to favor after the Restoration in 1660. That year, Cowley helped form the Royal Society, an organization that promotes the natural sciences, and became one of its first members.   Gary A. Stringer

See also **Metaphysical poets.**

Cowpea is a trailing or bushy vine widely cultivated in warm regions. One kind of cowpea, known as the *black-eyed* pea, grows wild in Africa but is cultivated in the United States. Another kind more common in tropical regions is called the *asparagus bean* or *yard-long bean.* The flowers of cowpeas are yellowish-white to purple, and they usually grow in pairs. In the Southern United States, cowpeas may be grown as food for livestock. Some kinds of cowpeas are eaten in the pod, shelled, or used in soups and stews.

Scientific classification. The cowpea belongs to the pea family, Fabaceae or Leguminosae. Its scientific name is *Vigna unguiculata.*   Daniel F. Austin

Cowper, *KOO puhr* or *KOW puhr,* **William** (1731-1800), was an English poet. He wrote simple poems about nature and rural domestic life. These poems became forerunners of the works of the English romantic poets of the early 1800's.

Cowper was born in Hertfordshire, near London. He studied law, and was admitted to the bar in 1754. But he did not like law and never practiced. A shy, gentle man, he suffered fits of melancholy that were perhaps intensified by his devotion to strict Calvinistic religious beliefs. Frequent attacks of spiritual despair led to recurrent periods of insanity and two suicide attempts. In 1765, Cowper went to live in Huntington with the family of Morley Unwin, a clergyman. Beginning in 1767, after Unwin's death, he lived in the country at Olney with Mrs. Mary Unwin and her children, who cared for him tenderly.

During his healthy periods, Cowper wrote many great hymns. The *Olney Hymns* (1779), written with John Newton, a minister, includes the famous "Oh! for a Closer Walk with God" and "God Moves in a Mysterious Way."

Much of the charm of Cowper's poetry comes from his gracious, kindly personality. Cowper also had a good sense of humor. His comic masterpiece is the merry ballad "The Diverting History of John Gilpin" (1782). Cowper was angered by the inhumanity shown in people's dealings with one another. "Minds are never to be sold!" he declared in his antislavery poem, "The Negro's Complaint." But Cowper typically wrote quiet, descriptive, thoughtful poems about nature and daily life. He liked tame, not wild nature. "Yardley Oak" (1791) does not describe the oak but the nostalgic feelings it arouses in the poet. His last poem, "The Castaway" (1799), powerfully evokes feelings of gloom and despair.

Cowper's major work was a 5,000-line poem called *The Task* (1785). This rambling poem was written in blank verse. It describes familiar rural sights and events, including the arrival of the mail and the countryside in the evening. The poem shows Cowper's love of the country and distaste for city life.   Karl Kroeber

Cowrie, *KOW ree,* also spelled *cowry,* is a sea snail with a shiny, colorful shell. It lives in the shallow waters of warm seas. Cowries may be from $\frac{1}{2}$ to 6 inches (1.3 to 15 centimeters) long. The top of the shell looks like a colorful egg, and the underside has a long, narrow opening bordered by many small teeth. There are more

Zig Leszczynski, Animals Animals

A cowrie has a glossy, richly colored shell. Cowries live in the shallow parts of warm seas. Some types of rare cowries are highly prized by shell collectors.

than 150 kinds of cowries. Some kinds are extremely rare and are worth hundreds of dollars to shell collectors. Cowries were once used as money in China, India, and Africa. One kind was worn as a badge of office by chieftains in the Fiji Islands. See **Shell** (pictures).

Scientific classification. Cowries belong to the cowrie family, Cypraeidae.   M. Patricia Morse

Cowslip is the name of four flowering plants. These plants are the *marsh marigold,* the *Virginia cowslip,* the *shooting star,* and the *European cowslip.*

The marsh marigold grows in swampy places. Its bright yellow flowers appear from April to June. People often eat the leaves and stems of this plant. The Virginia cowslip is also called the *Virginia bluebell.* Its bell-shaped flower clusters always seem to be nodding. The shooting star is the common name for a group of plants also known as *American cowslips.* The flowers of these plants have a distinctive shape. The petals of the American cowslip bend backward, and the pistil and yellow stamens form a pointed tip that seems to shoot out of the flower. The European cowslip grows in meadows throughout Europe. It has fragrant clusters of large yellow or purple flowers.

Scientific classification. The marsh marigold belongs to the crowfoot family, Ranunculaceae. It is *Caltha palustris.* The Virginia cowslip belongs to the borage family, Boraginaceae. It is *Mertensia virginica.* The shooting star and the European cowslip belong to the primrose family, Primulaceae. Shooting stars make up the genus *Dodecatheon.* The European cowslip is classified as *Primula veris.*   Melinda F. Denton

See also **Primrose.**

Cox, James Middleton (1870-1957), an American politician and newspaper publisher, was the Democratic candidate for President in 1920. He and his running mate, Franklin D. Roosevelt, were defeated by a Republican landslide that elected Warren G. Harding President and Calvin Coolidge Vice President.

Cox began his political career by serving in the U.S. House of Representatives from 1909 to 1913. He was elected governor of Ohio in 1912, 1916, and 1918. Cox owned newspapers and radio and television stations in Ohio, Georgia, and Florida. In 1933 he served as a delegate to the World Monetary and Economic Conference in London. He wrote an autobiography, *Journey Through My Years* (1946).

Cox was born in a log-cabin farmhouse near Jacksonburg, Ohio. He later became a teacher. Cox bought his first newspaper at the age of 28.   James S. Olson

Coxey, *KAHK see,* **Jacob Sechler** (1854-1951), organized *Coxey's Army,* a group of unemployed men, during the depression of the 1890's. He organized the "army" to attract national attention to his plan that the government create jobs through a road-improvement program. Coxey marched out of Massillon, Ohio, with 100 men and his infant son, Legal Tender Coxey. Coxey's Army paraded in Washington, D.C., on May 1, 1894, with nearly 500 men. The demonstration collapsed when Coxey was arrested for walking on the Capitol lawn. In 1932, he was the Farmer-Labor Party candidate for President of the United States. Coxey was born in Selinsgrove, Pa.

Edward A. Lukes-Lukaszewski

See also **Cleveland, Grover** (picture: "Coxey's Army").

Coyote, *KY oht* or *ky OH tee,* is a wild member of the dog family. It is known for its eerie howl, usually heard during the evening, night, or early morning.

Coyotes once lived primarily in western North America. However, they now inhabit much of the United States, Canada, and Mexico, and even parts of Central America. The coyote lives in a variety of environments, including deserts, mountains, and prairies. It is sometimes called the *prairie wolf* or *brush wolf.*

Adult coyotes vary in color from light yellow or yellowish-gray to brownish-yellow. Their fur may be tipped with black. The coyote has large, pointed ears and a bushy tail. An adult coyote measures about 4 feet (1.2 meters) long, including its 11- to 16-inch (28- to 41-centimeter) tail. It stands about 2 feet (0.6 meter) high and weighs from 25 to 30 pounds (11 to 14 kilograms). Most coyotes live alone or in pairs, but some form groups of three or more.

Most female coyotes first mate when they are about 2 years old. They have a pregnancy period of 60 to 63 days. In spring, the female usually gives birth to five or six pups. A newborn coyote weighs from 7 to 10 ounces (200 to 275 grams). It is born blind, but its eyes open within two weeks. The mother provides milk for her young until they are 6 or 7 weeks old. By that time, the pups have begun to eat prey and other foods supplied by their parents. Most coyote pups can care for themselves by late summer, when they leave the parents.

Coyotes feed chiefly on rabbits and on rodents, such as gophers, mice, prairie dogs, rats, and squirrels. Coyotes also prey on antelope, goats, sheep, and other animals. The coyote eats various insects and reptiles as well. During the winter, many coyotes in northern regions feed on the remains of large dead animals, such as cattle, deer, and elk. In some areas, coyotes eat juniper berries, mesquite beans, watermelons, and other fruits for a few weeks of the year.

© Alan G. Nelson, Animals Animals

The coyote lives in most areas of the United States, Canada, and Mexico and in some parts of Central America. Unlike most animals, the coyote has expanded its range through the years.

Some ranchers dislike coyotes because the animals kill cattle, sheep, and other livestock. Other people, however, think coyotes help keep rodent populations under control and are valuable for that reason. Some people hunt and trap coyotes for sport. Coyote pelts are used to make coats and to trim parkas or other clothing.

Scientific classification. The coyote belongs to the dog and wolf family, Canidae. Its scientific name is *Canis latrans.*

Frederick F. Knowlton

Coypu. See Nutria.

Coysevox, *kwaz VAWKS,* **Antoine,** *ahn TWAHN* (1640-1720), was the leading French sculptor during the latter part of the reign of Louis XIV. Coysevox produced much of the sculpture that decorated the gardens and Palace of Versailles. Much of his work reflected the tastes of Louis XIV. Its rich, ornamental style reflects a desire for dignity and grandeur.

Coysevox also made many portrait busts. Several of those he did later in his career are more informal and lively than his earlier decorative sculpture. This informality reflected the developing taste of the 1700's. Coysevox was born in Lyon. A picture of his statue *Mercury* is in the **Sculpture** article.   Douglas K. S. Hyland

Cozzens, *KUHZ uhnz,* **James Gould,** *goold* (1903-1978), an American author, became best known for his novels of upper-class manners. Cozzens' fiction shows his fascination with social roles and forms. His typical hero is a professional man who distrusts emotion and believes in reason and self-discipline. Cozzens' style is analytical and filled with realistic detail.

Cozzens won the 1949 Pulitzer Prize for fiction for his novel *Guard of Honor* (1948), which concerns military life on an Air Force base. Cozzens' most popular novel is *By Love Possessed* (1957). The work investigates how a lawyer's life and principles are shaken by discoveries he makes about his friends and family. *Men and Brethren* (1936) is a study of a liberal clergyman. *The Just and the Unjust* (1942) describes the impact of a murder trial on the various participants.

Cozzens was born in Chicago. He wrote his first novel in 1924, but his first notable work was the novelette *S.S. San Pedro* (1931).   Samuel Chase Coale

CPA. See Accounting; Certified public accountant.
CPR. See Cardiopulmonary resuscitation.
Crab is a type of animal with a hard shell and jointed legs. Some crabs live in shallow waters along seashores, and some are found in deeper waters. Others live in burrows on sandy beaches or muddy shores. Only a few species of crabs live in fresh water or on land. Certain species of crabs are popular seafood.

Crabs belong to a group of invertebrate animals called *crustaceans.* A crab's abdomen, unlike that of other crustaceans, lies folded under the body. The male crab has a narrow abdomen, but the female's abdomen occupies the entire space between the legs. A crab's shell, called the *carapace,* covers the upper side of the body.

A crab has five pairs of legs. The first pair bear large claws called *chelae.* The shape and size of the chelae vary greatly among species and even in the same individual. In male *fiddler crabs,* for example, one chela is much larger than the other. The male waves this large chela about to attract female crabs and to threaten smaller male crabs (see **Fiddler crab**). Most crabs prowl sandy or muddy shores by walking or running sideways on the tips of their last four pairs of legs. In crabs that swim, the last pair of legs are modified into paddles.

Top view of a blue crab
WORLD BOOK illustrations by Lloyd P. Birmingham

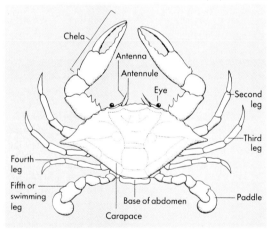

Underside view of a blue crab

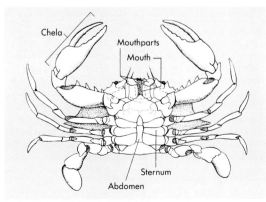

Some kinds of crabs

Crabs make up part of the animal life along many seashores. The ghost crab, *left,* lives in burrows on sandy beaches. Its color blends so well with sand that a motionless ghost crab seems to disappear. The rock crab, *right,* dwells on rocky seashores.

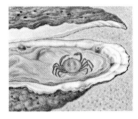

WORLD BOOK illustrations by James Teason

Several crabs live in unusual places. The female pea crab, *left,* lives in the shell of a live oyster. The pine crab, *right,* makes its home in bromeliad plants that grow on tropical trees. It lives in water that collects at the bottom of the plant.

Crabs feed on many kinds of water organisms or the remains of organisms. Some species of crabs eat chiefly algae and plants. Almost all species of crabs *spawn,* (lay eggs) in salt water. A newly hatched crab cannot survive in fresh water.

The *coral gall crab* is the smallest crab known. It measures about $\frac{1}{10}$ inch (2.5 millimeters) long and $\frac{1}{12}$ inch (2.1 millimeters) wide. The coral gall crab lives in cagelike formations of coral in the Caroline Islands of the Pacific Ocean just north of the equator. The *giant spider crab* of Japan is the largest crab. The giant spider crab measures as much as 12 feet (3.7 meters) long between outstretched claws.

The *blue crab* is the most common crab sold as food in eastern North America. It is caught with nets or hooks. After blue crabs *molt* (shed their shell) and before the new shell hardens, they are sold as *soft-shelled crabs.*

Two types of edible crabs are found along the Pacific coast of North America. The huge *red king crab* lives in deep waters from the Gulf of Alaska to the Bering Sea. It weighs about 12 pounds (5.5 kilograms). The *Dungeness crab* is found in shallow waters from California to Alaska. Fishing crews catch both these species with nets or traps.

Scientific classification. Crabs are in the subphylum Crustacea of the phylum Arthropoda. They belong to the order Decapoda.   Jonathan Green

Related articles in *World Book* include:
Animal (picture: Coconut crab)
Arthropod
Blue crab
Crustacean
Fiddler crab
Hermit crab

Crab apple is any of a wide variety of small trees that bear apples less than 2 inches (5 centimeters) in diameter. About 25 species of crab apple trees grow wild in the Northern Hemisphere. Most of them originated in

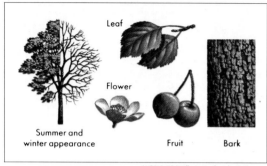

Leaf

Flower

Summer and winter appearance

Fruit

Bark

WORLD BOOK illustration by John D. Dawson

The crab apple tree has large white to deep pink flowers. Its fruit can be eaten fresh or used in jellies, butter, and pickles.

Asia. About 7 species are native to North America. In addition, hundreds of *cultivars* (cultivated varieties) of crab apple trees have been produced. Most of these cultivars are grown for use as landscape trees, especially in urban areas. Some are raised for their edible fruits, which are mostly used for making jellies.

Most crab apple trees measure less than 30 feet (9 meters) high. The trees produce white to deep pink flowers in the spring. Some bear red or yellow fruits that remain colorful through autumn and early winter. Some crab apple cultivars are particularly resistant to diseases and insects. Such cultivars have made the crab apple the chief flowering landscape tree in most parts of the United States.

Scientific classification. Crab apple trees belong to the rose family, Rosaceae. They are genus *Malus*.   Harrison L. Flint

Crack. See Cocaine.

Cradles of civilization. See Asia (History).

Craft. See Handicraft.

Cramp is a painful, uncontrolled contraction of one or more muscles. Cramps may involve any muscular area of the body. There may be only a single *spasm* (contraction) of the muscle, but usually it is followed by more intense cramping that begins and ends quickly and abruptly. A severe muscle spasm may continue for several hours or even days if untreated.

Cramps can occur either in skeletal muscles or in smooth muscles. When work is unusually hard and repetitious over long periods, the involved skeletal muscles often will cramp. Also, cramping is more likely to develop when one works or performs physical activity in the heat. This condition is called *heat cramp* and is associated with heavy sweating and loss of salt from the body. For example, foundry workers and fire fighters do heavy work in the heat and may develop cramps in their arms and legs.

Athletes often develop cramps in the muscles they use most strenuously. For example, runners may develop cramps in their legs. Cramps also can develop when certain muscles are used too much in performing ordinary, daily tasks. For instance, a person who writes for a long time may develop writer's cramp.

Perhaps the best-known cramps are those of the smooth muscles of the stomach and intestines. These may result from poor eating habits or from chilling the stomach. They often cause common stomachaches. Cramps are also characteristic of many diseases.

Doctors treat cramps with heat and massage, and give medicines to relieve pain. They may also administer drugs that relax the muscles.   Paul A. Molé

Cranach, *KRAH nahk,* **Lucas, the Elder** (1472-1553), was one of the leading German painters of the Renaissance. In his duties as court painter at Wittenberg, Cranach painted many of the great people of his time. He painted portraits of the Protestant leader Martin Luther and Luther's family, but also filled many commissions for religious paintings for Roman Catholic patrons. In addition, Cranach became known for his humorous versions of Greek mythology.

Like other German artists of his time, Cranach was active in printmaking. He invented the *chiaroscuro* woodcut, which uses two woodblocks to create a picture, one for lines and one for areas of color.

Cranach was born in Kronach, Bavaria. He took his name from the town and his real name is unknown. His three sons were minor artists.   Ann Friedman

Cranberry is a red, tart, round or oval fruit that grows on an evergreen vine. In the United States, cranberry sauce is a traditional Thanksgiving food. Many people also drink cranberry juices. Cranberries contain vitamin C. In the 1800's, many American sailors on long voyages ate cranberries to prevent *scurvy,* a disease caused by a lack of vitamin C. Some North American Indians have traditionally used the berries as a medicine and as a dye.

The cranberry vine grows low to the ground and produces white or pink flowers. It has oblong leaves and woody trailing stems called *runners.* The berries develop on *uprights,* stems that rise from the runners. Cranberry vines are native to North America. They grow wild in swampy areas of cool regions. In the United States, commercial growers cultivate cranberries in Massachusetts, New Jersey, Oregon, Washington, and Wisconsin. Cranberry production in Canada takes place in British Columbia, Quebec, and Nova Scotia.

Commercial growers prepare special *bogs* (swampy areas) for cranberries. The growers clear and level the land for quick flooding and drainage. They then cover the soil with 3 to 4 inches (8 to 10 centimeters) of sand. Cranberries grow best in acidic soil that contains some *organic matter* (material produced by plants and animals). The bogs must have a large supply of water nearby. Growers flood the bogs repeatedly to protect the plants from frost, insects, and disease and also when the berries are ready to harvest. If correctly prepared, a bog can produce fruit for more than 60 years.

Growers start new cranberry vines from cuttings 6 to 8 inches (15 to 20 centimeters) long. The cuttings are spread over the sand, then pressed into the sand by machine. Growers sometimes plant the cuttings by hand, placing the vines about 1 foot (30 centimeters) apart. As the cuttings grow, they form a matlike covering over the floor of the bog. The vines begin producing fruit after about three years.

Cranberries are harvested in September and October. To harvest berries for processing into juice or sauce, workers flood the bog. A harvesting machine then rakes

WORLD BOOK illustration by Kate Lloyd-Jones, Linden Artists Ltd.

Cranberries grow on evergreen vines in cool regions of North America. The berries have a tart taste and are used in cranberry sauce and other foods.

or knocks the berries from the vines. The berries float to the surface of the water, where workers collect them. To gather berries to be sold whole, mechanical rakes or scoops pick the berries off the vines. This method better preserves the firmness of the berries.

Scientific classification. Cranberries belong to the heath family, Ericaceae. The scientific name for the American cranberry is *Vaccinium macrocarpon.*   Max E. Austin

See also **New Jersey** (picture: Workers harvest cranberries).

Crandall, Prudence (1803-1890), was an American teacher who played an important role in the abolitionist movement. She won much support from abolitionists when she opened a Connecticut boarding school for black girls despite community opposition.

In 1831, Crandall established the Canterbury Female Boarding School for white girls in Canterbury, Conn. Two years later, she admitted a black girl for the first time. The parents of the other students threatened to withdraw their daughters from the school, and Crandall closed the institution in February 1833.

Department of Manuscripts and Archives, Cornell University, Ithaca, N.Y.

Prudence Crandall

Crandall reopened the school in April 1833 with 20 black girls as students. Many citizens of Canterbury objected and tried to discourage Crandall and her students. Later in 1833, Crandall was arrested and charged with breaking a new state law that prohibited the education of blacks who did not come from Connecticut. Leading abolitionists contributed money for her defense in court. She was convicted, but a higher court reversed the decision in 1834. A local mob then attacked the school, and Crandall closed it for the final time. She was born in Hopkinton, R.I.   Nancy Woloch

Crane is the name of a family of large birds with long legs and a long neck. Cranes live in marshy areas in many parts of the world. South America and Antarctica are the only continents with no cranes. Cranes resemble herons, but the two birds can be distinguished in flight. Cranes extend their head and neck straight ahead when they fly, but herons bend theirs into an S-shape.

Appearance. Cranes have long and slender legs, necks, and bills. The tallest cranes stand about 5 feet (1.5 meters) high, and the shortest are about $2\frac{1}{2}$ feet (0.8 meter) tall. A crane's wingspan can measure up to $7\frac{1}{2}$ feet (2.3 meters). The male and female look alike. They range in color from white to dark gray and brown. Most adult cranes have a patch of red skin on the head.

Habits. Most cranes that live in the Northern Hemisphere migrate south each fall from nesting grounds in the north. They return to their nesting ground each spring. Other cranes remain the year around in warm areas. A crane's powerful, buglelike voice carries for a great distance. The birds call to each other in flight, perhaps to keep the flock together during migration.

Cranes mate after they reach their nesting grounds. The male and female perform a dance before mating. The birds alternately circle around each other with opened wings, bow their heads, and leap into the air.

Cranes build nests in shallow water in a marsh, swamp, or other wet, open area. Both the male and the female help pile grasses, weeds, and other plants into a mound. A female crane usually lays only two eggs in a season. Both parents care for the eggs and young.

Cranes eat a variety of foods, including frogs, insects, snails, and grain and other plants. They are a pest in some areas because they take grain from farmers' fields.

Kinds. There are 15 species of cranes. Only two species are native to North America—the rare *whooping crane* and the more common *sandhill crane.*

Whooping cranes, or *whoopers,* once nested on the prairies of the United States and Canada. They began to die out during the 1800's, when settlers disturbed their nesting grounds. By 1954, only one flock of 21 birds remained. Laws now protect whoopers and their habitat. Scientists are breeding whoopers in captivity and have started two more flocks in the wild. Today, about 240 whooping cranes are alive. But they remain one of the rarest birds in North America. See **Whooping crane.**

Sandhill cranes nest in northern Russia, Canada, and the northern United States, as well as in Florida, Georgia, Mississippi, and Cuba. Only the sandhill cranes that nest in the north migrate. They winter mostly in Texas, New Mexico, and Mexico. Migrating sandhill cranes travel in enormous flocks, which may include more than 100,000 birds.

More species of cranes live in Africa, Asia, and Europe than in North America. Africa's elegant *crowned-cranes* have an ornamental tuft that resembles a shaving brush on top of their head. The *sarus cranes* of southern Asia are prized by Hindus, who believe that seeing a pair of these birds brings good luck. The *common crane* is a familiar bird throughout the northern parts of Asia and Europe.

Several species of cranes have become rare because

The whooping crane, *right,* is the tallest bird of North America. The bird has a wingspread of 6 to 8 feet (1.8 to 2.4 meters). It stands 4 to 5 feet (1.2 to 1.5 meters) tall. The largest flock of whooping cranes nests in northern Canada and spends the winter in Texas.

WORLD BOOK illustrations by Walter Linsenmaier

Fred W. Lahrman, Saskatchewan Museum of Natural History

Sarus crane
Grus antigone
Found in southern Asia
from India to the Philippines
Body length: 60 inches
(152 centimeters)

Demoiselle crane
Anthropoides virgo
Found in
south-central Eurasia
Body length: 38 inches
(97 centimeters)

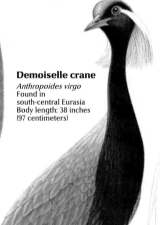

Sandhill crane
Grus canadensis
Found in northern and
southeastern North America
and northern Russia
Body length: 44 inches
(112 centimeters)

marshes in many areas have been drained for farming and for settlements. Destruction of their breeding ground is the chief threat to these cranes' survival.

Scientific classification. Cranes make up the crane family, Gruidae. The scientific name for the whooping crane is *Grus americana*. The sandhill crane is *G. canadensis;* the sarus crane, *G. antigone;* and the common crane, *G. grus*. The black crowned-crane is *Balearica pavonina*.   James J. Dinsmore

See also **Bird** (Bird refuges; Endangered species).

Crane is a machine that hoists, transports, and sets down heavy objects. Cranes are used in such workplaces as factories, shipyards, and construction sites. A crane picks up a load by means of an *attachment* such as a hook, bucket, or platform. On most cranes, the attach-ment is connected to a *block and tackle,* a system of pulleys and a cable. The end of the cable winds around a *winch* (rotating drum). Turning the winch raises or lowers the load.

There are three types of cranes: (1) *mobile cranes,* (2) *stationary cranes,* and (3) *traveling cranes.* In mobile and stationary cranes, the cable that leads from the block and tackle passes around a pulley at the end of a *boom* (long arm), then winds around the winch. The entire boom can swing about to move the load along an arc. In addition, all mobile cranes and some stationary cranes can raise and lower the boom. Raising the boom moves the load toward the base of the crane. Lowering the boom moves the load away from the base.

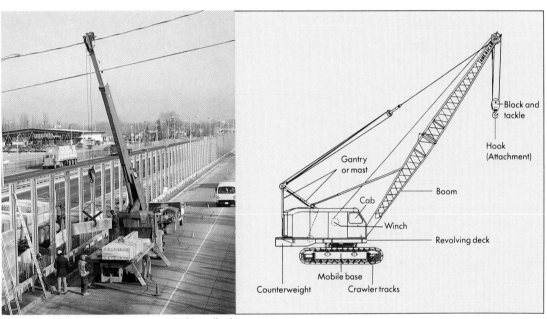

John McGrail, Wheeler Pictures   David Tarrant, Shostal

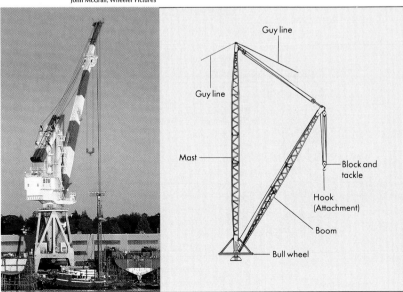

Cranes grasp the load with an *attachment* such as a hook. A *block and tackle,* a system of pulleys and a cable, lifts the load. A long arm called a *boom* moves the load about. Various devices prevent the weight of the load from tipping the crane. The *truck crane,* a mobile crane mounted on a truck, *upper left,* uses legs that extend from the base. The *crawler crane,* a mobile crane on a crawler base, *above,* uses a counterweight. Stationary cranes use a counterweight, *far left,* or long cables called *guy lines, left.*

On most mobile cranes, the base is mounted on wheels or crawler tracks. To prevent tipping when the boom is extended, mobile cranes use counterweights, rollers, or long legs that extend outward from the base.

Stationary cranes also use these devices to prevent tipping. In addition, they use *guy lines,* long cables connecting the crane with a massive object such as a concrete column that has been driven into the ground.

A traveling crane has no boom. Its hoisting equipment is mounted in a *trolley,* a device that travels on wheels along a horizontal *bridge* (beam). In *overhead cranes,* which are permanently installed in buildings, the bridge extends the entire width of a room. On the ends of the bridge are wheels that travel along elevated, horizontal tracks. These tracks extend the length of the room. In *straddle carries,* the ends of the bridge are attached to long, vertical columns. The columns are on wheels.   LeRoy T. Boyer

See also **Block and tackle.**

Crane, Hart (1899-1932), was an American poet best known for his complex work *The Bridge* (1930). Crane used the Brooklyn Bridge in New York City as his major symbol of the meaning and texture of modern life in the United States. Crane incorporated history, geography, and technology into an abstract, mythological vision of America's past, present, and future.

In *The Bridge,* Crane interwove legendary figures from American history with modern inventions. For example, he portrayed Rip Van Winkle as a passenger on a New York City subway. The subway itself is a vehicle that carries the reader backward into America's past and forward into a vision of the future. Although Crane was optimistic about life in the United States, his poem shows his awareness of the problems created by an industrial society. Crane published one other book of poems during his lifetime, *White Buildings* (1926).

Harold Hart Crane was born in Garrettsville, Ohio. He had an unhappy personal life and committed suicide at the age of 32.   Bonnie Costello

Crane, Stephen (1871-1900), was an American novelist, short-story writer, poet, and journalist. Although he died of tuberculosis at the age of 28, Crane produced a vast number of newspaper articles, more than 100 stories and sketches, two volumes of poetry, and six novels. He pioneered in psychological realism, often exploring thoughts of fictional characters facing death.

Crane's greatest novel is *The Red Badge of Courage* (1895), a story set during the Civil War (1861-1865). It portrays a young Union soldier who undergoes a transformation from cowardice to heroism amidst the noisy confusion and "crimson roar" of the battlefield. Crane based the youth's experiences on conversations with veterans of combat, fictional works, histories of military campaigns, and his vivid imagination. The novel remains a masterpiece of literature about war.

Crane was born in Newark, N.J. In 1891, he moved to New York City to work as a free-lance newspaper writer. Crane's observations of slum life inspired his first novel, *Maggie: A Girl of the Streets* (1893), about a young prostitute driven to suicide. Its subject matter discouraged publishers from accepting the manuscript, so Crane published it at his own expense.

Following a trip to the Great Plains and the South in 1895, Crane wrote two of his finest short stories. "The Bride Comes to Yellow Sky" (1898) is an unconventional Western showdown between a gunman and a Texas marshal. "The Blue Hotel" (1898) is an ironic account of an immigrant's death in Nebraska. After 1896, Crane traveled widely, covering two wars and accepting newspaper assignments. On Jan. 2, 1897, he was shipwrecked off the coast of Florida. The experience provided material for his classic story "The Open Boat" (1897).

Crane's poetry was collected in *The Black Riders and Other Lines* (1895) and *War Is Kind* (1899). His cynical poems anticipate the free verse style of the 1900's.
            Alan Gribben

Additional resources

Colvert, James B. *Stephen Crane.* Harcourt, 1984.
Crane, Stephen. *Prose and Poetry.* Ed. by J. C. Levenson. Literary Classics, 1984.

Crane, Walter (1845-1915), was an English artist who became famous for his illustrations for children's books. Crane's illustrations are noted for their flat colors and attention to details of clothing and objects. The artist's bold, simple compositions reflect his interest in Japanese prints.

Crane was best known for his pictures for more than 30 *toy books,* which were small volumes of nursery rhymes and fairy tales for young children. His toy books include *Sing a Song of Sixpence* (1866), *Beauty and the Beast* (1874), *Little Red Riding Hood* (1875), and *Aladdin* (1875). Crane created some of his best illustrations for two books of nursery rhymes set to music by his older sister, Lucy. The books were called *The Baby's Opera* (1877) and *The Baby's Bouquet* (1878).

Crane also created illustrations for adult books, as well as oil paintings, murals, and posters. In addition, he designed tapestries and wallpaper. He was born in Liverpool.   Marilyn Fain Apseloff

Crane fly. See **Daddy longlegs.**

Cranium. See **Head.**

Cranmer, Thomas (1489-1556), was the first Protestant archbishop of Canterbury, the leader of the Church of England. He became a leading figure of the English Reformation, which was the movement that led to the establishment of Protestantism in England.

Cranmer was born at Aslockton, in Nottinghamshire. He attended Cambridge University, became a fellow of Jesus College, and was ordained to the priesthood by 1520. Cranmer came to the attention of King Henry VIII in 1529, when he met with the king's advisers concern-

Alfred A. Knopf, Inc.
Stephen Crane

Bettmann Archive
Thomas Cranmer

ing Henry's divorce proceedings against Catherine of Aragon. Henry's wish to divorce Catherine conflicted with doctrines of the Roman Catholic Church. Cranmer suggested that the divorce question be put to theologians at the universities for judgment rather than to the pope. In 1532, Cranmer was sent as part of a delegation to Europe, which met with political leaders and theologians. In Germany, Cranmer also married the niece of a religious reformer. Cranmer kept the marriage secret because it violated his priestly vows. In 1533, Cranmer became archbishop of Canterbury. He supported Henry's efforts to divorce Catherine and to separate the Church of England from the Catholic Church. See **Henry** ([VIII] of England).

During Henry's reign, Cranmer authorized using an English language Bible in parish churches and published an English version of a *litany,* a form of prayer. In the reign of Edward VI, Cranmer organized the preparation of the *Book of Common Prayer* (1549). He also shaped a statement of doctrine that eventually became the Thirty-Nine Articles of the Church of England.

In 1553, Mary, the daughter of Henry VIII and Catherine of Aragon, came to the English throne. Mary, a devout Roman Catholic, had Cranmer imprisoned. In 1554, he was charged with heresy. Two years later, he was burned at the stake.   Dale A. Johnson

Cranston, Alan MacGregor (1914-   ), a Democrat from California, was a United States senator from 1969 to 1993. He served as Democratic *whip* (assistant leader) of the Senate from 1977 to 1990. In 1991, the Senate Ethics Committee reprimanded Cranston for his dealings with Charles H. Keating, Jr., an American banker. An investigation by the committee had concluded that Cranston acted improperly by using his political influence on Keating's behalf at the same time the senator was accepting large campaign contributions from Keating. Cranston denied that he had done anything improper. Cranston also was an unsuccessful candidate for the 1984 Democratic presidential nomination. He served as chairman of the Senate Veterans' Affairs Committee from 1987 to 1993.

Cranston was born in Palo Alto, Calif., and graduated from Stanford University in 1936. He worked as a correspondent in Europe and Ethiopia for the International News Service (INS) until 1938. In 1942, Cranston became chief of the foreign language division of the Office of War Information. From 1947 to 1958, Cranston headed a real estate firm in Palo Alto. He helped found the California Democratic Council in 1953 and served as its first president until 1957. Cranston held office as controller of California from 1959 to 1967.   William J. Eaton

Crappie, *KRAP ee,* is a freshwater fish closely related to sunfish and black bass. It is found in sluggish, shallow waters of the Midwestern and Southern United States. The crappie is silvery olive with dark-green spots. It is about 1 foot (30 centimeters) long when full grown. It has a high fin on its back and a similar one on its belly. The *white crappie* has up to six spines in the back fin, and the *black crappie* has seven or more spines in the back fin. Crappies have large mouths. They feed on insects, small fishes, and other animals. They are an excellent food fish and one of the most important game fish in their region. Crappies are called by many other names, including bridge perch, bachelor perch, chin-

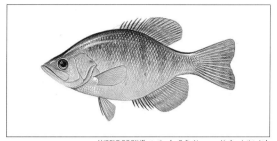

WORLD BOOK illustration by Colin Newman, Linden Artists Ltd.

The white crappie is a popular freshwater game fish and food fish. It measures about 1 foot (30 centimeters) long.

quapin perch, strawberry bass, calico bass, and sacalait.

Scientific classification. The crappie is in the sunfish family, Centrarchidae. The white crappie is *Pomoxis annularis.* The black crappie is *P. nigromaculatus.*   Robert D. Hoyt

Crassus, *KRAS uhs,* **Marcus Licinius,** *MAHR kuhs lih SIHN ee uhs* (112?-53 B.C.), was a Roman statesman, financier, and military leader. In 60 B.C., Crassus, Caesar, and Pompey formed the *First Triumvirate,* a three-man political alliance that attempted to dominate Rome (see **Caesar, Julius; Triumvirate**). Crassus had previously held the high government posts of praetor, consul, and censor. He was called *the Rich* because he made much money through real estate investments.

In 71 B.C., Crassus had crushed the revolt of the gladiator Spartacus (see **Spartacus**). Seeking further glory, Crassus attacked Parthia, an empire in central Asia. In 53 B.C., Parthian archers trapped his army and killed Crassus and most of his troops.   Arthur M. Eckstein

Crater is a funnel- or bowl-shaped depression on the surfaces of planets and other bodies in the solar system. Most craters on the earth are formed by volcanic activity. Some of these craters result from explosions that blast cinders and other debris from volcanic vents. Such craters are rarely larger than $1\frac{1}{4}$ miles (2 kilometers) across. Other craters form when the ground surface collapses following the withdrawal of lava from below. The depression occupied by Crater Lake in Oregon and the crater of Kilauea in Hawaii were both formed by collapse. Collapse craters larger than $\frac{3}{5}$ mile (1 kilometer) across are called *calderas.* Smaller collapse craters are called *pit craters.* Craters are common on the moon and on planets other than the earth. But almost all the craters on these bodies are *impact craters* that were formed by the impact of large meteorites. See also **Meteor** (Meteorites; picture); **Moon.**   Michael H. Carr

Crater Lake is the deepest lake in the United States. It lies in the crater of Mount Mazama, an inactive volcano in the Cascade Mountains of Oregon. The lake is almost 6 miles (10 kilometers) across at its widest point. It covers 20 square miles (52 square kilometers). Its surface is about 6,200 feet (1,900 meters) above sea level. Its greatest depth is 1,932 feet (589 meters). There are no known outlets and no streams flowing into it.

The lake was formed about 7,700 years ago when the top of Mount Mazama, then about 12,000 feet (3,660 meters) high, collapsed. This left a huge "bowl" which gradually filled with water. A small volcano called Wizard Island formed in the lake when lava erupted later from the interior of Mount Mazama.

Crater Lake, in the Cascade Mountains of southwestern Oregon, is the deepest lake in the United States. It reaches 1,932 feet (589 meters) at its greatest depth. The lake lies in the crater of Mount Mazama, an inactive volcano. It is part of Crater Lake National Park.

George Schwartz, FPG

The Klamath Indians believed the lake's waters had healing qualities. John Hillman, a mining prospector, arrived at Crater Lake in June 1853. He named it Deep Blue Lake. The area was made a national park in 1902. Originally, there were no fish in Crater Lake. But the lake was stocked with several varieties of fish from the late 1800's until 1941. Some rainbow trout and kokanee salmon still survive there.   Gary H. Searl

See also **Oregon** (picture); **Volcano** (Composite volcanoes).

Crater Lake National Park was created in southwestern Oregon to preserve Crater Lake and the forests around it. The walls of an ancient volcano, Mount Mazama, rise from 500 to 2,000 feet (152 to 610 meters) above the surface of the lake. They have been changed by the weather into fantastic forms. Several peaks of the Cascade Mountains, including Mount Scott, Cloud Cap, and Llao Rock, rise near Crater Lake. Coniferous trees cling to broken rocks around the lake and are often reflected by the waters. There are more than 500 kinds of flowering plants, ferns, and flowers in the meadows and on the slope of the volcano. Animals and birds are plentiful. President Theodore Roosevelt set 10 Oregon townships aside in 1902 to create the park. For its area, see **National Park System** (table: National parks).

Critically reviewed by the National Park Service

Crawford, William Harris (1772-1834), an American politician and statesman, became a Southern leader in United States politics. His Democratic-Republican Party believed in an extreme form of states' rights, the idea that the states retain all powers not given to the national government.

Crawford was a U.S. senator from Georgia from 1807 to 1813. He served as U.S. secretary of the treasury under Presidents James Madison and James Monroe from 1816 to 1825. In 1824, he ran for President but lost to Secretary of State John Quincy Adams. Crawford was born in Amherst County, Virginia.   James C. Curtis

Crayfish, also called *crawfish*, is a freshwater crustacean that is closely related to the lobster. It lives in and along lakes and rivers and is found on every continent except Africa and Antarctica. The crayfish seldom grows over 6 inches (15 centimeters) long. It varies in color from white through pink, orange, and brown, to greenish-black and dark blue. The clear white crayfish is a blind animal that lives in underground rivers.

A hard structure called the *exoskeleton* covers the body of the crayfish. This serves as a suit of armor to protect the soft tissues of the body from injury. The body is divided into sections, or segments. The front part of the body is rigid, but the back part, or abdomen, has movable segments. The crayfish has five legs on each side of the body. The two front legs are shaped into large, sharp claws, or pincers. They are similar to those of the lobster and are used to capture and hold the prey. The four other pairs of legs are used for walking. *Swimmerets* (leglike structures used in reproduction) are located under the abdomen. The crayfish also has two long feelers, or antennae, and two shorter ones.

The crayfish feeds on snails, small fish, tadpoles, or the young of insects. It is most active at nightfall and at daybreak, when it comes out of its burrow or from under a stone. It has burrowing habits which may destroy cropland or weaken levees and milldams. One kind digs down to water in damp meadows and throws up clay "chimneys" in the process. The crayfish is a fighter. If it loses a limb or claw in battle, a new one grows in its place.

The crayfish is considered good food in Europe and North America. In the United States, large numbers of crayfish are raised on fish "farms."

Scientific classification. Crayfish belong to the family Astacidae. American crayfish are *Cambarus virilis* and *C. bartoni.* European crayfish are *Astacus fluviatilis.*

J. Laurens Barnard

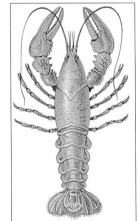

WORLD BOOK illustration by James Teason
Crayfish

See also **Crustacean; Lobster.**

Crayon is a stick of colored wax shaped like a short pencil. Colored pencils, colored chalk, and *pastels* (sticks made of a chalky paste) are sometimes called crayons. This article discusses wax crayons.

Children use crayons to create bright, colorful drawings. Crayons are often a child's first drawing tool. Artists sometimes use crayons to add texture to their works, by melting the wax or by other techniques.

To make crayons, manufacturers add natural or synthetic *pigments* (coloring materials) to heated wax. The mixture is then poured into molds. After the crayons harden, they are wrapped in paper.

No one knows exactly when wax crayons were invented, but they were used in Europe by the 1700's. Crayons were first made in the United States by Binney & Smith in Easton, Pa., in 1903.   Eric Zebley

See also **Pencil** (Colored pencils).

Crazy Horse (1844?-1877) was an Oglala Sioux Indian chief. In 1875, the United States government ordered Crazy Horse and other Sioux to enter a reservation. They refused. In 1876, Crazy Horse led the Sioux and Cheyenne, who defeated General George Crook in the Battle of the Rosebud in Montana. Eight days later, he led the Indians in the Battle of the Little Bighorn, where Lieutenant Colonel George A. Custer and his command were wiped out (see **Custer, George Armstrong**).

As a boy, Crazy Horse was named Curly. After his first great war deed, his father, who was himself named Crazy Horse, gave his name to the boy. Crazy Horse had light skin and hair. He had a quiet manner. He had unusual spiritual powers. The Sioux called him their "Strange One."

In 1877, Crazy Horse voluntarily surrendered to American troops. Crazy Horse was killed in 1877 at Fort Robinson, Nebr., by a soldier while the chief was being forced into a jail cell. A gigantic figure of Crazy Horse is being sculptured out of a mountain in the Black Hills of South Dakota.   Jerome A. Greene

Cream. See Milk (table); **Butter.**

Creasey, John (1908-1973), an English author, became one of the best-known writers of detective stories of the 1900's. He published more detective fiction than any other writer of his time—almost 600 novels written under 28 names. Most critics consider Creasey's stories uneven in quality but have praised his best ones for their fast-paced action and clever plots.

Creasey created several detectives. Under his own name, he wrote three separate series of novels about Inspector Roger West of Scotland Yard and two amateur detectives, Dr. Stanislaus Palfrey and Richard Rollison. Rollison is known as the Toff, an English slang word for a stylishly dressed man. Perhaps Creasey's most popular detective is Commander George Gideon of Scotland Yard. Under the name of J. J. Marric, Creasey wrote the Gideon series, the best example of the British police procedural novel. Creasey's other pen names include Gordon Ashe, Norman Deane, Michael Halliday, Kyle Hunt, and Jeremy York. Creasey was born in the county of Surrey.   David Geherin

Creation. See Life (The origin of life).

Creationism is a set of beliefs based on the idea that a Supreme Being brought into existence the earth and all its life through a direct act of creation. Most creationists are conservative Christians who base their beliefs on the Bible's account of the Creation. Creationists include people of many different Christian faiths.

Creationist beliefs. There is considerable variation in creationist beliefs. *Strict creationists* take the Biblical story of the Creation literally. They believe that God created the universe just thousands of years ago, and that He created all life forms within six 24-hour days. Other creationists interpret the Bible more loosely. For example, some think the universe is millions or billions of years old, but that human beings were created only thousands of years ago. All creationists believe that each *species* (type of life form) on earth has remained relatively unchanged since the Creation, and that no species has evolved from any other. Most creationists base their beliefs on the Bible alone. Some, however, called *scientific creationists,* argue that there is scientific evidence supporting their viewpoint.

Creationists reject the theory of evolution, which nearly all scientists have adopted as a basic idea of modern biology. The theory of evolution first gained widespread attention when it was presented by British naturalist Charles R. Darwin in 1858. It states that the earth came into being about $4\frac{1}{2}$ billion years ago and that one basic life form evolved since then into the more than 2 million species that inhabit the world today. Modern human beings, according to the theory, first appeared about 100,000 years ago, after evolving from earlier human and prehuman ancestors. Most Christians who are not creationists accept the theory of evolution, believing the process was guided by God.

Early theories about the Creation. Modern Christian creationist belief stems from a time line published in the 1650's by James Ussher, an archbishop of the Church of Ireland. Ussher constructed the time line by interpreting literally the birth and death dates of figures in the Bible. According to Ussher, God created the earth and its life forms in 4004 B.C. Today, however, considerable disagreement exists among creationists concerning the date of what they believe was the Creation.

In the 1700's and 1800's, Ussher's ideas were called into question by the theory of evolution and other scientific developments. Christian leaders argued increasingly among themselves about the role of science in understanding Biblical accounts of the Creation. Some maintained the Bible should still be the basic source for information on the origin of the earth and its life.

The 1900's. In the early 1900's, public high schools in the United States began teaching evolution in science classes. In the 1920's, creationists proposed laws in 20 states to ban public schools from teaching evolution. They considered the teaching of the theory to be part of a dangerous trend toward the separation of religious beliefs from everyday life. Several states, including Arkansas and Tennessee, passed such legislation. The American Civil Liberties Union (ACLU) opposed the laws, saying that they violated the constitutional principle of the separation of church and state. The ACLU challenged the Tennessee law in 1925 by defending a teacher named John T. Scopes, who had volunteered to stand trial on the charge of teaching evolution.

The ACLU lost the Scopes case, and the laws against teaching evolution remained in effect. However, public opinion of creationism suffered as a result of the trial because the press portrayed creationists as uninformed and out of touch with mainstream science.

In the 1960's, more public schools again began to teach evolution, in part because of a fear that the United States was falling behind other nations in the teaching of science. In 1968, the Supreme Court of the United States ruled that laws banning the teaching of evolution were unconstitutional because they made religious considerations part of the curriculum. Despite these setbacks, the creationist movement gained strength in the 1960's.

In the 1970's and early 1980's, scientific creationists proposed laws that would have made creationism a required subject in classrooms that taught evolution. These people argued that creationism, like evolution, is based on science and so should be taught along with evolution. They also said that because evolution is "just a theory," it should be considered a religion. Thus they claimed that teaching only evolution would violate the Constitution both by limiting academic freedom and by supporting one religion over another.

In 1981, Arkansas and Louisiana passed laws that would have required the teaching of creationism in public schools. But the laws were declared unconstitutional—the Arkansas law by a U.S. district court in 1982 and the Louisiana law by the U.S. Supreme Court in 1987. The courts ruled that the theory of evolution was scientific rather than religious. They also concluded that creationism was essentially a religious explanation of life and that the Arkansas and Louisiana laws were therefore unconstitutional because they favored one religion over another.

After the Supreme Court's 1987 ruling, creationists began to shift their focus away from state legislatures and federal courts. Instead, they tried to strengthen their influence through increased political activity in local communities. They began to call for schools to teach theories of "abrupt appearances" and "intelligent design." These theories, without referring to God, state that instead of evolving, species appeared suddenly. Using this approach, creationists had, by the early 1990's, persuaded an increasing number of local school boards and teachers to teach creationism in science classrooms.   Raymond A. Eve

See also **Evolution** (Acceptance of evolution; Evolution and religion); **Scopes trial.**

Crécy, *KREHS ee* or *kray SEE,* **Battle of,** was the first important battle of the Hundred Years' War (1337-1453). It took place in 1346 at the site of the present village of Crécy, in the French department of Somme. English troops under Edward III defeated a much larger French army under Philip VI. Almost half the French force was killed in the battle, including more than a thousand knights. English archers on foot proved more effective than armor-clad French knights on horses. The hero of the battle was Edward, the Black Prince, son of Edward III of England.   C. T. Allmand

See also **Edward III; Edward** (the Black Prince); **Hundred Years' War.**

Credit, in education. See **Universities and colleges** (Curriculum).

Credit enables people to obtain goods or services even if they do not have enough money to pay for them right away. For example, a person who cannot immediately pay the full price of an automobile or a house may make the purchase on credit.

The word *credit* comes from the Latin word *credo,* meaning *I trust.* Moneylenders trust borrowers to pay them back. Sellers extend credit to buyers because it in-

creases sales and, ordinarily, the buyers pay interest. Buyers are willing to pay interest for credit because in this way, they can use things they want while they are still paying for them.

A *credit rating* establishes the extent to which a person or company can buy on credit or borrow money. Factors that contribute to a credit rating include income, financial reliability, and records of previous credit transactions. Organizations called *credit bureaus* compile credit ratings and provide this information to stores, business firms, and lending institutions.

Credit can promote economic growth and contribute to a nation's wealth. Business companies use credit to build factories or to buy equipment in order to increase the production of goods. Governments use credit to build schools, highways, and other public projects.

Types of credit. There are three major types of credit—*consumer, commercial,* and *investment.*

Consumer credit enables consumers to spend more money than they have at the time. A charge account is one kind of consumer credit. Most charge accounts involve no interest, but the full price of items bought through a charge account must be paid monthly. If the full amount is not paid by the specified date, many charge accounts require interest payments. Most businesses that provide charge accounts give their customers *credit cards* to make credit buying convenient. Banks also issue credit cards that can be used to charge purchases at many stores, restaurants, and other businesses. Another kind of consumer credit is an installment plan. Payments for a purchase on an installment plan are made over a stipulated period of time and, in most cases, include interest.

Commercial credit is used by companies to develop their business. They expect to repay the loans from their increased profit. Most of these loans are repaid within six months and so are called *short-term credit.*

Investment credit is a loan paid back over a period as long as 30 years, or even more. This kind of loan is called *long-term credit.* Examples include home mortgages and corporate bonds. Businesses use investment credit to undertake a major project, such as the construction of a factory.

Lending institutions take money received from savers and other customers and lend it on credit to those who need funds. Such institutions include banks, savings and loan associations, credit unions, finance companies, and insurance firms.

The terms of a loan are set forth in a loan contract. These terms include *interest, maturity,* and *collateral.* Interest is paid by the borrower to the lender. It serves as compensation for giving up the use of the money, for waiting for repayment of the loan, and for risking the loss of the money. Maturity is the date by which the loan must be completely repaid. Collateral is something of value that a borrower pledges to the lender in case the loan is not repaid as promised. For example, the title of a house is the collateral on a home mortgage.

Credit and the economy. The availability of credit affects both the rate of economic growth and the level of prices. When credit is easy to get, people are able to buy more, and their demand for goods and services grows. In response to the growing demand, business companies may try to hire more workers to increase output. Credit also enables firms to buy new equipment to boost production. However, if output does not keep pace with demand, prices will increase. A continuing increase in prices is called *inflation.*

During periods of inflation, moneylenders may hesitate to grant credit. Inflation drives down the purchasing power of money, and so the dollars that lenders get back buy fewer goods and services than those they lent. If lenders expect a period of inflation to continue, they may raise interest rates to make up for the loss in money value. When credit becomes harder to obtain, economic activity may decline, and inflation may slow down or even stop. Frank J. Bonello

Related articles in *World Book* include:

Bank	Finance company	Mortgage
Collection agency	Inflation	Pawnbroker
Credit card	Installment plan	Savings and loan
Credit union	Interest	association
Farm Credit System	Loan company	

Credit card allows people to charge goods and services at business places that accept the card. Many types of firms issue credit cards. To obtain one, a person must have a record of paying bills on time. Each credit card has the cardholder's name and account number. The cardholder presents the card when making a purchase.

Many oil companies and department and chain stores issue credit cards that may be used only at their own establishments. Travel and entertainment card companies and many banks issue cards that the cardholder may use at a variety of hotels, restaurants, stores, and other businesses. The banks and the card companies pay the businesses for purchases but deduct a fee for the service. In addition, travel and entertainment card companies and many banks charge cardholders an annual fee.

Cardholders receive a monthly bill. Most types of credit cards permit cardholders to pay only part of the bill if they wish. But cardholders then must pay a finance charge on the unpaid part.

Cards called *debit cards* resemble credit cards. But when a cardholder uses a debit card, the amount of the purchase is typically deducted directly from the cardholder's checking account. Frank J. Bonello

Credit Mobilier of America, *moh BEEL yuhr* or *moh BEEL yay,* was a joint-stock company responsible for a major political scandal in the United States. It was first chartered in 1859 as the Pennsylvania Fiscal Agency. In 1864, the agency came under the control of the Union Pacific Railroad Company, which renamed it Credit Mobilier and made it the railroad's construction company. In effect, the same men owned the Union Pacific and Credit Mobilier, and they awarded the railroad's construction contracts to Credit Mobilier. Under the Pacific Railroad Acts of 1862 and 1864, the federal government gave the Union Pacific large loans and land grants to build a transcontinental railroad to the West Coast. In building the railroad, the Union Pacific paid unreasonably high bills submitted by Credit Mobilier, and the Credit Mobilier owners benefited immensely.

The managers of Credit Mobilier tried to ensure that the U.S. Congress did not question the way the railroad managed its business. They did this by offering Credit Mobilier stock at far below market value to certain key congressmen and other federal government officials. The participants were even allowed to pay for the stock

out of dividends they expected to earn from it. Oakes Ames, the head of Credit Mobilier and a member of the U.S. House of Representatives, secured the participation of several important officials. Those accused of participating included Representatives Schuyler Colfax and James A. Garfield and Senator James W. Patterson. Colfax became Vice President of the United States in 1869. Garfield served as President in 1881.

Credit Mobilier's dealings were revealed in 1872. Congress investigated the company and issued two reports. But it did little more than to *censure* (officially condemn) Ames, Patterson, and Representative James Brooks, another participant in the scandal. Ames argued that Credit Mobilier should not be singled out for criticism because similar financial manipulation and bribing of congressmen were widespread. The scandal resulted in mounting criticism by reformers of the standards of public morality in the 1870's. Michael Perman

Credit union is a cooperative banking association operated exclusively for the benefit of its members. The members pool their savings and borrow money at a rate of interest sometimes lower than the interest charged by most banks. Credit unions are often organized among the employees of companies or members of farm groups, labor unions, and educational, religious, and social institutions. In the early 1990's, there were about 14,300 credit unions in the United States with a membership of about 62 million. The unions had assets of about $230 billion. Deposits are insured up to $100,000 per account by the federal government.

Cooperative credit societies originated in Germany during the 1840's. Alphonse Desjardins organized the first credit union in North America in 1900 in Lévis, Quebec. Desjardins helped set up the first credit union in the United States in Manchester, N.H., in 1908. In 1909, Massachusetts became the first state to legalize credit unions. Desjardins helped draft the new law. Boston merchant Edward A. Filene became a leader in the development of American credit unions. Today, more than half of all credit unions in the United States operate under federal charters and are supervised by the National Credit Union Administration. The others are chartered by individual states. William G. Dewald

Cree Indians are a people who live in Canada and in Montana in the United States. They form a number of bands that speak various dialects of a single Algonquian language. All Cree once lived in the forests of eastern and northern Canada. In the late 1600's, they began to trade furs to Europeans for weapons, traps, and other items. During the mid-1700's, some bands of Cree moved onto the grassy plains of Alberta and Saskatchewan. The Indians who moved west, called the Plains Cree, became buffalo hunters. Today, many Cree farm on reservations. Others live in Canadian cities.

The Cree who remained in the Canadian forests became known as the Woodlands Cree. They continued to take part in the fur trade. Until the 1950's, the Woodlands Cree lived in small groups of a few related families. They lived in tents covered with hides or birchbark or, later, canvas. Today, most Woodlands Cree live in cabins or frame houses in villages. They earn money by trapping animals for furs, by catching and processing fish, and by mining and other wage labor. The Canadian government employs some Cree as health-care workers, teachers, and clerks. The Cree believe in an almighty spiritual power, which they call *manito.*

At least 76,000 Cree live in Canada. About 2,000 Plains Cree live on a reservation in Montana.   Alice B. Kehoe

See also **Poundmaker; Saskatchewan** (picture: Cree Indians).

Creed, American's. See American's Creed.

Creed, Apostles'. See Apostles' Creed.

Creed, Nicene. See Nicene Councils.

Creek Indians belong to any of 19 tribal groups that once occupied much of what are now Alabama and Georgia. Today, most of the approximately 20,000 Creeks live in Oklahoma. The largest Creek tribes are the Alabama and the Muskogee. They were called the Upper Creeks because they lived farther north than other Creek groups. Most other Creeks belong to the Yuchi or Hitchiti tribes, called the Lower Creeks.

European explorers first came in contact with the Creeks in 1540. By that time, several Creek tribes had joined together and formed the Creek Confederacy. The Creeks farmed the land and lived in about 50 small settlements called *Creek towns,* some of which had more than 1,000 persons. The Creek Confederacy grew in power during colonial times as it expanded to include tribes displaced by European settlers.

During the early 1800's, the Creeks fought a series of wars with white settlers who wanted their lands (see **Indian wars** [In the South]; **Jackson, Andrew** [The Battle of Horseshoe Bend]). In the 1830's, the government forced the Creeks to move to the Indian Territory in what is now Oklahoma. Few received any payment for their land, and most had to leave their belongings behind.

The Creeks faced poverty and starvation in the Indian Territory. But they developed crops and farming methods suitable for their new land and soon became fairly prosperous. Laws passed in the 1890's broke up tribal landholdings into areas that were given to individual Indians. But many of these areas were too small to be farmed profitably, and the Creeks were forced back into poverty. Today, many Creeks are poor. But others work in a wide range of fields, including education, law, and medicine.   Don Whiteside

See also **Five Civilized Tribes.**

Creeley, Robert (1926-   ), an American poet, is one of a group of writers who are sometimes called the *Black Mountain poets.* This group, which includes Robert Duncan and Charles Olson, worked together at Black Mountain College, an experimental school in Black Mountain, N.C. Beginning in the 1950's, they developed a new kind of poetry based on Creeley's idea that "form is never more than an extension of content."

Creeley's poems are short and unrhymed, with few descriptive details. They often deal with "the tragedy of human relationships," such as strained communication between lovers, friends, or parents and children. Some poems suggest a playful or passionate struggle between the mind and body, and the self and world.

Robert White Creeley was born in Arlington, Mass. His poetry has been collected in *Collected Poems: 1945-1975* (1982) and *Selected Poems* (1991). A selection of his fiction and nonfiction was published as *The Collected Prose of Robert Creeley* (1984).   Steven Gould Axelrod

Creeper is the name of many species of small, woodland birds that live in most parts of the world. The *brown creeper* is the only species found in North America. The brown creeper ranges from central Canada south into Mexico. Creepers measure about 5 inches (13 centimeters) long and have a long, thin bill. The upper parts of the creeper's body are mainly brown, and the underparts are white.

Creepers eat insects and spiders found on and in the crevices of bark. These birds search for food almost continually. They "creep" up tree trunks in quick, jerky movements, using their long, stiff tail as a prop. After reaching the treetop, creepers fly down to a different tree trunk and begin their upward hunting movements again.

Creepers make their nests behind loose flaps of bark. They build the nests of twigs, strips of bark, and feathers. The female lays 5 to 8 eggs, which are white but speckled reddish-brown. In the fall, creepers that live in regions with cold climates may migrate to warmer areas. Those that stay in cold regions often huddle together in groups of from 2 to 15 birds to stay warm.

Scientific classification. North American creepers belong to the tree-creeper family, Certhiidae. The scientific name for the brown creeper is *Certhia familiaris.*   Richard F. Johnston

See also **Bird** (picture: Birds of Europe and Asia).

Cremation is burning a dead body to ashes. Burial is the most common method of disposing of the dead in most countries, but the practice of cremation is increasing in the United States, Canada, and Europe. Some people who request cremation consider burial in a cemetery to be undignified. Other people feel that burial is a wasteful use of land.

Most funeral directors can arrange a cremation. A funeral service may take place before or after the burning. The cremation is performed in a building called a *crematory* or *crematorium.* The body is put in a coffin or other container, which is burned in a special oven from one to four hours. The remaining bones are then crushed into white, powdery ashes. The ashes are placed in a container called an *urn* and given to the relatives of the dead person. The relatives may keep the ashes, bury them in a cemetery, or place them in a special burial vault called a *columbarium.* Some people request that their ashes be scattered in one particular place, such as a favorite lake.

Cremation has been practiced throughout history. It was not used by the ancient Chinese or Egyptians. But the ancient Greeks and Romans practiced it. They believed that burning the body purified the soul and released it from its earthly form. The early Christians believed in the eventual reuniting of the body and soul, and viewed cremation as a form of disrespect.

Cremation remained uncommon in Christian countries until the 1800's. Then concern about land use in urban areas and increasing opposition to church restrictions helped reawaken interest in cremation. The first legally recognized crematory for public use opened in Milan, Italy, in 1876. Crematories were first established in the United States in 1884. Today, cremations account for the disposal of about 10 percent of the dead in the United States, about 20 percent in Canada, and about 60 percent in the United Kingdom.   Robert Fulton

Creole, *KREE ohl,* in North or South America, is a person whose ancestors were early French or Spanish settlers of the New World. The word *Creole* comes from the Spanish word *criollo*, meaning *native to the place*. The term also refers to Creole foods and other aspects of Creole culture. In the United States, a Creole is a descendant of French and Spanish settlers of the Gulf States. Many Creoles speak a form of French, Spanish, or Portuguese. Creole foods include *gumbo*, a kind of soup; and *pralines*, a candy. See also **Cable, George Washington; New Orleans** (Ethnic groups).

James H. Dormon

Creosote, *KREE uh soht*, is a heavy, oily liquid made by distilling wood or coal tar. It has a penetrating, smoky smell and is nearly colorless when pure. Creosote as marketed is commonly a brownish color, and is a mixture of cresol and several other substances. Creosote oil taken from beechwood tar has been used in medicine. This oil is made chiefly of creosote and guaiacol. Creosote obtained by distilling coal tar is one of the most effective wood preservatives. It has been used for this purpose for more than 100 years. However, creosote is poisonous. In addition, tests have shown that the substance causes cancer in laboratory animals and may cause cancer in human beings. In 1986, the United States Environmental Protection Agency (EPA) began restricting the use of creosote as a wood preservative. See also **Cresol; Tar.**

Donald L. Stinson

Creosote bush, *KREE uh soht*, is a shrub that grows throughout the desert regions of the southwestern United States and Mexico. A number of closely related shrubs grow in the deserts of Argentina. Unlike most desert shrubs, the cresote bush is an evergreen. It grows about 5 to 8 feet (1.5 to 2.4 meters) high. It has many branches and produces a resin. The shrub has small yellow flowers. The fruit is round, with long, soft white or reddish-brown hairs. The creosote bush is sometimes called *greasewood*, but it is not a true greasewood.

Creosote bushes often grow in rings. Some botanists suggest that such rings are colonies of identical plants. According to this theory, all the bushes in a ring are offshoots of one plant and may be thousands of years old.

Scientific classification. The creosote bush is in the family Zygophyllaceae. Its scientific name is *Larrea tridentata*.

Philip W. Rundel

© K. H. Surtak, N.H.P.A.

The creosote bush is an evergreen that grows in North American deserts. It has many branches and tiny yellow flowers.

Crescent, *KREHS uhnt*, is a symbol that resembles the moon in its first quarter. In heraldry, the crescent is a symbol of the second son in a family.

The people of Byzantium (now Istanbul, Turkey) used the crescent of Diana, a moon goddess in Roman mythology, as their symbol. When the Turks conquered the city, they adopted it as their symbol. It appears on the flag of Turkey. In addition, many countries with large numbers of *Muslims* (followers of Islam) feature a crescent on their national flags. The state flag of South Carolina also includes a crescent.   Whitney Smith

Cresol, *KREE sohl*, is the common name for a group of chemicals that scientists called *hydroxytoluenes*. Creosote oil contains cresols, and is used to preserve railroad ties, fence posts, and other wood used outdoors. Antiseptic soaps and emulsions are made from a purified mixture of the known cresols: ortho-cresol, meta-cresol, and para-cresol. These soaps and emulsions are used as local antiseptics and disinfectants. See also **Creosote.**   Patrice C. Bélanger

Cress is any one of three green plants in the mustard family. They are used in salads and to garnish meats. The best-known cress plant is called *water cress* because it grows in water in sandy creek bottoms. It has smooth, bright-green leaves on long slender stems. *Garden cress*, or *peppergrass*, has a sharper taste than water cress. It grows in the Midwest. *Swedish cress*, sometimes called *upland cress* or *winter cress*, grows in Sweden. It is served as a vegetable there.

Water cress may be raised as a winter crop in greenhouses. It grows best in running water. Garden cress is usually planted in the early spring and harvested about six or seven weeks later. The cresses are rich in minerals, but are usually eaten in too small amounts to provide much food value.

Scientific classification. Cresses belong to the mustard family, Brassicaceae or Cruciferae. The scientific name for water cress is *Nasturtium officinale*. Garden cress is *Lepidium sativum*. Swedish cress is *Barbarea vulgaris*.   S. H. Wittwer

See also **Mustard.**

Cretaceous Period, *krih TAY shuhs*, is a period in the geologic time scale of the earth's history. Scientists believe that the Cretaceous Period began about 138 million years ago and lasted about 75 million years.

See also **Earth** (table: Outline of the earth's history).

Crete, *kreet* (pop. 502,165), is a Greek island in the Mediterranean Sea. The first important European civilization, the Minoan culture, began on Crete about 5,000 years ago. The island is located about 60 miles south of the Peloponnesus, the southern peninsula of mainland Greece. For the location of Crete, see **Greece** (map).

Crete covers 3,217 square miles (8,332 square kilometers) and is the largest island of Greece. Khania is the capital of Crete. Iraklion, the island's chief commercial center and port, is the largest city.

The people of Crete speak Greek, and most of them belong to the Eastern Orthodox Church of Crete. Cretans are proud of their historic past and follow many old customs. For example, they perform traditional dances and folk songs at weddings and baptisms and on saints' days. Early every evening, the people of Crete's towns put on their best clothes and stroll up and down one of the main streets.

Cretans have strong family ties, and many parents arrange marriages for their children. The men of Crete spend much of their time in cafes, where they chat and read newspapers.

Land and climate. A chain of mountains extends across the center of Crete in an east-west direction. The highest point is Mount Ida, which rises 8,058 feet (2,456 meters) in central Crete. Fertile valleys and plains lie among the mountains, which drop off sharply to the sea along most of the southern coast. The mountains slope more gradually in the north, and a narrow plain extends along the northern coast.

Crete has a mild, dry climate. Temperatures average 53° F. (12° C) in winter and 75° F. (24° C) in summer. Rain falls chiefly from October to March and is heavier in the mountains than on the plains and valleys. A number of Crete's farming areas require irrigation because they do not get enough rain. Windmills furnish power for the irrigation systems.

Economy. Most Cretans work on small farms and do much of the work by hand. The main crops are fruits, including grapes, olives, and oranges. The farmers also grow vegetables and nuts.

In the northern coastal cities, factories process food and make building materials. Plants in Iraklion make soap and leather goods. Many of the people work at such handicrafts as basketmaking and metalwork.

Tourism plays an important part in Crete's economy. The ancient Minoan relics at the Iraklion Museum, and the Minoan ruins at Knossos and Phaistos attract large numbers of modern visitors. Iraklion and other coastal cities have modern hotels and restaurants.

Government. Crete is governed by the central Greek government in Athens. The island is divided into four *nomoi* (departments), each headed by a *nomarch* (governor) appointed by the minister of the interior.

History. The first people to settle in Crete came from Asia Minor (now Turkey) about 6000 B.C. By about 3000 B.C., the Cretans had developed an advanced civilization. It is called the *Minoan* culture, after the legendary King Minos (see **Minos**). During the Minoan period, the Cretans made great advances in art, architecture, and engineering. They built beautiful palaces with spacious courtyards. They excelled at making pottery and jewelry and also used a system of writing. For more information, see the *World Book* article on **Aegean civilization** (The Minoan culture).

Fire destroyed many towns and palaces of Crete after about 1450 B.C., and the civilization gradually declined. The Romans invaded the island in 68 B.C. and made it a province in 66 B.C. After the division of the Roman Empire in A.D. 395, Crete came under Greek rule as part of the Byzantine Empire. Venice ruled the island from 1204 to 1669. The Ottoman Turks ruled it from 1669 to 1898.

A movement for union with Greece developed in Crete during the 1800's, and Crete became part of Greece in 1913. German forces conquered Crete in 1941, during World War II. The Germans controlled the island until several months before the war ended in 1945. After the war, Crete greatly improved its roads and tourist facilities. Today, it ranks as a major attraction for visitors to Greece.   Mortimer Chambers

See also **Architecture** (Minoan); **Clothing** (Ancient times; pictures); **Knossos; Painting** (Origins and early painting [Cretan painting]).

Cretinism, *KREE tuh nihz uhm,* is a condition in which babies are born with underdeveloped brains and poorly formed skeletons. Individuals afflicted with cretinism are called *cretins.*

Cretinism is caused by the failure of the thyroid gland to begin functioning during the early stages of the development of a *fetus* (unborn child). The thyroid gland produces hormones necessary for growth and maturation of the body and brain. It normally begins functioning during the 12th week of fetal development. The absence of thyroid hormones disrupts normal growth patterns.

Doctors treat cretinism with supplemental thyroid hormones. Treatment must begin in the first six weeks after birth to prevent both physical and mental retardation.   Charlotte H. Greene

See also **Thyroid gland.**

Creutzfeldt-Jakob disease, *KROYTS fehlt YAH kahb,* is a rare virus disease that destroys the cells of the brain. Two German neuropsychiatrists, Hans G. Creutz-

Jean-Claude Cochet, Explorer

Windmills furnish power for irrigation on farms throughout Crete. Most Cretan farmers must irrigate their land because of the dry climate. Their crops include wheat and potatoes.

feldt and Alfons M. Jakob, first described the disease in the early 1920's. In most cases, the earliest symptom of Creutzfeldt-Jakob disease is loss of memory or peculiar behavior. Within weeks, visual disturbances, lack of co-ordination, and muscular jerking occur. Intellectual ability and awareness continue to deteriorate, and the illness progresses rapidly to death, usually within a year.

Creutzfeldt-Jakob disease is caused by a *slow virus.* In diseases caused by slow viruses, symptoms do not appear until months or years after infection. Scientists do not know how the virus spreads among people, except for a few cases caused by accidental contact with virus-contaminated materials. The disease occurs throughout the world, affecting about 1 out of 1 million people. It afflicts both men and women, mainly between the ages of 50 and 75. No treatment or cure has been discovered.

Paul W. Brown

Crèvecoeur, *krehv KUR,* **Michel-Guillaume Jean de,** *mee SHEHL gee YOHM zhahn duh* (1735-1813), was a French-born essayist who portrayed rural life in colonial America. His descriptions of the attitudes and hopes of the colonists persuaded many Europeans to settle in America.

Crèvecoeur was born near Caen, France. When he was 19 years old, he went to Canada to fight with the French during the French and Indian War. In 1769, he bought a farm near Chester, N.Y., and began his literary career.

Crèvecoeur wrote under the pen name of J. Hector St. John. He became best known for 12 essays collected in *Letters from an American Farmer* (1782), written to an imaginary friend in England. The essays describe such scenes as children coming home from school during a snowstorm and families fleeing an Indian massacre.

Crèvecoeur supported the British during the Revolutionary War in America (1775-1783). In his *Sketches of Eighteenth Century America* (published in 1925, after his death), he accused the patriots of greed and the abuse of power in their struggle for independence. Crèvecoeur served as French consul to the United States from 1783 to 1790 and spent the rest of his life in France.

Edward W. Clark

Crewel, also called *crewelwork,* is a form of embroidery done with woolen yarn. Most crewel has designs stitched on a background of plain, sturdy cloth. The yarn, which consists of two woolen threads twisted to-

Crewel is a wool yarn used for embroidery. The yarn is stitched onto a plain cloth, following the design printed on the cloth.

WORLD BOOK photo

gether loosely, is also called crewel. Crewel can be used to create almost any design. Many crewel embroideries show flowers and vines arranged in graceful patterns. Crewel may include any embroidery stitch.

Historians believe the ancient Hebrews used crewel to decorate the Tabernacle, a tent in which they worshiped. During the A.D. 1000's or 1100's, French women stitched the Bayeux Tapestry, a famous crewel wall hanging. Crewel decorated curtains and upholstery in many American and English homes of the 1600's and 1700's. Today, many people stitch crewel pictures and other items.   Dona Z. Meilach

Crib death. See Sudden infant death syndrome.

Cribbage is a card game for two, three, or four people. Each player keeps score on a *cribbage board,* using two *pegs.* The object of the game is to *peg* (score) 121 points. The invention of the game is credited to Sir John Suckling, an English poet during the 1600's.

When two people play, they *cut* (divide) the pack and the one with the lower card deals. Each player is dealt six cards and places two of them face down. These cards form the *crib,* which is used at the end of the hand. The nondealer cuts the rest of the cards and turns up the top

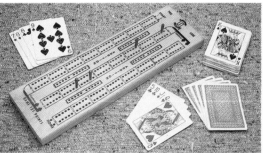

WORLD BOOK photo by Ralph Brunke

In a cribbage game, the players keep their own score by moving two pegs on the special cribbage board.

card of the lower part of the pack. This is the *turnup* or *starter.* If the turnup is a jack, the dealer pegs 2 points for *heels.*

The nondealer begins by laying down a card and calling its value. The dealer then lays down a card and adds its value to the first card. They continue until the value of the cards totals 31. The player who reaches 31 pegs 2 points. A player who cannot lay down a card without going beyond 31 must say "go." The other player then pegs 1 for *go* after playing as many cards as possible without passing 31. Whenever a *go* occurs, the opponent of the one who last played begins a new count. When the players have used all their cards, they peg the total points for their hands.

In scoring, face cards count 10, the ace counts 1, and the others count according to their spots. Points are scored both during the play and at the end of the hand. Each combination of 15 points and each pair counts 2 points. A *run* of three or more cards in sequence scores 1 for each card. Three cards of a kind count 6 and four of a kind count 12. Four cards of the same suit (or five, including the turnup) score a *flush,* worth 1 point per card. At the end of the hand, the nondealer's score is counted first. All players include the turnup in the count of their hands. A player holding a jack of the same suit as the turnup pegs 1 for *nobs.* The crib belongs to the dealer, and is scored in the same way, except that only five-card flushes count.   R. Wayne Schmittberger

Crick, Francis H. C. (1916-   ), is a British biologist. He shared the 1962 Nobel Prize in physiology or medicine with American biologist James D. Watson and biophysicist Maurice H. F. Wilkins, also of Great Britain. Crick and Watson built a model of the molecular structure of *deoxyribonucleic acid* (DNA), the substance that transmits genetic information from one generation to the next. The model, resembling a twisted ladder, is called the *Watson-Crick model.* Later, Crick helped explain how DNA determines the development of living things. See Cell (The 1900's; picture: A model of a DNA molecule); **Nucleic acid.**

Originally a physicist, Crick helped develop radar during World War II. He began research work in molecular biology at Cambridge University in 1949. In 1976, he became a research professor at the Salk Institute in San Diego. Born in Northampton, England, Crick studied at London and Cambridge universities.   Daniel J. Kevles

See also **Science** (picture: A ladderlike model of DNA); **Watson, James D.**

Cricket is a type of jumping insect related to grasshoppers. Crickets differ from grasshoppers in several ways. Crickets have a long, needlelike *ovipositor* that deposits eggs. The wings of most crickets lie flat over each other on top of their backs. Other crickets have only tiny wings or are wingless. The slender antennae are much longer than the body in most kinds of crickets.

Crickets are well known for their songs. These songs are produced primarily by the males. Each kind of cricket has a different song, usually trills or a series of chirps. Crickets produce sound by rubbing their two front wings together. They hear sound with organs in their front legs. Their songs help male and female crickets find each other.

Crickets are commonly found in pastures and meadows, and along roads. Sometimes crickets enter houses. Crickets eat plants and the remains of other insects.

The best-known crickets are the *house cricket* of Europe and the *common, black,* or *field cricket* of the United States. These black or brown insects are about 1 inch (2.5 centimeters) long. The *tree cricket* is a white or pale-green insect. It lives on trees and shrubs and feeds on small insects called *aphids.* Male tree crickets sing in chorus. Their song is a high pitched *treet-treet-treet.* The tiny *ant-loving crickets* are wingless and as broad as they are long. They live in ants' nests and eat ants' young. *Mormon crickets, camel (cave) crickets, mole crickets,* and *Jerusalem crickets* are not considered true crickets (see **Mole cricket; Mormon cricket**).

Scientific classification. Crickets are in the order Orthoptera and the cricket family, Gryllidae.   Betty Lane Faber

See also **Grasshopper; Insect** (picture: The "ears" of a cricket).

E. R. Degginger

The common North American field cricket, *above,* is known for its song. It grows about 1 inch (2.5 centimeters) long.

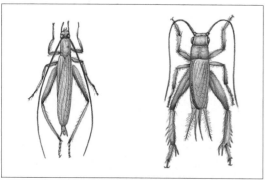

WORLD BOOK illustrations by Shirley Hooper, Oxford Illustrators Limited

Tree cricket   **House cricket**

E. R. Degginger

The camel cricket lives in caves and hollow trees.

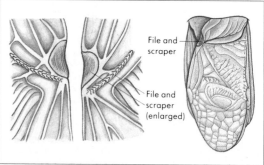

File and scraper

File and scraper (enlarged)

WORLD BOOK illustrations by Oxford Illustrators Limited

The organs with which the cricket "sings." At the right are shown the cricket's front wings, folded along its back so that the right wing nearly covers the left. At the left, portions of the wings are shown separated, with the sound-producing organs enlarged. Each wing has a "file," or thickened vein with cross-ridges, and a "scraper," or hard, sharp-edged portion. The scraper of either wing may be rubbed against the file of the other wing to produce the mating call.

Cricket is a game played with a bat and a ball by two teams of 11 players each. It is one of the most popular games in England and in many countries that once were British colonies. Cricket is played on a round or oval grass field. The action centers on two *wickets.* Each wicket consists of three wooden stumps and two sticks called *bails,* which rest on top of the stumps.

The teams take turns batting and fielding. A member of the fielding side called the *bowler* stands near one of the wickets. The bowler runs a few steps and *bowls* (delivers) the ball with a stiff-armed motion at the opposite wicket. The ball bounces once in front of the wicket on most deliveries. A fielder called the *wicketkeeper* stands behind the wicket.

Members of the batting side are called *batsmen.* A batsman called the *striker* stands at the far wicket, facing the bowler, and tries to hit the ball with a long, flatsided bat. If the ball gets by and knocks a bail off the wicket, the striker is out. If the ball is hit into the field, the striker and a batsman called the *nonstriker*—a teammate at the opposite wicket—may try to score a run.

The batsmen score each time they run to the opposite wicket before a fielder can knock off a bail with the ball. Sometimes they can run back and forth several times before a fielder can return the ball. The next striker is the batsman who is at the wicket opposite the bowler when the ball is returned. The two batsmen remain *in* (at bat) until one of them is put out. The batsman who is put out is then replaced by a teammate. Runs are also scored for hits that reach or cross the field's boundary line. A major cricket match may last from three to five days or more, and each team may score hundreds of runs. The team that scores the most runs wins.

The field and equipment

The field may vary in size. Most fields on which official matches are played measure about 450 feet (137 meters) wide and 500 feet (150 meters) long. The wickets are 22 yards (20 meters) apart in the center of the field. They stand opposite and parallel to each other. The area between the wickets is called the *pitch.*

Each wicket measures 9 inches (22.9 centimeters) wide. The stumps of each wicket are close enough together so the ball cannot pass between any two of them. The tops of the stumps stand 28 inches (71.1 centimeters) above the ground. The bails are $4\frac{3}{8}$ inches (11.1 centimeters) long and rest in grooves on the tops of the stumps. The bails do not rise more than $\frac{1}{2}$ inch (13 millimeters) above the stumps.

White lines made by chalk or lime mark certain boundaries called *creases.* A line called the *bowling crease* is drawn through the stumps of each wicket. It is 8 feet 8 inches (2.64 meters) long, with the middle stump of the wicket at its center. A line called the *popping crease* is marked 4 feet (1.22 meters) in front of the bowling crease. The popping crease extends at least 6 feet (1.83 meters) on either side of the center of the wicket but is considered to be unlimited in length. Lines called *return creases* are marked from each end of the bowling crease. The return creases extend forward to the popping crease and back at least 4 feet behind the bowling crease. However, the return creases are considered to be unlimited in length. The bowler must deliver the ball with some part of the front foot behind the popping crease. The back foot must be between the return creases.

Equipment. The rules of cricket do not specify the material to be used in making a cricket ball. The best balls have a cork center wrapped with twine, and a leather cover. The ball must be between $8\frac{13}{16}$ and 9 inches (22.4 and 22.9 centimeters) in circumference, and it must weigh between $5\frac{1}{2}$ and $5\frac{3}{4}$ ounces (155.9 and 163 grams).

The bat cannot be more than 38 inches (96.5 centime-

Cricket players must have quick reflexes. The bowler, *center,* delivers the ball to a batsman from the opposing team. The batsman hits the ball and races back and forth between the wickets, trying to score as many runs as possible before fielders retrieve the ball.

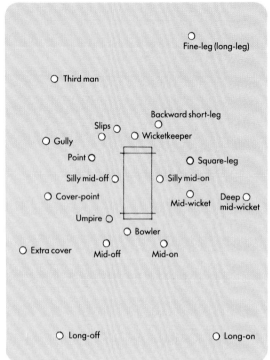

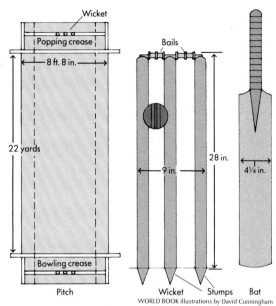

WORLD BOOK illustrations by David Cunningham

Cricket field and equipment. The fielding positions, *left,* are those often used for a right-handed batsman. The positions vary according to the skills of the batsman and the bowler. The pitch is marked by batting and bowling creases. Stumps are close together so the ball cannot go between them. Bats vary in length.

ters) long nor more than $4\frac{1}{4}$ inches (10.8 centimeters) wide at any point. It must be made of wood. The bat has a round handle and a flat, bladelike hitting surface.

Cricket players wear peaked caps or helmets, open-necked shirts, trousers, and spiked or crepe-soled shoes. Batsmen and wicketkeepers wear protective leg pads and gloves.

The game

A cricket match may consist of one or two periods, each called an *innings.* Important matches are played in two innings. A team's innings ends when 10 of its 11 players have been put out. But the captain of the batting side may declare the side's innings over at any time.

Team captains toss a coin to decide who will bat first. After the first innings of a two-innings match, the captain whose team batted first may order the opposing side to *follow-on* if the opposing side is behind by a certain number of runs. The opposing team must then bat its second innings immediately after its first innings. The opposing team may be ordered to follow-on if it is behind by 200 runs in a match of five days or more, by 150 runs in a three- or four-day match, by 100 runs in a two-day match, or by 75 runs in a one-day match. If the team that follows-on cannot catch up, the team that batted first wins *by an innings.* A team wins by an innings if it scores more runs in one innings than the opposing team scores in two innings. If the team that follows on takes the lead, the team that batted first can then bat its second innings.

A team may also win by a certain number of wickets. A team wins by wickets if it takes the lead during its second innings and the opposing team has already batted twice. If the team takes the lead after four batsmen have

been put out, for example, it wins by six wickets because six batsmen have not been put out. If a match is not won by an innings or by wickets, the outcome is expressed by the number of runs scored by each team.

Scoring. Most runs are scored by running from one wicket to the other. Each runner must safely cross the opposite popping crease to score one run. Batsmen also score runs when they hit the ball out of bounds, known as a *boundary.* They score four runs when the ball rolls or bounces across the boundary line. They score six runs if the ball lands out of bounds without bouncing.

Runs called *extras* or *sundries* may also be scored in various ways. Sundries are scored on *byes, leg byes, wide balls,* and *no balls.* A bye is a run scored when the ball passes the striker without touching the bat or any part of the striker's body and without knocking off a bail. A leg bye is a run scored when the ball hits the striker anywhere but on the hands. A ball that hits the hands is played as if it had hit the bat.

A wide ball is a delivery that the umpire rules is out of the striker's reach. One run is automatically scored for a wide ball. The batsmen may attempt to score more runs by running from one wicket to the other before the ball is returned. A no ball may be called for certain rules violations. The main violations occur when (1) the bowler throws the ball instead of bowling it or (2) the bowler's feet are not in the proper position when the ball is delivered. A penalty of one run is scored for a no ball. But if a striker hits a no ball and the batsmen score runs, these runs are counted instead of the penalty.

Outs. There are several ways to put out a batsman. The most direct way is bowling a bail off the striker's wicket. Strikers are also out if they are *caught*—that is, if they hit a ball that is caught by a fielder before it

Ways to be out

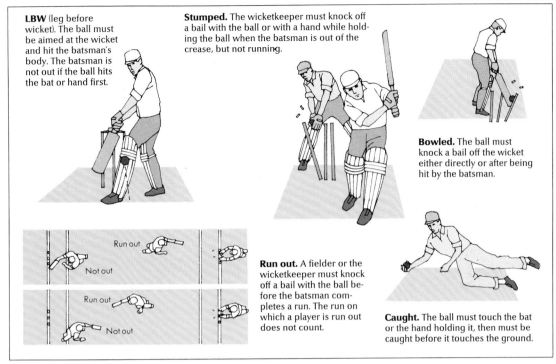

LBW (leg before wicket). The ball must be aimed at the wicket and hit the batsman's body. The batsman is not out if the ball hits the bat or hand first.

Stumped. The wicketkeeper must knock off a bail with the ball or with a hand while holding the ball when the batsman is out of the crease, but not running.

Bowled. The ball must knock a bail off the wicket either directly or after being hit by the batsman.

Run out

Not out

Run out

Not out

Run out. A fielder or the wicketkeeper must knock off a bail with the ball before the batsman completes a run. The run on which a player is run out does not count.

Caught. The ball must touch the bat or the hand holding it, then must be caught before it touches the ground.

bounces or that lands in a fielder's clothing without touching the ground. Either batsman may be *run out* when trying to score. A batsman is run out if a wicketkeeper or other fielder knocks a bail from the batsman's wicket while the batsman is between the popping creases. Strikers are out *stumped* if they step in front of the popping crease when not attempting a run and the wicketkeeper knocks off a bail. Strikers can be out *LBW* (leg before wicket) if they prevent a delivered ball from hitting the wicket by stopping it with any part of their body except the hands. They are also out if they *break the wicket* (knock off a bail) with their bat, clothing, or any part of the body while trying to hit the ball. In addition, strikers are out if they hit the ball a second time except to keep it from hitting the wicket. If the striker or the nonstriker intentionally prevents a player from fielding the ball, the striker is out. Either batsman may be called out for intentionally touching a ball in play with a hand that is not holding the bat.

Umpires make sure the game is played according to the rules, and they settle all disputes. One umpire stands behind the bowler's wicket to make decisions on whether the striker is caught or out LBW, and to rule on run outs at the bowler's end. A second umpire stands to the side of the striker's popping crease to rule on a stumping or run out at that end.

The umpire at the bowler's end also decides whether the ball is in play. The ball is in play from the moment the bowler begins the run-up to the popping crease. The ball is *dead* (not in play) when (1) it is finally settled in the hands of the wicketkeeper or bowler, (2) it lodges in the clothing or equipment of a batsman or umpire, (3) it lodges in a fielder's helmet, (4) it has been called lost, (5) a boundary is scored, (6) a batsman is out, (7) a penalty is awarded after a fielder intentionally stops the ball with something other than the body, (8) the umpire calls "over" or "time," (9) the umpire suspends play because of an injury to a player, or (10) the umpire calls a case of unfair play.

Playing cricket

The batting side. The order in which a team's batsmen will bat is decided by the captain. After a batsman is put out, a teammate takes a turn at bat until 10 players are out. One batsman always remains *not out.*

A batsman may hold the bat any way that is comfortable and effective. Batsmen should stand with their weight evenly distributed and the feet slightly apart. Most batsmen stand with one foot on each side of the popping crease. One of the great skills of batsmanship is the ability to hit the ball between the fielders.

The batting strokes may be divided into two categories, *forward play* and *back play.* Each may be used either (1) to attack and try to score runs or (2) defensively to protect the wicket. For both strokes, the batsman swings the bat back in a movement called the *back-lift,* then brings it forward and down past the feet to hit the ball.

On a forward stroke, the batsman moves the front foot forward near the path of the ball. When the ball is bowled slowly, the batsman may take two or three steps toward the ball, rather than one long step. A forward stroke is best for a ball that bounces near enough to the batsman to be hit on the *half-volley*—that is, as soon as it bounces off the ground. Forward strokes are usually made with the bat pointed down.

WORLD BOOK illustration by David Cunningham

The bowler looks over his shoulder at the point on which he wants to bounce the ball. He then brings his arm over, keeping it stiff to prevent jerking, and follows through after the release.

Roger Archibald, Shostal

Skillful bowlers deliver the ball at varying speeds. They try to confuse the batsman by changing speeds and making the ball change direction either before or after it bounces.

The back stroke is better for a ball that bounces so far in front of the batsman's wicket that the batsman can see which way the ball moves after it hits the ground. When playing defensively, the batsman brings the back leg into the path of the ball and points the bat down. There should be no space for the ball to pass between the bat and the batsman's body. In attacking on back play, batsmen use a wide variety of strokes, depending on where the ball bounces and in what direction it moves. For example, they may swing the bat at an angle to the path of the ball with a *hook* or a *cut* stroke.

As soon as the bowler delivers the ball, the nonstriker should be *backing up* (moving toward the opposite wicket) and ready to run. Batsmen do not have to try to score if the ball is hit. On most hits that go in front of the popping crease, the striker decides whether it is possible to score. If it looks like both batsmen can safely reach the opposite popping crease, the striker calls to the nonstriker that they should try for a run. When the ball goes behind the popping crease, the nonstriker decides whether the batsmen should try to score. Misun-

derstanding between the batsmen is the main cause of run outs. There are no foul balls in cricket.

The fielding side consists of the bowler, the wicket-keeper, and nine other fielders. The other fielders' positions vary in name and location. The most common positions are shown in the diagram of the field that appears in this article. The captain directs the fielders to various positions, depending on the bowler and on whether the striker is right-handed or left-handed.

After the bowler has delivered a certain number of balls, the umpire calls "over." An over consists of either six or eight legitimate deliveries. Wide balls and no balls do not count in the total. After each over, the striker becomes the nonstriker and the nonstriker becomes the striker. Two successive overs cannot be bowled from the same end in one innings. In *limited-over* cricket, the game ends after a certain number of overs rather than after one or two innings.

Good bowling is based on coordinated body, arm, and shoulder motion. The run-up to the bowling crease is designed to give the bowler enough power and balance to bowl the ball at the desired speed. At the final stride, a right-handed bowler's left shoulder should point toward the batsman. When the bowler's left foot has swung forward, the right shoulder should move forward and point in the direction the ball will travel. The bowler's wrist must be loose and the hand cocked back before releasing the ball. For the most power, the bowler continues the arm motion after the release.

Bowlers try to deliver the ball so it bounces a short distance in front of the batsman. Such a delivery is difficult to hit because the batsman is uncertain whether to play forward or back. In addition, bowlers try to get batsmen out by changing the direction of the ball. Bowlers change the direction by controlling the ball's speed and by gripping and spinning the ball in special ways. They can thus make the ball *curve* (change direction in flight) or *break* (change direction after it bounces).

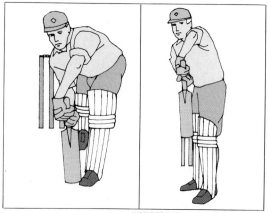

WORLD BOOK illustration by David Cunningham

Batting strokes are used either to try to score runs or to protect the wicket. The batsman at the left uses a forward stroke to try to hit the ball into the field. At the right, he uses a back stroke to keep the ball from hitting the wicket.

History

Cricket was probably first played in England, at least as early as the 1300's. It became a major sport there in the 1700's. The first printed rules appeared in 1744.

Out   Wide ball   No ball   Boundary, six   Boundary, four

WORLD BOOK illustrations by David Cunningham

The umpires stand at either end of the pitch. They use arm signals to indicate their decisions to players and spectators.

Since 1788, cricket rules have been made and published in England by the Marylebone Cricket Club (M.C.C.).

In the earliest forms of cricket, the ball was bowled underhand and bats were shaped like hockey sticks. In the mid-1800's, overhand bowling became legal and batsmen began using bats like those of today.

The highest level of cricket is international competition called *test matches.* The first test match was played in 1877 between England and Australia in Melbourne, Australia. Today, the International Cricket Conference regulates test matches. Official tests are played between seven teams, representing Australia, England, India, New Zealand, Pakistan, Sri Lanka, and the West Indies.

Since 1882, a series of test matches between England and Australia has been played for *the Ashes.* This term was first used after Australia had beaten England in a match in London. After that defeat, an English newspaper printed a death notice of English cricket. The last words were: "The body will be cremated, and the ashes taken to Australia." A year later, an English team went to Australia and won. Some Australian women burned part of a wicket, put the ashes in a small urn, and presented the urn to the English team captain. The urn was later sent to Lord's, a major cricket ground in London and the headquarters of the M.C.C. It is always kept there, no matter which country wins the Ashes.

Many countries in which cricket is popular hold one or more championship series. These series include the County Championship in the United Kingdom, the Sheffield Shield in Australia, the Shell Series in New Zealand, the Currie Cup in South Africa, and the Ranji Trophy in India.   Sir Donald George Bradman

See also **England** (picture: Cricket).

Additional resources

Andrew, Keith. *The Skills of Cricket.* Crowood, 1989.
Formhals, Hugh. *The Jolliest Game Under the Sun: A Beginner's Guide to Cricket.* Western Mountain, 1983.

Crile, George Washington (1864-1943), an American surgeon, made important contributions to the development of surgery, especially in the areas of shock, hemorrhage, and blood transfusion. He also pioneered the use of blood-pressure measurement in surgery and developed a nerve-block system of anesthesia. His books include *Diseases Peculiar to Civilized Man* (1934); *The Phenomena of Life* (1936); and *Intelligence, Power and Personality* (1941).

Crile was born in Chili, Ohio. He became professor of surgery at Western Reserve University (now Case Western Reserve University) in 1900. He founded the Cleveland Clinic Foundation in 1921.   Dale C. Smith

Crime is a term that refers to many types of misconduct forbidden by law. Murder—also called *homicide*—is a crime in all countries. In the United States, stealing a car is a crime. So is resisting arrest, possessing or selling illegal drugs, and using the mails to cheat someone. Other crimes include appearing nude on a public street and driving while under the influence of alcohol.

The list of acts considered crimes is constantly changing. For example, people in the United States no longer are charged with witchcraft, though many were accused of that crime in colonial Massachusetts. Today, it is becoming a serious crime to pollute the air and water. Pollution caused few problems and received little attention in colonial days. In England during the 1700's, it was not a crime for people to steal money entrusted to their care by an employer. Today, this type of theft, called embezzlement, is a crime.

From a legal standpoint, a crime is a violation of the *criminal law.* Such law deals with actions considered harmful to society. On the other hand, most harmful acts causing injury to another person are violations of the *civil law.* Some overlapping occurs in this classification. For example, murder and rape are committed against individuals, but the law considers them crimes because they threaten society. For this reason, a crime is regarded as an offense against the state.

Major crimes in the United States

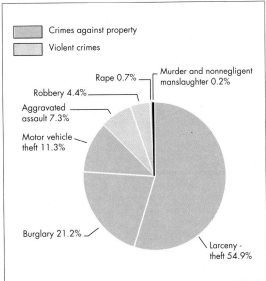

Crimes against property
Violent crimes

Rape 0.7%
Murder and nonnegligent manslaughter 0.2%
Robbery 4.4%
Aggravated assault 7.3%
Motor vehicle theft 11.3%
Burglary 21.2%
Larceny-theft 54.9%

Source: *Uniform Crime Reports for the United States: Crime in the United States, 1990,* FBI.

This chart shows the per cent of total major crimes in the United States by type of crime. The chart is based on the Crime Index compiled by the Federal Bureau of Investigation (FBI). The index covers seven crimes that the FBI considers serious offenses likely to be reported most accurately to the police. Murder and nonnegligent manslaughter, rape, robbery, and aggravated assault are *violent crimes.* Burglary, larceny-theft, and motor vehicle theft are *property crimes.*

An act is viewed as a crime if enough evidence exists to make a police officer, a prosecutor, or a judge believe that a violation of criminal law has taken place. However, the law does not consider accused people to be criminals unless a judge or jury finds them guilty. A criminal may be imprisoned or receive some other punishment, according to the laws of the community in which the crime was committed or the trial was held.

A person who commits any crime is called a criminal. But the term is sometimes used only for a person who commits such a serious crime as murder or robbery. At other times, the term refers only to habitual criminals.

The study of criminal behavior is called *criminology,* and experts in this field are called *criminologists.* Criminologists study crime and criminals for various reasons. They may try to determine where, when, and why different types of crime occur. They also seek the relationships between criminals and the victims, as well as the most effective ways to prevent crime. See **Criminology.**

Types of crimes

Crimes may be classified in various ways. For example, they sometimes are grouped according to the seriousness of the offense. For statistical purposes, many governments divide crimes into offenses against people, against property, and against public order or public morality. Some social scientists classify crimes according to the motives of the offenders. Such crimes might include economic crimes, political crimes, and crimes of passion. Other important kinds of crime include organized crime and white-collar crime.

Crimes are often divided between acts that most people would consider evil and acts that lawmakers decide should be regulated in the interest of the community. The first group includes such major crimes as arson, assault, burglary, kidnapping, larceny, murder, rape, and robbery. The second group of crimes includes violations of income tax laws, liquor-control regulations, pure food and drug laws, and traffic laws. Crimes in the first group are called *substantive offenses* and usually involve severe punishments. Most of these crimes have long been forbidden by the English *common law,* the source of criminal law codes in all states in the United States except Louisiana (see **Common law**). Offenses in the second group are called *regulatory offenses* and are generally punished by fines or notices to follow the court's orders.

Felonies and misdemeanors. Crimes are frequently classified according to their seriousness as *felonies* or *misdemeanors.* Generally, felonies are more serious than misdemeanors. Under federal and state criminal law systems, felonies are punishable by death, or by imprisonment for a year or more. A misdemeanor is punishable by a fine or by imprisonment for less than a year. Most people convicted of felonies serve their sentence in state or federal prisons. People convicted of misdemeanors serve their sentence in city or county jails or houses of correction.

The classification of crimes as felonies or misdemeanors is inexact. Not all courts draw the same distinction between felonies and misdemeanors. A felony in one state may be a misdemeanor in another.

Crimes against people or property. Crimes against people include assault, kidnapping, murder, and sexual attacks. Such crimes usually bring severe punishment. Crimes against property include arson, motor vehicle theft, burglary, embezzlement, forgery, fraud, larceny, and vandalism. In most cases, these crimes carry lighter penalties than do crimes against people.

Robbery is the crime most difficult to classify. The law generally considers robbery a crime against the person. Robbery involves taking property from a person by using force, such as a mugging or other strong-arm tactics.

Crimes against public order or morality include disorderly conduct, gambling, prostitution, public drunkenness, and *vagrancy* (having no permanent residence or visible means of support). These offenses generally involve lighter penalties than do crimes against people or property.

Criminologists question whether some offenses against public order or morality should be considered crimes. For example, many experts believe that habitual drunkenness is a medical problem and that the offender should be given medical help instead of being put in jail. There is also wide disagreement about whether certain practices hurt society and should be considered crimes. Such acts include gambling, marijuana use, and homosexuality between consenting adults.

Organized crime consists of large-scale activities by groups of gangsters or racketeers. Such groups are often called the *crime syndicate* or the *underworld.* Organized crime specializes in providing illegal goods and services. Its activities include gambling, prostitution, the illegal sale of drugs, and *loan-sharking* (lending money at extremely high rates of interest). Many of these activities are often called *victimless crimes* because both the buyer and the seller take part in them willingly.

Most activities of the crime syndicate are not reported to the police. People who use the illegal services try to avoid the police. When the crime syndicate invades a legitimate business or labor union, it uses terror, blackmail, and other methods to keep people from going to the police. Even when the illegal activities are discovered, prosecutors have difficulty convicting the gangsters because of the lack of reliable witnesses. In addition, the syndicate frequently tries to bribe witnesses or law officers and sometimes succeeds in doing so. The syndicate also furnishes bail money and lawyers for members who are arrested.

White-collar crime originally included only criminal acts committed by business and professional people while earning their living. The term referred to such crimes as stock market swindles and other kinds of fraud. Today, the term covers such acts as cheating in the payment of taxes—which may or may not be done in connection with one's business. It may apply to petty thefts by employees, as well as to million-dollar stock market swindles. It could also include a service station owner's charging for an automobile repair that was not made, or a physician's billing a patient for services that were not performed.

The increasing use of computers has created new opportunities for white-collar crime. Computer crimes are difficult to detect but easy to accomplish once a criminal learns the code or password to activate the system. Thus, automatic bank tellers increase the possibility of fraud or theft. Computer access by bank employees creates additional opportunities for embezzlement.

Many consumer protection laws are aimed at white-collar crime. These laws regulate business and professional activities to protect consumers. During the 1960's and early 1970's, consumer protection became one of the fastest growing fields of criminal law. In the United States, for example, the federal government developed new rules and penalties. The regulations were intended to control air and water pollution, to prevent fraudulent trade practices, and to alert people seeking loans about actual interest costs. See **Consumerism**.

Political crime became an increasingly serious criminal activity during the 1970's. It includes acts of terrorism against innocent people and assassinations of leading political figures throughout the world. Unlike many criminals who seek money or personal gain through crime, most terrorists and assassins commit crimes to show support for a political cause. Since the early 1970's, political crimes such as airplane hijackings, assassinations, bombings, and the taking of hostages have become more frequent. As a result, most governments have taken steps to guard against terrorists. For example, security at airports, embassies, and other potential targets has been increased, and specially trained law enforcement or military units have been formed.

The extent of crime

Crime is one of the world's oldest social problems. Almost every generation has felt itself threatened by increasing crime and violence. However, no country has yet developed completely reliable methods for measuring the volume and trend of crime.

Crime in the United States. The Federal Bureau of Investigation (FBI) serves as the main source of information about crime in the United States. The FBI has maintained national crime statistics only since 1930. Reporting procedures between 1930 and 1958 gave only a very inexact national estimate of crime. Since 1958, improved reporting methods have provided increasingly reliable figures. The FBI receives monthly and annual crime reports from law enforcement agencies throughout the country. It summarizes and publishes this information in semiannual reports and in its annual *Uniform Crime Reports for the United States.*

The FBI's Crime Index measures the amount and distribution of serious crime in the United States. The index covers seven crimes that the FBI considers serious of-

Crime rate in the United States

Rate per 100,000 population

Source: Federal Bureau of Investigation.

fenses likely to be reported most accurately to the police. Four of these offenses are classified as violent crimes—aggravated assault, forcible rape, murder and nonnegligent manslaughter, and robbery. The other three are crimes against property—burglary, larceny-theft, and motor vehicle theft.

FBI reports show that the U.S. crime rate per 100,000 population has gone up sharply since 1960. From 1960 to 1990, the crime rate for reported serious offenses rose more than 400 per cent. However, criminologists and police authorities find it difficult to determine how much of this increase actually occurred and how much resulted from improved crime-reporting procedures. In 1960, slightly more than $3\frac{1}{3}$ million serious crimes were reported in the United States. About $14\frac{1}{2}$ million serious crimes were reported in 1990. Crimes against property accounted for 87 per cent of the offenses reported in 1990. The remaining 13 per cent of the offenses reported in 1990 were for crimes of violence against the person.

Many people believe that most arrests are made for the same serious crimes covered by the FBI's crime index. But such crimes account for only about one-fifth of the arrests each year in the United States. Four offenses related to alcohol and drugs—driving under the influence, drug abuse, drunkenness, and liquor law violations—account for more than a third of all arrests.

Crime in other countries. Countries vary greatly in their definition of crime and in the reliability of their crime statistics. Conditions that affect the amount of crime also vary from one country to another. Such conditions include the proportion of people living in cities, the proportion of young and old people in the population, and the degree of conflict among various cultural, economic, and racial groups.

One basis of comparison is the homicide rate in various countries. Most murders are reported to the police, though their definition may vary. In 1988, the United States reported 8.3 homicides per 100,000 population.

Most frequent arrests in the United States*

Offense charged	Number of arrests	Rate of arrests per 100,000 population
Driving under the influence		
of liquor or narcotics	1,390,906	719
Larceny-theft	1,241,236	641
Drug abuse violations	869,155	449
Simple assault	801,425	414
Drunkenness	716,504	370
Disorderly conduct	579,674	300
Liquor law violations	552,039	285
Aggravated assault	376,917	195
Burglary	341,192	176
Fraud	279,776	145

*Data are not available for arrests for any traffic violations except driving under the influence.
Source: *Uniform Crime Reports for the United States: Crime in the United States, 1990,* FBI.

This rate was $1\frac{1}{2}$ times the rate of Canada, 4 times the rate of the United Kingdom, and 7 times the rate of Japan.

A comparison of the changing crime rates within a country proves more valuable than comparing the rates of two or more countries. Studies show that crime rates for both property crimes and violent crimes are rising in most countries. For example, from 1980 to 1988, the property crime rate in the United Kingdom increased about 30 per cent and the violent crime rate increased about 70 per cent. During this same period, the property crime rate in the United States went up 3 per cent and the violent crime rate went up 20 per cent. In Canada, the property crime rate increased about 30 per cent, but the violent crime rate decreased 7 per cent.

Comparisons of the crime rates of various nations indicate that increases in crime accompany increases in the rate of social change. The crime rate stays relatively stable in traditional societies where people believe their way of life will continue. Crime rates tend to rise in societies where rapid changes take place in where people live and what they do for a living—and in their hopes for their future well-being. Crime rates are particularly high in industrial nations that have large cities.

Unreported crime. Statistics about crime are based on complaints to the police, offenses observed by the police, and arrests of suspects. Much crime goes unreported. One national survey of 10,000 U.S. families has shown that family members were victims of major crimes in more than twice as many offenses as those covered by police statistics that year. Many other types of crimes also remain unreported, including offenses against businesses, organizations, and public agencies and against public order and morality.

The U.S. Bureau of the Census and the Bureau of Justice Statistics of the U.S. Department of Justice produce an annual survey called *Criminal Victimization in the United States.* This survey reveals that in the early 1990's, 61 per cent of all violent crime and 46 per cent of personal theft went unreported to the police.

The cost of crime to its victims is impossible to determine accurately. Any estimate based on existing data will probably underestimate the cost considerably. For example, a dishonest business scheme may cost consumers or investors millions of dollars, but no records are kept of such losses. Similarly, there is no way to determine the profits to the crime syndicate of gambling, loan-sharking, narcotics sales, and prostitution.

The cost of crime prevention and control measures is also difficult to determine. Expenditures for law enforcement and criminal justice agencies in the United States total about $30 billion annually. However, these agencies also deal with many noncriminal matters, such as traffic control. About 40 per cent of police costs can be directly charged to crime control. In addition, most courts handle both criminal and civil cases.

Causes of crime

People commit crimes for various reasons. For example, many people steal things they could not obtain otherwise. Others, such as drug addicts, steal to get money to buy narcotics or other things they need. Some shoplifters steal for excitement, but others do so because they are poor. Many automobile thieves take cars for

joy-riding, but others strip down the stolen autos and sell them. Many embezzlers take money from their employers to meet a personal emergency, intending to return the money.

The motives also vary in crimes of violence. A robber may kill the victim to avoid detection. Some gangsters torture people to obtain money. A man may beat his wife in a fit of rage during a quarrel.

Biological and psychological explanations. Many studies have sought to explain crime. Most of them compare habitual criminals with people who have not been convicted of crimes to try to find important differences between the two groups.

Since the late 1800's, for example, researchers trained in the biological sciences have searched for physical differences. Such studies involve differences in body type, the pattern of brain waves, and the formation of genes. None of these studies has proved that criminals have any physical traits that make them different from other people.

Research by psychiatrists and psychologists stresses personality differences resulting from experiences in childhood or later. This research shows that many people who became criminals were neglected by their parents or were given harsh or uncertain discipline. Such treatment left them insecure and demanding in their relations with others. Their own wants made them ignore the needs or rights of others. But researchers have had difficulty making a direct connection between emotional needs and crime because many people with emotional problems find acceptable ways of solving them.

Social conditions and crime. Sociologists have conducted crime studies that focus on the neighborhood and community rather than on the individual. Some of these studies deal with how a person becomes committed to a career of crime, and others try to explain differences in crime rates.

The highest crime rates occur in the most deprived sections of large cities. These are the areas where it is most difficult to train children to become law-abiding citizens. Such areas have the highest rate of broken homes. Even in many homes where both parents are present, emotional conflicts and health and financial problems affect family life. Slum areas usually have the poorest schools and the highest unemployment rates. These neighborhoods have much run-down, overcrowded housing and poor recreation facilities.

For many young people, the excitement of the streets provides the principal escape from boredom and seemingly unsolvable problems. These streets are also the scene of much vice and crime—gambling, prostitution, narcotics use and sale, public drunkenness, and acts of violence. Law enforcement in the inner city is difficult, partly because too few police officers patrol the neighborhoods. In addition, many of the people fear the police and refuse to cooperate with them.

Most residents of the high-crime slum areas of many large cities are blacks or members of other minority groups. As a result, the crime rate for such minorities is higher than that for the white majority. Nonwhites are also more likely to become the victims of crimes.

Most crimes in the United States are committed by boys and young men. People under 18 years of age account for 43 per cent of the arrests for motor vehicle

Arrests for major crimes by age in the U.S.

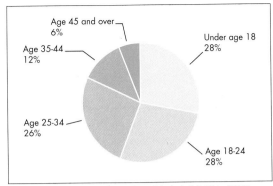

Age 45 and over
6%

Age 35-44
12%

Age 25-34
26%

Age 18-24
28%

Under age 18
28%

Source: *Uniform Crime Reports for the United States: Crime in the United States, 1990,* FBI.

theft; 33 per cent for burglary; 30 per cent for larceny-theft; and 24 per cent for robbery. This same group makes up about 15 per cent of all people arrested for murder, rape, and aggravated assault.

There are several reasons why young people commit most crimes. As people become older and settled in their jobs and families, they acquire a stake in society that they would not care to risk for momentary gain. On the other hand, young people have fewer job opportunities. The unskilled jobs available seem dull when compared to the quick and exciting returns from theft. Young people are also more willing to risk arrest because they have less stake in things as they are.

About 80 per cent of the people arrested for crimes are males. In 1989, men were arrested most often for driving under the influence of alcohol, which accounted for 13 per cent of all male arrests. Women were arrested most often for larceny-theft. This crime accounted for 19 per cent of all female arrests in 1989 and 77 per cent of female arrests for serious crimes reported in the FBI's Crime Index.

Many violent crimes are committed by people who are acquainted with their victims. In over half of all murders, for example, the killer and the victim knew each other. In fact, about a sixth of all murders are committed by a member of the victim's family. In numerous cases, because so many murderers know their victims, the police have a relatively easy time identifying the killer. As a result, the arrest and conviction rate for murders is high. Police have a much harder time identifying robbers and burglars, few of whom know the victims. Handguns were used in about 50 per cent of the murders reported during the early 1990's.

Crime prevention

For hundreds of years, the criminal law has been built around the idea that wrongdoers must be punished for their crimes. The most basic argument for punishment is that it preserves law and order and respect for authority. From this point of view, punishment does two things. It upholds the law, and it prevents others from thinking they can get away with doing the same thing without punishment. Punishment is based on the idea that many people have a barely controlled desire to act in forbidden ways.

Many criminologists stress the need for improving

the performance of criminal justice agencies—the police, the courts, and correctional institutions. For example, they point out that better educated, equipped, and coordinated police forces are more effective in controlling crime.

One of the best ways to reduce crime is to reform or rehabilitate habitual criminals. The fundamental problem is not the first offender or the petty thief but the repeated offender who commits increasingly serious crimes. According to criminologists, crime would decrease greatly if all such offenders could be turned away from wrongdoing. But United States prisons have had little success in rehabilitating inmates. About two-thirds of the people arrested in any year have a previous criminal record.

Rehabilitation of criminals could probably be improved greatly if experts could provide the right kind of program for different types of offenders. Criminals vary widely in the kinds of crimes they commit, their emotional problems, and their social and economic backgrounds. Not all offenders can be helped by the same course of treatment. Many require the aid of physicians, psychiatrists, or psychologists. Others respond well to educational or vocational training. In the late 1980's, there were about 850,000 criminals in U.S. city, county, state, and federal correctional institutions, and about 300,000 more were out on parole. Society spent about $6 billion to operate prisons and related institutions yearly, but only a small fraction of this sum goes to provide treatment. Nearly all the funds are used to feed and clothe prisoners and to keep them under control.

Since the late 1970's, however, there has been a trend toward punishment rather than rehabilitation of offenders. Prison sentences are longer. Capital punishments have been used more frequently since the U.S. Supreme Court lifted a death penalty ban in 1976. Nevertheless, crime prevention should aim to prevent people from becoming criminals in the first place. Such a goal probably would benefit from reform programs in urban slums. These programs would include improved housing, schools, and recreation programs and increased job opportunities.

There are many other ways to reduce crime. People can be educated or persuaded to take greater precautions against crime. They can be taught, for example, how to protect their homes from burglary. Automobile thefts would drop sharply if drivers removed their keys and locked their cars when leaving them. Better lighting helps discourage purse-snatchings and other robberies on city streets and in parks. Many experts believe that strict gun-licensing laws would greatly reduce crime.

George T. Felkenes

Related articles. See the *World Book* article on Criminology. See also the following articles:

Crimes

Arson	Counterfeiting	Homicide
Assassination	Desertion	Juvenile delin-
Assault and battery	Embezzlement	quency
Bigamy	Euthanasia	Kidnapping
Blackmail	Extortion	Larceny
Breach of the peace	Felony	Libel
Bribery	Forgery	Lynching
Burglary	Fraud	Manslaughter
Conspiracy	Gambling	Mayhem
Contempt	Hijacking	Misdemeanor

Murder	Robbery	Terrorism
Perjury	Sabotage	Treason
Polygamy	Shoplifting	Trespass
Rape	Slander	Vagrancy
Riot	Smuggling	Vandalism

Law enforcement procedures

Arrest	False imprisonment	Lie detector
Bail	Fingerprinting	Police
Bertillon system	Footprinting	Search warrant
Crime laboratory	Gun control	Voiceprint
Criminal justice system	Handcuffs	Warrant
	Indictment	Wiretapping
DNA fingerprinting	Inquest	

Punishment

Capital punishment	Forfeiture	Prison
	Garrote	Probation
Chain gang	Gas chamber	Rack
Deportation	Guillotine	Sentence
Ducking stool	Hanging	Stocks
Electrocution	Parole	Torture
Exile	Pillory	Whipping post
Fine		

Other related articles

Amnesty	Gang	Reprieve
Bandit	Mafia	Vendetta
Feud	Pardon	

See also *Crime and law enforcement* in the Research Guide/Index, Volume 22, for a *Reading and Study Guide.*

Additional resources

Currie, Elliott. *Confronting Crime: An American Challenge.* Pantheon, 1985.

LeVert, Marianne. *Crime in America.* Facts on File, 1991. Also suitable for younger readers.

Meltzer, Milton. *Crime in America.* Morrow, 1990. Also suitable for younger readers.

Pepinsky, Harold E., and Jesilow, Paul. *Myths That Cause Crime.* Rev. ed. Seven Locks, 1985.

Crime laboratory is a laboratory where experts analyze, identify, and interpret evidence connected with a crime. Glass splinters or a gun found on a suspect may be matched with broken glass or a bullet taken from the scene of a crime. The pattern of bloodstains near a body may indicate how a murder was committed. Other evidence includes documents, drugs and narcotics, fibers, fingerprints, hair, and soil.

The technique of using scientific methods in solving crimes is called *forensic science.* A person who examines evidence in a crime laboratory is known as a *forensic scientist* or a *criminalist.* The word *forensic* comes from a Latin word that means *forum* or *court of law.*

Forensic science includes such specialties as *forensic psychiatry, forensic toxicology,* and *forensic pathology.* A forensic psychiatrist examines persons suspected of a crime to determine if they are legally sane. A forensic toxicologist identifies drugs and poisons in body tissues and determines their effects. A forensic pathologist performs autopsies on victims to learn the cause of death.

How evidence is handled

Criminalists and other investigators protect all evidence according to a security process called a *chain of evidence.* This process involves keeping a record of each person who handles the evidence. The chain begins at the crime scene and ends when the evidence is presented in court. If any evidence is left unguarded, the

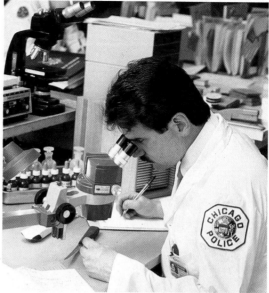

WORLD BOOK photo by Ralph Brunke

A crime laboratory investigates bloodstains, weapons, and other evidence. Experts in the laboratory use chemical tests, microscopic examinations, and a variety of special procedures.

judge may disallow its admission in court.

There are three steps in handling evidence: (1) collecting the evidence at the crime scene, (2) analyzing the evidence in the laboratory, and (3) presenting the evidence in court.

Collecting the evidence. In most crimes, the evidence is collected either by police officers or by technicians associated with a crime laboratory. But in such serious crimes as bank robbery and murder, criminalists often go to the scene of a crime. They gather the evidence and, if possible, try to reconstruct the crime.

After a crime is discovered, the police *freeze* the scene. They permit nothing to be disturbed and keep unauthorized people out of the area.

Police investigators follow certain procedures to make sure they miss no evidence. First, they photograph the scene from several angles to show the location of the evidence. Then a police artist or an investigator draws a *crime scene sketch,* which records the exact position of each piece of evidence according to precise measurement. The evidence is then collected.

Criminalists and other investigators use several methods to collect evidence. One of the most important methods is used to reveal fingerprints. First, the experts *dust* (brush) a surface with powder. The powder sticks to the oils left on a surface by one or more fingers. The print is photographed and then lifted from the surface with clear adhesive tape. The tape transfers the print to a piece of paper, which forms a permanent record. Fingerprints in blood, grease, or other visible material are photographed directly. See **Fingerprinting.**

To preserve other marks, such as footprints and tire tracks, criminalists first photograph them. Then a cast of the mark is made with plaster of Paris.

Criminalists sometimes use special instruments to collect evidence. For example, a plastic container called a *vacuum trap* fits on the end of a vacuum cleaner hose and gathers small particles called *trace evidence.* Trace evidence includes fibers, hairs, sand, wood splinters, and particles of glass and paint. Larger evidence, such as bullets and firearms, is also collected. Criminalists label each piece of evidence.

Analyzing the evidence. A crime laboratory uses a number of techniques to identify and analyze evidence. These techniques may involve the use of special instruments or chemical treatments.

Most crime laboratories have several types of microscopes. A *bullet comparison microscope* is used to compare two or more bullets and to examine tool marks and determine their source (see **Ballistics** [Forensic ballistics]). Criminalists identify minerals, drugs, and narcotics with a *polarizing microscope,* which enlarges the crystal forms of each material. A *stereoscopic binocular microscope* helps sort trace evidence and is used to examine handwriting, typewriting, and samples of paint.

Criminalists use chemicals to identify certain damaged evidence. For example, they use acid to restore partially erased serial numbers on stolen property, such as automobiles and bicycles. They also use chemicals to determine the cause of an explosion or a fire. These chemicals detect traces of flammable substances, including gasoline and kerosene, in the burned remains. Chemicals also help identify samples of blood.

Since the mid-1900's, many new instruments have been developed for use in crime laboratories. These instruments include the *spectrophotometer* and the *gas chromatograph.* A spectrophotometer records light and heat rays that the human eye cannot detect. This instrument shows the pattern of the rays when they strike an object. Criminalists can detect forgeries or illegal erasures on documents with a spectrophotometer by comparing the pattern of rays in ink. A gas chromatograph separates the various components of a substance. The amount of each component is then measured. Criminalists use a gas chromatograph to determine the amount of alcohol in a person's blood. See **Chromatography.**

One of the newest techniques of analyzing evidence is called *DNA fingerprinting.* In this method, investigators identify the persons to whom such biological substances as blood, hair, or semen belong by analyzing the genetic material that the substances contain. The genetic material, called *deoxyribonucleic acid* (DNA), is present in most cells. See **DNA fingerprinting.**

Presenting the evidence. Criminalists are responsible for accurately explaining the significance of evidence. They usually present their findings in written reports and may also testify in court. They are called *expert witnesses* because of their training and experience. Courts allow most witnesses to present only facts, but expert witnesses can give opinions based on evidence. They serve chiefly as witnesses for the prosecution.

Careers in forensic science

A person needs at least a B.A. degree in chemistry, criminalistics, or a related science to work in a crime laboratory in the United States. Some colleges and universities offer graduate programs in forensic science that lead to an M.S. or a Ph.D. degree. A student of forensic science takes many chemistry courses and survey courses in such areas as anatomy, botany, geology, physics, and physiology. Most criminalists in the United States work for agencies of the federal, state, or local government. A few are employed as private consultants for individuals, companies, or organizations.

A professional organization called the American Academy of Forensic Science promotes research and training in the forensic sciences. The academy issues a quarterly publication, the *Journal of Forensic Sciences,* which reports on original research conducted in all specialty areas of the profession.

History

One of the first crime laboratories was established in 1910 in Lyon, France, by Edmond Locard, a physician.

WORLD BOOK photo by Ralph Brunke

A laser beam reveals fingerprints on a handgun. A laboratory technician then photographs the prints.

WORLD BOOK photo by Ralph Brunke

A firearms expert looks for identifying marks on the bullets and weapons connected with a crime.

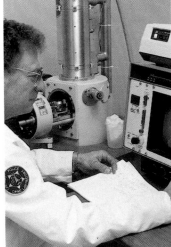

WORLD BOOK photo by Ralph Brunke

An electron microscope helps in examining *trace evidence,* which consists of hair and other small particles.

Locard helped work out scientific methods to investigate crimes. Alphonse Bertillon, a French statistician, developed a method of identifying persons according to their body measurements. This method, called the *Bertillon system,* was first used in Paris in 1879 and soon spread throughout the world. See **Bertillon system.**

Sir William J. Herschel, a British colonial administrator in India during the late 1800's, was probably the first person to devise a workable method of fingerprint identification. Historians credit Sir Francis Galton, a British scientist, with developing Herschel's methods into a modern system of fingerprint identification in the 1880's. By the late 1910's, fingerprinting had replaced the Bertillon system almost entirely as a more accurate method of identification. In the United States, the Federal Bureau of Investigation (FBI) established a fingerprint file in 1930.

Hans Gross, an Austrian judge, probably invented the word *criminalistics.* In his book *Criminal Investigation* (1893), Gross declared that criminalistics was a science that should use a systematic approach to investigate crimes and analyze evidence.

The first U.S. crime laboratory was set up in Los Angeles in 1923. Today, the nation has about 250 crime laboratories. The FBI crime laboratory, organized in 1932, is one of the finest in the world (see **Federal Bureau of Investigation**). FBI experts examine about 900,000 pieces of evidence yearly. Some crime laboratories examine only one type of evidence. For example, the U.S. Postal Inspector's Department Laboratory examines documents associated with such crimes as mail theft and forgery of money orders.   John I. Thornton

See also **DNA fingerprinting; Footprinting; Voiceprint.**

Crimea, *kry MEE uh,* a region of Ukraine, is a peninsula that juts from the southern part of Ukraine into the Black Sea and the Sea of Azov. It covers about 10,400 square miles (27,000 square kilometers) and is joined to the mainland by the narrow Isthmus of Perekop. The population of the Crimea is about 2,309,000. The capital is Simferopol. Other cities include Kerch, Sevastopol, historically important Balaklava, and Yalta, which served as the scene of the historic conference of Allied leaders during World War II (1939-1945).

The Crimea rises gradually from coastal plains to the low Crimean Mountains along the southern coast. The grassy plains furnish pasture for sheep and horses.

Tass from Sovfoto

The Crimean coast has many beautiful resort towns. Yalta, *above,* lies on the southern coast near the Crimean Mountains.

Crimea

★ Regional capital
• Other city or town
── Railroad
── Major road
✕ Crimean War battlefield

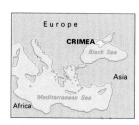

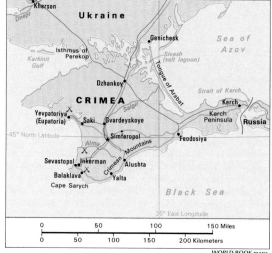

WORLD BOOK maps

Grapes from the vineyards are used to produce wine. Grains flourish in the northern lowlands of the peninsula. Important deposits of iron, marble, and limestone have been found in the Crimea, and salt is dried along the coasts. The chief industries are shipbuilding, mining, and fishing. Resorts and health centers line the coasts.

The Crimea was one of the strongholds of opposition to the Communist government after the Russian Revolution of 1917. In 1921, the Crimea became an autonomous republic within the Russian republic of the Soviet Union.

During World War II, German troops occupied the peninsula from 1941 to 1944. In 1944, Soviet authorities forcibly deported about 250,000 Turkic-speaking people called Tatars from Crimea to Siberia and Central Asia. The Crimean Tatars were falsely accused of collaborating with the Germans. In 1967, these charges were dropped, but the Tatars were prevented from returning to the Crimea in large numbers. The Crimea's autonomous status was removed in 1945, and it became a province of Russia. In 1954, the Soviet Union made the Crimea part of the Soviet republic of Ukraine. In 1991, following an upheaval in the Soviet Union, Ukraine declared itself an independent nation. It became part of the Commonwealth of Independent States, a loose association of former Soviet republics. In 1992, Russia declared the 1954 decision to give Crimea to Ukraine unconstitutional. However, Ukraine opposed this declaration.   Jaroslaw Bilocerkowycz

See also **Crimean War; Sevastopol; Tatars; Yalta.**

Crimean War, *kry MEE uhn* (1853-1856), was fought between Russian forces and the allied armies of Britain, France, the Ottoman Empire (now Turkey), and Sardinia. The war's name comes from the Crimean Peninsula, an area of present-day Ukraine where much of the fighting took place.

Causes of the war included religious, commercial, and strategic rivalries among Britain, France, and Russia in the Near East and political rivalries between France and Russia in Europe. A chief objection of the allies was Russia's expansion in the Black Sea region. Major battles in the Crimean Peninsula occurred along the River Alma and around the towns of Sevastopol, Balaklava, Inkerman, and Yevpatoriya (also spelled Eupatoria). Russia's lack of supplies, railroads, and reinforcements led to its defeat. The Treaty of Paris, signed on March 30, 1856, ended the war. It forced Russia to give up some territory it had taken from the Ottoman Empire and forbade warships on and fortifications around the Black Sea.

The Crimean War was the first war to be covered by newspaper reporters and photographers at the front. The English poet Lord Tennyson wrote a famous poem, "The Charge of the Light Brigade," about the Battle of Balaklava. The activities of Florence Nightingale, an English nurse, later helped bring about improvements in nursing and hospital care.　　A. P. Saab

See also **Balaklava, Battle of; Nightingale, Florence.**

Criminal justice system is the system used to enforce the laws established by society. It attempts to protect people from assault, murder, rape, robbery, and other crimes. It also tries to safeguard them from being falsely arrested, imprisoned, or fined.

Every nation has its own system of criminal justice. This article discusses how criminal laws are enforced in the United States. The U.S. system is divided into three areas: (1) the police, (2) the courts, and (3) the correctional system.

The police

The police have the primary responsibility for enforcing the nation's laws. Police officers work to protect the people and property of each community. They also regulate public behavior and act as public servants in ways unrelated to crime. For example, police officers direct traffic, assist motorists, and find lost children.

The main job of a police force is to try to prevent crime. To do this, police officers patrol the streets and parks of a community on foot, in automobiles, on motorcycles, or on horses.

After a crime has been committed, the police question the victim and any witnesses. They also gather such evidence as fingerprints, weapons, and stolen property. If the police have reason to believe that a certain person committed the crime, they arrest him or her. They often apprehend a suspect in the act of committing a crime or soon after the crime takes place. In some cases, police officers are required to obtain a court order called a *warrant* before they arrest a suspect.

Police detectives investigate crimes. These officers work in specialized fields that deal with such crimes as murder, robbery, or the illegal sale of drugs. Various technical units of a police department assist the detectives in investigations. These units examine all evidence that has been gathered. The reports of the detectives and the technical units are later used to support testimony given in court.

The police follow certain procedures when they investigate crimes, and when they arrest suspects and put them in jail. These procedures are governed by strict laws that protect the suspect. For example, the *Miranda rule* requires that before questioning a suspect, the police must inform the individual of his or her rights, including the right to remain silent (see **Miranda v. Arizona**). A person accused of a crime also has the right to have his or her attorney present during questioning.

The courts

Criminal courts decide the legal guilt or innocence of people accused of violating the law. The courts also determine the punishment for those who are convicted.

Pretrial procedures. In most cases, the suspect is brought to court for a hearing within 24 hours after being arrested. At this hearing, called *arraignment,* a judge reads the charges against the defendant. The judge also reads the person his or her rights concerning a fair trial. The most important right of any defendant is the right to be considered innocent until proved guilty "beyond a reasonable doubt." If the defendant pleads guilty to the charges, the judge may sentence the person immediately. If the individual pleads not guilty, the case goes to trial. The judge appoints a defense attorney to handle the defendant's case if the accused person cannot afford a lawyer.

The judge decides whether to keep the defendant in jail until the trial or to release the person on bail. The defendant or another person puts up bail to guarantee that the accused will return to the court to stand trial. A defendant who cannot put up bail must stay in jail until the trial. The courts cannot require bail so high that no one can furnish it. But the judge may deny bail to a person considered likely not to return for trial. Some states also prohibit bail for individuals who are accused of such serious crimes as espionage and murder.

Cases involving less serious crimes, such as disorderly conduct or driving without a license, may be completed in a single court session. In these cases, the judge hears the testimony, decides the guilt or innocence of the defendant, and sentences the guilty.

Cases of murder, kidnapping, or other especially serious crimes may be presented to a *grand jury.* This panel, which consists of 16 to 23 citizens in most states, decides if the evidence against the defendant justifies bringing the case to trial. The purpose of the grand jury is to protect the defendant from being accused of a crime with insufficient evidence.

Many cases are settled by *plea bargaining.* In this procedure, the accused agrees to plead guilty in exchange for being charged with a less serious crime or being promised a shorter prison sentence. About 90 per cent of all defendants plead guilty, most of them through plea bargaining.

The trial. When a criminal case goes to trial, the defendant chooses to have it heard either by a jury or by the judge alone. In most states, a trial jury consists of 12 citizens. However, the juries in some states may have as few as 6 members. The jury or judge hears the evidence for and against the defendant and then reaches a verdict. If the individual is found guilty, the judge pronounces sentence. If the defendant is found not guilty, he or she is released.

In most cases, the judge determines the sentence for a defendant convicted of a crime. The judge imposes punishment that he or she feels will best serve both the offender and society. Laws may provide a maximum and a minimum sentence according to the crime involved. In some cases, the recommendation of the jury determines the sentence that may be given to the offender.

The judge may put a convicted offender on probation to protect the individual from the harmful effects of being imprisoned with experienced criminals. A law-breaker who is on probation remains free but must follow certain rules. A probation officer assigned by the court supervises the individual's conduct. A probationer who violates any of the rules of his or her probation may be sent to prison. Some judges require offenders to repay their victims, either with money or by working for them without pay.

The correctional system

The correctional system, often called simply *corrections,* carries out the sentences given by the courts to convicted offenders. This system includes probation, imprisonment, and parole.

Criminologists—and people in general—disagree about the role of the correctional system. Some people believe the purpose of imprisoning offenders is to prevent them from committing more crimes. But this prevention may be only a temporary solution unless a criminal is imprisoned for life. Other individuals think the correctional system should punish convicted offenders so that a sense of justice in society can be maintained.

Many criminologists believe corrections should help criminals become law-abiding citizens. This goal is called *rehabilitation.* Prison programs rehabilitate inmates through vocational training and psychological counseling. These programs also help find jobs for men and women on probation or parole.

Some people feel the correctional system should serve as a *deterrent* to crime—that is, it should discourage people from breaking the law. The term *general deterrence* refers to the process of making an example of lawbreakers in order to dissuade other people from committing crimes. In *individual deterrence,* the experience of punishment convinces an offender to avoid breaking the law again.

Problems in criminal justice

Problems of the police. Traditionally, routine patrolling in police cars has been considered the most effective method of crime prevention. But studies conducted during the 1970's showed that such patrolling may have little effect on crime. Some police departments, in an effort to improve the effectiveness of their patrols, have assigned more officers to walk neighborhood beats. Foot patrols bring police officers into closer contact with a neighborhood and its people than patrolling in cars. This contact enables the police and neighborhood residents to become acquainted more easily and thus work better together in an effort to reduce crime.

Many police officials believe that efforts to convict criminals are hindered by the rules governing the investigation of crimes and the arrest of suspects. However, many other people insist that such rules are necessary to protect the rights of every person. The majority of police officials also are convinced that stricter gun controls would reduce crime (see **Gun control**).

Problems in the courts. A person accused of a crime has the right to be tried as soon as possible after being arrested. But in many cities, an overload of cases has caused serious delays in bringing defendants to trial. Defendants may have to wait more than a year before their cases go to court. Some people feel that inefficiency in the court system causes unnecessary delays. Others believe many cases that go to court could be settled by plea bargaining.

Plea bargaining itself has led to controversy. Critics of this practice believe it jeopardizes the defendant's right to be considered innocent until proved guilty. Others feel that plea bargaining enables some criminals to be punished less severely than they deserve. Supporters of plea bargaining argue that it helps relieve the courts of their overload of cases.

Sentencing may lead to still other problems because different judges often give different sentences to persons convicted of similar crimes. Each judge has his or her own belief about the most appropriate sentence in a given case. Many criminologists feel that differences in sentences imposed for similar crimes are unjust and also add to the problem of unrest in prisons. These experts believe specific, *fixed* sentences for particular crimes would be fairer. According to other criminologists, each defendant has special problems that should affect the sentence imposed by the judge.

Some communities have developed programs of *pretrial intervention.* Such programs offer some defendants counseling, vocational training, and a job before their cases go to trial. Many offenders have been rehabilitated, and the courts have then dismissed the charges against them. Pretrial intervention helps reduce the overload of cases in the courts and enables defendants to avoid prosecution and imprisonment.

Problems in the correctional system. Studies show that the correctional system has had little success. Many convicts return to crime after serving their sentences, and the threat of punishment has not prevented others from breaking the law. Probation and parole officers are overloaded with cases and cannot properly help or supervise all the people assigned to them. Many jails and prisons are severely overcrowded, and riots, beatings, and killings occur frequently. Most of the problems in the correctional system result from a lack of funds and from inadequate planning.

Some prisons allow certain inmates with favorable records to spend periods of time, called *furloughs,* at home or elsewhere with their families. Many criminologists favor *work-release programs,* which allow inmates to hold a job outside the prison and return to custody at night. Both these types of programs help prevent a person's life from being totally disrupted by imprisonment. Some criminologists believe such programs help rehabilitate offenders and so reduce the chance that they will return to crime after being released. Some prisoners are assigned to *halfway houses* or *community correctional centers* before their release. Counselors in these institutions help inmates readjust to life in the community.   James O. Finckenauer

Related articles in *World Book* include:

Arrest	Crime	Escobedo v. Illinois
Bail	Criminology	nois
Court	Due process of law	Evidence

Indictment	Parole	Sentence
Judge	Plea bargaining	Supreme Court of
Jury	Police	the United States
Juvenile	Prison	(Civil rights)
delinquency	Probation	Trial
Law enforcement	Reformatory	Warrant
Pardon		

Criminology is the scientific study of crime, criminals, criminal behavior, and the criminal justice system. Criminologists conduct research that examines factors related to crime. They also study individuals to learn how and why people become criminals. Most research in criminology involves such related fields as sociology, psychology, and psychiatry.

Criminology helps provide an understanding of the nature of crime. The results of criminological research help guide community leaders and law enforcement officials in crime prevention. Criminologists also help determine the best methods of treating offenders.

In the United States, criminology is taught chiefly in departments of criminology and criminal justice of colleges and universities. This instruction emphasizes social and environmental causes of crime. In Europe, criminology is generally taught in law or medical schools. European schools have traditionally emphasized the relationship of biological characteristics to criminal behavior. But today, social science research plays an increasingly important role in European criminology.

What criminologists study

Criminologists devote much research to personal and other factors that may cause crime. Most criminological research examines environmental conditions associated with crimes. Some studies concentrate on the connection between crime and such biological factors as brain structure and chemical imbalances. Others emphasize the role that people's emotions and motives play in criminal behavior.

Sociological theories and methods serve as the basis for most studies of environmental causes of crime. Many criminologists investigate the relationship between crime and other social problems, including poverty, poor housing, and overcrowding. Some study the ways in which individuals learn criminal behavior through association with people—including criminals—who have little regard for the law.

Criminologists also study *penology,* the science of the punishment and treatment of offenders. During the early 1900's, penologists began to stress *rehabilitation,* the treatment of criminals with the goal of restoring them to useful lives. However, studies during the 1970's showed that rehabilitation had little success. Today, criminologists recommend making punishment more certain than ever, bringing people to trial quickly, imposing fair and uniform sentences, and providing prisons that are more humane.

Most criminologists do not consider criminal investigation techniques as a part of criminology. People who analyze evidence and do other investigative police work are called *criminalists.* See **Crime laboratory.**

Methods of criminology

Criminologists use a wide variety of research techniques. The two most important methods of criminology

research are *statistical studies* and *case studies.*

Statistical studies help criminologists to formulate and test their theories. These experts use statistics to study the crime rate and the characteristics of criminals.

Crime statistics help criminologists find relationships between crime rates and certain physical or social conditions. For example, such studies may show that the crime rate increases when poverty and unemployment rise. Criminologists generally use statistics compiled by government agencies.

Criminologists also use statistics to learn about personality traits or social conditions that are more common among criminals than other people. Researchers usually compare a group of criminals with a group of noncriminals who are similar to the lawbreakers in most ways. Differences between the two groups can be measured in this manner. Any personality trait or social condition that occurs more frequently among criminals may be one of many causes of criminal behavior.

Case studies. In a case study, a criminologist examines all the personality traits and social conditions that affect one criminal. The researcher studies the person's family history, environment, physical condition, psychological state, and many other characteristics. All these details help determine how certain conditions produce criminal behavior in an individual. Some case studies are conducted on certain groups of criminals, such as rapists or juvenile gangs. A criminologist may use the results of a case history to work out a theory about the development of criminal behavior.

History

Criminology began to develop as a distinct area of study during the 1700's. In 1764, an Italian economist named Cesare Bonesana, Marchese di Beccaria, wrote *On Crimes and Punishments.* This book became the foundation of the *classical school* of criminology.

Beccaria and his followers protested the severe punishments that were common for criminals at that time. They argued that the only purpose of punishment should be to prevent future crime. Beccaria assumed that criminals had free will and that pleasure and pain

WORLD BOOK photo by Ralph Brunke

A criminologist interviews a criminal as part of a case study. Interviews help criminologists learn about personality traits and social conditions that may cause criminal behavior.

determined their actions. He believed crime could be prevented by the certainty and speed of punishment, rather than its severity. According to Beccaria, everyone who violated a specific law should receive the same punishment, regardless of age, sex, wealth, or social position. In modified form, the principles of the classical school are the basis of criminal law today in the United States, Canada, and many other nations.

The *positive school* of criminology, also known as the *Italian school,* developed during the late 1800's. In general, this school shifted the emphasis of criminology from crime itself to the study of criminals and the possible causes of their actions. The positivists believed criminal behavior resulted from conditions beyond the criminal's control. Cesare Lombroso, an Italian physician, was the most important leader of the positive school. He studied many criminals and concluded that certain physical traits made them different from other people. His ideas have been proved false, but his scientific approach to crime laid the basis for modern criminology.

During the 1900's, criminologists have proposed a wide variety of theories about crime. Edwin H. Sutherland, an American criminologist, developed the *theory of differential association.* It states that all criminal behavior is learned through association with criminals or people with unfavorable attitudes toward the law. Other criminologists believe the structure of society leads some people to choose criminal methods to achieve such socially approved goals as wealth and status. Still others argue that society produces crime, and so crime can be reduced or eliminated only by changing the organization of society.

Careers

Most criminologists have university training in criminal justice, criminology, sociology, psychology, psychiatry, or related areas. Requirements vary for a career, but most criminologists have a master's or doctor's degree. Many of these experts conduct research and teach criminology at universities and colleges.

Many social workers are employed in the general area of criminology. Parole and probation officers must have a knowledge of criminology. Personnel trained in criminology also work in crime prevention programs and in the treatment of offenders. Lawyers, judges, and prison superintendents also should have some knowledge of criminology.

In the United States, the major professional organization for criminologists is the American Society of Criminology, which was founded in 1941. The society issues a quarterly publication called *Criminology: An Interdisciplinary Journal.*   Charles F. Wellford

See also **Crime; Juvenile delinquency; Prison.**

Criticism is the analysis and judgment of works of art. It tries to interpret and to evaluate such works and to examine the principles by which they may be understood. Criticism attempts to promote high standards among artists and to encourage the appreciation of art. It also helps society remain aware of the value of both past and present works of art.

Criticism plays an important part in every art form. This article emphasizes literary criticism.

Kinds of literary criticism. Criticism can be divided into four basic types. They differ according to which as-

pect of art the critic chooses to emphasize. *Formal criticism* examines the forms or structures of works of art. It may also compare a work with others of its *genre* (kind), such as other tragic plays or other sonnets. Formal criticism is sometimes *intrinsic*—that is, it may seek to treat each work of art as complete in itself. *Rhetorical criticism* analyzes the means by which a work of art affects an audience. It focuses on style and on general principles of psychology. *Expressive criticism* regards works as expressing the ideas or feelings of the artist. It examines the artist's background and conscious or unconscious motives. *Mimetic criticism* views art as an imitation of the world. It analyzes the ways that artists show reality, and their thoughts about it.

The four types of criticism can also be combined. For example, a critic who looks at the form of a work might also study the way this form affects an audience.

History of literary criticism. The ancient Greek philosopher Plato was the first known literary critic. He accused poetry of imitating the mere appearance of things. Aristotle, his pupil, defended epic poetry and tragic drama. In his *Poetics,* Aristotle said that poetry is an instructive imitation, not of things but of actions. Other essays on criticism tended to be rhetorical handbooks that taught writers how to achieve certain effects. They included *Art of Poetry* by the Roman poet Horace and *On the Sublime* by the Greek writer Longinus.

During the late 1500's, such critics as the English poet Sir Philip Sidney praised literature as the image of an ideal world. During the 1600's and 1700's, critics turned their attention to defining the rules by which they thought works should be written and judged. The three most important English critics during this period were John Dryden, Samuel Johnson, and Alexander Pope.

At the end of the 1700's, critics in Germany and England began to regard literature as an expression of the author's imagination. These critics, called romantics, compared the forms of poems to those of living creatures, each with its own organic unity. Johann Wolfgang von Goethe, Friedrich Schiller, and the brothers August and Friedrich Schlegel were important German romantic critics. The greatest of the English romantic critics were Samuel Taylor Coleridge and William Hazlitt.

In the mid-1800's, critics stressed the relation between art and society. The English writer Matthew Arnold thought poetry should be "a criticism of life," which could help people attain a more accurate spiritual vision of the world, and correct the illusions of political propaganda. The American critics of the 1800's also related art to society. But they insisted that American experience was different from that of Europe and therefore required a different sort of art. Ralph Waldo Emerson, an influential American writer, called for a new, democratic breed of author who would look to the future rather than the past.

In the late 1800's and early 1900's, the novelist Henry James attempted a balance between American and European ideas of culture. James also wrote many essays on the craft of fiction. Later, such American critics as Edmund Wilson and Lionel Trilling continued the effort to relate American culture to its art.

In the early 1900's, the poet T. S. Eliot argued for a criticism that would be the servant of poetry, not of society. I. A. Richards, an English critic, developed methods of close reading. He asked readers to pay attention to the exact meaning of the text, not to impose their own ideas on it. In the mid-1900's, a movement called the *New Criticism* was popular in America. Such New Critics as Cleanth Brooks and John Crowe Ransom analyzed a work of literature as a self-contained whole, without reference to its historical period, the author's life, or other external influences.

Beginning in the 1950's, many critics turned from interpretative criticism to issues of theory. *Semiotics* approaches literature as a system of symbols that can be broken down like a language into parts for analysis. It is derived from the language theories of the American philosopher Charles Sanders Peirce and the Swiss linguist Ferdinand de Saussure. *Deconstructionism* is a theory based on the work of French philosopher Jacques Derrida. It states that every text dissolves into contradictions under close examination.

In the *reader-response theory,* critics attempt to understand how the audience plays a part in shaping the experience of literature. Some reader-response theorists stress how the psychological makeup of people causes them to read a work in different ways. *Feminist literary criticism* looks at the way the gender of the writer or the reader affects the writing or reading experience. Some feminist critics suggest that women's imagination and approach to language differ from men's. *New historicism,* based on the theories of French philosopher Michel Foucault and American anthropologist Clifford Geertz, emphasizes the historical analysis of literature. It insists that history, like literature, is not a matter of "hard facts," but of texts that need to be interpreted to be understood.   David H. Richter

Related articles in *World Book* include:

Aristotle	Naturalism
Arnold, Matthew	Plato
Boileau-Despréaux, Nicolas	Poe, Edgar Allan
Classicism	Ransom, John Crowe
Coleridge, Samuel Taylor	Realism
Dryden, John	Richards, I. A.
Eliot, T. S.	Romanticism
Emerson, Ralph Waldo	Ruskin, John
Frye, Northrop	Sainte-Beuve, Charles A.
Goethe, Johann W. von	Schiller, J. C. Friedrich von
Hazlitt, William	Shakespeare, William (Shake-
Horace	spearean criticism)
Howells, William Dean	Taine, Hippolyte Adolphe
James, Henry	Tate, Allen
Johnson, Samuel	Trilling, Lionel
Literature	Wilson, Edmund
Longinus	Wordsworth, William

Crittenden Compromise was a proposal submitted to the United States Senate in 1860 by Senator John Crittenden of Kentucky in an effort to keep the Southern States from leaving the Union. The Compromise proposed six amendments to the U.S. Constitution. Among other things it provided that slavery be protected south of 36° 30', and prohibited north of that line. The Compromise also denied the right of Congress to abolish slavery "in places under its exclusive jurisdiction." It protected the interstate slave trade, and it provided for compensation by the United States government to the owners of slaves who had been helped to escape. Defeat of the Compromise was due partly to President-elect Abraham Lincoln's opposition to any extension of slavery.   Robert F. Dalzell, Jr.

Logan Museum of Anthropology, Beloit College (Randall White)

Remains of Cro-Magnon culture include weapons and artwork. The Cro-Magnon spearheads at the right were made from reindeer antlers about 33,000 years ago. The engraving of a trotting horse, *above,* was cut into a limestone slab by a Cro-Magnon artist about 11,000 years ago. Both the engraving and the spearheads were found in southwestern France.

Randall White

Cro-Magnons, *kroh MAG nahnz,* were prehistoric human beings who lived in Europe, Asia, and North Africa from about 40,000 to 10,000 years ago. The name comes from the Cro-Magnon cave in Les Eyzies, in southwestern France. The first Cro-Magnon skeletons were discovered there in 1868, and more than 100 Cro-Magnon skeletons have since been found. The skeletons indicate that these people were strong and had a height of more than $5\frac{1}{2}$ feet (170 centimeters). The bone structure of the Cro-Magnons was similar to that of modern people. Scientists believe that the Cro-Magnons were an early form of modern human being.

Cro-Magnons hunted game on the cold, grassy plains of Europe. Ice sheets covered much of Europe when the Cro-Magnons lived there. Cro-Magnon hunters made weapons with tools of bone and stone. They also used such tools to scrape skins and to sew hides for clothing and shelter. The tools varied, and the people improved them through the centuries. Most Cro-Magnons lived in shelters built in the open, but some made shelters in caves. Some family groups may have wandered long distances. They probably exchanged such items as special rocks for toolmaking with other groups.

Some Cro-Magnons produced beautiful cave paintings. They painted animal pictures in caves in southwestern France and northern Spain. They also made bone carvings and modeled in clay.   Alan E. Mann

Croatan Indians. See Lumbee Indians.

Croatia, *kroh AY shuh,* is a country in southeastern Europe that declared its independence in June 1991. In 1918, Croatia had become part of the Kingdom of the Serbs, Croats, and Slovenes, later renamed Yugoslavia. In 1946, Yugoslavia became a federal state consisting of six republics, one of which was Croatia. War broke out in 1991 after Serbia, another Yugoslav republic, opposed Croatia's declaration of independence. Serbia seized about a third of Croatia's territory within a few months. A cease-fire in January 1992 ended most of the fighting, though some fighting has continued. Serbian troops continued to occupy about a third of Croatia.

Croatia covers 21,829 square miles (56,538 square kilometers) and has about 4,840,000 people. It borders on Slovenia and Hungary to the north, Serbia to the east, Bosnia-Herzegovina to the south, and the Adriatic Sea to the west. Zagreb, Croatia's capital and largest city, is the center of cultural and political life in the country. Other important towns in Croatia are, in order of size, Split, Rijeka, Osijek, and Dubrovnik. Osijek and Dubrovnik were heavily damaged during the war.

From 1945 to 1990, Communists held a monopoly on power in Croatia, as in all of what was then Yugoslavia. In 1990, non-Communists won a majority of seats in Croatia's first multiparty elections.

Government. Croatia adopted its first democratic constitution in December 1990, while it was still a Yugoslav republic. The 1990 Constitution guarantees freedom of speech, assembly, press, and religion. It also promises the right to form political parties and the right of minority groups to cultural independence.

The voters elect the president of Croatia to a five-year term. The president may be reelected only once. A two-house parliament makes the laws. The people elect the 199 members of parliament to four-year terms.

The most important political party in Croatia is the Croatian Democratic Union, an organization that promotes pride in Croatian culture. Other parties include the Social Liberal Party, the Social Democratic Party (formerly the Communist Party), the Croatian Democratic Party, and the Party of Rights.

The Supreme Court is Croatia's highest court. A spe-

Croatia

International boundary
Road
Railroad
National capital
Other city or town
Elevation above sea level

WORLD BOOK maps

Facts in brief

Capital: Zagreb.
Official language: Croatian.
Official name: Republika Hrvatska (Republic of Croatia).
Area: 21,829 sq. mi. (56,538 km²). *Greatest distances*—north-south, 290 mi. (465 km); east-west, 290 mi. (465 km).
Elevation: *Highest*—Mount Troglav, 6,276 ft. (1,913 m) above sea level. *Lowest*—sea level along the coast.
Population: *Estimated 1994 population*—4,840,000; density, 222 persons per sq. mi. (86 per km²); distribution, 51 percent urban, 49 percent rural. *1991 census*—4,784,265. *Estimated 1999 population*—4,916,000.
Chief products: *Agriculture*—apples, cattle, cherries, corn, grapes, olives, pears, pigs, plums, potatoes, poultry, sheep, soybeans, sugar beets, tobacco, wheat. *Manufacturing*—chemicals, petroleum, ships, textiles. *Mining*—bauxite, coal.
Flag: The flag has horizontal stripes of red, white, and blue. The coat of arms is in the center. See **Flag** (picture: Flags of Europe).
National anthem: "Lijepa naša domovino" ("Our Beautiful Homeland").
Money: *Basic unit*—dinar.

cial committee chosen by parliament appoints members of this court to life terms. Croatia also has a constitutional court. The parliament names the 11 judges of this court to eight-year terms. About 20,000 men and women serve in Croatia's armed forces.

People. Before the war, Croats (pronounced *KROH ats*) made up about 75 percent of the population of Croatia. Serbs made up more than 10 percent. Most of the Serbs lived in or around Knin, a town in southwestern Croatia. Pockets of other nationalities also lived in Croatia, sometimes in villages made up entirely of a single ethnic group. But many of these people fled after Serbian forces destroyed their villages.

The Croatian and Serbian languages are so similar that experts consider them two forms of a single language, often called Serbo-Croatian. Croatian is written in the Roman alphabet and Serbian usually employs the Cyrillic alphabet, the system of writing also used in Russian. After the war began, Croats began a campaign to further distinguish Croatian from Serbian. They sought to restore ancient Croatian words and to invent new words with Croatian roots. Many Croats, especially those in the major cities or along the Adriatic coast, speak either German or English in addition to Croatian. Most Croats are Roman Catholics. The traditional reli-

Zagreb is Croatia's capital and largest city. People shop for fruits and vegetables at an outdoor Zagreb market, *left.* The St. Etienne Cathedral rises in the background.

Alexander Boulat, Sipa Press

gion of the Serbs is the Serbian Orthodox faith.

Before the war, almost half the people of Croatia lived in rural areas, and the rest lived in cities. But the war destroyed many villages, forcing people to flee to Zagreb and other large cities.

Most rural families live in wooden houses with steep roofs. Many suburban residents have homes in modern high-rise apartment buildings. City dwellers often live in older houses or apartment buildings.

Croats value close family ties. Traditionally, the father holds the most authority in the family. Since the mid-1970's, however, a women's rights movement has grown in Croatia, especially in Zagreb. The movement has challenged the traditional ideas about authority in the family and called for women to have economic, political, and social equality with men.

Croatian cooking is similar to that of other central European countries. One of Croatia's best-loved dishes is *Zagreb veal cutlet,* breaded veal slices. Another traditional dish is *gibanica* (pronounced *GIHB bah niht sa*), a layered cheese pastry that may be eaten alone or with a meat dish. Croatia also makes some excellent wines.

Almost all adults in Croatia can read and write. Children are required to attend school between the ages of 6 and 14. Croatia has universities in Rijeka, Split, and Zagreb, and many other institutions of higher education.

Croatia has a lively cultural tradition. During the early 1900's, Croatian sculptor Ivan Meštrović became famous for his highly patriotic and religious works. Traditional dances of the Croats include the *kolo,* a fast-paced dance performed in a circle. Jazz festivals attract large audiences in Croatia, and classical music is also popular. Rock music, too, is extremely popular and has served as a means of expressing strong political views. During the 1970's and 1980's, many Croatian rock groups performed songs that criticized the Communist system or its policies. Since the 1980's, many rock groups have promoted Croatian pride and desire for independence.

Land and climate. Croatia consists of two land regions: (1) Dalmatia and (2) the Pannonian Plains. Dalmatia, a coastal region between the Adriatic Sea and Bosnia-Herzegovina, has rocky cliffs and little fertile soil.

The fertile Pannonian Plains, which include the historic region of Slavonia, border on Hungary. The Dinaric Alps extend through the center of Croatia. Croatia's two main rivers, the Drava and the Sava, flow into the Danube, one of the most important waterways in Europe.

Dalmatia has a mild climate. In winter, the temperature rarely falls below freezing. However, a cold, gusty wind called a *bora* sometimes blows down from the mountains into the northern areas in autumn and winter. Summers are sunny, hot, and dry. The Pannonian Plains have cold winters with a freezing wind called a *košava.* Summers are dry and hot. Temperatures often rise to about 100 °F (38 °C). Heavy rains in spring and autumn frequently cause floods along the Danube River and its tributaries.

Economy. Croatia had a high standard of living when it was part of Yugoslavia. Much of Croatia's wealth came from tourism and money sent home by Croats working in Germany and Austria. But Croatia also expanded its agriculture, cattle-breeding, and shipbuilding industries. In 1990, Croatia abandoned Communism and began to establish a free-enterprise system, in which businesses could operate without government control.

Zagreb is Croatia's leading manufacturing center. Major industries include chemicals, petroleum, shipbuilding, and textiles. Croatia is also an important producer of cement and steel. The most valuable mineral resources in Croatia are bauxite and coal.

Croatia's chief crops are corn, potatoes, soybeans, sugar beets, tobacco, and wheat. The major fruits are apples, cherries, grapes, olives, pears, and plums. Farmers also raise cattle, pigs, poultry, and sheep.

Tourism has contributed greatly to Croatia's economy. Resorts along the Adriatic coast and on the islands of Brač, Hvar, and Krk are popular tourist sites. The historic walled city of Dubrovnik also draws many sightseers. However, the tourist industry in Croatia has suffered from the war.

Croatia's major trading partners are Austria, Germany, and Italy. These countries and Great Britain provide most of the tourist traffic to Croatia.

Croatia has a good system of roads and railroads.

© Jonathan Blair, Woodfin Camp, Inc.

Croatia's dramatic coastline along the Adriatic Sea has traditionally drawn many tourists. Vacationers swim and sunbathe at a beach on the Makarska Rivieria, near Split, *above.* The war in the 1990's caused a sharp decline in tourism.

However, the war damaged parts of the transportation network and blocked access to much else. Serbian forces have occupied some roads leading to Bosnia-Herzegovina and have destroyed all bridges spanning the Sava River. In addition, some rail lines run through Serb-occupied areas and cannot be used.

Croatia has airports in Pula, Rijeka, Split, and Zagreb. The country's major seaports are Dubrovnik, Rijeka, Šibenik, and Split.

The leading daily newspapers in Croatia are *Večernji list* and *Vjesnik* of Zagreb and *Slobodna Dalmacija* of Split. *Danas,* a weekly magazine, and *Globus,* a weekly newspaper, are also popular.

History. Slavic tribes began to settle in what is now Croatia during the A.D. 600's. In 803, Croatian tribes accepted the rule of Charlemagne, a Germanic ruler who united much of western Europe to form a great empire. The Croats soon converted to Christianity. Croatia was an independent kingdom in the 900's and 1000's.

In 1102, Kálmán, the king of Hungary, also became king of Croatia, thus creating a political union between Croatia and Hungary that lasted for more than 800 years. Despite this union, the Croats always kept their own parliament, called the *Sabor.*

In 1526, the Ottoman Empire, based in present-day Turkey, defeated a Hungarian army in the Battle of Mohács. As a result, much of both Hungary and Croatia came under Ottoman rule. The Habsburgs, an Austrian royal family, gained control of the rest of Croatia at about the same time. Most of Croatia remained under Ottoman rule until it was transferred to the Habsburgs by the Treaty of Karlowitz in 1699.

In 1809, Croatia became part of the Illyrian Provinces of Emperor Napoleon I of France. In 1815, the Habsburgs once again took over Croatia. In 1867, the Habsburg Empire was restructured as the *Dual Monarchy* of Austria-Hungary. Austria and Hungary had equal political status within the restructured monarchy. Hungary took over Croatia. The following year, Croatia signed the *Nagodba* (agreement) with Hungary. The agreement guaranteed Croatia some of its historic rights.

Austria-Hungary fought on the side of the defeated Central Powers in World War I (1914-1918). After the war, it was broken into a number of pieces. In 1918, Croatia became part of a new state called the Kingdom of the Serbs, Croats, and Slovenes. The Croats hoped they would have full equality and regional *autonomy* (self-rule) within the kingdom. Instead, the Serbs used their greater military power to enforce centralized rule from Belgrade, the Serbian capital. In addition, taxation, military promotions, and banking policies discriminated against the Croats in favor of the Serbs.

In 1921, the Serbs passed a new constitution despite objections by the Croats. The Croatian Peasant Party—then the largest political party in Croatia—boycotted sessions of the legislative assembly held to draft the Constitution. The party continued its boycott of the assembly for several years. King Alexander I of Serbia took the throne of the combined kingdom under the Constitution. In 1929, the king changed the name of the kingdom to Yugoslavia and began to rule as dictator. He was assassinated in 1934 by a Bulgarian who had been hired by a Croatian terrorist group. Hostility between the Croats and Serbs continued.

In 1939, an agreement granted Croatia much control over its own affairs and those of Bosnia-Herzegovina. However, the outbreak of World War II later in the year ended this agreement.

In 1941, during the war, the Axis powers—led by Germany and Italy—invaded and occupied Yugoslavia. Croatia was proclaimed an independent state, but it was actually controlled by the Axis. Croatia was forced to turn over much of its coastal territory to Italy but was given control of Bosnia-Herzegovina.

After the war ended with the defeat of the Axis in 1945, Communists came to power in Yugoslavia. Josip Broz Tito, secretary-general of the Communist Party, became the country's prime minister and later became president. Under a constitution passed in 1946, Yugoslavia was organized as a federal state—that is, one in which the powers of government were shared between a central government and republics. Croatia then became one of Yugoslavia's six republics, as did Bosnia-Herzegovina. In 1947, most of Istria, which had belonged to Italy, became part of Croatia. In 1963, a new constitution was enacted. It gave the republics some control over their own affairs. After the passage of this Constitution, Croats began to press for greater independence.

Between 1967 and 1971, Croatian politics became increasingly liberal. Many Croatian leaders openly resented Serbia's influence in the federal government and demanded more control over Croatian affairs. In 1971, Tito forced many Croatian liberals to leave their posts, including Savka Dabčević-Kučar and Miko Tripalo, Croatia's leading political figures. From 1971 to the death of Tito in 1980, Croatia was ruled by conservatives who kept liberal economic reforms, but enforced a stricter line in political and cultural spheres.

After Tito's death, the federation that made up Yugoslavia began to unravel. Many Croats called for complete independence from Yugoslavia. They complained that the federal government took too much of Croatia's income and that Serbia sought to control Croatia and the other republics.

Croatia's relations with Serbia worsened dramatically in the late 1980's with the rise to power of Serbian leader Slobodan Milošević. Milošević, a strong supporter of Serbian unity and the expansion of Serbia's borders, began to rally the Serbian minority in Croatia against the Croatian government. Croatia and another Yugoslav republic, Slovenia, sought political reforms that would transform Yugoslavia into a union of independent states. Serbia and Montenegro, on the other hand, aimed to make Yugoslavia into a centralized state. After negotiations failed, Croatia and Slovenia each declared independence in June 1991.

In 1990, Milošević had begun smuggling large quantities of arms and other military equipment to Serbs living in Croatia. When war broke out between Croatia and Serbia in June 1991, these Serbs fought alongside the Yugoslav National Army against the Croats. Croatia lost more than 30 per cent of its territory to the Serbs within a few months. The war also destroyed about 40 per cent of Croatian industry, as well as many historic buildings and monuments. About 10,000 people were killed in the fighting.

In early 1992, the United Nations sent a peacekeeping force of about 14,000 to Croatia. But scattered fighting has continued to break out in Croatia, especially in the northeast. In April 1992, Serbia and Montenegro joined to form a new state of Yugoslavia, thus seeming to accept Croatia's independence. Sabrina P. Ramet

See also **Meštrović, Ivan; Split; Stepinac, Aloysius Cardinal; Yugoslavia** (History); **Zagreb.**

Croatoan. See **Lost Colony.**

Croce, *KRAW cheh,* **Benedetto,** *beh neh DEHT taw* (1866-1952), was probably the most distinguished Italian philosopher of the 1900's. He believed there are two kinds of knowledge: that which comes from understanding and that obtained from the imagination. For Croce, imagination rules art. He believed that art does not attempt to classify objects as a science does, but only feels and presents them.

Croce helped revive interest in the work of the Italian thinker Giambiattista Vico and influenced the reassessment of the ideas of the German philosopher G. W. F. Hegel. Croce had a major impact on British philosophy of art and history through his influence on the writings of the English philosopher and historian R. G. Collingwood. Croce founded and edited *La Critica,* a journal of literature, philosophy, and history. Croce's major books include *Aesthetic* (1902), *Philosophy of the Practical* (1908), *Logic* (1909), and *History as the Story of Liberty* (1938).

Croce was born in Pescasseroli, near Pescara. He was appointed a senator in 1910. Croce helped reform Italian schools in the 1920's. He was an opponent of the Fascist government of Benito Mussolini and was a leader in liberal intellectual circles in Italy. Karl Ameriks

Crocheting, *kroh SHAY ihng,* is a way of making lace by methods similar to those used in knitting. Crochet lace is heavy and inexpensive. Almost any yarn or thread may be crocheted, but the most common is a hard-twist cotton thread. The lace is made by looping a single yarn or thread into fabric or a chain by means of a needle called a *crochet hook.* This type of needle is a narrow piece of metal, bone, wood, or plastic about 6 inches (15 centimeters) long that ends in a barblike hook. The

French word *crochet* means *crook* or *crooked.*

A person can create many more variations of pattern with crochet stitches than with knitting needles. Variety in pattern is achieved by combining the three main stitches: chain, single crochet, and double crochet. The *chain* stitch is used to cast on and create pattern spaces.

WORLD BOOK photo by Ralph Brunke

Crochet lace is made with yarn or thread and a crochet hook. Crocheting produces a great variety of patterns. The illustrations below show how to make two stitches.

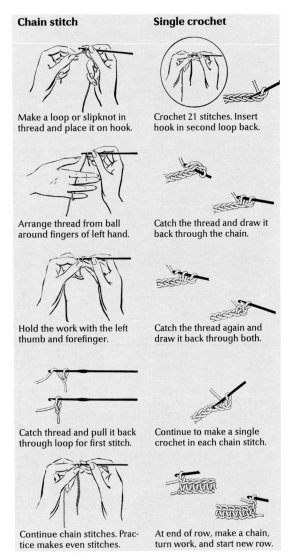

Chain stitch

Make a loop or slipknot in thread and place it on hook.

Arrange thread from ball around fingers of left hand.

Hold the work with the left thumb and forefinger.

Catch thread and pull it back through loop for first stitch.

Continue chain stitches. Practice makes even stitches.

Single crochet

Crochet 21 stitches. Insert hook in second loop back.

Catch the thread and draw it back through the chain.

Catch the thread again and draw it back through both.

Continue to make a single crochet in each chain stitch.

At end of row, make a chain, turn work, and start new row.

A loop of thread is placed upon the hook. The thread is wound over the needle, and drawn through this loop. *Single crochet* creates solid-pattern shapes and bars in an openwork pattern. *Double crochet* is used in the same way as single crochet, but is twice as wide. Other crochet stitches include *netting,* the *rose stitch,* and the *shell stitch.*

Crocheting is done with fine thread and a fine hook for lacy doilies and trimmings. A medium thread and needle are used for crocheting bedspreads, gloves, and potholders. With wool yarn and a needle of medium size, a person can crochet stoles, berets, sweaters, and afghans. Heavy yarns or fabric strips may be crocheted using a large crochet hook to make carpets or mats.

Crocheting is an ancient craft. Although the lace can be made by machine, workers in Belgium, Italy, France, and China continue to produce it by hand. An excellent Italian crochet work is called *Orvieto lace.*

The Irish are also famous for their beautiful crochet work. Crochet lace was introduced into Ireland about 1820. Using very fine thread, Irish women developed a type of lace using a series of three-leafed shamrocks, roses, and little rings surrounded by a lacy background of chain stitches with small *picots,* or knots. This type of lace can be recognized by the whiteness of the linen thread used.   Patrick H. Ela

Crockett, Davy (1786-1836), was one of the most famous frontiersmen in United States history. He became a first-rate hunter and Indian fighter who used his reputation to build a political career. Crockett succeeded Daniel Boone as the nation's best-known symbol of the American frontier. Many people felt the national spirit of the United States was reflected in Crockett's motto: "Be always sure you're right—then go ahead!" Crockett died fighting in the war for Texas independence. His colorful life and heroic death brought him lasting fame in both history and legend.

Early life. David Crockett was born in Greene County, Tennessee, on Aug. 17, 1786. The Crockett family moved to Jefferson County, where Davy's father opened a tavern in 1796. Davy started school at about the age of 13. He often played hooky, and he ran away from home for about $2\frac{1}{2}$ years to avoid being punished for missing class. In 1806, Crockett married Mary (Polly) Finley, the daughter of a farmer. They had three children.

In 1813, Crockett became a U.S. Army scout. He fought in the Creek Indian War in what is now part of Alabama and Florida until 1815. His wife died that year. In 1816, Crockett married Elizabeth Patton, a widow with two children. They moved to western Tennessee in 1817.

Political career. In Tennessee, Crockett developed a successful political career. He held several local positions, including justice of the peace, town commissioner, and colonel of the county militia. Crockett served in the Tennessee legislature from 1821 to 1824. He won a seat in the U.S. House of Representatives from Tennessee in 1827 and was reelected in 1829 and 1833.

In Congress, Crockett opposed President Andrew Jackson and other Tennessee members of Congress on several issues, including land reform and a bill to relocate Indian tribes. Whig Party leaders promoted Crockett as a presidential candidate for the election of 1836. But Crockett lost his reelection bid for Congress in 1835, and his presidential ambitions ended.

The Alamo. In November 1835, Crockett set out for Texas. He felt he could renew his political career there and become wealthy as a land agent. At the time, Texas was fighting to gain its independence from Mexico. In early February 1836, Crockett joined 188 men who had established a fort at the Alamo, an old Roman Catholic mission in San Antonio. When Mexican troops attacked the fort, the men held them off for nearly two weeks. But on March 6, the Mexican forces overran the Alamo. Some historians believe that a few men, perhaps including Crockett, survived the battle but were then executed by the Mexicans. Other scholars believe that all the defenders died in the battle.

The legends. Crockett excelled at *backwoods brag,* a type of country exaggeration, and he told many tall tales about himself. In one tale, a raccoon gives up when Crockett spots him while hunting. Crockett also may have been exaggerating when he claimed to have killed 105 bears in seven months.

Crockett became known for political antics as well. For example, he once memorized an opponent's standard speech and spoke it word for word as his own at a debate. Not being able to repeat the same speech, his confused rival was forced to make an unprepared reply.

Stories written after his death helped create the fictional legends of Davy Crockett. One description claimed that he could "run faster, jump higher, squat

Oil painting by John Chapman; Humanities
Research Center, University of Texas, Austin

Davy Crockett was a famous hunter, scout, soldier, and Congressman. He posed in hunting clothes for this portrait in 1834.

Detail of *Fall of the Alamo* (1903), oil painting on canvas by Robert Onderdonk; Governor's Mansion of Texas (Friends of the Governor's Mansion)

Crockett fought at the Alamo to help Texas win its independence from Mexico. In 1836, a Mexican army attacked the Alamo, an old Roman Catholic mission used by Texans as a fort. Although greatly outnumbered and low on ammunition, Crockett, *standing center left,* and 188 other defenders held off the Mexicans for nearly two weeks before losing the fort.

lower, dive deeper, stay under longer, and come out drier than any man in the whole country." Through the years, Crockett has been the subject of songs, books, TV programs, and movies.   Michael A. Lofaro

See also **Alamo; Pioneer life in America** (Places to visit).

Additional resources

Davy Crockett. Ed. by Michael A. Lofaro. Univ. of Tennessee Pr., 1985. For older readers.
Santrey, Laurence. *Davy Crockett: Young Pioneer.* Troll, 1983.
Shackford, James A. *David Crockett: The Man and the Legend.* Greenwood, 1981. First published in 1956. For older readers. The standard biography.
Townsend, Tom. *Davy Crockett: An American Hero.* Eakin, 1987.

Crocodile is one of the largest living reptiles. Crocodiles, alligators, gavials, and caymans look much alike, and are all called *crocodilians.* Both crocodiles and alligators have a long, low, cigar-shaped body, short legs, and long powerful tails with which they swim. They both have tough hides, long snouts, and sharp teeth to grasp their prey. In most crocodiles, however, the snout comes to a point in front, where an alligator's snout is rounded. The American crocodile is only about two-thirds as heavy as an old American alligator of the same length and can move much more quickly. The lower fourth tooth is extra long in both animals. It fits into a pit in the alligator's upper jaw. But the crocodile's fourth tooth fits into a groove in the side of the upper jaw, and

Marc & Evelyne Bernheim, Woodfin Camp, Inc.

A crocodile's body, *left,* is long, low, and cigar-shaped. It has a tough hide. The animal uses its short legs mainly for walking on land. It uses its long, powerful tail to swim.

Caulion Singletary

A baby American crocodile, *above,* hatches after about 105 days. At birth, it measures about 9 inches (23 centimeters) long.

E. R. Degginger

A crocodile's long snout has sharp teeth. Its teeth set in strong jaws, *above,* that can snap a heavy board in two.

it is visible when the animal's jaws are closed.

Crocodiles live in tropical countries throughout the world. They prefer large bodies of shallow water, sluggish rivers, open swamps, and marshes. Their webbed feet allow them to walk on the soft ground. Their eyes and nostrils are higher than the rest of the head. This arrangement fits in with the crocodile's life in the water, for it likes to float with only its eyes and nostrils above the surface. Its throat has a slitlike valve in front of the tube leading to its nostrils. This valve shuts tight when the animal is underwater. It keeps the water from entering through the mouth when the reptile seizes its prey.

Crocodiles eat many small animals, such as fishes, birds, and turtles, which they seize and swallow whole. Occasionally they attack large animals and people. A crocodile can twist a large animal into pieces by seizing it and then rapidly spinning lengthwise in the water. Crocodiles are more aggressive than American or Chinese alligators. Large wild crocodiles should be left alone.

Like most reptiles, crocodiles lay eggs. These look like hens' eggs, but are longer and have a less brittle shell. Crocodiles conceal their eggs in nests of rubbish and vegetation, or they bury them in sand beaches. The female of some types guards the nest until the young are hatched. When she can hear the young reptiles grunting, she digs them out of the nest. Some crocodiles help their young hatch and then carry them in their mouth to the water. Not much is known about the breeding habits and general behavior of crocodiles.

Most of the true crocodiles inhabit the Eastern Hemisphere, but four species live in North and South America. The *American crocodile* lives in the extreme south of Florida, on the larger West Indian islands, and in Cen-

tral America and areas near it. The usual length of adult American crocodiles is about 12 feet (3.7 meters).

The *Nile crocodile* is found widely in Africa. This animal lives almost everywhere on the continent except in the Sahara and on the northern coast. This reptile was known by ancient peoples and described by the Greek historian, Herodotus. The small, long-snouted crocodile of the Congo Basin grows no longer than 8 feet (2.4 meters). The two kinds of dwarf crocodilians of Africa, one of which is very rare, are closely related to true crocodiles.

The giant *saltwater crocodile* lives in many places from India to northern Australia, and even in the Solomon Islands. The *mugger* lives in India and Pakistan, and the *Siamese crocodile* inhabits Java, Thailand, and nearby parts of Asia. There is also an *Australian crocodile.* Sumatra and the Malay Peninsula have the *false gavial.* The false gavial has a narrower snout than most other crocodilians. It uses its long snout to catch fish.

The crocodilians are remnants of a large and ancient group of reptiles. Fossils show that these reptiles once reached a length of 50 feet (15 meters). This is more than twice as long as any crocodiles living today. There are now 12 species of crocodiles.

Crocodiles have been widely hunted for their hides, which manufacturers make into leather for shoes and handbags. Such hunting has caused three species—the American crocodile, Cuban crocodile, and Nile crocodile—to become endangered species. Laws now forbid crocodile hunting in many parts of the world, but these restrictions are difficult to enforce. Biologists in some areas have begun programs to collect crocodile eggs and hatch them in incubators. The baby crocodiles are then released into the wild.

Scientific classification. Crocodiles belong to the family Crocodylidae. The Nile crocodile is *Crocodylus niloticus.* The American crocodile is *C. acutus.*   D. Bruce Means

See also **Alligator; Gavial; Reptile.**

Crocodile bird. See Courser.

Crocus, *KROH kuhs,* is the name of a group of small flowering plants native to southern Europe and Asia and cultivated in many regions of the world. A crocus grows from a thick, bulblike stem called a *corm.* The leaves look like large blades of grass. The flower consists of six nearly equal segments and may be white, yellow, or purplish. Some crocuses bloom early in spring, and others in the autumn. A popular spring-blooming species, the *cloth-of-gold crocus,* has a bright orange-yellow flower. Most crocuses grow only about 3 or 4 inches (8 to 10 centimeters) high.

Gardeners plant crocuses about 3 inches (8 centimeters) deep in rich soil. After the plants bloom, the corms die and new ones grow in their place.

Crocus is the Latin word for *saffron.* Saffron was once used extensively to make a yellow dye and as a spice for food. Commercial saffron is obtained from the *saffron crocus,* which is

George Nelson, Artstreet

Crocuses

grown mainly in France, Italy, and Spain. See **Saffron.**

The *colchicum* is a flowering plant that closely resembles crocuses. It is often called *autumn crocus* or *meadow saffron* (see **Colchicum**). The *wild crocus,* or *pasqueflower,* is an anemone (see **Pasqueflower**).

Scientific classification. Crocuses make up the genus *Crocus* in the iris family, Iridaceae. The scientific name for the cloth-of-gold crocus is *Crocus angustifolius.* The saffron crocus is *C. sativus.*   Kenneth A. Nicely

See also **Flower** (picture: Garden perennials [Bulbs]).

Croesus, *KREE suhs* (reigned 560-546 B.C.), was the last king of Lydia, a country in what is now western Turkey. Croesus raised Lydia to the peak of its power, conquering Greek coastal cities and extending his empire to the Halys River (now called the Kizil River) in central Asia Minor. During Croesus' reign, Lydia achieved vast wealth through gold mining and extensive trade.

Croesus succeeded his father, Alyattes, as king. In 549 B.C., he formed an alliance with Babylonia, Egypt, and Sparta against Persia. He attacked the Persians in about 545 B.C., expecting help from his allies. But help could not reach him, and he withdrew to Sardis, his capital. Cyrus, the Persian leader, followed him there, defeated him, and made Lydia part of the Persian Empire.
          Clive Foss

Crohn's disease. See **Ileitis.**

Crompton, Samuel (1753-1827), was an English weaver and inventor. In 1779, he developed an improved spinning machine that led to major growth in the cotton industry. The new machine was called *the mule* because it was a cross between two machines, the spinning jenny and the water frame, just as a mule is a cross between two animals. The mule made the strong, uniform cotton yarn required for fine muslin and calico.

Crompton did not get a patent on his machine, and he received little of the money that cloth manufacturers promised him. But Parliament gave him a national gift of £5,000 in 1812 when he was able to show that the many mules in use had revolutionized the cotton industry. Crompton was born in Firwood, Lancashire.
          Richard F. Hirsh

Cromwell, Oliver (1599-1658), led the armed forces of Parliament to victory in the English Civil War in the 1640's and ruled England from 1653 to 1658. He had an iron will and was a military genius. Few leaders have inspired more love and respect or more fear and hatred.

Cromwell was born in Huntingdon, England, near Peterborough. He came from a wealthy and influential family. Cromwell studied at Sidney Sussex College in Cambridge, but his father's death forced him to leave before getting a degree. In 1628, he was elected to Parliament. During the 1630's, Cromwell became a dedicated Puritan. Puritans were Protestants who strongly believed in the right of people to follow more simple forms of worship and church organization than those of the Church of England (see **Puritans**).

Rise to power. In 1629, King Charles I dismissed Parliament. He believed that kings got their right to rule from God, not from the people. Charles showed little respect for Parliament and did not call it to meet until 1640, when he needed it to provide money. The struggle for power between the king and Parliament resumed, and civil war broke out in 1642. Cromwell had won election to Parliament in 1640, and he became its leading general. He had no military experience, but he turned out to be a brilliant cavalry leader. His forces, called the "Ironsides," never lost a major battle. In 1645, Cromwell won the decisive Battle of Naseby. The king surrendered in 1646.

Parliament's supporters split into two rival groups. These two groups were the Presbyterians and the Independents. The Presbyterians, who had the majority of the seats in Parliament, wanted Parliament and the king to share political power. Some of the independents,

The Mansell Collection Ltd.

Crayon drawing by Samuel Cooper; Sidney Sussex College, Cambridge, England (Stearn's and Sons, Ltd.)

Oliver Cromwell, *above,* ruled England from 1653 to 1658. He dismissed Parliament in 1653, *left,* because it failed to adopt major reforms. Cromwell is shown at the bottom of the left side of the drawing wearing a plumed hat and pointing a staff.

whose supporters included the chief officers of the army of Parliament, favored formation of a republic governed entirely by Parliament.

Fighting between the king's sympathizers and the Independents broke out in 1648. Cromwell supported the Independents and put down the revolt. Soon afterward, Parliament's army seized Charles and removed the Presbyterian members of Parliament. Cromwell was a leader in the king's trial and execution in 1649. England then became a republic called the Commonwealth of England. In the next two years, Cromwell crushed uprisings by Scottish and Irish forces and defeated an army loyal to Charles Stuart, son of the executed king.

The Protectorate. Parliament's failure to adopt major reforms upset Cromwell. In 1653, he dismissed Parliament and ended the Commonwealth. Cromwell's military officers then prepared a document that made England a Protectorate. Cromwell became its chief executive with the title of *lord protector.*

Cromwell limited freedom of the press, demanded rigid moral standards, and adopted other strict measures. He also strengthened England's navy and brought Scotland and Ireland under English control. In addition, Cromwell aided the development of English colonies in Asia and North America. In 1657, Parliament offered Cromwell the title of king, but he refused it.

After Cromwell died in 1658, his son, Richard, became lord protector. But Richard was an ineffective ruler and resigned in 1659. In 1660, Parliament invited Charles Stuart to rule as King Charles II.   Roger Howell, Jr.

See also **Charles (I; II) of England; England** (The civil war); **Long Parliament; Restoration; Rump Parliament.**

Cromwell, Richard (1626-1712), ruled England as lord protector from September 1658 to May 1659. He succeeded his father, Oliver Cromwell, as lord protector. But he could not govern effectively, and a group of political and army leaders forced him to resign. In 1660, Parliament invited Charles Stuart to return from the Continent and rule as Charles II. Cromwell fled to France. He returned to England about 1680 and lived under another name in Cheshunt until his death.

Cromwell was born in Huntingdon. He fought with Parliament's forces against King Charles I during the English Civil War in the 1640's. Cromwell was admitted to the Council of State and was named chancellor of Oxford University in 1657.   Vernon F. Snow

Cromwell, Thomas (1485?-1540), was a trusted adviser to King Henry VIII of England. A talented and ruthless administrator, Cromwell directed England's civil and religious affairs in the 1530's.

Cromwell is often called the architect of the English Reformation for his part in establishing Protestantism in England. Pope Clement VII had refused Henry's request for a divorce from Catherine of Aragon. Cromwell showed Henry that he could get the divorce by breaking with the Roman Catholic Church and by making himself head of an independent Church of England. Cromwell seized property belonging to monasteries for the king, and he demanded total obedience to the new religion. But later he fell from favor, and was beheaded.

Historians believe Cromwell was born in Putney, England. He became an assistant to Thomas Cardinal Wolsey in 1524. When Wolsey fell from power in 1529, Cromwell became principal secretary, vicar general, and lord privy seal. He was made Earl of Essex and lord chancellor in 1539.   Lacey Baldwin Smith

Cronin, A. J. (1896-1981), was a popular British novelist. He gained literary fame with his first novel, *Hatter's Castle* (1931), a story of country life in Scotland. Cronin developed a pattern of centering his novels on a single problem or profession, treating it with an engaging combination of realistic detail and romantic plotting. *The Stars Look Down* (1935) describes poor working conditions in an English mining community. *The Citadel* (1937) is the story of a young Scottish doctor and also a critical study of the medical profession. *The Keys of the Kingdom* (1941) is a moving story about a Roman Catholic missionary priest in China. Cronin's later novels include *A Thing of Beauty* (1956), *A Pocketful of Rye* (1969), and *The Lady with Carnations* (1976).

Archibald Joseph Cronin was born in Cardross, Scotland. He practiced medicine from 1919 to 1930. Cronin moved to the United States in the mid-1940's. His autobiography, *Adventures in Two Worlds* (1951), deals with his early years as a doctor.   Garrett Stewart

Cronkite, Walter (1916-   ), a television news reporter, was anchorman of the CBS evening news from 1962 to 1981. He won fame as one of the most trusted TV newscasters.

Walter Leland Cronkite was born in St. Joseph, Mo. He attended the University of Texas at Austin from 1933 to 1935 and worked as a reporter for the Scripps-Howard Newspapers while there. Cronkite joined the United Press (now United Press International) in 1937 and was a correspondent in Europe during World War II.

CBS News

Walter Cronkite

After the war, Cronkite remained in Europe as a reporter. He served as bureau manager of the United Press in Moscow from 1946 to 1948. Cronkite joined CBS in 1950 and worked as a Washington correspondent for four years. He was transferred to New York City as a correspondent in 1954 and became managing editor of the CBS evening news in 1963. He retired from the evening news in 1981, but remained with CBS, working on special assignments.   William L. Rivers

Cronus was the youngest child of Gaea, the earth; and Uranus, the sky, in Greek mythology. Unlike most gods, he did not represent a place, event, function, or quality. Cronus belonged to the race of gods known as Titans. The Roman god Saturn closely resembled him.

Uranus feared that his children would overthrow him, and so he confined them within Gaea's huge body. With Gaea's help, Cronus deposed Uranus and became king of the Titans. Cronus married his sister Rhea, and they had six children. Cronus feared that his children would depose him, too, and so he swallowed the first five of them at birth. Rhea hid the last child, Zeus, on the island of Crete. Then she tricked Cronus by giving him a large stone wrapped in baby clothes.

After Zeus grew to manhood, he helped his brothers and sisters escape Cronus. Together, they deposed their father, and Zeus then became the king of the gods.

C. Scott Littleton

See also **Mythology** (Greek mythology); **Titans.**

Crookes, Sir William (1832-1919), was a British chemist and physicist. Crookes discovered the chemical element thallium and determined its atomic weight. He also developed several devices that were widely used in scientific research for many years.

During the 1870's, Crookes constructed a vacuum tube for studying a form of radiation called *cathode rays.* This device, later known as the *Crookes tube,* contributed to the development of the modern *cathode-ray tube* that is used in electronic equipment (see **Crookes tube; Vacuum tube**). Crookes also invented the *radiometer,* a device that measures the intensity of radiant energy. In addition, he developed an instrument called the *spinthariscope* for observing high-energy particles emitted by certain radioactive substances.

Crookes was born in London, and graduated from the Royal College of Chemistry in 1851. In 1859, he founded the journal *Chemical News.* He was knighted in 1897.

Romualdas Sviedrys

Crookes tube is a type of vacuum tube. Sir William Crookes, an English physicist and chemist, developed the tube in the 1870's as part of his study of what came to be called cathode rays. His work led to the discovery that these rays consist of streams of electrons.

A Crookes tube has electrodes at or near each end, and low air pressure inside. When a strong electric current flows from the *cathode* (negative electrode) to the *anode* (positive electrode), a glow appears in the end of the tube opposite the cathode. Crookes concluded that invisible rays from the cathode caused the glow. To study the rays, Crookes placed small objects in the rays' path within the tube.

In 1879, Crookes suggested that the rays consisted of streams of negatively charged molecules. The English physicist Sir Joseph J. Thomson confirmed that the rays were charged particles of matter in 1897. Crookes tubes were forerunners of television picture tubes. Today, the Crookes tube is used only for classroom demonstrations.

Bernard S. Finn

See also **Cathode rays.**

Crop, in zoology. See **Bird** (The digestive system); **Insect** (Digestive system).

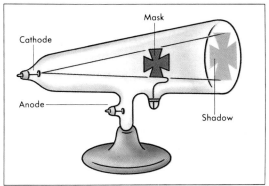

WORLD BOOK illustration by Sarah Woodward

A Crookes tube produces cathode rays. These rays cause glass at the opposite end of the tube to *fluoresce* (give off light). A metal mask blocks some of the rays and casts a shadow.

Crop is a large number of plants of any given kind that are grown for human use. Crops grown to feed people are called *food crops.* Crops that are consumed by animals are *feed crops.* Other crops, called *fiber crops,* produce fiber for use in clothing and other products. Certain other crops are grown to *ornament* (decorate) people's surroundings.

Food crops include fruits, vegetables, and grains such as barley, corn, oats, rice, and wheat. Animal feed crops include *forage,* such as grasses and certain herbs. Cotton, flax, and hemp provide fiber. Ornamental crops include flowers, lawn grasses, shrubs, and decorative trees. James D. Arnold

See also **Agriculture** (Chief agricultural products).

Crop insurance provides protection for a farmer's income in case bad weather or other unavoidable natural hazards cause crop losses. There are two main types of crop insurance sold in the United States—*multiperil insurance* and *hail insurance.* Both types are designed to provide coverage for only a fraction of a farmer's crop.

Multiperil insurance is sold by private agents. However, claims are paid by the Federal Crop Insurance Corporation (FCIC), an agency of the U.S. Department of Agriculture. Multiperil insurance covers losses due to almost all natural causes, including disease, drought, flood, and insects. It is available for corn, cotton, tobacco, wheat, and about 30 other crops.

Hail insurance is sold by private agents, whose companies also pay the claims on crop losses. Its coverage is limited to those losses caused by hail, wind, or fire. This insurance is restricted to only a few causes in order to offer some protection for the insurer. A private insurer, unlike a government agency, could be ruined if crop losses occurred over a wide area. Warren F. Lee

See also **Federal Crop Insurance Corporation.**

Crop rotation. See **Cropping system.**

Cropping system is a method of growing crops and producing high yields without weakening the soil. It involves the combination of different production techniques to provide for the best possible use of the land. In determining the crops and production methods best suited for their land, farmers must consider the composition of their soil; the slope, drainage, and *erosion* (wearing away) problems of their land; and the land's past cropping history. Production techniques such as different cultivation methods, rotation of crops, and the proper use of fertilizers and pesticides are used in different combinations to aid the farmer.

One of the oldest and most widely used ways of preserving the soil is through the *rotation of crops* (alternating the crops grown in a field from one year to the next). A single crop will use up vital minerals and organic matter in the soil if it is grown in the same field year after year. But different kinds of crops planted in the field on a regular schedule will replace lost minerals and organic matter and help break up plant disease and insect cycles. For example, corn takes nitrogen out of the soil, while crops such as alfalfa and clover put nitrogen into the soil. If corn is planted in a field one year, alfalfa or clover may be planted in it the next year to replace the nitrogen used by the corn crop. The nitrogen producing crop can also be plowed into the soil. When it rots, it replaces lost organic matter and enriches the soil. On sloping land, grasses and deep-rooted crops are often

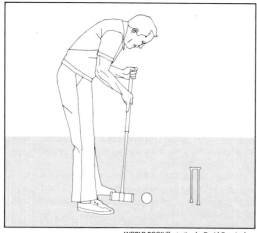

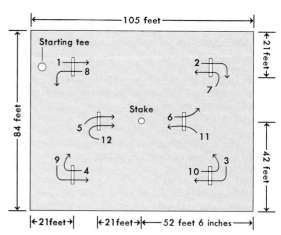

A croquet player scores a point by hitting the ball through a wicket with a mallet. The diagram shows the required course of the balls through the six wickets.

WORLD BOOK illustration by David Cunningham

WORLD BOOK diagram

alternated with other crops to hold the soil in place and prevent erosion.

The use of fertilizers is gradually replacing the crop rotation system as a means of producing the most profitable crops year after year while still keeping soil fertile. Nitrogen fertilizers and other fertilizers have been developed that can restore lost minerals to soil. When these fertilizers are added, and the proper cultivation and pest control methods are used, the same crop can be planted year after year without harming the soil.

Other developments that aid the farmer include chemical pesticides that kill harmful insects, weeds, and microorganisms.   James D. Arnold

Croquet, *kroh KAY,* is a popular outdoor lawn game in which the players use mallets to hit balls through narrow arches called *wickets.* Croquet originated in France during the late 1400's and was first played in the United States in the 1860's. Today, top players of several nations compete in the sport of croquet, but it is largely a backyard game in the United States. There are many versions of croquet. This article discusses the tournament version used by the U.S. Croquet Association.

The court and equipment. A standard croquet court measures 105 feet (32 meters) long and 84 feet (26 meters) wide. In a game, each side uses wooden mallets and two wooden balls. A croquet mallet weighs from 2 to 4 pounds (0.9 to 1.8 kilograms). It has a handle 2 to $3\frac{1}{2}$ feet (61 to 107 centimeters) long and a head 10 inches (25 centimeters) long. Each ball is blue, red, black, or yellow. The balls are played in this order throughout a game. A croquet ball has a diameter of $3\frac{3}{8}$ inches (9.2 centimeters) and weighs about 1 pound (0.5 kilogram).

A wooden stake stands in the center of the court. It has a diameter of $1\frac{1}{2}$ inches (3.8 centimeters). Six iron or aluminum wickets are at designated places on the court. They are 12 inches (30 centimeters) high and must be no more than 4 inches (10 centimeters) wide.

The game. Each of the two competing sides in a game of croquet has either one or two players. Each player scores points by hitting his or her ball along a required course through the wickets and back again. A player uses two balls in a singles game. A point is

scored each time a ball passes through a wicket or hits the stake at the end of the course. The first side to score 26 points wins the game.

Each ball must be played in turn. A player may hit his or her ball only once at the start of each turn. But if the ball goes through its wicket in its proper order, the player gets one additional stroke.

A player whose ball hits another ball earns two more strokes. For the first of these, he or she may take one of three shots. (1) The player may place his or her ball against the other ball, striking it so that both balls are driven away. (2) The player may hit his or her ball while holding it next to the other ball with one foot, thus driving the other ball away. (3) The player may hit his or her ball away after moving the ball the length of a mallet head from the other ball. A player takes one of these strokes before taking the second, or *continuation,* stroke. A player whose ball has hit another ball is considered *dead* on that ball. That is, the striker's ball cannot hit that same ball again until it has scored the next wicket point.   Jack R. Osborn

Crosby, Bing (1903-1977), was a popular American singer and motion-picture star. He became especially well known for his relaxed "crooning" style of singing. Crosby made about 60 movies, most of which were musicals and romantic comedies. He introduced his most famous song, "White Christmas," in the movie *Holiday Inn* (1942). Crosby won an Academy Award in 1944 for his performance as a singing priest in *Going My Way.* He also co-starred with Bob Hope and Dorothy Lamour in *Road to Singapore* (1940) and six later "Road" comedies.

Wide World

Bing Crosby

Crosby was born in Tacoma, Wash. His real name was Harry Lillis Crosby. He started his career in 1924 singing with a Los Angeles band. From about 1927 to 1930, he sang with a trio called the Rhythm Boys. Film and radio appearances and phonograph records made Crosby nationally famous in the 1930's. Crosby was married to actress Dixie Lee from 1930 until her death in 1952. They had four sons. In 1957, Crosby married actress Kathryn Grant. They had two sons and a daughter.   Roger Ebert

Cross is the most common symbol of Christianity. It represents the cross on which Jesus Christ was crucified. Christians believe that Jesus' Crucifixion played a central role in redeeming humanity from its sins, and they regard the cross as a sign of redemption. Various groups of Christians have adopted different styles of crosses. Roman Catholics and Protestants chiefly use the Latin cross. This cross is a vertical post with a shorter horizontal crosspiece above the center. Many Eastern Orthodox Churches use the Greek cross, which has four arms of equal length.

During the first 300 years after Christ's death, Christians feared persecution by the hostile Roman govern-

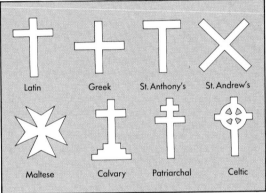

Latin   Greek   St. Anthony's   St. Andrew's

Maltese   Calvary   Patriarchal   Celtic

WORLD BOOK illustration by Arthur Grebetz

The cross is the most familiar symbol of Christianity. The illustration above shows eight styles of crosses that became famous in the history of the religion. The picture below shows a *crucifix*, which is a cross with an image of the crucified Jesus Christ.

Detail of a gilt bronze and lapis lazuli crucifix (1700's); The Art Institute of Chicago

ment and rarely displayed the cross in public. In the 300's, the Romans began to tolerate Christianity, and crosses were widely displayed. During the early Middle Ages, Christian artists made crosses as symbols of the Christian belief in the Resurrection of Christ. Many of these crosses portrayed the risen Christ wearing priestly clothes and a royal crown. Later, Christians began to emphasize the sufferings of Jesus in *crucifixes.* A crucifix is a cross with an image of the dying Jesus.

Crosses have a number of uses in Christian worship. A cross on a staff is carried in many processions. During some ceremonies, members of the clergy or worshipers trace the shape of a cross with a hand or certain fingers. Cathedrals and many churches have floor plans based on the shape of the Latin cross.   Jill Raitt

Cross-country is a type of long-distance racing. Unlike track and field races, cross-country competition is not held on a track. Runners usually race across fields or golf courses and often through woods and over hills. Because distances and terrains differ for each race, no national or world records exist for this event. In the United States, the National Federation of High School Associations has set a minimum distance of $1\frac{1}{2}$ miles (2.4 kilometers) and a maximum distance of 3 miles (4.8 kilometers) for races. The National Collegiate Athletic Association has set a distance of 5 kilometers ($3\frac{1}{10}$ miles) for women and between 8 and 10 kilometers (5 and $6\frac{1}{5}$ miles) for men. The Athletics Congress conducts championships at distances of 10 kilometers for men and 6 kilometers ($3\frac{3}{4}$ miles) for women.   Michael Takaha

Cross-examination. See Debate; Trial.

Cross-eye. See Strabismus.

Cross-reference is a method used in books, indexes, library catalogs, and filing systems to direct attention to additional information about a subject in another part of the book or index. Cross-references are widely used in encyclopedias, dictionaries, and textbooks. For instance, this article on **Cross-reference** mentions indexes. At the end of the article there is a cross-reference reading "See also **Index.**" The reader can find more information about indexes in that article. This type of cross-reference is sometimes called a *related subject* or a *related article.*

Cross-references may also appear within the text of an article or chapter. *The World Book Encyclopedia* article on the famous American author whose pen name was Mark Twain illustrates another kind of cross-reference. Because the author is best known as Mark Twain, his biography is given under **Twain, Mark.** But because his real name was Samuel Langhorne Clemens, there is an entry **Clemens, Samuel Langhorne,** which refers the reader to the article on Mark Twain in inverted form: Twain, Mark. This is a direct reference, and will be "See **Twain, Mark.**" Some publications use the symbols *cf.* (from the Latin *confer,* meaning *compare*), or *q.v.* (from the Latin *quod vide,* meaning *which see*).

Charles F. Sieger

See also **Index.**

Crossbill is the name of several species of small birds. The upper and lower parts of the bill of these birds cross each other at the ends.

The male *red,* or *American, crossbill* is colored brick red, with wings and tail of brown. It is about the size of a house sparrow. The plumage of the female is a slightly mottled, greenish yellow. This bird breeds from the

WORLD BOOK illustration by John Rignall, Linden Artists Ltd.

The crossbill uses the crossed ends of its bill to get seeds from fir cones. The male red crossbill, *above,* is brick red.

Detail of an illuminated manuscript by an unknown artist; Bibliothèque Nationale, Paris

Turkish forces fought with crossbows in 1480. Some archers used cranks to prepare their crossbows for shooting.

northern states northward. In the region of the Allegheny Mountains, it breeds as far south as the Carolinas. In winter, red crossbills migrate in small flocks to the Gulf of Mexico, and west as far as Idaho and Arizona. They build their nests in evergreens. The female lays three or four pale-greenish eggs with purple or lilac spots. Red crossbills feed chiefly on seeds of cone-bearing trees. They also eat small quantities of buds and a few insects. The bird uses its crossed bill to lift the scales from the cones to get the seeds.

The *white-winged crossbill* is similar in habits to the red crossbill. It breeds from the northern states northward. In winter, it migrates as far south as Virginia.

Scientific classification. The crossbills belong to the finch family, Fringillidae. The red crossbill is *Loxia curvirostra*. The white-winged crossbill is *L. leucoptera.* Sandra L. Vehrencamp

Crossbow was a weapon used for shooting arrows, especially during the Middle Ages. It had a stout bow mounted horizontally across the end of a handle called a *stock* or *tiller.* To load the crossbow, the archer drew

the bowstring back to a catch called a *nut.* To shoot, the archer pulled a trigger that released the string from the hook.

The most powerful crossbows needed a special cocking machine to draw the bowstring back. Archers could cock smaller crossbows by placing the bow against the feet and pulling the bowstring back by hand.

In ancient times, the Chinese used a simple kind of crossbow. During the Middle Ages in Europe, special infantry units consisted entirely of soldiers armed with crossbows. By the 1500's, the longbow had gained popularity because it was faster to operate. The development of weapons that used gunpowder also reduced the crossbow's value in war. Richard A. Sauers

Crossword puzzle is a popular word game. It is commonly played on a diagram of black and white

Harle Publications, Inc., 1973

Crossword puzzle clues have numbers corresponding to numbered squares in a diagram. When the puzzle is completed, each square will have a letter that helps to spell a word.

ACROSS

1. Lump of sugar
5. Galilee, for example
8. Batter's target
12. October birthstone
13. Used to be
14. Diva's specialty
15. Bogeymen
17. Penny
18. Printer's measures
19. Barnyard clucker
20. Play ice hockey
21. Cat, dog, or canary
22. Indian's greeting
23. Blossom
26. In the direction of
30. Lends a hand
31. That girl
32. Indianapolis 500, for example
33. Troublesome bureaucratic complexity: 2 words
35. Confess
36. Shed tears
37. Sale announcements

38. Diamond size
41. Before: prefix.
42. Spartan campus at East Lansing: abbr.
45. Winglike
46. Vegetables
48. Declared
49. Long past
50. Away from the wind
51. Book holders
52. Original
53. Four-posters

DOWN

1. Arrive
2. Atop
3. Prohibits
4. Kays, ____, ems
5. ____ sixteen
6. Deserve
7. Donkey
8. In a reverse direction
9. Neighborhood
10. Bit of fluff
11. Behind time
16. Those people

20. Scatter seeds
21. Greetings from vacationers
22. Till the soil
23. Snack counter
24. Fib
25. Peculiar
26. Nothing but ____ best
27. Ewe's mate
28. 601: Roman numerals
29. Solidify
31. Foreign agent
34. Museum treasure
35. Summer beverages
37. Direction indicator
38. Attorney's concern
39. Chester ____ Arthur
40. Surprise attack
41. Book segment
42. Distance measure
43. Scurried
44. Puts into operation
46. Pot's relative
47. Arrest

squares. A set of numbered definitions or clues is usually printed near the diagram. The object is to answer the clues with words interlocking across and down the diagram. The player writes in each answer word in the row of empty squares starting at the number corresponding to the number of the clue.

Arthur Wynne created the first modern crossword puzzle, which appeared in the Sunday *New York World* newspaper on Dec. 21, 1913. The puzzle became a fad in the United States and spread to other countries. Today, crosswords appear in many languages throughout the world. Puzzle championships are often held in the United States and other countries.   Will Shortz

Croton, *KROH tuhn,* is the name of a group of tropical shrubs or small trees. The best-known type is the *garden croton,* which grows about 3 to 8 feet (0.9 to 2.4 meters) high. Its smooth-edged leaves may be spotted, streaked, or banded with yellow, white, green, and red. Because of these colors, the leaves are often used in wreaths. On some garden crotons no two leaves have the same pattern. The white flowers are small and hardly noticeable. The fruits are round and split into three segments. Garden crotons grow best in good, moist soil. They can be kept indoors in pots. In tropical climates, they are often grown outdoors in lawns and parks.

Scientific classification. The garden croton belongs to the spurge family, Euphorbiaceae. Its scientific name is *Codiaeum variegatum pictum.*   Walter S. Judd

Croup, *kroop,* is an inflammation of the air passages of the throat and *trachea* (windpipe). During an attack of croup, the mucous membranes in these areas become inflamed and swollen, restricting the flow of air. A victim of croup feels hoarse, breathes with great difficulty, and wheezes when inhaling. The patient also develops a hollow, barking cough. Croup occurs most often among children who are 6 months to 3 years old. Their air passages are smaller and more easily blocked.

Most croup results from influenza, a cold, or some other respiratory infection caused by a virus. Attacks of viral croup last three or four days. In mild cases, physicians prescribe bed rest and breathing moist air from a vaporizer. In severe cases, the patient may receive oxygen and a mist of a drug that widens the breathing passages. If the air passages become completely blocked, the physician performs an *intubation* or a *tracheotomy.* An intubation involves inserting a tube into the nose or mouth and through the swollen throat to the lungs. In a tracheotomy, the doctor cuts an opening through the neck into the trachea below the blockage.

Croup may also be caused by allergic reactions or bacterial infections. Drugs used to treat asthma help relieve croup that results from an allergy. A kind of bacterial croup called *acute epiglottitis* can develop into a life-threatening blockage of the air passages within hours. Doctors treat this condition with antibiotics and perform an intubation or tracheotomy if necessary. Another bacterial infection causes *diphtheria,* also called *membranous croup,* a severe disease in which a membrane forms over the air passages.   Neil R. Blacklow

See also **Diphtheria.**

Crow is a type of large, black bird that lives in all parts of the world except Antarctica, New Zealand, and South America. Crows belong to the crow family, which also includes jays, ravens, magpies, rooks, and jackdaws. The

Karl Maslowski, Photo Researchers

The American crow is found in most parts of North America. Crows use different calls to communicate with one another.

American crow, also called the *common crow,* is a clever, alert bird that inhabits open areas, farmland, the edges of woodland, and parks throughout North America. It typically remains in the same region the year around. Only the northernmost populations of these crows migrate south for the winter.

The American crow measures about 17 to 21 inches (43 to 53 centimeters) long. It has glossy, black feathers and a strong, sharply pointed bill. Bristly feathers cover the nostrils and the base of the bill. The bird's strong feet are well adapted for walking. Male and female American crows look alike, but the female is slightly smaller.

Crows do not have musical voices. However, they use more than 23 calls to communicate with one another. For example, when crows see or hear a predator, they call other crows with repeated long, loud notes. The crows then gather together to drive away the predator.

Crows build nests of sticks and bark in shrubs and trees, and sometimes on the crossarms of telephone poles. The female lays four or five bluish-green eggs with olive-brown spots. Both the male and female care for the young.

Crows eat a wide variety of foods. They annoy farmers by eating corn, wheat, and sorghum. However, they also feed on many kinds of insects and thus help limit insect damage to crops. Crows also eat spiders, small birds, eggs, rodents, and the flesh of dead animals.

Scientific classification. Crows belong to the crow family, Corvidae. The scientific name for the American crow is *Corvus brachyrhynchos.*   Edward H. Burtt, Jr.

Related articles in *World Book* include:

Blue jay	Jay	Raven
Jackdaw	Magpie	Rook

Crow, Jim. See Jim Crow.

Crow Indians are a tribe of the northern Great Plains of the United States. About 4,000 of the tribe's members live on the Crow Indian Reservation in southeastern Montana. The Crow have strong ties to this area, which they have occupied for at least 300 years.

The Crow conduct their official business through a tribal council made up of all adult members of the tribe. The council elects a chairman and other officers. The Crow work in agriculture, cattle ranching, tourism, and other occupations. The Crow hold several traditional ceremonies, including the annual sun dance and Crow Fair and Rodeo. Tobacco-planting ceremonies, the sun dance, Christianity, and use of the drug peyote play an important part in their religion.

The Crow were originally farmers. They were once part of another Plains tribe, the Hidatsa, along the Missouri River in what is now North Dakota. About the early 1700's, the Crow moved westward and hunted buffalo on the northern plains. The people lived in tepees and moved often to follow the buffalo herds. The Crow called themselves the *Apsáalooke,* which means *children of the large-beaked bird.* They became wealthy horse traders and produced fine craftwork.

The Crow were frequently at war with neighboring tribes, including the Blackfeet and the Sioux. But they quickly became friends with the white settlers and soldiers. In 1825, the tribe signed a friendship treaty with the United States government. The government established the Crow reservation through a series of treaties that began in 1851. Peter Nabokov

See also **Indian, American** (Indians of the Plains; picture: Shield covers).

Crowfoot. See **Buttercup.**

Crowfoot (1830-1890), a Canadian Blackfoot Indian chief, prevented his people from joining the North West Rebellion against the Canadian government. The advance of white settlers into the Saskatchewan region disturbed many Indians. But Crowfoot realized that resistance would be foolish because the whites were so powerful. Government promises of food and other assistance to the Blackfoot helped influence Crowfoot to decide against joining the uprising.

Glenbow-Alberta Institute
Crowfoot

Crowfoot was born in southern Alberta. His Indian name was Isapomuxika. As a young man, Crowfoot became a noted warrior known for his bravery and scouting abilities. But he later urged his people to stop fighting the whites and other Indians. In 1866, Crowfoot became head chief of the Blackfoot. He settled on a reservation in 1877. Hartwell Bowsfield

Crown. See **Teeth** (Kinds of teeth; picture).

Crown. See **Tree** (The parts of a tree).

Crown is a British coin worth 25 pence, or one-fourth of a pound sterling. Although they were once widely used, crowns are now coined only for special occasions, such as the wedding of Prince Charles and Lady Diana Spencer in 1981. They are rarely seen in circulation. On one side, the crown bears a likeness of the king or queen who was reigning when the coin was minted.

A coat of arms or other symbolic design is imprinted on the other. The crown was first issued in gold in the 1500's during the reign of Henry VIII. The crown, as it is known today, dates from 1551. Early crowns were made of fine silver, called crown silver. Since 1951, crowns have been struck in copper-nickel alloy. Burton H. Hobson

Crown is a circular ornament worn on or around the head as a symbol of authority, merit, or distinction. A royal crown is a king's or queen's symbol of supreme authority, but is generally worn only on state occasions. Such crowns are usually made of gold, engraved, and ornamented with precious gems.

The British royal crown consists of a gold band studded with diamonds, pearls, and other precious stones. From the band rise crosses, fleurs-de-lis, and four

© Lee Boltin
Historic crowns include the Crown of the Andes, *left,* from Peru, and the Imperial Russian Nuptial Crown, *right.*

British Crown copyright
Historic British crowns include St. Edward's Crown, *left,* copied from a crown worn by Edward the Confessor; and the British Imperial State Crown, worn by the monarch on state occasions.

arches, topped by a jeweled gold cross. The crown of the British ruler is regarded to be priceless (see **Gem** [picture]; **Elizabeth II** [picture]). A few crowns made for princes in India have famous, valuable jewels.

The Crown is a term often used for a monarch in his or her official capacity. It also means a monarch's rule, position, or empire, of which the crown is a symbol.

The history of crowns. Various jeweled head-dresses were worn by rulers of ancient Egypt and Assyria. The Greeks gave a crown or diadem of olive leaves to their athletes as a symbol of victory. Later the Romans adopted this custom. Their crowns were made of metal, usually gold, and were worn by the Roman emperors. From the reign of Constantine (306-337), the diadem was regarded as the symbol of royal power. Later European rulers probably borrowed the practice of wearing a crown from the Romans.

Iron Crown of Lombardy was worn by the Lombard kings and the emperors of the Holy Roman Empire when they became kings of Lombardy. It is made of gold, decorated with jewels and cloisonné enamel. Its name comes from an inner iron circlet which tradition says was beaten from a nail of the cross of Christ. Artisans probably made it in the A.D. 500's. Charlemagne, Emperor Charles V of the Holy Roman Empire, and Napoleon I wore the Iron Crown. It is in the Cathedral of St. John the Baptist at Monza, Italy.   Whitney Smith

Crown colony. See **Commonwealth of Nations** (Dependencies).

Crucifixion. See **Jesus Christ** (The Crucifixion); **Andrew, Saint.**

Crude oil. See **Petroleum** (introduction).

Cruikshank, *KRUK shangk,* **George** (1792-1878), an English artist, became famous for his caricatures and illustrations. His more than 5,000 works range from caricatures to illustrations and historical paintings. He worked closely with Charles Dickens to produce the illustrations for *Oliver Twist.* For examples, see **English literature** and **Dickens, Charles.** Cruikshank also illustrated books by such writers as Oliver Goldsmith, Henry Fielding, and Miguel de Cervantes. In addition, he gained praise for his series of drawings on the evils of drunkenness. Cruikshank was born in London. His father, Isaac Cruikshank, was a noted political caricaturist.

Charles P. Green

Cruiser is a large warship used to escort aircraft carriers and for independent operations with destroyers. Modern cruisers, called *guided missile cruisers,* can fire missiles, rockets, and torpedoes. Some can also carry helicopters. Cruisers use radar, sonar, and electronic intercept equipment to detect enemy aircraft, surface ships, and submarines.

United States Navy cruisers built in the 1980's and 1990's belong to the *Ticonderoga* class. They are 567 feet (172.8 meters) long, and they have an advanced radar and weapon control system known as AEGIS.

Most cruisers have gas turbine engines. Some cruisers have nuclear reactors that provide steam power. Cruisers can travel at a speed of about 30 knots (30 nautical miles per hour).

During World War II (1939-1945), cruisers fought enemy ships and bombarded beaches in support of amphibious landings. After the war, the U.S. Navy built large destroyer-type ships to escort aircraft carriers. These ships were called *frigates* until 1975, when the Navy renamed them guided missile cruisers. That year, the Navy also decommissioned its last all-gun cruiser.

Norman Polmar

See also **Frigate.**

Crumb, George (1929-   ), is an American composer known for his innovative and highly individual

works. Crumb received the Pulitzer Prize for music in 1968 for his orchestral work *Echoes of Time and the River* (1967). This work incorporates elements of theater. Instrumentalists are asked to march and to whisper and shout various short phrases and magical incantations. In the third *movement* (section), a xylophone taps out Crumb's name in Morse code.

Among Crumb's important works are vocal compositions based on poems by Federico García Lorca of Spain. They include four books of *Madrigals* (1965-1969), *Songs, Drones, and Refrains of Death* (1969), and *Ancient Voices of Children* (1970). The latter piece reflects Crumb's fascination with unusual instruments. The work is written for soprano, boy soprano, and an ensemble including percussion instruments, musical saw, and amplified harp and piano. The trio *Vox Balanae* (*Voice of the Whale,* 1971) consists of an electronically amplified cello, flute, and piano played by musicians wearing masks. This composition was inspired by the composer's hearing recorded sounds of a whale. Crumb was born in Charleston, W. Va.   Stephen Jaffe

Crusades were Christian military expeditions organized mainly to recapture Palestine during the Middle Ages. Palestine, also called the Holy Land, was important to Christians because it was the region where Jesus Christ had lived. Palestine lay along the eastern coast of the Mediterranean Sea, and Muslims had taken control of it from Christians. The crusaders, who came from Western Europe, organized eight major expeditions between A.D. 1096 and 1270. This was a period when Western Europe was expanding its economy and increasing its military forces. The Crusades were a part of a broad Christian expansion movement.

Kings, nobles, and thousands of knights, peasants, and townspeople took part in the Crusades. They had two stated goals: (1) to gain permanent control of the Holy Land and (2) to protect the Byzantine Empire, a Greek Christian empire centered in southeastern Europe, from the Muslims (see **Byzantine Empire**). But many crusaders also fought to increase their power, territory, and riches. The crusaders won some battles and established a crusader kingdom along the eastern shore of the Mediterranean Sea, but their victories had no permanent effect. However, the Crusades increased already existing contacts between the West and the East. These contacts led to additional trade and commerce.

The Crusades were originally called armed pilgrimages. The word *crusade* comes from the Latin word *crux,* meaning *cross.* Members of the many expeditions sewed the symbol of the cross of Christ on their clothing. "To take up the cross" meant to become a crusader.

How the Crusades began. During the A.D. 500's, the Byzantine Empire controlled much of the land bordering the Mediterranean Sea. This area included southeastern Europe, Asia Minor (now Turkey), Palestine, Syria, Italy, and parts of Spain and North Africa. In the 600's, Arab Muslims conquered Palestine, which included Jerusalem and other places sacred to Christians. Most of the new Arab rulers allowed the Christians to visit the shrines. See **Jerusalem.**

During the 1000's, however, fierce Seljuk Turks from central Asia invaded the Near East and conquered Asia Minor, Palestine, and Syria (see **Seljuks**). The Turks crushed the Byzantines in the Battle of Manzikert in Asia

Minor in 1071. The Turks had become Muslims. But unlike the Arab Muslims, they made it difficult for Christian pilgrims to reach the holy places.

In 1095, Byzantine Emperor Alexius Comnenus asked Urban II, pope of the Roman Catholic Church, for assistance in fighting the Turks. Urban agreed to help. He wanted to defend Christianity against the Muslims and to recover the holy places. He also wished to gain power and prestige for himself at the expense of a rival claiming to be pope. Urban believed that a military expedition against the Turks would unite the Christian knights and nobles of Western Europe and end their continual fighting with one another.

In the autumn of 1095, Urban held a meeting of church leaders in Clermont, France. At this Council of Clermont, Urban called for a crusade. He gave a stirring sermon, urging European Christians to stop fighting among themselves and recapture the Holy Land from the Muslims. He promised the crusaders both spiritual and material rewards for their work. The crowd enthusiastically responded with shouts of "God wills it!" An intense desire to fight for Christianity gripped Western Europe, and thousands of people joined the cause.

Not all the crusaders joined the expeditions for religious reasons. The French knights wanted more land. Italian merchants hoped to expand trade in Middle Eastern ports. Many priests and monks wanted valuable religious relics. Large numbers of poor people joined the expeditions simply to escape the hardships of their normal lives.

The First Crusade (1096-1099). Following Pope Urban II's call for a crusade, an enthusiastic preacher known as Peter the Hermit and a knight called Walter the Penniless led a group that rushed ahead of the official expedition. This group, known as the Peasants' Crusade, was untrained and undisciplined. Its members demanded free food and shelter as they traveled through eastern Europe toward Constantinople (now Istanbul, Turkey). Because these crusaders often stole what they wanted, many of them were killed by angry Europeans. The Turks slaughtered most of the rest in Asia Minor. See **Peter the Hermit**.

The main armies sent by Pope Urban II consisted chiefly of well-trained French and Norman knights. The key leaders included Godfrey of Bouillon, Raymond of Toulouse, Robert of Flanders, and Bohemond of Taranto. At Constantinople, Byzantine forces joined the crusaders. In 1097, the combined army defeated the Muslims near Nicaea, in what is now northwest Turkey.

Then the army divided, and the Western Europeans marched toward Jerusalem, fighting many bloody battles along the way. The most difficult was the siege of Antioch, in northern Syria (now in Turkey). Many crusaders died there, in battle or from hunger, and many others deserted. After Antioch had been captured, the crusaders were attacked there by the Turks. However, the discovery of a lance said to be the one that wounded Jesus on the cross inspired the crusaders, and they won a great victory. The Europeans arrived at Jerusalem in the summer of 1099. They recovered the Holy City after six weeks of fighting. Most of the crusaders then returned home. The leaders who remained divided the conquered land into four states. These states, called the *Latin States of the Crusaders,* were the County of Edessa, the Principality of Antioch, the County of Tripoli, and the Kingdom of Jerusalem.

The Second Crusade (1147-1149). The Christian forces in the Holy Land grew weak. In 1144, the Turks conquered the County of Edessa. The threat to the other Christian states brought about the Second Crusade. The spirited preachings of the French religious leader Bernard of Clairvaux inspired Western Europeans to defend the Latin States against the Muslims.

King Louis VII of France and King Conrad III of Germany led the armies of the Second Crusade into Asia Minor. But their armies did not cooperate, and the Muslim forces defeated them before they reached Edessa.

The Third Crusade (1189-1192). The Muslims continued to attack the Christians in the Holy Land. By 1183, Saladin, the sultan of Egypt and Syria, had united the Muslim areas around the Latin States. In 1187, Saladin easily defeated a Christian army at the Battle of the Horns of Hattin, and triumphantly entered Jerusalem. Only the coastal cities of Tyre, Tripoli, and Antioch remained in Christian hands.

The loss of Jerusalem led to the Third Crusade. The important European leaders of the Third Crusade included the German emperor Frederick I (called Barbarossa), King Richard I (the Lion-Hearted) of England, and King Philip II (Augustus) of France.

Frederick drowned in 1190 on his way to the Holy Land. Quarrels among Richard, Philip, and other leaders limited the crusaders' success. The Europeans conquered the Palestinian port cities of Acre (now Akko)

Bruno Barbey, Magnum

A crusader's fortress, the Krak des Chevaliers, was powerfully built to withstand Muslim attacks. This castle, which stands in Syria, was built by the Knights Hospitallers in the 1100's. Such fortresses could house several thousand fighting men and their servants.

First and Third crusades

This map shows where the First and Third crusades started and the routes the crusaders followed to the Holy Land. The First Crusade began in 1096 and ended in 1099. The crusaders succeeded in capturing Jerusalem. They also established the Latin States of the Crusaders: *Edessa, Antioch, Tripoli,* and *Jerusalem.* The Third Crusade began in 1189 and ended in 1192. The crusaders failed to recapture Jerusalem, but won an agreement with the Turks to permit Christians to visit the city.

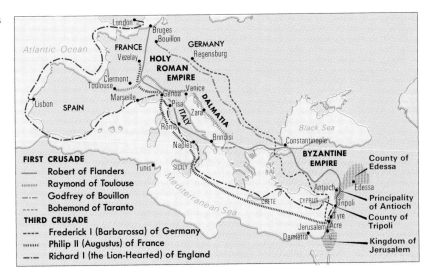

FIRST CRUSADE
—— Robert of Flanders
⋯⋯ Raymond of Toulouse
– – Godfrey of Bouillon
- - - - Bohemond of Taranto

THIRD CRUSADE
- - - - Frederick I (Barbarossa) of Germany
⋯⋯ Philip II (Augustus) of France
-·- Richard I (the Lion-Hearted) of England

County of Edessa

Principality of Antioch

County of Tripoli

Kingdom of Jerusalem

0   200   400 Miles
0 200 400 600 Kilometers

WORLD BOOK map

and Jaffa in 1191. But after the capture of Acre, Philip returned home to plot against Richard. Richard attempted to recapture Jerusalem, but failed. Before Richard left for home, however, he negotiated a treaty with Saladin. As a result of this treaty, the Muslims let Christian pilgrims enter Jerusalem freely.

The Fourth Crusade (1202-1204) resulted from the failure of the Third Crusade to recapture Jerusalem. The crusaders became involved in affairs of the Byzantine Empire, however, and never reached their original goal.

Pope Innocent III persuaded many French nobles to take part in the Fourth Crusade, which he thought should go to the Holy Land. But the crusade's leaders decided to attack Egypt instead in order to split Muslim power. The crusaders bargained with traders from Venice, a powerful Italian port city, to take them by ship to Egypt. Only about a third of the expected number of crusaders arrived at Venice, and they could not pay the costs of the ships. However, the Venetians offered to transport the crusaders if the crusaders helped them attack Zara, a city in what is now Croatia. The crusaders accepted the offer.

Meanwhile, a refugee Greek prince named Alexius claimed that his father, Isaac, was the rightful ruler of the Byzantine Empire. The crusaders agreed to help him regain the empire in return for money and other aid in reconquering the Holy Land. In 1203, they seized Constantinople and made Isaac and Alexius co-emperors. But Alexius could not fulfill his promises to the crusaders. In 1204, the crusaders captured Constantinople and put Count Baldwin of Flanders on the Byzantine throne. This Latin Empire of Constantinople lasted until 1261.

The Children's Crusade (1212) was one of the strangest and most tragic events in the history of the Crusades. Thousands of boys and girls from about 10 to 18 years old became convinced that they could recover Jerusalem. They believed God would deliver the Holy City to them because they were poor and faithful. Children from France formed one part of the group, and children from Germany the other. They expected God to part the waters of the Mediterranean Sea so that they could cross safely to Jerusalem.

None of the children reached the Holy Land. Many starved or froze to death during the long march south to the Mediterranean. When the expected miracle did not occur, the youngsters who survived the terrible journey to the sea returned home in shame. Others got aboard ships going to the East and either were drowned in storms at sea or sold into slavery by the Muslims.

Other Crusades continued in the 1200's. In the expedition known as the Fifth Crusade (1217-1221), the Christians captured the town of Damietta in Egypt. But other efforts failed, and they soon gave up Damietta in exchange for a truce.

Emperor Frederick II of the Holy Roman Empire led the Sixth Crusade (1228-1229). To the displeasure of the pope, he negotiated a peace treaty with the Muslim sultan. The sultan then gave Jerusalem to the Christians.

Jerusalem remained Christian until the Muslims seized it again in 1244. The fall of Jerusalem caused King Louis IX of France (Saint Louis) to lead the Seventh Crusade (1248-1254). Louis revived the idea of winning the Holy Land by attacking cities in Egypt. But his expedition became disorganized, and the Muslims captured Louis and his army. The Muslims freed the king in exchange for a huge ransom. Before returning to France, Louis spent four years in the Holy Land trying to strengthen the Christian forces there. In 1270, he led the Eighth Crusade against the Muslims. He landed his army at Tunis, in northern Africa. Louis died soon afterward, however, when a plague broke out among his troops.

Meanwhile, in the East, the Muslims continued to gain Christian territory. They captured Antioch in 1268. Finally, in 1291, they seized Acre, the last Christian center in Palestine. By this time, Europeans were losing interest in the Holy Land. Several weak attempts to organize crusades during the 1300's and 1400's failed. Europe was turning its attention westward to the Atlantic Ocean and beyond. In 1492, Christopher Columbus sailed to the New World. The European countries looked toward America to satisfy their ambitions to expand. They left the Holy Land to the Muslims.

Results of the Crusades. The crusaders failed to accomplish their main goals. They recaptured the Holy

Land for a time but could not establish lasting control over the area. Western and Eastern Christians united to fight the Muslims. But relations between the two groups of Christians, especially as a result of the Fourth Crusade, became so bitter that they led to a heritage of hate. The Byzantine Empire fell to the Ottoman Turks in 1453. Also, the pope's prestige declined because some popes used the Crusades for personal and political gain.

However, the Crusades also enriched European life. For example, they further stimulated economic growth by bringing increased trade between cities that bordered the Mediterranean Sea. The Italian cities of Venice, Genoa, and Pisa prospered and grew powerful by carrying crusaders and their supplies to the Middle East, where these cities gained privileges in territories conquered during the Crusades. Goods from Asia passed through these territories on the way to the cities in Italy.

Western Europeans also learned how to build better ships and make more accurate maps during the Crusades. They began to use magnetic compasses to tell directions. The Crusades were of only modest importance compared to the great commercial expansion or the rise of monarchies in Western Europe. In the minds of the people of the crusading era, however, the Crusades seemed very important.

Historians once thought the crusaders who returned to Europe acquainted Westerners with the goods and ways of life in the East and that this contact greatly influenced life in the West. As a result of the Crusades, historians once argued, Europeans were introduced to such items as sugar, silk, velvet, and glass mirrors.

Modern historians, however, reject these arguments. They say that Europeans had known of sugar, silk, velvet, and glass mirrors before the Crusades. These historians point to a wide amount of interchange between Muslims, Byzantines, and Europeans many years before the Crusades. Venice, above all, had served for many years as a link between the East and West.

Donald E. Queller

Related articles in *World Book* include:

Bernard of Clairvaux, Saint	Frederick II (Holy Roman emperor)	Louis (IX, of France)
Feudalism	Innocent III	Muslims
Flag (pictures: Historical flags of the world)	Knights and knighthood	Philip (II, of France)
Frederick I (Holy Roman emperor)	Knights	Richard (I, of England)
	Hospitallers	Saladin
	Knights Templars	Urban II

See also *Crusades* in the Research Guide/Index, Volume 22, for a *Reading and Study Guide.*

Additional resources

Level I

Buehr, Walter. *The Crusaders.* Putnam, 1959.
Theis, Daniel. *The Crescent and the Cross: The Early Crusades.* Thomas Nelson, 1978.

Level II

Billings, Malcolm. *The Cross & the Crescent: A History of the Crusades.* Sterling Pub., 1987.
Finucane, Ronald C. *Soldiers of the Faith: Crusaders and Moslems at War.* St. Martin's, 1983.
Mayer, Hans E. *The Crusades.* 2nd ed. Oxford, 1988.
Payne, Robert. *The Dream and the Tomb: A History of the Crusades.* Stein & Day, 1984.

Crusoe, Robinson. See Robinson Crusoe.

Crustacean, *kruhs TAY shuhn,* is an invertebrate animal with many jointed legs and a hard external shell. A crustacean has no bones. The external shell, called an *exoskeleton,* covers and protects the body. Crabs, crayfishes, lobsters, and shrimp are crustaceans, as are barnacles, water fleas, and wood lice.

There are more than 42,000 species of crustaceans. The largest species, the giant spider crab of Japan, measures up to 12 feet (3.7 meters) long between its outstretched claws. The smallest crustaceans, such as copepods and water fleas, may be less than $\frac{1}{24}$ inch (1 millimeter) long. Most crustaceans live in salt water, but some inhabit fresh water. A few species, including certain crabs and wood lice, live on land.

Crustaceans play a major role in *aquatic* (water) ecology. In most aquatic environments, small, floating organisms that make up the *phytoplankton* are the basic food producers (see **Plankton**). These organisms produce food from light by means of photosynthesis. Many small crustaceans feed on phytoplankton. These crustaceans then are eaten by larger crustaceans, fish, and even baleen whales. Crustaceans thus form an important link between the small food-producing organisms and the larger animals in the aquatic food chain.

People in many parts of the world eat lobsters, shrimp, and other crustaceans. On the other hand, some kinds of crustaceans cause problems for people. For example, certain aquatic wood lice burrow into, and eventually destroy, wooden wharves. Barnacles attach themselves to the hulls of ships and greatly reduce the vessels' speed. In some tropical regions where farms are near the sea, certain crabs and other crustaceans harm crops by burrowing into and damaging dikes that surround the fields or by eating the young plants.

The body of a crustacean

Outer body. The body of an adult crustacean typically has three main parts, each of which consists of many segments. These three parts are (1) the head, (2) the thorax, and (3) the abdomen.

The head of a crustacean has two pairs of antennae, a pair of eyes, and three pairs of accessory mouthparts. The eyes may be level with the surface of the exoskeleton or at the ends of stalks. The head also includes the mouth and a pair of jaws.

Each segment of the thorax has a pair of legs. The two pairs of legs closest to the head have *pincers* (claws), which are used for catching food and bringing it to the mouth, for fighting, and for other activities. Crustaceans use their other legs mainly for walking or swimming. In some crustaceans, gills for breathing develop at the base of the legs.

The abdomen of a crustacean varies greatly in size and appearance, depending on the species. The abdomen of a lobster is large and muscular and extends from the thorax like a tail. The abdomen of a crab, on the other hand, is thin and is folded beneath the thorax. Some species of crustaceans, such as lobsters and shrimp, have leglike appendages on their abdomen. These appendages usually are tiny, and the animal uses them primarily in swimming. A crustacean's abdomen ends in a flattened, taillike structure called a *telson.* Some crustaceans snap the telson rapidly to swim backward.

Giant spider crab

Orion Press from Bruce Coleman Ltd.

Spiny lobster

© Edward S. Ross

© F. Stuart Westmorland,
Tom Stack & Assoc.

Goose barnacles

© Paulette Brunner,
Tom Stack & Assoc.

Copepod

Crustaceans are invertebrate animals with an external shell. There are more than 42,000 species of crustaceans. Most of them live in salt water. The above photographs suggest the great variety of types of crustaceans.

Internal organs. In large crustaceans, a heart pumps blood throughout the body. Arteries carry blood away from the heart. The blood drains into cavities in the lower parts of the body and then returns to the heart through special openings. Some of the smaller crustaceans, such as certain copepods, have no heart. Their body movements promote circulation of the blood.

A crustacean's digestive system has three main parts: (1) the foregut, (2) the midgut, and (3) the hindgut. A crustacean has no teeth, and so it cannot chew. Instead, plates and spikes of shell in the foregut grind up food. The food is then directed to the midgut or the hindgut. The midgut produces enzymes and other substances that help digest the food. The hindgut stores undigested materials until they are eliminated from the body through an opening called the *anus.*

Crustaceans have a simple brain. It is connected to a nerve cord that extends along the underside of the body. Branches from the nerve cord enter each body segment and control various activities.

Most crustaceans breathe through gills. However, many small species have no gills. They breathe through their skin.

Senses. Most adult crustaceans have a pair of *compound eyes.* These eyes consist of many separate simple eyes. The entire group of eyes provides the crustacean with a mosaic image and can detect movement (see **Compound eye**). Adult copepods and a few other species of crustaceans have only *simple eyes,* which sense light but do not form an image.

Tiny hairlike *setae* cover various parts of the exoskeleton. Certain of them are sensitive to taste and touch. These sensory setae are concentrated on the antennae, mouthparts, and pincers.

The life of a crustacean

Reproduction. Among crustaceans, a new individual is created when a sperm of the male fertilizes the egg of a female. The male may deposit sperm on the female's shell or into sperm receptacles on her abdomen. The sperm then fertilize the eggs as the female lays them. The number of eggs produced at one time varies tremendously among species. The crayfish lays from about 50 to 150 eggs. The Chinese wool-handed crab produces as many as 900,000 eggs at a time. In most species of crustacean, the female carries the eggs on the abdomen and protects them until they hatch.

The body of a crustacean

A crustacean's body has three main parts: head, thorax, and abdomen. The animal's hard shell, called the *exoskeleton,* protects the body. The crustacean pictured below is a shrimp.

WORLD BOOK diagram by Patricia J. Wynne

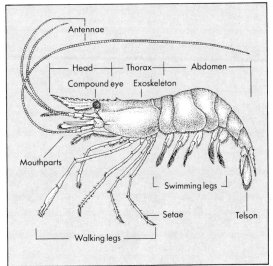

Interesting facts about crustaceans

WORLD BOOK illustrations by James Teason

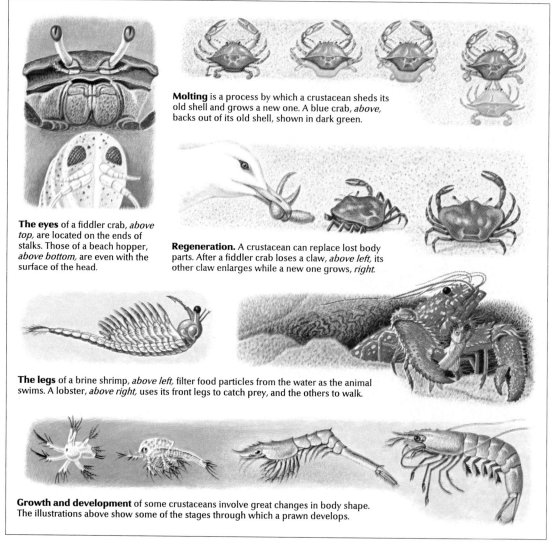

Molting is a process by which a crustacean sheds its old shell and grows a new one. A blue crab, *above,* backs out of its old shell, shown in dark green.

The eyes of a fiddler crab, *above top,* are located on the ends of stalks. Those of a beach hopper, *above bottom,* are even with the surface of the head.

Regeneration. A crustacean can replace lost body parts. After a fiddler crab loses a claw, *above left,* its other claw enlarges while a new one grows, *right.*

The legs of a brine shrimp, *above left,* filter food particles from the water as the animal swims. A lobster, *above right,* uses its front legs to catch prey, and the others to walk.

Growth and development of some crustaceans involve great changes in body shape. The illustrations above show some of the stages through which a prawn develops.

Growth and development. Most crustaceans hatch from the egg in an immature form known as a *larva.* At first, the larva does not look at all like the adult animal. The larva swims weakly in the sea for several weeks. During this time, it gradually changes form, adding new body segments and appendages until it looks like its parents. A few species of crustaceans, including beach hoppers and wood lice, have no larval stage. The young of these species hatch as miniature adults.

A crustacean's exoskeleton does not expand, and so the growing animal repeatedly sheds its old shell and grows a new, larger one. The shedding process is called *molting.* Many species of crustaceans continue to molt throughout life, but others stop after reaching maturity. Before molting begins, the crustacean absorbs some of the nutrients from its old shell. It uses these nutrients to form a soft, thin new exoskeleton beneath the old shell. The old exoskeleton then splits, and the animal works its

way out of it. The crustacean takes in water and swells to a larger size before the new shell hardens. A crustacean's muscles are connected to its shell. During molting, muscle attachments to the old shell are broken, and the animal has difficulty moving about. Until the new shell hardens, the animal often hides in a crevice or a small underwater cave.

If certain parts of a crustacean's body are damaged or lost, they may be repaired or replaced through a process called *regeneration.* The replacement part may appear during the next molt in a reduced size and then gradually enlarge to full size with successive molts. Some crustaceans, such as crabs and lobsters, can voluntarily detach a limb that has been caught by an enemy.

Food and habits. A few species of crustaceans live as parasites on other animals. Other species, including crabs, crayfishes, and lobsters, prey on various water creatures or eat the remains of animals and plants. Certain species, such as water fleas and some copepods, as well as many crustacean larvae, drift through the water and feed on floating microorganisms. In turn, these crustaceans are eaten by barnacles, krill, and other crustaceans, and by many kinds of fish. Krill are eaten by baleen whales, fish, and birds. Various other crustaceans become the prey of birds and land mammals.

Crustaceans live in a wide variety of habitats. Some drift continuously in the water as part of the plankton. Others prowl along the shore of a body of water and hide among rocks or weeds. Some find shelter in a sponge or coral, or inside an abandoned shell of a snail. Crabs and some other crustaceans burrow into mud or sand for safety. Barnacles attach themselves to rocks along the seashore as well as to turtles, whales, ships, and wharves. Most land crustaceans live under rocks or in burrows, rotting wood, or other damp places.

Scientific classification. Crustaceans make up the subphylum Crustacea in the phylum Arthropoda. Crabs, crayfishes, lobsters, shrimp, and wood lice belong to the class Malacostraca. Barnacles make up the class Cirripedia. Copepods make up the class Copepoda. Water fleas belong to the class Branchiopoda.

Jonathan Green

Related articles in *World Book* include:

Arthropod	Crab	Hermit crab	Shrimp
Barnacle	Crayfish	Krill	Water flea
Blue crab	Fiddler crab	Lobster	Wood louse
Copepod			

Cryobiology, *KRY oh by AHL uh jee,* is the study of how extremely low temperatures affect living things. Cryobiologists use temperatures that range from 32 °F (0 °C), the freezing point of water, down to just above −459.67 °F (−273.15 °C), which is absolute zero (see **Absolute zero**). The word *cryobiology* comes from the Greek *kryos* (cold) and *biology* (science of living things).

Cryobiologists are chiefly concerned with freezing living matter to preserve it for future use. The freezing must be done to keep the cells alive. Cryobiologists use a liquid gas, usually nitrogen, to obtain temperatures far below normal freezing. Cells kept cold in the gas stop working. But they stay alive and unchanged in a state of "suspended animation." They can remain in this state without harm for long periods. After thawing, the cells resume their normal work almost at once. Cryobiologists are experimenting with a technique called *vitrification* to preserve living cells that are normally damaged by other freezing techniques. Vitrification involves cooling specimens into glasslike solids using solutions that prevent ice crystals from forming.

The freezing of blood and tissues such as corneas and skin makes it possible to store these parts in "banks." Doctors may use skin from such a bank to graft onto a badly burned patient. They use stored corneas to replace diseased or damaged ones. Frozen red blood cells can be stored for many years. Frozen sperm, eggs, and embryos are commonly used for animal breeding and sometimes for human *in vitro fertilization* (see **Infertility** [Treatment]).

In *cryosurgery,* surgeons use extreme cold to destroy diseased tissue. For example, surgeons can perform a "bloodless" operation using instruments equipped with *freezing tips.*   David Mason Robinson

Cryogenics, *KRY uh JEHN ihks,* is the study of extremely low temperatures. It includes the development of techniques that produce and maintain such temperatures for industrial and scientific use. Temperatures of primary interest in cryogenics range from about −184 °F (−120 °C) to almost *absolute zero,* −459.67 °F (−273.15 °C). Absolute zero is, theoretically, the lowest temperature a gas can reach. Cryogenic temperatures are usually given on the *Kelvin scale,* the standard for scientific temperature measurement. Absolute zero has a value of zero on the Kelvin scale.

The word *cryogenics* comes from two Greek words meaning *cold* and *produce.* Physicists first produced extremely cold temperatures in the 1870's with the development of *liquid air* (see **Liquid air**).

In 1963, scientists cooled copper nuclei to the lowest temperature reached so far—almost one millionth Kelvin above absolute zero. The nuclei were magnetized at low temperatures in a magnetic field. When the magnetic field was removed, the nuclei became demagnetized and their temperature dropped to near absolute zero.

The first industrial use of cryogenics was the production of liquid air, a primary source of liquid oxygen and liquid nitrogen. Certain aircraft and spacecraft carry liquid oxygen that can be converted into gaseous form for crews to breathe on long flights. Other uses of liquid oxygen include the manufacture of synthetic gases and the treatment of waste water. Liquid oxygen and liquid hydrogen also are used in some rocket propellants and in fuel cells. Liquid nitrogen serves as a refrigerant. In addition, industry uses cryogenic techniques in the liquidizing, transportation, and storage of natural gas and the freezing, transportation, and storage of food.

Cryogenics has provided physicians with ways to freeze living parts of the body, such as blood and eye corneas, for future use. Other medical uses of cryogenic techniques include freezing organs during operations and destroying diseased tissue (see **Cryobiology**).

In physics research, the development of the liquid hydrogen bubble chamber provided a major tool for the study of subatomic particles (see **Bubble chamber**). Processing at cryogenic temperatures has made isotope-separation techniques more efficient for nuclear energy research. Cryogenics also contributed to the discovery of *superconductivity,* the ability of some materials to conduct electricity with no resistance at temperatures near absolute zero. Superconducting magnets cooled with liquid helium are used in medicine in *magnetic resonance imaging,* a technique that produces images of the internal organs of the body (see **Magnetic resonance imaging**).   Alan F. Clark

See also **Absolute zero; Superconductivity.**

Cryosurgery. See Cryobiology; Surgery (Technique); Medicine (picture: Cryosurgery).

Crypt, *krihpt,* is an underground room or vault. It usually refers to a vault under a church. The word comes from the Greek *kryptein* (to hide). Saints and martyrs were often buried in crypts. Chapels and altars were sometimes built over the spot where their bones were supposed to lie. One famous crypt is that of Saint Helena in Jerusalem. Legend says she found there the cross on which Christ died. Other famous crypts include those of Saint Peter's in Rome, of Saint Nicholas at Bari, of Canterbury Cathedral, and of Glasgow Cathedral.

Stanley K. Stowers

See also **Altar; Catacombs.**

Cryptology. See Codes and ciphers.
Crystal. See Glass.
Crystal is a solid that is composed of atoms arranged in an orderly pattern. Most nonliving substances are made up of crystals. For example, metals and rocks consist of crystals, as do snowflakes, salt, and sugar.

Well-developed crystals have a distinctly regular shape as a result of their geometrically ordered arrangement of atoms. Such crystals have smooth, flat surfaces, which intersect to form sharp edges. These surfaces, called *crystal faces,* show definite symmetrical relationships. The faces of crystals of the same substance always meet at the same angle regardless of the shape and size of the crystals.

The scientific study of crystals is called *crystallography.* Crystallographers measure the angles between crystal faces and analyze the symmetrical arrangements of such surfaces. They also examine and identify the atomic structures of crystals with the aid of *transmission electron microscopes* and *X-ray diffraction* techniques (see **X rays** [In scientific research]).

Crystallization is the process by which nonliving matter grows into crystals. Crystals may form from vapors, solutions, or *melts* (molten materials). When either temperature or pressure is lowered or evaporation occurs, certain atoms in such substances move close together and join. In most cases, they do so on a *crystallization nucleus,* an impurity or a tiny piece of crystal consisting of a particle or cluster of atoms. The atoms collect on the nucleus and arrange themselves into structural units called *unit cells* to form a crystalline solid. A crystal increases in size by adding atoms to its surfaces in an expanding network of unit cells. See **Mineral** (Inside minerals).

In a few cases, crystals develop smooth, mirrorlike faces. Such crystals are said to be *euhedral.* In nature, euhedral crystals rarely occur because they form only in an unconfined space where they can grow without touching other crystals. Most crystals are *subhedral*—that is, they have poorly formed faces that are rough or pitted. Some crystals, called *anhedral* crystals, have no faces at all. Most rocks are composed of anhedral crystals.

Classifying crystals. Crystals are classified according to *symmetry,* a balanced arrangement of faces. There are three basic types of crystal symmetry—plane of symmetry, axis of symmetry, and center of symmetry.

A *plane of symmetry* is an imaginary plane that divides a crystal into identical halves. An *axis of symmetry* is an imaginary line through the center of a crystal. When a crystal is rotated 360° about this axis, identical faces will appear from two to six times. If identical faces recur twice, the axis is a *twofold* axis of symmetry. If they reappear three times, the axis is a *threefold* axis. A crystal has a *center of symmetry* if opposite sides are identical. Most crystals have a center of symmetry.

All crystals can be grouped into one of 32 possible combinations of symmetry. These combinations, in turn, can be classified into seven general crystal systems. These systems are (1) isometric, (2) tetragonal, (3) hexagonal, (4) rhombohedral, (5) orthorhombic, (6) monoclinic, and (7) triclinic. Each system may be described in terms of three imaginary axes, called *crystallographic axes,* which intersect in the center of a crystal.

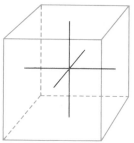

Isometric crystal

Pyrite

Isometric system. Crystals in this system have three axes of equal length that are perpendicular to one another. The simplest isometric crystal is a cube. Another form is the octahedron, which has eight sides consisting of equilateral triangles. Such minerals as galena, garnet, and pyrite crystallize in this system.

Tetragonal system. Tetragonal crystals have three axes that intersect at right angles. Two of the axes are of equal length. The simplest form of tetragonal crystal is a prism in which the sides are rectangular and the top and bottom are square. Other tetragonal crystals resemble

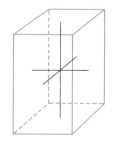

Tetragonal crystal

Rutile

eight-sided pyramids. Their sides are made up of identical *isosceles* triangles, which are triangles with two equal sides. The minerals cassiterite, rutile, and zircon crystallize in the tetragonal system.

Hexagonal system. Hexagonal crystals have four axes. Three of the axes are of equal length and lie in a horizontal plane with a 120° angle between one another. The fourth axis is perpendicular to the others and may be of any length. The simplest hexagonal crystal is a prism that has six rectangular faces parallel to the fourth axis. The

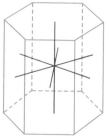

Hexagonal crystal

Field Museum of Natural History (WORLD BOOK photos)

Apatite

Rhombohedral crystal

Quartz

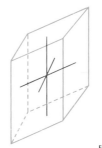

Triclinic crystal

Field Museum of Natural History (WORLD BOOK photos)

Plagioclase feldspar

minerals apatite, beryl, graphite, and molybdenite form in this system.

Rhombohedral system. Some crystallographers consider the rhombohedral system a subdivision of the hexagonal system because both systems can be defined in terms of the same axes. However, there is one major difference between them. The vertical axis of a rhombohedral crystal is a threefold symmetry axis, but that of a hexagonal crystal is a sixfold axis. The simplest crystal in the rhombohedral system has six rhomboidal faces, each consisting of an equal parallelogram. This system includes crystals of calcite, dolomite, and quartz.

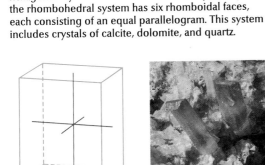

Orthorhombic crystal

Barite

Orthorhombic system. Orthorhombic crystals have three axes of unequal length that intersect at right angles. The simplest crystal of this type is an orthorhombic prism with three sets of unequal rectangular faces that meet at right angles. Aragonite, barite, topaz, and certain other minerals crystallize in this system.

Monoclinic system. Monoclinic crystals have three axes of different lengths. Two of the axes are perpendicular to each other, but the third is inclined. A simple

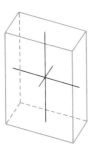

Monoclinic crystal

Gypsum

monoclinic crystal has two rhomboidal faces and four rectangular ones. The top and bottom surfaces are inclined. Many compounds, including the minerals gypsum, hornblende, orthoclase, and pyroxene belong to this system.

Triclinic system. Triclinic crystals have three axes of unequal length. None of the axes are perpendicular. The faces of these crystals are all different and do not meet at right angles. Plagioclase feldspars and a few other minerals form in this system.　　　William B. Simmons, Jr.

See also **Gem; Mineral; Snow.**

Crystal ball. See **Fortunetelling.**

Crystal set. See **Radio** (How radio programs are received; picture: A "crystal" radio).

Crystalline lens. See **Eye** (The uveal tract).

CT scan. See **Computerized tomography.**

Ctenophore, *TEHN uh fawr,* is a small transparent sea animal that lives in all the oceans of the world. Ctenophores are also called *comb jellies* and *sea walnuts.* The body of a ctenophore may be shaped like a ball, a thimble, or a belt. It looks somewhat like a jellyfish. The size of most *species* (kinds) varies from that of a pea to a thimble. One group of species, called *Venus's-girdle,* is shaped like a belt and may grow more than 3 feet (91 centimeters) long.

The word *ctenophore* means *a comb bearer.* The animal gets this name from the eight bands of comblike organs on the sides of its body. The combs are made of groups of *cilia* (tiny hairlike structures). Ctenophores move slowly through the water by beating these cilia. In some species, the combs give off flashes of light.

Scientific classification. Ctenophores make up the phylum Ctenophora.　　　P. A. McLaughlin

Cuauhtémoc, *kwow TEHM ohk* (1495?-1525), was the last Aztec Indian ruler of Mexico. He defended the Aztec capital, Tenochtitlan (now Mexico City), against the Spanish conqueror Hernando Cortés. The fall of Tenochtitlan in 1521, after a long siege, marked the end of the Aztec civilization.

Cuauhtémoc became ruler of the Aztec in 1520, four months after the death of his uncle, Emperor Montezuma II. In 1525, Cortés had Cuauhtémoc killed because he believed the Indian leader was plotting against the Spaniards.

Today, Mexicans honor Cuauhtémoc as a national hero because of his bravery in the defense of Tenochtitlan. Mexican Americans admire him as a symbol of their struggle for civil rights.　　　Feliciano M. Ribera

Cub. See **Bear; Lion; Tiger.**

Cub Scout. See **Boy Scouts.**

WORLD BOOK photo by Ron Laytner

Workers harvest sugar cane on a government-owned farm. Sugar is Cuba's chief crop.

J. A. Hancock, Photo Researchers

The José Martí Monument rises 450 feet (137 meters) above the Plaza de la Revolución in Havana.

Cuba

Cuba, *KYOO buh,* is an island country in the West Indies, about 90 miles (140 kilometers) south of Florida. It consists of one large island and more than 1,600 smaller ones. Few people live on the smaller islands except the Isle of Youth. Havana is the capital and largest city.

Cuba is one of the most beautiful islands in the Antilles, a part of the West Indies island group. Cubans call it the *Pearl of the Antilles.* Towering mountains and rolling hills cover about a fourth of the island. The rest of Cuba consists mainly of gentle slopes and broad grasslands. Cuba has a magnificent coastline marked with deep bays, sandy beaches, and colorful coral reefs.

Cuba has a long history of struggle for independence and social reform. For about 400 years, Spain ruled Cuba. During this period, many Cubans died in revolts against Spanish rule. In 1898, the United States helped defeat Spain in Cuba's struggle for independence. Spain then gave up all claims to Cuba, and a U.S. military government ruled the island until 1902. In the 1930's, Cuba was controlled by a dictator, Fulgencio Batista. In 1959, Fidel Castro and a band of rebels overthrew Batista. They later set up a socialist government, with Castro as its head. Today, the government is highly centralized, and Castro has strong control. The government allows only one political party, the Cuban Communist Party.

Robert Freeman Smith, the contributor of this article, is Distinguished University Professor of History at the University of Toledo and the author of Background to Revolution: The Development of Modern Cuba.

The Castro government provides many benefits for the people, including free medical care and free education. But Cuba's economy has developed slowly under Castro. The output of some industries has declined, and government attempts to increase agricultural production have been only partly successful.

Relations between Cuba and the United States became tense soon after the Castro revolution. In 1961, the United States ended diplomatic relations with Cuba. The United States maintains a naval base in Cuba at Guantánamo Bay. Cuban leaders resent the presence of the foreign naval base in their country, but the United States refuses to give it up.

Facts in brief

Capital: Havana.
Official language: Spanish.
Area: 42,804 sq. mi. (110,861 km²). *Greatest distances*—northwest-southeast, 759 mi. (1,221 km); north-south, 135 mi. (217 km). *Coastline*—2,100 mi. (3,380 km).
Elevation: *Highest*—Pico Turquino, 6,542 ft. (1,994 m). *Lowest*—sea level.
Population: *Estimated 1994 population*—10,991,000; density, 257 persons per sq. mi. (99 per km²); distribution, 78 per cent urban, 22 per cent rural. *1981 census*— 9,723,605. *Estimated 1999 population*—11,416,000.
Chief products: *Agriculture*—citrus fruits, coffee, milk, sugar cane, tobacco, vegetables. *Manufacturing*—cement, cigars, fertilizers, refined petroleum, refined sugar, rum, textiles. *Mining*—chromium, iron, nickel.
National anthem: "La Bayamesa."
National holiday: July 26, the anniversary of Fidel Castro's attack on the Moncada Army Barracks.
Money: *Basic unit*—peso. For the price of the peso in dollars, see **Money** (table: Exchange rates). See also **Peso.**

Under the Constitution of Cuba, adopted in 1976, the country is a socialist state and a *republic.* Actually, however, Cuba is a dictatorship that is controlled by Fidel Castro and the Communist Party of Cuba. According to Cuba's Constitution, the Communist Party is "the highest leading force of the society and of the state." The Communist Party is headed by Castro and has about 400,000 members.

The Cuban government has two major goals: (1) economic development of the nation and (2) economic and social equality among the people. Economic development has been slow in Cuba. But the government has made great progress toward its goal of economic and social equality.

National government. The most powerful position in Cuba's government is that of the president of the Council of State. This official is both the head of state and the head of government. The president of the Council of State also presides over a Council of Ministers, which enforces laws, directs government agencies, and conducts Cuba's foreign policy. The Council of State has the power to enact special laws, called *decree-laws,* when the country's legislature is not in session. All decree-laws are subject to the review and approval of the legislature.

The legislature of Cuba is called the National Assembly of People's Power. It is made up of deputies elected by the people to five-year terms. The National Assembly holds two regular sessions a year. It may also meet in special sessions called by the Council of State. The National Assembly elects from its members the 31 members of the Council of State, including the president. Then the president, with the approval of the National Assembly, appoints the members of the Council of Ministers.

Local government. Cuba is divided into 14 provinces that are further divided into about 170 *municipalities.* One municipality, the Isle of Youth, is not a part of any province and is responsible directly to the central government. Each province and municipality has its own assembly, which passes local laws and appoints administrators.

Cuban citizens who are over 16 years of age may vote. The people elect the members of municipal assemblies to $2\frac{1}{2}$-year terms. They also elect the delegates to the provincial assembly. Some provincial delegates also become deputies to the National Assembly.

Courts. The People's Supreme Court is the highest court in Cuba. Other courts may also be established under the Constitution, but all courts are controlled by the Council of State. The country's State Security Courts enforce laws that ban political dissent. People who break such laws often receive long prison sentences.

Armed forces. Cuba has one of the largest and best-equipped armies in Latin America. About 130,000 men and women serve in the country's regular armed forces, and about 135,000 men and women are in the regular reserves. The armed forces perform many nonmilitary services, such as harvesting sugar cane and clearing farmland. Cuban men must serve two years of active duty after they reach the age of 16, unless they volunteer for farm work.

Fred Mayer from Woodfin Camp, Inc.

Fidel Castro speaks to a large audience in Havana. A huge poster of Ché Guevara and Camilo Cienfuegos, leaders in the 1959 revolution, is displayed in the background.

Cuba's flag was officially adopted in 1902, shortly after Cuba became a republic. The star stands for independence.

Coat of arms. The key means Cuba is the key to the Gulf of Mexico. The stripes are from the flag.

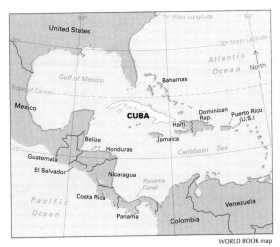

WORLD BOOK map

Cuba is an island country in the West Indies. It lies about 90 miles (140 kilometers) south of Key West, Fla.

Population and ancestry. Cuba has a population of about 11 million. About three-fourths of the people live in cities and towns. Havana, the capital and largest city, has more than 2 million people. One other city—Santiago de Cuba—has more than 300,000 people. See the separate articles on Cuban cities listed in the *Related articles* at the end of this article.

According to Cuban government records, about 75 per cent of the people are white and of Spanish descent. Most of the rest are blacks or *mulattoes* (people of mixed black and white ancestry). However, many of the people who are listed as white have a mixed ancestry. Almost all Cubans speak Spanish. Some people, especially in the cities, also speak English.

Way of life. About a fourth of the Cuban people live in rural areas. Many of them are poor. Before the Castro revolution, Cuba's government used much of the nation's economic resources to help make Havana one of the world's most luxurious and popular tourist centers. But little was done to improve life in rural areas, where many people lived largely on beans, rice, sugar cane, and such root crops as cassava and sweet potatoes. Castro's government turned some of its attention from Havana. Today, it spends large sums of money on food, housing, and education for the rural people.

Cuba has a housing shortage. In the cities, many people live in crowded apartment buildings that need repairs. Two or more families may share an apartment. A

Fred Mayer from Woodfin Camp, Inc.

Thatch-roofed houses are common in rural areas of Cuba. Many families use palm leaves to thatch their houses.

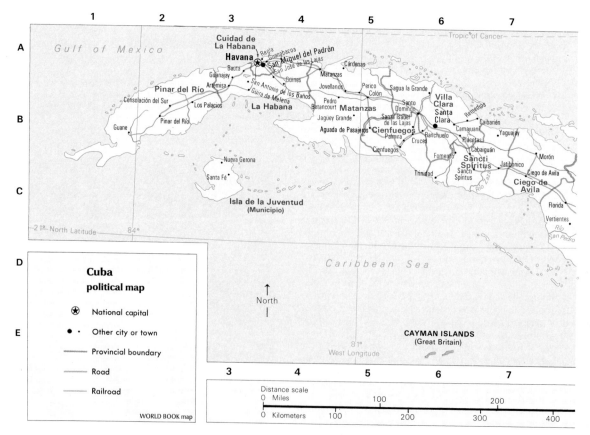

Cuba
political map

⊛   National capital

● ·   Other city or town

———   Provincial boundary

———   Road

———   Railroad

WORLD BOOK map

large number of country people live in thatch-roofed huts, many of which have cement floors. The government has built much new housing, but not enough to meet the demand. Rent for government-built apartments is set at 6 to 10 per cent of a family's income.

Many types of food are scarce in Cuba, and the country has a system of food rationing. The government issues coupons that entitle the holder to buy limited amounts of certain kinds of food at very low prices. Beans, beef, milk, potatoes, and rice are all sold this way. This system is intended to ensure that the poorest people can buy enough to eat. Additional amounts of the same kinds of food, except beef, may be purchased by those who can afford it, but at much higher prices. One or two free meals a day are provided to schoolchildren and to some workers.

Cubans have a strong love for their country and its traditions. In addition, the government encourages extreme *nationalism* (patriotism) among the people. Throughout Cuba, posters and neon lights display the revolutionary motto *Patria o Muerte, Venceremos* (Fatherland or Death, We Shall Conquer).

Most Cubans enjoy singing and dancing, especially to the lively folk music of the island. Popular Cuban dances include the cha-cha-cha, the mambo, and the rumba. Young Cubans enjoy rock music. Cubans are also enthusiastic sports fans. Favorite sports include baseball, basketball, swimming, and track and field.

Fred Mayer from Woodfin Camp, Inc.

Free hot lunches, often consisting of rice, beans, and meat, are served daily to Cuban schoolchildren.

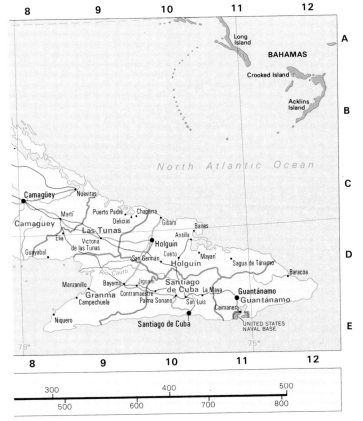

Provinces

Camagüey	......664,566.	.C 8
Ciego de Ávila	..........320,961.	.C 7
Cienfuegos	.......326,412.	.B 5
Ciudad de La Habana	........1,924,886.	.A 3
Granma	.......739,335.	.E 9
Guantánamo	.......446,609.	.E 11
Holguín	.......911,034.	.D 10
Isla de la Juventad†	.....57,879.	.C 3
La Habana	......586,029.	.A 3
Las Tunas	......436,341.	.D 9
Matanzas	.......557,628.	.B 5
Pinar del Río	...........640,740.	.B 2
Sancti Spíritus	.......399,700.	.C 6
Santiago de Cuba	..........909,506.	.E 10
Villa Clara	..........764,743.	.B 6

Cities and towns

Aguada de Pasajeros	......12,171.	.B 5
Artemisa	.........34,024.	.B 3
Banes	............31,282.	.D 10
Baracoa	.........35,538.	.D 12
Bauta	...........17,734.	.A 3
Bayamo	......100,543.	.D 9
Cabaiguán	......25,348.	.B 6
Caibarién	........32,094.	.B 7
Camagüey	......245,235.	.C 8
Camajuaní	......17,537.	.B 6
Campechuela	...14,151.	.E 9
Cárdenas	........59,501.	.A 5
Ciego de Ávila	....74,216.	.C 7
Cienfuegos	...102,426.	.B 5
Colón	........35,098.	.B 5
Consolación del Sur	...........16,995.	.B 2
Contramaestre	......22,204.	.D 10
Cruces	..........18,123.	.B 6
Cueto	...........13,552.	.D 10
Florida	..........39,700.	.C 8
Fomento	......14,925.	.B 6
Gibara	..........14,511.	.C 10
Guanajay	.........21,042.	.A 3

Guantánamo	.......167,405.	.E 11
Güines	..........41,552.	.A 4
Güira de Melena	......21,145.	.B 3
Havana (La Habana)	........1,924,886.	.A 3
Holguín	.......186,013.	.D 10
Jagüey Grande	.......15,540.	.B 5
Jatibonico	.....14,863.	.C 7
Jiguaní	...........15,042.	.D 10
Jovellanos	......20,899.	.B 5
La Maya	........13,939.	.E 10
Los Palacios	....13,928.	.B 2
Manzanillo	......87,471.	.D 9
Matanzas	.......99,194.	.A 4
Mayarí	...........21,139.	.D 10
Moa*	.........26,850.	.D 11
Morón	...........40,396.	.B 7
Niquero	........15,544.	.E 8
Nueva Gerona	......30,898.	.C 3
Nuevitas	......35,103.	.C 9
Palma Soriano	.......55,927.	.E 10
Palmira	...........9,856.	.B 5
Pedro Betancourt	............9,033.	.B 5
Pinar del Río	....95,476.	.B 2
Placetas	.........37,535.	.B 6
Puerto Padre	....23,239.	.C 9
Ranchuelo	.......14,644.	.B 6
Remedios	........16,176.	.B 6
Sagua de Tánamo	........15,327.	.D 11
Sagua la Grande	......42,741.	.B 6
San Antonio de los Baños	.........27,550.	.A 3
San José de las Lajas	......27,279.	.A 4
San Luis	.........23,638.	.E 10
Sancti Spíritus	.........71,959.	.C 6
Santa Clara	.....171,914.	.B 6
Santiago de Cuba	........345,772.	.E 10
Santo Domingo	......12,945.	.B 6
Trinidad	........32,809.	.C 6
Vertientes	.......22,440.	.C 8
Victoria de las Tunas	......84,749.	.D 9

*Does not appear on map; key shows general location.
†Municipality responsible to central government.
Source: 1981 census.

Education. Cuban law requires children to go to school for at least six years. The government controls the schools, and education is free. About 35,000 students go to the country's three national universities, located in Havana, Santa Clara, and Santiago de Cuba.

The government has set up various adult education programs. During the early 1960's, it recruited students to teach uneducated Cubans how to read and write. Later, other education projects were established. As a result of these programs, a great number of adults have completed elementary school. More than 95 per cent of Cuban adults can read and write. Many adults attend night school and job-training classes.

Religion. Most Cubans belong to the Roman Catholic Church. But the church has always been weak in Cuba, and few people attend services regularly. The government has taken over almost all church schools and has forced many priests to leave the country. Two religious groups, the Jehovah's Witnesses and the Seventh-Day Adventists, have been banned. People who attend religious services in the country cannot obtain good jobs or join the Communist Party.

Some Cubans believe in *Santería,* a religion that combines African tribal and Roman Catholic ceremonies. Its followers regard themselves as Catholics. They believe that Catholic saints represent African gods. Other religious groups include Episcopalians and Methodists.

The arts. The Cuban government strongly supports the arts and sponsors free ballets, plays, and other cultural events. It also provides scholarships for talented youths to the Cubanacan, a Havana fine arts center. The Casa de las Américas, a government-controlled publishing company, is the center of literary activity. It publishes a literary magazine, novels, poetry, and textbooks.

The works of many of Cuba's greatest writers have attacked political and social injustice. During the 1800's, Cuba's struggle for independence from Spain inspired such writers as José Martí and Rafael Mendive. During the 1900's, the poet Nicolás Guillén, the novelist Alejo Carpentier, and other writers have described the bitter hardships of the lower classes. Also during the 1900's, Fernando Ortiz became famous for his studies of customs of Cuban blacks and of the Cuban sugar and tobacco industries. Since the Castro revolution, several young writers have become popular. They include the novelist Edmundo Desnoes and the poet Roberto Fernández Retemar. Since the early 1960's, the Castro government has imprisoned some writers for expressing views contrary to government policy.

During the 1900's, Cuban sculptors and painters have produced many outstanding works. The best-known sculptors include Teodoro Ramos Blanco and Juan José Sicre. Cuban painters have become known for their landscapes and portrayals of daily life. Leading artists include Wilfredo Lam and Cundo Bermúdez.

Cuban composers have combined African and European musical traditions. Musicians use bells, bottles, castanets, and drums to produce the unusual beat of Cuban music. Famous composers of the 1900's include José Ardévol and Alejandro García Caturla.

WORLD BOOK photo by Ron Laytner

World-famous Havana cigars rank among Cuba's leading exports. The best cigars are made from tobacco grown in the Vuelta Abajo region in northwestern Cuba. Skilled workers, *left,* roll the cigars by hand, the traditional method of making high-quality cigars.

The land

Cuba lies about 90 miles (140 kilometers) south of Key West, Fla. The Cuban mainland is the largest and westernmost island in the West Indies. The mainland and its surrounding islands cover 42,804 square miles (110,861 square kilometers).

Surface features. Cuba has a varied landscape. Mountains and hills cover about a fourth of the island. The rest of Cuba consists chiefly of gentle slopes, rolling plains, and wide, fertile valleys.

Cuba has three main mountain ranges—the Sierra de los Órganos in the northwest, the Sierra de Trinidad in central Cuba, and the Sierra Maestra in the southeast. The highest point in Cuba, the Pico Turquino, rises 6,542 feet (1,994 meters) in the Sierra Maestra. Heavy forests, consisting chiefly of pine trees, cover the mountain regions of southeastern Cuba.

Rich croplands and pasturelands lie between the mountain ranges. This fertile soil consists mainly of red clay. Western and central Cuba have sandy areas. Stretches of lowlands and swamps lie along the coasts. Central Cuba has some limestone hills with large caves.

Rivers. Cuba has more than 200 rivers and streams. Most of them are short and narrow and too shallow for navigation. The longest river, the Cauto, flows about 150 miles (241 kilometers) through the southeastern part of the country. It is navigable for only about 75 miles (121 kilometers). Many of the rivers and streams in the mountain regions have waterfalls.

Coastline and islands. Cuba's coastline measures 2,100 miles (3,380 kilometers) long. It is marked with deep bays and sandy beaches and is fringed with coral islands and reefs. About 200 harbors lie along the coast.

Fred Mayer from Woodfin Camp, Inc.

A farmer tends his oxen in Pinar del Río, a province in western Cuba known for its rich soil and low, rolling hills.

Most of the harbors have narrow entrances, which protect the inner area against winds and waves. The most important harbors include Havana and Nuevitas on the north coast and Cienfuegos, Guantánamo, and Santiago de Cuba on the south coast.

More than 1,600 islands surround the Cuban mainland. The largest island, the Isle of Youth, lies about 40 miles (64 kilometers) off the southwest coast. It has an area of about 1,180 square miles (3,056 square kilometers). Forests cover the northern and southern parts of the Isle of Youth, and flat marshes lie in the center.

Cuba physical map

Numerous coral reefs and small islands form bays along the Cuban coast. Cuba also has many small rivers. Pico Turquino, the country's highest mountain, rises in the Sierra Maestra.

Geographical Terms	
Archipiélago	islands
Bahía	bay
Cabo	cape
Golfo	gulf
Pico	mountain
Río	river
Sierra	mountain range

⊛	National capital
•	Other city or town
▲	Mountain peak
	Swamp
	River

WORLD BOOK map

Distance scale
0 — 100 — 200 Miles
0 — 100 — 200 Kilometers

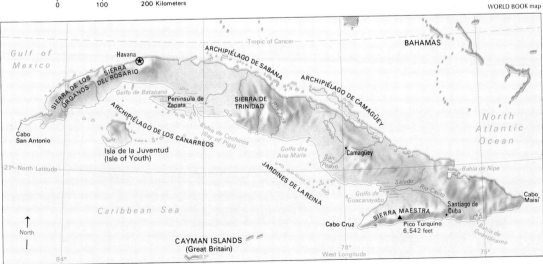

Cuba lies within the northern tropics and has a semi-tropical climate. Cool ocean breezes from the northeast during the summer and warm breezes from the southeast in the winter give the island a mild climate throughout the year. Average daily temperatures in Cuba range from about 70 °F (21 °C) in winter to about 80 °F (27 °C) in summer. The interior has a greater temperature range than the coastal regions. But temperatures in the interior rarely fall below 50 °F (10 °C) or rise above 90 °F (32 °C). Frosts sometimes occur in the mountains.

Cuba has a dry season and a rainy season. The dry season lasts from November through April, and the rainy season runs from May through October. The country has an average annual rainfall of 54 inches (137 centimeters). Thunderstorms occur almost daily in summer. Cuba has occasional dry periods during which not enough rain falls to produce sufficient juice in the country's sugar cane. Sugar is made from the juice of the sugar cane.

Violent hurricanes frequently hit the island, particularly the western half of the island, during August, September, and October. The strong winds occasionally destroy buildings and crops and create high waves that flood the coastal lowlands.

Economy

The government plans and controls Cuba's economy. It owns all industries, banks, and small businesses. The government also owns more than 70 per cent of the farmland. The remainder of Cuba's farmland is privately owned.

The Cuban economy has been developing slowly. In the early 1960's, the government began a program to industrialize the country. The program was only partly successful because of a lack of funds and raw materials. The government then shifted its emphasis to agriculture, especially sugar production. However, dry periods, hurricanes, and planning errors have limited the success of Cuba's agriculture.

Cuba's production

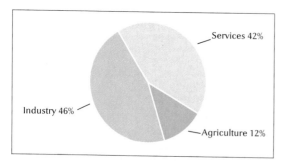

The net material product (NMP) is the total value of goods and services used in the production of goods produced by a country in a year. Such services include communication, trade, and transportation. NMP does not include financial services, government services, or community, social, and personal services. Cuba's NMP was $16,628,000,000 in 1989.

J. A. Hancock, Photo Researchers

Coffee trees, like many other tropical and subtropical plants, thrive in Cuba's mild climate and fertile soil.

Natural resources of Cuba include fertile soil and large mineral deposits. The best soil is in the center of the island, where farmers raise citrus fruits, rice, sugar cane, and vegetables.

Agriculture. The Cuban government controls all farming. It operates many large *state farms,* on which workers collect wages from the state. Many of these farms were estates owned by American companies before Castro's government took them over in 1959 and 1960. Private landowners receive financial help from the state and must sell their crops to the government. Their farms may not be larger than 166 acres (67 hectares).

Sugar cane has long been Cuba's chief crop. It is grown throughout the island, but the largest crops

Production and workers by economic activities

Economic activities	Per cent of NMP produced	Employed workers	
		Number of persons	Per cent of total
Manufacturing, mining, & utilities	37	757,200	22
Wholesale & retail trade	34	436,500	13
Agriculture	12	662,100	19
Construction	9	322,600	9
Transportation & communication	8	242,200	7
Community, social, & personal services*	—	1,024,800	30
Total	100	3,445,400	100

*Includes government and financial services.
Sources: International Labor Organization; United Nations.

come from eastern Cuba. Tobacco, the second most important crop, comes mainly from northwestern Cuba. Other farm products include bananas, cassava, citrus fruits, coffee, pineapples, potatoes, rice, sweet potatoes, and tomatoes. Cattle raising and milk production have increased because of the government's farm program.

Manufacturing. Before the Castro revolution, American companies owned most Cuban industries, and almost all factory machinery and raw materials came from U.S. suppliers. In 1960, the government seized all American-owned industries. The United States broke diplomatic and trade relations with the Cuban government in 1961. In the early 1960's, Cuba began depending primarily on the Soviet Union for its industrial needs. In 1991, however, the Soviet Union was dissolved.

Cuba's chief industry is food processing, especially the processing of sugar, dairy products, and flour. Cuban refineries process imported petroleum. Other manufactured products include cement, farm tools, fertilizer, iron and steel, paper, rum, shoes, textiles, tobacco products, and wood products.

Cuba has labor unions, but the government controls them. Members use the unions primarily to present complaints to factory managers. Worker assemblies handle such problems as job dismissals, job transfers, and workloads. The government sets the workers' salaries.

Mining is a growing industry in Cuba. The government owns all the mines and mineral reserves. One of the world's largest nickel ore reserves lies in northeastern Cuba. The country also has large deposits of limestone, used in making cement and fertilizer. Other minerals include chromium, copper, and silver.

Fishing. Cuba's fishing industry is growing rapidly. The government owns a fleet of large fishing boats. It also has organized *fishing cooperatives,* in which the members share in the profits. Important Cuban fishing ports include Caibarién, Cienfuegos, and Havana.

Trade. Cuba's chief exports are sugar and refined nickel ore. It also exports cigars, citrus fruits, fish, and rum. The country's main imports include machinery, petroleum, and grains.

Cuba spends more on imports than it collects on exports. From the early 1960's to 1991, Cuba depended on its main trading partner, the Soviet Union, for loans or gifts of billions of dollars to make up the difference. But when the Soviet Union was dissolved in 1991, Cuba lost this important source of economic aid.

Transportation and communication. Cuba has a good road system. The main road, the Central Highway, extends from Pinar del Río to Santiago de Cuba. Few Cubans have automobiles. There are more than 50 people for each car in Cuba. Most Cubans travel by bus. Railroads link Cuba's main cities, but many more people ride buses than trains. About 65 per cent of Cuba's railroad track consists of short lines that connect sugar mills to the main lines. The state airline, Cubana, flies within Cuba and to several other countries. José Martí International Airport in Havana is the largest airport.

Telegraph and telephone lines connect the major Cuban cities. Many homes do not have telephones, but the government has installed free public telephones in many cities. Cuba has an average of about 1 radio for every 5 people and 1 television set for every 13 people. About 15 daily newspapers are published in the country.

The government controls all Cuban newspapers and radio and TV broadcasts. But Cubans can pick up radio and TV broadcasts from the United States. Radio Martí, a U.S. government radio station that broadcasts to the Cuban people, began operating in Miami, Fla., in 1985.

Pineapples are picked by a Cuban farmworker. Central Cuba produces the nation's largest pineapple crops.

Early years. Christopher Columbus landed in Cuba in 1492 and claimed it for Spain. Spaniards began to settle the island in 1511, and Cuba soon became one of the richest colonies in the West Indies. Most of the settlers took up farming. They grew sugar and tobacco on large plantations and forced the native American Indians to work in the fields. Many Indians died from diseases and harsh treatment. As the Indian population declined, the Spaniards began to import African slaves. The first African slaves arrived in Cuba in 1517.

From the mid-1500's to the late 1700's, Cuba developed slowly. Pirates raided the coasts frequently, and many colonists moved to South America.

During the late 1700's, Cuba grew prosperous again. Havana became a commercial center as its port developed into a shipyard and naval base. Sugar and tobacco production increased, and Cuba began to sell its products to the British colonies of North America.

Cuban plantation owners imported more and more slaves during the late 1700's and early 1800's. Many owners treated their slaves brutally. In 1812, a group of slaves, headed by José Antonio Aponte, planned a revolt. The Spaniards discovered the plot and hanged Aponte and his followers.

Struggle against Spain. During the 1800's, various Cuban groups plotted revolts against the Spanish rule of their country. In 1821, José Francisco Lemus organized the first important revolutionary movement. But it collapsed by 1826. About the same time, Simón Bolívar, a South American general, and several Mexican leaders organized an army to invade Cuba and Puerto Rico and free them from Spain. The United States warned that it would support Spain against the invasions, and the military leaders dropped their plans.

During the mid-1800's, some Cubans and Americans supported a movement to *annex* (join) Cuba to the United States. A slave uprising had occurred in Cuba in 1844. Cuban and American slaveholders, fearing that Spain would end slavery in Cuba, supported the annexation movement. Other groups in Cuba and the United States favored American control of the island for economic and military reasons. The United States made several offers to buy Cuba, but Spain rejected them.

Cuba's struggle against Spanish rule led to the outbreak of the Ten Years' War in 1868. Carlos de Céspedes, a wealthy planter, headed a revolutionary group that demanded independence and the abolition of slavery. Spain rejected the group's demands, and fighting followed. The war ended with the signing of the Pact of Zanjón in 1878. This treaty provided for political reforms and for the gradual abolition of slavery.

Slavery was ended in Cuba in 1886, but many Cubans still wanted independence for their country. A revolution, led by José Martí, broke out in 1895. Thousands of Cubans died in the fighting. But by 1898, Spain controlled only the major coastal cities of Cuba.

President William McKinley of the United States believed that the fighting on the island threatened

The U.S. battleship *Maine* arrived in Havana in 1898 to protect Americans during Cuba's fight for freedom from Spain. The ship exploded mysteriously, triggering the Spanish-American War.

American interests. He told the Spanish government to either crush the revolution or give up Cuba. In February 1898, the U.S. battleship *Maine,* which was sent to Havana to protect Americans in Cuba, exploded mysteriously. The United States blamed Spain for the explosion and, in April, declared war on Spain. Cuba's struggle for independence thus became known as the Spanish-American War. The Spanish army surrendered in August. Under the Treaty of Paris, signed on December 10, Spain gave up all rights to the island. The United States then set up a military government in Cuba. The presence of U.S. forces angered many Cubans and Americans. See **Spanish-American War.**

United States control. Cuba experienced some development under U.S. military rule. General Leonard Wood governed Cuba from 1899 to 1902. He began an important public works program.

For many years, a deadly disease called yellow fever had plagued the Cuban people. In 1881, Carlos Finlay, a Cuban physician, said he believed mosquitoes carried the disease. In 1900, a U.S. Army commission in Cuba proved that Finlay was right. Mosquito-control programs were then begun to wipe out the disease.

Under strong pressure from the Cuban people for immediate independence, the United States decided to let them govern themselves. In 1901, Cuba adopted a constitution. The constitution included a set of provisions,

Important dates in Cuba

1492 Christopher Columbus landed in Cuba and claimed the island for Spain.

1517 The first African slaves arrived in Cuba.

1868-1878 Cuban revolutionaries fought Spanish rule in the Ten Years' War. Under the Pact of Zanjón, which ended the war, Spain promised reforms.

1886 Slavery was abolished in Cuba.

1895 A revolution, led by José Martí, broke out in Cuba against Spanish rule.

1898 The United States defeated Spain in the Spanish-American War. Spain gave up all claims to Cuba.

1898-1902 A U.S. military government controlled Cuba.

1902 Tomás Estrada Palma became the first president of the Republic of Cuba.

1906-1909 American forces occupied Cuba for the second time, after opposition to Palma's government grew into open rebellion.

1933 A revolutionary group led by Fulgencio Batista took control of the government.

1934-1959 Batista controlled the government, except for the years 1944 and 1952.

1953 Fidel Castro led an unsuccessful attack on the Moncada Army Barracks in Santiago de Cuba.

1959 Castro's forces overthrew Batista's government, and Castro became ruler of the country.

1961 Cuban exiles invaded Cuba at the Bay of Pigs and were quickly defeated by Castro's army.

1962 The Soviet Union agreed to U.S. demands that it remove its missiles and missile bases from Cuba.

1976 Cuba adopted a new constitution. The constitution declared the nation to be a socialist state and a republic.

1991 The Soviet Union, which had been an important source of economic aid to Cuba, was dissolved.

called the *Platt Amendment,* which the United States insisted must be part of the document. The amendment limited Cuban independence by permitting the United States to intervene in Cuban affairs. It also allowed the United States to buy or lease land for naval bases in Cuba. Under a treaty with Cuba in 1903, the United States received a permanent lease on Guantánamo Bay and began to build a large naval base there.

In 1902, the Cuban people elected Tomás Estrada Palma as the first president of the Republic of Cuba. American troops then left the country. But they returned in 1906, after opposition to Palma's government developed into open rebellion. A civil-military government, headed by Charles E. Magoon of the United States, ruled Cuba from 1906 to 1909.

The Second Republic of Cuba was established after American forces left the country in 1909. But the new Cuban government did little to help the lower classes. A black uprising broke out in 1912. In 1917, a workers' revolt threatened to destroy the sugar mills. American companies owned many mills, plantations, and other businesses in Cuba. During both uprisings, the United States sent military forces into the country to protect American property.

The Cuban people elected Gerardo Machado president in 1924. During his campaign, Machado had attacked the Platt Amendment and had promised reforms. But after becoming president, he ruled as a dictator. In July 1933, an army revolt forced Machado out of office. Two months later, an army sergeant named Fulgencio Batista and a group of university students and professors led a revolt that overthrew the new government. They named a five-member committee, which was

United Press Int.

Fulgencio Batista, famous for his fiery speechmaking, ruled Cuba as dictator from 1934 to 1944 and from 1952 to 1959.

headed by Ramón Grau San Martín, to govern Cuba.

The Grau San Martín government wanted to reduce U.S. influence in Cuba and make far-reaching changes. The United States thought the new government was too extreme and refused to support it.

The Batista era. Batista felt that his best hope for power lay in winning U.S. support. He removed Grau San Martín from office in 1934. Until 1940, Batista ruled Cuba as dictator through presidents who served in name only. The United States supported Batista's government. In 1934, the United States and Cuba signed a treaty that canceled the Platt Amendment, except for the Guantánamo Bay lease.

In 1940, Cubans adopted a new constitution and elected Batista president. The constitution prevented Batista from seeking reelection in 1944, and Grau San Martín became president again. Carlos Prío Socarrás won the 1948 election.

In 1952, Batista overthrew Prío's government and again became dictator. Cuba grew prosperous under Batista. He stressed the development of light industry and encouraged foreign companies to build businesses in Cuba. Batista also established badly needed public works. But most Cubans continued to live in poverty.

The Castro revolution. On July 26, 1953, Fidel Castro, a young lawyer, tried to start a revolution against Batista by attacking the Moncada Army Barracks in Santiago de Cuba. Castro and many of his followers were captured and imprisoned. After his release in 1955, Castro organized the *26th of July Movement,* a revolutionary group named after the date of his first revolt. He then went to Mexico. Castro's forces landed in Cuba in December 1956. Most of the rebels were soon killed. However, Castro and 11 of his followers escaped to the Sierra Maestra mountains. In the mountains, they formed a guerrilla band to carry out surprise attacks against the Cuban government.

In 1957, Castro's forces began to attack army units and to blow up bridges and railroad tracks. Attempts by the government to crush the revolution increased the people's support of the rebels. By mid-1958, Cubans had lost confidence in Batista's government. On Jan. 1, 1959, Batista fled the country. Castro's forces then took control of the government. Later, Castro became premier of Cuba. Manuel Urrutia was named president. The revolutionary leaders did away with the political and military structure of Batista's government. Many former political officials and army officers were tried and executed.

At first, the United States supported the Castro government. But the leading revolutionaries did not welcome U.S. support. In 1959 and 1960, the Cuban government seized American-owned sugar estates and cattle ranches, and relations between the two countries declined sharply.

Immediately after the revolution, many Cubans who opposed Castro left the country. Most of them moved to the United States. In late 1959, a group of these exiles hired American planes and flew over Cuba, dropping anti-Castro leaflets and small fire bombs. Cuban leaders criticized the United States for not stopping the flights. The Castro government grew more hostile toward the United States after Western European nations, under U.S. pressure, refused to sell arms to Cuba. Cuba then turned to the Soviet Union for economic and military as-

Fidel Castro became the head of the Cuban government in 1959 after he and his supporters overthrew the dictatorship of Fulgencio Batista. Here Castro waves as he appears before a crowd of Cubans after he took power.

sistance. The Soviet aid became substantial, and Cuba's economy depended on it heavily.

In June 1960, the Castro government took over American oil refineries in Cuba. The United States then stopped buying sugar from Cuba. The Castro government responded by taking over all of the remaining American businesses in Cuba. In January 1961, the United States ended diplomatic relations with Cuba. The United States government also severely restricted travel to Cuba by American citizens.

The Bay of Pigs invasion. In April 1961, Cuban exiles invaded Cuba at the Bay of Pigs on the south coast. They had been promised direct U.S. military action, including air cover, to ensure the success of the invasion. President John F. Kennedy had approved the invasion, but he refused to send military aid. Castro's forces crushed the invasion and captured most of the exiles. His government later released many of the exiles to the United States in exchange for nonmilitary supplies.

The Cuban missile crisis. In 1962, Cuban leaders became convinced that the United States was planning an attack on Cuba. They asked the Soviet Union for more military aid. The Soviet Union responded by sending missiles and materials to build launch sites. In October, the United States learned that Cuba had missile bases that could launch nuclear attacks on American cities. President Kennedy ordered a naval blockade to halt the further shipment of arms and demanded that the Soviet Union remove all missiles and missile bases from the island. For several days, the world stood on the brink of nuclear war. Finally, the Soviet Union removed the weapons under protest from Castro. But several thousand Soviet troops remained in Cuba.

Recent developments. The Cuban government resents the presence of a United States naval base at Guantánamo Bay. Cuban leaders claim that the base threatens Cuba's security. But the United States refuses to give up the Guantánamo location. In 1964, Castro shut off the naval base's fresh water supply. The United States then moved a plant that turns ocean water into fresh water to Guantánamo.

Castro has tried to spread revolution throughout Latin America and has supplied military aid to guerrilla groups in several Latin-American countries. At first the guerrillas were not successful. Ché Guevara, a leader in the Castro revolution, was killed during a guerrilla operation in Bolivia in 1967. In the 1970's, Cuba trained and supplied weapons to members of the Sandinista National Liberation Front, then a guerrilla organization in Nicaragua. The Sandinistas won control of Nicaragua's government in 1979 and held power there until 1990.

In the 1970's, Cuba began to aid groups in Africa that favor Communist principles. Cuban troops and civilian and military advisers were sent to several African countries. In 1975 and 1976, Cuban troops fought alongside a pro-Communist group in a civil war in Angola. When this group took over Angola's government in 1976, Cuban troops remained in the country to support government troops in their fight against antigovernment guerrillas. Cuban troops began to withdraw from Angola in 1989. By mid-1991, Cuban troops had completely withdrawn from the country. Cuban troops also aided Ethiopia's Socialist government in that country's war with Somalia in 1977 and 1978.

Relations between Cuba and the United States have remained strained since the early 1960's. But from time to time, there have been signs of improved relations between the two countries. For example, in 1977, the U.S. government ended its restrictions on travel to Cuba by American citizens. In 1982, however, the United States government reinstated severe travel restrictions to Cuba. Cuba and the United States also established diplomatic offices in each other's country in 1977. But the two nations did not resume full diplomatic relations.

Since the revolution, hundreds of thousands of Cubans have left the country because of their opposition to Castro or because of dissatisfaction with their social and economic conditions. Most of these people have settled in the United States. Others have settled in such Spanish-speaking countries as Mexico and Spain. An especially large emigration wave took place between April and September of 1980, when about 125,000 Cubans moved to the United States.

In the late 1980's, the Soviet Union and other European Communist countries began programs to give their people more political and economic freedom. Castro criticized these reform efforts. Non-Communist governments replaced Communist governments in most of the Eastern European countries, including the Soviet Union in 1991. But Castro vowed that Cuba would remain a Communist country. Some Cubans protested against Communist control of Cuba's government. Many of them were arrested. Also in 1991, the Soviet government announced it would remove its troops from Cuba. In the early 1990's, all the Soviet troops were removed from Cuba. In December 1991, the Soviet Union was dissolved, and Cuba lost its most important source of aid. This loss of aid harmed Cuba's economy.

Robert Freeman Smith

Study aids

Related articles in *World Book* include:

Cities

Guantánamo	Santiago de Cuba
Havana	

History

Batista y Zaldívar, Fulgencio	Guevara, Ché
Castro, Fidel	Kennedy, John F. (Cuba)
Columbus, Christopher	Martí, José Julián
Finlay, Carlos Juan	Reed, Walter
García Íñiguez, Calixto	Spanish-American War
Guerrilla warfare (History)	Wood, Leonard

Other related articles

Organization of American States
West Indies

Outline

I. **Government**
II. **People**
    A. Population and ancestry   D. Religion
    B. Way of life   E. The arts
    C. Education

Questions

What was the Platt Amendment?
What are the two major goals of Cuba's government?
What are Cuba's two most important crops?
What was the 26th of July Movement?
How has Cuba promoted adult education?
What are *state farms*?
What was the Cuban missile crisis?
Why does Cuba have a mild climate the year around?
What is *Santería*?
Why has Cuba's economy developed slowly under Fidel Castro?

Additional resources

Crouch, Clifford W. *Cuba.* Chelsea Hse., 1991. Also suitable for
   younger readers.
Pérez, Louis A. *Cuba: Between Reform and Revolution.* Oxford,
   1988.
Smith, Wayne S. *The Closest of Enemies: A Personal and Diplomatic Account of U.S.-Cuban Relations Since 1957.* Norton,
   1987.
Suchlicki, Jaime. *Historical Dictionary of Cuba.* Scarecrow, 1988.
   Cuba: From Columbus to Castro. 3rd. ed. Pergamon, 1990.

Cube, in geometry, is a solid bounded by six square
faces of equal size. A cube has 12 edges, all of which are
equal to one another. The *volume* of a cube, or the
space it fills, is expressed
in cubic inches, cubic feet,
cubic centimeters, or some
other cubic unit. The volume is found by multiply-
ing the number that represents the length of one of
the edges by itself, then
multiplying by the length
again. For example, if the
edge of a cube is 4 meters
long, the volume of the
cube is 4×4×4, or 64,
cubic meters. In arithmetic,
the *cube* of a number is
the product obtained when
a number is used as a factor three times. Thus, the
cube of 4 is 4×4×4, or 64.
This can be indicated by 4^3.

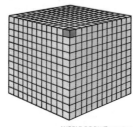

WORLD BOOK illustration
by Sarah Woodward
A cube is bounded by six
square faces. Each face of a
cube of one cubic foot is 12
inches long and 12 inches
wide. The volume is 12×12×
12, or 1,728, cubic inches. The
small red cube is $\frac{1}{12}$ of the
length, width, and height.

See also **Archimedean solid** (picture); **Cube root; Root.**

    Mary Kay Corbitt

Cube root is one of three equal factors of a number
(see **Factor**). The same number (*m*) taken as a factor
three times will be the cube root of another number (*n*).
Thus, $m \times m \times m = n$. For example, 2 is the cube root of
8, because 2×2×2=8, and −5 is the cube root of
−125, because −5×−5×−5 = −125. A real number
has only one real cube root, which is positive or negative, according to whether the given number is positive
or negative. When a cube root or any other root of a
number is to be *extracted* (determined), another symbol
is placed over the number. This symbol is written $\sqrt{}$,

and is called the *root sign,* or *radical sign.* If the root to
be extracted is a cube root, a small figure 3 is added to
the root sign. Thus, $\sqrt[3]{8}$ indicates that the cube root of 8
is to be determined.

    Finding cube roots by tables. Perhaps the easiest
way of finding cube roots is to use a *table of cube roots,*
a *table of cubes,* or a *table of logarithms.* These tables
provide correct answers and eliminate tedious calculations. In most cases, the numbers will not have exact
cube roots. In these cases, tables are especially helpful.

    Calculating cube roots. Sometimes tables may not
be available. Or, if they are, they will not be accurate
enough for a particular purpose. In this case, a person
must make his or her own calculations.

    One procedure, called *Newton's method,* is easy to
use with a calculator. It can be used to calculate the
cube root of a number between 1 and 1,000. For example, a person might wish to find the cube root of 200.
Since 5×5×5=125, and 6×6×6=216, it is easy to see
that 6 is the closest *integral,* or whole number, cube
root of 200. A closer complete approximation can be
made by dividing 200 by the square of 6, or 6×6, which
equals 36. To the nearest tenth, this gives 5.6. Thus,
6×6×5.6 is approximately 200.

    To get the second approximation of the cube root of
200, average the three factors 6, 6, and 5.6. This will
give $\frac{6+6+5.6}{3}$ = 5.9. This procedure is repeated to
obtain a still better approximation. Thus,
$\frac{200}{5.9 \times 5.9} = \frac{200}{34.81} = 5.74$, and the next approximation is
given by $\frac{5.9+5.9+5.74}{3}$ = 5.85. Repeating once more
gives $\frac{200}{5.85 \times 5.85} = \frac{200}{34.2225} = 5.8441$, which gives the
next approximation $\frac{5.85+5.85+5.8441}{3}$ = 5.8480.

    This process may be continued indefinitely. In each
approximation beyond the second, you can retain a
number of digits that is one less than twice the number
of digits found in the previous approximation. For example, the second approximation, 5.9, contains two digits.
The third approximation may retain three digits, and the
fourth approximation may retain five digits.

    If the number whose cube is desired is not between 1
and 1,000, either multiply or divide it successively by
1,000 to bring it within this range. The cube root of this
number will lie between 1 and 10. After finding the cube
root, either divide or multiply it successively by 10 as
many times as necessary to give the cube root of the
original number.   John M. Smith

See also **Cube; Logarithms; Root.**

Cubeb, *KYOO behb,* is the dried, unripe berry of a
climbing vine belonging to the pepper family. It grows
in Pinang, Sumatra, New Guinea, and neighboring islands. It resembles black pepper. Cubebs are used as
spices in Asia, and as medicine in Europe and America.
Drugs prepared from cubebs are used as kidney stimulants, urinary antiseptics, and expectorants. Cubebs, in
the form of cigarettes, were formerly used to treat hay
fever, asthma, and pharyngitis.

    Scientific classification. The cubeb belongs to the family
Piperaceae. Its scientific name is *Piper cubeba.*

    W. Dennis Clark

Cubic measure. See Weights and measures.

Cubism was the most influential movement in the history of modern art. The cubists introduced radically new approaches to rendering form and space.

Cubism began in France, where it flourished as a movement between 1907 and 1914. The leaders of the movement were the Spanish-born artist Pablo Picasso and the French artist Georges Braque. Other cubists included Juan Gris of Spain and Robert Delaunay and Fernand Léger of France. The aims of the movement were first expressed in a 1912 book by two other French cubist painters, Albert Gleizes and Jean Metzinger.

The cubist painters shunned conventional treatment of space and form. A typical cubist painting analyzes the subject in basic geometric shapes and elementary signs. By reorganizing these elements and freeing them from direct reference to objects seen in nature, the cubists developed a new language of representation.

Many cubist paintings and sculptures are still lifes that represent such commonplace objects as tabletops, musical instruments, bottles, and glassware. Cubist painters and sculptors were often inspired by everyday subject matter, such as the mass media and popular materials including advertisements, cartoons, and songs. Artists often included numbers and fragments of words in their pictures. The cubists also made *collages,* which are paintings that incorporate real objects, such as newspaper clippings, wallpaper, or oilcloth (see **Collage**). In addition, many of the cubists were strongly influenced by the formal simplification and expressive power of black African sculpture.

Cubist paintings are traditionally described in terms of *analytic cubism* and *synthetic cubism.* Analytic cubism refers to the style that emerged about 1910. Its name suggests the way artists broke down, or *analyzed,* and

Museum of Modern Art, New York, acquired through the Lillie P. Bliss Bequest

Early cubism grew from Pablo Picasso's *Les Demoiselles d'Avignon,* of 1907, *above.* Black African sculpture influenced it.

The Bottle of Banyuls (1914), a gouache and pencil with paper collage on canvas by Juan Gris; Kunstmuseum Bern, Hermann and Margrit Rupf Collection © COSMOPRESS, Genf

Synthetic cubism began in 1912. This style of cubism was more realistic and colorful than the earlier analytic cubist style.

Museum of Modern Art, New York, acquired through the Lillie P. Bliss Bequest

Analytic cubism divided objects into many fragments and planes, as in Georges Braque's *Man with a Guitar* of 1911, *above.*

then reassembled observed forms in various ways. Synthetic cubism refers to the style of 1912 and later, in which artists tried to *synthesize* (combine) imaginative elements into new representational structures.

Although no single painting can be identified as the first cubist picture, Picasso's *Les Demoiselles d'Avignon* (1907) is a landmark in the movement. The series of landscapes Braque painted in the town of l'Estaque, near Marseilles, had a strong geometric character typical of early cubism.   Nancy J. Troy

For other examples of cubist painting, see **Painting** (Cubism); **Duchamp, Marcel; Léger, Fernand.** See also **Braque, Georges; Cézanne, Paul; Gris, Juan; Picasso, Pablo; Sculpture** (Cubism and futurism).

Additional resources

Daix, Pierre. *Cubists and Cubism.* Rizzoli, 1982.
Roskill, Mark W. *The Interpretation of Cubism.* Art Alliance, 1985.

Cubit, *KYOO biht,* is a measure of length used by several early civilizations. It was based on the length of the forearm from the tip of the middle finger to the elbow. No one knows when this measure was established. The length of the arm, or cubit, was commonly used by many early peoples, including the Babylonians, Egyptians, and Israelites. The royal cubit of the ancient Egyptians was about $20\frac{3}{5}$ inches (52.3 centimeters) long. That of the ancient Romans was $17\frac{1}{2}$ inches (44.5 centimeters). The Israelite's cubit at the time of Solomon was $25\frac{1}{5}$ inches (64 centimeters).   Richard S. Davis

Cuchulainn, *koo KUHL ihn,* also spelled Cuchulain, is a great hero of Irish mythology and folklore. He is the main character in *The Cattle Raid of Cooley,* the oldest epic of western Europe in a native language. It is the central story of the Ulster cycle of ancient Irish tales. Said to have taken place about the time of Jesus Christ, the story has a slim base in fact, but the details are mythological. Cuchulainn's reputation as a warrior grew in Irish folk tales until he came to be treated as a defender of all Ireland. Cuchulainn became a favorite character among writers of the Irish Literary Renaissance of the late 1800's.

Cuchulainn had extraordinary powers because his father was *Lugh (loo),* an important Celtic god. He won the name Cuchulainn (Hound of Culan) by offering to take the place of a ferocious watchdog he had killed at the house of Culan.   Janet Egleson Dunleavy

See **Irish literature** (Heroic tales, romances, and sagas); **Mythology** (The Irish cycles).

Cuckoo is any one of a group of related birds found throughout most of the world. The name *cuckoo* comes from the song of the Old World common cuckoo. This song also serves as the basis for the well-known sound of the cuckoo clock. Cuckoos have rather long and slightly curved beaks. They differ from most birds because two of their toes point forward and two backward. In most species of birds, three toes point forward and one toe points backward.

Two common kinds of cuckoos in North America are the black-billed cuckoo and the yellow-billed cuckoo. Their songs consist of a series of low, mournful, quivering notes. These cuckoos are slender birds about 1 foot (30 centimeters) long. They have long, rounded tails, olive-brown backs, and white breasts. They differ chiefly

WORLD BOOK illustration by Trevor Boyer, Linden Artists Ltd.

The black-billed cuckoo has a long, slightly curved black beak and red circles around its eyes. This species is found in North America east of the Rockies.

in the color of the bill. The black-billed cuckoo has a red circle around its eyes, and the yellow-billed cuckoo has larger white marks on its tail.

Black-billed and yellow-billed cuckoos make their homes in woods, thickets, and orchards. They build untidy nests. There may be two to seven eggs in one nest. The eggs are green-blue with a dull surface. The American cuckoos feed on hairy caterpillars and other insect pests that are shunned by other birds. These cuckoos migrate to the tropics for the winter.

The Old World common cuckoo is about the same size as American cuckoos. Males and females both have white breasts with dark bars. The head and back of the males are gray, but those of the females are gray or brown. The Old World common cuckoo is found throughout Europe and most of Asia, and in Africa south of the Sahara.

The common cuckoo, like many other Old World species of cuckoos, does not care for its own young. It lays its eggs in another bird's nest and leaves them to be hatched and cared for by the other bird.

Scientific classification. The cuckoos belong to the cuckoo family, Cuculidae. The scientific name for the yellow-billed cuckoo is *Coccyzus americanus.* The black-billed cuckoo is *C. erythropthalmus.* The Old World common cuckoo is *Cuculus canorus.*   Richard C. Banks

See also **Ani; Bird** (pictures: Birds of forests and woodlands; Birds of Africa; Birds' eggs); **Roadrunner.**

Cuckoo-shrike is the name of a family of about 70 species of songbirds. Cuckoo-shrikes live in Africa, Asia, Australia, and the Pacific Islands. They are not related to either shrikes or cuckoos. But they have notched bills like those of shrikes, and some have barred feathers like those of many cuckoos.

Cuckoo-shrikes range from $5\frac{1}{2}$ to $12\frac{1}{2}$ inches (14 to 32 centimeters) in length. They have a thick cluster of stiff feathers on their rumps. These feathers fall out easily and so help protect cuckoo-shrikes from hawks and other birds that prey on them. A hawk that strikes a

The mature fruits are tough and contain many hard seeds. They are sometimes pickled or served as a hot vegetable. Cucumbers are a good low-calorie salad item. They are also a good source of iron and calcium, and they provide a moderate amount of vitamins.

Cucumbers grow best in warm weather and are easily killed by frost. Gardeners grow them from seed. They sow the seed in small hills of loam or light soil as soon as warm weather comes. They form the hills about 4 feet (1.2 meters) apart to allow room for the vines to grow. When the plants start to grow, they are thinned so only four or five remain in a hill. The plants grow rapidly in warm weather and if they have enough moisture. Small fruits suitable for pickles appear quite soon. Gardeners pick them every two or three days.

Some cucumbers, particularly the seedless type, are grown in greenhouses. The plants grow much as they do in fields. But usually, because of the limited space, the gardener trains the vines on cords or wires. A cucumber plant frequently yields 100 or more fruits.

WORLD BOOK illustration by John Dawson

A **cuckoo-shrike** has a notched bill. Most species have long wings and tails, and feathers that are white and black or gray. The ground cuckoo-shrike, *above,* lives in Australia.

cuckoo-shrike on the rump may catch only a mass of feathers instead of the bird itself.

Most cuckoo-shrikes have long wings and tails. The majority of species are varying shades of gray or black, and white. However, some African cuckoo-shrikes have bright areas of yellow, orange, or red. Males of most kinds of minivets—a group of cuckoo-shrike species found in Asia—are black, and bright red or orange.

Most cuckoo-shrikes live in tropical woodlands. They eat caterpillars and other insects, and fruit. Flocks of cuckoo-shrikes continually fly from one tree to another in search of food. However, the ground cuckoo-shrike, which lives in the dry interior of Australia, searches for food on the ground.

Cuckoo-shrikes build cup-shaped nests in trees, and, in most cases, lay from two to three eggs. The eggs of most species are greenish, with brown, gray, or violet spots or blotches.

Scientific classification. Cuckoo-shrikes make up the family Campephagidae. The ground cuckoo-shrike is *Pteropodocys maxima.* David M. Niles

Cucumber is a common garden vegetable native to southern Asia, but cultivated as an annual in many parts of the world. The cucumber plant is a hairy-stemmed vine that bears many tendrils. Its triangular leaves may have three pointed lobes. The plant bears yellow or whitish flowers on short stems. Its edible fruit, which is commonly called *cucumber,* may grow from 1 to 36 inches (2.5 to 91 centimeters) long. The pulpy fruit generally contains many seeds, though some types, such as the English type, are seedless. It is covered by a thin, smooth or prickly skin. The flesh of the fruit is usually white or yellowish.

Small cucumbers used for pickling are often called *gherkins.* But the true gherkin is another plant closely related to the cucumber. It bears many little spiny fruits shaped like olives.

People eat the young cucumber fruits raw or pickle them. The raw fruits are eaten in salads and sandwiches.

WORLD BOOK illustration by Christobel King

Cucumbers grow on vines that have many coiled growths called *tendrils.* The plant has triangular leaves and yellow or whitish flowers. Cucumbers are eaten raw or pickled.

Several kinds of beetles attack young cucumber plants. Gardeners often spray the plants with rotenone dust to destroy the insects. The *melon aphid* also attacks cucumber plants and spreads *mosaic,* a virus disease.

Scientific classification. The cucumber belongs to the gourd family, Cucurbitaceae. It is *Cucumis, sativus.* Gherkins are *C. anguria.* Albert Liptay

Cud is a small mass of food that animals called *ruminants* bring up from their stomachs for a second chewing. Ruminants include antelope, camels, cattle, deer, and goats. See also **Ruminant; Cattle** (Stomach).
C. Richard Taylor

Cudahy, *KUHD uh hih,* **Michael** (1841-1910), an American meat packer, developed and introduced cold-storage facilities in packing plants. This made possible year-round meat curing and livestock marketing. Cudahy went to work for a meat packer in Milwaukee, Wis., at the age of 14. In 1875, he became a partner in Armour and Company. With P. D. Armour, he formed the Armour-Cudahy Company in 1887. In 1890, he founded the Cudahy Packing Company, one of the largest such companies in the United States, in Omaha, Nebr. Cudahy was born in Callan, Ireland, and came to the United States with his parents in 1849.   William R. Childs

Cuenca, *KWEHNG kah* (pop. 227,212), is a city in the Andes Mountains of southern Ecuador. For Cuenca's location, see **Ecuador** (political map). Cuenca, a commercial center, leads Ecuador in the production of Panama hats. Other important products include cinchona bark, which is used to make drugs; gold; hides of alligators and other animals; and tires. The city has a modern cathedral and a picturesque market where Indians of the region sell their goods. Spaniards founded Cuenca in 1557.   Murdo J. MacLeod

Cuernavaca, *KWEHR nuh VAHK uh* (pop. 232,355), is the capital of the state of Morelos in Mexico. It lies about 37 miles (60 kilometers) south of Mexico City (see **Mexico** [political map]). The city's mild climate and beautiful scenery have made it a popular resort. The city has many beautiful estates and ancient buildings. Tourist attractions include the Palace of Cortes and the Borda gardens. The Spaniards founded the city in 1521.

James D. Riley

Cuffe, Paul (1759-1817), an American seaman and merchant, encouraged the colonizing of blacks in Sierra Leone, Africa, after sailing there in 1810. He financed the voyage of 38 free blacks in 1815. He also sought to strengthen the legal position of blacks in the United States. His efforts led to a law in 1783 that gave blacks in Massachusetts the right to vote. Cuffe, part black and part Indian, was born on Cuttyhunk Island, Massachusetts. He also preached among his fellow Quakers.

Richard D. Brown

Cuisenaire Method, *KWIHZ uh NAIR,* is a teaching system designed to help students discover basic mathematical principles by themselves. The method uses rods of 10 different colors and lengths that are easy to handle. By using the rods, students can prove numerical relationships and understand principles of proportion. Students can also use the colored rods in learning addition, subtraction, multiplication, division, factoring, and fractions.

The rods help the student understand mathematical principles rather than merely memorize them. For example, two white rods placed end to end are the same length as a red rod. The red rod then stands for the number 2 if the white rod represents 1. A red rod and a white rod placed end to end are as long as a light-green rod. The light-green rod then stands for 3, because it is as long as three white rods. The rods can also be used to represent different sets of numbers. For example, if the white rod is assigned a value of 3, the red rod becomes 6.

Students can discover many facts about mathematical relationships by working with the rods. For example, three red rods placed end to end are as long as one dark-green rod. The dark-green rod is two-thirds as long as a blue rod. Students can see that the three red rods equal two-thirds of a blue rod.

The rods also can be used to teach such elementary arithmetic properties as the associative, commutative,

and distributive properties. For instance, to help students understand that $3 \times 2 = 2 \times 3$, an example of the commutative property, two light-green rods can be placed on top of three red rods, as shown below.

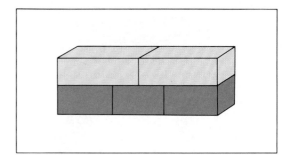

To show that $4 \times (2 + 3) = (4 \times 2) + (4 \times 3)$, an example of the distributive property, a set of four red rods and four light-green rods can be split into two sets. One of the two sets would have four red rods. The other would have four light-green rods. See the illustration below.

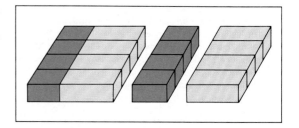

Schoolteachers use the Cuisenaire Method in the United States, Canada, and parts of Europe. Emile-Georges Cuisenaire, a schoolteacher from Thuin, Belgium, developed the method.   Jeffrey C. Barnett

Cukor, *KOO kuhr,* **George** (1899-1983), was an American motion-picture director. He became noted for his ability to draw superior performances from many of Hollywood's leading actresses. Cukor directed Greta Garbo in *Camille* (1937), Katharine Hepburn in *The Philadelphia Story* (1940), Judy Holliday in *Born Yesterday* (1950), and Judy Garland in *A Star Is Born* (1954). He won an Academy Award for directing *My Fair Lady* (1964). Cukor directed or co-directed about 50 films from 1930 to 1981.

Cukor was born in New York City. He directed plays on Broadway before going to Hollywood in 1929. During the 1930's, he made several films based on literary classics, including *Little Women* (1933) and *David Copperfield* (1935). Cukor also directed the popular comedies *Adam's Rib* (1949) and *Pat and Mike* (1952), both of which co-starred Katharine Hepburn and Spencer Tracy. Cukor's other films include *A Bill of Divorcement* (1932), *Holiday* (1938), *The Women* (1939), and *Travels with My Aunt* (1972).   John F. Mariani

Cullen, Countee, *kown TAY* or *kown TEE* (1903-1946), was a black poet and novelist known for his lyrical poetry. He established his reputation with his first published collection of poems, *Color* (1925). His other books of poetry include *Copper Sun* (1927) and *The Black Christ* (1929). He collected the poems by which he wished to be remembered in *On These I Stand* (1947). Cullen's novel *One Way to Heaven* (1932) satirizes high society in Harlem. He and Arna Bontemps, a black American author, wrote the musical play *St. Louis Woman* (1946). Cullen also wrote two children's books, *The Lost Zoo* (1940) and *My Lives and How I Lost Them* (1942).

Cullen was born in New York City. He graduated from New York University and earned an M.A. in English literature from Harvard University. He spent much of his later life teaching.   William L. Andrews

Cult is the term commonly used for a new religious group devoted to a living leader and committed to unusual teachings and practices. Such groups range in size from a few followers to worldwide organizations directed by a complex chain of command. Members of these groups generally consider them to be legitimate religions and rarely call them cults. Most historians of religion use the more neutral term *new religious movement* instead of *cult.*

Because there is no one definition of cults, their number and membership today cannot be accurately measured. According to some estimates, 3,000 cults exist throughout the world, claiming a membership of more than 3 million people, mostly young adults.

Kinds of cults. Traditionally, the term *cult* referred to any form of worship or ritual observance, or even to a group of people pursuing common goals. Many groups accepted as religions today were once classified as cults. Christianity began as a cult within Judaism and developed into an established church. Other groups that began as cults and developed into organized churches include the Quakers, Mormons, Swedenborgians, Christian Scientists, Methodists, Jehovah's Witnesses, and Seventh-day Adventists. The Amish, who trace their history to the 1500's, are an example of a cult that has changed little over the centuries. For a discussion of cults in the ancient world, see **Mysteries.**

Since the mid-1900's, publicity about cults has altered the meaning of the term. Today, the term is applied to groups that follow a living leader who promotes new and unorthodox doctrines and practices. Some leaders demand that members live apart from everyday society in communities called *communes.* Leaders claim that they possess exclusive religious truth, and they command absolute obedience and allegiance from their followers. Some cults require that members contribute all their possessions to the group.

Modern cults. Probably the most notorious United States cult of the late 1900's was the People's Temple, a group led by Jim Jones, a Protestant clergyman. Hundreds of his followers moved into a rural commune called Jonestown in the South American country of Guyana. They lived under Jones's absolute rule. In 1978, cult leaders killed a U.S. congressman and three journalists investigating activities in Jonestown. Jones then ordered his followers to commit suicide, resulting in the deaths of over 900 people. See **Guyana** (History).

Another notorious cult was the Branch Davidians, led by a self-proclaimed prophet named David Koresh. In 1993, a 51-day confrontation between the cult and federal forces near Waco, Tex., ended with the apparent mass suicide of over 80 cult members, including Koresh.

Some movements regarded as cults did not begin as religious groups. A movement called Synanon was originally organized in California to rehabilitate drug addicts. It changed into a commune that won legal recognition as a religion. Another movement, called Scientology, uses scientific language as it encourages its members to progress through various spiritual stages toward a state called *Clear.* See **Scientology.**

Two of the largest groups regarded as cults in the United States began in Asia. The International Society for Krishna Consciousness, commonly called the Hare Krishna movement, came from India in 1954. During the 1960's and 1970's, its leader, Swami Bhaktivedaria, established many centers in the United States and other countries. Members of Hare Krishna wear orange robes similar to those worn by Indian holy men. The men shave their heads, and members meditate in strictly regulated communes.

The Unification Church, led by its Korean founder, the evangelist Sun Myung Moon, is an adaptation of Christianity. Its members, commonly called "Moonies," believe in a cosmic struggle between the forces of good and the forces of evil, represented by international Communism. The Unification Church has been aggressive in seeking conversions. Like many other cults popular in the 1970's, however, they began to adopt a more moderate tone in the 1980's.

Less aggressive and more loosely organized cults tend to stress personal, individual meditation. Transcendental Meditation and Zendo are forms of meditation. See **Transcendental Meditation.**   Mark Juergensmeyer

See also **Divine, Father.**

Additional resources

Deikman, Arthur J. *The Wrong Way Home: Uncovering the Patterns of Cult Behavior in American Society.* Beacon Pr., 1991.
Galanter, Marc. *Cults: Faith, Healing, and Coercion.* Oxford, 1989.
Johnson, Joan J. *The Cult Movement.* Watts, 1984. Also suitable for younger readers.
Melton, J. Gordon. *Encyclopedic Handbook of Cults in America.* Garland, 1986.

Cultural anthropology. See **Anthropology.**

Cultural lag is the failure of certain parts of a culture to keep up with other, related parts. William F. Ogburn, an American sociologist, introduced the term in the 1920's. He noted that the development of technology caused rapid changes in *material culture,* including housing, machinery, and industrial processes. But he observed that *nonmaterial culture,* including ideas, values, and social systems, often lagged behind material culture.

According to Ogburn, many social problems result from cultural lag. For example, new inventions may replace many workers. The time it takes these workers to learn new skills and find other jobs is a cultural lag that results in unemployment.

Today, social scientists realize that changes in ideas and social systems may sometimes occur before changes in technology. They refer to the condition that results when related parts of a culture change at different rates as *cultural dissonance.*   Jennie Keith

See also **Culture** (How culture changes).

Cultural Revolution. See **China** (The Cultural Revolution).

Bruce McAllister, Black Star   James Sugar   Charles Moore, Black Star

Different cultures have different customs. A bride and groom in Poland, *left,* kneel as a priest says Mass. Among the Dorze in Ethiopia, *center,* the groom's friends pretend to kidnap the bride. At a Hindu wedding in Singapore, *right,* a priest sprinkles the couple with holy water.

Culture

Culture is a term used by social scientists for a people's whole way of life. In everyday conversation, the word *culture* may refer to activities in such fields as art, literature, and music. But to social scientists, a people's culture consists of all the ideas, objects, and ways of doing things created by the group. Culture includes arts, beliefs, customs, inventions, language, technology, and traditions. The term *civilization* is similar, but it refers mostly to scientifically more advanced ways of life. A culture is any way of life, simple or complex.

Culture consists of learned ways of acting, feeling, and thinking, rather than biologically determined ways. Some simple animals act on the basis of information carried in their *genes,* the parts of a cell that determine inherited traits. This biologically inherited information even includes the animal's ways of obtaining food and shelter. But human beings can experiment, learn, and work out their ways of doing these things, a process that never ends.

Culture is a set of simple extensions of various parts of the body. The Austrian psychologist Sigmund Freud compared it to such devices as artificial limbs, eyeglasses, and false teeth. Like these devices, culture enables people to do things their muscles and senses alone would not allow them to do. For example, human

Paul Bohannan, the contributor of this article, is Professor Emeritus of Anthropology at the University of Southern California.

beings do not need fangs if they have arrows. They need not be able to run fast if they have tamed the horse. Without culture, the astronauts could not have reached the moon nor survived there. The human body needs oxygen and a certain range of temperature to live. However, cultural devices have enabled human beings to overcome some of the limitations of their bodies and stay alive in harsh environments.

Early culture was a means to extend the ability to obtain food, seek protection, and raise offspring. The ancestors of modern human beings had an advantage in the struggle for survival because they developed tools and other culture. They became more likely to live and reproduce than creatures that lacked such advantages. As a result, the ability to create culture grew from generation to generation.

Characteristics of culture

The British anthropologist Sir Edward Burnett Tylor introduced the term culture as scientists use it today. In his book *Primitive Culture* (1871), Tylor defined culture as "that complex whole which includes knowledge, belief, art, morals, law, custom, and any other capabilities and habits acquired by man as a member of society." Tylor's definition includes three of the most important characteristics of culture: (1) Culture is acquired by people, a process called *enculturation.* (2) A person acquires culture as a member of society. Social life would be impossible without understandings and practices shared by all people. (3) Culture is a complex whole. Its units are called *cultural traits.* They may include a customary burial place for the dead; a device, such as a plow; or a gesture, such as a handshake. A group of related traits is called a *culture pattern*. For example, the related customs of dating, courtship, and marriage form a culture pattern.

Most large groups have a set of cultural traits that meet the group's needs and ensure its survival. Such a set of traits can be called *a culture*. Nations, most tribes, and even some villages have a culture in that sense.

However, every family has a cultural tradition of its own. This tradition includes many traits that the family shares with others who live in the same area and belong to the same social class. In addition, the family has its own set of cultural traits. Business companies, villages, and other social groups also have their own cultural traditions. Social scientists sometimes use the term *subculture* for a set of cultural traits found only in one group. Many occupational groups, such as physicians and truckdrivers, and ethnic groups, such as Chinese Americans and Mexican Americans, have their own subculture and also share American culture.

Culture must be in two places at once. First, it must be in the environment, where it appears as *artifacts* (things made by human beings) or as behavior. Some of the culture in the environment, such as a gesture or the telling of a story, is short-lived. But other culture, such as a stone ax or a written story, lasts for a very long time. Secondly, culture must be in some person's mind as a set of ideas for understanding and evaluating artifacts and behavior. An "artifact" that nobody "understands" is incomplete culture. An idea that is not shared is not culture at all. Things from the environment get into people's minds through learning and enculturation. Things move from people's minds to the outside world through behavior, discussion, and invention.

How cultures resemble one another

All cultures have features that result from basic needs shared by all people. Every culture has methods of obtaining food and shelter. It has an orderly means of distributing the food and other goods to its people. Each culture has systems for assigning power and responsibility, including social ranks and governments. There also is a way to keep order and settle disputes—for example, a system of police, courts, and prisons.

Every culture has ways to protect itself against invaders. It also has family relationships, including forms of marriage and systems of kinship. A culture has religious beliefs and a set of practices to express them. All societies have forms of artistic expression, such as carving, painting, and music. In addition, each culture has some type of scientific knowledge. This knowledge may be folklore about the plants people eat and the animals they hunt, or it may be a highly developed science.

How cultures differ

Cultures differ in their details from one part of the world to another. For example, eating is a biological need. But what people eat, when and how they eat, and how food is prepared differ from culture to culture. A geographical region in which the people share many cultural traits and patterns is called a *culture area*.

Environmental differences are related to cultural variation. Such factors as climate, land forms, mineral resources, and native plants and animals all influence culture. For example, most people in tropical regions wear

A subculture is a group of people whose cultural traits set them apart within a culture or society. The people shown above are Amish. Many members of this Protestant group wear plain clothes and use horses rather than cars. Their simple way of life makes them a subculture within modern society.

draped clothing, which consists of one or more long pieces of cloth wrapped around the body. People who live in colder parts of the world wear tailored clothing, which is cut and sewn to fit the body. Tailored clothing provides more warmth than draped clothing.

People do not realize how greatly culture influences their behavior—until they come across other ways of doing things. Only then can they see that they have been doing things in a cultural way rather than in a "natural" way. For example, many Westerners believe it is natural to look directly into a person's eyes while talking. But the people of some Asian nations think it is rude to do so.

People feel most comfortable within their own culture, and they prefer the company of others who share their culture. When people have to deal with persons of another culture, even small differences in behavior may make them uneasy. The difficulty or uneasiness that people undergo when they leave their own culture and enter another is called *culture shock*. The attitude that a person's own culture is the best and most natural is called *ethnocentrism*.

The history of human culture

The foundations for human culture developed in prehistoric times. Important steps in the growth of culture include (1) the development of tools, (2) the start of farming, (3) the growth of cities, and (4) the development of writing.

The development of tools began about 2 million years ago. At this time, the first human beings lived by gathering fruit, insects, and edible leaves and by catching small animals with their hands. They learned to make and use tools, thus taking the first steps toward the development of culture. Many of these tools were sharp-edged rocks used for cutting and scraping. The sharp edge was made by hitting or chipping one rock with another. Prehistoric people probably also made articles of bone, hair, hides, and wood.

The early human beings learned to make stone tools

and kill game for food. To hunt large animals, they had to work together as a group. Leaders developed if one member of the group gave orders and the others obeyed. Groups that developed rules of behavior and systems of rank and authority had an advantage over groups that did not.

The hunters also learned the habits of the animals they hunted. Such learning is a simple kind of scientific knowledge. When science cannot explain natural events, people devise explanations. After centuries, these explanations may become part of religion.

The earliest human beings became increasingly skilled at hunting. Therefore, with better hunting, the food supply improved and the population increased. To feed the growing population, the hunters killed more game. After large animals became scarce, some people had to turn to planting crops and raising animals for food. They became the first farmers.

The start of farming, which occurred about 9000 B.C., was one of the most important steps in the growth of human culture. After about 2 million years as hunters, moving about in search of large game, some people could now settle in one place to produce their food.

The farmers could produce enough crops that many people could be freed from the task of raising food. These people developed new skills, such as pottery making, weaving, and other crafts. They distributed food and other products through systems of markets and by paying taxes to their leaders, who then redistributed the wealth. Populations continued to grow. The growing populations and permanent settlements required new methods of managing community affairs and providing services for people. As a result, various new forms of government developed.

The growth of cities. By about 3500 B.C., cities had appeared. City dwellers developed increasingly specialized occupations. Some became artists and builders. Others became judges and priests. All their new knowledge and skills made up the growth of culture.

The cities also attracted people from a variety of cultural backgrounds. These people mixed and learned from one another by exchanging ideas. Cultural exchange is one of the most important elements in the history of civilization.

The development of writing ranks as one of the most important steps in the growth of human culture. The first system of writing was developed about 3500 B.C. in what is now southeastern Iraq. Others developed in China at about the same time. Writing enabled people to record their thoughts and discoveries for later use and to communicate over long distances. They also began to record aspects of their culture and to hand it down in written form from generation to generation.

How culture changes

Every culture changes continually. The rate of change may be slow or rapid. Because a culture consists of many related parts, a change in one part affects many others. Some social scientists believe that many social problems come about because some parts of a culture change more slowly than others. The term *cultural lag* refers to this tendency of certain parts of a culture to fall behind other related parts.

In United States history, much cultural lag has oc-

curred in customs, ideas, and other nonmaterial parts of the nation's culture. Science and technology change so rapidly that they sometimes have outrun nonmaterial culture. For example, the development of power-driven machinery during the 1700's and 1800's led to the establishment of factories. The working conditions in the early factories were bad. Not until the 1900's did social changes catch up with the technological changes that had built the factories. These social changes included labor unions, safety regulations, a shorter workday, and the abolition of child labor.

In other societies and at other times, however, changes in ideas have come before changes in the material culture. For example, physicians had the knowledge to perform some operations for thousands of years. But little surgery was possible until the discovery of antiseptics and painkillers in the 1800's.

A number of factors may cause a culture to change. The chief ones include (1) changes in the environment, (2) contact with other cultures, (3) invention, and (4) further development of the culture itself.

Changes in the environment. Any change in the environment of a group will result in changes in the group's culture. For example, after the Ice Age ended about 10,000 years ago, the climate in what is now Nevada and Utah gradually became drier and warmer. As the climate changed, the culture of the Indians who lived in that area also changed. The Indians had to eat more and more plants because large game became scarce. The area eventually grew so dry that it became desertlike. The Indians began to roam in small bands,

Ray Cranbourne, Black Star

Cultures change through contact with one another. For example, Hong Kong blends Eastern and Western ways of life. This fast-food restaurant in Hong Kong sells American-style hamburgers and soft drinks.

People borrow devices from other cultures, particularly if a new device seems better than a traditional one. These men are using a traditional dugout canoe—powered by a modern outboard motor.

James Nachtwey, Black Star

searching for things to eat. They learned to eat insects and roots for the first time.

Contact with other cultures. Any contact between two societies with different cultures causes change in both societies. Each borrows cultural traits from the other, particularly if a newly learned trait seems better than a traditional one. As a result, cultural traits and patterns tend to spread from the society in which they originated. This spreading process is called *diffusion.*

Diffusion is one of the most common causes of cultural change. Christianity, which originated in the Middle East, spread throughout the world by means of diffusion. Corn, sweet potatoes, and tobacco all originated in the New World, but people in many places now use them. Spanish explorers introduced horses into Mexico during the 1500's. The use of the animals spread so rapidly that many Indian tribes rode horses for years before they first saw a European.

Prolonged contact between cultures brings *acculturation,* a process in which people of one culture adopt traits from another. In many cases, acculturation results from conquest. For example, the Romans conquered Greece in the 100's B.C. During the centuries that followed, the Romans adopted many features of Greek culture, including Greek art, literature, and religion.

In most cases of acculturation, both cultures borrow from each other. For example, many cultures adopted dog sleds, fur parkas, and snowshoes from the Eskimos.

In turn, Eskimos adopted motorboats, rifles, and snowmobiles from other cultures.

Another process, called *assimilation,* involves borrowing that is more one-sided. Assimilation takes place when immigrants or other newcomers adopt the culture of the society in which they have settled. Assimilation may lead to the disappearance of a minority group. The minority group disappears because its members lose the cultural characteristics that had set them apart.

Invention is the creation of a new device, process, or product. Throughout history, many inventions have changed human culture. For example, the Industrial Revolution of the 1700's and early 1800's brought such inventions as the power loom and the steam engine. These machines produced great changes in people's way of life. See **Invention.**

Further development of a culture also brings change. For example, a society may switch from food gathering to farming as a result of population growth and the disappearance of game. A still larger population, in turn, brings even greater specialization and division of labor. Different systems of social organization and other changes follow. A culture changes whenever environmental changes or other pressures make new ways of doing things desirable.

After people adopt new and better ways of doing things, they rarely go back to their old ways. For example, after people have learned to use money, they never

Cultural diffusion is the process by which cultural traits and patterns spread from the cultures in which they originated. This map shows how one trait, wheat growing, spread throughout the world from the Fertile Crescent in Southwest Asia.

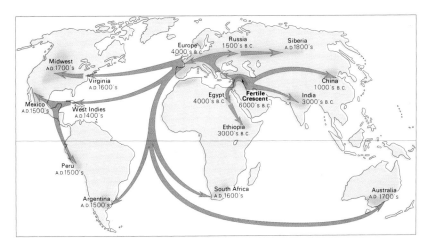

WORLD BOOK map

will lack a medium of exchange. After they have learned to make fire, they never will live without it. Such devices as coins and tinderboxes may be replaced. But money and the controlled use of fire will always be present.

Cultural change today

The rate of cultural change has increased rapidly since the mid-1800's. This increase has occurred largely because of many advances in science and technology. Exchanges between cultures also have become more rapid and widespread since the mid-1800's. Because of airplanes, motion pictures, and radio and TV, most of the cultural traditions in the world are continually in touch with one another. A person can find American jazz and Japanese kimonos in any large city.

Today, a common culture of all human beings is emerging because people travel widely, and television has spread throughout the world. In addition, many types of music, sports, and industrial processes are the same in all areas of the world. Some people fear that such similarities will make all cultures alike. But people create new local cultures as quickly as they learn this "world culture." Though the "world culture" covers only a limited range of known culture, many of its triumphs enable new local cultures to develop and flourish.

The culture of animals

Scientists once thought that only human beings had culture. But most of them now believe animals also have some elements of culture. For example, some animals make and use tools, and the members of many species communicate with one another by means of signs.

Toolmaking consists basically of taking something found in the environment and using it for a purpose other than its original function. Elephants break off tree branches and wave them with their trunks to whisk away flies. Chimpanzees catch termites by peeling a twig and inserting the sticky, sappy end of the twig into a termite mound. When a chimpanzee pulls the twig out of the mound, termites stick to it. Young chimpanzees learn this method from older members of their group. The technique is a cultural trait that has been passed along from one generation of chimpanzees to the next.

Many animals use various kinds of signs to communicate. For example, dogs bark and lay their ears back. Dolphins communicate with one another by means of barks, clicks, whistles, and other sounds. Scientists have taught chimpanzees to "speak" to people in sign language. However, most scientists agree that any culture must include the use of symbols to be considered a true culture.   Paul Bohannan

Related articles in *World Book* include:

Acculturation	Assimilation	Etiquette
Anthropology (Cultural anthropology; Social anthropology)	Civilization	Folklore
	Cultural lag	Mores
	Custom	Social change
	Ethnocentrism	Socialization

Outline

I. **Characteristics of culture**
II. **How cultures resemble one another**
III. **How cultures differ**
IV. **The history of human culture**
    A. The development of tools
    B. The start of farming
    C. The growth of cities
    D. The development of writing

V. **How culture changes**
    A. Changes in the environment
    B. Contact with other cultures
    C. Invention
    D. Further development of a culture

VI. **Cultural change today**
VII. **The culture of animals**

Questions

What basic elements do all cultures have in common?
What is culture shock?
How did the development of farming contribute to the growth of human culture?
Why is the spread of Christianity an example of cultural diffusion?
What is ethnocentrism?
How does assimilation differ from acculturation?
What are the chief causes of cultural change?
What is an example of cultural lag?
What are two cultural traits of animals?
How does a trait differ from a culture pattern?

Additional resources

Concise Histories of American Popular Culture. Ed. by M. Thomas Inge. Greenwood, 1982. Essays from *Handbook of American Popular Culture,* 1978-1981.
Great Ages of Man. Time-Life Books. Each book in this series focuses on one of the world's great cultural areas, such as *African Kingdoms* (1971) and *Rise of Russia* (1967).
Harris, Marvin. *Cannibals and Kings: The Origins of Cultures.* Random Hse., 1978. First published in 1977.
Reader, John. *Man on Earth.* Univ. of Texas Pr., 1988.

Culture, in biology, is a growth of microorganisms or cells produced under controlled conditions in a laboratory. Microorganisms grown in cultures include bacteria, viruses, and yeasts. A culture of plant or animal cells is known as a *cell culture.*

Cultures require sterile conditions to prevent contamination, and a suitable *culture medium* (substance that provides nutrients). A cell culture will grow and multiply if the culture medium meets its nutritional needs. If the *primary culture* becomes too crowded, the scientist can transfer part of the cells to a *secondary culture.* Cells ordinarily divide only a limited number of times and then die. Occasionally, however, a mutation occurs that enables them to grow indefinitely.

Cell cultures show how cells grow and function normally and thus help scientists understand more about cell abnormalities that occur in cancer and other diseases. Cultures of microorganisms help doctors diagnose diseases. For example, bacteria or viruses found in mucus or body tissue can be grown in a culture for identification. Cultures also are used to produce antibiotics, vaccines, and other drugs.   Mary Lee S. Ledbetter

Culture shock. See Culture (How cultures differ).
Cum laude. See Degree, College.
Cumberland Gap is a natural pass in the Appalachian Mountains, near the meeting point of Kentucky, Tennessee, and Virginia. The gap cuts a notch about 600 feet (180 meters) deep into Cumberland Mountain. The gap is about 1,600 feet (490 meters) above sea level. Pioneers used the gap as a passage into the Cumberland Mountains and the Appalachian Plateau to the west.

An exploring party led by the pioneer scout Thomas Walker used the Cumberland Gap in 1750. In 1775, the famous pioneer Daniel Boone blazed the Wilderness Road through the gap (see **Boone, Daniel**). Between 1775 and 1800, about 200,000 people passed through the gap. The gap was controlled alternately by the Confederate and Union armies during the American Civil War (1861-1865). Cumberland Gap National Historical Park covers about 20,000 acres (8,000 hectares) and is one of the country's largest historical parks. Karl B. Raitz

Cumberland Mountains, part of the Appalachian Mountain system, extend across part of eastern Tennessee and Kentucky, and form the boundary between Virginia and Kentucky. Some geographers call this mountain region the Cumberland Plateau. Streams have carved a complex pattern of narrow, steep-sided valleys into the mountains. The Cumberlands rise from 2,000 to 3,000 feet (610 to 910 meters) above sea level. The mountains contain rich coal fields. See also **Appalachian Mountains**. E. Willard Miller

Cumberland River, a branch of the Ohio River, rises in the Cumberland Mountains in eastern Kentucky. From there, it winds southwestward into central Tennessee, then northwestward into western Kentucky. It empties into the Ohio at Smithland, Ky. The Cumberland is about 690 miles (1,100 kilometers) long and drains an area of about 18,000 square miles (46,600 kilometers). It drops 68 feet (21 meters) at Cumberland Falls, now part of a state park in southern Kentucky. Below the falls, the river is dammed by Wolf Creek Dam. The river is navigable from the dam to the Ohio, a distance of about 460 miles (740 kilometers). The main cities on the Cumberland are Nashville and Clarksville, Tenn. The Big South Fork National River and Recreation Area lies along the river's South Fork. See also **Ohio River** (map). Karl B. Raitz

Cumberland Road. See National Road.

Cumin, *KUHM uhn,* is a small herb grown for its fruit. The dried fruit, commonly called *cumin seed,* is primarily used to season foods. The plant, native to the Mediterranean region, is cultivated commercially in Europe, the Middle East, Africa, and Asia. The cumin plant grows about 6 inches (15 centimeters) high. It bears clusters of white or rose-colored flowers and yellowish-brown fruit. The plant grows best in a mild climate and in rich, well-drained soil. As an *annual,* it lives for only one growing season.

Cumin seeds have a strong, spicy taste similar to that of caraway seeds. Cumin provides the main flavor in most Egyptian, Indian, and Turkish curries. It also is used to flavor many Mexican dishes, cheeses, sausages, stews, soups, pickles, meats, and dressings. The fruit yields an oil used in perfumes and alcoholic beverages.

Scientific classification. Cumin belongs to the parsley family, Apiaceae or Umbelliferae. The scientific name for cumin is *Cuminum cyminum.* Lyle E. Craker

WORLD BOOK illustration by Lorraine Epstein
The cumin plant bears clusters of small flowers, *left.* The fruit, *right,* is dried and used to season foods.

Cummings, E. E. (1894-1962), was one of the most innovative poets in American literature. He is especially known for violating the rules of composition, rejecting punctuation and capitalization, distorting *syntax* (sentence structure), and experimenting with *typography* (the arrangement of printed matter). He wrote his own name as e. e. cummings.

However, Cummings' themes and even many of his forms are traditional. Beneath his poems' complex surfaces are relatively simple, straightforward ideas. Cummings emphasized the supremacy of the individual over society, and he criticized the tendency of people to conform to socially accepted values and opinions. His poems show him to be joyous and childlike, a believer in love and spontaneity.

Marion Morehouse
E. E. Cummings

Edward Estlin Cummings was born in Cambridge, Mass. He studied at Harvard University, earning a B.A. degree in 1915 and an M.A. degree in 1916. During World War I (1914-1918), Cummings served as a volunteer ambulance driver in France. French authorities suspected him of expressing treasonous views and held him in a French detention camp for three months. Cummings vividly described this experience in his book *The Enormous Room* (1922). Cummings published his first book of poems, *Tulips and Chimneys,* in 1923. In addition to his poetry, Cummings wrote verse plays such as *Him* (1928); *Eimi* (1933), an account of a visit to the Soviet Union; and *i: six nonlectures* (1953), lectures originally delivered at Harvard. His *Complete Poems 1913-1962* was published in 1972. Bonnie Costello

See also **Poetry** (Rhythm and meter).

Additional resources

E. E. Cummings: A Collection of Critical Essays. Ed. by Norman Friedman. Prentice-Hall, 1972.
Kennedy, Richard S. *Dreams in the Mirror: A Biography of E. E. Cummings.* Norton, 1980.
Kidder, Rushworth M. *E. E. Cummings: An Introduction to the Poetry.* Columbia Univ. Press, 1979.
Marks, Barry A. *E. E. Cummings.* Twayne, 1964.

Cumulus. See Cloud.

Cunard, Sir Samuel (1787-1865), founded the Cunard line of steamships. In 1838, he became the chief founding investor of the North American Royal Mail Steam Packet Company, commonly known as the Cunard line. The company provided semimonthly mail and passenger service between England and America. The *Britannia* made the company's first voyage in 1840. Cunard was made a baronet for services the Cunard lines rendered to Great Britain in the Crimean War (1853-1856). He was born in Halifax, N.S. James C. Bradford

Examples of cuneiform writing

MEANING	Outline Character about 3000 B.C.	Cuneiform about 2000 B.C.	Assyrian about 700 B.C.	Babylonian about 500 B.C.
The Sun				
God or Heaven				
Mountain				
Man				
Ox				
Fish				

Cuneiform, *kyoo NEE uh fawrm,* was a system of writing used by the people of ancient Middle Eastern civilizations. It became widespread long before the development of modern alphabets. The word *cuneiform* comes from the Latin word *cuneus,* meaning *wedge.* Cuneiform characters are shaped like a wedge—broad at one end and pointed at the other. Most cuneiform writings were inscribed in rectangular clay tablets. The characters were made with a wedge-shaped tool called a *stylus,* while the clay was still wet. The tablets were then dried in the sun until they hardened. The characters also were inscribed in metal and stone.

Scholars have had difficulty translating cuneiform writing because many of the characters represent either words or syllables. In addition, many ancient peoples developed their own interpretations of cuneiform symbols, and so one character may have several meanings.

Cuneiform was probably developed by the Sumerian people as a shortened form of picture writing. The earliest known cuneiform inscriptions were found in the lower Tigris-Euphrates Valley in what is now southeastern Iraq. They date from about 3000 B.C. The most recent cuneiform clay tablet was written about A.D. 75, near the beginning of the Christian Era.

Sumerian cuneiform symbols are more complex than those of other peoples. The Sumerians and Babylonians used about 600 characters, which ranged from a single wedge to complicated signs consisting of 30 or more wedges. The Hittites used about 350 characters, the Elamites about 200, and the Persians only 39.

Scholars first attempted to translate cuneiform writing in the late 1700's. At that time, European travelers became interested in a cuneiform inscription discovered in western Iran. This inscription was written in three languages—Persian, Babylonian, and Elamite—and measured about 300 feet (91 meters) long. It was carved in a cliff called Behistun Rock. During the mid-1800's, Sir Henry Rawlinson, an English diplomat, first translated the Persian portion and later the Babylonian portion. They described the accomplishments of the Persian king Darius I in the late 500's B.C. The Elamite section was translated much later. The translations helped scholars decipher other cuneiform inscriptions.

Since 1800, several hundred thousand cuneiform clay tablets and stone inscriptions have been discovered. These inscriptions, which are on exhibit in museums throughout the world, help scholars broaden their knowledge about early human history.   John W. Snyder

See also **Communication** (picture: Cuneiform writing).

Cunha, *KOO nyuh,* **Euclides da** (1866-1909), a Brazilian newspaper reporter, wrote perhaps the greatest work in Brazilian literature. The book, *Os Sertões* (1902), has been translated as *Rebellion in the Backlands.*

In *Os Sertões,* da Cunha realistically described an armed rebellion that occurred in 1896 and 1897. In this rebellion, Brazilians of the poverty-stricken *sertão* (backlands) fought against the government. Da Cunha witnessed the rebellion as a newspaper correspondent. *Os Sertões* combines journalistic reporting with certain features of a novel, such as characterization, drama, and pacing. The book gives a vivid account of guerrilla warfare. It also provides a sociological study of Brazilian society and its problems. In particular, the author attacked Brazilian society for its neglect of the people of the sertão. *Os Sertões* aroused public support for these people. It helped the wealthy residents of the coastal region understand the people of the sertão. Da Cunha was born in the state of Rio de Janeiro.   Earl E. Fitz

Cunningham, Merce (1919-   ), is an American dancer and *choreographer* (dance creator). Cunningham often creates dances without advance knowledge of the

Martha Swope

Merce Cunningham, *center,* is a dancer and choreographer who leads one of the major modern dance companies in the United States.

music and the set designs that will accompany them. He became particularly known for his methods of *chance composition.* For example, in choreographing a dance, he would write the name of a movement, the name of a dancer, a length of time, and a space on the stage. Cunningham would then toss dice or dip into a grab bag to determine which dancer would do what movement for how long and where.

Cunningham was born in Centralia, Wash. From 1939 to 1945, he was a soloist with the Martha Graham company. In 1944, Cunningham began presenting dances in collaboration with the American composer John Cage. In 1953, Cunningham formed his own company with

Cage as musical director. Cunningham has choreographed about 100 works. Selma Landen Odom

Cuomo, *KWOH moh,* **Mario Matthew** (1932-), gained national attention as the governor of New York. Cuomo, a Democrat, was first elected to the governorship in 1982. He was the first Italian-American elected to that office. A powerful orator, Cuomo established himself as a potential presidential candidate when he delivered a stirring address at the 1984 Democratic National Convention.

State of New York
Mario Cuomo

Cuomo was born in New York City. He received a bachelor's degree in 1953 from St. John's College (now St. John's University). In 1956, Cuomo received a law degree from St. John's. From 1956 to 1958, he served as a legal assistant to Judge Adrian Burke of New York's Court of Appeals, the state's highest court. Cuomo then entered private law practice.

Cuomo first attracted public attention in 1972, when he settled a bitter housing dispute between blacks and Jews in Queens, N.Y. Governor Hugh L. Carey of New York appointed him secretary of state in 1975. Cuomo won election as lieutenant governor of New York in 1978. Four years later, Cuomo defeated Republican Lewis Lehrman to become governor. Cuomo was reelected in 1986 and 1990. Gerald Benjamin

Cupid was the god of love in Roman mythology. He was also called *Amor.* Cupid was identified with the Greek god Eros. The Romans portrayed Cupid as a son of the goddess Venus.

Cupid had both a cruel and a happy nature. His cruelty appears in his treatment of his wife, the beautiful princess Psyche. Cupid forbade Psyche ever to try to see what he looked like. He refused to be with her except at night in the dark. One night while Cupid was asleep, Psyche lit a lamp so she could look at him. Cupid awoke and fled in anger. But other myths describe Cupid as a happy lad who united lovers. See **Psyche.**

The earliest images of Cupid show him as a handsome, athletic young man. By the mid-300's B.C., he was portrayed as a chubby, naked infant with wings, holding a bow and arrows. A person shot with one of Cupid's gold-tipped arrows supposedly fell in love. His lead-tipped arrows had the opposite effect. E. N. Genovese

Cuquenán Falls, *koo kay NAHN,* also spelled *Kukenaam,* is one of the highest waterfalls in the world. The water drops 2,000 feet (610 meters). Cuquenán stands on the Cuquenán River in Venezuela near the Guyana border. See also **Waterfall** (chart). Gregory Knapp

Curaçao, *KYOOR uh SOH* or *koo rah SAH oh,* is the largest island of the Netherlands Antilles—two groups of islands in the West Indies. The Netherlands Antilles is part of the Kingdom of the Netherlands (see **Netherlands** [Government]). For location, see **West Indies** (map).

Curaçao covers 171 square miles (444 square kilometers) and has a population of about 150,000. Willemstad, the largest city on the island, is the capital of the Nether-

lands Antilles. A dry, nearly flat island, Curaçao has lovely beaches, warm weather the year around, and picturesque cities and towns. These features attract many tourists. Most of Curaçao's people are blacks, or have mixed black and white ancestry. Oil refineries process crude oil from nearby Venezuela. Oil refining, tourism, and trade are the island's main economic activities.

American Indians were Curaçao's first inhabitants. The Netherlands gained control of the island in 1634. From the 1600's to the 1800's, the Dutch brought many black African slaves to Curaçao. Gary Brana-Shute

See also **Netherlands Antilles; Willemstad.**

Curare, *kyu RAH ree,* is the name for various substances used as arrow poison by Indians in South America. It is derived mainly from varieties of the plants *Chondodendron tomentosum* and *Strychnos toxifera.* Curare also is used by doctors to relax skeletal muscles during certain medical procedures.

South American Indians have used curare-poisoned arrows for hunting for hundreds of years. When curare enters an animal's bloodstream or body tissues, it paralyzes the skeletal muscles, including those necessary for breathing. The animal suffocates as a result.

In 1856, the French physiologist Claude Bernard showed that curare works by blocking the passage of nerve impulses to skeletal muscles. In the second half of the 1800's, some doctors used curare in treating epilepsy and tetanus. Today, the drug is used along with anesthetics to relax the patient's abdominal muscles during abdominal surgery. Doctors also use curare to relax the throat muscles during certain kinds of throat examinations. Doctors administer curare *intravenously* (into a vein) in appropriate doses. Edwin S. Munson

Curassow, *KYUR uh soh,* is the name of a group of large birds that live in forests of tropical America. The *great curassow* is found from Mexico to Ecuador. The male is mostly black with a green or blue sheen to its feathers and looks somewhat like a turkey. The female is usually brown. Like most other curassows, the great curassow has a crest of feathers on top of the head. The crest can be raised forward or lowered. In many males, the bill is brightly colored and has a raised knob on top.

Curassows make nests of twigs and leaves in bushes

WORLD BOOK illustration by John F. Eggert
A male great curassow has a brightly colored beak. Its crest of feathers on the head can be raised or lowered.

or trees. The female typically lays two eggs. Curassows feed mainly on nuts and fruits from the forest floor.

Curassows can be tamed, and their flesh is good to eat. These birds are poor flyers and make easy targets for hunters. Hunting of curassows and destruction of their habitat have endangered some species.

Scientific classification. Curassows belong to the family Cracidae. The scientific name for the great curassow is *Crax rubra.*   Stuart D. Strahl

Curfew is the time of day which once brought with it evening and the end of work. The word comes from the French expression *couvre-feu* which means *cover the fire.* At curfew, a bell was rung, telling people to put out their lights, cover their fires, and get off the streets until daybreak. William the Conqueror introduced the curfew in England during the 1000's. In 1103 Henry I repealed the curfew law, but the bell continued to be rung. It is still rung in some parts of Britain.

In the United States, some communities have a curfew hour after which children may not be on the streets or in public places. The custom began long ago, but in Omaha, Nebr., about 1880, a curfew law was passed. Children under 15 had to be indoors after 8 p.m. unless they were with an adult or had written permission from their parents or guardians to be away from home. Many U.S. cities passed similar laws. Some communities have curfew laws for adults during wartime. Persons of an enemy nationality must often be in their homes after a certain hour in wartime.   Park Dixon Goist

Curia regis, *KYOOR ee uh REE jihs,* was a group that helped kings govern during the Middle Ages. The group was often called the *King's Council* or *King's Court.* It consisted of leading barons, churchmen, and other officials. The court advised the king on important affairs of state, agreed to taxation and legislation, and served as a high court to settle difficult legal cases. The English Parliament and Cabinet, and European systems of administration and law, developed from it.

For normal government business, the king depended on his household officials and a few trusted barons and churchmen. This small group, also called *curia regis,* met daily.   Bryce Lyon

Curie, *KYUR ee,* is a unit of radioactivity. Its symbol is *Ci.* One curie equals 37 billion *spontaneous nuclear transformations* per second. These transformations involve the emission of particles and rays by atomic nuclei. The radioactivity of 1 gram of radium equals about 1 curie. The curie was named for French physicist Pierre Curie. One *millicurie* is 1 one-thousandth of a curie. The curie has been largely replaced by the *becquerel.* One becquerel equals 1 spontaneous nuclear transformation per second.   John W. Poston

Curie, Irène Joliot-. See Joliot-Curie, Irène.

Curie, *KYOO ree,* **Marie Skłodowska,** *sklaw DAWF skah* (1867-1934), was a French physicist who became famous for her research on radioactivity. She received two Nobel Prizes—one in physics and one in chemistry.

Curie and her husband, Pierre, also a physicist, worked together in studying the radiation given off by radioactive substances. They found that uranium ore contained much more radioactivity than could be accounted for by the uranium itself. The Curies then began to search for the source of the radioactivity. They separated minute amounts of two new highly radioactive

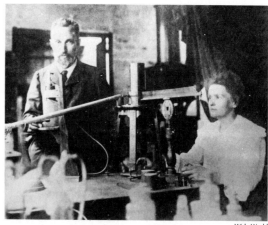

Wide World

Pierre and Marie Curie became famous for their research on radioactivity. The husband-and-wife team and a co-worker isolated the radioactive element radium in 1898.

chemical elements from tons of uranium ore, called *pitchblende.* The Curies named the elements *radium* and *polonium.* For this work, they and Antoine Henri Becquerel, a French physicist who discovered natural radioactivity, received the 1903 Nobel Prize in physics. In 1911, Marie Curie won the Nobel Prize in chemistry for her discovery of the new elements, and for her work in isolating radium and studying its chemical properties.

Curie helped found the Radium Institute (now the Curie Institute) in Paris in 1914 and served as its first director. She was born in Warsaw, Poland. Her maiden name was Marie Skłodowska. She studied mathematics, physics, and chemistry in Paris, where she became acquainted with Pierre Curie.   Romualdas Sviedrys

Additional resources

Curie, Ève. *Madame Curie: A Biography.* Da Capo, 1986. First published in 1937. A classic work.
Pflaum, Rosalynd. *Grand Obsession: Madame Curie and Her World.* Doubleday, 1989.

Curie, *KYOO ree,* **Pierre,** *pyair* (1859-1906), was a French physicist known for his work in radioactivity. He and his wife, Marie, shared the 1903 Nobel Prize in physics with another French physicist, Antoine Henri Becquerel, for research on the radioactivity of uranium. The Curies, while studying uranium, discovered two highly radioactive chemical elements, *radium* and *polonium.* A co-worker, Gustave Bémont, helped in the work with radium.

Curie was born in Paris and studied and taught physics at the University of Paris. His early work involved research on the magnetic properties of metals. The temperature at which such properties suddenly change became known as the *Curie point.* In 1880, Curie and his brother Jacques published a paper about their discovery of the piezoelectric properties of crystals (see **Piezoelectricity**).   Romualdas Sviedrys

Curium, *KYUR ee uhm,* is an artificially created radioactive element. Its atomic number is 96 and its chemical symbol is Cm.

Curium has 14 known isotopes, the most stable of which has a mass number of 247 and a half-life of 10 million years (see **Radioactivity** [Half-life]). However, this isotope occurs in amounts too small for most experiments. Two other isotopes of the element are more readily available. One has a mass number of 244 and a half-life of 18 years. The other has a mass number of 248 and a half-life of 340,000 years. Curium melts at 1340° C. At 20° C, it has a density of 13.51 grams per cubic centimeter (see **Density**).

Curium was discovered in 1944 by the American scientists Glenn T. Seaborg, Ralph A. James, and Albert Ghiorso. They produced it by bombarding plutonium with helium ions in a cyclotron. The element is named for the French chemist Marie Curie.   Richard L. Hahn

See also **Element, Chemical** (table); **Transuranium element; Seaborg, Glenn T.**

Curlew, *KUR loo,* is a long-legged bird that is related to sandpipers and snipes. It is found from Patagonia, in the far south of South America, to the Arctic in North America. It also lives in Europe and Asia. Curlews have long, slender bills which curve downward. They are

WORLD BOOK illustration by John Rignall, Linden Artists Ltd.
The long-billed curlew is a wading bird. It has long, bare legs, a short, rounded tail, and a long, slender bill.

wading birds, but they nest on dry ground, often far from water.

The *long-billed curlew* is one of the most common. It is 2 feet (61 centimeters) long and has a short, rounded tail. Its back is pale brown and spotted with black and dark-brown marks. The bird's breast is rusty brown and is more or less streaked. It has slender, bare legs. It gets its name from its slender bill, which is about 8 inches (20 centimeters) long. It uses its bill to catch small crabs, shellfish, snails, worms, and beetles.

The *whimbrel,* or Hudsonian curlew, is a smaller member of the group. Commonly found on the eastern coast of North America, it migrates to South America in the winter. The rare *Eskimo curlew* is still smaller.

Scientific classification. The curlew is in the sandpiper family, Scolopacidae. The long-billed curlew is *Numenius americanus.* The whimbrel is *N. phaeopus,* and the Eskimo curlew is *N. borealis.*   George L. Hunt, Jr.

See also **Sandpiper; Snipe.**

Curley, James Michael (1874-1958), a colorful American politician, was best known as mayor of Boston. He

also served as a Democratic state legislator, member of the U.S. House of Representatives, and governor of Massachusetts.

Curley served four terms as mayor (1914-1918, 1922-1926, 1930-1934, and 1946-1950). His methods and honesty were disputed, but he was popular among Boston's poor. When he was fined $30,000 in a fraud case in 1938, thousands of citizens donated money to pay the fine. In 1947, while serving as mayor, Curley went to prison for mail fraud. He served five months. President Harry S. Truman pardoned him in 1950. Curley was born in Boston.   Charles B. Forcey and Linda R. Forcey

Curling is a game played on a level sheet of ice sprayed with water droplets. Two four-player *rinks* (teams) compete on a sheet of ice 146 feet (45 meters) long and 15 feet 7 inches (5 meters) wide. The players slide stones on the ice toward a target. Curling probably began in Scotland and the Netherlands about 400 years ago. It has become popular in Canada and in more than 20 states in the United States.

The game. Each player slides two stones toward the *house* (target), a 12-foot (3.7-meter) circle at the far end of the ice. The competitors deliver one stone at a time, alternating with their opponents. When all 16 stones have been delivered, a period called an *end* or *inning* has been played. A game usually consists of 8 or 10 ends and lasts 2 to $2\frac{1}{2}$ hours. The stones of one rink that are closer to the house's center than any stones of the opposing rink score one point each. The opposing rink receives no points in that end.

Players deliver the stones from a *hack* (foothold) 126 feet (38 meters) from the center of the house at the far end of the ice. The stones used in most regulation matches weigh $42\frac{1}{2}$ pounds (19.3 kilograms). Each stone has a handle on top.

To deliver the stone, the player puts one foot in the hack, then crouches with the feet together. The stone rests on the ice to the player's side. Grasping the handle, the player slides the stone straight back and rises from a crouching position. The stone comes up off the ice during the backswing. Then, as the arm and stone swing forward, the player turns the hand either in or out. This

Eric Carle, Shostal
Curling players sweep the ice ahead of a sliding stone delivered by a teammate. Sweeping enables the stone to travel farther on the ice. The player on the right directs the sweepers.

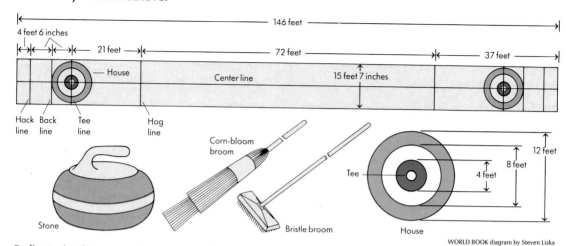

WORLD BOOK diagram by Steven Liska

Curling is played in a rectangular area on a level sheet of ice. A player stands on the *hack line* and slides a granite stone down the ice toward a target called the *house.* A team scores points by placing its stones closer to the *tee,* the center of the house, than those of its opponents.

action causes the stone to turn as it is released, and it *curls* (curves) to the right or left as it slides along. The game gets its name from this action.

The rink. In club competition, a rink is composed of a *lead,* a No. 2 player, a No. 3 player, and the *skip* or captain. They deliver the stones in that order. The lead, who is usually the least experienced player, goes first because it is simpler to deliver with no stones on the ice. In curling tournaments, called *bonspiels,* and in national and international competition, a rink consists of four experienced players.

Before the first player delivers, the skip moves to the house at the far end of the ice. The skip indicates with a broom the spot at which the stones should be aimed. After each stone is delivered, the skip judges its speed. If it appears that the stone will fall short of the target, the skip shouts, "Sweep." The other two players then move ahead of the sliding stone, sweeping the ice with their brooms. Sweeping alters the ice surface and lessens resistance to the stone. It can add 6 to 10 feet (1.8 to 3 meters) to a delivery. Players may use brooms with short, fine bristles or ones with long, stiffer bristles. The skip shouts "Brooms up" to command the sweepers to stop sweeping. After delivering two stones, a player joins a teammate in sweeping for the other members of the rink. Critically reviewed by the United States Curling Association

Curly-coated retriever is a dog trained to bring back game that has been shot. It gets its name from its black or liver-colored coat, which is a mass of thick, tight curls. This coat keeps the dog from getting chilled while swimming. The dog will work in cold water for a long time. It stands about 26 inches (66 centimeters) high at the shoulder and weighs from 50 to 80 pounds (23 to 36 kilograms). A curly-coated retriever is fairly easy to train, and makes a good watchdog.

Critically reviewed by the Curly-Coated Retriever Club of America

See also **Retriever.**

Currant is a small berry that grows on a low, bushy shrub. Currants are round and smooth, and they have a sour flavor. Their colors include black, red, gold, and white. Currant plants grow best in northern regions where the weather is generally cool and humid.

There is little commercial production of currants in the United States, but the berries are grown in many home gardens. Red currants and black currants are popular in northern Europe, where they grow wild. Red currants are used for jellies, jams, wines, and pies. Black currants, which are popular in Canada as well, have a sharper flavor and are used mainly for making juice.

Currant plants serve as host plants for a disease called *white pine blister rust fungus.* This disease is harmful to white pines and similar trees. For this reason, the growing of currant plants is banned in many areas of the United States where white pine forests are of commercial value.

Scientific classification. Currants belong to the saxifrage family, Saxifragaceae. The red currant and white currant are *Ribes rubrum.* The black currant is *R. nigrum;* the golden currant, *R. aureum.*   Max E. Austin

See also **Gooseberry; Saxifrage.**

Currency. See Money.

Current, Electric. See Electric current.

Currents, Ocean. See Ocean (How the ocean moves).

WORLD BOOK photo

The curly-coated retriever is named for its dark coat of thick, tight curls. The animal makes a good hunting dog and pet.

Curriculum, *kuh RIHK yuh luhm,* generally refers to the teaching and learning experiences provided by a school. But educators use the term in a variety of ways. Curriculum may refer to the subject matter taught or to the sequence of classes students follow. It may also describe a school's planned educational program or the educational experiences of students. Educators often distinguish between the curriculum as taught and the curriculum as learned. The term *hidden curriculum* refers to the total of experiences, attitudes, values, and behaviors a student learns in school. The hidden curriculum may or may not be intentionally taught by teachers.

Curriculum content. The United States, unlike other nations, has no standard national curriculum for public schools. However, most public schools have similar curriculums. In elementary schools, the curriculum emphasizes the basic skills of reading, writing, and arithmetic. Instruction is also provided in art, music, social studies, science, and physical education. The curriculum of junior high schools is a transition from elementary school to high school. Students study basic skills along with *disciplines,* or recognized branches of knowledge, such as social studies or humanities.

High school curriculums center around disciplines. They usually offer broad choices in courses of study called *tracks.* Tracks guide students into a sequence of classes, such as college preparatory or vocational classes. High schools also offer *electives,* which are non-required courses. Various activities are offered as *extracurricular,* or voluntary, beginning in junior high schools. These activities include sports teams, bands, drama, and a wide variety of clubs.

Most private and specialized schools have curriculums similar to those of public schools. However, these schools usually adopt a specialized approach to subject matter depending on the character and function of the school. For example, some private schools add a significant religious orientation to the overall curriculum. Also, many special public or private schools design curriculums to meet the needs of particular groups, such as disabled or intellectually gifted students.

Colleges offer a number of specialized curriculums. Students at community and technical colleges usually study for particular careers. Some junior colleges also have a general education curriculum. Four-year colleges offer curriculums for careers, such as nursing, engineering, or education, along with a general or liberal arts curriculum. Students following the liberal arts curriculum choose a *major,* or special area of study, such as philosophy, history, or biology. Graduate schools provide the most specialized curriculums. Some offer advanced work in a number of disciplines. Others, such as medical and law schools, focus on professional study.

Curriculum planning operates differently in the various educational institutions. School administrators and teachers usually develop the specific curriculum in public elementary and secondary schools. Their planning is influenced by such concerns as community expectations, broad national policies, and the teaching materials available. Curriculum planning is individualized at most colleges. However, departments within colleges play an important role in determining curriculums. College curriculums are also influenced by social and cultural institutions and concerns.

Curriculum changes occur as knowledge expands into new fields or as social problems force the development of new ideas and attitudes. During the late 1950's and the 1960's, for example, the exploration of space and the growth of computer technology caused a demand for more engineers, mathematicians, and scientists. This need led to the development of new content and methods in science and mathematics courses.

The 1960's and 1970's were times when traditional curriculums were challenged. For example, minority groups and others demanded changes that would reflect their particular concerns and traditions. Intense social concerns over human rights and foreign policy resulted in pressure on schools to deal with the moral and value issues involved in education. Parents and teachers also urged schools to help students cope with such issues as sexuality and drug and alcohol abuse.

In addition, many educators focused on the major social, economic, and moral aspects of curriculums. Some stressed the question of curriculum regarding the purpose of education. Others focused on the values reflected in particular curriculum practices. Still others discussed how curriculums could be designed to provide for the freedom and dignity of all people.

In the early 1980's, educators and parents began to demand more stress on achievement. This concern is reflected in the *back-to-basics* movement, which emphasizes basic reading and arithmetic skills. As a result, elementary and secondary schools have renewed their stress on traditional disciplines, such as English, history, mathematics, and science. Many schools have also become interested in *public accountability.* They emphasize *competency tests* or other forms of periodic testing to ensure specific types of learning have taken place. Colleges have also followed the back-to-basics trend by increasing requirements and reducing electives.

As schools limit what is taught, however, many educational theorists continue to challenge curriculums. Some theorists urge educators to consider the esthetic, moral, and political implications of their work.

David E. Purpel

See also **Education** (What should be taught?); **Elementary school; High school; Junior high school; Universities and colleges** (Selecting courses).

Currier and Ives was an American firm that specialized in publishing lithographs. The company flourished in the mid- and late 1800's, producing more than 7,000 images. The lithographs provided a broad view of American life, showing fashions of the time in sports, clothing, and transportation. The firm also published images of fires, shipwrecks, historical events, and portraits of celebrities. The prints were originally produced at modest cost and were widely used for interior decoration and for illustrations. Today, many of the images have become rare, highly prized, and valuable.

Nathaniel Currier (1813-1888) was born in Roxbury, Mass., and served as an apprentice in a Boston lithography shop before establishing his business in New York City. He issued his first prints in 1835.

James Merritt Ives (1824-1895), Currier's brother-in-law, served first as the bookkeeper and later as an artist and the art director for the firm. After 1857, all the prints published by the firm carried the joint name. Currier retired from the company in 1880, and Ives carried on the business with Nathaniel's son, William Currier. Ives was born in New York City.   Charles C. Eldredge

For examples of Currier and Ives lithographs, see **Baseball; Brooklyn Bridge; United States, History of.**

Curry is a blend of spices that is used to flavor a variety of fish, meat, vegetable, and grain dishes. *Curry* also refers to a stewlike dish flavored with curry spices. The curry blend is generally prepared by grinding and mixing from 2 to 20 different spices. In the United States, this ground mixture is called *curry powder.* The selection of curry seasonings varies with the dish but usually includes chili peppers, coriander, cumin, and turmeric. Some curries also include cardamom, cinnamon, cloves, fennel seeds, fenugreek seeds, ginger, and mustard seeds. Curries range in taste from hot and tangy to mild and sweet. Curry is believed to have originated in India and Pakistan.   James E. Simon

Curry, Jabez Lamar Monroe (1825-1903), an American statesman and educator, worked for 60 years to make education possible for all black and white children in the South. He administered the George Peabody Fund for public education in the South after 1888, and served as agent of the Slater Fund for Negro Schools after 1890. In 1899, he became president of the Southern Educational Board.

Curry served in the U.S. House of Representatives (1857-1861), in the Confederate Congress (1861-1863 and 1864), and in the Confederate Army (1864-1865). He was president of Howard College—now Samford University—(1865-1868), and United States minister to Spain (1885-1888 and 1902). Alabama placed a statue of him in the U.S. Capitol in Washington, D.C.

Curry was born in Lincoln County, Georgia. He graduated from the University of Georgia and from Harvard Law School.   Richard N. Current

Curry, John Steuart (1897-1946), an American painter, became famous for his dramatic scenes of Mid-

western rural life. He admired this life for what he considered its enduring goodness and simplicity. The best known of his works include *Baptism in Kansas* (1928) and *Tornado over Kansas* (1929). Curry belonged to the art movement of the 1930's known as *regionalism.* This movement attempted to portray the American scene during the hard times of the Great Depression. He painted murals for the U.S. Department of Justice and the Department of the Interior buildings in Washington, D.C., and for the Kansas Capitol in Topeka.

Curry was born in Dunavant, Kans. He studied at the Kansas Art Institute, at the Art Institute of Chicago, and then for a year in Paris.   Sarah Burns

Curtis, Charles (1860-1936), served as 31st Vice President of the United States under President Herbert Hoover. He had served in the U.S. House of Representatives from 1893 to 1907, and in the U.S. Senate from 1907 to 1913 and 1915 to 1929. Curtis was an experienced parliamentarian as a member of the Senate Rules Committee. He became majority leader of the Senate during the Administration of President Calvin Coolidge. Curtis became known for his ability to have the Senate complete its work without extra sessions.

Curtis, whose mother was part Kaw Indian, was born in North Topeka (now Topeka), Kans. As a youth, he worked as a jockey. But his interest turned to law, and he was admitted to the bar in 1881. He practiced law successfully, and became the attorney for Shawnee County.   James S. Olson

See also **Vice President of the United States** (picture).

Curtis, Cyrus Hermann Kotzschmar (1850-1933), an American publisher, founded the Curtis Publishing Company in 1890. He started his first publication, *Young America,* as a 12-year-old newsboy. Later he moved to Boston and, in 1872, founded a magazine called *The People's Ledger.* Four years later, he took this publication to Philadelphia. There, Curtis started another maga-

University of Nebraska, Lincoln, F. M. Hall Collection

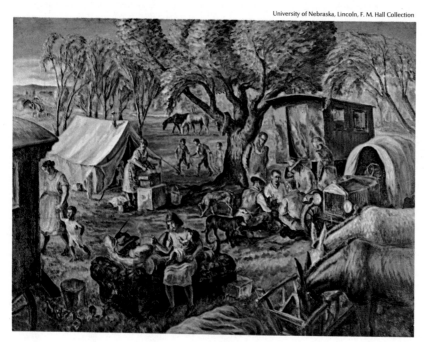

John Steuart Curry's paintings portray rural Midwestern life. The artist painted *The Roadmenders' Camp* in 1929.

zine, *The Tribune and Farmer,* which became the *Ladies' Home Journal* in 1883. Curtis bought *The Saturday Evening Post* in 1897 and *The Country Gentleman* in 1911.

Curtis also owned and published eight large daily newspapers. They included the *Philadelphia Public Ledger,* which he bought in 1913. Curtis purchased the *Philadelphia Press* in 1920, the *New York Post* in 1924, and the *Philadelphia Inquirer* in 1930. He organized Curtis-Martin Newspapers, Inc., a newspaper chain, in 1925. Curtis was born in Portland, Me. He engaged in many philanthropic activities.   Joseph P. McKerns

Curtis Institute of Music in Philadelphia prepares gifted students for professional careers. All students are on full scholarships. The institute was founded and endowed in 1924 by Mary Louise Curtis Bok, and named for her father, Cyrus H. K. Curtis. It grants degrees of Bachelor of Music and Master of Music in Opera and Accompanying. The faculty has included such distinguished musicians as Leopold Auer, Jorge Bolet, Todd Duncan, Josef Hofmann, Max Rudolf, Rudolf Serkin, Leopold Stokowski, and Efrem Zimbalist.

Critically reviewed by the Curtis Institute of Music

Curtiss, Glenn Hammond (1878-1930), an American inventor, made important contributions to the development of aircraft. He manufactured airplanes, and made thousands of planes during World War I (1914-1918). His Wasp held a number of records. In 1919, a Navy-Curtiss flying boat, commanded by Albert C. Read, made the first flight across the Atlantic Ocean.

Curtiss was born in Hammondsport, N.Y., and educated in the town's elementary schools. An interest in bicycle racing as a boy led to his flying career. From bicycles he turned to building motorcycles, one of which he raced at 137 miles (220 kilometers) per hour. In 1904, he began building engines for the first U.S. dirigibles, designed by Thomas Scott Baldwin. Curtiss built his airplane engine in 1907, as a member of Alexander Graham Bell's Aerial Experiment Association. In 1908, he helped design an airplane called the *June Bug.* It had a box tail and was controlled by *ailerons* (hinged flaps on the wings). Orville and Wilbur Wright had obtained a patent on a method of twisting wings to control flight. They claimed Curtiss' ailerons violated their patent. They won a court suit against Curtiss.

In 1910, Curtiss won $10,000 by flying one of his planes from Albany, N.Y., to New York City in 2 hours 51 minutes. He built the first planes for the United States Navy in 1911 after demonstrating that planes could land and take off from ships.   Bobby H. Johnson

See also **Airplane** (picture: The *June Bug*).

Curve. See Parabola; Circle; Baseball (Pitching); Bowling; Railroad (The roadbed and route).

Curzon Line was the eastern boundary of Poland proposed by the Allies in 1919, after World War I. It was named for Lord George Curzon, a British diplomat. Before the war, Poland had been divided among Austria-Hungary, Germany, and Russia. The Curzon Line was to be the frontier between Russia and a new Poland. The two countries had already been at war over territory in 1919, and both rejected the plan. The Treaty of Riga in 1921 moved the border east of the Curzon Line. The line is now the boundary separating Poland from Belarus and Ukraine.   William A. Jenks

Cusa, Nicholas of. See Nicholas of Cusa.

Cusco, *KOOS koh* (pop. 255,300), also spelled *Cuzco,* is a city in the southern Andes Mountains of Peru. For location, see **Peru** (political map). The city lies about 11,200 feet (3,400 meters) above sea level. Cusco was the capital of the Inca Empire. Francisco Pizarro, a Spanish soldier, took it in 1533. Cusco has many Inca and Spanish colonial buildings, and the ancient Inca city of Machu Picchu is nearby. Cusco is a trading center for nearby farmers. The city is also a center of tourism.

Jerry R. Williams

Cuscus, *KUHS kuhs,* is a possum that lives on the northern tip of Australia and in New Guinea and nearby islands. It grows about 2 feet (61 centimeters) long, not including the tail. Cuscuses have large eyes, tiny ears, and woolly fur. The fur may be entirely brown, gray, or

Fleay's Fauna Reserve

The cuscus is a mammal of Australia, New Guinea, and nearby islands. The lower part of its tail is hairless and has scales.

white, or it may be spotted or striped. The rear part of the tail is hairless and has scales.

Cuscuses move slowly and are most active at night. They live in trees and eat chiefly fruits and leaves. Cuscuses are *marsupials.* Female marsupials give birth to tiny, poorly developed offspring. Like most marsupials, young cuscuses are carried in a pouch on the mother's belly until they develop more completely.

Scientific classification. Cuscuses belong to the family Phalangeridae.   Michael L. Augee

See also **Possum.**

Cush. See Kush.

Cushing, Harvey (1869-1939), an American physician and surgeon, was one of the world's greatest brain surgeons. He won fame for his achievements in neurosurgery and for experimental work on the brain, nervous system, and pituitary gland. As a result of Cushing's work, neurological surgery became a respected medical subspecialty.

Cushing was born in Cleveland. He attended Yale College and Harvard Medical School before joining the surgical staff of Johns Hopkins Hospital in 1896. In 1912, he returned to Harvard as a professor of surgery. In 1926, Cushing won a Pulitzer Prize in biography for *The Life of Sir William Osler* (1925), the life story of his friend and fellow physician.   Dale C. Smith

Cuspid. See Teeth (Permanent teeth).

Custer, George Armstrong

Custer, George Armstrong (1839-1876), was a United States Army officer who won fame as a Civil War general and an Indian fighter in the West. Custer is best known for his role in the Battle of the Little Bighorn on June 25, 1876, in the Montana Territory. In this battle, which is also known as "Custer's Last Stand," Sioux and Cheyenne Indians killed Custer and all of the men under

Brown Bros.

George A. Custer

his direct command. The battle became famous because of disagreement over the reasons for Custer's defeat.

Early career. Custer was born in New Rumley, Ohio. As a boy, he wanted to be a soldier. He graduated from the U.S. Military Academy in 1861, ranking last in his class. But during the Civil War, which had just begun, Custer quickly gained attention as a fearless cavalry leader. In 1863, at the age of 23, he was made a brigadier general, and in 1865, a major general, both temporary ranks.

Many who served with the bold "boy general" admired his bravery and success. Many others felt that Custer was overly proud and too sure of his abilities. Some of his enemies were jealous of him and called Custer a "glory hunter." But he captured the public's attention and became a hero in the North.

After the Civil War ended in 1865, the Army dropped Custer to his regular rank of captain. He joined the Seventh Cavalry Regiment in 1866 as a lieutenant colonel. Custer won greater fame and made more enemies while fighting Indians in the southern Great Plains region and in the Dakota and Montana territories.

The 1876 campaign. In early 1876, Custer's regiment joined troops organized to force the Sioux and Cheyenne Indians onto reservations. General Alfred H. Terry commanded the expedition. In June, the main part of the army force reached an area in the Montana Territory where Terry expected to find the Sioux Indians. Terry ordered Custer's regiment to get in a position south of the Indians.

On the morning of June 25, Custer's scouts found an Indian village about 15 miles (24 kilometers) away. It lay in the valley along the Little Bighorn River. Custer expected to find about 1,000 warriors. He believed his 650 soldiers could easily capture the village. But the camp really had at least 2,000 Sioux and Cheyenne warriors. This group, whose leaders included Crazy Horse, Gall, and Sitting Bull, was probably the largest gathering of Indian warriors in Western history.

The battle. Custer decided to attack immediately. He split his regiment into three main groups—one under Captain Frederick W. Benteen, one under Major Marcus A. Reno, and one under himself. He sent Benteen to the south to prevent Indians from escaping in that direction. He ordered Reno to cross the river and attack the village. Custer's group turned north and went downstream, probably to attack a weak point in the village.

After intense fighting in the valley, Reno's badly beaten troops retreated up the hills on the other side of

the river. Benteen's group joined Reno's men there. About 4 miles (6.5 kilometers) away from this site, the Indians killed Custer and his entire unit of approximately 210 soldiers. The fighting may have lasted only one hour. The Indians fought Benteen and Reno's troops until June 26. Later that day, the Indians disbanded their camp and left the territory. Terry arrived with his soldiers on June 27.

The controversy. Americans found it almost impossible to believe that any group of Indians could have killed such a well-known officer and all his men. Custer's enemies accused him of disobeying Terry by attacking the Indians without waiting for the main body of soldiers. Custer's supporters charged that Reno had been a coward, and could have rescued Custer if he had not retreated. Others blamed Terry and his aides for not knowing the size of the Indian force. Historians still argue about the reasons for Custer's defeat, but no one really knows.   Brian W. Dippie

See also **Crazy Horse; Gall; Indian wars** (The Sioux wars); **Reno, Marcus A.; Sitting Bull.**

Additional resources

Level I

Halliburton, Warren J. *The Tragedy of Little Bighorn.* Watts, 1989.
Reynolds, Quentin J. *Custer's Last Stand.* Random Hse., 1964. First published in 1951.
Stein, R. Conrad. *The Story of the Little Bighorn.* Childrens Pr., 1989. First published in 1983.

Level II

Connell, Evan S. *Son of the Morning Star: Custer and the Little Bighorn.* Harper, 1988. First published in 1984.
The Custer Reader. Ed. by Paul A. Hutton. Univ. of Nebraska Pr., 1992.
Gray, John S. *Custer's Last Campaign: Mitch Boyer and the Little Bighorn Reconstructed.* Univ. of Nebraska Pr., 1991.
Monaghan, Jay. *Custer: The Life of General George Armstrong Custer.* Univ. of Nebraska Pr., 1971. First published in 1959.
Utley, Robert M. *Cavalier in Buckskin: George Armstrong Custer and the Western Military Frontier.* Univ. of Oklahoma Pr., 1988.

Custer Battlefield National Monument. See Little Bighorn Battlefield National Monument.

Custis, George Washington Parke (1781-1857), grandson of Martha Washington, became the adopted son of George Washington. He is known for his *Recollections of Washington* (1860) and for his plays. One of them, *Pocahontas,* told the story of the Indian princess and Captain John Smith. In another play, Custis brought a locomotive steam carriage onto the stage.

Custis was born in Mt. Airy, Md. His mansion became the home of his son-in-law, General Robert E. Lee. The mansion stands in Arlington National Cemetery, across the Potomac River from Washington, D.C.

Kathryn Kish Sklar

See also **Washington, George** (picture: The Washingtons).

Custis, Martha. See Washington, Martha Custis.

Custom is a practice or a way of doing things that has been handed down from one generation to the next. Customs are part of the culture shared by members of a social group. Many customs begin because people like to know what to expect in social situations. Like all cultural traits, customs are a form of learned behavior and differ among different peoples. For example, eating is a biological requirement for all people, but table manners and customs of food preparation vary among groups.

Practices that change frequently are called *fashions*. They include social dances, styles of dress, and slang expressions. Fashions that quickly come and go are called *fads*. A fashion may become a custom through long usage. For example, eating with a fork was a fashion in Europe during the 1500's, but it is now a custom throughout the Western world.

Customs last partly because people often find it easier to conform than to face the disapproval of their social group. Such disapproval may range from mild ridicule to severe punishment. Many customs produce only mild reactions when broken. Such customs include many wedding and funeral traditions and rules of etiquette. A person who departs from such customs may encounter surprise, annoyance, or scorn.

Important customs that reflect a society's ideas of right and wrong are called *mores*. Examples include the reaction of people to murder or cannibalism, which produce anger and shock.

In isolated, nonindustrial communities, most customs remain unchanged from generation to generation. The majority of people in such societies believe the old ways are best—and what was good for the parents is good for the children. In modern industrial societies, however, customs change more easily. A number of factors, including new inventions and contact with other cultures, may lead to such changes.   Hanan C. Selvin

Related articles. See the country articles in which customs are discussed, such as **India** (Way of life). See also:

Clothing (Clothing around the world)	Folklore (Superstitions and customs)	Holiday
Etiquette	Food	Mores
Fashion	Funeral customs	Rite of passage
Feasts and festivals		Taboo

Customs are duties paid to a nation's government on items that people bring in from another country. Each nation has its own regulations regarding the quantity and kinds of articles that may be imported.

Customs inspectors examine the baggage of all travelers returning to a country. All articles acquired abroad must be *declared*—that is, they must be identified and their value given to an inspector. If a person fails to declare an article or understates its value, the article may be taken away and the individual may be fined.

In the United States, articles totaling up to $400 are *exempt* (free from any duty) if they meet certain regulations. For example, the articles must be for personal use, and the person's trip must have lasted at least 48 hours. Also, the articles cannot be prohibited or restricted by federal regulations. The $400 exemption can be claimed by a person once every 30 days. The 48-hour rule does not apply to trips to Mexico or the Virgin Islands.

If a traveler cannot claim the $400 exemption because of the 48-hour or 30-day restriction, he or she may claim a $25 exemption. However, a person must pay duties on all articles if their total value exceeds $25. Duty rates depend on the type, value, and quantity of the articles.

Prohibited items include illegal narcotics and dangerous drugs, obscene publications, and switchblade knives. Certain items, such as firearms, fruit, meat, and vegetables, are either prohibited or require an import permit. Federal laws allow the importation of up to 1 liter (1.06 quarts) of alcoholic beverages and up to 200 cigarettes and 100 cigars for personal use.

Canadian customs laws differ from U.S. customs laws. For example, when returning to Canada after a 48-hour absence, a resident may claim an exemption of up to $100. After any 24-hour absence, an exemption of up to $20 is allowed. Once a year, after a seven-day absence, a traveler may claim an exemption of up to $300.

Critically reviewed by the United States Customs Service

See also **Customs Service, U.S.; Smuggling.**

Customs Court, United States. See **Court of International Trade, United States.**

Customs Service, United States, is an agency of the Department of the Treasury that assesses and collects taxes on imported merchandise. These taxes, also called *tariffs,* include customs duties, excise taxes, and penalties. The service collects about $20 billion a year, more than any other federal agency except the Internal Revenue Service, which collects income taxes.

The Customs Service processes goods, people, and vehicles entering or leaving the United States. For example, customs inspectors examine the baggage of travelers returning to the country. The agency works to prevent smuggling and to enforce many other federal laws, including those governing environmental protection and motor vehicle safety. It also works to protect U.S. business and labor by enforcing copyright, patent, and trademark regulations.

The service administers seven customs regions in the United States, Puerto Rico, and the Virgin Islands. These regions are divided into 44 districts with about 300 *ports of entry.* Ports of entry are cities with customs facilities where goods may enter the country legally. The commissioner of customs directs the agency.

The service was established in 1789 by the First Congress. The headquarters of the Customs Service are at 1301 Constitution Avenue NW, Washington, DC 20229.

Critically reviewed by the United States Customs Service

See also **Customs; Airport** (picture: Customs officials).

Customs union is an association of two or more countries to encourage trade. The countries making such an arrangement agree to eliminate duties and other restrictive regulations on trade among them. Members of the union apply a single set of tariffs to all countries outside the union. A *free trade area* is like a customs union, except that the members of a free trade area may apply separate tariffs against nonmembers.

The best-known customs unions have included the Zollverein, Benelux, and the European Economic Community (EEC). The Zollverein was formed by German states in the 1830's. These states became the German nation in 1871. Belgium, the Netherlands, and Luxembourg established Benelux in the 1940's. Belgium, France, Italy, Luxembourg, the Netherlands, and West Germany set up the European Economic Community in 1957. Britain, Denmark, and Ireland joined the EEC in 1973, Greece joined in 1981, and Portugal and Spain joined in 1986.

Robert M. Stern

See also **Benelux; European Community; European Free Trade Association.**

Cutch. See **Catechu.**

Cuticle. See **Hair** (The structure and growth of hair).

Cutlassfish is a type of saltwater fish with a long, slender body that tapers to a hairlike tail. Cutlassfish live in all warm seas and are abundant in the Caribbean and the Gulf of Mexico. These fish have a large mouth with four large barbed fangs in the upper jaw and two in the lower jaw. Most cutlassfish measure about $2\frac{1}{2}$ feet (75 centimeters) long, but some grow as long as 5 feet (150 centimeters). Cutlassfish living off the coast of Japan lay their eggs in fairly shallow waters. The fish are caught for food in some areas.

Scientific classification. Cutlassfish belong to the cutlassfish family, Trichiuridae. Tomio Iwamoto

Cutting. See Plant (Vegetative propagation).

Cuttlefish is a *mollusk* (soft boneless animal) in the same class as the squid. It is found in most seas except those surrounding the Americas. It usually lives in deep water, but it is sometimes found near the shore. It ranges in size from about 3 inches (8 centimeters) to about 6 feet (1.8 meters) long. The body is brown with crossbands and purple spots. It is brilliantly metallic in the sunlight and often changes color. The cuttlefish's oval body is surrounded with a frilled fin.

The cuttlefish has eight short arms and two long *tentacles* (feelers) that surround the mouth. Both the arms and the tentacles have four rows of hard and rough suckers. The tentacles can be pulled into pockets behind the eyes. The cuttlefish uses its arms to attach itself to objects, and to capture marine life for food.

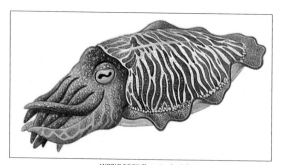

WORLD BOOK illustration by Colin Newman, Linden Artists Ltd.

The cuttlefish has a broad head with two large eyes. It has eight short arms and two long tentacles surrounding the mouth.

The cuttlefish has an internal shell called the *cuttlebone.* The broad cuttlebone is spongy and chalky. It is fed to canaries and parrots because of its lime food value. It is also used in making toothpaste.

The cuttlefish moves by forcing water in or out of the space between the cuttlebone and body. To hide from its enemies, the cuttlefish can darken the water as it moves by pouring out an inky substance containing the brown *pigment* (coloring matter) called sepia. Ink made from sepia was widely used in ancient times.

Scientific classification. The common cuttlefish is in the cuttlefish family, Sepiidae. The scientific name for it is *Sepia officinalis.* M. Patricia Morse

See also **Mollusk; Nautilus; Octopus; Squid.**

Cutworm is the caterpillar of certain dull-colored, night-flying moths. Cutworms have a smooth skin and vary in color from light gray to black. Some are striped or spotted. Cutworms are quite destructive. Groups of cutworms have been known to destroy entire fields of young wheat, corn, or garden vegetables overnight. Cutworms also may cause a great deal of damage to tobacco, cotton, and various kinds of fruit trees. From one to four generations of cutworms may grow each year.

Some spend the winter as pupae, others as larvae. Solitary cutworms feed beneath the soil. Climbing cutworms crawl up the plants at night to feed. Gardeners kill both kinds of cutworms with poisoned baits and sprays. See **Moth.**

Scientific classification. Cutworms are in the owlet moth family, Noctuidae. John R. Meyer

Cuvier, *KYOO vee AY* or *koov YAY,* **Baron** (1769-1832), was a French naturalist who studied *comparative anatomy,* a branch of zoology that compares the differences and similarities in the body structure of different animals. Cuvier included investigations of the remains of prehistoric animals in his comparisons. He wrote *The Animal Kingdom* (1817), which became an authoritative reference on the classification of animals.

Cuvier began his work by dissecting marine *invertebrates* (animals without backbones). He later studied many large land mammals, including the rhinoceros and the elephant. Cuvier proposed the theory of *geological catastrophe* to explain why many fossil animals no longer exist. This theory held that great volcanic upheavals and similar catastrophes destroyed many forms of life. Cuvier believed that the distinctive anatomical characters of various animal groups was proof that they had not evolved from the same ancestor. Cuvier also believed that species did not change over time.

Georges Léopold Chrétien Frédéric Dagobert Cuvier was born in Montbéliard, France. He taught at the College of France. He contributed to reform of the French educational system and helped to found some of the French provincial universities. G. J. Kenagy

See also **Biology** (The origins of scientific classification); **Geology** (Experimental geology).

Cuzco. See Cusco.

Cyanide, *SY uh nyd,* is the name given to metal salts containing the CN group (a carbon atom linked to a nitrogen atom). Sodium cyanide (NaCN) and potassium cyanide (KCN) are important industrial chemicals. Both are used in the cyanide process of separating gold and silver from their ores, and in the hardening of steel. Both forms also are very poisonous if swallowed or absorbed through injured skin. Strong acids react with metal cyanides to make hydrogen cyanide (HCN), a deadly poison gas. Organic cyanides are *nitriles.* Acrylonitrile, important in the manufacture of fabrics, plastics, and synthetic rubber, is made from cyanide. Chemists use cyanide in solutions for electroplating and in the production of drugs and other chemicals. See also **Gas chamber; Prussic acid.** Marianna A. Busch

Cyanite. See Kyanite.

Cyanobacteria. See Algae; Moneran.

Cyanosis, *SY uh NOH sihs,* is a medical condition involving a bluish tint of the skin and mucous membranes. Cyanosis results if the blood flowing through vessels in the skin and mucous membranes contains too much *reduced hemoglobin*—that is, hemoglobin not combined with oxygen. Hemoglobin is the compound in red blood cells that carries oxygen. When combined with oxygen, hemoglobin makes blood bright red. Blood containing large amounts of reduced hemoglobin appears bluish when seen through the skin and mucous membranes.

Cyanosis may occur among people who live at high altitudes, where the air pressure is low and less than the normal amount of oxygen is available. It may result from abnormalities in hemoglobin or heart and lung ailments that prevent blood from combining properly with oxygen. For example, *blue babies* have cyanosis because a heart defect prevents some blood from entering their lungs to receive oxygen (see **Blue baby**). Cyanosis also can occur when blood circulates poorly after a person goes into shock or suffers heart failure.

Cyanosis resulting from too little oxygen may be treated by improving the patient's respiration or by using an oxygen tent or mask. Physicians treat cyanosis caused by poor circulation by increasing the rate of the blood flow.   G. David Roodman

Cybernetics, *sy buhr NEHT ihks,* is the study of control and communication in machines and animals. Norbert Wiener, an American mathematician, introduced the term *cybernetics* in his book of the same name, first published in the United States in 1948.

Wiener's book described the similarities in the functioning of human beings and machines. Wiener and others had observed that both people and machines were purposeful and orderly, sought stability, and used information. One of their most important shared characteristics, according to Wiener, was the use of *feedback.* Feedback involves the circling back of information to a control device to adjust behavior. For example, when the body temperature of a human being is too high or too low, this information is *fed back* to the brain. The brain then acts to correct the temperature. A household thermostat uses feedback when it corrects the operation of a furnace to maintain a set temperature.

Cybernetics has prompted attempts to build machines that imitate human behavior, including decision-making and analysis of data. Because such machines accomplish more than the simple mechanization of work, some theorists argue that cybernetics has started a second industrial revolution. Since the 1940's, the ideas of cybernetics have influenced such fields as biochemistry, computer science, and psychology. Today, many specialized terms have replaced the word *cybernetics.* In business fields, the term is no longer used.

    David McComb

See also **Wiener, Norbert.**

Cycad, *SY kad,* is a large subtropical and tropical seed plant. It is related to *conifers* (cone-bearing trees), such as the pine and spruce, but looks like a palm or fern. Some cycads have unbranched, erect stems that may be 60 feet (18 meters) high. Others have a partially underground stem, called a *tuber,* that resembles a potato. Some species reach ages of nearly a thousand years.

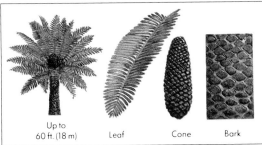

Up to 60 ft. (18 m)   Leaf   Cone   Bark

WORLD BOOK illustration by John D. Dawson

The cycad plant bears its seeds in cones.

The cycad's leathery, fernlike leaves grow in a circle at the end of the stem. New leaves emerge every year and live several years. The cycad has a *strobilus* (large cone) that contains seeds. The cone grows erect in the center of the circle of leaves. When the seeds mature, part of the strobilus shrivels, allowing the seeds to drop.

Scientists have found fossils which show that cycads were common during prehistoric times. The cycads are the most primitive seed plants, but not necessarily the most ancient. They grow in only a few small areas. One kind of cycad, called *Zamia,* is common in tropical America.

Scientific classification. Cycads belong to the cycas family, Cycadaceae.   Thomas B. Croat

See also **Conifer; Gymnosperm; Seed.**

Cyclamen, *SIHK luh mehn,* is the name of a group of attractive plants that grow wild in the Mediterranean region of Europe. Cyclamens are cultivated outdoors in areas where the climate permits or indoors in pots. The leaves are heart- or bean-shaped and have long *petioles* (leafstalks). The flowers are white, rose, or purple and have no fragrance. They measure up to $2\frac{1}{2}$ inches (6.4 centimeters) long.

Cyclamens are cultivated from seed and grow best at temperatures from 50 °F to 60 °F (10 °C to 16 °C) in rich, moist soil. Some species flower in the spring, and others bloom in the summer or autumn. Cyclamen plants that are cultivated indoors or in greenhouses may flower in the winter. See also **Primrose.**

Scientific classification. Cyclamens belong to the primrose family, Primulaceae. They make up the genus *Cyclamen.*

Melinda F. Denton

Cycling. See **Bicycle racing.**

Cyclone is a low-pressure area in the atmosphere in which winds spiral inward. A cyclone may cover an area half as large as the entire United States. A special, intense kind of cyclone from about 300 to 8,000 feet (90 to 2,400 meters) across is a *tornado.*

All cyclones have two characteristics: (1) the atmospheric pressure is lowest at the center, and (2) the winds spiral in toward the center. In the Northern Hemisphere, the winds blow counterclockwise. In the Southern Hemisphere, they blow inward in a clockwise direction.

Some parts of the world have so many cyclones that their average atmospheric pressure is below that of the rest of the world. For example, in the *Aleutian low* in the North Pacific Ocean and the *Icelandic low* of the North Atlantic, the pressure is low most of the winter. Such regions may be called *semipermanent* low-pressure centers or *centers of action.*

Storms usually occur with cyclones. Falling atmospheric pressure generally indicates that bad weather is coming. But sometimes cyclones do not bring bad weather, because the kind of air also has much to do with the weather. For example, if a cyclone forms in dry air, there may not be any clouds.

A *tropical cyclone* develops over tropical or subtropical waters. Severe tropical cyclones, with winds of 74 miles (119 kilometers) per hour or more are called *hurricanes* or *typhoons,* depending on where they form. Hurricanes form in the North Atlantic or eastern North Pacific, and typhoons form in the western Pacific. These storms may bring winds up to 180 miles (290 kilometers) an hour, terrific rains, violent thunder, and lightning.

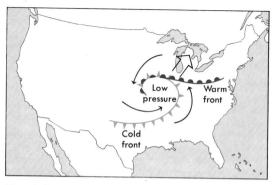

The winds of a cyclone spiral in toward a low-pressure center. In the Northern Hemisphere, they blow counterclockwise as the low-pressure center moves from southwest to northeast.

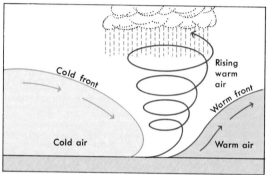

WORLD BOOK diagrams

A cyclonic storm develops at a low-pressure center. The heavy cold air along an advancing cold front lifts the lighter, warmer air along a warm front. Clouds form, and rain begins to fall when the water vapor in the warm air condenses.

They measure 200 to 300 miles (320 to 480 kilometers) across.

Cyclones may be either warm-core or cold-core types. *Warm-core* cyclones are warmer at the center than near the edges. They are fairly shallow and become weaker in the upper atmosphere. They often occur over especially warm land areas. *Cold-core* cyclones are coldest near the center and warmer near the edges. These cyclones may be very deep, and are more intense several thousand feet in the air than they are at the surface of the earth.   Wayne M. Wendland

See also **Hurricane; Tornado; Weather; Wind.**

Cyclonite. See RDX.

Cyclopedia. See Encyclopedia.

Cyclops, *SY klahps,* in Greek mythology was any member of a race of giants with one eye in the middle of the forehead. Three Cyclopes—Arges, Brontes, and Steropes—were sons of the sky god Uranus and the earth goddess Gaea. The three made the thunderbolts carried by Zeus, king of the gods.

The best-known of the Cyclopes was Polyphemus. The epic poem *Odyssey* describes how the Greek hero Odysseus and his men sailed to an island inhabited by Polyphemus. The Cyclops imprisoned the Greeks and ate six of them. After Odysseus made Polyphemus drunk, he and his surviving men put out the giant's eye

with a burning stake and escaped. The blind Polyphemus prayed to his father, the sea god Poseidon, to punish Odysseus. As a result, Odysseus suffered many hardships and delays before reaching his home. Another story tells how Polyphemus killed the Sicilian youth Acis, his rival for the love of the sea nymph Galatea.   Robert J. Lenardon

Cyclosporine, *sy kloh SPAWR een,* is a drug that fights the rejection of transplanted body tissues and organs. It is produced from cultures of a fungus, *Tolypocladium inflatum.* Jean Borel, a Swiss immunologist, discovered the medicinal properties of cyclosporine in 1972. The drug has been proven effective in operations in which the heart, liver, pancreas, bone marrow, a kidney, or a lung of one person is transferred to another person. Cyclosporine was first used in transplant operations in 1981. Such use has lowered the frequency of complications and deaths resulting from transplants.

Cyclosporine works by suppressing the functioning of a person's immune system. The drug is believed to block production of a type of white blood cells called *T-helper cells.* These blood cells attack invading or unfamiliar substances and thus cause the body to reject transplanted tissues or organs. In addition to its use during and after transplant operations, cyclosporine has shown promise in the treatment of certain diseases involving the immune system.

Patients may take cyclosporine orally by mixing it in orange juice or milk. The drug also may be injected into the bloodstream. Cyclosporine may produce a number of side effects. The most serious of these include high blood pressure, reduced kidney function, liver damage, and abnormal growth of hair. To reduce its toxic effect, cyclosporine is often given in association with several other drugs.   Bruce A. Reitz

Cyclotron, *SY kluh trahn,* is a machine that accelerates electrically charged atomic particles to high energies. It is a type of *particle accelerator* that makes the particles travel in circles. Cyclotrons accelerate particles ranging in mass from protons to heavy nuclei. Most reach energies of from 10 million to 50 million electronvolts. A few attain even higher energies.

In a cyclotron, the particles travel in a vacuum chamber located between the poles of a powerful electromagnet. The electromagnet creates a magnetic field that forces the particles to follow a circular path. The vacuum chamber also contains two *D*-shaped electrodes, called *dees,* that have a gap between them. An alternating electric field is applied across this gap. It acts on the electric charge of the particles and gives them a slight "push" each time they cross the gap. As a result, the particles gradually speed up. The diameter of their path grows in proportion to their speed, and so they spiral outward. When the particles approach the edge of the magnetic field, they are traveling at their maximum speed. The particles are then directed to a target, or they are extracted from the machine in the form of a particle beam. For a diagram of a cyclotron, see **Particle accelerator.**

The cyclotron was invented in 1930 by the American physicist Ernest O. Lawrence. Lawrence received the 1939 Nobel Prize for physics for his achievement. The cyclotron was originally developed for use in studying the atomic nucleus, but today it has many functions.

Some of the cyclotrons built in recent years can accelerate the atomic nuclei of any of the elements that occur naturally in or on the earth.   Robert H. March

Cygnet. See Swan.

Cylinder, in geometry, is a solid figure with two identical bases that lie on parallel planes. Each base is bounded by a curved edge, called the *directrix.* The *lateral surface* (side) of a cylinder consists of parallel lines that join corresponding points on each base. When the directrixes of a cylinder are circles, the figure is called a *circular cylinder.* A *right circular cylinder* is a circular cylinder with a lateral surface that is perpendicular to the bases. Circular cylinders with a lateral surface not perpendicular to the bases are called *oblique circular cylinders.* A cylinder whose directrixes are ellipses is called a *cylindroid.*

The *height (h)* of a cylinder is the perpendicular
distance between the
planes of the bases. The
volume (V) of a cylinder
can be calculated by multiplying the height by the
area (B) enclosed by either
of the two bases: $V=Bh.$ If
the bases of a cylinder are
circles, then $B = \pi r^2$,
where r stands for the radius of either of the circles.
The formula for the volume
of the cylinder can then be
written: $V = \pi r^2 h.$ An approximate value for π (pi) is
3.1416.

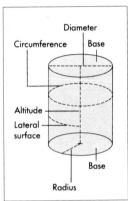

WORLD BOOK diagram by Linda Kinnaman
Parts of a cylinder

The area of the lateral
surface in a right circular cylinder is equal to the circumference of the base times the height. It can be found
using the formula $L = 2 \pi rh.$ In the formula, L stands
for the lateral surface area. The *total surface area (A)* of a
right circular cylinder, therefore, can be calculated by
adding together the lateral surface area and the areas of
the two bases: $A = 2 \pi rh + 2 \pi r^2$ or $2 \pi r (h + r).$

John K. Beem

Cymbal is a brass percussion instrument shaped like a broad-brimmed hat. The center of a cymbal resembles the crown of a hat. A musician may hold the cymbal by a leather handle attached to the center or hang the instrument on a stand. A player can produce tones that vary in quality by striking two cymbals together or by striking one cymbal with a mallet. The mallet may be made of metal or wood, and some mallets are covered with felt or yarn.

Cymbals are made in many sizes. Most musicians prefer cymbals that measure from 12 to 22 inches (30 to 56 centimeters) in diameter. Cymbals vary in thickness as well as diameter, and no two sound exactly alike. See Music (picture: Percussion instruments).

Cymballike objects were found in the ruins of the Indus Valley civilization, which arose in what are now Pakistan and northwestern India about 2500 B.C. The cymbal was first used by an orchestra in an opera in 1680 that was held in Hamburg, Germany.

The Zildjian Company in the United States manufactures the most widely used cymbals in the world. The

company has been making cymbals by a secret method since 1623.   John H. Beck

Cynic philosophy, *SIHN ihk,* was established in the 300's B.C. by Antisthenes, a disciple of Socrates. He took as his starting point the doctrine of his great teacher that virtue rather than pleasure is the chief end of life, and constitutes true happiness. He argued that the wise person is the one who looks with contempt on all the ordinary pleasures of life, and lives without regard for riches or honors. Continued happiness, he declared, is not possible if a person has wants and desires which may not be satisfied. A person is bound by no obligations to society, state, or family, because these things give rise to desires that cannot be satisfied.

Among the enthusiastic followers of Antisthenes was Diogenes, who carried the principles of the Cynics to an extreme. It is said that he lived on the coarsest bread and slept at night in a tub. Zeno of Citium, a Cynic of the late 300's and early 200's B.C., founded Stoic philosophy (see **Stoic philosophy**).

Some authorities say that the name *cynic* refers to *Cynosarges,* the name of the building in Athens where the Cynics first met. Others say that the name comes from the Greek word for dog, and refers to the rude manners of the Cynics. In ordinary speech, a person who sneers at the idea that goodness exists in human nature is often called a *cynic.*   S. Marc Cohen

See also **Diogenes; Zeno of Citium.**

Cypress, *SY pruhs,* is any one of a group of evergreen trees and shrubs that grow in North America, Europe, and Asia. There are about 13 species of cypresses, six of which grow naturally in the Southwestern United States. The *baldcypress* is not a true cypress but is related to the sequoia.

Cypresses adapt readily to warm climates, and gardeners often use them as ornamentals. The trees have small, scalelike leaves that grow in dense fan-shaped sprays. Their globe-shaped cones are covered by woody scales that look like small shields. The wood is light brown, durable, and has a strong cedarlike odor.

The *Monterey cypress* is one of the most picturesque trees in North America. It is named for the Monterey Peninsula of California, its native region. Its trunk is rarely more than 20 inches (50 centimeters) in diameter. The tree has long, strong, massive limbs that spread and grow in unusual shapes. It often grows near the ocean shore, where its branches are gnarled and bent by strong ocean winds. The Monterey cypress is a favorite subject for artists.

Scientific classification. Cypresses belong to the cypress family, Cupressaceae. The scientific name for the Monterey cypress is *Cupressus macrocarpa.*   Douglas G. Sprugel

See also **Baldcypress; Cedar; Conifer; Tree** (Familiar broadleaf and needleleaf trees [picture]).

Cyprus, *SY pruhs,* is an island country in the northeast corner of the Mediterranean Sea. It lies about 40 miles (64 kilometers) south of Turkey and 60 miles (97 kilometers) west of Syria. Geographically, Cyprus is part of Asia. But its people live much like southern Europeans and have a relatively high standard of living. Cyprus is a scenic country noted for its hilltop castles, old churches, beaches, and rugged mountains.

About four-fifths of the people in Cyprus are of Greek origin, and most of the rest are of Turkish origin. Nearly

Cyprus

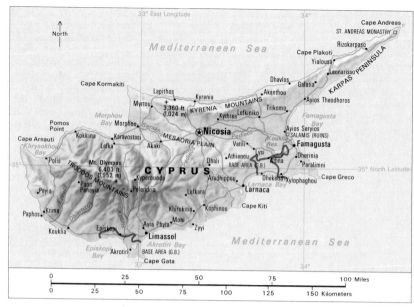

▬▬▬	Base area boundary
────	Road
⊛	National capital
•	Other city or town
+	Elevation above sea level

WORLD BOOK maps

all of the people regard themselves as Greeks or Turks rather than as Cypriot nationals. Conflicts between the two groups have caused problems in Cyprus. Problems have also been caused by the interference of other countries in Cyprus' affairs. In 1974, Turkish troops invaded the island. The Turkish government claimed the troops were sent to support the Turkish Cypriots. The Turks captured a large part of northeastern Cyprus, and thousands of Greek Cypriots fled to the southwestern part of the country. Today, most of the Greeks live in southwest Cyprus, and most of the Turks live in northeast Cyprus.

Cyprus became independent in 1960, after being ruled by Britain since 1878. Its official name is Kypriaki Dimokratia in Greek and Kibris Cumhuriyeti in Turkish. Both mean Republic of Cyprus. Nicosia is the capital and largest city. Most of Nicosia lies in the Greek area, but part is in the Turkish area (see **Nicosia**).

Government. Cyprus is a republic. According to Cyprus' 1960 Constitution, the president serves as head of state and government. The president must be a Greek Cypriot, elected by Greek Cypriots. The vice president must be a Turkish Cypriot, elected by Turkish Cypriots. The Constitution also provides for a division of power between Greek and Turkish Cypriots in the legislature and in other government institutions.

The Turkish invasion in 1974 caused a split in the country's government. Following the invasion, the Turks established a separate government, but the Cypriot government continued to exist under Greek Cypriot control. See the *History* section of this article for details on the government split.

People. Many people in the cities of Cyprus live in large Western-style apartment buildings. Most of the village people live in simple stone or brick houses built around a courtyard. Some older Cypriot men in rural areas wear richly decorated vests and baggy black trousers called *vrakas*. Some of the women wear long skirts and short blouses called *sarkas*.

About 90 percent of Cypriot adults can read and write. Children from 6 to 12 years of age must attend school. Cyprus has technical schools and a teacher training academy.

Most Greek Cypriots are Christians and belong to the independent Orthodox Church of Cyprus. Most Turkish Cypriots are Muslims.

Land. Cyprus has great scenic beauty. Both rugged rock formations and golden sandy beaches line its coast. The broad, fertile Mesaoria Plain separates its two mountain ranges, Troodos and Kyrenia. Troodos, in southwestern Cyprus, is the larger range. Parts of this range are thickly forested. Mount Olympus, its highest peak, rises 6,403 feet (1,952 meters) above sea level. The Kyrenia range stretches along Cyprus' northern coast.

Cyprus has a pleasant, sunny climate all year. Snow falls high in the Troodos Mountains early in the year. Winters are mild in the Mesaoria Plain, but tempera-

Facts in brief

Capital: Nicosia.
Official languages: Greek and Turkish.
Area: 3,572 sq. mi. (9,251 km²). *Greatest distances*—east-west, 128 mi. (206 km); north-south, 75 mi. (121 km).
Elevation: *Highest*—Mount Olympus, 6,403 ft. (1,952 m) above sea level. *Lowest*—sea level.
Population: *Estimated 1994 population*—727,000; density, 204 persons per sq. mi. (79 per km²); distribution, 56 percent urban, 44 percent rural. *1976 census*—612,851. *Estimated 1999 population*—756,000.
Chief products: *Agriculture*—barley, grapefruit, grapes, lemons, olives, oranges, potatoes. *Manufacturing*—cement, cigarettes, olive oil, shoes, textiles, wines. *Mining*—asbestos, chromium.
National anthem: "Imnos pros tin Eleftherian" ("The Hymn to Liberty").
Flag: The flag is white with a map of Cyprus in copper-yellow (for copper) in the center above two green crossed olive branches (for peace). See **Flag** (picture: Flags of Asia and the Pacific).
Money: *Basic unit*—Cyprus pound. See **Money** (table).

Ciganovic, FPG

Nicosia is the capital and largest city of Cyprus. The city's skyline, *above,* shows the Turkish influence on its architecture. The Kyrenia Mountains rise in the background.

tures sometimes go over 100 °F (38 °C) there during the summer. Rainfall averages from 12 to 16 inches (30 to 41 centimeters) a year on the plain. Parts of the Troodos receive more than 40 inches (100 centimeters).

Economy. Tourism ranks as an important industry of Cyprus. Many people visit the country to enjoy its scenery, historic sites, and climate. Chief products include cement, cigarettes, olive oil, shoes, textiles, and wines. Farmers grow barley, grapefruit, grapes, lemons, olives, oranges, potatoes, and wheat. The island's chief minerals are asbestos and chromium. In ancient times, Cyprus produced much copper, but the mines are now almost worked out. Cyprus has a good highway system but no railroad. Limassol and Larnaca are the chief ports. The main airport is at Larnaca.

History. The earliest known people to live in Cyprus date back to about 6000 B.C. Greek settlers arrived there about 1200 B.C., and started city-states similar to those in ancient Greece (see **Greece, Ancient** [The city-state]). Before the time of Christ, the Assyrians, Egyptians, Persians, Greeks, and Romans conquered Cyprus. Saint Paul and Saint Barnabas brought Christianity to the island in A.D. 45. In A.D. 330, Cyprus became a part of the Byzantine Empire. Richard the Lion-Hearted of England captured Cyprus in 1191, but he sold it to a French nobleman. The Ottoman Turks invaded in the 1570's and ruled Cyprus until they turned it over to Britain in 1878. Britain declared the island a crown colony in 1925.

In the 1950's, Greek Cypriots, under the leadership of Archbishop Makarios, started a campaign for *enosis* (union with Greece). A Greek Cypriot secret organization called *EOKA* started guerrilla attacks on the British. Britain declared a state of emergency on the island in 1955, and in 1956 exiled Makarios to Seychelles in the Indian

WORLD BOOK map

Turkish troops invaded Cyprus in 1974, capturing the dark area shown on this map. Greeks control the light-colored area.

CYPRUS

Turkish Section

Nicosia

Greek Section

Mediterranean Sea

Ocean. Greece and Turkey met in Zurich, Switzerland, in 1959. The two countries agreed that Cyprus should become independent. Britain accepted the agreement.

Cyprus became independent on Aug. 16, 1960, under a Constitution written by Britain, Greece, and Turkey and agreed upon by the leaders of the Greek and Turkish Cypriots. Britain, Greece, and Turkey signed an agreement that guaranteed Cyprus' independence. Britain kept control of two military base areas along the southern coast, at Akrotiri and Dhekelia.

Archbishop Makarios became president of the new state. In 1963, Makarios suggested 13 amendments to the Constitution, arguing that they would result in better administration of the country. He claimed that certain provisions of the Constitution threatened to paralyze the operations of the government. Turkey and the Turkish Cypriot leaders opposed the changes, arguing that the changes would eliminate many of the Turkish Cypriots' rights and safeguards. Fighting broke out between Greek and Turkish Cypriots. In 1964, the United Nations sent a peacekeeping force to Cyprus.

In 1967, another clash between the two groups caused a new crisis. Between 1967 and 1974, Greek and Turkish Cypriots held talks in an effort to reach agreement on the Constitution. Progress was made, but disagreements remained.

Makarios was reelected president in 1968 and 1973. In July 1974, Cypriot national guard forces led by Greek officers overthrew Makarios, who then fled from Cyprus. Nikos Sampson, a newspaper publisher, became president. But he resigned after a week, and Glafcos Clerides, president of the Cypriot House of Representatives, took over the presidential duties.

After the overthrow of Makarios, Turkey invaded Cyprus. Widespread fighting occurred between the Turks and Greek Cypriots, and the Turks captured large amounts of territory in northeastern Cyprus. Thousands of Greek Cypriots fled to southwestern Cyprus. Ceasefire negotiations ended the fighting in August. Makarios returned to Cyprus as president late in 1974. Makarios died in 1977, and Spyros Kyprianou, president of the Cypriot House of Representatives, succeeded him. Kyprianou remained president until 1988, when George Vassiliou was elected president. In 1993, Clerides was elected president. But Turkey and the Turkish Cypriots have refused to recognize the Cypriot government.

Representatives of the Greek and Turkish Cypriots, and of Greece and Turkey, have met off and on since 1974 in an effort to reach new constitutional arrangements for the whole of Cyprus. But strong disagreements over control of the country have remained. In 1975, Turkey and Turkish Cypriot leaders declared the northeastern territory captured by the Turks an *autonomous* (self-governing) region called the Turkish Cypriot Federated State. In 1983, the Turkish Cypriots declared the territory an independent nation called the Turkish Republic of Northern Cyprus. However, the United Nations and all countries except Turkey recognize Cyprus as a single nation under the authority of the Greek Cypriot government in the southwest.   Theofanis G. Stavrou

See also **Makarios III.**

Cyrano de Bergerac, *SIHR uh* NOH *duh BUR juh* RAK, **Savinien de,** *sa vee* NYAN *duh* (1619-1655), was a French author and soldier. He was also known for his skill in swordfighting and for his long nose. Edmond Rostand's famous play *Cyrano de Bergerac* (1897) contains a somewhat fanciful account of Cyrano's life.

Culver

Cyrano de Bergerac

Cyrano wrote a comedy *The Ridiculous Pedant* (1653) and a tragedy *The Death of Agrippina* (1654). But his most famous books are two science-fiction works published after his death. They are *The Other World, or the States and Empires of the Moon* (1657) and *The States and Empires of the Sun* (1662). A freethinker, Cyrano questioned traditional religious beliefs and the church's authority. He also said matter is made up of atoms.

Cyrano was born in Périgord. Twice wounded in battle, he left military life in 1642 to study science and literature in Paris.   Robert B. Griffin

Cyril of Alexandria, *SIHR uhl,* **Saint** (378?-444), was the most outstanding Christian theologian of the early 400's. Cyril formulated what became known as the orthodox doctrine of the Incarnation. This doctrine deals with Jesus as both divine and human. For Cyril, salvation depended upon the proper understanding of how God made Himself human in the person of Jesus.

Cyril was born in Alexandria, Egypt. Little is known of his early life. In 412, Cyril succeeded his uncle, Archbishop Theophilus, in the *see* (bishop's seat) of Alexandria. Cyril attacked Jews, Christian heretics, and pagans with great vigor, and quarreled with the Roman urban prefect. He had the Jews expelled from Alexandria.

In 429, Cyril attacked Nestorius, bishop of Constantinople, for denying that the Virgin Mary was the mother of God. He believed Nestorius was denying that Jesus was both human and divine. In 431, with the support of Pope Saint Celestine I, Cyril persuaded the Council of Ephesus to condemn Nestorius and to accept Cyril's interpretation of the doctrine of Jesus (see **Nestorian Christians**). His feast day is February 9.   Richard R. Ring

Cyrillic alphabet. See Alphabet (Other systems of writing); **Russian language.**

Cyrus the Great, *SY ruhs* (? -530 B.C.), founded the Persian Empire about 550 B.C. He extended this empire to include most of southwestern Asia.

Cyrus was born into a noble Persian family, the Achaemenids. In 559 B.C., he became ruler of Anshan, a part of the Median Empire. About 550 B.C., Cyrus overthrew King Astyages of Media and made the Median Empire the center of what became the Persian Empire. Cyrus seized control of western Asia Minor (now western Turkey) after defeating King Croesus of Lydia about 545 B.C. and then overcoming the Greek cities along the coast of Asia Minor. In 539 B.C., he conquered Babylonia and took control of much of the Middle East, including Palestine.

Cyrus respected local customs and religions in his empire. He freed the Jews from captivity in Babylonia and let them rebuild their temple at Jerusalem. He died in a battle in central Asia.   Jack Martin Balcer

See also **Persia, Ancient** (The Achaemenid Empire).

Cyst, *sihst,* is a sac in the body that contains fluid and has no outside opening. Cysts of the skin occur more often than others. These usually form when the opening of an oil gland or *hair follicle* (baglike structure that surrounds a hair) becomes blocked. Some cysts form around a foreign substance that gets into the body. Others form around blood, after an injury. A cyst that forms in the salivary gland under the tongue is called a *ranula.* Cysts of internal organs are usually caused by abnormal development of the organ. Cysts may be removed by surgery. See also **Wen.**   Paul R. Bergstresser

Cystic fibrosis, *SIHS tihk fy BROH sihs,* often abbreviated as *CF* and also called *mucoviscidosis,* is a common hereditary disease in which the cells of certain glands in the body secrete large amounts of abnormally thick mucus. Accumulation of the mucus can block the ducts of these glands and eventually may block the passageways of organs into which the ducts empty. Many organs may be damaged by this accumulation of mucus, particularly the lungs, pancreas, and liver.

The first symptoms of cystic fibrosis usually occur during infancy or early childhood. Infant deaths from cystic fibrosis are often caused by a blockage in the intestines. Patients who survive early infancy develop breathing difficulties because the thick mucus blocks their air passages. Many patients also suffer from frequent lung infections. Lung problems are the most common cause of death of CF patients. Cystic fibrosis patients may not be able to digest their food completely because plugs of mucus may prevent the pancreas from secreting digestive enzymes. Physicians can diagnose CF by testing the patient's perspiration. People with the disease have much salt in their perspiration.

In 1989, researchers identified the abnormal gene that causes cystic fibrosis. This gene is located on *chromosome 7,* one of the 23 pairs of chromosomes in human cells. A person who has two CF genes on this pair has the disease. People who carry one normal gene and one CF gene do not have the disease themselves. They are called *carriers.* A child of two carriers has a one in four chance of inheriting cystic fibrosis. Because doctors know the gene that causes CF, they can often predict which child will get the disease. In the future, doctors may be able to replace the abnormal genes with copies of normal genes.

Cystic fibrosis cannot yet be cured. Doctors use antibiotics to fight the lung infections. Digestion can be improved by special diets and by pills that contain the missing enzymes. Physical therapy, anti-inflammatory drugs, exercise, and special aerosol mists inhaled by the patient can help loosen the mucus from the air passages so that it can be coughed up. A drug called *DNase* is being tested for treatment of CF. The drug is genetically engineered from an enzyme that occurs naturally in the human body. DNase helps break up the mucus in the airways.   Michael G. Levitzky

See also **Races, Human** (Susceptibility to genetic disease).

Cytoplasm. See Cell (Inside a living cell); **Protoplasm.**

Czar, *zahr,* also spelled *tsar,* was the title used by the emperors of Russia. *Czar* comes from *Caesar,* the name used by the emperors of Rome. The first Russian ruler to adopt the title was Ivan the Terrible, in 1547. The last one was Nicholas II (1868-1918). See also **Caesar; Kaiser.**

Travelpix from FPG

Prague, the capital and largest city of the Czech Republic, is one of the most beautiful cities in central Europe. The Charles Bridge, *above,* is a major tourist attraction.

Czech Republic

Czech Republic is a country in central Europe that became independent on Jan. 1, 1993. It is bordered by Poland to the north, Slovakia to the east, Austria to the south, and Germany to the west. Prague is the capital and largest city. From 1918 until Dec. 31, 1992, the area that is now the Czech Republic was united with Slovakia in a larger nation called Czechoslovakia.

Most of the people in the Czech Republic belong to a Slavic group called *Czechs.* Two regions—Bohemia in the west and Moravia in the east—make up most of the republic. The country also includes a small part of a region called Silesia, which extends from the northern section of the Czech Republic into Poland.

The area that is now the Czech Republic has been an industrial center since the 1800's. From 1948 until 1989, when Communists ruled Czechoslovakia, the people in the region had one of the highest standards of living in Communist central and eastern Europe. However, their prosperity declined in the 1980's, and dissatisfaction with the Communist government grew. In 1989, following mass protests, the country's top Communist leaders resigned. Non-Communists took over the government.

Soon after the Communists left office, tensions began to build between Czechoslovakia's two main ethnic

Sharon L. Wolchik, the contributor of this article, is Director of Russian and East European Studies at George Washington University and author of Czechoslovakia in Transition.

groups, the Czechs and the Slovaks. In mid-1992, Czech and Slovak leaders decided to split Czechoslovakia into two nations, one for Czechs and one for Slovaks. On Jan. 1, 1993, the Czech Republic and Slovakia were formed to replace Czechoslovakia.

This article deals with the area that is now the Czech Republic from its early history to the present. For more information on Czechoslovakia, see **Czechoslovakia.**

Government

National government. The Czech Republic is a parliamentary democracy. A two-house Parliament makes the country's laws. The 81 members of the smaller house, called the Senate, serve six-year terms. Voters

Facts in brief

Capital: Prague.
Official language: Czech.
Official name: Česká Republika (Czech Republic)
Area: 30,450 sq. mi. (78,864 km²). *Greatest distances*—east-west, 305 mi. (491 km); north-south, 175 mi. (282 km).
Elevation: *Highest*—Sněžka, 5,256 ft. (1,602 m) above sea level. *Lowest*—377 ft. (115 m) along the Elbe River near the German border.
Population: *Estimated 1994 population*—10,470,000; density, 344 persons per sq. mi. (133 per km²). *1980 census*—10,291,927. *Estimated 1999 population*— 10,661,000.
Chief products: *Agriculture*—barley, cattle, corn, hogs, hops, oats, potatoes, poultry, rapeseed, rye, sheep, sugar beets, wheat. *Manufacturing*—footwear, glass, iron and steel, textiles. *Mining*—coal.
National anthem: "Kde domov můj?" ("Where Is My Home?")
Money: Basic unit—koruna. See **Money** (table: Exchange rates).

elect one-third of the senators every two years. The 200 members of the larger house, called the Chamber of Deputies, are elected to four-year terms. The Parliament elects a president, who serves as head of state. The president appoints a prime minister, who heads the government and oversees its day-to-day operations. The prime minister names a cabinet to help carry out the executive functions of government.

Local government. The Czech Republic is divided into seven regions, excluding Prague, which is a separate administrative unit. Each region is governed by an elected council. Cities, towns, and villages also have their own local governments.

Politics. The Czech Republic has many political parties. The Civic Democratic Party and the Christian Democratic Union, two moderate non-Communist parties, form a coalition in the government. Together, they are the strongest parties. The Left Bloc, a group that includes former Communists, is the next most important party. Several smaller parties also hold seats in the Chamber of Deputies. All Czech citizens 18 years of age and older may vote.

Courts. The Supreme Court is the Czech Republic's highest court. The Czech Republic also has a constitutional court and high, regional, and district courts.

Armed forces. Men are required to serve for one year in the armed forces of the Czech Republic after reaching the age of 18. Women serve in the military on a voluntary basis.

People

Population. The Czech Republic has a population of about $10\frac{1}{2}$ million. About 80 percent of the people are Czechs and about 15 percent are Moravians. Slovaks make up the largest minority group. Small numbers of Germans, Gypsies, Hungarians, and Poles also live in the Czech Republic.

Before World War II (1939-1945), Czechoslovakia had a large Jewish population. But almost all the Jews were killed by Nazis during the war. Today, between 15,000 and 18,000 Jews live in the Czech Republic. Most of the Jews make their homes in Prague, which has a well-preserved Jewish synagogue and cemetery.

Ancestry. The Czechs are descendants of Slavic tribes who settled in the region by about A.D. 500. Bohemia gets its name from the Boii, a Celtic tribe that probably lived in the region in about the 400's B.C. There have been large German settlements in what is now the Czech Republic for much of the region's history.

Language. The official language of the Czech Republic is Czech. Moravians speak a form of Czech that is slightly different from that spoken in Bohemia. Slovaks speak Slovak, a language closely related to Czech. Gypsies speak Romany, which belongs to the Indo-Iranian group of languages. Other minority groups speak their own languages at home but generally also speak Czech.

Way of life

City life. Most of the people in the Czech Republic live in towns and cities. Prague, with a population of more than 1 million, is the largest city. Other cities with more than 150,000 people are Brno, Ostrava, and Plzeň.

The Czech Republic has a severe housing shortage. Most people in urban areas live in apartment buildings,

many of which are poor quality high-rises built during the Communist era.

Air pollution is a health threat in the Czech Republic, especially in the cities. Alcoholism, crime, and drug abuse are also serious problems.

The Czech government is working to move the country from a Communist state-controlled economy to one based on private enterprise. Despite disruptions caused by the shift, the people of the Czech Republic still have one of the highest standards of living in post-Communist central and eastern Europe. Most households have automobiles, refrigerators, televisions, and washing machines. Many city families have country cottages.

Rural life. People in rural areas usually work in agriculture or travel to cities or nearby factories to work. Rural families often live in single-family homes.

Food and drink. The Czech diet is close to that of Germany. Pork is a popular dish, as are sliced, boiled dumplings and pickled cabbage. Carp with potato salad is a traditional Christmas menu. Apple strudel is a favorite dessert. World-famous Czech beer is the main alcoholic beverage consumed in the Czech Republic. Several fine wines are made in Moravia.

Recreation. Favorite forms of recreation in the Czech Republic include attending and playing in soccer matches and other sporting events, and watching motion pictures and television. Many people gather in pubs

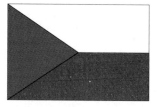 

Symbols of the Czech Republic include a flag adopted in 1993. It is the same flag that Czechoslovakia used. The coat of arms features a white lion with a double tail on a red field. The Holy Roman emperor granted it to Bohemia in the 1100's.

WORLD BOOK map

The Czech Republic is in central Europe. It borders four countries including Slovakia, its former partner in Czechoslovakia.

to chat, play games, and drink. Outdoor activities, including gardening, hiking, and such winter sports as skiing and skating, are also popular.

Religion. The Communist rulers of Czechoslovakia tried to keep people from practicing religion. But Czechoslovakia's new government granted the people full religious freedom in 1990. About 40 percent of the people are Roman Catholics. Other active churches include the Orthodox Church and Protestant denominations such as the Czech Brethren and the Czechoslovak Church. The country's Jewish population is working to revive Jewish culture and customs.

Education. Czech law requires children to attend nine years of elementary school. A student may then attend a vocational or technical secondary school, a teacher training institute, or a general education school.

Charles University in Prague is one of the oldest universities in Europe. It was founded in 1348. Other universities are in Brno, Olomouc, and Opava. Most schools and all universities are state-owned.

The arts. The composers Antonín Dvořák and Bedřich Smetana, who wrote their major works in the late 1800's, are considered the founders of the Czech national school of music. Composer Leoš Janáček created operas in the early 1900's that show his interest in Moravian folk music. Today, popular music, including country, jazz, and rock, is also popular in the Czech Republic.

The first major works of literature in Czech were written in the 1300's. Czech literature flowered during an awakening of national identity that began in the late 1700's and continued into the early 1900's. Outstanding authors from the later period include Karel Čapek; Jaroslav Hašek; and Franz Kafka, who wrote in German.

Czechoslovakia's Communist government attempted to limit artistic expression. However, many Czech artists, filmmakers, and writers resisted political control. Miloš Forman, Jiří Menzel, and other Czech *New Wave* filmmakers achieved worldwide acclaim during the 1960's for motion pictures that criticized social and political conditions. A large number of Czech writers became known outside of Czechoslovakia for their works. These writers include the novelist Milan Kundera; the playwright Václav Havel, who later became president of Czechoslovakia and of the Czech Republic; and the poet Jaroslav Seifert, who won the Nobel Prize for literature in 1984. The non-Communist government removed restrictions on art in 1990.

Land and climate

The Czech Republic consists of five main geographic regions: (1) the Bohemian Mountains; (2) the Sudeten Mountains; (3) the Bohemian Basin; (4) the Bohemian-Moravian Highlands; and (5) the Moravian Lowlands.

The Bohemian Mountains are a series of mountain ranges in the western part of the Czech Republic. These ranges include the Ore Mountains in the northwest and the Bohemian Forest in the west and southwest. This region, which rises more than 2,500 feet (762 meters) above sea level, is known for its ski slopes and *spas* (health resorts). Many people visit the spas at Karlovy Vary (also called Karlsbad) and Mariánské Lázně (also called Marienbad) to drink waters from the mineral springs there or bathe in them. Coal mining in the Ore Mountains and industrial pollution have damaged the

region's environment. The Bohemian Forest is an important source of lumber and wood products.

The Sudeten Mountains form much of the Czech Republic's northern border. The *Krkonoše* (Giant) Mountains of the Sudeten system have one of the country's largest nature preserves. But acid rain and other kinds of pollution threaten the animal and plant life there.

The Bohemian Basin lies in north-central Bohemia. This region of low plains and rolling hills has much fertile farmland. Prague and Hradec Králové are among the region's industrial centers. Several major rivers, including the Elbe, Ohře, and Vltava, flow through the basin.

The Bohemian-Moravian Highlands cover much of the central part of the Czech Republic. High plains, plateaus, and low hills make up this largely agricultural region. Plzeň, the largest city in the area, is a major manufacturing center noted for automaking and beer brewing. The city's breweries produce a famous pale beer called Pilsner. The Sázava, the Vltava, and several smaller rivers drain the highlands.

The Moravian Lowlands occupy the southeastern part of the country. Farmers grow a variety of crops in the fertile valley of the Morava River. Many farmers also raise cattle there. The city of Ostrava is an industrial and mining center. Important coal fields lie nearby. The Morava and Oder are the chief rivers of the lowlands.

Climate. The Czech Republic has warm summers and cold winters. Temperatures vary greatly by elevation. They range from an average of 23 °F (−5 °C) in winter to 68 °F (20 °C) in summer. Annual *precipitation* (rain, melted snow, and other forms of moisture) ranges from 18 to 41 inches (45 to 103 centimeters).

Economy

After the Communists came to power in Czechoslovakia in 1948, they began managing all aspects of the economy. They put all factories and almost all farms under state control. They changed the economy's focus from light industry, such as glass and textiles, to heavy industry, such as machinery and steel. The economy thrived until the 1960's, when poor planning, labor shortages, and other problems caused it to decline. After the Communist government resigned in 1989,

STR from Bavaria

The Sudeten Mountains form most of the northern border of the Czech Republic. The natural beauty of the region draws many hikers, mountain climbers, and other outdoor enthusiasts.

Czechoslovakia's new leaders moved quickly to create a free-enterprise economy, in which businesses could operate without extensive government control. Many new businesses were established, especially in retail trade and other service industries.

Service industries. About 45 percent of the workers of the Czech Republic hold jobs in service industries. During the Communist period, the service sector was largely undeveloped. But it is growing rapidly today. There are many new, privately owned insurance and real estate firms, medical and other professional services, repair shops, and retail stores. Hotels and travel agencies have expanded to meet a large increase in tourism since the late 1980's.

Manufacturing and mining. Manufacturing employs about 40 percent of the labor force of the Czech Republic. Although heavy industry is still important today, light industries such as footwear, glass, and textiles are reemerging as important producers for export. The main manufacturing centers are Brno, Hradec Králové, Ostrava, Plzeň, Prague, and Ústí nad Labem.

The Czech Republic has large deposits of brown coal. The Ore Mountains contain large deposits of uranium and small amounts of antimony, mercury, and tin.

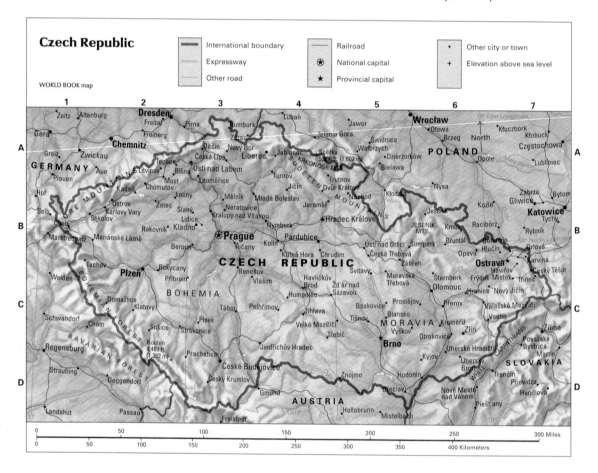

Czech Republic map index

Agriculture employs about 10 percent of the workers of the Czech Republic. About 40 percent of the country's land is suitable for farming. Major crops are barley, corn, fruits, hops, oats, potatoes and other vegetables, rapeseed, rye, sugar beets, and wheat. Farmers also raise cattle, hogs, poultry, and sheep.

When Communists ruled Czechoslovakia, almost all the farms were either state farms or *collectives.* State farmworkers earned a salary from the government, while collective farmworkers received a share of the farm's profits, some of its products, and a small wage. Legislation was passed in 1991 that began to allow farmland to be returned to private farmers. But most farmland remains under state control.

Trade. The Czech Republic's main trading partners are Austria, France, Germany, Hungary, Italy, Poland, Russia, Slovakia, and the United States. Chief exports include automobiles, coal, footwear, iron and steel, and machinery. The country depends heavily on imports of natural gas and petroleum. Other major imports include iron ore, other ores, and automobiles.

Transportation and communication. The Czech Republic has a well-developed system of roads and railroads. There are about 35,000 miles (56,000 kilometers) of highways and 5,900 miles (9,500 kilometers) of railroads. Prague has a subway system and an international airport.

There are about 30 daily newspapers and some 1,800 other journals, newspapers, and magazines in the Czech Republic. Radio and television stations operate under both private and state ownership. Foreign news broadcasts, such as Cable News Network, are also available.

History

Early days. Celtic tribes probably lived in what is now the Czech Republic in about the 400's B.C. Germanic tribes arrived about 10 B.C. Various Slavic tribes, including the ancestors of the present-day Czechs, settled in the region by about A.D. 500. The Slavs were conquered by the Avars in the 500's. The Slavs drove the Avars from the region in the 600's. Several of the Slavic tribes united to create their own state in the 800's. The state formed the core of the Great Moravian Empire, which eventually included Bohemia, southern Poland, Slovakia, and parts of western Hungary. Hungarian tribes conquered the Great Moravian Empire in 907.

The rise of Bohemia began during the 900's. The Přemyslid dynasty ruled Bohemia for almost 400 years. Under its rule, Bohemia expanded its territory and came under the protection of the Holy Roman Empire, a German-based empire that also included Austria and parts of Belgium, Italy, and the Netherlands. In 1212, Holy Roman Emperor Frederick II made Bohemia a semi-independent kingdom within the empire. Many German craftworkers and merchants settled in Bohemia in the 1200's, contributing to the region's prosperity.

Bohemia's political and economic power continued to grow in the 1300's. Prague flourished under Charles IV, who became king of Bohemia in 1346 and ruled as Holy Roman emperor from 1347. In 1348, Charles founded Charles University, the first university in central Europe, in Prague. He also brought foreign artists to Prague to make the city a major European cultural center.

The death of a priest named John Hus in 1415 triggered a series of religious wars in Bohemia. Hus led a movement to reform the Roman Catholic Church and was burned at the stake as a heretic. The wars ended in 1436 with a compromise. In 1458, Hus supporters elected Jiří of Poděbrady, a Protestant, king of Bohemia. Jiří thus became the first Protestant king in Europe. In the late 1400's, most of the Czech nobility became Protestants, and the power of the nobles increased.

Habsburg rule. In 1526, the Austrian Habsburgs (or Hapsburgs), a Catholic family, began ruling Bohemia. Bohemia remained partially independent, though the nobles lost some power. In 1618, a group of Czech Protestant nobles revolted against the Habsburgs. This revolt touched off the Thirty Years' War, a series of wars that spread through Europe.

In 1620, the Habsburg armies defeated the nobles in the Battle of White Mountain. Almost all the nobles were killed or forced into exile. Bohemia then lost most of its self-governing powers. The Habsburgs made the people convert to Catholicism. They also forced most Czechs to give up their own language and culture and adopt German.

German culture dominated Bohemia until the late 1700's. At about this time, industries began to develop in Bohemia and Moravia, and many Czech peasants moved to cities. Czech writers and other intellectuals worked to create a greater sense of national identity among Czechs. By the mid-1800's, a movement for self-government had gathered strength. But Austria continued to rule Bohemia and Moravia. In 1867, Austria and Hungary formed a monarchy called Austria-Hungary.

The creation of Czechoslovakia. During World War I (1914-1918), Tomáš G. Masaryk and other Czech leaders sought support abroad for their idea of an independent state made up of Czechs and Slovaks. At the end of the war, Austria-Hungary collapsed, and Czechoslovakia was created from a part of it. The Czechoslovak Constitution established a democratic republic.

Masaryk served as president of Czechoslovakia from 1918 until 1935, when Eduard Beneš succeeded him. The 1920's and early 1930's were generally a period of political stability and prosperity in Czechoslovakia. However, the Czech-dominated government was less successful in dealing with the country's minority groups. Many Slovaks began calling for broader powers of self-government. The *Sudeten Germans*—Germans living in the Sudetenland, the border regions of western Czechoslovakia—were also dissatisfied with Czech rule.

The Munich Agreement. In 1938, German dictator Adolf Hitler used the dissatisfaction of the Sudeten Germans to pressure Czechoslovakia to give the Sudetenland to Germany. He threatened to declare war on Czechoslovakia if his demand was not met. In an attempt to avoid war, British and French leaders gave in to Hitler's demand. They signed the famous Munich Agreement forcing Czechoslovakia to turn over the Sudetenland to Germany. Later that year, Poland and Hungary claimed parts of Czechoslovakia. In March 1939, a few months before World War II broke out, Germany seized the rest of Czechoslovakia. Slovakia became a separate state under German control, and German troops occupied Bohemia and Moravia. Beneš, who had resigned as president in 1938, established a government-in-exile in London.

The people of Bohemia and Moravia suffered greatly under German occupation. Nazis killed almost all the Jewish population. By 1945, Soviet troops had freed most of Czechoslovakia from the Germans. After World War II ended in 1945, the government-in-exile returned.

Communist rule. Beneš formed a coalition government to lead postwar Czechoslovakia. Leaders of the Communist Party held many important positions in the new government. In national elections in 1946, the Communists won more votes than any other party. In 1948, they caused a crisis that led to the resignation of non-Communist government ministers. The Communists then formed a government dominated by Communists. Beneš soon resigned and was replaced by Communist Party chairman Klement Gottwald.

Czechoslovakia's Communist leaders copied the Soviet model of Communist rule. The Communist Party became the only powerful political party. The government controlled the planning and production of all important goods. It took over nearly all the country's land and forced most farmers to join state farms or collectives. Censorship became widespread. The power of the secret police grew, and Czechoslovakia became one of the Soviet Union's most loyal allies.

The 1960's. During the 1960's, economic performance in Czechoslovakia dropped. In addition, many Slovaks wanted greater recognition of Slovak rights. In 1968, Alexander Dubček became head of the Communist Party. Under Dubček, the government introduced a program of liberal reforms known as the "Prague spring" or "socialism with a human face." The press was granted greater freedom, and citizens were given a limited role in politics. But leaders of the Soviet Union and other European Communist nations feared that Dubček's programs would weaken Communist control in Czechoslovakia. They also feared that people in other Communist countries would demand similar reforms. As a result, troops from the Soviet Union, Bulgaria, East Germany, Hungary, and Poland invaded Czechoslovakia in August 1968. Gustáv Husák replaced Dubček as head of the Communist Party in April 1969 and reversed most of the reforms. A small number of *dissidents* (political protesters) continued to oppose the government.

The Velvet Revolution. During the late 1980's, the standard of living in Czechoslovakia fell. Support for the Communist system also declined. The dissident movement grew, inspired by the democratic reforms that were taking place in the Soviet Union under Mikhail S. Gorbachev. In November 1989, large numbers of Czechs and Slovaks gathered in the streets of Prague to call for an end to Communist rule. Less than a month after the protests began, the Communist government resigned. Non-Communist leaders gained control of the government. The Federal Assembly elected Václav Havel, a non-Communist playwright, to succeed Husák as president. The end of Communist rule in Czechoslovakia occurred so smoothly and peacefully that it became known as the *Velvet Revolution.*

In free elections held in June 1990, Civic Forum—the Czech party that had emerged in 1989 to lead the Velvet Revolution—and its Slovak ally, Public Against Violence, won a majority of seats in the Federal Assembly. The Assembly reelected Havel president in July 1990.

Czechoslovakia's new leaders restored such basic civil liberties as freedom of religion, speech, and the press. New laws were passed to change the legal system, restore property rights, and establish a free-enterprise economy. Czechoslovakia also reestablished friendly relations with Western nations, including the United States.

The breakup of Czechoslovakia. After the non-Communist government took office, Czechs and Slovaks began to disagree over political and economic issues. The disagreements blocked the adoption of a new constitution and slowed economic reform. In mid-1992, Czech and Slovak leaders began to discuss splitting the country into two separate nations. Havel resigned, saying that he did not want to preside over the breakup of Czechoslovakia.

On Jan. 1, 1993, the Czech Republic and Slovakia were created to replace Czechoslovakia. Later in January, the Czech legislature elected Havel president of the Czech Republic.   Sharon L. Wolchik

Related articles in *World Book* include:

Biographies

Beneš, Eduard	Hus, John
Čapek, Karel	Janáček, Leoš
Comenius, John A.	Kafka, Franz
Dvořák, Antonín	Masaryk (family)
Havel, Václav	Smetana, Bedřich

Cities

Brno	Ostrava
Karlovy Vary	Prague

History

Austria (History)	Thirty Years' War
Czechoslovakia	Warsaw Pact
Habsburg, House of	World War II (The failure of
Munich Agreement	appeasement)

Other related articles

Bohemia	Ruthenia	Slovakia
Elbe River	Silesia	Sudetenland
Moravia		

Outline

I. Government
- A. National government
- B. Local government
- C. Politics
- D. Courts
- E. Armed forces

II. People
- A. Population
- B. Ancestry
- C. Language

III. Way of life

A. City life	E. Religion
B. Rural life	F. Education
C. Food and drink	G. The arts
D. Recreation	

IV. Land and climate
- A. The Bohemian Mountains
- B. The Sudeten Mountains
- C. The Bohemian Basin
- D. The Bohemian-Moravian Highlands
- E. The Moravian Lowlands
- F. Climate

V. Economy

A. Service industries	D. Trade
B. Manufacturing	E. Transportation and
and mining	communication
C. Agriculture	

VI. History

Czechoslovakia was a country in central Europe from 1918 until 1992. On Dec. 31, 1992, Czechoslovakia ceased to exist, and the Czech Republic and Slovakia were formed in its place.

Czechoslovakia was home to two closely related Slavic peoples, the Czechs and the Slovaks. Most of the Czechs lived in the western part of the country, in the regions of Bohemia and Moravia. The Slovaks lived primarily in Slovakia, an area in the east.

In 1948, Communists began ruling Czechoslovakia. In 1989, hundreds of thousands of citizens participated in demonstrations calling for an end to Communist rule. In response, the Communist government resigned and a non-Communist government came to power.

Disagreements soon broke out between Czechs and Slovaks over how to reform the country's government and economy. In mid-1992, Czech and Slovak leaders decided to break Czechoslovakia into two separate nations. On Jan. 1, 1993, the Czechs formed the Czech Republic and the Slovaks formed Slovakia to replace Czechoslovakia.

Early history. Celtic and Germanic tribes lived in what became Czechoslovakia more than 2,000 years ago. Slavic tribes settled in the region by about A.D. 500. Several of the tribes united to form a state in the 800's. The state became the core of the Great Moravian Empire, which soon covered much of central Europe. Hungarian tribes conquered the empire in 907. Hungarians then ruled Slovakia for about the next 1,000 years.

In 1212, Bohemia became a semi-independent kingdom within the Holy Roman Empire, a German-based empire in western and central Europe. In 1526, the Austrian Habsburgs (or Hapsburgs) began ruling Bohemia. In time, Bohemia lost most of its self-governing powers. In the late 1700's, Czech intellectuals worked to create a greater sense of national identity among Czechs. By the mid-1800's, a movement for self-government had gathered strength. A similar movement grew in Slovakia. But Hungarian rulers put down the Slovak movement. In 1867, Austria and Hungary formed a monarchy called Austria-Hungary.

The formation of Czechoslovakia. During World War I (1914-1918), two leading Czech nationalists—Eduard Beneš and Tomáš G. Masaryk—worked to gain foreign support for the idea of an independent nation made up of Czechs and Slovaks. At the end of World War I in 1918, Austria-Hungary collapsed, and Czechoslovakia was created from part of it. The Czechoslovak Constitution established the country as a democratic republic. Masaryk served as president from 1918 until 1935, when Beneš succeeded him. In 1919, Ruthenia, a region east of Slovakia, became part of Czechoslovakia.

Although Czechs made up less than 50 percent of the population of Czechoslovakia, they dominated the economy and government. During the 1920's and 1930's, many Slovaks grew resentful of Czech control. The *Sudeten Germans* (Germans who lived in the Sudetenland, the border regions of western Czechoslovakia) also became dissatisfied with Czech dominance.

The Munich Agreement. German dictator Adolf Hitler encouraged the Sudeten Germans to demand self-rule. He threatened war with Czechoslovakia if the demand was not met. In 1938, the leaders of Britain and France agreed to Hitler's demand and signed the Munich Agreement, a pact that forced Czechoslovakia to give the Sudetenland to Germany. Later that year, Hungary and Poland claimed other parts of Czechoslovakia. In March 1939, a few months before World War II broke out, Germany seized the rest of Czechoslovakia. Slovakia became a separate republic under German control. Hitler made Bohemia and Moravia a German protectorate.

German occupation during the war brought widespread suffering to Czechoslovakia. More than 250,000 people, including almost all the country's Jews, were killed.

Eduard Beneš, who had resigned as president in 1938, formed a government-in-exile in London during the war. He cooperated with both Western powers and the Soviet Union. In 1943, he signed a treaty of friendship and cooperation with the Soviet government. By 1945, the Soviet army had freed most of Czechoslovakia from the Germans. United States troops liberated parts of Bohemia. After World War II ended in 1945, the government-in-exile returned, and all foreign troops were withdrawn from Czechoslovakia. The same year, Czechoslovakia gave Ruthenia to the Soviet Union.

Communist rule. Beneš formed a coalition government to lead postwar Czechoslovakia. Communists held many important positions in the new government. With popular support, the government put many of the country's major industries under state control. It also forced hundreds of thousands of Germans and Hungarians living in Czechoslovakia to leave.

WORLD BOOK map

Czechoslovakia was a country in central Europe that existed from 1918 until 1992. It consisted of three main regions—Bohemia, Moravia, and Slovakia. Germany took over the Sudetenland in 1938 and seized the rest of Czechoslovakia in 1939.

In national elections in 1946, the Communist Party received more votes than any other party. The Communist Party chairman, Klement Gottwald, became prime minister of Czechoslovakia. In February 1948, the Communists caused a crisis that led to the resignation of non-Communist government ministers. The Communists then formed a government dominated by Communists. Beneš resigned a few months later, and Gottwald succeeded him.

Czechoslovakia's Communist leaders copied the Soviet model of political organization and economic development. The Communist Party became the only powerful political party. The government managed all aspects of the economy. Farmers were forced to join either state farms or *collectives.* The government owned and operated state farms. On collective farms, farmworkers jointly owned the farm equipment and property.

Gottwald remained president of Czechoslovakia until 1953, when Antonín Zápotocký succeeded him. Antonín Novotný became president in 1957.

The 1960's. During the early 1960's, Czechoslovakia's agricultural and industrial production dropped, and there were shortages of food and other goods. Even members of the Communist Party criticized the government's inability to reverse the economic decline. At the same time, the country's intellectuals called for more freedom of expression, and many Slovaks renewed their efforts to gain recognition for Slovak rights. In 1968, the Communists removed Antonín Novotný as party leader. Alexander Dubček, a Slovak, became the party leader, and Ludvík Svoboda became the country's president.

Under Dubček, the government introduced a program of liberal reforms. These reforms included more freedom of the press and increased contacts with non-Communist countries. Dubček won popularity among Czechoslovakia's people for the reforms, known as the "Prague spring." But leaders of the Soviet Union and other European Communist nations feared that Dubček's program would weaken the party's control in Czechoslovakia. They also feared that people in other Communist countries would demand similar reforms. The reform movement ended when troops from the Soviet Union, Bulgaria, East Germany, Hungary, and Poland invaded Czechoslovakia in August 1968. The Soviet troops remained, but the other troops withdrew by late 1968.

In April 1969, the Czechoslovak Communist Party replaced Dubček with Gustáv Husák, another Slovak Communist. Thousands of people who had been active in the reform movement either resigned or were removed from the party. In 1975, Husák succeeded Svoboda as president and also continued to serve as Communist Party leader. Under Husák, Czechoslovakia remained a tightly controlled Communist state and a loyal ally of the Soviet Union.

The Velvet Revolution. In 1987, Husák resigned as Czechoslovakia's Communist Party leader. He remained president. Miloš Jakeš succeeded Husák as party leader. In November 1989, hundreds of thousands of people gathered in the streets of Prague to demand changes in the government and greater political, economic, and civil freedoms. The demonstrations were followed by general strikes and demonstrations by people across the country. In response to the protests, Communist Party leader Jakeš resigned and Karel Urbánek replaced him. In addition, Czechoslovakia's Communist-controlled Federal Assembly voted to end Communism's leading role in the Czechoslovak government and society.

In December, Marián Calfa, a liberal Communist, became prime minister and later left the Communist Party. Non-Communists gained control of most key Cabinet ministries. Husák then resigned under pressure. The Federal Assembly elected Václav Havel, a non-Communist playwright, to succeed Husák. The end of Communist rule was so smooth and peaceful that it became known as the *Velvet Revolution.*

The new government worked to increase free enterprise in Czechoslovakia. It restored such civil liberties as freedom of religion, speech, and the press. It also called for free elections, which were held in June 1990. In the elections, the Civic Forum—the Czech party that had emerged in November 1989 to lead the Velvet Revolution—and its Slovak ally, Public Against Violence, won a majority of seats in the Federal Assembly. The Assembly reelected Havel president in July 1990. The Soviet Union withdrew its troops from Czechoslovakia in June 1991, six months before it broke apart.

In 1992, Czechoslovakia's government took a large step toward establishing an economy based on free enterprise. It began to sell shares of stock in companies it had owned. As a result, more than 1,000 companies became privately owned. In addition, hundreds of thousands of new privately owned businesses were established.

However, the move toward a free-enterprise economy caused far more unemployment in Slovakia than in the Czech areas. Tensions between the Czechs and Slovaks prevented the adoption of a new constitution and slowed economic reform. Although many Czechs and Slovaks wanted to remain united, the prime ministers of the Czech Republic and Slovakia began negotiating the breakup of Czechoslovakia in June 1992. Havel resigned, saying he did not want to preside over the breakup of his country. On Jan. 1, 1993, the independent nations of the Czech Republic and Slovakia were created to replace Czechoslovakia.   Sharon L. Wolchik

Related articles. See Czech Republic and Slovakia and their lists of *Related articles.* See also:

Czerny, *CHEHR nee,* **Karl** (1791-1857), was an Austrian composer, teacher, and pianist. He composed more than 1,000 works in a wide variety of instrumental and vocal forms. He also arranged many works by other composers for piano. His reputation rests largely on his many instructional compositions for piano, called *études.*

Czerny was born in Vienna. He was a friend of the German composer Ludwig van Beethoven and studied with him from 1800 to 1803. Early in his career, Czerny gave frequent piano recitals. But he gradually gave up public performing and concentrated on teaching and composing. Czerny became a highly successful teacher of many pupils.   Daniel T. Politoske

Czolgosz, Leon. See McKinley, William (Assassination).